5300	Audit Evidence	CAS 500	Audit Evidence
5301	Analysis	CAS 520	Analytical Procedures
5303	Confirmation	CAS 505	External Confirmations
5305	Audit of Accounting Estimates	CAS 540	Auditing Accounting Estimates, including Fair Value Accounting Estimates, and Related Disclosures
5306	Auditing Fair Value Measurements and Disclosures	CAS 540	Auditing Accounting Estimates, including Fair Value Accounting Estimates, and Related Disclosures
5310	Audit Evidence Considerations when an Entity Uses a Service Organization	CAS 402	Audit Considerations Relating to an Entity Using a Service Organization
5365	Communications with Actuaries	Appendix to CAS 500	Joint Policy Statement Concerning Actuaries Involved in the Preparation of Financial Statements and Auditors*
5370	Management Representations	CAS 580	Written Representations
5400	The Auditor's Standard Report	CAS 700	Forming an Opinion and Reporting on Financial Statements
5405	Date of the Auditor's Report	CAS 560	Subsequent Events
5510	Reservations in the Auditor's Report	CAS 705	Modifications to the Opinion in the Independent Auditor's Report
5600	Auditor's Report on Financial Statements Prepared Using a Basis of Accounting Other than Generally Accepted Accounting Principles	CAS 706	Emphasis of Matter Paragraphs and Other Matter Paragraphs in the Independent Auditor's Report
		CAS 800	Special Considerations—Audits of Financial Statements Prepared in Accordance with Special Purpose Frameworks
5701	Other Reporting Matters	CAS 706	Emphasis of Matter Paragraphs and Other Matter Paragraphs in the Independent Auditor's Report
		CAS 710	Comparative Information—Corresponding Figures and Comparative Financial Statements
5750	Communication with Management of Matters Identified During the Financial Statement Audit	Aspects of communications with management is dealt with in various CASs*	
5751	Communications with Those Having Oversight of the Financial Reporting Process	CAS 260	Communications with Those Charged with Governance
5800	Special Reports — Introduction	CAS 800	Special Considerations—Audits of Financial Statements Prepared in Accordance with Special Purpose Frameworks
5805	Special Reports — Audit Reports on Financial Information Other Than Financial Statements	CAS 805	Special Considerations—Audits of Single Financial Statements and Specific Elements, Accounts or Items of a Financial Statement
6010	Audit of Related Party Transactions	CAS 550	Related Parties
6030	Inventories	CAS 501	Audit Evidence—Specific Considerations for Selected Items
6550	Subsequent Events	CAS 560	Subsequent Events
6560	Communications with Law Firms Regarding Claims and Possible Claims (including the Joint Policy Statement)	CAS 501	Audit Evidence—Specific Considerations for Selected Items
6930	Reliance on Another Auditor	CAS 600	Special Considerations—Audits of Group Financial Statements (Including the Work of Component Auditors)

* Please see notes on disposition of other existing *Handbook* Sections dealing with the audit of financial statements.

Source: Reprinted [or adapted] with permission from *The CICA Handbook—Assurance Sections Related to Audits of Financial Statements Concordance* (2009: The Canadian Institute of Chartered Accountants, Toronto, Canada). Any changes to the original material are the sole responsibility of the author [and/or publisher] and have not been reviewed or endorsed by the CICA.

Auditing
AN INTERNATIONAL APPROACH

Fifth Edition

Wally J. Smieliauskas, Ph.D., C.P.A., C.F.E.
Joseph L. Rotman School of Management
University of Toronto

Kathryn Bewley, Ph.D., C.A.
York University

McGraw-Hill Ryerson
Connect. Learn. Succeed.

The McGraw-Hill Companies

McGraw-Hill
Ryerson
Connect. Learn. Succeed.

Auditing: An International Approach
Fifth Edition

ISBN-13: 978-0-07-096829-5
ISBN-10: 0-07-096829-2

1 2 3 4 5 6 7 8 9 10 TCP 1 9 8 7 6 5 4 3 2 1 0

Printed and bound in Canada.

Care has been taken to trace ownership of copyright material contained in this text; however, the publisher will welcome any information that enables them to rectify any reference or credit for subsequent editions.

VICE-PRESIDENT AND EDITOR-IN-CHIEF: Joanna Cotton
EXECUTIVE SPONSORING EDITOR: Rhondda McNabb
EXECUTIVE MARKETING MANAGER: Joy Armitage Taylor
DEVELOPMENTAL EDITOR: Rachel Horner
SENIOR EDITORIAL ASSOCIATE: Christine Lomas
SUPERVISING EDITOR: Jessica Barnoski
COPY EDITOR: Julie van Tol
PROOFREADER: Carol Fordyce
PRODUCTION COORDINATOR: Lena Keating
COVER DESIGN: Katherine Strain
INTERIOR DESIGN: Katherine Strain
PAGE LAYOUT: Aptara, Inc.
PRINTER: Transcontinental Printing Group

Library and Archives Canada Cataloguing in Publication

Smieliauskas, Wally

Auditing : an international approach / Wally J. Smieliauskas, Kathryn Bewley.—5th ed.

Includes index.

First Canadian ed. published under title: Auditing & other assurance engagements / Jack C. Robertson, Wally J. Smieliauskas. 2nd Canadian ed. published under title: Auditing / Jack C. Robertson, Wally J. Smieliauskas.

ISBN 978-0-07-096829-5

1. Auditing—Textbooks.   I. Bewley, Kathryn, 1955-   II. Title.

HF5667.S567 2010   657'.45   C2009-904167-7

W. J. Smieliauskas dedicates this book to
Adrian and Fabrice

Kathryn Bewley dedicates this book to
my mother Joanne and my father Bill Bewley

About the Authors

Wally J. Smieliauskas is a professor of accounting at the University of Toronto, where he has been a member of the faculty since 1979. He has published articles on a variety of auditing, accounting, and education issues.

At the University of Toronto, Professor Smieliauskas developed the first degree-credit introductory auditing course (in 1981) and the first advanced auditing course (in 1990). In 1988 he was the first director of the MBA Co-op Program in Professional Accounting, a position he held until 1993. The program is designed to facilitate the entry of undergraduates from various fields into the profession, and to provide a broader management education as well as specialized training in accounting, auditing, and tax topics. It has evolved to become the Master of Management & Professional Accounting (MMPA) program now offered through the University of Toronto's Mississauga campus.

Kathryn Bewley has been a professor of accounting and auditing at York University since 1991. As well, she is a member of the Institute of Chartered Accountants of Ontario. Professor Bewley began her career in auditing with Clarkson Gordon in Toronto.

Professor Bewley has her Ph.D. from the University of Waterloo. Her main research focus is on the impact of regulations, including auditing standards, on the information companies report and how people use that information, with a particular interest in environmental reporting. Her work has been published in several professional and academic journals.

Brief Contents

Contents

PART II

BASIC AUDITING CONCEPTS AND TECHNIQUES

PART III

PERFORMING THE AUDIT

PART IV

OTHER PROFESSIONAL SERVICES

Preface to the Fifth Edition

In this our fifth edition, we have updated the many professional developments that have taken place in the first decade of the 21st century. These include adoption of new Canadian Audit Standards (CASs), the further development of public accountability boards and their monitoring activities, and increasing emphasis on corporate governance, internal controls, risk-based auditing, independence, and quality controls. In this edition, we summarize these developments through mid-2009, offering our perspective on their significance. We refer to this dramatically altered corporate landscape as the "post-Enron audit environment."

In this new environment, we see not only radical changes in audit standards and the regulatory environment, but also significantly revised expectations of the auditor's role in corporate governance and capital markets. This environment is characterized by more risks for auditors and their clients than ever before, as well as more restrictions on non-audit services for audit clients. However, we find the broadening adoption of internationalized auditing standards in Canada and other countries opens the door on a exciting new era for the auditing profession. With a high quality globalized set of audit standards, developed by an international standards board, and based on codes of conduct that encompass ethical conduct and independence as key requirements, a new bar is set for quality in audit practice.

Fraud, corporate governance, independence risk, the role of audit committees, global convergence of audit and accounting standards, and information technology have all become more prominent since the fourth edition; consequently, all these issues have been updated for the fifth edition. As in past editions, we continue to provide thorough coverage of auditing at the conceptual and procedural levels. Overall, we hope that students come away with a well-rounded and forward-looking learning experience in the field of auditing, and a thorough introduction to the new Canadian Auditing Standards coming into effect for financial statements for periods ending on or after December 14, 2010. We hope this edition's coverage of the introduction of the new CAS in Canada may also be a helpful reference and resource during this transition stage in auditing practice.

WHAT'S NEW IN THE FIFTH EDITION

This fifth edition has been developed to make the learning experience enjoyable and straightforward for students, while still fostering essential critical thinking skills that challenge students as they learn. Key updates and ongoing approaches include:

- updated referencing to Canadian Auditing Standards (CASs) based on International Standards on Auditing (ISAs) as part of the process of international convergence of auditing standards
- extensive *CICA Handbook* changes through mid-2009 that incorporate a risk-based approach to auditing
- understanding the audit client's business, its operating environment, and risks
- assessing the risk of material misstatement in the financial statements on an assertion-by-assertion basis
- developing auditing objectives and gathering evidence with auditing procedures
- making judgments about the fair presentation of financial statement assertions

- a sequencing of topics placing professional, ethical, and legal responsibilities at the beginning of the text, and integration of the business risk-based auditing approach and information technology (IT) throughout

- an innovative introduction of critical-thinking concepts integrating ethical, accounting, as well as auditing theory to help structure professional audit decision making and analysis in financial reporting

- an introduction to the accounting risk concept as a way of helping implement critical thinking in audited financial reporting

- a pioneering chapter on fraud awareness, of which fraud detection procedures are integrated in the rest of the text

- strategic systems auditing, seen in previous editions, is now used throughout the text to help explain business risk and risk-based auditing

- information systems and information technology topics integrated with the coverage of internal control and control evaluation in audit planning

- comprehensive coverage of the assurance engagement concept as it applies now to internal auditing, audits of internal control, as well as to external and public sector auditing

- website appendices on the more technical aspects of statistical sampling in auditing, corporate governance, information technology, internal control, critical thinking, integrating auditing, accounting, and ethical reasoning

- various updated anecdotes, asides, short cases, and new application cases with suggested solutions at the end of each chapter that all enrich the text material

- several new critical-thinking and Internet assignment questions complement the preceding changes

KEY FEATURES

. . . .

CICA Handbook Assurance Recommendation Updates: Canadian Auditing Standards (CASs) and the Convergence to International Auditing

This edition provides complete referencing to CASs that go into effect for audits from December 14, 2010, on. It thus provides essential guidance for auditors in the 21st century and makes all previous Canadian audit texts largely obsolete. CASs introduce new fundamental concepts such as acceptable reporting frameworks in the form of compliance and fair presentation frameworks. CASs continue the incorporation of international standards started in earlier editions of this text. Since the last edition, the rigour and acceptability of International Standards on Auditing (ISAs) as issued by the International Federation of Accountants (IFAC) has continued to grow. This edition provides both CAS references (following the naming of the section titles as of July 2009) and the corresponding original CICA Handbook Assurance section references whenever these exist. The inside front cover provides a complete cross referencing between the new CASs and the Canadian Handbook assurance sections dealing with audits of financial statements. Students, and practitioners, may find this cross referencing summary useful for quick reference. At the time of writing (July 2009), the CICA plans to continue to use the old Handbook sections for other assurance engagements and association rules.

References to U.S. auditing standards, issued by the PCAOB for public companies and the AICPA for non-public companies, are also included when these are important in the Canadian environment. This brings students to the leading edge of auditing and responds to the increasing focus on international auditing and accounting standards in the real world of business management.

Risk-based Auditing

The major change in *CICA Handbook* Assurance Recommendations in the last edition was the introduction of *CICA Handbook*, sections 5141 and 5143, requiring a risk-based approach to auditing. These changes brought the CICA Assurance Recommendations closer to international auditing standards. This edition completes the transition to include the full set of CASs to be used in financial statement audits from December 14, 2010, on, including the new audit report format and the concept of acceptability of reporting frameworks. In addition, the risk-based audit approach builds on the idea of the strategic systems approach to auditing, developed in the 1990s, stressing that the auditor needs to understand the auditee's business as management runs it in order to conduct an effective audit. By formally placing these business risk assessment requirements into the standards, the CICA has linked these requirements more clearly to the generally accepted auditing standards (GAAS), which outline the required procedures and judgments supporting the auditor's opinion on whether the financial statements are materially misstated.

A novel feature of this edition is the introduction of the new concept of accounting risk. Accounting risks extend the risk-based approach to financial reporting issues. This approach provides a more complete explanation of auditee information risks, a clearer link between audit and accounting theory, and thus an improved basis for making operational the words "present fairly" in the audit report. Under our critical thinking approach auditing and accounting standards are increasingly viewed as an integrated framework. We believe that such or related approaches represent the future of 21st century audited financial reporting.

Fraud Auditing

This text was the first to contain full-chapter coverage of fraud awareness auditing, a crucial topic in the new millennium. With the rapid global growth in white-collar crime, especially that of fraudulent financial reporting, auditors have had to take more responsibility for fraud detection, particularly in the area of premature revenue recognition. The basic purpose of the fraud chapter (Chapter 17) is to create awareness of, and sensitivity to, the signs of potential errors, irregularities, frauds, and corruption. The chapter contains some unique insights on extended auditing, investigation procedures, and detection of fraudulent accounting estimates. In addition, fraud coverage is integrated throughout the text, consistent with the increased need for auditors to detect fraud.

Post-Enron Environment

A continuation from the previous edition, this perspective includes the changes to the auditing standards, the regulatory environment, and society's expectations, as well as an analysis of the significance of these changes. Specific post-Enron topics include: increased monitoring of the profession by accountability boards such as CPAB, increased emphasis on good corporate governance, the increased importance of audit committees, independence guidance, fraud risk assessments, the risk-based audit approach, increased liability due to statutory law, and increased risks associated with fair value estimates and accounting estimates in general.

Critical Thinking

The pioneering coverage of skepticism and logical argumentation in auditing has been expanded to the broader concept of critical thinking. Such an expanded approach to a more formalized skepticism incorporates assessments of the character of individuals with whom the auditor deals, the language used in the reasoning, as well as the logic of the reasoning. Such an approach to skepticism and ethical reasoning is increasingly important in detecting fraudulent financial reporting. Critical thinking provides an improved framework for tackling issues that require integration of ethical, accounting, as well as audit reasoning.

Critical-thinking concepts are first introduced in Chapter 2, and then are found integrated throughout the text where appropriate, as well as in new critical-thinking discussion and application case questions. The accounting risk concept is a major innovation in this edition to help make critical thinking more operational in a financial reporting setting.

Learning Aids

Each chapter and section in *Auditing: An International Approach* contains a number of pedagogical features that both enhance and support the learning experience. They include the following:

- **Learning Objectives.** Each chapter opens with a new presentation of pertinent learning objectives for the following chapter material. These are repeated as marginal notes throughout the chapters. In addition, all Exercises and Problems and Discussion Cases are cross-referenced to their corresponding Learning Objectives to assist student learning.
- **Professional Standards References.** Each chapter references the relevant professional standards for the chapter topics.
- **Anecdotes and Asides.** Illustrative anecdotes and asides are found throughout the text and have been updated considerably with this new edition. Some are located within the chapter text, while others stand alone (in boxes) to add realism and interest for students. The result is a real-world flavour to the treatment of auditing.
- **Exhibits.** To assist in the learning process, we have included several more exhibits in this edition to visually illustrate teaching concepts.
- **Icons for Critical Thinking, Fraud/Ethics, International Standards, and Internet Assignments.** For quick and easy identification purposes, we have included these icons to flag the text material dealing with these major issues.

Application Cases

Each chapter now has an application case at the end illustrating the application of concepts introduced in the chapter. The purpose of the application cases is to enliven the study of auditing by introducing the professional judgments involved in the practice of auditing. They replace a lengthy exposition of auditing fundamentals with illustrative situations based on real events. The application cases in the chapters of Parts II and III follow the experiences of a new auditor joining a firm of public accountants. Many of the application cases deal with what might be considered advanced material by many. Nevertheless they can serve as a useful basis for class discussion. The solutions provided are not the only ones possible.

Key Terms

Throughout the text, key terms are highlighted in boldface print. Understanding these terms is crucial to success in auditing; therefore, an alphabetical glossary is in the back of the text.

ORGANIZATION
. . . .

Part I—Introduction to Auditing and Public Practice

Part I consists of five chapters covering the basic orientation to auditing as a profession. Chapter 1 introduces the concept of auditing and the role of the public accounting profession. Chapter 2 introduces generally accepted auditing standards, assurance standards, and quality control standards, providing an overview of the audit process. Chapter 3 covers audit reports. Chapter 4 discusses professional ethics including a technical appendix on critical thinking. Chapter 5 covers professional legal responsibilities, including technical appendices on the effects of recent legislation.

Part II—Basic Auditing Concepts and Techniques

Part II is organized to present financial statement audit planning from a business risk perspective. Chapter 6 starts this off with a discussion of how auditors obtain an understanding of the auditee's business, its environment, and its risks, and how this knowledge is used to assess the risk that the financial statements are materially misstated. It explains the link from the business strategy to its business processes and the related accounting cycles that create the financial statements, the fundamental auditing concepts of materiality, and management's assertions contained in the financial statements. Chapter 7 presents the conceptual audit risk model used to plan the audit, and expands on the business understanding by describing the relation between the business strategy and its risks, the business processes in place to reduce these risks, including an overview of information systems controls used by management to reduce risks of materially misstating this information. Chapter 8 presents the fundamental concepts of audit evidence and the evidence-gathering procedures used to develop the detailed audit plan and programs, and describes working paper documentation. Chapter 9 elaborates on internal control consideration in an audit engagement, describing control risk assessment and control testing.

The topics presented in Chapters 6 to 9 provide a basis for developing an appropriate overall strategy for the audit, the detailed audit plan, and specific programs used to perform the audit. Chapter 10 covers the pervasive concept of audit testing, how testing is affected by the audit risk model, and how representative testing can be implemented using the most simple formulas and tables from statistical sampling. An extensive appendix to Chapter 10 provides more details on the technical aspects of statistical sampling, and is located in the Online Learning Centre. Application cases are used to provide practical perspectives on the planning issues covered in Part II.

Part III—Performing the Audit

Part III contains four chapters that address performing the work set out in a detailed audit plan for the main business processes that will need to be managed in every organization, and a fifth chapter that wraps it all up with audit completion considerations. The processes covered are as follows: the Revenues, Receivables, and Receipts Process (Chapter 11); the Purchases, Payables, and Payments Process (Chapter 12); the Production and Payroll Processes (Chapter 13); and the Finance and Investment Process (Chapter 14). Each of these chapters provides an overview of the transactions, balances, and risks of misstatement in the business process, the relevant controls, and auditing procedures. Application cases are used to illustrate the application of concepts and techniques in practice, and examples of audit programs are provided to demonstrate the kinds of audit procedures that can be used. Each of these chapters also provides an overview of the balance sheet approach as a basis for the overall analysis of the financial statements. Chapter 15 presents various activities involved in completing the audit work such as the audit of the revenue and expense accounts, overall analytical review, lawyer's letters, management representation letters, subsequent events, adjustments to the financial statements, and the auditor's formation of the opinion to be expressed in the audit report.

Part IV—Other Professional Services and Responsibilities

The two chapters in Part IV (Chapters 16 and 17) can stand alone or be integrated with the preceding chapters. Chapter 16 deals with other assurance and some non-assurance services offered by public accounting firms. Chapter 17 covers fraud awareness auditing in more detail. It gives students a better understanding of the mindset and specialized procedures needed to more effectively detect frauds. This chapter has benefited from our association with the Association of Certified Fraud Examiners. Chapter 18 of the 4th edition has been replaced by a new section in chapter 16 as part of the other assurance engagements coverage. It was decided that more thorough coverage of public sector auditing is best left for a different type of book. Note that Part IV and the advanced material of earlier chapters (often located on the Online Learning Centre) can be used to develop the core topics for advanced auditing courses, if preferred.

PROFESSIONAL STANDARDS

This text contains numerous references to authoritative statements on auditing standards and to standards governing other areas of practice. Even so, the text tries to avoid the mere repetition of passages from the standards, concentrating instead on explaining their substance and operational meaning in the context of making auditing decisions. Instructors and students may wish to supplement the text with current editions of pronouncements published by the International Federation of Accountants (IFAC), the Canadian Institute of Chartered Accountants (CICA), the Certified General Accountants Association of Canada (CGA-Canada), and the Institute of Internal Auditors (IIA).

INNOVATIVE TECHNOLOGY SOLUTIONS

Connect Accounting

McGraw-Hill Ryerson's **Connect Accounting** is a Web-based assignment and assessment platform that gives students the means to better connect with their coursework, with their instructors, and with the important concepts they will need to know for success now and in the future.

In partnership with Youthography, a Canadian youth research company, and hundreds of students from across Canada, McGraw-Hill Ryerson conducted extensive student research on student study habits, behaviours, and attitudes—we asked questions and listened . . . and we heard some things we didn't expect. We had two goals: to help faculty be more efficient in and out of the classroom by providing a study tool that would help them improve student engagement and to help students learn their course material and get better grades. Through this research, we gained a better understanding of how students study—and how we could make vast improvements to our current online study tools. The result is a study tool that students overwhelming said is *better* and there's *nothing else like it out there*. Included is:

Study Plan

An innovative tool that helps students customize their own learning experience. Students can diagnose their knowledge with a pre and post test, identify the areas where they are weak, search contents of the entire learning package for content specific to the topic they're studying and add these resources to their study plan. Students told us the act of creating a study plan is how they actually study and that having the opportunity to have everything in one place, with the ability to search, customize and prioritize the class resources, was critical. No other publisher provides this type of tool and students told us without a doubt, the "Study Plan" feature is the most valuable tool they have used to help them study.

eText

Now students can search the textbook online, too! When struggling with a concept or reviewing for an exam, students can conduct key word searches to quickly find the content they need

Homework Assessment

Connect Accounting assessment activities don't stop with students. Instructors can deliver assignments, quizzes, and tests online. They can edit existing questions and add new ones; track individual student performance—by question, assignment, or in relation to the class overall—with detailed grade reports; integrate grade reports easily with Learning Management Systems such as WebCT and Blackboard; and much more.

Connect really is the first study tool built by students for students. Getting better grades really is only a click away! Please contact your iLearning Sales Specialist for additional information on Connect Accounting.

Online Learning Centre

(**www.mcgrawhill.ca/olc/smieliauskas**): The Online Learning Centre serves as an extension of the text, providing additional content and self-study quizzing.

OTHER RESOURCES
. . . .

Instructor Resources:

The Instructor Area of the Online Learning Centre (www.mcgrawhill.ca/olc/smieliauskas) includes a variety of resources for faculty including:

- *Solutions Manual*— The solutions manual, created by the authors, provides the answers to problem and assignment material that is featured throughout the text.
- *Computerized Test Bank*—The Computerized Test Bank contains numerous multiple choice, short-answer, and essay questions.
- *Microsoft® PowerPoint® Slides*—The PowerPoint® Slides offer a summary of chapter concepts for lecture purposes.

CourseSmart

CourseSmart brings together thousands of textbooks across hundreds of courses in an e-textbook format providing unique benefits to students and faculty. By purchasing an e-textbook, students can save up to 50 percent off the cost of a print textbook, reduce their impact on the environment, and gain access to powerful Web tools for learning including full-text search, notes and highlighting, and e-mail tools for sharing notes between classmates. For faculty, CourseSmart provides instant access to review and compare textbooks and course materials in their discipline area without the time, cost, and environmental impact of mailing print exam copies. For further details contact your *i*Learning Sales Specialist or go to www.coursesmart.com.

iLearning Sales Specialist

Your Integrated Learning Sales Specialist is a McGraw-Hill Ryerson representative who has the experience, product knowledge, training, and support to help you assess and integrate any of the following products, technology, and services into your course for optimum teaching and learning performance. Whether it's helping your students improve their grades, or putting your entire course online, your *i*Learning Sales Specialist is there to help you do it. Contact your local *i*Learning Sales Specialist today to learn how to maximize all of McGraw-Hill Ryerson's resources!

ACKNOWLEDGEMENTS

. . . .

The International Federation of Accountants (IFAC), the Certified General Accountants Association of Canada (CGA-Canada), and the Canadian Institute of Chartered Accountants (CICA) have generously given permission for liberal quotations from official pronouncements and other publications, all of which lend authoritative sources to the text. In addition, several publishing houses, professional associations and accounting firms have granted permission to quote and extract from their copyrighted material. Their co-operation is much appreciated because a great amount of significant auditing thought exists in this wide variety of sources.

We are also very grateful to the staff at McGraw-Hill Ryerson who provided their support, management skills, and ideas—especially our editorial team, whose hard work and attention to detail kept us on track and transformed what we wrote into a book.

A special acknowledgement is due Joseph T. Wells, former chairman of the Association of Certified Fraud Examiners. He created the Certified Fraud Examiner (CFE) designation. Mr. Wells is a well-known authority in the field of fraud examination education and his entrepreneurial spirit has captured the interest of fraud examination professionals throughout North America.

Special acknowledgement is also due to Steven E. Salterio of Queen's University. Steven contributed greatly to the strategic systems approach to auditing used in this text. This text could not have been completed without the co-operation and input of our many auditing students over the years. Special thanks go to Enola Stoyle for material that was adapted in various forms in this text.

We are grateful to many people involved in the auditing profession in various roles who generously shared their time and ideas with us over the years as the new materials for the book took shape in our minds and on paper, including Jean Bédard, Janne Chung, Susan McCracken, Steve Fortin, Genviève Turcotte, John Carchrae, James Sylph Alan Willis, Robert Langford, Andre de Haan, Joy Keenan, Sylvia Smith, Dianne Hillier, Jan Munro, Greg Shields and the AASB staff, Karen Duggan, Rand Rowlands, Mark Davies, Mark Lam, and Vaani Maharaj. We would like to acknowledge our appreciation for the great academics and practitioners, who influenced us in various ways as we developed this text, including Ron Gage, Al Rosen, Randy Keller, Don Cockburn, Dagmar Rinne, Morley Lemon, Ingrid Splettstoesser-Hogeterp, Don Leslie, Larry Yarmolinsky, Bill Scott, Efrim Boritz, Joel Amernic, Donna Losell, Ulrich Menzefricke, Russell Craig, Kevin Lam, Yoshihide Toba, Takatoshi Hayashi, Ping Zhang, Hung Chan, Len Brooks, Manfred Schneider, and Irene Wiecek. Also, we have been inspired often by Rod Anderson's 1984 text, *The External Audit*, which set out a logical, conceptual framework for auditing that still stands the test of time.

And lastly, our sincere thanks go out to all the reviewers for their careful review and many detailed and candid comments that were extremely useful in revising this new edition:

Maria Belanger, Algonquin College

Olga Soukhovtseva, Carleton University

William Gough, Centennial College

Patrick Delaney, Concordia University

Sandra Robinson, Concordia University

Bruce MacLean, Dalhousie University

Don Hutton, Durham College

Susan Deakin, Fanshawe College

Rand Rowlands, George Brown College

Don Smith, Georgian College

Brad Sacho, Kwantlen University College

Joan Wallwork, Kwantlen University College
Ralph Cecere, McGill University
Susan McCracken, McMaster University
Peggy Coady, Memorial University of Newfoundland
Bill Waterman, Mount Allison University
Michael Malkoun, St. Clair College
Vincent Durant, St. Lawrence College
Dan Simunic, University of British Columbia
Douglas Yee, University of British Columbia
Janet Morrill, University of Manitoba
Chi Ho Ng, University of Ontario Institute of Technology
Merridee Bujaki, University of Ottawa
Manfred Schneider, University of Toronto
Linda Robinson, University of Waterloo
Janne Chung, York University

Wally Smieliauskas and Kate Bewley
July 2009

CHAPTER 1

Introduction to Auditing

Chapter 1 is an introduction to auditing, especially financial statement auditing. Other accounting courses helped you learn the principles and methods of accounting, but here you will begin to study the ways and means of auditing—the verification of accounting and other information.

LEARNING OBJECTIVES

After completing this chapter, you will be able to do the following:

1. Explain the importance of auditing.

2. Distinguish auditing from accounting.

3. Explain the role of auditing in information risk reduction.

4. Describe the current audit environment, including regulatory oversight.

5. Describe the other major types of audits and auditors.

6. Outline how public accountants (PAs) are regulated.

7. Provide an overview of international auditing and its impact on Canadian audit standards.

8. Apply and integrate the chapter topics to analyze a practical auditing situation/case/scenario.

9* Research websites on the accounting and auditing activities of PA organizations. (Appendix 1A)

10* Chronicle the historical development of auditing standards, including the criticisms and responses of the profession. (Appendix 1B)

11* Describe alternative theories of the role of auditing in society. (Appendix 1C)

* This is considered advanced material. Note: Appendices 1A, 1B, and 1C are located on this text's Online Learning Centre (OLC).

INTRODUCTION: THE CONCEPT OF AUDITING

LEARNING OBJECTIVE

1 Explain the importance of auditing.

Auditing is a field of study that has received considerable media attention lately. In the business press, audit-related issues are mentioned daily. Headlines such as "Auditors: The Leash Gets Shorter," "The Betrayed Investor," "Dirty Rotten Numbers," and "Accounting in Crisis" indicate that the attention has not all been positive. This reality arises from the fact that auditing is critical to the proper functioning of capital markets, and, if audits are perceived to fail, then capital markets can do the same. Without effective audits, modern capital markets cannot fulfill their role as efficient economic systems leading to high living standards. An example of an effective auditor is shown in the box below.

AN EFFECTIVE AUDITOR

Molex Incorporated is a $2.2 billion electronics manufacturer headquartered in Chicago. In late 2004 Molex's auditor, Deloitte & Touche, complained that CEO J. Joseph King and his chief financial officer had not disclosed that they allowed a bookkeeping error worth 1% of net income into the audited results. When the auditor demanded on Nov. 13 that King be removed from office, the board initially stood behind the CEO with a unanimous vote.

Then Deloitte did something unexpected: It quit. Two weeks later the firm wrote a blistering and detailed account of the affair for public disclosure at the SEC. That virtually assured that no auditor would work for Molex again as long as King was in charge. Within 10 days the directors had eaten crow: They ousted King, promised to hire a new director with financial expertise for their audit committee, and agreed to take training classes in proper financial reporting.

Source: "The Boss on the Sidelines," *BusinessWeek*, April 25, 2005, p. 94.

The preceding example illustrates the work of effective auditors in the new business environment of the early twenty-first century. In modern business, the role of auditing is so critical that references can be made to **audit societies**. In audit societies, economic activities (and other politically important ones) are extensively monitored to ensure market efficiency. In these societies, auditors also monitor the effectiveness and efficiency of government. For example, the political uproar surrounding Canada's Gomery commission inquiry (www.gomery.ca) in 2005 was the result of an audit of questionable sponsorship payments that yielded "no value" for taxpayer money spent. As a result of this and similar events, auditing is increasingly recognized as part of a broader process of social control. This expanding role is at the heart of the audit society concept.[1]

But what is auditing, exactly? Simply put, **auditing** is the verification of information by someone other than the one providing it. Since there are many types of information, there are many types of audits. Most of this text focuses on audits of financial statement information, or *financial statement auditing* for short. Before describing auditing in more detail, we will try to make financial statement auditing more intuitive through a simple illustration.

A Simple Illustration of the Importance of Auditing

Assume you have always wanted to run your own business, say, a Thai food restaurant. After some searching, you find an owner who wants to retire and is willing to sell his

---

[1] M. P. Power, *The Audit Society* (New York: Oxford University Press, 1997).

busy restaurant in a choice location of a major metropolitan area for $3 million. One of the first things you ask yourself is whether the business is worth the $3 million asking price. How can you answer that?

You could find out the price of similar properties—comparison shop. But, ultimately, you must decide on the value of this particular business. Accounting information is useful in answering these types of questions: What is the business's net worth (Assets – Liabilities)? What is its profitability?

The owner of the restaurant may claim annual profits of $600,000. First, you want to reach an agreement on how that profit is calculated: on a cash basis? before tax? after tax? under generally accepted accounting principles? Those are the criteria you might use in measuring the profitability (earnings) of the business.

Having decided on the criteria for measurement, you need to use a decision rule with your measurement. Businesses are frequently valued on some multiple of earnings. For example, if you are willing to pay five times current earnings (calculated using your agreed criteria) and the current owner reports $600,000 in earnings annually, you would be paying five times $600,000 or $3 million for the business. You need accounting information to establish that $600,000 is the current earnings number.

But the owner prepares the accounting records. How do you know they are accurate? There may be errors or, worse, the owner might inflate earnings to get a higher price than the business is worth. For example, if the owner is overstating the earnings and they are only $500,000, the most the business is worth to you is five times $500,000, or $2.5 million rather than $3 million. In other words, you are concerned about the risk of overpaying for your investment.

What can you do to minimize this risk and give yourself assurance? Hire an auditor! The auditor can help you by verifying that the $600,000 figure reported by the current owner is accurate. The earnings can be on whatever basis you agree to, usually **generally accepted accounting principles (GAAP)**. The auditor can independently and competently verify the earnings so that you will have more confidence (assurance) in the numbers you base your decision on. The auditor increases the reliability, or reduces the risk, of using inaccurate information in your decision making. For example, if the auditor finds that earnings are really $400,000, you would be unwilling to pay more than five times $400,000 or $2 million for the restaurant. The difference between the original asking price ($3 million) and what you should actually pay ($2 million) is the value of the audit—in this case $1 million. If the audit fee is under $1 million you would, therefore, be better off having an audit.

This simplified example illustrates the value of auditing in investment decision making. But it also shows how auditing can provide other, more general, social services. For example, the restaurant owner can retire with a fair price for his business, and you can achieve your dreams of owning a restaurant and being your own boss. These are accomplished by using a fair exchange price based on reliable (accurate, trustworthy) information.

The transaction entries that you learn in your accounting courses are part of the raw data auditors deal with. The summarization of all the transactions over a period is achieved through the financial statements. When auditors verify the reliability of this information, they reduce the **information risk** associated with the financial statements. Now, imagine this illustration extended to all investors contemplating even partial ownership of a business—for example, investors in the stock market—and you will have some idea of how auditing can facilitate efficient economic activities by reducing financial information risk. And when auditors fail to do a proper job of verification (i.e., fail to reduce information risk), the type of headlines noted at the beginning of this section can result.

When you make an investment, you agree to enter into a contract to purchase from another party. The auditor can be called the first party and the seller the second party. Notice, however, that there is a third party—you the investor. The auditor is an independent party hired to verify information provided by the second party. The auditor is hired because you, the third party, do not trust the information provided by the second party. You feel the information risk is too high; therefore, the first party will provide you with independent verification. We refer to this relationship throughout the text as **three-party accountability**.

In an audit society, three-party accountability is so institutionalized that regulators require certain second parties to pay for the audit. In particular, companies whose shares are traded on regulated stock exchanges (public companies) are required to hire an independent auditor to verify the annual financial statements. The accountability is still three party, because the audit's purpose is to reduce information risk for the third party, but the public company second party pays the audit fee. It is important to note that three-party accountability is not determined by who pays the fee.

Exhibit 1–1 indicates how three-party accountability applies to the Molex and Thai restaurant examples. In the Exhibit, accountability is represented as a triangle with the auditor of the financial information, the management preparing the financial information, and the users of the financial information at the apexes. The triangle reflects an **accountability relationship** because management is accountable to the users. However, the users cannot rely on the financial statements as they do not trust management sufficiently; they demand that the financial statements be verified by a competent, independent auditor. Thus, the auditor is also accountable to the user. Three-party accountability is an important distinguishing feature of auditing.

Note that the concept of three-party accountability means that the auditor is expected to act in the interests of the user of the financial statements. If the owner of the Thai restaurant gives you an audited set of financial statements, you are entitled to assume that the auditor has not misled you. This is an important point, because, if you could not assume the auditor is trustworthy, the relevance of the audit would largely disappear, leaving little if any role for the audit in society. Thus, it is extremely important to the audit profession that the auditor be perceived as acting in the interest of the financial statement users, also referred to as **acting in the public interest**. Later in this text, you will see how the public interest is reflected in the objectives of the audit engagement, in auditors' legal liability, and in the professional rules of conduct that determine the auditor's professional role.

Three-party accountability is also important because it distinguishes the type of services that only licensed practitioners can provide (in some parts of Canada) from other services, such as tax work and business advisory services that anyone can provide. Audits are part of a broader class of services called *assurance engagements* that are licensed to professionals (in some parts of Canada). Three-party accountability applies to all assurance engagements. We will clarify these important concepts throughout the rest of the text, especially in Chapters 2 and 16. For now, think of three-party accountability as reducing the risk on information created by the second party, the preparer of the information.

EXHIBIT 1–1   THREE PARTIES INVOLVED IN AN AUDITING ENGAGEMENT (THREE-PARTY ACCOUNTABILITY)

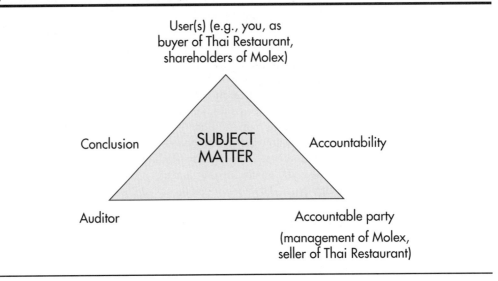

Reducing information risk is synonymous with improving the credibility of, or providing assurance on, information produced by the second party.

We hope you have found the preceding illustrations useful. Next, we further clarify the roles of accounting and auditing in the financial reporting environment.

USER DEMAND FOR RELIABLE INFORMATION

Accounting

LEARNING OBJECTIVE
2 Distinguish auditing from accounting.

The following three underlying conditions affect users' demand for accounting information:

1. *Complexity.* A company's transactions can be numerous and complicated. Users of financial information are not trained to collect and compile it themselves. They need the services of professional accountants.

2. *Remoteness.* Users of financial information are usually separated from a company's accounting records by distance and time, as well as by lack of expertise. They need to employ full-time professional accountants to do the work they cannot do for themselves.

3. *Consequences.* Financial decisions are important to the state of investors' and other users' wealth. Decisions can involve large dollar amounts and massive efforts. The consequences are so important that good information, obtained through the financial reports prepared by accountants, is an absolute necessity.

Accounting is the process of recording, classifying, and summarizing into financial statements a company's transactions that create assets, liabilities, equities, revenues, and expenses. It is the means of satisfying users' demands for financial information that arise from the forces of complexity, remoteness, and consequences. The function of **financial reporting** is to provide statements of financial position (balance sheets), statements of results of operations (income statements), cash flows statements, and accompanying disclosure notes (footnotes) to outside decision makers. A company's accountants are the producers of such financial reports. In short, accounting tries to record and summarize economic reality for the benefit of economic decision makers (the users).

Because of advances in **information technology (IT)**, the form in which accounting records are stored has changed dramatically over the past few decades. Although these changes have affected the form of audit evidence, the basic role of verification for users and their decision-making needs has not changed.

The goal of generally accepted accounting principles (GAAP), which you study in your financial accounting courses, is to yield financial statements that represent as faithfully as possible the economic conditions and performance of a company. This is why GAAP are the most common criteria used in preparing financial statements. However, as illustrated in the introduction, auditors are independent financial reporting experts who are frequently asked to verify that these goals are met.

REVIEW CHECKPOINTS

1 Explain how the auditor can help you in your investment decision making.

More on Auditing

Financial decision makers usually obtain their accounting information from companies wanting loans or selling stock. This is a potential **conflict of interest**, a condition that leads to society's demand for audit services. Users need more than just information; they need reliable, error-free information. Preparers and issuers (directors, managers, accountants, and others employed in a business) might benefit from giving false, misleading, or overly optimistic information. The potential conflict is real enough to generate a natural skepticism on the part of users. Thus, users depend on **external professional auditors** to serve as objective intermediaries and to lend some credibility to financial information. This "lending of credibility" is also known as **providing assurance**, and external auditing of financial statements is described as an **assurance engagement**.

Auditing does not include financial report production. That function is performed by a company's accountants under the direction of management. Auditors determine whether the information in the financial statements is reliable, and they communicate this conclusion to the users by reporting that the company's presentation of financial position, results of operations, and cash flows statement are in accordance with GAAP, or some other disclosed basis of accounting. This is the assurance provided by the assurance function, as it relates to the traditional financial statements. Assurance always requires three-party accountability, as discussed previously. To achieve three-party accountability, auditors must not be involved in production of the information audited. Such **external auditors** can provide a range of services in addition to audits, causing them to be referred to frequently as **public accounting (PA) firms.**

External auditors work for clients. A **client** is the person (company, board of directors, agency, or some other person or group) who retains the auditor and pays the fee. In financial statement audits, the client and the auditee are usually the same economic entity. The **auditee** is the company or entity whose financial statements are being audited. Occasionally, the client and the auditee are different entities. For example, if Conglomerate Corporation hires and pays the auditors to audit Newtek Company in connection with a proposed acquisition, Conglomerate is the client and Newtek is the auditee.

As explained previously, reliable financial information helps make capital markets efficient and helps people understand the consequences of a wide variety of economic decisions. External auditors practicing the assurance function are not, however, the only auditors at work in the economy. Bank examiners, Canada Revenue Agency auditors, provincial regulatory agency auditors (e.g., auditors with a province's Commissioner of Insurance), internal auditors employed by a company, and the Office of the Auditor General of Canada (or a provincial equivalent) all practise auditing in one form or another. There are many acronyms associated with various auditing associations and auditors. The acronyms are part of the jargon of the profession.

Professional judgment is a widely used concept in accounting and auditing. It is defined in CAS 200 as "the application of relevant training, knowledge, and experience, within the context provided by auditing, accounting, and ethical standards, in making informed decisions about the courses of action that are appropriate in the circumstances of the audit engagement." Professional judgment includes consideration of key principles and concepts of disciplines underlying the professional standards, such as economics, psychology, law, finance, statistics, philosophy, and other social sciences. This integration of diverse areas helps explain why a university education is now required of external auditors. Specialized concepts and language integrate the disciplines in order to provide appropriate justification for audit decisions. We refer to the basic concepts and principles of justification as **critical thinking**. Critical thinking concepts are covered in some of the more difficult exercises throughout the book, and aspects of it are applied in cases analyzed at the end of most chapters.

REVIEW CHECKPOINTS

2 What is auditing? What condition creates demand for audits of financial reports?

3 What is the difference between a client and an auditee? What are the three parties in three-party accountability?

4 What is the difference between auditing and accounting?

5 What conditions create demand for financial reports, and who produces financial reports for external users?

DEFINITIONS OF AUDITING

. . . .

Definitions of Auditing

In 1971, the American Accounting Association (AAA) Committee on Basic Auditing Concepts prepared a comprehensive definition of auditing as follows:

> Auditing is a systematic process of objectively obtaining and evaluating evidence regarding assertions about economic actions and events to ascertain the degree of correspondence between the assertions and established criteria and communicating the results to interested users.

This definition contains several ideas important in a wide variety of audit practices. The first and most important concept is the perception of auditing as a systematic process that is purposeful, logical, and based on the discipline of a structured approach to decision making. Auditing is not haphazard, unplanned, or unstructured.

The audit process, according to this definition, involves obtaining and evaluating evidence consisting of all the influences that ultimately guide auditors' decisions, and it relates to assertions about economic actions and events. When beginning an audit engagement, an external auditor receives financial statements and other disclosures by management that are management's assertions about economic actions and events (assets, liabilities, revenues, expenses). Evidence is then gathered to either substantiate or contradict these management assertions.

External auditors generally begin work with explicit representations from management—assertions of financial statement numbers and information disclosed in the notes to the financial statements. When these assertions are made explicit in writing by the accountable party (the asserter), the resulting audit engagement is referred to as an **attest engagement**. Financial statements are an example of written assertions, and thus the audit of financial statements is an attest engagement. Not all auditors are provided with such explicit representations. An internal auditor, for example, may be assigned to evaluate the cost-effectiveness of the company's policy to lease rather than purchase equipment. A governmental auditor may be assigned to determine whether the goal of creating an environmental protection agency has been met by the agency's activities. Often, these latter types of auditors must develop the explicit standards of performance for themselves. This type of engagement is called **direct reporting**.

The purpose of obtaining and evaluating evidence is to determine the degree of correspondence between the assertions and the established criteria. The findings will ultimately be communicated to interested users. To communicate in an efficient and understandable manner, there must be a common basis, or established criteria, for measuring and describing financial information. These established criteria appear in a variety of sources. For external auditors, government auditors, and Canada Revenue Agency inspectors, the criteria largely consist of the GAAP. Canada Revenue Agency inspectors also rely heavily on criteria specified in federal tax acts. Government auditors may rely on criteria established in legislation or regulatory agency rules. Bank examiners and provincial insurance board auditors look to definitions and rules of law. Internal and governmental auditors rely extensively on financial and managerial models of efficiency and economy, as well as on GAAP. All auditors rely to some extent on the elusive criteria of general truth and fairness.

Exhibit 1–2 (page 8) depicts an overview of financial statement auditing.

Audit Objective and the Auditor's Report

The AAA definition of accounting is broad and general enough to encompass external, internal, and governmental auditing. The **Canadian Institute of Chartered Accountants (CICA)** sets forth the main objective of a financial audit as follows:

EXHIBIT 1-2   OVERVIEW OF FINANCIAL STATEMENT AUDITING

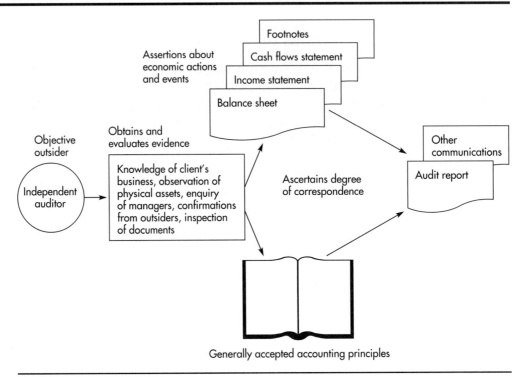

The objective of the audit of financial statements is to enable the auditor to express an opinion whether the financial statements are prepared, in all material respects, in accordance with an applicable financial reporting framework.[2]

The CICA statement of objective restricts auditing interest to external auditors' audit of the traditional financial statements and accompanying notes. However, as the needs of users change, new audit objectives and reports are created to meet them. Thus, the *CICA Handbook* also offers guidance on such divergent topics as reporting on control procedures at service organizations, solvency issues, and examining a financial forecast in a prospectus. A set of evolving "assurance standards" (presented in Chapter 2) provides a framework governing a wide range of assurance services, including audit services. These expanding standards indicate a corresponding demand for new types of audits and an expanded social role for auditing. This is consistent with an evolving audit society. Historically, the demand for an expanded role for auditing has grown faster than standard setters' ability to meet these public expectations. As a result, an **expectations gap** has developed between what the public expects of auditors and what auditors can actually deliver. For example, historically, the public has expected auditors to take on more responsibility for fraud detection than the standards required.

The auditor's opinion on financial statements is expressed in the last paragraph of the audit report. A standard report is shown in Exhibit 1–3. (Chapter 3 explains this and other audit reports in more detail.)

In this book, we refer to a **Canadian Audit Standard** as **CAS.** Unless otherwise indicated, the equivalent International Standard on Auditing (ISA) is the same number as the CAS number. For example, CAS 700 and ISA 700 refer to the same standard, except for some minor variations explained later. We refer to each CAS by the number associated with it, and give the equivalent, original *CICA Handbook* Recommendation number in parentheses. For example, CAS 700 is the equivalent of the original Recommendation 5400 so we present it as CAS 700 (5400).

---

[2] Canadian Audit Standard (CAS) 200, "General Objective of the Independent Auditor." The Canadian Audit Standards of the *CICA Handbook* are the authoritative CICA pronouncements on auditing theory and practice.

EXHIBIT 1-3   INDEPENDENT AUDITOR'S REPORT

To the Shareholders of.............

Report on the Financial Statements

We have audited the accompanying financial statements of ABC Company, which comprise the balance sheet as at December 31, 20X1, and the income statement, statement of changes in equity and cash flows statement for the year then ended, and a summary of significant accounting policies and other explanatory notes.

Management's Responsibility for the Financial Statements

Management is responsible for the preparation and fair presentation of these financial statements in accordance with Canadian generally accepted accounting principles; this includes the design, implementation, and maintenance of internal control relevant to the preparation and fair presentation of financial statements that are free from material misstatement, whether due to fraud or error.

Auditor's Responsibility

Our responsibility is to express an opinion on these financial statements based on our audit. We conducted our audit in accordance with Canadian generally accepted auditing standards. Those standards require that we comply with ethical requirements and plan and perform the audit to obtain reasonable assurance whether the financial statements are free from material misstatement.

An audit involves performing procedures to obtain audit evidence about the amounts and disclosures in the financial statements. The procedures selected depend on the auditor's judgment, including the assessment of the risks of material misstatement of the financial statements, whether due to fraud or error. In making those risk assessments, the auditor considers internal control relevant to the entity's preparation and fair presentation of the financial statements in order to design audit procedures that are appropriate in the circumstances, but not for the purpose of expressing an opinion on the effectiveness of the entity's internal control. An audit also includes evaluating the appropriateness of accounting policies used and the reasonableness of accounting estimates made by management, as well as evaluating the overall presentation of financial statements.

We believe that the audit evidence we have obtained is sufficient and appropriate to provide a basis for our audit opinion.

Opinion

In our opinion, the financial statements present fairly, in all material respects, the financial position of ABC Company as of December 31, 20X1, and of its financial performance and its cash flows for the year then ended in accordance with Canadian generally accepted accounting principles.

[Auditor's signature]

[Date of auditor's report]

[Auditor's address]

Source: © CAS 700.

A Definition of Auditing Relating to "Risk Reduction"

LEARNING OBJECTIVE

③ Explain the role of auditing in information risk reduction.

Although it is sometimes difficult to distinguish between a definition and a theory, most statements of theory begin with a definition. The theory that auditing is a "risk-reduction activity" is gaining popularity, and the following definition supports this view:

> Auditing in financial reporting is a process of reducing (to a socially acceptable level) the information risk to users of financial statements.

Economic activity takes place in an atmosphere of **business risk**. Business risks result from significant conditions, events, circumstances, or actions that might adversely affect the entity's ability to achieve its objectives and execute its strategies. Auditors do not directly influence a company's business risk, but they are responsible for ensuring proper disclosure of these risks by the auditee in the financial statements. As the business world becomes more complex, auditors are finding that they must increasingly focus on understanding the client's business risks in order to judge whether the financial statements reflect them properly. It is emphasized in auditing that risk is an important part of economic substance that should be reflected in financial reporting. A good illustration of the effects of business risks related to the economic crisis that began in 2008 is given in the box on page 10.

ACCOUNTING BLAMED FOR GLOBAL CREDIT CRISIS

Wall Street executives and lobbyists say they know what helped push the nation's largest financial institutions over the edge in recent months. The culprit, they say, is accounting.

Companies including American International Group Inc., the insurer that accepted $85 billion in a U.S. takeover, have said the rule by the U.S. Financial Accounting Standards Board requires them to record losses they don't expect to incur. Financial service companies have reported more than $520 billion in write-downs and credit losses since last year. Supporters of the rule say companies seeking the exemption are citing fair value as a way to cover their poor performance.

Fair value "is an accounting issue that's too important to be left just to accountants," former SEC Chairman Harvey Pitt said in an interview today. Economists, academics and regulators from outside FASB, in addition to accountants, should be involved in considering a new approach to fair value, he said.

"What the banks are telling everyone is that the accounting has caused the problem," former SEC chief accountant Lynn Turner said. "The only thing fair-value accounting did is force you to tell investors you made a bunch of very bad loans."

". . . The banking lobby is also confusing the role of accounts. These should simply be a true and fair record of management's stewardship of the business. How the owners, regulators, and tax authorities that read accounts choose to interpret them is their choice. Complaining about what the accounts show, when we're talking about a system supported by such users of accounts as investors and regulators, is akin to blaming a torch for shining a light on the mess in your cupboard."

As an example of recent accounting challenges, analysts cite Merrill Lynch's sale of $30.6 billion of collateralized debt obligations, or pools of mortgage-linked assets, to the investment company Lone Star Funds for only 22 cents on the dollar in July. Jessica Oppenheim, a spokeswoman for Merrill, which this month agreed to be purchased by Bank of America, declined to comment.

Advocates for leading financial institutions, including the Financial Services Roundtable and the American Bankers Association, have been raising the issue with government officials in Washington and New York for months. Arizona Sen. John McCain, the GOP presidential candidate, mentioned fair-value accounting as a problem in a recent stump speech.

Lobbyists have been seeking temporary relief from the accounting measure, which they say establishes bargain-basement prices for assets that would be valued far higher during more normal trading conditions. The events of last week raised fresh concerns among industry executives who fear that investments sold to the government as part of the $700 billion bailout plan will set a bargain-basement precedent for the rest of the market.

Banks also have been fighting their auditors, some of which have reasoned that downmarket conditions have persisted for so long that assets are no longer "temporarily impaired" but now require write-downs and capital infusions. Banking trade association officials are scheduled to meet with SEC regulators this week to discuss the issue, which could prompt some banks to attract new capital to meet regulatory requirements.

"The accounting rules and their implications have made this crisis much, much worse than it needed to be," said Ed Yingling, president of the bankers' association. "Instead of measuring the flame, they're pouring fuel on the fire."

Source: Excerpts from *Washington Post*, Sept. 23, 2008: D01 (Carrie Johnson); Bloomberg.com, Ian Katz, Sept. 23, 2008; and jennifer.hughes@ft.com, www.ft.com/accountancy, *The Financial Times* Limited, 2008.

Information risk refers to the possible failure of financial statements to appropriately reflect the economic substance of business activities, including risks and uncertainties. It thus includes failure to properly disclose business risk. For example, if a company fails to disclose that it plans to file for bankruptcy, the risk of bankruptcy is a business risk, and failure to disclose it is an information risk. Note that information risk is influenced by the evidence of bankruptcy gathered by the auditor and by the rules (i.e., GAAP) for appropriately disclosing this.

Information risk from the auditor's perspective is the risk (probability) that the financial statements distributed by a company will be materially false and misleading. **Materiality**, as used in auditing, means the same thing as it does in your accounting courses. Basically, a material misstatement is one that would affect user decision making.

Financial analysts and investors depend on financial reports for stock purchase and sale decisions; creditors (suppliers, banks, and so on) use them to decide whether to give trade credit and bank loans; labour organizations use them to help determine a company's ability to pay wages; and government agencies and Parliament use them in preparing analyses of the economy and making laws concerning taxes, subsidies, and the like. All these users cannot determine whether financial reports are reliable and, therefore, low on the information risk scale. They do not have the expertise, resources, or time to enter thousands of companies to satisfy themselves about the veracity of financial reports. Auditors assume the social role of attesting to published financial information, offering users the valuable service of assurance that the information risk is low. This role of auditors has been institutionalized through laws and regulations.

It is important to be aware that, from the auditor's perspective, there are two major categories of information risk. One is the risk of insufficient evidence being gathered on the facts concerning the client's (auditee's) economic circumstances. This is referred to as **audit risk**. The other category is the risk that errors associated with forecasts used in GAAP accounting estimates are not properly disclosed. We refer to this second category of information risk as **accounting risk**. Forecasts are a distinguishing feature of GAAP and are what separate GAAP accounting from cash basis accounting. Accounting risk is primarily the responsibility of accounting standards. However, while the term audit risk is a key part of auditing standards, accounting risk is dealt with only indirectly in accounting standards. You likely did not encounter the accounting risk concept in your financial accounting courses because accounting theory is not as risk oriented as auditing theory currently is. This makes controlling information risk in financial reporting a major challenge for auditors. The accounting risk concept used in this book addresses this challenge.

The risk-reduction definition may appear very general. As your study of auditing continues, you will find that the primary objective of many auditing tasks is reducing the risk of giving an inappropriate opinion on financial statements. Auditors are careful to work for trustworthy clients, to gather and analyze evidence about the data in financial statements, and to take steps to ensure audit personnel report properly on the statements when adverse information is known. Subsequent chapters will have more to say about these activities. We begin the process with the Application Case and Analysis discussion at the end of this chapter.

REVIEW CHECKPOINTS

6 What would you say if asked by an anthropology major, "What do auditors do?"

7 What is the essence of the risk-reduction definition of auditing?

THE CURRENT ENVIRONMENT OF AUDITING

· · · · · · · · · · · · · · · ·

LEARNING OBJECTIVE

4 Describe the current audit environment, including regulatory oversight.

The audit environment has undergone profound changes as a result of spectacular corporate failures, such as Enron and WorldCom, starting in 2001. This process of rapid change is continuing with the economic crisis of 2008/2009. The integrity of capital markets is being questioned all over the world. WorldCom's failure in 2002 led to the passage of the most drastic legislation affecting the accounting profession since 1933. This section briefly summarizes these changes in the current audit environment. Later chapters explain the significance of these changes in more detail, and Appendix 1B on the text's Online Learning Centre provides a brief overview of the history of the profession leading up to them.

The Sarbanes-Oxley Act

On July 30, 2002, President Bush signed the *Sarbanes-Oxley Act* (SOX) into law. This legislation began its progress through Congress after the fall of Enron, and the WorldCom failure catalyzed the legislative process and guaranteed quick passage and approval by Bush. For auditors of public companies, SOX created a five-member **Public Company Accounting Oversight Board (PCAOB)** with the authority to tighten quality control of audit practices and report on the results of inspections of audit firm practices. Key features of SOX include the following:

- increased oversight of auditors, including audit standard setting by PCAOB
- increased penalties for corporate wrongdoers
- more timely and extensive financial disclosures
- more timely and extensive disclosure on the way the firm is governed
- new options of recourse for aggrieved shareholders, including increased legal liability for auditors

Canadian companies listed on the American stock exchanges, as well as their auditors, are subject to these SOX rules. SOX and the financial disasters that preceded it have had a huge impact on corporate governance and the regulation of accounting and auditing around the world. For example, in Canada, the CICA helped organize the creation of its own **Canadian Public Accountability Board (CPAB)** to oversee the auditors of public companies. The CPAB also tightens quality control of audit practice and reports on inspections of audit firm practices. In addition, several of Canada's largest pension and mutual funds banded together in 2002 to form the **Canadian Coalition for Good Governance**. This organization controls $400 billion in assets and monitors executives, audit committees, auditors, and boards of directors in corporate Canada for compliance with what they consider good corporate governance and financial reporting practices. However, in Canada, for the time being at least, the profession continues to be self-regulating. Through SOX, in the United States, the profession is more constrained under the PCAOB.

The PCAOB's composition was finalized in April 2003. Its first actions included the following: (1) conducting an inspection of the Big Four accounting firms, (2) creating a registry system for **PA** firms, (3) conducting a review of existing audit standards, and, most importantly, (4) taking on the task of setting future audit standards in the United States. The last action is noteworthy as it represents the first time American auditing standards are not set by its professional institute, the **American Institute of Certified Public Accountants (AICPA)**. The AICPA, however, still sets audit standards for non-public companies whose shares are not traded on the stock markets.

The corporate failures, the fall of Arthur Andersen, and the resulting passage of SOX dramatically changed the corporate environment. We refer to this changed world as the **post-Enron world**. The PCAOB's actions reflect the dramatically increased regulation of the profession. The Canadian, American, and other accountability boards around the world will likely make this second-guessing of professional judgment a fixture of the post-Enron world. That world is now more complicated for auditors and the profession, and the implications will become more clear as it unfolds. However, auditing will likely become more important to accounting firms and to society. Specific effects evident through 2009 are included in this text.

Until 2002, the accounting profession was largely self-regulating. By **self-regulation** we mean the profession itself established the rules governing audit practice and monitored compliance with them. This reliance on self-regulation changed with the perceived failure of the profession to detect the problems leading to the corporate scandals of 2002/2003. The crucial role of auditing in well-functioning capital markets became clear as never before.

But this increased attention came at a price: the extensive impact on the markets of the profession's perceived failures means it is no longer acceptable to leave monitoring of the profession to the professionals themselves. The stock markets hit multi-year lows in 2002, coinciding with WorldCom's bankruptcy and resultant speedy passage of the SOX legislation with its increased external monitoring and control of the profession. The monitoring process now involves groups representing the broader public interest as well as the government, but the exact mix of monitors depends on the country. Since most of the corporate failures prompting the changes took place in the United States, America tends to lead in promoting new ways of providing oversight of auditors, and the instrument of the changes is SOX.

SOX's impact can be seen throughout the world, but it also had consequences for broader areas of corporate activities. Following is a quick overview of its main impact on auditors:

- management certification of all its publicly issued financial information
- evaluation of internal control in statements made by management
- closer regulation of the profession, including regular monitoring of its activities
- greater responsibilities assigned to client audit committees
- increased importance of the role of the internal auditor

Internal control statements deal with the reliability of the system or process that creates the financial statements.[3] **Audit committees** monitor management's financial reporting responsibilities, including meeting with the external auditors and dealing with various audit and accounting matters that may arise during an audit. We will discuss audit committees and the evolving concept of internal control in much greater detail throughout the rest of this text.

Perhaps the most important result of SOX for the auditor has been the increased monitoring of the profession, in the form of accountability boards. The board in Canada has authority and responsibilities that are quite different from those of its American counterpart, as the legal systems and political institutions of the two countries are quite different.

In the United States, the PCAOB has nationwide legislative backing for its monitoring and enforcement activities. PCAOB has final authority on auditing, ethical, and independence standards, as well as on the quality control criteria that will be used to monitor the profession. Detailed monitoring reports identifying specific audit firms are available to the public at www.pcaob.org/inspection.

In Canada, on the other hand, the CPAB does *not* have legislative backing. This means that if an accounting firm claims the legal privilege of client confidentiality, the CPAB cannot review those client documents. This constrains the CPAB's monitoring activities. Also, the CPAB is directly funded by the audit firms, leading to questions about its independence from the profession itself. In contrast, the PCAOB is directly funded by the Securities and Exchange Commission (SEC). Finally, the CPAB uses the profession's auditing, ethics, independence, and quality control standards in performing its monitoring. However, like the PCAOB, the CPAB issues reports on its monitoring that are made public at www.cpab-ccrc.org.

The first two consequences of SOX identified above relate to management's increased responsibility for financial reporting and the requirement of an external audit of management's internal control statement. Management's certification of financial reporting

---

[3] We deviate from official terminology by always referring to "reports" as auditor-prepared and "statements" as management-prepared communications.

means that it must state in writing that it is not aware of any factual errors or omissions of facts that would make the financial and internal control statements misleading. These are all best summarized as attempts to strengthen the system of corporate governance. **Corporate governance** describes how well a company is run in the interests of shareholders and other stakeholders. Corporate governance principles are covered in Appendix 7F. Audit committees and internal auditing are also covered in more detail later.

Canadian regulations, especially those in Ontario, have been influenced by the SOX requirements. There is now greater emphasis on more timely disclosures of material information and more disclosure of corporate governance practices. Management is now required to disclose its conclusions about the effectiveness of internal control in the management discussion and analysis (MD&A) section of the annual report. In Canada it is not required that this disclosure on internal control be audited. In contrast, the SEC requires audits of internal control disclosures by registrant companies. In Ontario, the Toronto Stock Exchange (TSX) companies do not need to follow best corporate governance practices, but failure to do so by the largest companies must be disclosed. The Ontario Securities Commission (OSC) specifies the duties and authority of audit committees, including providing a definition of independence of its members.

· ·

R E V I E W
C H E C K P O I N T S

8   What is meant by self-regulation? How is self-regulation for the profession being affected in the post-Enron environment?

9   What are the differences between Canadian and U.S. accountability boards? Compare the differences in their monitoring reports. Which ones do you think are better?

· ·

OTHER KINDS OF AUDITS AND AUDITORS

· · · · · · · · · · · · · · ·

LEARNING OBJECTIVE

5 Describe the other major types of audits and auditors.

The AAA, the CICA, and the risk-reduction definitions apply to the financial statement audit practice of independent external auditors who practice in public accounting firms. The word *audit*, however, is used in other contexts to describe broader kinds of work.

The variety of audit work performed by different kinds of auditors causes problems with terminology. Hereafter in this text, the terms independent auditor, external auditor, **chartered accountant (CA)**, **certified general accountant (CGA)**, and **public accountant (PA)** refer to people doing audit work with public accounting firms. In governmental and internal contexts, auditors are identified as governmental auditors, operational auditors, and internal auditors. While many of these are chartered accountants or certified general accountants, in this text the initials PA, CA, and CGA will refer to auditors in public practice. We will use the neutral term PA as much as possible.

Internal and Operational Auditing

The **Institute of Internal Auditors (IIA)** defines **internal auditing** and its purpose as follows:

> Internal auditing is an independent, objective assurance and consulting activity designed to add value and improve an organization's operations. It helps an organization accomplish its objectives by bringing a systematic, disciplined approach to evaluate and improve the effectiveness of risk management, control, and governance processes.[4]

Internal auditing is practiced by auditors employed by organizations such as banks, hospitals, city governments, or industrial companies. Some internal auditing activity is known as **operational auditing**. Operational auditing (also known as **performance auditing** and **management auditing**) is the study of business operations in order to make recommendations

---

[4] www.theiia.org.

about the economic and efficient use of resources, effective achievement of business objectives, and compliance with company policies. The goal of operational auditing is to help managers discharge their management responsibilities and improve profitability.

Internal and operational auditors also perform audits of financial reports for internal use, much as external auditors audit financial statements distributed to outside users. Thus, some internal auditing work is similar to the auditing described elsewhere in this text. In addition, the expanded-scope services provided by internal auditors include (1) reviews of control systems for ensuring compliance with company policies, plans, procedures, and laws and regulations; (2) appraisals of the economy and efficiency of operations; and (3) reviews of program results in comparison with their objectives and goals.

Internal auditors need to be independent of the organization's line managers, much like the external auditors need to be independent of the company management. Independence helps internal auditors be objective and achieve three-party accountability. As noted earlier, you as a user of audited information expect the auditor to be unbiased and impartial, as well as competent, in verifying the accuracy of the information you rely on in making your decision. Internal auditors can recommend correction of poor business decisions and practices, and they can praise good decisions and practices. If they were responsible for making the decisions or carrying out the practices themselves, they would hardly be credible in the eyes of upper-management officers they report to. Consequently, the ideal arrangement is to have internal auditors whose only responsibilities are to audit and report to a higher level in the organization, such as a financial vice-president and the audit committee of the board of directors. This arrangement offers an independence that enhances the appraisal function (internal audit) within a company. Internal audit can be an important aspect of auditee internal controls as they monitor auditee operations year round. When such internal independence exists, external auditors may also be able to rely quite a bit on internal audit work as a valuable source for evidence. In the SOX world, internal auditor reports to independent audit committees are increasingly viewed as indispensable for good corporate governance. In addition, in the SOX world, if an external auditor performs internal audit functions he or she is deemed to be insufficiently independent and prohibited from auditing for external reporting. Again, this helps preserve external auditor independence.

Public Sector (Governmental) Auditing

The Office of the Auditor General of Canada (OAG) is an accounting, auditing, and investigating agency of Parliament, headed by the Auditor General. In one sense, OAG auditors are the highest level of internal auditors for the federal government. Many provinces have audit agencies similar to the OAG answering to provincial legislatures and performing the same types of work as we describe in this section. In another sense, the OAG and equivalent provincial auditors are really external auditors with respect to government agencies they audit because they are organizationally independent.

Many government agencies have their own internal auditors and inspectors: for example, federal ministries such as the Department of National Defence or Canada Revenue Agency and provincial education, welfare, controller agencies. Well-managed local governments (cities, regions, townships) also have internal audit staff. Activities of all levels of government are frequently referred to as the **public sector**.

Internal and public sector auditors have much in common. The OAG and internal auditors share elements of expanded-scope services. The OAG, however, emphasizes the accountability of public officials for the efficient, economical, and effective use of public funds and other resources. The CICA sets accounting and auditing standards for all public sector audit engagements, including those of the federal, provincial, and local levels of government.

In the public sector, you can see the audit function applied to financial reports and a compliance audit function applied with respect to laws and regulations. All government organizations, programs, activities, and functions were created by law and are surrounded by regulations governing the things they can and cannot do. For example, in some provinces there are serious problems of health card fraud by ineligible persons. A hospital cannot simply provide free services to anyone as there are regulations about eligibility of tourists and visitors from other countries. A compliance audit of services involves a study of the hospital's procedures and performance in determining eligibility and treatment of patients. Nationwide, such programs involve millions of people and billions of taxpayers' dollars.

Also, in the public sector you see **value-for-money (VFM) audits,** a category that includes economy, efficiency, and effectiveness audits. Government is always concerned about accountability for taxpayers' resources, and VFM audits are a means of improving accountability for the efficient and economical use of resources and the achievement of program goals. VFM audits, like internal auditors' operational audits, involve studies of the management of government organizations, programs, activities, and functions. The following box indicates the range of activities that VFM audits can cover.

SOME EXAMPLES OF RECOMMENDATIONS BASED ON VALUE-FOR-MONEY AUDITS CONDUCTED BY THE ONTARIO OFFICE OF THE PROVINCIAL AUDITOR

Health care. Stronger efforts are needed in using available data to identify pharmacies overcharging the Ontario Drug Benefit Plan. Ontario is unprepared for a flu pandemic despite 44 deaths from 2003 SARS crisis.

Archives. Hundreds of historically significant items, including a valuable Group of Seven painting, have gone missing. Inventory control practices need to be strengthened.

Education. Ontario university buildings are in need of $1.6 billion in repairs. Capital asset management systems need to be enforced.

Environment. Monitoring of hazardous waste shipment has been lax. Hundreds of tonnes of hazardous waste have gone missing. The Ministry's own standards need to be better enforced.

Transportation. New drivers are more likely to be involved in collisions if they take the province's beginning driver education course than if they do not. Inappropriate handling of driver education certificates by unscrupulous driving schools is suspected. Systems and procedures for assuring the public's money is properly spent are inadequate.

Criminal law. Several hundred names are missing from the sex offender registry. Amendments to legislation are needed.

Source: 2007 annual report by the Office of the Provincial Auditor of Ontario as summarized by the authors.

Comprehensive governmental auditing involves financial statement auditing, compliance auditing, and VFM auditing. It goes beyond an audit of financial reports and compliance with laws and regulations to include economy, efficiency, and effectiveness audits. The public sector standard on the elements of comprehensive auditing is similar to the internal auditors' view. Public sector standards do not require all engagements to include all types of audits. The scope of the work is supposed to be determined by the needs of those who use the audit results.

Regulatory Auditors

For the sake of clarity, other kinds of auditors deserve separate mention. You probably are aware of tax auditors employed by the Canada Revenue Agency. These auditors take the "economic assertions" of taxable income made by taxpayers in their tax returns and audit these returns to determine their correspondence with the standards found in the *Income Tax Act.* They also audit for fraud and tax evasion. Their reports can either clear a taxpayer's return or claim that additional taxes are due.

Federal and provincial bank examiners audit banks, trust companies, and other financial institutions for evidence of solvency and compliance with banking and other related laws and regulations. In 1985 these examiners as well as external auditors made news with the failures of two Alberta banks—the first Canadian bank failures in over 60 years.

Fraud Auditing and Forensic Accounting

Fraud is an attempt by one party (the fraudster) to deceive someone (the victim) for gain. Fraud falls under the Criminal Code and includes deception based on manipulation of accounting records and financial statements. Recently, auditor responsibilities to detect fraud have significantly increased. Financial statement auditors are now responsible for detecting material financial reporting fraud. They can no longer presume that management is honest. The PA needs to look for fraud risk factors. Some firms are beginning to screen clients before any wrongdoing is even suspected. The screening is done by specialist auditors who may do sensitive interviews or review unusual transactions and suspicious circumstances. In a normal audit the procedures are diagnostic, not investigative. This is a distinction we will make more clear later in the text.

Fraud auditing is a separate engagement that might be done on behalf of the audit committee—a special in-depth investigation of suspected fraud by those with specialized training, and often involving a specialist auditor. It is a proactive approach to detecting financial statement deception using accounting records and information, analytical relations, and awareness of fraud perpetration and concealment in developing investigative procedures.

Fraud auditing and forensic accounting are huge growth areas for PA firms in the post-Enron world. The main reason for this is that white-collar crime is one of the fastest-growing areas of crime, and police and regulators need the expertise of auditors to carry out these investigations. But there are other factors, and these relate to the broader category of forensic accounting. **Forensic accounting** includes fraud auditing and uses accounting and/or auditing skills in investigations involving legal issues. The legal issues might be criminal (e.g., fraud) or civil (e.g., commercial disputes). Common examples of civil legal disputes are insurance claims for business losses of various types and valuation of spousal business assets in a divorce proceeding.

Two specialist designations are available for investigative engagements. One for CAs is referred to as CA-IFA for investigative and forensic accounting. See the website at www.rotman.utoronto.ca/difa for details. There is also an older association of certified fraud examiners (CFEs) providing training for an internationally recognized designation that does not require any other accounting designation. See its website at www.cfenet.com for details.

Some people feel all PAs should take more responsibility to detect fraud, especially financial statement fraud, and that this may be the main reason for the existence of the profession. The controversies generated by the economic crisis of 2008/2009 may strengthen this perspective. Appendix 1C on the Online Learning Centre discusses this increasingly influential view in more detail. Chapter 17 also gives more details on forensic accounting and fraud auditing.

· ·

REVIEW CHECKPOINTS

10 Distinguish between forensic accounting and fraud auditing.

11 What is fraud?

12 What is operational auditing? How does the CICA view operational auditing?

13 What are the elements of comprehensive auditing?

14 What is compliance auditing?

15 Name some other types of auditors in addition to external, internal, and governmental auditors.

16 Are financial statement audits intended to find fraud?

· ·

PUBLIC ACCOUNTING
. . . .

The Accounting Profession

There are professional accounting associations at the national and international levels. For example, in Canada, there are the Canadian Institute of Chartered Accountants (CICA), the Certified General Accountants Association of Canada (CGA-Canada), and the **Society of Management Accountants of Canada (SMAC)**. Internationally, there is the International Federation of Accountants (IFAC), and in the United States there is the American Institute of Certified Public Accountants (AICPA), whose members are referred to as Certified Public Accountants or CPAs.

Within a single country there may be a number of professional designations representing auditors. For example, in Canada there are the provincial Institute of Chartered Accountants (known in Quebec as the Order of Chartered Accountants of Quebec), the Certified General Accountants Associations, the Societies of Management Accountants, and the Institute of Internal Auditors. Each of these organizations has developed its own professional designation as follows: Chartered Accountants (CAs), Certified General Accountants (CGAs), Certified Management Accountants (CMAs), Certified Internal Auditors (CIAs), and Certified Fraud Examiners (CFEs). The requirements for obtaining these various designations vary greatly, so it is best to consult each organization for the details. A list of websites with education and certification requirements is provided in Appendix 1A on the Online Learning Centre.

Each designation has its distinguishing features: CAs are oriented to providing auditing and related public accounting services for large companies, CMAs primarily aim to provide private management and internal accounting services, CIAs provide private internal audit services to larger organizations, and CGAs aim to provide all types of services. In virtually all provinces, CGAs can be public accountants like CAs, but they tend to service smaller audit clients. There is considerable overlap among all these accounting professionals. They all provide accounting, tax, and management advisory work, with CAs and CGAs largely providing these services to the public while CMAs and CIAs provide these services to their full-time employer companies.

CGAs and CMAs have public practice rights throughout Canada, therefore making it appropriate to refer to public accountants as PAs rather than CAs in a text about external auditing. Although we use the more generic term PA throughout the text, many of our illustrations are based on standards set by the CICA, as these standards have legal standing in the courts through the various federal and provincial Corporation Acts, and through regulatory policy statements. In addition, when CGAs and CMAs practise public accounting, their guides refer to the *CICA Handbook* standards.

Public Accounting Firms

Many people think of public accounting in terms of the "big" accounting firms. As of 2009, there are four such firms, often referred to as the "Big Four": Ernst & Young, Deloitte & Touche, KPMG, and PricewaterhouseCoopers. Notwithstanding this perception, public accounting is carried out in hundreds of practice units ranging in size from sole proprietorships (individuals who "hang out a shingle") to international firms employing thousands of professionals. Many students look upon public accounting as the place to begin a career; they gain intimate knowledge of many different business enterprises for the first three to ten years, and then they select an industry segment to pursue their interests in. Public accounting experience is an excellent background to almost any business career.

Public accountants do business in a competitive environment. They perform audit services in the public interest, but they also need to make a living at it, so they have a profit motive just like other professionals. This duality—profit motive and professional responsibility—creates tensions in their work. As a result of increased litigation against them in the 1990s, the profession lobbied for legislation making it harder to sue professional accounting firms. In 1995, in the United States, legislation was passed allowing public accounting firms to take on the **limited liability partnership (LLP)** form of organization. The LLP structure, which will be covered in Chapter 5, is now commonplace in Canada and around the world.

The United States and Canada went through an economic boom in the second half of the 1990s. This was also a time of unprecedented growth in non-audit services for the public accounting firms. However, by the late 1990s, this growth had led to concerns about the independence of audit services provided by accounting firms that also engaged in extensive, possibly conflicting, non-audit services for the same client. Many cite this lack of independence as the primary cause of the profession's problems in the post-Enron world.

Public accounting services involve many PAs employed in assurance, tax, and consulting work. Although structures will differ, Exhibit 1–4 shows the organization of a typical larger PA firm. Some firms include additional departments, such as small-business advisory or compensation consulting departments, while others might have different names for their staff and management positions.

In Exhibit 1–4 you see the various staffing levels within a PA firm. A recent graduate will most likely start work as a staff accountant. This typical entry-level position involves working under the supervision of more senior people. As auditors need to verify virtually everything the auditee claims in his financial reporting, there is much mundane work to be done verifying the math and the extensions of financial data and reconciling the physical amounts with recorded amounts. How does a user know the balance sheet balances? Someone needs to verify the seemingly obvious, and that someone is the auditor. One should look upon this experience as a form of apprenticeship. In most firms your responsibilities will increase quickly once you demonstrate your reliability.

Depending on the firm, there may be several levels of staff accountants. Individuals who have just passed the professional exams are usually the most senior staff accountants and are ready to be promoted to manager once they've had a few years of experience and demonstrated leadership potential. Leadership means having people management skills that are successful with both clients and staff accountants. Technical skills alone are

EXHIBIT   1–4   TYPICAL ORGANIZATION OF A PA FIRM

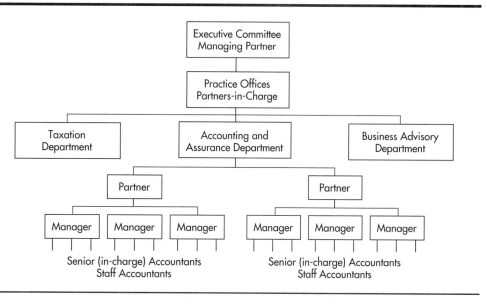

usually not sufficient for a manager. The ability to expand the firm's practice becomes increasingly important. Getting along comfortably with client personnel is a high priority, as otherwise it is difficult to get the information an auditor needs. These personal dynamics become more important at the higher levels in a PA firm. Keep this context in mind as you read descriptions of the various procedures in subsequent chapters. Managers supervise most of the details of the audit engagement as explained throughout this text. They are the backbone of the audit at the technical level.

Partners, working closely with managers, take overall responsibility for the audit and lead meetings with auditee's management and its audit committee. Partners usually have at least ten years' experience and are the only permanent employees in a PA firm. About 5 percent of those with a PA designation become partners, while the rest go into industry or other PA firms. For more information on these positions, career opportunities, and the latest salary trends for PAs in North America, see the websites at www.mcintyre-smith.com and www.roberthalffinance.com.

Assurance Services

Audits of traditional financial statements are the most frequent type of assurance services for public companies and for most large and medium nonpublic companies. Auditing amounts to 20–60 percent of the business of larger PA firms. Most of this text is about the audit of traditional financial statements.

Accounting and review services are the "nonaudit" or other services performed frequently for medium and small businesses and not-for-profit organizations. A great deal of nonaudit work is done by small public accounting practice units. PAs can be associated with clients' financial statements without giving the standard audit report. They can perform compilations, which consist of writing up the financial statements from a client's books and records, without performing any evidence-gathering work. They can perform reviews, which are lesser in scope than audits but include some evidence-gathering work. (Compilation and review standards are explained in more detail in Chapter 16.)

Assurance services are also performed on information in presentations other than traditional financial statements. Since assurance is the lending of credibility by an independent party (assurer, auditor) to representations made by one person or organization to another, demand for a greater variety of PA engagements has grown. Public accountants provide assurance to vote counts (e.g., for the Academy Awards), to dollar amounts of prizes claimed to have been given in lottery advertisements, to investment performance statistics, and to claims made about the capabilities of computer software programs. These nontraditional services are governed by professional standards.

In this text we reference three sets of professional standards—Canadian, international, and, to a lesser extent, American—which all influence each other. For example, the CICA's Assurance and Auditing Standards Board influences international standards by providing commentary on exposure drafts of new international standards. Once a new international standard is adopted, the CICA issues an exposure draft any unique-to-Canada modifications that must be made before they can be incorporated into the CICA standards. Other countries follow similar processes. Increasingly, the trend is convergence to a common set of standards. For example, the CICA is to adopt international standards with minor modifications by 2010. These **Canadian Auditing Standards (CAS)** are the main professional standards we refer to in this text.

Convergence is a defining characteristic of the post-Enron world and makes it more important to be aware of the similarities, as well as the differences, among the standards. International standards reference IFAC's **International Standards on Auditing (ISAs)**; American PCAOB standards are referenced to its **Auditing Standards (ASs)**.

Taxation Services

Local, provincial, national, and international tax laws are often called "full-employment acts" for accountants and lawyers; they are complex, and PAs perform tax planning and tax return preparation services in the areas of income, sales, property, and other taxation. A large proportion of small accounting firm work is tax practice. Tax laws change frequently, and tax practitioners have to spend considerable time in continuing education and self-study to keep current.

Consulting or Management Advisory Services (MAS)

All accounting firms handle a great deal of consulting and management advisory services (some firms refer to these as management ancillary services). These are the great "open end" of public accounting practice that puts accountants in direct competition with the non-PA consulting firms. The field is virtually limitless, and no list of consulting activities could possibly include all of them. Indeed, accounting firms have created consulting units with professionals from other fields—lawyers, actuaries, engineers, and advertising executives, to name a few. Until Enron, many of the large accounting firms had tried to become "one-stop shopping centres" for clients' auditing, taxation, and business advice needs. However, through the chilling effect of the SOX, these activities have been greatly restricted whenever the engagement includes assurance services.

Nevertheless, consulting work for nonaudit clients may continue to expand to new non-conflicting areas, such as eldercare where PAs provide a package of services ranging from assurance to consulting, bill paying, and financial planning for the elderly. In large PA firms, the consulting department is quite often independent from the auditing and accounting departments, performing engagements that do not directly interact with the audits. PA firms are greatly restricted in the types of consulting or business advisory services they can provide to audit clients, but there are no such restrictions for nonaudit clients.

REGULATION OF PUBLIC ACCOUNTING

· · · · · · · · · · · · · · · ·

LEARNING OBJECTIVE
6 Outline how public accountants (PAs) are regulated.

Regulation of public accounting in Canada, as with most professional groups, is a provincial matter. Most provinces have laws—public accountancy acts—that specify who is allowed to practise public accounting in the province. For example, for many years Ontario's *Public Accounting Act* licensed only CAs to perform assurance engagements. However, as part of the post-Enron reform process, this legislation was amended in 2004 to allow any accounting organization meeting the Public Accountants Council (PAC) of Ontario's educational and experience standards to perform what they describe as public accounting functions that meet the public interest. (See their website at www.pacont.org for more details on their activities and requirements.) For PAC, the public interest is effectively represented by the third-party users of the financial statements. These reforms were linked to the creation of the new Accountability Board (CPAB), which provides oversight for all PAs in the province. Similar regulatory reforms are evolving in other provinces.

In recent years, the trend in provincial public accountancy legislation has been to open public accounting to CGAs and CMAs, as well as CAs. The goal is to increase accessibility to reasonably priced public accounting services while maintaining standards. Public interests, particularly those of vulnerable third parties, must be protected. Quality control standards and CPAB monitoring implemented in recent years to ensure this are further explained in Chapter 2.

In addition to the system of regulation outlined previously, other factors greatly influence the profession. These include the legal system the profession operates in (discussed in Chapter 5) and the impact of regulators on practising auditors. Regulators include, at the federal level, the Superintendent of Financial Institutions, whose prime responsibility is regulating the financial services industry under the jurisdiction of the *Federal Bank Act*.

At the provincial level, there are the securities commissions with responsibility for investor protection and ensuring the fairness and efficiency of the province's capital markets. There are securities commissions in every province and territory, but, because of the division of powers between the provinces and the federal government, there is no national-level securities commission in Canada comparable to the SEC in the United States. However, since 1999 the Joint Forum of Financial Market Regulators, consisting of provincial securities commissioners and various national regulators, has coordinated and streamlined the regulation and services in Canadian financial markets through voluntary agreement between participants.

The Ontario Securities Commission (OSC) has responsibility for the biggest and most developed capital markets in Canada. We will use it here to illustrate the impact a regulator can have on public accounting. Three principal activities of the OSC ensure the orderly functioning of capital markets within its jurisdiction, such as the Toronto Stock Exchange:

1. registering issuers, dealers, and advisers trading in securities and commodity futures contracts

2. monitoring the full extent of reporting requirements, including those related to prospectuses, takeovers, and continuous disclosure of material information

3. enforcing the provisions of the *Securities Act* and the *Commodity Futures Act*

Prospectuses are the information, usually including financial information, about a firm that accompanies any new issuance of shares in a regulated securities market. The staff of the OSC includes the chief accountant and a chief forensic accountant who work under the director of enforcement. The Office of the Chief Accountant is responsible for formulating financial reporting policy and for monitoring the application of accounting principles and auditing standards by report issuers and their auditors. Financial statements are reviewed on a selective basis, and up to one-quarter of companies reviewed receive comment letters relating to inadequacies in their financial reports. The companies' auditors are also informed of problems. If the financial reporting problems are severe enough, the Enforcement Branch is notified. In 2001, the OSC found revenue recognition to be a significant problem area for high-tech firms.

An example of an Enforcement Branch action affecting an auditor is given in the following box. This OSC action followed an investigation of Nortel's accounting launched in April 2004 by the SEC and OSC. Nortel, then one of Canada's premiere high-tech companies in the telecommunications industry, had to restate its financial results for quarterly periods going back through 2003, 2002, and 2001. The restated 2003 results reduced earnings by 41 percent. By January 2005, Nortel's stock price had gone down to the $4 range from a July 2000 high of $124. The earlier 2003 earnings had triggered millions of dollars of bonus payments to management. Twelve senior executives agreed to return $10.4 million of these bonuses, but Nortel is still seeking repayment of 2003 bonuses from managers fired in April 2004.

OSC COMMISSIONERS CONTINUE MANAGEMENT CEASE-TRADE ORDER AGAINST NORTEL INSIDERS, MAY 31, 2004

TORONTO—Following a hearing held today, a panel of Ontario Securities Commission (OSC) Commissioners has made a final order under paragraph 2 of subsection 127(1) of the *Securities Act* that all trading by certain directors, officers, and insiders of Nortel Networks Corporation and Nortel Networks Limited in securities of Nortel Networks Corporation and Nortel Networks Limited cease until two full business days following the receipt by the Commission of all filings, including financial statements, the corporations are required to make pursuant to Ontario securities law. This order continues the temporary order made by the Director on May 17, 2004.

Source: www.osc.gov.on.ca/About/NewsRelease/2004/nr_20040528_osc-nortel-cont-cease-trade.jsp.

An independent review by Nortel's audit committee concluded that the corporate culture encouraged financial manipulation through weak internal controls. In January 2005, the board of directors went through a major reorganization, with half of the board members leaving. In addition, a high-profile ethics watchdog and compliance officer was hired to help change the corporate culture. The ongoing saga of lawsuits and investigations at Nortel that continued is covered in subsequent chapters. This example illustrates why good corporate governance principles need to be followed. (Corporate governance principles are explored in more detail in Appendix 7F.)

The OSC also monitors auditing and accounting standards setting of the CICA, and it provides input on emerging issues as well as commentary on proposed standards. In addition, since 1989 the OSC has issued Staff Accounting Communiqués (SACs) intended to explain the OSC staff's views on specific reporting issues. Although the SACs have no official OSC approval, OSC staff are likely to challenge any treatment that is inconsistent with an SAC. By publishing the results of its monitoring program, by filing complaints to provincial disciplinary committees, and through its representation on CICA standard-setting boards, in recent years the OSC has made a significant, ongoing impact on the profession.

There are other regulators affecting the profession. For example, the Canadian Investor Protection Fund, which is sponsored by the Toronto and the Montreal stock exchanges, the Canadian Venture Exchange, the Toronto Futures Exchange, and the Investment Dealers Association of Canada, is a trust established to protect customers from the financial failure of a member firm (any member of a sponsoring organization, and some American bond dealers that trade in Canada). In recent years, Fund staff have taken a more active supervisory role by overseeing regular monthly, quarterly, and annual reporting, paying surprise visits to offices of member firms, and conducting at least one financial questionnaire a year. The Fund can fine or set sanctions against a member firm that violates capital, reporting, or other requirements. It develops policy statements that address standards for internal control within member firms. Auditors must be aware of these standards when auditing member firms. Internal control reports are discussed in more detail in Chapter 16.

Another regulator, the **Securities and Exchange Commission (SEC)**, affects Canadian auditors whose client firms have dealings with U.S. securities markets. In recent years, many Canadian companies have gone to American and other international markets to raise cash through **initial public offerings (IPOs)**. Because they need to file regulatory documents in each province, which increases the cost of financing, many Canadian companies are finding it cheaper to raise money through public markets in other countries. The Canadian Department of Finance has for a number of years explored the idea of creating a national securities regulator (like the SEC in the U.S.), or some national coordinator of provincial securities commissions, to improve the quality and competitiveness of Canadian securities markets.[5] The impact of the SEC on auditors is discussed in more detail in Appendix 1B.

An important development in the regulation of the Canadian accounting profession was the creation of the Canadian Public Accountability Board (CPAB) on July 17, 2002. The Board represents the public interest through being dominated by non-CA members (seven of the eleven Board members are to be non-CAs). The Board monitors audit practice and conducts annual inspections of accounting firms to assess their ability to protect the public interest. It has the power to sanction any auditor that fails to protect the public interest, and is viewed as the first in a series of major structural reforms to protect the integrity of Canada's financial accounting systems. Other steps include the CICA's evolving standard for auditor independence and the creation of provincial boards to oversee the professional conduct and peer-review systems.

Finally, there are regulators, such as provincial ministries of the environment and natural resources, that indirectly impact the profession by placing restrictions on

[5] A. Freeman and K. Hawlett, "Keep IPO's at Home: Martin," *The Globe and Mail*, March 8, 1996, B1.

activities that the clients themselves may need to disclose as part of the client's business risk.

It should be clear from this brief review that the profession is facing an increasingly complex regulatory environment and that auditors must be sensitized to regulatory concerns in order to do a proper audit. Auditors also need to be concerned with meeting the demands of regulators in different countries. One part of the solution is using worldwide standards whenever feasible.

· ·

REVIEW
CHECKPOINTS

17 Identify several types of professional accountants and their organizations.

18 What are some examples of assurance services rendered on representations other than traditional financial statements?

19 What are the three major areas of public accounting services?

20 Locate Nortel's audit committee report on the Internet. Is the OSC or the SEC website more user-friendly for investors?

· ·

INTERNATIONAL AUDITING

· · · · · · · · · · · · · · ·

LEARNING OBJECTIVE

7 Provide an overview of international auditing and its impact on Canadian auditing standards.

Many of the large public accounting firms are worldwide organizations that grew rapidly in the last few decades, in parallel with the increased economic integration of their global clientele. Developments such as the North American Free Trade Agreement (NAFTA), the evolution of the European Economic Union and other free trade zones, and the pervasive effects of technological change are all contributing to increased global harmonization of auditing and accounting standards. For these reasons the **International Federation of Accountants (IFAC)**, created in 1977, mirrors at an international level what national institutes have been doing. In particular, IFAC publishes its own handbook on auditing standards that recommends International Standards on Auditing (ISAs). ISAs cover basic principles of auditing, auditor's reports, professional independence, reliance on other auditors abroad, and professional qualifications.

The issue is when ISAs will achieve worldwide acceptance. On April 1, 2002, the **International Auditing and Assurance Standards Board** was created with resources commensurate with its responsibilities. This Board now has probably the largest group of technical audit standard-setting support staff in the world, making future ISAs more rigorous. ISAs are increasingly becoming the dominant standards worldwide. The CICA's policy is to adopt ISAs as is, unless Canadian conditions require a different standard. The sources of auditing standards in Canada are the *CICA Handbook,* whose standards were traditionally referred to as the *Handbook* Recommendations, and the Audit Guidelines (AuGs), which provide additional guidance on implementing the standards. The CICA adopted the revised and redrafted ISAs as well as the International Standard on Quality Control on December 15, 2009, effective for fiscal periods after December 14, 2010. It will decide at a future date what, if any, other international standards it will adopt. We provide more details in later chapters. The goal of convergence, or **international harmonization** as it is frequently called, is a key focus of Canadian standard setters in the post-Enron world.

As the world becomes more interdependent, many concepts and terms used in other countries will become increasingly accepted in Canadian practice. Indeed, many large firms already use manuals and training materials reflecting international practice. This text makes use of those terms and concepts and does not restrict itself to those used in the *CICA Handbook* or CASs.

REVIEW 21 Find the IFAC Handbook on the IFAC website and review its table of contents.
CHECKPOINTS

APPLICATION CASE AND ANALYSIS
MEANING OF THE WORDS "PRESENT FAIRLY" IN THE AUDITOR'S REPORT

Discussion Case

Your client, Margo N., has prepared financial statements that she feels are in conformity with Canadian GAAP, but she notes that in your report you use the words "present fairly, in all material respects . . . in accordance with Canadian GAAP." She asks you to explain what these words mean so that she can fulfill her responsibilities to prepare the financial statements appropriately.

Analysis

"Present fairly" is one of those widely used accounting terms that is never defined in any standard. As auditor, you must provide an intuitive, reasonable, if not authoritative, explanation of its meaning. A good starting point is telling Margo that fair presentation means not to mislead, but to tell the truth about economic reality, including appropriate disclosure of business risks. Failure to disclose appropriately business risks and economic reality leads to information risk in financial reporting. Defining fairness of presentation in financial reporting so that it includes a risk orientation will lead to acceptable levels of information risk.

But what is "economic reality" then? Obviously, there should be no deliberate errors concerning the economic facts of Margo's reporting entity. This is implicit in both GAAP and your studies of financial accounting, and it is worth remembering as an auditor. By verifying those facts, as an auditor, you will determine which ones are correct and which are misleading. Hence, fair presentation includes an understanding that an auditor will be able to verify the facts through the records kept by Margo's accounting or information system by gathering independent corroborating evidence of the information. This way the risk of errors in that information will be reduced to a level you as auditor find acceptable for financial reporting. This is the low audit risk component of information risk that auditors aim to achieve. However, auditors also need to keep track of the accounting risks associated with forecasting in GAAP estimates. Forecasts are based on assumptions, and if those assumptions are unrealistic or unreasonable, the accounting risks associated with the accounting estimates increase. And increased accounting risks, in turn, lead to increased information risks in financial reporting. Thus, fairness of presentation also includes appropriately disclosing business risks through accounting entries and perhaps through appropriate note disclosures as well.

A specific example of this could be the proper accounting for accounts receivable that you studied in your financial accounting course. To determine the appropriateness of the presentation of accounts receivable in the balance sheet, it must be verified that the receivables exist, that they are owed to Margo's company, and that they have been properly recorded and classified, per GAAP, as of the balance sheet date. All of this is factual information based on past events that can be verified by various audit procedures that you will be studying in this book. Verification is, therefore, the process of assuring yourself and others that these facts are accurately recorded. As an auditor, you will gather evidence from Margo's accounting system that the facts regarding receivables are accurate.

However, auditors in fact rarely find it an economical use of their time to exhaustively gather evidence on accounts receivable. So they do less than that, and instead accept that the less-than-perfect evidence creates a risk of undetected material factual errors regarding receivables. It is important to remember that audit risk for receivables is the risk of failing to detect material factual errors in the records for receivables. Audit risk is, therefore, an evidence gathering risk.

The other component of information risk is accounting risk. This risk considers the question of whether all the receivables will be collected at their face amounts, regardless of how accurately the amounts were recorded. This uncertainty is unavoidable because it relates to the future and there is little that is certain about the future. Neither you the auditor nor Margo can predict with certainty, as of the balance sheet date, which receivables will be collected at face value. You might recall from your accounting course that there are techniques for calculating bad debt expense that don't seem to involve forecasting. However, such techniques are based on assumptions from past experience. If these assumptions are wrong, the resulting estimate will be wrong as well. Some common assumptions are that percentage collection experienced in the past will continue to apply, that interest rates won't change, or that other economic factors will remain the same. Only the passage of time and actual collection of payments on the receivables can eliminate the uncertainty around these things. But, in the meantime, under the periodic reporting system of GAAP accounting you do not have the luxury of waiting for these future events to take place; you need an estimate of these future events now! An estimate of amounts to be realized as future cash flows is made by estimating the amount that will be uncollectible. The forecast of uncollectible amounts is the basis for adjustments to the allowance for doubtful accounts that will help you estimate the realizable value of receivables. This is necessary for proper valuation of receivables and also for proper matching.

LEARNING OBJECTIVE

8 Apply and integrate the chapter topics to analyze a practical auditing situation/case/scenario.

Because there is no guarantee that the estimates will be accurate, it is likely that there will be a deviation between the estimate for bad debt expense and what will actually be realized as uncollectible. We call this the forecast error. A forecast error has the same impact on financial reporting as a recorded factual error—it is the difference between what is recorded and what is ultimately realized. Thus, material forecast errors have the same impact as material factual errors in financial reporting. This means that accounting risk is just as important as audit risk to users of financial statements. The problem, as we will see later, is that GAAP is largely silent on the acceptability of accounting risks for various accounts. GAAP does not normally consider the reasonableness of specific assumptions in making some forecasts. This forecast evaluation task is left to the professional judgment of the auditor. We introduce subjective concepts like accounting risk to facilitate the decision making that goes into them. Thus, a logical aspect of fairness of presentation within GAAP is that accounting risk is kept to some "acceptable" level—at least as it concerns the amounts recorded as line items in the financial statements. This helps determine which assumptions to treat as reasonable. By keeping accounting risks appropriately low, we help keep information risk low and thereby make operational the concept of fairness of presentation.

Unless otherwise indicated, in this textbook we use the term "GAAP" to mean "presented fairly within Canadian GAAP." In the auditor's report, this wording can be viewed as a reminder to auditors that in applying GAAP they need to consider the reasonableness of assumptions for making accounting estimates (leading to acceptable accounting risk), as well as the importance of an acceptably low level of risk of factual errors in financial statements. (If we assume that auditors correct all material factual errors upon detection, then the latter risk corresponds to audit risk.) With both conditions satisfied, a more comprehensive risk-oriented approach to achieving "fairness of presentation in conformity with GAAP" is possible. This is the approach we follow throughout this text.

Summary

. . . .

This chapter began by illustrating and defining auditing, distinguishing it from accounting. The practice of public accounting is rooted in the history of auditing. The accounting profession has been undergoing radical changes since the bankruptcy of Enron in December 2001. These changes are being accompanied by broad corporate governance and regulatory reforms.

Auditing is practiced in numerous forms by various practice units including PA firms, the Canada Revenue Agency, the OAG, companies' internal audit departments, and several types of regulatory auditors. Fraud examiners, many of whom are internal auditors and inspectors, have found a niche in auditing-related activities.

Many auditors aspire to become CGAs, CAs, CPAs, CIAs, CFEs, or CMAs; this involves passing rigorous examinations, obtaining practical experience, and maintaining competence through continuing professional education. Each of these groups has a large professional organization that governs the professional standards and quality of practice of its members.

This chapter has given you a broad overview of auditing. Being aware of the bigger picture of the context of auditing is increasingly important for effective auditing. This is the main reason the concept of critical thinking in professional judgment is being introduced in this text. We end this introduction with a brief overview of what you can expect from this text. Part I, consisting of the first five chapters, introduces you to the most fundamental concepts you will need to consider as an auditor. Part II introduces you to evidence-based concepts and refines the important concept of internal control. In Part III, you will learn to apply the concepts studied thus far to the various accounts in the financial statements. This part concludes with the opinion that ends the audit report and reflects an evaluation of financial statements as a whole. Part IV covers other assurance engagements and specialized types of auditors and auditing.

When you begin a study of auditing, you may be eager to attack the nitty-gritty of financial statement audit work. Although this text will enable you to learn about auditing, instructors are seldom able to duplicate a practice environment in a classroom setting. You may feel frustrated about knowing "how to do it." This frustration is natural, because auditing is done in the field under pressure of time limits and in the surroundings of client personnel, paperwork, and accounting information systems. This text can provide a foundation and framework for understanding auditing, but nothing can substitute for the first few months of work when the classroom study comes alive in the field.

Refer to the text Online Learning Centre (OLC) for Appendices 1A through 1C.

MULTIPLE-CHOICE QUESTIONS FOR PRACTICE AND REVIEW

MC 1 When people speak of the assurance function, they are referring to the work of auditors in
   a. lending credibility to a client's financial statements.
   b. detecting fraud and embezzlement in a company.
   c. lending credibility to an auditee's financial statements.
   d. performing a program results audit in a government agency.

MC 2 Company A hired Sampson & Delila, CAs, to audit the financial statements of Company B and deliver the audit report to Megabank. Which is the client?
   a. Megabank
   b. Sampson & Delila
   c. Company A
   d. Company B

MC 3 According to the CICA, the objective of an audit of financial statements is
   a. an expression of opinion on the fairness with which they present financial position, results of operations, and cash flows in conformity with generally accepted accounting principles.
   b. an expression of opinion on the fairness with which they present financial position, results of operations, and cash flows in conformity with accounting standards promulgated by the Financial Accounting Standards Board.
   c. an expression of opinion on the fairness with which they present financial position, results of operations, and cash flows in conformity with accounting standards promulgated by the CICA Accounting Standards Committee.
   d. to obtain systematic and objective evidence about financial assertions and report the results to interested users.

MC 4 Bankers who are processing loan applications from companies seeking large loans will probably ask for financial statements audited by an independent PA because
   a. financial statements are too complex for them to analyze themselves.
   b. they are too far away from company headquarters to perform accounting and auditing themselves.
   c. the consequences of making a bad loan are very undesirable.
   d. they generally see a potential conflict of interest between company managers who want to get loans and their needs for reliable financial statements.

MC 5 Operational audits of a company's efficiency and economy of managing projects and of the results of programs are conducted by whom?
   a. Management advisory services departments of PA firms in public practice
   b. The company's internal auditors
   c. Governmental auditors employed by the federal government
   d. All of the above

MC 6 Independent auditors of financial statements perform audits that reduce and control
   a. the business risks faced by investors.
   b. the information risk faced by investors.
   c. the complexity of financial statements.
   d. quality reviews performed by other PA firms.

MC 7 The primary objective of compliance auditing is to
   a. give an opinion on financial statements.
   b. develop a basis for a report on internal control.
   c. perform a study of effective and efficient use of resources.
   d. determine whether auditee personnel are following laws, rules, regulations, and policies.

EXERCISES AND PROBLEMS

EP 1
LO.2 **Controller as Auditor.** The chair of the board of Hughes Corporation proposed that the board hire as controller a PA who had been the manager on the corporation's audit performed by a firm of independent accountants. The chair thought that hiring this person would make the annual audit unnecessary and consequently save the company the fee paid to the auditors. The chair proposed giving this new controller a full staff to conduct such investigations of accounting and operating data as necessary. Evaluate this proposal.

EP 2
LO.2 **Controller as Auditor.** Put yourself in the position of the person hired as controller in the above situation. Suppose the chair of the board moves to discontinue the annual audit because Hughes Corporation now has your services on a full-time basis. You are invited to express your views to the board. Explain how you would discuss the nature of your job as controller and your views on the discontinuance of the annual audit.

EP 3
LO.3 **Logic and Method.** Identify four major factors affecting information risk that make the need for independent audits important in today's business world. Give two examples for each.

EP 4
LO.3 **Logic and Method.** Auditors must have a thorough knowledge of generally accepted accounting principles (GAAP) if they are to properly perform an audit of the financial statements of a company. Explain why this is so. Use capital leases as an example of the need for this knowledge.

EP 5 **Operational Auditing.** Bigdeal Corporation manufac-
LO.5 tures paper and paper products and is trying to decide
whether to purchase and merge Smalltek Company. Smalltek has developed a process for manufacturing boxes that
can replace other containers that use fluorocarbons for ex-
pelling a liquid product. The price may be as high as $45
million. Bigdeal prefers to buy Smalltek and integrate its
products, while leaving the Smalltek management in
charge of day-to-day operations. A major consideration is
the efficiency and effectiveness of the Smalltek management. Bigdeal wants to obtain a report on the operational
efficiency and effectiveness of the Smalltek sales, production, and research and development departments.

Required:
Whom can Bigdeal engage to produce this operational
audit report? Several possibilities exist. Are there any
particular advantages or disadvantages in choosing
among them?

EP 6 **Auditor as Guarantor.** Your neighbour invited you to
LO.1 lunch yesterday. Sure enough, it was no "free lunch,"
because he wanted to discuss the annual report of the
Dodge Corporation. He owns Dodge shares and has just
received the report. He says, "PricewaterhouseCoopers
prepared the audited financial statements and gave an
unqualified opinion, so my investment must be safe."

Required:
What misconceptions does your neighbour seem to have
about the auditor's role with respect to Dodge Corporation?

EP 7 **Identification of Audits and Auditors.** Audits may be
LO.5 characterized as (*a*) financial statement audits, (*b*) compliance audits—audits of compliance with control
policies and procedures and with laws and regulations,
(*c*) economy and efficiency audits, and (*d*) program results audits. The work can be done by independent
(external) auditors, internal auditors, or governmental auditors. Below is a list of the purposes or products of various audit engagements.

1. Render a public report on the assumptions and compilation of a revenue forecast by a sports stadium/
   racetrack complex.
2. Determine the fair presentation in conformity
   with GAAP of an advertising agency's financial
   statements.
3. Report on how better care and disposal of vehicles
   confiscated by drug enforcement agents might save
   money and benefit law enforcement.
4. Determine costs of municipal garbage pickup services
   compared with comparable service subcontracted to a
   private business.
5. Audit tax shelter partnership financing terms.
6. Study a private aircraft manufacturer's test pilot performance in reporting on the results of test flights.
7. Conduct periodic examination of a bank for
   solvency.
8. Evaluate the promptness of materials inspection in a
   manufacturer's receiving department.

Required:
Prepare a three-column schedule showing: (1) each of
the engagements listed above; (2) the type of audit
(financial statement, compliance, economy and efficiency, or program results); and (3) the kind of auditors
you would expect to be involved.

EP 8 **Analysis and Judgment.** As part of your regular year-
LO.3 end audit of a publicly held client, you must estimate the
probability of success of its proposed new product line.
The client has experienced financial difficulty during the
last few years and, in your judgment, a successful introduction of the new product line is necessary for the client
to remain a going concern.

There are five steps, all of which are necessary for
successful introduction of the product: (1) successful labour negotiations between the building trades unions and
the construction firms contracted to build the necessary
addition to the present plant, (2) successful defence of
patent rights, (3) product approval by the Health Branch,
(4) successful negotiation of a long-term raw material
contract with a foreign supplier, and (5) successful conclusion of distribution contract talks with a large national
retail distributor.

In view of the circumstances, you contact experts who
have provided your firm with reliable estimates in the past.
The labour relations expert estimates that there is an 80
percent chance of successfully concluding labour negotiations before the strike deadline. Legal counsel advises that
there is a 90 percent chance of successfully defending patent rights. The expert on Health Branch product approvals
estimates a 95 percent chance of approval. The experts in
the remaining two areas estimate the probability of successfully resolving the raw materials contract and the distribution contract talks to be 90 percent in each case.
Assume these estimates are reliable.

Required:
What is your assessment of the probability of successful
product introduction? (*Hint:* You can assume the five
steps are independent of each other.)

EP 9 **Role of Auditing Questions.** What do you think manage-
LO.4 ment certification of financial statements means? Has
management's responsibility changed since the inception of SOX? Why do we need auditors if management
"certifies" its financial statements? Discuss in class.

EP 10 What do you think "meeting the public interest" should
LO.10 mean for a PA? Discuss in class.

EP 11 Identify the three-party accountability in a CRA tax audit.
LO.10

EP 12 Until recently, auditors took less responsibility for detecti
LO.10 ng fraudulent reporting than for detecting unintentional
misstatements. Which do you think is more important for
investors, detecting intentional misstatements or unintentional ones? (*Hint:* Ask your family and friends who have
not studied auditing.) Why do you think the profession
did not take more responsibility earlier?

CHAPTER 2

Audit, Assurance, and Quality Control Standards

Chapter 2 explains three sets of interrelated practice standards for audit services offered by PAs: audit, assurance, and quality control standards.

PRACTICE STANDARDS

LEARNING OBJECTIVE

1 List the various practice standards for independent audits of financial statements.

Practice standards are general guides for the quality of professional work, and the accounting and auditing profession has many sets of standards to choose from. This chapter deals directly with four sets: (1) generally accepted auditing standards (GAAS), issued by the CICA Assurance and Auditing Standards Board; (2) assurance standards, as suggested by section 5025 of the *CICA Handbook*; (3) the CICA's General Standards of Quality Control for Firms Performing Assurance Engagements (CSQC-1); and (4) quality control standards as reflected in firm peer reviews and provincial institutes' practice inspection manuals. As noted in Chapter 1, several countries have created accountability boards in the post-Enron world. These boards can influence standards through monitoring public company audits and identifying weaknesses in them. In most countries, public companies are those listed on stock exchanges. As noted in Chapter 1, the PCAOB can set its own standards for public companies; other standards are covered later in this text. Chapter 4 covers the rules of professional ethics, and the CICA Recommendations for compilation and review services are explained in Chapter 16.

You will find relatively few references to the accounting Recommendations in this text. The CICA issues accounting standards, but this text concentrates on auditing and the practice of accounting, not on the accounting rules themselves. An overview of generally accepted auditing standards is provided in the next section.

GENERALLY ACCEPTED AUDITING STANDARDS (GAAS)

LEARNING OBJECTIVE

2 Determine whether the CICA generally accepted auditing standards (GAAS) were followed in specific fact situations.

The CICA's **generally accepted auditing standards (GAAS)** were first written as a short statement of eight standards. Since 1975, these eight have been augmented by additional explanations and requirements in the assurance Recommendations of the *CICA Handbook*, section 5100. Beginning in 2010, *CICA Handbook* section 5100 was largely replaced by CAS 200 (5100, 5021, 5090, and 5095), and professional ethical requirements of the relevant professional accounting organizations were added. These changes are in line with convergence to international standards. CAS 200 is entitled "Overall Objective of the Independent Auditor, and the Conduct of the Audit in Accordance with Canadian Auditing Standards." CAS 200 establishes auditors' overall responsibilities when conducting an audit in accordance with CAS standards. It lists the objectives of the audit and a series of principles and concepts fundamental to financial statement auditing, as they are shown in Exhibit 2–1.

The importance of GAAS is that they identify the objectives and key principles of the financial statement audit. Every CAS is written so that it identifies the subject and objectives of the standard, provides new definitions wherever applicable, states the requirements for meeting the objective, and provides further explanation for carrying out those requirements. This may include examples of procedures that are appropriate in specific contexts. As we will see in Chapter 4, organizing the standards in this way more closely parallels the concepts of critical thinking within professional judgment. The goal is to have a more logically organized set of standards, and to communicate the reasoning behind these to the auditor.

If a relevant CAS objective cannot be achieved in an audit, the auditor has to consider whether the overall objectives of the audit, as stated in CAS 200, can be met. The CASs are issued from time to time, and the objective of each is consistent with the overall objective of CAS 200. For all practical purposes, this consistency of objectives makes all CASs part of GAAS. Any financial statement auditor who does not follow *Handbook* CASs can be judged as performing a deficient audit.

The auditing standards literature also includes a series of Canadian Audit Practice Statements (CAPSs) or **Audit Guidelines (AuGs)**. Although officially considered less

EXHIBIT   2–1   GENERALLY ACCEPTED AUDITING STANDARDS ARE AS FOLLOWS
(A SUMMARIZATION OF CASs 200, 300, AND 315):

Objective of an Audit of Financial Statements

The overall objective of the audit is to enable the auditor to express an opinion on whether the financial statements are prepared, in all material respects, with an applicable (acceptable) financial reporting framework. Most of this text deals with fair presentation frameworks.

General standard

The auditor should comply with relevant professional ethical requirements relating to audit engagements.

Examination standards

1. The auditor should conduct an audit in accordance with Canadian Audit Standards (CASs).
2. In determining the audit procedures to perform in accord with CAS's "scope of an audit," the auditor should comply with each CAS relevant to the audit.
3. The auditor should obtain reasonable assurance that the financial statements taken as a whole are free from material misstatement, whether due to fraud or error.
4. The auditor should plan and perform an audit to reduce audit risk to an acceptably low level that is consistent with the objective of an audit.

Reporting standards

1. The report should identify the financial statements and distinguish between the responsibilities of management and the responsibilities of the auditor.
2. The auditor should determine whether the financial reporting framework adopted by management in preparing the financial statements is acceptable.
3. The auditor should refer to CASs 700, 705, and 706 when expressing an opinion on a complete set of general purpose financial statements prepared in accordance with a financial reporting framework that is designed to achieve fair presentation.

Skepticism

The auditor should plan and perform an audit with an attitude of professional skepticism, recognizing that circumstances may exist that cause the financial statements to be materially misstated.

Source: © *CICA Handbook*, CASs 200, 300, and 315.

authoritative and less binding than the CAS standards, auditors still must justify any departures from them. For the most part, the guidelines give technical help.

Appendix 2A in the Online Learning Centre lists the American GAAS. Note the similarities to GAAS of Exhibit 2–1.

 Auditing standards are audit quality recommendations that remain the same over time and for all audits. Auditing procedures, on the other hand, are quite different and include the particular and specialized actions auditors take to obtain evidence in a specific audit engagement. Audit procedures may vary, depending on the complexity of an accounting system (whether manual or computerized), the type of company, and other situation-specific factors. These differences explain why audit reports refer to an audit "conducted in accordance with generally accepted auditing standards," rather than "in accordance with auditing procedures." As such, considerable judgment is required to apply audit procedures in specific situations.

GAAS: Objectives of the Audit of Financial Statements

The overall objective of a financial statement audit is to enable the auditor to express an opinion as to whether the financial statements are prepared, in all material respects, in conformity with an applicable framework. Note how this objective implies three-party accountability. Statements are prepared, and an auditor expresses an opinion on whether the statements conform to an applicable, also known as acceptable, framework. The CICA and international standards view the terms "applicable" and "acceptable" as equivalent, but "acceptable" better reflects both the need for the reporting to be appropriate to third parties and the evaluative component in auditor professional judgment.

CAS 200 offers a very broad financial reporting framework. In this book we focus primarily on Canadian generally accepted accounting principles (GAAP) as the reporting framework. This reporting includes a balance sheet, income statement, cash flows statement, statement of retained earnings, and notes made up of a summary of significant accounting policies as well as any other explanations.

GAAS: Ethical Requirements Relating to an Audit of Financial Statements

This section of GAAS relates to the personal integrity and professional qualifications of auditors. Until 2009, section 5100 included what was called a general standard. This general standard has been replaced by the rules of professional ethics that will be covered in Chapter 4. For now, we will summarize these under four headings.

Competence

The rules of professional ethics require competence—adequate technical training and proficiency—in auditors. This competence begins with an education in accounting, since auditors hold themselves out as experts in accounting standards and financial reporting. It continues with on-the-job training in developing and applying professional judgment in real-world audit situations. This stage provides practice in performing the assurance function, in which auditors learn to (1) recognize the underlying assertions being made by management in each element (account) in the financial statements, (2) decide which evidence is relevant for supporting or refuting the assertions, (3) select and perform procedures for obtaining the evidence, and (4) evaluate the evidence and decide whether management assertions correspond to reality and GAAP. Auditors must be thoughtfully prepared to encounter a wide range of judgments on the part of management accountants—judgments varying from the truly objective to the subjective, and occasional deliberate misstatement within either extreme.

Objectivity

The ethics rules also require that auditors have an objective state of mind—that is, intellectual honesty and impartiality. Auditors must be unbiased with respect to the financial statements and other information they audit. They are expected to be fair not only to the companies and executives who issue financial information, but also to the outside persons who use it. This type of objectivity in assurance services is achieved by maintaining professional independence, in appearance as well as in fact. The appearance of independence—avoiding financial and managerial relationships with auditees—is important because this is what public users of audit reports can see. They cannot see an auditor's state of mind or attitude. Independence must be carefully guarded because the public will only recognize the professional status of auditors if they perceive them to be independent. Independence in appearance is addressed in more detail in Chapter 4.

Some critics of the public accounting profession find it undesirable that auditors are paid by their auditees. They argue that it is impossible to be independent from the party paying the fee. The alternative would be some form of public or government control of accounting fees, and very few PAs want government involvement. Auditing is unique in that, although a company pays the auditor, the real clients are the third-party users of financial statements. This concept of public interest increasingly guides standard setting and regulators in all aspects of the audit environment. An auditor, therefore, needs to differentiate between responsibilities to the company and responsibilities to third parties. Addressing such ethical conflicts in a competent manner is part of what makes public accounting a profession. (See Chapter 4 for more details.)

Due Professional Care

The exercise of due professional care requires observance of the rules of professional ethics and GAAS. Auditors must be competent and independent, exercising proper care in planning and supervising the audit, in understanding the auditee's control structure, and in obtaining sufficient appropriate evidence. Their training should include computer auditing techniques because of the importance and pervasiveness of computers in the business world.

Many social science theories incorporate the idea of a prudent professional practitioner—for example, the "economic person" of economic theory and the "reasonable person" in law. The qualities of a "prudent auditor," as summarized by Mautz and Sharaf, might be used to demonstrate the concept of due care in an audit:

> A prudent practitioner [auditor] is assumed to have a knowledge of the philosophy and practice of auditing, to have the degree of training, experience, and skill common to the average independent auditor, to have the ability to recognize indications of irregularities, and to keep abreast of developments in the perpetration and detection of irregularities. Due audit care requires the auditor to acquaint himself with the company under examination, the accounting and financial problems of the company . . . to be responsive to unusual events and unfamiliar circumstances, to persist until he has eliminated from his own mind any reasonable doubts he may have about the existence of material irregularities, and to exercise caution in instructing his assistants and reviewing their work.[1]

LESSONS AUDITORS IGNORE AT THEIR OWN RISK

Litigation is an exacting and uncompromising teacher, but it provides auditors with some hard and useful lessons. The tuition is the high cost of malpractice insurance, legal fees, adverse court decisions, embarrassing publicity and stress.
- There is no substitute for knowledge of the client's business.
- There is no substitute for effective, ongoing, substantial supervision of the work of people assigned to the engagement.
- The partner-in-charge of the engagement must constantly emphasize the importance of integrity, objectivity, and professional skepticism in carrying out the audit.

Source: W.D. Hall and A.J. Renner, "Lessons That Auditors Ignore at Their Own Risk," *Journal of Accountancy*, July 1988, pp. 50–58.

*All material from the *Journal of Accountancy* appearing in this text is reprinted with permission by the American Institute of Certified Public Accountants, Inc. Opinions of the authors are their own and do not necessarily reflect policies of the AICPA.

Due professional care is a matter of what auditors do and how well they do it. A determination of proper care must be reached based on all facts and circumstances in a particular case. When an audit firm's work becomes the subject of a lawsuit, the question of due audit care is frequently at issue (as you will see in the law cases in Chapter 5).

R E V I E W
C H E C K P O I N T S

1 What is the difference between auditing standards and auditing procedures?

2 By what standard would a judge determine the quality of due professional care? Explain.

3 What are the three specific aspects of independence that an auditor should carefully guard in the course of a financial statement audit?

GAAS Examination Standards

The examination standards are covered by CAS 315 (5100) and CAS 300 (5100), as well as by CAS 200 (5100). These standards set general quality criteria for conducting an audit

---

[1] R. Mautz and H. Sharaf, *The Philosophy of Auditing* (American Accounting Association, 1961), p. 140.

and also relate to the sufficiency and appropriateness of evidence gathered to support the audit opinion. Auditors cannot effectively satisfy the general standard requiring due professional care if they have not also satisfied the examination standards.

The CAS 200 concepts and principles that influence the examination standards include conduct of an audit; scope of an audit; reasonable assurance; audit risk and materiality; planning and supervision; internal control assessment; and sufficient, appropriate evidential matter. All of these are extensively covered in later chapters. Here we will only provide an overview.

Conduct of an Audit of Financial Statements

In order to meet the overall objective of the audit of financial statements, the auditor in Canada must comply with the CASs and the Canadian Audit Practice Statements (CAPSs). While this might seem to state the obvious, it serves to make the requirement explicit so that there are no excuses for failing to comply.

Scope of an Audit of Financial Statements

This principle refers to exercising professional judgment when deciding, based on CASs, on the type and extent of audit procedures to perform in the particular circumstance. The procedures performed must be documented during the audit engagement.

Reasonable Assurance

The evidence gathered during the audit procedures should allow the auditor to have reasonable assurance that the financial statements as a whole are free of material misstatements, whether due to fraud or error. Reasonable assurance means the same as high assurance; that is, assurance should not be too low for an audit engagement. On the other hand, it does not mean certainty or absolute assurance. If assurance were represented as the degree of confidence in the audit opinion, then a range of 90–99 percent confidence, with 95 percent being the most common, would be normal. Reasonable assurance is closely related to the concepts of audit risk and materiality.

Audit Risk and Materiality

The risk that an auditor expresses an inappropriate audit opinion when the financial statements are materially misstated is **audit risk**. As introduced in Chapter 1, this risk relates to evidence gathering. The most serious form of audit risk is failing to detect a material misstatement. These misstatements would affect the decisions of third-party users of the financial statements. Reasonable or high audit assurance can only be obtained when audit risk is acceptably low. Thus, the objective of the audit is only achieved when audit risk is reduced to an acceptably low level. This is done through performing effective audit procedures—the means auditors use to obtain evidence for their opinion. The audit opinion must be supported by sufficient appropriate evidence. This is the only acceptable way to meet the overall audit objective. An important means of controlling audit risk is through proper training, planning, and supervision. As noted in Chapter 1, the focus of audit standards is controlling audit risk, whereas accounting standards primarily deal with accounting risk.

Planning and Supervision

CAS 300 (5150) of the *Handbook* contains several considerations for planning and supervising an audit. They are all concerned with (1) preparing an audit program and supervising the audit work, (2) obtaining knowledge of the auditee's business, and (3) dealing with differences of opinion among the audit firm's own personnel.

A written audit program is desirable. An **audit program** lists the audit procedures the auditors will perform to produce the evidence needed for good audit decisions. The procedures in an audit program should include enough detail to instruct the assistants about the work to be done. (You will see detailed audit programs later in this text.)

An understanding of the auditee's business is an absolute necessity. An auditor must be able to understand the events, transactions, and practices that are characteristic of the business and its management and that may have a significant effect on the financial statements.

This knowledge helps auditors identify areas for special attention (the places where errors, irregularities, or frauds might exist), evaluate the reasonableness of accounting estimates made by management, evaluate management's representations and answers to enquiries, and make judgments about the appropriateness of accounting principles chosen.

Where does an auditor get this understanding of a business? By being there; working in other companies in the same industry; conducting interviews with management and other auditee personnel; reading extensively—accounting and audit guides of various accounting bodies, the practice manuals of the various accounting organizations, industry publications, other companies' financial statements, business periodicals, and textbooks; getting a thorough familiarization presentation from the partner-in-charge of the audit before beginning the engagement; and being observant and letting on-the-job experience sink into long-term memory. Auditors are increasingly building their understanding of the auditee's business through knowledge acquisition frameworks from strategic management. These frameworks (covered in more detail in Chapters 6 and 7) provide a structured approach to gaining deep knowledge of the auditee's business and industry.

There is no guarantee that the auditors on an audit team will always agree among themselves on audit decisions, which range from inclusion or omission of procedures to conclusions about the fair presentation of an account or the financial statements as a whole. When differences of opinion arise, audit personnel should consult with each other and with experts in the firm to try to resolve the disagreement. If resolution is not achieved, the audit firm should have procedures allowing an audit team member to document the disagreement and to dissociate himself or herself from the matter. Particularly where there are disagreements, the basis for the final audit decision on the matter should be documented in the working papers for later reference.

Timing is important for audit planning. To have time to plan an audit, auditors should be engaged before the auditee's fiscal year-end. An early appointment benefits both auditor and auditee. The audit team may be able to perform part of the audit at an **interim date**, a date some weeks or months before the fiscal year-end, and thereby make the rest of the audit work more efficient. It could include preliminary analytical procedures, preliminary assessment of internal control risk, testing the controls, and auditing some account balances. Advance knowledge of problems can enable auditors to alter the audit program so that year-end work (performed on and after the fiscal year-end date) can be more efficient. Advance planning for the observation of physical inventory and for the confirmation of accounts receivable is particularly important.

Too Late

FastTrak Corporation was angry with its auditor because the partner in charge of the engagement would not agree to let management use operating lease accounting treatment for some heavy equipment whose leases met the criteria for capitalization. FastTrak fired the auditors ten weeks after the company's balance sheet date, then began contacting other audit firms to restart the audit. However, the audit report was due at the OSC in six weeks. Every other audit firm contacted by FastTrak refused the audit because it could not be planned and performed properly with such a tight deadline.

Internal Control Assessment

The examination standard CAS 315.12–23 (5100) requires an understanding of the auditee's internal control. This consists of a company's control environment, accounting system, and control procedures. The existence of a satisfactory internal control system reduces the probability of errors and irregularities in the accounts. Auditors need to know enough about the auditee's control system to assess the control risk. Control risk is the probability that a material misstatement (error or irregularity) could occur and not be prevented or detected on a timely basis by the internal control structure, as is discussed in CAS 200 (5220).

The primary purpose of control risk assessment is to help the auditors develop the audit program. This standard presumes two necessary relationships: (a) good internal control reduces the control risk, minimizing the extent of subsequent audit procedures; (b) conversely, poor internal control produces greater control risk, increasing the necessary extent of subsequent audit procedures. If auditors saw no relationship between the quality of controls and the accuracy of output, then an assessment of control risk would be pointless. Audit efficiency would be lost in many cases. (Chapters 7 and 9 explain the work involved in control risk assessment.)

Sufficient Appropriate Evidential Matter

Examination standard CAS 200 (5100) recognizes that evidence is the heart of audits of financial statements and it requires auditors to obtain enough to justify opinions on those statements. Evidence is the influence on auditors that ultimately guides their decisions. It includes the underlying accounting data and all available corroborating information as discussed in CAS 330 (5143) and CAS 500 (5300). Appropriate evidence—that is, reliable and relevant—may take many forms: quantitative or qualitative, objective or subjective, absolutely compelling or mildly persuasive. The audit team's task is to collect and evaluate sufficient appropriate evidence in order to afford a reasonable and logical basis for audit decisions.

CONTROL LAPSE CONTRIBUTES TO DUPLICATE PAYMENTS

All Points Trucking processed insurance claims on damages to shipments in transit on its trucks, paying them through a self-insurance plan. After payment, the claim documents were not marked "paid." Later, the same documents were processed again for duplicate payments to customers, who kicked back 50 percent to a dishonest All Points employee. When the auditors learned that the claims were not marked as paid, they concluded that the specific control risk of duplicate payments was high and extended their procedures to include a search for duplicate payments in the damage expense account. They found the fraudulent claims and traced the problem to the dishonest employee. Embezzlements of $35,000 per year were stopped.

The standard refers to sufficient rather than absolute evidence. In most cases, not all of a company's transactions and events are audited, and audit decisions are made by inference based on data samples. The standard gives broad outlines for procedures for gathering evidence—inspection, observation, enquiry, and confirmation. Chapter 8 gives a more thorough explanation of audit objectives and procedures.

· ·

REVIEW CHECKPOINTS

4 What three elements of planning and supervision are considered essential in audit practice?

5 Why does the timing of an auditor's appointment matter in the conduct of a financial statement audit?

6 Why does an auditor obtain an understanding of the internal control system?

7 Define audit evidence.

· ·

GAAS Reporting Standards

LEARNING OBJECTIVE
3 Interpret the standard unqualified audit report.

The ultimate objective of independent auditors—the report on the audit—is guided by the GAAS reporting standards. The three that are identified in CAS 200 deal with acceptability of the financial reporting framework, auditor and management responsibilities, and report content. Auditing standards dictate the use of a "standard report" when the auditor is expressing an opinion on a complete set of general purpose financial statements prepared to achieve fair presentation. Detailed guidance on these reports is given in CAS 700 and 705. These standards cover audit reports using a fair presentation reporting framework, as well as audit reports using a compliance financial reporting framework. Special considerations for reporting on special purpose financial statements, or financial information other than a full set of financial statements, are covered in CAS 800 and 805. In this chapter we provide an overview of the CAS 700 audit report on fair presentation for a set of general purpose financial statements. Chapter 3 gives more indepth coverage.

An unqualified report, or a report without reservation, means that the auditors are not calling attention to anything wrong with the audit work or the financial statements. The standard unqualified audit report is shown in Exhibit 2–2 (on page 38), and you should review it in relation to the discussion that follows. A qualified report means that either the financial statements contain a departure from GAAP or the scope of the audit work was limited. (You will study qualified audit reports in Chapter 3.)

All standard unqualified reports contain the following features:

1. **Title.** The title should refer to the auditor, thus indicating that the report is based on an audit examination and not some other types of engagement.

2. **Address.** The report is normally addressed to those it is prepared for; this may be the shareholders or those chargsed with governance of the auditee organization.

3. **Introductory paragraph.** This should identify the financial statements and declare that they were audited.

4. **Responsibilities.** The second paragraph should state management's responsibility for the financial statements and a third should describe the auditor's responsibility for the audit report.

5. **Description of the audit.** The fourth and fifth paragraphs should declare that the audit was conducted in accordance with generally accepted auditing standards and describe the principal characteristics of an audit. This covers what is traditionally referred to as the scope of the audit.

6. **Opinion.** The report's sixth paragraph should contain an opinion (opinion paragraph), stating whether the financial statements present fairly, in all material respects, . . . in accordance with generally accepted accounting principles.

7. **Signature.** The auditor should sign the report, manually or otherwise.

8. **Date.** The report should be dated no earlier than the date when the auditor obtained sufficient appropriate audit evidence supporting the auditor's opinion on the financial statements; this will be after those with recognized authority (e.g., board of directors) have taken responsibility for (i.e., approved) the financial statements. The engagement quality control review discussed later in this chapter (CSCQ-1, CAS 220) also needs to be completed before the date of the auditor's report.

9. **Auditor's Address.** The report should name the location in the country or jurisdiction where the auditor practices.

Generally Accepted Accounting Principles (GAAP)

In the audit report, the opinion sentence shows the GAAP standard has been met: "In our opinion, the financial statements . . . present fairly in all material respects the financial position . . . and the results of operations and cash flows . . . in accordance with Canadian

EXHIBIT 2-2   INDEPENDENT AUDITOR'S REPORT

To the Shareholders of.............

Report on the Financial Statements

We have audited the accompanying financial statements of ABC Company, which comprise the balance sheet as at December 31, 20X1, and the income statement, statement of changes in equity, and cash flow statement for the year then ended, and a summary of significant accounting policies and other explanatory notes.

Management's Responsibility for the Financial Statements

Management is responsible for the preparation and fair presentation of these financial statements in accordance with Canadian generally accepted accounting principles; this includes the design, implementation, and maintenance of internal control relevant to the preparation and fair presentation of financial statements that are free from material misstatement, whether due to fraud or error.

Auditor's Responsibility

Our responsibility is to express an opinion on these financial statements based on our audit. We conducted our audit in accordance with Canadian generally accepted auditing standards. Those standards require that we comply with ethical requirements and plan and perform the audit to obtain reasonable assurance whether the financial statements are free from material misstatement.

An audit involves performing procedures to obtain audit evidence about the amounts and disclosures in the financial statements. The procedures selected depend on the auditor's judgment, including the assessment of the risks of material misstatement of the financial statements, whether due to fraud or error. In making those risk assessments, the auditor considers internal control relevant to the entity's preparation and fair presentation of the financial statements in order to design audit procedures that are appropriate in the circumstances, but not for the purpose of expressing an opinion on the effectiveness of the entity's internal control. An audit also includes evaluating the appropriateness of accounting policies used and the reasonableness of accounting estimates made by management, as well as evaluating the overall presentation of financial statements.

We believe that the audit evidence we have obtained is sufficient and appropriate to provide a basis for our audit opinion.

Opinion

In our opinion, the financial statements present fairly, in all material respects, the financial position of ABC Company as of December 31, 20X1, and of its financial performance and its cash flows for the year then ended in accordance with Canadian generally accepted accounting principles.

[Auditor's signature]

[Date of auditor's report]

[Auditor's address]

Source: © CICA Handbook, CAS 700.

generally accepted accounting principles." Here, the auditors make a statement of fact about their belief (opinion). Auditors are the professional experts, and users of financial statements rely upon the audit opinion.

However, determining the appropriate GAAP in a company's circumstances is not always easy. Students often think of *CICA Handbook* Recommendations on accounting standards as the complete body of GAAP. This is not so, as GAAP actually consists of all the accounting methods and procedures that have substantial authoritative support. The *CICA Handbook* is only one source of such support, albeit the most powerful. It is widely recognized that the meaning of the expression "present fairly in accordance with GAAP" in the audit report establishes a hierarchy of authoritative support for various sources of GAAP.

Handbook Recommendations cover many accounting issues and problems, and its standards for these are generally compelling. However, the *Handbook* does not cover all conceivable accounting matters. When a conclusion about GAAP cannot be found in *Handbook* Recommendations, auditors follow a hierarchy to find the next highest source of support for an entity's accounting solution to a financial reporting problem. Reference can be made to positions taken by provincial securities commissions, international standards, authoritative pronouncements by other countries' standards boards, industry audit and accounting guides, consensus positions of the CICA's Emerging Issues Committee, and other accounting literature.

The unqualified opinion sentence contains implicit messages: (a) the accounting principles in the financial statements have general acceptance—that is, authoritative support; (b) the accounting principles used by the company are appropriate in the circumstances; (c) the financial statements and notes are informative of matters that may affect their use, understanding, and interpretation—that is, full disclosure accounting principle; (d) the classification and summarization in the financial statements is neither too detailed nor too condensed for users; and (e) the financial statements are accurate within practical materiality limits covered in CAS 320 (5142). This last feature refers to both materiality and accuracy. Auditors and users do not expect financial account balances to be absolutely accurate, as accounting is too complicated and includes too many estimates to expect this. After all, many financial reports use numbers rounded to the thousands, even millions, of dollars! Financial figures are "fair" as long as they are not materially misstated—that is, misstated enough to make a difference in users' decisions. All of these issues in applying GAAP involve professional judgment, which can be defined very generally as making a decision using professional standards and other criteria while maintaining professional ethics responsibilities. (Chapter 4 covers auditors' professional ethics responsibilities.)

Consistency

The reporting standards call for explicit reporting in accordance with GAAP, except in special circumstances. Prior to 1991, all audit reports contained a sentence confirming that GAAP had been "consistently applied" when no changes in the application of accounting principles had been made. This sentence referred to a company's use of the same accounting procedures and methods from year to year. However, *CICA Handbook*, section 1506, governs the accounting and disclosure of a company's change of accounting principles. In 1991 the reporting standards were changed to allow the audit report to be silent—that is, implicit—about consistency when no accounting changes had been made or when any changes that were made were properly disclosed in the financial statements.

Adequate Disclosure

The reporting standards include a second implicit element. They require auditors to use professional judgment in deciding whether the financial statements and related disclosures contain all the important accounting information users need. It may be necessary to disclose information not specified in authoritative support sources, for instance, if there is an unusual fact situation not encountered before. Using this standard, auditors have latitude to determine what is important and what is not. Likewise, users of financial statements also have the right to claim that certain information is necessary for adequate disclosure. In fact, many lawsuits are brought forward on this issue, and auditors must show reasons for the lack of disclosure. As noted in Chapter 1, disclosures are an important means of dealing with accounting risk and a significant aspect of auditor professional judgment, as many aspects of implementing accounting and auditing standards are not covered by them.

When auditors believe that certain information is necessary for adequate disclosure but the company refuses to disclose it, a departure from GAAP exists. Usually, a qualified opinion is written, and the reason for the departure (missing disclosure) is described in the audit report. Sometimes the missing disclosure is added to the audit report itself.

Report Content

The reporting standard of CAS 700 and 705 states the requirements for an opinion. Two types of modifications to the report are relevant: those that affect the audit opinion and those that do not. In this section we provide an overview of matters that affect the audit opinion. Chapter 3 provides more details on these and other modifications.

CAS 700 provides guidance for the standard audit report, while CAS 705 provides guidance on reservations in the auditor's report and requires that the report must contain either the opinion on the financial statements or an assertion that an opinion cannot be given. This means that there are two classes of opinion statements: all opinions on statements (i.e., unqualified, adverse, and qualified opinions) and the disclaimer of opinion. An **adverse opinion** is the opposite of an unqualified opinion. It states that the financial statements are not in accordance with GAAP. A **disclaimer of opinion** is an auditor's declaration that no opinion is given. The standard applies to financial statements as a whole; that is, the standard applies equally to the set of financial statements and footnotes and to each individual financial statement and footnote.

According to CAS 705, an explanation is required whenever there is a report reservation. Thus, when an adverse opinion, qualified opinion, or disclaimer of opinion is rendered, all the substantive reasons for doing so must be given in an additional paragraph(s).

Other reporting standards relate to auditor responsibilities and identifying the financial statements covered by the opinion. Every time PAs (even when acting as accountants associated with unaudited financial statements) are associated by name or by action with financial statements, they must report on their work and responsibility. The character of the work is usually described by the standard reference to an audit in accordance with generally accepted auditing standards. But, if an audit has been restricted in some way, or if the statements are simply unaudited, the auditor must say so.

The "degree of responsibility" is indicated by the form of the opinion. Auditors take full responsibility for their opinion about conformity with GAAP when they give either an unqualified or an adverse opinion. They take no responsibility whatsoever when they give a disclaimer of opinion. When they give qualified opinions, they take responsibility for all matters except those that are the reasons for the qualification. (Qualified and adverse opinions and discaimers of opinion are discussed more fully in Chapter 3.) These are part of the association rules that cover information the PA is associated with. The association rules will be covered in Chapter 3, after you have been introduced to other types of PA engagements.

REVIEW CHECKPOINTS

8   What are the nine important features of a standard unqualified audit report?

9   Identify various authoritative supports for GAAP, with an indication of their ranking.

10   Do auditors take any responsibility for auditees' choices of accounting principles?

11   What four kinds of audit opinion statements are identified in this chapter? What is the message of each one?

12   What messages are usually implicit in a standard audit report?

Professional Skepticism and Critical Thinking

LEARNING OBJECTIVE
4 Outline the characteristics of professional skepticism and critical thinking.

Professional skepticism, a phrase that appears frequently in auditing literature and speech, is an auditor's tendency to not believe management assertions, but instead to find sufficient support for the assertions through appropriate audit evidence. Professional skepticism is inherent in applying due care in accordance with the general standards. The business environment that has seen errors and fraud in financial reports dictates this basic level of professional skepticism: "A potential conflict of interest always exists between the auditor and the management of the enterprise under audit."

The belief that the potential for conflict of interest always exists causes auditors to perform procedures in search of errors and frauds that would have a material effect on financial statements. This tends to make audits more extensive and expensive. The extra work is not needed in the vast majority of audits where there are no material errors, irregularities, or frauds. Nevertheless, auditors approach all audits with a mindset framed by the actions of a minority of people, and they must be careful, therefore, to also control their professional skepticism. Once audit procedures give them evidence that there have been no errors or fraud, the audit team must be willing to let go of their skepticism and accept that fact.

Still, due audit care does call for a degree of professional skepticism—an inclination to question all material assertions made by management whether oral, written, or contained in the accounting records. However, this attitude must be balanced by a willingness to respect the integrity of management. Auditors should neither blindly expect that every management is dishonest nor thoughtlessly assume management to be totally honest. The key lies in auditors' objectivity and in the audit requirement of gathering sufficient appropriate evidence and evaluating financial statement disclosures to reach reasonable and supportable audit decisions.

With the adoption of international standards with their greater emphasis on the most basic principles of accounting and auditing, the role of critical thinking in professional judgment will become more important. For example, critical thinking and skepticism become more important when the auditor takes an equal responsibility for detecting fraud as he does for detecting unintentional errors. In addition, there is an increased need for auditors to use critical thinking skills in meeting the objectives of the broader assurance engagement concept that are being developed. Critical thinking considers how, when, *and whom* management is trying to persuade in making its assertions. This is necessary in evaluating the appropriateness of how the assertions are presenteed to third parties. As noted in Chapter 1, the economic crisis of 2008/2009 is creating new concerns about the limits of the audit process and the financial reporting that it verifies. When combined with new concepts like accounting risk, critical thinking can be used to help address these concerns. A framework for critical thinking is introduced in Chapter 4, and the next section provides an overview of the audit process along with the development of a broader assurance engagement concept.

R E V I E W
C H E C K P O I N T S

13 Why should auditors act as though there is always a potential conflict of interest between the auditor and the management of the enterprise under audit?

14 Can the auditor detect deception without being skeptical? Explain.

OVERVIEW OF THE AUDIT PROCESS

LEARNING OBJECTIVE
⑤ Summarize the audit process.

The audit process itself is outlined in Exhibit 2–3, and in this section we give an overview of each of the steps involved. Subsequent chapters provide much more detail.

1. The Auditor Should Plan on an Effective Audit Engagement

CAS 300, entitled "Planning An Audit of the Financial Statements," starts by stating that in planning an engagement the audit objective is to carry out an effective audit. The rest of the steps indicate how to accomplish this objective.

2. Are Preconditions for an Audit Present?

The auditor must determine the acceptability of the financial reporting framework used, as is outlined in CAS 210. For example, in considering the needs of third-party users, the auditor must decide if general purpose or special purpose financial reports need to be used.

EXHIBIT 2-3   OVERVIEW OF THE AUDIT PROCESS

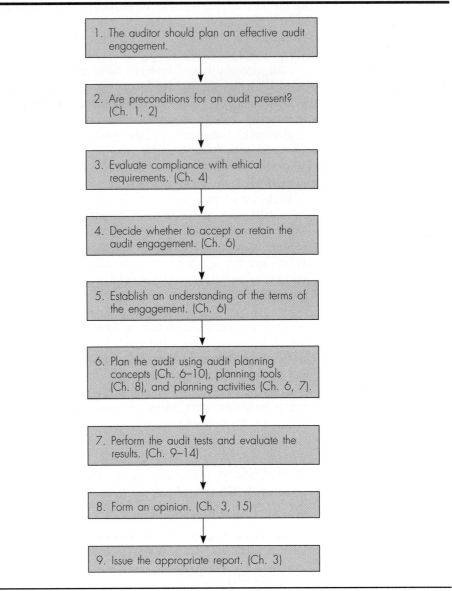

The auditor also must determine whether management and those charged with governance understand their responsibilities, and whether there are any scope limitations being imposed by the engagement.

3. Evaluate Compliance with Ethical Requirements, Including Independence

Auditors also need to assess whether they are independent of the auditee, as without this the audit cannot be effective in meeting the public interest. This is a key consideration in quality control standards for audits of financial statements. Factors that might affect the auditor's independence include having any significant financial interest in the auditee or having performed other services for the auditee that will put them in the position of auditing their own work. The point of independence rules is preventing actions that will constitute conflicts of interest, or be perceived as such, by users of financial statements. As you will see, independence and conflict-of-interest rules can become quite technical, but all of these need to be resolved before accepting the audit engagement.

A final major issue to consider before accepting an engagement is competence. Does the auditor have the business and industry expertise to carry out the audit effectively? Does the auditor have the resources to perform an effective audit in the available time? Does the auditor have enough staff to take on the audit engagement and realistically meet reporting deadlines? Large organizations tend to be audited by larger PA firms that have resources in place, such as offices and staff experienced in areas where the auditee has significant activities. Economies of scale are a major factor for global audits. For example, in auditing a large airline company, auditors need to be available to examine widely dispersed operations, they need specialized expertise on local safety regulations that may require extensive technical monitoring reports, and a control system is needed to perform the necessary inspections and file timely reports with local regulators. Failure to do these things can cause the airline to be shut down. To effectively assure proper disclosure of these risks and uncertainties in financial reporting, the auditor needs to have the necessary expertise and resources.

4. Decide Whether to Accept or Retain the Audit Engagement

There are additional factors to consider in accepting or retaining an engagement. One important decision is whether to do an audit in the first place. About half of all PA firms in Canada who did audits before the creation of the Canadian Public Accountability Board (CPAB) no longer do so as they feel it is not worthwhile to be monitored by the CPAB or to adhere to the new quality control standards for listed companies.

The consequences of an auditor leaving an engagement can be serious in the SOX world, where the departing auditor must within 24 hours publicly report to the SEC as to why they left. Under this system, other PA firms can quickly learn what they are getting into. Recall from Chapter 1 the example of a $2 billion electronics manufacturer being forced to replace their CEO, and the board promising to take training classes in proper financial reporting and to hire a financially literate director for the audit committee before they could find a replacement auditor! This illustrates that auditors have much more leverage under SOX than they did previously.

Several issues need to be considered in accepting an engagement. Why is the audit requested? Does the client actually need an audit? What are the client's expectations? Answering such questions helps manage expectations on both sides and reduces problems later on. The above example from Chapter 1 included some dramatic changes in expectations with the new auditor.

Assuming this is not the very first audit engagement for an auditee, an important issue for a first-time audit engagement is obtaining the auditee's permission to contact the predecessor auditor. Rules of professional ethics require getting such permission. The predecessor auditor has unique insights and knowledge that a successor auditor would find invaluable in building their understanding of the auditee. On the other hand, an auditee's failure to give permission for this is a warning sign that they may be a risk or have something to hide.

Increasingly, PA firms are paying more attention to the risks all auditees bring to an engagement. If those risks prove to be too great, the PA firm will decline the engagement. When the PA firm turns down an engagement with a long-existing auditee, it is sometimes referred to as "firing the client." As the demise of Arthur Andersen proved, firms should not keep risky auditees, no matter how lucrative their fees. Fortunately, the recent improvements in corporate governance have reduced these risks for auditors. Some other questions the auditor must consider when entering an engagement are the likelihood of being sued, the risk of fraud, whether management is trustworthy and competent, and the risk that the auditee will fail soon after the financial statements are issued. Some auditors are more risk averse than others; therefore, this is, in large part, a decision based on risk preferences. The acceptance decision issues are summarized in the following box.

ISSUES TO CONSIDER WHEN DECIDING TO ACCEPT OR RETAIN THE AUDITEE

1. Why is the auditee requesting an audit?
2. Will the auditee allow the auditor to contact the predecessor auditor, if applicable?
3. Is the auditee in financial difficulties?
4. Is the auditor independent for this engagement?
5. Is the auditee trustworthy?
6. Is the auditor competent for this engagement?

---

5. Establish an Understanding of the Terms of the Engagement

If the auditor decides to accept the audit engagement, the auditor should document the understanding with the auditee management about the expectations and limitations of the engagement. The auditor next needs to obtain a better understanding of the auditee's overall control environment and related risks, along with a better understanding of the auditee's business for the period under audit.

Understand the Auditee's Business

To gain an understanding of the auditee's business, the auditor performs preliminary analytical procedures. These include asking management questions and analyzing the relationships of financial data for the period under audit. These procedures help identify unusual and risky areas that the auditor may want to target for more detailed audit work. Enquiries can also be made with outsiders who deal with the auditee—including bankers, lawyers, outside analysts, and business associations—to help assess its overall reputation.

Use of industry, auditee, and competitor websites as well as Internet searches are proving to be powerful tools in gaining an understanding of the auditee's business. Web logs (blogs) include comments from customers, rivals' employees, and even management (see GM's vice-chairman Bob Lutz's FastLaneBlog). These are a free and growing source of very current information on just about any topic. Blogs are estimated to be the fastest growing use of the Internet. They tend to be linked by topic, so they may soon become an invaluable information source for auditors. During the 2008/2009 economic crisis, blogs often provided the earliest information about company cost cutting and layoffs. Blogs are bringing more transparency to company activities. One caution is that the information is frequently biased, anecdotal, and speculative. Although unreliable on their own, when combined with other information, blogs can be useful in identifying company risks and potential financial statement disclosures.

An important new development in audit preparation is placing forensic accountants within regular audit teams to screen for fraud risks. The forensic specialists talk to management and audit committees, especially when there are concerns about internal controls or information from whistle-blowers. Audit standards since 2003 do not allow auditors to assume that management is honest. Instead, auditors must assess the risk of management fraud, and if it is too high (rarely is there certainty of no risk), they may call in the forensic specialists. The risks must be continually reassessed throughout the engagement as more evidence is gathered. Chapters 7 and 8 cover assessment of risks in auditing in more detail.

6. Plan the Audit

Assess Materiality

With sufficient understanding of the auditee's business and user needs, the auditor can further plan for the audit. The most basic planning decision is establishing the materiality level—that is, the amount of misstatement beyond which user decisions would be affected. Clearly, a one-penny overstatement in office supplies will not affect any user's decision. But there is a level at which such overstatements will make a difference—think back to the restaurant illustration at the beginning of Chapter 1. What amount of misstatement would be important in that case?

Auditors need to make this assessment on every audit. The materiality discussed in your financial accounting courses is the same materiality used in planning the audit. You may wonder, why not just set materiality at zero? That would be too costly, and impossible as well, as estimates involving forecasts of future events must be used in GAAP—otherwise everything would have to be realized before financial statements could be produced. So auditors and users must settle for a materiality amount greater than zero. How much greater will depend on user needs and other circumstances—part of the context of the engagement, covered in Chapter 1.

There are both qualitative and quantitative aspects to materiality assessment. Examples of qualitative aspects include whether a misstatement will result in a change in an earnings trend, a change from a loss to a positive income, or a breach of a bond covenant. An intentional misstatement is much more serious than a random or unintentional one. An example of quantitative materiality is some rule of thumb based on a fixed percentage. One example from the earlier restaurant scenario is to use 5 percent of reported earnings as the quantitative materiality assessment.

The assessment of materiality has a pervasive impact on the audit and is, therefore, a key judgment made in audit planning. The engagement partner normally makes this decision near the beginning of the engagement. The materiality judgment and its consequences are further discussed in Chapters 3 and 6.

Assess Audit Risk

After identifying the materiality level, the auditor needs to assess the acceptable risk of material misstatement in the financial statements after the audit. This risk is called **audit risk**. As noted in Chapter 1, audit risk is <u>fundamentally</u> the audit's failure to detect <u>material</u> factual errors in the auditee's financial statements. The acceptable level of audit risk is based on the possible consequences of the failure. Significant consequences include client dissatisfaction, lawsuits, and auditor loss of reputation. Arthur Andersen's failure was primarily due to its lost reputation over the Enron prosecution when its clients left in droves. In fact, the whole profession's reputation was tarnished, and it is now living with the consequences in the form of the CPAB, SOX, and other regulatory fallout.

The auditor takes these things into account by planning an appropriate level of audit risk for the engagement. The assessment also considers the auditor's tolerance for risk—the higher the tolerance, the higher the planned audit risk. Guidance for audit risk is generally a matter of firm policy as all partners feel the consequences of this decision. As with materiality, it is not normally possible to reduce the risk to zero, and the auditor must, therefore, decide on a maximum acceptable level, which is referred to as planned audit risk, or audit risk for short. Also like materiality, the audit risk has a pervasive impact on audit planning, which explains why it is important to identify the risk level early in the planning process. Generally, the greater the materiality or audit risk levels are, the less evidence the auditor needs to gather. If either level is decreased, the auditor must do more work.

Make Preliminary Assessment of Inherent and Control Risk

In the post-SOX environment, a decision needs to be made early on whether the internal controls are providing sufficiently reliable data. A review of prior year's audit working papers can be very valuable for this. But auditors are increasingly interested in the auditee's capacity to maintain good controls, as now the auditee's management needs to take more explicit responsibility for them. For new audits, auditors ask for evidence that the underlying accounting records reconcile to the general ledger and that ending balances flow to the financial statements. Auditors also frequently ask for copies of prior-year financial statements and all adjusting journal entries as part of the process of initially assessing the auditee's internal control capabilities.

In planning the audit, audit risk can be viewed as consisting of several components, with two important ones being inherent risk and control risk. **Inherent risk** is the susceptibility to material misstatement before considering the effects of controls. **Control risk** is the risk that the internal controls will fail to detect and correct the material misstatements that do occur. Many auditors combine the evaluation of inherent and control risks because they feel this simplifies audit planning. For example, strong controls—that is, control risk is low—might have a deterrent effect on inherent risk so that inherent risks are lower when controls are strong.

Inherent and control risks are not set at some planned level by the auditor, as audit risk is. Inherent and control risks are part of the auditee characteristics, part of the context of the audit. There is nothing the auditor can do to change these risks during the audit. The auditor's responsibilities are to assess them for audit planning purposes and to report on fairness of presentation of the auditee's financial statements.

Decide on Audit Approach for Gathering Evidence

For the audit of financial statements, the level of inherent and control risks can greatly influence the remainder of the audit approach for gathering evidence. The biggest impact is on the mix of testing of controls and testing of account balance procedures. The timing of the audit work can also be affected. When auditors rely more on tests of controls, the audit work can be spread more evenly over the period under audit. When auditors do not rely as much on controls, most of the audit work is concentrated in the period immediately following the balance sheet date. More details on audit approach decisions are provided in Parts II and III of this text.

There can be considerable overlap between testing of controls as part of the audit of financial statements and testing of controls as part of the audit of internal control statements. The major difference between them, however, is that in the latter case the focus is on design of internal controls at a point in time, whereas in financial statement audits the focus of testing is on the performance of the system of control over the period of time covered by the financial statements. Another way to characterize the difference is that control statements require more extensive tests of the design of the system whereas financial statement audits focus on testing the operations, assuming the design is good. (For more details, see Part II of the text.) These planning issues are summarized in the following box.

PLANNING THE AUDIT

1. Establish materiality.
2. Identify acceptable audit risk.
3. Make preliminary assessment of inherent and control risks.
4. Decide on audit approach for gathering evidence.

---

7. Perform the Audit Tests and Evaluate the Results

There are three broad categories of audit testing:

1. tests of internal control
2. substantive tests using analytical procedures
3. other substantive tests

The difference between control testing (item 1) and substantive testing (items 2 and 3) is that control tests are indirect tests of the dollar accuracy of the financial statement amounts whereas substantive tests are direct tests of the accuracy of the financial statement numbers. At the planning stage, the decision on approach will either concentrate most of the audit work in the months after the balance sheet date (the balance sheet approach or substantive approach) or spread the audit work over a much longer period, including the months well before the balance sheet date (the income statement approach or combined approach). There are fewer audit staffing problems when the audit work can be spread over a longer period, but the combined approaches tend to be more complex and limited to audits in larger organizations.

Regardless of the strategy, the auditor must collect sufficient appropriate evidence to support the audit opinion. The objective is the same, but the efficiency with which the audit can be conducted can vary with the approach chosen. The effectiveness of an audit should not be influenced by the type of audit approach followed.

PERFORM THE AUDIT TESTS AND EVALUATE THE RESULTS

- Tests of controls for
  (a) verifying that control risk is acceptably low
  (b) finding indirect evidence that the risk of material misstatement is acceptably low
  (c) issuing an opinion on management's report on internal controls
- Analytical procedures as substantive tests
- Other substantive procedures, tests of details of balances

---

8. Form an Opinion

At the end of the audit, after all the evidence has been gathered, the auditor should be able to reach a conclusion about the fairness of the financial statements presentation. If not, he or she must be willing to state that they cannot reach an opinion. A conclusion on fairness of presentation requires the auditor to consider how well the reporting framework applied in the auditee's circumstances. This decision is quite different from deciding whether sufficient appropriate evidence has been gathered. Because of this important difference, the audit can be viewed as involving two major stages: (1) evidence gathering and (2) deciding on the appropriateness of the financial reporting given the evidence and the reporting framework. The second part is more of an interpretive stage and your financial accounting courses have focused on preparing you to make decisions at this stage. This book concentrates on the first aspect because this is the focus of the audit risk concept and auditing standards. There are, however, some significant gaps in auditing and accounting standards, and critical thinking plays a role in helping to bridge these gaps in a reasonable way.

9. Issue the Appropriate Report

The audit report is the most important part of the audit process because it is the only part that is visible to the public. If the report did not reflect the auditor's true belief, the auditor would be guilty of producing a fraudulent document. The SEC has made such accusations against some of the major accounting firms. Hence, it is extremely important that the auditor's belief be accurately reflected in the report. This need to reveal beliefs is the reason auditor independence and integrity are so important. Users of the report need be confident that it reflects the auditor's true beliefs before they will accept it. Conflicts of interest that can arise when the auditor is paid by the auditee to verify its performance should not get in the way of truthfulness. The rules of professional ethics help assure this.

There are two major types of reports issued by the auditor: the auditor's report on the financial statements, and the auditor's reports that are restricted to management and the audit committee. The first report is public when the auditee is a listed company. The second is a by-product of that audit and indicates how the auditee's operations can be improved. The first report is further explained in Chapter 3 and the second in Chapters 16 and 17. Most of this text deals with evidence gathering for the first report.

REVIEW CHECKPOINTS

15   What factors should the auditor consider in accepting an audit engagement?

16   What are the auditor responsibilities in detecting fraud?

ASSURANCE STANDARDS

LEARNING OBJECTIVE

6 Explain the importance of general assurance standards, using examples of assurance matters.

A special framework in the IFAC Handbook covers the international standards for assurance engagements. It was issued in 2005 and was heavily influenced by the *CICA Handbook*, section 5025. However, ISA standards for some assurance engagements have not yet been integrated with its framework. As a consequence, the CICA continues to use its original assurance standard. Thus, the *CICA Handbook* assurance standard section 5025 is not part of CAS.

In March 1997, the CICA issued section 5025, "Standards for Assurance Engagements." The standard, the first of its kind in the world, is significant because it is intended to provide an umbrella for all existing and future audit-type engagements, including many that don't involve financial statements. Section 5025 also contemplates different levels of assurance.

An *assurance engagement* is defined in paragraphs 5025.03–.04 as follows:

> An engagement where, pursuant to an accountability relationship between two or more parties, a practitioner is engaged to issue a written communication expressing a conclusion concerning a subject matter for which the accountable party is responsible. An *accountability relationship* is a prerequisite for an assurance engagement. An *accountability relationship* exists when one party (the "accountable party") is answerable to and/or is responsible to another party (the "user") for a subject matter, or voluntarily chooses to report to another party on a subject matter. The accountability relationship may arise either as a result of an agreement or legislation, or because a user can be expected to have an interest in how the accountable party has discharged its responsibility for a subject matter.

The assurance standard does not supercede existing audit and review standards, but it is influencing changes to more specific standards. It is designed to provide guidance for expanding assurance services to subject matters not currently covered in the *Handbook*. For example, it is the assurance standard that introduced the three-party accountability concept. The general relationships in assurance engagements are given in Exhibit 2–4.

An assertion is a statement about some aspect of a subject matter—for example, that a building exists as of a certain point in time. The assurance standards in section 5025 are quite broad in that they can be applied to assertions that are only implied—**direct reporting engagements**—as well as to written assertions, called **attestation engagements**. *Handbook* paragraphs 5025.05–.06 state the following:

> In an attest engagement the practitioner's conclusion will be on a written assertion prepared by the accountable party. The assertion evaluates, using suitable criteria, the subject matter for which the accountable party is responsible. In a direct reporting engagement, the practitioner's conclusion will evaluate directly using suitable criteria, the subject matter for which

EXHIBIT 2–4   UNIVERSE OF PA ENGAGEMENTS

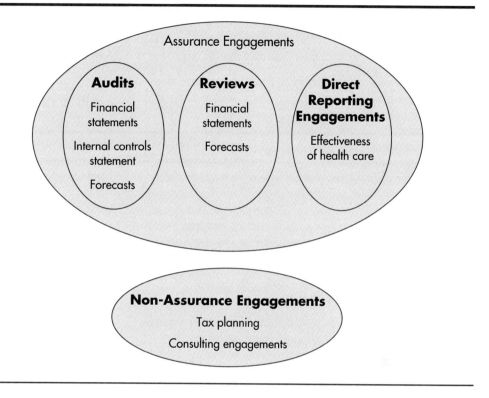

the accountable party is responsible. . . . In these standards, the accountable party is referred to as management. Depending on the circumstance, the user could include a variety of stakeholders such as shareholders, creditors, customers, the board of directors, the audit committee, legislators, or regulators. The practitioner is the person who has overall responsibility for the assurance engagement.

These relationships are illustrated in Exhibit 2–5. For example, the practitioner in paragraph 5025.06 of the exhibit has traditionally been referred to as an **external auditor** in a financial statement assurance engagement. Since most of this text deals with financial statement audits, we will continue using this terminology. After we have become

EXHIBIT 2–5   THREE PARTIES INVOLVED IN AN ASSURANCE ENGAGEMENT
(THREE-PARTY ACCOUNTABILITY)

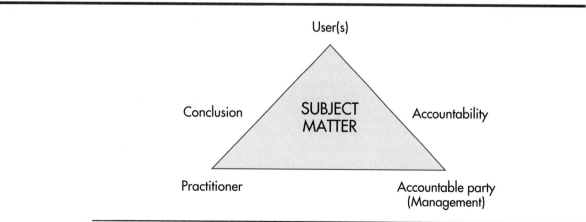

Source: © *CICA Handbook*, paragraph 5025.07.

familiar with other assurance services in Chapter 16, we will explain the assurance standards in more detail. In this chapter, we focus on existing auditing standards and provide an overall comparison between GAAS and the assurance standard.

The assurance standard was written long after GAAS for financial statement audits. In Exhibit 2–6 you can see the ideas borrowed from the pre-existing GAAS of section 5100.

EXHIBIT   2–6   COMPARISON OF ASSURANCE (5025) AND AUDIT STANDARDS (5100)
(The numbers are in the sequence of the more familiar and specific GAAS of section 5100.)

Assurance Standards	Auditing Standards
1. The practitioner should seek management's acknowledgment of responsibility for the subject matter as it relates to the objective of the engagement. If the practitioner does not obtain management's acknowledgment, the practitioner should: (a) obtain other evidence that an accountability relationship exists, such as a reference to legislation or a regulation; (b) consider how the lack of management's acknowledgment might affect his or her work and conclusion; and (c) disclose in his or her report that acknowledgment of responsibility has not been obtained. The assurance engagement should be performed with due care and with an objective state of mind. The practitioner and any other persons performing the assurance engagement should have adequate proficiency in such engagements. The practitioner and any other persons performing the assurance engagement should collectively possess adequate knowledge of the subject matter. In addition, when a specialist is involved, the practitioner should consider whether the practitioner's involvement in the engagement and knowledge of the subject matter elements involving the specialist is sufficient to enable the practitioner to discharge his or her responsibilities.	1. The examination should be performed and the report prepared by a person or persons having adequate technical training and proficiency in auditing, with due care and with an objective state of mind.
2. The work should be adequately planned and the practitioner should ensure that any other persons performing the assurance engagement are properly supervised.	2. The work should be adequately planned and properly executed, using sufficient knowledge of the entity's business as a basis. If assistants are employed they should be properly supervised.
	3. A sufficient understanding of internal control should be obtained to plan the audit. When control risk is assessed below maximum, sufficient appropriate audit evidence should be obtained through tests of controls to support the assessment.
4. The practitioner should consider the concept of significance and the relevant components of engagement risk when planning and performing the assurance engagement. Sufficient appropriate evidence should be obtained to provide the practitioner with a reasonable basis to support the conclusion expressed in his or her report.	4. Sufficient appropriate audit evidence should be obtained, by such means as inspection, observations, enquiry, confirmation, computation, and analysis, to afford a reasonable basis to support the content of the report.
5,6,7,8. As a minimum the practitioner's report should: (a) identify to whom the report is directed; (b) describe the objective of the engagement and the entity or portion thereof, the subject matter, and the time period covered by the engagement; (c) in an attest report, identify management's assertion; (d) describe the responsibilities of management and the practitioner; (e) identify the applicable standards in accordance with which the engagement was conducted; (f) identify the criteria against which the subject matter was evaluated;	5. The report should identify the financial statements and distinguish between the responsibilities of management and the responsibilities of the auditor. 6. The report should describe the scope of the auditor's examination.

EXHIBIT 2-6   COMPARISON OF ASSURANCE (5025) AND AUDIT STANDARDS (5100) (continued)

Assurance Standards	Auditing Standards
(g) state a conclusion that conveys the level of assurance being provided and/or any reservation the practitioner may have; (h) state the date of the report; (i) identify the name of the practitioner (or firm); and (j) identify the place of issue. 7. The reservation should be expressed in the form of a qualification of conclusion, or a denial of conclusion when the practitioner is unable to obtain sufficient appropriate evidence to evaluate one or more aspects of the subject matter's conformity with the criteria. When the practitioner: (a) in a direct reporting engagement, concludes that the subject matter does not conform with criteria; or (b) in an attest engagement, concludes that the assertion prepared by management does not present fairly the criteria used or the conformity of the subject matter with the criteria or essential information has not been presented or has been presented in an inappropriate manner, he or she should express a reservation in the form of a qualification of conclusion or an adverse conclusion. 8. A reservation should be expressed when the practitioner: (a) is unable to obtain sufficient appropriate evidence to evaluate one or more aspects of the subject matter's conformity with the criteria; (b) in a direct reporting engagement, concludes that the subject matter does not conform with the criteria; or (c) in an attest engagement concludes that (i) the assertion prepared by management does not present fairly the criteria used, (ii) the assertion prepared by management does not present fairly the subject matter's conformity with the criteria, or (iii) essential information has not been presented or has been presented in an inappropriate manner. A reservation should provide an explanation of the matter giving rise to the reservation and, if reasonably determinable, its effect on the subject matter. A. Before undertaking an assurance engagement, the practitioner should have a reasonable basis for believing the engagement can be completed in accordance with the standards in this Section. B. The practitioner should identify or develop criteria that are suitable for evaluating the subject matter. When generally accepted criteria consistent with the objective of the engagement exist, the practitioner should use them in forming his or her conclusion except when, and only when, the intended users of practitioner's report are an identifiable limited group of users and he or she is satisfied such users agree their needs are met by using criteria other than generally accepted criteria. In such cases, the practitioner's report should not include a reservation with respect to generally accepted criteria but should include a caution that the report is intended only for the use of the intended users. In no circumstances should the practitioner perform the engagement using criteria which, in his or her judgment, would result in a report that would be misleading to intended users. C. The practitioner should document matters that in his or her professional judgment are important in providing evidence to support the conclusion expressed in his or her report.	7. The report should contain either an expression of opinion on the financial statements or an assertion that an opinion cannot be expressed. In the latter case, the reasons therefor should be stated. 8. Where an opinion is expressed, it should indicate whether the financial statements present fairly, in all material respects, the financial position, results of operations, and changes in financial position in accordance with an appropriate disclosed basis of accounting, which, except in special circumstances, should be generally accepted accounting principles. The report should provide adequate explanation with respect to any reservation contained in such opinion.

A, B, C, designates section 5025 standards that are not directly comparable to a GAAS standard.

The main differences lie in the areas of practitioner competence, internal control, and reporting. With respect to practitioner competence, GAAS presume knowledge of accounting and require training and proficiency as an auditor (meaning an auditor of financial statements, since that was the only kind of assurance engagement being performed when the GAAS were first written). On the other hand, the assurance standards are more general, requiring training and proficiency in assurance engagements and knowledge of the subject matter of the engagement. The assurance service refers to the ability to recognize the information being asserted, to determine the relevant evidence, and to make decisions about the correspondence and the suitablilty of its criteria. The knowledge of the subject matter is not confined to accounting and financial assertions because assurance engagements may cover a wide variety of information. Note, however, that the first assurance standard allows auditors to provide assurance only on assertions within their level of competence.

The assurance standards, unlike GAAS, have no requirement regarding an understanding of the internal control structure for an information system. Considerations of internal control are implicit in the task of obtaining sufficient evidence for financial statement audits. However, some kinds of assured information may not have an underlying information control system in the same sense as a financial accounting and reporting system.

Reporting is different because assurance engagements on nonfinancial information do not depend upon generally accepted accounting principles. The assurance standards speak of "evaluation against suitable criteria" and "accordance with generally accepted criteria" and they leave the door open for assurance engagements on a wide variety of assertions. An illustration of how far assurance engagements can go is provided in the Wall Street Journal article entitled "Fore!" Many people appreciate the value of auditors' assurance to historical financial statements, and they have found other representations for PAs to assure, as illustrated in the box "Other Examples of Assurance Engagements."

An important assurance engagement now required by SOX is the audit of internal control statements prepared by management. Like audits of financial statements, these internal control audits verify the accuracy of management's internal control statement; the difference is the subject matter.

A main objective in developing the assurance standards is to provide a general framework for, and set reasonable boundaries around, the assurance services offered by public accountants. The assurance standards shown in Exhibit 2–6 provide guidance and a broad framework for a wide variety of assurance engagements PAs can perform in public practice. Whether these standards actually set boundaries remains to be seen. After all, before the assurance standards were published, PAs were using the GAAS audit standards as a point of departure for other assurance engagements. Now they must use the assurance standards as the point of departure.

FORE!

An interesting example of an assurance engagement subject matter is the distance a particular brand of golf balls can hit on a driving range. This type of assurance engagement was requested by Wilson Sporting Good Company to prove that amateur golfers could drive Wilson golf balls farther than competing brands of golf balls. The assurance engagement required PAs to measure the average distance of golf drives at 30 driving ranges. The PAs reported that Wilson's brand of golf balls could be hit farther by an average of 5.7 yards per drive. In addition to walking off the distances of the golf drive, the PA verified that all participants were amateurs, that the participants were not paid by Wilson, and that Wilson's records of the results were accurate.

OTHER EXAMPLES OF ASSURANCE ENGAGEMENTS

- GST and real estate tax bases
- political contributions and expenditures
- financial feasibility of a rapid transit system
- cost justification for a utility rate increase
- regulator's questionnaire on business ethics and conduct
- reliability of drinking water surveillance program
- quality of nursing home care
- effectiveness of student loan programs in meeting needs of students
- effectiveness of research and development activities
- labour data for union contract negotiation
- newspaper and magazine audience and circulation data
- integrity and security of a computer network
- investment performance statistics
- insurance claims data
- pollution emissions data (e.g., greenhouse gas emissions)

Assurance standards are explained in more detail in Chapter 16.

REVIEW CHECKPOINTS

17 What are the major differences between assurance standards and GAAS?

18 Define assurance engagements.

19 What is the theoretical essence of an assurance service?

20 **CRITICAL THINKING QUESTION:** In the "Fore!" feature, identify the assertion, the three parties to the engagement, and the criteria being used. Is a high level of assurance being provided? Explain.

QUALITY CONTROL STANDARDS

LEARNING OBJECTIVES

7 Explain how requirements of quality control standards are monitored for PA firms.

Generally accepted auditing standards must be observed in each audit engagement conducted by a PA firm. Thus, PA firms need to observe GAAS in their entire audit practice. While GAAS relate to the conduct of each audit engagement, quality control standards govern the quality of a PA firm's audit practice as a whole. Quality control can be defined as actions taken by a public accounting firm to evaluate compliance with professional standards. And a "system of quality control" is designed to provide reasonable assurance of conforming with professional standards. Professional standards include GAAS as covered in the *CICA Handbook*, as well as provincial rules of ethical conduct.

Elements of Quality Control

The International Federation of Accountants (IFAC) has identified at least four basic elements of quality control. These are listed and explained briefly in Exhibit 2–7. In comparison, the AICPA has identified a more detailed set of nine basic elements of quality control: independence, assignment of personnel to engagements, consultation, supervision, hiring, professional development, advancement, acceptance and continuation of engagements, and inspection. These may be further refined by the PCAOB.

EXHIBIT 2-7   ELEMENTS OF QUALITY CONTROL

1. Quality control policies and procedures should be implemented both at the level of the audit firm and on individual audits.
2. The audit firm should implement quality control policies and procedures designed to insure that all audits are conducted in accordance with ISAs or relevant national standards of practices.
3. The firm's general quality control policies and procedures should be communicated to its personnel in a manner that provides reasonable assurance that the policies and procedures are understood and implemented.
4. The auditor should implement those quality control procedures which are, in the context of the policies and procedures of the firm, appropriate to the individual audit. In particular, delegated work should be properly directed, supervised, and reviewed.

Source: ISA 220. This text is an extract from International Standard of Auditing 220 of the International Auditing and Assurance Standards Board, published by the International Federation of Accountants (IFAC) in February 2006 and is used with permission of IFAC.

Both the 1978 Adams Report (*Report of the Special Committee to Examine the Role of the Auditor*) and the 1988 Macdonald Commission Report (*Report of the Commission to Study the Public's Expectations of Audits*) recommended the development of quality control standards to guide PA firms. More recently, several regulatory agencies initiated discipline for substandard performance by professional staff in PA firms and criticized the individual-level focus of the provincial disciplinary process. In response, provincial institutes are amending their bylaws to bring firms, as well as individuals, within the disciplinary process. This expanded disciplinary process will require new guidelines for evaluating systems of quality control. Increasing litigation is also putting pressure on firms to develop good systems of quality control so that they can demonstrate compliance with professional standards and thus minimize the loss from litigation. A CICA study entitled "Guide for Developing Quality Control Systems in Public Accounting" proposed detailed guidance based on five key components or areas: clients, personnel, engagement procedures, practice administration, and a quality control review program.

Exhibit 2–8 illustrates the implementation of a quality control system using the five key components included in the CICA study. The study proposed that the areas of client relationships (including independence from the clients) and engagement procedures be given top priority when implementing a system in stages. The right-hand columns in Exhibit 2–8 suggest priority in setting up a firmwide quality control system. Note in Exhibit 2–8 that the five areas have each been subdivided into series of elements that allow firms to better articulate all the different aspects of quality control. While the exhibit framework is not a standard right now, it indicates where Canadian guidance may be headed. Note that tax and management advisory services could be included in the framework, but the extent to which they should be considered in the quality control system is controversial.

The International Federation of Accountants (IFAC) issued a standard on quality control, ISCQ-1. As a result, the CICA added to its *Handbook* the section, Canadian Standard on Quality Control, CSCQ-1 (was CGSF-QC), for firms performing assurance engagements. This standard is outlined in Exhibit 2–9. There are only minor differences between CSCQ-1 and the international equivalent ISCQ-1.

Firms can use the evolving quality control standards in developing their own policies and procedures, along with the related documentation. When peer or quality reviews are conducted, the reviewers "audit" the PA firm's policies and procedures designed to ensure compliance with the elements of CSQC-1 and perhaps additional criteria. The statements of policy and procedures may vary in length and complexity, depending on the size of the PA firm and the regulatory system affecting them. (Students who wish to know these policies and procedures in detail when interviewing for a job should ask for a copy of the firm's quality control document.)

EXHIBIT   2-8   IMPLEMENTING A QUALITY CONTROL SYSTEM

Quality Control Area/Elements	First Priority	Second Priority
A. Clients		
1. Independence and Objectivity	✓	
2. Prohibited Investments	✓	
3. Conflicts of Interest	✓	
4. Confidentiality	✓	
5. Acceptance and Continuance	✓	
6. New Client Proposals	✓	✓
B. Personnel		
1. Hiring		✓
2. Assignment		✓
3. Performance Evaluation		✓
4. Advancement		✓
5. Continuing Professional Education	✓	
6. Restriction of Professional Staff Activities	✓	
C. Engagement Procedures		
1. Engagement Letters	✓	
2. Planning and Execution	✓	
3. Documentation	✓	
4. Supervision and Review	✓	
5. Resolution of Differences of Opinion		✓
6. Consultation with Peers		✓
7. Independent Review	✓	
8. Management Letters	✓	
D. Practice Administration		
1. Use of Firm Name		✓
2. Access to Client Files	✓	
3. Security of Confidential Information	✓	
4. Retention of Files		✓
5. Software Usage and Security		✓
6. Technical Reference Materials	✓	
7. Litigation and Professional Conduct		✓
8. Advertising and Promotion		✓
9. Solicitation of Clients	✓	
E. Quality Control Review Program		
1. Internal Review		✓
2. Monitoring Client Services		✓
3. Monitoring Quality Control		✓
4. Premerger Review		✓
Total Elements	17	16

*© Same as Exhibit 4–2 in CICA's *Guide for Developing Quality Control Systems in Public Accounting*, p. 35.

Accountability Boards Quality Control

As noted in Chapter 1, accountability boards have been created in the Canada and the United States to help preserve the integrity of the financial reporting system. Most countries in the European Union were supposed to have equivalents of a CPAB by 2009, but many did not meet this deadline. The boards have been pressing for new rules in the monitoring of quality control and audit practice, most of these geared to improving auditor independence. These rules include five-year rotations of partners and strict limits on consulting services that have the potential to create conflicts of interest with the auditing role. The list of conflicting services would include valuation services, legal services, information technology systems

EXHIBIT   2-9   CICA CANADIAN STANDARDS ON QUALITY CONTROL FOR FIRMS (CSQC-1)

.005 • *The firm's system of quality control should include policies and procedures addressing each of the following elements:*

  (a) leadership responsibilities for quality within the firm;

  (b) ethical requirements;

  (c) acceptance and continuance of client relationships and specific assurance engagements;

  (d) human resources;

  (e) engagement performance; and

  (f) monitoring.

The quality control policies and procedures should be documented and communicated to the firm's personnel. [Nov. 2006]

Source: © The *CICA Handbook* CSQC-1.

design, and internal audits for auditees with more than $10 million in assets or market capitalization. In addition, the PCAOB would study the requirements of audit firm rotation and the potential conflict created when audit firm personnel leave to work for auditees. These are primarily issues of professional ethics and are covered in more detail in Chapter 4.

In monitoring PA firm quality control practices, the boards would need to consider implementation controls. The quality control elements listed in Exhibits 2–7, 2–8, and especially 2–9 are examples of criteria that could be used to implement the monitoring. In future, the accountability boards may issue their own standards for accounting firms' quality controls, including monitoring of ethics and independence, internal and external consulting on audit issues, audit supervision, hiring, development and advancement of audit personnel, client acceptance and continuance, and internal inspections.

The PCAOB has indicated that it will set future auditing independence and quality control standards. In contrast, the CPAB has indicated that it will let the profession decide on these standards. Hence, CPAB uses CSQC-1 as outlined in Exhibit 2–9 as its primary criteria.

Monitoring of Quality Control: Practice Inspection, Peer Reviews, and Quality Inspections

Practice inspections, peer reviews, and quality inspections are "audits of the auditors." **Practice inspection** is the system of reviewing and evaluating practice units' audit files and other documentation by an independent external party. The main objective of practice inspection is to evaluate conformity of the work with the *CICA Handbook* and with the professional, ethical principles and rules of conduct (covered in Chapter 4). The practice unit can be an individual or an entire office, in which case the individual members of the office are evaluated relative to their level of responsibility. Provincial practice inspection programs apply to all members of the relevant institutes, orders, or associations and consist of several steps:

1. selection of practice unit for inspection (can be a PA firm, an office of a firm, or a sole practitioner)

2. completion of questionnaires to gather general information about the practice and quality control systems of the practice unit

3. assignment of inspector

4. inspection of a sample of engagement files

5. report of inspection—each report focuses on an individual in a practice unit

6. follow-up review of corrective actions, if applicable

7. a report to the professional conduct committee if necessary[2]

[2] CICA, *Guide for Developing Quality Control Systems in Public Accounting* (CICA, 1993), p. 17.

There are some minor variations among provincial practice inspection programs relating to types of engagements reviewed and the way the inspection reports are prepared. The overall focus is on individual member's performance, and the orientation is more educational than disciplinary, although serious deficiencies could lead to a complaint with a professional conduct committee, as is further explained in Chapter 4. Practice inspections are a useful complement to a firm's system of quality control. Their success is reflected in the fact that many countries have followed the Canadian model, including Ireland, Norway, China, and Australia.

Peer reviews are a practice inspection, usually done as a special engagement by another audit firm hired for the task by the firm reviewed. The reviewers issue a report on the firm's compliance with quality control standards and make recommendations for improvements to the audit practice.

Quality inspections are an examination and evaluation of the quality of the overall practice. They are thus aimed at the firm level rather than at individuals. A quality inspection involves an extensive study of a firm's quality control document and includes interviews with audit personnel as well as detailed study of quality of work, adherence to GAAS, and quality control standards on a selection of audit engagements. A quality inspection has the same objective as a peer review but is less extensive. They are usually requested by the smaller PA firms.

The new accountability boards have taken on the job of regulating inspections of firms' audit operations to ensure compliance with the various quality control criteria outlined in the preceding section. The inspection reports for CPAB and PCAOB can be found at their websites, www.cpab-ccrc.org, and www.pcaobus.org, respectively.

The first CPAB report dealt with inspections of the Big Four firms in Canada (issued October 6, 2004). The most common problems cited were lack of documentation for work said to have been done and independence violations. But the CPAB indicated that these problems did not represent negligent work. The SEC requires that any litigation alleging audit deficiencies and involving public companies or regulated financial institutions or their personnel be reported to them by the auditors. The SEC obtains documents related to the litigation in order to determine whether the case has any bearing on quality control deficiencies in the PA firm. In Canada, sometimes a regulator such as the OSC will ask that a PA firm or individual be reviewed by the CPAB and a provincial institute reviewer. This is usually in response to a complaint, but it sometimes arises from regular monitoring of annual reports and filings submitted to the regulator.

The extent of work involved in practice inspections, peer reviews, or quality inspections is greatly influenced by the quality of documentation concerning the quality control system. Generally, if the quality control documentation is good and the reviewer can rely on extensive internal monitoring of quality control, less work is required than if documentation is poor and the reviewer must rely more on her own detailed inspection of files.

- -

REVIEW
CHECKPOINTS

21 Consider the following quality control policy and identify the quality control element it relates to: "Designate individuals as specialists to serve as authoritative sources; provide procedures for resolving differences of opinion between audit personnel and specialists."

22 What is a practice inspection, and what roles does it play in the quality control self-regulation of the profession?

23 Compare the quality inspection reports of the CPAB and PCAOB. Do the PA firms in the U.S. and Canada have similar quality control problems?

24 What is the meaning of quality control as it relates to a PA firm?

- -

APPLICATION CASE AND ANALYSIS
AN ILLUSTRATION OF THE DIFFERENCE BETWEEN AUDIT RISK AND ACCOUNTING RISK

A horse business example: Part I

A man bought a horse for $600 and sold it for $700. Then he bought it back for $800 and again sold it, this time for $900. How much money did he make in the horse business? Was it $100, $200, $300, or none of these?

Analysis Part I

LEARNING OBJECTIVE

8 Apply and integrate the chapter topics to analyze a practical auditing situation/case/scenario.

If you did not get the correct answer of $200, do not feel too bad as numerous psychology studies show that 55 percent of all university students get this problem wrong. This example illustrates how the natural process of reasoning can sometimes lead us astray. Something about buying back the same horse confuses people.

Of course, accounting students will have an advantage in solving this problem because they have both the tools of arithmetic and the rules of accounting available to them. We know that the profit is the difference between revenues and expenses, regardless of whether the same horse is involved. Thus, accounting students would subtract total costs from total revenues to get $1600 (700 + 900) – $1400 (600 + 800) = $200, which is the correct answer.

If you were the auditor you would verify that this calculation is 100 percent accurate. You would then also need to obtain evidence that these transactions took place at the amounts indicated, but getting exhaustive evidence for such a simple business should not be difficult, so the risk of having erroneous facts after obtaining all the evidence would be zero. In other words, for all practical purposes, audit risk is zero after corroborating these transactions, and we can be certain that the profit is $200. This is an example of accounting under no uncertainty.

In this example there is no need to make forecasts, so correct facts are the only things that matter. Part II of this case introduces forecasts in accounting and the consequent appearance of accounting risk.

The horse business example: Part II—Introduction of Accounting Risk

Assume the same facts as in Part I except that now the horse is sold the first time for a lottery ticket having the following payoffs: $2800 at probability of 0.25 and $0 at probability of 0.75. How much was earned in the horse business now, assuming the profit needs to be calculated before the lottery payoff date?

Analysis: Part II

Again, if the auditor can verify that these facts, including the probabilities and payoffs from the lottery corporation, are 100 percent true, then the audit risk is zero. But what is the profit under GAAP?

Under contingency accounting, we cannot recognize a contingent gain from the lottery ticket; therefore the profit is $900 – $1400 = –$500, in other words, a $500 loss. There is 0.25 probability that this loss is wrong, however. This 0.25 is the accounting risk associated with recording a $500 loss. This loss is the way the business risk associated with the lottery ticket is disclosed in financial reporting via accounting for contingencies. We would probably want to disclose the contingent gain in the notes to the financial statements. But this raises a deeper question of whether fairness of presentation requires that every contingent gain should be disclosed in the notes no matter how unlikely the gain. Or, should there be a cutoff probability for such disclosures?

An added complexity associated with accounting risk is that there may be a conflict between accounting standards. For example, under fair value accounting, treating the lottery ticket as a "financial instrument" would give us an expected value of $700 for the lottery ticket, the result being that the profit becomes what it was in Part I of the Analysis—$200. But note that the accounting risk associated with recording $200 is a probability of 1.00; that is, it is guaranteed to be wrong! This is because, assuming the lottery ticket is not sold before the payoff date, only two profit states are possible: there is a $2800 payoff yielding a profit of $2300 (at 0.25 probability, so if you record $2300 then the accounting risk is 0.75) or a loss of $500 (at 0.75 probability of being correct, so accounting risk is 0.25). These results contrast greatly with that in Part I, where only one profit state is possible because there is no accounting risk.

The question is, therefore, which profit calculation should be acceptable to the auditor? The answer is that it depends on which accounting risk is acceptable. Note that in both cases the facts are known with 100 percent certainty. The only issue is proper disclosure of the facts. The point is then that accounting risk needs to be properly disclosed and that this is a financial accounting issue. If GAAP are unclear it creates challenges for the auditor when deciding what presents fairly, and he must use professional judgment when deciding what is fair presentation in the particular circumstance. Note, too, that the additional complexity of Part II is due entirely to the need to forecast future events and the decision on proper disclosure of this in financial reporting. This complexity is what the accounting risk concept attempts to address. We will continue to explore this professional judgment in reporting issue in subsequent chapters.

SUMMARY

The assurance standard is the general framework for applying assurance engagements to a wide range of subjects. They are the quality guides for general assurance work. Theoretically, they could serve as quality guides for independent audits of financial statements. However, they were created long after GAAS for audits of financial statements, and, therefore, GAAS remains the predominant framework for most engagements.

Financial statement auditors are most concerned with GAAS standards because they are the direct guides for the quality of everyday audit practice. The goal of the audit is to provide high assurance that the financial statements present fairly. The general standard consists of the code of professional ethics, and it sets requirements for auditors' competence, objectivity, and due professional care. The examination standards set requirements for planning and supervising each audit, obtaining an understanding of the auditee's internal controls, and obtaining sufficient appropriate evidence to serve as a basis for an audit report. The reporting standards cover the requirements for an acceptable framework of financial reporting (usually GAAP), auditor and management responsibilities, adequate disclosure, and report content. We briefly reviewed the financial statement audit process to show how GAAS concepts relate to this process.

In all matters relating to financial statement audits, auditors are advised to have a sense of professional skepticism. This attitude is reflected in a "prove it with evidence" response to management representations, to answers for enquiries, and to financial statement assertions themselves. Critical thinking is a broader idea covered in Chapter 4 that considers not only the evidence, but also the effects of the reporting framework that should be applied. Critical thinking and skepticism consider how management's reporting may mislead users.

While assurance standards and GAAS govern the quality of work on each individual engagement, the quality control elements guide a PA firm's audit practice as a whole. Quality control is the foundation of the self-regulatory system of peer review, practice inspection, and quality inspection. It also serves as the basis for monitoring by accountability boards. The elements of independence, assigning personnel, consultation, supervision, hiring, professional development, advancement, acceptance and continuance of audit engagements, and inspection are usually the objects of a firm's policies and procedures for assuring that GAAS are followed faithfully in all aspects of the firm's practice.

As an auditor, you must have a thorough understanding of these practice standards, especially GAAS. All practical problems can be approached by beginning with a consideration of the practice standards in question. Auditing standards do not exist in a vacuum. They are put to work in numerous practical applications. Practical applications of the standards will be shown in subsequent chapters on audit program planning, execution of auditing procedures, gathering evidence, and auditing decisions.

MULTIPLE-CHOICE QUESTIONS FOR PRACTICE AND REVIEW

Check the website, www.mcgrawhill.ca/olc/smieliauskas, for additional end-of-chapter material.

MC 1 It is always a good idea for auditors to begin an audit with the professional skepticism characterized by the assumption that
  a. a potential conflict of interest always exists between the auditor and the management of the enterprise under audit.
  b. in audits of financial statements, the auditor acts exclusively in the capacity of an auditor.
  c. the professional status of the independent auditor imposes commensurate professional obligations.
  d. financial statements and financial data are verifiable.

MC 2 When Auditee Company prohibits auditors from visiting selected branch offices of the business, this is an example of interference with
  a. reporting independence.
  b. investigative independence.
  c. auditors' training and proficiency.
  d. audit planning and supervision.

MC 3 After the auditors learned of Auditee Company's failure to record an expense for obsolete inventory, they agreed to a small adjustment to the financial statements because the Auditee president told them the company would violate its debt agreements if the full amount were recorded. This is an example of a lack of

a. auditors' training and proficiency.
b. planning and supervision.
c. audit investigative independence.
d. audit reporting independence.

MC 4 The primary purpose for obtaining an understanding of the company's internal controls in a financial statement audit is to

a. determine the nature, timing, and extent of auditing procedures to be performed.
b. make consulting suggestions to the management.
c. obtain direct, sufficient, and appropriate evidential matter to afford a reasonable basis for an opinion on the financial statements.
d. determine whether the company has changed any accounting principles.

MC 5 Auditors' activities about which of these generally accepted auditing standards are not affected by the auditee's utilization of a computerized accounting system?

a. The audit report shall state whether the financial statements are presented in accordance with GAAP.
b. The work is to be adequately planned and assistants, if any, are to be properly supervised.
c. Sufficient appropriate evidential matter is to be obtained . . . to afford a reasonable basis for an opinion regarding the financial statements under audit.
d. The audit is to be performed by a person or persons having adequate technical training and proficiency as an auditor.

MC 6 Which of the following is not found in the standard unqualified audit report on financial statements?

a. An identification of the financial statements that were audited
b. A general description of an audit
c. An opinion that the financial statements present financial position in conformity with GAAP
d. An emphasis paragraph commenting on the effect of economic conditions on the company

MC 7 The assurance standards do not contain a requirement that auditors obtain

a. adequate knowledge in the subject matter of the assertions being examined.

b. an understanding of the auditee's internal control structure.
c. sufficient evidence for the conclusions expressed in an attestation report.
d. independence in mental attitude.

MC 8 Auditor Jones is studying a company's accounting treatment of a series of complicated transactions in exotic financial instruments. She should look for the highest level of authoritative support for proper accounting in

a. provincial securities commissions' staff position statements.
b. CICA industry audit and accounting guides.
c. CICA recommendations in the *Handbook*.
d. Emerging Issues Committee consensus statements.

MC 9 Which of the following is not an example of a quality control procedure likely to be used by a public accounting firm to meet its professional responsibilities to auditees?

a. Completion of independence questionnaires by all partners and employees
b. Review and approval of audit plan by the partner in charge of the engagement just prior to signing the auditor's report
c. Evaluating professional staff after the conclusion of each engagement
d. Evaluating the integrity of management for each new audit client

MC 10 Which of the following concepts is not included in the wording of the auditor's standard report?

a. Management's responsibility for the financial statements
b. Auditor's responsibility to assess significant estimates made by management
c. Extent of auditor's reliance on the auditee's internal controls
d. Examination of evidence on a test basis

MC 11 Which of the following is not mandatory when performing an audit in accordance with GAAS?

a. Proper supervision of assistants
b. Efficient performance of audit procedures
c. Understanding the auditee's system of internal controls
d. Adequate planning of work to be performed

EXERCISES AND PROBLEMS

EP 1
LO.5

Audit Independence and Planning. You are meeting with executives of Cooper Cosmetics Corporation to arrange your firm's engagement to audit the corporation's financial statements for the year ending December 31. One executive suggests the audit work be divided among three staff members to minimize audit time, avoid duplication of staff effort, and curtail interference with company operations. One person would

examine asset accounts, a second would examine liability accounts, and the third would examine income and expense accounts.

Advertising is the corporation's largest expense, and the advertising manager suggests that a staff member of your firm, whose uncle owns the advertising agency handling the corporation's advertising, be assigned to examine the Advertising Expense account. The staff member has a thorough knowledge of the rather complex contact between Cooper Cosmetics and the advertising agency.

Required:
a. To what extent should a PA follow the auditee management's suggestions for the conduct of an audit? Discuss.
b. List and discuss the reasons why audit work should not be assigned solely according to asset, liability, and income and expense categories.
c. Should the staff member of your PA firm whose uncle owns the advertising agency be assigned to examine advertising costs? Discuss.

EP 2
LO.2
Examination Standards. You have accepted the engagement of auditing the financial statements of the C. Reis Company, a small manufacturing firm that has been your auditee for several years. Because you were busy writing the report for another engagement, you sent a staff accountant to begin the audit, with the suggestion that she start with the accounts receivable. Using the prior year's working papers as a guide, the auditor prepared a trial balance of the accounts, aged them, prepared and mailed positive confirmation requests, examined underlying support for charges and credits, and performed other work she considered necessary to obtain evidence about the validity and collectibility of the receivables. At the conclusion of her work, you reviewed the working papers she prepared and found she had carefully followed the prior year's working papers.

Required:
The opinion rendered by a PA states that the audit was made in accordance with generally accepted auditing standards.

List the three generally accepted standards of field work. Relate them to the above illustration by indicating how they were fulfilled or, if appropriate, how they were not fulfilled.

(ICAO adapted)

EP 3
LO.5
Time of Appointment and Planning. Your public accounting practice is located in a town of 15,000 people. Your work, conducted by you and two assistants, consists of compiling clients' monthly statements and preparing income tax returns for individuals from cash data and partnership returns from books and records. You have a few corporate clients; however, service to them is limited to preparation of income tax returns and assistance in year-end closings where bookkeeping is deficient.

One of your corporate clients is a retail hardware store. Your work for this company has been limited to preparing the corporation income tax return from a trial balance submitted by the bookkeeper. On December 26 you receive a letter from the president of the corporation with the following request:

> We have made arrangements with the First National Bank to borrow $500,000 to finance the purchase of a complete line of appliances. The bank has asked us to furnish our auditor's certified statement as of December 31, which is the closing date of our accounting year. The trial balance of the general

ledger should be ready by January 10, which should allow ample time to prepare your report for submission to the bank by January 20. In view of the importance of this certified report to our financing program, we trust you will arrange to comply with the foregoing schedule.

Required:
From a theoretical viewpoint, discuss the difficulties that are caused by such a short-notice audit request.

(AICPA adapted)

EP 4
LO.3
Reporting Standards. PA Musgrave and his associates audited the financial statements of North Company, a computer equipment retailer. Musgrave conducted the audit in accordance with the general and field work standards of generally accepted auditing standards and therefore wrote a standard audit description in his audit report. Then he received an emergency call to fill in as a substitute tenor in his barbershop quartet.

No one else was in the office that Saturday afternoon, so he handed you the complete financial statements and footnotes saying, "Make sure it's OK to write an unqualified opinion on these statements. The working papers are on the table. I'll check with you on Monday morning."

Required:
In general terms, what must you determine in order to write an unqualified opinion paragraph for Musgrave's signature?

EP 5
LO.2
GAAS in a Computer Environment. The Lovett Corporation uses an IBM mainframe computer system with peripheral optical reader and high-speed laser printer equipment. Transaction information is initially recorded on paper documents (e.g., sales invoices) and then read by optical equipment that produces a magnetic disk containing the data. These data file disks are processed by a computer program, and printed listings, journals, and general ledger balances are produced on the high-speed printer equipment.

Required:
Explain how the audit standard requiring "adequate technical training and proficiency" is important for satisfying the general and field work standards in the audit of Lovett Corporation's financial statements.

EP 6
LO.3
Audit Report Language. The standard unqualified report contains several important sentences and phrases. Give an explanation of why each of the following phrases is used instead of the alternative language indicated.
1. Address: "To the Board of Directors and Stockholders" instead of "To Whom It May Concern."
2. "We have audited the balance sheet of Anycompany as of December 31, 1997, and the related statements of income, retained earnings, and cash flows for the year then ended" instead of "We have audited the attached financial statements."
3. "We conducted our audit in accordance with generally accepted auditing standards" instead of "Our

audit was conducted with due audit care appropriate in the circumstances."

4. "In our opinion, the financial statements referred to above present fairly . . . in conformity with generally accepted accounting principles" instead of "The financial statements are true and correct."

EP 7
LO.7
Public Oversight of the Accountancy Profession. The Canadian Public Accountability Board (CPAB) and the Public Company Accounting Oversight Board (PCAOB) in the U.S. will provide oversight for public accountants who audit public companies. What are the objectives of these boards? What factors should these boards consider in assessing public accountants' work?

EP 8
LO.4
Scope of an Audit, Requirement for Specialist Expertise. Consider the following two situations.

1. The auditor discovers during the audit that the auditee company has entered a complex legal contract that involves transferring assets to another company if that company performs certain future services by obtaining supplies from a foreign country. The auditor is unable to establish whether the contract imposes any financial liability or has any other financial impact on the auditee company.

2. The auditor learns that the auditee company is required to comply with environmental standards requiring it to monitor various emissions using complex scientific techniques. The amounts of the financial penalties that can be imposed by the government are determined by the nature and extent of noncompliance with these scientific standards.

Required:
Contrast these two situations in terms of the auditor's responsibility to perform audit procedures and issue a report. Include a recommendation on which form of report would be issued in each case, based on your analysis.

EP 9
LO.5
Assurance Engagements, General Assurance Standards. A radio advertisement for a new software management product included the following statement: "According to ITR, Knovel's new software product will pay back in three months."

ITR is an information technology (IT) research firm that is hired by various companies in the IT industry to provide reports on IT usage and sales in the IT market. As soon as ITR's president heard the ad on his car radio, he immediately phoned Knovel and told them to stop using the ad.

Required:
Discuss whether ITR's statement is the result of an assurance engagement. Consider the parties involved, the subject matter, the accountability relationships, the nature of the report, and any other relevant aspects of the situation. Why do you think ITR's president wanted the ad stopped?

EP 10
LO.3
Fair Presentation in Accordance with GAAP. The third reporting standard of GAAS states that the auditor's opinion on the financial statements should indicate whether they present fairly the financial position, results of operations, and changes in financial position in accordance with GAAP. The *CICA Handbook* Recommendations are an important source of GAAP. However, the Recommendations may allow for different interpretations and choices in how they are applied, or they may be silent.

Required:
a. How does the auditor assess whether financial statements are in accordance with GAAP when a conclusion on GAAP is not found in the *CICA Handbook* Recommendations? Give an example of an accounting issue that may not be covered in the Recommendations.

b. How does the auditor assess whether financial statements are in accordance with GAAP when the *CICA Handbook* Recommendations allow for different accounting methods to be acceptable? Give an example of an accounting issue for which alternate acceptable accounting treatments are provided in the Recommendations.

EP 11
LO.3
Missing Disclosure Described in Auditor's Report. Bunting Technology Corporation is a large public company that manufactures the IXQ, a telecommunications component that speeds up Internet transmission over fibre optic cable. Subsequent to its current year-end, but, before the audited financial statements are issued, a competitor of Bunting launches a new product that increases transmission speed one hundred times more than Bunting's IXQ and sells for one-tenth of the price. Bunting has approximately 11 months of inventory of the IXQ in inventory, based on the current year's sales levels.

Bunting's auditors, Ditesmoi & Quail (DQ), have determined that this subsequent event warrants a write-down of Bunting's year-end inventory to reflect technological obsolescence. Given that the IXQ is Bunting's main product, the write-down will be highly material. DQ argues that this development will result in a permanent change in Bunting's future earnings potential and cash flows, and it would be misleading users if it is not included in the current year financial statements.

Bunting's management refuses to record the inventory write-down, arguing that the event occurred after the year-end and therefore does not relate to the current year's results. Also, since the competitor's product is brand new, management argues that there is significant uncertainty about whether it will perform as well in actual use as the competitor claims. Thus, it is premature to assume it will have an impact on IXQ sales, and it is impossible to estimate a dollar amount of the impact. Management is also concerned that, by publicly reporting information about the competing product in Bunting's annual report, DQ will jeopardize several large sales contracts that Bunting is currently negotiating, and this may lower sales even more than if the information were withheld.

DQ issues a qualified audit report that spells out its estimate of the material impact of the technological obsolescence on Bunting's assets, net income, and retained earnings.

Required:

Discuss the issues raised by DQ's decision to issue a qualified report in this situation. Consider the impact of DQ's audit report qualification on Bunting, on users of the audited financial statements, and on DQ as Bunting's auditor.

EP 12 **Auditor's Professional Scepticism.** Auditors are required
LO.4 to have professional scepticism, but an auditor must also rely on management representations in order to complete the audit. Discuss the inherent conflicts in these two requirements and how they may be resolved.

EP 13 **Assurance Engagement other than Audit or Review.**
LO.6 During 2002 and 2003, United Nations weapon inspectors entered Iraq to search for "weapons of mass destruction." These include chemical, biological, and nuclear weapons. It has been reported that these weapons and equipment for manufacturing them may be concealed in public buildings such as schools, hospitals, or apartment buildings.

Required:

Identify the subject matter and design an approach for assessing risks and probabilities of weapons existing, and for implementing the inspection. Use basic audit definitions and approaches from financial statement auditing. For example, compare the weapons inspectors' objectives to the approach to looking for a material understatement of a financial statement liability.

EP 14 **Audit Weaknesses Found in CPAB Inspections.** Access
LO.7 the CPAB website at www.cpab-ccrc.ca and find the most common weaknesses in Canadian audit practice as identified in their reports.

CHAPTER

Reports on Audited Financial Statements

This chapter covers the most frequent variations in audit reports. Management has primary responsibility for the fair presentation of financial statements in conformity with generally accepted accounting principles. Auditors have primary responsibility for their own audit reports of the financial statements. As a starting point, you must have knowledge of the standard unqualified report. This chapter then discusses changes necessary to the standard language when auditors cannot give a "clean opinion."

LEARNING OBJECTIVES

After completing this chapter, you will be able to do the following:

1. Describe the association framework.

2. Determine whether a PA is associated with financial statements.

3. Describe the three levels of assurance.

4. Compare and contrast the scope and opinion paragraphs in a standard unqualified audit report.

5. For a given set of accounting facts and audit circumstances, analyze qualified, adverse, and disclaimer audit reports.

6. Write an unqualified audit report containing additional explanation or modified wording for specific issues allowed by GAAS.

7. Determine the effects of materiality on audit report choices.

8. Apply and integrate the chapter topics to analyze a practical auditing situation/case/scenario.

9* Explain the differences in the American auditor's report. (Appendix 3A)

10* Explain why auditors have standards for reporting on the application of accounting principles. (Appendix 3B)

11* Write an audit report in which the principal auditor refers to the work of another auditor. (Appendix 3C)

12* Write the required modifications to the audit report when prior-year comparative financial statements are changed. (Appendix 3C)

13* Identify the type of audit report issued when an audit engagement is limited. (Appendix 3C)

14* Explain auditors' reporting responsibilities with respect to "other information" and supplementary (including pro forma) information. (Appendix 3C)

15* Describe the reporting requirements involved in auditors' association with summarized financial information. (Appendix 3C)

* Learning Objectives marked with an asterisk (*) and their corresponding topics are considered advanced material. Note: Appendix 3C is located in the text's Online Learning Centre.

THE ASSOCIATION FRAMEWORK

· · · · · · · · · · · · · · · ·

LEARNING OBJECTIVE
1 Describe the association framework.

The public accounting services covered in this chapter are part of the broadest concept of auditor involvement with a business enterprise's information—that of association. **Association** is a term used within the profession to indicate a public accountant's involvement with an enterprise or with information issued by that enterprise. General standards for association are covered in section 5020 of the *CICA Handbook*. At the time of writing, there were comparable international standards on association but they are not in the CASs.

Association can arise in three ways:

1. Through some action, the PA associates himself or herself with information issued by the enterprise.

2. Without the PA's knowledge or consent, the enterprise indicates that the PA was involved with information issued by them.

3. A third party assumes the PA is involved with information issued by an enterprise.

According to paragraph 5020.04, a public accountant associates himself or herself with information when they either perform services or consent to the use of their name in connection with that information. When associated with information, a PA's professional responsibilities include the following:

1. Applicable standards in the *CICA Handbook* must be met.

2. The PA complies with their provincial institute's rules of professional conduct.

3. There is appropriate communication of the extent of their involvement with the information.

The PA should ensure that the information they are associated with is accurate, accurately reproduced, and not misleading. If the client attempts to make inappropriate use of his name, the PA should amend the information or get legal advice.

Exhibit 3–1 provides a framework illustrating the relationships between various types of engagements and *CICA Handbook* sections, including CASs. As a result of the changes to public accounting brought on by section 5025, the concept of association had to be revised to incorporate the assurance framework. Further revisions were required with adoption of CASs. CASs are for now viewed outside the association framework. The association responsibilities are illustrated in section 5020.A.

EXHIBIT 3–1   OVERVIEW OF THE ASSURANCE HANDBOOK

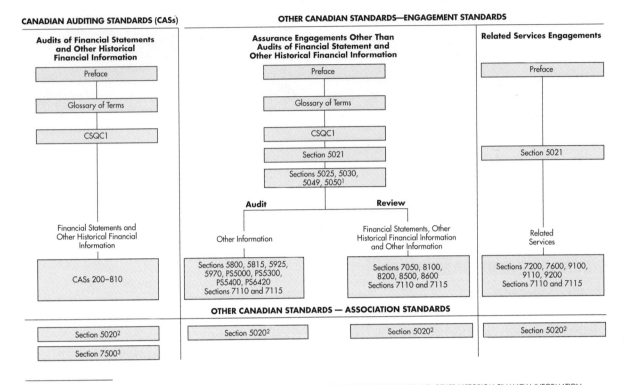

¹ USING THE WORK OF INTERNAL AUDIT IN ASSURANCE ENGAGEMENTS OTHER THAN AUDITS OF FINANCIAL STATEMENTS AND OTHER HISTORICAL FINANCIAL INFORMATION. Section 5050, provides guidance on using the work of internal audit in carrying out an audit engagement other than an audit of financial statements and other historical financial information. The guidance may be useful for other types of engagements.

² ASSOCIATION, Section 5020, provides guidance on the public accountant's association with information, which may occur irrespective of the type of engagement.

³ AUDITOR ASSOCIATION WITH ANNUAL REPORTS, INTERIM REPORTS, AND OTHER PUBLIC DOCUMENTS. Section 7500, provides guidance on the auditor's responsibilities, after the completion of the audit of the entity's financial statements, when the auditor agrees to consent to the use of the auditor's report in connection with a designated document.

Source: © Preface to *CICA Handbook*, Appendix 4.

Revising the concept of association meant that changes to PAs' responses to various client actions were also necessary. Their responsibilities concerning information or subject matters they are inappropriately associated with is summarized on the decision tree in the second box relating to section 5020.A.

Exhibit 3–1 provides a preliminary version of the evolving association framework for all assurance engagements. The CASs are also part of an assurance framework like that covered in section 5025. Many of the other types of engagements are covered in Chapter 16. In the next section we deal with determination and obligations of association.

Association with Financial Statements

LEARNING OBJECTIVE

② Determine whether a PA is associated with financial statements.

Auditing standards require a report in all cases where a PA's name is **associated with financial statements**. As a PA, you are associated with financial statements when (1) you have consented to the use of your name in connection with them; or (2) you have prepared or performed some other services with respect to them, even if your name is not used in any written report. This is covered in the *Handbook*, paragraph 5020.04.

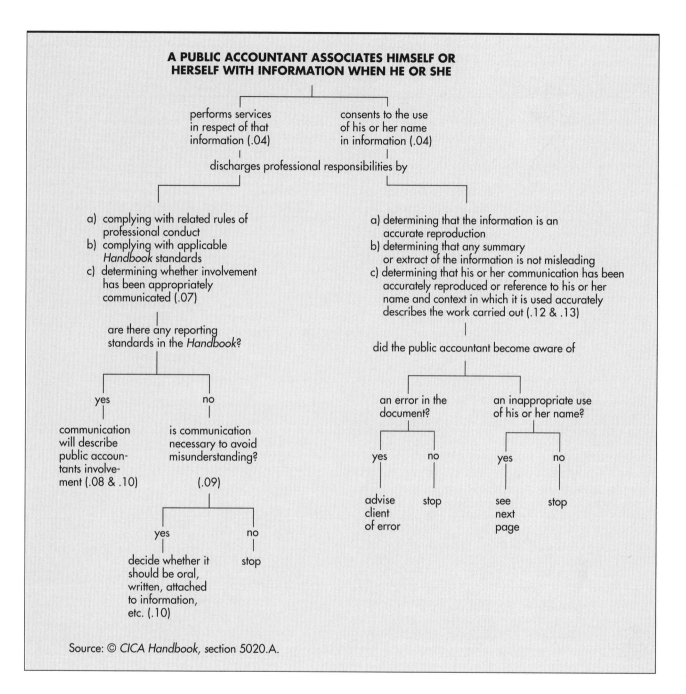

A PUBLIC ACCOUNTANT ASSOCIATES HIMSELF OR HERSELF WITH INFORMATION WHEN HE OR SHE

performs services in respect of that information (.04) — consents to the use of his or her name in information (.04)

discharges professional responsibilities by

a) complying with related rules of professional conduct
b) complying with applicable *Handbook* standards
c) determining whether involvement has been appropriately communicated (.07)

are there any reporting standards in the *Handbook*?

yes — communication will describe public accountants involvement (.08 & .10)

no — is communication necessary to avoid misunderstanding? (.09)

yes — decide whether it should be oral, written, attached to information, etc. (.10)

no — stop

a) determining that the information is an accurate reproduction
b) determining that any summary or extract of the information is not misleading
c) determining that his or her communication has been accurately reproduced or reference to his or her name and context in which it is used accurately describes the work carried out (.12 & .13)

did the public accountant become aware of

an error in the document?

yes — advise client of error

no — stop

an inappropriate use of his or her name?

yes — see next page

no — stop

Source: © *CICA Handbook*, section 5020.A.

The concept of association is far reaching with respect to financial statements. A PA is associated with them when (1) these are merely reproduced on their letterhead, (2) they are produced by their computer as part of a bookkeeping service, or (3) a document containing financial statements merely identifies them as the public accountant or auditor for the company. A report is required in these cases of association because most users of financial statements will assume that an audit has been conducted and that "everything is OK" on the basis of the involvement. Consequently, an obligation exists to inform the users about the nature of the work performed, if any, and the conclusions the PA has made about the financial statements. These responsibilities are summarized in the preceding and following boxes.

The next section outlines the various levels of assurance that are possible in PA engagements. We then discuss the audit reports that result from an audit of financial statements—the main audit covered in this text.

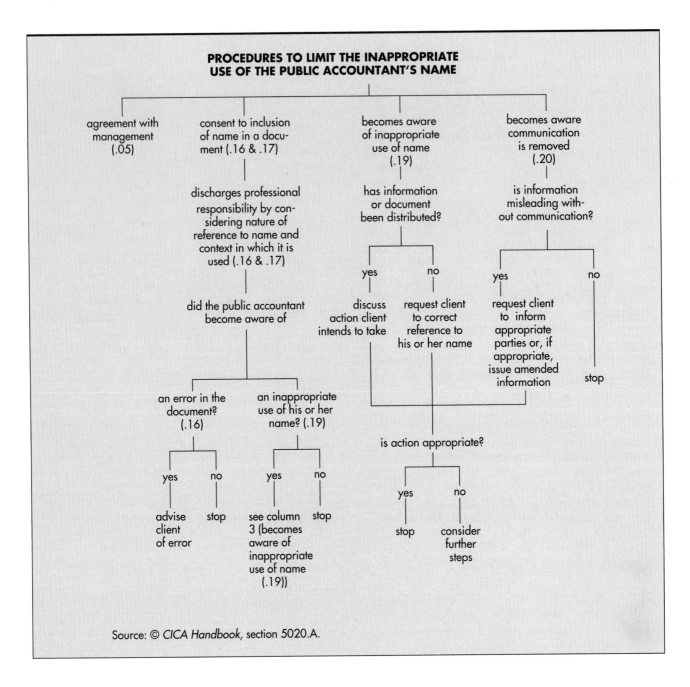

PROCEDURES TO LIMIT THE INAPPROPRIATE USE OF THE PUBLIC ACCOUNTANT'S NAME

Source: © *CICA Handbook,* section 5020.A.

....

REVIEW CHECKPOINTS

1 Why should PAs issue a report whenever they are associated with financial statements?

....

LEARNING OBJECTIVE
3 Describe the three levels of assurance.

Levels of Assurance

In practice, accountants and auditors can render three types of conclusions, or **levels of assurance**, about financial statements. The highest level of assurance is the standard unqualified report, sometimes referred to as the **clean opinion**. Its opinion sentence reads, "In our opinion, the accompanying financial statements present fairly, in all material respects." This opinion sentence is sometimes called **positive assurance** because it is a forthright and factual statement of the PA's opinion based on an audit. Positive assurance is also frequently referred to as **reasonable** or **high assurance** in the *Handbook*. The IFAC

International Framework for Assurance Engagements refers to reasonable assurance also, noting that it is higher than moderate assurance.

Current CASs cover only high assurance engagements; hence the old *CICA Handbook* sections still apply for the other engagement conclusions. The middle level, known as **moderate** or **negative assurance**, is typical in the review report of unaudited financial statements. Its opinion would read, "Based on my review, nothing has come to my attention that causes me to believe that these financial statements are not, in all material respects, in accordance with Canadian generally accepted accounting principles," as per paragraph 8200.42 of the *Handbook*. This conclusion is called negative because it uses the backdoor phrase "nothing has come to my attention" to give assurance about conformity with GAAP. Auditing standards prohibit the use of negative assurance in reports on audited financial statements because it is considered too weak a conclusion for the audit effort involved (section 5400.15). However, it is permitted in reviews of unaudited financial statements, in letters to underwriters, and in reviews of interim financial information. (More details about review reports on unaudited financial statements are found in Chapter 16.)

The lowest level of assurance is a **no assurance** engagement. The most common examples are compilation engagements and specified procedures engagements. Compilation engagements are not considered to be assurance engagements because the practitioner is not required to audit, review, or otherwise attempt to verify the accuracy or completeness of the information provided by management. The practitioner is, therefore, not expressing a conclusion on the reliability of the statements. Their involvement presumably adds accounting credibility to the financial statements, however, even though there is no supporting evidence or audit assurance provided. For example, accounting credibility includes the use of correct account titles and format in the financial statements, but there is no verification of the accuracy of the underlying accounting records. (More details about compilation reports on unaudited financial statements are in Chapter 16.)

The professional credibility in accounting and tax services provided by PAs is the main reason for the rules of association. These rules provide guidance on avoiding association with misleading information and, thereby, assist in maintaining the reputation of the public accounting profession. The levels of assurance are shown in Exhibit 3–2. It should be noted that audit, review, and compilation engagements are intended to provide the specified assurance levels given in Exhibit 3–2. As we will see when discussing the disclaimer of opinion, under some conditions not even an audit engagement can provide much assurance.

The most important aspect of the concept of assurance levels is that it reflects the separate levels of evidence the PA has gathered to support the conclusions in the various types of assurance engagements. The reason there is less assurance in a review engagement is because the PA is required to gather less evidence. The reason compilations are considered a no assurance engagement is because PAs are not required to gather any evidence

EXHIBIT   3-2   LEVELS OF ASSURANCE

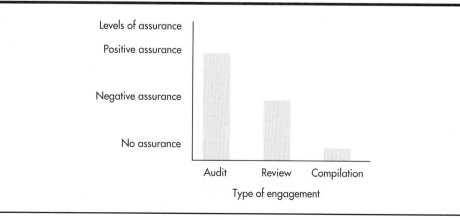

on the financial information. In any of these engagements, however, a PA's responsibility is to not be associated if they become aware that there is a reporting deficiency associated with the financial information. We cover PA responsibilities for review and compilations in more detail in Chapter 16.

REVIEW CHECKPOINTS

2 What is the most important distinction between an auditor's opinion on financial statements and other PA communications?

3 What is negative assurance? When is negative assurance permitted?

4 What is the difference between assurance and accounting credibility?

STANDARD UNQUALIFIED REPORT AND VARIATIONS

LEARNING OBJECTIVE
4 Compare and contrast the scope and opinion paragraphs in a standard unqualified audit report.

In this section we cover the various audit reports on management's financial statements. There are two broad categories: the standard unqualified report covered in CAS 700 (5400) and report reservations.

The standard unqualified report contains four basic segments: (1) introductory paragraph, (2) management (or other preparer) responsibility paragraph, (3) auditor responsibility paragraphs, and (4) opinion paragraph. An example is given in Exhibit 3–3. The technical

EXHIBIT   3–3   AUDITOR'S REPORT

To the Shareholders of.........................

We have audited the accompanying financial statements of ABC Company, which comprise the balance sheet as at December 31, 20X1, and the income statement, statement of changes in equity, and cash flow statement for the year then ended, and a summary of significant accounting policies and other explanatory notes.

Management is responsible for the preparation and fair presentation of these financial statements in accordance with Canadian generally accepted accounting principles; this includes the design, implementation, and maintenance of internal control relevant to the preparation and fair presentation of financial statements that are free from material misstatement, whether due to fraud or error.

Our responsibility is to express an opinion on these financial statements based on our audit. We conducted our audit in accordance with Canadian generally accepted auditing standards. Those standards require that we comply with ethical requirements and plan and perform the audit to obtain reasonable assurance whether the financial statements are free from material misstatement.

An audit involves performing procedures to obtain audit evidence about the amounts and disclosures in the financial statements. The procedures selected depend on the auditor's judgment, including the assessment of the risks of material misstatement of the financial statements, whether due to fraud or error. In making those risk assessments, the auditor considers internal control relevant to the entity's preparation and fair presentation of the financial statements in order to design audit procedures that are appropriate in the circumstances, but not for the purpose of expressing an opinion on the effectiveness of the entity's internal control. An audit also includes evaluating the appropriateness of accounting policies used and the reasonableness of accounting estimates made by management, as well as evaluating the overall presentation of financial statements.

We believe that the audit evidence we have obtained is sufficient and appropriate to provide a basis for our audit opinion.

In our opinion, the financial statements present fairly, in all material respects (or "give a true and fair view of,") the financial position of ABC Company as of December 31, 20X1, and of its financial performance and its cash flows for the year then ended in accordance with Canadian generally accepted accounting principles.

City

Date

(signed).....................

CHARTERED ACCOUNTANT

Source: © CICA Handbook, CAS 700 (5400.22).

details of this report were introduced in Chapter 2. The equivalent report used in the U.S. is given in Appendix 3A and is quite similar to the report used in Canada for audits before December 14, 2010.

Meaning of the Introductory, Scope, and Opinion Paragraphs

Many users understand the audit report by counting the paragraphs! Crude as this may seem, it makes some sense because each of the six standard paragraphs is supposed to convey the same message on all audits. The first place most analysts look in the client's annual report is the audit report, as any major problems in using the financial statements should be identified there.

Introductory Paragraph
The introductory paragraph declares that an audit has been conducted and identifies the financial statements. These identifications are important because, if a financial statement is not identified in this introductory paragraph, the opinion paragraph at the end likewise does not offer any opinion on it.

Management's Responsibility Paragraph
The second paragraph gives notice of management's (or other preparer's) responsibility to prepare the financial statements in conformity with a fair presentation reporting framework. This includes designing, implementing, and maintaining internal control; selecting and applying appropriate accounting policies; making accounting estimates that are reasonable in the circumstances; and primary responsibility for avoiding fraudulent financial reporting.

Auditor's Responsibility Paragraphs
Auditors must render a fair presentation of their own work, as well as an opinion on the financial statements. These paragraphs, also referred to as the scope paragraphs, are the auditor's report of the character of the work in the audit. This portion of the report is vitally important for disclosure of the quality and extent of the audit itself. Note that it makes explicit the auditor's responsibility to detect fraudulent reporting, abide by ethical standards, and appropriately support the opinion with audit evidence.

The sentence "We conducted our audit in accordance with Canadian generally accepted auditing standards" refers primarily to the general and the examination standards. Its message is that (1) the auditors were trained and proficient, (2) the auditors were independent, (3) due professional care was exercised, (4) the work was planned and supervised, (5) a sufficient understanding of the internal control structure was obtained, and (6) sufficient appropriate evidential matter was obtained. To the extent that one or more of these standards is not actually satisfied during an audit, the scope paragraphs must be qualified. A qualification means that an explanation of exactly which standard was not satisfied is added. In practice, auditors always change the standard opinion paragraph language when the scope paragraph is qualified.

The scope paragraphs contain general descriptions of the audit work in addition to the reference to Canadian auditing standards. They make special mention of the auditors' assessment of the choice of accounting principles and the evaluation of the overall financial statement presentation. It also lists any conditions that prevented the auditor from getting sufficient appropriate evidence, things that might also be areas for improvement in the client's system of recordkeeping.

Opinion Paragraph
Users of audited financial statements are generally most interested in the opinion paragraph, which is actually one long sentence. This sentence contains the auditors' conclusions about the financial statements. It is the public manifestation of the private audit decision process.

The following reporting standards are incorporated in the opinion sentence:

1. The standard report states that the financial statements are presented fairly in all material respects in accordance with Canadian generally accepted accounting principles. Under CAS 700, general purpose financial statements such as Canadian GAAP are deemed capable of achieving fairness of presentation under certain conditions. General purpose financial reporting implies broad principles that are a basis for developing and applying policies consistent with the concepts underlying the requirements of the framework. Such a framework is also referred to as an "acceptable financial reporting framework," and it provides a proper context for evaluating fairness of presentation. Note that, in the Exhibit 3–3 version of the report, the opinion paragraph has two options regarding fairness of presentation—the traditional one (present fairly) and the "true and fair" wording common in Europe.

2. The standard report, by its silence, regards the financial statement disclosures as reasonably adequate. This is part of the fairness criteria noted in item 1.

3. The standard report contains an expression of opinion regarding the financial statements.

4. An overall opinion is expressed in the standard report, so reasons for not doing so need not be stated.

The above points illustrate the importance of critical thinking and professional judgment in determining the acceptability of a financial reporting framework. Essentially, auditors are expected to be familiar with both the detailed accounting rules and the basic principles and concepts underlying them. These allow the auditor to determine if the rules are applicable in a specific auditee context. In particular, auditors must be sure that the particular rule applied is appropriate and not misleading in the context. This is the essence of the fairness of presentation framework of CAS 700.

With regard to the opinion reservations of CAS 705, other examples later in this chapter will show how auditors assert that an opinion cannot be expressed (disclaimer of opinion) or how audit responsibility can be limited (qualified opinion).

When reading the reporting standards, the term financial statements includes not only the traditional balance sheet, income statement, and cash flows statement but also all the footnote disclosures and additional information (e.g., earnings per share calculations) that are integral to the basic financial presentation required by GAAP. The report comments on consistency only when accounting principles have been changed and disclosures are considered inadequate. The adequacy of disclosures may be judged by GAAP requirements, but auditors also must be sensitive to the information needs of investors, creditors, and other users when considering information that is not explicitly required by GAAP. Disgruntled investors often use the "lack of informative disclosure" criterion as a basis for lawsuits. Users feel they have been misled in that case, and auditors need to be sensitized to these expectations. This is part of the context of financial reporting discussed in CAS 700.

The context of financial reporting usually impacts the audit report decision in two ways. First, additional disclosures beyond those required by specific accounting rules may be needed in order for the financial reporting not to be misleading. Second, mechanical application of a specific accounting rule may give misleading results in some circumstances, causing the auditor to insist on deviating from that rule in order to get a presentation that is not misleading. In both cases, the aim is to be consistent with the fairness of presentation framework.

Reservation in the Audit Report

The following sections of this chapter explain major variations on the standard report, often referred to as **reservations**. There are two basic reasons for giving a report that is other than the standard unqualified audit report. When the financial statements contain a departure from GAAP, including inadequate disclosure, the auditors must choose between a qualified opinion and an adverse opinion. The choice depends on the materiality (significance) and pervasiveness of the effect of the GAAP departure. This is frequently referred to as an **accounting deficiency reservation**. When there is a scope limitation (extent of audit work has been limited), and the auditors have not been able to obtain sufficient appropriate evidence on a particular account balance or disclosure, the auditors must choose between a qualified opinion and a disclaimer of opinion. The choice depends on the materiality of the matter for which evidence is not sufficient. Scope limitation reservations are also frequently referred to as **audit deficiency reservations**.

REVIEW CHECKPOINTS

5   Think about the standard unqualified introductory and scope paragraphs. What do they identify as the objects of the audit? What is meant by this sentence: "We conducted our audit in accordance with Canadian generally accepted auditing standards"?

6   What are the major reasons for departures from the standard unqualified report?

AUDIT REPORT RESERVATIONS

LEARNING OBJECTIVE

5 For a given set of accounting facts and audit circumstances, analyze qualified, adverse, and disclaimer audit reports.

Audit reports other than the standard unqualified audit report are called audit report reservations. The most common report reservations are called **qualified reports** because they contain an opinion paragraph that does not give the positive assurance that everything in the financial statements is in conformity with GAAP. There are two basic types of qualified reports: GAAP departure reports and scope limitation reports.

GAAP Departure Reports

For various reasons, a company's management can decide to present financial statements containing an accounting treatment or disclosure that is not in conformity with GAAP. They may not wish to capitalize leases and show the related debt, may calculate earnings per share incorrectly, may not accrue unbilled revenue at the end of a period, may make unreasonable accounting estimates, or may be reluctant to disclose all the known details of a contingency. Whatever the reason for the departure from GAAP, the auditor must decide on the type of opinion to render.

If the departure is immaterial or insignificant, it can be treated as if it did not exist and the audit opinion can be unqualified. What is considered immaterial under the circumstances is a matter of the auditor's professional judgment. Critical thinking can help structure this decision.

If, in the auditor's judgment, the departure is material enough to potentially affect users' decisions based on the financial statements, the opinion must be qualified. In this case, the qualification takes the "except for" language form. The opinion sentence begins, "In my opinion, except for the [nature of the GAAP departure], the financial statements present fairly, in all material respects . . . in accordance with Canadian generally accepted accounting principles." This style of qualification identifies the particular departure but says that the financial statements are otherwise in conformity with GAAP. The nature of the GAAP departure can be explained in a separate paragraph (called the reservation paragraph) between the scope paragraphs and the opinion paragraph, as covered by CAS 705 (5510.28). The introductory and scope paragraphs are the same as in the standard unqualified report. After all, the audit was performed without limitation, and the auditors have sufficient appropriate evidence about the financial statements, including the GAAP departure.

EXHIBIT   3-4

Departure from generally accepted accounting principles—no depreciation recorded.
When the auditor has determined that a qualification is the type of reservation required, the following wording may be appropriate.

AUDITOR'S REPORT

To the Shareholders of....................

(The introductory, management responsibility, and auditor responsibility paragraphs are the same as in the unqualified report [see Exhibit 3–3]. A new paragraph may be added after the scope paragraphs to provide more details immediately preceding the opinion paragraph as follows.)

Note .... describes the depreciation policy with respect to the company's manufacturing plants and equipment. The note also indicates that the company is not depreciating its head office building, which it acquired 5 years ago, on the grounds that it is not a producing asset and is maintaining its value as a potential rental or resale property. In this respect the financial statements are not in accordance with generally accepted accounting principles. The estimated useful life of similar buildings is usually considered to be between 30 and 40 years. If depreciation had been provided on the basis of an estimated useful life of, say, 35 years, depreciation for the current year would have been increased by $.......... (20....$..........), net income after taxes would have been decreased by $..........(20....$..........), accumulated depreciation would have been increased by $..........(20....$..........) and the balance of deferred income taxes and the closing balance of retained earnings would have been reduced by $..........(20....$..........) and $..........(20....$..........) respectively.

In my opinion, except for the effects of the failure to record depreciation as described in the preceding paragraph, these financial statements present fairly, in all material respects, the financial position of the company as at ...., 20...., and the results of its operations and the cash flows for the year then ended in accordance with Canadian generally accepted accounting principles.

(signed)....................
CHARTERED ACCOUNTANT

Source: © CICA Handbook, CAS 705 (modified 5510.A, Example A).

GAAP-departure report examples are hard to find in published financial statements. Most published statements come under the jurisdiction of the provincial securities commissions, which require public companies to file financial statements without any departures from GAAP. Exhibit 3–4 shows a GAAP departure due to a failure to record depreciation.

If the GAAP departures are either (1) much more material, or "so significant that they overshadow the financial statements," or (2) pervasive, affecting numerous accounts and financial statement relationships, there is a condition of **pervasive materiality** and an adverse opinion should be given. An adverse opinion is exactly the opposite of the unqualified opinion. In this type of opinion, auditors say the financial statements do not present the financial position, results of operations, and changes in financial position in conformity with generally accepted accounting principles. When this opinion is given, all the substantive reasons for it must be disclosed in the reservation paragraph(s), as covered by *Handbook* CAS 705 (5510.28). The introductory and scope paragraphs should not be qualified because, in order to decide to use the adverse opinion, the audit team must possess all evidence necessary to reach the decision.

Because of the securities commission requirements, adverse opinions are hard to find. The example in Exhibit 3–5 is due to a disagreement between the auditor and management on the carrying value of a long-term investment. That departure from GAAP is considered to be highly or pervasively material, or well in excess of what would be considered material for an "except for" qualification.

Practically speaking, auditors require more evidence to support an adverse opinion than to support an unqualified opinion. Perhaps this can be attributed to auditors' reluctance to be bearers of bad news. However, audit standards are quite clear that, if an auditor has a basis for an adverse opinion, the uncomfortable position cannot be relieved

EXHIBIT 3-5   ADVERSE REPORT

Departure from generally accepted accounting principles—disagreement on carrying value of a long-term investment. When the auditor has determined that an adverse opinion is the type of reservation required, the following wording may be appropriate. (For an adverse opinion, "present fairly" in the opinion paragraph, need not be modified with the phrase "in all material respects.")

AUDITOR'S REPORT

To the Shareholders of....................

(The introductory, management responsibility, and auditor responsibility paragraphs are the same as in the unqualified report [see Exhibit 3–3]. A new paragraph may be added after the scope paragraphs to provide more details immediately preceding the opinion paragraph as follows.)

The company's investment in X Company Ltd., its only asset, which is carried at a cost of $10,000,000, has declined in value to an amount of $5,850,000. The loss in the value of this investment, in my opinion, is other than a temporary decline and in such circumstances generally accepted accounting principles require that the investment be written down to recognize the loss. If this decline in value had been recognized, the investment, net income for the year, and retained earnings would have been reduced by $4,150,000.

In my opinion, because the write-down has not been made for the significant decline in value of the investment described in the preceding paragraph, these financial statements do not present fairly the financial position of the company as at ...., 20...., and the results of its operations and the cash flows for the year then ended in accordance with Canadian generally accepted accounting principles.

City

Date

(signed)....................

CHARTERED ACCOUNTANT

Source: © CICA Handbook, CAS 705 (modified 5510.A, Example H).

by giving a disclaimer of opinion. GAAP departure reports cover those situations where the auditor knows the true state of affairs—there is or there is not an accounting deficiency. The next section will outline situations where the auditor does not know the true state of affairs. These are situations where there are limitations on the scope of the auditors' work.

REVIEW CHECKPOINTS

7 With reference to evidence, what extent of evidence is required as a basis for the unqualified opinion? for an adverse opinion? for an opinion qualified for GAAP departure?

8 What effect does the materiality of a GAAP departure have on the auditors' reporting decision?

Scope Limitation Reports

Auditors are in the most comfortable position when they have all the evidence needed to make a report decision—whether the opinion is to be unqualified, adverse, or qualified. There are two kinds of situations, however, that can result in **scope limitations**—conditions where the auditors are unable to obtain sufficient appropriate evidence: (1) management deliberately refuses to let auditors perform some procedures or (2) circumstances, such as late appointment of auditor, make it impossible for some procedures to be performed.

If management's refusal or the circumstances affect the audit in a minor, immaterial way, or if sufficient appropriate evidence can be obtained by other means, the audit can be considered to be unaffected, and the report can be unqualified as if the limitation had never occurred.

EXHIBIT   3–6A   SCOPE LIMITATION REPORTS

PANEL A: QUALIFIED OPINION

Scope limitation—The auditor is appointed during the year and is unable to observe the inventory count at the beginning of the year. (It is assumed that the prior year's figures were unaudited and that the auditor was satisfied with respect to all other aspects of inventories and all other opening figures.) When the auditor has determined that a qualification is the type of reservation required, the following wording may be appropriate.

AUDITOR'S REPORT

To the Shareholders of....................

(The introductory and management responsibility paragraphs are the same as in the unqualified report [see Exhibit 3–3 on page 70].)

Our responsibility is to express an opinion on these financial statements based on our audit. Except as discussed in the following paragraph, we conducted our audit in accordance with .... (The remaining words are the same as illustrated in the auditor's responsibility paragraphs [see Exhibit 3–3].) Because we were appointed auditor of the company during the current year, we were not able to observe the counting of physical inventories at the beginning of the year nor satisfy ourselves concerning those inventory quantities by alternative means. Since opening inventories enter into the determination of the results of operations and cash flows, I was unable to determine whether adjustments to cost of sales, income taxes, net income for the year, opening retained earnings, and cash provided from operations might be necessary.

In our opinion, except for the effect of adjustments, if any, which we might have determined to be necessary had we been able to examine opening inventory quantities as described in the preceding paragraph, the statements of income, retained earnings, and cash flows present fairly, in all material respects, the results of operations and cash flows of the company for the year ended ...., 20...., in accordance with Canadian generally accepted accounting principles. Further, in my opinion, the balance sheet presents fairly, in all material respects, the financial position of the company as at ...., 20...., in accordance with Canadian generally accepted accounting principles.

City	(signed)....................
Date	CHARTERED ACCOUNTANT

Source: © *CICA Handbook*, CAS 705 (modified 5510A, Example J).

Management's deliberate refusal to give access to documents or to otherwise limit audit procedures is the most serious condition. It casts doubt on management's integrity. (Why is management refusing access or limiting the work?) In most such cases, the audit report is qualified or an opinion is disclaimed, depending upon the materiality of the financial items affected.

Exhibit 3–6 shows two reports that illustrate the auditors' alternatives. The failure to take physical counts of inventory, as shown, might have been a deliberate management action, or it might have resulted from other circumstances, such as the company's not anticipating the need for an audit and appointing the auditor after the latest year-end.

In Panel A, the opinion is qualified, using the except-for language form. Here the lack of evidence is considered material, but not pervasively or highly material enough to overwhelm the meaning of qualified audit opinion and the usefulness of the remainder of the financial statements. The proper qualification phrase here is, "In our opinion, except for the effects of adjustments, if any, as might have been determined to be necessary had we been able to examine evidence regarding the inventories, the financial statements present fairly, in all material respects, . . . in conformity with Canadian generally accepted accounting principles." This report "carves out" the inventory from the audit reporting responsibility, thus taking no audit responsibility for this part of the financial statements.

Notice that the introductory paragraph in Panel A is the same as for an unqualified report. However, the first scope paragraph is qualified because the audit was not completed entirely in accordance with generally accepted auditing standards. Specifically, sufficient

EXHIBIT   3-6B   SCOPE LIMITATION REPORTS

PANEL B: DISCLAIMER OF OPINION

Scope limitation—the physical inventory count was not observed by the auditor and there are serious deficiencies in the accounting records and in the system of internal control over inventory. When the auditor has determined that a denial of opinion is the type of reservation required, the following wording may be appropriate. (For a disclaimer of opinion, "presented fairly" in the opinion paragraph need not be modified with the phrase "in all material respects.")

AUDITOR'S REPORT

To the Shareholders of....................

(The introductory and management responsibility paragraphs are the same as in the unqualified report [see Exhibit 3–3]. Omit the sentence stating the responsibility of the auditor.)

(The paragraph discussing the scope of the audit would be either omitted or amended according to the circumstances.)

(Add a paragraph discussing the scope limitations as follows.)

We were not able to observe all physical inventories due to limitations placed on the scope of our work by the Company.

Because of the significance of the matters discussed in the preceding paragraph, we do not express an opinion on the financial statements.

City

Date

(signed).....................

CHARTERED ACCOUNTANT

Source: © *CICA Handbook, CAS 705.*

---

appropriate evidence about the inventories was not obtained. Whenever the scope paragraph is qualified for an important omission of audit work, the opinion paragraph should also be qualified.

The Panel B situation is considered fatal to the audit opinion. In this case, the inventories are too large and too important to say "except for adjustments, if any." The audit report then must be a disclaimer of opinion.

It is important to remember that scope limitation reservations arise only when it is not possible to obtain compensating assurance from alternative audit procedures. If, for example, in Panel A and Panel B the auditor had been able to satisfy himself through alternative procedures that the inventory was materially accurate, then an unqualified opinion could have been issued for both panels. Thus, scope limitation reports are issued only if, in the auditor's judgment, the alternative procedures do not compensate for the restriction.

To summarize, we can view audit reservations as arising from two types of circumstances: audit deficiencies, or scope limitations, and accounting deficiencies resulting from a GAAP departure. Audit deficiencies can result in either a qualification or a disclaimer of opinion, depending on the significance of the scope limitation. In an audit deficiency reservation, both the scope and opinion paragraphs are affected. When there is an audit deficiency, the auditor does not have enough evidence or does not know the true state of affairs. An accounting deficiency, on the other hand, can result in either a qualification or adverse opinion, depending on the significance of the GAAP departure. In an accounting deficiency reservation, only the opinion paragraph is affected. To reach a conclusion about an accounting deficiency, the auditor must have sufficient appropriate evidence to support the conclusion. The auditor is in a position to know the true state of affairs.

It should be stressed that both auditor and client work to avoid a report reservation. It may take much discussion and negotiation between the auditor and client management to do this. This negotiation is discussed in more detail in Chapter 15, after we have considered the topic of available evidence at the end of the engagement.

> ## OTHER RESPONSIBILITIES WITH A DISCLAIMER
>
> A disclaimer of opinion because of severe scope limitation or because of association with unaudited financial statements carries some additional reporting responsibilities. In addition to the disclaimer, these rules should be followed:
> - If the PA should learn that the statements are not in conformity with generally accepted accounting principles (including adequate disclosures), the departures should be explained in the disclaimer.
> - If prior years' unaudited statements are presented, the disclaimer should cover them as well as the current-year statement.

Exhibit 3–7 summarizes the audit decision process in arriving at either some type of reservation (far right column) or an unqualified opinion (far left column). Make sure you understand the reasoning behind the paths shown in this exhibit.

EXHIBIT   3-7   AUDIT REPORT DECISION PROCESS

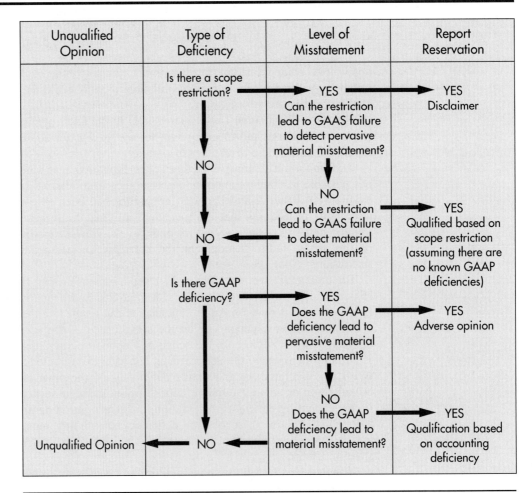

R E V I E W
CHECKPOINTS

9 What are the differences between a report qualified for a scope limitation and a standard unqualified report?

10 What are the differences between a report in which the opinion is disclaimed because of scope limitation and a standard unqualified report?

11 The auditor knows about the client's situation for which opinions? Explain.

Effects of Lack of Independence

Independence is the foundation of the audit function. When independence is lacking, an audit in accordance with generally accepted auditing standards is impossible, and the auditors should resign or not accept an audit engagement. An audit does not simply require the application of the tools, techniques, and procedures of auditing, it also requires independence in mental attitude of the auditors. This idea is reflected in the general standard and codes of professional ethics, an example of which is Rule 204, entitled "Independence."

204.1 (INDEPENDENCE IN) ASSURANCE AND SPECIFIED AUDITING PROCEDURES ENGAGEMENTS

A member or firm who engages or participates in an engagement (a) to issue a written communication under the terms of an assurance engagement, or (b) to issue a report on the results of applying specified auditing procedures shall be and remain independent such that the member, firm and members of the firm shall be and remain free of any influence, interest or relationship which, in respect of the engagement, impairs the professional judgment or objectivity of the member, firm or a member of the firm or which, in the view of a reasonable observer, would impair the professional judgment or objectivity of the member, firm or a member of the firm.

This rule applies to the auditors of financial statements. The criteria for determining independence are discussed in Chapter 4.

Source: Institute of Chartered Accountants of Ontario (ICAO).

R E V I E W
CHECKPOINTS

12 If an auditor is not independent with respect to a public company client, what should she do?

13 Why is independence important for auditors?

UNQUALIFIED OPINION WITH EXPLANATION OR MODIFICATION

LEARNING OBJECTIVE

6 Write an unqualified audit report containing additional explanation or modified wording for specific issues allowed by GAAS.

Several circumstances may permit an unqualified opinion paragraph, but they raise the need to consider information and paragraphs that are additional to the standard report. Four such situations are covered in this section.

- **Consistency** The effects of various changes in accounting and the appropriate disclosure

- **Uncertainty** A paragraph that draws attention to accounting and disclosure for contingencies

- **Emphasis paragraph(s)**   Additional explanatory paragraphs that "emphasize a matter" of importance
- **Going Concern**   A paragraph that draws attention to problems of being able to continue as a going concern

Consistency

As long as changes are properly disclosed in the financial statements, there is no need to make reference to consistency, even when there are changes in accounting principles. Consistency references are not required in the audit report for (1) changes in accounting estimates; (2) error corrections that do not involve a change in accounting principles; (3) changes in the classification or aggregation of financial statement amounts; (4) changes in the format or basis of the statement of cash flows (e.g., from a balancing format to a net change format); and (5) changes in the subsidiaries included in consolidated financial statements as a result of forming a new subsidiary, buying another company, spinning off or liquidating a subsidiary, or selling a subsidiary. However, failure to disclose any of these changes could amount to a GAAP departure and, therefore, perhaps present a different reason for qualifying the opinion.

When evaluating a change in accounting principle, auditors must be satisfied that management's justification for the change is reasonable. In the United States, there is an additional requirement that the change be to a "preferable" principle—one that provides a better measure of business operations. The U.S. standard "Accounting Changes" states:

> The presumption that an entity should not change an accounting principle may be overcome only if the enterprise justifies the use of an alternative acceptable accounting principle on the basis that it is preferable.

For example, a change from accelerated depreciation to straight-line in order to increase profits may be preferable from management's viewpoint, but it is not reasonable justification for most auditors. If the U.S. auditors cannot agree that a change in accounting principle is preferable, then an opinion qualification based on a departure from GAAP is appropriate. In the U.S., the SEC requires auditors to submit a letter stating whether the change is to a preferable principle.

Uncertainty

Previously in this chapter, you studied scope limitations in which either management or circumstances prevented the auditors from obtaining sufficient appropriate evidence about a part of the financial statements. A different type of problem arises when client uncertainties exist. We will refer to these as accounting uncertainties because they do not arise from scope restrictions. Instead, they are related to accounting measurement uncertainties. A good example of an accounting uncertainty is an accounting contingency, which is defined in the *Handbook*, paragraph 3290.02:

> A contingency is . . . an existing condition, or situation, involving uncertainty as to possible gain ("gain contingency") or loss ("loss contingency") to an enterprise that will ultimately be resolved when one or more future events occur or fail to occur. Resolution of the uncertainty may confirm the acquisition of an asset or the reduction of a liability or the loss or impairment of an asset or the incurrence of a liability.

Handbook section 3290 sets forth accounting and disclosure standards for contingencies. One of the most common ones involves the uncertain outcome of litigation pending against a company. Accounting uncertainties include not only lawsuits, but also such things as the value of fixed assets held for sale (e.g., a whole plant or warehouse facility) and the status of assets involved in foreign expropriations. Auditors may perform procedures in accordance with generally accepted auditing standards, yet the uncertainty and lack of evidence may persist. The problem is that it is impossible to obtain audit "evidence" about the future. The concept of audit evidence includes information knowable at the time a reporting decision is made and does not include predictions about future resolution of uncertainties. Consequently, auditors should not change (modify or qualify) the introductory, scope, or opinion paragraphs of the standard unqualified report when contingencies and uncertainties exist. When the audit has been performed in accordance with generally accepted auditing standards, and the auditor has done all things possible in the circumstances, no alteration of these standard paragraphs is necessary as long as the uncertainty has been properly disclosed. Whether the disclosure is proper, however, can be a major financial reporting issue and a key professional judgment of the auditor.

Under Canadian audit standard CAS 706, however, the auditor may decide to place a "red flag" paragraph drawing attention to the uncertainty in the report. If there is material uncertainty about the going concern assumption, for example, then CAS 706 requires that an emphasis of matter paragraph be added even when there is proper disclosure in the financial statements.

Uncertainty situations may cause audit reports to be qualified for departures from GAAP, if (1) management's disclosure of the uncertainty is inadequate, (2) management uses inappropriate accounting principles to account for the uncertainty, or (3) management makes unreasonable accounting estimates in connection with the effects of the uncertainty. The audit report also may be qualified because of a scope limitation regarding available evidence about an uncertainty.

A Historical Note: "Subject to" Opinions Prior to 1980

From the early 1960s until 1980, auditors gave "subject to" opinions for accounting uncertainty situations. The opinion sentence was qualified with these words: "In our opinion, subject to the effects of such adjustments, if any, as might have been determined had the outcome of the uncertainty discussed in the preceding paragraph been known . . ." The explanatory paragraph was placed before the opinion paragraph, and the opinion was considered qualified. You may see this form of "subject to" opinion when you use reports issued in 1980 and earlier. However, the audit standards were changed in 1980, and now the "subject to" wording is prohibited, the explanatory paragraph is no longer used, and the opinion sentence itself is unqualified.

The inclusion of significant matter paragraphs discussed below appears to be one way that the basic red-flagging objective of "subject to" opinions may be resurrected.

Significant Matter Paragraph(s): Modifications That Do Not Affect the Audit Opinion

Sometimes auditors opt to add additional information in the audit report. There are two types of additions possible under CAS 706: emphasis of matter (EOM) paragraphs or other matter (OM) paragraphs. These are used for enriching the information content beyond the standard unqualified report wording. Under CAS 706, the EOM paragraph can be used for a much broader range of issues than allowed previously. One or more paragraphs can be added in the audit report regarding something the auditor believes readers should consider important or useful, or when the auditor intends to write an unqualified opinion paragraph. Indeed, the matter emphasized is not supposed to be mentioned in the standard unqualified opinion sentence. Exhibit 3–8 illustrates such a paragraph.

EXHIBIT 3-8   EXAMPLE OF AN EMPHASIS OF A MATTER PARAGRAPH

Without qualifying our opinion we draw attention to Note X to the financial statements. The Company is the defendant in a lawsuit alleging infringement of certain patent rights and claiming royalties and punitive damages. The Company has filed a counter action, and preliminary hearings and discovery proceedings on both actions are in progress. The ultimate outcome of the matter cannot presently be determined and no provision for any liability that may result has been made in the financial statements.

Source: © *CICA Handbook, CAS 706.*

As noted above, EOM paragraphs are required when there is material uncertainty regarding the going concern assumption.

OM paragraphs are distinguished from EOM paragraphs by the information they reference. EOMs refer only to information presented or disclosed in the financial statements, whereas OMs relate to information which is not required to be disclosed in the financial statements. For example, OMs can refer to other information included with the financial statements, such as MD&A or comparative information from other periods, especially when there appear to be discrepancies between the two.

Going Concern

Generally accepted accounting principles are based on the going-concern concept, which means the entity is expected to continue operations and meet its obligations as they become due, without substantial disposition of assets outside the ordinary course of business, restructuring of debt, externally forced revisions of its operations (e.g., a bank reorganization forced by the Superintendent of Financial Institutions), or similar actions. Thus, an opinion that financial statements are in conformity with GAAP means that continued existence may be presumed for a "reasonable time"—at least one year beyond the date of the financial statements.[1] This one-year time horizon was reiterated in the CICA's December 2008 "Risk Alert" on audit considerations during the economic crisis that began in 2008/2009.

Dealing with questions of going concern is difficult because auditors are forced to evaluate matters of financial analysis, business strategy, and financial forecasting. Most managements are unwilling to give up and close their businesses without strong attempts to survive. Sometimes, survival optimism prevails until the creditors force bankruptcy proceedings and liquidation, and auditors are generally reluctant to puncture any balloons of optimism. Managers and auditors both view news of financial troubles in an audit report (an attention-directing paragraph or a disclaimer based on going-concern doubt) as a "self-fulfilling prophecy" that causes bankruptcy. However debatable this view might be, it still prevails and inhibits auditors' consideration of going-concern questions.

Auditors are responsible for determining whether there is a significant doubt about a company's ability to continue as a going concern. No careful auditor should ignore signs of financial difficulty and operate entirely on the assumption that the company is a going concern. Financial difficulties, labour problems, loss of key personnel, litigation, and other such things may be important signals. Likewise, elements of financial flexibility (salability of assets, lines of credit, debt extension, dividend elimination) may be available as survival strategies. (In U.S. auditing standards, these elements of financial flexibility and management strategy are known as **mitigating factors** that may reduce the financial difficulties.)

Accounting and finance research efforts have produced several bankruptcy prediction models. These models use publicly available financial information to classify companies into "fail" and "nonfail" categories. An auditing firm might use such a model as an analytical review tool. Auditing standards, however, make no mention of research models and instead suggest many company-specific considerations and elements of internal information for analysis. (One bankruptcy prediction model is described briefly in Chapter 7 of this text.)

Since the going concern assumption is so fundamental to financial reporting, it becomes a good example of how GAAP and GAAS can overlap. An important CICA research study,

[1] "The Going-Concern Assumption," CICA Research Report (Boritz, 1991).

"The Going-Concern Assumption," gives recommendations based on key threshold probabilities. The key audit recommendations of the study are as follows:

1. Require auditors on every audit to perform procedures that provide reasonable assurance about the validity of the going-concern assumption.
2. Evaluate results of procedures performed.
3. If significant (20–50 percent probability) or substantial (50 percent or greater probability) doubts are raised, assess management's plans to address these matters, considering if they can be effectively implemented. (*Note:* The very existence of such plans should call "going concern" into question.)
4. Expand the auditor's reporting responsibilities when in doubt about the validity of the going-concern assumption becomes substantial. Include an explanatory paragraph even if doubt is adequately disclosed in the notes.
5. Issue an adverse opinion where substantial doubt exists and disclosure is inadequate.
6. Issue an adverse opinion if virtually certain, and GAAP no longer applies.

According to this study, five types of audit reports may be used when going-concern problems exist. The first is a standard report with no additional explanatory paragraphs as long as doubts are minor or significant but properly disclosed in the notes to the financial statements. The second type is a standard report with an unqualified opinion paragraph and an additional explanatory paragraph(s) to direct attention to management's disclosures about the problems. This would be used when there are substantial doubts and the company has properly disclosed these problems in the notes. The third type of report is an adverse opinion that arises from failure to disclose substantial doubts, or when it is virtually certain that the company will fail to continue as a going concern and GAAP no longer applies. A fourth type of report is a qualification for a GAAP departure if the auditor believes the company's disclosures about financial difficulties and going-concern problems are inadequate. Such a report is shown in Exhibit 3–9. The fifth type of report is one qualified for a scope limitation if evidence that might or might not exist is not made available to the auditors, leading

---

EXHIBIT   3-9   A QUALIFIED REPORT EXPLAINING GOING-CONCERN PROBLEMS

Departure from generally accepted accounting principles—inadequate disclosure of matters affecting the company's ability to continue as a going concern. When the auditor has determined that a qualification is the type of reservation required, the following wording may be appropriate.

AUDITOR'S REPORT

To the Shareholders of.........................

The introductory, management responsibility, and auditor responsibility paragraphs are the same as in the unqualified report (see Exhibit 3–3 on page 70). A new paragraph is added after the scope paragraphs to provide more details immediately preceding the opinion paragraph as follows.

The accompanying financial statements, in my opinion, do not draw attention explicitly to doubts concerning the company's ability to realize its assets and discharge its liabilities in the normal course of business. These doubts arise because it is uncertain whether the company will be able to refinance long-term debt in the amount of $.................... due on ...., 20X2 in view of the existence of recurring operating losses in the past five years and the deficiency in working capital of $................. as at ...., 20X1. If refinancing cannot be arranged, it is not known whether the company can sell its hotel property for an amount sufficient to realize its carrying value of $...................., and to generate adequate funds to repay this debt.

In my opinion, except for the omission of the disclosure described in the preceding paragraph, these financial statements present fairly, in all material respects, the financial position of the company as at ...., 20X1 and the results of its operations and its cash flows for the year then ended in accordance with generally accepted accounting principles.

City

Date

(signed)....................

CHARTERED ACCOUNTANT

Source: © *CICA Handbook*, CAS 706 (section 5510.A, Example F).

to the "except for adjustments, if any" type of qualified opinion explained earlier in this chapter. These different reports arise from the refined classification scheme reflected by the going-concern study recommendations. Note that, to be consistent, both accounting and auditing standards should use similar criteria. Unfortunately, on issues like going concern, these standards do not use the same terminology so it is unclear whether the same criteria are intended. The auditor is left to rely on his or her professional judgment to resolve such incompatibility in standards. This is when a systematic approach like critical thinking can help come up with the most appropriate decision in the circumstances.

In summary, the current *Handbook* recommendation that applies is CAS 706, which effectively states that if there is a going-concern problem, an unqualified opinion is given as long as the problem is adequately disclosed. If there is material uncertainty about going concern, then an emphasis paragraph is also required even when the facts are adequately disclosed. If the facts are not adequately disclosed, the auditor should issue a reservation of the audit opinion. An illustration of an "except for" qualification reservation is shown in Exhibit 3–9 (page 83).

The above discussion on accounting uncertainties and going concern suggests that the audit process can be viewed as a two-stage process. In stage one, the auditor gathers enough audit evidence to reduce audit risk to acceptable levels. This stage deals with what we can call audit evidence uncertainties, those related to the amount of evidence gathered. The significance of evidence uncertainties is that they distinguish between high, moderate, and no assurance engagements. If the purpose of the engagement is to obtain high assurance, then the PA needs to gather extensive detailed data to support the PAs audit report, and we get all the audit report issues discussed in this chapter. If, on the other hand, the purpose of the engagement is not to supply high assurance, then new evidence considerations come into play that we discuss in Chapter 16.

The accounting uncertainties discussed above have little to do with evidence gathering as they reflect the business risks of the client. Audit evidence gathering procedures can do little to alleviate most client business risks. These are best dealt with by proper disclosure of them in the client's financial reporting. This brings us to stage two of the audit process.

In stage two the auditor uses the evidence obtained in stage one to make a determination of the appropriateness of financial reporting relative to GAAP and fairness of presentation criteria. The two steps reflect the two major categories of audit report reservations: audit deficiency reservations based on stage one, and accounting deficiency reservations based on stage two. Thus the distinction between audit and accounting uncertainties is critical for audit report reservations. One of the reasons critical thinking in professional judgment is important is that it focuses on the link between your study of auditing and your study of financial reporting in your accounting courses. Specifically, critical thinking helps integrate professional judgment in accounting with professional judgment in auditing.

REVIEW CHECKPOINTS

14 Why is the going concern assumption of financial reporting important for auditors?

15 Why might "opinion shopping" be suspect? beneficial? (See Appendix 3B.)

SUMMARY

LEARNING OBJECTIVE

7 Determine the effects of materiality on audit report choices.

This chapter began with setting forth the requirement that auditors must report whenever they are associated with financial statements. This report can take different forms in different circumstances—audit assurance, negative assurance, and no assurance. These levels of assurance are further explained in terms of (1) reports qualified for scope limitations and departures from GAAP, (2) adverse reports resulting from GAAP departures, and (3) disclaimers of opinion resulting from lack of independence and lack of sufficient appropriate evidence.

EXHIBIT 3–10   INFLUENCE OF MATERIALITY ON AUDIT REPORTS

	Required Type of Report	
Circumstances for Departure from Standard Report	Materiality	Pervasive Materiality
Departure from GAAP	Qualified "except for": separate paragraph discloses reasons and effects*	Adverse Opinion: separate paragraph discloses reasons and effects
Limitation on Scope (lack of evidence)	Qualified Opinion: refers to possible effects on financials	Disclaimer of Opinion: separate paragraph explains limitations
Uncertainty	Unqualified Opinion**	Unqualified Opinion**

*Where the departure is necessary to make the financials not misleading, an unqualified opinion is issued with an explanation of the circumstances.
**Unless there is a failure to properly disclose the uncertainty

Throughout this chapter's explanation of the auditors' choices of reports, the materiality dimension played an important role. When an auditor makes decisions about the audit report, immaterial or unimportant information can be ignored and treated as if it does not exist. However, when inaccuracies, departures from GAAP, accounting changes, and uncertainties have a large enough financial impact, the standard audit report must be changed. In practice, when an auditor decides a matter is material enough to make a difference, a further distinction must be made between misstatements of "materiality" and those of "pervasive materiality." Materiality means that the item in question is important and needs to be disclosed or that the opinion for it needs to be qualified—the information cannot simply be ignored. Pervasive materiality means that the item is important and has a significant impact on the reporting decision. The biggest distinction between the two materialities is the number of users affected by the potential misstatements: pervasive materiality affects many more users than does materiality. In the post-Enron environment, the amount of misstatement that is considered acceptable has been reduced in many audits so that both materialities have also been reduced. As you will see, this effectively increases the amount of audit work in the engagement.

Auditing standards refer to several basic circumstances that cause departures from the standard unqualified audit report. These circumstances are shown in Exhibit 3–10 in relation to the influence of materiality. You can see that each report is qualified when the situation involves materiality, but becomes a disclaimer or an adverse report when the situation involves pervasive materiality. The exception is the lack of independence issue, where materiality does not make a difference.

Audit reports can also be modified and expanded with additional paragraphs. Such additions to the audit report arise from the need for EOM and EM paragraphs in certain situations. Appendix 3B of this chapter covers "shopping" for accounting principles and auditors. Standards exist to raise the public perception that auditors are careful about competing with each other on the basis of professional opinions.

REVIEW CHECKPOINTS

16 Explain the effect of materiality or pervasive materiality on an auditor report when the client uses an accounting method that departs from generally accepted accounting principles.

17 Explain the effect of pervasive materiality on an auditor report when there is a scope limitation.

18 Explain the effect of pervasive materiality on an auditor report when there is a material uncertainty associated with the financial statements.

19 Identify the levels of assurance associated with auditor reports.

20 Under what conditions would an auditor use an emphasis of a matter paragraph?

APPLICATION CASE AND ANALYSIS:
GOING CONCERN AND ACCOUNTING RISK

A recent CICA study shows that only 46 percent of companies that failed had any indication of going-concern problems in the previously audited financial statements.[2] Do you think this is acceptable? What does this say about accounting risks associated with failing companies?

Analysis

LEARNING OBJECTIVE

8 Apply and integrate the chapter topics to analyze a practical auditing situation/case/scenario.

The going-concern assumption is crucial in measuring assets and liabilities as though they will be realized in the normal course of business. According to Recommendation 1400 of the *CICA Handbook*, the auditee should disclose in the financial statements uncertainties (material uncertainties) which "may cast significant doubt" on the auditee's ability to continue as a going concern. Under CAS 570, the auditor needs to evaluate, based on the evidence obtained, the appropriateness of the auditee's going-concern assumption in the preparation and presentation of the financial statements. The auditor does this by evaluating whether the evidence "casts significant doubt" on the auditee's ability to continue as a going concern. This involves a forecast of the period at least one year after the date of the financial statements. If there is significant doubt but, in the auditor's opinion, appropriate disclosure is made, the auditor expresses an unqualified opinion but includes an EOM paragraph in the report. If appropriate disclosure is not made, the auditor expresses a qualified or adverse opinion and states that there is a material uncertainty possibly casting significant doubt about the auditee's ability to continue as a going concern. For example, on March 31, 2009, there were headlines to the effect, "General Motors' new CEO says bankruptcy possible." Should this business risk be disclosed as a going-concern issue in financial reporting?

Unfortunately, the standards are not as clear as the Boritz (1991) criteria given in the text. Using those criteria, significant doubt is a 20–50 percent probability of failure. Thus, if audit firms tended to use the upper end of this range, the average results would be those indicated at the beginning of this case. Is this a good enough track record for the profession? If half the failing companies gave no indication of going-concern problems, would you as an investor feel that the financial statements "presented fairly"?

Note that accounting risk for such failed companies corresponds to the 50 percent failure-to-warn rate. More generally, acceptable accounting risk level corresponds with the significant risk level of auditee failure, assuming auditors interpret significant risk to be at similar levels of about 50 percent. Thus, if you feel 50 percent is too high, you would want auditors to interpret significant risk to be a lower probability, say 20 percent. At 20 percent acceptable risk, auditors would, on average, fail to indicate going-concern problems only 20 percent of the time. This assumes auditors follow a decision rule based on acceptable accounting risk levels. We amplify this discussion in Chapter 10, after you have learned a bit more about how risks are controlled in auditing. But, hopefully, the above logic is largely intuitive.

[2] See Alison Arnot, "Reporting a Going Concern," *CGA Magazine*, July–August 2004, pp. 26–31.

MULTIPLE-CHOICE QUESTIONS FOR PRACTICE AND REVIEW

MC 1 A PA developed a system for clients to enter transaction data by remote terminal into the PA's computer. The PA's system processes the data and prints monthly financial statements. When delivered to the clients, these financial statements should include a(n)

a. standard unqualified audit report.

b. adverse audit report.

c. report containing a description of the character of the engagement and the degree of responsibility the PA is taking.

d. description of the remote terminal system and of the controls for ensuring accurate data processing.

MC 2 According to the CICA, what is the objective of an audit of financial statements?

a. An expression of opinion on the fairness with which they present financial position, results of operations, and cash flows in conformity with GAAP

b. An expression of opinion on the fairness with which they present financial position, results of operations, and cash flows in conformity with FASB

c. An expression of opinion on the fairness with which they present financial position, results of operations, and cash flows in conformity with GAAS

d. To obtain systematic and objective evidence about financial assertions and report the results to interested users

MC 3 Some of the GAAS require certain statements in all audit reports ("explicit") and others require statements only under certain conditions ("implicit" basis). Which of the following combinations correctly describes these features of the reporting standards?

Standards	(*a*)	(*b*)	(*c*)	(*d*)
1. GAAP	Explicit	Explicit	Implicit	Implicit
2. Consistency	Implicit	Explicit	Explicit	Implicit
3. Disclosure	Implicit	Implicit	Explicit	Explicit
4. Report	Explicit	Explicit	Implicit	Implicit

MC 4 A PA finds that the client has not capitalized a material amount of leases in the financial statements. When considering the materiality of this departure from GAAP, the PA's reporting options are

a. unqualified opinion or disclaimer of opinion.

b. unqualified opinion or qualified opinion.

c. emphasis paragraph with unqualified opinion or an adverse opinion.

d. qualified opinion or adverse opinion.

MC 5 An auditor has found that the client is suffering financial difficulty and that the going-concern status is seriously in doubt. Even though the client has placed good disclosures in the financial statements, the PA must choose among the following audit report alternatives:

a. Unqualified report with a going-concern explanatory (EOM) paragraph

b. Disclaimer of opinion

c. Qualified opinion or adverse opinion

d. Standard unqualified report

MC 6 A company accomplished an early extinguishment of debt, and the auditors believe that recognition of a huge loss distorts the financial statements and causes them to be misleading. The auditors' reporting choices are to

a. explain the situation and give an adverse opinion.

b. explain the situation and give a disclaimer of opinion.

c. explain the situation and give an unqualified opinion, relying on rules of professional conduct not to be associated with misleading financial statements.

d. give the standard unqualified audit report.

MC 7 Which of these situations would require an auditor to insert an explanatory paragraph about consistency in an unqualified audit report?

a. Client changed its estimated allowance for uncollectible accounts receivable

b. Client corrected a prior mistake in accounting for interest capitalization

c. Client sold one of its subsidiaries and consolidated six this year compared with seven last year

d. None of the above

MC 8 Phil became the new auditor for Royal Corporation, succeeding Liz, who audited the financial statements last year. Phil needs to report on Royal's comparative financial statements and should write in his report an explanation about another auditor having audited the prior year

a. only if Liz's opinion last year was qualified.

b. describing the prior audit and the opinion, but not naming Liz as the predecessor auditor.

c. describing the audit but not revealing the type of opinion Liz gave.

d. describing the audit and the opinion, and naming Liz as the predecessor auditor.

MC 9 When other independent auditors are involved in the current audit on parts of the client's business, the principal auditor can write an audit report that

a. mentions the other auditor, describes the extent of the other auditor's work, and gives an unqualified opinion.

b. does not mention the other auditor and gives an unqualified opinion in a standard unqualified report.

c. places primary responsibility for the audit report on the other auditors.

d. names the other auditors, describes their work, and presents only the principal auditor's report.

MC 10 An "emphasis of a matter" paragraph inserted in an audit report causes the report to be characterized as

a. unqualified opinion report.

b. divided responsibility.

c. adverse opinion report.

d. denial of opinion.

MC 11 When will an auditor express an opinion containing the phrase "except for"?

a. The client refuses to provide for a probable income tax liability that is very material, or super-material.

b. There is a high degree of uncertainty associated with the client company's future.

c. He or she did not perform procedures sufficient to form an opinion on the valuation of accounts receivable which are material.

d. The auditor is basing his or her opinion in part on work done by another auditor.

EXERCISES AND PROBLEMS

EP 1
LO.1
Association with Financial Statements. For each of the situations described below, state whether the PA is or is not associated with the financial statements. What is the consequence of being associated with financial statements?

a. PA audits financial statements and his or her name is in the corporate annual report containing them.

b. PA prepares the financial statements in the partnership tax return.

c. PA uses the computer to process client-submitted data and delivers financial statement output.

d. PA uses the computer to process client-submitted data and delivers a general ledger printout.

e. PA lets client copy client-prepared financial statements on the PA's letterhead.

f. Client issues quarterly financial statements and mentions PA's review procedures but does not list PA's name in the document.

g. PA renders consulting advice about the system to prepare interim financial statements but does not review the statements prior to their release.

EP 2
LO.8
Reports and the Effect of Materiality. The concept of materiality is important to PAs in audits of financial statements and expressions of opinion on these statements. How will materiality influence an auditor's reporting decision in the following circumstances?

a. The client prohibits confirmation of accounts receivable, and sufficient appropriate evidence cannot be obtained using alternative procedures.

b. The client is a gas and electric utility company that follows the practice of recognizing revenue when it is billed to customers. At the end of the year, amounts earned but not yet billed are not recorded in the accounts or reported in the financial statements.

c. The client leases buildings for its chain of transmission repair shops under terms that qualify as capital leases. These leases are not capitalized as leased property assets and lease obligations.

d. The client company has lost a lawsuit. The case is on appeal in an attempt to reduce the amount of damages awarded to the plaintiffs.

EP 3
LO.4
Scope Limitation, Auditor Independence. Crow Corporation, a public company, has set up a number of limited partnerships to pursue some risky development projects. The limited partnerships borrow money from various financial institutions to support the development projects, and Crow guarantees these loans. Crow's interest in each limited partnership is set at a level just below the percentage that would require the partnerships, and their debts, to be included in Crow's consolidated financial statements. These percentages are set out specifically in the professional accounting recommendations that form the basis of GAAP for the purpose of Crow's financial reporting.

Zilch Zulch, LLP (ZZ) has been the auditor of Crow since its incorporation thirty years ago. The current CFO of Crow was formerly an audit partner in ZZ and was in charge of the Crow audit for five years before Crow hired her as its CFO. Because of her familiarity with ZZ's approach to setting materiality for its audits, the CFO was able to suggest the amount of a loan that could be guaranteed in each limited partnership without being material. If an individual loan was material, it would need to be disclosed as a contingency in Crow's consolidated financial statements even if the partnership was not required to be consolidated. Approximately 1,000 limited partnerships were set up, since a large sum of money was required to fund Crow's development activities. Because of the way the limited partnerships were structured, none of them was consolidated and no disclosure of Crow's loan guarantees to the partnerships was made in Crow's 2000 financial statements, despite the fact that in total they exceeded the reported long-term debt and shareholders' equity of Crow.

Zero Mustbe, the audit partner in charge of the audit of Crow's 2000 consolidated financial statements, was somewhat puzzled as to why there were so many limited partnerships, since only one development project was being undertaken. However, he was assured by Crow's CFO that the structure was appropriate and in accordance with GAAP because, in her words, "It was all set up by financial engineers with Ph.D.s in ZZ's consulting group. These people know all about GAAP and are much smarter that you are, Zero, so there is nothing to be concerned about."

As a result of his audit work, Zero provided a clean audit opinion on Crow's 2000 consolidated financial statements. During 2001, adverse events resulted in Crow's being unable to meet its obligations under the loan guarantees and it went bankrupt.

Required:
Comment on the adequacy of Zero's audit, the independence and scope issues raised, and the appropriateness of issuing a clean audit report in this scenario.

EP 4
LO.2
Negative and Positive Assurance and Users' Needs. Ellen Eagle is a banker in a small town. Her customers, Dave and Dot Dauber, are the owners of a franchised candy store in town. They have an opportunity to buy a second franchised store in a nearby town, and are requesting that Ellen increase their bank loan from $300,000 to $2,000,000 to finance this acquisition. The Daubers are two of Ellen's best customers and have always made their loan payments on time during the ten years they have been customers of her bank. Currently, Ellen is requiring the Daubers to provide annual financial statements with a review report of a PA. To approve the requested loan increase, the bank's head office will require them to provide audited annual financial statements.

Required:
Distinguish between a review report and an audit report. Why would the bank require an audit instead of a review in this case? Do you think the bank's policy is reasonable?

EP 5
LO.4
Arguments with Auditors. Officers of the company do not want to disclose information about the product liability lawsuit filed by a customer asking $500,000 in damages. They believe the suit is frivolous and without merit. Outside counsel is more cautious. The auditors insist upon disclosure. Angered, the Kingston Company chairman of the board threatens to sue the auditors if a standard unqualified report is not issued within three days.

Required:
Explain the issues raised in the preceding situation. What actions do you recommend to the company's auditor?

EP 6
LO.10
Errors in a Comparative Report with Change from Prior Year (Appendix 3A). The following audit report was drafted by an assistant at the completion of the audit of Cramdon Inc., on March 1, 2005. The partner in charge of the engagement has decided the opinion on the 2004 financial statements should be modified only with

reference to the change in the method of computing sales. Also, because of a litigation uncertainty, an uncertainty paragraph was included in the audit report on the 2003 financial statements, which are included for comparative purposes. The 2003 audit report (same audit firm) was dated March 5, 2004, and on October 15, 2004, the litigation was resolved in favour of Cramdon, Inc.

Auditor's Report

To the Board of Directors of Cramdon Inc.:

We have audited the accompanying financial statements of Cramdon Inc., as of December 31, 2004 and 2003. These financial statements are the responsibility of the Company's Management. Our responsibility is to express an opinion on these financial statements based on our audits.

We conducted our audits in accordance with generally accepted auditing standards. Those standards require that we plan and perform the audit to obtain reasonable assurance about whether the financial statements are free of material misstatement. An audit includes examining, on a test basis, evidence supporting the amounts and disclosures in the financial statements. An audit also includes assessing the accounting principles used and significant estimates made by management, as well as evaluating the overall financial statement presentation. We believe that our audit provides a reasonable basis for our opinion.

As discussed in Note 7 to the financial statements, our previous report on the 2003 financial statements contained an explanatory paragraph regarding a particular litigation uncertainty. Because of our lawyer's meritorious defence in this litigation, our current report on these financial statements does not include such an explanatory paragraph.

In our opinion, based on the preceding, the financial statements referred to above present fairly, in all material respects, the financial position of Cramdon Inc., as of December 31, 2004, and the results of its operations and its cash flows for the period then ended in conformity with generally accepted accounting principles consistently applied, except for the changes in the method of computing sales as described in Note 14 to the financial statements.

/s/ PA Firm
March 5, 2005

Required:

Identify the deficiencies and errors in the draft report and write an explanation of the reasons they are errors and deficiencies. Do not rewrite the report.

EP 7   **Negative and Positive Assurance and Users' Needs.**
LO.2   One of your neighbours, Hans House, is a minority shareholder of Grackle Corporation, a private company. Grackle is also the company that employs Hans. Recently Hans and the other Grackle Corporation shareholders were asked to approve a resolution that would waive the requirement for the company to have its financial statements audited. The company has been audited in past years, but would have a review instead of an audit

if the resolution is passed unanimously by the shareholders. Hans knows that you are an advanced accounting student and has asked for your advice on whether he should vote for or against the audit waiver.

Required:

List the factors that Hans should consider in making this decision. What fact situations would support voting for the audit waiver, and what fact situations would indicate he should vote against the waiver?

EP 8   **Distinguishing Forms of Assurance.** Explain the difference between "negative assurance" and an "adverse
LO.2   opinion."

EP 9   **GAAS General Standard, Audit Scope.** Give three ex-
LO.4   amples of fact situations in which the General Standards of GAAS are not met. For each example, explain the impact of the violation on the scope of the audit and the audit report.

EP 10   **GAAS Examination Standard, Audit Scope.** Give one
LO.4   example of a fact situation in which each of the three Examination Standards of GAAS are not met. For each example explain the impact of the violation on the scope of the audit and the audit report.

EP 11   **Audit Opinion on Financial Statements.** The unquali-
LO.3   fied audit opinion states that the financial statements ". . . present fairly . . . in accordance with Canadian generally accepted accounting principles."

Required:

a. Explain, from the perspective of the auditing profession, reasons why the auditor's opinion on fair presentation of financial statements is given in reference to Canadian generally accepted accounting principles.

b. Explain, from the perspective of financial statement users, the contrasting view that the auditor's responsibility to assess the fair presentation goes beyond a literal interpretation of whether the statements meet the requirements of Canadian GAAP.

c. Which position, part (a) or part (b), do you agree with? Why?

EP 12   **Audit Scope Limitations—Auditor Appointed Late**
LO.4   *a.* What alternative procedures can an auditor perform to determine whether the inventory balance is not materially misstated when he or she is appointed in the middle of the year and did not observe the inventory count at the end of the prior year?

b. What alternative procedures can an auditor perform to determine whether the inventory balance is not materially misstated when he or she was appointed after the year end under audit and was not able to observe the count of either the opening or the ending inventory.

c. What are the reporting implications if alternative procedures can be performed and provide sufficient audit evidence in situations (a) and (b) above?

d. What are the reporting implications if alternative procedures cannot be used to satisfy audit evidence requirements in situations (a) and (b) above?

EP 13 Audit Scope Limitations—Client Imposed

LO.4 *a.* What alternative procedures can an auditor perform to determine whether the accounts receivable balance is not materially misstated when client management will not permit audit confirmations to be used?

b. What are the reporting implications if alternative procedures can be performed and provide sufficient audit evidence in situation (a)?

c. What are the reporting implications if alternative procedures cannot be used to satisfy audit evidence requirements in situation (a)?

EP 14 Reporting on Contingencies. Describe the pre-2011

LO.5 requirements of Canadian GAAS for reporting for contingencies and uncertainties. Identify the pros and cons of the current approach, contrasting these with the pros and cons of the "subject to" opinions that were used in Canada prior to 1980.

EP 15 Reporting Going-Concern Uncertainties. Current

LO.5 Canadian GAAS through 2010 did not permit the auditor to refer to a going-concern uncertainty in the audit report when the uncertainty was properly disclosed in the financial statement notes.

Required:

a. Describe the strengths and weaknesses of this approach, taking into consideration the perspectives of the company, its financial statement users, and its auditor.

b. Identify one or more alternative reporting methods that may be more beneficial to financial statement users.

c. You have been invited to comment to the Canadian assurance standards-setting board on its current audit reporting standards. What comment would you make to the standard setters on the issue of audit reporting when there is substantial doubt about a company's ability to continue as a going concern?

EP 16 Going-Concern Assumption—One Year Limitation.

LO.5 For the purpose of assessing the going-concern assumption it is presumed that the auditor will consider whether the company will continue in existence for a "reasonable time" that does not exceed one year beyond the date of the financial statements. Give reasons that auditors are not required to consider the entity's ability to continue as a going concern for a period longer than one year. In your opinion, is this one-year limitation reasonable? Explain and evaluate possible alternative approaches to support your opinion.

EP 17 Standard-Setting Research. Investigate the history and

LO.5 current status of the CICA Exposure Draft on the going-concern assumption that was originally issued in 1996. Use the CICA website, *CA Magazine,* and other professional publications to conduct this research. Explain how the due process involved in setting Canadian auditing standards is illustrated by the history of this Exposure Draft.

EP 18 Going-Concern Issue. PA is the auditor of Jayhawk Inc.

LO.5 Jayhawk's revenues and profitability have decreased in each of the past three years and, as of this year end, 2003, its retained earnings will fall into a deficit balance. Jayhawk's long-term debt comes due in 2004, and its management is currently renegotiating the repayment date and terms with its bondholders. According to PA's discussions with management, the renegotiation is not going well and there is a significant risk that the bondholders will put Jayhawk into receivership and liquidate its assets. Jawhawk's CFO has provided draft 2003 financial statements to PA that are prepared in accordance with GAAP.

Required:

a. Discuss the audit reporting implications of the preceding situation.

b. Assume the long-term debt repayment date was not until 2005. Would your response differ?

EP 19 Going-Concern Audit Reporting. Before 2011, *CICA*

LO.5 *Handbook,* paragraph 5510.53, provided guidance for audit reporting when there is a going-concern problem.

Required:

a. Critique the audit reporting required by paragraph 5510.53 from the perspective of a financial statement user who owns shares of the auditee company.

b. Assume the role of the company's auditor. How would you respond to the criticisms raised in (a)?

EP 20 Report on the Application of Accounting Principles.

LO.7 *CICA Handbook* section 7600 sets out procedures relating to requests for advice from a PA from parties other than the PA's audit clients.

Required:

a. What are the purposes of section 7600?

b. Describe the requirements of section 7600 and explain how effective they are in achieving the purposes described in part (a).

EP 21 Report on the Application of Accounting Principles. Kite Corporation's auditor, PA1, formed the opinion that

LO.7 Kite should accrue for estimated future costs to clean up an environmental problem on one of Kite's properties in its 2003 financial statements. Kite requested a second opinion from PA2 on this issue. PA2 gave an opinion that the estimated liability amount is contingent on various future events that are highly uncertain, such as changes in environmental regulations and environmental cleanup technologies. Thus it is a contingency that is too uncertain to accrue and, in accordance with GAAP, it should only be disclosed. Kite's management sides with the opinion of PA2 because it prevents the company from reporting a loss, allows Kite's management to receive bonuses for 2003, and, in their view, it is a more appropriate application of GAAP.

Required:

a. Assume that Kite is a public company and PA1 and PA2 are Big Four audit firms. What public perception of auditors may arise if disputes on the application of GAAP can be resolved by the public company's obtaining an opinion from another auditor?

b. Take the role of PA1. What issues arise by Kite's taking this action in your dispute over the accrual of the contingent liability?

c. Take the role of PA2. What considerations should you make before issuing your opinion?

d. Take the role of one of Kite's Directors. What issues arise by Kite's management's taking this action in resolving its dispute with PA1 over the accrual of the contingent liability?

EP 22 **Audit Evidence from Specialists.** Lark Limited reports
LO.9 a material balance of deferred development costs in its
current financial statements. The cost relates to the development of a mobile robot that can be used to monitor
temperature, humidity, and security in large warehouses.
Lark's auditor obtained an engineers' report to support
the technological feasibility of the robotics project and a
market research consultant's report to determine the selling prices and volumes likely to be achieved over the first
ten years that the product is marketed.

Required:

Explain the nature of audit evidence obtained in this
case. How would this audit evidence affect the auditor's

report? Compare the use of these specialists' reports in
the audit with using the reports of other auditors.

EP 23 Find Nortel's 2004 annual report on its website or SEC
LO.4 filings, and review the audit reports for 2001–2004. In
light of Nortel's history (as indicated in Chapter 1), do
you think these reports are appropriate? Discuss.

EP 24 Explain auditor responsibilities re-
LO.5 garding going-concern disclosures-
under GAAS. Contrast these with
GAAP requirements and discuss
ways of reconciling the two.

APPENDIX 3A

LEARNING OBJECTIVE
9 Explain the differences
in the American audi-
tor's report.

The PCAOB/AICPA Standard Unqualified Report

AU Section 508 (paragraph .08) Reports on Audited Financial Statements

Independent Auditor's Report

We have audited the accompanying balance sheet of X Company as of December 31, 20X1,
and the related statements of income, retained earnings, and cash flows for the year then
ended. These financial statements are the responsibility of the Company's management. Our
responsibility is to express an opinion on these financial statements based on our audit.

We conducted our audit in accordance with auditing standards generally accepted in
the United States of America. Those standards require that we plan and perform the audit
to obtain reasonable assurance about whether the financial statements are free of material
misstatement. An audit includes examining, on a test basis, evidence supporting the
amounts and disclosures in the financial statements. An audit also includes assessing the
accounting principles used and significant estimates made by management, as well as
evaluating the overall financial statement presentation. We believe that our audit provides
a reasonable basis for our opinion.

In our opinion, the financial statements referred to above present fairly, in all material
respects, the financial position of X Company as of [at] December 31, 20X1, and the
results of its operations and its cash flows for the year then ended in conformity with
accounting principles generally accepted in the United States of America.

Signed,
Date,

APPENDIX 3B

LEARNING OBJECTIVE
10 Explain why auditors
have standards for re-
porting on the applica-
tion of accounting
principles.

Reporting on the Application of Accounting Principles

The subject of reporting on the application of accounting principles touches a sensitive
nerve in the public accounting profession. It arose from clients' "shopping" for an auditor
who would agree to give an unqualified audit report on a questionable accounting treatment. Shopping often involved auditor–client disagreements, after which the client said,

"If you won't agree with my accounting treatment, then I'll find an auditor who will." These disagreements often involved early revenue recognition and unwarranted expense or loss deferral. A few cases of misleading financial statements occurred after the shopping resulted in clients' switching to more agreeable auditors. However, the practice is not entirely undesirable, because complex accounting matters often benefit from consultation with other PAs. Note that these situations illustrate the importance of a variety of perspectives on a financial reporting issue—a key aspect of critical thinking in professional judgment. It is clear from such situations that the application of accounting standards in specific circumstances is not always straightforward. Critical thinking helps to deal with such situations in a systematic, more defensible way.

Handbook section 7600 established procedures for dealing with requests for consultation from parties other than an auditor's own clients. These parties can include other companies (nonclients who are shopping), lawyers, investment bankers, and perhaps other people. Section 7600 is applicable in these situations:

- when preparing a written report or giving oral advice on specific transactions, either completed or proposed
- when preparing a written report or giving oral advice on the type of audit opinion that might be rendered on specific financial statements
- when preparing a written report on hypothetical transactions

The standard does not apply to conclusions about accounting principles offered in connection with litigation support engagements or expert witness work, nor does it apply to advice given to another PA in public practice. It also does not apply to an accounting firm's expressions of positions in newsletters, articles, speeches, lectures, and the like, provided that the positions do not give advice on a specific transaction or apply to a specific company.

The basic requirements are to consider the circumstances of the request for advice, its purpose, and the intended use of the report of the advice; to obtain an understanding of the form and substance of the transaction in question; to review applicable GAAP; to consult with other professionals if necessary; and to perform research to determine the existence of creditable analogies and precedents (e.g., find the authoritative support). When the request for advice comes from a business that already has another auditor, the consulting PA should consult with the other auditor to learn all the facts and circumstances.

Written reports are required and should include these elements:

- description of the nature of the engagement and a statement that it was performed in accordance with standards for such engagements
- statement of relevant facts and assumptions, and the sources of information
- statement of the advice—the conclusion about appropriate accounting principles or the type of audit report, including reasons for the conclusions, if appropriate
- statement that a company's management is responsible for proper accounting treatments, in consultation with its own auditors
- statement that any differences in facts, circumstances, or assumptions might change the conclusions

The purpose of the section 7600 standards is to impose some discipline on the process of shopping/consultation and to make it more difficult for companies to seek out a "willing" auditor.

CHAPTER 4

Professional Ethics and Auditor Responsibilities

This chapter highlights the regulation of auditors and PAs. As you will see, regulation and discipline depend on published codes of ethics and effective enforcement practices.

LEARNING OBJECTIVES

After completing this chapter, you will be able to do the following:

1 Explain the importance of professional ethics in audit decision making.

2 Analyze whether a PA's conduct conforms to provincial rules of professional ethics.

3 Explain the importance of an independence framework for auditors.

4 Outline the types of penalties that various provincial associations and government agencies can impose on PAs when enforcing rules of professional conduct.

5 Apply and integrate the chapter topics to analyze a practical auditing situation/case/scenario.

6* Evaluate an ethical decision problem using the critical thinking framework. (Appendix 4A)

* Learning Objectives marked with an asterisk (*) and their corresponding topics are considered advanced material. Note: Appendix 4A is located on the Online Learning Centre.

LEARNING OBJECTIVE

1 Explain the importance of professional ethics in audit decision making.

As part of a privileged profession, auditors are responsible to society. This responsibility can be divided into three categories of responsibility: moral, professional, and legal. Morality deals with character and "doing the right thing" as is determined largely by social norms. Thus, auditors have a responsibility to conform to social norms. However, social norms change and a study of ethics is helpful in preparing for lifelong adaptation. Auditors' **moral responsibilities** can be summarized as "public accountants should be upright, not kept upright." Ethics relates to proper conduct in life, and a study of ethics helps the auditor develop a set of principles by which to live.

Professional responsibilities refer to the more formal ethical responsibilities of auditors. These responsibilities (or **professional ethics**) are the rules and principles for the proper conduct of an auditor in her work. Professional ethics are necessary for a number of reasons: to obtain the respect and confidence of the public, to distinguish the professional from the general public, to achieve order within the profession, and to provide a means of self-policing the profession. This chapter will focus on ethics that are particular to accountants and auditors in relation to the responsibilities of the profession.

Legal responsibilities are covered in the next chapter (Chapter 5).

General Ethics

A pervasive sense of proper ethical conduct is critical for professional accountants. Two aspects of ethics operate in the professional environment—general ethics (the spirit) and professional ethics (the rules). Mautz and Sharaf have contributed the following thoughts to the link between general and professional ethics:

> The theory of ethics has been a subject of interest to philosophers since the beginnings of recorded thought. Because philosophers are concerned with the good of all mankind, their discussions have been concerned with what we may call general ethics rather than the ethics of small groups such as the members of a given profession. We cannot look, therefore, to their philosophical theories for direct solutions to our special problems. Nevertheless, their work with general ethics is of primary importance to the development of an appropriate concept in any special field. *Ethical behaviour in auditing or in any other activity is no more than a special application of the general notion of ethical conduct devised by philosophers for men generally. Ethical conduct in auditing draws its justification and basic nature from the general theory of ethics. Thus, we are well advised to give some attention to the ideas and reasoning of some of the great philosophers on this subject.*[1]

Overview

What is ethics? Wheelwright defined ethics as "that branch of philosophy which is the systematic study of reflective choice, of the standards of right and wrong by which it is to be guided, and of the goods toward which it may ultimately be directed."[2] In this definition, you can detect three key elements of ethics: (1) it involves questions requiring reflective choice (decision problems), (2) it involves guides of right and wrong (moral principles), and (3) it is concerned with the consequences of decisions.

What is an ethical problem? A problem exists when you must make a choice among alternative actions and the right choice is not absolutely clear. It is an ethical problem because the alternative actions affect the well-being of other people.

What is ethical behaviour? There are two standard philosophical answers to this question: (1) it is that which produces the greatest good, and (2) it is that which conforms to moral rules and principles. Problem situations arise when two or more rules conflict or when a rule and the criterion of "greatest good" conflict. Some examples of these are given later in this chapter.

Why does an individual or group need a code of ethical conduct? While it has been said that a person should be upright and not kept upright, a code serves as a useful reference or benchmark and specifies the criteria for conduct of a profession. Thus, codes of professional

---

[1] R. K. Mautz and H. A. Sharaf, *The Philosophy of Auditing* (American Accounting Association, 1991). [Emphasis added.]
[2] P. Wheelwright, *A Critical Introduction to Ethics*, 3rd ed. (Indianapolis, Ind.: Odyssey Press, 1959).

ethics provide some solutions that may not be available in general ethics theories, it allows individuals to know what the profession expects, and it publicly declares the profession's principles of conduct so these standards can be enforced.

A Variety of Roles

The decision maker role does not fully describe a professional person's entire ethical obligation. Each person acts as an individual, a member of a profession, and a member of society. Hence, accountants and auditors are also spectators (observing the decisions of colleagues), advisers (counselling with co-workers), instructors (teaching accounting students or new employees on the job), judges (serving on disciplinary committees of provincial associations), and critics (commenting on the ethical decisions of others). All of these roles are important in the practice of professional ethics.

An Ethical Decision Process

Your primary goal in considering general ethics is arriving at a set of acceptable methods for making ethical decisions. Consequently, you will only behave according to the rules of professional conduct if you understand the general principles of ethics.

In the previous definition of ethics, one of the key elements was reflective choice. This involves an important sequence of events beginning with recognizing decision problems. Collecting evidence, in the ethics context, refers to thinking about rules of behaviour and outcomes of alternative actions. The process ends with analyzing the situation and taking an action. Ethical decision problems almost always involve projecting yourself into the future to live with your decisions. Professional ethical decisions usually turn on these questions: What written and unwritten rules govern my behaviour? What are the possible consequences of my choices? Principles of ethics can help you think about these two questions in real situations.

TO TELL OR NOT TO TELL?

In your work as an auditor, you discover that the cashier, who has custody over the petty cash fund, has forged several payment records in order to cover innocent mistakes and make the fund balance each month when it is replenished. Your investigation reveals that the amount involved during the year is $240. The cashier is a woman, age 55, and the president of the company is a man who can tolerate no mistakes, intentional or otherwise, in the accounting records. In fact, he is unyielding in this respect. He asks you about the results of your audit. Not doubting that the cashier would be fired if the forgeries were known, should you remain silent or the truth?

Philosophical Principles in Ethics

A discussion of ethical theories would be unnecessary if we accepted a simple rule: "Let conscience be your guide." Such a rule is appealing because it calls on an individual's own judgment, which may be based on wisdom, insight, or adherence to custom or an authoritative code. However, it might also be based on self-interest, caprice, immaturity, ignorance, stubbornness, or misunderstanding.

In a similar manner, relying on the opinions of others or a social group is not always enough, as they may perpetuate a custom or habit that is wrong (e.g., smoking). Adhering blindly to custom or group habits is abdicating individual responsibility. Titus and Keeton summarized this point succinctly: "Each person capable of making moral decisions is responsible for making his own decisions. The ultimate locus of moral responsibility is in the individual."[3] Thus, ethical principles not only provide a simple and sure rule, they also provide some guidelines for taking individual decisions and actions. The earlier illustration

[3] H. H. Titus and M. Keeton, *Ethics for Today*, 4th ed. (New York: American Book-Stratford Press, 1966), p. 131.

("To Tell or Not to Tell?") and the one that follows demonstrate some ethical problems that, for most people, would present difficult choices. Consider them in light of the ethical principles discussed in the following box.

CONFLICTING DUTIES

Because of your fine reputation as a public accountant, you were invited to become a director of a local bank and were pleased to accept the position. While serving on the board for a year, you learned that a bank director is under a duty to use care and prudence in administering the affairs of the bank, and that failure to do so in such a way that the bank suffers a financial loss means that the director(s) may be held liable for damages. This month, in the course of an audit, you discover a seriously weakened financial position in a client who has a large loan from your bank. Prompt disclosure to the other bank directors would minimize the bank's loss, but, since the audit report cannot be completed for another three weeks, such disclosure would amount to divulging confidential information gained in the course of an audit engagement (prohibited by confidentiality principles). You can remain silent and honour confidentiality principles (and fail to honour your duty as a bank director), or you can speak up to the other directors (thus violating confidentiality principles). Which should you choose?

Ethical theories can be subdivided into two types: monistic and pluralistic. **Monistic theories** assume that universal principles apply regardless of the specific facts. **Pluralistic theories**, on the other hand, assume that there are no universal principles and that the best approach is to use the principles that are most relevant in a particular case.

There are a number of monistic theories. The most important are deontological (or duty based) theories dominated by the ideas of Immanuel Kant, and utilitarianism. **Deontological (Kantian) ethics** assumes that there are universal principles (**imperatives**) such as the biblical Ten Commandments that must always be followed regardless of the consequences. Kant maintained that motive and duty alone define a moral act, not the consequences of the act.

Some object to the imperative principle because so-called universal rules always turn out to have exceptions. Others respond that, if the rule is stated properly to include the exceptional cases, then the principle is still valid. But the human experience is complicated, and the rules would be very complex if they had to cover all possible cases.[4] This problem is not unique to ethics, as identifying the universal or primary principles and concepts of anything is a challenge for anyone trying to justify some action or conclusion. Universal principles are generally easier to identify in mathematics and the physical sciences than they are in social sciences such as accounting and auditing. Nevertheless, auditors must try to give the best reasons they can for their professional judgments and conclusions (claims).

Another major problem with duty-based ethics is that duties can conflict; one then needs to sort out which duty is most important, depending on the specific context. The professional rules of conduct for accountants have been greatly influenced by duty-based Kantian ethics and can be viewed as duties. Thus, there is also a potential conflict of professional rules, most notably the rules of confidentiality and of not being associated with misleading information. These rules are discussed in more detail later in the chapter.

Utilitarianism indicates that, when we have a choice, we pick the one that results in the best outcome (that is, has the highest utility). Decisions based on **consequentialism** aim to achieve the greatest good for the greatest number of people. A minority, however, might suffer as a consequence of this.

---

[4] Several rules of professional conduct to be discussed shortly are explicitly phrased to provide exceptions to the general rules (for example, rules 210 and 204 of the ICAO Rules of Professional Conduct). Imperative rules also seem to generate borderline cases, so the ethics divisions of PA professional bodies issue interpretations and rulings to explain the applicability of the rules.

These monistic theories are not sufficient on their own to handle the complexities of most real-life ethical problems, including those of practical, professional ethics. Nevertheless, they can be important principles when providing reasons for a claim or decision. For example, standard economic theory is based on utilitarianism, the same theory used in cost-benefit analysis. However, exclusive reliance on one principle can lead to problems. The cost-benefit analysis approach was used by many PA firms in the 1990s when they decided to put more emphasis on developing the management consulting side of their practices rather than on auditing. In some cases, auditing was viewed as a "loss leader" in creating more lucrative consulting practices. At the time, the big PA firms were also the largest consulting firms in the world.[5] The resulting increase in consulting revenues was so large that the appearance of independence was affected. In fact, overreliance on consulting led to Arthur Andersen's demise. This focus on utilitarianism thus caused the profession a great deal of grief. With the passage of SOX and other reforms, the pendulum is now swinging the other way—the focus on quality control puts emphasis on auditors' duties toward the public interest. Ethical reasoning is different from other types of reasoning because it includes consideration for the perspective of others.

The consequences of a decision for others and the ability to imagine others' feeling about these must be part of ethical reasoning. This ability to imagine is frequently referred to as **moral imagination**. For example, a moral imagination helps in finding the incentives that could be indicators of fraud. It also allows understanding of user needs in financial reporting. Had the CEO at Molex (the company described at the beginning of Chapter 1) used his moral imagination, he might not have been fired. The same is true of the former CEO of Boeing Corp. discussed in Appendix 4A.

Auditors cannot rely on standards for detailed rules in all possible situations. IFAC's international code of professional ethics recognizes that every engagement is unique and, consequently, auditors must tailor their moral imaginations to the specific circumstances of the engagement. It is part of being a professional, rather than just a technician mechanically following standards and rules of conduct. It will not be sufficient to merely follow detailed rules of GAAP and GAAS and rules of ethics on an engagement in order to meet audit objectives, just as it doesn't work to rely too much on one broad principle of morality, such as utilitarianism, to resolve all ethical conflicts.

A framework for structured thinking will prepare you to deal with the ethical and other issues of professional judgment in the post-Enron audit environment. A **critical thinking framework** is one that consists of principles, concepts, and their application, and ethics is an important concept within the framework. In the end, the auditor must have good reasons other than "it feels right" to support a position. (For a good example at the professional level, see Appendix 3B.)

Reliance on detailed rules of GAAS and GAAP may not be enough either. Standards should not be seen as a recipe to memorize. True professionalism means being aware of how and why the standards have evolved the way they have. Basic principles underlie all the standards and the standard-setting process. Some of these principles are more obvious than others, and critical thinking helps identify the less obvious ones. For example, Appendix 1C discusses the reasoning and theories behind the important concept of meeting the public interest. Ultimately the auditor relies on the fundamental principles such as fairness of presentation in the circumstances, meeting the public interest, and maintaining the reputation of the profession. There are no rules for achieving these in all situations, and the auditor must think through each case in a systematic way. A critical thinking framework is a guide to achieving the most well-supported conclusion possible.

A brief description of the framework follows in Exhibit 4–1, with more detail provided in Appendix 4A on the text Online Learning Centre.

Critical thinking means involving principles in your analysis of an issue. Unless the principle is logic based, it will have an important ethical component. In particular, note

---

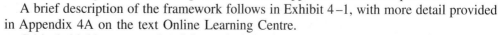

[5] For a good review of the history of the profession during this period, see A. R. Wyatt, "Accounting Professionalism—They Just Don't Get It!" *Accounting Horizons*, March 2004, pp. 45–54.

EXHIBIT   4-1   A FRAMEWORK OF CRITICAL THINKING PRINCIPLES: ACHIEVING A GOAL WITH AN
                      ENQUIRING MIND

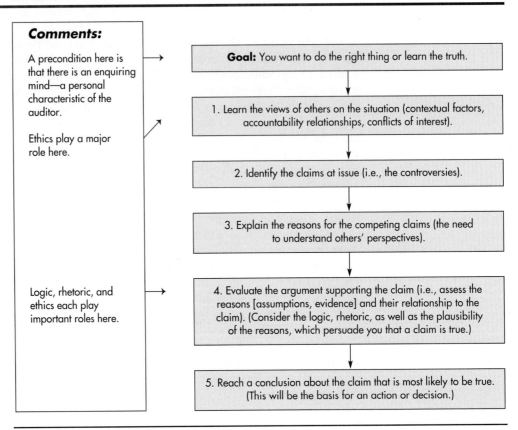

Comments:

A precondition here is that there is an enquiring mind—a personal characteristic of the auditor.

Ethics play a major role here.

Logic, rhetoric, and ethics each play important roles here.

Goal: You want to do the right thing or learn the truth.

1. Learn the views of others on the situation (contextual factors, accountability relationships, conflicts of interest).

2. Identify the claims at issue (i.e., the controversies).

3. Explain the reasons for the competing claims (the need to understand others' perspectives).

4. Evaluate the argument supporting the claim (i.e., assess the reasons [assumptions, evidence] and their relationship to the claim). (Consider the logic, rhetoric, as well as the plausibility of the reasons, which persuade you that a claim is true.)

5. Reach a conclusion about the claim that is most likely to be true. (This will be the basis for an action or decision.)

the principle of a questioning mind, or skepticism, which represents a mental attitude incorporating all the rest of the critical thinking principles. Thus, critical thinking extends traditional audit virtues to a more holistic approach to judgment.

Steps 4 and 5 in the framework reflect the role of logic, or the need for justification in critical thinking. Applying logic essentially means identifying reasons supporting a claim or conclusion. There must be a link between reasons and a conclusion, and on an audit engagement we want that link to be strong. A second condition, that of truth or substantial truth, should be met before we can say that an audit conclusion is justified by the reasons given. If both these conditions are satisfied, then we can say that our conclusion is justified by the reasons. The term "sound reasoning," the essence of being objective on an issue, can be used when our conclusions are justified this way. Thus, for example, CAS 700 requires the auditor to identify the broad principles and concepts serving as a basis for applying accounting policies to meet the general reporting objectives of a framework such as Canadian GAAP. These broad principles and concepts are the basis for sound reasoning regarding fairness of presentation in particular circumstances.

Critical thinking involves questioning the application of a standard, the concepts and principles underlying it, and the consistency of standards to one another. Questioning of standards may go back to questions about the goals of financial reporting, as is becoming evident with the CAS's new classification of financial reporting frameworks as general purpose versus special purpose, and fairness of presentation versus compliance objectives.

Whereas logic is concerned with the link between reasons and conclusion, the truthfulness of reasons is determined by the source of the reasons, in this case accounting and auditing theory and their underlying concepts, assumptions, and principles. These concepts, along with the words used to state them, affect the persuasiveness of your reasons as an auditor. A critical thinker uses language to clarify, not cloud or bias, the reasoning.

For example, an auditor uses the words "present fairly" to persuade the user of the acceptability of the audited financial statements.

Professional judgment in auditing is essentially critical thinking on accounting issues and the evidence related to them. The critical thinking framework can be used for deciding when an audit conclusion is sufficiently justified. When this reasoning is documented in an audit, there is no basis for questioning the sufficiency of audit documentation. The continuing problems found by the CPAB in auditor documentation suggest insufficient critical thinking in professional judgment on the part of practising auditors. These CPAB findings are reviewed later in this chapter. For a more complete discussion of this critical thinking framework, along with illustrations of its application, see Appendix 4A.

This brief review of the principles of ethics and critical thinking provides some background on the way people approach difficult decision problems. The greatest task is to take general ethical principles and apply them to a real decision. Applying them through codes of professional ethics is a challenge. In this book we suggest that the minimal critical thinking issues auditors should consider are the following: it is important to supply good reasons for conclusions (claims); the reasons should be acceptable to capital providers in the broadest sense of that term; and the reasons should ultimately be based on materiality and the various risk concepts introduced in this book. Later chapters illustrate application of the critical thinking framework, especially steps 4 and 5, on specific audit and accounting issues.

The rest of this chapter is devoted to the more practical rules of professional ethics, related concepts and principles, and their application in relevant situations. However, these professional rules and principles rely on the various ethical theories discussed in this section, especially duty-based theories, for their justification.

REVIEW CHECKPOINTS

1 What is a professional accountant's role with regard to ethical decision problems?

2 When might the rule "Let conscience be your guide" not be a sufficient basis for your personal ethical decisions? for your professional ethical decisions?

3 Assume that you accept the following ethical rule: "Failure to tell the whole truth is wrong." In the illustrations about (a) your position as a bank director and (b) your knowledge of the cashier's forgeries, what would this rule require you to do? Why is an unalterable rule like this considered an element of duty-based ethical theory?

4 How do utilitarian ethics differ from duty-based ethics?

5 Why are simplified monastic theories of ethics not sufficient for professional decision making?

6 Why is critical thinking becoming more important in the post-Enron environment?

7 How does professional ethics relate to critical thinking?

CODES OF PROFESSIONAL ETHICS

LEARNING OBJECTIVE

2 Analyze whether a PA's conduct conforms to provincial rules of professional ethics.

All the Canadian PA bodies (CAs, CGAs, CMAs) and the International Federation of Accountants (IFAC) have their own rules of professional conduct for their members and students, either provincially or nationally. Generally, these rules are published as a part of a member's handbook identifying the various activities and regulations of the PA associations, and include a section on professional conduct. Codes of conduct need to develop a balance between detailed rules and more general principles. They also need to be practical, and as a result they tend to have similar frameworks, as indicated in the next box.

The codes of professional conduct are usually organized hierarchically, moving from general principles at the beginning, to rules, and on to specific interpretations of the rules. The general principles are sometimes referred to as "ideal standards" and the more specific rules and related interpretations as "minimum standards."

The various codes of professional conduct are meant to apply to all members, with exceptions for students and members not in public practice. Generally, codes for CAs and CMAs are the responsibility of provincial institutes or societies. CGAs have a national code set by CGA-Canada; however, provincial CGA associations may add modifications to this. Recently, the CA provincial institutes have substantially harmonized their codes so that the CA code can be viewed as more of a national one. The CASs do not refer to the IFAC's code of ethics. Instead, Canadian PAs use the code of the provincial accounting organization to which they belong.

An example of a code is the ICAO Member's Handbook, which identifies the various activities and regulations of the Ontario Institute, including a section on professional conduct which is divided into three parts: the Foreword, the Rules of Professional Conduct, and the Interpretation of the Rules. Many people consider the Foreword the most important part of the professional conduct regulations because it contains principles that provide guidance in the absence of specific rules.[6] The Foreword is essential reading for CA members and students as the Members' Handbook specifically advises that all the rules in it "are to be read in the light of the Foreword to the rules." In this sense, the Foreword is analogous to the conceptual framework of accounting; for example, section 1000 of the *CICA Handbook* and the rules themselves are like the Recommendations in the *CICA Handbook*.

The Foreword has clearly defined sections. The first section sets out the purpose of the rules, which is to guide the profession in serving the public. The second reviews the key characteristics that mark a profession and a professional, concluding that "chartered accountancy is a profession." The third section identifies the six "fundamental statements of accepted conduct" around which all the rules are centred. These six principles can be summarized as follows:

1. The member should act to maintain the profession's reputation.
2. The member should use due care and maintain his or her professional competence.
3. The member should maintain the appearance of independence as well as the fact of independence of his or her professional judgment.
4. The member should preserve client confidentiality.
5. The member should base his or her reputation on professional excellence—in particular, advertising should inform, not solicit.
6. The member should show professional courtesy to other members at all times.

These principles are ideals every professional aspires to. The rules themselves are more specific because they are intended as guides to action and enforceable. However, adherence to the rules represents only a minimum acceptable level of performance for CAs. On the other hand, because they are more detailed, the rules are more specific benchmarks that a member's performance can be measured against.

The Foreword singles out several principles requiring additional guidance: (a) sustaining professional competence (principle 2 above), (b) avoiding conflicts of interest in respect of a client's affairs (principle 3), and (c) practice development based on professional excellence rather than self-promotion (principle 5). It is evident from the space devoted to them that these particular principles require the most detailed guidance. However, as the Foreword makes clear, as ethical decision making becomes more complex yet indispensable for maintaining the public interest, the absence of specific rules makes the principles that much more important. As a result, some writers have concluded that the six principles should be given much more prominence and used more frequently.[7]

After the Foreword are the rules of conduct themselves. The ICAO Council also publishes "Council Interpretations" of these rules—detailed explanations to help members understand particular applications of them. Anyone departing from Council interpretations has the burden of justifying that departure in any disciplinary hearing.

---

[6] K. Gunning, "Required Reading," *CA Magazine*, November 1992, pp. 38–40.
[7] Ibid.

The CMAs have a similar set of rules for each provincial society. For example, the Society of Management Accountants of Ontario (SMAO) Handbook on Ethics predominantly contains general principles of ethics; the more detailed rules and interpretations are covered in the remainder. Where CMAs have the right to perform assurance engagements, the rules require that they comply with local legislation.

The CGA's national code of conduct provides the basic framework for each of the provincial association rules. It consists of a preamble that explains why a code is necessary and who is affected; a statement of ethical principles; rules of conduct, with guidance concerning their application to certain specific situations; and a set of definitions of terms used throughout the code.

The IFAC includes a code of ethics for PAs as part of their standards as well. It avoids preparing detailed rules or interpretations as these will be influenced by national laws, culture, and the particular circumstances of the engagement. Part A of the IFAC code provides general concepts and a conceptual framework, while part B illustrates how the framework is applied by PAs in specific situations. IFAC feels that specific rules can be arbitrary and not represent the public interest in all cases, justifying a conceptual approach. The framework identifies threats against conformity to the general principles, evaluates their significance, and, if warranted, applies safeguards eliminating or reducing them to acceptable levels. This framework is summarized in the box below and the principles are discussed in more detail in the rest of the chapter.

Elements of the critical thinking (CT) framework of Exhibit 4–1 (page 98) that closely correspond to this one are also indicated in the box to show the similarities between them. However, the CT framework is broader and allows extension to auditing and accounting issues. We have illustrated the potential for such integration in prior discussion cases and will continue to do so in future chapters.

IFAC FRAMEWORK FOR A CODE OF CONDUCT FOR PROFESSIONAL ACCOUNTANTS

- Objective: to serve the public interest (this cannot be accomplished by mere conformity to detailed rules—this dedication to serve is more like a state of mind) (CT: Goal)

- Principles necessary to attain objective (CT: step 3)
  - Integrity
  - Ojectivity
  - Professional competence and due care
  - Confidentiality
  - Professional behaviour

- Conformity is achieved by identifying, evaluating, and controlling threats to non-conformity to an acceptable level. (CT: step 4)

- Part B provides examples, but these are not exhaustive as this is impossible. Therefore, a principles approach should be followed (as indicated by the above principles). (CT: step 3)

There is much similarity in the concepts of all professional codes. These are reviewed in the next section, along with the related rules.

Rules of Professional Conduct

The rules of professional conduct derive their authority from the bylaws of the various PA professional organizations (or those that strive to be recognized as such). Members of these groups (CAs, CGAs, CMAs) are responsible for compliance with the rules by all employees and partners associated with them. Further, members may not have other people to carry out prohibited acts on their behalf.

The various PA institutes and associations have detailed rules of conduct that have much in common, and we cannot list all of them, so those of the Institute of Chartered Accountants of Ontario (ICAO) are given in the next box and will serve as an illustration. (Full access to the ICAO handbook is at www.icao.on.ca/ICAO.) In terms of the critical thinking framework, these rules can be viewed as important reasons for taking (or not taking) a particular action. Specifically, the rules follow the logic of Kantian imperatives or duties, although there is also an element of utilitarianism, as is indicated in the discussion following a second box.

This second box summarizes IFAC's conflict resolution process. The rest of this chapter discusses ethical and critical thinking principles, and their related rules, in more detail. However, you should refer to the appropriate CAs, CGAs, or CMAs members' handbooks for more extensive guidance on rules related to these professional groups.

THE INSTITUTE OF CHARTERED ACCOUNTANTS OF ONTARIO (ICAO)

RULES OF PROFESSIONAL CONDUCT

TABLE OF CONTENTS

400 – ORGANIZATION AND CONDUCT OF A PROFESSIONAL PRACTICE

401	Practice names
404.1	Use of descriptive styles
404.2	Operation of members' offices
404.3	Proprietary interest with non-members
405	Association with firms
406	Member responsible for a non-member in practice of public accounting
407	Related business or practice, and member responsible for non-member in such business or practice
408	Association with non-member in public practice
409	Office by representation
410	Practice of public accounting in corporate form

500 – RULES OF PROFESSIONAL CONDUCT APPLICABLE ONLY TO FIRMS

501	Firm's maintenance of policies and procedures for compliance with professional standards
502	Firm's maintenance of policies and procedures: competence and conduct of firm members
503	Association with firms

APPENDIX A

Former Rule of Professional Conduct 204 (Objectivity)

Source: The Institute of Chartered Accountants of Ontario "Rules of Professional Conduct." These materials are produced by permission of the Institute of Chartered Accountants of Ontario, and may not be further reproduced without the prior written permission of the Institute of Chartered Accountants of Ontario. These Rules are as of the date January 1, 2009, and are subject to revision and change at any time.

IFAC CONCEPTUAL FRAMEWORK FOR RESOLVING A CONFLICT IN THE APPLICATION OF FUNDAMENTAL PRINCIPLES

- Step 1: Members should consider the following: (CT step 2)
  - Identify the relevant facts. (CT steps 1, 3)
  - Identify ethical issues involved. (CT step 3)
  - Identify fundamental principles related to the matters in question. (CT steps 2, 3)
  - Identify established internal procedures. (CT step 3)
  - Identify alternative courses of action. (CT steps 2, 3)

- Step 2: Identify appropriate course of action consistent with fundamental principles. (CT steps 4, 5)

- Step 3: If conflict cannot be resolved consistent with fundamental principles, then the auditor should refuse to be associated with the conflict whenever possible. (CT step 5)

Serving the Public Interest

The single most important principle for accountants is to serve the public interest; they can only do so if the profession maintains a good reputation. "The phrase 'at all times' is significant because the public will view any serious transgression of a professional accountant, including those outside business or professional activity, as a black mark against the profession as a whole. Consequently, if a professional accountant is convicted of a minimal offense or fraud, his or her certification is usually revoked."[8] The remaining principles all serve to support this first one.

Serving the public interest primarily means to competently fulfill the role expected by the public. This is succinctly captured in Rule 205, which prohibits the PA from being associated with false or misleading information. As stated in the auditor's report, the role of the auditor is to express an opinion based on the audit of the financial statements prepared by management. In fulfilling this responsibility, the auditor reduces the risk of the

[8] L. J. Brooks, *Professional Ethics for Accountants* (Minneapolis/St. Paul: West Publishing, 1995), p. 120.

financial statements being false or misleading to an appropriately low level. Terms such as present fairly, in all material respects, audit risk, materiality, and risk of material misstatements used throughout the text capture this concept.

If the audit fails to detect a material misstatement, then the audit fails. The rapid demise of Arthur Andersen as a result of the failure of their Enron audit illustrates this. The profession is now particularly sensitized to the importance of not being associated with misleading information. And Rule 205 now probably represents the most important rule, particularly in light of responsibilities placed on auditors by SOX and the CPAB, as discussed in Chapter 1.

Integrity

Integrity is the duty to be honest and conscientious in performing professional services. Integrity relates to the basic character of the professional—a PA must be upright, not kept upright. Without integrity among its members, the profession cannot maintain its good reputation and serve the public interest.

INDEPENDENCE AND OBJECTIVITY

· · · · · · · · · · · · · · · ·

LEARNING OBJECTIVE

3 Explain the importance of an independence framework for auditors.

Rule 204.1 dealing with independence was introduced to you in Chapter 3. Independence and objectivity are closely related terms. In this case, independence is a way of achieving objectivity, and it is the term given to the objectivity required in the special case of assurance engagements. The term independence is also used in the *Canadian Business Corporations Act*, in some provincial corporations acts, and in various professional rules of conduct. Canadian legislation requires that the auditor be "independent"—presumably, the fact of independence must be determined by the courts.

The *Canadian Business Corporations Act*, section 161, defines independence as a key qualification of an auditor, as indicated in the following box.

---

161. (1) Qualification of auditor. Subject to subsection (5), a person is disqualified from being an auditor of a corporation if he is not independent of the corporation, of any of its affiliates, or of the directors or officers of any such corporation or its affiliates.

(2) Independence. For the purpose of this section,

(a) independence is a question of fact; and

(b) a person is deemed not to be independent if he or his business partner

(I) is a business **partner**, a director, an officer or an employee of the corporation or any of its affiliates, or a business partner of any director, officer or employee of any such corporation or any of its affiliates;

(II) **beneficially** owns or controls, directly or indirectly, a material interest in the securities of the corporation or any of its affiliates; or

(III) has been a receiver-manager, liquidator, or trustee in bankruptcy of the corporation or any of its affiliates within two years of his proposed appointment as auditor of the corporation.

(3) Duty to resign. An auditor who becomes disqualified under this section shall, subject to subsection (5), resign forthwith after becoming aware of his disqualification.

Source: Canadian Business Corporations Act, section 161.1.

The term independence is internationally recognized. For example, the International Federation of Accountants' *Technical Standard on Ethics*, section 8, specifies that "professional accountants in public practice when undertaking a reporting assignment should be independent in fact and appearance." Similar wording regarding the need for independence is used in the SMAO's code of conduct.

Clearly, independence is an important concept for PAs. For this reason we discuss both independence and objectivity. However, since the focus of this text is on audits, and independence is the term used to indicate objectivity in assurance engagements, our focus will be on independence.

The CICA, IFAC, and CGA-Canada all have standard frameworks for independence based on the five following threats or risks to a PA's independence:

1. self-review—providing assurance on his or her own work

2. self-interest—for example, benefiting from a financial interest in a client

3. advocacy—promoting a client's position or opinion

4. familiarity—becoming too sympathetic to a client's interests

5. intimidation—being deterred from acting objectively by actual or perceived threats from a client

Under all the independence standards, the PA must identify and evaluate the significance of any independence threat. If threats are other than clearly insignificant, the PA must apply safeguards to eliminate the threats or take action to reduce them to a level that would pose no real or perceived compromise. If no safeguards are adequate to preserve independence, the PA must eliminate the activity, interest, or relationship that is creating the threat, or refuse to perform or continue the particular engagement.[9]

We refer to the need to control independence threats as the independence principle. Principles like this one assist sound, structured ethical reasoning by auditors. As noted in Chapter 2, independence issues continue to be a problem for even the largest firms, according to the CPAB's 2004 monitoring report.[10]

The Canadian legislation referred to previously requires independence for financial statement audit services. However, review services of unaudited financial statements, such as engagements to report on prospective financial statements (forecasts and projections) and expressing opinions on representations other than financial statements (e.g., reports on internal control), all require independence as well. The definition of public practice is significant here. A member is considered to be in the public practice of accounting if he or she (1) lets it be known publicly that he or she is a PA, and (2) offers the types of services rendered by other PAs. The latter part of the definition is very broad because PAs perform a wide range of accounting, audit, taxation, and consulting services.[11] This means that most PAs who seek clients from the general public are in the practice of public accounting. For example, the PAs who work for H&R Block, the tax preparation corporation, are in public practice if they let themselves be known as PAs.

Since the purpose of independent financial auditing is to lend credibility to financial statements, auditors must be impartial and unbiased with respect to both the client management and the client entity itself. Auditors must be independent in fact and also independent of outside decision makers who rely on their assurance services. Independence is, in fact, a mental condition and difficult to demonstrate by physical or visual means. Thus, some things that give the appearance of lacking independence may be prohibited in specific interpretations of the independence principle. Note how awareness of other perspectives is crucial in correctly assessing the various independence risks (step 1 of Exhibit 4–1, page 98).

---

[9] As modified from "Proposed new independence standards for auditors," *CA Magazine*, October 2002, p. 51.

[10] See www.cpab_ccrc.org for the latest reports.

[11] The CICA's definition of public accountant in its *Terminology for Accountants*, 4th ed. (1992), is as follows: "1. The perfomance of services for clients, the purpose of which is to add credibility to financial information that may be relied upon by interested parties. 2. The performance of independent professional accounting and related services for clients. 3. Any service so defined by a particular statute or authority."

The rest of the critical thinking framework is also useful for deciding if the independence risks are appropriately low for a specific situation. For example, the IFAC's conceptual framework approach to ethics consists of compliance with their fundamental principles, identification of threats to achieving those principles, and safeguarding against these threats. The safeguards include training, professional standards, regulatory monitoring, and corporate governance. They are implemented using a process similar to that outlined in Exhibit 4–1. In brief, achieving the objective of independence is accomplished through understanding users' perspectives, taking actions that address the risk of threats against their interests, and reducing those risks of threats to acceptable levels. Thus, critical thinking and the independence principle have a great deal of overlap, not surprising as independence risks are a significant category at issue on engagements for which critical thinking provides a broad reasoning process framework.

To further develop perspectives on independence, the box below identifies the concepts of programming, investigative, and reporting independence that are useful in avoiding influences that might bias judgment.

THREE ASPECTS OF PRACTICAL INDEPENDENCE

Programming Independence
Auditors must remain free from interference by client managers who try to restrict, specify, or modify the procedures auditors want to perform, including any attempt to assign personnel or otherwise control the audit work. Occasionally, client managers try to limit the number of auditors permitted in a location.

Investigative Independence
Auditors must have free access to books, records, correspondence, and other evidence. They must have the co-operation of management without any attempt to interpret or screen evidence. Sometimes, client managers refuse auditors' requests for access to necessary information.

Reporting Independence
Auditors must not let any feelings of loyalty to the client or auditee interfere with their obligation to report fully and fairly. Neither should the client management be allowed to overrule auditors' judgments on the appropriate content of an audit report. Disciplinary actions have been taken against auditors who go to a client management conference with a preliminary estimate for a financial adjustment and emerge after agreeing with management to a smaller adjustment.

Observing the rules regarding prohibited activities is an important way of maintaining the independence principle. The fact that they vary with the circumstances is a complication. A member may divest a prohibited financial interest before the first work on a new client begins, and, if the engagement continues, it is improper to reinvest. Direct or indirect financial interests are allowed up to the point of materiality, that is, until they make significant contributions to the PA's wealth. This provision permits members to hold mutual fund shares and have some limited business transactions with clients.

As noted previously, SOX is an influence globally in determining which threats to independence are against the public interest. The currently prohibited activities seem to focus on the self-review threat. Other threats will likely be identified as the SEC and PCAOB establish regulations required by SOX. Earlier standards and rules of professional conduct focused on self-interest and intimidation threats through rules on financial interests and those related to conflicts of interest. The more detailed rules are reviewed next.

Permitted Loans

If the client is a bank or other financial institution, the codes of conduct generally allow home mortgages, immaterial loans, and secured loans, all made under a client's normal lending terms. Neither is independence considered impaired if a member obtains the following types of personal loans from assurance service clients: auto loans and leases, insurance policy loans based on policy surrender value, loans collateralized by cash deposits at the same financial institution, and credit card balances and cash advances equivalent to those of other customers in the normal course of business. For insurance company clients, the PA can borrow against the cash surrender value of a life insurance policy. However, the loans should have the same terms as granted to other customers of the institution in the normal course of business. Potentially, these kinds of permitted loans could be abused in spirit, as apparently happened in the United States. The key ethical judgment is understanding "the normal course of business" and, more basically, awareness of the types of loans that could lead to even the perception of impairment of auditor independence.

Other Issues Related to the Independence Principle

Broadly defined, the codes of conduct collectively prohibit activities that amount to having the ability to make decisions for the client or to act as management. The appearance of independence is impaired if such a connection existed at any time during the period covered by the financial statements, regardless of whether the association was terminated prior to the beginning of the audit work. The presumption is that members cannot be independent and objective when attesting to decisions they took part in or are connected with.

In terms of ethical principles, these rules may be justified on a utilitarian theory basis as far as direct financial interests are concerned. The logic is something like this: The greatest good is created by making a situation free of any suspicious circumstances, no matter how innocent they may be in truth. The goodwill of public reliance and respect is greater than the PA's sacrifice of the opportunity to invest in securities of clients or participate in their management.

In addition to the issues previously discussed, there are other rules relevant to the independence principle, now briefly described.

Honorary Positions in Nonprofit Organizations

Ordinarily, independence is impaired if a PA serves on an organization's board of directors. However, members can be honorary directors of charity hospitals, fund drives, symphony orchestra societies, and other nonprofit organizations so long as (1) the position is purely honorary, (2) the PA is identified as an honorary director on letterheads and other literature, (3) the only form of participation is the use of the PA's name, and (4) the PA does not vote with the board or participate in management functions. When all these criteria are satisfied, the PA/board member can perform assurance services because the appearances of independence will have been preserved.

Retired Partners

Independence problems do not end when partners retire, resign, or otherwise leave an accounting firm. A former partner can impair independence by association with a client of the former firm. However, the problems are solved and independence is not impaired if (1) the person's retirement benefits are fixed, (2) the person is no longer active in the accounting firm (some retired partners remain "active"), and (3) the former partner is not held out to be associated with the accounting firm by a reasonable observer. Regulators may have stricter rules relating to former partners.

Accounting and Other Services

If a PA performs the bookkeeping and makes accounting decisions for a company and the management does not know enough about the financial statements to take primary responsibility for them, the PA cannot be considered independent for assurance services. It might be perceived that the PA has both prepared the financial statements or other data and given an audit report or other assurance on his own work. The PA can perform the bookkeeping and counsel the client management about the accounting principle choices, but in the final analysis the management must be able to say, "These are our financial statements (or other data); we made the choices of accounting principles; we take primary responsibility for them." Again, regulators may have stricter rules relating to such bookkeeping services.

SOX prohibits the following services for auditors of publicly traded companies: internal audit services for the client, financial-information-system design and implementation, and even tax services. All of these services must be pre-approved by the client's audit committee and disclosed to regulators.

Rotation of Partners and Second Partner Review

CPAB and SOX require rotation of the lead audit partner and/or concurring review partner (but not the audit firm) every five years. The five-year period includes time spent providing professional services as a non-partner (for example, manager) and includes years before 2002. The intent of the rule is to prevent auditors from becoming too complacent and not sufficiently skeptical with the client relationship. A second partner review is now mandated by both CPAB and SOX.

Actual or Threatened Litigation

When a PA and a client move into an adversary relationship and away from the cooperative one needed in an assurance engagement, independence is threatened by appearances of the PA trying to serve her own best interests. PAs are considered not independent when (1) company management threatens or actually starts a lawsuit against them, alleging deficiencies in audit or other assurance work, or (2) the PA threatens or starts litigation against the company management, alleging fraud or deceit. Such cases may be rare, but auditors get out of such difficult audit situations by ending the assurance engagement. Essentially, the PA–client relationship ends, and the litigation begins a new relationship.

Investor or Investee Relationships

In this context, the terms investor and investee have the same meaning as in rules about accounting for investments in the equity method, covered in *Handbook* section 3050. The *investor* is the party that has significant influence over a business, and the *investee* is the business in which the investor has the significant influence.

When the PA's client is the investor, the PA's direct or material indirect financial interest in a nonclient investee impairs their independence. The reasoning is that the client investor, through its ability to influence a nonclient investee, can materially increase or decrease the PA's financial stake in the investee. If, on the other hand, the nonclient investee is immaterial to the investor, independence is not considered impaired when the PA's financial interest in a nonclient investee is immaterial in relation to the PA's wealth.

When a PA has an investment in a nonclient investor, (a) this investment may be a direct or material indirect financial interest that will diminish independence with respect to a client investee; (b) independence is not impaired, as long as the PA does not have significant influence over the actions or financial statements of the nonclient investor; but (c) independence is impaired when the PA's investment gives him significant influence over the actions of the nonclient investor, which might in turn influence the client investee. In any of these relationships, the independence of the PA is impaired because it puts him in a position similar to that of a member of management of the client investee.

Effect of Family Relationships

The codes of conduct and all the interpretations apply to members, but being a member of a professional accounting institute, society, or association shouldn't be confused with the use of the word "member" in the rule. For purposes of independence, the terms member and member's firm generally include:

- all partners in the accounting firm
- all professional employees participating in the engagement, including audit, tax, and management consulting personnel
- all other manager-level employees located in a firm office that does a significant part of the audit
- any PA-firm personnel formerly employed by or connected with the audit client in a managerial capacity unless the person (a) is disassociated from the client and (b) does not participate in the engagement
- any PA-firm professional (e.g., partner, manager, staff) who is associated with the client in a managerial capacity and is located in an office of the PA firm that does a significant part of the engagement

The term "member" excludes students registered under the bylaws of the professional body. However, the codes of conduct generally apply to students as well as to members.

All this is rather complicated, but the bottom line is that it is rare for any partners or shareholders in the firm to be able to have any of the financial or managerial relationships. It is possible for managers and staff to have such relationships, provided they are far removed from the actual work on the audit engagement.

Financial interests of spouses and dependent persons (whether related or not) and some financial interests of close relatives are attributed to the member. Thus, for example, independence would be impaired if (a) a spouse or dependent of a member had a direct financial interest in an audit client or (b) a member on an engagement knew about a brother's or nondependent child's material financial interest in a client.

Employment relationships of spouses, dependent persons, and close relatives can be attributed to a member. Positions that are "audit sensitive" or can exercise significant influence over the operating, financial, or accounting policies of the client are attributed to the member and impair independence. Positions that are "audit sensitive" (e.g., cashier, internal auditor, accounting supervisor, purchasing agent, inventory warehouse supervisor) are attributed to the member and impair independence. However, such employment poses no problem when it cannot influence the audit work (e.g., secretarial, nonfinancial positions).

The code of conduct rules are the minimum criteria relating to independence. PA firms can make more limiting rules. The anecdote in the next box shows some rules given to job applicants of a Big Four accounting firm.

IF EMPLOYED BY "ANONYMOUS FIRM," I UNDERSTAND THAT:

Professional staff members of the firm, their spouses, and dependents are prohibited from owning or controlling investments in any of our clients and certain related nonclients, and I will be required to dispose of any such investments before commencing employment with the firm.

I will be prohibited from disclosing nonpublic information regarding clients or other entities to anyone, other than for firm business, or using it for any personal purpose.

I will be expected to devote my energies to the firm to the fullest extent possible and refrain from other business interests that might require significant time or that could be considered a conflict of interest.

Neither an offer of employment nor employment itself carries with it a guarantee of tenure of employment, and my employment, compensation, and benefits can be terminated, with or without cause or notice, at any time at the option of the firm or me.

Analysis of Independence Rules

Generally, the rules of professional conduct and corporate acts legislation imply a fine distinction between independence, integrity, and objectivity. The spirit of the rules is that integrity and objectivity are required in connection with all professional services and, in addition, independence is required for assurance services. In this context, integrity and objectivity are the larger concepts, and independence is a special condition largely defined by the matters of appearance specified in the codes or their interpretations. Conflicts of interest, for example as cited in ICAO Rule 204, refers to avoiding business interests in which the accountant's personal financial relationships or relationships with other clients might tempt him not to serve the best interests of a client or the public that uses the results of the engagement.

The issue of independence gained even more prominence on January 6, 2000, when the SEC published a report citing thousands of violations by one of the Big Four firms of rules requiring PAs to remain independent from companies they audit. This occurred despite concerns about independence that led to the May 1997 creation of a new private sector body, the Independence Standards Board. In 1999, the Board issued its first standard, requiring auditors to confirm their independence annually to audit committees. Other items on the Board's agenda included an official definition of independence as well as a conceptual framework for it. The Board was disbanded and replaced in 2002 by the PCAOB created under SOX. Fully operational since 2003, PCAOB has even more demanding objectives. It is clear that maintenance of independence is a continuing and growing concern within the profession.

Phrases such as "shall not knowingly misrepresent facts" and "[shall not] subordinate his or her judgment to others" emphasize conditions people ordinarily identify with the concepts of integrity and objectivity. PAs who know about a client's lies in a tax return, false journal entries, material misrepresentations in financial statements, and the like, have violated both the spirit and the letter of the rules of conduct.

Professional Competence and Due Care

The professional competence and due care rules of the codes of conduct can be summarized as follows:

A. *Professional competence.* Undertake only those professional services that the member or the member's firm can reasonably expect to be completed with professional competence.

B. *Due professional care.* Exercise due professional care in the performance of professional services.

C. *Planning and supervision.* Adequately plan and supervise the performance of professional services.

D. *Sufficient relevant data.* Obtain sufficient relevant data to afford a reasonable basis for conclusions or recommendations in relation to any professional services performed.

Analysis of Competence and Due Care Rules

The professional competence and due care principles are a comprehensive statement of general standards that PAs are expected to observe in all areas of practice. These are the principles that enforce the various series of professional standards. For example, there is usually a specific rule relating to compliance with professional standards.

Compliance with Professional Standards

A member engaged in the practice of public accounting shall perform his professional services in accordance with generally accepted standards of practice of the profession, (from Rule 206 of ICAO).

Analysis of Compliance Rule

This rule may be viewed as an extension and refinement of the due care principle. It implies adherence to technical standards in all areas of professional service, including review and compilation (unaudited financial statements), consulting, tax, and other professional services. The practical effect of this rule is to make noncompliance with all technical standards subject to disciplinary proceedings. Thus, failure to follow auditing standards, accounting and review standards, as well as assurance, compilation, and professional conduct standards is a violation of this rule.

Accounting Principles

The compliance rule requires adherence to official pronouncements of accounting principles, but with an important exception related to unusual circumstances where adherence would create misleading statements. The rule itself concedes that unusual circumstances may exist; it permits PAs to decide for themselves how applicable the official pronouncements are and makes them responsible for ethical decisions. The rule also allows PAs to exercise a utilitarian calculation for circumstances when adherence would be misleading. Misleading statements would result in financial harm for outside decision makers, so presumably the greater good would be realized by explaining a departure.

Note that the compliance rule requires the coherent integration of accounting, auditing, and ethical concepts, assumptions, rules, and principles. But, if there is a conflict, how should it be resolved? Critical thinking is helpful in these situations of dealing with the logical gaps and inconsistencies of professional standards in specific applications. These are illustrated in questions throughout the text. On some issues, such as confidentiality, discussed next, the courts have helped resolve the ethical conflicts. But, in other situations, the auditor will need to resolve conlicts in some reasonable way. This is the essence of professional judgment. Interestingly, lawyers and the courts use critical thinking to assist in their deliberations, and critical thinking courses are common in law schools.

Confidentiality

The general principle of confidentiality is that a PA must not disclose any confidential information without the specific consent of the client. This principle does not allow a PA to ignore the obligation to comply with a validly issued subpoena or summons or not to comply with applicable laws and government regulations.[12] Neither do confidentiality principles prohibit review of a PA's professional practice under member's handbook bylaws. In spite of the principles, a PA still must initiate necessary complaints to, and respond to enquiries by, their professional group (CAs, CMAs, or CGAs). Members of any professional association involved with professional practice reviews may not disclose any confidential client information that comes to their attention in carrying out those reviews, but neither should it restrict any exchange of information that is necessary for the review. Confidential information is information that should not be disclosed to outside parties unless demanded by a court or an administrative body with the power to do so. Privileged information, on the other hand, is information that cannot even be demanded by a court. Common law privilege exists for husband–wife, attorney–client, and physician–patient relationships. In all the recognized privilege relationships, the professional person is obligated to observe the privilege, which can be waived only by the client, patient, or penitent—the holders of the privilege. ICAO Council Interpretation 210.1, paragraph 1 states:

---

[12]C. Chazen, R. L. Miller, and K. I. Solomon, "When the Rules Say: See Your Lawyer," *Journal of Accountancy*, January 1981, p. 70.

> The duty to keep a client's affairs confidential should not be confused with the legal concept of privilege. The duty of confidentiality precludes the member from disclosing a client's affairs without the knowledge or consent of the client. However, this duty does not excuse a member from obeying an order of a court of competent jurisdiction requiring the member to disclose the information.

> A court will determine whether or not a member should maintain the confidentiality of client information depending on the facts of each case.

PAs and clients have attempted to establish privilege for tax file workpapers to shield them from Canada Revenue Agency summons demands (tax file workpapers contain accountants' analyses of "soft spots" and potential tax liability for arguable tax positions), but have so far been unsuccessful. As noted in Chapter 2, privilege was invoked by a number of PA firms when the CPAB attempted to access audit files as part of its monitoring of quality control practices.

The rules of privileged and confidential communication are based on the belief that they facilitate a free flow of information between parties to the relationship. The nature of accounting services makes it necessary for the PA to have access to information about salaries, products, contracts, merger or divestment plans, tax matters, and other data required for the best possible professional work. Managers would be less likely to reveal such information if they could not trust the PA to keep it confidential. If PAs were to reveal such information, the resultant reduction of the information flow might be undesirable, so no PAs should break the confidentiality rule without a good reason.

Problems arise over auditors' obligations to "blow the whistle" on clients' shady or illegal practices. Generally, the codes indicate that confidentiality in such cases can be overridden through obtaining or following legal advice. If a client refuses to accept an audit report that has been modified because of illegal activities and their effects, the audit firm should withdraw from the engagement and give the reasons in writing to the board of directors. In such an extreme case, the withdrawal amounts to whistle-blowing, but the action results from the client's decision not to disclose the information. For all practical purposes, information is not considered confidential if disclosure of it is necessary to make financial statements not misleading.

Auditors are not, in general, legally obligated to blow the whistle on clients. However, circumstances may exist where auditors are legally justified in making disclosures to a regulatory agency or a third party. Such circumstances include when a client (1) has intentionally and without authorization associated or involved a PA in its misleading conduct, (2) has distributed misleading draft financial statements that were prepared by a PA for internal use only, (3) prepares and distributes in an annual report or prospectus containing misleading information for which the PA has not assumed any responsibility, or (4) the situation falls under the requirements of anti-money laundering legislation.

Analysis of the Confidentiality Principle

PAs should not view the rules on confidential information as a license or excuse for inaction where action may be appropriate to right a wrongful act committed or about to be committed by a client. In some cases, auditors' inaction may make them an accessory to a wrong. Such situations are dangerous and potentially damaging. A useful initial course of action is to consult with a lawyer about possible legal pitfalls of both whistle-blowing and silence. Then, decide for yourself.

Contingency Fees and Service Without Fees

ICAO Rule 215 states, "A member engaged in the practice of public accounting or a related function shall not offer or agree to perform a professional service for a fee payable only where there is a specified determination or result of the service. . . . A member engaged in the practice of public accounting or a related function shall not represent that he or she performs any professional service without fee except services of a charitable, benevolent, or similar nature. . . ."

For a fee to be considered a contingency fee, two characteristics need to be met:

1. its terms must be contracted for before any services are performed
2. the amount paid for the performance must be directly affected by the results obtained

Generally, if one of these characteristics is not present, the fee is not a contingency fee and therefore does not violate the ICAO's Rule 215 or similar rules by other accounting bodies, such as the CGA-Canada's Rule 508.[13] Fees are not contingent if they are fixed by a court or other public authority, determined as a result of the finding of judicial proceedings or government agencies, or when they are based on the work's complexity or time required. The current Rule 215 is quite restrictive, conflicting with some statutes such as the *Federal Bankruptcy Act* and *Provincial Trustee Acts*, which allow fees based on the results of the PA's work. Because of these conflicts with statutory law, some have called for modifications of the rules to apply to assurance engagements only.[14]

Rule 215 prohibits contingent fees in assurance engagements where users of financial information may be relying on the PA's work. Acceptance of contingent fee arrangements while engaged to perform any type of assurance engagement is considered an impairment of independence.

Fee Quotation

ICAO Rule 214 states that "a member shall not quote a fee for any professional services unless requested to do so by a client or prospective client, and no quote shall be made until adequate information has been obtained about the assignment." It is thus against Rule 214 to quote a fee over the phone or to quote a fixed charge for all audits. There is extensive anecdotal evidence that, particularly during economic downturns, some firms practice "low balling" or charging a fee that is below cost in order to obtain an engagement. This is at least in violation of the spirit of Rule 214, since presumably the need for the information about the assignment is to ensure that an adequate audit is done, in which the costs are recovered (no service should be provided for free unless for charitable purposes). The real concern is that auditors may cut back on audit procedures to the point of reducing the quality of audits.[15]

Discreditable Acts

CGA-Canada's Rule R101 states that "a member shall not permit the member's firm name or the member's name to be used with, participate in, or knowingly provide services to any practice, pronouncement, or act which would be of a nature to discredit the profession." Generally, we will refer to this and related rules as discreditable act rules.

Analysis of Discreditable Act Rules

The discreditable act rules may be called the moral clauses of the codes, but they are only occasionally the basis for disciplinary action. Penalties usually are invoked automatically under the bylaws, which provide for expulsion of members found by a court to have committed any fraud, filed false tax returns, been convicted of any criminal offence, or been found by a disciplinary committee to be guilty of an act discreditable to the profession. Discreditable acts can include (a) withholding a client's books and records when the client has requested their return; (b) practising employment discrimination in hiring, promotion, or salary practices on the basis of race, colour, religion, sex, or national origin; (c) failing to follow government audit standards and guides in governmental

---

[13] C. Schultz, "When Talk Turns to Contingency Fees," *CA Magazine*, May 1988, p. 29.
[14] Ibid., p. 33.
[15] M. C. Carscallen, "Fee Completion Hurts Integrity of Accounting Services," *The Bottom Line*, April 1991, p. 20.

audits; and (d) making, or permitting others to make, false and misleading entries in records and financial statements. An extreme example of an actual discreditable act is given in the box following.

EXTREME EXAMPLE OF A DISCREDITABLE ACT

The Enforcement Committee found that Respondent drew a gun from his desk drawer during a dispute with a client in his office in contravention of section 501.41 [discreditable acts prohibition] of the [Texas] Rules of Professional Conduct. Respondent agreed to accept a private reprimand to be printed . . . in the Texas State Board Report.

Source: *Texas State Board* Report (February 1986).

Advertising and Other Forms of Solicitation

The rules relating to solicitation state that a member shall not attempt to obtain clients by advertising or other forms of solicitation that are false, misleading, or deceptive. Solicitation through coercion, overreaching, or harassing conduct is prohibited as well.

Analysis of Solicitation Rules

The current rules apply only to PAs practising public accounting and relate to their efforts to obtain clients. The rules permit advertising with only a few limitations, and basic guidelines include the following:

- Advertising may not create false or unjustified expectations of favourable results.
- Advertising may not imply the ability to influence any court, tribunal, regulatory agency, or similar body or official.
- Advertising may not contain a fee estimate when the PA knows it is likely to be substantially increased, unless the client is notified.
- Advertising may not contain any representation that is likely to cause a reasonable person to misunderstand or be deceived, or that contravenes professional good taste.

Advertising consists of messages designed to attract business and are broadcast widely (e.g., through print, radio, television, billboards, and pop-up ads on various websites) to an undifferentiated audience. The guidelines basically prohibit false, misleading, and deceptive messages.

Solicitation, on the other hand, generally refers to direct contact (e.g., in person, email, telephone) with a specific potential client. The rules regarding solicitation basically prohibit extreme bad behaviour that brings disrepute on the profession.

The advertising rules have undergone many changes over the last three decades. Long ago, all advertising by PAs was prohibited. Then, institutional-type advertising on behalf of PAs in general was permitted. In 1979, in response to the Charter of Rights guarantee to members, the ICAO approved advertising "in good taste," with limitations on style, type size, and the like. The other professional bodies followed suit.

Most PAs carry out only modest advertising efforts, and many do no advertising at all. According to a recent article, advertising so far has been precisely targeted—for example, at chief financial officers of wholesalers in the food industry. Firms have generally used local rather than national advertising. The biggest problem so far is of members making claims they are unable to substantiate.

Firms rarely obtain new clients through advertising, but it can be effective in generating business in the form of new services for existing clients or from referrals. Overall, except for some isolated examples of creative advertising by some firms, the profession has not pursued advertising aggressively. Nevertheless, we see PA firm advertisements in an increasing variety of formats and media.[16] This seems to be especially true as websites by PA firms continue to proliferate (see Chapter 8).

THE ART OF ADVERTISING

In 1987, three charges were brought against "a partner of Ernst&Whinney" in Ontario under subsections (c), (a), and (d). The discipline committee found the member "not guilty" on the first charge, but "guilty" on the second and third. Both guilty charges concerned a 1985 ad he had placed in *The Globe and Mail* which stated, in part, "Canada's Fastest Growing Firm of Business Advisors Announces Its Newest Partners."

The committee found the ad misleading in two ways. First, "accountants do not have a monopoly on the term 'business advisors.' " Second, the claim was made on the basis of statistics that were "accurate as they relate to the participating chartered accountant firms [but] without disclosure of the necessary parameters or basis for the statement, it is misleading."

The member received a written reprimand, was assessed court costs of $6,000, and was fined $5,000.

Source: Tim Falconer, *CA Magazine*, October 1993, p. 46.

Public practice is generally marked by decorum and a sense of good taste. However, there are exceptions, and they tend to get much attention, most of it disapproving, from other PAs and the public in general. The danger with bad advertising is that the advertiser may develop a professional huckster image, which may backfire on efforts to build a practice.

Communications Between Predecessors and Successors

Successor auditors are required to make certain enquiries of predecessor auditors when a new client is obtained (e.g., Rule 302 of Professional Conduct of ICAO). Rule 302 and similar rules of other accounting bodies apply to all public accounting engagements, including compilation and review work.

Interpretation to Rule 302 gives advice to PAs when communicating with the predecessor. First, the successor PA should ask the new client to notify the predecessor (incumbent) PA of the proposed change. The successor should then ask the predecessor "whether there are any circumstances that should be taken in account which might influence the potential successors' decision whether to accept the appointment," per Interpretation 302. Normally, the successor should wait for the reply before commencing work for the new client. The interpretation also requires the predecessor to reply promptly. When enquiries are made, the successor must have the client's permission for the predecessor to disclose confidential information. When confidentiality is in doubt, legal advice should be obtained. The effort the predecessor should make in supplying information to the successor is an important issue. The interpretation suggests that, as a minimum, "reasonable information about the work being assumed" should be discussed, and it then gives advice on what constitutes "reasonable."

In addition to the rules of professional conduct, PAs should be aware of any federal and provincial legislation, including securities legislation, regulating changes in professional appointments.

---

[16] T. Falconer, "The Art of Advertising," *CA Magazine*, October 1993, pp. 43–46.

Commissions and Referral Fees

A practicing PA must not accept a commission for recommending or referring any product or service to a client, or accept a commission for recommending or referring any product or service offered by a client. Neither should a member PA receive a commission when another member of his firm performs public accounting for that client. These prohibitions apply during the period in which the PA performs public accounting services and the period covered by any historical financial statements involved in these services. A member in public practice may, however, receive a commission from the sale or purchase of an accounting practice.

Analysis of Commissions Rules

A **commission** is a percentage fee charged for professional services related to executing a transaction or performing some other business activity. Examples are insurance sales commissions, real estate sales commissions, and securities sales commissions. Such fees are an impairment of independence when received from assurance engagement clients, just like ICAO's Rule 215 treats contingent fees.

However, many PAs perform financial planning for businesses and individuals, and they have seen commissions for insurance, securities, mergers and acquisitions, and other transactions go to other professionals. They want some of this action. The rules permit such commissions, provided the engagement does not involve assurance services.

Most commission fee activity takes place in connection with personal financial planning services. PAs often recommend insurance and investments to individuals and families. When the rule change was under consideration, critics pointed out that commission agents (e.g., insurance salespersons, securities brokers) cannot always be trusted to have the best interests of the client in mind when their own compensation depends in large part on client's buying the product that produces their commissions. Critics made the point that fee-only planning advisers, who do not work on commission, were more likely to have the best interests of the client in mind, directing them to investment professionals who handle a wide range of alternatives. Because of this, some PAs make it a point to provide financial planning services on a fee-only basis. This is also the position of the Financial Planners Standards Council of Canada, which is dedicated to maintaining a licensing system for certified financial planners (CFPs) in Canada. This organization is sponsored by the CICA, CGA-Canada, and SMAC, among other associations.

The rules also include fee arrangements related to commissions. Referral fees are those a PA receives for recommending another PA's services, or fees a PA pays to obtain a client, and they may or may not be based on a percentage of the amount of any transaction. Referral involves the practice of sending business to another PA and paying other PAs or outside agencies for drumming up business. These activities are banned by the rules of conduct on the basis that they impair the principle of objectivity. The sole exception is sale or purchase of an accounting practice, covered in Rule 216.

Form of Organization and Name

The general rule relating to PA organization is that each practice office should be under the personal charge of a member who is a public accountant. The name of the public accounting firm should not be misleading. Names of one or more past owners may be included in the firm name of a successor organization.

Analysis of PA Organization Rules

The rules allow members to practise in any form of organization permitted by provincial laws and regulations—proprietorships, partnerships, professional corporations, limited liability partnerships, limited liability corporations, and ordinary corporations. Most provincial accountancy laws prohibit the general corporate form of organization for PAs, but, because of increased legal risk, there has been a recent push for the limited liability partnership structure. In the traditional form of partnership, all partners' personal assets are at risk. Under the limited liability partnership (LLP) form of organization, the only partners with personal assets at risk are those involved in the litigated engagement, while the others risk only their investment in the partnership. Thus, the limited liability partnership is a great improvement at a time of increased litigation, and many PA firms are now LLPs.

In 1992, the AICPA approved a move to permit PAs to practise in limited liability corporations and ordinary corporations. This has led to non-PA firms such as American Express owning PA firms.

PAs have experienced lawsuits for damages in which they and their insurers are the only persons left with any money (e.g., in cases of business failure), and multimillion-dollar damages have been awarded to plaintiffs against them. In the proprietorship, partnership, and professional corporation forms of business, all the business and personal assets of PAs are exposed to plaintiffs. Many PAs think the tort liability litigation process has gotten out of hand, and so they seek some protection through new forms of organization. See the following box for some consequences that can arise from an attempt at innovative forms of PA firm organization.

PAs (ALMOST) SELL SHARES TO PUBLIC

Nearman & Lents, a Florida PA firm, formed a corporation named Financial Standards Group, Inc., and filed a registration statement with the Securities and Exchange Commission to sell shares to the public. The accounting firm wanted to "go national on a large scale, and . . . raise $3 million or $4 million capital."

The registration became effective, and some shares were actually sold. However, Nearman & Lents withdrew the offering and gave the money back to the purchasers. Florida regulators had raised questions about the company practising public accounting without a license with non-PA ownership, which was prohibited. Financial Standards Group did not become the first publicly held PA firm.

The venture met resistance. Accounting traditionalists and lawyers who specialize in suing accountants for misconduct have generally frowned on letting accountants avail themselves of the limited legal liability provided by a corporation. Regulators have also discouraged accounting firms from issuing shares to outsiders for fear that outside equity partners might taint a firm's ability to judge [audit] a client's books impartially.

Source: *The New York Times*, June 14, 1990, and SEC.

The Canadian rules of conduct effectively block persons who are not PAs from being owners. This rule section creates problems for tax and management consulting services personnel who are not PAs. They cannot be admitted to full partnership or become shareholders without causing the other owners who are PAs to be in violation of the rule. Thus, an accounting firm may employ non-PAs who are high on the organization chart, but these persons may not be unrestricted partners or shareholders under current rules.

Rules of Conduct and Ethical Principles

Specific items in the rules of conduct may not necessarily be based on one of the ethics principles, but instead they may involve various elements of different ethical theories. As is typical in a code of conduct, the rules take the form of duties or imperatives, but elements of various theories seem to be part of their rationales. If this perception is accurate, then pluralistic theories may be used by auditors in difficult decision problems where adherence to a rule would produce an undesirable result. Appendix 4A discusses other factors to consider in audit decision making and justification.

8 What ethical responsibilities do members of the provincial associations/institutes have for acts of nonmembers who are under their supervision (e.g., recent university graduates who are not yet PAs)?

9 Is an incorporated accounting practice substantially different from an accounting practice organized in the form of a partnership? in the form of a limited liability partnership?

10 Define the term contingency fee, explaining how such fees apply to PAs. Do you feel a change is necessary to rules for contingency fees in Canada?

11 Do auditors need to report suspicious activities to the police? Explain.

REGULATION AND QUALITY CONTROL

LEARNING OBJECTIVE

4 Outline the types of penalties that various provincial associations and government agencies can impose on PAs when enforcing rules of professional conduct.

As a PA, you will be expected to observe the rules of conduct published in several codes of ethics. If you are a PA and have a client who is a public company, you will be subject to the following:

Examples of Rules of Conduct	Applicable to:
Members' Handbook ICAO, CGA-Canada's Code of Ethical Principles and Rules of Conduct	Persons licensed by provinces to practice accounting or, if no licence is required in the province, persons belonging to provincial institutes, societies, or organizations
Business Corporations Acts, Securities Acts at federal and provincial levels, and CGA requirements	PAs (usually PAs performing public accounting services) within the various jurisdictions
U.S. Securities and Exchange Commission and PCAOB	Persons who practise before the SEC as accountants and auditors for SEC-registered companies (including auditors of many large Canadian corporations)

If you are an internal auditor, you are expected to observe the rules of conduct of the Institute of Internal Auditors. As a management accountant, you are expected to observe the Society of Management Accountants' standards of ethical conduct. Certified fraud examiners are expected to observe the Association of Certified Fraud Examiners' code of ethics.

Regulation and professional ethics go hand in hand. Codes of ethics provide the underlying authority for regulation. Quality control practices and disciplinary proceedings provide the mechanisms of self-regulation. **Self-regulation** refers to quality control reviews and disciplinary actions conducted by fellow PAs—professional peers. Elements of PAs' self-regulation have been explained in terms of the quality control standards in Chapter 2.

Self-Regulatory Discipline

Accounting firms, as well as individuals, are subject to the rules of professional conduct of the institutes, associations, or societies only if they choose to join these organizations. But anyone wishing to practise public accounting finds that the added credibility of belonging to a professional group greatly improves the chances of establishing a successful practice. Thus, enforcing the rules of conduct is an important means of regulating the profession. Regulators can suspend a member's activities on certain exchanges, and the professional bodies can initiate other disciplinary proceedings.

FRAUD EXAMINER EXPELLED FOR FRAUD

Curtis C was expelled by the board of regents at its regular meeting on August 4, 1991. Mr. C, formerly an internal auditor employed by the City of S, was a member from February 1989 until his expulsion. He was the subject of an investigation by the trial board for falsifying information.

Mr. C wrongfully represented himself as a certified internal auditor, when in fact he did not hold the CIA designation. Such conduct is in violation of Article 1.A.4 of the CFE Code of Professional Ethics.

L. Jackson Shockey, CFE, CPA, CISA, chairman of the board of regents, said: "We are saddened that a member has been expelled for such conduct. However, in order to maintain the integrity of the CFE program, the trial board vigorously investigates violations of the Code of Professional Ethics. When appropriate, the board of regents will not hesitate to take necessary action."

Source: *CFE News*. Reprinted with permission from the September 1991, issue of *CFE News*, a publication of the Association of Certified Fraud Examiners, Inc., in Austin, Texas © 1991.

An Illustration of Self-Regulation: A Provincial Institute's Disciplinary Process

A provincial institute's bylaws and rules of professional conduct in its members' handbook provide the basis for self-regulation. The institutes have a duty to investigate all written complaints received about their members and students, as well as review information from the media that may indicate professional misconduct. While anyone can initiate a complaint, this is most frequently done by a client, and sometimes the provincial institute will do so.[17] The Professional Conduct Committee, which represents a cross-section of the membership, investigates the complaints and decides whether further action is necessary. The committee considers the respondent's reply and all relevant data in making its decision.

Three general conclusions are possible:

1. The member did not breach the rules and the process is ended.
2. The member did breach or may have breached the rules, but the infraction is not serious enough to prosecute before the discipline committee; the respondent is informally admonished in writing or at a committee meeting.
3. Charges are laid and the matter is brought up before the discipline committee where a process similar to a civil trial procedure is followed. The discipline committee can reach a decision of not guilty or guilty. There is also an appeal process, which is headed by the Appeal Committee.

In a guilty verdict the penalties can include any one or more of the following:

- reprimand
- suspension from the institute
- stricken from the student register in the case of students
- expulsion from membership in the institute
- completion of a professional development course(s) and/or an examination(s) and/or engagement of an adviser or tutor
- a period of supervised practice
- reinvestigation by the professional conduct committee

[17] S. Arihara, "The importance of being ethical," *CA Magazine*, August 2008, p. 25

- charged with costs and/or fined
- discipline as determined by the committee
- publication of the decision, order(s), and member's or student's name

These penalties cover a range of severity. In many cases a discipline committee can admonish or suspend a PA and require additional **continuing professional education (CPE)** to be undertaken. The goal is to help the PA attain an appropriate level of professional competence and awareness. Although intended as a constructive resolution, the CPE requirement is similar to "serving time." Persons who fail to satisfy CPE conditions will find themselves charged with "actions detrimental to the profession," for violations of rules such as CGA-Canada's Rule R606 or ICAO's Rule 201, and expelled as second offenders. What PAs dread most is having their guilty verdict made public, as it can destroy their careers.[18]

The expulsion penalty, while severe, does not prevent a PA from continuing to practice accounting. Membership in a professional group, while beneficial, is not required. However, a PA must have a valid licence in order to practise public accounting in certain provinces.

CGAs are subject to disciplinary action for any offence that constitutes a breach of professional conduct. This disciplinary action is brought on by the member's association or professional corporation, or, if the action is outside these groups, by the board of directors of CGA-Canada, per Rule R602.1.

Public Regulation Discipline

Some provincial institutes of chartered accountants, associations of CGAs, and societies of CMAs are self-governing agencies. Depending on the province's *Public Accounting Act*, they issue licences to practise accounting in their jurisdictions or certificates indicating that standards to be a PA have been met. Most provinces require a licence or certification procedure to use the CA, or *Chartered Accountant*, designation, and some limit the assurance (audit) function to license holders. Most provinces do not regulate work in areas of management consulting, tax practice, or bookkeeping services.

Provincial institutes, associations, and societies have rules of conduct and disciplinary processes as outlined above. Through the disciplinary process, these organizations can admonish a licence holder; but, more importantly, they can suspend or revoke the licence to practice in some provinces, severe penalties because a person then can no longer use the PA title or sign audit reports. When candidates have successfully passed the PA examination or fulfilled other requirements and are ready to become PAs, some provincial institutes administer an ethics examination or an ethics course intended to familiarize new PAs with the rules of professional conduct.

This traditional self-regulatory system is supplemented by CPAB, established in 2002. (Recall that the CPAB is a national body that reviews public company audits and the auditors' quality control systems.) This new system doubles the amount spent nationally on practice inspection. A review of the first report was provided in Chapter 2 and is publicly available on CPAB's website at www.cpab-ccrc.org. CPAB's February 2008 report indicates that the most common problems in professional audit practice are as follows:

Failure to properly document the audit and thereby support the audit opinion

Failure to consult partners on complex accounting matters

Failure of PA firms to internally monitor the quality of their audits[19]

Note that the first two points relate to failures of critical thinking and professional judgment. Recall that an improperly supported audit opinion can be construed as misleading because it indicates that the auditor does not have sufficient reasons to believe that the opinion is true. At the extreme, such as when no audit work supports the audit opinion, the

---

[18] Ibid., pp. 26–28

[19] J. Middlemiss, "From there to here," *CA Magazine*, June/July 2008, p. 26.

audit report is a fraudulent document. The comparable PCAOB's quality inspection report of PA firms in the U.S. can be found at its website, www.pcaobus.org.

The goal of these accountability boards is to prevent problems arising from audits of public companies in both countries. Their initial round of inspections focused on compliance with quality control standards, similar to practice inspections and peer review discussed in Chapter 2. It also put the spotlight on the four largest PA firms with the largest clients. Subsequent inspections have been extended to many more PA firms and will increasingly stress the quality of the audit output. This will be done by analyzing the results of specific engagements. Thus, there will be increased stress on monitoring questionable accounting practices allowed by auditors, and on the effect that problems of independence and competence in clients' internal audit functions have on the external audit.

The results of the monitoring will be made public. In addition, all auditors will be subject to disciplinary actions by the accountability boards, including restrictions on their ability to perform audits of public companies. Further disciplinary action may be taken by the PA institutes or associations. CPAB is hoping that its inspection process of PA firms will be acceptable to PCAOB. In Canada, the profession will continue to set auditing, independence, and quality control standards, whereas in the United States the PCAOB has taken over this role for public company audits.

Exhibit 4–2 summarizes the disciplinary system in Canada arising from the creation of CPAB. **AASOC** and **AcSOC** stand for the **Auditing and Assurance Oversight Council** and the **Accounting Standards Oversight Council**, respectively, and **PICA** stands for **Provincial Institutes of Chartered Accountants** (or other relevant professional accounting bodies). The exhibit illustrates that standard setting (right side of exhibit) is separate from the monitoring of audit process (left side of exhibit). As noted, this is not the case in the U.S. Note also that the CPAB can report PA firms to a professional body, which can then subject the firm to a provincial institute/association disciplinary process, as described previously.

EXHIBIT   4-2   PUBLIC OVERSIGHT MODEL (CANADA)

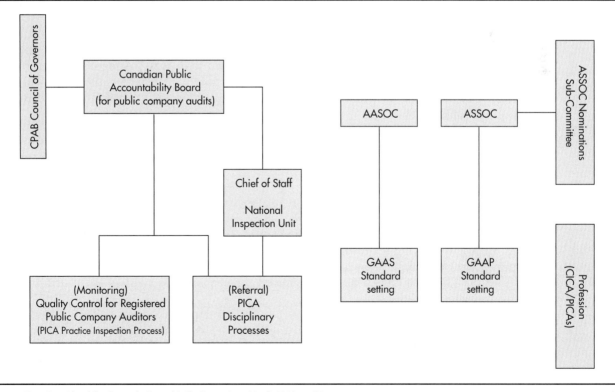

Source: "Busy Year Ahead for Oversight Council," *The Bottom Line*, March 2003, p. 21.

As noted in Chapter 2, the provincial securities commissions sometimes file complaints with the Professional Conduct Committees of the provincial institutes or associations. In addition, some securities commissions, notably the OSC, have been assertive in not accepting financial statements that they consider at odds with GAAP. The OSC issues staff accounting communiqués (SACs) in which it highlights major problem areas. Any company attempting to use the disfavoured technique may find that its financial statements are unacceptable to the OSC even though there is no reservation in the auditor's report.

The OSC is going even further: it plans to increase its supervision of auditors and other financial advisers and to gain the power to take disciplinary action against them. Although these proposals have yet to be enacted, the OSC already exerts some control over firms via out-of-court settlements, as indicated in the box below.

Public regulation disciplinary actions are also conducted by the SEC. Its authority comes from its rules of practice, one of which, Rule 2(e), provides that the SEC can deny, temporarily or permanently, the privilege of practice before the SEC to any person (1) not qualified to represent others, (2) lacking in character or integrity or having engaged in unethical or improper professional conduct, or (3) having willfully violated any provision of the federal securities laws or their rules and regulations. When conducting a "Rule 2(e) proceeding," the SEC acts in a quasi-judicial role as an administrative agency.

The SEC penalty bars an accountant from signing any documents filed by an SEC-registered company and effectively stops the accountant's SEC practice. In a few severe cases, Rule 2(e) proceedings have resulted in settlements barring not only the individual accountant but also the accounting firm or certain of its practice offices from accepting new SEC clients for a period.

PREVENTIVE MEDICINE

In response to problems arising from the audit of National Business Systems, Inc., the OSC agreed that the partner in charge of that audit would not act as the senior or second partner in charge of the audit of a public company for a year. It was also agreed that procedures and systems would be reviewed by an auditor from another firm and that the results would be resubmitted to the OSC. Moreover, arrangement was made to have the Toronto office inspected by a partner from outside Canada to ensure professional standards were met. The firm agreed to pay $70,000 to cover OSC expenses.

Source: J. Bedard and L. LeBlanc, *CA Magazine*, November 1991, p. 42.

The OSC and other Canadian regulators have been pushing to have similar disciplinary powers. Clearly, if the self-regulating process of the institutes is not deterring bad practices, regulators are willing to step in. In 1991, members of the ICAO approved a proposal giving the institute the power to subject firms to disciplinary action. In 2002, the Ontario legislature passed legislation that not only opened up public practice rights to CGAs and CMAs but also increased the penalties for auditors associated with misleading reporting.

In the next chapter, we will see how, in reaction to a Supreme Court of Canada ruling in the *Hercules v. Ernst & Young* Case, new securities laws that have been passed in some provinces hold auditors firmly liable for any negligence in financial statement audits. Other regulatory developments include greater independence and enforcement powers for Ontario and Quebec securities commissions, and increased harmonization procedures between the Alberta and British Columbia commissions. These structural changes in the regulatory climate are likely to increase regulatory disciplinary actions against PAs in the future.

The Canada Revenue Agency can also discipline PAs as a matter of public regulation. It can suspend or disbar from practice before it any PA shown to be incompetent or disreputable or who has refused to comply with tax rules and regulations, as well as levy fines for improper practices. The Revenue Ministry has made public its willingness to prosecute those accountants it suspects of "deliberate attempt to defraud the federal treasury."[20]

According to a study by Brooks and Fortunato, most disciplinary actions by the ICAO stem from violating the standards affecting the public interest (200 level).[21] Over a roughly three-year period (1988–90), most violations involved just four rules:

Rule 201: Good Reputation of Profession representing
20 percent of all violations   36 violations
Rule 202: Integrity and Due Care representing 16 percent
of all violations   29 violations
Rule 205: False and Misleading Representations representing
11 percent of all violations   20 violations
Rule 206: Expressing an Opinion Without Complying with
GAAS representing 12 percent of all violations   21 violations

EXAMPLE OF PUBLIC DISCIPLINARY NOTICE

Member Found Guilty of Breaching Rule of Professional Conduct 215
Re: Contingent Fees
A member has been found guilty of a charge of professional misconduct, laid by the professional conduct committee, under Rule of Professional Conduct 215, for agreeing to render professional services for a fee contingent on the results.

It was ordered that
- the member be reprimanded in writing by the chairman of the hearing
- the member be assessed costs of $1,500 to be paid within a specified time
- the decision and order be published in *Check Mark*

It was determined that the publication of the member's name was not necessary in the circumstances, as there was no evidence of any intent to breach the rules of professional conduct or of moral turpitude on the part of the member, and this was a matter of first instance.

This same study also found that "all but one of the ICAO convictions we examined resulted in disclosure of the convicted member's names, and 95 percent resulted in levying the costs of hearing on that person. Of those convicted 78 percent were reprimanded, of which 44 percent were also suspended; 17 percent of the total convicted were expelled from the profession." The average fine levied for these cases was $5,695.[22] An updated list from a more recent survey indicates that the findings in the Brooks and Fortunato study have not changed much in the last 20 years.[23]

[20]J. Middlemiss, "Too Many Accountants Guilty of Fraud, Liberals Vow Crackdown on Shady Advisers," *The Bottom Line*, March 1994, p. 1.
[21]L. Brooks and V. Fortunato, "Disciplines at the ICAO," *CA Magazine*, May 1991, p. 45.
[22]Ibid, pp. 42–43.
[23]S. Arihara, "The importance of being ethical," *CA Magazine*, August 2008, p. 26.

REVIEW
CHECKPOINTS

12   What options does the Canada Revenue Agency have for disciplining PAs?

13   What organizations and agencies have rules of conduct that must be observed when practising public accounting? internal auditing? management accounting? fraud examination?

14   What penalties can be imposed on CAs by provincial institutes in their "self-regulation" of ethical code violators?

15   What penalties can be imposed by the CPAB on PAs who violate rules of conduct?

CONSEQUENCES OF UNETHICAL/ILLEGAL ACTS

Ethics is serious business. Several sectors of professional and public activity exist under general clouds of suspicion. Even though many practitioners of accounting, business management, finance, journalism, law, medicine, and politics conduct themselves in an exemplary fashion, some people hold generally unfavourable perceptions of them. PAs used to rank near the top of trustworthy professions, but in the post-Enron environment since 2002 one could argue they have moved down in the rankings (see Chapter 1). This is a major problem because, without the public's confidence, the accounting profession cannot meet the public interest.

However, conforming to rules of ethical behaviour is not always easy. A reason for this is the potential conflicts in the rules. The most troublesome potential conflict lies between the rules related to confidentiality on the one hand, and the prohibition against association with misleading information on the other. Whenever there is a conflict of interest situation for the auditor, there is a potential to create a threat to the auditor's independent state of mind. Brooks identified the following deficiencies in professional codes of conduct:

- No or insufficient prioritization is put forward to resolve conflicting interests.
- Consultation on ethical matters is encouraged for some members, but is inhibited for others.
- A fair reporting/hearing process is not indicated, so members are uncertain whether to come forward.
- Protection is not offered to a whistle-blower.
- Sanctions are often unclear, and their applicability is not defined.
- Resolution mechanisms for conflicts between professionals and firms, or employers, or employing corporations are not put forward.[24]

According to an article by Sandra Rubin, the latest round of mergers among the accounting firms is making these deficiencies even more critical to the integrity of the financial reporting system.[25] The problem is the perception of increased conflict of interest and the fact is the problem, along with the fact that the merged firms will be so big that no single nation (or national body) will be able to regulate them. The role of the International Organization of Securities Commissions (IOSCO) will likely increase the future regulation of the huge international PA firms.

CHAPTER APPLICATION CASE

LEARNING OBJECTIVE
5 Apply and integrate the
chapter topics to analyze
a practical auditing situ-
ation/case/scenario.

There are two boxes near the beginning of this chapter. One is entitled "To Tell or Not to Tell?" and the other is called "Conflicting Duties." How would you resolve the ethical dilemmas presented in these cases?

[24]L. J. Brooks, *Professional Ethics for Accountants* (Minneapolis/St. Paul: West Publishing Company: 1995), p.126.
[25]S. Rubin, *Financial Post*, November 13, 1997.

APPLICATION CASE AND ANALYSIS:
TO TELL OR NOT TO TELL?

The key issue in the first scenario is the "innocent mistake." It does not take much moral imagination to sympathize with the cashier's plight. The president of the company, on the other hand, has a reasonable expectation to keep the risk of mistakes acceptably low. Rather than blaming the cashier, the root of the problem might be in the petty cash system. Has the cashier been properly trained in the way petty cash funds work? Is the petty cash fund too large or replenished too infrequently. Are there proper reconciliation procedures for the fund? By focusing on the system rather than on the cashier, the auditor can minimize mistakes and save the cashier's job. The critical thinking steps from Exhibit 4–1 involved here are steps 3, 4, and 5. The claims made by the various parties are as follows: cashier—innocent mistakes are impossible to avoid; the president—innocent mistakes can be avoided; and the auditor—innocent as well as intentional mistakes can be avoided with proper procedures, training, and controls.

APPLICATION CASE AND ANALYSIS:
CONFLICTING DUTIES

For the second case, we can apply the IFAC framework as it relates to auditor effectiveness. This case is an example of a false dilemma, as it is a situation that could easily have been avoided through the use of some forward thinking and moral imagination. Although IFAC does not mention it, moral imagination is at the heart of the thinking process behind identifying threats to fundamental principles. If the public accountant had warned the board of the confidentiality principle and its consequences to them, there would be no dilemma as the public accountant would not have to reveal confidential information. As it stands now, the public accountant should reveal that she or he has a conflict, without revealing the confidential information. The board can then decide if it is willing to keep the accountant as a director.

The problem remaining for the PA is then one of integrity and possible association with misleading information by not revealing the problem loan. IFAC argues for avoiding the conflict entirely, most likely through resigning from the board once the PA is aware of the confidential information.

In some cases it may be too late to resign, and then the accountant may have a conflict of principles. The framework would be improved if it contained a hierarchy of principles so that, in cases such as this one, when a conflict is unavoidable, the hierarchy would determine which principle has "conceptual primacy," to borrow a term from accounting frameworks. In this chapter, we have suggested that the primary principle should be that of not being associated with misleading information. That means either avoiding such associations, or making sure the misleading information has been corrected.

SUMMARY
. . . .

This chapter began with considerations of moral philosophy, explained the provincial rules of professional conduct, and ended with the agencies and organizations that enforce the rules governing PAs' behaviour.

Professional ethics for PAs is not simply a matter covered by a few rules in a formal code of professional conduct. Concepts of proper professional conduct permeate all areas of practice. Ethics and its accompanying disciplinary potential are the foundation for PAs' self-regulatory efforts.

Your knowledge of philosophical principles in ethics will help you make decisions about the provincial rules of professional conduct. This structured approach to thoughtful decisions is important not only when you are employed in public accounting but also when you work in government, industry, and education. The ethics rules may appear to be restrictive, but they are intended for the benefit of the public as well as for the discipline of PAs.

PAs must be careful in all areas of practice. Regulators' views on ethics rules may differ in several aspects from the provincial institute views. As an accountant, you must not lose sight of the nonaccountants' perspective. No matter how complex or technical a decision may be, a simplified view of it always tends to cut away the details of special technical issues to get directly to the heart of the matter. A sense of professionalism coupled with sensitivity to the impact of decisions on other people is invaluable in the practice of accounting and auditing.

Finally, it should be noted that there is a strong link between codes of conduct and GAAS. In fact, codes of conduct can be viewed as a means of fulfilling auditor responsibilities for GAAS and assurance standards. For example, the first GAAS standard, which relates to the personal attributes of the auditor (see Chapter 2), closely corresponds to the ethical principles of integrity, objectivity, independence, professional competence, and due care discussed previously. The dominance of ethical issues over accounting or auditing techniques is increasingly being recognized throughout the profession. Most audit failures appear to be attributable to poor professional judgment, at least in hindsight, that arise from improper consideration of conflicts of interest on various disclosure and measurement issues.[26] Critical thinking helps address this problem, at least for the most contentious issues.

MULTIPLE-CHOICE QUESTIONS FOR PRACTICE AND REVIEW

MC 1 Auditors are interested in having independence in appearance because
  a. they want to impress the public with their independence in fact.
  b. they want the public at large to have confidence in the profession.
  c. they need to comply with the standards of field work of GAAS.
  d. audits should be planned, and assistants, if any, need to be properly supervised.

MC 2 If a PA says she always follows the rule that requires adherence to CICA pronouncements in order to give a standard unqualified audit report, she is following a philosophy characterized by
  a. the imperative principle in ethics.
  b. the utilitarian principle in ethics.
  c. the generalization principle in ethics.
  d. reliance on one's inner conscience.

MC 3 Which of the following "committees" have been authorized to discipline members in violation of the rules of professional conduct?
  a. CICA Committee on Professional Ethics
  b. Appeals Committee
  c. Discipline Committee
  d. Professional Conduct Committee

MC 4 Which of the following bodies does not have any power to punish individual members for violations of the rules of professional conduct?
  a. CICA
  b. Canada Revenue Agency
  c. OSC
  d. ICAO

MC 5 Phil Greb has a thriving practice in which he assists lawyers in preparing litigation dealing with accounting and auditing matters. Phil is "practising public accounting" if he
  a. uses his PA designation on his letterhead and business card.
  b. is in partnership with another PA.
  c. practises in a limited partnership with other PAs.
  d. never lets his clients know that he is a PA.

MC 6 The ICAO should remove its general prohibition against PAs taking commissions and contingent fees because

  a. CAs prefer more price competition to less.
  b. commissions and contingent fees enhance audit independence.
  c. the Charter of Rights will force the change anyway.
  d. objectivity is not always necessary in accounting and auditing services.

MC 7 PA Smith is the auditor of Ajax Corporation. Her audit independence will not be considered impaired if she
  a. owns $1,000 worth of Ajax shares.
  b. has a husband who owns $2,000 worth of Ajax shares.
  c. has a sister who is the financial vice-president of Ajax.
  d. owns $1,000 worth of the shares of Pericles Corporation, which is controlled by Ajax as a result of Ajax's ownership of 40 percent of Pericles's shares, and Pericles contributes 3 percent of the total assets and income in Ajax's financial statements.

MC 8 When a client's financial statements contain a material departure from a *CICA Handbook* Accounting Recommendation and the PA believes that disclosure is necessary to make the statements not misleading, the PA
  a. must qualify the audit report for a departure from GAAP.
  b. can explain why the departure is necessary, and then give an unqualified opinion paragraph in the audit report.
  c. must give an adverse audit report.
  d. can give the standard unqualified audit report with an unqualified opinion paragraph.

MC 9 Which of the following would not be considered confidential information obtained in the course of an engagement and for which the client's consent would be needed for disclosure?
  a. Information about whether a consulting client has paid the PA's fees on time
  b. The actuarial assumptions used by a tax client in calculating pension expense
  c. Management's strategic plan for next year's labour negotiations
  d. Information about material contingent liabilities relevant for audited financial statements

MC 10 Which of the following would probably not be considered an "act discreditable to the profession"?
  a. Numerous moving traffic violations
  b. Failing to file the PA's own tax return

---

[26] L. J. Brooks, *Professional Ethics for Accountants* (Minneapolis/St. Paul: West Publishing Company, 1995), p. 69; also see S. Gunz and J. McCutcheon, "Some Unresolved Ethical Issues in Auditing," *Journal of Business Ethics*, 1991.

c. Filing a fraudulent tax return for a client in a severe financial difficulty

d. Refusing to hire Asian Canadians in an accounting practice

MC 11 The U.S. Securities and Exchange Commission would consider an audit firm's independence not impaired in which of the following situations?

a. A partner completed the client's audit in January, retired from the firm in March, and became a member of the former client's board of directors in August.

b. A partner who had been in charge of the firm's national audit co-ordination office retired in May 2000, and became a member of the board of directors of one of the firm's clients in August 2002.

c. A partner in the firm has a father-in-law who is the warehouse supervisor for an audit client.

d. The audit firm helped the client perform data processing for three months during the current year in connection with preparing financial statements to be filed with the SEC.

MC 12 A PA's legal licence to practice public accounting can be revoked by which organization?

a. the CICA

b. provincial institute of PAs

c. Auditing Standards Board

d. provincial securities commissions

MC 13 A PA's independence would not be considered impaired if he had

a. owned common shares of the audit client but sold them before the company became a client.

b. sold short his common shares of an audit client while working on the audit engagement.

c. served as the company's treasurer for six months during the year covered by the audit but resigned before the company became a client.

d. performed the bookkeeping and financial statement preparation for the company, which had no accounting personnel, and a president with no understanding of accounting principles.

MC 14 When a PA knows that a tax client has skimmed cash receipts and not reported the income in the federal income tax return, but he signs the return as a PA who prepared the return, that PA has violated which rule of professional conduct?

a. Confidential Client Information

b. Integrity and Objectivity

c. Independence

d. Accounting Principles

Exercises and Problems

EP 1
LO.3
Independence, Integrity, and Objectivity Cases.
Knowledge of the rules of conduct and related interpretations on independence, integrity, and objectivity will help you respond to the following cases. For each case, state whether or not the action or situation shows violation of the rules of professional conduct, explain why, and cite the relevant rule or interpretation.

a. R. Stout, PA, performs the audit of the local symphony society. Because of her good work, she was elected an honorary member of the board of directors.

b. N. Wolfe, a retired partner of your PA firm, has just been appointed to the board of directors of Palmer Corporation, your firm's client. Wolfe is also an ex officio member of your firm's income tax advisory committee, which meets monthly to discuss income tax problems of the partnership's clients, some of which are competitors of Palmer Corporation. The partnership pays Wolfe $100 for each committee meeting attended and a monthly retirement benefit, fixed by a retirement plan policy, of $1,000.

(AICPA adapted)

c. Archie Goodwin, PA, performs significant day-to-day bookkeeping services for Harper Corporation and supervises the work of the one part-time bookkeeper employed by Marvin Harper. This year, Marvin wants to engage PA Goodwin to perform an audit.

d. PA Fritz's wife owns 20 percent of the common shares of Botacel Company, which wants Fritz to perform the audit for the calendar year ended December 31, 2007.

e. Fritz's wife gave her shares to their 10-year-old daughter on July 1, 2007.

f. Fritz's daughter, acting through an appropriate custodian, sold the shares to her grandfather on August 1, 2007. His purchase, as an accommodation, took one-half of his retirement savings.

g. Fritz's father managed to sell the shares on August 15 to his brother, who lives in Brazil. The brother fled there 20 years ago and has not returned.

h. Clyde Brenner is a manager in the Regina office of a large national PA firm. His wife, Bonnie, is assistant controller in ATC Corporation, a client of the firm whose audit is performed by the New York office. Bonnie and Clyde live in Rhode Island and commute to their respective workplaces.

i. Clyde Brenner just received word that he has been admitted to the partnership.

j. The Rockhard Trust Company, a client of your firm, privately told your local managing partner that a block of funds would be set aside for home loans for qualified new employees. Rockhard's president is well aware that your firm experiences some difficulty hiring good people in the midsize but growing community and is willing to do what he can to help while mortgage money is so tight. Several new assistant accountants obtained home loans under this arrangement.

EP 2   **Independence, Integrity, and Objectivity Cases.**
LO.3   Knowledge of the rules of conduct, interpretations thereof, and related rulings on independence, integrity, and objectivity will help you respond to the following cases. For each case, state whether or not the action or situation shows violation of the rules of professional conduct, explain why, and cite the relevant rule or interpretation.

a. Your client, Contrary Corporation, is very upset over the fact that your audit last year failed to detect an $800,000 inventory overstatement caused by employee theft and falsification of the records. The board discussed the matter and authorized its lawyers to explore the possibility of a lawsuit for damages.

b. Contrary Corporation filed a lawsuit alleging negligent audit work, seeking $1 million in damages.

c. In response to the lawsuit by Contrary, you decided to start litigation against certain officers of the company, alleging management fraud and deceit. You are asking for a damages judgment of $500,000.

d. The Allright Insurance company paid Contrary Corporation $700,000 under fidelity bonds covering the employees involved in the inventory theft. Both you and Contrary Corporation have dropped your lawsuits. However, under subrogation rights, Allright has sued your audit firm for damages on the grounds of negligent performance of the audit.

e. Colt & Associates, PAs, audit Gore Company. Ms. Colt and Bill Gore (president) found a limited real estate partnership deal that looked too good to pass up. Colt purchased limited partnership interests amounting to 23 percent of all such interests, and Gore personally purchased 31 percent. Unrelated investors held the remaining 46 percent. Colt and Gore congratulate themselves on the opportunity and agree to be passive investors with respect to the partnership.

f. A group of dissident shareholders filed a class-action lawsuit against both you and your client, Amalgamated Inc., for $30 million. They allege there was a conspiracy to present misleading financial statements in connection with a recent merger.

g. PA Anderson, a partner in the firm of Anderson, Olds & Watershed (a professional accounting corporation), owns 25 percent of the common shares of Dove Corporation (not a client of AO&W). This year Dove purchased a 32 percent interest in Tale Company and is accounting for the investment using the equity method of accounting. The investment amounts to 11 percent of Dove's consolidated net assets. Tale Company has been an audit client of AO&W for 12 years.

h. Durkin & Panzer, PAs, regularly perform the audit of the North Country Bank, and the firm is preparing for the audit of the financial statements for the year ended December 31, 2007.

i. Two directors of the North Country Bank became partners in D&P, PAs, on July 1, 2007, resigning their directorship on that date. They will not participate in the audit.

j. During 2007, the former controller of the North Country Bank, now a partner of D&P, was frequently called on for assistance regarding loan approvals and the bank's minimum chequing account policy. In addition, he conducted a computer feasibility study for North Country.

(AICPA adapted)

k. The Cather Corporation is indebted to a PA for unpaid fees and has offered to give the PA unsecured interest-bearing notes. Alternatively, Cather Corporation offered to give two shares of its common stock, after which 10,002 shares would be outstanding.

(AICPA adapted)

l. Johnny Keems is not yet a PA but is doing quite well in this first employment with a large PA firm. He's been on the job two years and has become a "heavy junior." If he passes the PA exam in September, he will be promoted to senior accountant. This month, during the audit of Row Lumber Company, Johnny told the controller about how he is remodelling an old house. The controller likes Johnny and has a load of needed materials delivered to the house, billing Johnny at a 70 percent discount—a savings over the normal cash discount of about $300. Johnny paid the bill and was happy to have the materials, which he otherwise would not have been able to afford on his meager salary.

m. PA Lily Rowan inherited $1 million from her grandfather, $100,000 of which was the value of shares in the North Country Bank. Lily practices accounting in Hamilton, and several of her audit clients have loans from the bank.

n. Groaner Corporation is in financial difficulty. You are about to sign the report on the current audit when your firm's office manager informs you that the audit fee for last year has not yet been paid.

o. Your audit client, Glow Company, is opening a plant in a distant city. Glow's president asks that your firm's office in that city recruit and hire a new plant controller and a cost accountant.

EP 3   **General and Technical Rule Cases.** Knowledge of the
LO.2   rules of conduct, interpretations thereof, and resolutions of Council related to general and technical standards will help you respond to the following cases. For each case, state whether or not the action or situation shows violation of the ICAO rules of professional conduct, explain why, and cite the relevant rule or interpretation.

a. P. Stebbins, PA, helped Price Corporation prepare a cash flow forecast of hospital operations. The forecast was presented by Stebbins at a city council hearing for approval under the city's health services ordinance. Stebbins's report, which accompanied the forecast, consisted entirely of a full description of the sources of information used and the major assumptions made but did not include a disclaimer on the achievability of the forecast.

b. Kim Philby of Philby & Burgess, PAs, received a telephone call from his friend John, who is financial vice-president of U.K. Auto Parts. U.K. distributes parts over a wide area and does about $40 million of business a year. U.K. is not a client but is audited by Anderson, Olds & Watershed CAs, a venerable firm in the city. Kim has been hoping that John would switch auditors. Today John wants to get Kim's opinion about accounting for lease capitalizations related to a particularly complicated agreement with franchise dealers. Kim makes notes and promises to call John tomorrow.

c. PA Maclean gave a standard unqualified audit report on the financial statements of Anglo Korp. The annual report document did not contain supplementary oil and gas reserve information required by the *Handbook*.

d. Saul Panzer is a former university football player. Saul is a PA who works for Aggregate Corporation, which owns controlling interests in 42 other corporations. Theodolinda Bonner, president of Aggregate, has assigned Saul the task of performing audits of these corporations and submitting audit opinions directly to her for later presentation to the board of directors.

e. PA Blunt audits the Huber Hope Company. Huber's controller, also a PA, has conducted his own audit of Little Hope, Inc., Huber's single subsidiary, which amounts to 10 percent of the total assets, revenue, and income of the consolidated entity. Blunt has written an audit report that carefully explains reliance on "part of examination made by other independent auditors," with added language to explain the controller's role.

EP 4 **Responsibilities to Clients' Cases.** Knowledge of the
LO.3 rules of conduct and interpretations thereof on confidential client information and contingent fees will help you respond to the following cases. For each case, state whether or not the action or situation shows violation of the ICAO rules of professional conduct, explain why, and cite the relevant rule or interpretation.

a. PA Sally Colt has discovered a way to eliminate most of the boring work of processing routine accounts receivable confirmations by contracting with the Cohen Mail Service. After the auditor has prepared the confirmations, Cohen will stuff them in envelopes, mail them, receive the return replies, open the replies and return them to Sally.

b. Cadentoe Corporation, without consulting its PA, has changed its accounting so that it is not in conformity with generally accepted accounting principles. During the regular audit engagement, the PA discovers that the statements based on the accounts are so grossly misleading that they might be considered fraudulent. PA Cramer resigns from the engagement after a heated argument. Cramer knows that the statements will be given to John Cairncross, his friend at the Last National Bank, and knows that John is not a very astute reader of complicated financial statements. Two days later, Cairncross calls Cramer and asks some general questions about Cadentoe's statements and remarks favourably on the very thing that is misrepresented. Cramer corrects the erroneous analysis, and Cairncross is very much surprised.

c. A PA who had reached retirement age arranged for the sale of his practice to another public accountant. Their agreement called for the transfer of all working papers and business correspondence to the accountant purchasing the practice.

d. Martha Jacoby, PA, withdrew from the audit of Harvard Company after discovering irregularities in Harvard's income tax returns. One week later, Ms. Jacoby was telephoned by Jake Henry, PA, who explained that he had just been retained by Harvard Company to replace Ms. Jacoby. Mr. Henry asked Ms. Jacoby why she withdrew from the Harvard engagement. She told him.

e. Amos Fiddle, PA, prepared an uncontested claim for a tax refund on Faddle Corporation's amended tax return. The fee for the service was 30 percent of the amount that the Canada Revenue Agency rules to be a proper refund. The claim was for $300,000.

f. After Faddle had won a $200,000 refund and Fiddle collected the $60,000 fee, Jeremy Faddle, the president, invited Amos Fiddle to be the auditor for Faddle Corporation.

EP 5 **Other Responsibilities and Practices Cases.** Knowledge
LO.2 of the rules of conduct and interpretations thereof regarding various other responsibilities and practices will help you respond to the following cases. For each case, state whether or not the action or situation shows violation or potential for violation of the ICAO rules of professional conduct, explain why, and cite the relevant rule or interpretation.

a. R. Stout, PA, completed a review of the unaudited financial statements of Wolfe Gifts. Ms. Wolfe was very displeased with the report. An argument ensued, and she told Stout never to darken her door again. Two days later, she telephoned Stout and demanded he return (1) Wolfe's cash disbursement journal, (2) Stout's working paper schedule of adjusting journal entries, (3) Stout's inventory analysis working papers, and (4) all other working papers prepared by Stout. Since Wolfe had not yet paid her bill, Stout replied that provincial law gave him a lien on all the records and that he would return them as soon as she had paid his fee.

b. The PA firm of Durkin & Panzer had received promissory notes in payment of the Henshaw Hacksaw company tax return preparation fee. Six months after the notes were due, PA Durkin notified Dave Henshaw that the notes had been turned over to the North Country Bank for collection.

c. PA Panzer has been invited to conduct a course in effective tax planning for the City Chamber of Commerce. The C. of C. president said a brochure would be mailed to members giving the name of Panzer's firm, his educational background and degrees held, professional society affiliations, and testimonials from participants in the course held last year comparing his excellent performance with that of other PAs who have offered competing courses in the city.

d. PA Philby is a member of the provincial bar. Her practice is a combination of law and accounting, and she is heavily involved in estate planning engagements. Her letterhead gives the affiliations: Member, Provincial Bar of —, and Member, CICA.

e. The PA firm of Burgess & Maclean has made a deal with Cairncross & Company, a firm of management consulting specialists, for mutual business advantage. B&M agreed to recommend Cairncross to clients who need management consulting services. Cairncross agreed to recommend B&M to clients who need improvements in their accounting systems. During the year, both firms would keep records of fees obtained by these mutual referrals. At the end of the year, Cairncross and B&M would settle the net differences based on a referral rate of 5 percent of fees.

f. Sturm & Drang, PAs, conduct an aggressive, growing practice in Middle City. The firm pays 20 percent of first-year fees to any staff member (below partner) who brings in a new client.

g. Jack Robinson and Archie Robertson (both PAs) are not partners, but they have the same office, the same employees, and a joint bank account, and they work together on audits. A letterhead they use shows both their names and the description "Members, ICAO."

h. PA Dewey retired from the two-person firm of Dewey & Cheatham. One year later, D&C merged practices with Howe & Company, to form a regional firm under the name of Dewey, Cheatham & Howe Company.

i. Fritz Brenner, PA, died and widow Brenner inherited the interest he had in the PA firm of Brenner & Horstmann, P.C. Can widow Brenner share in the partnership as a passive investment? She is not a PA.

EP 6   Rules of Professional Conduct

LO.2

Required:

For each of the following completely independent situations, describe the rules of professional conduct that are relevant. Have they been violated? Support your conclusion.

Situation A

Randi Woode, PA, was working on the year-end audit of her client, Pads N' Pens (PNP). PNP is an office stationery retailer with a July 31 year-end. She was having difficulty completing the audit because some accounting records for the months of April and May had been destroyed in a fire. She told the owner-manager of PNP, Joe Smith, that she might have to qualify her audit report because of her inability to substantiate some of the balances on the financial statements. Joe pointed out that he had been her client for eight years and that she knew him to be honest and trustworthy. He also said a qualified report would harm his negotiations with the bank for additional loans. After considering PNP's need for

additional financing, as well as their long-standing relationship, Randi agreed to issue an unqualified report.

Situation B

Lori Wilkes is an audit senior with a large PA firm in Toronto. She has learned that one of her largest clients, Superior Motors Ltd. (SML), is planning to acquire Steelco Inc. SML is Canada's largest automobile manufacturer, and Steelco is one of SML's biggest steel suppliers. Lori is confident that SML's acquisition of Steelco will reduce SML's costs dramatically, and that, as a result, SML's share price will rise. She has, therefore, encouraged her boyfriend, Tom, to buy some shares while being careful not to divulge the real reasons behind her recommendation.

Situation C

After obtaining his PA designation, Larry Wilde decided to set up his own public accounting practice. He reasoned that naming his practice "Quality Chartered Accountancy Services" would best attract new clients.

(ICAO adapted)

EP 7   Rules of Professional Conduct. In mid-May, Aileen

LO.2 Macdonald, PA, received a phone call from one of her largest clients, a manufacturer. The client wanted to know more details about the impact that the GST would have on his 2001 operations and financial statements. When Aileen and the client had discussed the results of the 1999 audit last February, part of their conversation had dealt with the tax. Aileen had indicated that she would be sending a newsletter about the tax by July 1.

Since February there had been more changes to the legislation, which Aileen and her partners hadn't had time to absorb. However, Aileen had registered for the annual June provincial conference, where she would attend the four technical sessions on the GST. She planned to ask questions about her client's situation during the question-and-answer periods that followed each session.

Aileen explained to the client that she would have more information within a month and would contact him then. At that time, she will ask the client for names of firms that might be interested in receiving her newsletter.

Required:

Which rules of professional conduct are relevant in the above situation? Discuss the rules with which Aileen Macdonald is in compliance as well as those she may have violated.

(ICAO adapted)

DISCUSSION CASES

DC 1   General Ethics. Is there any moral difference between a

LO.1 disapproved action in which you are caught and the same action that never becomes known to anyone else? Do many persons in business and professional society make a distinction between these two circumstances? If you respond that you do (or do not) perceive a difference while persons in business and professional society do not (or do), then how do you explain the differences in attitudes?

DC 2   Ethics Decision Problem. You are treasurer of a church.

LO.1 A member approaches you with the following proposition: "I will donate shares to the church on December 31, if, on January 1, you will sell them back to me. All you will need to do is convey the certificate with your signature to me in return for my cheque, which will be for the asking price of the shares quoted that day without reduction for commissions."

The member's objective, of course, is to obtain the income tax deduction as of December 31, but he wants to maintain his ownership interest. The policy of the church board is not to hold any shares but to sell shares within a reasonably short time.

Consider:

a. Should the treasurer accommodate the member? Would you if you were treasurer?

b. Would your considerations and conclusions be any different if the church
1. was financially secure and the gift was small?
2. was financially secure and the gift was large?
3. would be in deficit position for the year were it not for the gift?

DC 3
LO.2

Competition and Audit Proposals. Accounting firms are often asked to present "proposals" to companies' boards of directors. These proposals are comprehensive booklets, accompanied by oral presentations, telling about the firm's personnel, technology, special qualifications, and expertise in hope of convincing the board to award the work to the firm.

Dena has a new job as staff assistant to Michael, chairman of the board of Granof Grain Company. The company has a policy of engaging new auditors every seven years. The board will hear oral proposals from 12 accounting firms. This is the second day of the three-day meeting. Dena's job is to help evaluate the proposals. Yesterday, the proposal by Anderson, Olds & Watershed was clearly the best.

Then Dena sees Michael's staff chief, a brash go-getter, slip a copy of the AOW written proposal into an envelope. He tells Dena to take it to a friend who works for Hunt and Hunt, a PA firm scheduled to make its presentation tomorrow. He says, "I told him we'd let him glance at the best proposal." Michael is absent from the meeting and will not return for two hours.

What should Dena do? What should PA Hunt do if he receives the AOW proposal, assuming he has time to modify the Hunt and Hunt proposal before tomorrow's presentation?

DC 4
LO.2

Engagement Timekeeping Records. A time budget is always prepared for audit engagements. Numbers of hours are estimated for various segments of the work—for example, internal control evaluation, cash, inventory, report review, and the like. Audit supervisors expect the work segments to be completed within budget, and staff accountants' performance is evaluated in part on ability to perform audit work efficiently within budget.

Sarah is an audit manager who has worked hard to get promoted. She hopes to become a partner in two or three years. Finishing audits on time weighs heavily on her performance evaluation. She assigned the cash audit work to Craig, who has worked for the firm for 10 months. Craig hopes to get a promotion and salary raise this year. Twenty hours were budgeted for the cash work. Craig is efficient, but it took 30 hours to finish because the company had added seven new bank accounts. Craig was worried about his performance evaluation, so he

recorded 20 hours for the cash work and put the other 10 hours under the internal control evaluation budget.

What do you think about Craig's resolution of his problem? Was his action a form of lying? What would you think of his action if the internal control evaluation work was presented "under budget" because it was not yet complete, and another assistant was assigned to finish that work segment later?

DC 5
LO.2

Audit Overtime. All accountants' performance evaluations are based in part on their ability to do audit work efficiently and within the time budget planned for the engagement. New staff accountants, in particular, usually have some early difficulty learning speedy work habits, which demand that no time be wasted.

Elizabeth started work for Anderson, Olds & Watershed in September. After attending the staff training school, she was assigned to the Rising Sun Company audit. Her first work assignment was to complete the extensive recalculation of the inventory compilation, using the audit test counts and audited unit prices for several hundred inventory items. Her time budget for the work was six hours. She started at 4 p.m. and was not finished when everyone left the office at 6 p.m. Not wanting to stay downtown alone, she took all the necessary working papers home. She resumed work at 8 p.m. and finished at 3 a.m. The next day, she returned to the Rising Sun offices, put the completed working papers in the file, and recorded six hours in the time budget/actual schedule. Her supervisor was pleased, especially about her diligence in taking the work home.

What do you think about Elizabeth's diligence and her understatement of the time she took to finish the work? What if she had received help at home from her husband? What if she had been unable to finish and had left the work at home for her husband to finish while he took off a day from his job interviews?

EP 6
LO.2

Form of Practice, Technical Standards, and Confidentiality. Knowledge of the rules of conduct and interpretations thereof will help you respond to this case problem.

Gilbert and Bradley formed a corporation called Financial Services Inc. Each took 50 percent of the authorized common shares. Gilbert is a PA and a member of the provincial institute. Bradley is a CPCU (Chartered Property Casualty Underwriter). The corporation performs auditing and tax services under Gilbert's direction and insurance services under Bradley's supervision. The opening of the corporation's office was announced in a full-page advertisement in the local newspaper.

One of the corporation's first audit clients was the Grandtime Company. Grandtime had total assets of $600,000 and total liabilities of $270,000. In the course of the audit, Gilbert found that Grandtime's building with a book value of $240,000 was pledged as a security for a 10-year term note in the amount of $200,000. The client's statement did not mention that the building was pledged as security for the 10-year term note. However, as the failure to disclose the lien did not affect either the value of the assets or the amount of the liabilities, and the audit was satisfactory in all other respects, Gilbert rendered an unqualified opinion on Grandtime's financial statements. About two months after the date of his opinion, Gilbert learned that an insurance company was planning to lend Grandtime $150,000 in the form of a first-mortgage note on the building. Realizing the insurance company was unaware of the existing lien on the building, Gilbert had Bradley notify the insurance company of the fact that Grandtime's building was pledged as security for the term note.

Shortly after the events described above, Gilbert was charged with several violations of professional ethics.

Required:
Identify and discuss the rules of professional conduct violated by Gilbert and the nature of the violations.

(AICPA adapted)

DC 7
LO.2
Rules of Professional Conduct. You and Laura Cooper are the two partners of a PA firm in Ottawa. After your two-week Caribbean vacation, you return to the office to discover that your secretary is busily preparing to mail some brochures. You have never seen the brochures before and your secretary explains that Laura had them printed during your absence. The brochures are colourful and glossy and the name of your firm is boldly displayed on the front cover. You pick up a brochure and notice that it describes your firm as "the PA firm where clients always come first." On the last page of the brochure, readers are advised that new audit clients will not be charged a fee for any management consulting services provided in the first full year.

You ask Laura about the brochures, and she tells you that she had them specially designed and printed to increase the firm's profile and competitiveness. She believes that mailing these brochures to all the top companies in Ottawa will not only increase the firm's client base but will also help it develop a high-quality image by getting a reputation for obtaining the "best clients." Furthermore, she plans to contact all recipients of the brochure in a few weeks to arrange a follow-up meeting to discuss their accounting and auditing needs.

Required:
Describe which rules of professional conduct may have been violated, and indicate your professional responsibilities and course of action.

(ICAO adapted)

DC 8
LO.3
Conflict of Clients' Interests. Jon Williams, PA, has found himself in the middle of the real-life soap opera "Taxing Days of Our Lives."

The cast of characters:
Oneway Corporation is Jon's audit and tax client. The three directors are the officers and also the only three shareholders, each owning exactly one-third of the shares.

President Jack founded the company and is now nearing retirement. As an individual, he is also Jon's tax client.

Vice-president Jill manages the day-to-day operations. She has been instrumental in enlarging the business and its profits. Jill's individual tax work is done by PA Phil.

Treasurer Bill has been a long-term, loyal employee and has been responsible for many innovative financial transactions and reports of great benefit to the business. He is Jon's close personal friend and also an individual tax client.

The conflict:
President Jack discussed with PA Jon the tax consequences to him as an individual of selling his one-third interest in Oneway Corporation to vice-president Jill. Later, meeting with Bill to discuss his individual tax problems, Jon learns that Bill fears that Jack and Jill will make a deal, put him in a minority position, and force him out of the company. Bill says, "Jon, we have been friends a long time. Please keep me informed about Jack's plans, even rumours. My interest in Oneway Corporation represents my life savings and my resources for the kids' university. Remember, you're little Otto's godfather."

Thinking back, Jon realized that vice-president Jill has always been rather hostile. Chances are that Phil would get the Oneway engagement if Jill acquires Jack's shares and controls the corporation. Nevertheless, Bill will probably suffer a great deal if he cannot learn about Jack's plans, and Jon's unwillingness to keep him informed will probably ruin their close friendship.

Later, on a dark and stormy night:

Jon ponders the problem. "Oneway Corporation is my client, but a corporation is a fiction. Only a form. The shareholders personify the real entity, so they are collectively my clients, and I can transmit information among them as though they were one person. Right? On the other hand, Jack and Bill engage me for individual tax work, and information about one's personal affairs is really no business of the other. What to do? What to do?

Required:
Give Jon advice about alternative actions, considering the constraints of the ICAO's Rules of Conduct.

DC 9
LO.3
Independence and Management Responsibility for Financial Statements. PA has been engaged by Pinto Inc. for several years. His work involves compiling the monthly financial reports for Pinto's management and providing advice to Pinto's president on cost controls, taxes, and other financial reporting matters. PA has also performed a review engagement on the annual GAAP financial statements that are provided to the company's shareholders and its banker. As Pinto's business was growing rapidly, two years ago it hired a full-time CFO to handle the expanding accounting and reporting requirements. The CFO is a former banker who was laid off by the bank and was recommended for the job by Pinto's COO, an old school friend, even though he had never previously worked as a CFO. Over the two years that CFO has held the position, he has sought advice from PA on many accounting, tax, and reporting issues.

At first, PA thought the CFO was learning the job by asking all these questions. However, after two years the PA began to realize that the CFO was merely implementing whatever PA suggested, without questioning it. When PA insisted that the CFO complete various accounting and tax analyses for the current-year financial statements on his own, the CFO stalled at first and then finally admitted that he couldn't do the analyses. PA needed to work over the weekend to provide the required information so the company could file its tax returns and payroll tax information forms on time. As a result of these events, PA has become concerned that Pinto's management does not know enough about its own financial statements to take primary responsibility for them.

Just prior to the current year-end, the Pinto shareholders met to approve the appointment of PA as the company's independent accountant for another year. Pinto has three shareholders who each own 30 percent of the common shares, while 20 current and former employees own the remaining 10 percent. At this meeting, some of the shareholders expressed concern about the financial management at Pinto, and demanded that PA be engaged to audit the company's financial statements rather than just doing a review.

Required:

Discuss the professional issues raised in the above case. Assess whether or not PA should accept the audit engagement, and recommend an appropriate course of action for PA.

DC 10 CGA Code of Ethics. The issue of ethical conduct is becoming more and more important in the professional practice of PAs.

LO.1

Required:

a. Identify the sequence of steps that have been proposed for an auditor to follow in attempting to resolve an ethical dilemma.
b. What are the two broad aims of the CGA Code of Ethical Principles and Rules of Professional Conduct?
c. Briefly describe the three mechanisms by which the CGA Code of Ethical Principles and Rules of Professional Conduct work.

(CGA-Canada adapted)

DC 11 Independence. You are an audit manager with the firm of Wu, Potter and McKinley, PAs. You and Ray St. Claire, a manager with another PA firm, are having a discussion about auditor independence. Ray says, "On the one hand, the public seems to be demanding more and more assurance from us about more and more aspects of a client's operations, but to maintain our practice in today's environment we have to be competitive to be able to attract new clients."

LO.3

Required:

a. Identify and briefly explain the competitive practice on the part of auditors to which Ray is referring.
b. Why is this perceived as a threat to auditor independence and the quality of audits?

c. With reference to parts *a.* and *b.*, what could a client do, at least in theory, to take advantage of this situation? What is the reason this strategy might not work?
d. What does the CGA-Canada Code of Ethics say about this issue?

(CGA-Canada adapted)

DC 12 Audit Proposals. Smith and Mulberry (S&M) were asked by Behometh Ltd. to submit a proposal for its audit. This involved a 30-minute presentation to the board of directors and a written submission. The submission included a fixed-fee quote for the first two years, a detailed outline of the proposed audit strategy, and a list of the qualifications of the audit team to be assigned. Five other PA firms were invited to bid on the engagement. S&M put in a "lowball" bid because the partners saw this as a golden opportunity to get exposure in this industry.

LO.2

Several weeks later, Edgar Brown, chairman of the board, telephoned Mike Mulberry, congratulating him on being awarded the audit. The conversation went as follows:

Edgar: I'm pleased to offer you the engagement, Mike, and I want you to know you weren't the lowest bid. What really impressed us was your attitude and promise to give us personal attention. It's so refreshing to find an auditor who openly states there needs to be a completely harmonious relationship between auditor and client.

Mike: We're really pleased to be your auditors, Edgar. We were a little apprehensive about not having any experience in your industry.

Edgar: Well Mike, since you did indicate you would hire someone experienced to oversee the engagement, I really see no problem. I certainly support your idea of Stan Biggs, since he knows the industry inside out. We're a little sorry to lose him. He had only been with us two years since obtaining his PA and was a fine controller.

Mike: Yes, his knowledge of your operations should allow us to complete the audit in the minimal time.

Edgar: There is one favour you can do FOR us right away, Mike. We would like to start a national ad campaign that depicts our auditor slashing prices to the bone on our products. We would like you to be the auditor in that ad.

Mike: Acting's not really my strong suit, Edgar, but I'm sure we can accommodate you on that.

Edgar: By the way Mike, to show how much we value our auditors, I want to give you a key to the executive washroom, a special pass that allows you to park in restricted zones, and a letter that will give you folks an additional 25 percent off our employee store prices.

Mike: Thanks very much, Edgar.

(ICAO adapted)

The following week Mike went out to review the working papers of the predecessor auditors. He was shocked at the poor quality of work evident in these files. However, given the rule against criticism of fellow members, he believed it would be inappropriate to mention this to Behometh.

The audit went very smoothly. In fact, with Biggs in charge, S&M even managed to turn a profit on the job.

Several months later some information came to light, about which Mike was not sure he should worry. Although Biggs had severed all employment ties with Behometh prior to joining S&M, apparently he still retained 1,000 shares of voting stock in the company.

Required:

Discuss the ethical issues in this case.

(ICAO adapted)

DC 13 **Rules of Professional Conduct.** The Canada Revenue
LO.2 Agency was recently granted the power to impose new "preparer penalties" on individuals who have received payment for preparing a tax return in which the taxpayer is found to have understated its taxes payable. Tax preparers are liable for penalties of up to $100,000 if the CRA finds that the preparer was aware that the taypayer was under-reporting its taxes payable. Formerly, only the taxpayer could be penalized.

Required:

Given that the rules of conduct for professional accountants already prohibit PAs from being associated with false or misleading information and require them to conduct themselves with integrity, why do you think these preparer penalties were considered necessary by federal law makers?

DC 14 **Contingency Fees.** PA provides assurance on a forecast
LO.2 income statement included in a the prospectus for a public offering of shares of Mustang Inc. PA's engagement letter with Mustang states that the fee for the assurance report will be 10 percent of the proceeds of the share issue.

Required:

Discuss the appropriateness of this fee arrangement in light of the rules of professional conduct.

DC 15 **Forms of Public Accountants' Organizations.** Three
LO.2 forms of organization for public accountants are unlimited liability partnership, limited liability partnership, or limited liability professional corporation.

Required:

What are the pros and cons of each form from the perspective of public accountants in these firms and from the perspective of users of public accountants' assurance reports? In particular, consider the implications of these different organizational forms for public accountants' incentives to perform their functions with due care and with objectivity.

DC 16 **Public Accounting as a Career.** A and B, two 40-some-
LO.2 thing PAs, are raising a few glasses at the local pub to celebrate their 15 years in partnership, and are taking the opportunity to reflect over their choice of career.

A: All in all, I think public accounting has been a good career choice for me. I've been able to do very challenging, analytical work. I've had the opportunity to be very helpful to many business owners and have seen a number of my clients become millionaires—and I think I can give some of the credit for that to the good financial advice I gave them, especially in those really tough times when they didn't know how they were going to cover the next payroll! And I think my assurance reports added value to financial reports and were helpful to the people using them, even if I didn't even know specifically who those people were a lot of the time. But, at the same time, it's been really hard work and long hours, and I probably could have made more money with less effort if I had become a lawyer or a doctor.

B: I think you are probably right about that. Sometimes I think being a public accountant is like taking some kind of "vow of poverty." Our clients get rich, but we are only allowed to charge by the hour because otherwise, say if we took shares in our client's companies instead of fees or took a percentage of the tax savings we identify for them, we would lose our appearance of independence. To me the big irony of being a public accountant is that our duty is to serve the public, and so we need to stay independent of the clients we report on, but the public doesn't pay us—our clients do! If we are going to make a living at this we need to maximize our profitability, and yet it seems the rules of professional conduct are designed to prevent us from ever making a lot of money at this!

Required:

Discuss the views of the two PAs, that public accountants' duty to the public and operating a profit-oriented business are incompatible. Do you agree? Generate some possible solutions that would resolve the dilemma they see. Evaluate the solutions you have generated in terms of their effectiveness and practicality, given the context in which public accounting is practised and the public needs that it fills. Which of your possible solutions do you think would be the most practical and effective?

DC 17 Use the critical thinking framework to explain why serv-
LO.2 ing the public interest should be the most important principle for PAs.

DC 18 Explain how the independence principle can be derived
LO.3 from the critical thinking framework.

DC 19 Explain how insufficient reasons in audit documentation
LO.6 can lead to a fraudulent audit opinion.

DC 20 Use classical problems in moral theory to illustrate why, even with critical thinking, it may not always be possible to come up with good reasons for all actions.

CHAPTER

Legal Liability

In this chapter we will focus on the legal responsibilities of auditors. This chapter will help you understand PAs' legal liability for professional work, as dictated by the courts.

LEARNING OBJECTIVES

After completing this chapter, you will be able to do the following:

1. List some examples of potential civil and criminal litigation facing PAs.

2. Outline the various types of common law liability for PAs, citing specific case precedents.

3. Outline the various types of statutory law liability for PAs.

4. Apply and integrate the chapter topics to analyze a practical auditing situation/case/scenario.

5*. Recognize U.S. SEC, SOX, and other (statutory) law liability issues. (Appendix 5A)

* Learning Objectives marked with an asterisk (*) and their corresponding topics are considered advanced material. Note: Appendix 5A is located on the text Online Learning Centre.

THE LEGAL ENVIRONMENT

· · · · · · · · · · · · · · · ·

LEARNING OBJECTIVE

1 List some examples of potential civil and criminal litigation facing PAs.

In order to get our bearings on how the law affects auditors, we begin with an overview of the legal system. Law is essentially a social system for resolving conflicts. Conflicts between individuals (and corporations) that are settled in court are part of what is called private law or civil law. Disputes between an individual and the state, as well as those between states, or different levels of government, are settled in the part of the legal system called public law. Public law includes criminal law, administrative law, and constitutional law. All public law is codified by statute, passed by some level of government.

Common law refers to the system of law based primarily on previous judicial decisions; unlike public law, its laws have not been codified in statutes via legislation (statutory law). It is a distinctive part of the Anglo-American system of private/civil law used in Canada, the U.S., and most former colonies of the British Empire. There are several major categories of civil law: contracts (agreements or promises that create expectations for others), torts (civil wrongs such as negligent actions which create obligations for the offending party), and property (rights over goods and land). Common law liabilities for auditors arise from the law of contracts or, torts. Statutory law liabilities for auditors arise from administrative law related to economic regulation, and from criminal charges.

Because common law has been the main source of auditor liability in the past, most of this chapter is devoted to legal liability under common law. However, we also introduce you to the increasingly important liability arising from statutory law. SOX is an example of statutory law. This U.S. law is proving to be very influential in shaping legislation in Canada and around the world in the post-Enron environment, as we saw through some of the effects of SOX discussed in Chapter 1. In Canada, we have nothing like the Securities and Exchange Commission (SEC) Acts that were passed in the U.S. in the 1930s, but, as we will discuss in this chapter, we may be moving towards that. Other statutory law affecting accountants is the legislation prohibiting money laundering and payment of bribes. Under this legislation, PAs also have responsibilities to disclose such activities once they are aware of them. These responsibilities are also covered in this chapter and in Appendix 5A located on the text Online Learning Centre. The chapter ends with Appendix 5A, which introduces you to the SEC Acts and some influential court cases, both of which affect auditor liability. We review the U.S. experience because it is useful for providing some perspective on the likely future impact of recent Canadian securities legislation.

Legal liability has been increasing for all professionals, not just PAs. "Tort reform" has been a hot topic in the business and popular press. Record-setting damages have been awarded and professional liability insurance premiums have increased dramatically, or insurance is difficult to obtain. The problems affect everyone, from manufacturers to rock concert promoters and PAs. In the 1990s, payments for litigation were over four times greater than in the 1980s. Payments in the U.S. now run into the billions. Twenty-seven medium-sized accounting firms formed their own offshore captive insurance company in Bermuda to get adequate liability insurance.

PAs are potentially liable for monetary damages and even subject to criminal penalties (e.g., under SEC rules), including fines and jail terms, for failure to perform professional services properly. They can be sued by clients, clients' creditors, investors, and the government. Exposure to large lawsuit claims is possible through class actions permitted under federal rules in Canada and the United States. In a class action suit, any number of plaintiffs with small individual claims can bring suit for large damages in the name of an extended class. After a bankruptcy, for example, 40 bondholders who lost $40,000 might decide to sue, and they can sue on behalf of the entire class of bondholders for all their alleged losses (say $40 million). In some jurisdictions, lawyers will take such suits on a contingency fee basis (a percentage of the judgment, if any). The size of the claim and the zeal of the lawyers make the class action suit a serious matter. In the United States, class action suits have become such a problem that they threaten the existence of many firms. Arthur Andersen and some regional firms were forced into bankruptcy as a result of such litigation.

Lawsuit Causes and Frequency

One study of law cases showed that accountants' and auditors' legal troubles arose from five major types of errors. In 129 cases, 334 errors were found, classified as follows: (a) 33 percent involved misinterpretation of accounting principles, (b) 15 percent involved misinterpretation of auditing standards, (c) 29 percent involved faulty implementation of auditing procedures, (d) 13 percent involved client fraud, and (e) 7 percent involved fraud by the auditor.[1] These data suggest that accountants and auditors are exposed to liability for failure to report known departures from accounting principles, for failure to conduct audits properly, for failure to detect management fraud, and for actually being parties to frauds. Threat of lawsuits has also affected how PAs conduct their work in consulting services and tax practice; about 60 percent of civil damage suits arise from tax practice disputes. However, lawsuits related to audits tend to be "high cost" resulting in much higher claims.[2]

All litigation is serious and results in expenses for defence, but not all cases result in payments for damage. In fact, about 40 percent of the lawsuits in the period 1960–85 were dismissed or settled with no payment by the accounting firm. Another 30 percent were settled by payment of approximately $1 million or less. This leaves about 30 percent of the cases where the auditors paid significant damage awards. All these data relate exclusively to lawsuits over audit services.[3]

Audit Responsibilities

Many users of audit reports expect auditors to detect fraud, theft, and illegal acts, and to report them publicly. Auditors take responsibility for detecting material misstatements in financial statements; however, they are very cautious about taking responsibility for detecting fraud, and are especially cautious about accepting a public reporting responsibility. Fraud and misleading financial statements are large concerns of financial statement users. They are afraid of information risk due to intentional misstatements, and they want it reduced, even eliminated. Some of their expectations are very high, resulting in an expectation gap between the diligence users expect and the diligence auditors are able to accept.

The audit responsibility for detection of fraud in financial statements is a complex topic, as seen in Chapters 7 and 17. Auditors take some responsibility but not as much as many users expect. For example, see CAS 240, 250 (5135, 5136). This disparity leads to lawsuits, even when auditors have performed well.

REVIEW CHECKPOINTS

1   What are class action lawsuits, and why should auditors be concerned about them?

2   What are some causes of auditors becoming defendants in lawsuits?

3   What proportion of lawsuits against accountants relate to tax practice?

The next parts of this chapter cover PAs' legal liabilities under common law and statutory law. The principle of *stare decisis*, or to stand by a previous decision, is important to common law. The practical problem in many cases, however, is whether

---

[1] K. St. Pierre and J. Anderson, "An Analysis of Audit Failures Based on Documented Legal Cases," *Journal of Accounting, Auditing, and Finance,* Spring 1982, pp. 236–237.

[2] S. Andersen and J. Wolfe, "A Perspective on Audit Malpractice Claims," *Journal of Accountancy,* September 2002, p. 59.

[3] Z. Palmrose, "An Analysis of Auditor Litigation and Audit Service Quality," *Accounting Review,* January 1988, pp. 55–73.

the facts in a given case are similar enough to a precedent-setting one. Rarely are the facts exactly the same. Common law is "common knowledge," in the sense that judges tend to follow the collective wisdom of past cases. In contrast, statutory law is prohibitions enacted in statutes by a legislature—for example, the *Canada Business Corporations Act* and related provincial Corporations Acts. Most countries' laws arise from legislation (statutory law) rather than precedent (common law). Such legal systems are called Code-Law systems.

Until Enron, the major source of liability for PAs was under common law, but Enron changed all that. The fatal damage to Arthur Andersen seems to have been caused by the SEC, which charged the audit firm with securities fraud two years previous to Enron over its audit of Waste Management Company. It should be noted that SEC prosecutions are under statutory law. Andersen ultimately paid a $7 million fine in June 2001. This set the stage for Arthur Andersen's rapid loss of reputation when the Enron audit problems surfaced six months later. Andersen had already lost most of its big clients by the time of its conviction, which was overturned by the U.S. Supreme Court in 2005, and the accounting world was shocked and dazed by the speed of its disintegration.

Since Enron, the SEC appears to have become much more aggressive in imposing statutory legal liability. For example, on January 29, 2003, the SEC sued one of the Big Four firms for securities fraud, alleging that it let Xerox Corp. inflate pretax earnings by over $3 billion from 1997 to 2000. Xerox agreed to a record $10 million penalty to settle the SEC charges. By this point Xerox had also dropped the PA firm as its auditor. After an investigation, this became SEC's first fraud case against a major accounting firm since Enron's collapse. The SEC alleged that, "Instead of putting a stop to Xerox's fraudulent conduct, the PA firm defendants themselves engaged in fraud by falsely representing to the public that they had applied professional auditing standards to their review of Xerox's accounting." The PA firm vigorously and publicly defended its work, but the case illustrates that statutory law may become a bigger threat to the profession than common law liability, especially if reputational effects are taken into consideration.

It should be noted that, under SEC law, securities fraud puts a greater burden of proof on the defendant PA, as outlined in Exhibit 5A–1 of Appendix 5A, than is generally the case for fraud defendants, as discussed in this chapter. In addition, the SEC doctrine of "fraud on the market," discussed later in this chapter, increases PA liability to broader classes of potential plaintiffs.

In Ontario, Bill 198 was passed December 9, 2002, giving the Ontario Securities Commission potentially greater power in setting rules for appointing auditors than even SOX does. These events also suggest that statutory law liability may become a far greater threat to the profession than common law liability. This was also indicated in Appendix 1B, which noted that some influential public officials already feel self-regulation of the profession to be a failure.

However, there are few precedents to go by other than those already outlined. So, other than noting the potential changes in future liability in this introduction, this chapter focuses on the more traditional sources of auditors' legal liability.

LIABILITY UNDER COMMON LAW

LEARNING OBJECTIVE

2 Outline the various types of common law liability for PAs, citing specific case precedents.

Legal liabilities of PAs arise from lawsuits brought on the basis of the law of contracts or as tort actions for negligence. Most lawsuits stem from a breach of contract claim that accounting or auditing services were not performed in the manner agreed.

Tort refers to a private or civil wrong or injury (e.g., fraud, deceit, and injury), actions normally initiated by users of financial statements. The rule of the law of torts is to compensate victims for harm suffered from the activities of others. The problem for tort law is to identify the actions creating a right to compensation. The law takes into account the fault or blame of the defendant (breach of duty) and whether the defendant's conduct could be considered the cause of the harm (causation), both of which must be established in order for the defendant to be found liable for damages. However, the burden of proof for tort actions varies depending on social policy. For example, under "no fault" schemes, the burden of compensation is spread widely to all automobile owners.[4]

Suits for civil damages under common law usually result when someone suffers a financial loss after relying on financial statements later found to be materially misleading. In the popular press, such unfortunate events are called audit failures. While a business failure is a bankruptcy or other serious financial difficulty arising from many kinds of adverse economic events, an audit failure is based on an auditor's faulty performance, a failure to conduct an audit in accordance with GAAS so that misleading financial statements get published.

Characteristics of Common Law Actions

When an injured party considers herself damaged by a PA and brings a lawsuit, she generally asserts all possible causes of action, including breach of contract, tort, deceit, fraud, or whatever else may be relevant to the claim.

Burden of Proof on the Plaintiff

Actions brought under common law place most of the burdens of affirmative proof on the plaintiff, who must prove (1) that he or she was damaged or suffered a loss, (2) that there was a beneficiary relationship with the defendant, (3) that the financial statements were materially misleading or that the accountant's advice was faulty, (4) that he or she relied on the statements or advice, (5) that they were the direct cause of the loss, and (6) that the accountant was negligent, grossly negligent, deceitful, or otherwise responsible for damages. Appendix 5A reviews the U.S. Securities Acts, U.S. statutory law regulating the PA profession. There you will find that some of the U.S. statutes shift some of these burdens of affirmative proof to the PA.

Clients may bring a lawsuit for breach of contract. The relationship of direct involvement between parties to a contract is also known as *privity*. When privity exists, a plaintiff usually need only show that the defendant accountant was negligent— showed lack of reasonable care in the performance of professional accounting tasks. If negligence is proved, the accountant may be liable, provided the client did not contribute to his own harm.

Smith v. London Assurance Corp. (1905)

> This was the first North American case involving an auditor. The auditor sued for an unpaid fee, and the company counterclaimed for a large sum that had been embezzled by one of its employees, which they claimed would not have occurred except for the auditor's breach of contract. The evidence indicated that the auditors indeed failed to audit cash accounts at one branch office as stipulated in an engagement contract. The court recognized the auditors as skilled professionals and held them liable for embezzlement losses that could have been prevented by non-negligent performance under the contract.

Fifty years ago, it was very difficult for parties, other than contracting clients, to succeed in lawsuits against auditors. Other parties not in privity had no cause of action for breach of contract. However, the court opinion in the case known as *Ultramares* expressed the view that, if negligence is so great that it constitutes gross negligence—lack of minimum care in performing professional duties, indicating reckless disregard for duty and responsibility—grounds might exist for concluding that the accountant had engaged in constructive fraud. Actual fraud, on the other hand, is an intentional act designed to deceive, mislead, or injure the rights of another person.

---

[4] J. E. Smyth, D. A. Soberman, and A. J. Easson, *The Law and Business Administration in Canada*, 7th ed. (1995), pp. 76–79.

Ultramares Corporation v. Touche (1931)

The *Ultramares* decision stated criteria for an auditor's liability to third parties for deceit (a tort action). In order to prove deceit, (1) a false representation must be shown, (2) the tort-feasor must possess scienter—either knowledge of falsity or insufficient basis of information, (3) intent to induce action in reliance must be shown, (4) the damaged party must show justifiable reliance on the false representation, and (5) there must have been a resulting damage. The court held that an accountant could be liable when he did not have sufficient information (audit evidence) to lead to a sincere or genuine belief. In other words, an audit report is deceitful when the auditor purports to speak from knowledge when he has none. The court also wrote that the degree of negligence might be so gross, however, as to amount to a constructive fraud. Then the auditor could be liable in tort to a third-party beneficiary.

An important result of the *Ultramares* case was that the accountants were not liable to third parties for ordinary negligence under common law for the next 35 years. As a result of this case, U.S. Congress was influenced in its passage of the SEC Acts of 1933 and 1934 so that a statutory responsibility to third parties was created where none existed under common law (see Appendix 5A).

Most auditor **legal responsibilities** arise from the law of negligence, the part of the common law known as the law of torts. Negligence is the failure to perform a duty with the requisite standard care (due care as it relates to one's public calling or profession). Under the common law of torts for negligence, all of the following four elements of negligence must be established by the plaintiff if he is to successfully sue the audit.

Four Elements of Negligence

1. There must be a legal duty of care to the plaintiff.
2. There must be a breach in that duty (e.g., failure to follow GAAS and GAAP).
3. There must be proof that damage resulted (otherwise the plaintiff is limited to the amount of audit fee).
4. There must be a reasonably proximate connection between the breach of duty and the resulting damage (e.g., losses must occur subsequent to firm's audit).

The auditor's defence is to demonstrate that at least one of the preceding elements is missing. The auditor may also argue that the plaintiff contributed to his own loss by, for example, not correcting internal control weaknesses. However, this defence applies only to parties having a contractual relationship with the auditor. Just to keep things straight, the auditor is the first party, the contractual client (who hires the auditor for the audit engagement and thus has privity of contract with the auditor) is the second party, and other audited financial statement users are third parties.

I. Due Care to Whom?

A key issue in establishing liability against auditors is to whom do they owe a duty of care? The contractual client (the second party to the contract) is owed a duty of care due to privity of contract. The client is the organization (corporation, proprietorship, partnership) that appoints the auditor. The engagement letter is critical in specifying the contractual obligation, particularly for nonaudit engagements. This explains the importance of having the engagement letter in the first place—it is the basis for establishing the liability of the auditor to second parties.

Under the *Foss* v. *Harbottle* (1842) principle, financial stakeholders cannot sue for losses simply because the corporation they hold a stake in has suffered losses. This is the flipside of the protection that the stakeholder has against suits by the corporation's creditors. The corporation itself, as a "legal person," has to claim any damages. In the case of auditors, the owners are not viewed as having privity of contract with the auditors; only the corporation has privity of contract. Thus, shareholders can take action only as third parties, and then they must establish damages separate from that to the corporation.

Establishing separate damages has greatly limited legal liability to Canadian accountants from shareholders (even though the audit report is addressed to the shareholders).

The most significant source of liability to auditors, however, is from third parties. This relates to a principle of common law that was transplanted from third-party liability for acts causing injury or physical damage (*Heaven* v. *Pender*, [1883]). Until recently, courts were unwilling to compensate for pure economic losses—that is, where there was no physical injury or damage to a plaintiff's person or property. The *Ultramares* v. *Touche* (1931) case confirmed that there is no third-party liability for financial losses caused by ordinary auditor negligence. Only if the auditors had committed fraud or constructive fraud (gross negligence) could they be held liable to third parties. However, that situation has changed dramatically. The leading case for extending tort law to cover pure economic loss is *Hedley Byrne* v. *Heller and Partners*, which is described in the following box.

HEDLEY BYRNE & CO. LTD. V. HELLER & PARTNERS LTD. (1964) A.C. 562 (H.L.)

In this case, a bank acting on behalf of its client, Hedley Byrne, asked Heller & Partners if one of that company's customers was financially healthy. Heller & Partners replied in the affirmative but disclaimed all responsibility. On the basis of this, Hedley Byrne then entered into a contract with that customer, suffering losses when the customer subsequently filed for bankruptcy. The UK's highest court (House of Lords) decided that Heller & Partners would have owed a duty of care to Hedley Byrne had they not made the disclaimer of responsibility. The duty arises from professional advisers whose negligence gives rise to third-party damages.

Another reason that *Hedley Byrne* v. *Heller* is so important to the public accounting profession is that it established the precedent of third-party liability for (ordinary) negligence to "reasonably foreseeable third-parties." These third parties would eventually include, as a result of subsequent cases, present shareholders and lenders as well as limited classes of prospective shareholders and prospective lenders.

This precedent-setting decision was upheld by the Supreme Court of Canada in *Haig* v. *Bamford* (1976). The Supreme Court concluded that auditors owe a duty to third parties of which they have "actual knowledge of the limited class that will use and rely on the statements." The details of this are given in the following box.

HAIG V. BAMFORD ET AL. (1976) 72 D.L.R. (3D) 68

In *Haig,* the accountants were asked by Saskatchewan Development Corporation to prepare financial statements for Bamford. On the basis of these statements, Saskatchewan Development Corporation gave a loan to Bamford. The negligently prepared financial statements showed a profit that should have been reported as a loss. The court held that, where an accountant has negligently prepared financial statements and a third party relies on them to his or her disadvantage, a duty of care in an action for negligent misstatement will arise in the following circumstances: the accountant knows that the results will be shown to and relied on by the plaintiff, who is also a member of a known limited class; the statements have been prepared primarily for guidance of that limited class and for purposes the plaintiff did in fact rely on them for; the fact that the accountant did not know the identity of the plaintiff is not material as long as the accountant was aware that the person intended to supply them to others of this very limited class.

The contemporary *Toromont* v. *Thorne (1975)* case also upheld the *Hedley Byrne* precedent, as it applied to Canada, of liability to known third parties (in this case a prospective investor, Toromont). Auditor's liability in Canada was further extended to prospective investors (reasonably foreseeable third parties) in *Dupuis* v. *Pan American Mines* (1979), the details of which are given in the following box.

DUPUIS V. PAN AMERICAN MINES

On June 15, 1971, a draft prospectus pertaining to Pan American Mines Ltd. and its wholly owned subsidiary, Central Mining Corporation, was filed with the Quebec Securities Commission. Included in the prospectus was a consolidated balance sheet of Pan Am and its subsidiary, which had been audited by the accounting firm of Thorne, Gunn, Helliwell & Christenson, and upon which Thorne, Gunn had expressed an unqualified opinion. On June 16, 1971, the securities commission authorized trading in Pan Am shares and distribution of the prospectus. Pan Am was then listed on the Canadian Stock Exchange, but in November 1971 trading in the shares was suspended, and in February 1972 Pan Am was delisted.

The plaintiff, Albert Dupuis, brought an action claiming that he had suffered a loss on shares of Pan Am purchased between the time the shares were listed and the time trading was suspended. His action was based on the alleged falsity of some of the information contained in the prospectus, including the auditors' report and the notes to the consolidated financial statement.

The judge's decision was worded in part as follows: "when an auditor prepares a balance sheet which he knows is going to be inserted in a company prospectus offering stock for sale, *I believe he has a duty to make sure that the contents of that balance sheet are accurate* so that prospective investors will not be led into error by it." In conclusion, the judge gave the plaintiff judgement against Thorne, Gunn for $89,266.91, with interest from October 15, 1971, and costs.

Source: H. Rowan, "Legal Cases," *CA Magazine*, August 1979, pp. 36–39. Reproduced by permission from *CA Magazine*, published by the Canadian Institute of Chartered Accountants, Toronto, Canada. [Emphasis added.]

CAPARO INDUSTRIES PLC. V. DICKMAN ET AL. (1991) 2. W.L.R. 358 (H.L.)

Caparo acquired Fidelity based on its audited financial statements. Fidelity's financial statements were misstated to show a profit of £1.3 million instead of a loss of £400,000. Caparo sued the auditors for negligence. The UK's highest court decided that the auditor owed no duty of care to Caparo, primarily because the auditor had no knowledge of Caparo's intended use of the financial statements to acquire Fidelity.

In summary, Canadian courts had gradually widened auditor's liability under common law to include limited classes of third parties through 1979. The *Caparo Industries Plc.* v. *Dickman* case in the UK, however, began a reversal of the increasing liability to third parties by limiting liability to those third parties the auditors had knowledge of.[5] This reversal was largely completed in the *Hercules Managements Ltd.* v. *Ernst & Young* (1997) case when the Supreme Court of Canada ruled that "an audit is not prepared in order to assist shareholders in making investment decisions but rather 'to assist the collectivity of shareholders of the audited companies in their task of overseeing management' (paragraph 49)." This controversial decision is described in the box that follows.

[5] M. Paskell-Mede, "Duty of Care Revisited," *CA Magazine*, December 1993, pp. 34–35.

AUDITORS NOT LEGALLY LIABLE TO INVESTORS, TOP COURT RULES

An auditor who signs a company's financial statements has no legal liability to shareholders or investors. That's the thrust of a ruling by the Supreme Court of Canada brought down Thursday in the case of *Hercules Managements Ltd. et al.* v. *Ernst & Young et al.*

The court's concern, observers say, is to protect auditors from unlimited liability to thousands of investors who may use the audit opinion for many different purposes.

The annual financial statement is now a joke, says Al Rosen, a professor of accounting at York University in Toronto and a partner in Rosen & Vettese Ltd., forensic accountants.

"Public accountants may think this is a wonderful win for them," Rosen added. "But in the long run I see this as a disaster. Who really needs an audit of financial statements that is not useful for investor decisionmaking?"

The court's ruling was applauded by Michael Rayner, president of the Canadian Institute of Chartered Accountants. "The decision leaves the profession in a legal environment in which it can maximize its contribution to the capital markets," Rayner said yesterday.

The court has "tried to provide a reasonable amount of liability for auditors," he added.

"We believe the responsibility of auditors is important . . . and there are still significant redresses available through the courts for auditors who are engaged in a situation where there is clear negligence on their part."

The effect of the court's ruling could be shortlived. Brenda Eprile, executive director of the Ontario Securities Commission—Canada's leading securities regulator—says provincial regulators are working on a legal framework that will re-establish the legal liability of auditors to investors.

Hercules Managements was the 80 percent shareholder of Manitoba-based Northguard Acceptance Ltd., which lent money on mortgages in the 1970s and early 1980s. Ernest & Young was the auditor.

In 1984, Northguard went into receivership. Hercules sued Ernst & Young, alleging negligence. The action was dismissed by the Manitoba Court of Queen's Bench, and by the Manitoba Appeal Court. It was heard by the Supreme Court on December 6. The Canadian Institute of Chartered Accountants gained status with the court to argue in favour of protecting auditors from liability.

The court's ruling does not declare whether Ernst & Young was negligent.

On the issue of liability, the court said audited financial reports only call for "a duty of care" by the auditors when they are used "as a guide for the shareholders, as a group, in supervising or overseeing management."

For this reason, there appears to be no direct liability to the shareholders for any reduction in value of their equity, jointly or individually.

"The law in Canada in respect of the responsibility of auditors is basically consistent with the United Kingdom, the United States and many other countries," Rayner said.

"I feel that I have been run over by a truck," said Mark Schulman, of the Winnipeg law firm of Schulman and Schulman, who acted for Hercules.

He points out that one motions judge, three judges of the court of appeal, and seven judges in the Supreme Court all ruled against Hercules, and thoroughly entrenched the principle of no general auditor liability.

Eprile pointed out that auditors are already liable, under securities acts, to investors, in the narrow case when the audited financial statements appear in a prospectus.

"We are recommending that we amend our securities legislation . . . to call for liability in the [entire] secondary market," she said.

That would mean that the public company, the auditor, the directors, and possibly the underwriters would be liable for any negligent disclosure when investors buy a company's shares through a stock exchange.

The legislation has been drafted, Eprile said. It would be uniform across Canada and may take a year or two to get through provincial legislatures, she said.

Source: Philip Mathias, "Auditors Not Legally Liable to Investors, Top Court Rules," *The Financial Post,* May 24, 1997, p. 3. Material reprinted with the express permission of "The National Post Company," a CanWest partnership.

The legislation referred to at the end of the *Hercules* box is Bill 198. The intent of Bill 198 (and similar legislation) is to make it easier for investors to recover damages from accountants, directors, and others associated with misleading financial reporting. We discuss these developments under statutory law liability.

It should be noted that, despite the *Hercules* case's precedent under common law, auditors may still be liable under common law to third parties if the specific reliance of the third parties is made known to the auditors at the beginning of the engagement and the third parties can be said to be a "limited class" as per *Haig* v. *Bamford.* This is shown in the following cases.

State Street Trust Co. v. Ernst (1938)

Accountants, however, may be liable to third parties, even without deliberate or active fraud. A representation certified as true to the knowledge of the accountants when knowledge there is none, a reckless misstatement or an opinion based on grounds so flimsy as to lead to the conclusion that there was no genuine belief in its truth, are all sufficient upon which to base liability. A refusal to see the obvious, a failure to investigate the doubtful, if sufficiently gross, may furnish evidence leading to an inference of fraud so as to impose liability for losses suffered by those who rely on the balance sheet. In other words, heedlessness and reckless disregard of consequences may take the place of deliberate intention. In this connection we are to bear in mind the principle already stated, that negligence or blindness, even when not equivalent to fraud, is nonetheless evidence to sustain an inference of fraud. At least, this is so if the negligence is gross.

Primary beneficiaries are the third parties the audit or other accounting service is primarily performed for. A beneficiary will be identified, or reasonably foreseeable by the accountant prior to or during the engagement, and the accountant will know that her work will influence the primary beneficiary's decisions. For example, an audit firm may be informed that the report is needed for a bank loan application. Many cases indicate that proof of ordinary negligence may be sufficient to make accountants liable for damages to primary beneficiaries.

CIT Financial Corp. v. Glover (1955)

Auditors are liable to third parties for ordinary negligence if their reports are for the primary benefit of the third party. Thus, the privity criterion may not serve as a defence when third-party beneficiaries are known.

PAs may also be liable to foreseeable beneficiaries—creditors, investors, or potential investors who rely on accountants' work. If the PA is reasonably able to foresee a limited class of potential users of his work (e.g., local banks, regular suppliers), liability may then be imposed for ordinary negligence. This, however, is an uncertain area, and liability in a particular case depends entirely on the unique facts and circumstances. These types of beneficiaries and all other injured parties may recover damages if they are able to show that a PA was grossly negligent and perpetrated a constructive fraud.

Rusch Factors, Inc. v. Levin (1968)

With respect to the plaintiff's negligence theory, this case held that an accountant should be liable in negligence for careless financial misrepresentations relied upon by actually foreseen and limited classes of persons. According to the plaintiff's complaint in the case, the defendant knew that his certification was to be used for, and had as its very aim and purpose, the reliance of potential financiers of the Rhode Island corporation.

Rosenblum, Inc. v. *Adler* (1983)

Giant Stores Corporation acquired the retail catalogue showroom business owned by Rosenblum, giving stock in exchange for the business. Fifteen months after the acquisition, Giant Stores declared bankruptcy. Its financial statements had been audited and had received unqualified opinions on several prior years. These financial statements turned out to be misstated because Giant Stores had manipulated its books.

In finding for the plaintiffs on certain motions, the New Jersey Supreme Court held that independent auditors have a duty of care to all persons whom the auditor should reasonably foresee as recipients of the statements from the company for proper business purposes, provided that the recipients rely on those financial statements . . . It is well recognized that audited financial statements are made for the use of third parties who have no direct relationship with the auditor . . . Auditors have responsibility not only to the client who pays the fee but also to investors, creditors, and others who rely on the audited financial statements.

[The case went back to the trial court for further proceedings.]

In summary, the current status of auditor third-party legal liability under common law appears to be as follows: The courts have attempted to strike a fair balance between reliable information for users of financial statements and unreasonable risk to the auditor. This balance has resulted in Canadian auditors currently being liable for negligent error to limited classes of third parties. Third parties are often classified in the following categories:

(*a*) known third parties

(*b*) reasonably foreseeable third parties

(*c*) all third parties relying on financial statements

The trend in litigation suggests the courts will most likely draw the line between categories (a) and (b) for purposes of deciding who auditors owe a duty of care to under common law. This summary applies to ordinary negligence. For gross negligence or fraud on the part of the auditor the third-party liability is much broader.

Fraudulent misrepresentation is a basis for liability in tort (established in *Haig* v. *Bamford*), so parties not in privity with the accountant may have causes of action when negligence is gross enough to amount to constructive fraud. These other parties include primary beneficiaries, actual foreseen and limited classes of persons, and all other injured parties.

II. Due Care: Its Meaning

A key aspect to the second element of negligence is due care. Due professional care implies the careful application of all the standards of the profession (GAAS, GAAP) and observance of all the rules of professional conduct. The courts have interpreted due care to be reasonably prudent practice; therefore, neither the highest possible standards nor the minimum standards would be considered due care. This suggests that following the rules of professional conduct or the *Handbook* may not always be sufficient as these would be minimum standards. In fact, over the years the courts have helped shape audit practice by their interpretation of due care. For example, the concept of testing (less than 100 percent examination of the accounts) was first accepted as reasonable by the precedent-setting decision in *London* v. *General Bank* (1895). This case was also the first to acknowledge that there is some limit on the auditor's responsibility for the detection of fraud and the duty to take increased care in the presence of suspicious circumstances. This case influenced the development of later professional announcements and hundreds of subsequent cases (e.g., *1136 Tenants* [1967]). However, the general legal standard is that an auditor is "a watchdog not a bloodhound" (in *Kingston Cotton Mill Company* [1896]). This means that it is reasonable for auditors to assume management's honesty as a working hypothesis as long as the auditor can provide documented reasons for this assumption.

Nonetheless, auditors need to be alert to factors (evidence) that conflict with this hypothesis, in which case auditors must take additional precautions under the due care requirement, as discussed in Chapters 9 and 17. CAS 240 (5135) characterizes this approach as presuming the possibility of management's dishonesty, but that such presumption is refutable by the evidence. Of course, such evidence must be documented in the audit file.

The courts have also influenced auditing standards (and therefore influenced due care provisions) in the requirement that the auditor corroborate management assertions with his own evidence. The auditor cannot just rely on management's words; he must justify reliance through checking, testing, and other audit procedures. This practice, following from the third examination standard, has been shaped by decisions in many court cases, such as *Continental Vending* (1969) and the Canadian *Toromont* v. *Thorne* (1975).

Another example of court influence in determining what constitutes auditor due care is *McKesson Robbins* (1939) discussed in Appendix 5A, which also ultimately influenced the creation of the *Handbook*, CAS 501 (6030), and similar sections in U.S. standards. In that case, the auditor failed to observe inventory or confirm receivables. It is evident that the due care provision of negligence has significantly shaped and probably will continue to influence the development of audit standards. One impact of the *Continental Vending* case (Appendix 5A) rests on the courts' decision not to accept the auditor's defence that he followed GAAP (i.e., the auditor was able to establish that the footnote in the financial statement was in accordance with GAAP); instead, the courts expected the auditor to use some higher standard of fairness in deciding on proper disclosure. This has led to greater diligence on the part of standard setters designing disclosure standards for various types of information. In the meantime, it may help for auditors to take a more structured framework such as critical thinking to deal with such situations.

A sense of the importance on this issue of fairness was introduced to Canadian courts via the *Kripps* case discussed in the following box.

ACCOUNTING PROFESSION HAS A DUTY TO SHAREHOLDERS

Before buying shares in a company, investors usually rely on an important safeguard—the auditor's opinion of its financial statements. And that opinion usually declares that the statements are both "presented fairly" and are "in accordance with generally accepted accounting principles (GAAP)." For decades though, auditors have tried to duck legal liability to the investors they serve. Auditors appear to want what doesn't exist: authority without responsibility.

Two Canadian lawsuits promise to clarify the trust that investors can place in auditors. One case, *Stephen Kripps et al.* v. *Touche Ross* (now Deloitte & Touche) *et al.*, emerged from the B.C. Court of Appeal. In 1985, Kripps et al. relied on the audited financial statements of a mortgage company to buy $1.9 million of its debentures. The company went into receivership and the investors lost $2.7 million including interest. The investors sued the auditor, lost in a lower court, and won at appeal.

A 2-to-1 appeal court majority ruled that "Touche had actual knowledge that a simple application of GAAP would . . . lead to financial statements that could not be said to have fairly represented the financial position" of the company. "Auditors cannot hide behind [the formula] 'according to GAAP,' " the court declared, "if the auditors know . . . that the financial statements are misleading." It ruled against Touche. The court's point is correct—GAAP is too loose a standard to be a sufficient safeguard by itself. That's why the financial statements must also be "presented fairly," to use the actual language of the auditor's opinion. Despite the ruling's validity, some accountants want the Canadian Institute of Chartered Accountants (CICA) to support an appeal by Touche to the Supreme Court.

Postscript: On November 6, 1997, the Supreme Court of Canada denied Deloitte & Touche's right to appeal the negligence ruling against it by the B.C. Court of Appeal. However, as discussed earlier, the Supreme Court made it much more difficult for investors to sue Canadian auditors under common law in its *Hercules* decision.

Source: "Accounting Profession Has a Duty to Shareholders," *The Financial Post*, May 20, 1997, p. 14. Material reprinted with the express permission of "The National Post Company," a CanWest partnership.

Auditor's Liability When Associated with Misleading Financial Information

If the courts conclude that the auditor is associated with misleading financial statements, even if these statements are in conformity with GAAP, they may conclude that the auditors are fraudulently negligent. If auditors are found guilty of a fraudulent misrepresentation, then there are no limits on third-party liability. In U.S. courts, through common law and in statutory law via the U.S. Securities Acts, the concept of gross negligence (constructive fraud) has expanded auditor liability to larger classes of third parties. As a result, there have been several cases in the United States in which auditors have been found guilty of fraud when they otherwise would have been found only negligent (e.g., *Continental Vending* in Appendix 5A).

The Ontario Securities Commission appears to be interested in increasing auditors' legal responsibility to shareholders by revising the Securities Acts in Ontario. This is a way of expanding auditor liability to wider classes of third parties. This, combined with the increasing influence of the Charter of Rights and Freedoms legislation on the courts, may make the Canadian legal environment more comparable to that of the United States in the near future. In addition, class action legislation has been approved in Quebec (1979), Ontario (1993), and British Columbia (1995). Contingency fees are another issue being considered by the Ontario Law Society; implementing them would also make the Ontario environment more comparable to that of the United States. Thus, many of the problems of high litigation rates and insurance premiums and costly court decisions may soon be imported to at least parts of the Canadian legal environment. Other requirements that expand auditor responsibilities for detecting money-laundering schemes further add to the liabilities burden.

Legal Liability for Failure to Disclose Illegal Acts

CAS 250 (5136, "Misstatements—illegal acts") provides expanded guidance on detecting and disclosing illegal or possibly illegal acts with the objective of reducing the auditor's exposure to legal liability. It does this by (1) reducing the risk that GAAS will be misinterpreted by auditors and the courts, (2) establishing recommendations that reduce the likelihood of an audit's failing to detect a material misstatement arising from the consequences of an illegal act, and (3) providing a defence for the auditor if he or she fails to detect a material misstatement despite conducting the audit in accordance with the standards.[6]

Illegal acts is another area where potential ethical and legal conflicts may be expected to grow. According to an article by M. Paskell-Mede, the whistle-blowing responsibility of the auditor to third parties may grow even in the absence of a regulator, since plaintiffs are raising the issues of association more frequently in lawsuits. It is Paskell-Mede's impression that plaintiffs whose lawyers recognize that their case is weak—as a result of inability to demonstrate either actual reliance on the financial statements or that a direct duty of care was owed with respect to those statements—are now compensating for this weakness by presenting the claim as one based on association. The plaintiff's lawyer will argue that their client relied on the auditor's reputation. However, the courts so far have upheld the obligation for auditors to maintain client confidentiality. For example, in *Transamerica Financial Corporation, Canada* v. *Dunwoody & Company*, the judge decided that client confidentiality overrode whistle-blowing to a third-party plaintiff, especially since the plaintiff was already aware of irregularities at the client. For Paskell-Mede, this is evidence that the courts are becoming more careful about assigning blame to auditors—that they are becoming more sophisticated in analyzing the causal connection between the illegal misrepresentation and damages.[7]

Liability in Compilation and Review Services

You may find it easy to think about common law liability in connection with audited financial statements, but PAs also render compilation and review services and are associated with unaudited financial information (see Chapter 16). People expect PAs to perform

---

[6] V. Murusalu, "Drawing the Line," *CA Magazine*, January/February 1995, pp. 68–69.
[7] M. Paskell-Mede, "Tales of Sherwood Forest," *CA Magazine*, August 1994, pp. 47–48.

these services in accordance with professional standards, and courts can impose liability for accounting work judged to be substandard. PAs have been assessed damages for work on such statements, as shown in *1136 Tenants' Corporation* v. *Max Rothenberg & Co.* Approximately 11 percent of losses in the AICPA professional liability insurance plan involve compilation and review engagements relating to unaudited financial statements.

1136 Tenants' Corporation v. *Max Rothenberg & Co.* (1967)

Despite defendant's claims to the contrary, the court found that he was engaged to audit and not merely write up plaintiff's books and records. The accountant had, in fact, performed some limited auditing procedures including preparation of a worksheet entitled "Missing Invoices 1/1/63–12/31/63." These were items claimed to have been paid but were not. The court held that, even if accountants were hired only for write-up work, they had a duty to inform plaintiffs of any circumstances that gave reason to believe that a fraud had occurred (e.g., the record of "missing invoices"). The plaintiffs recovered damages of about $237,000.

One significant risk is that the client may fail to understand the nature of the service being given. Accountants should use a meeting and an engagement letter to explain clearly that a compilation service (write-up) involves little or no investigative work, and that it is lesser in scope than a review service. Similarly, a review service should be explained as being less extensive than a full audit service. Clarity at the outset can prevent later disagreements between accountants and clients.

Even with these understandings, public accountants cannot merely accept unusual or misleading client-supplied information. A court has held that a PA's preparation of some erroneous and misleading journal entries without sufficient support was enough to trigger common law liability for negligence, even though the PA was not associated with any final financial statements. CICA standards for compilations require PAs to obtain additional information if client-supplied accounting data are incorrect, incomplete, or otherwise unsatisfactory. Courts may hold PAs liable for failure to obtain additional information in such circumstances.

When financial statements are reviewed, PAs' reports state, "Based on my review, nothing has come to my attention that causes me to believe that these financial statements are not, in all material respects, in accordance with generally accepted accounting principles" (*Handbook*, paragraph 8200.42). Courts can look to the facts of a case and rule on whether the review was performed properly. Generally, the same four elements of negligence must be met, both for review engagements and for audit engagements. The only difference is that "due care" in review engagements should follow the standards for review engagements rather than the standards for audits. Generally, it would appear that third-party liability continues to flow to the same classes of persons who would be relying on the financial statements.[8] Some courts might decide a PA's review was substandard if necessary adjustments or "material modifications" should have been discovered. These risks tend to cause PAs to work beyond superficial enquiry procedures.

A 1987 New York case, however, may create an attitude more favourable for PAs' review work on unaudited financial statements. In 1985, William Iselin & Company sued the Mann Judd Landau (MJL) accounting firm, claiming damages for having relied on financial statements reviewed by MJL. Iselin had used the financial statements of customers for its factoring–financing business. A customer had gone bankrupt, and Iselin's loans became worthless. A New York appeals court dismissed the case, saying that third parties (Iselin) cannot rely on reviewed, rather than audited, financial statements for assurance that a company is financially healthy. The court observed that MJL expressed no opinion on the reviewed financial statements. Iselin's lawyer was reported to have observed, "Accountants and their clients will find that reviews are useless, since no one can rely on them."

---

[8] "The Jury's Still Out on Review Engagement Liability," *CA Magazine*, June 1988.

4 What must the plaintiff prove in a common law action seeking recovery of damages from an independent auditor of financial statements? What must the defendant accountant do in such a court action?

5 What legal theory is derived from the *Ultramares* decision? Can auditors rely on the *Ultramares* decision today?

6 Define and explain *privity*, *primary beneficiary*, and *foreseeable beneficiary* in terms of the degree of negligence on the part of a PA that would trigger the PA's liability.

7 What proportion of lawsuits against PAs relate to compilation and review (unaudited financial statements) practice?

Confidentiality versus Misleading Financial Statements

In Chapter 4, we noted that there may be a potential conflict between rules dealing with confidentiality and rules dealing with association with misleading financial statements. A conflict between similar rules in the U.S. code has been the focus of two court cases there: *Consolidata Services* v. *Alexander Grant* (1981) and *Fund of Funds* v. *Arthur Andersen* (1982). In *Consolidata*, the courts ruled that auditors should have preserved confidentiality, and, in *Fund of Funds*, the courts ruled that the confidential information should have been used to prevent misleading reports. The inconsistent legal results from these two cases illustrate that the rules can be just as difficult for the courts to resolve as they are for practicing auditors. In both cases, however, it was the auditors who lost—and paid. (The court awarded $80 million in damages to Fund of Fund's shareholders, the largest judgment ever made against a public accounting firm until that time.)

III. (Third) and IV. (Fourth) Elements of Negligence

The two remaining elements of negligence have also proven to be material issues in various court cases. The third element is that some damage must occur to the third party—otherwise only the audit fee can be recovered. This was the situation in *Toromont* v. *Thorne*.

The last element of negligence requires that there be a causal link between the breach of duty and the resulting damage. Thus, for example, if losses occur before the time of the audit, or if it can be proven that the plaintiff did not rely on the audited information to any significant degree, the lawsuit will fail. A Canadian case illustrating the need for a causal link to damages suffered is given in the following box:

FLANDERS V. MITHA

In August 1992, Justice Holmes of the B.C. Supreme Court ruled in *Flanders* v. *Mitha* (1992) that "disgruntled investors suing a BC accounting firm Buckett & Sharpley for negligently preparing a housing co-op's financial statements must show that they actually relied on those statements when making their investment decision." During the court proceedings none of the plaintiffs was found to have actually relied on the financial statements in purchasing an apartment. They either relied on the realtor or had made the purchase decision prior to requesting and receiving the financial statements from the realtor. *Flanders* v. *Mitha* (1992) thus limits the auditor's liability when his or her work is used by a client to solicit investments from the public.

The interesting questions are whether the Canadian courts will continue to take this narrow approach (other British Columbia decisions suggest so), and whether regulatory agencies, such as the Ontario Securities Commission (OSC), will succeed in convincing legislatures to make companies, their directors, and auditors legally responsible to share-holders under revised securities acts for all misleading documents (as in the United States). Currently, Canadian auditors' legal liability to third parties follows largely from common law (e.g., *Toromont* v. *Thorne et al.*). Nevertheless, financial press articles during the 1990s made it clear that litigation against auditors in Canada was reaching alarming proportions. There are several major lawsuits against PAs outstanding in Canada. It will take years to resolve them.

At this point it is perhaps useful to note the relationship between the fourth element of evidence, the causal link between breach of duty and damages, and something known as joint and several liability. In Canada and the United States **joint and several liability** means any of several defendants that have caused part of the damages are liable to the plaintiffs for the entire amount of damages. This system was set up to protect plaintiffs from having to sue several different parties to recover the full amount of damages. Under joint and several liability, the courts can force the defendant with the "deepest pockets" to pay all the damages even though he may have contributed, say, only 1 percent to the losses. It is, of course, then up to the defendant auditor to recover shares of the losses from the others. If the other defendants are in bankruptcy, however, this can leave the auditor with all the losses. The following box, from a *National Post* article, indicates the problems that joint and several liability have caused in Canada.

OUTDATED LIABILITY LAWS HARMING ECONOMY: ICAO

TRANSACTIONS "JUST DON'T GET DONE" AS AUDITORS TURN AWAY BUSINESS

Canada's antiquated liability laws are badly hurting the economy, according to the country's largest accounting body, which is spearheading demands for liability reform.

The Institute of Chartered Accountants of Ontario—with 35,000 members—said the laws lag behind those in other parts of the world and the failure to make crucial reforms could force an exodus of investment to more attractive jurisdictions.

The ICAO estimates the amount of litigation against the big accounting firms has increased by more than 300% since 1988. The cost of liability insurance for auditors is as much as three times higher than it was in 2001, and the number of firms offering audit services in Canada has dropped by 50% in the past two years, from 400 to just over 200.

Brian Hunt, president and chief executive officer of the ICAO, said failure to fully reform the laws could result in a worst-case scenario where individuals and business ask, "Why would I do business in Canada, when I could get more protection south of the border?"

A recent ICAO survey of more than 500 small and mid-sized accounting firms in Ontario showed that almost three-quarters of the firms surveyed say they have faced a moderate to significant increase in professional liability costs over the past five years. Two-thirds also said liability-related issues are deterring them from taking on client engagements.

Joel Cohen, executive audit partner at mid-tier Canadian accounting firm RSM Richter LLP, said the current regime also restricts access to the capital markets, even for well-governed companies operating in stable industries, because audit firms are unwilling to take on the risk of providing accounting and auditing services.

"We are at a competitive disadvantage," Mr. Cohen said.

Mr. Cohen said the current liability environment has forced RSM Richter to turn down engagements on five or six transactions in the past six months alone. He said it is doubtful the companies involved will find an audit firm in Canada willing to help them.

"We are limiting liability anyway by limiting access to our service," he said.

In one case, RSM Richter needed to enlist another department auditor for a client of its firm. But, Mr. Cohen said, no one was willing to take on the risk, even though the client was a "solid company, making profits, where the business was not risky."

Canada's liability laws "inhibit the completion of transactions. They just don't get done," he added.

Len Crispino, president and chief executive officer of the Ontario Chamber of Commerce, said he has heard anecdotal evidence among his members to support the accountants' position. "It's becoming tougher and tougher to get an accounting firm," he said, "and, in a sense, we all lose."

The key issue is Canada's "joint-and-several" liability laws, which mean an auditor who is only 1% to blame for a corporate bankruptcy can be forced to pay out 100% of the costs associated with any litigation.

Mr. Cohen said the main problem with Canada's joint-and-several liability laws is that they make the risks of providing audit and accounting services "unquantifiable."

That is not the same in other countries. In Australia, legislators recently enacted laws to cap the amount of liability that audit firms could be forced to suffer. In the United States, federal legislators introduced a form of proportionate liability—the costs of losing in litigation are proportionate to the attributed blame—as far back as 1995, and 39 states have eliminated or significantly amended their joint-and-several liability laws. The U.K. and the European Union have also indicated plans to move away from joint-and-several liability.

The Ontario government has recognized the issue and has passed legislation to put some limits on professional liability. However, joint-and-several liability continues to apply in many cases, including civil suits involving audited documents such as prospectuses, take-over bid circulars, and issuer bid circulars, which are generally considered higher risk.

The ICAO is pushing for further changes to fully eliminate joint-and-several liability, Mr. Hunt said. He said he expects resistance from the legal community and from shareholder activists who might perceive reform as something that only favours the big accounting firms. But, he said, these groups do not understand the magnitude of the problem.

Mr. Hunt said not only would the number of firms offering audit services in Canada continue to decline, but there could be a drain of qualified and experienced accountants to countries where the risks of performing audits is much lower. He said this will all add up to audit costs that will be higher in Canada than in other countries.

One sign of the increased risks, Mr. Cohen said, is the cost of professional indemnity insurance for audit firms, which tripled in Canada between 2001 and 2004.

The big accounting firms are also feeling the pinch of rising costs due to Canada's liability regime, said Lou Pagnutti, chairman and chief executive officer for Canada at big four accounting firm Ernst & Young LLP. Since the collapse of Arthur Andersen, the big accounting firms are finding it increasingly difficult to obtain professional indemnity insurance in Canada, he said. "Even if you can get it," he said, "the premiums have increased." Premiums here for the big firms have risen by as much as 30% to 40% a year, forcing them to arrange expensive self-insurance, Mr. Pagnutti said. "Absent liability reform," he said, "there will be further cost increases."

Source: Duncan Mavin, "Outdated liability laws harming economy: ICAO: Transactions 'just don't get done' as auditors turn away business," *The National Post*, Wednesday, June 29, 2005, p. FP7. Material reprinted with the express permission of "The National Post Company," a CanWest partnership.

In light of these potential legal liabilities, a recent development has been the creation of **limited liability partnerships** (LLPs). In 1998, Ontario was the first province to enact legislation allowing the use of the LLP form of organization, followed by Alberta in 1999. With the traditional partnership form of organization, the partners themselves are liable for all debts and liabilities incurred by their firm. In an LLP, the negligent partner is still liable to the extent of his or her own personal assets, while the personal assets of non-negligent partners are not threatened.

Thus, the LLP form of organization can generally reduce the risk to partners of legal liability. However, the LLP form of organization did not prevent the demise of Arthur Andersen, so there are now obvious limits to its benefits. In particular, the LLP form may have less impact under a system where the primary source of legal liability is from statutory law via a high profile regulator, something that can affect the LLP's reputation in the marketplace—a system that looks increasingly likely in the post-Enron environment.

EXTENT OF LIABILITY FOR STAFF OF PA FIRMS

You may be interested in knowing about who suffers exposure and penalties in lawsuits—accounting firms, partners, managers, senior accountants, staff assistants, or all of these. Most lawsuits centre attention on the accounting firm and on the partners and managers involved in the audit or other accounting work. However, court opinions have cited the work of senior accountants, and there is no reason that the work of new staff assistant accountants should not also come under review. All persons involved in professional accounting are exposed to potential liability.

U.S. Auditing Standards titled "Planning and Supervision" offer some important thoughts for accountants who question the validity of some of the work being done in an audit. Accountants can express their own positions and let the working paper records show the nature of the disagreement and the resolution of the question. SAS 22 expressed the appropriate action as follows:

"The auditor with final responsibility for the examination [partner in charge of the audit] and assistants should be aware of the procedures to be followed when differences of opinion concerning accounting and auditing issues exist among firm personnel involved in the examination. Such procedures should enable an assistant to document his disagreement with the conclusions reached if, after appropriate consultation, he believes it necessary to disassociate himself from the resolution of the matter. In this situation, the basis for the final resolution should also be documented."

Defences of the Accountant

The defendant accountant in a common law action presents evidence to counter the plaintiff's claims and evidence. For example, the accountant might offer evidence that the plaintiff was not in privity or not foreseen, that the financial statements were not misleading, or that the plaintiff contributed to the negligence. The primary defence against a negligence claim is to offer evidence that the audit had been conducted in accordance with GAAS with due professional care.

Some courts hold plaintiffs to a strict privity criterion in order to have a standing in court. In New York courts, the general rule is that the accountants must have been aware that the financial reports were to be used for a particular purpose, that a particular third party was going to rely on the reports, and that there is a link between the accountants and the third party demonstrating that the accountants knew of the reliance on the reports. This has prompted some users of financial statements to request a **reliance letter**, in which accountants sign that they have been notified that a particular recipient of the financial statements and audit report intends to rely upon them for particular purposes. The AICPA has warned accountants to be careful when signing such letters as they might become an automatic proof of users' actual reliance.

In several Canadian cases, the auditors successfully argued that clients should not have relied on the financial statements to make their investment decision.[9] A good example is banks' claims that they have been mislead by the financial statements. The fourth element of negligence is key here: Did the banks' losses follow from the auditor's breach of duty with regard to auditing the financial statements? Paskell-Mede notes that "the courts carefully review the degree of reliance plaintiff bankers have on misleading financial statements. Banks usually have available to them not only their customers' financial statements but a great deal of other information as well. Their decision to continue a loan is very

---

[9] "Auditing in Crisis," *The Bottom Line*, March 1990.

often based on considerations quite apart from any reliance they may place on the opinion of the customer's auditors. In these circumstances the auditors ought not to be found liable—or at least not entirely—for the bank's losses." In general, "it's refreshing to see a court carefully reviewing the degree of reliance plaintiff bankers place on misleading financial statements."[10]

AUDITOR'S LIABILITY UNDER STATUTORY LAW

· · · · · · · · · · · · · · · ·

LEARNING OBJECTIVE

3 Outline the various types of statutory law liability for PAs.

A great deal of liability for American auditors arises from statutory law under the SEC. These laws give the SEC the legal right to decide what is GAAP. There is nothing comparable in Canadian legislation, yet increasingly the OSC and Quebec regulators are seeking more enforcement power over professionals such as PAs operating in the capital markets. We discuss the latest Canadian developments in this section.

What is unique about Canadian statutory law is the *Canada Business Corporations Act* (CBCA) and related provincial corporation acts. The highlights of the CBCA are as follows (to be covered in more detail in your business law course):

1. The CBCA identifies conditions under which the auditor is not considered independent in Section 161.

2. It identifies conditions of appointing and retiring the auditor in sections 162 and 163.

3. It identifies the auditor's rights and responsibilities in section 168:

   (*a*) to attend shareholder meetings,

   (*b*) to provide a written statement of reasons for a resignation, and

   (*c*) to make an audit examination unimpeded and gain access to data the auditor considers necessary.

4. The CBCA identifies the financial statements subject to audit, and specifies that the financial statements must be in conformity with the *CICA Handbook*. (Note that this represents a stark contrast with U.S. securities law, which allows the SEC to decide what is GAAP. Thus the ultimate authority on accounting issues in the U.S. is the SEC, whereas in Canada it is CICA via the *Handbook*. This gives *Handbook* standards much higher legal status than comparable standards in the United States.)

5. Until 1994, the CBCA requirements for audited financial statements applied to all companies incorporated under the act with revenues in excess of $10 million or assets greater than $5 million. Under amendments to the CBCA made in 1994, privately held companies are no longer required to have their financial statements audited or disclosed. The *Ontario Business Corporations Act* requires audits only for companies having $100 million of either assets or revenues; other provincial corporations acts vary in their reporting requirements.

In December 1995 the American accounting profession was successful in having the U.S. Congress pass (over President Clinton's veto) the *Private Securities Litigation Reform Act*, which changed auditor liability under SEC section 10b (discussed in Appendix 5A). There were three objectives to the Act. First, it was intended to "discourage abusive claims of investors' losses due to fraudulent misstatements or omissions by issuers of securities" (and professionals associated with the misstatements or omissions, such as auditors). Second, the Act provided more protection against securities fraud. Third, the Act increased the flow of forward-looking financial information. The Act met these objectives by imposing specific pleading requirements, by reducing discovery's effectiveness in coercing

---

[10] H. Rowan, "Are Banks Looking to Pin the Blame?" *CA Magazine*, June 1988.

settlements, mandating sanctions for frivolous claims, giving the plaintiff class far more control of class actions, providing for proportionate liability except in cases of knowing fraud, creating a safe harbour for forward-looking information, and codifying auditor's responsibilities to search for and disclose fraud.[11]

For the purposes of this chapter, the most important feature of the Act concerns the reform of "joint and several liability," which, under SEC law, now applies only to auditors who knowingly commit a violation of the security law. "A defendant (auditor) whose conduct is less culpable is liable only for a percentage of the total damages corresponding to the percentage of responsibility allocated to the defendant (auditor) by the jury . . . Thus, for example, if a PA firm is found 10 percent responsible for an injury and insolvent corporate management is allocated 90 percent, the PA firm no longer will have to make up all of the management's share (as long as the PA firm did not engage in knowing fraud)."[12] This type of liability is referred to as **proportionate liability**.

The CBCA was amended in 2001 to change the liability associated with financial statement misrepresentations from one of joint and several liability to modified proportionate liability. Auditors in Canada are now liable under the CBCA to the extent of their degree of responsibility for the loss (proportionate liability). However, the proportionate liability is modified in that, if other defendants in the lawsuit are unable to pay, the auditor is then liable for additional payments capped at 50 percent of his own original liability. Under some conditions, the courts can revert to the joint and several liability, in which case the auditor may be required to pay up to 100 percent of the damages.[13]

Post-Enron provincial legislation in Canada under the leadership of the **Canadian Securities Administrators (CSA)** is influencing a whole new set of auditor liabilities. These are response to decreased liabilities resulting from the *Hercules* case discussed earlier that did away with most third-party liability under common law.

The *Hercules* case along with post-Enron developments prompted Ontario to pass its Bill 198 in December 2002. Bill 198 is similar to SEC laws discussed in Appendix 5A. The CSA is promoting passage of similar legislation throughout all of Canada's provinces in an effort to demonstrate that Canadian regulators are as concerned in preserving the integrity of their capital markets as the SEC is in the U.S.

This legislation creates a statutory law civil liability for PAs and others accused of misleading the public. It allows class action lawsuits against PAs, placing the burden of proof that a drop in the client's share price was not due to a financial statement misrepresentation (the "fraud on the market" theory used by the SEC in the U.S.) on the defendant PA. In other words, once a misrepresentation has been identified, it is up to the auditor to show that any losses suffered by investors were not due to the misrepresentation. However, the legislation puts caps on the PA's liability and uses the proportionate rather than the joint and several liability rule. These limitations on liability, however, do not apply if the PA knowingly deceived the market.[14]

Although Bill 198 was passed in December 2002, it was not proclaimed (put into force) until late 2004 and went into effect December 2005. The article opposite discusses the significance of this legislation.

These legislative initiatives seem to be inspired by U.S. statutory law covered in Appendix 5A. It should be noted that PAs in Canada already had similar liabilities for initial public offerings of securities. The newer legislation extended the liability to subsequent financial statements of companies already listed on the TSE, and such an extension exposes the Canadian PA to far more potential legal liability.

---

[11] A. R. Andrews and G. Simonette Jr., "Tort Reform Revolution," *Journal of Accountancy*, September 1996, p. 54.

[12] Ibid., p. 50.

[13] See M. Paskell-Mede, "Fair Shares," *CA Magazine*, November 2001, pp. 31–32; G. McLennan, "Trust Not," *CA Magazine*, June/July, 1993, pp. 40–43; and M. Paskell-Mede, "Adviser Relationships," *CA Magazine*, May 1995, pp. 27–32.

[14] See M. Paskell-Mede, *CA Magazine*, June/July, 2003, pp. 34–36 for more details.

LAW TO MAKE IT EASIER FOR INVESTORS TO SUE

"MORE GROUNDS FOR SUITS"

So you lost money on a stock and want to sue the company for misleading statements.

What's already a common practice in the United States is coming to Canada. Canadian public companies are readying themselves for broad new legislation that will greatly increase investors' ability to file civil lawsuits against them.

The new civil liability legislation will come out by the end of the year and substantially widens the type of disclosure investors can use as a basis for litigation.

This means that false or misleading information in press releases and financial statements will soon be fair game. It can even extend to public oral statements, such as conference calls or speeches, made by authorized company representatives. Currently, investor lawsuits are limited to information in a prospectus.

This new addition to the *Ontario Securities Act* was actually introduced by the provincial government in late 2004. But the clock is now ticking for companies to get their disclosure models in order, since it comes into effect Dec. 31. . . .

"This may constitute the biggest change to Canadian securities law in the last 25 years," according to a report by law firm Borden Ladner Gervais LLP.

One of the most significant parts of the new law is how plaintiffs will no longer have to prove they relied on the misrepresentation when investing in a company. For example, under the current legislation, an investor would have to say "I bought this stock reliant on XX amount of earnings, and it turns out they were really XXX . . . I relied on this information and I can prove it," said Paul Findlay, a lawyer at Borden Ladner who co-wrote the report.

This was a significant stumbling block to class-action suits in Ontario, since they typically involve groups of shareholders and it was pretty much impossible to prove that each investor had looked at and relied on the information in question, he added.

With this impediment removed, there's little doubt there will be an increase in securities class-action lawsuits in the province. Plus, it could make it more attractive for shareholders to file suits against cross-listed Canadian companies here, Mr. Findlay said. In the past, these actions have often taken place in the United States, which already has some provisions for materially false and misleading information in continuous disclosure.

Source: Lori McLeod, "Law to make it easier for investors to sue: More grounds for suits," *The National Post*, Friday, November 15, 2005, p. FP12. Material reprinted with the express permission of "The National Post Company," a CanWest partnership.

The auditors defence under Bill 198 is to show that they acted with due professional care and they had no reasonable basis for believing the financial statements are false. To prove due diligence, auditors need to document their work in the audit file—a topic discussed in later chapters.

An additional feature of Bill 198 that is relevant to auditors is the restriction of the amount of liability to the proportionate liability. This amount is also capped at the greater of $1 million or the amount of revenues earned from the client "during the 12 months preceding the misrepresentation."[15]

[15] Ibid, p. 35.

Auditor's Liability in Foreign Corrupt Practices

Numerous other laws affect accountants and business, but two of them deserve special mention. The Foreign Corrupt Practices Act of 1977 (FCPA) and the Racketeer Influenced and Corrupt Organization Act (RICO) in the United States have changed the landscape of much audit practice and have influenced the nature of lawsuits. There are two Canadian counterparts to these laws. They are the Proceeds of Crime (Money Laundering) and Terrorist Financing Act (PCMLTFA) and Corruption of Foreign Officials Act. These two laws are modelled after RICO and the FCPA, respectively.

A rising tide of public indignation and impatience with wrongdoing prompted enactment of the Foreign Corrupt Practices Act of 1977 (FCPA). This law—an amendment of the Securities Exchange Act of 1934—makes it a criminal offence for American companies to bribe a foreign official, a foreign political party, or a candidate for foreign political office for the purpose of influencing decisions in favour of the business interests of the company. Companies may be fined up to $2 million; individuals may be fined up to $100,000 and imprisoned up to five years for violations. In 1997, Canada signed a convention with the OECD to fight foreign corruption, and in 2001 Canada passed legislation similar to FCPA.

The FCPA is a law directed at company managements. Independent auditors have no direct responsibility under the law. They may advise clients about faulty control systems, but they are under no express obligation to report on deficient systems. The law cast a spotlight on companies and their internal auditors. It had the effect of making internal audit departments more important and more professional. The internal auditors often got the assignment to see that their companies complied with FCPA. Under SOX this has become a more urgent task and this is one reason internal auditors have become more important after SOX.

Under antibribery legislation, auditors are responsible to detect foreign bribes insofar as they have a material effect on financial statements. Materiality here needs to consider not only the amount of the bribe but also any fines, jail terms for guilty executives, and related consequences for the reputation of the firm and business risk. The auditor is responsible for disclosing material contingencies, disclosing findings to management and the audit committee, and proper consultation with lawyers (the client's, the auditor's, or both).

Bill C-22 and the Racketeer Influenced and Corrupt Organization Act (RICO)

The important Canadian statutory law based on Bill C-22 met with controversy when it was first proposed, as is described in the following box. It gives auditor responsibility in fraud and illegal act detection, as these are covered in Chapter 17. If client organizations do not comply with the legislation, they risk fines of up to $2 million and their management and employees can be imprisoned. Auditors should be aware of these risks, their reporting responsibilities to outside agencies, and the need to avoid being considered accomplices under the legislation. Bill C-22 had been influenced by RICO and similar legislation in the U.S. RICO is a general federal law, not administered by the SEC, and it has both civil and criminal features. Lawsuits are often characterized as "civil RICO" or "criminal RICO." The original intent of the law was to provide an avenue for criminal prosecution of organized crime activities. However, clever lawyers have found ways to apply it in other cases, including malpractice lawsuits against accountants.

The civil RICO provisions permit plaintiffs to allege (a) fraud in the sale of securities and (b) mail or wire (e.g., telephone) fraud related to audit or tax practice. But RICO provides a perverse twist; if the plaintiffs can prove a "pattern of racketeering activity," they can win triple damages, court costs, and legal fees' reimbursement. These potential losses raise the risk of the lawsuit considerably.

You might think that accountants may not be in great danger of being found to have participated in a "pattern of racketeering activity." Think again! Such a "pattern" can be established if a defendant accountant has engaged, whether convicted or not, in two racketeering acts—fraud in the sales of securities, mail fraud, wire fraud—within the past 10 years. An accounting firm can meet this test by losing a malpractice lawsuit that involved clients' mailing misleading financial statements and using the telephone during the audit. Since all the major PA firms have lost malpractice lawsuits, they are exposed to civil RICO lawsuits. In fact, RICO has been included among the charges in numerous lawsuits against accountants, and one accounting firm lost such a lawsuit, resulting in a judgment of about $10 million.

RICO is hated and feared not only because of the monetary effect on a lawsuit. Being characterized as "racketeers" is not good for a PAs business. When the RICO threat is included in a lawsuit, PAs are more eager to settle with the plaintiffs before trial, paying damages that might not be won in a courtroom.

PROPOSED FEDERAL CRIME LEGISLATION PUTS ACCOUNTANTS AT RISK OF BEING PROSECUTED

Vancouver: Amendments to Canada's Criminal Code could jeopardize unwary financial professionals, legal experts warn.

Bill C-22, known informally as the "proceeds of crime" legislation, is so sweeping that unsuspecting accountants could be guilty of a criminal offence for simply giving advice, the lawyers say.

The proceeds of crime legislation, which is now contained in Part XII.2 of the Criminal Code, is based on American antiracketeering statutes and is designed to deprive criminals of their ill-gotten gains.

But, although the new law may seem well intentioned, Bill C-22 is so broadly worded that, if accountants know or even suspect that a client has illegal profits, they could be guilty of a crime if they act for that client.

The amendments contained in the Bill create two new offences—money laundering and possession of property derived through drug trafficking.

Money laundering is defined as dealing with any property with intent to conceal or convert it while knowing that it was derived as a result of a "designated drug offence" or an "enterprise crime."

The Criminal Code describes "designated drug offences" as virtually any drug infraction other than simple possession. "Enterprise crimes" are generally profit-motivated offences and include things such as bribery, fraud, gambling, and stock manipulation.

Under the criminal law doctrine of "wilful blindness," people are deemed to know they are dealing with the proceeds of crime if they are suspicious about the source of any property but choose to remain ignorant rather than make further inquiries.

The effect of the legislation is that accountants who accept any property, including fees, from a client, knowing or being wilfully blind to the fact the property was obtained illegally, could be charged with possession or laundering.

Problems could also arise if accountants become suspicious about a client's finances during an ongoing engagement. If they continue to act and their advice relates to property obtained through a crime, they could be committing an offence.

Accountants will be particularly vulnerable because they are often aware of the intimate details of a client's financial dealings.

Source: Brad Dusley, "Proposed Federal Crime Legislation Puts Accountants at Risk of Being Prosecuted," *The Bottom Line*, November 1990, p. 6. Reprinted with permission.

Other Issues

1. Fiduciary Duty of Accountants

According to an article by G. McLennan, a unique feature of Canadian common law that may precipitate a litigation crisis here is the expanding concept of accountants' fiduciary duty. An accountant may be a fiduciary when he or she acts as a trustee, receiver, auditor, or simply an adviser to a vulnerable client. Simply assisting someone who is a fiduciary to another might make a PA liable, although this would only be the case where a PA knows the fiduciary relationship and knows it is being dishonestly breached.

Allegations of a breach of fiduciary duty have become increasingly common in lawsuits against accountants in Canada. If a court concludes that an accountant is a fiduciary, he or she may be held responsible for damages, even though (1) the PA's conduct did not cause the damage, (2) the plaintiff failed to take reasonable steps to mitigate those damages, or (3) the plaintiff was partially at fault or other third parties contributed to the damages suffered. Thus, a PA's common defences to a negligence action, such as contributory negligence, remoteness of damages, failure to mitigate, and no duty of care, do not apply to an action in breach of fiduciary duty.

Literally, fiduciary means "trust-like," but the term has been used in so many contexts in the courts that it is applied as if it related to, among other things, all breaches of duty by accountants. The closest thing to legal definition is that set forth in the Supreme Court of Canada decision concerning *LAC Minerals* v. *Corona Resources*. Here the court stated there were three factors to consider when determining if a fiduciary duty exists:

1. The fiduciary has scope for the exercise of some discretion or power.

2. The fiduciary can unilaterally exercise that power or discretion so as to affect the beneficiary's legal or practical interests.

3. The beneficiary is peculiarly vulnerable to or at the mercy of the fiduciary, who is holding the discretion or power.

All three factors must exist to prove a fiduciary duty. An article by M. Paskell-Mede reviews several cases when such duty exists. Generally, when an accountant acts as a receiver/manager or trustee in insolvency situations, he or she owes a fiduciary duty to creditors of an insolvent corporation. If an accountant has an established relationship with one lender, it may be that it is a breach of fiduciary duty to also act as a trustee or receiver of the insolvent borrower. Accountants that act as financial advisers or tax advisers also have a fiduciary duty. Accountants that have successfully defended themselves in lawsuits involving breach of fiduciary duty have done so by showing that either factors 1 or 3 in the definition were not present.[16]

2. Legal Liability Implications for Auditor Practice

As a result of the increasingly litigious climate, auditors ought to

(*a*) be wary of what kind of clients are accepted,

(*b*) know (thoroughly) the client's business (KNOB), and

(*c*) perform quality audits:

    (*i*) use qualified personnel, properly trained and supervised, and motivated;

    (*ii*) obtain sufficient evidence (including proper elicitation of oral evidence and documentation of client's oral evidence);

    (*iii*) prepare good working papers;

    (*iv*) obtain engagement and representation letters.

---

[16] G. McLennan, "Trust Not," *CA Magazine*, June/July, 1993, pp. 40–43; M. Paskell-Mede, "Adviser Relationships," *CA Magazine*, May 1995, pp. 27–32.

Increased litigation has also caused improvements in audit working paper files through use of

(*a*) forceful management letters that are "unambiguous and couched in terms of alarm with respect to problematic internal controls or sloppy bookkeeping,"

(*b*) detailed memos in the working papers describing the conversation with the client and accompanied by a follow-up letter to the client, and

(*c*) a letter to the client or note to the file documenting discussions to reduce audit fees or changing to a review engagement.[17]

The business press provides much anecdotal evidence that there are sometimes serious problems in many auditor-client relationships. For example, according to a vice-president of finance of a major Canadian company, "it's very easy for management to browbeat an auditor at any time in the audit," and "anything goes unless there is a rule to the contrary (in the *Handbook*)."

To combat these problems, auditors should report to a company's audit committee (or equivalent), standard setters should reduce the number of accounting alternatives in GAAP, auditors need more guidance on how to report on a company's ability to continue, and auditors need to better document high-risk clients and be ready to take immediate defensive measures. Some firms now even "fire" their troublesome clients. Some warning signs of potentially troublesome clients include financial or organizational difficulty, involvement in suspicious transactions, uncooperativeness, fee pressures, refusal to sign engagement and representation letters, and frequent involvement in litigation.

Before accepting clients, PAs should ask why clients are changing accountants, visit the client's business, meet their accounting and tax personnel, and check their references. A useful client acceptance checklist could be used that documents whether a client should be accepted for an engagement. This form should be prepared before the engagement letter is submitted. If this screening does not result in rejection of an existing or prospective client, it may also be used to identify engagements that require extra precautions, such as very precise engagement letters and advance collection of fees.[18] In the post-Enron environment, these recommendations have become standard practice and will likely be mandatory once the various new accountability boards and newly empowered regulators develop their own tightened requirements.

[17] M. Paskell-Mede, "So Sue Me," *CA Magazine*, February 1991, pp. 36–38; M. Paskell-Mede, "What Liability Crisis," *CA Magazine*, May 1994, pp. 42–43.
[18] M. F. Murray, "When a Client Is a Liability," *Journal of Accountancy*, September 1992, pp. 54–58.

APPLICATION CASE AND ANALYSIS:
BURDEN OF PROOF CONCEPT IN LAW AND AUDITING

In law, the "burden of proof" concept helps decide who wins at trial. The burden is normally on the plaintiff party. The reasoning in law is similar to that of critical thinking used in this book. In fact, legal reasoning has had a great impact on the argumentative aspects of critical thinking (step 4 in Exhibit 4–1 on page 98). Under critical thinking, auditors have a burden of proof that must be satisfied on every audit engagement in order to be prepared to defend challenges to their decisions. This burden is reflected in auditing standards. What is the burden of proof on an audit engagement?

Analysis

Auditors claim to provide high or reasonable evidential assurance on an audit engagement. In other words, they gather sufficient evidence so as to keep the risk of failing to detect material factual misstatements to an acceptable level.

The audit evidence responsibility to be in conformity with audit evidence standards is satisfied when evidence risk is acceptably low, and assurance (= 1 minus risk) is therefore acceptably high. This responsibility parallels burden of proof in civil law, which looks for "the balance of probabilities" or the "preponderance of evidence." The meaning of these terms of civil law varies, depending on the context.

LEARNING OBJECTIVE

4 Apply and integrate the chapter topics to analyze a practical auditing situation /case/scenario.

For example, in commercial disputes, balance of probabilities means that, if the evidence makes the plaintiff's position more likely to be true than the defendant's, then the plaintiff wins the case. On the other hand, the auditor's burden of proof is determined by the audit standards.

Civil burdens of proof are in sharp contrast to criminal law procedures where the state must prove the guilt of the defendant "beyond a reasonable doubt" for a conviction. Applying both the concept of beyond a reasonable doubt and the courts' operating presumption that all are presumed innocent until proven guilty will result in an extremely remote chance of sending an innocent person to jail.

These distinctions can be important in defining auditor responsibility for detecting fraud since fraud is a criminal act that falls under the criminal code. The O. J. Simpson trials can be used to illustrate the distinction. At his first trial in 1995, a criminal trial, Simpson was found not guilty of the charge of murdering his wife and her friend. That is, the jury was not convinced "beyond a reasonable doubt" that Simpson was guilty. The burden of proof was not met by the prosecution and the presumption of innocence was not overturned by the evidence presented at trial. But, at a civil trial in 1997, Simpson was found responsible for the wrongful deaths of both individuals and required to pay a settlement of US$33.5 million. The facts and evidence were substantially the same but the burden of proof is much lower for a plaintiff in a civil trial, so Simpson lost that case.

These cases have implications for auditors: even if they were able to meet the burden of proof of an audit engagement and provide high assurance that fraud took place, it does not mean the auditor can make an accusation of fraud. The fraud must be proved in criminal court. Moreover, auditors must be careful in the language they use to describe suspicions of fraud based on audit evidence. Auditors should always refer to the risks or evidence of fraud, not to proven fraud, lest they be sued for libel or slander. This is an important aspect of the context of audit engagements and the amount of responsibility auditors can take for detecting fraud. These responsibilities are discussed further in Chapter 17.

SUMMARY

Litigation against accountants has virtually exploded in the United States and to a lesser extent in Canada. Damage claims of hundreds of millions of dollars have been paid by PA firms and their insurers. Insurance is expensive and hard to obtain. The SEC has sued several of the largest accounting firms for securities fraud within the last decade. One of these firms, Arthur Andersen, paid fines of $7 million and later was convicted of "obstructing justice" and forced into bankruptcy. Accountants are not alone in this rash of litigation, which affects manufacturers, architects, doctors, and people in many other walks of life. The professional accounting organizations have joined with other interest groups pushing for "tort reform" of various types (e.g., limitation of damages, identification of liability) in an effort to stem the tide. Other effects of this climate take the form of changing the nature of organizations in which public accountants practise (such as to LLPs).

Accountants' liability to clients and third parties under common law has expanded. Fifty years ago, a strict privity doctrine required other parties to be in a contract with and known to the accountant before they could sue for damages based on negligence.

Of course, if an accountant was grossly negligent in such a way that his or her actions amounted to constructive fraud, liability exists as it would for anyone who committed a fraud. Over the years, the privity doctrine was modified in many jurisdictions, leading to liability for ordinary negligence to primary beneficiaries (known users) of the accountants' work product, and then to liability based on ordinary negligence to foreseen and foreseeable beneficiaries (users not so easily known). While the general movement has been to expand accountants' liability for ordinary negligence, some jurisdictions have held closer to the privity doctrine of the past. The treatment can vary from province to province. The *Kripps* v. *Touche Ross* case discussed in this chapter has also called into question the sufficiency of conformity with GAAP defence in Canada, but it is unclear what alternative standards auditors will be held to. Future court cases will likely clarify this issue.

Accountants' liability under statutory law is also growing rapidly, especially the potentially wide influence of Ontario's Bill 198 on other Canadian provinces, the changes in the CBCA, and the PCMLTFA legislation, which can label accountants as "racketeers." Regulatory laws in the United States greatly changed the obligations of public accountants. Canadian PAs whose clients obtain financing from the United States may be affected by these laws, and these laws also have had an influence on Canadian laws such as Bill 198.

Under common law, a plaintiff suing an accountant had to bring all the proof of the accountant's negligence to the court and convince the judge or jury. In the case of a public offering of securities registered in a registration statement filed under a U.S. Securities Act or Ontario's Bill 198, the plaintiff only needs to show evidence of a loss and that the financial statements were materially misleading; case rested. Then, the accountant shoulders the burden of proof of showing that the audit was performed properly or that the loss resulted from some other cause. The burden of proof has thus shifted from the plaintiff to the defendant. The securities acts also impose criminal penalties in some cases. As indicated throughout the chapter, many commentators feel that the profession is in the midst of a liability crisis that imposes major changes in auditor responsibilities.

This chapter also outlines the PCMLTFA legislation and other statutory laws affecting accountants and corporate governance. Appendix 5A located on the OLC reviews U.S. statutory law in some detail because many court cases setting legal precedents for accountants were launched as a result of this legislation.

MULTIPLE-CHOICE QUESTIONS FOR PRACTICE AND REVIEW

MC 1 Under the Foreign Corrupt Practices Act,
   a. companies must refrain from bribing foreign politicians for commercial advantage.
   b. independent auditors must audit all elements of a company's internal control system.
   c. companies must establish control systems to keep books, records, and accounts properly.
   d. independent auditors must establish control systems to keep books, records, and accounts properly.

MC 2 The management accountants employed by Robbins, Inc., wrongfully charged executives' personal expenses to the overhead on a government contract. Their activities can be characterized as
   a. errors in the application of accounting principles.
   b. irregularities of the type independent auditors should plan an audit to detect.
   c. irregularities of the type independent auditors have no responsibility to plan an audit to detect.
   d. illegal acts of a type independent auditors should be aware might occur in government contract business.

MC 3 Which of these laws does the U.S. Securities and Exchange Commission not administer?
   a. Securities Act of 1933
   b. Securities and Exchange Act of 1934
   c. Racketeer Influenced and Corrupt Organization Act
   d. Foreign Corrupt Practices Act of 1977

MC 4 Good Gold Company sold $20 million worth of preferred shares. The company should have registered the offering under the Securities Act of 1933 if it were sold to
   a. 150 accredited investors.
   b. one insurance company.
   c. 30 investors all resident in one state.
   d. diverse customers of a brokerage firm.

MC 5 When a company registers a security offering under the Securities Act of 1933, the law provides an investor with
   a. an SEC guarantee that the information in the registration statement is true.
   b. insurance against loss from the investment.
   c. financial information about the company audited by independent PAs.
   d. inside information about the company's trade secrets.

MC 6 A group of investors sued Anderson, Olds & Watershed, PAs, for alleged damages suffered when the company they held common shares in went bankrupt. In order to avoid liability under the common law, AOW must prove which of the following?
   a. The investors actually suffered a loss.
   b. The investors relied on the financial statements audited by AOW.
   c. The investors' loss was a direct result of their reliance on the audited financial statements.
   d. The audit was conducted in accordance with generally accepted auditing standards and with due professional care.

MC 7 The Securities and Exchange Commission document that governs accounting in financial statements filed with the SEC is
   a. Regulation D.
   b. Form 8-K.
   c. Form S-18.
   d. Regulation S-X.

MC 8 Able Corporation plans to sell $10 million worth of common shares to investors. The company can do so without filing an S-1 registration statement under the Securities Act (1933) if Able sells the shares
   a. to an investment banker who then sells them to investors in its national retail network.
   b. to no more than 75 investors solicited at random.
   c. only to accredited investors.
   d. only to 35 accredited investors and an unlimited number of unaccredited investors.

MC 9 A "public company" subject to the periodic reporting requirements of the Exchange Act (1934) must file an annual report with the SEC known as
   a. Form 10-K.
   b. Form 10-Q.
   c. Form 8-K.
   d. Form S-3.

MC 10 When investors sue auditors for damages under Section 11 of the Securities Act (1933), they must allege and prove

a. scienter on the part of the auditor.

b. that the audited financial statements were materially misleading.

c. that they relied on the misleading audited financial statements.

d. that their reliance on the misleading financial statements was the direct cause of their loss.

EXERCISES AND PROBLEMS

EP 1
LO.2
Responsibility for Errors and Irregularities. Huffman & Whitman, a large regional PA firm, was engaged by the Ritter Tire Wholesale Company to audit its financial statements for the year ended January 31. Huffman & Whitman had a busy audit engagement schedule from December 31 through April 1, and they decided to audit Ritter's purchase vouchers and related cash disbursements on a sample basis. They instructed staff accountants to select a random sample of 130 purchase transactions and gave directions about the important deviations, including missing receiving reports. Boyd, the assistant in charge, completed the working papers, properly documenting the fact that 13 of the purchases in the sample had been recorded and paid without the receiving report (required by stated internal control procedures) being included in the file of supporting documents. Whitman, the partner in direct charge of the audit, showed the findings to Lock, Ritter's chief accountant. Lock appeared surprised but promised that the missing receiving reports would be inserted into the files before the audit was over. Whitman was satisfied, noted in the work papers that the problem was solved, and did not say anything to Huffman about it.

Unfortunately, H&W did not discover the fact that Lock was involved in a fraudulent scheme in which he diverted shipments to a warehouse leased in his name and sent the invoices to Ritter for payment. He then sold the tires for his own profit. Internal auditors discovered the scheme during a study of slow-moving inventory items. Ritter's inventory was overstated by about $500,000 (20 percent)—the amount Lock had diverted.

Required:

a. With regard to the 13 missing receiving reports, does a material weakness in internal control exist? If so, does Huffman & Whitman have any further audit responsibility? Explain.

b. Was the audit conducted in a negligent manner?

EP 2
LO.2
Responsibility for Errors and Irregularities. Herbert McCoy is the president of McCoy Forging Corporation. For the past several years, Donovan & Company, PAs, has done the company's compilation and some other accounting and tax work. McCoy decided to have an audit. Moreover, McCoy had recently received a disturbing anonymous letter that stated: "Beware, you have a viper in your nest. The money is literally disappearing before your very eyes! Signed: A friend." He told no one about the letter.

McCoy Forging engaged Donovan & Company, PAs, to render an opinion on the financial statements for the year ended June 30, 2003. McCoy told Donovan he wanted to verify that the financial statements were "accurate and proper." He did not mention the anonymous letter. The usual engagement letter providing for an audit in accordance with generally accepted auditing standards (GAAS) was drafted by Donovan & Company and signed by both parties.

The audit was performed in accordance with GAAS. The audit did not reveal a clever defalcation plan. Harper, the assistant treasurer, was siphoning off substantial amounts of McCoy Forging's money. The defalcations occurred both before and after the audit. Harper's embezzlement was discovered by McCoy's new internal auditor in October 2003, after Donovan had delivered the audit report. Although the scheme was fairly sophisticated, it could have been detected if Donovan & Company had performed additional procedures. McCoy Forging demands reimbursement from Donovan for the entire amount of the embezzlement, some $40,000 of which occurred before the audit and $65,000 after. Donovan has denied any liability and refuses to pay.

Required:

Discuss Donovan's responsibility in this situation. Do you think McCoy Forging would prevail in whole or in part in a lawsuit against Donovan under common law? Explain your conclusions.

(AICPA adapted)

EP 3
LO.2
Common Law Liability Exposure. A PA firm was engaged to examine the financial statements of Martin Manufacturing Corporation for the year ending December 31. Martin needed cash to continue its operations and agreed to sell its common share investment in a subsidiary through a private placement. The buyers insisted that the proceeds be placed in escrow because of the possibility of a major contingent tax liability that might result from a pending government claim against Martin's subsidiary. The payment in escrow was completed in late November. The president of Martin told the audit partner that the proceeds from the sale of the subsidiary's common shares, held in escrow, should be shown on the balance sheet as an unrestricted current account receivable. The president was of the opinion that the government's claim was groundless and that Martin needed an "uncluttered" balance sheet and a

"clean" auditor's opinion to obtain additional working capital from lenders. The audit partner agreed with the president and issued an unqualified opinion on the Martin financial statements, which did not refer to the contingent liability and did not properly describe the escrow arrangement.

The government's claim proved to be valid, and, pursuant to the agreement with the buyers, the purchase price of the subsidiary was reduced by $450,000. This adverse development forced Martin into bankruptcy. The PA firm is being sued for deceit (fraud) by several of Martin's unpaid creditors who extended credit in reliance on the PA firm's unqualified opinion on Martin's financial statements.

Required:

a. What deceit (fraud) do you believe the creditors are claiming?

b. Is the lack of privity between the PA firm and the creditors important in this case?

c. Do you believe the PA firm is liable to the creditors? Explain.

(AICPA adapted)

EP 4
LO.2

Common Law Liability Exposure. Risk Capital Limited, an Alberta corporation, was considering the purchase of a substantial amount of treasury shares held by Sunshine Corporation, a closely held corporation. Initial discussions with the Sunshine Corporation began late in 2002.

Wilson and Wyatt, Sunshine's accountants, regularly prepared quarterly and annual unaudited financial statements. The most recently prepared financial statements were for the year ended September 30, 2002.

On November 15, 2002, after extensive negotiations, Risk Capital agreed to purchase 100,000 shares of no par, class A capital shares of Sunshine at $12.50 per share. However, Risk Capital insisted on audited statements for calendar year 2002. The contract that was made available to Wilson and Wyatt specifically provided:

"Risk Capital shall have the right to rescind the purchase of said shares if the audited financial statements of Sunshine for the calendar year 2002 show a material adverse change in the financial condition of the corporation."

The audited financial statements furnished to Sunshine by Wilson and Wyatt showed no such material adverse change. Risk Capital relied on the audited statements and purchased the treasury shares of Sunshine. It was subsequently discovered that, as of the balance sheet date, the audited statements were incorrect and that in fact there had been a material adverse change in the financial condition of the corporation. Sunshine is insolvent, and Risk Capital will lose virtually its entire investment.

Risk Capital seeks recovery against Wilson and Wyatt.

Required:

Assuming that only ordinary negligence is proved, will Risk Capital prevail

a. under the Ultramares decision?

b. under the Rusch Factors decision?

EP 5
LO.2

Common Law Liability Exposure. Smith, PA, is the auditor for Juniper Manufacturing Corporation, a privately owned company that has a June 30 fiscal year. Juniper arranged for a substantial bank loan, which was dependent on the bank's receiving, by September 30, audited financial statements showing a current ratio of at least 2 to 1. On September 25, just before the audit report was to be issued, Smith received an anonymous letter on Juniper's stationery indicating that a five-year lease by Juniper, as lessee, of a factory building that was accounted for in the financial statements as an operating lease was in fact a capital lease. The letter stated that there was a secret written agreement with the lessor modifying the lease and creating a capital lease.

Smith confronted the president of Juniper, who admitted that a secret agreement existed but said it was necessary to treat the lease as an operating lease to meet the current ratio requirement of the pending loan and that nobody would ever discover the secret agreement with the lessor. The president said that, if Smith did not issue his report by September 30, Juniper would sue Smith for substantial damages that would result from not getting the loan. Under this pressure and because the working papers contained a copy of the five-year lease agreement supporting the operating lease treatment, Smith issued his report with an unqualified opinion on September 29. In spite of the fact that the loan was received, Juniper went bankrupt. The bank is suing Smith to recover its losses on the loan and the lessor is suing Smith to recover uncollected rents.

Required:

Answer the following, setting forth reasons for any conclusions stated:

a. Is Smith liable to the bank?

b. Is Smith liable to the lessor?

c. Was Smith independent?

(AICPA adapted)

EP 6
LO.2

Common Law Liability Exposure. Farr and Madison, PAs, audited Glamour Inc. Their audit was deficient in several respects:

1. Farr and Madison failed to audit properly certain receivables, which later proved to be fictitious.

2. With respect to other receivables, although they made a cursory check, they did not detect many accounts that were long overdue and obviously uncollectible.

3. No physical inventory was taken of the securities claimed to be in Glamour's possession, which in fact had been sold. Both the securities and cash received from the sales were listed on the balance sheet as assets.

There is no indication that Farr and Madison actually believed the financial statements were false. Subsequent creditors, not known to Farr and Madison, are now suing based on the deficiencies in the audit described above. Farr and Madison moved to dismiss the lawsuit against it on the basis that the firm did not have actual knowledge of falsity and therefore did not commit fraud.

Required:

May the creditors recover without demonstrating that Farr and Madison had actual knowledge of falsity? Explain.

EP 7 **Liability in a Review Engagement.** Mason and
LO.2 Dilworth, PAs, were the accountants for Hotshot Company, a closely held corporation owned by 30 residents of the area. M&D had been previously engaged by Hotshot to perform some compilation and tax work. Bubba Crass, Hotshot's president and holder of 15 percent of the shares, said he needed something more than these services. He told Mason, the partner in charge, that he wanted financial statements for internal use, primarily for management purposes, but also to obtain short-term loans from financial institutions. Mason recommended a "review" of the financial statements. Mason did not prepare an engagement letter.

During the review work, Mason had some reservations about the financial statements. Mason told Dilworth at various times he was "uneasy about certain figures and conclusions," but that he would "take Crass's word about the validity of certain entries since the review was primarily for internal use in any event and was not an audit." M&D did not discover a material act of fraud committed by Crass. The fraud would have been detected had Mason not relied so much on the unsupported statements made by Crass concerning the validity of the entries about which he had felt so uneasy.

Required:

a. What potential liability might M&D have to Hotshot Company and other shareholders?

b. What potential liability might M&D have to financial institutions that used the financial statements in connection with making loans to Hotshot Company?

(AICPA adapted)

EP 8 **Regulation D Exemption.** One of your firm's clients,
LO.3 Fancy Fashions Inc., is a highly successful, rapidly
and expanding company. It is owned predominantly by the
LO.5 Munster family and key corporate officials. Although additional funds would be available on a short-term basis from its bankers, this would only represent a temporary solution of the company's need for capital to finance its expansion plans. In addition, the interest rates being charged are not appealing. Therefore, John Munster, Fancy's chairman of the board, in consultation with the other shareholders, has decided to explore the possibility of raising additional equity capital of approximately $15 million to $16 million. This will be Fancy's first public offering to investors, other than the Munster family and the key management personnel.

At a meeting of Fancy's major shareholders, its lawyers and a PA from your firm spoke about the advantages and disadvantages of "going public" and registering a share offering in the United States. One of the shareholders suggested that Regulation D under the Securities Act of 1933 might be a preferable alternative.

Required:

a. Assume Fancy makes a public offering for $16 million and, as a result, more than 1,000 persons own shares of the company. What are the implications with respect to the Securities Exchange Act of 1934?

b. What federal civil and criminal liabilities may apply in the event that Fancy sells the securities without registration and a registration exemption is not available?

c. Discuss the exemption applicable to offerings under Regulation D, in terms of two kinds of investors, and how many of each can participate.

(AICPA adapted)

EP 9 **Applicability of Securities Act and Exchange Act.**
LO.3 1. The partnership of Zelsch & Company, PAs, has been
and engaged to audit the financial statements of Snake
LO.5 Oil Inc., in connection with filing an S-1 registration statement under the Securities Act (1933). Discuss the following two statements made by the senior partner of Zelsch & Company.

   a. "The partnership is assuming a much greater liability exposure in this engagement than exists under common law."

   b. "If our examination is not fraudulent, we can avoid any liability claims that might arise."

2. Xavier, Francis & Paul is a growing, medium-sized partnership of PAs located in the Midwest. One of the firm's major clients is considering offering its shares to the public. This will be the firm's first client to go public. State whether the following are true or false. Explain each.

   a. The firm should thoroughly familiarize itself with the securities acts, Regulation S-X, and Regulation S-K.

   b. If the client is unincorporated, the Securities Act (1933) will not apply.

   c. If the client is going to be listed on an organized exchange, the Exchange Act (1934) will not apply.

   d. The Securities Act (1933) imposes an additional potential liability on firms such as Xavier, Francis & Paul.

   e. So long as the company engages in exclusively intrastate business, the federal securities laws will not apply.

EP 10 **Section 11 of Securities Act (1933) Liability Exposure.**
LO.3 The Chriswell Corporation decided to raise additional
and long-term capital by issuing $20 million of 12 percent
LO.5 subordinated debentures to the public. May, Clark & Company, PAs, the company's auditors, were engaged to examine the June 30, 1993, financial statements, which were included in the bond registration statement.

May, Clark & Company submitted an unqualified auditor's report dated July 15, 1993. The registration statement was filed and became effective on September 1, 1993. On August 15 one of the partners of May, Clark & Company called on Chriswell Corporation and had lunch with the financial vice-president and the controller. He questioned both officials on the company's operations since June 30 and enquired whether there had been any material changes in the company's financial position since that date. Both officers assured him that everything had proceeded normally and that the financial condition of the company had not changed materially.

Unfortunately, the officers' representation was not true. On July 30 a substantial debtor of the company failed to pay the $400,000 due on its account and indicated that it would probably be forced into bankruptcy. This receivable was shown on the June 30 financial statements as a collateralized loan secured by shares of the debtor corporation, which at the time the financial statements were prepared had a value in excess of the loan but was virtually worthless at the effective date of the registration statement. This $400,000 account receivable was material to the financial condition of Chriswell Corporation, and the market price of the subordinated debentures decreased by nearly 50 percent after the foregoing facts were disclosed.

The debenture holders of Chriswell are seeking recovery of their loss against all parties connected with the debenture registration.

Required:

Is May, Clark & Company liable to the Chriswell debenture holders under Section 11 of the Securities Act (1933)? Explain. (*Hint:* Review the BarChris case in Chapter 5.)

(AICPA adapted)

EP 11 **Rule 10b-5 Liability Exposure under the Exchange**
LO.3 **Act (1934).** Gordon & Groton, PAs, were the auditors
and of Bank & Company, a brokerage firm and member of
LO.5 a national stock exchange. G&G examined and reported on the financial statements of Bank, which were filed with the Securities and Exchange Commission.

Several of Bank's customers were swindled by a fraudulent scheme perpetrated by Bank's president, who owned 90 percent of the voting shares of the company. The facts establish that Gordon & Groton were negligent in the conduct of the audit but neither participated in the fraudulent scheme nor knew of its existence.

The customers are suing G&G under the antifraud provisions of Section 10(b) and Rule 10b-5 of the Exchange Act (1934) for aiding and abetting the fraudulent scheme of the president. The customers' suit for fraud is predicated exclusively on the negligence of G&G in failing to conduct a proper audit, thereby failing to discover the fraudulent scheme.

Required:

Answer the following, setting forth reasons for any conclusions stated:
a. What is the probable outcome of the lawsuit?
b. What might be the result if plaintiffs had sued under a common law theory of negligence? Explain.

(AICPA adapted)

EP 12 **Foreign Corrupt Practices Act.** Major Manufacturing
LO.3 Company is a large diversified international corpora-
and tion whose shares trade on the New York Stock Exchange.
LO.4 The U.S. Department of Justice and the SEC have

investigated the Global Oil Well Equipment Company, a subsidiary of Major. The agencies allege that Global has engaged in activities clearly in violation of the Foreign Corrupt Practices Act.

Tobias (Global president), Wilton (vice-president), and Clark (regional manager of operations in Nogoland) have conspired to make payments to influential members of Nogoland's Parliament in order to influence legislation in Global's favour. The agencies allege that Tobias, Wilton and Clark met secretly in Geneva and decided to give inducements to Mr. Rock, the Speaker of Nogoland's Parliament. They made a $750,000 loan to Mr. Rock's manufacturing business at a 2 percent interest rate. They gave a $10,000 diamond to Mrs. Rock as a memento of the Rock's wedding anniversary. They paid Jeremy Rock's tuition to medical school. These expenditures were classified as investments, commissions and promotion expenses in the Global financial statements. Their nature and purpose were not otherwise disclosed.

Required:
a. What provisions of the FCPA have apparently been violated by these actions by Global and its officers?
b. What penalties might be assessed on the corporation, if convicted? on Tobias, Wilton and Clark?

(AICPA adapted)

EP 13 **Management Fraud Probability Assessment.** This is
LO.3 an exercise designed to reveal some facts of reasoning
and and decision making. The "fraud involvement test" is
LO.5 fictional.

A team of accountants and psychologists has developed a procedure to test for management involvement in fraudulent activities. The procedure consists of developing a personality profile of key managers and comparing each profile with a master profile of a number of individuals who have perpetrated material frauds. If the manager's profile is sufficiently similar to the master profile, the test signals "fraud." In the last 18 months, the procedure has been tested extensively in the field by a national public accounting firm, and the test has found the following:

- If a key manager has been involved in a material fraud, the test procedure indicates "fraud" 8 times out of 10.
- If a key manager has not been involved in a material fraud, the test will nonetheless indicate "fraud" 20 times out of 100.
- The evidence indicates that about 10 key managers in 100 have been involved in material fraud.

Based on these results, what is your assessment of the probability that a key manager who receives a "fraud" test signal is actually involved in fraudulent activities?

EP 14 **Audit Report and Legal Liabilities.** The auditor's
LO.2 report below was drafted by Smith, a staff accountant at the firm of Wong & Wilson, PAs, at the completion of the audit of the financial statements of PPC Ltd., a publicly held company, for the year ended March 31, 2003. The report was submitted to the engagement partner, who reviewed the audit working papers and properly concluded that an unqualified opinion should

be issued. In drafting the report, Smith considered the following:

- During the fiscal year, PPC changed its amortization method for capital assets. The engagement partner concurred with this change in accounting principles and its justification, and Smith included an explanatory paragraph in the auditor's report.
- The 2003 statements were affected by an uncertainty concerning a lawsuit, the outcome of which cannot presently be estimated. Smith has included an explanatory paragraph in the auditor's report.
- The financial statements for the year ended March 31, 2002, are to be presented for comparative purposes. Wong & Wilson had previously audited these statements and expressed an unqualified opinion.

The report which Smith drafted appears below:

Independent Auditor's Report
To the Board of Directors of PPC Ltd.:
We have audited the accompanying balance sheet of PPC Ltd., as of March 31, 2003 and 2002, and statements of income and retained earnings for the year then ended. These financial statements are the responsibility of the company's management.

We conducted our audits in accordance with generally accepted auditing standards. Those standards require that we plan and perform the audit to obtain reasonable assurance about whether the financial statements are fairly presented. An audit includes examining, on a test basis, evidence supporting the amounts and disclosures in the financial statements. An audit also includes assessing significant estimates made by management, as well as evaluating the overall financial statement presentation. We believe that our audits provide a basis for determining whether any material modifications should be made to the accompanying financial statements.

As discussed in Note X to the financial statements, the company changed its method of computing amortization in fiscal 2003.

In our opinion, except for the accounting change, with which we concur, the financial statements referred to above present fairly, in all material respects, the financial position of PPC Ltd. as of March 31, 2003, and the results of its operations for the year then ended in conformity with generally accepted accounting principles.

As discussed in Note Y to the financial statements, the company is a defendant in a lawsuit alleging infringement of certain copyrights. The company has filed a counteraction, and preliminary hearings on both actions are in progress. Accordingly, any provision for liability is subject to adjudication of this matter.
Wong & Wilson, PAs
May 5, 2003

Required:
Identify the deficiencies in the order in which they appear in the auditor's report as drafted by Smith. Do not redraft the report.

(CGA-Canada adapted)

EP 15 **Liability for Auditor Negligence.** You have been called
LO.2 to testify as an expert witness in a negligence action brought against another public accounting firm, Muss, Tache & Co. (Muss). Briefly, the facts of the case are:

- Muss's client is insolvent.
- A major cause of the insolvency was overvaluation of the net assets of a wholly owned subsidiary, which led to its failure.
- The subsidiary was audited by another PA firm, Able & Co. (Able).
- The primary auditor (Muss) accepted the work of Able without examination of either the subsidiary's accounting records or Able's working papers.
- The action was initiated by the bank that was the primary creditor.
- Muss's defence hinged on these factors:
  (a) There was no need to examine the other auditor's working papers, since the other firm was in good standing with the Institute.
  (b) Since the subsidiary constituted only 12 percent of consolidated net income, it was not material anyway.

Required:
a. Discuss whether or not the bank will be successful in its suit for damages, with reference to the factors the court would consider in arriving at its decision.
b. If Muss, Tache & Co. had made an internal quality control review several weeks after the issuance of the audit report and the review indicated that Muss should have performed some work on the subsidiary, what action should Muss, Tache & Co. have taken at the time? Assume that the review had occurred before Muss's client's insolvency became known and before that bank's negligence action was initiated.
c. Discuss the factors that Muss, Tache & Co. should have considered when determining the materiality for this engagement.

(ICAO adapted)

EP 16 **Liability in a Prospectus Engagement.** Alex P. Keaton
LO.2 Jr. has just returned to the office after an exhausting "busy season." His partner, Malory Dowell, called Alex into her office.

"Alex, I have good news and bad news. First the good news! I've just returned from Expansion Exploration Ltd. and they are going public to help finance their Arctic activities. Therefore, you finally get a chance to work on a prospectus engagement! The bad news is that they want to have the prospectus and the underwriting agreement signed by next Friday, the 31st of March.

"Fortunately, we have been their auditors for the past five years, so we won't have any problems there. Also, I'm quite certain that all five years have had "clean" opinions.

"They have provided me with a copy of their interim financial statements for the five months ended February 28, 1999. As you may recall, their last year-end was September 30, 1998.

"What I would like you to do now, is to provide me with a memo for our planning file briefly outlining what our involvement is to be on this prospectus and describing what communications we are going to have to provide to the securities commission as a result of this involvement."

Required:

a. Assume the role of Alex P. Keaton Jr. and prepare the memo requested by Malory Dowell.

b. Indicate the parties to whom it could be shown that the auditors owe a legal duty of care in this particular situation, and discuss the implications.

(ICAO adapted)

EP 17 **Litigation Resulting from Bankruptcy of Client.** A
LO.2 bank that lent considerable funds to a "high-flying" and, until its recent bankruptcy, highly successful real estate development company has hired your firm to investigate the company's long-time auditors, a medium-sized PA firm. The bank has claimed that the financial statements did not fairly represent the company's financial position. The senior partner in your firm in charge of the investigation has been provided with full access to the complete working papers of the initial auditor in order to complete the investigation. If the matter ultimately goes to court, the case will likely be very high in profile and will likely receive significant media coverage.

The senior partner in your firm has assigned you, a manager with considerable auditing experience, to assist him in evaluating the auditors' quality of work and actions.

Required:

a. Outline what you would do to help your senior partner prepare for the investigation. You should give details of those items he should consider in his preparation as well as the guidelines that would be used to develop an opinion as to the appropriateness of the auditors' actions.

b. On what basis (bases) will the court decide the auditors' liability in this situation?

(ICAO adapted)

EP 18 **Money Laundering, Auditor Responsibilities.** PA is
LO.3 the audit intermediate on the current year's audit of
and Bluroot Inc., a publicly traded sugar importer and
LO.4 refiner. During the audit of Bluroot's cash records and bank account reconciliations, PA notes numerous instances where a large dollar amount was deposited into one of the company's bank accounts and then an identical amount was transferred out, usually on the same or the next day. PA presents a list of these "unusual transactions" to the company treasurer for further explanation. The treasurer, who is very busy, takes the list and says she will get back to PA as soon as possible. Several hours later, the treasurer tosses the list on PA's desk and says, somewhat impatiently, "I don't know why you wasted expensive audit time making up this list. All of these transactions offset, so there is no net effect on

our cash balance. Most of them relate to intercompany transfers with our many foreign subsidiary companies, for cash management purposes. As you note, we have 12 bank accounts with four different banks in order to facilitate cash transfers with our subsidiaries. Also, some of these are probably just bank errors that the bank discovered and subsequently corrected. That happens quite frequently because of the complexity of our banking arrangements. For your audit purposes, all you need to record in your audit file is that the transactions offset and all our intercompany balances agree at year-end. What happens between year-ends is of no significance to your audit! So please get on with completing the necessary audit tests and stop wasting your time and our money!"

PA is upset by this response. Of particular concern is that several of the sugar-cane producing countries where Bluroot has subsidiaries are listed on a list of "Non Cooperating Countries and Territories" issued by the OECD's Financial Action Task Force on Money Laundering, a topic that PA covered in a recent staff training course. And, in other audit tests of the management travel expenses, PA noticed that the treasurer and two of her assistants travelled to these countries on numerous occasions during the year.

PA records all of the details of this investigation in the audit working papers, and discusses the situation with the audit manager the following morning. The audit manager says she will take PA's concerns to the audit partner and also with the PA firm's forensic audit specialists. Several months later, PA learns that the RCMP has undertaken a confidential investigation of Bluroot's financial transactions under suspicion of illegal money laundering activities and PA is asked to answer some questions by the officers investigating the case.

Required:

a. Evaluate the actions of PA and other members of the PA firm in the above case in dealing with the possible illegal acts that they discovered during their audit. What actions and procedures did PA take that uncovered this situation? What different actions might PA have taken that would have allowed the potential money laundering to go undetected?

b. What are the difficulties that can arise for an auditor in whistle-blowing as illustrated in the above case? Can you identify other difficulties that might arise when an auditor suspects illegal acts at a client, more generally?

EP 19 Use the critical thinking framework to help resolve the confidentiality versus misleading financial statements conflict discussed in this chapter.

EP 20 Do you think Ontario's Bill 198 appropriately
LO.3 limits PA legal liability to protect the public interest? Discuss the pros and cons within an umbrella framework like critical thinking that is principles based.

PRELUDE TO PART II

BASIC AUDITING CONCEPTS AND TECHNIQUES

In Part II we describe the activities, concepts, and tools used in the planning stage of the audit engagement, explaining their significance and how they are applied. In practice, experienced auditors use each concept and tool as needed during performance of their audit fieldwork activities, but for study purposes we present these topics linearly, as set out in the Learning Objectives of each chapter. The topics related to audit fieldwork will be explained in Part III. The text mainly uses the terms "auditee" or "organization" to refer to the entity whose financial statements are being audited; in practice, auditors commonly refer to these entities as "audit clients."

EXHIBIT PII–1   OVERVIEW OF THE AUDIT PROCESS AS COVERED IN PARTS II AND III

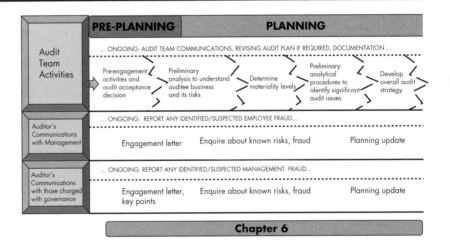

OVERVIEW OF THE AUDIT PROCESS

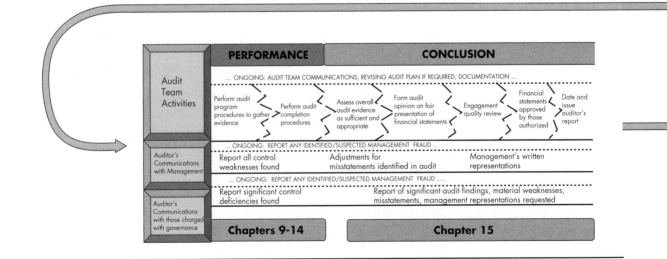

An Overview of the Audit Engagement

Chapter 6 starts off with the pre-engagement arrangements made as the public accountant takes on the role of independent auditor, and then outlines the preliminary analytical procedures involved in developing an understanding of the organization's business and environment. The chapter explains how this helps the auditor both to understand the business performance being communicated by management to stakeholders in its financial statements and to assess the risk of material misstatements. The next topic introduces the business and accounting processes that generate financial statements, followed by an outline of the form and content of management's financial statements. The fundamental concept of materiality is then explained, along with the methods auditors use to determine appropriate materiality levels for audit planning. Finally, the chapter presents the concept of management assertions, explaining how these are used to assess the risk of material misstatements and to establish audit objectives.

To keep things simple, Parts II and III of this text will focus mainly on the audits of financial statements of typical profit-oriented business entities that are prepared in accordance with generally accepted accounting principles (GAAP) as set out in IFRS or the

EXHIBIT PII–1 OVERVIEW OF THE AUDIT PROCESS Continued

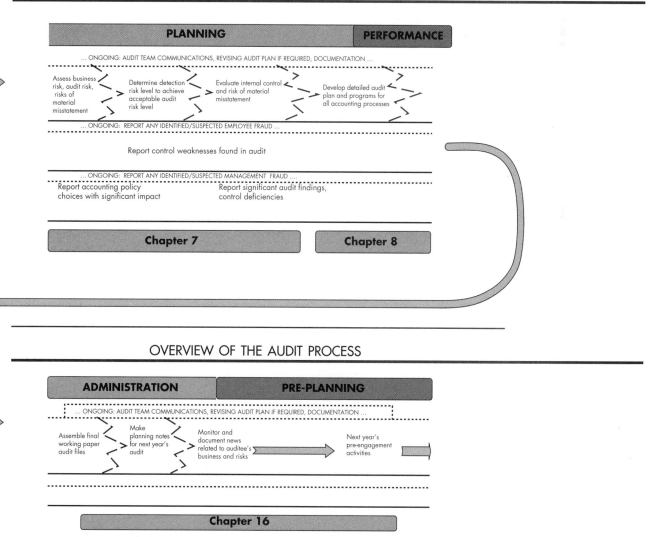

CICA Handbook. As noted in Chapter 3, management can use different acceptable frameworks to present financial statements, but we will just focus on a framework that provides fair presentation in accordance with GAAP. While the text focuses mainly on audits of profit-oriented business entities, the concepts, tools, and procedures covered also apply to audits of other types of entities, such as governments, schools, hospitals, and charities.

Looking ahead, the remaining chapters in Part II take you through the audit planning process and then apply your knowledge and understanding in creating a preliminary audit plan. Chapter 7 (Assessing Risks and Internal Control) expands on the knowledge needed to plan the audit by describing the relation between the business strategy and its risk, the role of business processes in reducing these risks, and the related information systems and control activities used to capture, summarize, and present reliable financial information. Understanding the systems and controls helps auditors to decide on key areas to audit. Chapter 8 (Audit Evidence and Assurance) explains how risk assessment helps the auditor identify relevant audit evidence, and explains the fundamental concepts and tools used to develop the audit plan and specific audit programs. An audit program identifies the procedures needed to provide the evidence supporting the audit opinion. Chapter 9 (Control Assessment and Testing) expands on the understanding required to evaluate and test controls, and Chapter 10 (Audit Sampling) presents sampling techniques used in audit testing.

Overall, in Part II we look at how the auditor integrates business understanding with the key auditing concepts to create an overall strategy and a preliminary audit plan for obtaining evidence supporting the audit opinion. Throughout Part II, the ongoing and iterative nature of the audit planning process is illustrated. Part III moves on to explain the actual audit work, and how to apply the concepts and tools in specific accounting processes in the auditee's business. You will learn how auditors gather evidence from different components of the auditee's systems and processes by testing controls and balances and by performing analytical procedures. These audit procedures generate new knowledge used to refine the preliminary plan. Part III will also explain how auditors synthesize their knowledge and evidence to decide whether the financial statements are fairly presented in accordance with GAAP. The critical activities of documenting the audit planning, the evidence gathered, and the basis of the opinion at the conclusion of the work will also be discussed.

Refer to the following overview of the audit process in Exhibit PII–1, which shows the audit team activities to be covered in Parts II and III. The overview also shows two key ongoing activities that auditors perform throughout the engagement. One such activity is the ongoing communication and reconsideration of planned audit work based on the knowledge gained as the audit proceeds. The other is the critical activity of documenting the work into a working paper file that provides an accurate record of the results of the audit work as support for the auditors' opinion. After working through Parts II and III, you should be ready to join an audit team out in the field and fully appreciate the tasks you will be trained to do under the supervision of more experienced auditors. Experience shows that most of the learning about how to audit happens on the job.

CHAPTER

Preliminary Auditing Planning: Understanding the Auditee

Chapter 6 will take you through the start-up stage of the audit of an organization's general purpose financial statements. You will study the activities, concepts, and tools seen in a typical audit engagement. The first thing to decide is whether to undertake the audit engagement at all. Not every organization is desirable as an auditee! Once the audit has been accepted, the auditors learn about the auditee organization's business, operations, industry, and the economic and regulatory environment it operates in to identify riskier areas of the business that might have led to misstatements in the statements. From drafts of management's financial statements, the auditors identify key elements to examine, and determine a materiality level that reflects what is important to financial statement users. The chapter then presents the concept of management assertions, used as focal points for assessing the risk of material misstatements and establishing audit objectives. Based on these preliminary investigations, the chapter ends by discussing how auditors develop an overall audit strategy for the work required to determine whether the financial statements are fairly presented in accordance with generally accepted accounting principles.

The rest of the chapters in Part II will expand on these planning decisions and the steps in gathering the evidence to support their opinion. Chapter 7 expands on how the auditor's business risk assessment is used to assess the risk of material misstatements. Chapter 7 also explains how auditors gain an understanding of the internal control that management puts in place to reduce those risks, and stresses the close relation between risk and control. Chapter 8 explains how auditors develop detailed audit programs for gathering sufficient appropriate evidence to respond to the assessed risks. Chapter 9 elaborates on how auditors evaluate the auditee's internal control and the important role this evaluation plays in developing the detailed audit plan and programs. Chapter 10 explains the sampling decisions that go into designing tests to collect audit evidence.

LEARNING OBJECTIVES

After completing this chapter, you will be able to do the following:

1 Describe the activities auditors undertake before starting a financial statement audit engagement.

2 Explain why auditors need to understand the auditee organization's business, its environment, and risks at the start of a financial statement audit.

3 Explain the purpose of preliminary analytical procedures and business risk analysis in the audit planning process.

4 Apply preliminary analytical procedures to management's draft financial statements in

order to identify areas where misstatements are most likely.

5 Explain the materiality concept, the materiality levels used for planning the audit, and how these amounts are determined.

6 Describe the principal assertions in management's financial statements and their application in establishing audit objectives.

7 Explain how the preliminary planning activities are integrated in the overall audit strategy.

8 Apply and integrate the chapter topics to analyze a practical auditing situation/case/scenario.

Note: The following Appendix accompanies this chapter:
6A   Selected Financial Ratios

PRE-ENGAGEMENT ARRANGEMENTS

· · · · · · · · · · · · · · ·

LEARNING OBJECTIVE
1 Describe the activities auditors undertake before starting a financial statement audit engagement.

Auditors undertake several activities, called the **pre-audit risk management activities**, before beginning any audit work on an organization's financial statements. Auditors try to reduce risk by carefully managing the engagement. Risk in an audit engagement generally refers to the probability that something will go wrong that might lead to the financial statements being misstated. The flip side of risk management is quality management, which was explained in Chapter 2 under "Quality Control Standards." The topics covered next are understood in the context of risk management and quality management.

Audit Engagement Acceptance and Continuance

An important element of a public accounting firm's quality control policies and procedures is a system for deciding to accept a new audit engagement or to continue with current engagements. Public accounting firms are not obligated to accept undesirable audit clients or to continue when relationships deteriorate or the auditee's management comes under a cloud of suspicion. For example, an auditor may think twice about accepting an engagement with management that has a poor business reputation or questionable integrity.

Acceptance and continuance decisions involve the following policies and procedures.

1. Obtain and review financial information about the prospective auditee organization (e.g., annual reports, interim financial statements, registration statements, annual information forms, and reports to regulatory agencies) to determine the purpose and main users of the financial statements and the basis of accounting being used.

2. Evaluate the public accounting firm's and individual auditors' independence and ability to comply with other relevant ethical requirements with regard to the prospective auditee.

3. Consider whether the public accounting firm has the competency and resources to perform the audit, including any need for special skills (e.g., information systems auditing or specialized industry knowledge).

4. Obtain information from the prospective auditee's management in order to understand the business and its risks and to assess whether the organization's managers and those charged with its governance are willing and able to accept responsibility for preparing financial statements in accordance with an acceptable financial reporting framework and for implementing adequate controls to reduce risk of error and fraud.

5. Consider whether the engagement requires special attention or involves unusual risks (e.g., financial statement users rely heavily on the general purpose financial statements for important financial decisions and/or have no access to other information about the company's financial condition and performance; if there is high media interest in the organization; management competence or integrity is questionable; etc.).

6. Search for information about the organization by looking for news reports and, when possible, asking the prospective auditee's banker, legal counsel, underwriter, or other business associates about the organization, giving particular attention to any indicators relating to the integrity of principal owners, managers, or those charged with its governance.

7. For new audits, communicate with the previous auditor, if possible, for information on the integrity of management, on disagreements with management about accounting principles and procedures or similar matters, and on the reasons for a change of auditors.

Further details and guidance on the matters to consider prior to accepting the audit are provided in CSQC-1 and CAS 210.

Determining Auditability

Through discussions with the prospective auditee's management personnel (as well as those charged with governance; e.g., the board of directors), the auditor must determine whether the organization is "auditable." This involves determining whether the financial statements will be presented in accordance with GAAP or another acceptable reporting framework. Without an acceptable framework, the auditor lacks suitable criteria for evaluating whether the statements are properly presented, and the audit engagement must be declined.

The auditor must be satisfied that the prospective auditee's management understands their responsibilities for preparing financial statements in accordance with the acceptable financial reporting framework and for implementing and maintaining internal control adequate to ensuring financial statements are free of misstatements due to either error or fraud; otherwise, the risk of misstatements may be too high. Management also must be willing to provide all required information and to grant the auditor unrestricted access to records, documentation, and any other needed sources.

The auditor will also want management's commitment to providing written representations at the end of the audit that they have given this information. If management will not do these things, or if it imposes some limitation on the scope of the auditor's work that could lead to a disclaimer of audit opinion, it is usually not appropriate to accept that engagement.

Decisions to continue auditing an organization are similar to acceptance decisions, except that the public accounting firm will have more first-hand experience with the company. *Retention reviews*, done annually, take many possible changes into account: management, directors, ownership, legal counsel, financial condition, litigation status, nature of the auditee's business, scope of the audit engagement, uses of the financial statements, and auditors' independence issues. Conditions causing an audit firm to reject a prospective auditee may develop at any time. For example, an auditee may expand and diversify on an international scale so that a small auditing firm does not have the competence to continue. It is not unusual to see newspaper stories such as the ones summarized in the box below about auditors dropping auditees.

REASONS WHY AN AUDITOR QUITS

These news stories relate situations in which auditors needed to reconsider whether to continue engagements.

QUESTIONABLE MANAGEMENT INTEGRITY

Ernst and Young resigned early in 2001 as auditors of Cinar Corp., after Cinar management refused to assist in determining whether the company's books contain evidence of fraud, illegal acts, or related-party transactions, Cinar said. Cinar said it plans to issue unaudited financial statements for 1999 and the first six months of 2000. It would normally have had these financial statements audited. However, when Cinar informed its independent auditors Ernst and Young LLP that its management would not be able, until at least the completion of fiscal 2001, to make the necessary representations regarding the accuracy of the company's financial statements, Ernst and Young then resigned. In March 2000, Cinar fired founders and co-chief executives Micheline Charest and Ron Weinberg after auditors discovered $20 million in company funds had been invested in off-shore accounts without the knowledge of the board of directors.

AUDITOR FIRM'S INDEPENDENCE MAY BE IMPAIRED

In July 2003, PricewaterhouseCoopers LLP resigned as one of two auditors for Royal Bank of Canada. PwC had provided non-audit services to one of the bank's subsidiaries in July and August of 2003, RBC said. Though providing such services did not violate any Canadian requirements, a review of the matter by RBC and PwC concluded such services may have impaired PwC's independence under the much more rigid U.S. rules on auditor independence. These toughened rules resulted in May 2003 when the U.S. Securities and Exchange Commission adopted revised independence standards brought forward by the Sarbanes-Oxley Act. RBC said it must comply with U.S. rules because its shares are listed on the New York Stock Exchange and it files reports with the SEC. Although the fees for the non-audit work by PwC came to less than $200,000, the amount is irrelevant under the SEC rules, RBC said. A financial analyst praised RBC for its handling of the issue. "While everyone is concerned when auditors resign," the analyst said in a research note, "this is an occasion when a company is showing its highly professional attitude toward corporate governance."

MANAGEMENT FRAUD

In February 2007, the Institute of Chartered Accountants of Ontario found three Deloitte & Touche LLP accountants guilty of professional misconduct in connection with the disastrous audit of Livent's books in 1998. The auditors failed to uncover the alleged fraud in the financial statements of Livent Inc. and must each pay $100,000 in fines and $417,000 in costs following the longest disciplinary hearing on record for the ICAO. "The auditors knew this was a high-risk audit yet they failed to exercise the required degree of professional scepticism," the ICAO disciplinary panel wrote in its decision. Livent, the theatre company that produced shows such as *Phantom of the Opera* and *Ragtime*, collapsed amid allegations of widespread accounting fraud. Criminal charges have been laid against former members of Livent's management. A fourth Deloitte accountant who was originally included in the complaint disagreed with the accounting treatment of key elements of the audit and argued that Deloitte should resign after Livent managers allegedly lied to the auditors. His warnings were ignored, with devastating results for the other three auditors who were handed down the largest fines the ICAO has ever charged.

Sources: Adapted from "Ernst and Young resign as auditors of Montreal-based Cinar, management says," *Canadian Press NewsWire*, January 26, 2001; Keith Kalawsky, "PricewaterhouseCoopers resigns as RBC auditor," *CanWest News*, September 23, 2003, p. 1; John Gray, "Accountants get the hook," *Canadian Business*, 80 (21), October 22, 2007, p. 19.

Communication between Predecessor and Successor Auditors

When organizations change auditors, the former auditor is called the **predecessor**, and the new auditor the **successor**. Experience has shown that auditors are fired because of arguments about the scope of the audit or the acceptability of accounting principles. Sometimes these arguments involve auditors' access to necessary evidence, questions of early revenue recognition, or disputes over deferral of expenses and losses. Often, however, a change in business ownership or a concern over fees is the reason.

As discussed in Part I of the text, professional conduct rules for public accountants require a successor auditor to initiate contact and attempt to obtain basic information directly from the predecessor. The former auditor knows a great deal about the auditee and can give information that will be useful in (1) deciding whether to accept the new auditee and (2) planning the audit. The rules of conduct require the predecessor to respond promptly to communications from the successor.

It is common practice for the successor to explain the situation and the rules to the auditee's management, asking them to give the predecessor consent to speak to the successor and allow the successor to review the prior year's audit files. This consent will determine the amount of auditee information conveyed to the successor. Note that the audit files belong to the auditor, not the auditee, but confidentiality must be respected, even after the auditor-auditee relationship ends. The prospective auditee management's refusal to consent would raise serious concerns about their integrity, and the successor may decide it is too risky to accept this engagement.

With consent, the predecessor can speak freely. It is not unusual to have a cordial change-over, with the successor interviewing the predecessor's staff and obtaining copies of the predecessor's working papers, thus greatly facilitating the successor's first-time audit.

A change of auditors might cause the successor's report to be modified from the standard form. It is important to note that the predecessor-successor situation is not the "using the work and reports of other independent auditors" topic explained in Appendix 3B. That situation involved the engagement of two or more audit firms auditing the financial statements for the same year. This predecessor-successor situation involves the topic "reporting on comparative statements" in Appendix 3B. In this case, the successor auditor is reporting on the current year, but the prior-year comparative financial statements were audited by the predecessor. The successor's report should disclose this fact in a separate paragraph following the opinion paragraph.[1]

Engagement Letters

When a new audit is accepted, the auditor must obtain an **engagement letter** (Exhibit 6–1). Auditing standards require that the auditor and auditee management establish a mutual understanding of, and agreement on, the terms of the engagement.[2] The agreement is documented to reduce the risk that either the auditor or the auditee misinterprets the needs or expectations of the other party. For continuing auditees, the auditor confirms the terms of the engagement annually, preferably in writing. Every year, the auditor must take into account whether there are any new circumstances that would require the terms to be revised, such as a significant change in the nature or size of the entity's business.

The engagement letter is, in effect, the contract. The letter should cover the objective, scope, and limitations of the audit as well as respective responsibilities of both parties. It should specify the applicable financial reporting framework to be used, explain the form of audit report expected to be given, and indicate that the form of report may change if circumstances require that. The letter may list special requests and assignments the auditors will undertake, or it may be a standard letter stating that an audit of financial statements will be performed in accordance with generally accepted

---

[1] CAS 710 (5701).
[2] CAS 210 (5110).

auditing standards. An engagement letter can head off claims that the auditors did not perform the work promised. For example, agreeing on a completion date can reduce disappointments later on.

The engagement letter also may set forth the auditor's fee, which normally is based on the time required to perform the services. Such time estimates require some familiarity with the accounting system. Also, changes in fees and services from the previous year would be communicated.

Auditing standards provide a template for an engagement letter. Every letter needs to be adapted to the circumstances of the auditee organization and the audit. Exhibit 6–1 shows an engagement letter for the audit of a privately held real estate development company.

EXHIBIT 6–1   EXAMPLE OF AN ENGAGEMENT LETTER

November 6, 2010

Ms. Harriet Liu, President
Real Estate Development Limited
600 Paree Street
Richmond, BC

Dear Ms. Liu:

You have requested that we audit the financial statements of Real Estate Development Limited ("the company"), which comprise the balance sheet as at December 31, 2010, and the income statement, statement of changes in equity, and cash flow statement for the year then ended, and a summary of significant accounting policies and other explanatory notes. Our audit will be conducted with the objective of expressing an opinion on the financial statements. Our understanding is that the intended purposes of the financial statements are to report to the Real Estate Development Limited shareholders and to satisfy the requirements of Real Estate Development Limited's credit agreement with the Regal Bank of British Columbia. We are pleased to confirm our acceptance and our understanding of this audit engagement by means of this letter.

Our Responsibilities

As auditors, our responsibility is to conduct the audit in accordance with Canadian generally accepted auditing standards. Those standards require that we comply with ethical requirements and plan and perform the audit to obtain reasonable assurance whether the financial statements are free from material misstatement. An audit involves performing procedures to obtain audit evidence about the amounts and disclosures in the financial statements. The procedures selected depend on the auditor's judgment, including the assessment of the risks of material misstatement of the financial statements, whether due to fraud or error. An audit also includes evaluating the appropriateness of accounting policies used and the reasonableness of accounting estimates made by management, as well as evaluating the overall presentation of the financial statements.

Because of the test nature and other inherent limitations of an audit, together with the inherent limitations of any accounting and internal control system, there is an unavoidable risk that even some material misstatements may remain undiscovered.

In making our risk assessments, we consider internal control relevant to the entity's preparation and fair presentation of the financial statements in order to design audit procedures that are appropriate in the circumstances, but not for the purpose of expressing a separate opinion on the effectiveness of the entity's internal control. However, if we identify any of the following matters, they will be communicated to you.

(a) misstatements, resulting from error, other than trivial errors
(b) fraud or any information obtained that indicates that a fraud may exist
(c) evidence obtained that indicates that an illegal or possibly illegal act, other than one considered inconsequential, has occurred
(d) significant weaknesses in the design or implementation of internal control to prevent and detect fraud or error
(e) related party transactions identified by our audit team that are not in the normal course of operations and that involve significant judgments made by management concerning measurement or disclosure

The matters communicated will be those that we identify during the course of our audit. Audits do not usually identify all matters that may be of interest to management in discharging its responsibilities. The type and significance of the matter to be communicated will determine the level of management to which the communication is directed.

One of the underlying principles of the profession is a duty of confidentiality with respect to client affairs. Accordingly, except for information that is in or enters the public domain, we will not provide any third party with confidential information concerning the company's affairs without the company's prior consent, unless required to do so by legal authority, or the rules of professional conduct/code of ethics of the provincial public accountancy council.

Company responsibilities

Our audit will be conducted on the basis that you, your management team, and the company's Board of Directors who are charged with governance acknowledge and understand that you are responsible for

(a) preparation and fair presentation of the financial statements in accordance with Canadian generally accepted accounting principles. This includes the design, implementation, and maintenance of internal control relevant to the preparation and fair presentation of financial statements that are free from material misstatement, whether due to fraud or error.

EXHIBIT 6-1   Continued

(b) providing us with all information, such as records, documentation and related data, copies of all minutes of meetings of shareholders, directors, and committees of directors, and other matters that are relevant to the preparation and fair presentation of the financial statements.

(c) providing us with any additional information we may request from the company, such as

- information relating to any known or probable instances of noncompliance with legislative or regulatory requirements, including financial reporting requirements;
- information relating to any illegal or possibly illegal acts, and all facts related thereto;
- information regarding all related parties and related party transactions;
- an assessment of the risk that the financial statements may be materially misstated as a result of fraud;
- information relating to fraud or suspected fraud affecting the entity involving management, employees who have significant roles in internal control, or others, where the fraud could have a non-trivial effect on the financial statements;
- information relating to any allegations of fraud or suspected fraud affecting the entity's financial statements communicated by employees, former employees, regulators, or others;
- significant assumptions underlying fair-value measurements and disclosures in the financial statements, and management's assessment of their reasonableness;
- any plans or intentions that may affect the carrying value or classification of assets or liabilities;
- information relating to the measurement and disclosure of transactions with related parties;
- an assessment of all areas of measurement uncertainty known to management that are required to be disclosed in accordance with Canadian generally accepted accounting principles;
- information relating to claims and possible claims, whether or not they have been discussed with Real Estate Development Limited's legal counsel; other liabilities and contingent gains or losses, including those associated with guarantees, whether written or oral, under which Real Estate Development Limited is contingently liable;
- information on whether Real Estate Development Limited has satisfactory title to assets, whether any liens or encumbrances on assets exist, and whether any assets are pledged as collateral;
- information relating to compliance with aspects of contractual agreements that may affect the financial statements; and
- information concerning subsequent events.

(d) providing us with unrestricted access to those within the company from whom we determine it is necessary to obtain audit evidence.

As part of our audit process, we will request from management and, where appropriate, those charged with governance, written confirmation concerning representations provided to us during the audit on matters that are

- directly related to items that are material, either individually or in the aggregate, to the financial statements;
- not directly related to items that are material to the financial statements but are significant, either individually or in the aggregate, to the engagement; and
- relevant to your judgments or estimates that are material, either individually or in the aggregate, to the financial statements.

Reporting

Unless unanticipated difficulties are encountered, at the conclusion of my audit we will submit to you a report containing our opinion on the financial statements. We expect to report as shown in the Appendix to this letter:

[Include Standard Audit Report as an Appendix.]

If during the course of my work it appears for any reason that we will not be in a position to render an unqualified opinion on the financial statements, we will discuss this with you.

Other Matters

We will ask that your personnel, to the extent possible, prepare various schedules and analyses, and make various invoices and other documents available to the audit team members. This assistance will facilitate our work and minimize your audit costs. We look forward to full cooperation from your staff during our audit.

We may also submit to you a memorandum containing our comments on the adequacy of existing systems of internal control, accounting policies and procedures, and other related matters which come to our attention during the course of the audit.

We ask that our firm name be used only with our consent, and that any information to which we have attached a communication be issued with that communication unless otherwise agreed to by our firm.

Our charges to the company for the audit services will be made at our regular rates plus out-of-pocket expenses. Bills will be rendered on a regular basis with payment to be made upon presentation.

The above terms of this engagement will be effective from year to year until amended or terminated in writing. If you have any questions about the contents of this letter, please raise them with Mo Kelley, the audit partner assigned to your audit. If the services outlined are in accordance with your requirements and if the above terms are acceptable to you, please sign the copy of this letter in the space provided and return it to us. We appreciate the opportunity to be of service to your company.

Yours very truly,

....

Kelley and Randu, LLP, PUBLIC ACCOUNTANTS

Acknowledged and agreed on behalf of Real Estate Development Limited by

....
Harriet Liu   [date]

Source: Adapted from *CICA Handbook* (2006 ed.), section 5110, appendix, and proposed CAS 210.

Staff Assignment and Time Budgets

When a new audit engagement is obtained, most public accounting firms assign a full-service team to it. For audits of larger organizations, this team usually consists of the audit engagement partner (the person with final responsibility for the audit), the audit manager, one or more senior audit staff members, staff assistants or public accounting students, information systems or industry experts (if needed), a tax partner, and a second audit partner. For smaller auditees, the team may consist of only one or two people, for example the partner and one staff assistant.

Firm policy, particularly for public company audits, will require that a second audit partner review the work of the audit team to ensure firm quality standards are met. This partner is expected to have a detached professional point of view, because he or she is not directly responsible for keeping friendly relations with the auditee's personnel. The partner and manager in charge of the audit prepare a time budget as a plan for the timing of the work and the number of hours each segment of the audit is expected to take. The budget is based on last year's performance for continuing auditees, taking into account any changes in the auditee's business. In a first-time audit, it may be based on a predecessor auditor's experience or on general experience with similar companies. A simple time budget is shown in Exhibit 6–2.

This particular budget is illustrative only and not complete. Real-time budgets are much more detailed. Some specify the expected time by level of team member (partner, manager, in-charge accountant, staff assistant, specialists). This table shows time at interim and at year-end.

Interim audit work covers procedures performed several weeks or months before the balance sheet date. The exact timing of the interim work depends on the circumstances, such as when enough transaction data will be available making it efficient for the auditor to start performing procedures; when auditee reconciliations or count procedures are available for audit purposes; when auditee staff has time to accommodate and assist the auditors; and other practical issues.

Year-end audit work refers to procedures performed shortly before and after the balance sheet date. As many auditees have year-ends on the same date (December 31 is common), audit firms typically ensure they will have time and people available by spreading the workload over the year. For many audit firms, the "busy season" runs from October

EXHIBIT 6–2   A SIMPLE TIME BUDGET

	Audit Time Budget (hours)	
	Interim	Year-End
Knowledge of the business	15	
Assessment of risk of material misstatement	10	
Control testing	30	10
Audit program planning	25	
Related parties investigation	5	15
Auditor-auditee conferences	10	18
Cash	10	15
Accounts receivable	15	5
Inventory	35	20
Accounts payable	5	35
Other accounts		10
Representation letters		10
Financial statement review		25
Report preparation		12
Total	160	175

through June of the following year. The interim work can consist of both internal control risk assessment and auditing balances as they exist at an early date, or examination of documents or electronic information only available for a certain period during the year.[3]

The time taken to perform procedures for each segment of the audit work is recorded by budget category so that (1) there is a record for billing the auditee, (2) the efficiency of the audit team members can be evaluated, and (3) there is a record for planning the next audit. This may cause some staff members to feel pressured to "meet the budget." Beginning auditors in particular can get frustrated before they learn how to work efficiently. They may be tempted to understate the actual time they spent, with the result that not enough time is budgeted for future audits. Firms can lessen the problem by building learning time for less experienced staff into the budgets.

REVIEW CHECKPOINTS

1 What sources of information can an auditor use in deciding whether to accept a new audit engagement?

2 Why does the successor auditor need to obtain the auditee's consent in order for the predecessor auditor to provide the successor with information about the auditee?

3 What benefits are obtained by having an engagement letter?

4 What is the purpose of a time budget and what information does it contain?

5 What is interim audit work? year-end audit work?

PRELIMINARY UNDERSTANDING OF AUDITEE'S BUSINESS, ENVIRONMENT, AND RISKS

LEARNING OBJECTIVE

2 Explain why auditors need to understand the auditee organization's business, its environment, and its risks at the start of a financial statement audit.

The objective of a financial statement audit is to render an opinion on whether the financial statements, taken as a whole, are fairly presented in accordance with generally accepted accounting standards. Understanding the auditee's business and its operating environment is very important in starting out the audit, as it helps to assess the risk that the auditee's financial statements might contain material misstatements and therefore not be fairly presented. The term "material" in the preceding sentence refers to the key auditing concept of materiality—a misstatement significant enough to affect an important decision someone might make on the basis of that information. How auditors determine what is material is discussed in more detail later in this chapter.

The auditor attempts to understand the auditee's business and risks in order to establish an **overall audit strategy** for the engagement and to guide the design of a detailed **audit plan** containing a set of **audit programs** that effectively address all the significant risks of financial statement misstatements. An audit program is a list of the procedures believed necessary to obtain sufficient appropriate evidence about significant components of the financial statements. This evidence is the basis for the opinion stated in the auditor's report. Auditing standards require the auditor to document the overall strategy, audit plan, audit programs, and evidence that support the report.[4] A program "in my head" is not sufficient. Audit programs are explained more fully in the remaining chapters of Part II and detailed examples are provided in Part III.

Early in the engagement, the auditor must ascertain the auditee's business risks. First the auditor investigates the management's understanding of its business risks, and then he or she independently assesses both the business risk and management's risk assessment process to determine how likely a material misstatement of the financial statements is. The auditing standards explain the risk assessment procedures for obtaining an understanding

---

[3] CAS 315 (5141).

[4] CAS 300 (5150), CAS 230 (5145).

of the auditee as well as sources of information about the auditee entity and its environment, including its internal control.

The standards also require the audit team to discuss the susceptibility of the auditee's financial statements to material misstatement. Based on its shared understanding, the audit team can identify what can go wrong at the financial statement level.[5] The risk assessment also considers classes of transactions, account balances, and disclosures in the financial statements. These financial statement elements are made up of specific "assertions" or fundamental claims by management. There are five principal assertions: the element exists, it is properly owned or owed by the entity, it is complete, its value is measured appropriately in accordance with the financial reporting framework, and it is presented appropriately in terms of classification, description, and disclosure. The auditor assesses risk in the financial statement elements assertion by assertion. (Assertions will be explained in detail later in this chapter.) The standards also require the auditor to determine the significance and likelihood of these risks. This chapter will focus on understanding the auditee's business with its environment and risks, as well as the assertions contained in its financial statements, to develop the overall audit strategy. Chapter 7 will expand on the procedures auditors use to analyze and assess risks through understanding internal control and the information systems that produce the financial statements.

In order to design the audit, auditors must understand the broad economic environment the auditee operates in, including such things as the effects of national economic policies (e.g., price regulations and import/export restrictions), the geographic location and its economy (e.g., Alberta's resource-based economy, or Ontario's manufacturing-based economy), and developments in taxation and regulatory areas (e.g., deregulation in agriculture and telecommunications, approval processes in the drug and chemical industries). For example, an increase in the Canadian dollar relative to the U.S. dollar negatively affects Canadian firms that rely on exports to the United States because their products become more expensive and thus less competitive in the U.S. market. A rapid, unexpected increase in energy prices, such as occurred during 2008, negatively impacts businesses such as manufacturing, through increased costs, and retail or tourism, by reducing disposable incomes of consumers. In response to climate change concerns, a global initiative to reduce carbon emissions by imposing carbon taxes or emissions caps creates uncertainty and risk affecting many business models, particularly those whose energy needs result in high levels of carbon emissions.

At the time of writing, a credit crisis in the global financial system resulted in a deep worldwide economic recession affecting many sectors of the economy. Such economic events can require business managers to make drastic changes to operating plans in order to survive and succeed. Some businesses benefit from economic turmoil but many are not able to continue as going concerns. Clearly, auditors must have a strong grasp of the potential impact of economic events on a company's business in order to ensure its financial information fairly presents its underlying economic condition.

Industry characteristics also affect business risks. There are great differences in the production and marketing activities of banks, insurance companies, mutual funds, supermarkets, hotels, oil and gas, agriculture, manufacturing, and so forth. No auditors are experts in all these businesses. Audit firms typically have people who are expert in one or two industries and rely on them to manage audits in those industries. Indeed, some public accounting firms have a reputation for having many auditees in particular industries.

An example of industry-related risk in the forestry industry is presented in the box opposite. This is an example of a strategic risk faced by businesses in industries that depend on foreign sales where high, unexpected duties could put some companies into financial distress if profits fall. Auditors need to be aware of such risk to understand the business performance and how it affects the financial statements. Alternatively, financial statements indicating growth in profitability while heavy duties were being imposed go against expectations and need to be investigated carefully. It may suggest a misstatement.

---

[5] CAS 315 (5141).

B.C. SOFTWOOD LUMBER INDUSTRY IN CRISIS

From May 22, 2002, to December 20, 2004, most Canadian softwood lumber exported to the United States was subject to a combined countervailing and anti-dumping duty of 27 percent, collected by U.S. Customs. As of December 20, 2004, the duty had been reduced to 20 percent. Committees of the North American Free Trade Agreement (NAFTA) and World Trade Organization (WTO) both ruled in 2005 that these duties are not justified, but U.S. Customs continued to collect them.

The Canadian defence involved federal and provincial governments and the forest industry. The federal government has the overall responsibility for coordinating national activities related to the countervailing duty, while provincial governments have the lead in addressing the allegations that relate to provincial programs. The forest industry has the lead in the anti-dumping duty case.

In a poll of its members taken in June 2003, the Canadian Federation of Independent Businesses found that 70 percent of British Columbia's small forestry businesses reported being significantly or somewhat harmed by the lumber dispute. The graph below shows the magnitude of the duties paid by the industry.

SOFTWOOD LUMBER DUTIES COMPARISON

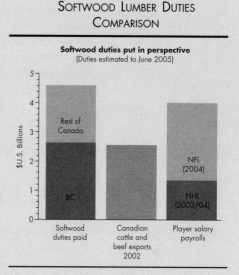

Sources: Adapted from "2006 softwood lumber agreement," Ministry of Forests and Range, Province of British Columbia website, www.for.gov.bc.ca/HET/Softwood (accessed February 23, 2008), based on "Softwood lumber export duties: BC Stats estimate"; Industry Canada, "Cattle and beef exports," Strategis website, www.ic.gc.ca (data from Statistics Canada converted to U.S. dollars); "Player salary payrolls," *USA Today*.

Note: NHL payroll excludes incentives and salaries of players appearing in fewer than 30 games; NFL payroll may not include short-term and practice squad players.

While the duty crisis described in the box above was resolved by an agreement between Canada and the U.S. in 2006, in late 2008 another risk for the forestry industry reared its head when AbitibiBowater Inc. decided to shut a money-losing newsprint mill in Newfoundland. The provincial government took action to expropriate the company's timber cutting rights. These rights had been granted in 1905 to a company that eventually became AbitibiBowater, in exchange for creating jobs and making investments in Newfoundland. The government also took steps to expropriate the company's hydroelectricity rights, which are even more valuable. Taking the view that the company has reneged on its side of the agreement by throwing the newsprint workers out of their jobs, the government's position was that the deal was no longer valid. As AbitibiBowater was planning to sell these rights to try to turn its struggling business around, this extraordinary event could have a significant impact on results in its financial position and future prospects. The company's auditors need a good understanding of this situation involving the ownership of these rights to ensure the financial statements present it fairly to users.[6]

---

[6] See the Ministry of Forests and Range, Province of British Columbia website, www.for.gov.bc.ca/HET/Softwood (accessed December 23, 2008); "NL government to expropriate most AbitibiBowater assets," *Fort McMurray Today*, December 16, 2008, p. 2; "Premier Williams takes on pulp giant; but AbitibiBowater threatens legal action as Newfoundland seizes hydro and timber assets," *The Toronto Star*, December 17, 2008, p. B01; "AbibitiBowater calls expropriation 'hostile'," *Waterloo Region Record*, December 20, 2008, p. F3.

These events illustrate why greater knowledge of business is required than in the past. Auditors are expected to use integrative reasoning to draw together many complex and rapidly changing factors in reaching their conclusions. Accounting is supposed to reflect the economic substance of an entity's transactions, events, and conditions. Auditing in this dynamic world requires asking management the right questions, which calls for strong understanding of the auditee's business, environment, and risks.

The following box illustrates the kinds of risks a high-technology business faces. Intellectual property rights and patents raise a possibility that certain liabilities might be understated in the financial statements. In this case, the company faced significant risks related to development and patenting of its technology and the existence of other, similar patents. Management needs a process for managing these risks, and auditors need to assess whether these risks and liabilities have been reported fully in the statements.

TECH COMPANY MAY NEED FURTHER $550 MILLION TO SETTLE BLACKBERRY PATENT INFRINGEMENT CLAIM

Research In Motion Ltd. may have to pay $550-million (U.S.) more than it has set aside to settle claims that its BlackBerry e-mail device infringes another company's patents.

Liability for infringement could reach $1 billion, said ThinkEquity analyst Pablo Perez-Fernandez. RIM has reserved only $450-million to cover damages for infringement and licensing fees until the patents run out in 2012. The $1-billion estimate followed the refusal on Oct. 7 by a U.S. appeals court to overturn an August jury finding of infringement of the patents, which are owned by a closely held company, NTP Inc.

RIM faces a court order halting BlackBerry service in the United States if it can't get the verdict thrown out. More than 70 percent of the company's $1.35 billion in annual revenue comes from the United States. It has $2.5 billion in cash, marketable securities, short- and long-term investments, and the money set aside for the litigation, Mr. Perez-Fernandez said.

"They can come up with a billion if they have to," said Mr. Perez-Fernandez, who rates the Waterloo, Ont.–based company's shares "sell" and does not own them. "When the $450-million settlement was announced, it was clear it was a discount."

Investors are likely to accept a higher settlement price if it means an end to the litigation, analysts said. A payment of more than $450-million would be "positively received by RIM investors," said Mike Abramsky, an RBC Dominion Securities analyst in Toronto, in an Oct. 10 note to clients. Mr. Abramsky has a "sector perform" rating on the shares. "Every $200-million additionally paid to NTP equates to only $1 a share."

RIM's U.S. shares have fallen 19 percent since the company announced an impasse in the settlement June 9 and are down 22.3 percent this year.

In June, RIM co-chief executive officer James Balsillie said his company has "backup technology" to work around the patented inventions in dispute if it can't come to an agreement with NTP. The company will do what it takes to continue selling BlackBerrys, which are now owned by more than three million people, Mr. Balsillie said.

In the meantime, the U.S. Patent and Trademark Office is reviewing the NTP patents to see if they should have been issued. A decision against NTP would end the litigation in favour of RIM.

6 Why does the auditor need a good understanding of the auditee's business and environment?

7 How do changes in the economic environment affect a business's risks?

8 How do changes in the industry environment affect a business's risks?

9 What specific risks exist in high-tech companies? in the forestry industry?

PRELIMINARY ANALYTICAL PROCEDURES FOR AUDIT PLANNING

The Auditee's Risks and Their Impact on Audit Planning

LEARNING OBJECTIVE

3 Explain the purpose of preliminary analytical procedures and business risk analysis in the audit planning process.

Auditors use the planning tools of business risk assessment, analytical procedures, materiality decisions, overall audit strategy, audit risk assessment, and audit plans to guide and direct their work. Based on the preliminary analysis and on understanding the auditee's financial reporting and its business risks, auditors establish the overall audit strategy for the engagement; set out the basic scope, nature, and timing of the work to be performed; and identify any key risk areas requiring special attention by the audit team.[7]

The overall audit strategy guides the development of the audit plan, which contains more specific procedures for assessing risk of material misstatements and detailed audit programs listing procedures for providing evidence to support the auditor's conclusion. The audit plan includes the audit team's decision on whether to use a "substantive approach" or a "combined approach" to the audit. A substantive audit approach focuses on gathering evidence directly substantiating the balances, transactions, and disclosures in the financial statements. In a combined approach, some of the required assurance is obtained indirectly through evidence that controls are likely to have prevented or corrected any material misstatements. A combined approach will include testing the controls in the auditee's information systems and substantive testing. The audit plan will be discussed further in Chapter 7, after we have covered audit risk assessment in more depth.

Even though auditing standards do not require particular analytical procedures, their application is required at two points in the audit. At the beginning of an audit, the planning stage risk assessment discussed in this chapter [CAS 315 (5141)] is required, and at the end of an audit it is required that the partners in charge review the overall quality of the audit work and look for problems by analyzing the financial statements [CAS 520 (5301)]. Auditors may also decide to include analytical procedures as a way of providing substantive evidence about specific financial statement assertions [CAS 330 (5143)]. Examples of this use are provided in Part III.

Analytical procedures are powerful techniques for identifying unusual changes and relations in financial statement data. The purpose of doing analysis at the beginning of the engagement is "attention directing"—to alert the audit team to problems (errors, fraud) that may exist in the account balances, transactions, and disclosures and to guide the design of further audit work. The auditor's understanding of the business risks is important in identifying the changes and relations expected based on how the business performed during the audited period and what might indicate the financial information is misstated.

Five types of general analytical procedures performed on financial statement data are listed below. The first three types involve comparisons with other relevant data and the last two involve studying relationships.

1. Compare current-year account balances with balances for one or more comparable periods.

2. Compare current-year account balances and financial relationships (e.g., ratios) with similar information for the industry the company operates in.

[7] CAS 300 (5150).

3. Compare the current-year account balances with the company's anticipated results as found in the budgets and forecasts.

4. Evaluate the relationships of current-year account balances to other current-year balances for conformity to predictable patterns based on the company's experience.

5. Study the relationships of current-year account balances to relevant nonfinancial information (e.g., physical production statistics).

Horizontal analysis (type 1), comparison of changes of financial statement numbers and ratios across two or more years, and **vertical analysis** (type 4), comparison of financial statement amounts expressed each year as proportions of a base (e.g., sales for the income statement accounts and total assets for the balance sheet accounts), are often used.

Research finds that analytical procedures are most effective when integrated with other sources of information, especially when accompanied by a strong knowledge of the auditee's business. "Auditors must combine different types of knowledge (accounting, general business, industry, and auditee-specific) and issues (operating, financing, and investing) into a whole. This skill is needed whether analytical procedures are used for planning, substantive testing, or overall review purposes, but it appears to be most critical at overall review, where the auditor's goal is to examine the financial statements to determine whether they make sense taken as a whole."[8]

Analytical procedures can also take other forms, ranging from simple to complex. A wide range of early information-gathering activities can be defined as "analytical procedures," including the following:

- review of accounting misstatements discovered in prior year audits and any adjustments proposed to management;
- conversations with auditee personnel regarding developments affecting the organization, such as changes in strategy, business processes, information technology, key management, ownership, industry conditions, economic conditions, legal environment, etc.;
- review of the corporate charter and bylaws or partnership agreement;
- review of contracts, agreements, and legal proceedings; and
- reading and study of the **minutes** of meetings of the board of directors, the group charged with governance of the organization, as well as of any sub-committees of the board (e.g., executive committee, finance committee, compensation committee, audit committee).

The box below outlines some of the key knowledge that auditors obtain from reading minutes.

WHAT'S IN THE MINUTES OF MEETINGS?

Boards of directors are supposed to monitor the auditee's business. The minutes of both their meetings and those of their committees (e.g., executive committee, finance committee, compensation committee, audit committee) contain information of vital interest to the independent auditors. Some examples are as follow:
- declared amount of dividends
- authorization of officers' salaries and bonuses
- authorization of stock options and other "perq" compensation
- acceptance of contracts, agreements, and lawsuit settlements
- approval of major purchases of property, plant and equipment, and investments
- discussions of any acquisitions, mergers, and divestitures in progress
- authorization of financing by share issues, long-term debt, and leases

---

[8] E. Hirst, L. Koonce, and F. Philipps, "First, Know the Business," *CA Magazine*, August 1998, p. 41.

- approval to pledge assets as security for debts
- discussion of negotiations on bank loans and payment waivers
- approval of accounting policies and accounting for estimates and unusual transactions
- authorizations for individuals to sign bank cheques

Auditors take notes on or make copies of important parts of the minutes and compare them with information in the accounting records, financial statements, and note disclosures (e.g., compare the amount of dividends declared with the amount paid and reported in the financial statements, etc.). Because the minutes are so important in determining what needs to be reported in order to obtain fair presentation, denying access to the board of directors meeting minutes constitutes a major scope restriction by an auditee. In such a case, because of the pervasive impact that boards of directors' decisions can have on financial statement measurements and disclosures, a disclaimer of audit opinion is likely. When the auditor expects to issue a disclaimer of opinion, the audit firm will usually resign from the audit engagement since the audit would add little value.

Other types of analytical procedures can be complex, including mathematical time series and regression calculations, comparisons of multi-year data, and trend and ratio analyses. In the sections that follow, two of the general analytical procedures are emphasized: (1) comparison of current-year account balances with balances for one or more comparable periods, and (4) evaluation of the relationships of current-year account balances with other current-year balances for conformity with predictable patterns based on the company's experience. Exhibit 6–3 below illustrates an approach that combines analysis of relationships (financial ratios) and trends (current year versus prior year).

EXHIBIT   6–3   ANYCOMPANY INC. SELECTED FINANCIAL RATIOS

	Prior Year	Current Year	Percent Change
Balance Sheet Ratios			
Current ratio	4.57	2.23	–51.29%
Days' sales in receivables	18.40	30.91	67.98
Doubtful accounts ratio	0.0800	0.0556	–30.56
Days' sales in inventory	80.00	80.00	0.00
Debt/equity ratio	0.40	0.49	21.93
Operations Ratios			
Receivables turnover	19.57	11.65	–40.47
Inventory turnover	4.50	4.50	0.00
Cost of goods sold/sales	75.00%	72.73%	–3.03
Gross margin percentage	25.00%	27.27%	9.09
Return on beginning equity	6.62%	12.76%	92.80
Financial Distress Ratios (Altman, 1968, Appendix 6A)			
Working capital/total assets	0.49	0.30	–38.89
Retained earnings/total assets	0.22	0.26	17.20
EBIT/total assets	0.09	0.14	54.87
Market value of equity/total debt	2.59	1.89	–27.04
Net sales/total assets	2.22	2.04	–7.92
Discriminant Z score	4.96	4.35	–12.32

10   What is the purpose of performing analytical procedures at the beginning of the audit engagement?

11   What is the role of the auditor's understanding of the business and its risks in performing analytical procedures?

12   What are five types of general analytical procedures?

13   What official documents and authorizations should an auditor read when performing preliminary analytical procedures?

14   What important information can be found in directors' minutes about officers' compensation? business operations? corporate finance? accounting policies and control?

15   What is the role of business risk analysis in the audit planning process?

APPLYING ANALYTICAL PROCEDURES TO MANAGEMENT'S DRAFT FINANCIAL STATEMENTS

LEARNING OBJECTIVE

Apply preliminary analytical procedures to management's draft financial statements in order to identify areas where misstatements are most likely.

One of the first things the auditor receives is management's draft financial statements. Depending on the organization, these financial statements may be virtually complete and final (e.g., in a large company with many professionally qualified accountants on staff) or preliminary statements that still require adjustments for items such as bonuses and income taxes (e.g., in a small company with few in-house accountants). Even when the audit begins with a set of draft statements still requiring final adjustments, the auditor must remember that all financial reporting decisions are management's responsibility. Particularly in smaller organizations, an auditor may identify appropriate adjustments or accounting entries, but, to maintain independence, the auditor must ensure that management approves and takes responsibility for all the accounting choices made.

Analysis Procedures for Attention Directing

Auditors perform analytical procedures on the draft statements looking for relationships that do not make sense, as these may indicate problem areas where the accounts do not faithfully represent the underlying economic substance. Faithful representation is a fundamental accounting concept relating to the claims, or assertions, that management makes in its financial statements. Analysis of the financial statements' assertions is very important in the business risk approach to auditing, as we will discuss in more depth later in this and later chapters. Here in the planning stage, analytical procedures are primarily attention directing; they do not provide direct evidence about the numbers in the financial statements, but their main purpose is to help the audit team plan effective audit programs maximizing the probability of finding any material misstatements. They identify potential problem areas so that the subsequent work can be designed to reduce the risk of missing something important. The analysis application explained here illustrates this attention-directing aspect—the pointing out of accounts that may contain misstatements.

Use an Organized Approach

By following an organized approach—using a standard starting place—preliminary analytical procedures can provide considerable familiarity with the auditee's business. Many auditors start with comparative financial statements and calculate common-size statements (vertical analysis) and year-to-year change in balance sheet and income statement accounts (horizontal analysis). This is the start of describing the financial activities for the current year under audit.

Exhibit 6–4 contains financial balances for the prior year (consider them audited) and the current year (consider them draft numbers not yet audited). Common-size statements (vertical) are shown in parallel columns, and the dollar amount and percentage change (horizontal) are shown in the last two columns. These analytical procedures generate basic analytical data that is the starting point for the auditors' further evaluation and enquiry.

EXHIBIT 6-4 ANYCOMPANY INC.: PRELIMINARY ANALYTICAL PROCEDURES DATA

	Prior Year		Current Year		Change	
	Balance	Common Size Analysis	Balance	Common Size Analysis	Amount	Percent Change Analysis
Assets						
Cash	$ 600,000	14.78%	$ 200,000	4.12%	($ 400,000)	–66.67%
Accounts receivable	500,000	12.32	900,000	18.56	400,000	80.00
Allowance doubtful accounts	(40,000)	–0.99	(50,000)	–1.03	(10,000)	25.00
Inventory	1,500,000	36.95	1,600,000	32.99	100,000	6.67
Total current assets	2,560,000	63.05	2,650,000	54.63	90,000	3.52
Equipment	3,000,000	73.89	4,000,000	82.47	1,000,000	33.33
Accumulated amortization	(1,500,000)	–36.95	(1,800,000)	–37.11	(300,000)	20.00
Total assets	$4,060,000	100.00%	$4,850,000	100.00%	$ 790,000	19.46%
Liabilities and Equity						
Accounts payable	$ 500,000	12.32%	$ 400,000	8.25%	($ 100,000)	–20.00%
Bank loans, 11%	0	0.00	750,000	15.46	750,000	
Accrued interest	60,000	1.48	40,000	0.82	(20,000)	–33.33
Total current liabilities	560,000	13.79	1,190,000	24.53	630,000	112.50
Long-term debt, 10%	600,000	14.78	400,000	8.25	(200,000)	–33.33
Total liabilities	1,160,000	28.57	1,590,000	32.78	430,000	37.07
Share capital	2,000,000	49.26	2,000,000	41.24	0	0.00
Retained earnings	900,000	22.17	1,260,000	25.98	360,000	40.00
Total liabilities and equity	$4,060,000	100.00%	$4,850,000	100.00%	$ 790,000	19.46%
Income						
Sales (net)	$9,000,000	100.00%	$9,900,000	100.00%	$ 900,000	10.00%
Cost of goods sold	6,750,000	75.00	7,200,000	72.73	450,000	6.67
Gross margin	2,250,000	25.00	2,700,000	27.27	450,000	20.00
General expense	1,590,000	17.67	1,734,000	17.52	144,000	9.06
Amortization	300,000	3.33	300,000	3.03	0	0.00
Operating income	360,000	4.00	666,000	6.46	306,000	85.00
Interest expense	60,000	0.67	40,000	0.40	(20,000)	–33.33
Income taxes (40%)	120,000	1.33	256,000	2.59	136,000	113.33
Net income	$ 180,000	2.00%	$ 370,000	3.74%	$ 190,000	105.56%

Describe the Financial Activities

After generating these basic financial data, the next step is to describe the financial changes and relationships visible in them. According to the draft financial statements in Exhibit 6–4, the company increased the net income through increasing sales by 10 percent, reducing cost of goods sold as a proportion of sales, and controlling other expenses. At least some of the sales growth appears to have been prompted by easier credit (larger accounts receivable) and more service (more equipment in use). The company also used much of its cash and borrowed to purchase the equipment, make its payment on the long-term debt, and pay dividends.

Ask Relevant Questions

The next step is to ask, "what could be wrong?" and "what errors, fraud, or legitimate explanations might account for these financial results?" For this explanation we will limit our attention to the accounts receivable and inventory, while other ratios can help support the analysis. (Exhibit 6–5[*] contains several familiar ratios and Appendix 6A includes a list

* Same as Exhibit 6–3.

EXHIBIT   6-5   ANYCOMPANY INC.: SELECTED FINANCIAL RATIOS

	Prior Year	Current Year	Percent Change
Balance Sheet Ratios			
Current ratio	4.57	2.23	-51.29%
Days' sales in receivables	18.40	30.91	67.98
Doubtful accounts ratio	0.0800	0.0556	-30.56
Days' sales in inventory	80.00	80.00	0.00
Debt/equity ratio	0.40	0.49	21.93
Operations Ratios			
Receivables turnover	19.57	11.65	-40.47
Inventory turnover	4.50	4.50	0.00
Cost of goods sold/sales	75.00%	72.73%	-3.03
Gross margin percentage	25.00%	27.27%	9.09
Return on beginning equity	6.62%	12.76%	92.80
Financial Distress Ratios (Altman, 1968, Appendix 8A)			
Working capital/total assets	0.49	0.30	-38.89
Retained earnings/total assets	0.22	0.26	17.20
EBIT/total assets	0.09	0.14	54.87
Market value of equity/total debt	2.59	1.89	-27.04
Net sales/total assets	2.22	2.04	-7.92
Discriminant Z score	4.96	4.35	-12.32 *

of commonly-used ratios with their formulas.) Here are two examples of the kinds of questions auditors should ask about these financial statements.

- *Are the accounts receivable collectible?* (Or, is the allowance for doubtful accounts large enough?) Easier credit can lead to more bad debts. The company has a much larger amount of receivables (Exhibit 6–4), days' sales in receivables has increased significantly (Exhibit 6–5), receivables turnover has decreased (Exhibit 6–5), and allowance for doubtful accounts is smaller in proportion to the receivables (Exhibit 6–5). If the prior-year allowance for bad debts at 8 percent of receivables was appropriate, and conditions have not become worse, perhaps the allowance should be closer to $72,000 than to $50,000. The auditors should work carefully on the evidence related to accounts receivable valuation.

- *Could the inventory be overstated?* (Or, could the cost of the goods sold be understated?) Overstatement of the ending inventory would cause the cost of goods sold to be understated. The percentage of cost of goods sold to sales shows a decrease (Exhibits 6–4 and 6–5). If the 75 percent of the prior year represents a more accurate cost of goods sold, the income before taxes may be overstated by $225,000 (75 percent of $9.9 million minus $7.2 million unaudited cost of goods sold). The days' sales in inventory and the inventory turnover remained the same (Exhibit 6–5), but you might expect them to change in light of the larger volume of sales. Careful work on the physical count and valuation of inventory is needed.

Other questions can be asked and other relationships derived when industry statistics are available. Industry statistics from services such as Statistics Canada, FPinformart.ca, Dun & Bradstreet, Investext Plus, and Mergent Online typically include industry averages for important financial yardsticks such as gross profit margin, return on sales, current ratio, and debt/ net worth. A comparison with auditee data may reveal out-of-line statistics, indicating company strength, a weak financial position, or possibly an error or misstatement in the statements. However, remember that averages may not be representative of a particular company.

Comparing reported financial results with internal budgets and forecasts also can be useful. If a budget or forecast represents management's estimate of probable future outcomes, items that fall short of or exceed the estimates become audit-relevant questions. If a company expected to sell 10,000 units of a product but sold only 5,000, the auditors will plan a careful lower-of-cost-and-market study of the inventory of unsold units. If 15,000 were sold, they will plan a careful audit for sales validity. Comparisons can be tricky, however. Some companies use budgets and forecasts as goals rather than as expressions of probable outcomes. Also, the avoidance of shortfall or excess might be the result of managers' manipulating the numbers to "meet the budget." Auditors must be careful to know something about a company's business conditions from sources other than the internal records when analyzing comparisons with budgets and forecasts.

Look at the Cash Flows

The analysis of changes in cash flows from operating, investment, and financing activities is a very informative tool. A cash flow deficit from operations may signal financial difficulty. Companies fail when they run out of cash (no surprise) and are unable to pay their debts when they become due. In a small business audit, the auditee may not have prepared a cash flow statement. In that case, the auditors can use the comparative financial statements to prepare one providing this important part of their preliminary analysis.

R E V I E W
C H E C K P O I N T S

16 What are management's draft financial statements?

17 What steps can auditors use to apply comparison and ratio analysis to management's financial statements?

18 What can the auditor learn from a vertical analysis?

19 What can the auditor learn from a horizontal analysis?

20 What are some of the ratios that can be used in preliminary analytical procedures?

21 How can computing the accounts receivable turnover ratio indicate potential misstatement in the accounts receivable balance?

22 How can computing the number of days of sales in inventory indicate potential misstatement in the inventory balance?

23 Is anything questionable about the relationship between retained earnings and income for the Anycompany data shown in Exhibit 6–4?

24 What is the operating cash flow for the current year for Anycompany shown in Exhibit 6–4?

25 Why don't preliminary analytical procedures provide direct evidence about financial statement misstatements?

MATERIALITY LEVELS FOR AUDIT PLANNING

LEARNING OBJECTIVE

5 Explain the materiality concept, the materiality levels used for planning the audit, and how these amounts are determined.

Materiality is one of the first important judgments the auditor must make, since it affects every other planning, examination, and reporting decision. The materiality decision is an important application of professional judgment and is based on the auditor's knowledge about the organization's business risks, identification of the likely users and uses of its audited general purpose financial statements, preliminary analysis of its draft financial statements, and experience in prior audits. When planning a financial statement audit, auditors should think of materiality as the largest amount of uncorrected dollar misstatement that might exist in published financial statements that still fairly present the company's financial position and results of operations in conformity with GAAP. The concept of fair presentation comes from the accounting standards and generally means that the financial statements do not contain misstatements or omissions significant enough to mislead users into making inappropriate economic decisions based on those financial statements.

Financial Statement Materiality

So what is materiality, and how can you deal with it? In financial accounting and reporting, information is material and should be disclosed if it is likely to influence the economic decisions of financial statement users. Auditing standards provide guidance intended to help auditors with these judgments.[9] The emphasis is on the users' point of view, not that of accountants or managers. Thus, "material" means important or significant.

An analogy placing the materiality concept in a more everyday context may be helpful. Imagine you are planning to get your car repaired, and the mechanic tells you it will most likely cost $500, but the actual amount could be between $490 and $510. Would you decide to go ahead with the repairs, given the range in estimates? Most people probably would not let a $10 difference on $500 affect their decision; that is to say, $10 is not "material." If the mechanic said the actual price could be between $100 and $900, most people would find that range too big to accept. The possible $400 variation (in either direction) from the likely cost of $500 is an amount that does affect the decision and is highly material. If a mechanic said the repair would be $500 and it ended up being $900, most people would say that the $500 number was materially misstated! What if the mechanic gave a range of $450 to $550? Some people might be okay with this range, while others would find another mechanic who could give a more precise amount. This analogy illustrates how materiality is viewed as an amount that a typical user of the information finds significant to their decision making. It also illustrates how materiality is a judgment call, because the exact amount cannot be specified, and it can vary from user to user.

It is a challenge for an auditor to reach a judgment about what amount is material to users. To some extent, the auditor guesses what a typical financial statement user would consider significant to his or her decisions. It is even more challenging to apply materiality in performing the audit and evaluating the audit results. Financial statement measurements and information in disclosures are not perfectly accurate. However, do not conclude that financial reports are inherently imprecise and inaccurate. Some numbers will contain mistakes, and some are imprecise because they are based on estimates. Everyone knows that people make mistakes (for example, billing a customer the wrong amount or using the wrong price to value inventory), and many financial measurements are based on estimates (for example, the estimated depreciable lives of fixed assets or the estimated amount of uncollectible accounts receivable). However, this is not an excuse to be sloppy about clerical accuracy or negligent in accounting judgments. As an example of applying materiality to auditing accounting numbers that involve a high degree of management judgment, the box below illustrates the auditor's approach for assessing management's estimates.

Auditors are limited by the nature of accounting. Some amount of inaccuracy is unavoidable in financial statements for the following reasons:

1. Unimportant inaccuracies do not affect users' decisions and hence are not material.

2. The cost of finding and correcting small errors is too great.

3. The time taken to find them would delay issuance of financial statements.

Accounting numbers are never perfectly accurate, but public accountants and auditors want to ensure that financial reports do not contain material misstatements that could make them misleading.

AUDIT CONSIDERATIONS FOR ACCOUNTING ESTIMATES

An accounting estimate is an approximation of a financial statement number, and estimates are often included in financial statements (see CAS 540). Examples include net realizable value of accounts receivable, fair values of assets and liabilities, amortization expense, lease capitalization criteria, percentage-of-completion contract revenues, pension expense, and warranty liabilities.

---

[9] CAS 320 and 450 (5142).

Management is responsible for making accounting estimates. Auditors are responsible for determining that all appropriate estimates have been made, that they are reasonable, and that they are presented and disclosed in conformity with GAAP.

As part of the audit process, the auditors produce their own estimate and compare it with management's. Often, a range for an amount is considered. For example, management may estimate an allowance for doubtful accounts at $50,000, and the auditors may estimate it at $40,000 to $55,000. In this case management's estimate is within the auditors' range of reasonableness. However, the auditors should take note that the management estimate leans toward the conservative side (more than the auditors' $40,000 lower estimate, but not much less than the auditors' higher $55,000 estimate). If other estimates exhibit the same conservatism, and the effect is material, the auditors will need to evaluate the overall reasonableness of the effect of all estimates taken together.

If the auditors develop an estimate that differs (e.g., a range of $55,000 to $70,000 for the allowance that management estimated at $50,000), the difference between management's estimate and the closest end of the auditors' range is considered a misstatement (in this case, misstatement = $5,000 = auditors' $55,000 minus management's $50,000). The remaining difference to the farthest end of the range ($15,000 = $70,000 − $55,000) is noted and reconsidered in combination with the findings on all management's estimates.

Some evidence of the reasonableness of estimates is the actual experience of the company with financial amounts estimated at an earlier date. Tracking the accuracy of management's earlier estimates can provide the auditor with information on the expected accuracy of future estimates.

In the setting out the overall audit strategy, the auditor determines a materiality level for the financial statements as a whole. However, just as accounting may have limitations, there are also limitations in performing an audit. Since every item can't be tested and totally conclusive evidence is never available, auditors may misinterpret or overlook evidence that could reveal misstatements. To leave room for error and reduce the probability that the total of uncorrected and undetected misstatements exceeds materiality for the financial statements, auditors will determine an amount, referred to as **performance materiality**, that is somewhat less than the materiality for the financial statements as a whole. For example, imagine you are going on a four-day holiday that you expect will be sunny and warm. You have $600 to spend and know your hotel will be $100 per night. You could spend all your remaining $200 on meals and entertainment, but if you are cautious you will keep some of it aside for unexpected events such as a lost camera or a medical emergency.

The difference between the whole materiality level and the performance materiality level is a cushion against misstatements, unknown to the auditor, that could make the financial statements materially misstated, just as holiday cash is kept aside for unexpected events. The smaller performance materiality is used for identifying and assessing risks, for determining audit procedures to be done in response to the assessed risks, and for evaluating the materiality of the total misstatements discovered during the audit. How much smaller should it be? Again, we see the need for auditors to use their judgment. Hints for making your decision can be found in the amount of misstatements found in previous audits, or in the average in similar organizations if it is a new audit.

Since the materiality decisions must be made very early, auditors will reconsider these decisions whenever new information that might affect the materiality decision surfaces during the audit. Note that if the materiality is revised to a smaller amount the auditor will probably have to extend any testing that was done based on the larger materiality level.

Materiality Judgment Criteria

Materiality is both a quantitative and a qualitative judgment, made in the context of the auditee's specific circumstances. There is renewed interest in the qualitative aspects of materiality in the post-Enron environment because of the perception that the materiality concept has been "abused." For example, under SEC regulations auditors are not allowed to rely exclusively on quantitative benchmarks. In particular, any quantitatively small misstatements resulting from intentional misstatement, intentional violation of the law, or intentional earnings manipulation must be considered material. Generally, a quantitatively immaterial misstatement is now considered material if it

- masks a change in earnings or other trends,
- hides a failure to meet analysts' consensus expectations for the auditee,
- changes a loss into net income or vice versa,
- concerns a segment of the business that is considered significant,
- affects the auditee's compliance with regulatory requirements,
- involves concealment of an unlawful transaction or fraud, and
- has the effect of increasing management compensation—for example, satisfies requirements for the award of bonuses or other forms of incentive compensation.[10]

The next section covers some traditional quantitative materiality guidelines, and it also will show how even these considerations include qualitative aspects. Auditors consider these factors as well as professional judgment in determining materiality levels.

Materiality Judgment Criteria—Quantitative

Accountants might prefer that definitive, quantitative materiality guides could be issued, but understand the drawbacks of having guidelines that are too rigid. Appropriate materiality levels are based on auditor judgment on an audit-by-audit basis. The auditing standards offer some guidance on quantitative measures of materiality that might be appropriate when making a preliminary assessment of what is material to the financial statements.[11] Some common rules of thumb are as follows:

- 5 to 10 percent of income from continuing operations
- 5 to 10 percent of net income before bonus (for an owner-managed enterprise with a tax-minimization objective where net income is consistently nominal)
- industry-specific measures of materiality that have become generally accepted in practice may also be used; examples include

    a. not-for-profit entity, ½ percent to 2 percent of total expenses or total revenues

    b. mutual fund industry, ½ percent to 1 percent of net asset value

    c. real estate industry, when an entity owns income-producing properties, 1 percent of revenue

The auditor must use professional judgment in selecting alternative financial statement items when making a quantitative determination of materiality. Depending on circumstances, other items used could include total revenues (for start-up companies), net assets, total assets, gross profit, and cash flows from operations. An averaging technique based on several items may be useful in some situations.

If income is used, it should be adjusted for abnormal or extraordinary items. If it is negative, close to zero, or fluctuates significantly from year to year, an average could be used. "Normalizing" income should be done with caution and, if it is difficult to justify normalized income, such as when income is negative or too small relative to other items, then use a different basis altogether. Auditors cannot apply the rules of thumb mechanically and other factors, such as those discussed below, must be considered. Note the role of qualitative factors in these, even though the main issue is quantitative in nature.

---

[10] SEC SAB 99.
[11] CAS 320 (5142).

Absolute Size   A potential misstatement may be important because of its size, regardless of any other considerations. Not many auditors use absolute size alone as a criterion, because a given amount may be appropriate in one case but not in another. Yet some auditors have been known to say that $1 million (or some other large number) is material, no matter what. Even in a very large company, people may find it hard to believe that a large dollar amount of error could be missed first by management, and then by auditors!

Relative Size   The relationship of potential misstatement to a relevant base number is often used. Potential misstatements in income statement accounts are usually related to net income before taxes. In balance sheet accounts, they may be related to a subtotal number, such as current assets or net working capital. A misstatement in segment information may be small in relation to the total business but important for analysis of the segment.

As an example of the complexity of setting materiality, in a particular audit an auditor may decide that certain classes of transactions, account balances, or disclosures should be audited to a lower amount than the amount being used as the materiality level for the financial statements as a whole. The auditor might expect that users' decisions based on these items might be affected by a lower amount of misstatement than the level for the financial statements as a whole. The facts that certain measures or disclosures are required by law (for example, executive compensation and related party transactions), and that there are disclosures key to a particular industry (such as research and development costs for a pharmaceutical company) are indicators of the need to do this. Using an amount lower than whole materiality for a certain account relates to audit sampling decisions, as it can be the basis for setting a **tolerable misstatement** for that account.[12] In this text we will just consider the materiality level and the performance materiality for the financial statements as a whole.

Materiality Judgment Criteria—Qualitative

The quantitative materiality guidelines are a good starting point for qualitative judgments, as they can be applied fairly objectively in every audit. Having the result of the mechanical quantitative calculation, the auditor needs to stand back to take a broad perspective and consider other factors that may be informative about the consequences of the materiality level used. New information that causes revision to materiality during the audit is usually a qualitative consideration.

User-related Factors   Certain users may require more precise financial information: it might be the only information available for a new business; it contains the profit information that shareholders' dividend income is based on. Some users might scrutinize financial reports to determine whether specific laws or practices, such as anti-competitive practices or environmental protection agreements, are being followed.

Nature of the Item or Issue   Small items may be considered material because of what they suggest about management's character or how they interact with a specific user decision or evaluation. For example, an illegal payment is important because of what it is, not because of its absolute or relative amount. Other qualitative factors include whether a misstatement affects the trend of earnings, whether analysts' forecasts are met, and whether a loan covenant is violated. Generally, potential errors in the more liquid assets (cash, receivables, and inventory) are considered more important than potential errors in other accounts (such as fixed assets and deferred charges) because of their impact on liquidity ratios that are often included in debt covenants.

Circumstances   Auditors generally use a smaller materiality level, and thus smaller permitted misstatement, for auditees whose financial statements will be widely used (publicly held companies) or used by important outsiders (bank loan officers) than they do for auditees whose financial statement users are closer to management and may have access to other sources of information. When management exercises discretion over an accounting treatment and important

---

[12] CAS 530, and further discussion in Chapter 10.

decisions will be based on the financial statement information, auditors tend to exercise more care and use a more stringent materiality criterion. Troublesome events, such as the string of corporate and audit failures of the post-Enron environment, have also led auditors to lower materiality and audit measurement and disclosures with more precision. These matters relate as much to risks as they do to financial statement materiality, as the two concepts are closely related in planning the nature, timing, and extent of the auditor's work. The relationship between materiality and audit risk decisions are further explained in Chapter 7.

Exhibit 6–6 (pages 196 and 197) illustrates a materiality worksheet that could be used to summarize the quantitative and qualitative factors that go into an auditor's decision on both the materiality level for financial statements as a whole and the performance materiality.

The materiality judgment for the current-year financial information of Anycompany Inc. shown in Exhibit 6–4 involves focusing on the most important financial decisions made based on the financial statements. The centre of attention will be different for different audits. For example, the focus may be the current asset–liability position for a company in financial difficulty seeking to renew its bank loans. This company may be experiencing operating losses, and the balance sheet, rather than the income statement, will be the most important information. In other cases, when a company is growing and issuing shares to the public, decisions based on income performance are the focus, so the income statement and the net income number may be the most important. The box below shows a calculation of overall materiality based on an assumed effect of income misstatement on a share price. If the auditors decide the shares could be mispriced by 10 percent and nobody would be disadvantaged, the income before taxes and interest could be overstated (or understated) by as much as $71,000.

DETERMINATION OF POSSIBLE RELATIVE SIZE MATERIALITY

Suppose the auditors have decided the influence of earnings per share (EPS) on share price is an important consideration in determining materiality, and they choose a simple EPS multiple as the model for share price determination. (This is not to suggest that share prices are actually determined by such a simple method as multiplying the EPS. Analysts and investors use other models not considered in this simplified illustration.)

Assume that Anycompany Inc. (Exhibit 6–4) has 100,000 shares outstanding and its shares trade at a 14 price-earning multiple, thus indicating a share price of $51.80.

(Share price = EPS ($3.70 = $370,000/100,000) × 14 = $51.80)

The auditors make a judgment about how much investors could overpay for the shares without its making any difference to them—say 5 to 10 percent.

	Low (5%)	High (10%)
Indicated share price (14 × $3.70)	$ 51.80	$ 51.80
Price materiality judgment	2.59	5.18
Adjusted share price	49.21	46.62
Adjusted earnings per share (divide by 14 multiple)	3.52	3.33
Indicated net income (multiply by 100,000 shares)	352,000	333,000
Add pre-tax accounts that can be audited completely		
Interest expense	40,000	40,000
Income tax expense (40%)	234,667	222,000
Indicated pre-tax income*	626,667	595,000
Unaudited pre-tax income	666,000	666,000
Indicated planning materiality based on pre-tax income	39,333	71,000

*Calculate the pre-tax income, which, when reduced by interest expense and 40 percent income taxes, produces the indicated net income (after-tax).

At this point it is useful to review the reason for determining materiality. First, materiality levels determined at the planning stage are used to decide how much work to do on each financial statement account. At the completion stage of the audit, as discussed in Chapter 15, auditors use them to evaluate the cumulative effects of known or potential misstatements. If the audit work discovered five different $15,000 mistakes that all increase net income, it is not appropriate to consider these as immaterial when the net income-based materiality limit is $50,000. While misstatements may be discovered in auditing an income statement account, the misstatement's materiality must be considered in relation to one or more balance sheet accounts. This is because income misstatements in the double-entry bookkeeping system can leave a **"dangling debit"** or a "dangling credit" somewhere in the balance sheet accounts, and the audit challenge is to find it. (For example, if fictitious credit sales were recorded, setting up fictitious accounts receivable will balance the accounts.) If there is no dangling debit or credit, the other side of the misstatement transaction has gone through the income statement, probably causing misstatement in two accounts (opposite directions), with no net effect on the net income bottom line. (In the previous example, if the fictitious accounts receivable were written off as bad debt expense, both the revenue and expense would be overstated, but the income would not be misstated.) The articulation of the balance sheet and income statement shown here support setting materiality/performance materiality at the financial statement level, since then what is material in the balance sheet is also material in the income statement, and vice versa.

REVIEW CHECKPOINTS

26 Why is the materiality decision one of the first decisions made in the audit?

27 What is material information in accounting and auditing?

28 What limitations of accounting affect auditors?

29 How is the materiality level applied in auditing an accounting estimate?

30 What do you think is the best objective evidence of the reasonableness of an accounting estimate? Use the allowance for doubtful accounts receivable as an example.

31 Why are qualitative criteria important in the auditor's materiality decision?

32 Do auditing standards require auditors to use a specific quantitative criterion to determine planning materiality?

33 How do fraud considerations relate to the auditor's materiality decision?

34 What are the advantages of using the same overall materiality level for planning the audit instead of assigning a part of the overall materiality to each account balance?

35 How does materiality for the financial statements as a whole differ from performance materiality in the auditing standards?

36 What issues arise if an auditor realizes part way through the audit that a smaller materiality level is appropriate?

FINANCIAL STATEMENT ASSERTIONS AND AUDIT OBJECTIVES

LEARNING OBJECTIVE

6 Describe the principal assertions in management's financial statements, and their application in establishing audit objectives..

This section explains the concept of the financial statement **"assertions"** that are the claims management makes. Keep the following things in mind as you study this:

- Management's accounting system produces a trial balance.
- Management arranges the trial balance in financial statements and thereby makes certain assertions about how the financial statements represent the underlying economic data in the accounting system.

EXHIBIT   6-6   MATERIALITY ASSESSMENT

Auditee:_____ **Year end:**_____

Materiality assessment

1. Qualitative factors

	Comments
a) Identify the specific users of the financial statements for this engagement.	
b) Identify what expectations the users may have for the financial statements for this engagement.	
c) Identify any possible situations or misstatements that would affect a user now or at some future point, regardless of the materiality level. (e.g., Consider environmental matters, policies, statutes, safety issues, etc.)	

2. Quantitative factors

a) Planning data

	This year actual (adjusted)	This year anticipated	Last year	2nd preceding year
Assets				
Liabilities				
Equity				
Sales/revenue				
Gross profit				
Expenses				
Income before tax				
Previous materiality				

b) Normalized pre-tax income

	This year actual (adjusted)	This year anticipated	Last year	2nd preceding year
Estimated pre-tax income	$			
Adjustment for nonrecurring items or unadjusted errors brought forward _____				
Normalized pre-tax income	$			

Date & initials	Prepared	Reviewed	Index

EXHIBIT 6-6   Continued

Auditee:_____   **Year end:**_____

3. Materiality considerations

a) Profit-oriented enterprises

Identify financial statement users	Measurement base	Factor applied*	Possible materiality	Comments
	Normalized pre-tax income		$	
	Assets		$	
	Equity		$	
	Revenue		$	
	Gross profit		$	
	Other		$	

*Materiality guidelines

Normalized pre-tax income	5–10%
Assets	½–1%
Equity	½–5%
Revenue	½–1%
Gross profit	½–5%

These materiality factors are provided as guidelines only, and should be used only as an aid in the development of your professional judgment. The materiality level should represent the largest amount of a misstatement or group of misstatements that would not, in your judgment, influence or change a decision based on the financial statements.

Often, normalized pre-tax income is used as an initial reference point for businesses although it may not be sufficient for businesses with little or no income. Weighted averages are also used at times. Revenue is often used for NPOs. See AUG-41 for more guidance.

b) Not-for-profit enterprises

Identify financial statement users	Measurement base revenue/expenses	Factor applied*	Possible materiality	Comments
Governmental authorities				
Funding organizations				
Directors				
Other				

*Materiality factors

Total expenses or total revenues ½ to 2%

c) Other factors considered in determining materiality for this engagement

_____

_____

_____

Preliminary planning materiality assessment for financial statements as a whole

Based on the anticipated financial statement amounts and on the other factors described above, preliminary materiality for this engagement is:

$_____ Misstatements below this threshold, if not corrected, will be accumulated on the Possible Adjustments Sheet unless such misstatements are deemed trivial (below $ ____). Note: The auditor may designate an amount below which misstatements are deemed trivial and need not be accumulated because the auditor expects that the accumulation of such amounts clearly will not have a material effect on the financial statements. In so doing, the auditor considers the fact that the determination of materiality involves qualitative as well as quantitative considerations and that misstatements of a relatively small amount could nevertheless have a material effect on the financial statements. The summary of uncorrected misstatements included in or attached to the management representation letter need not include trivial misstatements.

Performance materiality assessment

Based on expected misstatements in current period financial statements of $_____, and on other factors noted above, performance materiality for planning the auditee

$_____.

	Prepared	Reviewed		Index
Date & initials				

EXHIBIT 6–7   MANAGEMENT ASSERTIONS ABOUT INVENTORY

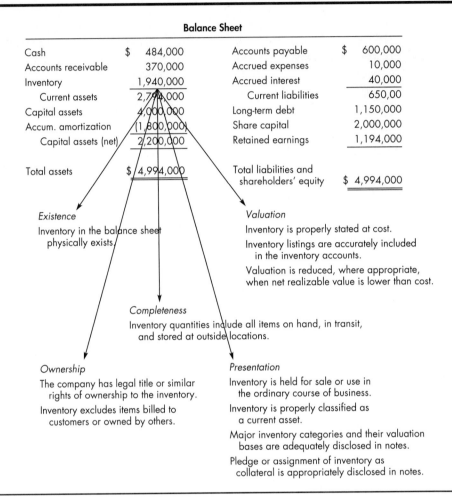

Balance Sheet

Cash	$ 484,000	Accounts payable	$ 600,000
Accounts receivable	370,000	Accrued expenses	10,000
Inventory	1,940,000	Accrued interest	40,000
Current assets	2,794,000	Current liabilities	650,00
Capital assets	4,000,000	Long-term debt	1,150,000
Accum. amortization	(1,800,000)	Share capital	2,000,000
Capital assets (net)	2,200,000	Retained earnings	1,194,000
Total assets	$ 4,994,000	Total liabilities and shareholders' equity	$ 4,994,000

Existence
Inventory in the balance sheet physically exists.

Valuation
Inventory is properly stated at cost.
Inventory listings are accurately included in the inventory accounts.
Valuation is reduced, where appropriate, when net realizable value is lower than cost.

Completeness
Inventory quantities include all items on hand, in transit, and stored at outside locations.

Ownership
The company has legal title or similar rights of ownership to the inventory.
Inventory excludes items billed to customers or owned by others.

Presentation
Inventory is held for sale or use in the ordinary course of business.
Inventory is properly classified as a current asset.
Major inventory categories and their valuation bases are adequately disclosed in notes.
Pledge or assignment of inventory as collateral is appropriately disclosed in notes.

- Auditors take these assertions as focal points for the audit work.
- The practical audit objectives are to obtain and evaluate evidence about the assertions made by management in financial statements.

We will start with five principal assertions that, while broadly defined, are distinct and comprehensive descriptions of the claims in financial statement elements:

1. Existence
2. Completeness
3. Ownership (rights and obligations)
4. Valuation (measurement and allocation)
5. Presentation (classification and disclosure)

Exhibit 6–7 illustrates these assertions in relation to the inventory in the balance sheet. Various sets of assertions used in audit practice provide finer definitions and make it easier to relate to financial statement information and auditing procedures. For example, CAS 315 classifies assertions into a framework the auditor uses to identify and assess the risks of material misstatement at the financial statement and assertion levels when designing the audit plan. The detailed assertions as set out in the audit standards are shown in the following box, with cross-references to the five principal assertions. The five assertions will next be described in more detail in the context of audit objectives and procedures.

ASSERTIONS FOR CLASSES OF TRANSACTIONS, ACCOUNT BALANCES, AND PRESENTATION AND DISCLOSURE

Auditing standards require the auditor to assess risk of material misstatement assertion by assertion at the levels of transactions and events, account balances, and presentation/disclosure. In planning and performing the audit, an auditor may use the assertions as described in the standards, or he may express them differently as long as all aspects described in the standards above have been covered. Some auditors may prefer to combine assertions about transactions and events with those about account balances, or to cover proper cutoff of transactions and events under occurrence and completeness assertions rather than as a standalone assertion.

Assertion terms used at the transaction, account balance, and disclosure levels are shown with links to the five principal assertions.

Detailed assertions per CAS 315	Principal assertion(s) linked to detailed assertion
1. Assertions about classes of transactions and events	
(i) Occurrence—transactions and events that have been recorded have occurred and pertain to the entity	Existence
(ii) Completeness—all transactions and events that should have been recorded have been recorded	Completeness
(iii) Accuracy—amounts and other data relating to recorded transactions and events have been recorded appropriately	Valuation
(iv) Cutoff—transactions and events have been recorded in the correct accounting period	Existence Completeness -depending on direction of testing
(v) Classification—transactions and events have been recorded in the proper accounts	Presentation
2. Assertions about balance sheet items	
(i) Existence—assets, liabilities, and equity interests exist	Existence
(ii) Rights and obligations—the entity holds or controls the rights to assets, and liabilities are the obligations of the entity	Ownership
(iii) Completeness—all assets, liabilities, and equity interests that should have been recorded have been recorded	Completeness
(iv) Valuation and allocation—assets, liabilities, and equity interests are included in the financial statements at appropriate amounts, and any resulting measurement or allocation adjustments are appropriately recorded	Valuation
3. Assertions about presentation and disclosure	
(i) Occurrence and rights and obligations—disclosed events, transactions, and other matters have occurred and pertain to the entity	Existence Ownership
(ii) Completeness—all disclosures that should have been included in the financial statements have been included	Completeness

(iii) Classification and understandability—financial information is appropriately presented and described, and disclosures are clearly expressed	Presentation
(iv) Accuracy and valuation—financial and other information are disclosed fairly and at appropriate amounts	Valuation

Source: Adapted from CAS 315.

Existence

The audit objective related to *existence* establishes with evidence that balance-sheet assets, liabilities, and equities actually are real. For revenue and expense transactions, the existence assertion is also described as *occurrence*, as the auditor requires evidence that transactions are valid and actually occurred. Both terms relate to whether a recorded amount is genuine, not fictitious. An account balance overstatement, for example, is an existence error. In determining whether cash, inventory, receivables, insurance in force, and other assets actually exist, auditors will count cash and inventory, confirm receivables and payables, and perform other procedures. Beginning students must be careful at this point, however, because finding evidence of existence alone generally proves little about the other four assertions.

Completeness

Completeness establishes with evidence that all valid transactions and accounts that should be presented in the financial reports are included. A completeness error exists when a transaction total or account balance is understated. Thus, auditors gather evidence that, for example, inventory on hand is included, inventory consigned out is included, sales that occurred have been recorded, and so forth. Auditing this assertion means auditing what is not there, so it creates special difficulties for the auditor. Management's written representation that all transactions are included in the accounts is always obtained by the auditor, but this alone is not sufficient. Auditors also need to gather corroborating evidence, often from several sources.

Cutoff

Proper *cutoff* means accounting for all transactions that occurred during a period without postponing some recordings to the next period or accelerating next-period transactions into the current-year accounts. Cutoff errors result in accounts being overstated or understated and, therefore, relate to either the existence or the completeness assertions.

Simple cutoff errors occur in the revenue accounting process when late-December sales invoices are recorded for goods not actually shipped until January, or when cash receipts are recorded through the end of the week (e.g., Friday, January 4) and the last batch for the year should have been processed on December 31. They can occur in the purchases process when there is a failure to record accruals for expenses incurred but not yet paid, thus understating both expenses and liabilities. A failure to record materials purchased but not yet received, and therefore not included in the ending inventory, results in understating both inventory and accounts payable.

In a financial statement audit, the cutoff date usually refers to the auditee's year-end balance sheet date; however, it can be required at other times, for example when one accounting system is converted to a new system during the year.

Ownership (Rights and Obligations)

The objective related to *ownership* is establishing, with evidence, the ownership (rights) for assets, "ownership" (obligations) for liabilities, and the propriety of revenue and expense transactions. Ownership, however, can include assets (rights) the company does not actually hold title to. For example, an auditor will specifically gather evidence about the amounts capitalized for leased property. Likewise, ownership includes accounting liabilities that a company may not yet be legally obligated to pay. For example, an auditor would gather evidence about the obligations under a capitalized lease, estimated liability for product warranties, or estimated future environmental clean up. This assertion links to the fundamental "entity" concept you are familiar with from the conceptual framework of financial accounting. The auditor's knowledge of the boundaries of the auditee entity are important in setting the scope of the audit and in assessing the appropriate application of accounting principles in the financial statements.

Valuation (Measurement and Allocation)

The objective related to *valuation* (also stated as measurement, or allocation) is determining whether proper dollar amounts have been assigned to the assets, liabilities, equities, revenue, and expense recognized in the financial statements. It can involve the measurement approach used (historic cost, fair value, present value) or the method of allocating joint costs. Auditors obtain evidence about specific dollar measurements by reconciling bank accounts, comparing vendors' invoices to inventory prices, obtaining lower-of-cost-and-market data, evaluating collectibility of receivables, and so forth. Many valuation and allocation decisions involve determining the proper application of GAAP.

Presentation (Classification and Disclosure)

Auditors also must determine whether accounting principles are properly selected and applied, whether financial information is presented in accordance with the underlying economic reality, whether disclosures are adequate, and whether any GAAP that apply have been followed—all aspects of financial statement *presentation*. Specific objectives of presentation include proper balance sheet classification (e.g., current versus long-term), proper income statement classification (e.g., cost of sales components, unusual items, discontinued operations items, extraordinary items), and note disclosure of accounting policies and account details. The presentation assertion is the meeting place between accounting principles and audit reporting standards.

Compliance Assertion

Although it is not normally listed as a separate assertion, *compliance* with laws and regulations is very important for a business, and disclosure of known noncompliance is necessary for presentation of financial statements in conformity with generally accepted accounting principles. The compliance assertion will increase in importance as new laws and regulations come into force to improve governance and accountability (in response to corporate scandals). Auditors gather evidence related to laws and regulations that can have financial implications, such as provincial securities acts, tax withholding regulations, minimum wage laws, wage and price guidelines, credit allocation regulations, income tax laws, environmental regulations, and specialized industry regulations. Compliance with legal terms of the company's private contracts (e.g., merger agreements and bond indentures) is also important for financial statement presentation, as failures to comply may be a warning sign that the company is not a going concern, which requires financial statement disclosure and must be emphasized in the auditor's report. CAS 570, "Going Concern," has elevated the importance of this assertion and provides additional guidance on dealing with it in the audit of financial statements.

When the sole purpose of an engagement is to audit compliance with various laws, regulations, or rules, it is called a **compliance audit**. These are discussed in Chapter 16. Compliance with laws and regulations is part of governmental audits, such as those by the Auditor General and provincial auditors. It is generally an objective for internal auditors with respect to managerial policies. These types of audits are covered in advanced auditing courses.

Assertions and Audit Objectives

Financial statement assertions are the fundamental management claims to be audited and the focal points for all audit procedures. In an audit program, the evidence produced by each procedure relates to one or more specific objectives linked to specific assertions. When you have a list of audit procedures (e.g., from last year's audit), begin planning by asking the following questions:

- What are the assertions management is making by reporting this financial information?
- What are the risks of material misstatement in these assertions?
- Which assertion(s) does this procedure produce evidence about?
- Does the list of procedures (the audit program) address the risk of material misstatement in all the assertions?

Qualitative factors, cost of the procedure, risk level associated with each assertion, and materiality determine the extent that a particular procedure is used.

You can simplify the five major assertions by thinking of them as existence, completeness, ownership, valuation, and presentation. Each of them has additional aspects, depending on the financial items you are auditing and the audit evidence available. How procedures are linked to assertions is covered in more detail in Chapters 8 and 9, and in Part III.

R E V I E W
CHECKPOINTS

37 Briefly explain the five principal assertions that can be made about assets and liabilities, and auditors' objectives related to each.

38 How do financial statement assertions relate to audit procedures?

39 Why is it particularly challenging to obtain audit evidence about the completeness assertion?

40 Why should auditors think about a compliance assertion that is not listed in the auditing standards about assertions?

41 How are assertions used in audit planning?

DEVELOPING THE OVERALL AUDIT STRATEGY

Overall Audit Strategy

LEARNING OBJECTIVE
7 Explain how the preliminary planning activities are integrated in the overall audit strategy.

As discussed throughout Part II of the text, audit planning is an ongoing, iterative process where information gained as the audit is performed may result in revisions to the plan. The preliminary planning activities are the basis for the **overall audit strategy**, which documents information about (1) investigation or review of the prospective or continuing engagement and client relationship; (2) staff, and special technical or industry expertise required; (3) preliminary materiality levels; (4) assessment of significant industry or company risks and related audit issues; (5) identification of unusual accounting principles; (6) use of substantive or combined audit approach; (7) nature and extent of resources required; (8) staff assignment and scheduling of team communications and field work; and (9) special considerations for intitial or group audit engagments.

This overall audit strategy guides development of the detailed audit plan, which contains the specific programs. The programs include specific audit objectives and procedures for determining inherent and control risk, obtaining the sufficient competent evidence that is the basis for the audit report, and producing the required documentation. These programs are discussed in the next chapter, and their contents are covered in more detail in Part III.

Exhibit 6–8 below provides a checklist of considerations auditors include in developing the overall audit strategy for a typical continuing audit engagement. The checklist is a questionnaire form that could be used to document the planning, as required by the auditing standards. The first part lists considerations that are usually relevant in ongoing audits, and the following two parts relate to specific circumstances such as intitial engagements or audits of consolidated financial statements. Many of these matters will influence the auditor's detailed audit plan, which will be further discussed in Chapter 8 after we have more fully assessed the auditee's business risks and related internal control. The examples cover a broad range of matters applicable to many engagements. While some of the matters referred to below may be required by other CASs, not all matters are relevant to every audit engagement, and the list is not necessarily complete.

A key purpose of the overall audit strategy is to pull together all relevant preliminary planning activities to guide the development of the detailed audit plan. The audit plan details the nature, timing, and extent of the audit procedures for each component of the audit. The "nature" of audit procedures refers to evidence techniques they will use. The "timing" refers to when they will be performed, whether before (interim date), at, or after the auditee's year end. Timing may have other aspects, such as surprise procedures (unannounced to auditee personnel) or the need to observe periodic auditee procedures, such as rotating inventory counts during the year. The "extent" usually refers to the sample sizes of data examined, such as the number of customer accounts receivable to confirm, or the number of inventory categories/products to count.

EXHIBIT 6-8   CONSIDERATIONS IN ESTABLISHING THE OVERALL AUDIT STRATEGY

Matters relevant to planning financial statement audits	
Document the following information based on enquiries of appropriate auditee personnel:	**Response/File Documentation Reference**
Considerations applicable on most continuing audits of standalone financial statements	

Engagement Characteristics
- Entity's reporting requirements and deadlines.
- Financial reporting framework used in financial information to be audited a "GAAP" framework or otherwise acceptable per CAS 210?
- Any requirement to reconcile to another financial reporting framework?
- Any additional specific reporting requirements; e.g., industry, regulatory, legislated (e.g., in public sector) requirements?
- Expected audit coverage, including the number, locations, and nature of business components.
- Reporting currency to be used; need for currency translation in the financial information audited.
- Existence of related parties and extent of any related party transactions and balances.
- Impact of information technology on data available for audit procedures; potential to use computer-assisted audit techniques.
- Organizational structure, key auditee personnel, information systems, and availability of data relevant to audit
- Need to use work of others for audit evidence, such as other auditors, experts with specialized knowledge, internal audit work, service organizations; audit reports on effective design or operation of controls performed by them?

Audit Timing and Communications
- Schedule of meetings with management and those charged with governance to discuss the nature, timing, and extent of the audit work; expected type and timing of auditor's report; management letters; and other communications, both written and oral, throughout the engagement.
- Expected nature and timing of communications and meetings among engagement team members.
- Expected timing for performing and reviewing audit work.
- Plan for communicating to engagement team members on the need to question management and exercise professional skepticism in gathering and evaluating audit evidence throughout the audit

EXHIBIT 6-8   Continued

Preliminary Audit Activities
- Initial determination of appropriate materiality and performance materiality level for financial statements as a whole for planning purposes (and lower levels for specific financial statement elements, if required).
- Reconsideration of materiality levels based on new information as audit procedures are performed during the course of the audit.
- Identification of material business components and financial statement account balances.
- Preliminary identification of significant audit issues (areas where there may be a higher risk of material misstatement).
- Consider results of previous audits, including evaluation of internal control operating effectiveness, management's commitment to effective internal control, nature and magnitude of misstatements identified by the auditor, any restatements and corrections made by management
- Consider volume of transactions, complexity of information systems, availability of records, importance of internal control to successful business operations, and other relevant factors to determine whether it is more efficient for the auditor to test internal control effectiveness to obtain audit assurance.
- Preliminary decision on whether a combined approach (using both control testing evidence and substantive evidence) should be used for any aspects of the audit.

Identification of Significant Audit Issues
- Consider significant business developments such as changes in information technology and business processes; key management changes; and acquisitions, mergers, and divestments.
- Consider significant industry developments such as changes in industry regulations, new reporting requirements, and the legal environment affecting the entity.
- Consider significant changes in the applicable financial accounting standards.

Nature, Timing, and Extent of Required Resources
- Consider impact of assessed risk of material misstatement at the overall financial statement level on engagement staffing, direction, supervision, and review.
- Selection of, and audit work assignment to, engagement team members; assigning appropriately experienced team members to areas with higher risks of material misstatement.
- Engagement time budgeting, including considering adequate time for high risk areas, supervision, and review of less experienced team members.

Additional Considerations for Specific Circumstances	**Response/ File Documentation Reference**

Initial audits
- Consider:
  - if entity previously audited, consider matters raised in communications with predecessor and accessibility of previous audit working papers.
  - impact on engagement and audit report of availability of evidence regarding opening balances, consistency of accounting policies, and comparative figures if these are reported.

Group audits of consolidated entities
- Consider:
  - nature of the control relationships between a parent and its components that determine how the group is to be consolidated.
  - extent to which components are audited by other auditors.
  - need for a statutory audit of standalone financial statements in addition to an audit for consolidation purposes.
  - communication with auditors of components, regarding things such as the expected types and timing of reports to be issued and other communications.
  - setting and communicating materiality for auditors of components.
  - nature, timing, and extent of resources needed for engagement team to assess understanding, group-wide risks and controls, and consolidation process.

Source: Adapted from CAS 300, 510, 600.

REVIEW CHECKPOINTS

42 What audit planning activities are documented in the overall audit strategy?

43 How does the overall audit strategy relate to the audit plan and detailed programs?

APPLICATION CASE AND ANALYSIS
Audit Engagement Acceptance Decision

LEARNING OBJECTIVE

8 Apply and integrate the chapter topics to analyze a practical auditing situation/case/scenario.

Discussion Case

About a year ago, Jack joined a medium-sized local public accounting firm as a junior auditor. Early in his first year Jack got the opportunity to work on a new audit client acceptance decision with Hilda, one of the firm's top audit managers. The prospective client is a local company called Sweet Dreams Inc. Hilda had gathered information about Sweet Dreams as required to comply with the firm's quality control standards, and she asked Jack to review it and comment on her recommendation that the firm accept the audit engagement. Hilda saw this as a way for Jack to get familiar with the client as he was the junior member of the Sweet Dreams audit team, but it was also a way for Jack to learn the firm's procedures for new client acceptance decisions. Some of the key points Jack noted in reviewing the information Hilda had gathered follow.

- Sweet Dreams operates a chain of retail mattress stores across the city. It is privately owned by three sisters who inherited the company from their parents, the company's founders. The owners are not involved in managing the business, but it pays quarterly dividends that are their main source of income. The three sisters are all highly involved in local charitable associations and are well respected in the community.

- Sweet Dream's predecessor auditor, a partner in a small local firm, resigned from the audit because she is planning to retire from practice soon. Since all her partners also plan to retire in a few years, she felt it would be in Sweet Dreams' best interest to switch to another firm that could continue the audit for a longer time.

- The predecessor's response letter to Hilda also indicated that Sweet Dreams had been an excellent audit client over twenty years. Management is very competent and control conscious, ensuring employees keep accurate records and follow all control procedures. Misstatements uncovered by the auditor, even immaterial ones, have always been promptly corrected, and they have always paid the audit fees in full, promptly. The predecessor also noted that management has given its permission for her to give its new auditors access to her prior year's audit files to facilitate their familiarization to the company.

- The company is very profitable and the owners receive audited financial statements annually, as well as quarterly profit reports. Management provided Hilda with the company's most recent financial statements, and she notes that it uses an appropriate acceptable basis of accounting. Management and senior employees participate in a profit sharing plan that gives them above average earnings.

- The company participates in many community fundraising events, such as supplying new mattresses to homeless shelters. Sweet Dreams was the first business in the city to undertake a comprehensive waste and energy reduction program. Employees are proud to work for Sweet Dreams, and it has won awards from the city for its community and environmental initiatives.

After his review of Hilda's documentation, Jack felt he had a good introduction to Sweet Dreams and that he fully understood why Hilda recommended that the firm accept it as a new audit client.

Later that year, Hilda assigned Jack to assist on another new client acceptance decision, this time for Grouse Mines Limited. She was very impressed with Jack's progress, and decided to give him a little more rope this time by letting him gather some of the background information required. Jack was instructed not to contact Grouse management, as that would have to be done by one of the firm's partners, but to do any other information gathering that could be relevant to the firm's acceptance decision. Jack was happy to have this challenge and set about his work, gathering the following points.

- Grouse is a mining company that owns and operates several mines outside the city. Grouse also owns mining properties in South America and Indonesia, which are operated by local managers.

- Its shares are publicly traded on the over-the-counter market.

- After three attempts, Grouse's predecessor auditor responded to Jack by telephone. He explained that his firm has resigned from all its public company audits because "we are sick and tired of CPAB breathing down our necks about trivial issues like documentation." Further, he "can't give any reason why your firm shouldn't accept the audit. They always paid their audit fees, and we plan to continue to do consulting work for them on financing, management compensation, and environmental disclosure issues. Now that we don't have CPAB tying our hands, we should be able to provide much more valuable business advice to Grouse's management." When Jack enquired about the possibility of reviewing prior year working papers, the predecessor said it would not be possible since his firm's staff is "far too busy to spend the time it would take to get those old files ready for your firm to see."

- In reviewing Grouse's regulatory filings on SEDAR, Jack notes Grouse's profitability had been declining until two years ago when it hired a mining veteran as its new CEO to implement serious cost-cutting measures. The company's profits have increased modestly in the last two years, but it is late in filing its most recent quarterly report. The CEO and her management team have stock options that will vest next year.

- Grouse's recent annual report includes several pages of disclosure about its environmental management policies and its compliance with all environment regulations.

- News stories have appeared reporting that residents living near the mines in Canada and the other countries have organized protests after noting an increase in breathing problems as well as several serious fish kills in the rivers downstream of the mines' tailings ponds.

- Grouse issued a recent press release announcing it has preliminary assays indicating that one of the world's largest reserves of platinum exists in one of its South American mining properties. Further testing is being done and more certain estimates of the platinum reserve quantities are expected to be available some time next year.

In trying to apply what he learned in his prior experience with Sweet Dreams, Jack is amazed at how different the Grouse situation is in just about every aspect. He is looking forward to a meeting with Hilda to discuss all the information. As he prepares for the meeting, what do you think are the key points for Jack to consider in this case?

* * * * * * *

Analysis

Let's now consider the key points Jack has learned about these two different prospective audit clients by applying the list of acceptance decision procedures provided in this chapter.

1. *Obtaining and reviewing financial information about the prospective auditee organization to determine purpose, main users, and basis of accounting*

Sweet Dreams provided Jack's firm with relevant reports, indicating its management has a good sense of the role and responsibilities of an auditor. Hilda also learned that the purpose and main users are the three sisters who own the shares, and she determined the basis of accounting appropriate for this purpose and these users.

Grouse is publicly traded and Jack was thus able to obtain relevant information from the regulatory filings, which are available online. But additional information is needed from Grouse management in order to assess all the purposes and users of its financial statements. As a mining company, Grouse's basis of accounting may be complex, and discussions with management are needed to learn more details and establish the appropriateness of its accounting policies for estimates related to mineral reserves, revenue recognition, environmental liability estimates, etc.

2. *Evaluating the public accounting firm's and individual auditors' independence from the prospect*

This would be done at the firm level as part of quality control procedures. Hilda and Jack can only know about their own independence: close relatives who are employees of these companies or holding shares or debts that could create a conflict of interest (self-interest threat). These factors need to be considered for all audit staff.

Other independence threats relating to acceptance decisions need to be considered at the firm level. For example, any prior association with these companies involving promoting their position (assisting the company with obtaining a bank loan = advocacy threat), personal or business relations making it difficult to exercise professional skepticism (a former audit partner now being on the prospect's management team = familiarity threat), or any risk for intimidation of an auditor with respect to the financial statements or the conduct of the audit (management seems very aggressive and motivated to manipulate the financial statements = intimidation threat).

Jack might have a concern about the likelihood of a Grouse management attempt at intimidation of the auditor, as there are indicators that their cost-cutting actions may have increased their risk of environmental liability (news reports), and there is motivation related to the stock options that will vest next year (reports of a huge platinum find would increase Grouse's share price at the time these options vest, and history has shown that such findings can easily be falsified or overstated). Not enough information is given in this case to go any further on these independence aspects, but remember they are critical to the firm's acceptance decision. Independence threats were explained in more detail in Chapter 4.

3. *Considering whether the public accounting firm has competency, resources, any special skills required*

Sweet Dreams is a local business in a fairly straightforward industry, and its basis of accounting was appropriate, so it seems reasonable to assume Jack's firm has the staff and competency to do the job. Any specific information systems or tax expertise required would also be typical, so the required competencies would be readily available within the firm.

Grouse is in a specialized industry with more complex operations to account for. Jack's firm may have other audits of mining companies in the area, and thus have the expertise to handle the mining-specific accounting issues. Grouse also has operations in foreign countries. If these are material, Jack's firm will need to obtain knowledge of foreign laws and regulations and be able to do audit work in those locations. Using the work of foreign auditors will increase the complexity and risk of this engagement. Jack's mid-sized local firm may not be able to manage that aspect of auditing Grouse.

4. *Obtaining information from management as to whether the prospect's management accepts responsibility for the financial statement preparation and implementing adequate controls to reduce risk of errors and fraud*

The case suggests Sweet Dreams' management are aware of and have accepted their responsibilities for (1) preparing financial statements in accordance with an acceptable financial reporting framework and (2) implementing adequate internal control to reduce risk of error and fraud. Their most recent financial statements and information indicate strong control awareness at the management level and throughout the whole organization. Employee pride and community involvement suggest that integrity and responsibility, which are desirable qualities in an auditee, are part of the corporate culture at Sweet Dreams. Jack did not meet with Grouse management so information on these issues is missing, but there are hints in information Jack obtained from other sources, as is seen below.

5. *Considering whether the engagement would require special attention or involve unusual risks*

Sweet Dreams does not appear to present any special concerns, but it is important that the owners depend on the audited financial statements for information about the financial position of the business. The preliminary analysis shows that Grouse presents many risks, such that the firm may already find the company and the engagement too risky to accept just on the basis of what Jack has learned.

6. *Searching for news reports and, when possible, asking business associates about the organization*

Some key information about both companies was obtained from news reports. These can be searched quite easily online using a search tool like Google. A firm partner may ask business associates about the prospective client, but this must be done carefully and in compliance with confidentiality rules of the profession or the firm. Partners often have a wide network of business associates where a lot of useful information can be obtained informally, possibly over a game of golf or a dinner, without breaking any confidence.

7. *For new audits, communicating with the previous auditor*

Sweet Dreams' predecessor audit has provided Hilda with much useful information. The predecessor has good reasons for resigning and the fact that her partners are not taking over does not reflect badly on the integrity of management or the risk of Sweet Dreams as an auditee. She reports there were no disagreements with management about accounting matters in many years as the company's auditor. We also learn that management will be very cooperative and helpful to the auditor, which is a sign the audit can be done well within a reasonable amount of audit time.

The information obtained from Grouse's predecessor auditor paints a rather risky picture. The predecessor appears to have lacked competence to do the audit, as evidenced by deficiencies in documentation found by CPAB's inspectors. The fact that it was doing consulting work on executive compensation, financing, and disclosure means it lacked independence. Public company auditors cannot consult on these areas as they will be involved with reporting decisions and, therefore, not be objective in assessing the company's financial statements. The fact that the auditor resigned and was not dismissed by the auditee suggests that management did not object to the predecessor's lack of competence and independence, further bringing management's integrity and competence into question. The predecessor's reluctance to respond to Jack's request and failure to do so in writing also cast doubt on the quality of that firm and its audits of Grouse. Since his only reply was by telephone, it is important that Jack make detailed notes right away so there is reliable documentation of the predecessor's responses. The refusal to provide Jack's firm with access to any working papers also suggests a poor quality audit, increasing the risk that Grouse's opening balance sheet is misstated—creating audit difficulties for the current year and potentially a scope limitation.

Based on all the factors given, it seems likely that Sweet Dreams will be a great audit client, but Grouse appears at this stage to be a very undesirable one. Jack's firm may want one of its partners to obtain further information by contacting Grouse's management and enquiring in the local community, but it seems likely these will only confirm its undesirability.

As a further exercise, we briefly give some thought to how these considerations might be different if these were decisions about continuing with existing audit client relationships instead of about new engagements.

- There would be no predecessor.
- Jack's firm would need to consider whether any changes in the economy, operating environment, ownership structure, accounting standards, or other factors could affect the risk of the auditee, the firm's ability to complete the audit, independence, appropriateness of the financial reporting framework, and adequacy of internal control, etc. Such changes could affect the risk of material misstatement at the financial statement level, or at the assertion level.
- The information would be obtained from the same sources as those used above: management enquiry, research, and enquiries to associates. The main difference is that now the firm is starting with a high level of knowledge of the auditee and factoring in new information about any significant changes to assess acceptability.

SUMMARY

This chapter covered three major topics. The first was a set of activities auditors undertake when beginning an audit engagement. These pre-engagement activities start with the work of deciding whether to accept a new auditee as a client and, on an annual basis, deciding whether to continue as auditor for existing clients. Public accounting firms are not obligated to provide audits to every organization that asks for one, and they regularly exercise discretion about the organizations they wish to associate with. The investigation may involve the cooperative task of communicating with the predecessor auditor. Once an audit engagement is accepted, the pre-engagement work continues with the preparation of an engagement letter. The planning works starts with obtaining an initial understanding of the auditee's business, its environment, and its risks; a preliminary analysis of its draft financial statements to identify potential risk areas; and a preliminary decision about what amount of financial statement misstatement would affect user decisions, to determine appropriate materiality levels for auditing purposes.

Next, the financial statements were explained in terms of the primary assertions management makes in them. These assertions were identified as the focal points of the auditors' procedural evidence-gathering work.

The chapter then presented the process of integrating the results of these initial planning activities into an overall audit strategy document setting out the preliminary decision that guides further planning and execution. The overall audit strategy summarizes key considerations regarding the engagement and client relationship; materiality levels for the audit and assessment of risks involved; expected audit approach; and the nature, timing, and extent of resources expected to be required to perform a competent audit.

At this point in the audit process, the auditor has a broad, high-level understanding of the auditee and has made some important preliminary decisions, set out in the overall audit strategy, on how to operationalize the audit. The chapter finishes with a practical application case analysis that provides an opportunity to think about how these planning activities matter in real audit engagements.

MULTIPLE-CHOICE QUESTIONS FOR PRACTICE AND REVIEW

MC 1 An audit engagement letter should normally include the following matter of agreement between the auditor and the auditee:
  a. schedules and analyses to be prepared by the auditee's employees
  b. methods of statistical sampling the auditor will use
  c. specification of litigation in progress against the auditee
  d. auditee representations about availability of all minutes of meetings of the board of directors

MC 2 When a successor auditor initiates communications with a predecessor auditor, the successor should expect
  a. to take responsibility for obtaining the auditee's consent for the predecessor to give information about prior audits
  b. to conduct interviews with the partner and manager in charge of the predecessor audit firm's engagement
  c. to obtain copies of some or all of the predecessor auditor's working papers
  d. all of the above

MC 3 Generally accepted auditing standards require that auditors prepare and use
  a. a written engagement letter for new audits
  b. a written engagement letter for continuing audits
  c. a written overall audit strategy
  d. all of the above

MC 4 The revenue process of a company generally includes these accounts:
  a. inventory, accounts payable, and general expenses
  b. inventory, general expenses, and payroll
  c. cash, accounts receivable, and sales
  d. cash, notes payable, and capital stock

MC 5 Understanding the client's business environment is important to the auditor because
  a. it helps distinguish interim audit work from year-end audit work
  b. management's draft financial statements contain assertions about the business environment
  c. it helps the auditor to assess the risks that the financial statements contain misstatements
  d. it eliminates the need for the auditor to understand the auditee's internal controls

MC 6 Management's general purpose financial statements
  a. are the responsibility of the auditor
  b. include only non-routine transactions
  c. make assertions that are the focal point of audit procedures
  d. can rarely be reconciled to the auditee's trial balance

MC 7 Auditors are not responsible for accounting estimates with respect to
  a. making the estimates
  b. determining the reasonableness of estimates
  c. determining that estimates are presented in conformity with GAAP
  d. determining that estimates are adequately disclosed in the financial statements

MC 8 If the XYZ company reports a $355,000 balance of accounts receivable, the existence assertion means
  a. there are no accounts receivable by XYZ that have not been included in the balance
  b. all the amounts making up the $355,000 balance will be collected in full, in cash
  c. all the amounts included in the $355,000 balance represent valid sales on account that are still outstanding and due to the company
  d. the receivables have not been sold to another company

MC 9 Auditors perform analytical procedures in the planning stage of an audit for the purpose of
a. deciding the matters to cover in an engagement letter
b. identifying unusual conditions that deserve more auditing effort
c. determining which of the financial statement assertions are the most important for the auditee's financial statements
d. determining the nature, timing, and extent of audit procedures for auditing the inventory

MC 10 Analytical procedures used when planning an audit should concentrate on
a. weaknesses in the company's internal control procedures
b. predictability of account balances based on individual transactions
c. five major management assertions in financial statements
d. accounts and relationships that may represent specific potential problems and risks in the financial statements

MC 11 When a company that has $5 million current assets and $3 million current liabilities pays $1 million of its accounts payable, its current ratio will
a. increase
b. decrease
c. remain unchanged

MC 12 When a company that has $3 million current assets and $5 million current liabilities pays $1 million of its accounts payable, its current ratio will
a. increase
b. decrease
c. remain unchanged

MC 13 When a company that has $5 million current assets and $5 million current liabilities pays $1 million of its accounts payable, its current ratio will
a. increase
b. decrease
c. remain unchanged

MC 14 When a company that sells its products for a (gross) profit increases its sales by 15 percent and its cost of goods sold by 7 percent, the cost of goods sold ratio will
a. increase
b. decrease
c. remain unchanged

MC 15 Which of the following is not a benefit claimed for the practice of determining materiality in the initial planning stage of starting an audit?
a. Being able to fine-tune the audit work for effectiveness and efficiency
b. Avoiding the problem of doing more work than necessary (overauditing)
c. Being able to decide early what kind of audit opinion to give
d. Avoiding the problem of doing too little work (underauditing)

MC 16 Tolerable misstatement in the context of audit planning means
a. amounts that should be disclosed if they are likely to influence the economic decisions of financial statement users
b. the largest amount of uncorrected dollar misstatement that could exist in published financial statements while still fairly presenting the company's financial position and results of operations in conformity with GAAP
c. part of the overall materiality amount for the financial statements assigned to a particular account
d. a dollar amount of materiality assigned to an account as required by auditing standards

EXERCISES AND PROBLEMS

EP 1   **Analytical Review Ratio Relationships.** The following
LO.3   situations represent errors and irregularities that can occur in financial statements. Your requirement is to state how the ratio in question would compare (greater, equal, or less) to what the ratio "should have been" had the error or irregularity not occurred.
a. The company recorded fictitious sales with credits to sales revenue accounts and debits to accounts receivable. Inventory was reduced and cost of goods sold was increased for the profitable "sales." Is the current ratio greater than, equal to, or less than what it should have been?
b. The company recorded cash disbursements paying trade accounts payable but held the cheques past the year-end date—meaning that the "disbursements" should not have been shown as credits to cash and debits to accounts payable. Is the current ratio greater than, equal to, or less than what it should have been? Consider cases

in which the current ratio before the improper "disbursement" recording would have been (1) greater than 1:1, (2) equal to 1:1, and (3) less than 1:1.
c. The company uses a periodic inventory system for determining the balance sheet amount of inventory at year-end. Very near the year-end, merchandise was received, placed in the stockroom, and counted, but the purchase transaction was neither recorded nor paid until the next month. What was the effect on inventory, cost of goods sold, gross profit, and net income? How were these ratios affected, compared with what they would have been without the error: current ratio, return on beginning equity, gross margin ratio, cost of goods sold ratio, inventory turnover, and receivables turnover?
d. The company is loath to write off customer accounts receivable, even though the financial vice-president makes entirely adequate provision for uncollectible

amounts in the allowance for bad debts. The gross receivables and the allowance both contain amounts that should have been written off long ago. How are these ratios affected compared with what they would be if the old receivables were properly written off: current ratio, days' sales in receivables, doubtful account ratio, receivables turnover, return on beginning equity, working capital/total assets?

e. Since last year, the company has reorganized its lines of business and placed more emphasis on its traditional products while selling off some marginal businesses merged by the previous go-go management. Total assets are 10 percent less than they were last year, but working capital has increased. Retained earnings remained the same because the disposals created no gains, and the net income after taxes is still near zero, the same as last year. Earnings before interest and taxes remained the same, a small positive EBIT. The total market value of the company's equity has not increased, but that is better than the declines of the past several years. Proceeds from the disposals have been used to retire long-term debt. Net sales have decreased 5 percent, because the sales decrease resulting from the disposals has not been overcome by increased sales of the traditional products. Is the discriminant Z score (see Appendix 6A) of the current year higher or lower than that of the prior year?

EP 2
LO.4 **Understand the Business—Transactions and Accounts.** In the table below, the left column names several "classes of transactions." The right column names several general ledger accounts.

Classes of Transactions	General Ledger Accounts
Cash receipts	Cash
Cash disbursements	Accounts receivable
Credit sales	Allowance for doubtful accounts
Sales returns and allowances	
Purchases on credit	Inventory
Purchase returns	Capital assets
Uncollectible account write-offs	Accounts payable
	Long-term debt
	Sales revenue
	Investment income
	Expenses

Required:
Identify the general ledger accounts that are affected by each class of transactions.

Approach:
Match the classes of transactions with the general ledger accounts where their debits and credits are usually entered.

EP 3
LO.5 **Auditing an Accounting Estimate.** Suppose management estimated the lower-of-cost-and-market valuation of some obsolete inventory at $99,000, and wrote it down from $120,000, recognizing a loss of $21,000. The auditors obtained the following information: the inventory in question could be sold for an amount between $78,000 and $92,000. The costs of advertising and shipping could range from $5,000 to $7,000.

Required:
a. Would you propose an audit adjustment to the management estimate? Write the appropriate accounting entry.
b. If management's estimate of inventory market (lower than cost) had been $80,000, would you propose an audit adjustment? Write the appropriate accounting entry.

EP 4
LO.5 **Risk of Misstatement in Various Accounts.** Based on information you have available in Chapter 6:
a. Which accounts may be most susceptible to overstatement? To understatement?
b. Why do you think a company might permit asset accounts to be understated?
c. Why do you think a company might permit liability accounts to be overstated?
d. Which direction of misstatement is most likely: income overstatement or income understatement?

EP 5
LO.3
and
LO.6 **Audit Planning.** Walter Wolf was pleased. He had been with the firm of Riding, Hood & Co. less than a year-and-a-half since graduation from university and had received excellent performance reviews on every engagement. Now he was being given "in charge" responsibility on an audit. It was a small client, but it felt good to have the firm show such confidence in him. He planned to show that the firm had made the right decision.

Walter thought back to some of the advice his seniors had given him. Two comments in particular stood out as key steps to a successful audit:
• Careful attention to planning the audit pays dividends. Time spent on audit planning is never wasted.
• Avoid being a mechanical auditor. Focus on the assertions embodied in the financial statements and the related audit objectives when planning audit tests.

Required:
a. Develop a list of tasks Walter should perform in planning this audit engagement, before any audit testing begins.
b. *Handbook* section CAS 315 lists management assertions embodied in financial statements. List and briefly describe the audit objectives that relate to these assertions.

(ICAO adapted)

EP 6
LO.6 **Assertions.** The assertions listed in CAS 315 (see text box titled: "Assertions for Classes of Transactions, Account Balances, and Presentation and Disclosure" — pages 199–200) are each cross-referenced to the five principal assertions.

Required:
Why are these different terms used to describe assertions in different audit guidance materials?

EP 7
LO.7
Experts' Work as Audit Evidence. If expertise in a field other than accounting or auditing is necessary to obtain sufficient appropriate audit evidence, an auditor may need to use the work of an auditor's expert. The need for special expertise may include such matters as:

- the valuation of complex financial instruments, land and buildings, plant and machinery, jewellery, works of art, antiques, intangible assets, and business combinations and conducting impairment reviews.
- the actuarial calculation of liabilities associated with insurance contracts or employee benefit plans.
- the estimation of oil and gas reserves.

- the valuation of environmental liabilities, and site clean-up costs.
- the interpretation of contracts, laws, and regulations.
- the analysis of complex or unusual tax compliance issues.

Required:

How does an auditor determine the need to use an expert when developing the overall audit strategy? What additional work does an auditor need to perform if planning to use an expert's work as audit evidence to form an audit opinion?

DISCUSSION CASES

DC 1
LO.1
Communications Between Predecessor and Successor Auditors. Your firm has been contacted by the president of Lyrac Inc. about becoming the company's auditor. Lyrac was audited last year by PA Diggs and, while generally pleased with the services provided by Diggs, the president of Lyrac thinks the audit work was too detailed and interfered excessively with normal office routines. You have asked Lyrac's president to inform Diggs of the decision to change auditors, but he does not wish to do so.

Required:

List and discuss the steps to follow in dealing with a predecessor auditor and a new audit client before accepting the engagement. (*Hint*: Use the independence rules of conduct for a complete response to this requirement.)

DC 2
LO.1
Audit Engagement Acceptance. You are a PA in an accounting firm that has 10 offices in three provinces. Mr. Shine has approached you with a request for an audit. He is president of Hitech Software and Games Inc., a five-year-old company that has recently grown to $40 million in sales and $20 million in total assets. Mr. Shine is thinking about going public with a $17 million issue of common shares, of which $10 million would be a secondary issue of shares he holds. You are very happy about this opportunity, because Mr. Shine is the new president of the Symphony Society board and has made quite a civic impression since he came to your medium-size city seven years ago. Hitech is one of the growing employers in the city.

Required:

a. Discuss the sources of information and the types of enquiries you and the firm's partners can make in connection with accepting Hitech as a new client.
b. Does the profession require any investigation of prospective clients?
c. Suppose Mr. Shine also told you that 10 years ago his closely held hamburger franchise business went bankrupt, and you learn from its former auditors (your own firm) that Shine played fast and loose with franchise

fee income recognition rules and presented such difficulties that your office in another city resigned from the audit (before the bankruptcy). Do you think the partner in charge of the audit practice should accept Hitech as a new client?

DC 3
LO.1
Predecessor and Successor Auditors. The president of Allpurpose Loan Company had a genuine dislike for external auditors. Almost any conflict generated a towering rage. Consequently, the company changed auditors often.

Wells & Ratley, PAs, was recently hired to audit the 2003 financial statements, the firm succeeding the firm of Canby & Company which had obtained the audit after Albrecht & Hubbard had been fired. A&H audited the 2002 financial statements and rendered a report that contained an additional paragraph explaining an uncertainty about Allpurpose Loan Company's loan loss reserve. Goodbye, A&H! Canby & Company then audited the 2003 financial statements, and Art Canby started the work. But, before the audit could be completed and an audit report issued, Canby was fired, and W&R was hired to complete the audit.

Required:

Does Wells & Ratley need to initiate communications with Canby & Company? with Albrecht & Hubbard? with both? Explain your response in terms of the purposes of communications between predecessor and successor auditors.

DC 4
LO.1
LO.2
LO.3
LO.4
LO.5
LO.6
Pre-engagement and Preliminary Analysis Activities. Sunrise Solar Inc. (SS) is a medium-sized company that is developing solar energy systems for private residences and small businesses. It is privately owned, with the majority of the shares held by the company's president, Shu Mingfei. Started up two years ago, to date it is mostly involved in research and development, but this year it completed its first customer sales and installation. Ms. Shu has engaged your firm to do the current year's audit because she plans to obtain $20 million in debt financing from outside investors to

allow further commercialization of the SS systems. You are now reviewing SS's preliminary general ledger trial balance in order to begin preparing the audit planning.

The following is a summary of the accounts that appear in this trial balance as at year end:

Account	Balance dr/(cr)
Cash	$ 101,209
Accounts receivable	85,019
Allowance for bad debts	(15,000)
Inventory, finished goods	900,550
Inventory, work-in-progress	44,666
Inventory, raw material	67,890
Deferred development costs	34,445
Property, plant, and equipment	3,700,990
Accumulated amortization, PPE	(901,108)
Patents, at cost	1,010,000
Accounts payable	(198,009)
Warranty provision	(30,000)
Shareholder loan, non interest bearing	(11,000,000)
Share capital, common shares	(1,000)
Retained earnings	1,261,558
Revenue	(812,202)
Cost of goods sold	666,502
General and administration expenses	1,002,500
Research and development expenses	3,990,000
Other expenses	89,990

Required:
a. Identify three factors that your firm should consider before agreeing to conduct the audit.
b. What are the economic and industry risks affecting this business? How would these risks affect the company's financial statements and your overall audit strategy?
c. State the dollar amount you would consider an appropriate materiality level for planning this audit, giving your supporting reasons. Explain why the materiality judgment is one of the first important decisions your team must make in planning this audit.
d. List two analytical procedures you could perform using the trial balance data above (you are not required to calculate any ratios). Explain what each procedure can tell you about the risks in SS's financial statements. Give one example of additional information you would want to obtain to perform analytical procedures in this audit, and a reason why it would be useful.

DC 5   **Preliminary Analysis, Materiality, Assertions.** Your
LO.2   firm has been engaged to do the current year's audit of
LO.3   Dawood Ltd., a medium-sized business involved in man-
LO.4   ufacturing television screens and monitors. Dawood is
LO.5   privately owned and its two shareholders have requested
LO.6   that the annual financial statements be audited for the first time this year. One of the shareholders manages the business; the other is not involved. You are now reviewing Dawood's preliminary general ledger trial balance, shown below, to begin the audit planning.

Account	Balance dr/(cr)
Cash	$ 10,009
Accounts receivable	167,090
Allowance for bad debts	(25,000)
Inventory, finished goods	200,550
Inventory, work-in-progress	94,601
Inventory, purchased components	199,800
Inventory, parts	34,400
Property, plant, and equipment	9,700,100
Accumulated amortization, PPE	(3,607,597)
Accounts payable	(222,400)
Warranty provision	(87,000)
Bank loan, long term	(1,000,000)
Share capital, common shares	(1,500,000)
Retained earnings	(1,738,442)
Revenue	(9,005,800)
Cost of goods sold	4,696,600
General and administration expenses	1,902,500
Other expenses	180,589

Required:
a. When planning this audit, explain why it is important for Dawood's auditor to understand its business, its environment, and its risks.
b. List two analytical procedures you could perform using the trial balance data above. Explain what each procedure can tell you about the risks in Dawood's financial statements, and what further investigation the analytical results may suggest.
c. Identify two accounts that you feel would have a high risk of material misstatement. Use the five principle assertions as the basis for your assessment. Give the reasons supporting your assessment.
d. Determine an appropriate materiality level for preliminary audit planning purposes. Explain your reasons for selecting this materiality level.

DC 6   **Calculate a Planning Materiality Amount.** The audi-
LO.5   tors were planning the work on the financial statements of the Mary Short Cosmetics Company. The unaudited financial statements showed $515,000 net income after providing an allowance of 35 percent for income taxes. The company had no debt and no interest expense. Mary Short's shares are traded over the counter, and investors have generally assigned a price-earnings multiple of 16 to the shares. Press releases by the company have enabled analysts to estimate the income for the year at about $515,000, which was forecast by the company at the beginning of the year. There are 750,000 shares outstanding, and the last quoted price for them was $11.

The auditors have decided that a 6 percent mispricing error in the shares would not cause investors to change their buying and selling decisions.

Misstatements totalling $13,000 were discovered in the previous year's audit but were not corrected.

Required:
Calculate the materiality for the financial statements as a whole and the performance materiality the auditors might use in the current year audit, based on the income before income taxes.

DC 7 **Materiality Level Reduced.** Your firm has done the audit
LO.5 of Rhea Fashions Inc. for many years. You are in charge
of the fieldwork for the current year's audit. Rhea is a
manufacturer of high-fashion clothing. Its shares are publicly traded, but a majority of the common shares are held
by the members of the family that started the business
during the 1950s. During the current year, Rhea's business shrank substantially because of losing a major customer, a country-wide department store chain that went
out of business. Rhea has not been able to replace the lost
business. Since many of Rhea's long-time employees
were happy to take an early retirement offer, Rhea management's strategy now is to continue to operate only a
few unique clothing brands that represented about 50 percent of its sales volume in prior years. The materiality
level used in the prior years was $80,000. The audit part-
ner has determined that the appropriate materiality for the
current year financial statement audit is $40,000.

Required:

a. Discuss the factors that the audit partner would have
considered in deciding to reduce the materiality level.

b. What impact will the lower materiality level likely
have on your audit procedures in the current year?

c. While reviewing the previous year's audit file, you
note that last year's staff uncovered one error. Rhea
had failed to accrue approximately $50,000 of cus-
tomer volume discounts because of a calculation
error in computing the customer's total sales. Since
the error was less than materiality, no adjustment was
made to the prior year's financial statements. Explain
the impact this error had on the prior year's financial statements, the impact it will have on the current
year's financial statements when it reverses, and on
your audit, given your new materiality level.

DC 8 **Materiality Approaches in Audit Practice.** Three BCom
LO.5 classmates are meeting for dinner to celebrate completing
their first year as junior auditors at three different public
accounting firms. After reminiscing about the time they all
skipped their auditing class to go to a playoff hockey game,
one of them recalls, "It was great the Canucks won that
game, even though they didn't make it to the next round.
But the auditing class we missed that night was on materiality. I have learned a lot on the job, but materiality is still
the one decision we make at work that makes no sense to
me. And that makes me nervous because materiality is such
a key factor in deciding what accounts to focus our audit
work on and how much testing to do."

During the ensuing discussion they realize that their
three firms use three different approaches to setting materiality for planning purposes. In Firm 1, the level of
materiality is set for the whole audit based on 5–10% of
normal earnings, or other benchmarks if earnings are not
useful. In Firm 2, a similar method is used to come up
with the starting materiality amount but then adjustments
are made for anticipated misstatements and prior year
misstatement reversals, resulting in using a smaller
amount for the purpose of planning the audit. In Firm 3,
a similar starting point is used but the amount is then allocated to different accounts based on their size and any

special user-based considerations such as whether the
amount is used in a debt covenant.

Required:

Discuss the implications for audit practice of having so
much variability in setting materiality. What is the impact of the new CAS 320 on the three different approaches described in this scenario?

DC 9 **Materiality and Misstatements in Estimates.** The au-
LO.5 ditors of Letron Inc. have set an overall materiality level
of $900,000 and a performance materiality level
of $800,000 for the current year audit, 20X2. They used the
same materiality levels in their 20X1 audit. Letron is in
the telecommunication equipment business and its inventory value is subject to fluctuations due to changes in
supply and demand as well as technological obsolescence, creating considerable measurement uncertainty.
Management's point estimate of the inventories' value
as of the end of 20X2 is $15.9m, after reversal of a write-
down that was taken in 20X1. The auditors have established a range of estimates for the inventory value of
$14–16m, so management's point estimate is within the
auditors' range. In 20X1, poor market conditions pre-
vailed and Letron wrote down its inventory to net realizable value, estimated to be $12.3. Management and the
auditor had a disagreement regarding inventory valuation for 20X1, because it fell outside of the auditors'
range of $13–15m. However, this difference and the ag-
gregated misstatements for 20X1 were less than the performance materiality, so these misstatements were not
corrected. Letron initiated a bonus plan in 20X0 that
would reward top management if the company reported
positive profits. Letron reported losses in 20X0 and
20X1. In 20X2 Letron reported a small profit, giving
rise to a substantial bonus to its management team.

Required:

Assume the role of Letron's auditor, and explain the actions you would take in this situation, based on applying
the requirements and guidance in CAS 450 and CAS 540.

DC 10 **Overall Audit Strategy, Retail Industry.** Using the
LO.7 SEDAR database (www.sedar.com), find the most recent
annual reports for two Canadian retailers (e.g. Loblaw,
Rona, Danier Leather).

Required:

a. Based on the information provided in the companies'
audited financial statements and the Management Discussion and Analysis (and, optionally, other Internet
research you may wish to do), use the planning document shown in Exhibit 6–8 to identify and list key
information items that should be documented in the
"Engagement Characteristics" section of the overall
audit strategy for each these companies.

b. What do you think would be the most significant audit
issues in each company? Explain issues that would be
similar in each audit. For any issues you identify that
would differ between the companies, explain why you
think these differences would exist.

APPENDIX 6A

SELECTED FINANCIAL RATIOS

Balance Sheet Ratios	Formula*
Current ratio	$\dfrac{\text{Current assets}}{\text{Current liabilities}}$
Days' sales in receivables	$\dfrac{\text{Ending net receivables}}{\text{Credit sales}} \times 360$
Doubtful account ratio	$\dfrac{\text{Allowance for doubtful accounts}}{\text{Ending gross receivables}}$
Days' sales in inventory	$\dfrac{\text{Ending inventory}}{\text{Cost of goods sold}} \times 360$
Debt ratio	$\dfrac{\text{Current and long-term debt}}{\text{Shareholder equity}}$

Operations Ratios	
Receivables turnover	$\dfrac{\text{Credit sales}}{\text{Ending net receivables}}$
Inventory turnover	$\dfrac{\text{Cost of goods sold}}{\text{Ending inventory}}$
Cost of goods sold ratio	$\dfrac{\text{Cost of goods sold}}{\text{Net sales}}$
Gross margin ratio	$\dfrac{\text{Net sales} - \text{Cost of goods sold}}{\text{Net sales}}$
Return on beginning equity	$\dfrac{\text{Net income}}{\text{Shareholder equity (beginning)}}$

Financial Distress Ratios (Altman, 1968)	Formula*
(X_1) Working capital ÷ Total assets	$\dfrac{\text{Current assets} - \text{Current liabilities}}{\text{Total assets}}$
(X_2) Retained earnings ÷ Total assets	$\dfrac{\text{Retained earnings (ending)}}{\text{Total assets}}$
(X_3) Earnings before interest and taxes ÷ Total assets	$\dfrac{\text{Net Income} + \text{Interest expense} + \text{Income tax expense}}{\text{Total assets}}$
(X_4) Market value of equity ÷ Total debt	$\dfrac{\text{Market value of common and preferred shares}}{\text{Current liabilities and long-term debt}}$
(X_5) Net sales ÷ Total assets	$\dfrac{\text{Net sales}}{\text{Total assets}}$
Discriminant Z score (Altman, 1968)	$1.2 \times X_1 + 1.4 \times X_2 + 3.3 \times X_3 + 0.6 \times X_4 + 1.0 \times X_5$

*These ratios are shown to be calculated using year-end, rather than year-average, numbers for such balances as accounts receivable and inventory. Other accounting and finance reference books may contain formulas using year-average numbers. As long as no dramatic changes have occurred during the year, the year-end numbers can have much audit relevance because they reflect the most current balance data. For comparative purposes, the ratios should be calculated on the same basis for all the years being compared. In the Anycompany example in Exhibits 6–3 and 6–4, the market value of the equity in the calculations is $3 million.

CHAPTER ⑦

Assessing Risks and Internal Control

Chapter 7 will allow you to develop a detailed plan for performing an effective audit of an organization's financial statements. We start with a key tool of audit fieldwork planning: a conceptual audit risk model that defines and relates the main types of risks an auditor must manage. Next we discuss the business risk–based approach to auditing, a key component of GAAS. This chapter will also introduce internal control by describing the components the organization's management has put in place. The chapter stresses that management is responsible for identifying and assessing business risk, and for implementing effective internal control to reduce business risk to an acceptable level. Thus risk and control are closely related and auditors must consider them together. While the need to integrate the concepts of risk and control makes this chapter very challenging, this integration is essential to understanding the business risk–based approach to auditing. Auditors must understand the auditee's risks and controls to assess the risks of a material misstatement occurring because of error or fraud. This risk assessment is used to develop a detailed audit plan that includes procedures needed to address the assessed risks and provide reasonable assurance that the financial statements are not materially misstated. Assurance is the complement of audit risk.

LEARNING OBJECTIVES

After completing this chapter, you will be able to:

① Describe the conceptual audit risk model and its components, and explain its usefulness and limitations in conducting the audit.

② Explain how auditors assess the auditee's business risk through strategic analysis and business process analysis.

③ Outline the relationships among business processes, accounting processes/cycles, and management's general purpose financial statements.

④ Illustrate how business risk analysis is used in a preliminary assessment of the risk that fraud or error has led to material misstatement at the overall financial statement level.

⑤ Describe the basic components of internal control: control environment, management's risk assessment process, information systems and communication, control activities, and monitoring.

⑥ Explain how the auditor's understanding of an organization's internal control helps to assess the risk that its financial statements are misstated.

⑦ Apply and integrate the chapter topics to analyze a practical auditing situation/case/scenario.

Note: The following Appendices accompany this chapter. An asterisk (*) indicates those located on the Online Learning Centre:

7A*   Risk and Internal Control Frameworks
7B*   Strategic Systems Audit Approaches to Understanding Business Risk
7C   Business Risk Factors
7D   Audit Risk and Accounting Risk
7E*   Ecommerce: Implications for Auditors
7F*   Corporate Governance

AUDIT RISK ASSESSMENT

· · · · · · · · · · · · · · · ·

LEARNING OBJECTIVE

① Describe the conceptual audit risk model and its components, and explain its usefulness and limitations in conducting the audit.

Auditing is fundamentally a risk management process. Audit risk is related to the information risk (discussed in Chapter 1) that audited financial statements that are materially misstated will go out to users. Assurance is the complement of audit risk. Auditors strive to lower audit risk by performing audit work that gives a high level of assurance that the statements are fairly presented. Audit risk is associated with gathering evidence on the facts of the auditee's economic reality—it is created by having less than all the possible corroborating audit evidence. This is why Chapter 3 noted that review engagements are viewed as a lesser assurance engagement: with less corroborating evidence in a review engagement, the risk associated with it is higher than it is for an audit engagement. Similarly, compilation engagements provide no assurance because the evidence risk associated with having no corroborating evidence is 100 percent.

Understanding the auditee's business and performing preliminary analytical procedures help auditors to identify problem areas and make an overall business risk assessment. The organization's management is responsible for addressing business risk by implementing effective internal control. Thus, business risk and internal control are inseparable concepts that exist within an auditee organization. To develop the audit work programs, auditors need to assess risk specifically in audit-related terms: inherent risk, control risk, and detection risk. The term "risk" should always be used with a modifier (inherent, control, and so on) to specify the one you mean. We will discuss audit risk and the conceptual model in more detail after first considering each of the components.

Inherent Risk

Inherent risk is the probability that material misstatements have occurred in transactions within the accounting system used to develop financial statements, or that material misstatements have occurred in an account balance.[1] Put another way, inherent risk is the risk of material misstatements occurring in the first place. It is a characteristic of the auditee's business, the major types of transactions, and the effectiveness of its accountants, so understanding the auditee's business risk is important for assessing inherent risks. Auditors do not create or affect inherent risk, they can only try to assess its magnitude. It is important to understand that audit care should be greater where inherent risk is greater.

[1] CAS 315 (5141), CAS 200.

EXHIBIT   7–1   REVENUE REPORTING RISK

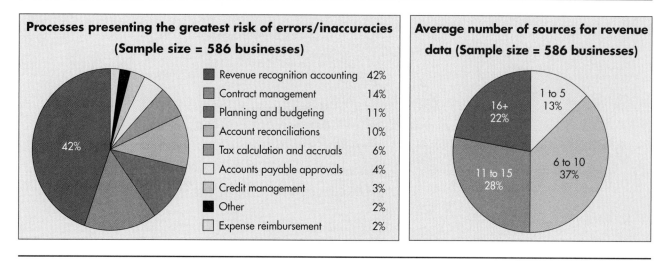

Source: Gerry Murray, "Revenue reporting risk remains high," *CA Magazine*, December 2008, p.10.

An assessment of inherent risk can be based on a variety of information. If material misstatements were discovered during the last year's audit, inherent risk will be considered higher than it would be if last year's audit had no material misstatements. Auditors may believe that the organization's accounting clerks tend to misunderstand GAAP and the organization's own accounting policies, thus suggesting a significant probability of mistakes in transaction processing. The nature of the auditee's business may produce complicated transactions and calculations known for data processing and accounting treatment error (e.g., real estate, franchising, oil and gas transactions). Some kinds of inventories (e.g., coal, grain, cocoa) may be harder to count, value, and keep accurately in perpetual records than are others (e.g., cars, jewellery). Some accounts (e.g., cash and inventory) are more susceptible to embezzlement, theft, or other losses than are other accounts (e.g., land or prepaid expenses).

Revenue accounting can have high inherent risk. Exhibit 7–1 shows the main results of a survey of 586 businesses that finds revenue recognition is the process most vulnerable to material errors; this is because of the complexity of revenue accounting. Businesses often use information from many sources and compile the revenue numbers in spreadsheets rather than by an automated system, which increases the inherent risk of material errors and inaccuracies.

Auditor experience has also shown that, because of management optimism and bias, asset and revenue accounts tend to have a higher inherent risk of overstatement than understatement, while liability accounts have a higher inherent risk of understatement than overstatement. Because of this, auditors tend to use procedures that are more effective in detecting overstatements for auditing revenues and assets, as you will see later in the chapter. At the same time, audit procedures that are more effective in detecting understatements are more likely to be used with liability and expense accounts. Thus, the inherent risks determine the importance of various procedures for different accounts.

Control Risk

Control risk is the probability that the auditee's internal control policies and procedures will fail to detect or prevent material misstatements. Auditors do not create or affect the control risk. They can only evaluate an organization's control system and assess the probability of material misstatements. Auditors are mainly concerned with "internal control relevant to the audit"—those policies and procedures established and maintained by management that affect control risk relating to specific financial statement assertions at the account balance or class of transactions level.

EXHIBIT 7-2   INTERNAL CONTROL FRAMEWORK

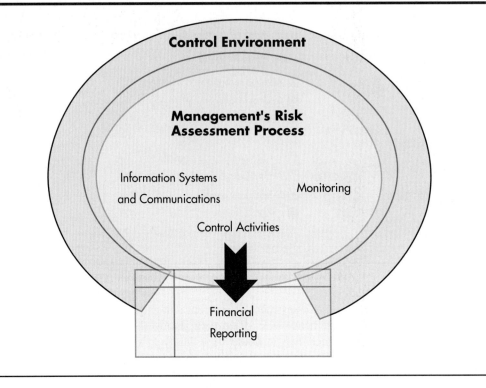

Internal control is a key component of an organization's overall risk management framework. Auditors use the risk management frameworks for assessing risks at the company level, as well as for auditing controls over financial reporting. These risk and control frameworks include CICA's *Criteria of Control Committee (COCO)*, *Committee of Sponsoring Organizations of the Treadway Commission (COSO)*, *Internal Control—Integrated Framework and Enterprise Risk Management—Integrated Framework, and Control Objectives for Information and Related Technology (COBIT)*, published by the IT Governance Institute. These frameworks are all further described in Appendix 7A on the OLC. An overview of the internal control framework that will be used in this text is given in Exhibit 7–2. The internal control components will be discussed later in the chapter, and again in Chapter 9. Frameworks are a useful tool to help improve audit quality.[2]

The control frameworks define control broadly. In the COCO framework, it includes an organization's resources, systems, processes, culture, structure, and tasks that work together to support the organization's objectives. Effective management, therefore, needs an integrated structure of control processes—processes for strategic control, management control, and business process control. Strategic and management control processes encompass controls for that entity as a whole. These controls often rely on long-term and strategically relevant criteria to evaluate overall corporate performance of division and units by management. Business process controls operate at the specific process level.

Thus, management control systems are much broader than are "internal controls relevant to the audit." Internal controls relevant to the audit would be a subset of this broader view of controls. Auditors are mainly concerned with accounting controls and systems. There are many other controls present in organizations that may not be relevant to the auditor.

---

[2] For audits of internal control that are integrated with a financial statement audit, use of a control framework is mandated by PCAOB Auditing Standard No. 5 and by *CICA Handbook* s.5925.

EXHIBIT 7-3 INTERNAL CONTROL CONDITIONS AND CONCLUSIONS

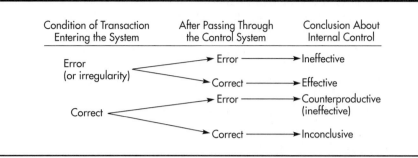

Source: Adapted from Lynford. E. Graham, "Audit Risk-Part III," *CPA Journal*, October 1985, p. 39. Reprinted from *The CPA Journal*, October 1985, © 1985 with permission from the New York State Society of Certified Public Accountants.

An auditor's assessment of control risk is based on the study and evaluation of the company's control system. Exhibit 7–3 illustrates the function of controls by showing the combinations of original errors and control effectiveness, or lack thereof.

Preliminary control effectiveness conclusions and risk assessments are made for planning purposes. Auditors often carry preconceived notions about control risk when they audit the same organization year after year. Starting with knowledge of last year's conclusions on control risk assessment is known as **anchoring**, and it represents (1) a useful continuity with the auditee and (2) a potential pitfall if conditions worsen and the auditor fails to acknowledge the deterioration of control.

Note that control risk assessment provides only an indirect assessment of the monetary amount of misstatement of financial statements. As a result, special labels such as **control testing** or **compliance testing** are given to the procedures used in the control risk assessment. You will study this process in detail in Chapter 9. Control risk should not be assessed so low that auditors place complete reliance on controls and do not perform any other audit work. Many auditors conclude their control risk assessment decisions with descriptive assessments (e.g., high, moderate, low), and some auditors put probability numbers on them (e.g., 1.0, 0.50, 0.30).

Combined Inherent and Control Risk: The Risk of Material Misstatement

As seen above, inherent risk and control risk are different in nature but related, so auditors can combine their assessment of these two risks into what is called the **risk of material misstatement**.[3] The standards emphasize understanding an auditee's business and assessing the risk of material misstatement in planning the audit. Inherent and control risks can be difficult to assess separately because some internal controls "work" only when errors, irregularities, and other misstatements occur, while others are preventive in nature and so tend to reduce inherent risk. An auditor may make separate or combined assessments of inherent and control risk depending on preferred audit procedures and practical considerations.

The risks of material misstatement at the financial statement and assertion level are a basis for designing further audit procedures. When the auditor's assessment of the risk of material misstatement includes an expectation of the operating effectiveness of controls, the standards state that there must be supporting tests of those controls. Internal control is a complex and critical consideration in every audit; thus, control evaluation and testing will be explained in more detail in Chapters 9 and 10.

Changes in the economic environment can affect the risk of material misstatement. The CICA issues *Risk Alert* notices on its website that highlight current risk areas that PAs should take into account in their risk assessments and audit planning. An example of a *Risk Alert* issued in February 2008 concerning the credit crunch related to asset backed commercial paper (ABCP) is found in the following box.

[3] CAS 315 (5141).

Risk Alert, **February 2008**
AUDITING IN THE CREDIT CRUNCH ENVIRONMENT

THE CREDIT CRUNCH IN CANADA

The global financial markets have been in turmoil over the last few months. In Canada, there has been particular concern about non-bank-sponsored asset-backed commercial paper (ABCP) for which the market remains suspended as at the date of this *Risk Alert*.

In January 2008, the staff of the Canadian Performance Reporting Board issued a *CPR Alert* titled "MD&A Disclosures about Non-bank Asset-Backed Commercial Paper." As noted in the *CPR Alert*, non-bank trusts in Canada have issued approximately $33 billion in ABCP. Largely because of the deepening of the US sub-prime credit crisis, many non-bank trust issuers of ABCP have been unable to repay maturing paper, causing a liquidity crisis. In addition, the terms of the derivative transactions have placed further constraints on some trusts' operations. The mix of assets and exposures (e.g., collateral calls) in the trusts differs from trust to trust and the extent to which any impairment in value exists could vary significantly among the population of trusts.

The purpose of this *Risk Alert* is to highlight matters for auditors to consider when responding to higher risks of material misstatement of financial statements of entities that have invested in ABCP and other financial instruments affected by the credit crunch. Related matters, including the entity's statutory disclosures and auditor independence, are also noted.

AUDITING FINANCIAL INSTRUMENTS IN THE CREDIT CRUNCH

The fundamental question for an auditor to address is whether the reporting entity's financial statements have been prepared in accordance with Canadian GAAP. In January 2008, the staff of the Accounting Standards Board (AcSB) published a financial reporting commentary Non-bank-sponsored Asset-Backed Commercial Paper: Year-End Reporting Issues (AcSB staff commentary). That commentary describes how GAAP applies to ABCP held by investors, and expands upon earlier material published by the AcSB staff in October 2007. It discusses, among other things, issues related to accounting and disclosure of financial instruments in the credit crunch environment. An impact of the credit crunch may be a severe curtailment or even cessation of trading in a particular investment. In such an event, management may have difficulty in establishing the value of the instruments, increasing the risk that such valuation may be materially misstated.

Auditing Fair Value Measurements and Disclosures, paragraphs 5306.22-.32[*], provide requirements and supporting guidance related to matters such as:
• obtaining audit evidence about management's intent to carry out specific courses of action (when intent is relevant to the use of fair value measurements) and management's ability to carry out its intended courses of action; and
• evaluating whether the method of measurement is appropriate, considering changes in the environment or circumstances affecting the entity.

Due to the impact of the credit crunch on valuation of financial instruments, entities holding ABCP may be required to have more extensive disclosures compared to prior years. For example, such entities may have to disclose the extent of measurement uncertainty if it is reasonably possible that the recognized amount of ABCP could change by a material amount in the near term. The AcSB staff commentary discusses such disclosure requirements in more detail.

In some cases, the auditor may need to use a specialist possessing particular knowledge in the valuation of the financial instruments. The auditor would follow the Recommendations and guidance in Section 5049, *Use of Specialists in Assurance Engagements.*[*]

CONCERNS ABOUT GOING CONCERN

In the credit crunch environment, banks face rising loan defaults and are becoming more cautious when considering whether to provide or renew finance facilities. They may also establish new criteria or increase interest rates. As a result, the audited entity's prior ability to obtain necessary financing may not be a reliable indicator of an entity's ability to obtain financing in the future.

Reservations in the Auditor's Report, paragraphs 5510.51-.53,[*] note conditions that may cast doubt on the ability of an enterprise to continue as a going concern. Two of the conditions that are particularly relevant to the credit crunch environment are an entity's inability to obtain financing sufficient for continued operations and an inability to comply with terms of existing loan agreements. Other such conditions listed include:
• recurring operating losses;
• serious deficiencies in working capital;

- the possibility of an adverse outcome of one or more contingencies;
- insufficient funds to meet liabilities;
- a plan to significantly curtail or liquidate operations; and
- external factors that could force an otherwise solvent enterprise to cease operations.

In assessing whether the entity's financial statements are in accordance with GAAP, the auditor would refer to *General Standards of Financial Statement Presentation*, paragraphs 1400.08A-.08C, which discuss the concept of going concern in relation to the preparation of financial statements.

OTHER MATTERS

MD&A disclosures (for reporting issuers)

National Instrument 51–102 *Continuous Disclosure Obligations* requires a reporting issuer to file MD&A relating to its annual and interim financial statements. The *CPR Alert* includes suggested MD&A disclosure around ABCP. Management is responsible for the preparation of the MD&A which may contain information regarding the impact of a credit crunch on the entity's valuation of financial instruments, ability to meet its debt covenants, and liquidity.

The auditor is associated with information in the MD&A, and would comply with Section 7500, *Auditor Association with Annual Reports, Interim Reports, and Other Public Documents*[*]. This Section contains standards and guidance with respect to the auditor's statutory reporting responsibility in relation to the other public documents.

INDEPENDENCE ISSUES

In the credit crunch environment, auditors need to be alert to the possibility of prohibitions and self-review threats. For example, the auditor may be asked to perform a valuation of the entity's financial instruments including ABCP. If the auditor undertakes such an engagement, his or her objectivity and independence may be impaired, or may be perceived to be impaired.

Quality Control Procedures for Assurance Engagements, paragraph 5030.15,[*] requires the auditor to form a conclusion on compliance with independence requirements that apply to the assurance engagement.

IN CONCLUSION

This *Risk Alert* does not address all issues that might arise when auditing in the environment of a credit crunch. Auditing in this environment will present challenges and higher risks. The auditor needs to ensure that those assigned to the engagement team collectively have the necessary competencies, resources, and time to meet these challenges and risks. Appropriate and timely consultations on complex or contentious matters, as well as clear communications with management and those having oversight responsibility for the financial reporting process, will also be particularly important when auditing in this environment.

[*]Note that, effective in 2010, these *CICA Handbook* sections will have been replaced, respectively, by the following CAS: 540, 620, 705 (also relevant is 570), 720, 220.

Source: http://www.aasb.ca/index.cfm/ci_id/43007/la_id/1 (accessed on July 11, 2008).

Detection Risk

Detection risk is the risk that any material misstatement that has not been prevented or corrected by the auditee's internal control will not be detected by the auditor.[4] In contrast to the inherent and control risks, it is the auditor's responsibility to reduce detection risk to an acceptably low level by performing evidence-gathering procedures. These substantive audit procedures are the auditors' opportunity to detect material misstatements that can cause financial statements to be misleading.

You will study substantive audit procedures in subsequent chapters. These procedures provide a direct assessment of the monetary amount of misstatement in the auditee's proposed accounting. As a result, they are highly effective in detecting material misstatements, and are therefore considered the most important audit procedures. The two categories of substantive procedures are (1) tests of the details of transactions and balances and (2) analytical procedures applied to produce circumstantial evidence about dollar amounts in the accounts. Detection risk is the probability that these substantive procedures will fail to detect material misstatements.

[4] CAS 315 (5141), CAS 200.

At this point it may be helpful to use an analogy to compare the auditor's risk assessment to something you are probably more familiar with, like a hockey game, as set out in the following box.

THE RISK OF MATERIAL MISSTATEMENT—THEY SHOOT! THEY SCORE!

Think of a "material misstatement" in audited financial statements as the unfortunate event of the opposing team getting the puck into a hockey team's net. The "risk of material misstatement" is the probability of the opposing team's getting a shot on the defending team's net. The "inherent risk" of this happening depends on the skill, effort, and luck of the opposing team's forwards in shooting the puck towards the net. The defending team can't affect this inherent risk—it can only try to prevent it. The team's defencemen provide the "internal control," skating backwards furiously and swinging their sticks to prevent the puck from getting through to the net. The "control risk" is the probability that the defencemen will fail to stop the puck from getting through. If they fail, the goalie is there to detect the incoming puck and stop it. The risk of the goalie's failing to stop the puck after it gets through the defence is like the "detection risk," and if the goalie works effectively this risk is reduced. To be successful, the team needs a goalie that can lower the risk of the puck's getting into the net. The goalie in this analogy is like the auditor, the final line of defence to detect the incoming "puck"—material misstatement—and stop it. If the puck gets past the goalie, the analogy to financial statement auditing is that audited statements go out containing a material misstatement, which is referred to as "audit risk." Bringing the analogy back to the audit context, we see that audit risk is realized when a material misstatement exists (inherent risk), controls fail to stop it (control risk), and the auditor's work fails to discover it (detection risk).

Note that this illustration is based on an objective fact—a goal, or a misstatement. This illustration says nothing about subjective facts like possible future misstatements or possible goals before the end of the hockey game. Such forecast errors are not explicitly covered in the misstatements concept of current auditing standards. It is important to keep this distinction in mind when thinking about audit risk and its components in the audit risk model. Forecast errors are a distinguishing feature of GAAP financial reporting (e.g., see J. C. Glover, Y. Ijiri, C. B. Levine, and P. J. Liang, "Separating Facts from Forecasts in Financial Statements," *Accounting Horizons*, December 2005, pp. 267–282), and we discuss some implications of this for auditors after reviewing the current audit risk model.

Audit Risk

In an overall sense, **audit risk** is the probability that an auditor will fail to express a reservation that financial statements are materially misstated. Audit risk can at best be controlled at a low level but not eliminated, even when audits are well planned and carefully performed. The risk of audit failure is much greater in poorly planned and carelessly performed audits. Planned audit risk varies according to auditee circumstances. Generally, the more risky the auditee or the more users rely on the audited financial statements, the lower the planned audit risk. As the risk of being sued for material misstatement increases, an auditor will decrease planned audit risk to compensate for the increased risk associated with the engagement. Many auditing firms have developed internal guidelines for setting planned levels of audit risk.

The auditing profession has no hard standard for an acceptable level of audit risk, except that it should be "appropriately low" and involve the exercise of professional judgment.

At one time, CICA guidance suggested that most auditors should strive to limit such risks to no more than 5 percent. However, auditors would be appalled to think that even 1 percent of their audits would be bad. For a large auditing firm with 2,000 audits per year, accepting 5 percent audit risk makes it look as though the firm will have 100 failed audits every year! But that would only be the case if every auditee had financial statements that were materially misstated, and not all do. So, even with using 5 percent planned audit risk on every engagement, it is likely there will be audit failures much less than 5 percent of the time. As an example, if we assumed there is a material misstatement in 6 percent of a firm's audit engagements, then, with 5 percent audit risk, the percentage of failed audits would be $0.06 \times 0.05 = 0.003 = 0.3$ percent.

The concept of audit risk also applies to individual account balances, transactions, and disclosures. Here the risk is that material misstatement is not discovered in an account balance (e.g., the inventory total), transaction stream (e.g., total revenues), or in a disclosure (e.g., pension liability). Audit risk is often used in practice with regard to individual balances and disclosures. You should keep this context in mind when you study the risk model summary presented next.

In summary, audit risk is the same whether applied to financial statements as a whole or to individual accounts. Thus, for example, if audit risk is set at 5 percent, it is used for all accounts as well as for financial statements as a whole.

The Audit Risk Model

These audit-related risks can be expressed conceptually by using a simple model that assumes the elements of audit risk are independent. Thus, the risks are multiplied as follows:

Audit risk (AR) = Inherent risk (IR) × Control risk (CR) × Detection risk (DR)

Intuitively, audit risk is the probability that the audit fails to detect a material misstatement. This will occur when (1) there is a material misstatement to start with (inherent risk), (2) the internal controls fail to detect and correct the material misstatement (control risk), and (3) the audit procedures also fail to detect the material misstatement (detection risk). The audit fails only if all three events occur. Audit risk is thus the probability that the audit fails. The probability of audit success is one minus the probability that it fails; therefore, audit assurance equals 1 – audit risk. Thus, reducing acceptable (or planned) audit risk, say from 5 percent to 1 percent, is equal to increasing acceptable (or planned) audit assurance, from 95 percent to 99 percent, in this example.

In their work, auditors want to hold the audit risk (AR) to a relatively low level (e.g., 0.05, or an average 5 percent of audit decisions when there is a material misstatement will be wrong). As such, AR is a quality criterion based on professional judgment. All the other risk assessments are estimates based on professional judgment and evidence.

For example, an auditor thought an inventory balance had a high inherent risk of material misstatement (say, IR = 0.90) and that the auditee's internal control was not very effective (say, CR = 0.70). If the auditor wanted audit risk at a 5 percent level (AR = 0.05), planned audit procedures would need to achieve detection risk (DR) that did not exceed 0.08 (approximately). The model can be used for planning the audit work by rearranging it to solve for DR.

AR = IR × CR × DR

DR = AR / (IR × CR)
   = 0.05 / (0.90 × 0.70)
   = 0.08

It is difficult to know if the audit has been planned and performed well enough to hold the detection risk as low as 0.08. Despite its simplicity, the risk model is only a conceptual tool. Auditors have few ways to calculate detection risk, and this model is more a way to think about audit risks than a way to calculate them. However, some auditors in practice use this model to calculate risks and the related extent of audit testing. Chapter 10 gives more details on the audit risk model as applied to audit sampling.

The model produces some insights, including these:

1. Auditors cannot rely on an estimate of zero inherent risk without other evidence-gathering procedures, which would appear as follows:

   $$AR = IR\ (=0) \times CR \times DR = 0$$

2. Auditors cannot rely only on internal control, which would appear as follows:

   $$AR = IR \times CR\ (= 0) \times DR = 0$$

3. Audits would not be exhibiting due audit care if the risk of failure to detect material misstatements were too high, for example:

   $$AR = IR\ (= 0.80) \times CR\ (= 0.80) \times DR\ (= 0.50) = 0.32$$

4. Auditors could rely almost exclusively on evidence produced by substantive procedures, even if they think inherent risk and control risk are high. For example (provided AR = 0.05 is acceptable),

   $$AR = IR\ (= 1.00) \times CR\ (= 1.00) \times DR\ (= 0.05) = 0.05$$

Even though the conceptual audit risk model appears to be precise when presented this way, in reality applying it is difficult and highly judgmental. However, it can help auditors decide whether they have obtained sufficient appropriate audit evidence. The objective in an audit is to limit audit risk (AR) to a low level, as judged by the auditor. This is done by assessing inherent risk (IR) and control risk (CR) along a spectrum, often presented as three levels: high, moderate, or low risk. The greater the inherent and control risks are, the lower the detection risk needs to be, resulting in more audit procedures (more in number, effectiveness, and extent). The objective is to limit audit risk (AR) to an appropriately low level, thereby achieving reasonably high assurance that the financial statements are free of material misstatement. As noted earlier, the concept of assurance is the complement of risk. For example, if audit risk of 5 percent was achieved, then the assurance obtained would be 95 percent. Put another way, the auditor would be 95 percent sure that the financial statements don't contain a material misstatement. Remember, too, that the audit risk model incorporates the concept of materiality and that materiality enters throughout the risk assessment process, as further explained in the next section.

How Materiality and Audit Risk Are Related

Materiality refers to the magnitude of a misstatement, while audit risk refers to the level of assurance that material misstatement does not exist in the financial statements. The materiality decision is based on how misstatements will affect financial statement users. Understanding the business and its environment helps the auditor to identify financial statement users and assess what is significant to their decisions. For example, the shareholders of a medium-sized private company may be relying on the audited income number for calculating the managers' bonuses. A smaller misstatement might affect them more than would be the case in a large public company where a user's decision is less directly related to the audited income figure. An auditor decides on the materiality level independently of audit risk considerations.

Acceptable audit risk is determined by how much assurance the auditor requires. For example, if there is a high risk the auditor will be sued if the audit fails to uncover a material misstatement because venture capital investors are basing their financing conditions on the audited information, high assurance is required. High profile companies such as banks require high assurance, as audit failure affects many people and generates a lot of bad news coverage, seriously damaging the auditor's reputation as well. As audit risk is the complement of audit assurance, requiring a high level of assurance means setting audit risk low. The auditor is only willing to accept a small risk of missing a material misstatement.

Audit risk and materiality thus both deal with the sufficiency of evidence, covered in Chapter 8. Both audit risk and materiality levels will be planned early in the engagement. These planned levels are used throughout the audit for financial statements as a whole, as well as for individual accounts, unless situations discovered during performance of the audit indicate they should be adjusted. Inherent risk, control risk, and detection risk, on the other hand, will vary assertion by assertion for each account balance, transaction stream, and disclosure, depending on the conditions for each assertion. Nonetheless, as long as the risk model is used so that the audit risk for each financial statement assertion is at or below the planned levels, the auditor is reasonably certain that sufficient appropriate evidence has been obtained to support the audit opinion. However, there are practical limits to the evidence decision; not all the evidence can be obtained at a reasonable cost or quickly enough to provide a timely audit report, and not all has the same level of reliability, so trade-offs have to be made. The concepts of materiality and audit risk are important elements in exercising professional judgment about the sufficiency and appropriateness of audit evidence.

The materiality and audit risk decision's main impact is on the extent of audit evidence that needs to be gathered. To be systematic and consistent, auditors try to keep the planning for the users' materiality separate from the assurance level decision. But when an auditor believes a high level of assurance is needed, choosing a low audit risk level or a low materiality level have the same impact, both increasing the amount of evidence the audit will need to gather. The underlying considerations of materiality and audit risk concepts are, however, different in nature, so it is good practice to keep these decisions separate in planning an audit.

Business Risk and Extensions of the Audit Risk Model

Business risk is any event or action adversely affecting an organization's ability to achieve its business objectives and execute its strategies. For example, the development of the PC and its word-processing capabilities in the 1980s dramatically reduced the market for electric typewriters and threatened the business objectives of many firms in the typewriter business. More recently, the capability for downloading music and video files over the Internet severely challenged business models of the music and movie industries and their methods of making profits. Auditing standards emphasize the financial statement auditor's need to understand and respond to business risk.[5]

The current business risk–based audit approach of the auditing standards emerged in the 1990s in response to increasingly complex businesses, operating environments, systems, and financing techniques. In the past, audit partners' personal experience, knowledge, and practice skills were sufficient to perform effective audits for relatively simple businesses. As businesses became more complex, it became evident that auditors, especially less experienced ones, needed more guidance and formalized structure for exercising good auditor judgment. Auditors were not always able to assess the many ways that events and conditions of a business increase the risk that its financial statements do not fairly present the business's financial realities. **Strategic Systems Auditing (SSA)** was developed in the 1990s as rigorous top-down business risk–based audit methodology to meet this need (see further description in Appendix 7B on the OLC). SSA presented quite radical changes for auditors used to the traditional, more bottom-up process of verifying transactions in the search for processing errors. Some people believe that the new SSA philosophy was not properly implemented, or even

[5] CAS 315 (5141).

that its intent was to increase audit profitability by justifying doing little substantive testing. Some attribute grave audit failures like Enron and WorldCom to the ineffectiveness of SSA.[6]

Still, supporters of SSA's risk-based philosophy believe that its goal was always to improve audit effectiveness. The use of a risk-based audit approach in Canadian and international auditing standards places business risk assessment at the heart of the audit process. Appendix 7C provides a summary of the risk factors set out in the auditing standards as an example of the comprehensive aspects of business risk that a financial statement auditor considers when assessing the risk of material misstatement.

This debate about SSA's value has led to recent research within the audit profession to better understand how auditors address business risk to manage audit risk. Being familiar with the traditional simple audit risk model, it is useful to look at what researchers are exploring through further analysis of the risks in a financial statement audit.

We saw that AR is a function of the risk of material misstatement (RMM) after application of internal control (RMM = IR × CR) and the risk that the auditor does not detect it (DR). As noted above, DR is a difficult risk to assess, and we can view it as having several layers. The first layer shows that detection can be achieved either by analytical procedures or by tests of details. With both substantive approaches, there is risk that the procedures will not detect a material misstatement.

In the case of tests of details, auditors recognize that when using samples there is a risk, called sampling risk. This is the risk that the sample result will not truly reflect the population the sample was taken from. (Chapter 10 will explain audit sampling in detail, but for our purposes a few basic ideas are introduced here.) Even with a rigorously selected random sample, bad luck can still strike and only correct items are selected when in fact there is a very high rate of errors. There are techniques for ensuring that sampling risk is reduced to a reasonable level, so there should be only a small

EXHIBIT 7–4   THE AUDIT RISK MODEL EXPANDED—ILLUSTRATING AUDITOR'S BUSINESS-RISK-BASED JUDGMENTS

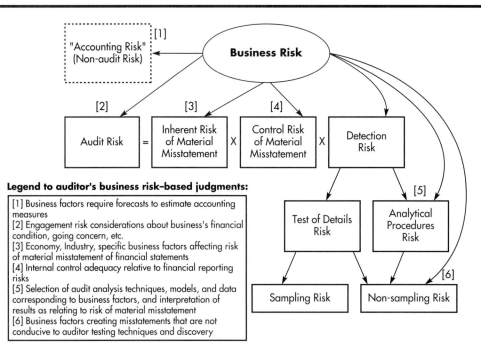

Legend to auditor's business risk–based judgments:

[1] Business factors require forecasts to estimate accounting measures
[2] Engagement risk considerations about business's financial condition, going concern, etc.
[3] Economy, Industry, specific business factors affecting risk of material misstatement of financial statements
[4] Internal control adequacy relative to financial reporting risks
[5] Selection of audit analysis techniques, models, and data corresponding to business factors, and interpretation of results as relating to risk of material misstatement
[6] Business factors creating misstatements that are not conducive to auditor testing techniques and discovery

[6] See W. R. Knechel, "The business risk audit: Origins, obstacles, and opportunities," *Accounting, Organizations, and Society*, 32 (2007) pp. 383–408 for a full exploration of this issue.

sampling risk if it is done properly. If reducing sampling risk to get to the desired DR was the only concern, the limitations of audits would be tiny. But there is also non-sampling risk—the risk that the wrong conclusion will be reached from a sample, for other reasons that don't relate to sampling risk. For example, the auditor may be careless in performing the test and misinterpret the results, or the test procedure may not be relevant to the audit objective. A similar type of non-detection risk also exists for analytical procedures, since these may use inappropriate methods or ignore relevant data and fail to pick up significant indicators of misstatement. Exhibit 7–4 on page 226 summarizes and illustrates how business risks and an auditor's judgments based on them can permeate every aspect of the risk modelling exercise.

This extention of the audit risk model to incorporate business risk and accounting risk is discussed further in the box below.

NEW PERSPECTIVES ON BUSINESS RISK, ACCOUNTING RISK, AND AUDIT RISK*

Knechel (2007) proposes a non-sampling risk concept that includes many risks of material misstatement that simply can never be identified through substantive testing, and argues that these risks can be reduced by incorporating business risk analysis in audits to provide insight into how significant non-detectible misstatements might be. If the auditor assesses such risks as unacceptably high, effectively the scope of the audit is too limited to allow the auditor to provide reasonable assurance on the financial statements.

A further perspective on this problem is the concept of accounting risk discussed in Smieliauskas (2008). Accounting risk arises mainly from forecasting used to generate accounting estimates. For example, an estimate of the fair value of a financial instrument can require forecasts of factors such as future interest or exchange rates. The limits and deficiencies that audit detection work cannot remove from the underlying accounting are accounting risk. If management must make accounting estimates under a great deal of measurement uncertainty, there is a risk these estimates are misstated, and increasing the extent of audit testing or analytical procedures cannot reduce this risk. Appendix 7D explains the accounting risk concept in more depth, and gives a critical thinking exercise illustrating how it relates to but differs from audit risk. Again, business risk analysis is a way for the auditor to distinguish accounting risk from audit risk.

Perhaps if Enron's auditors had realized that accounting risk for Enron's special-purpose entities was extremely high, they could have realized that deficiencies in GAAP were allowing billions of dollars of liabilities to go unreported such that Enron's financial statements were not fairly stated. Their audit evidence might not have been sufficient to support an adverse opinion, but they could have realized that their scope was too limited to provide the clean opinion they issued! The important point is that, when accounting risks are too high for GAAP to provide fair presentation, the auditor is not doing anyone any favours by effectively accepting this as higher audit risk and issuing a clean opinion anyway. The audit profession has always had a crucial public interest role in promoting high-quality financial reporting. Auditors' professional duty to the protect the public can at times require auditors to refuse to provide assurance when accounting risk is too high to provide reliable financial information to users. Some people argue that IFRS's current trend toward providing more fair value accounting information for many types of assets and liabilities may produce unacceptably high accounting risks in some cases. If an auditor concludes the fair value accounting risk is too high, the responsibility is to flag the estimation uncertainty in the audit report so that financial statement users are not misled. This perspective also relates to the debate about whether the audit opinion is a two-part assertion on fair presentation and compliance with GAAP, or a one part statement only on GAAP compliance. Accepting the accounting risk as a real problem makes it impossible to see the audit opinion as anything but a two-part assertion. New audit reporting standards (CAS 706, Emphasis of Matter Paragraphs and Other Matter(s) Paragraphs in the Independent Auditor's Report) address this problem to some extent by giving auditors the option of using extra paragraphs in the audit report to provide (1) further emphasis on matters contained in the financial statements or (2) information on other matters the auditor believes are important for users in interpreting financial statements.

You might be wondering if non-detectible misstatement risk and accounting risk make effective audits impossible. Reasonable assurance can be perplexing (even to experienced auditors!) but these perspectives on risk can make the limitations more concrete and easier to conceptualize. These viewpoints might also help outsiders understand the limitations better, and reduce the expectation gap discussed in Chapter 1. Overall, a fuller appreciation of business risk and its relation to both audit and accounting risk shows how business risk analysis can enhance audit effectiveness.

*This discussion on expanding the audit risk model is based on W. R. Knechel, "The business risk audit: Origins, obstacles, and opportunities," *Accounting, Organizations, and Society*, 32 (2007), pp. 383–408; W. Smieliauskas, "A framework for identifying (and avoiding) fraudulent financial reporting," *Accounting Perspectives*, 7(3) (2008), pp. 189–226; and M. E. Peecher, R. Schwartz, and I. Solomon, "It's all about audit quality: Perspectives on strategic-systems auditing," *Accounting, Organizations and Society* 32 (2007), pp. 463–485.

The remainder of this chapter, and Part II of the text, will focus primarily on how the auditor's business understanding is used to assess inherent risk, and how understanding internal control and information systems helps to assess control risk. These risk assessment procedures are the basis of developing a detailed plan to gather evidence to reduce the risk of material misstatement to an acceptable level given the level of audit risk the auditor has decided is acceptable for the engagement.

REVIEW CHECKPOINTS

1   What are the four risks included in the simple conceptual audit risk model? How are they related?

2   Give an example of one account with high inherent risk and one with low inherent risk.

3   What factors influence the auditor's decision on an acceptable audit risk level?

4   In the hockey game analogy used to explain the audit risk factors, whom do the hockey team's fans represent?

5   What is the purpose of a control framework?

6   Describe two control frameworks that can help in the auditor's preliminary control risk assessment.

7   How are auditors' judgments about the quality or effectiveness of internal control affected by anchoring?

8   How do bad economic times increase the risks that auditors should be alert to in auditees' financial statements?

9   What is the difference between "audit risk in an overall sense" and "audit risk applied to individual account balances"?

10   How does the auditor's decision on materiality relate to audit risk?

11   What is the relationship between business risk and audit risk?

12   How can the risk model be expanded to incorporate limitations to the audit that arise from accounting and other business risks?

BUSINESS RISK–BASED APPROACH TO AUDITING

LEARNING OBJECTIVE

2 Explain how auditors assess the auditee's business risk through strategic analysis and business process analysis.

The **business risk–based approach** to auditing requires the auditor to understand the auditee's business risks and strategy and its related internal control to assess the risks of material misstatement and to both design and perform procedures that address the assessed risks. Business risk analysis allows auditors to learn about the risks the business faces, management's strategy for addressing those risks to meet organization goals, and the business processes it uses to implement the strategy. There are two parts of business risk analysis: strategic analysis and business process analysis.

At the end of the business risk analysis the auditor should be able to answer the following questions:

1. What is the entity's strategy?

2. Is it sustainable?

3. What are the business risks/threats that can prevent the entity from achieving its strategic goals?

4. What business processes, internal controls, and information systems does the entity management use to manage those risks?

5. What are the gaps or weaknesses in the entity's risk management approach?

6. Do those gaps affect the financial statements?

Answers to these questions allow the auditor to identify significant risks that could result in material misstatements. In particular, the answer to question 4 requires an in-depth evaluation of the design and implementation of internal controls during the audit period— also known as assessing the **entity's risk assessment process**. Management uses the entity's risk assessment process to deal with uncertainty and associated risks and opportunities, thereby allowing the organization to meet its goals. A useful guide to entity risk assessment is COSO's *Enterprise Risk Management—Integrated Framework*, which provides the following definition:

> Enterprise risk management is a process, effected by an entity's board of directors, management, and other personnel, applied in strategy setting and across the enterprise, designed to identify potential events that may affect the entity, and manage risk to be within its risk appetite, to provide reasonable assurance regarding the achievement of entity objectives.[7]

The auditor's first step is understanding the entity management's own process for identifying business risks affecting financial reporting objectives and for deciding on actions to minimize these risks. Organizations approach risk assessment in various ways, and understanding management's assessment process helps the auditor, in turn, to assess the risk that the financial statements could be materially misstated. In this text, the need for the auditor to understand the auditee's business risks and strategy is called the business risk–based approach to auditing.

Having an understanding of business risks, auditors exercise professional judgment by using mental models and systems thinking. A mental model "consists of organized knowledge, integrated data about the patterns and cues, and rules for linking knowledge and cues."[8] These are used throughout the audit and updated continuously for new information. Systems thinking involves viewing the organization in a complex web of relationships between the auditee and relevant features of the auditee's external environment. In systems thinking, the auditor considers not only cause-and-effect relationships that affect the auditee's business but also how random shocks, such as the softwood lumber duties example in Chapter 6, can change its dynamics. This allows the auditor to get a deep

---

[7] Source: COSO website: www.coso.org/Publications/ERM/COSO_ERM_ExecutiveSummary.pdf (accessed December 2008).

[8] T. Bell and I. Solomon, *Cases in Strategic-Systems Auditing* (KPMG and University of Illinois, 2002).

understanding of the business risks facing the auditee organization and their potential consequences. The next part of this section explains a systems thinking–based methodology for analyzing business risk.

Strategic Analysis

The audit team begins the strategic analysis by learning from senior auditee management (for example, the chief executive officer or chief operating officer) about the business objectives and the key strategies and risks in achieving those objectives. In for-profit entities, objectives are normally some combination of profitability and growth. In a not-for-profit entity, objectives might be, for example, an inner city health clinic's goal of providing medical services to homeless people underserved by the mainstream medical service delivery.

Strategies are the systems and processes an organization implements to achieve the business objectives. Common strategies include being an industry cost leader (i.e., having the lowest costs), or differentiating your products from your competitor's (i.e., deliver an element of the product that purchasers value).

The following box illustrates the risks faced by a company that enjoys market leadership from selling the most popular hand-held email devices. Competitors are constantly in the wings looking for ways to take away some of BlackBerry's market share. Different aspects of its strategy will present a variety of risks to the company, so auditors must take a broad view of the business environment to identify all important risks. The more successful the company, the more complex and varied its risks may be.

APPLE iPHONE LATEST THREAT TO BLACKBERRY

Apple may have been planning to use its iPhone for a major assault on Research In Motion (RIM), the dominant maker of the BlackBerry smartphones for business users. RIM stock fell about 8 percent after Apple CEO Steve Jobs introduced the iPhone at the company's annual technology showcase in January 2007, saying it would eventually surpass the BlackBerry.

The iPhone has a touch screen instead of a keyboard, plays music like the popular Apple iPod, surfs the Internet, does email, and runs the Macintosh computer operating system. It went on sale in the U.S. in June 2007, in Europe in late 2007, and Asia in 2008, at prices ranging from U.S. $499 to $599, depending on the model.

Some analysts say the long-term impact on RIM of Apple's entry into the market is uncertain. While RIM is expected to keep a solid hold on its traditional business market share, on the consumer side things are more competitive. The iPhone's innovative design and features, and its move to 3G technology, made it a strong competitor to RIM in the consumer segment of the market, which is expected to be the next source of growth for RIM.

Throughout July 2008, Apple's media blitz over its first 3G iPhone mobile device dominated the news. The battle for higher-end consumers has seen RIM sprucing up the multimedia handling abilities of its plain, but functional, BlackBerry business phones. The BlackBerry Pearl and Curve models began the trend. The BlackBerry Bold, available in August 2008, challenged Apple's new 3G iPhone as RIM's first 3G offering, complemented by a set of consumer-oriented features including a 2-megapixel camera with video recording capability, a music player, GPS, and Wi-Fi.

However, Apple's other innovations in the smartphone market include a business model that Apple presented in August 2008; instead of paying Apple part of the subscription fee, wireless network companies will subsidize the devices upfront to make them cheaper. Analysts say this aggressive pricing is likely to change smartphone pricing across the industry, seeing wireless carriers pricing BlackBerrys much lower and putting more pressure on other competitors like the Palm Treo.

Auditors of companies in the smartphone industry will need to understand the business risks that arise in an industry with fierce competition on technological innovations, pricing models, and market segmentation. They need to understand the strategic plans and business processes management has in place to address these risks. The risk of material misstatement in this business environment rise mainly in the valuation of inventory, patents, and other technology-based intangible assets.

Sources: David Paddon, The Canadian Press, "Apple Handset Gives BlackBerry New Battle," *The Daily Herald-Tribune*, (Grande Prairie, Alberta), January 12, 2007. Computers, p. 48. © Sun Media Corporation. All rights reserved; Matt Walcoff, Record Staff, "Apple Won't Take Big Bite out of RIM—yet; analysts; Shares of BlackBerry maker rebound after initial fears over new iPhone," *The Record* (Kitchener-Waterloo, Ontario) Business, p. D8. © 2007 Toronto Star Newspapers, Ltd. All rights reserved; "RIM Begins BlackBerry Bold Release," EWeek.com, August 11, 2008, Mobile and Wireless, © 2008 Ziff Davis Media Inc.; Jonathan Spicer, Reuters, "Investors Keep Faith in Maker of the BlackBerry," *The International Herald Tribune*, Finance, p.15, © 2008 International Herald Tribune.

The strategic analysis begins the auditor's understanding of management's process for identifying business risks and making decisions about actions to address those risks. The business risk approach requires the auditor to enquire about business risks that management has identified and consider whether they may result in material misstatement.

In smaller businesses where management may not have a formal risk assessment process, the auditor should discuss with management how risks to the business are identified and how they are addressed.

Business Process Analysis

Management tries to minimize business risks by designing well thought-out business processes. Business processes are a structured set of activities designed to produce a specific output that matches business strategy. Examples include customer relations management in a consumer products distribution firm or processing income tax returns in the Canada Revenue Agency's operations. If the business process produces value-added output according to the strategy, it is more likely that the business will achieve its objectives and not fall prey to the various risks.

The business process view of the firm has become an important perspective in management in recent years. Interest in business processes follows the understanding that a firm's success ultimately depends on how well its management can execute the main aspects of its strategy, such as cost leadership, differentiation, or focus. (Appendix 7B on the OLC includes details of types of strategies.)

Business processes work to create value for customers and thus achieve strategic objectives. Typically, they will cross boundaries between an organization's functional departments, such as sales, marketing, manufacturing, and research and development, and involve groups of employees from the different areas working together to complete the work. Exhibit 7–5 shows examples of some simplified business processes for an airline company and a manufacturing company, illustrating how the different functions combine to achieve the overall goal.

Business processes are each organization's unique ways of coordinating work, information, and knowledge to produce a value-added product or service. This business process–based management approach has been facilitated by the development of powerful information systems, called **enterprise resource planning systems (ERPS)**, that can integrate enterprise-wide resource and accounting information. These information systems can help organizations achieve efficiencies by automating parts of their business processes, but this still requires careful analysis and planning. More complex systems might

EXHIBIT 7-5   EXAMPLES OF BUSINESS PROCESSES

Business Processes in a Passenger Airline Company

Market and sell services.

1. Develop a marketing plan.
2. Form and continue alliances with other airlines.
3. Establish positive customer contact.

Provide transportation services.

1. Acquire, maintain, and manage assets: airplanes, parts, hangers.
2. Manage safety and risk.

Business Processes in a Manufacturing Company

Production Processes

Planning production.

1. Schedule production.
2. Order materials.

Manufacturing products.

1. Assemble product.
2. Test product.
3. Record costs of materials, labour, and overhead used.

Shipping products.

1. Ship product ordered.
2. Record inventory used.

Order Fulfillment Processes

Process sales orders.

1. Receive the order.
2. Enter the order.
3. Clear the order once shipped.

Account for the sale.

1. Check and approve credit.
2. Generate invoice upon shipment.
3. Post sales journal entry.

---

strengthen the wrong process of business model, and the business can become more efficient at things it should not be doing. As a result, the business's strategy will not be achieved and it will become vulnerable to competitors with better models. The most important strategic decisions involve understanding what business processes need improvement and how information systems can improve them, not simply buying the latest information technology.

The business process view also highlights the fact that business organizations differ in terms of the kinds of activities they perform and the technology they use. Some organizations use mainly routine tasks that can easily be reduced to simple formal rules that require little judgment (e.g., inventory ordering in a grocery business). These types of tasks can easily be programmed, and these organizations are more likely to be run hierarchically. In contrast, organizations with activities that are non-routine and require judgment (e.g., an engineering firm designing specifications for office towers) would have complex functions in their operation and thus would be run less hierarchically.

Effects of Information Technology and eCommerce on Business Risk

Changes in information technology and ecommerce can affect business risks and processes. Business risk analysis includes analyzing the effects of ecommerce in the entity's business strategy. As a business becomes more involved with ecommerce, and as its information systems become more integrated and complex, it will change its business processes and introduce new business risks that could affect the financial statements. Managers responsible for the entity's ecommerce activities, such as the chief information officer, are a useful source of the necessary knowledge. Ecommerce activities may be complementary to an entity's traditional business, such as an online order entry system run over the Internet, or it may represent a new line of business, such as when the firm uses its website to both sell and deliver digital products via the Internet. In an industry significantly affected by ecommerce, such as those in the box below, the business risks that can affect the financial statements may be greater.

BUSINESS RISKS AND ECOMMERCE

Many industries, in all business sectors, have been significantly affected by ecommerce. The following are some key industries being transformed:

a. computer software
b. financial services
c. travel services
d. books and magazines
e. recorded music and movies
f. advertising
g. news media
h. education

To understand management's strategy and risk assessment process for ecommerce, the auditor would consider factors such as
- alignment of ecommerce activities with the entity's overall business strategy.
- sources of revenue for the entity and how these are changing (for example, whether the entity will be acting as a principal or agent for goods or services sold).
- management's evaluation of how ecommerce affects the earnings of the entity and its financial requirements.
- the extent to which management has identified ecommerce opportunities and risks in a documented strategy that is supported by appropriate controls, or whether ecommerce is subject to ad hoc development responding to opportunities and risks as they arise.
- management's commitment to relevant codes of best practice or web-trust programs.
- the IT skills and knowledge of entity personnel.
- the risks involved in the entity's use of ecommerce and its approach to managing those risks, particularly the adequacy of the internal control system, including the security infrastructure and related controls, as it affects the financial reporting process.
- information security issues arising from the firm's website, which can provide an access point to the entity's financial records. The security infrastructure and related controls can be expected to be more extensive where the website is used for transacting with business partners, or where systems are highly integrated.

Source: Adapted from *CICA Handbook*, Assurance Guideline AuG-32, and IAPS 1013.

Further details on the impact of ecommerce activities on an organization's business processes and risk, the security of its payments made over the Internet, and the impact on the audit work and need for IT expertise are provided in Appendix 7E on the OLC.

Summary

The business process analysis deepens the auditor's understanding that began in the strategic analysis. It should allow the auditor to identify risk areas that may affect the amounts and relations among the numbers recorded in the accounting system and the financial statements. The process analysis may also suggest disclosures that should be present in the notes to the financial statements. Business risks and audit risk assessment are an important consideration in applying the audit risk model components discussed above, in relation to developing the detailed audit plan (discussed in Chapter 8), and in testing the internal controls (discussed in Chapter 9).

REVIEW CHECKPOINTS

13 Explain the business risk–based approach to the audit. What is its purpose?

14 What are the two parts that make up business risk analysis? What is the goal of business analysis?

15 How does understanding the business's strategy help the auditor to assess business risk?

16 What is a business process?

17 How do business processes relate to strategy and business risk?

18 Give an example of one business risk that affects the airline industry and one that affects a manufacturing business.

19 How do organizational differences relate to strategies and business processes?

20 How do risks of IT and ecommerce affect the risks of financial statement misstatements?

21 What are the implications of a business using ecommerce on its business analysis?

Business Performance Analysis and Management's Financial Statements

This section expands on how the auditor applies an understanding of the business, its environment, and risks, as well as management's process for managing those risks, in assessing the risk of material misstatement of the financial statements.

The auditor's concern is that the financial statements will not capture the underlying business reality fairly and in accordance with GAAP because errors or fraud have occurred. The auditor considers whether the analysis of business performance is consistent with the performance portrayed in the financial statements. Business performance analysis ideally will consider financial and nonfinancial performance measures and the interrelationships between the two. The auditor should also consider how performance measures are used, both externally (e.g., key performance indicators reported to analysts, creditors, and shareholders) and internally (e.g., for personnel review and incentive programs). Pressures on the business managers increase the risk that they are motivated to misstate the financial statements, as illustrated by the audit guidance in the following box.

POTENTIAL TROUBLE SPOTS

Fraud is usually concealed, making it very challenging for an auditor to detect. When planning the audit, the auditor may notice certain events or conditions referred to as "fraud risk factors." These are events or conditions that suggest management has an incentive, pressure, or opportunity leading them to commit fraud. Some examples of risk factors often present in situations where frauds have occurred are

a. <u>pressures</u> to meet earnings expectations or existing debt covenants to obtain additional debt financing;

b. <u>incentives</u> arising from the availability of significant bonuses when profit targets are met; and

c. <u>opportunities</u> provided by an ineffective control environment with poor access controls.

While fraud risk factors may not always lead to the occurrence of fraud, they should be considered in the auditor's assessment of the risks of material misstatement if they are present.

Source: CAS 315 (25–27, A116) and CAS 240 (3.A1).

Financial Performance Analysis

Financial performance analysis continues the analytical procedures discussion presented in Chapter 6. It includes examining key sets of financial statement ratios (e.g., short-term liquidity ratios—see Appendix 6A for details), examining trends over time in those ratios, and considering the interrelationships among the ratios for consistency. Based on previous audit findings and the business risk assessment, the auditor forms expectations about what the financial analysis should discover.

Financial performance analysis includes a review of management's significant accounting policy choices and benchmarking those with significant industry competitors. Here the auditor is attempting to gain an understanding of the degree of conservatism of management's accounting policy selection. In particular, the auditor considers the revenue recognition policy in for-profit entities, as this has been a key area of abuse when apparently successful companies suddenly fail.[9] See Exhibit 7–6 for examples. If the accounting policies vary significantly from industry norms, the auditor adjusts the accounting policies to those normal to the industry and "reperforms" the quantitative financial performance analysis. The results are then compared with industry benchmarks. This may suggest areas of additional audit work to reduce audit risk to an appropriately low level, or that management should modify its accounting policies and practices.

Part of the financial analysis in for-profit companies involves considering the quality of the earnings. **Quality of earnings** refers to the auditee's ability to replicate its earnings, both the amounts and the trends, over relatively long periods. Exhibit 7–7 lists factors indicative of high earnings quality. Indications of low-quality earnings may result in the auditor's performing additional audit procedures to reduce risk to

EXHIBIT 7-6 ACCOUNTING "GIMMICKS" FOR EARNINGS MANIPULATION

- Recording revenue before it is earned
- Creating fictitious revenue
- Boosting profits with nonrecurring transactions
- Shifting current expenses to a later period
- Failing to record or disclose liabilities
- Shifting current income to a later period
- Shifting future expenses to an earlier period

[9] CAS 240 (5135).

EXHIBIT 7-7   HIGH-QUALITY EARNINGS

1. Earnings management practices that are not used by firms with high-quality earnings:
   a. Using accounting accruals to smooth income increases over time
   b. Structuring business transactions to ensure an outcome desired by management on accounting income for the period
   c. Making management choices based primarily on short-term profitability
2. High-quality earnings have operating cash flows and income recognized closely together over time.
3. Indicators of high-quality earnings include:
   a. Consistency of accounting accruals from year to year.
   b. Accounting policy changes reduce income.
   c. Short time lag between income recognition and the related cash being received by the business.

an appropriately low level or suggest changes to the financial statements prepared by management.

Auditing standards require the auditor to communicate on a timely basis with the audit committee, or those having oversight responsibility for the financial reporting process, on matters that are significant qualitative aspects of the entity's accounting practices, including accounting policies, estimates, and disclosures.[10] This communication should be open and frank discussions among the auditor, audit committee, and management on all items that have a significant effect on the understandability, relevance, reliability, and comparability of the financial statements, including the

- impact on earnings of implementing changes in accounting policies;
- effect of significant accounting policies in controversial or emerging areas, or those unique to an industry;
- estimates, judgments, and uncertainties;
- existence of acceptable alternative policies and methods, the acceptability of the particular policy or method used by management, the financial statement amounts that are affected by the choice of principles, as well as information concerning accounting principles used by peer group companies, and the auditor's views on whether management has chosen the most appropriate practice;
- unusual transactions; and
- timing of transactions that affect the recognition of revenues or avoid recognition of expenses.

The auditor must also ask management and those charged with governance about any known or suspected frauds affecting the auditee.[11] The auditor has an ongoing responsibility to communicate any suspicions or evidence of fraud to a level of management higher than the employees involved, or with those charged with governance if high-level managers are suspected.

Nonfinancial Performance Analysis

Through the key business process analysis discussed previously, the auditor has developed a deep understanding of the nonfinancial performance measures employed in various business processes. Nonfinancial performance analysis builds on that, by analyzing the relationships among the business's resources, the processes for using those resources, and the firm's ability to compete in the markets for its products or services. Based on the business analysis, the auditor already has information about the business's processes and available resources. The auditor collects information on the entity's market

[10] CAS 260.
[11] CAS 240 (5135).

EXHIBIT 7-8   THE BALANCED SCORECARD

The balanced scorecard is a strategic planning and management system that is used extensively in business and industry, government, and nonprofit organizations worldwide to align business activities to the vision and strategy of the organization, improve internal and external communications, and monitor organization performance against strategic goals. It is a performance measurement framework that adds strategic nonfinancial performance measures to traditional financial metrics to give managers a more "balanced" view of organizational performance.

The balanced scorecard contains measures related to four perspectives: financial performance, customer relations, internal business processes, and measures related to learning and growth in the organization. Each of these is explained in the table below.

Balanced Scorecard Perspectives	Relevant Measures
Financial	
To meet its financial goals, how should the organization report performance to its stakeholders?	Measures relevant to each business unit (e.g., revenues per employee for a sales unit, or research and development expense for a pharmaceutical division)
Customers	
To achieve its strategic goals, how should it relate to its customers?	Customer surveys, sales from repeat customers, and customer profitability
Internal business processes	
What business processes must the organization perfect to satisfy stakeholders and customers?	Measures specific operational processes of each business unit (e.g., investment in product development and dealer quality for a petroleum distributor)
Learning and growth	
To achieve its strategic goals, how will it sustain the ability to change and improve?	Employee capabilities, information systems capabilities, and employee motivation and empowerment

The scorecard is a strategic management tool that should reveal the drivers of performance, as well as provide measures of performance.

Source: http://www.balancedscorecard.org/BSCResources/AbouttheBalancedScorecard/tabid/55/Default.aspx (accessed on December 29, 2008).

performance. For this analysis, the auditor can develop a **"balanced scorecard"** for the entity and benchmark with others in the industry. Exhibit 7–8 explains the concept of a balanced scorecard, and your management accounting classes will provide more in-depth understanding. The scorecard reflects measures of resources (learning and growth), processes (internal business), and markets (customer related), and relates all three to financial performance.

A key part of the nonfinancial performance analysis is determining if the resources available to the entity and the relative efficiency and effectiveness of the business processes are consistent with marketplace results. For example, a business entity is competing in a technological industry with a high rate of change. The entity does not have up-to-date equipment or top engineers (both examples of resources). Its business processes are bench-marked as below industry average in performance. Therefore, the entity should have below-average market performance in terms of market share or customer satisfaction. This pattern would reflect a set of consistent results and increase the auditor's confidence in the assessment of business risk.

Interrelationships between Financial and Nonfinancial Performance
The auditor considers whether the financial results and the nonfinancial performance measures each portray the same picture of the auditee's business. If the auditee's

EXHIBIT   7-9   RELATING NONFINANCIAL AND FINANCIAL PERFORMANCE

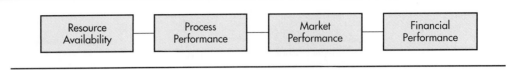

financial statements show increasing sales and increasing gross margins, there should be market share increases, resource advantages, or process efficiencies in the nonfinancial measures that support these financial results. If discrepancies are found, there is a risk of material misstatement, and additional substantive audit work may be needed to lower this risk to an acceptable level. This analysis also allows the auditor to consider going-concern issues and other areas of completing the audit, as are covered later in Chapter 15.

The process of relating nonfinancial and financial performance can be illustrated with a simple theoretical model like the one in Exhibit 7–9. For example, consider an auditee company with limited financial resources and minimal investment in new production capability (Resource Availability). The company is producing its products with the technology that the company founder used ten years ago. An analysis of the nonfinancial performance measures is made; for example, measures of machine downtime are increasing each year (Process Performance), the company's sales of the product remain as strong as in the last two years (Market Performance), but the financial statements show a lower percentage of repairs and maintenance expense to gross fixed assets than in previous years (Financial Performance). This is an inconsistency that needs to be resolved through additional substantive audit of details of repair expenses and additions to productive asset balances.

To determine the acceptable level of audit risk, business risk needs to be considered. The higher the business risks, the greater the need to report them accurately. As a consequence, the higher the auditee's business risk, the less chance that the auditor can take that the financial statements do not adequately communicate those business risks to users and decision makers. As explained earlier, when the auditor cannot take a lot of risk of giving a clean opinion on financial statements that are misstated, the auditor sets the acceptable audit risk at a low level.

Summary

The business risk–based approach to auditing starts with a business risk analysis that provides an understanding of the auditee's business, its environment, and the risks it faces. The auditor's strategic and business process analyses involve a critical assessment of the strategic goals of the business, the risks of not meeting those goals, and the process the entity's management uses to manage those risks. The auditor then examines the financial and nonfinancial performance of the entity to assess whether the performance reported in management's financial statements is consistent with the auditor's strategic and business process analyses. The link from the business risk to the financial statements is covered in the next section. Internal control, the main aspect of an entity's risk management process, and the auditor's procedures to understand risks related to internal control are discussed in the following section.

REVIEW CHECKPOINTS

22   What are some examples of external and internal business performance measures? How can these performance measures motivate management to misstate the financial statements?

23   What are some "gimmicks" that management can use to manipulate earnings?

24   What is earnings quality and what are some indicators of high-quality earnings?

25 What are the auditor's responsibilities when they suspect or find evidence of fraud? How do their responsibilities differ if the fraud involves low-level employees or high-level managers?

26 What are the three components of business performance analysis? Why does the auditor conduct business performance analysis?

27 What are the activities in a financial performance analysis? When would the auditor design and carry out additional substantive audit procedures as a result of performance analysis?

28 What are the activities of nonfinancial performance analysis?

29 Why does the auditor examine the relationship between financial and nonfinancial performance measures?

ACCOUNTING PROCESSES AND THE FINANCIAL STATEMENTS

LEARNING OBJECTIVE

3 Outline the relationships among business processes, accounting processes/cycles, and management's general purpose financial statements.

After performing preliminary analysis of the financial statements and expanding this with an in-depth analysis of the entity's business risk, we can consider how management's financial statements are created with a more informed perspective. Two points need to be stressed about management's financial statements: (1) the management of the organization is responsible for preparing them; thus they contain management's assertions about economic actions and events, and (2) the numbers in them are produced by the organization's control system, which includes the accounting system that generates the trial balance. The relationship between the accounting system and the trial balance is shown in Exhibit 7–10, and the relationship between the trial balance and the financial statements is illustrated in Exhibit 7–11.[12] These exhibits show the trial balance of the Kingston Company, a fictional company that will be used in various examples throughout Parts II and III of this text.

The Kingston trial balance is shortened and simplified; real trial balances are more complex, with hundreds of accounts. To simplify the audit plan, auditors apply one of a fairly standard set of business processes, each of which has a set of accounts and an **accounting process** related to it. Four simplified accounting processes are

1. revenue process dealing with accounting for the sales activities of the firm,
2. purchasing process dealing with accounting for purchasing,
3. production process dealing with accounting for manufacturing and inventory costing, and
4. financing process dealing with the accounting for all the financing activities of the firm.

An accounting process can be thought of as a cycle. The accounts go together in the accounting information system because they record transaction information from the same business activity and run through the same accounting process over and over, in a cycle. These routine transactions are recorded by the organization's accountants using journal entries involving the same set of accounts. The cycle perspective looks at accounts grouped according to the routine transactions by which all are normally affected. The revenue cycle starts with a sale and the recording of an account receivable, which is later collected

---

[12] The term *amortization*, as used in the *CICA Handbook*, is the general term for allocating capital asset costs over the years benefited. Historically and internationally, specialized names for amortization have evolved in practice. Depreciation is amortization applied to tangible capital assets, such as machinery and buildings, while the term depletion tends to be used for natural resources. In practice, amortization tends to be used in the more restricted sense of applying to intangible assets and premium or discount on long-term debt. Consistent with the *CICA Handbook*, however, in Exhibit 7–10 and thereafter, we treat all these allocations as specialized names for amortization.

EXHIBIT 7-10 KINGSTON COMPANY TRIAL BALANCE, DECEMBER 31, 20X2

Revenue process	Purchasing process	Production process	Financing process		Debit	Credit
X	X	X	X	Cash	484,000	
X				Accounts receivable	400,000	
X				Allowance for doubtful accounts		30,000
X				Sales		8,500,000
X				Sales returns	400,000	
X				Bad debt expense	50,000	
	X	X		Inventory	1,940,000	
	X			Capital assets	4,000,000	
	X			Accum amortization		1,800,000
	X			Accounts payable		600,000
	X			Accrued expenses		10,000
	X			General expense	1,955,000	
		X		Cost of goods sold	5,265,000	
		X		Amortization expense	300,000	
			X	Bank loans		750,000
			X	Long-term notes		400,000
			X	Accrued interest		40,000
			X	Share capital		2,000,000
			X	Retained earnings		900,000
			X	Dividends declared	0	
			X	Interest expense	40,000	
			X	Income tax expense	196,000	
					15,030,000	15,030,000

in cash, provided for in an allowance for doubtful accounts, or written off. The typical journal entries used in this cycle are as follows:

dr   Accounts Receivable
     cr   Sales Revenue
To record sales made on account

dr   Cash
     cr   Accounts Receivable
To record collection of receivables

dr   Bad Debt Expense
     cr   Allowance for Bad Debts
To provide for accounts receivable likely to be uncollectible

dr   Allowance for Bad Debts
     cr   Accounts Receivable
To write off uncollectible accounts receivable previously provided for

Auditors find it easier to audit the related accounts with a coordinated set of procedures instead of attacking each account as if it stood alone, as predictable relationships should exist among these accounts. For example, if sales decrease but accounts receivable increase it may be a warning sign of financial difficulties. Also, the audit evidence available for one part of the accounting process often also contains information for other parts; for example, recording collection of a receivable involves recording the invoice information as well as the information about the cash collected. The cycle concept is part of the relation-based analytical procedures discussed in the following section.

In Exhibit 7–10, to illustrate the idea of the accounting processes, the Kingston accounts are put into an order not normally seen in a trial balance. Some accounts are in more than one process. For example, the cash account is represented in all the processes, because

EXHIBIT 7-11   KINGSTON COMPANY UNAUDITED FINANCIAL STATEMENTS

BALANCE SHEET

Cash	$ 484,000	Accounts payable	$ 600,000
Accounts receivable	370,000	Accrued expenses	10,000
Inventory	1,940,000	Accrued interest	40,000
Current assets	$2,794,000	Current liabilities	$ 630,000
Capital assets (gross)	$4,000,000	Long-term debt	$1,150,000
Accum amortization	(1,800,000)		
		Share capital	$2,000,000
Captial assets (net)	$2,000,000	Retained earnings	1,194,000
		Total Liabilities	
Total Assets	$4,994,000	and Shareholder Equity	$4,994,000

STATEMENT OF INCOME

Sales (net)	$8,100,000
Cost of goods sold	5,265,000
Gross Profit	$2,835,000
General expenses	$2,005,000
Amortization expense	300,000
Interest expense	40,000
Operating Income	
Before Taxes	$ 490,000
Income Tax Expense	196,000
Net Income	$ 294,000

CASH FLOWS

Operations:	
Net Income	$ 294,000
Amortization	300,000
Decrease in Accounts receivable	90,000
Increase in Inventory	(440,000)
Increase in Accounts payable	150,000
Decrease in Accrued expenses	(40,000)
Decrease in Accrued interest	(20,000)
Cash Flow from Operations	$ 334,000
Investing Activities:	
Purchase Capital assets	$ (1,000,000)
Financing Activities:	
Bank Loan	$ 750,000
Repay Notes payable	(200,000)
Financing Activities	$550,000
Increase (Decrease) in Cash	$ (114,000)
Beginning Balance	600,000
Ending Balance	$ 484,000

NOTES TO FINANCIAL STATEMENTS
1. Accounting Policies
2. Inventories
3. Plant and Equipment
4. Long-term Debt
5. Stock Options
6. Income Taxes
7. Contingencies
8. Etc.

(a) cash receipts are involved in cash sales and collections of accounts receivable (revenue process), (b) cash receipts arise from issuing shares and loan proceeds (finance process), (c) cash disbursements are involved in buying inventory and capital assets and in paying for expenses (purchases process), and (d) cash disbursements are involved in paying wages and overhead expenses (production process).

When placed in the financial statements, the accounts and their descriptive titles contain the assertions that are the focal points of audit procedures. Exhibit 7–11 carries the accounts forward to the financial statements. Exhibit 7–12 illustrates the relationships among business activities, accounting processes, and the financial statements. These accounting processes will be covered in more detail in Chapters 11 through 14.

To summarize the business process view of an organization, Exhibit 7–13 provides a big picture overview showing how all the entity's activities and business processes flow through to its financial statements.

EXHIBIT   7-12   RELATIONSHIPS AMONG BUSINESS PROCESSES, ACCOUNTING CYCLES, AND FINANCIAL STATEMENTS

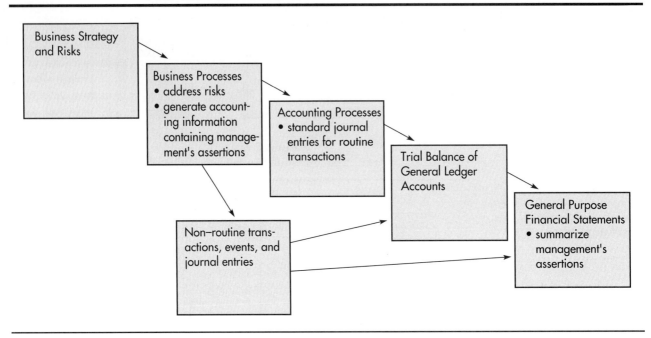

EXHIBIT   7-13   CAPTURING AN ORGANIZATION'S BUSINESS PROCESSES IN ITS FINANCIAL STATEMENTS

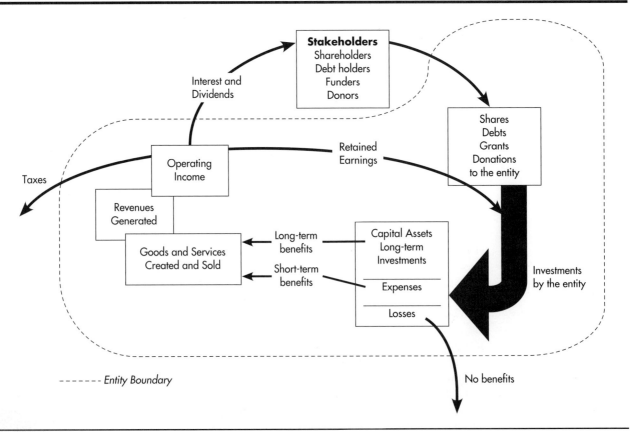

. . . .

R E V I E W
CHECKPOINTS

30 What are four of the major accounting processes? What accounts can be identified with each? Why can an accounting process be described as a cycle?

31 Why is the cash account involved in more than one accounting process?

32 Why do auditors tend to find it easier to look at accounting processes rather than individual trial balance accounts?

. . . .

BUSINESS RISK AND THE RISK OF MATERIAL MISSTATEMENT

. . . .

LEARNING OBJECTIVE

4 Illustrate how business risk analysis is used in a preliminary assessment of the risk that fraud or error has led to material misstatement at the overall financial statement level.

The ultimate objective of a financial statement audit is to render an opinion on whether the financial statements, taken as a whole, are materially in accordance with generally accepted accounting principles. The term "materially" in auditing refers to a misstatement that is significant enough to affect an important decision that someone might make based on the financial statement information, as explained in Chapter 6. That is, a misstatement is material if it could lead someone to make a poor decision and suffer a loss from it, when they probably could have made a good decision if they used information that was not misstated. To determine the risk that the financial statements could be materially misstated, the auditor learns about management's understanding of the business and its risks, and independently assesses the business risk and management's risk assessment process. This section describes a process the auditor may use to make this risk assessment.

The auditor knows that management has to take certain risks to achieve rewards in the marketplace. Those are the risks management accepts from being in business; in effect, these risks are tolerated on a cost-benefit basis. Risks can be managed in any of four ways:

- avoided by not performing those business activities that would cause the risk to occur
- monitored to ensure costs continue to be less than benefits
- reduced to an acceptable level via management controls embedded in business processes
- transferred to another party via a contract (e.g., insurance)

After understanding the business risks, the auditor needs to consider which risks are high. He examines two factors in this analysis: the likelihood the risk will occur and the magnitude of the risk. Each risk is qualitatively judged according to a three-point scale on likelihood of occurrence (unlikely, possible, or likely) and magnitude of risk (insignificant, moderate, and significant). When considered together, these two assessments allow the auditor to classify a risk as low, medium, or high.

Exhibit 7–14 is a graphical representation of the assessment process. For example, point A indicates a business risk that will probably occur and, if so, will have a significant effect. Therefore, the auditor would classify point A as a high risk. Using a smartphone company like RIM as an example, point A could be the risk of technological obsolescence of smartphones. Point E indicates a business risk that is unlikely to occur, and if it did it would be insignificant in size. Hence, the auditor would classify this risk as low. For a smartphone company, point E might be the risk that it will be required to change its packaging materials to comply with new environmental regulations.

Most business risks are managed through an effective risk-management process and well-designed business processes, although some fall into the transferred category. The auditor considers any of the risks threatening to prevent the entity from carrying out its processes effectively, and then identifies the controls in place to ensure efficient and effective functioning of those business processes. Here, controls can be broadly defined as the

EXHIBIT   7-14   INITIAL RISK ASSESSMENT

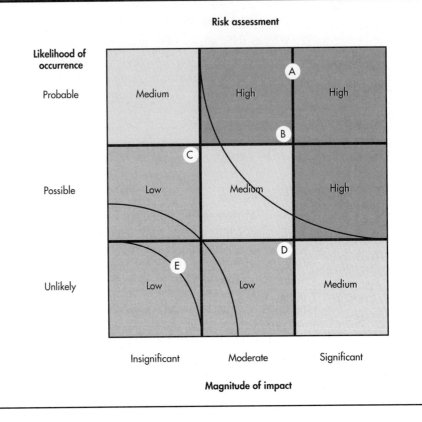

elements of an organization, including its resources, culture, structure, processes, systems, and tasks, that work together to help its people achieve the organization's objectives. See Exhibit 7–15 for examples of management controls.

The auditor can consider these management controls by determining if the key performance indicators are effective at controlling the process and if management is actually using these controls. At this point the auditor makes a preliminary assessment of whether management controls are appropriate for producing reliable financial statements. Controls are explained further throughout the chapters in Parts II and III of the text because they are a pervasive consideration in all stages of planning and performing the audit.

After considering the management controls, the auditor evaluates the results that effective functioning of controls have on the original risk analysis. Exhibit 7–16 shows the auditor reassessing business risk after examining management controls. The auditor has reclassified point A from a high risk to a medium-to-high risk. For the smartphone company example, say the auditor finds the company's product development process is effective in staying ahead of the technological developments in the industry, and its sales forecasting is linked closely to production to ensure slow-moving models are taken out of

EXHIBIT   7-15   EXAMPLES OF MANAGEMENT CONTROLS

- Budget systems
- Forecasting systems
- Physical measures of process performance (e.g., defect rates)
- Quality enhancement programs
- Performance indicators (both financial and nonfinancial)
- Process monitoring activities
- Traditional accounting internal controls

EXHIBIT 7-16   RISK ASSESSMENT AFTER CONSIDERING MANAGEMENT CONTROLS

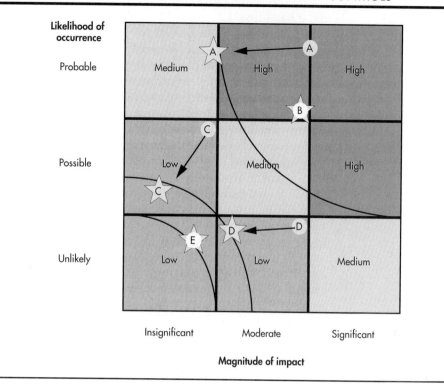

production quickly. This lowers the assessed risk of obsolescence in inventory valuation. Note, however, that controls did not reduce the risks associated with point B. Point B might be the risk that smartphone production equipment assets will not last as long as planned. If the management has not addressed this risk, it increases the risk that the value of those assets is impaired. Risks that are not moved into the low category by management controls represent categories for which the controls fail to reduce the risks that the financial statements do not portray the actual business performance. These are areas that need to be audited with the greatest care.

To illustrate how risk assessment works in practice, let's consider the case of a business in the food manufacturing industry. The story in the box below illustrates the kinds of risks that a food manufacturing company has to manage, and the potential financial impact.

BUSINESS RISK IN THE FOOD INDUSTRY

On Sunday, August 17, 2008, Canada's largest food processing company announced it was recalling two types of packaged roast beef products because of concerns they may have been contaminated with bacteria known as Listeria monocytogenes. By August 29, there were 29 confirmed and 35 suspected cases of Listeriosis, nine confirmed deaths, another six deaths under investigation, and more than 200 different products pulled from store shelves across the country. Ultimately, the deaths of 20 people were attributed to this outbreak.

Consumption of food contaminated with Listeria monocytogenes may cause Listeriosis, a food-borne illness that can be fatal in as many as one in three cases. Listeria is very common in the environment, and fortunately it is not dangerous to most people. Very young children, the elderly, pregnant women, and people with weakened immune systems are at the greatest risk. Listeria is a particular concern in refrigerated meat-packing plants because, unlike other types of bacteria, it has adapted to survive in colder temperatures. Using a genetic identification technique called pulsed field gel electrophoresis, health officials were able to match the strain of Listeria people got sick from to meat products produced in Maple Leaf's Toronto plant.

Recalls can be disastrous for a company that processes food, potentially damaging its brand equity and sales volumes, but they are not uncommon. The Canadian Food Inspection Agency website lists dozens of recalls and alerts. Maple Leaf's president is credited with saving his company from ruin by responding quickly and candidly. He held new conferences and accepted responsibility for the situation, noting that the company has excellent systems and processes in place, but in this crisis its best efforts had failed to ensure food safety. He stressed that the company's priority at this time was not cost or market share, its priority was to do the right thing for its customers. The Toronto plant was immediately shut down to be fully sanitized and all aspects of the processing system were examined by outside experts. It voluntarily expanded the recall of products manufactured at in this plant (Establishment No. 97B) as a precautionary measure.

The company reported that its protocol is to test the Toronto plant's surfaces for contamination 3,000 times a year. If any contamination is found, the area would be sanitized and then retested until three negatives in a row are found. While positive results for Listeria inside a food plant are common, the president told reporters at the time that nothing out of the norm had been reported in the period leading up to the outbreak in the Toronto plant.

Stock market analysts who cover Maple Leaf remained positive about the company in the midst of the crisis, finding the company's transparency and prompt handling of the situation to be consistent with best practices in crisis management and corporate public relations. Reported estimates indicated the company spent around $5 million to deal immediately with the crisis, the company's massive recall is thought to cost $20 million, and the potential class action suits may cost even more.

Maple Leaf's trend to consolidate into larger processing plants can be a strength as new efficiencies can be leveraged. On the other hand, it can sometimes create a weakness, especially when something like a Listeria outbreak occurs. Centralization can increase the impact of a bacterial outbreak because any breakdown in control can affect more products. Instead of recalling 20 or 30 products, Maple Leaf had to recall hundreds that may have been affected.

Improvements in information technology that allow products to be tracked through a meat-packing plant have made recalls more effective in the meat industry. A bar code is given to each individual cut and it can be used to trace back to the animal and the farm it came from. This can help companies to manage food safety risks. This also can help reassure the public, as many customers can now be expected to look for greater assurance about where their food originates.

Sources: Steve Buist, "From Food Recall to Deadly Outbreak," *The Hamilton Spectator* (Ontario, Canada), August 30, 2008, p. A01 © 2008 Toronto Star Newspapers, Ltd. All rights reserved; Robert Cribb, Record News Service, "Listeriosis Reporting Rule Dropped Before Deadly Outbreak," Front, p. A1, *Waterloo Region Record,* October 6, 2008, © Toronto Star Newspapers, Ltd. All rights reserved; Market News Publishing, "Expands Product Recall from Toronto Plant as a Precautionary Measure," August 25, 2008, © 2008 Market News Publishing, Inc. All rights reserved; Peter Epp, "Food Origin Questions Arise Again," *Chatham This Week* (Canada) September 3, 2008, Editorial/Opinion, p. 6, © 2008 Sun Media Corporation; CP Toronto, "Maple Leaf Foods CEO Admits Even After Intensive Sanitization of the Plant, 'We Will Never, Never Eliminate It...,'" *London Free Press* (Ontario, October 10, 2008, © 2008 Sun Media Corporation. All rights reserved.

As the story shows, a food manufacturing company's success depends on delivering wholesome, tasty foods at reasonable prices for consumers and a cost that ensures the company remains profitable. Since food products spoil very easily, if management does not implement effective controls, the risk of delivering spoiled food would be assessed as probable. Since spoiled food can make people ill, and even be fatal, this risk would have very significant negative impact on the company. In the Risk Assessment matrix, this risk would be assessed as high. It would affect the financial statements because of the product liability contingency if consumers decide to sue the company's. If the brand reputation is damaged, this could even result in the company's being unable to continue as a going concern.

Management's risk assessment needs to ensure appropriate management controls are embedded in the business processes; in the Maple Leaf case this includes its safety inspection protocols and its product identification and tracking processes. The company also uses insurance as a risk transferring management tool, though it is unlikely that all its risks can be fully insured because of the uncertainty of when food contamination or other business risks might occur. The auditor of a food manufacturing company would look for strong management controls related to these risk   would obtain first hand information to verify them. If strong controls are in plac   ssed risk would be lower. How much lower? This is a judgment call, but ther   h uncertainty about these risks it is unlikely it can be reduced below a mod

Another business risk in this industr   others, arises from the use of commodity product as raw materials. Comm   luctuate significantly, making it difficult to budget accurately. This can result   runs that make inventory costs higher than market values, affecting the financia   t inventory valuation. A management control to reduce this risk is entering forwa   acts with fixed prices for commodities, effectively transferring this risk to the other   y in the contract.

Summary

In the business risk–based approach to auditing, the auditor must understand both the auditee's business risk and the related management controls to assess the risk of material misstatement in the financial statements. The examples above illustrate how business risk and internal control are linked, and how auditors develop a full understanding of the auditee's business by considering them together. To provide a better understanding of the procedures companies use to implement control over financial reporting, the next section of the chapter gives an overview of the entity's internal control structure. Here we start thinking about designing audit work so that it gives reasonable assurance that the financial statements are not materially misstated.

R E V I E W C H E C K P O I N T S

33 How can business risks be managed?

34 What is the relationship between business risks and business processes?

35 What are some examples of management controls? What are the purposes of management controls?

36 Why does the auditor consider management's controls of business processes?

37 How does business analysis relate to the auditor's goal of assessing the risk that the financial statements are materially misstated?

UNDERSTANDING INTERNAL CONTROL

LEARNING OBJECTIVE
5 Describe the basic components of internal control, control environment, management's risk assessment process, information systems and communication, control activities, and monitoring.

So far this chapter has covered the business risk–based approach to auditing by explaining the audit risk model and how auditors analyze the auditee's business risk to assess the risk of material misstatement. This is the most challenging part of financial statement auditing, requiring integration of complex concepts and the application of professional judgment. Congratulations for sticking it out to this point in the chapter! The chapter has also stressed that business risk and internal control are so tightly linked that auditors need to consider them together. At this point in an audit, the audit team would begin considering internal control in relation to their understanding of the business risk in order to assess the risk of material misstatement for the purpose of designing audit procedures that respond appropriately to the assessed risks. For study purposes, we will conclude this chapter's discussion of risk and control by giving an overview of internal control as it exists in most organizations, and then consider how internal control relates to the risk that the financial statements are materially misstated. In Chapter 8, we will introduce you to some key audit tools: the concepts of evidence and the types of audit procedures used to gather it. With these tools in hand, you will be ready for Chapter 9, where we will discuss how auditors assess control risk and test controls.

Internal Control Components

For financial statement audit purposes, internal control is defined as the process designed, implemented, and maintained by management and other auditee personnel to provide reasonable assurance about the reliability of financial reporting, effectiveness and efficiency of operations, and compliance with applicable laws and regulations. As shown in the internal control framework introduced in Exhibit 7–2 (page 218), the auditing standards describe internal control as consisting of the following components:[13]

(a) control environment

(b) management's risk assessment process

(c) information system, including the related business processes, relevant to financial reporting and communication

(d) control activities

(e) monitoring of controls

These provide a useful basis for considering how different aspects of an entity's internal control may affect the financial statements. Control components (a), (b), (c), and (e) comprise the **management controls** that operate at the company level. As discussed earlier, management controls are implemented to assess adherence to management policy, promote operational efficiencies, and address strategic risks. These **company-level controls** permeate the organization and can have a big impact on whether its financial reporting and disclosures objectives are met.

Component (d), the control activities, are controls over processes, applications, and transactions more closely related to accounting information; we will refer to these as **internal controls relevant to the audit**. The auditor is primarily interested in the accounting controls, as these help a company safeguard its assets and prepare financial statements in conformity with generally accepted accounting principles.[14]

Audits of small entities may require different control considerations than audits of large ones do. In a small entity there is a concentration of ownership and management in one person or a small number of people. There are likely also few sources of income, unsophisticated record-keeping, and limited internal controls together with the potential for management override of controls.[15]

The five control components are illustrated in Exhibit 7–17, and further described below. Special internal control considerations of small entities are also addressed.

Control Environment

Management's and directors' attitudes, awareness, and actions concerning the company's internal controls set the tone for the control environment. The way that integrity and ethical values are communicated and enforced in the company are also part of the control

---

[13] CAS 315 (5141), and COSO Framework.

[14] As noted in previous chapters, the regulations in SOX 404 and PCAOB Auditing Standard 5 for audits of management's internal control reporting and the similar standards now introduced in Canada for audits of control effectiveness (CICA *Handbook* 5925, "An Audit of internal control over financial reporting that is integrated with an audit of financial statements") require the internal control assessment at the company level and the control activity level.

[15] IFAC *Handbook* glossary, 2008.

EXHIBIT 7-17   CONTROL FRAMEWORK FOR RISK ASSESSMENT

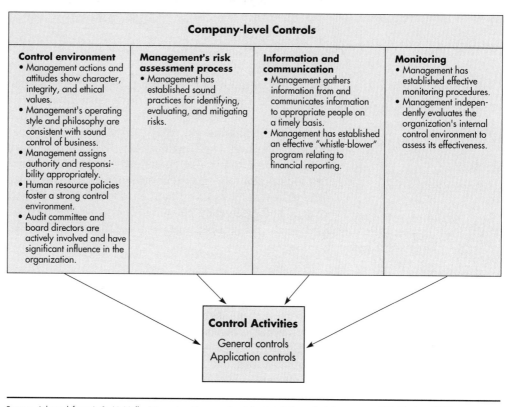

Company-level Controls

Control environment	**Management's risk assessment process**	**Information and communication**	**Monitoring**
• Management actions and attitudes show character, integrity, and ethical values. • Management's operating style and philosophy are consistent with sound control of business. • Management assigns authority and responsibility appropriately. • Human resource policies foster a strong control environment. • Audit committee and board directors are actively involved and have significant influence in the organization.	• Management has established sound practices for identifying, evaluating, and mitigating risks.	• Management gathers information from and communicates information to appropriate people on a timely basis. • Management has established an effective "whistle-blower" program relating to financial reporting.	• Management has established effective monitoring procedures. • Management independently evaluates the organization's internal control environment to assess its effectiveness.

Control Activities

General controls
Application controls

Source: Adapted from J. S. McNally, "Assessing Company-Level Controls," *Journal of Accountancy* 199 (6), June 2005, pp.65–68. © 2005 by the American Institute of Certified Public Accountants Inc. All rights reserved. Used with permission.

environment, because the controls cannot be more effective than the integrity levels and ethical values of the people who create, administer, and monitor them. Management must act to remove or reduce incentives and temptations motivating people in the organization to act unethically. It must assess requisite skills and knowledge for particular jobs, ensuring that people in those positions are competent. Directors or others charged with governance of the organization should be independent from management and experienced and knowledgeable enough to pursue difficult questions with management as well as internal and external auditors. They should be responsible for the design and effective operation of whistle-blower procedures, and engaged in a process for assessing internal control effectiveness.

Management's approach to taking and monitoring business risks, attitudes toward financial reporting (conservative or aggressive selection of accounting principles and use of accounting estimates), and controls are critical to the strength of the control environment. To set the right example, management should react immediately and appropriately to control violations. Clear policies relating to appropriate business practices, knowledge and experience of key personnel, and resources for carrying out duties should be in place. Policies should ensure that all personnel understand the entity's objectives, know how their individual actions interrelate, contribute to those objectives, and are aware of what they will be held accountable for.

The control environment is concerned with management attitudes, structure (organization chart), effective communication of control objectives and supervision of personnel and activities, as noted previously. The elements of internal control environments are summarized in the following box.

KEY ELEMENTS OF THE INTERNAL CONTROL ENVIRONMENT

- management's philosophy and operating style
- entity's organization structure
- functioning of the board of directors, particularly its audit committee
- methods of assigning authority and responsibility
- management's monitoring methods, including internal auditing
- personnel policies and practices
- external influences (e.g., examinations by bank regulatory agencies)
- control environment for computerized systems, which includes the organizational and logical controls of system development, access to computers and computer files, authorization of changes to program and data files, storage and maintenance of data, and emergency planning for backup and recovery of systems and data

---

Two categories of controls are preventive controls and detective/corrective controls. Generally, environmental controls can be characterized as preventive controls since they are there to prevent misstatements from arising in the first place. Preventive controls are more effective than controls designed to detect and correct misstatements after they have entered the system. Auditors tend to focus their preliminary evaluation on environmental controls for this reason, and also because they have such a pervasive impact on the accounting cycles affected.

Since the mid-1980s when management fraud in financial statements became an acceptable topic for discussion, "tone at the top" has become a catchphrase for the foundation of good internal control; company tone is virtually identical to control environment. A wide variety of activities characterize the control environment, some of them obvious, such as who has the immediate responsibility to authorize payments in payroll processing. Other aspects of the control environment, such as management's philosophy, are hard for auditors to understand and document. The following box illustrates some criteria to consider in evaluating the human factor in the control environment.

TONE AT THE TOP

All control rests ultimately on people assuming responsibility for their decisions and actions. Organizational values that people find acceptable encourage them to assume responsibility for the continuous improvement of their organization.

Shared ethical values influence all behaviour in an organization. Together with an understanding of mission and vision, they constitute the basic identity that will shape the way an individual, group, organization, or board will operate, and they provide stability over time. Shared values contribute to control because they provide a guide for individual, group, or team decision making, action, and policy.

The values and preferences of senior management and the board of directors greatly influence an organization's objectives and systems. These values and preferences address issues such as

- good corporate citizenship
- commitment to truth and fair dealing
- commitment to quality and competence
- leadership by example

- compliance with laws, regulations, rules, and organizational policy
- respect for the privacy of auditee, organization, and employee information
- fair treatment of and respect for individuals
- fair relationships with competitors
- integrity of transactions and records
- a professional approach to financial reporting

Ethical values are part of an organization's culture and provide an unwritten code of conduct against which behaviour is measured. A formal written code of conduct offers a means for consistent communication of the standards of ethical behaviour. People can periodically be asked to confirm their understanding and observance of the code.

Source: COCO, *Guidance on Control* (November 1995), pp. 14–15.

The board of directors and the audit committee are critical corporate governance elements of high-level internal control. Among the board's key functions is monitoring that traditionally least-monitored group of employees—top management. In the post-Enron environment, the role of the board and audit committee in monitoring management and financial reporting rose to unprecedented levels. The audit committee, usually a subcommittee of the board's members, helps the board by overseeing the financial reporting as well as external and internal auditing functions. The audit committee's prime role is to act as intermediary between management and the auditor in the external audit, helping make it function more independently. Appendix 7F on the OLC further explains the traditional responsibilities of the board and audit committee, as well as their expanded corporate governance responsibilities in the post-Enron environment.

Small entities may use the control environment elements differently than larger entities; for example, rely on oral communication and personal relations to establish ethical standards, rather than use more formal methods. Directors of small entities are less likely to be independent of management, and owners are more likely to be involved in managing day-to-day operations.

Management's Risk Assessment Process

As explained earlier, management's risk assessment process is used to identify risks relevant to misstatements occurring in the preparation of financial statements and to estimate the risks' significance and likelihood. This is the starting point of the auditor's business risk analysis discussed at the start of the chapter. It helps management to decide how to manage the business risk efficiently and effectively. Risks can arise or change with changing circumstances, so risk assessment is a continuous process. The operating environment, personnel changes, growth, new technologies, new business lines, structural changes in the organization, and new accounting pronouncements can affect the risk assessment.

Even small entities are expected to have a risk assessment process, but it is likely to be quite basic and informal. Management may be aware of risks related to financial reporting mainly through personal involvement with employees and outside parties.

Information System, Related Business Processes, and Communication

An information system can be broadly defined as a set of interrelated functions that collect, process, store, and distribute information in an organization. They are used to support management decisions and to help people in the organization perform analysis, develop models, collaborate on projects, and create knowledge. An information system has three main activities: input, processing, and output. The input is mainly data, the raw facts collected from the environment. Processing coverts data into output in an understandable and useful form referred to as information. Many information systems are highly automated, making extensive use of **information technology (IT)**. The components of an information system consist of hardware, software, people, procedures, and data.

Information Systems and Business Processes

The information system is related to all of the key business processes. It is important that the auditor understands how the information system relates to financial reporting, and how it is used to communicate information within the organization. In organizations with enterprise resource planning systems, the information inputs and outputs from many or all the business processes will be processed in an integrated manner, so the accounting component of the information system will be closely related to many other functional areas such as sales, inventory, human resources, cash management, etc. Within the business process view, logical links exist between information generated in various processes and the accounting component of the information system.

The quality of system-generated information affects management's ability to make appropriate decisions in managing and controlling the entity's activities and in preparing reliable financial reports. The auditor needs to understand how the auditee's information system is used in its financial reporting process, and identify the risk associated with IT use. Financial reporting objectives rely on information system procedures and records established to initiate, record, process, and report entity transactions (and events and conditions) as well as to maintain accountability for the related assets, liabilities, and equity. These functions will be discussed in detail in Chapter 9.

Communications

Communication helps ensure that information system control procedures are implemented correctly and exceptions are reported and acted on appropriately. Good communications procedures help ensure that important tasks do not just "fall between the cracks" because no one was sure whose job it was to do them.

The auditor must understand how the information system facilitates communications within the organization, in particular those aspects that relate to implementation of internal control. Internal control involves activities, policies, and procedures ensuring that threats that may prevent the business from achieving its strategy are addressed. Control activities occur within both IT and manual processes, have various objectives, and are applied at various organizational and functional levels; thus, effective communication is essential for internal control to work properly.

Open communications enhance internal control effectiveness. Employees involved in financial reporting must understand their individual roles and responsibilities in implementing internal control, as well as how their activities relate to the work. Communications policies show the importance of employees reporting and acting on control exceptions immediately, and establish appropriate channels for reporting these to appropriate levels within the organization. Communication media include accounting and financial reporting manuals, policy manuals, and internal memoranda. Communications can be performed electronically, orally, and through management's actions.

Business processes and information systems in small entities are likely to be less formal than in larger organizations, but they are just as important. In small entities, accounting procedures, records, or controls may not be in writing but will exist informally if the organization has a good risk assessment process and related internal controls. If management is highly involved in the business processes, there may be no need for extensive written descriptions of company policies or accounting procedures. Communication also may be less formal and easier to achieve as fewer people are involved and management tends to be more accessible to other employees than is the case in a larger, more hierarchical organizations.

REVIEW
CHECKPOINTS

38 What are the five basic components of internal control?

39 What are the basic functions of an information system?

40 How does the information system facilitate communications within an organization? Why are these communications important?

Control Activities

Companies have many policies and procedures that help achieve and ensure necessary actions are taken against risks threatening the entity's financial reporting objectives. As explained previously in this chapter, the auditor uses a control framework to understand and evaluate the auditee's internal control. Control policies and procedures make up the control activities component of the company's control framework. All control procedures are directed, one way or another, toward preventing, detecting, and correcting errors, irregularities, frauds, and misstatements. The two broad groups of control activities are **general controls** and **application controls**. These will be introduced briefly here and described in more detail in the context of testing controls in Chapter 9.

General Controls

General controls include organizational features such as capable personnel, segregation of responsibilities, controlled access, and periodic comparison. Like environmental controls, general controls are primarily preventive and have a pervasive impact on the various accounting processes. For these reasons, auditors' preliminary evaluation of internal controls tends to focus on environmental and general controls.

Application Controls

Application controls are viewed in terms of whether they relate to input, processing, or output of the accounting system. They help ensure that all recorded transactions really occurred, are authorized, and are completely and accurately entered and processed through the system. The different accounting processes—revenues/receivables/receipts, purchases/payables/payments, production/payroll, and investing/financing—will each have their own risks that lead to errors or make the business susceptible to fraud or other illegal acts. Thus, specific control procedures are designed to address the risks and control objectives for each accounting process.

Examples of application controls include

(a) authorization checks prior to data input

(b) arithmetical checks of the accuracy of records

(c) maintenance and review of accounts and trial balances

(d) automated controls such as edit checks of input data and numerical sequence checks

(e) manual follow-up of exception reports

Application controls are explained in more detail in Chapter 9 where we look at control testing, and in Chapters 11 through 14 where they form part of the audit programs applied to the accounting processes.

Higher-level policies established by management or those charged with governance are the basis for certain control activities. For example, authorization controls may be delegated under established guidelines, or non-routine transactions such as major acquisitions may require specific high-level approval, in some cases that of shareholders. This further illustrates the relationship between the control environment, other company-level controls, and the specific control activities that auditors may test and rely on for audit evidence purposes.

Control activities in small entities are likely to be similar to those in larger entities, but less formal. Certain types of control activities are not relevant in a small entity because of controls applied by management. For example, if management retains authority for approving credit sales, significant purchases, and draw-downs on lines of credit, this can provide strong control over those activities, reducing the need for more detailed control activities. An appropriate segregation of duties often presents difficulties in small entities. Even companies with only a few employees, however, may be able to assign responsibilities so that there is appropriate segregation or, if that is not possible, use management oversight of the incompatible activities to achieve control objectives.

Monitoring Controls

An important management responsibility is establishing and maintaining internal control on an ongoing basis. This includes considering whether controls are operating as intended and modifying them as appropriate for changes in conditions. It may include reviews of the timeliness of bank reconciliations, evaluation of sales personnel's compliance with entity policies by internal auditors, and oversight of compliance with entity ethical or business practice policies by the legal department.

Monitoring of controls assesses the quality of internal control performance over time and involves considering the design and operation of controls, including taking necessary corrective actions to ensure their continued effective operation. For example, if the timeliness and accuracy of bank reconciliations are not monitored, personnel are likely to stop preparing them. Monitoring of controls is accomplished through ongoing monitoring activities, separate evaluations, or a combination of the two.

These activities are built into an entity's regular, recurring activities and include regular management and supervisory activities. Managers of sales, purchasing, and production at divisional and corporate levels stay in touch with operations and question reports that differ significantly from what they know of operations. Internal auditors or personnel performing similar functions may contribute to the monitoring of an entity's controls through separate evaluations of the design and operation of internal control. They communicate information about strengths, weaknesses, and recommendations for improving internal control.

Information from external parties may be part of monitoring activities if it indicates problems or highlights areas in need of improvement. Customers corroborate billing data by either paying their invoices or complaining about their charges. Outside regulators may communicate with the entity concerning matters affecting the functioning of internal control; for example, examinations by bank regulatory agencies. Management monitoring activities may consider information relating to internal control from external auditors.

Ongoing monitoring activities of smaller entities are likely to be informal and performed as a part of the overall management of the entity's operations. Through close involvement in operations, management might identify significant variances from expectations and inaccuracies in financial data, and ensure corrective action to the control.

REVIEW CHECKPOINTS

41   What are the components of internal control?

42   What is the auditor's main purpose in understanding the auditee's internal control?

43   What are monitoring controls?

44   How can management meet its responsibility for establishing and maintaining an internal control system and assist the auditors at the same time?

45   What are some of the important characteristics of "tone at the top" and control environment?

46 Are environmental controls preventive or detective/corrective? Explain.

47 Distinguish among environmental controls, general controls, and application controls.

48 What organizational features can act as general controls?

49 What is the purpose of application controls? How does it differ from the purpose of general controls?

. . . .

HOW INTERNAL CONTROL RELATES TO THE RISK OF MATERIAL MISSTATEMENT

. . . .

LEARNING OBJECTIVE

6 Explain how the auditor's understanding of an organization's internal control helps to assess the risk that its financial statements are misstated.

Audit work related to internal control involves understanding control in the context of the business and its risks, assessing significant risks of financial statement misstatement, and performing tests of controls if needed to further assess risks or provide audit evidence. This section discusses how the auditor's understanding of internal control helps in assessing the overall risk of material misstatement. It reviews the key components of internal control with a particular focus on the controls that relate to financial reporting and disclosure.

As discussed above, the internal control framework includes company-level controls (control environment, risk assessment process, information systems and communication, and monitoring) and control activities (general and application). Exhibit 7–17 (page 249) showed how these components are related and work to support each other.

To assess the risk of material misstatement at the financial statement level, the auditor needs a detailed knowledge of internal control components relevant to financial reporting; these components are the control environment elements that affect financial reporting, and the information system.

The auditor gains knowledge mainly by making enquiries of auditee personnel. This provides an understanding of the flow of transactions through the accounting information system and the elements of the control environment that affect it. The auditor gathers information about the following features: (a) the organizational structure, (b) the methods used by the auditee to communicate responsibility and authority, (c) the methods used by management to supervise the accounting information systems, including the existence of an internal audit function, and (d) the accounting information system. A questionnaire is sometimes used to guide the enquiries. An example of a questionnaire summarizing some key questions an auditor asks is provided in Exhibit 7–18 below.

Through the enquiries noted in Exhibit 7–18, the audit team gains an understanding of the control environment, the accounting information system, and the flow of transactions. Auditors consider the auditee's methods for processing significant accounting information, including the use of outside organizations such as data-processing service centres. The auditee's methods influence the design of the accounting system, the nature of its control procedures, and the extent to which its internal control effectively reduces its financial reporting risks. This in turn affects the auditors' assessment of the risk of material misstatement and how they plan to conduct their audit.

This section concludes the introduction to the business risk–based audit approach and the knowledge-gathering work auditors perform to identify the main risks of material misstatement at the overall financial statement level. Exhibit 7–19 summarizes the components of the financial reporting process explained in Chapter 7. It illustrates how the auditee's business risk, processes, information systems, and controls result in production of the information reported in management's financial statements. The auditee's business and its environment generate the activities that are captured, monitored, and controlled by the information systems, which include manual and automated processes. The information systems are based on a financial reporting framework, usually GAAP, and internal control elements related to financial reporting.

EXHIBIT 7-18   INTERNAL CONTROL QUESTIONNAIRE

	Response/File Documentation Reference
Purpose: This questionnaire is used to document information gathered through enquiries about the key internal control elements related to financial reporting. This information supports an assessment of the risk of material misstatement at the overall financial statement level.	

Consider the effectiveness of the following internal control elements to reduce the risk of material misstatement of the financial statements.Consider the impact of internal control effectiveness on the audit plan to obtain evidence.

The Organizational Structure

The organizational structure defines how the organization plans, executes, controls, and reviews the activities that it undertakes to achieve its strategic objectives.

Obtain information about the key organizational structure aspects that relate to accounting information systems:

- the corporate structure, whether there are subsidiaries or other components in different locations and how their information systems are integrated
- management's attitudes and actions toward financial reporting, information processing, accounting functions, and personnel
- ownership and relations between owners and other parties; how the information system identifies related party transactions
- how authority and responsibility for information system operating activities are assigned
- how reporting relationships and authorization hierarchies are established
- policies and practices for hiring, training, evaluation, promotion, and compensation as well as for remedial actions for accounting and IT personnel
- a description of the company's information system and IT resources, including personnel within the IT department, interaction with personnel in other departments, details of computer equipment used, the use of an outside services centre, if any, and locations from which the computer resources can be accessed

    Consider
    - is access to information systems used to process accounting information controlled; are the company policies regarding access only by authorized personnel adequate?
    - are responsibilities segregated appropriately between systems and programming staff and operations personnel?
    - is the information systems function integrated with the overall organization structure?

Methods Used to Communicate Responsibility and Authority

Obtain information about

- accounting and other policy manuals, including IT operations and user manuals
- formal job descriptions for accounting and IT personnel
- related user personnel job descriptions that may also be helpful
- how information system resources are managed and how priorities are determined
- how other nonaccounting departments within the company understand how they must comply with financial information processing-related standards and procedures

    Consider
    - are communications between user departments and the information systems department open and adequate to determine whether system controls are effective and to detect and correct any processing errors that arise?

Methods Used by Management to Supervise the System

Obtain information about the procedures used to supervise the information system, including

- existence of systems design and documentation standards and the extent to which they are used
- existence and quality of procedures for system and program modification, systems acceptance approval, and output modification (such as changes in reports or files)
- procedures limiting access to authorized information, particularly with respect to sensitive information
- availability of financial and other reports, such as budget/performance reviews for use by management
- existence of an internal audit function and the degree of its involvement in reviewing computer-produced accounting records and related controls, and its involvement in systems development control evaluation and testing

EXHIBIT   7-18   INTERNAL CONTROL QUESTIONNAIRE   (Continued)

	Response/File Documentation Reference
Consider • are management supervision procedures adequate to maintain the overall accuracy and authorization of the information processed and reports generated by information systems? **The Accounting Information System** The accounting information system includes the accounting processes as well as procedures and records that the organization uses to meet its financial reporting objectives. These objectives include reporting financial transactions, events, and conditions, and maintaining records needed for accountability for the organization's assets, liabilities, and equity, and compliance with laws and regulations. Obtain information about the accounting information system and the flow of transactions to understand the information systems relevant to financial reporting, including • significant classes of transactions arising from the organization's business processes, such as selling, purchasing, producing goods and services, and recording financial and nonfinancial information for reporting and management control purposes • IT and manual procedures that initiate, record, process, and report transactions, including period end cutoff procedures • electronic or manual accounting records and supporting information supporting transactions • use of information system to capture significant events and conditions other than transactions • financial reporting processes, significant accounting estimates and disclosures • procedures to transfer information from processing systems (e.g., accounts receivable subledger) to general ledger or financial reporting systems • use of standard, recurring journal entries to record transactions such as sales, purchases, and cash disbursements in the general ledger (e.g., daily sales journal entries), or to record periodic accounting estimates (e.g., amortization). • use of nonstandard journal entries to record nonrecurring, unusual transactions, or adjustments (e.g., changes in estimated uncollectible accounts receivable, asset disposals or asset impairment estimates, consolidating adjustments) for manual, paper-based general ledger systems identified through inspection of ledgers, journals, and supporting documentation or for automated general ledger systems where such entries may exist only in electronic form identified through the use of computer-assisted audit techniques • procedures that ensure information for disclosures required by the applicable financial reporting framework is accumulated, recorded, processed, summarized, and appropriately reported • how the incorrect processing of transactions is resolved (e.g., a suspense file, how it is cleared on a timely basis) • how authorized system control overrides are processed and accounted for • risks of material misstatement associated with inappropriate override of controls over journal entries and the controls surrounding nonstandard journal entries, including automated journal entries that produce no visible evidence of intervention in the information systems Consider • is the accounting system designed and operated to ensure the organization's financial reporting objectives are met, such that all relevant financial transactions, events, and conditions are captured and reported, accurate records needed for accountability for assets, liabilities, and equity, and to comply with laws and regulations are maintained?	

. . . .

REVIEW CHECKPOINTS

50   What kinds of knowledge does the auditor gather to understand internal control and assess the risk of material misstatement?

51   Compare and contrast company-level controls to internal control relevant to the audit.

52   What are the two main types of control activities that are used in information systems?

53   What aspects of the accounting system are relevant to financial reporting objectives?

EXHIBIT 7-19   THE FINANCIAL REPORTING PROCESS IN AN AUDITEE COMPANY

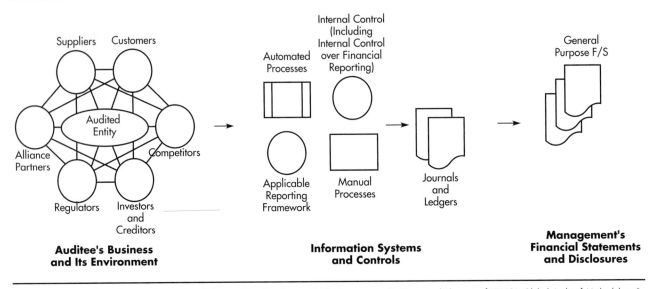

Source: Timothy B. Bell, Mark E. Peecher, and Ira Solomon, *"The 21st Century Public Company Audit:* Conceptual Elements of KPMG's Global Audit of Methodology," p. 4, (KPMG International © 2005).

54 What misstatement risks might not be eliminated by automated control procedures? How does this possibility affect the audit?

55 Why do auditors seek information about the use of nonstandard journal entries?

· ·

APPLICATION CASE AND ANALYSIS
BUSINESS RISK ANALYSIS AND AUDIT IMPLICATIONS

Discussion Case

Jack has recently joined your public accounting firm as a junior auditor and has been assigned to the audit team for SOL Technologies Corporation (SOL). Based on a review of previous years' audit working papers and permanent files, SOL's 20×7 quarterly reports, and its draft 20×7 Management Discussion and Analysis, Jack learned the following.

SOL is a Canadian-based solar energy technology company that currently has three distinct operations focusing on (i) development and commercialization of photovoltaic (PV) cell technology, (ii) development of a PV silicon processing technology, and (iii) sales and installation of PV systems. SOL's goal is to make solar energy a cost-effective, mainstream energy solution. The company was incorporated in October 1993 and began trading on the TSX Technology Exchange in 20×3. In March 20×6, SOL started trading on the Frankfurt Open Market System. Jack's firm has audited the company since 20×2.

LEARNING OBJECTIVE
7 Apply and integrate the chapter topics to analyze a practical auditing situation/case/scenario.

Governance

SOL currently has a six-member board of directors. The president and CEO is the only officer or employee of the company on the Board and is also a member of the Audit Committee. In April 20×7, the company hired a chief financial officer who had previously worked as chief accountant for another technology company. Prior to this, the company had a limited number of qualified accounting staff and relied mainly on an outside accounting firm to prepare its financial statements. The key employees are scientists and engineers, and most of the financial forecasts have been generated by them, not the accounting staff.

Operations

According to Photon Consulting, a leading solar energy industry research company, the solar energy market is growing at 40% annually and with an upward trend that management expects will continue. Details of SOL's three main business lines are:

PV Cell Technology

SOL's PV cell technology operation is currently developing a high-efficiency silicon wafer PV solar cell. The company's wholly owned German subsidiary SOL Technologies Deutschland GmbH (SOL Germany) is constructing a PV cell manufacturing plant in Germany with an initial capacity of 80MW per year. The PV cell manufacturing plant is expected to commence operations in the second fiscal quarter of 20×8. The plant is sized for three fully automated process lines that start with silicon wafers and finish with PV cells ready to be sold to PV module manufacturers. SOL's manufacturing strategy is to initially build two production lines. The first line will use turnkey, "off the shelf," technology to produce PV cells with a targeted efficiency of 15%. The second line will produce PV cells based on SOL's proprietary technology with a targeted efficiency of 18%.

PV Silicon Processing Technology

SOL's PV silicon operation is developing a new PV silicon processing technology to produce solar grade silicon (also known as polysilicon). PV silicon is currently in tight supply worldwide and it is a key input required for manufacturing PV cells. In 20×6, SOL received funding from the Canadian government to build and equip a pilot plant on the campus of a top engineering university and formed a consortium with other technology firms to conduct this research and development. Provided the current research and development is completed and funding is sourced, the silicon processing operation is expected to remove a barrier to growth (silicon wafer shortage) for the company's PV technology operation.

PV Systems

SOL's systems operation focuses on the design, distribution, installation, and support of PV systems on residential, industrial, commercial, and institutional buildings as well as the installation of PV systems on open land, so-called solar parks. The availability of 20-year fixed-price energy supply contracts in Ontario under the Ontario Power Authority's standard offer program has increased interest in solar energy generation facilities. SOL's systems operation has entered into six nonbinding letters of interests related to supplying PV systems for proposed solar park developments.

Business Strategy

SOL's ability to successfully manufacture PV cells depends on securing silicon wafers, a key raw material input. In the current tight silicon market, well-positioned companies will have an advantage. SOL's strategy is to pay higher prices for silicon and to secure silicon supply in the spot market, because of its highly efficient use of it. The larger competitors in the industry are expected to rely on buying power and strong relationships with feedstock suppliers for their supply and, thus, market share. Other well-capitalized competitors may be able to quickly expand non-silicon technologies (such as cadmium telluride) and thereby gain market share. Industry experts estimate that production of non-silicon based solar power products will increase from 150MW in 20×5 to 1.1GW in 20×8, a 22% market share.

In the short term, SOL is planning to secure a supply of silicon wafers for 20×8 with a combination of supply contracts, proprietary refining, and spot market purchases. Several industry estimates suggest a significant increase in silicon supply during 20×8. No contracts for silicon supplies are in place at this time in anticipation of falling prices. In the long term, the company expects to produce its own silicon.

There is a trend toward vertical integration in the solar industry. SOL is targeting the high-efficiency end of the market and believes that it will have a competitive cost advantage. Downstream module manufacturers and system integrators appear to be willing to pay a premium for high-efficiency cells. Management believes that this combination is a unique approach which will generate superior margins once the German plant is operational. SOL's value proposition is the combination of high-efficiency cells produced at a lower cost, with a focus on selling to existing module manufacturers by demonstrating that they can increase their profit with SOL's product. SOL has a thin-film technology approach that reduces risk and provides the potential for a broader product line. It gives SOL the option to produce a lower efficiency thin-film-only product in the face of continued silicon shortages.

The systems operation functions in a highly competitive market, both in Ontario and the rest of North America—especially in terms of ecommerce competition. The competitors are very fragmented in both location and size, creating niche opportunities that can be exploited through developing strategic supply and customer relationships.

Intellectual Property

SOL relies on a combination of patents, internally developed know-how, and trade secrets to protect its proprietary technology and PV cell prototypes. Much intellectual property and expertise is being created at the laboratory and manufacturing levels.

Marketing and Distribution Methods

The main distribution channel is a value-added distributor of solar products and solutions with a limited web presence. Under direction of its new Vice-President of Business Development (hired in 20×7), the company plans to market its own brand of key solar technology components and services (including repairs) on the Internet. The target market is solar professionals (e.g., knowledgeable power end users, dealers, and trades people), commercial customers taking advantage of the Ontario Standard Offer Program (e.g., solar farms), and energy efficient home builders, primarily in Ontario, taking advantage of various government incentives to bring solar options to mainstream building developments.

The SOL name is well known to customers desiring a broad assortment of PV products, within its home market of southern Ontario. The company has an extensive contact database of customers, channel partners, builders, and government bodies.

Financial performance

SOL has incurred losses since its inception and may be unable to generate net sales that achieve or sustain profitability for the future. For example, the company's cash requirements increased significantly in 20×7 and construction costs of the German plant will increase them in 20×8. In addition, operating expenses will increase as it expands its operations.

The company's ability to reach and sustain profitability depends on factors such as the growth rate of the solar energy industry, market demand for solar modules, competitiveness of its products and services, and its ability to increase production volumes. The solar energy market is at a relatively early stage of development, and the extent of its acceptance is uncertain. Many factors may affect the demand for solar modules, including the following:

- cost-effectiveness, performance, and reliability of solar modules compared with conventional and other non-solar energy sources and products;
- government incentives that support the solar energy industry;
- success of other renewable energy generation technologies, such as hydroelectric, wind, geothermal, solar thermal, concentrated photovoltaic, and biomass;
- economic and market conditions such as change in fossil fuel prices; and
- capital expenditures by end-users of solar modules, which tend to decrease when the economy slows and interest rates increase.

In September 20×7, SOL issued 21 million additional common shares for cash, to raise approximately $28 million in new equity. The net proceeds of the offering will be used primarily for (i) securing additional supplies of silicon wafers; (ii) accelerating the research and development on silicon processing; and (iii) providing additional working capital to the company's systems operating unit. In the interim, the $28 million will be invested in government securities or other short-term, interest-bearing, investment-grade securities as approved by the company's Audit Committee.

Regulatory Actions

On May 28, 20×4, and May 9, 20×5, the Ontario Securities Commission issued Cease Trade Orders (CTO) against SOL for failing to file annual statements within the required time frame. The CTOs were lifted in each case within two weeks, once the audited statements were filed.

To analyze SOL's business, environment, and risks, Jack organizes his information with these steps:

(a) Identify the key business factors, explaining why auditors must understand each factor to assess the risks of material misstatements. As a guide, consider the following categories:
 - industry, regulatory, other external risk factors
 - nature of SOL's business (operations, investments, financing)
 - SOL's objectives and strategy to address business risks

(b) Link these business risk factors to specific risks of material misstatement of the SOL financial statements. Explain clearly how the risks could lead to material misstatements.

(c) A key item in SOL's draft 20×7 balance sheet assets is patents with a cost of $439,000 and accumulated amortization of $310,000. The financial statement notes state that "Patent costs include legal fees incurred to obtain patents for technology developed or acquired by the company, and are being amortized over a period of five years." Assess the inherent risk for the patents balance, basing the assessment on the five principle assertions and giving the reasons supporting the assessment. How does this inherent risk assessment relate to the auditor's expectations regarding management's risk assessment processes and internal controls over patent assets, as well as to the planned approach for obtaining audit evidence for this account?

Analysis

Note: The following is one way to analyze the case, but other valid approaches and points are possible.

(a) <u>Risk factors</u>
Governance—The CEO is on the audit committee. There is little financial expertise on the Board and in the accounting department. The new CFO's competency and qualifications are not known yet. The corporate culture is dominated by scientists so finances may not be well managed.

<u>Controls over financial reporting</u>
There have been two CTOs for late filing; thus financial reporting control weakness is a major risk factor. Control risk appears high. CFO/CEO certifications on financial statements and internal control effectiveness may be misstated.

<u>Industry, regulatory, other external risk factors</u>
The company operates in a highly competitive technological market.

New Product Market Acceptance Risk: Market risk exists for new products such as the PV cell technology and solar grade silicon technology. There is no assurance that new products will be accepted, desired volumes will be realized, or product will not become obsolete. In addition, new product offerings will also require significant marketing and sales efforts to gain market acceptance.

Competition: Many of SOL's current and potential competitors have greater financial, marketing, technical, and other resources. There can be no assurance that SOL will be able to compete successfully with its existing or new competitors.

Availability of Solar Grade Silicon and Manufacturing Inputs: Inability to secure raw materials and other inputs to meet sales demands could negatively impact sales and earnings. The current shortage of silicon has increased the price significantly. There may be shortages of solar grade silicon, wafers, and certain specialized manufacturing tools and fixtures at any time, especially in periods of strong market demand. Few suppliers and quickly changing demand may also limit availability of inputs. With commercialization of the SOL PV cell technology, the inconsistent supply of solar grade silicon could seriously impact SOL's sales and prospects.

Government Subsidies for Solar Products: The solar market is somewhat dependent on government subsidies and programs that change with the political situation, with resultant changes in demand and pricing.

Foreign Exchange Risk: SOL's effort to sell its PV cells and solar grade silicon in foreign markets will create exposure to exchange rates, primarily the U.S. dollar and the euro, which may negatively impact SOL's future financial performance.

Operations—risks and uncertainties associated with operations:

Product Development Risk: SOL PV technology and solar grade silicon technology development are expending research resources but are not yet commercialized. There is no guarantee that the PV technology will achieve the solar cell efficiency necessary for success in the market. Commercializing any product includes the risk that full-scale production may not be at an acceptable cost level. In addition, the solar grade silicon technology is in early stages of development and there is no guarantee that technical milestones can be achieved.

Limited Protection of Patents and Proprietary Rights: The company relies on a combination of patents, trademarks, trade secrets, and know-how to protect its proprietary technology and rights. The company might not have resources to repair or protect current or future patents against infringements and challenges. Its trade secrets might be independently developed by competitors.

Expansion Risk: Bringing the SOL PV cells to market may require SOL to invest in new production equipment and systems and put manufacturing plants on tight time schedules, often without guaranteed revenue volumes. Bringing investments into production quickly may expose SOL to integration risks, depending on the size of the investment, the schedule, the technology involved, and the nature of the products to be produced.

Manufacturing Risk: SOL's production of PV cell manufacturing operations in Germany will require acquisition of land, development of manufacturing plans and production equipment, hiring of managerial personnel and skilled labour, and adequate financing arrangements. There is no assurance the company will be able to obtain these input factors or meet its implementation timeline.

Dependence on Key Personnel: SOL's success depends on attracting and retaining highly skilled personnel in key areas, including management. Unexpected loss of SOL's key employees could be detrimental to future operations. There is no assurance that the company will be able to engage or retain necessary personnel.

Financial Position: While SOL has raised additional capital in 20×6 and early 20×7, additional funds are required to complete the commercialization of the SOL PV technology and the SOL solar grade silicon technology.

Dependence on Government Funding: SOL's short-term business plan is based on securing government funding, including from SDTC and the Province of Ontario's OCE. Its plan for a manufacturing plant in Germany depends on government funding as well. Failure to finalize the funding agreements would have a materially adverse impact on the company's short-term plans.

(b) Link Business Risks to RISK OF MATERIAL MISSTATEMENT (RMM)

Industry, regulatory, other external risk factors
   –RMM: commodity prices and currency fluctuations are risk factors that may affect inventory valuation (LCM), contingent losses due to regulatory violations are probable and require disclosure (There may be other points linked to industry and external risk factors.)

Nature of SOL's business (operations, investments, financing)
   –RMM: inventory valuation affected by changes in costs imposed by suppliers and marketability; valuation of PPE and intangibles may be affected negatively by poor investment management risk or inadequate capitalization to complete construction, or inability to protect intellectual property rights; contingent liability disclosures may be incomplete if unreported product liability or patent infringement issues occur (There may be other points linked to operating/investing/financing risk factors.)

SOL's objectives and strategy to address business risks
   –RMM: strategies to address its risks may fail and the company may go bankrupt given the risky nature of its industry; alternate energy market is at very early stage; other points related to management's strategic risk assessment factors

(c) The inherent risk assessments take into consideration the nature of the item and the risk that an error can have occurred in accounting for that item in the first place. The assessment will indicate low, moderate, and high levels.

Patents are a critical asset in solar technology, so development businesses tend to have higher inherent risks. Thus, auditors expect management to have strong risk assessment processes and strong controls in place to offset and reduce these risks.

Referring to the five principle assertions

Existence—low IR because unlikely a patent would be set up in books unless it existed, and this can be verified quite reliably by examining legal documents, cash disbursements, etc.

Completeness—moderate IR as management may have patents that it didn't inform accounting staff about; some R&D expenses may have actually been to create patents; little reliable audit evidence is available for this

Valuation—very high IR because if the technology is not successful it creates high risk that the patent is worthless or overvalued; future earnings potential is very subjective and management could be biased; cost itself has fairly low IR since the payments to create patents are quite objectively determined and clearly linked to creation of legal patent rights

Ownership—high IR related to the legal enforceability and protection of patents from infringement by others; relates to the valuation of the patents as well

Presentation—low to moderate IR, appropriate policies for Intangibles tend to be set out in *Handbook* so it is clear what presentation is acceptable, but appropriate amortization may be an issue as it is subjective (useful life, etc.), increasing IR

If there are strong controls, it may be feasible and efficient for the auditor to test these controls and get some assurance from them that will lower the amount of assurance required from substantive tests. On the other hand, if the controls are not very strong, the RMM will be very high for high inherent risk items and the auditor will need a lot of substantive evidence to be able to get reasonable assurance to form an opinion about whether the financial statements are fairly stated.

SUMMARY

Chapter 7 extended the preliminary understanding of the auditee's business introduced in Chapter 6. It explained the concept of audit risk, the probability that audited financial statements contain a material misstatement. It covered the components of audit risk that can be viewed as a conceptual model for managing audit risk in an audit engagement. The relation of business risk to audit risk was explained to show various important judgments that auditors must make and that are supported by a deep understanding of the auditee's business and its risk. The relation between materiality and audit risk were also explained in terms of the different nature of these two concepts and their similar impact on the extent of audit work planned.

Chapter 7 provided a description of businesses processes, how they are used to implement the business strategy, and how auditors can assess the auditee's business risk through strategic analysis and business process analysis. The chapter described the relationships among business processes, accounting processes/cycles, and management's general purpose financial statements. The chapter also introduced internal control, an important component of the auditor's understanding of the auditee's business: the information systems that management has in place for running the business and meeting its information needs. This understanding is critical to assessing the possibility that management controls have not addressed the business risks that could lead to the financial statements being misstated. This is because the financial statements result from its business processes and information systems, and thus they are vulnerable to any control deficiencies and weaknesses that might exist.

A conceptual framework useful for understanding internal control was introduced. This framework consists of company-level controls and specific control activities. Company-level controls include the control environment, management's risk assessment processes, information systems related to business processes and communications policies, and management's monitoring activities. Control activities, a component of internal control which consists of general and application controls, were also briefly introduced here for completeness but will be explained in more detail in Chapter 9. Chapter 7 also addressed issues that auditors need to consider in understanding internal control in small entities. All aspects of controls will be explained in more detail in Chapter 9, where internal control concepts are integrated with the overall audit planning considerations concerning the design of tests of controls and other audit procedures to be performed. The chapter finished up with a discussion of how auditors use their internal control understanding to make a preliminary assessment of the risk of material misstatement at the financial statement level, including an integrated overview of the business, its processes, and how these are captured in financial statements through the internal control and information systems.

The chapter concluded with an application case and analysis illustrating how business risk assessment is performed in a practical example of using the business risk-based approach to auditing financial statements.

MULTIPLE-CHOICE QUESTIONS FOR PRACTICE AND REVIEW

MC 1   Business risk is related to business strategy because:
   a. auditors assess business risk so they can provide their auditees with a business strategy.
   b. business risks are events or actions that cause changes in technology.
   c. managers frequently change their businesses risks in response to changes in the business strategy.
   d. business risks are events or actions that will have a negative effect on the audit client's ability to achieve its strategic objectives.

MC 2   Information technology changes affect business risk when:
   a. they result in a need to change business processes.
   b. they involve entering ecommerce activities.
   c. systems become more integrated and complex.
   d. all of the above.

MC 3   The auditor assesses a business risk as high when:
   a. it is unlikely and moderate.
   b. it is likely and significant.
   c. it is possible and insignificant.
   d. it is likely and insignificant.

MC 4   Which of the following is not likely to be an important source of information the auditor can use to understand a client's business :
   a. geologist's reports on mineral reserves.
   b. internal auditors.
   c. retail sales statistics.
   d. Monday night football scores.

MC 5   The risk that the auditors' own work will lead to the decision that material misstatements do not exist in the financial statements, when in fact such misstatements do exist, is:
   a. Audit risk.
   b. Inherent risk.
   c. Control risk.
   d. Detection risk.

MC 6   Auditors are responsible for the quality of the work related to management and control of:
   a. Inherent risk.
   b. Relative risk.
   c. Control risk.
   d. Detection risk.

MC 7   The auditors assessed a combined inherent risk and control risk at .67 and said they wanted to achieve a .15 risk of failing to detect misstatements in an account with a material balance. What audit risk are auditors planning to accept for this audit?
   a. .20
   b. .10
   c. .75
   d. .05

MC 8   The cash account is included in more than one accounting process because:
   a. all the business processes involve either receiving or paying out cash at some point.
   b. cash is the most difficult asset to control.
   c. cash is the easiest asset to steal.
   d. cash can be either an asset or a liability.

MC 9   Analytical procedures are generally used to produce evidence from:
   a. confirmations mailed directly to the auditors by auditee customers.
   b. physical observation of inventories.
   c. relationships among current financial balances and prior balances, forecasts, and nonfinancial data.
   d. detailed examination of external, external-internal, and internal documents.

MC 10   Which of the following match-ups of types of analytical procedures and sources of information makes the most sense?

Type of Analytical Procedure	Source of Information
a. Comparison of current account balances with prior-periods statistics	Physical production
b. Comparison of current account balances with expected balances	Company's budgets and forecasts
c. Evaluation of current account balances with relation to predictable historical patterns	Published industry ratios
d. Evaluation of current account balances in relation to nonfinancial information	Company's own comparative financial statements

MC 11   Analytical procedures can be used in which of the following ways?
   a. As a means of overall review at the end of an audit
   b. As "attention directing" methods when planning an audit at the beginning
   c. As substantive audit procedures to obtain evidence during an audit
   d. All of the above

MC 12   The primary purpose for obtaining an understanding of an auditee's internal control structure is to:
   a. provide a basis for making constructive suggestions in a management letter.
   b. determine the nature, timing, and extent of tests to be performed in the audit.
   c. obtain sufficient appropriate evidential matter to afford a reasonable basis for an opinion on the financial statements under examination.
   d. provide information for a communication of internal control structure-related matters to management.

MC 13 What do management's internal control objectives include?

a. Reducing the amount of testing done by the auditors

b. Allowing the auditor to assess control risk

c. Preventing and detecting fraud

d. Implementing policies and procedures such that auditors can assess control risk as being low

EXERCISES AND PROBLEMS

EP 1
LO.1
and
LO.2

Business risk understanding. Super Natural Foods Limited manufactures, distributes, and sells all-natural grocery products.

Required:

Describe three business risks for this company and explain why they are important considerations for the auditor of its financial statements.

EP 2
LO.1
and
LO.2

Significant audit issues, audit risk decision. You are the auditor of Royal Health Limited (Royal). Royal is a public company that grows medicinal plants and sells them across North America, Europe, and the Far East. Its largest expense is marketing. All its marketing is done by another company that is owned by one of Royal's directors.

Required:

Identify three (3) key audit issues in this company and explain how these will affect your audit risk, using the audit risk model.

EP 3
LO.3

Business processes, accounting processes/cycles. Explain what an accounting process/cycle is and how it relates to business processes and to the entity's financial statements. Why is the approach of identifying accounting processes/cycles useful in planning an audit?

EP 4
LO.3

Business Processes, Different Industries. What business processes would be related to each of the four accounting processes in the following businesses?

a. a bicycle manufacturing business

b. an architectural firm

c. a retail grocery store

DISCUSSION CASES

DC 1
LO.1

Audit Risk Model. Audit risks for particular accounts and disclosures can be conceptualized in this model: Audit risk (AR) = Inherent risk (IR) × Internal control risk (CR) × Detection risk (DR). Use this model as a framework for considering the following situations and deciding whether the auditor's conclusion is appropriate.

1. Ohlsen, PA, has participated in the audit of Limberg Cheese Company for five years, first as an assistant accountant and the last two years as the senior accountant. He has never seen an accounting adjustment recommended. He believes the inherent risk must be zero.

2. Jones, PA, has just (November 30) completed an exhaustive study and evaluation of the internal control system of Lang's Derfer Foods, Inc. (fiscal year ending December 31). She believes the control risk must be zero because no material errors could possibly slip through the many error-checking procedures and review layers used by Lang's.

3. Fields, PA, is lazy and does not like audit jobs in Toronto, anyway. On the audit of Hogtown Manufacturing Company, he decided to use detail procedures to audit the year-end balances very thoroughly to the extent that his risk of failing to detect material errors and irregularities should be 0.02 or less. He gave no thought to inherent risk and conducted only a very limited review of Hogtown's internal control system.

4. Shad, PA, is nearing the end of a "dirty" audit of Allnight Protection Company. Allnight's accounting personnel all resigned during the year and were replaced by inexperienced people. The controller resigned last month in disgust. The journals and ledgers were a mess because the one computer specialist was hospitalized for three months during the year. Shad thought thankfully, "I've been able to do this audit in less time than last year when everything was operating smoothly."

DC 2
LO.2
and
LO.3

Planning, Inherent and Control Risk, Manufacturing Business. Darter Ltd. is a medium-sized business involved in manufacturing and assembling consumer electronic products such as DVD players, radios, and satellite receivers. It is privately owned. Its minority shareholders requested that the annual financial statements be audited for the first time this year. Your firm is engaged to do the current year's audit. You are now reviewing Darter's preliminary general ledger trial balance in order to begin preparing the planning memorandum. Consider the following accounts that appear in this trial balance:

Cash
Inventory, finished goods
Inventory, work-in-progress
Inventory, unassembled components
Inventory, spare parts
Property, plant and equipment
Deferred development costs
Goodwill
Accounts payable
Warranty provision

Bank loan, long term
Share capital, common shares
Retained earnings
Revenue
Cost of goods sold
General and administration expense

Required:

a. Evaluate the inherent risk for each of the above accounts. Give the reasons that support your assessment and state any assumptions you need to make.

b. How will inherent risk level relate to the types of controls that Darter's management implements for each of these accounts? Consider costs and benefits of implementing effective controls.

c. For each account describe the procedures you would use to assess the control risk.

d. How would you expect the company's accounts to differ and how would your inherent risk assessment differ if the company's business was:

- an iron mine
- a piano manufacturer
- a bank
- a shipping line

DC 3
LO.2 and LO.3   **Business Risk Analysis.** Assume you have recently been assigned to the audit team working on the financial statement audit of Town Groceries Limited ("TGL"). As a member of the team you are now in the process of gaining an understanding of the company's business, environment, and risks.

From the 20x4 Town Groceries Limited Annual Report you have learned the following about this business and its strategy:

TGL is Canada's largest food distributor and a leading provider of general merchandise products and services. TGL is committed to providing Canadians with a one-stop destination in meeting their food and everyday household needs. This goal is pursued through a portfolio of store formats across the country.

It operates across Canada under various operating banners (including Maritime Grocery, Western Groceries, and other banners). These banners are set up as 658 corporate-owned stores, 400 franchised stores, and 519 associated stores. The store network is supported by 32 warehouse facilities located across Canada. Some 130,000 full-time and part-time employees execute its business strategy in more than 1,000 corporate and franchised

stores from coast to coast. TGL is known for the quality, innovation, and value of its food offering. It also offers a strong private label program, including the unique Choice of Choice and OurTown brands.

While food remains at the heart of its offering, TGL stores provide a wide, growing range of general merchandise products and services. In addition, their Town Financial Inc. offers personal banking, a popular credit card, auto and home insurance, plus the Town Points loyalty program.

TGL seeks to achieve its business objectives through stable, sustainable, and long-term growth. It seeks to provide superior returns to its shareholders through a combination of dividends and share price appreciation. Its willingness to assume prudent operating risks is equalled by its commitment to the maintenance of a strong balance sheet position.

In executing its strategies, TGL allocates the resources needed to invest in and expand its existing markets. It also maintains an active product development program.

TGL is highly selective in its consideration of acquisitions and other business opportunities. Given the competitive nature of its industry, TGL also strives to make its operating environment as stable and as cost effective as possible. It works to ensure that its technology systems and logistics enhance the efficiency of its operations.

It strives to contribute to the communities it serves and to exercise responsible corporate citizenship.

Required:

a. Based on the preceding information, list the industry, regulatory, and other external factors that are relevant in understanding TGL's business and its environment. Use the risk factors outlined in Appendix 7C as a guide.

b. Link the risk factors you identified in part (a) to the risks in TGL's operations. Link these operating risks to risks of TGL's financial statements being materially misstated.

c. Outline TGL's strategy and describe, in general terms, the business processes you expect to find the company using to achieve its strategy.

d. While reading through the business section of the newspaper, you also came across the following article on TGL's third-quarter results for 20X5. What strategic risks are illustrated in the results being described in the article? Speculate on what strategic errors and/or business process deficiencies at TGL have contributed to these "woes." What impact do you expect these events to have on TGL's financial results for 20X5?

TGL PROFIT SLUMPS, CEO VOWS TO CONTINUE RETOOLING THE GROCERY OPERATIONS

July 30, 20X5

TGL Cos. Ltd. will stick to its current retooling strategy, the grocery chain CEO said yesterday, even though its third-quarter profit slumped by 26%. Profit was dragged down by supply-chain hiccups,

and higher-than-expected costs related to TGL's retooling strategy.

Thr supermarket operator reported its summer-quarter profit fell to $192-million, or 7 cents a share, from $258-million or 9.4 cents, a year ago. Analysts were expecting a profit of 10 cents per share, even though the company had previously warned that its planned retooling of supply chains, systems, and administration would likely result in some short-term profit decreases.

TGL's CEO said that retooling the national supply chain and converting to a common-information systems platform has taken longer and been more disruptive than planned, negatively affecting TGL's performance in the short term. The CEO expressed disappointment with the progress to date, but vows that the company is taking strong action to resolve the problems, and will be a stronger and much more competitive player as a result of these changes.

Another issue affecting profit arose from TGL's new third-party-operated general merchandise warehouse and distribution centre for the western region failing to reach the planned operating efficiency and capacity on schedule.

The profit declines come despite TGL's sales growing 6.4 per cent from a year earlier, to $8.7-billion from $8.1-billion, with growth across all regions. Sales at older stores, and sales of the general and beauty product lines tended to be flat, however, as they were most affected by the supply-chain disruptions.

TGL reported that $30-million of the profit decline was due to the flat sales; restructuring and other charges reduced it by another $27-million; and a special charge relating to a re-assessment by the Canada Revenue Agency relating to sales taxes on certain new lines of merchandise brought it down by another $20-million.

DC 4 **Business Understanding, Retail Industry.** The newspaper article following discusses strategic issues related to two large Canadian retailers: HBC and Winners. Based on the information provided (and, optionally, other Internet research you may wish to do), identify the strategies being followed in these two businesses. Apply the strategic systems approach outlined in the chapter, as follows:

LO.2 and LO.3

a. Explain management's objectives, strategies, and risks in the two businesses. What similarities and differences did you notice?

b. In your opinion, did the managers in both businesses fully analyze the risks involved and take action to address them? Support your opinions with facts from the article (and your additional research, if any).

c. Do you think it is possible that any of the risks you have identified might have a material effect on the businesses? If so, what financial implications might these risks have, and could they affect the financial statements?

COST-CONSCIOUS STRATEGY SCORES WINNER FOR HBC

Hudson's Bay Co., in the midst of an unfriendly takeover battle, appears to be having success in at least one area: its push to woo the value-conscious shopper. Indeed, the efforts may even be hurting a key competitor.

Winners, the discounter known for big-box stores and brand-name goods at lower prices, has experienced a drop in same-store sales at outlets open a year or more—an indication that the business is suffering. And some observers say it may be getting a bit more difficult for Winners to find quality goods from suppliers.

Why? Because a few years ago, HBC chief executive officer George Heller decided to take aim at Winners' thriving "off-price" business. He wanted to ensure that his regular suppliers provided HBC with the same type of low-priced, end-of-season, and excess goods that have made Winners such a destination.

"They've choked off the supply a little bit to Winners," says David Howell, president of consultancy Associate Marketing International. "It's probably one of the smarter things that George has done. It's a good strategy and it seems to be working."

HBC, which owns the Bay, Zellers, and Home Outfitters, has increased its selection of the so-called off-price products—everything from jackets to housewares—and marketed them heavily through flyers and in-store signs as "power buys." It opened special in-store boutiques called Style Outlets for discount items and, last year, began opening separate Designer Depot outlets similar to Winners stores.

In the midst of the push, late last month, HBC became the target of a $1.1-billion hostile takeover bid from U.S. financier and HBC shareholder Jerry Zucker, who is unhappy with the company's performance and says he can run it better.

Despite HBC's struggles, its off-price strategy stands out as a rare glimmer of hope. Executives didn't like to see their vendors supplying their stores with full-price products under well-known labels and then selling those very items—perhaps a little later in the season—to Winners at a fraction of the price.

"There's such a big appetite in the Canadian marketplace for off-price product and it's so underserviced," says Marc Chouinard, chief operating officer at HBC. "It's not surprising that this strategy is giving us what we want."

Sherry Lang, vice-president of investor relations at TJX Cos., the large U.S.-based parent of Winners, rejects any suggestion of overly tough competition with HBC for supplies. "Winners has enormous clout in sourcing globally," she says.

Rather, Winners' difficulties began in the last half of 2004 when its buyers purchased too much inventory too far in advance of the season, she says. It was forced to mark down prices heavily after other retailers began to do so, she says.

The weak results continued into the first half of 2005 as Winners' merchants attempted to correct the situation, she says. They purchased less inventory, and lowered all pricing at the stores, although she wouldn't say to what extent.

The results this year are soft, as well, because they are being compared to an "exceptionally" strong first half of last year, she adds.

Last week, TJX reported that October same-store sales at its Canadian division, which also includes HomeSense, fell 5 per cent and in the third quarter 4 per cent.

Ms. Lang says Winners' latest sales were short of expectations and hurt by unseasonably warm fall weather. She says the outlook is better for the remainder of the year.

Robert Johnston, a vice-president at Mr. Zucker's U.S. company, says Mr. Zucker is pleased that HBC is making inroads in its off-price strategy. But it took too long to get it off the ground, he says, adding Mr. Zucker would accelerate the off-price program if he took over HBC.

And while TJX has faltered of late, it has been vastly more successful over the past few years in its financial performance, compared with that of HBC, he adds.

Winners and sister off-price chain HomeSense still enjoy a comfortable lead in the category, generating more than $1.3-billion (U.S.) in annual sales.

HBC has about $250-million (Canadian) of annual "power buy" sales today, and aims to double that over the next three years, Mr. Chouinard says.

Source: Marina Strauss, Cost-Conscious Strategy Scores Winner for HBC, *The Globe and Mail*, November 14, 2005, p. B4. Reprinted with permission from The Globe and Mail.

DC 5 **Business Risk and Risk of Material Misstatement.** You
LO.2 have joined a public accounting firm as a junior auditor,
LO.4 and have been assigned to the audit team for one of your
LO.5 firm's largest audit engagements, Cold Beverages Corp.
LO.6 Cold Beverages Corp. (CB), a large public company, was incorporated in Canada in 1955. Your firm has audited CB for many years. Based on your review of previous years' audit working papers, CB's 2007 quarterly reports, and its draft 2007 Management Discussion and Analysis, you have learned the following.

CB is one of the world's largest non-alcoholic beverage producers, providing about 65% of the world's retailer branded soft-drinks, bottled water, juice drinks, and teas. Approximately 90% of its output is sold to retailers for sale under the retailers' brands, with the remainder sold under CB's own brand names. The company operates in North America, Mexico, the U.K., and Europe. In the past four years, CB has expanded its production and distribution capabilities mainly through acquisitions of other businesses. It plans to grow in future mainly by leveraging existing customer relationships, developing new products and distribution channels, and obtaining new

customers in new markets. During 2005 and 2006, CB rationalized its business by focussing on its highest performing production facilities, resulting in plant and warehouse closures in North America.

CB's products are sold primarily to a small group of very large customers, including large grocery and retail chains. One customer, Tram-Mart, accounts for about 40% of CB's total 2007 revenues, and its nine next largest customers account for about 30% of 2007 revenues. Products are delivered by third party carriers or are picked up by customers at CB's plants.

The main raw material used in production is water. Other materials required are mainly plastic bottles, aluminum cans, packaging materials, sweeteners, and flavourings. CB typically enters into annual arrangements with its suppliers rather than long-term contracts. At the end of each one-year period CB must renegotiate with the suppliers or find new suppliers. The prices of these materials fluctuate on world markets, but generally there are adequate supplies available and this is expected to continue in future. During 2006 the price of aluminum cans increased substantially and CB's management decided to enter a 5-year agreement with a supplier at a fixed cost. During 2007 the price of aluminum fell quite substantially. Because of growing demand for corn-based products, the costs of the main sweeteners used by CB have increased substantially in 2007. CB does not use derivatives to manage the risks of these price changes.

A key to CB's success is its intellectual property, consisting of trade secrets, beverage formulas, and trademarks for its beverage brands. These intangibles are protected mainly by registration, contractual agreements, employee confidentiality agreements, and rigorous prosecution of any infringements using all available common and statutory laws.

Competition in the soft-drinks industry is fierce. Three huge multinationals control about 85% of the consumer sales, and spend heavily on promotion. Other competitors are local independent producers who sell at aggressively discounted prices, and some large U.S. retail chains that manufacture their own soft-drinks and actively seek new customers to expand their sales. CB's management addresses these competitive threats by offering efficient distribution choices, top-quality products, attractive packaging, effective marketing strategies, and superior service.

CB's business is subject to many federal, state, provincial, and local laws and regulations that govern product manufacturing, distribution, labelling, and safety. It is also subject to a number of environmental laws relating to fuel use and storage, water use and treatment, waste disposal, and employee safety. Failure to comply with these laws and regulations can have very negative consequences including penalties and fines. Currently, CB is not in compliance with the Ontario Environmental Protection Act requirements that set a minimum percentage of its products that must be sold in refillable containers. At this time, the Ontario government is not enforcing this law. CB's management believes that none of its main competitors is in compliance either, and so it could not remain competitive if it attempted to comply.

During 2007, CB's management identified material weaknesses in the company's internal controls over financial reporting. The main issues related to controls over periodic inventory counts and credit notes. Inventory counting procedures were not properly executed because employees were not properly trained and supervised, resulting in an inability to produce a complete and accurate physical count. Lack of segregation of duties in the issuing of credit notes to customers permitted a fraud to occur. An accounts receivable clerk was discovered to be colluding with a warehousing employee to divert cases of high value beverages from legitimate customer orders, and cover up the shortages by issuing phony credit notes. The stolen beverages were sold by the warehouse employee to small local restaurants and variety stores. Both employees have been fired and management is in the process of redesigning its inventory control and credit note issuing procedures. Another weakness was found in the global material acquisition function, where supplier contracts were not being properly authorized,

resulting in improper agreements being entered into, and increased risk of employees in different countries accepting bribes from suppliers or engaging in other illegal acts.

Early in 2008, CB reported its fourth-quarter of 2007 performance, a large loss that was worse than financial analysts expected and much worse than the fourth quarter of 2006. CB management blames the poor performance on price competition, and declining soft-drink consumption in developed countries. Over the 2007 year, the company has reported very poor quarterly results and its share price has fallen dramatically all year. The analysts have also expressed concern that CB is close to violating its debt covenants and may have difficulty obtaining the financing it will require to succeed unless its profitability improves substantially in the early part of 2008. To try to please investors, CB's new CEO, a respected industry veteran, recently held a press conference to show off the company's new head office in Arizona and its innovative new products, and to explain how it is changing the company culture to focus on a turnaround strategy.

Required:

a. Identify key business factors in the CB case and explain why its auditors must understand each factor to assess the risks of material misstatements. As a guide, consider the following categories:
   - Industry, regulatory, other external risk factors
   - Nature of CB's business (operations, investments, financing)
   - CB's objectives and strategy to address business risks
b. Link the business risk factors you identified in part (a) to some specific risks of material misstatement of the CB financial statements. Explain clearly how the risks could lead to the financial statements being materially misstated.
c. What information relevant to understanding internal control is indicated in the case? Consider control environment and accounting controls relevant to financial reporting. How would you assess the effectiveness of CB's internal control to reduce the risk of material misstatement?

DC 6
LO.5
and
LO.6

Obtaining a "Sufficient" Understanding of Internal Control. The 12 partners of a regional PA firm met in special session to discuss audit engagement efficiency. Jones spoke up, saying:

"We all certainly appreciate the firmwide policies set up by Martin and Smith, especially in connection with the audits of the large companies that have come our way recently. Their experience with a large national firm has helped build up our practice. But I think the standard policy of conducting reviews and tests of internal control on all audits is raising our costs too much. We can't charge our smaller clients fees for all the time the staff spends on this work. I would like to propose that we give engagement partners discretion to decide whether to do a lot of work on assessing control risk. I may be an old mossback, but I think I can finish a competent audit without it."

Discussion on the subject continued but ended when Martin said, with some emotion: "But we can't disregard generally accepted auditing standards like Jones proposes!"

Required:

What do you think of Jones's proposal and Martin's view of the issue? Discuss.

DC 7 **Management Controls, Impact on Audit.** Jabiru Inc.'s
LO.5 senior management recently obtained a new decision-
and support database system that allows the managers to gen-
LO.6 erate standard reports and also customize enquiries that use data from all functional areas of their company. Before this system was in place, reports to senior managers were generated manually by the operations managers in the various departments, such as purchasing, marketing, inventory control, production, human resources, and administration. The senior managers are much happier with the new system because now they can generate reports as

soon as the period ends; they can draw the data directly from the company's computer databases; they can control the content and format of the reports; and the operating managers have less opportunity to manipulate the information in the reports. For example, in the first two months of the new system, senior managers were able to identify a discrepancy in the production department that was resulting in significant shrinkage and were able to correct the control weakness quickly. The previous report, which had been designed and produced by the production manager, did not include the data needed to identify the shrinkage problem.

Required:

a. Discuss how the new decision-support database system affects Jabiru's internal control and its risk of material mistatement.

b. Comment on the potential audit planning implications of the new decision-support database system.

APPENDIX 7C

BUSINESS RISK FACTORS

Business risks that the auditor considers when assessing the risk of material financial statement misstatement include the following:

UNDERSTANDING THE ENTITY AND ITS ENVIRONMENT, INCLUDING INTERNAL CONTROL

Industry, regulatory, and other external factors, including the applicable financial reporting framework

Industry conditions
a. The market and competition, including demand, capacity, and price competition
b. Cyclical or seasonal activity
c. Product technology relating to the entity's products
d. Energy supply and cost

Regulatory environment
a. Accounting principles and industry-specific practices
b. Regulatory framework for a regulated industry
c. Legislation and regulation that significantly affect the entity's operations
  (i) Regulatory requirements
  (ii) Direct supervisory activities
d. Taxation (corporate and other)
e. Government policies currently affecting the conduct of the entity's business
  (i) Monetary, including foreign exchange controls
  (ii) Fiscal

  (iii) Financial incentives (e.g., government aid programs)
  (iv) Tariffs, trade restrictions
f. Environmental requirements affecting the industry and the entity's business

Other external factors currently affecting the entity's business
a. General level of economic activity (e.g., recession, growth)
b. Interest rates and availability of financing
c. Inflation, currency revaluation

Nature of the entity

Business operations
a. Nature of the business
  (i) Profit-oriented (e.g., financial or other services, manufacturer, wholesaler, importer, exporter)
  (ii) Government (e.g., federal, provincial, territorial, local)

(iii) Government organization (e.g., department/ministry, Crown corporation, fund, agency)

(iv) Not-for-profit organization (e.g., an entity established for social, educational, religious, health, or philanthropic purposes)

b. Nature of revenue sources (e.g., manufacturer, wholesaler, banking, insurance or other financial services, import/export trading, utility, transportation, technology products and services)

c. Products or services and markets (e.g., major customers and contracts, terms of payment, profit margins, market share, competitors, exports, pricing policies, reputation of products, warranties, order book, trends, marketing strategy and objectives, manufacturing processes)

d. Conduct of operations (e.g., stages and methods of production, business segments, delivery of products and services, details of declining or expanding operations)

e. Alliances, joint ventures, and outsourcing activities

f. Involvement in electronic commerce, including Internet sales and marketing activities

g. Geographic dispersion and industry segmentation

h. Location of production facilities, warehouses, and offices

i. Key customers

j. Important suppliers of goods and services (e.g., long-term contracts, stability of supply, terms of payment, imports, methods of delivery such as "just-in-time")

k. Employment (e.g., by location, supply, wage levels, union contracts, pension and other post-employment benefits, stock option or incentive bonus arrangements, and government regulation related to employment matters)

l. Research and development activities and expenditures

m. Transactions with related parties

n. Nature of expenditures, including programs and activities of not-for-profit and government entities

Investments

a. Acquisitions, mergers, or disposals of business activities (planned or recently executed)

b. Investments and dispositions of securities and loans

c. Capital investment activities, including investments in plant, equipment, and technology, and any recent or planned changes

d. Investments in nonconsolidated entities, including partnerships, joint ventures and special-purpose entities

Financing

a. Group structure—major subsidiaries and associated entities, including consolidated and nonconsolidated structures

b. Debt structure, including covenants, restrictions, guarantees, and off-balance sheet financing arrangements

c. Leasing of property, plant, or equipment for use in the business

d. Beneficial owners (local, foreign, business reputation, and experience)

e. Related parties

f. Use of derivative financial instruments

g. Form of ownership (e.g., private company, public company, partnership, joint venture, government owned or controlled, member owned)

Financial reporting

a. Accounting principles and industry-specific practices

b. Revenue recognition practices

c. Accounting for fair values

d. Inventories (e.g., locations, quantities)

e. Foreign currency assets, liabilities, and transactions

f. Industry-specific significant categories (e.g., loans and investments for banks, accounts receivable and inventory for manufacturers, research and development for pharmaceuticals)

g. Accounting for unusual or complex transactions including those in controversial or emerging areas (e.g., accounting for stock-based compensation)

h. Financial statement presentation and disclosure

Objectives and strategies and related business risks

a. Existence of objectives (e.g., how the entity addresses industry, regulatory, and other external factors) relating to, for example, the following:

(i) Industry developments (e.g., the entity might not have the personnel or expertise to deal with the changes in the industry)

(ii) New products and services (e.g., potential for increased product liability)

(iii) Expansion of the business (e.g., demand might not have been accurately estimated)

(iv) New accounting requirements (e.g., potential incomplete or improper implementation, or increased costs)

(v) Regulatory requirements (e.g., there might be increased legal exposure)

(vi) Current and prospective financing requirements (e.g., potential loss of financing due to the entity's inability to meet requirements)

(vii) Use of IT (e.g., systems and processes may be incompatible)

b. Effects of implementing a strategy, particularly any effects that will lead to new accounting requirements (e.g., potential incomplete or improper implementation)

Measurement and review of the entity's financial performance	**Internal control components**
a. Key ratios and operating statistics	a. Control environment
b. Key performance indicators	b. Risk assessment process
c. Employee performance measures and incentive compensation policies	c. Information system, including the related business processes relevant to financial reporting and communication
d. Trends	d. Control activities
e. Use of forecasts, budgets, and variance analysis	e. Monitoring of controls
f. Analyst reports and credit rating reports	Source: Adapted from CAS 315 (5141).
g. Competitor analysis	
h. Period-on-period financial performance (revenue growth, profitability, leverage)	

APPENDIX 7D

AUDIT RISK AND ACCOUNTING RISK: ANOTHER ILLUSTRATION OF THE CRITICAL THINKING PROCESS

As noted in this chapter, the audit risk model deals with risks associated with gathering sufficient appropriate evidence and is the heart of auditing theory. But, as noted in Chapters 2 and 3, after deciding there is sufficient appropriate evidence, the auditor must decide on how best to report the verified facts within GAAP. This interpretive decision based on the evidence introduces an important new risk which we call accounting risk—the uncertainty associated with the need to make forecasts for the many estimates used in GAAP. Accounting risk is the main uncertainty in the estimation uncertainty concept of CAS 540.

The definition of inherent risk seems to suggest that accounting risk is already covered in this component of audit risk. To think this means you do not fully grasp the audit risk concept. Critical thinking allows you to understand the limitations of the audit risk model and to apply it properly in practice. To help you understand this, consider the following example.

Your client has made an investment of $10 million with the following projected cash flows:

$ 1 billion with probability 0.01
$ 0 with probability 0.99

The following questions cover the items a critical thinker would consider. State your conclusion to each issue given. Give supporting reasons. For each response, answer the question "Why is my answer to this question true?"

1. Is this $10 million investment an asset that should be reported in the financial statements?

2. What is the business risk associated with this investment?

3. What is the audit risk associated with this investment? (You can assume that the auditor is convinced that the above facts are true.)

4. What is the inherent risk?

5. What is the accounting risk?

6. What is the information risk?

7. What is the amount that can be recorded under the assets definition of *Handbook* section 1000? Does this agree with your response to question 1?

8. What is the best way to record this investment so that it "presents fairly" the economic reality of the investment? Explain why this differs or does not differ from your responses to 1 and 7.

9. What is the recorded amount for this investment that minimizes accounting risk? What is the information risk using this recorded amount? Do these values agree with your answer to 8? Why or why not?

10. As auditor, would you approve your client's recording this investment at $10 million? What would you document in your working papers?

Brief suggested solutions to above

1. No, because of reasons given below

2. The amount of the investment at risk here is 99% as there is only 1% chance this investment will recover its costs.

3. If the auditor is convinced that the facts are true, then he or she must have all the evidence needed. Effectively, the audit risk is zero. Now it's a question of deciding how to record these facts relative to GAAP requirements. Note that this is a situation typical in your financial accounting courses: audit risk is zero because the facts are presumed to be known with certainty, and the only issue is to how to properly report these facts in financial statements.

4. Inherent risk can be anything between 0 and 1 because that relates to evidence gathering assessment and we know from item 3 that CR and DR in the audit risk model must have compensated so that audit risk is 0. Specifically, either CR or DR, or both, are zero.

5. Accounting risk is dependent on what is recorded, as discussed below.

6. Since audit risk is 0, the accounting risk is the only source of information risk. So, if we want to minimize information risk we now need to focus on minimizing the accounting risk, or at least getting it to acceptable levels.

7. Under the *Handbook* 1000 definition, an asset must have "probable" future benefits. Many interpret this as meaning expected future benefits, especially in the case of fair value accounting for financial assets. Under this reasoning, the expected value, which also happens to be the amount of the investment, is $10 million, and most accountants would probably say this is the amount to record. A skeptical auditor, however, would have problems with this reasoning because a skeptical risk-oriented auditor would realize that GAAP largely ignores accounting risk.

8. A risk-oriented auditor would consistently consider risks in accounting as well as in auditing; otherwise, the auditor is violating a most basic rule of logic related to consistency in reasoning. Inconsistency is the basis of lies and misleading financial reporting. To better understand the problems of dealing inconsistently with risks, consider the following. Would you accept recording the investment at $ 1 billion and allowing management to record a $990 million profit by simply putting down the cost of $10 million? Most of you would say no. The rest of you would need to do a lot more explaining about the realization rules you are following, and convince the rest of us that they are acceptable for financial reporting. We will assume that you say no. This is probably based in large part on the fact that, if you record a $1 billion asset, the accounting risk for it is 99%. But, if you think this risk is too high, then you should also have problems with recording a $10 million asset because its accounting risk is 100%. (This is assuming you don't sell this investment on a complete, efficient market before the cash flows start coming in. We assume here that management will hang on to this investment until its realization date—you can think of this investment as a type of lottery ticket that can't be sold before the payoff date. If the auditor were sufficiently sure that it would be sold before the payoff date, then recording at $10 million makes sense. Note, however, how

important it is to make all your assumptions clear in justifying your conclusion. Critical thinking reminds you of both this and the need to document your reasoning in working papers.) By contrast, recording 0 has an accounting risk of 1%.

9. The accounting risk is minimized at recording a value of zero for investment. To make this more concrete, assume materiality here is $1 million. Thus, anything outside an immaterial range of zero has an accounting risk of 99% within a material amount of $1 billion, and 100% everywhere else.

10. In light of the above, if the auditor wishes to control accounting risk to acceptable levels, then recording a $10 million asset is unacceptable. To get the accounting risks down to acceptable, say, 1%, the auditor would insist on an adjusting entry crediting the investment asset $10 million and debiting either a loss or expense account. Further discussion of these possibilities, along with existing obligations for disclosing this investment in the notes to the financials, are discussed in the critical thinking question of Chapter 15.

CHAPTER 8

Audit Evidence and Assurance

Chapter 8 expands on the concepts of audit evidence, the auditor's source of reasonable assurance that financial statements are not materially misstated. It covers evidence gathering procedures and how these are used for risk assessment, control testing, and substantive testing. Most of the auditor's work involves designing and performing audit procedures to obtain sufficient appropriate audit evidence, and evaluating that evidence to draw reasonable conclusions on which to base the audit opinion. Chapter 8 explains how auditors apply judgment to determine the sufficiency and appropriateness of evidence as a source of reasonable assurance and to develop detailed evidence gathering procedures in the audit plan. Finally, the chapter describes how audit working papers are used to document the nature and extent of the audit work performed, the evidence gathered, and the conclusions the auditors reached based on their work. Documentation is essential to provide a complete, accurate record of the auditor's work, judgments, and decisions supporting the audit opinion.

LEARNING OBJECTIVES

After completing this chapter, you will be able to do the following:

1 Outline six general audit techniques for gathering evidence.

2 Identify the procedures and sources of information auditors can use to obtain evidence for understanding an auditee's business and industry, assessing risk, and responding to assessed risk.

3 Explain audit evidence in terms of its appropriateness and relative strength of persuasiveness.

4 Describe the content and purpose of the audit plan as well as the specific audit programs and detailed procedures it contains.

⑤ Explain the purpose of audit documentation and review an audit working paper for proper form and content.

⑥ Apply and integrate the chapter topics to analyze a practical auditing situation/case/scenario.

EVIDENCE-GATHERING AUDIT PROCEDURES

LEARNING OBJECTIVE

① Outline six general audit techniques for gathering evidence.

Auditors obtain six basic types of evidence and use six general techniques to gather it. The six techniques are (1) recalculation/reperformance, (2) observation, (3) confirmation, (4) enquiry, (5) inspection, and (6) analysis. One or more of these techniques may be used no matter what account balance, class of transactions, control procedure, or other information is under audit. In Chapters 6 and 7 we showed how one of the evidence gathering techniques, enquiry, is used to obtain information from auditee personnel or external sources for understanding the auditee's business and assessing the risk of material misstatement. Enquiry generates important audit evidence, but enquiry alone does not provide sufficient audit evidence that there is no material misstatement, or that internal control is effective. Auditors use a combination of evidence gathering techniques to look for corroborating evidence since that is more persuasive than a single piece of evidence. Auditors cannot obtain absolute assurance because of the limitations of audit procedures and accounting itself, so professional judgment is required in deciding when the evidence gathered is enough to provide reasonable assurance.

In practice, the general techniques are usually subdivided into more specific procedures. Auditors arrange these specific procedures into an audit program, basically a list of procedures. Exhibit 8–1 shows the six general techniques matched to the types of evidence each provides and gives some examples of specific procedures that could be included in an audit program.

EXHIBIT 8–1   AUDIT TECHNIQUES AND RELATED TYPES OF EVIDENCE

Audit Techniques	Types of Evidence	Examples of Specific Procedures
1. Recalculation/ Reperformance	1. Auditor's calculations	1. Recompute amortization expense using declining balance method. Recompute "price times quantity" on invoices. Recompute sales tax as a percentage of total sale amount on invoices. Reperform data entry procedure with automated missing data control.
2. Observation	2. Auditor's observations	2. Observe data entry procedures. Observe petty cash control procedures. Observe auditee's inventory counting procedures.
3. Confirmation	3. Statements by independent parties	3. Obtain written confirmation of A/R balance and detail from customer. Obtain written confirmation of loan amount, interest, collateral, and payment dates from lender.
4. Enquiry	4. Statements by auditee personnel	4. Enquire about frequency of bank reconciliation procedures. Enquire about which employee totals cash receipts and deposits them to the bank.
5. Inspection	5a. Documents prepared by independent parties	5a. Read terms of lease agreement for lessee.
	5b. Documents prepared by the auditee	5b. Review inventory variance analysis report prepared by production department.
	5c. Physical inspection of tangible assets	5c. Auditor's test counts of physical inventory quantities on hand at year end. Auditor's examination of damaged inventory on hand.
6. Analysis	6. Data interrelationships	6. Analyze monthly gross margin by product line. Compare inventory turnover rate to previous year.

Recalculation/Reperformance

Recalculation is redoing calculations already performed by auditee personnel. This produces compelling mathematical evidence as the auditee calculation is either right or wrong. Calculations made using computer programs can be recalculated using auditing software, with differences being pointed out for further audit investigation. Mathematical evidence can serve the objectives of both existence and valuation for financial statement amounts that result from calculations; for example, depreciation, pension liabilities, actuarial reserves, statutory bad debt reserves, and product guarantee liabilities. Recalculation, in combination with other procedures, is also used to provide evidence of valuation for all other financial data. It provides highly reliable evidence of mathematical accuracy, but the product is only as good as the components; the auditor must audit every significant part of the original computation if recalculation is to provide strong, persuasive evidence.

A related type of evidence is called *reperformance*. Usually applied in control testing, the auditor independently executes a procedure of the organization's internal control. This can provide compelling evidence about the effectiveness of a control procedure.

Observation

Observation consists of looking at how policy or procedures are applied by others. It provides highly reliable evidence as to performance or conditions at a given point in time, but it does not necessarily reflect performance at other times or over long periods. The technique is used whenever auditors take an inspection tour, watch personnel carry out accounting and control activities, or participate in a surprise petty cash count or payroll distribution. Physical observation also produces a general awareness of events in the auditee's offices.

External Confirmation

Confirmation consists of an enquiry, usually written, to verify accounting records. Direct correspondence with independent external parties is a confirmation procedure widely used in auditing. For example, external confirmation is recommended for accounts receivable by CAS 505 (5303). It can produce evidence of existence, ownership, valuation, and cut-off. Most transactions involve external parties and, theoretically, confirmation could be conducted even on such items as pay cheques. Auditors do, however, limit their use of confirmation to major transactions and balances that external parties can provide information about. A selection of confirmation applications includes

- banks—account balances
- customers—receivables balances
- borrowers—note terms and balances
- agents—inventory or consignment or in warehouse
- lenders—note terms and balances
- policyholders—life insurance contracts
- vendors—accounts payable balances
- registrar—number of shares of stock outstanding
- legal counsel—litigation in progress
- trustees—securities held, terms of agreements
- lessors—lease terms

The important general points about confirmations are as follows:

- Confirmation letters should be printed on the auditee's letterhead, or a facsimile, and signed by a auditee officer.
- Auditors should be very careful that the recipient's address is reliable and not altered by auditee personnel so that it misdirects the confirmation.

- The request should seek information the recipient can supply, such as the amount of a balance or the amounts of specified invoices or notes.
- Confirmations should be controlled by the audit firm, not given to auditee personnel for mailing.
- Responses should be returned directly to the audit firm, not to the auditee. Direct communication is required by auditing standards so there is no opportunity for auditee personnel to alter the confirmation responses.

Confirmations of receivables and payables may take several forms. Two of these are positive confirmation and negative confirmation. Positive confirmation requests a reply in all cases, whether the account balance is considered correct or incorrect. Negative confirmations request replies only if the account balance is considered incorrect. Auditors make second and third attempts to nonresponders of requests for positive conformation. If no response to a positive confirmation request appears, or if the response to either type of confirmation varies from the auditee's records, the auditors should investigate with other audit procedures, such as subsequent activity on the account or internal evidence supporting the recording of the receivable. The uses and limitations of confirmations, as well as issues arising from procedures for obtaining them, are explained more fully in Chapter 11.

Enquiry

Enquiry generally involves collecting oral evidence from independent parties, auditee officials, and employees. Auditors use enquiry procedures during the early office and plant tour and when conferences are conducted. Evidence gathered by formal and informal enquiry of auditee personnel generally cannot stand alone and must be corroborated by the findings of other procedures. Further enquiries could be made from other appropriate sources within the entity. Consistent responses provide an increased degree of assurance. Sometimes, however, conflicting evidence will come in the form of a negative statement by someone volunteering adverse information, such as an admission of theft, irregularity, or use of an accounting policy that is misleading. The auditor will have to use considerable judgment in reconciling the conflicting evidence or in deciding what additional evidence to gather. Skepticism and a critical attitude are, again, important aspects of professional judgment.

Enquiries, interviews, and other oral evidence are significant within the profession because management's explanations are an important part of obtaining an understanding of the business and the nature of specific transactions.[1] Management's explanations can be compared with those of other auditee employees, industry experts, and other sources of evidence. Oral evidence has always been viewed as critical evidence in public sector auditing. Auditors must obtain statements from management in the written representation letter acknowledging all important enquiries. (Representation letters are covered in detail in Chapter 15.)

The audit standards rely heavily on audit enquiry evidence, and the CICA research report entitled *Audit Enquiry* identifies ways of making it more reliable. For example, for the assessments required by the balanced scorecard as discussed in Exhibit 7–8, an auditor's primary source of information is enquiries to auditee management, other employees, and perhaps others outside the auditee organization, such as regulators, former employees, or suppliers. Assessing the reliability of the auditee's accounting estimates process frequently involves discussions with senior management. The CICA report provides an illustration involving enquiries of senior management in customer service, manufacturing, quality controls, marketing, and finance to assess the adequacy of an allowance for warranty claims.

Team discussions required by audit standards at the planning and risk assessment stages of the audit enhance integration and synthesis of the whole range of audit evidence obtained by audit team members.[2] Timely, well organized audit discussions facilitate sharing of enquiry evidence and other corroborating evidence to identify

---

[1] "A Matter of Evidence," *CA Magazine*, October 1994, pp. 57–58.
[2] CAS 300 (5150), 315 (5141).

inconsistencies that may indicate material misstatement due to error, and particularly to detect fraud.[3] A CICA research report makes this note about team meetings: "Debriefings following interviews and site visits should encourage perceptions and intuitive feelings to be brought out, and information challenged to help identify inconsistencies and gaps . . . and answer colleagues' questions about their findings and impressions . . . The objective, of course, is an integration of findings, capitalizing on the synergy that can come from focused group effort."[4] Junior auditors have the opportunity to learn from more experienced auditors how to apply judgment in evaluating evidence, and they can also benefit the team by bringing in their own objective viewpoints.

Inspection

Inspection consists of looking at records and documents or at assets with physical substance. The procedures are of varying degrees of thoroughness: examining, perusing, reading, reviewing, scanning, scrutinizing, and vouching. Physically inspecting tangible assets provides reliable evidence of existence and may give some evidence of condition, and hence valuation, but it does not provide reliable evidence of ownership. Physical inspection of formal documents with intrinsic value, such as securities certificates, also provides reliable evidence about existence. Records and documents that don't have an intrinsic market value, such as invoices or purchase orders, have varying degrees of reliability for different assertions, depending on their source. Much auditing work involves examining authoritative documents prepared by independent parties and by the auditee. These documents can provide at least some evidence regarding all the assertions.

Documents Prepared by Independent External Parties
A great deal of documentary evidence is external-internal; that is, convincing documentation prepared or validated by other parties and sent to the auditee. The signatures, seals, engravings, and other distinctive aspects of formal authoritative documents make them difficult to alter and, therefore, more reliable than ordinary documents prepared by outsiders. Some examples of both types of documents are listed below:

Formal Authoritative Documents	**Ordinary Documents**
1. Bank statements	1. Suppliers' invoices
2. Cancelled cheques	2. Customers' purchase orders
3. Insurance policies	3. Loan applications
4. Notes receivable	4. Notes receivable (on standard bank forms)
5. Securities certificates	5. Insurance policy applications
6. Indenture agreements	6. Simple contracts
7. Elaborate contracts	7. Correspondence
8. Title papers (e.g., autos)	

Documents Prepared and Processed within the Entity Under Audit
Documentation of this type is internal evidence. Some of these documents may be quite informal and not very authoritative or reliable. Generally, the reliability of these documents depends on the quality of internal control they were produced and processed under. Some of the most common of these documents are as follows:

1. Sales invoice copies

2. Sales summary reports

3. Cost distribution reports

4. Loan approval memos

5. Budgets and performance reports

6. Documentation of transactions with subsidiary or affiliated companies

---

[3] CAS 240 (5135).
[4] CICA, *Audit Enquiry* (CICA, March 2000), p. 24.

7. Shipping documents
8. Receiving reports
9. Requisition slips
10. Purchase orders
11. Credit memoranda
12. Transaction logs
13. Batch control logs

A Particular Inspection Procedure: Vouching—Examination of Documents

In vouching, an auditor selects an item of financial information from an account (e.g., the posting of a sales invoice in a customer's master file) and goes backward through the accounting and control system to find the source documentation supporting that item. For the sales invoice, the auditor finds the journal entry or data input list, sales summary, sales invoice copy and shipping documents, and, finally, customer purchase order. Vouching helps auditors decide if all recorded data are adequately supported (the existence/occurrence assertion), but it does not provide evidence that all events were recorded. This latter problem is covered by tracing.

A Particular Inspection Procedure: Tracing—Examination of Documents

Tracing takes the opposite direction to vouching. In tracing, the auditor selects samples of basic source documents and goes forward through the accounting and control system (whether computer or manual) to find the final record of the accounting transactions. For example, samples of payroll payments are traced to cost and expense accounts, sales invoices to the sales accounts, cash receipts to the accounts receivable subsidiary accounts, and cash disbursements to the accounts payable subsidiary accounts. Using tracing, an auditor can decide whether all events were recorded (the completeness assertion) and complement the evidence obtained by vouching. However, you must be alert to events that may not have been captured in the source documents and not entered into the accounting system.

A Particular Inspection Procedure: Scanning

Scanning makes use of auditors' alertness to unusual items and events in auditee documentation. A typical scanning directive in an audit program is "Scan the expense accounts for credit entries; vouch any to source documents."

Scanning is looking for anything unusual. The procedure usually does not produce direct evidence itself, but it can raise questions for which other evidence must be obtained. Scanning can be accomplished on computer records, online or printed out, using computer audit software. Typical items discovered by the scanning effort include debits in revenue accounts, credits in expense accounts, unusually large accounts receivable write-offs, unusually large pay cheques, unusually small sales volume in the month following the year-end, and large cash deposits just prior to year-end. Scanning can give some evidence of existence of assets and completeness of accounting records, including proper cutoff of material transactions.

Scanning is valuable when sampling methods are applied in audit decisions. When a sample is the basis for selecting items for audit, there is always the risk of choosing a sample that does not reflect the entire population of items, resulting in a decision error. Auditors subjectively reduce this detection risk by scanning items not selected in the sample.

Analysis

Auditors obtain evidence about financial statement accounts by methods of study and comparison called **analysis**. Auditing standards provide guidance on using analysis at the risk assessment and overall conclusion stages of the audit, and also for when auditors use analysis as an evidence-gathering procedure during the audit. Analysis is the "other" category in the list of six auditing techniques, and includes "everything else an auditor can think to do" that does not meet the definitions of recalculation/reperformance, observation, confirmation, structured enquiry, or inspection. Analytical procedures range from simple comparisons to complex mathematical estimation models. They can be used to obtain evidence on any of the management assertions, but they are most useful for assertions of completeness, valuation, and presentation.[5]

Analysis consists of

(a) identifying the components of a financial statement item so the characteristics of these can be considered in designing the nature, timing, and extent of other audit procedures; and

(b) performing analytical procedures, which are techniques by which the auditor

   (i) studies and uses meaningful relationships among elements of financial and nonfinancial information to form expectations about what amounts recorded in the accounts should be;

   (ii) compares expected with recorded amounts to identify fluctuations and relationships that are not consistent with other relevant information or that deviate significantly from expected amounts; and

   (iii) uses the results of this comparison to help determine what, if any, other audit procedures are needed for obtaining sufficient appropriate audit evidence that the recorded amounts are not materially misstated.[6]

The difference between part (a) above and scanning is that analysis relates to a higher level of aggregation—a comparison of financial statement components—whereas scanning relates to the detailed records about a particular component.

Analytical procedures can be classified into the five general types discussed in Chapter 6. When analysis is used to provide substantive evidence, auditors need to be careful to use independent, reliable information for comparison purposes. Thus, the sources of information used in analytical procedures need to be assessed for independence and objectivity. Quantitative information must be verified by the auditor if a high level of reliance is placed on the evidence provided by analysis. Examples of the types of independent information sources, and how their reliability can be verified, are as follows:

Information Source	Evidence of Reliability of Information Source
Financial account information for comparable prior period(s)	Information agrees with audited financial statements, or information in prior year audit working papers (e.g., monthly results).
Company budgets and forecasts	Budgeting or forecasting process is reviewed by the auditor and found to be based on realistic assumptions and methods, and targets are achievable under normal business conditions. Budget and forecast information is produced by the company's information systems under internal controls monitored by senior management; auditor has assessed these controls to be strong. Budgets and forecasts are used by board of directors for decision making.
Financial relationships among accounts in the current period	Account balances used in analysis should be agreed/referenced to audit working papers in current year file where they are verified substantively.
Industry statistics	Sources should be well-known industry analysis services (e.g., Moody's, Standard and Poors) and reports used should be obtained directly by the auditors.
Nonfinancial information, such as physical production statistics	Nonfinancial information is prepared by the company's information systems under internal controls monitored by senior management; auditor has assessed these controls to be strong. The nonfinancial information is used by senior management and the Board for decision making.

---

[5] D. G. Smith, Analytical Review (CICA, 1983), Chapter 2.
[6] CAS 520 (5301).

Because analytical procedures are loosely defined, it is tempting for auditors, as well as professors and students, to consider the evidence produced to be "soft." Therefore, they may tend to concentrate more on recalculation, observation, confirmation, inspection of assets, and vouching of documents that are perceived to produce "hard" evidence. However, analytical procedures can be very effective because they integrate evidence from a variety of sources and often provide an independent way of gathering evidence about whether the financial statement assertions hold true. Some examples of using analytical procedures to detect misstatements are given in the following box.

FINDING MISSTATEMENTS WITH ANALYTICAL PROCEDURES

Auditors noticed large quantities of rolled steel in the company's inventory. Several 30,000-kilogram rolls were entered in the inventory list. The false entries were detected because the auditor knew the company's fork-lift trucks had a 10,000 kilogram lifting capacity.

———

Auditors compared the total quantity of vegetable oils the company claimed to have inventoried in its tanks to the storage capacity reported in national export statistics. The company's "quantity on hand" amounted to 90 percent of the national supply and greatly exceeded its own tank capacity.

———

Last year's working papers showed that the company employees had failed to accrue wages payable at the year-end date. A search for the current accrual entry showed it had been forgotten again.

———

Auditors programmed a complex regression model to estimate the electric utility company's total revenue. They used empirical relations of fuel consumption, meteorological reports of weather conditions, and population census data in the area. The regression model estimated revenue within close range of the reported revenue.

Auditing researchers studied a large number of audits where misstatements requiring financial statement adjustment were found.[7] They were interested primarily in describing the audit procedures used to detect the misstatements. Their definition of analytical procedures was broad and included data comparisons, predictions based on outside data, analyses of interrelationships among account balances, "reasonableness tests," "estimates," and cursory review of financial statements in the audit planning stage. They also had two procedure categories called expectations from prior years (which involve the carry-over of analytical and detail knowledge about continuing audit clients) and discussions with auditee personnel.

They found that auditors gave analytical procedures credit for discovery of 27.1 percent of all misstatements. They gave credit to "expectations" and "discussions" for another 18.5 percent. Altogether, the so-called soft procedures accounted for detection of 45.6 percent of the misstatements. All of these procedures are typically applied early in the audit, so we cannot infer whether other kinds of audit procedures would or would not have detected the same misstatements. The detection success of other procedures depends on the results of the early applied procedures because, as this study was designed, even a good physical

---

[7] R. E. Hylas and R. H. Ashton, "Audit Detection of Financial Statement Errors," *The Accounting Review*, October 1982, pp. 751–765.

observation procedure did not get credit for discovery of a misstatement that already had been discovered using analytical procedures.

Analytical procedures are a good value since they are usually less costly than more detailed, document-oriented procedures. Also, the "hard evidence" procedures have their own pitfalls. Auditors may not be competent to "see" things they are supposed to observe. Auditee personnel can manipulate confirmations. The following box illustrates problems that can arise in evaluating evidence obtained with "hard evidence" procedures. An audit program makes use of several different types of procedures, and analytical procedures deserve a prominent place.

POTHOLES IN THE AUDIT PROCEDURE ROAD

Recalculation:
An auditor calculated inventory valuations (quantities times price) thinking the measuring unit was gross (144 units each), but the auditee had actually recorded counts in dozens (12 units each), thus causing the inventory valuation to be 12 times the proper measure.

Inspection of Assets:
While inspecting the fertilizer tank assets in ranch country, the auditor was fooled when the manager was able to move the tanks to other locations and place new numbers on them. The auditor "inspected" the same tanks many times.

Confirmation:
The insurance company executive gave the auditor a false address for a marketable securities confirmation, intercepted the confirmation, and then returned it with no exceptions noted. The company falsified $20 million in assets.

Enquiry:
Seeking evidence of the collectibility of accounts receivable, the auditors "audited by conversation" and took the credit manager's word about the collection probabilities on the over-90-day past-due accounts. They sought no other evidence, and did not discover that reported "net realizable value" of accounts receivable was materially overstated.

Inspection by Examination of Documents:
The auditors did not notice that the bank statement had been crudely altered. (Can you find the alteration in the bank statement in Exhibit 17–3 in Chapter 17?)

Inspection by the Scanning Procedure:
The auditors extracted a computer list of all the bank's loans over $1,000. They neglected to perform a similar scan for loans with negative balances, a condition that should not occur. The bank had data processing problems that caused many loan balances to be negative, although the trial balance balanced!

REVIEW CHECKPOINTS

1 List six audit techniques used to gather evidence and the types of evidence related to them.

2 What are the strengths and limitations of recalculation-based audit evidence?

3 What are the strengths and limitations of observation-based audit evidence?

4 Why must the entire confirmation process be controlled by the audit firm?

5 What can auditors do to improve the effectiveness of confirmation requests?

6 Differentiate between authoritative and ordinary externally produced documents.

7 What is meant by each: vouching, tracing, and scanning?

8 What does analysis consist of?

9 What are three stages in an audit engagement when analysis is used?

10 What sources of information are useful for performing analysis?

11 If analysis is used to provide substantive audit evidence, what steps must be taken regarding the source information used in the analysis?

12 Discuss the effectiveness of analysis for discovering errors and irregularities.

. . . .

Effectiveness of Audit Procedures

Audits are supposed to provide reasonable assurance of detecting misstatements that are material to the financial statements. When misstatements exist, and auditors do a good job of detecting them, adjustments will be made to management's unaudited financial statements before an audit report is issued. How often does this happen? Audit firms do not often give auditing researchers access to their audit working papers, to protect auditee confidentiality and also to protect themselves from risk of litigation or loss of reputation. However, early audit research by Wright and Ashton does provide relevant insights into the nature and causes of misstatements and the role of audit procedures in detecting these.[8] The researchers obtained information on 186 audits performed by a large auditing firm and the reported frequency of audit adjustments is shown in Exhibit 8–2.

What kinds of misstatements did the auditors find? Wright and Ashton reported the data for 23 accounts. A selection of them is shown in Exhibit 8–3. The misstatements consisted of both understatements and overstatements. (Remember that these are not "good" and "bad" descriptions. Overstatement of assets and understatement of liabilities both cause shareholders' equity to be overstated.) Since they come from respondents in one public accounting firm, these data may not be generalized to all audits. In this case, however, problems within the current assets were a mix of overstatements and understatements; in the noncurrent assets the majority were understatements, while in the liabilities understatements were in the majority, and in the expense accounts most were understatements.

As you can see, discovery of misstatements in management's unaudited financial statements is not unusual. How do the auditors do it? What procedures do they find effective? Wright and Ashton also compiled data on seven "initial events" that identified misstatements in financial statements. They were called initial events instead of audit procedures because they were the first work that identified misstatements, and all of them did not correspond exactly with specific procedures auditors would list in an audit program. Exhibit 8–4 shows the initial events indicating misstatements.

EXHIBIT   8–2   FREQUENCY OF AUDIT ADJUSTMENTS (SAMPLES OF AUDITS FROM ONE AUDIT FIRM)

Number of Audit Adjustments*	Number of Audits	Percent of Audits
Zero or 1	22	12%
2–5	30	16
6–10	45	24
More than 10	89	48
Total	186	100%

*Total number of adjustments detected regardless of size or nature.

[8] Data for Exhibit 8–2 and the other related exhibits come from Wright, Arnold, and Robert H. Ashton, "Identifying Audit Adjustments with Attention-Directing Procedures," *The Accounting Review*, October 1989, pp. 710–728.

EXHIBIT 8–3 SUMMARY OF MISSTATEMENTS (SELECTED ACCOUNTS)

Account	Number of Misstatements	
	Overstatement	Understatement
Cash	6	10
Securities	21	17
Accounts receivable	48	22
Inventory	24	32
Property, plant	14	23
Other noncurrent	11	24
Accounts payable	21	25
Accrued liabilities	17	40
Other current liabilities	10	13
Long-term liabilities	12	24
Revenue	32	30
Cost of goods sold	38	45
Selling expense	11	16
Gen and admin. expense	39	52

Note: The effect of adjustments on income was that 43 percent of the adjustments reduced the reported income, while 28 percent increased the reported income. The other 29 percent of the adjustments were reclassifications that neither reduced nor increased income.

EXHIBIT 8–4 INITIAL EVENTS THAT IDENTIFIED ADJUSTMENTS

Initial Event	Number of Adjustments	Percent
Tests of details: examination of transaction amounts and descriptions, account balance details, workups to support account balances, data on various reconciliations	104	28.7%
*Expectations from the prior year	78	21.5
*Analytical procedures: comparison of current unaudited balances with balances of prior years, predictions of current balances based on exogenous data, analyses of interrelationships	56	15.5
*Auditee enquiry	48	13.3
Test of detail: checks for mathematical accuracy	35	9.7
General audit procedures	8	2.2

*These were the three "attention-directing procedures" that accounted for 50.3 percent of the identified adjustments.

The so-called "soft" information from expectations based on prior-year experience, analytical procedures, and auditee enquiry accounted for 50 percent of the discovered misstatements. Nevertheless, detail audit procedures also were effective. Wright and Ashton note that the "ordering effect" (the fact that the attention-directing procedures come first) biases the results against showing that detail procedures might have detected the misstatements if they had not already been detected. They note further that (1) few adjustments were initially signalled by confirmations or inventory observation and (2) simple methods of comparison and auditee enquiry detected many misstatements.

The research findings are consistent with the continuing emphasis in auditing standards on understanding the auditee's business, its environment, and its business risks by using analysis for risk assessment at the early stages of the audit.

REVIEW CHECKPOINTS

13 In auditors' experience, is there any pattern in finding overstatements and understatements in accounts?

14 List several types of audit work (initial events, audit procedures) and discuss their likely effectiveness for identifying financial statement misstatements.

BUSINESS INFORMATION SOURCES AND METHODS

· · · · · · · · · · · · · · · ·

LEARNING OBJECTIVE

2 Identify the procedures and sources of information auditors can use to obtain evidence for understanding an auditee's business and industry, assessing risk, and responding to assessed risk.

This section summarizes the application of audit procedures to obtain evidence in the four main stages of the audit process that were set out in Exhibit PII-1 (pages 168–169). The audit process begins by obtaining an understanding of the auditee and its risks. Then the auditor performs risk assessment procedures to identify the risk of material misstatement at the overall financial statement level and the assertion level. From this, the auditor determines what procedures are necessary to address the assessed risks and reduce the risk of material misstatement to an acceptable level. These further procedures may include tests of controls, if the auditor deems it necessary. The auditor always performs some substantive procedures so that there are reasonable conclusions to base the audit opinion on. Substantive procedures give direct evidence about the financial amounts reported in the financial statements, while risk assessment procedures and control tests only provide indirect evidence about dollar misstatements. Substantive procedures can be either tests of details or substantive analytical procedures. The box below matches up these stages of the audit with the main procedures used for evidence gathering.

Stage of the Audit Process	Audit Evidence Gathering Procedures
Understanding the auditee and its risks	Enquiries of auditee personnel, including study of prior-audit working paper information Enquries of external parties, including industry, and other research sources
Assessing the risk of material misstatement (inherent and control risks)	Enquiry of auditee personnel Observation, including operation of accounting information system and internal control
Tests of control	Enquiry of auditee personnel Observation of controls performed by auditee personnel Recalculation/Reperformance of controls
Dual purpose tests of controls and substantive details of transactions	Recalculation/Reperformance of controls and recording Inspection of documents and records
Substantive tests of details of transactions and account balances	Inspection of documents, records, and assets Observation, including scrutiny External confirmation Recalculation/Reperformance
Substantive analytical procedures	Analysis of relations to other financial and non-financial information

How do auditors obtain evidence? The following discussion of some information sources and methods auditors use to obtain evidence expands on audit procedures given above. These are examples of the wide variety of information sources auditors use to understand the auditee's business, industry, and environment in order to assess risks of material misstatement and respond to them with further auditing procedures.

Enquiry, including prior working papers

Enquiry and interviews with the company's management, directors, and audit committee brings auditors up to date on changes in the business and industry. Interviews with auditee personnel (which include observations about the cooperation and integrity of auditee managers) build personal working relationships and develop auditors' understanding of problem areas in the financial statements. In specialized industries, management may have experts on staff or consultants who are important sources of an understanding of the business and its risks.

Information gathered in prior audits, and documented in the working papers, can also provide relevant and reliable information as follows:

- The nature of the organization, its environment, and its internal control

- Significant changes that the entity or its operations may have undergone since the prior financial period, which help the auditor identify and assess new risks of material misstatement

- Misstatements discovered in past audits and the timeliness of their correction

To use prior-period information in the current year, the auditor has to determine its relevance. For example, changes in the control environment may cause information obtained in the prior year to be irrelevant, so the auditor needs to make enquiries and possibly perform other procedures, such as walk-throughs of relevant systems.

For first-time audits there is often no prior working paper information, so this can require more work than in a repeat engagement. If this is a company's first audit but not its first year of operation, additional work includes establishing a starting place with reliable opening account balances for the audit. Inventory, fixed assets, and intangible assets accounts affect the current-year income and cash flows statements. If this information cannot be obtained, the scope of the current-year audit would be limited, and the opening balances and all the income statement amounts affected by them would require an audit report qualification.[9]

Enquiry also brings a fuller understanding of the needs of the users of the auditee's financial statements than was obtained when assessing whether to accept the engagement. The information obtained from enquiries of management, when combined with analysis of management's draft financial statements, helps the auditor to assess what is significant to users.

Observation

At the same time that enquiries and interviews take place, the audit team can take a tour of the company's physical facilities to look for activities and things that should be reflected in the accounting records. For example, an auditor might notice a jumbled pile of materials and parts in the warehouse and make a mental note to check how these items are valued in the inventory account balance. The tour is the time for auditors to get personal knowledge by seeing company personnel doing their normal day-to-day tasks. Later, the auditors will meet these same people in more directed evidence-gathering circumstances.

Research databases

Most industries have specialized trade magazines and journals, which are valuable for acquiring and maintaining industry expertise. Specific information about public companies can be found in registration statements and annual report filings with the provincial securities commissions. The CICA, IFAC, and AICPA industry accounting and auditing guides explain the typical transactions and accounts used by various kinds of businesses and not-for-profit organizations.

General business magazines and newspapers often contribute insights about an industry, a company, and individual corporate officers. Many are available, including *Canadian Business*, *Report on Business Magazine*, *Business Week*, *Forbes*, *Harvard Business Review*, *Barron's*, *The Wall Street Journal*, and the business sections of newspapers such as *The Globe and Mail* and the *National Post*. Practising auditors typically read several of these regularly. A selection of other public information sources is shown in the following box.

---

[9] CAS 620 (5049).

> # SOURCES OF GENERAL BUSINESS AND INDUSTRY INFORMATION
>
> Statistics Canada (including economic forecasts)
> D & B Principal International Businesses
> Hoover's
> Standard & Poor's Register of Corporations, Directors, and Executives
> CICA Audit *Risk Alert*s
> Value Line Investment Survey
> Moody's Investors Services (moodys.com)
> *CFO Magazine*
> Analysts' reports
> D & B Key Business Ratios
> Audit-firm libraries, universities, dissertations on specialized industry topics
> Lexis-Nexis
> Auditee websites, trade associations, conferences

The Internet is a very important information source for auditors. An organization's website might have financial statements and other information. Using effective search engines like Google, industry information and comparisons can also be obtained, allowing the auditor to improve his knowledge of business and thus design more effective analytical procedures. For larger companies, analyst and credit rating coverage are invaluable sources of information. Many articles in the business press are based on changes in credit ratings or analyst recommendations concerning specific companies and industries. Brokerage firms' websites contain analysis of lists of companies. There are also investor websites, such as Motley Fool (www.fool.com), that can provide valuable clues of potential problems in an auditee's (or potential auditee's) business. Be aware, however, that Internet information may not always be reliable, and must be used with caution. A minimum knowledge of the auditee and its industry is necessary to properly interpret such information.

Internal Auditors

Audit efficiency can be realized by working in tandem with internal auditors. Independent auditors should understand a company's internal audit activities as they relate to the internal control system. Internal auditors can also assist by providing information for understanding the business and its systems and controls, and even by performing control or substantive testing under the supervision of the independent audit team.[10]

Auditor's Experts

Auditors are not expected to be experts in all areas that may contribute information to the financial statements. In some cases, as noted above, enquiries to management experts hired by the auditee can offer key evidence. However, the auditor's understanding of the business can signal a need for the audit firm to use its own experts on the audit. Experts are persons skilled in fields other than accounting and auditing, such as actuaries, appraisers, legal counsel, engineers, chemists, and geologists who are needed for obtaining the understanding and evidence necessary for a particular account or assertion. When external experts are engaged, they must have appropriate professional qualifications and good reputations. They are not part of the audit team, but still should be unrelated to the auditee, if possible, in order to provide objective evidence. Auditor's experts may be employees of the audit firm, in which case they are subject to all the firm and engagement quality control standards like any other audit team member. Auditors must obtain an understanding of the experts's

---

[10] CAS 500 (5300).

methods, assumptions, and source data and be able to evaluate whether the expert's work is adequate for the purposes of the audit, and whether the findings are reasonble.[11]

R E V I E W
CHECKPOINTS

15 What are some of the methods and sources of information the auditor can use to understand an auditee's business?

16 When does an auditor need to use the work of an expert? What additional requirements must the auditor meet to use an expert's work as evidence?

SUFFICIENT APPROPRIATE EVIDENCE IN AUDITING

LEARNING OBJECTIVE

3 Explain audit evidence in terms of its appropriateness and relative strength of persuasiveness.

After assessing the risk of material misstatement in the assertions in management's draft financial statements, auditors proceed to the task of planning specific procedures for gathering evidence related to these assertions. However, before studying these procedures, you need to understand some features of evidence in auditing.

Auditing standards require auditors to obtain sufficient appropriate evidence to be the basis for an opinion on financial statements.[12] The accounting records (journals, ledgers, accounting policy manuals, computer files, and the like) are evidence of the bookkeeping/accounting process but not sufficient appropriate supporting evidence for the financial statements. The auditor must find evidence corroborating these records through direct personal knowledge, examination of documents, and enquiry of company personnel. Evidence is gathered and analyzed in support of the decision on whether the financial statements are fairly presented and conform to GAAP.

Identifying audit evidence is a key critical thinking activity in exercising professional audit judgment. To form an opinion on the fair presentation of the financial statements, the auditor requires evidence to (a) judge rationally whether the financial statement assertions are true and (b) provide logical support for the opinion expressed in the audit report.

Appropriateness of Evidence

Appropriateness of evidence relates to the qualitative aspects of evidence. To be considered appropriate, evidence must be relevant and reliable. Relevant audit evidence assists the auditor in achieving the audit objectives. This means that it must relate to at least one of the financial statement assertions; otherwise it is not relevant to the auditor.

The box below lists general audit procedures and indicates the financial statement assertion that each procedure may provide relevant evidence about. Note that most evidence is not conclusive and corroborating evidence is often required to provide reasonable assurance, especially when the assessed risk of material misstatement is high. So the comparison below should be viewed as only a rough guide, subject to the specific considerations in each audit.

The reliability of audit evidence depends on its nature and source. The following hierarchy of evidential matter shows the relative reliability and, when combined with relevance, the overall persuasive power or appropriateness of different kinds of evidence. The hierarchy starts with the strongest form of evidence and proceeds to the weakest.

1. An auditor's direct, personal knowledge, obtained through physical observation and his or her own mathematical recalculations or reperformance, is generally considered the most reliable evidence.

2. Documentary evidence obtained directly from independent external sources (external evidence) is considered very reliable.

[11] CAS 300, 230.
[12] CAS 230 (5145).

GENERAL AUDIT PROCEDURES	FINANCIAL STATEMENT ASSERTIONS EVIDENCE MAY BE RELEVANT TO
Recalculation	Existence Valuation
External Confirmation	Existence Ownership/Rights and Obligations Valuation; partially, usually requires corroborating evidence Cutoff; partially, usually requires corroborating evidence
Enquiry	All assertions; partially, but responses typically yield more assertions, in turn subject to audit with corroborating evidence
Inspection of documents	Existence; vouching direction Completeness; tracing direction Valuation; partially Ownership/Rights and Obligations Presentation and Disclosure
Inspection of physical assets	Existence Valuation; partially, usually requires corroborating evidence Ownership; partially, usually requires corroborating evidence Presentation and Disclosure
Analysis; Scanning	All assertions; partially, but raises questions that may be relevant to all assertions, but may not produce actual "evidence"; when performed on recorded amounts, evidence may be relevant to Existence, Valuation, Ownership, and Presentation/Disclosure; when performed on source documents, evidence may be relevant to the completeness assertion
Analysis; Analytical Procedures on Financial Relationships	Existence; partially, usually requires corroborating evidence Completeness; partially, usually requires corroborating evidence Valuation; partially, usually requires corroborating evidence

3. Documentary evidence originating outside the auditee's data processing system but received and processed by the auditee (external-internal evidence) is generally considered reliable. However, the circumstances of internal control quality are important.

4. Internal evidence consisting of documents that are produced, circulated, and finally stored within the auditee's information system is generally considered low in reliability. However, internal evidence is used extensively if internal control is satisfactory. Sometimes internal evidence is the only kind available. It is also generally easy to obtain and, therefore, tends to be less costly than other evidence.

5. Analysis using specific data that the auditor has verified is considered fairly reliable. While broad analytical procedures of a general nature are not considered highly reliable as substantive evidence, they are often used for preliminary risk identification and attention directing early in an audit.

6. Spoken and written representations given by the auditee's officers, directors, owners, and employees are generally considered the least reliable evidence. Such representations should be corroborated with other types of evidence.

Exhibit 8–5 below illustrates this hierarchy.

EXHIBIT 8–5   HIERARCHY OF AUDIT EVIDENCE RELIABILITY

MOST RELIABLE
Physical inspection
Confirmation
External documentation
Recalculation, Reperformance

LESS RELIABLE
External-internal documentation
Internal documentation
  (with good internal controls)
Observation
Analytical procedures with specific
  data

LEAST RELIABLE
Internal documentation (if poor
  internal controls)
Inquiry
Broad analytical procedures

Auditors must be careful about the appropriateness of evidence and choose the audit procedure providing that which is the most reliable. If physical observation and mathematical calculation are not relevant to the account, impossible, or too costly, then auditors move down the hierarchy to the procedure that will give the best evidence available—best in the sense of most appropriate or persuasive under the circumstances. It should be the most reliable evidence that can be obtained in a cost-effective manner, relative to a particular audit objective.

There may be situations, however, where no highly reliable source of evidence is available, such as cash donations received by a charity or ecommerce sales transactions that leave no visible trail. In these cases there may be two or more less reliable pieces of evidence that together may support the assertion. If the pieces of evidence are consistent with each other and are from two independent sources, the evidence may be persuasive enough. For example, observe employee procedures and test controls of these, plus review summarized sales reports prepared for marketing purposes. Another example is given in the following box.

RELATED PARTIES—A PERFECT STORM IN AUDITING

The existence of related parties poses considerable auditing challenges and can increase risks of material misstatement of the financial statements due to error and fraud. This note deals with the audit planning and evidence issues created by related parties.

Because the related party may have control or significant influence over the entity's operating, investing, and financing policies, transactions with them might not always be conducted under normal market terms. For example, assets could be transferred from the entity to a related party, such as a shareholder, for either no consideration or for an amount considerably below the assets' fair value, perhaps with no business justification. Related party relationships might also limit an audit, as the relationships may be complex, the entity's information systems may not be designed to flag transactions with related parties (management may not even know about them!), and reliable audit evidence about the transactions may not exist.

The fact that the different financial reporting frameworks have different accounting standards for related party transactions makes things even more complex. For example, Canadian GAAP (*CICA* section 3840) sets out recommendations for both measurement and disclosure, while IFRS (IAS 24) only deals with disclosure of related party transactions. GAAS (CAS 550) requires auditors to understand the entity's related-party relationships and transactions well enough to be able to assess the risk of misstatement and to conclude whether the financial statements are fairly presented in accordance with the framework's requirements. For example, selling an asset to a controlling shareholder for far more than its fair value and then reporting the gain as a profit when it was intended as an equity contribution by the shareholder is not fair presentation. Not disclosing that an entity's ability to continue as a going concern is dependent on continuing financial support from a related party would also be misleading.

Finally, related parties can increase fraud risk as these relationships may present a greater opportunity for collusion, concealment, manipulation, or falsification of evidential records and documents by management.

How do auditors defend against this "perfect storm"? Maintaining professional skepticism throughout the audit is the auditor's strongest weapon in noticing the unusual transactions and relationships that have no apparent business purpose and may not be reflected appropriately in the financial statements. Another key tool is frequent discussion among audit team members where observations and management enquiry responses are compared so that inconsistencies needing follow-up are highlighted. Inconsistent stories can indicate that the entity's financial statements are more susceptible to material fraud or error because of its related-party relationships and transactions, and the auditor has to dig deeper to find them. The audit problem with related parties is that evidence obtained from them should not be considered highly reliable in terms of persuasiveness. The source of the evidence may be biased. Hence, auditors should obtain evidence of the purpose, nature, and extent of related-party transactions and their effect on financial statements. Evidence should extend beyond management enquiry, and corroborating evidence should be obtained to increase persuasiveness.

Sources: CAS 550; *CICA Handbook* section 3840 "Related party transactions"; IAS 24 "Related party disclosures."

Sufficiency of Evidence

Sufficiency considers how much appropriate evidence is enough. The auditing profession has no official standard, leaving the matter of sufficiency to auditors' professional judgment. Realistically, however, audit decisions must be based on enough evidence to stand the scrutiny of other auditors (supervisors and reviewers) and outsiders (such as critics, judges, or CPAB inspectors). The real test of sufficiency is whether your evidential base allows someone else to reach the same conclusions you reached. The fact that important evidence is difficult or costly to obtain is not an adequate reason for failing to obtain it. If an auditor has not been able to obtain sufficient appropriate audit evidence about a material financial statement assertion, CAS 330 (5143) states that the auditor should express a qualified opinion or a disclaimer of opinion, as was discussed in Chapter 3.

With these aspects of evidence in mind, you will be ready to study the general processes for designing specific procedures in the detailed audit plan, to be covered next.

REVIEW
CHECKPOINTS

17 What is the relationship between assertions and audit evidence?

18 What factors determine whether audit evidence is appropriate? What types of audit evidence are most reliable? least reliable?

19 How is an auditor's professional judgment applied in assessing the appropriateness of audit evidence?

20 How are external, external-internal, and internal documentary evidence generally defined?

21 What is the problem with evidence obtained from related parties?

22 Distinguish between the appropriateness of audit evidence and the sufficiency of audit evidence.

23 What action is required if an auditor cannot obtain sufficient appropriate audit evidence?

. . . .

Exhibit 8–6 shows the interrelationships among the auditing concepts discussed in this chapter and how these concepts underlie the auditor's decision about what audit evidence is required. The materiality considerations are shown along the left side of the exhibit, the audit risk model components are in the centre, and the characteristics of potential audit evidence are on the right side. Notice that the evidence decision must take into account practical limitations—not all evidence can be obtained at a reasonable cost or quickly enough to provide a timely audit report. Not all evidence has the same level of reliability. Trade-offs have to be made because of these limitations. The concepts of materiality and audit risk guide these trade-offs. This diagram shows the kind of complex analysis that is at the heart of professional judgment about the sufficiency and appropriateness of audit evidence.

EXHIBIT   8–6   AUDITOR JUDGMENTS ON SUFFICIENCY AND APPROPRIATENESS OF EVIDENCE

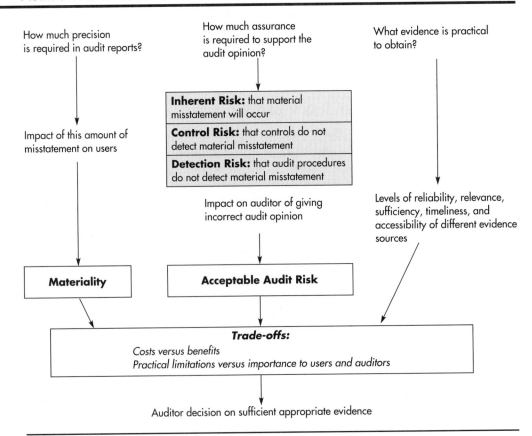

AUDIT PLAN AND DETAILED PROGRAMS

· · · · · · · · · · · · · · · ·

LEARNING OBJECTIVE

4 Describe the content and purpose of the audit plan as well as the specific audit programs and detailed procedures it contains.

As discussed throughout Part II of the text, audit planning is an on-going process. Planning is done at the start of the audit but continues throughout as new information results in revisions to the plan. Before, during, and after the field work period, the auditor responsible for an audit engagement constantly monitors events that may affect an auditee's business risk, the client relationship, or the engagement. The box below gives an example of why auditors must read the news and consider the impact of new developments on their audit engagements—significant changes in an auditee's business risk can occur any time!

MONEY LAUNDERERS SPREAD THEIR NET

It was reported that automated teller machines (ATMs) located in small retail shops have become a prime vehicle for money laundering by organized crime gangs in the suburban areas around a major city. The shop's revenue is a percentage of the service charge paid by anyone taking cash out of the ATM, with the balance of the service fee going to the bank that provides the ATM. Shop employees are responsible for refilling the machine with cash taken in legitimately from customer sales. It was suspected that some employees would accept "dirty cash" (i.e., proceeds of crime) from criminals and use that to refill the ATMs instead of the clean cash from the cash register, which was given to the criminals. The dishonest employees receive a portion of the cash exchanged as their cut of the deal.

Now put yourself in the shoes of the auditor of a company that owns a chain of small retailers operating ATMs in this area. How does this development affect the business risk of this auditee? The auditor needs to determine if management has identified this risk and responded appropriately by ensuring employees are adequately screened before hiring and are trained to be aware of the money-laundering laws and criminal penalties. Are there controls over employee activities, and is management monitoring them to ensure they are working? Even if the auditor discovers this situation six months before the audit is set to start, the information should be documented in the planning file. The auditor also should contact the auditee management as soon as possible to discuss the impact of this development on their business risk and what actions they are taking. Management may be too busy running the day to day operations to monitor business risks continuously!

THE PLANNING DOCUMENT

· · · · · · · · · · · · · · · ·

All the planning activities are recorded and summarized in a planning document, sometimes referred to as the **planning memorandum**. While audit firms can use a variety of planning and documentation practices, specific planning steps and documents are outlined in the auditing standards and are likely to be commonly used, so they are discussed here.[13]

Auditors may prepare a memorandum, called the overall audit strategy, summarizing the preliminary planning procedures and key decisions, as was introduced in Chapter 6. This document contains the results of analytical review, the decision on materiality levels, and the risk assessment. It gives specific attention to the effect of these on the nature, extent, and timing of audit resources needed to perform the work. The auditor's understanding of the business helps to assess inherent risk, and understanding the information systems and controls helps to assess control risk. These also aid in identifying what kinds of evidence are available and at what cost, the third component of the evidence decision

[13] CAS 300.

outlined above in Exhibit 8–6. The next planning decision to be documented is whether to use a combined approach or a substantive approach. As was discussed in Chapter 6, a combined audit approach involves testing effective controls to reduce risk of material misstatement, which can reduce the extent of substantive testing required. A substantive approach will assess controls for the purpose of the overall risk assessment, but will not test the controls as a component of the audit evidence.

The risk assessment and audit approach decisions guide the development of the **audit plan**, which summarizes the details of how the work is to be done. An audit plan lists specific detailed audit programs. The practical considerations and the trade-offs between the risk components and materiality guide decisions on what and how much evidence to gather through control tests, analytical procedures, and other tests of balances—the evidence gathering techniques discussed above. These evidence decisions are the basis of the audit programs that make up the audit plan. These procedures are designed to result in sufficient appropriate evidence that addresses the audit objectives set out in the program. The programs usually look like a to-do list for audit staff, some of whom may have little prior audit experience. Also included in the planning document are the audit team's understanding of the auditee's business and risks that were relevant in developing the decisions.

Auditors use two types of audit programs: the **internal control program** and the **balance audit program**. The internal control program lists the specific procedures for gaining understanding of the auditee's business transaction processing systems and controls, as well as for assessing the inherent risks and the control risks. The risks are assessed for the assertions in financial account balances and transaction streams that result from the information system processes. The balance audit program lists the substantive procedures for gathering direct evidence on the assertions (i.e., existence, completeness, valuation, ownership, presentation) about dollar amounts in the account balances and related disclosures.

These audit programs combine all the considerations of audit planning discussed up to this point, including:

- understanding the auditee's business, its environment and risks, its information systems, and its internal control
- assertions and objectives contained in the auditee's financial statements
- preliminary analytical procedures for identifying specific risk areas in the unaudited financial statements
- preliminary materiality decisions
- preliminary risk assessments
- persuasive strengths of evidence
- audit procedures for obtaining evidence: control testing, substantive detail testing, and substantive analytical procedures

In actual field situations these audit programs are very lengthy. Program documents may include separate listings of procedures and questionnaires on the company's internal control environment, management controls, and control procedures. To put the sequence of topics you have read about up until now into perspective, the following box summarizes elements of audit programs. The technical parts of internal control risk assessment programs are explained more fully in Chapter 9.

UNDERSTAND THE BUSINESS RISK, INHERENT RISK, CONTROL RISK

- Communicate with predecessor auditors.
- Study prior-year audit working papers, professional audit and accounting guides, and industry publications concerning the company and its industry.

- Interview management with regard to business and accounting policies.
- Evaluate the competence and independence of the company's internal auditors.
- Determine the need for specialists on the engagement.
- Determine the extent of significant computer applications in the company's accounting system.
- Obtain the financial statements and make decisions about the planning materiality appropriate in the circumstances.
- Perform preliminary analytical procedures to identify risk areas in the financial statement accounts.
- Assess the inherent risk in general and also with respect to particular accounts.

- Obtain an understanding of the company's internal control through interviews, observations, and tests of controls (see Chapter 9).
- Perform detailed test of control procedures, if necessary (see Chapters 9 and 10).
- Assess the control risk (see Chapters 9 and 10).
- Use the control risk assessment to design the nature, timing, and extent of substantive audit procedures (see Chapters 9 and 10).

The balance audit program consists of several programs, each applicable to a particular account. Auditors first subdivide the financial statements into accounting processes or cycles (as explained in Chapter 6), then turn attention to the accounts in each. The procedures in these audit programs are designed to obtain evidence about the existence, completeness, valuation, ownership, and presentation assertions implicit in each account title and balance. The following box contains a partial program in the revenue process, with brief specifications of procedures for auditing accounts receivable. The procedures contain many of the elements of the general techniques that were explained in the previous section (e.g., confirmation, recalculation, enquiry, inspection, and the assertions toward which they are directed). Audit programs are presented in more detail in Chapters 10 to 14.

BALANCE AUDIT PROGRAM IN REVENUE, RECEIVABLES, RECEIPTS PROCESS

ACCOUNTS RECEIVABLE

- Prepare and send confirmations on a sample of customers' accounts receivable. Analyze the returns.
- Obtain an aged trial balance of the receivables. Calculate and analyze the age status of the accounts and the allowance for uncollectible accounts.
- Interview the credit manager concerning the past-due accounts. Obtain credit reports and financial statements for independent analysis of overdue accounts.
- Vouch receivables balances to cash payments received after the confirmation date.
- Read loan agreements and make note of any pledge of receivables, sales with recourse or other restrictions, or contingencies related to the receivables.
- Read sales contracts for evidence of customers' rights of return or price allowance terms.
- Obtain written representations from the auditee concerning pledges for collateral, related party receivables, collectibility, and other matters related to accounts receivable.

24 What information is summarized in the audit planning document or memorandum? How does it relate to the preparation of audit programs?

25 What are the two kinds of audit programs and what is the purpose of each?

26 What is meant by the terms nature, timing, and extent of audit procedures?

AUDIT WORKING PAPERS

LEARNING OBJECTIVE

5 Explain the purpose of audit documentation and review an audit working paper for proper form and content.

An audit is not complete without proper working paper documentation. The planning document described above is a key component of the audit documentation, and additional documentation is required for the rest of the audit work. Documentation provides a record of the auditor's work for the purpose of file reviews, practice and regulatory inspections, or in some cases to defend against a law suit. Working papers are the auditors' record of compliance with generally accepted auditing standards. They should contain support for decisions on procedures deemed necessary and all other important decisions made during the audit.[14] Even though the auditor is the legal owner of the working papers, professional ethics requires that there is auditee consent before tranferring them because of the confidential information in them. Audit files must be retained for several years as required by professional accounting association rules and practice inspection procedures. Last year's file is a rich resource for the current year's engagement team on continuing audits. It provides valuable insights into key entity characteristics, likely risk areas, findings, and evidence relevant to the current year's financial statements, such as the audited opening balances.

The following box outlines the impact that destroying audit working papers has on the value of the audit and the reputation of the audit firm. The Andersen document shredding scandal was a key driver for development of more rigorous auditing standards. It shows why documentation is considered important by audit firms and the auditing standard setters.

SHREDDED AUDIT PAPERS....SHREDDED AUDITOR REPUTATION

In 2001, Andersen was the fifth largest auditing firm in the world, employing 85,000 people in 84 countries, and reporting revenues of U.S. $9.3 billion. In a crippling blow, in March 2002, the U.S. Justice Department indicted Andersen on criminal charges of obstruction of justice. The indictment alleged that the audit firm had shredded tons of documents sought by investigators who were probing financial problems at Andersen's client, the energy giant Enron Corp. These criminal charges were the first to come out in the Enron case, and they struck a blow that eventually led to the demise of the nearly 90-year-old auditing firm that had long enjoyed a solid reputation for integrity. The events that led to the destruction of Andersen are related below.

Signs of trouble at Enron first arose in the summer of 2001, when Enron vice-president Sherron Watkins warned chairman Kenneth Lay that the company might be overcome by a wave of accounting scandals unless it took quick action to correct a series of questionable transactions that its auditors, Andersen, had helped it to devise. Despite this warning, Enron's stock price collapsed amid questions about its accounting practices, and in December 2001 it declared bankruptcy. Thousands of employees lost their jobs, and current as well as former employees lost their

---

[14] CAS 230 (5145).

retirement savings as they had been encouraged to invest them in Enron shares. As rumours began to circulate that Andersen should not have given a clean audit opinion on Enron's financial statements, its reputation fell under suspicion and lawsuits against it began to pour in. Andersen's reputation declined further in January 2002, when it announced publicly that it had shredded documents related to Enron's audit.

The indictment against Andersen, issued by a federal grand jury in Houston, alleged a widespread effort to destroy audit documentation related to questionable transactions at Enron. It alleged that shortly after the SEC informed Andersen, on October 19, that it was launching a preliminary investigation of whether Enron had filed misleading financial reports, document shredding on a massive scale began. "The shredder at the Andersen office at the Enron building was used virtually constantly and, to handle the overload, dozens of large trunks filled with Enron documents were sent to Andersen's main Houston office to be shredded," the indictment alleged. Andersen undertook "an unparalleled initiative . . . to shred physical documentation and delete computer files. . . . Tons of paper relating to the Enron audit were promptly shredded as part of the orchestrated document destruction." As the indictment proceeded, prosecutors piled more pressure on Andersen by revealing damaging emails between auditors in the middle of the mass destruction of Enron documents, including one that read, "Argh, send more shredding bags."

As stories of the document shredding covered the front pages of newspapers, Andersen began to lose some of its biggest clients, casting doubt on whether the firm would be able to survive the crisis. The jury trial began on May 2, 2002, and on June 15, 2002, a guilty verdict was handed down. Andersen was found guilty of obstruction of justice and was barred from auditing SEC-registered companies after August 31, 2002. By then a large number of Andersen's 2,300 public-company clients had already replaced Andersen. As a result of these events, Andersen's ability to continue as an auditing firm was effectively destroyed, and it ceased operations on August 31, 2002.

Accounting researchers found that, in the days following Andersen's January 2002 announcement that it shredded Enron audit documents, the share prices of Andersen's other clients experienced a significant drop, indicating that investors downgraded the quality of the audits performed by Andersen. These findings show the importance of the auditor's reputation to investors. If investors believe the audit is of low quality, they have less assurance that the company's financial statements reflect its real business performance and financial position. They assess a higher likelihood that its income and net book value are overstated and that the auditor has failed to report this.

On May 31, 2005, the Supreme Court overturned the 2002 criminal conviction of Andersen on the grounds that the Houston jury was given overly broad instructions by the federal judge who presided at the trial that found it guilty of obstruction of justice. But, by then, Andersen, its reputation, and its business were long gone.

When asked whether the destruction of a firm with 85,000 employees and thousands of commercial clients was an appropriate price for Andersen to pay, one of the prosecuting attorneys suggested that Andersen had only itself to blame. "It should not come as a surprise that serious charges have serious consequences," the deputy attorney general said.

Sources: S. English, "Auditor overtime 'used for shredding'," *Daily Telegraph*, May 22, 2002, p. 32, © Telegraph Group Limited; C. Mondics and S. M. Hopkins, "Andersen Indicted in Enron Shredding," *The Record*, March 15, 2002, p. a01, © 2002 North Jersey Media Group Inc.. All rights reserved; K. Bewley, J. Chung, and S. McCracken, "An Examination of Auditor Choice Using Evidence from Andersen's Demise," *International Journal of Auditing*, (2008) 12, pp. 89–110; P. Chaney and K. Philipich, "Shredded Reputation: The Cost of Audit Failure," *Journal of Accounting Research*, 40 (4), pp. 1221–1245, © 2002, Blackwell Publishing.

Working papers can be classified into three categories: (1) permanent file papers, (2) audit administrative papers, and (3) audit evidence papers. The last two categories are often called the **current file** because they relate to the audit of one year.

Permanent File Papers

The **permanent file** contains information of continuing interest over many years' audits of the same auditee. This file can be used year after year, whereas each year's current audit evidence papers are filed away after they have served their purpose. Documents of permanent interest and applicability include (1) copies or excerpts of the corporate charter and bylaws or partnership agreements; (2) copies or excerpts of continuing contracts, such as leases, bond indentures, royalty agreements, management bonus contracts, etc.; (3) a history of the company, its products, and its markets; (4) excerpts of minutes of shareholders' and directors' meetings on matters of lasting interest; and (5) continuing schedules of accounts whose balances are carried forward for several years, such as share capital, retained earnings, partnership capital, and the like. Copies of prior years' financial statements and audit reports may also be included. The permanent file is a ready source of information for new auditors on the engagement who must familiarize themselves with the auditee.

Audit Administrative Papers

Administrative papers contain the documentation of the early planning phases of the audit. They usually include the engagement letter, staff assignment notes, conclusions related to understanding the auditee's business, results of preliminary analytical procedures, initial assessments of audit risks, and initial assessments of audit materiality. Many accounting firms follow the practice of summarizing these data in an engagement planning memorandum.

Audit planning and administration also includes work on the preliminary assessment of control risk and preparation of a written audit program. The following items are usually among the administrative working papers in each year's current file:

1. Engagement letter
2. Staff assignments
3. Auditee organization chart
4. Memoranda of conferences with management, board of directors, audit committee
5. Overall audit strategy
   (a) preliminary analytical review notes
   (b) initial risk assessment notes
   (c) initial materiality assessment notes
   (d) audit engagement time budget
6. Internal control questionnaire and control analyses
   (a) management controls questionnaire
   (b) IT controls questionnaire
   (c) internal control system flowcharts
7. Audit plan and specific programs
8. Working trial balance of general ledger accounts
9. Working paper record of preliminary adjusting and reclassifying entries
10. Review notes and unfinished procedures (all cleared by the end of the field work)

Audit Evidence Papers

The current-year audit evidence working papers are typically organized in sections: major accounting processes or cycles and balance sheet accounts. Each section contains a lead sheet that shows the dollar amounts reported in the financial statements, summary of the audit objectives in relation the account's assertions, procedures performed, evidence obtained, and conclusions reached for that section overall. The lead sheet is like an index, or table of contents, that provides references to all the audit working paper pages relating to the audit work on that section (see Exhibit 8–7 following). These papers communicate the quality of the audit, so they must be clear, concise, complete, neat, well indexed, and informative. Each separate working paper (or multiple pages that go together) must be complete in the sense that it can be removed from the working paper file and considered on its own, with proper cross-reference available to show how the paper fits in with the others. Working papers may be hard copy (handwritten, typed, printed from computer files) or stored electronically. Exhibit 8–8 provides an example working paper: a printout of bank reconciliation from the auditee's accounting system supporting the cash account amount recorded in the company's trial balance. The auditor

EXHIBIT 8–7   CURRENT WORKING PAPER FILE

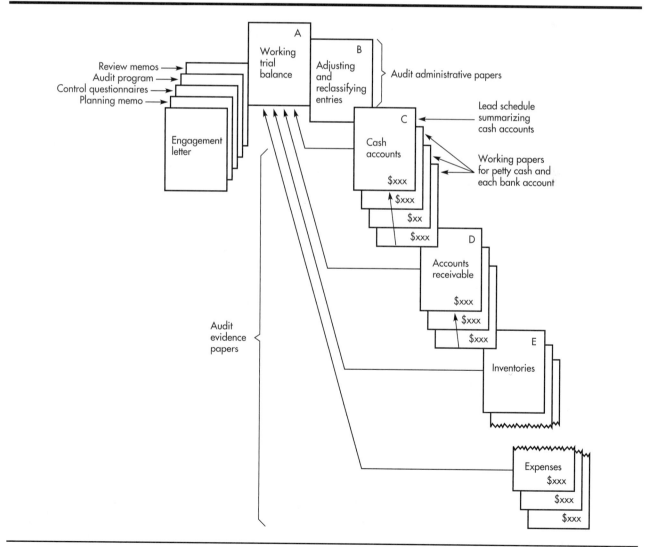

EXHIBIT 8-8   ILLUSTRATIVE WORKING PAPER

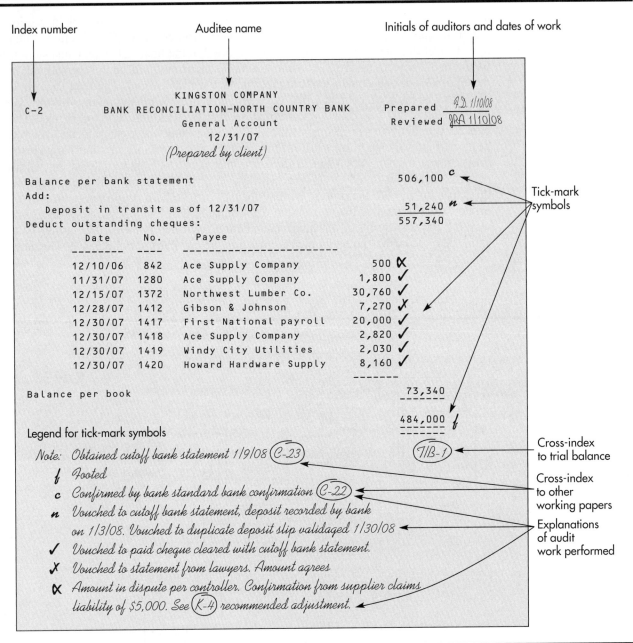

Index number   Auditee name   Initials of auditors and dates of work

KINGSTON COMPANY
C-2   BANK RECONCILIATION-NORTH COUNTRY BANK   Prepared   *J.D. 1/10/08*
General Account   Reviewed   *JRA 1/10/08*
12/31/07
(Prepared by client)

Balance per bank statement   506,100 *c*   Tick-mark
Add: symbols
  Deposit in transit as of 12/31/07   51,240 *n*
Deduct outstanding cheques: 557,340
        Date   No.   Payee
      --------   ----   --------------------
      12/10/06   842   Ace Supply Company   500 *X*
      11/31/07   1280   Ace Supply Company   1,800 ✓
      12/15/07   1372   Northwest Lumber Co. 30,760 ✓
      12/28/07   1412   Gibson & Johnson   7,270 *X*
      12/30/07   1417   First National payroll 20,000 ✓
      12/30/07   1418   Ace Supply Company   2,820 ✓
      12/30/07   1419   Windy City Utilities   2,030 ✓
      12/30/07   1420   Howard Hardware Supply 8,160 ✓

Balance per book   73,340

                                              484,000 *f*

Legend for tick-mark symbols   Cross-index
*Note: Obtained cutoff bank statement 1/9/08 (C-23)   to trial balance (TB-1)
  f   Footed
  c   Confirmed by bank standard bank confirmation (C-22)   Cross-index
  n   Vouched to cutoff bank statement, deposit recorded by bank to other
       on 1/3/08. Vouched to duplicate deposit slip validaged 1/30/08 working papers
  ✓   Vouched to paid cheque cleared with cutoff bank statement. Explanations
  X   Vouched to statement from lawyers. Amount agrees   of audit
  X   Amount in dispute per controller. Confirmation from supplier claims work performed
       liability of $5,000. See (K-4) recommended adjustment.*

has used the auditee-prepared report to document audit work results by making hand-written notes on the paper.

The current audit evidence papers must show the auditors' decision problems and conclusions. The papers must record the management assertions that were audited (book values or qualitative disclosures), the evidence gathered about them, and the final decisions. Auditing standards recommend that the working papers show (1) evidence that the work was adequately planned and supervised, (2) a description of audit evidence obtained, (3) evidence of the evaluation and disposition of misstatements, and (4) copies of letters or notes concerning audit matters reported to the auditee. Common sense also dictates that the working papers show that the financial statements conform to GAAP and that the disclosures are adequate. The working papers also should explain how exceptions and unusual accounting questions were resolved or treated. (Notice in

Exhibit 8–8 the auditor's confirmation of the disputed account payable liability.) Taken altogether, these features should demonstrate that all the auditing standards were observed.

Working Paper Arrangement and Indexing

Auditing organizations use different methods of arranging and indexing working papers. Usually, the papers are grouped behind the trial balance, ordered according to balance sheet and income statement captions. The current assets usually appear first, followed by fixed assets, other assets, liabilities, equities, revenue, and expense accounts. A typical arrangement is shown in Exhibit 8–7.

The quality of the finished product depends on the working papers following specific preparation formats. The following points are also shown in the illustrative working paper in Exhibit 8–8.

- Indexing. Each paper is given an index number, like a book page number, so it can be found, removed, and replaced without loss. An index number might consist of a section letter (e.g., C) and a page number within that section (e.g., C-2). Each section could be given to a different audit team without affecting other sections.
- Cross-indexing. Numbers or memoranda related to other papers carry the index of other paper(s) so that the connections can be followed.
- Heading. Each paper is titled with the name of the company, the period under audit date, and a descriptive title of the contents of the working paper. If the paper was created by auditee personnel (rather than the auditor) this is noted in the title.
- Signatures and initials. The auditor who performs the work and the supervisor who reviews it must sign the papers so that personnel can be identified.
- Dates of audit work. The dates of performance and review are recorded on the working papers so that reviewers can tell when the work was performed.
- Tick marks and explanations. Tick marks are the auditor's shorthand for indicating the work performed. They must always be accompanied by a full explanation of the auditing work.

Audit Working Paper Software

Specialized working paper software is common in public practice. Electronic working papers boost productivity by automating many tasks, such as carrying adjustments over to related working paper documents and the financial statements. Good working paper software integrates the audit information and makes it easy to access, review, and change the format, content, or order of the files. Because most organizations' data are already in electronic form, it is logical to integrate this data with electronic working paper files. In addition, the volume of paper required for file documentation is reduced or eliminated, and with laptop computers there is better communication and information sharing among team members, as well as continuous monitoring and review of the work, even from a distance, by a supervisor. The entire audit process can make use of the software's efficiencies, such as standard templates and electronic questionnaires.

Audit working paper software can also facilitate analysis. Links can be established to other databases or even websites so that data or information can be cross-referenced or transferred to the working papers. Thus, audit staff work and various other sources of information can be integrated to support the auditor's opinion.

There are, however, costs associated with computer-generated working papers, including costs of hardware, software, training, document scanning, and continual upgrades with advances in technology. Also, some copies of original source documents such as important contracts may still need to be kept in hard copy form. An example of a working paper software program used in public practice is CaseWare.

. . . .

R E V I E W
CHECKPOINTS

27 Why do audit firms and auditing standards require auditors to prepare and retain specific documentation of their audit work?

28 What information would you expect to find in a permanent audit file and how would auditors use this information?

29 What audit administration working papers are included in the current audit evidence working paper files?

30 What is considered the most important content of the current audit working papers?

31 What is the purpose of indexing and cross-referencing audit working papers?

32 What techniques can auditors use to improve the quality of working paper documentation?

33 How can software be used to prepare audit working papers?

. . . .

Audit documentation's key role is to help in revising the audit plan as the work proceeds, to allow for quality control reviews to be done effectively, and to help with planning the subsequent year's audit work. As the discussion in Part II up to now has shown, audit planning is a process of learning, feedback, and continuous improvement, as is depicted in Exhibit 8–9 below.

EXHIBIT   8–9   AUDIT PLANNING—A PROCESS OF CONTINUOUS IMPROVEMENT

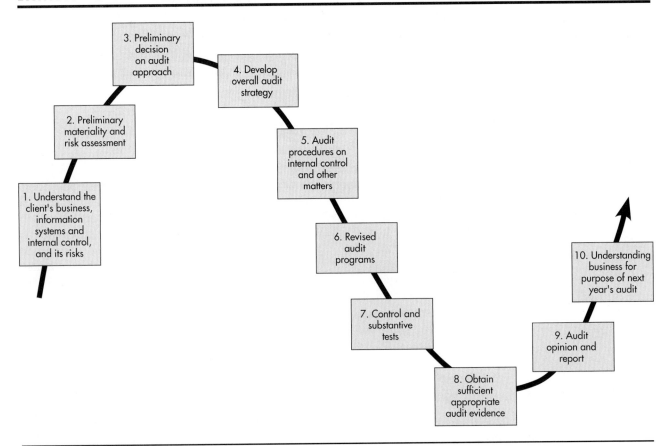

LEARNING OBJECTIVE

6 Apply and integrate the chapter topics to analyze a practical auditing situation/case/scenario.

APPLICATION CASE AND ANALYSIS
Review of an Audit Plan

Discussion Case

Towards the end of his first year in public accounting, Jack is assigned to the audit team for Foyer Properties Inc. (Foyer). Foyer's main activity is development and leasing of commercial real estate properties, such as shopping malls and office towers. In the past few years, Foyer has developed a niche residential property business: building university residences and nursing homes and leasing them under a head lease with a public sector organization, such as a university or municipal government. The public sector organization handles collection from the individual residents. Foyer is a private company, with the chairman holding 60 percent of the shares and the president and chief operating officer holding the remaining 40 percent.

Foyer has been a long-time audit for Jack's firm. The previous audit manager, Hank, just left the firm after ten years to be CFO at a local mining company and Hilda has taken over from him for the 20X8 audit. Hank had been on the Foyer audit since joining the firm and had managed the audit for the past six years. Looking over the previous audit files, Hilda noted that Hank had not changed the audit approach for years: a substantive approach focusing primarily on verifying existence and valuation of all the major real estate properties and all large transactions, such as the major purchase or sale of a property. Since accounts receivable from the universities and governments were always received by the time the audit was being done, they were verified by vouching subsequent receipts, not by confirmation. Revenues and expenses from the property leasing operations were audited entirely by analytical procedures.

Hilda is confident that the past audits obtained sufficient appropriate evidence to support the audit opinion, which has always been unqualified, but feels that the audit planning should be updated to follow a risk-based approach. This may identify areas where a more effective audit approach could be applied. Since Jack has had experience using risk-based audit plans in several of his other audits this year, Hilda thought it would be a good learning experience for Jack to apply the risk-based approach in Foyer's audit planning.

Hilda has asked Jack to develop a risk-based overall audit strategy and preliminary audit plan for the current year audit of Foyer. She would then like him to compare this plan with the plan used in previous years to identify and justify any differences.

The first thing Jack does is get out Foyer's prior year audit files (for its year ended December 31, 20X7) and study the final financial statements and the planning memorandum that Hank had prepared. Jack notices that Hank's planning memo has been copied and carried forward for several years, with any new information tacked on at the end. Extracts from Foyer's prior year audited financial statements and planning memorandum are provided below. What are the steps Jack will go through to create a risk-based audit plan?

FOYER PROPERTIES INC.
CONSOLIDATED BALANCE SHEET AS
AT DECEMBER 31, 20X7

	20X7	20X6
	(in thousands of dollars)	
Assets		
Rental properties (note 4)	$ 32,180	$ 36,211
Cash and short term investments	8,296	8,910
Deferred charges (note 7)	2,031	2,052
Other (note 8)	929	528
Construction in progress	857	402
Corporate taxes recoverable	28	—
	$ 44,321	$ 48,103
Liabilities		
Mortgages and other loans payable (note 10)	$ 26,362	$ 31,247
Accounts payable and accrued liabilities	968	870
Pension obligation (note 11)	768	828
Tenant deposits	297	393
	28,395	33,338
Shareholders' Equity		
Share capital (note 12)	5,850	5,850
Retained earnings	10,076	8,915
	15,926	14,765
	$ 44,321	$ 48,103

STATEMENT OF INCOME AND RETAINED EARNINGS FOR THE YEAR ENDED DECEMBER 31, 20X7

Real estate operations	20X7	20X6
	(in thousands of dollars)	
Revenue		
Rental income	$ 4,847	$ 4,600
Property management and other fees	902	1,137
	5,749	5,737
Operating expenses		
Municipal taxes	586	874
Repairs and maintenance	472	411
Utilities	251	356
Property management	201	164
Insurance	44	50
	1,554	1,855
	4,195	3,882
Interest	2,044	1,656
Amortization	999	828
	3,043	2,484
Net income from real estate operations	1,152	1,398
Other income (loss)		
Gain on disposition of real estate assets	1,518	2,806
Interest and other investment income	368	450
	1,886	3,256
General and administrative expenses		
Salaries and benefits	275	290
Office	355	274
Capital taxes	71	99
Professional fees	42	32
	743	695
Net income for the year	2,295	3,959
Dividends paid during the year	(1,134)	(798)
Retained earnings, beginning of the year	8,915	5,754
Retained earnings, end of the year	$ 10,076	$ 8,915

Note 4. Rental properties and other capital assets (in thousands of dollars)

	20X7			20X6
	Cost	Accumulated amortization	Net book value	Net book value
Buildings	$ 25,738	$ 2,763	$ 22,975	$ 28,028
Land	8,870	–	8,870	7,826
Parking lots and roadways	192	40	151	161
Furniture, fixtures, and equipment	370	187	183	196
	$ 35,170	$ 2,990	$ 32,180	$ 36,211

Note 10. Mortgages and other loans payable (in thousands of dollars)

	20X7	20X6
Mortgages and loans secured by rental properties and bearing interest at fixed rates ranging from 5.45% to 7.28%, blended monthly payments	$ 24,404	$ 30,524
Loan secured by rental property and bearing interest at prime plus 1.25%, blended monthly payments, due on demand	1,958	723
	$ 26,362	$ 31,247

Interest paid on this debt during the year totalled $2,043.

Foyer Properties Inc.

Planning Memorandum

Prepared by: Hank Grouse, Senior Manager

Knowledge of the auditee business

Private corporation, provincial incorporation on April 1, 20X0. Two shareholders, one (holds 40%) is the general manager of the business; the other (holds 60%) is chair of the corporation's board. Both have access to monthly financial reports and other information they require. Main reason for audit is to support borrowing for construction financing—the shareholders feel audited financial statements show the company is solid. Main operations are developing and leasing commercial shopping malls and office buildings, focus on high quality properties and tenants (e.g. banks, pharmacies)

Materiality

Materiality = $90,000 (10% normal pre-tax profit)

Risk analysis

Audit risk: Can accept the highest level
Reasons for Conclusion: Private company, few shareholders have access to all financial reports, other users are creditors with property securing loans, company is profitable and in strong financial position.

Inherent risk: LOW
Reasons for Conclusion: Operations and accounting not complex, previous audit work good, typically find only small (less than $3000) misstatements which management always corrects, low volume of high value transactions not susceptible to error and easily monitored by management.

Control risk: HIGH—won't rely on controls, will test substantively
Reasons for Conclusion: Controls appear strong, management control attitudes good, senior management monitors financial results closely, president is a major shareholder, clear job descriptions and lines of authority, rigorous human resource policies re hiring and evaluation and compensation, no fraud indicators noted.

Detection risk: MODERATELY HIGH
Reasons for Conclusion: Substantive evidence will verify key assertions for all significant financial statement amounts.

Other planning point

- commercial real estate market values tend to be stable
- environmental liabilities—management is on top of this, no problems to date over 25 purchase deals
- management policy is to retain adequate cash reserves to have flexibility to pay for unexpected repairs, or to be able to seize good acquisition opportunities that can arise at any time
- communications between shareholders are open, any shareholder loans or other related party transactions are agreed and approved by both
- all accounting policies used are acceptable in real estate industry
- management's key performance measure is cash flow from operations (net revenue from properties less debt service, so risk of manipulation of accruals is minimal—only cash is considered)

Systems notes

Control environment is strong, will not rely on systems and application controls, substantive approach will be used.

An industry standard financial reporting package (REMR) used—provides reliable monthly operating information (actuals vs. budgets)—summary data from REMR manually transferred to G/L.

Logins used for access, no systems changes required as operation is quite stable.

REMR system is behind firewall from the office IS network, so Internet interface has minimal security risk.

Significant financial statement accounts, audit approach to verify to assertions:

R/R/R Key assertions—CEV

Rent roll (rent revenue journal) is updated regularly, management reviews reports monthly, rent entries are easily auditable by matching to lease agreements.

P/P/P Key assertions—CEV

Management closely monitors monthly financial reports and follows up discrepancies.
Expenditures are largely regular and predictable so variances are easily detected.
Two signatures (CFO and Operations Manager) required on all cheques.
Audit will be by analytical procedures: Detailed comparison to prior years, by property, by month, and compare to budgets.

Rental Properties—EOV

Purchase agreements and lease agreement terms will be verified. Property tax bills will be inspected to verify Foyer retains ownership of each property. Loans and collateral agreements will be confirmed, analysis of interest and property taxes will be based on these inputs. Lease agreements and lease receipts will be analyzed in relation to properties leased. Management representations will be obtained to ensure no property sales are unrecorded, all purchases and new leases are recorded.

Additions to Planning Memorandum:

Note new information for 20X5 audit:
Company has entered a specialized residential real estate leasing business. Residential properties such as student residences and nursing homes are developed to order for public sector organizations such as universities and municipal governments—risks seem low, Foyer's management has capability to handle this type of operation, so no impact on audit for now.

Note for planning 20X6 audit:
Asset sale transactions can be complex, we were asked to review the agreement terms and management's proposed accounting entry prior to finalizing so there are no surprises when it comes to reporting sale in year-end financial statements and determined a $300,000 adjustment was required to management's proposed entry to account for the stepped up rent payments over the term of the lease per GAAP.

Notes for planning 20X7 audit:
Hank met with Foyer president to discuss the audit plan. He noted that construction project cost overruns on the public sector residential property have been a problem, as public sector officials get involved and demand various changes to the agreed plans. Foyer has hired a new construction project manager with experience in the public sector so these demands can be handled better. The construction manager reviews and approves all expenditures, and the two cheque-signing officers will not sign unless this approval is received. Construction changes and cost overruns are a potential risk area, since the lease payments are set prior to construction and may not be adequate to recover a higher investment in the property.

Note for planning 20X8 audit:
Hank had lunch with the Foyer President and learned that ten public sector residential properties are now leased, and six more are under construction. The company's strategy is to grow the public sector residential business, as commercial real estate leasing is mature and harder to grow. Most of Foyer's commercial properties can be sold now for good gains, so the new strategy is to begin to divest the commercial buildings when market conditions are optimal and buyers are found.

Analysis

After reviewing all the planning notes, Jack realizes that Hank had obtained a very thorough knowledge of the company and its risks and controls, and had assessed the risks of material misstatement appropriately. He had also developed a reasonable response to the assessed risks by deciding to use a substantive audit approach.

However, the effectiveness of the audit can be improved by implementing a more strategic analysis of the business risk factors, explicitly linking these to risk of material misstatement at the financial statement level and at the assertion level for the significant classes of transactions, account balances, and disclosures. Jack could reorganize the information from the planning notes and preliminary analysis of Foyer's financial statements to follow the risk-based planning steps, and develop more fully the links between the business risks and specific risks of material misstatement, and the audit responses that should be performed. The risk assessment must also consider fraud risk more explicitly. Management's related controls to reduce those risks could be considered and the remaining risks that the audit plan needs to respond to identified. This analysis would more likely draw the audit team's attention to the potential increase in risk from the company's new strategy in the public sector residential leasing business. The audit team will develop appropriate responses by planning further audit procedures related to this business line. The materiality determination and qualitative factors considered should also be more fully explained and documented.

Jack could document the business-risk analysis by type of factor, as follows.

Understanding the entity and its business, environment, risks, and controls

Nature of entity
Private corporation, provincial incorporation on April 1, 20X0. Two shareholders, one (holds 40%) is the general manager of the business, the other (holds 60%) is chair of the corporation's board. Both have access to monthly financial reports and other information they require. Main reason for audit is to support borrowing for construction financing; the shareholders feel audited financial statements show the company is solid. Main operations are developing and leasing commercial shopping malls and office buildings, focus on high-quality properties and tenants (e.g. banks, pharmacies).

Industry risk factors
No significant risks: local operation, very minimal and noncomplex regulatory environment, simple valuation measurements.

Legal regulatory risk factors
For land/property purchases need to do due diligence re environmental liabilities. Management is on top of this, no problems to date, over 25 purchase deals closed.

Economic risk factors
Real estate values have stopped increasing in current year, but expected to be stable, not crash in near term. Fair values exceed carrying values so no impairment expected, no financial instruments or complex financing is used, just standard mortgage loans.

Business relations
No key competitors/suppliers. Key customers are city government and universities involved in residential properties.

Strategy and related processes
Develop and lease profitable buildings.
– Select unique locations for targeted tenants—high quality businesses, public sector residential.
– Plan construction and monitor project costs closely to keep investment at level where required return can be achieved.
– Structure leases to ensure adequate rate of return on investment and recovery of operating cost and any increases; e.g., energy, property taxes, insurance.
– Implement effective collection procedures to ensure cash flows are on time and as planned.
– Arrange loans from large financial institutions, using specific assets as collateral, to obtain low cost financing.
– Retain adequate cash reserves to have flexibility in paying for unexpected repairs or seizing good acquisition opportunities that can arise at any time.

Internal control factors
Control environment
    – management is experienced and successful in industry
    – management works as team
    – clear job descriptions and lines authority
Management's risk assessment process
    – conservative risk takers, focus on rates of return on investment
    – budgeting for new property developments, and ongoing operations
Information system, related business processes, financial reporting, and communication
    – use industry standard information system (REMR)
    – accounting policies follow real estate industry guidelines, re depreciation assumptions, etc.
    – cash and straight line revenue recognition for stepped rent leases (per *CICA Handbook*)
Control activities
    – access controls, regular reporting
Monitoring of controls
    – top management actively involved and monitoring all aspects of the operation

Key financial statement accounts and underlying business processes

Revenue process
    – rent roll is updated regularly, system controls are strong, management reviews and rent entries are easily auditable as they will match to lease agreements
    – will depend on good entity controls, substantive test so IT general controls N/A
Purchasing process
    – management closely monitors monthly financial reports and follows up discrepancies
    – expenditures are largely regular and predictable so variances are easily detected
    – two signatures required on all cheques

Key performance measure
Cash flow operations show net revenue from properties less debt service (so risk of manipulation of accruals is minimal—only cash is considered)

Systems
Industry standard financial reporting package (REMR) used
    – provides reliable monthly operating information (actuals vs. budgets)
    – summary data from REMR manually transferred to G/L
    – logins used for access, no systems changes required as operation is quite stable
    – REMR system is behind firewall from the office computer network, reduces Internet security risk

Materiality determination

Users—Shareholders, lenders
Qualitative considerations—Very profitable business, well capitalized, well managed, low transaction volume; we have audited it problem free for many years, no management or operating changes this year

Worksheet:

	Anticipated current year	Prior year
NIBT	$2.95m	$2.3m
Total Assets	$50m	$44m
Nonrecurring items in income – Gain on sale	$2m	$1.5m
NIBT—normal, continuing	$.95m	$0.8m
Typical percentage – NIBT 5–10%, use 10% due to qualitative factors	$95,000	$80,000
Comparison with alternative base, Total Assets .5–1%	$250,000	$220,000
Materiality for financial statement as a whole	$95,000	$80,000
Anticipated misstatements based on previous audits – Less than $5000, most years misstatements negligible	$5,000	$5,000
Performance materiality	$90,000	$75,000

A matrix such as the one below could be used to organize the planning considerations. The key risk revealed by Jack's review is entered as an example, and the other business risks in Foyer can be analyzed and entered similarly.

Describe business risks with financial reporting implications or fraud risks	Describe related risks of material misstatement by account and assertion	Rate risks as High/Medium/Low	Describe management control(s) addressing the risk	Rate control effectiveness to reduce risk as High/Medium/Low	Are risks adequately controlled? Yes/No	Audit implications; e.g., control testing required, further audit procedures required to address remaining risk
– public sector residential projects fix future lease payments prior to construction – construction cost overruns can occur to meet public sector official's demands	– rental property costs can exceed recoverable values – fraud risk of kickbacks to public sector officials	M	– project costs approved – monitoring project cost overruns – leasing agreements structured to provide required ROI	M	Y	– observe and enquire as to monitoring effectiveness – examine project costs, approvals – analyze lease agreement, verify recovery of investment and operating costs
Etc.						

Overall Audit Strategy—Other preliminary conclusions

Financial Reporting Framework is GAAP, acceptable fair presentation framework
Preliminary risk assessment at financial statement level: LOW
–It appears risks of material misstatement are low initially, and management risk assessment is adequate to reduce these. Some further procedures needed to verify conclusions based on management control effectiveness via observation and enquiry of management.

Preliminary audit strategy to respond to assess risk at financial statement level:
Consider—Business processes involve small number of large transactions for property sales, planned and monitored construction project costs for development process, lease-driven revenue streams, predictable cost patterns for rental process. Substantive approach is most effective to obtain sufficient appropriate evidence.

Preliminary risk assessment at assertion level:
– Main identified risks affect following account/assertion
        Rental property/Valuation (costs incurred and recoverability of investment)
        Rental revenue/Existence (public sector leases)

Preliminary audit plan to respond to assessed risks:
(a) Timing
    Year end balance audit—not efficient to do interim work
(b) Nature
    Rental property valuation—Detailed analysis of budget and actual costs; any changes in project costs (overruns); changes in economic factors that can suggest investment not recoverable.
    Revenues Detailed analysis based on comparison with lease agreements, verify cash receipts. For new public sector residential business, external confirmation should be obtained of terms and payments from appropriate counterparty, to ensure no fraudulent scheme is occurring.
    Expenses—predictable, we have a history for comparison, so analysis of reasonability sufficient, can also indicate any misstatements/fraud in revenues.
(c) Extent
    Plan to confirm all revenue amounts that are material in total from one counterparty.
    Analysis will cover all significant accounts on balance sheet and income statement.

Staffing:
    – Experienced staff should be assigned to perform the bulk of the audit work as the analysis requires careful judgment and preparation. One junior staff member should be assigned to get experience but needs close supervision. A team meeting should be held prior to beginning audit preparations. Daily meetings should be held during field work to cross reference findings. A final meeting should be held after the files are completed for the partners' review and to clear any outstanding issues, if possible, or ensure they are documented clearly for the partner to follow up.

Summary:
Overall, the auditee presents a low risk of misstatement, and the substantive verification of year-end balances of Rental property (vouching costs), Loan balances and terms (confirmation), Public sector residential lease revenues (confirmation), combined with detailed analytical procedures, will provide sufficient appropriate evidence that material misstatement does not exist in the financial statements.

Summary

This chapter continued the explanation of audit planning started in Chapters 6 and 7 by describing the general procedures for obtaining audit evidence and the main sources of evidence. It then covered the underlying theory of evidence and its persuasiveness by discussing the fundamental auditing concept of sufficient appropriate audit evidence along with the reliability of various techniques for gathering it. This explanation of procedures was enriched with additional notes about the ways in which procedures can be misapplied. Analytical procedures were introduced, and their power was illustrated with some empirical research findings based on actual audit results. The chapter provided an overview of the audit plan and specific programs for collecting evidence. Programs were categorized as internal control programs and balance audit programs. The chapter described some key considerations about audit documentation by looking at planning documentation: the form, content, and purpose of audit working papers. Now the stage is set to, in Chapter 9, pursue a more detailed examination of the auditor's review, understanding of the auditee's information systems, and evaluation and testing of internal control.

The chapter finishes with an application case that provides an opportunity to review a risk-based audit plan for the audit of a real estate business.

Multiple-Choice Questions for Practice and Review

MC 1 An audit program contains:
a. specifications of audit standards relevant to the financial statements being audited.
b. specifications of procedures the auditors believe appropriate for the financial statements under audit.
c. documentation of the assertions under audit, the evidence obtained, and the conclusions reached.
d. reconciliation of the account balances in the financial statements with the account balances in the auditee's general ledger.

MC 2 When auditing the existence assertion for an asset, auditors proceed from the:
a. financial statement numbers back to the potentially unrecorded items.
b. potentially unrecorded items forward to the financial statement numbers.
c. general ledger back to the supporting original transaction documents.
d. supporting original transaction documents to the general ledger.

MC 3 The objective in an auditor's review of credit ratings of a auditee's customers is to obtain evidence related to management's assertion about:
a. compliance.
b. existence.
c. ownership.
d. valuation.

MC 4 Jones, PA, is planning the audit of Rhonda's Company. Rhonda verbally asserts to Jones that all the expenses for the year have been recorded in the accounts. Rhonda's representation in this regard:
a. is sufficient evidence for Jones to conclude that the completeness assertion is supported for the expenses.
b. can enable Jones to minimize his work on the assessment of control risk for the completeness of expenses.
c. should be disregarded because it is not in writing.
d. is not considered a sufficient basis for Jones to conclude that all expenses have been recorded.

MC 5 The evidence considered most reliable by auditors is:
a. internal documents, such as sales invoice copies produced under conditions of strong internal control.
b. written representations made by the president of the company.

c. documentary evidence obtained directly from independent external sources.
d. direct personal knowledge obtained through physical observation and mathematical recalculation.

MC 6 Confirmations of accounts receivable provide evidence primarily about these two assertions:
a. Completeness and valuation
b. Valuation and ownership
c. Ownership and existence
d. Existence and completeness

MC 7 When planning an audit, which of the following is not a factor that affects auditors' decisions about the quantity, type, and content of audit working papers?
a. The auditors' need to document compliance with generally accepted auditing standards
b. The existence of new sales contracts important for the auditee's business
c. The auditors' judgment about their independence with regard to the auditee
d. The auditors' judgments about materiality

MC 8 An audit working paper that shows the detailed evidence and procedures regarding the balance in the accumulated depreciation account for the year under audit will be found in the:
a. current file evidence working papers.
b. permanent file working papers.
c. administrative working papers in the current file.
d. planning memorandum in the current file.

MC 9 An auditor's permanent file working papers would most likely contain:
a. internal control analysis for the current year.
b. the latest engagement letter.
c. memoranda of conference with management.
d. excerpts of the corporate charter and by-laws.

EXERCISES AND PROBLEMS

EP 1
LO.1
Audit Procedures. Auditors frequently refer to the terms *standards* and *procedures*. Standards deal with measures of the quality of performance. Standards specifically refer to the generally accepted auditing standards expressed in the CASs. Procedures specifically refer to the methods or techniques used by auditors in the conduct of the examination. Procedures are also expressed in the CASs.

Required:
List six different types of procedures auditors can use during an audit of financial statements and give an example of each.

EP 2
LO.1
Potential Audit Procedure Failures. For each of the general audit procedures of (*a*) recalculation, (*b*) physical observations, (*c*) confirmation (accounts receivable,

securities, or other assets), (*d*) verbal enquiry, (*e*) inspection of internal documents, and (*f*) scanning, discuss one way the procedure could be misapplied or the auditors could be misled in such a way as to render the work (audit evidence) misleading or irrelevant. Give examples different from the examples in Chapter 8.

EP 3
LO.1
and
LO.2
Confirmation Procedure. A PA accumulates various kinds of evidence on which to base the opinion on financial statements. Among this evidence are confirmations from third parties.

Required:
a. What is an audit confirmation?
b. What characteristics of the confirmation process and the recipient are important if a PA is to consider the confirmation evidence competent?

EP 4 **Audit Procedure Terminology.** Identify the types of
LO.1 procedures(s) employed in each situation described
and below (vouching, tracing, recalculation, observation,
LO.2 and so on):

1. An auditor uses audit software to select vendors' accounts payable with debit balances and compares amounts and computation with cash disbursements and vendor credit memos.

2. An auditor examines property insurance policies and checks insurance expense for the year. The auditor then reviews the expense in light of changes and ending balances in capital asset accounts.

3. An auditor uses audit software to test perpetual inventory records for items that have not been used in production for three months or more. The auditee states that the items are obsolete and have already been written down. The auditor checks journal entries to support the auditee's statements.

4. An auditor tests cash remittance advices to see that allowances and discounts are appropriate and that receipts are posted to the correct customer accounts in the right amounts and reviews the documents supporting unusual discounts and allowances.

5. An auditor watches the auditee take a physical inventory. A letter is also received from a public warehouser stating the amounts of the auditee's inventory stored in the warehouse. The company's cost flow assumption, FIFO, is then tested by the auditor's computer software program.

EP 5 **General Audit Procedures and Financial Statement**
LO.3 **Assertions.** The six general audit procedures produce evidence about the principal management assertions in financial statements. However, some procedures are useful for producing evidence about certain assertions, while other procedures are useful for producing evidence about other assertions. The assertion being audited may influence the auditors' choice of procedures.

Required:
Prepare a two-column table with the six general procedures listed on the left. Opposite each one, write the financial statement assertions most usefully audited by using each procedure. Then provide a specific example of an account that would be found in the audit of a real estate company, and expand the general procedures to explain specifically how the evidence would be obtained for this auditee.

EP 6 **Relative Appropriateness of Evidence.** The third gener-
LO.3 ally accepted standard of audit fieldwork requires that auditors obtain sufficient appropriate evidential matter to afford a reasonable basis for an opinion regarding the financial statements under examination. In considering what constitutes sufficient appropriate evidential matter, a distinction should be made between underlying accounting data and all corroborating information available to the auditor.

Required:
What presumptions can be made about:
a. the relative appropriateness of evidence obtained from external and internal sources.

b. the role of internal control with respect to internal evidence produced by a auditee's data processing system.

c. the relative persuasiveness of auditor observation and recalculation evidence compared with the external, external-internal, and internal documentary evidence.

(AICPA adapted)

EP 7 **Relative Appropriateness of Evidence.**
LO.3 1. Classify the following evidential items by type (direct knowledge, external, and so on), and rank them in order of appropriateness:
   a. Amounts shown on monthly statements from creditors
   b. Amounts shown on "paid on account" in the accounts payable register
   c. Amount of "discounts lost expense" computed by the auditor from unaudited supporting documents
   d. Amounts shown in letters received directly from creditors

2. Classify the following evidential items by type (direct knowledge, external, and so on), and rank them in order of appropriateness.
   a. Amounts shown on a letter received directly from an independent bond trustee
   b. Amounts obtained from minutes of board of directors' meetings
   c. Auditors' recalculation of bond interest and amortization expense when remaining term and status of bond are audited
   d. Amounts shown on cancelled cheques

EP 8 **Audit Working Papers.** The preparation of working pa-
LO.5 pers is an integral part of a PA's audit of financial statements. On a recurring engagement, PAs review their audit programs and working papers from their prior audit while planning the current audit to determine usefulness for the current-year work.

Required:
a. (1) What are the purposes or functions of audit working papers? (2) What records may be included in audit working papers?

b. What factors affect the PA's judgment of the type and content of the working papers for a particular engagement?

c. To comply with generally accepted auditing standards, a PA includes certain evidence in his or her working papers; for example, "evidence that the audit was planned and work of assistants was supervised and reviewed." What other evidence should a PA include in audit working papers to comply with generally accepted auditing standards?

d. How can a PA make the most effective use of the preceding year's audit programs in a recurring audit?

(AICPA adapted)

DISCUSSION CASES

DC 1
LO.2
Financial Assertions and Audit Procedures. You were engaged to examine the financial statements of Kingston Company for the year ended December 31.

Assume that on November 1 Kingston borrowed $500,000 from North Country Bank to finance plant expansion. The long-term note agreement provided for the annual payment of principal and interest over five years. The existing plant was pledged as security for the loan.

Because of the unexpected difficulties in acquiring the building site, the plant expansion did not begin on time. To make use of the borrowed funds, management decided to invest in stocks and bonds, and on November 16 the $500,000 was invested in securities.

Required:
Describe a complete audit program for collecting relevant evidence for the audit of investments in securities at December 31.

Approach:
Develop specific assertions related to investments in securities at December 31 based on the five principle assertions.

DC 2
LO.3
Financial Assertions and Audit Procedures. You were engaged to audit the financial statements of Karachi Company for the year ended December 31, 20X1.

On June 1, 20X1, Karachi initiated a product warranty program to help it stay competitive with other companies in its industry. The warranty covers parts, labour, and shipping to repair any defect within one year of purchase.

During 20X1 Karachi paid $50,000 in warranty costs on product sales of $4,000,000 (approximately 80,000 units). Based on this, management estimates its warranty liability at December 31 is $80,000.

Required:
Describe a complete audit program for collecting relevant evidence for the audit of the estimated warranty liability.

Approach:
Develop specific assertions related to warranty liability based on the five principle assertions.

DC 3
LO.3
Appropriateness of Evidence and Related Parties. Johnson & Company, PAs, audited the Guaranteed Trust Company. M. Johnson had the assignment of evaluating the collectibility of real estate loans. Johnson was working on two particular loans: (1) a $4 million loan secured by the Smith Street Apartments and (2) a $5.5 million construction loan on the Baker Street Apartments now being built. The appraisals performed by the Guaranteed Appraisal Partners, Inc., showed values in excess of the loan amounts. Upon enquiry, Mr. Bumpus, the trust company vice president for loan acquisition, stated: "I know the Smith Street loan is good because I myself own 40 percent of the partnership that owns the property and is obligated on the loan."

Johnson then wrote in the working papers: (1) the Smith Street loan appears collectible; Mr. Bumpus personally attested to knowledge of the collectibility as a major owner in the partnership obligated on the loan, (2) the Baker Street loan is assumed to be collectible because it is new and construction is still in progress, (3) the appraised values all exceed the loan amounts.

Required:
a. Do you perceive any problems with related party involvement in the evidence used by M. Johnson? Explain.
b. Do you perceive any problems with M. Johnson's reasoning or the appropriateness of evidence used in that reasoning?

DC 4
LO.1
and
LO.4
Audit Plan with Weaknesses in Revenue Controls, Not-for-Profit Auditee. Kindness Home (KH) is a not-for-profit organization that operates a nursing home in a town near a major city. You are auditing the revenue and receivables at KH. The nursing home has a reputation for delivering excellent patient services, but its accounting department is understaffed and does not have time for internal verification or other accuracy checks. Your assessment of controls over cash receipts indicates there are effective management supervision and monitoring procedures in place, and you have found no indication of fraud risk, but past audits have found misstatements in recording the patient invoices and accounts receivable. In confirming the accounts receivable from patients in past audits, you have had a very low response rate. Furthermore, those patients who did respond did not appear to know what information they were being asked to provide or what their correct outstanding balance actually was. You have had the same experience in confirming receivables at other nursing homes. The nursing home has a large bank loan payable which is up for renewal two months after year end. The bank's loan officer has told management the bank's head office may not approve a renewal. The bank is concerned about its exposure to non-for-profit nursing homes because many new government-funded nursing homes are expected to open over the new few years. These new long-term care facilities will be more modern and will be located closer to many large hospitals than KH.

Required:
a. Identify the business risks in KH.
b. Assess the risk of material misstatement at the overall financial statement level. Identify the inherent and control risk factors in the organization to support your assessment.
c. In the audit of the revenues, explain the overall audit approach you would use to obtain sufficient appropriate evidence in this situation. Give clear reasons for the mix of control and substantive work you would plan to do. Describe the substantive tests you would

perform to audit the revenue transactions in this organization. Be specific and show how the tests tie in to the relevant assertions.

DC 5 **Working Paper Review.** The schedule in Exhibit DC 5
LO.5 was prepared by the controller of World Manufacturing, Inc., for use by the independent auditors during their examination of World's financial statements. All procedures performed by the audit assistant were noted in the bottom "Legend" section, and it was initialled properly, dated and indexed, and then submitted to a senior member of the audit staff for review. Internal control was reviewed and is considered to be satisfactory.

Required:

a. What information essential to the audit of marketable securities is missing from the schedule?

b. What essential audit procedures were not noted as having been performed by the audit assistant?

Approach:

Write specific assertions based on the five general assertions; then look to the working paper for documentation of evidence related to each one.

(AICPA adapted)

EXHIBIT DC 5   MARKETABLE SECURITIES (WORLD MANUFACTURING, INC., YEAR ENDED DECEMBER 31, 20X2)

Description of Security	Serial No.	Face Value of Bonds	General Ledger 1/1	Purchased in 20X2	Sold in 20X2	Cost	General Ledger 12/31	12/31 Market	Dividend and Interest Pay Date(s)	Amt. Received	Accruals 12/31
Corp. Bonds % Yr. Due											
A 6 09	21-7	10,000	9,400**a**				9,400	9,100	1/15 7/15	300**b,d** 300**b,d**	275
D 4 03	73-0	30,000	27,500**a**				27,500	26,220	12/1	1,200**b,d**	100
G 9 06	16-4	5,000	4,000**a**				4,000	5,080	8/1	450**b,d**	188
R**c** 5 03	08/2	70,000	66,000**a**		57,000**b**	66,000					
S**c** 10 07	07-4	100,000		100,000**e**			100,000	101,250	7/1	5,000**b,d**	5,000
			106,900	100,000	57,000	66,000	140,900	141,650		7,250	5,563
			a,f	**f**	**f**	**f**	**f,g**	**f**		**f**	**f**
Stocks											
P 1,000 shs Common	1,044		75,00**a**				7,500	7,600	3/1 6/1 9/1 12/1	750**b,d** 750**b,d** 750**b,d** 750**b,d**	250
U 50 shs Common	8,530		9,700**a**				9,700	9,800	3/1 2/1 8/1	750**b,d** 800**b,d** 800**b,d**	667
			17,200				17,200	17,400		4,600	917
			a,f				**f,g**	**f**		**f**	**f**

Legends and comments relative to above:
a = Beginning balances agreed to 20X1 working papers.
b = Traced to cash receipts.
c = Minutes examined (purchase and sales approved by the board of directors).
d = Agreed to general ledger entry to income account.
e = Confirmed by tracing to broker's advice.
f = Totals footed.
g = Agreed to general ledger.

CHAPTER ⑨

Control Assessment and Testing

Chapter 9 expands on the auditor's internal control work by describing the activities of internal control assessment and highlighting the role of control risk assessment and testing in planning the audit. Chapters 6, 7, and 8 discussed the need to understand internal control before making a preliminary assessment of the risk of material misstatement and designing the overall audit strategy and audit plan. In Chapter 9 these planning activities, concepts, and tools are used to identify and evaluate key controls that can detect or prevent material misstatements. Management assertions and their related audit objectives are applied to identify specific control risks in the auditee's information systems and processes, and to indicate the objectives of the auditee's control procedures. These control objectives are then used to assess the strengths and weaknesses in the auditee's internal control systems. The control strengths and weaknesses guide the auditor's plans on whether to test control procedures.

Internal control evaluation and control risk assessment are essential components of every financial statement audit and must be considered in planning the audit work. Generally accepted auditing standards emphasize internal control and the controls relevant to the audit.[1] The standards require the auditor to understand the auditee's controls related to significant risks and to assess the risk of material misstatement. When controls must operate effectively for the auditor to lower the assessed risk of material misstatement, the auditor is required to test the effectiveness of those controls.

---

[1] CAS 315 (5100).

LEARNING OBJECTIVES

After completing this chapter, you will be able to do the following:

1 Distinguish between management and auditor's responsibilities regarding an auditee organization's internal controls.

2 Explain why the auditor evaluates an auditee's internal controls.

3 Define seven internal control objectives, relating them to the assertions in management's financial statements.

4 Describe general and application control activities, document accounting systems, identify key controls and weaknesses, and write key control tests for an audit program (3 phases).

5 Outline the auditor's responsibility when internal control evaluation work detects or indicates a significant control weakness or a high risk of fraudulent misstatement.

6 Explain reasonable assurance and cost benefit in the context of control risk assessment and development of the audit approach.

7 Apply and integrate the chapter topics to analyze a practical auditing situation/case/scenario.

Appendix 9A, Understanding Information Systems and Technology for Risk and Control Assessment, is located on the text Online Learning Centre.

MANAGEMENT VERSUS AUDITOR RESPONSIBILITY FOR CONTROL

· · · · · · · · · · · · · · · ·

LEARNING OBJECTIVE

 Distinguish between management and auditor's responsibilities regarding an auditee organization's internal controls.

A company's management deals with rapidly shifting economic and competitive conditions and changes in customer demand, and it must respond to these changes to ensure survival and growth. Internal controls are put in place to keep the company on course toward achieving its goals, and to help anticipate changes that can affect their plans. In this dynamic and risky environment, internal controls help management improve operating efficiency, minimize risks of asset loss, enhance the reliability of financial statements, and monitor compliance with laws and regulations. This broad concept of internal control is exemplified by the definition set out by COSO in the following box.

COSO Internal Control Definition

Internal control is broadly defined as a process, effected by an entity's board of directors, management, and other personnel, designed to provide reasonable assurance regarding the achievement of objectives in the following categories:
• Effectiveness and efficiency of operations
• Reliability of financial reporting
• Compliance with applicable laws and regulations
   The first category addresses an entity's basic business objectives, including performance and profitability goals, and safeguarding of resources. The second relates to the preparation of reliable published financial statements, including interim and condensed financial statements and selected financial data derived from such statements, such as earnings releases reported publicly. The third deals with complying with those laws and regulations to which the entity is subject. These distinct but overlapping categories address different needs and allow a directed focus to meet the separate needs.

> Internal control systems operate at different levels of effectiveness. Internal control can be judged effective in each of the three categories, respectively, if the board of directors and management have reasonable assurance that they understand the extent to which the entity's operations objectives are being achieved, published financial statements are being prepared reliably, and applicable laws and regulations are being complied with.
>
> While internal control is a process, its effectiveness is a state or condition of the process at one or more points in time. In small and mid-size companies, controls may be less formal and less structured than in large companies, yet a small company can still have effective internal control.
>
> Source: "COSO Definition of Internal Control," Executive Summary of the COSO Internal Control Integrated Framework, Committee of Sponsoring Organizations of the Treadway Commission, 1992, page 3. © 1992 by Committee of Sponsoring Organizations of the Treadway Commission (COSO). Reprinted with permission.

Management balances the cost of controls with the benefit of risk reduction. At some point, the costs will exceed the benefits because it is not possible to reduce risks to zero. Managers need to decide what level of risk is acceptable. If they understate the risks through ignorance, poor analysis, or an attempt to cut costs, it becomes a source of control risk.

Controls could be made nearly perfect, but at great expense. A fence could be erected, locks installed, lighting used at night, television monitors put in place, and guards hired. Each successive safeguard costs money, as does extensive supervision of clerical personnel in an office. At some point the cost of protecting the inventory from theft, or of catching every clerical error, exceeds the benefit of the control. Hence, control systems generally do not provide absolute assurance that the objectives of internal control are satisfied. Reasonable assurance is enough, recognizing that the cost of an entity's internal controls should not exceed the expected benefits.

Business managers can estimate the expected benefits of controls and weigh them against the costs. They make their own judgments about how much control is necessary and how much business risk they are willing to accept. However, auditors should be aware that the "cost-benefit" justification might be used loosely by management to tolerate control deficiencies.

External auditors are not responsible for designing effective internal control for auditees. They are responsible for evaluating existing internal controls and assessing the risk of a material misstatement related to them. They use their assessment to determine the audit work required and develop appropriate audit programs to support their opinion. Public accountants may help design internal control systems as consulting engagements for nonaudit clients. Such design work must be separate and apart from an audit engagement because it could impair the public accountant's objectivity in assessing those controls in an audit. This is a threat to auditor independence.

Given the realities of reasonable assurance, auditors must carefully determine whether a system contains any internal control weakness. The auditor's primary purpose for this evaluation of internal control is to guide the design of the final audit plan. For this reason, the auditor's understanding of the auditee's internal control and the control risk assessment must be documented.

External auditors' documentation of control weaknesses can help management carry out its responsibility for maintaining effective internal control. However, external auditors' observations and recommendations are usually limited to external financial reporting matters. Their basis for knowing about control weaknesses comes from familiarity with the types of errors, frauds, and misstatements that can occur in an account balance or class of transactions. Clearly, hundreds of innocent errors and not-so-innocent fraud schemes are possible. (Many of these are discussed in Chapter 17, on fraud awareness auditing.) Rather than discuss hundreds of possible errors and frauds, Exhibit 9–1 shows seven general categories along with some examples. The external auditors' task of control risk assessment involves

EXHIBIT   9–1   GENERAL CATEGORIES AND EXAMPLES OF MISSTATEMENTS

1. Invalid transactions are recorded: Fictitious sales are recorded and charged to nonexistent customers.
2. Valid transactions are omitted from the accounts: Shipments to customers never get recorded.
3. Unauthorized transactions are executed and recorded: A customer's order is not approved for credit, yet the goods are shipped, billed, and charged to the customer without requiring payment in advance.
4. Transaction amounts are inaccurate: A customer is billed and the sale is recorded in the wrong amount because the quantity shipped and the quantity billed are not the same, and the unit price is for a different product.
5. Transactions are classified in the wrong accounts: Sales to a subsidiary company are recorded as sales to outsiders instead of as inter-company sales, or the amount is charged to the wrong customer account receivable record.
6. Transaction accounting is incomplete: Sales are posted in total to the accounts receivable control account, but some are not posted to individual customer account records.
7. Transactions are recorded in the wrong period: Shipments made in January are backdated and recorded as sales and charges to customers in December (previous year); shipments in December are recorded as sales and charges to customers in January (next year).

finding out what the company does to prevent, detect, and correct these potential errors and irregularities. You will encounter the flip side of these when you study control objectives later in this chapter.

REVIEW CHECKPOINTS

1   List the responsibilities of management regarding their organization's internal control.

2   Why does management have to trade off between costs and benefits of internal controls?

3   How does management's cost-benefit trade-off decision affect control risk?

4   What are auditors' responsibilities in relation to an auditee's internal controls?

5   Why is being involved in designing internal controls considered a risk to auditor independence?

6   How do external auditors help managers meet their responsibilities for internal control?

7   Define control risk and list seven general categories of misstatements that controls are intended to prevent, detect, and correct.

REASONS FOR CONTROL EVALUATION

LEARNING OBJECTIVE

2 Explain why the auditor evaluates an auditee's internal controls.

The primary reason for evaluating a company's internal control and assessing control risk is to have a basis for planning the audit and determining the nature, timing, and extent of audit procedures in the detailed audit plan. The auditor is concerned with the impact that controls have on safeguarding the company's assets and the accuracy of the accounting records (accounting controls), financial reporting, and disclosures. From this, the auditor prepares a preliminary audit program and thinks about the work that needs to be done, considering even the extreme possibility that the organization may not be auditable. This preliminary program might be last year's audit program or a template program that will need to be modified on the basis of auditee-specific preliminary analytical review findings, materiality, and risk assessments. Exhibit 9–2 outlines the process.

As introduced in Chapter 7, control risk is the risk that internal control will fail to prevent or detect a material financial statement misstatement. In the business risk approach, the auditor's main goal is to assess the risk of the financial statements' being misstated, and assessing both inherent and control risk is a key step in performing this assessment.

EXHIBIT 9-2   ROLE OF INTERNAL CONTROL IN ASSESSING RISK OF MATERIAL MISSTATEMENT

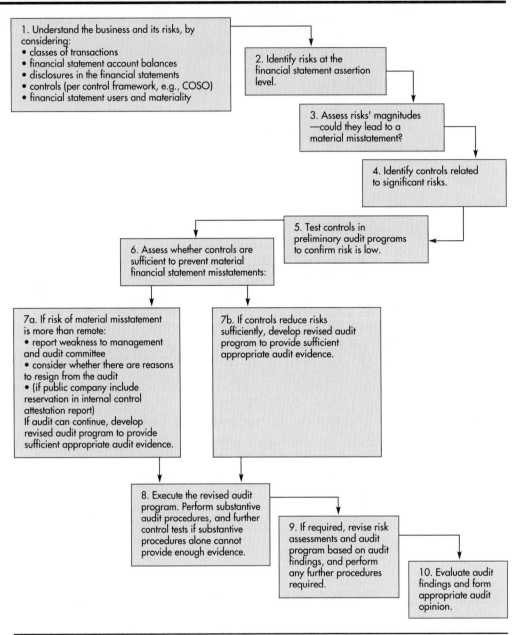

The standards do not give a specific definition of control risk, and they allow for inherent and control risk assessments to be combined since they are closely related. For example, consider an item with high inherent risk, such as an inventory of Rolex watches in a jewellery business. The inherent risk is high because these items are easy to pick up and conceal, have a high dollar value, and are easy to sell illegally. The auditor would expect management to have strong controls in place against these risks; otherwise the company could not survive. So, the auditor will expect to observe effective and continuous controls over the Rolex inventory in the management's risk assessment process. If this is not found, further procedures would need to be planned to address the risk that the inventory is materially misstated.

Control risk is a characteristic of the auditee's internal control, and the auditors' task is to assess it; that is, to assign an evaluation to it. Auditors may document their internal control risk assessment decisions with descriptions (e.g., high, moderate, low), and some auditors assign probability numbers to them (e.g., 1.0, 0.50, 0.30).

The role of internal control evaluation is one of the more difficult topics in an audit course. Perhaps the easiest way to understand this role is to imagine two extreme audit situations: the "clean" audit and the "dirty" audit. In a **clean audit**, the accounting records are easy to verify and accurate. In a dirty audit, however, the accounting records may be incomplete, riddled with misstatements, and harder to verify. Most people find it intuitive that a clean audit should require less work than a dirty audit, as the controls are likely to be good at meeting their objective of lowering the risk of material misstatement. Conversely, a dirty audit is associated with poor or nonexistent controls. So auditors evaluate internal controls because these are a good indicator of the accuracy of the accounting records and therefore reduce the amount of work needed to verify their accuracy more directly. Thus, evaluating internal controls creates efficiencies in clean audits and can provide assurance that the risk of material misstatement is low, so less substantive audit work is required.

Auditors rely on controls for more than just efficiencies. There may be risks of misstatements that substantive procedures alone cannot remove. For example, a completeness assertion is virtually impossible to verify without some evaluation of control effectiveness, as that gives auditors assurance on whether items that they might not know about, such as accrued liabilities, get recorded. It is possible that controls are so bad, leading to such a dirty audit situation, that an organization is not auditable. The following box describes a situation where the control risks are so great that the auditor cannot develop compensating audit procedures to reduce the risk of material misstatement to an acceptable level. This extreme case is a fairly rare occurrence. In many cases, if controls are weak, more substantive procedures can be performed to provide sufficient evidence about whether the financial statements contain a material error.

UNDERSTANDING THE AUDITABILITY OF THE ACCOUNTS: BAD BOOKS BLOCK A MUNICIPAL GOVERNMENT AUDIT

Officials of a municipal government kept such poor financial records for four non-profit corporations they controlled that the public accountant appointed to audit the corporations reported to the municipal council that the audits could not be done. The four corporations were conduits for more than $630 million in low-interest financing provided by the municipal government to local businesses. A public inquiry was called to investigate and report on the situation. The public accountant declared to the inquiry that the four corporations' records were beyond horrid—in fact he found there were virtually no records at all.

The inquiry found that (1) no records were kept of purchases and redemptions of certificates of deposit worth hundreds of thousands of dollars, (2) there might be certificates of deposit that the municipal officials did not know existed, (3) bank statements were not kept, and (4) chequing accounts were not reconciled.

The former treasurer of the corporations reported to the inquiry that the corporations used a very simple bookkeeping system; money went in and went out. The system wasn't sophisticated because, in the former treasurer's view, it wasn't needed. The public accountant, and the taxpayers who provided the funds, would see it differently.

In business risk–based audits, as explained in Chapters 6 and 7, the auditor begins the preliminary risk evaluation by understanding the organization's overall control environment, management's risk assessment process, the business processes along with related information systems and communication, and the monitoring procedures in place. Exhibit 7–17 (page 249) shows a sample framework for this.[2] The auditor identifies any significant risks related to financial reporting, and then he evaluates whether effective controls are in place to address them. The auditor also evaluates control activities—the specific procedures that are used to control processes, application, and transactions.

The auditor's understanding of the accounting information systems is key to evaluating control over financial reporting and planning further audit procedures. Important information systems functions include processes, records, and controls that can be directly related to the assertions and audit objectives that guide the auditor in planning audit evidence-gathering procedures, as follows:

Information System Function Related to Financial Reporting	Relation to Principal Financial Statement Assertions
Identify and record all valid and authorized transactions	Existence (valid) Completeness (all) Ownership (authorized)
Describe the transactions on a timely basis and in sufficient detail to permit their proper classification for financial reporting	Presentation (proper classification)
Measure the value of transactions in a manner that permits recording their proper monetary value in the financial statements	Valuation (proper monetary value)
Determine the period in which transactions occurred to permit recording in the proper accounting period	Existence (proper accounting period) Completeness (proper accounting period)
Present properly the transactions and related disclosures in the financial statements	Presentation (present properly; related disclosures)

A properly functioning information system will reduce risk of misstatement at the financial statement assertion level. Identifying and recording all valid transactions, and ensuring that they are recorded in the proper accounting period, satisfies the existence and completeness assertions. Procedures ensuring that recorded transactions are authorized as proper rights or obligations achieves the ownership assertion. The valuation assertion is addressed when the dollar values of transactions are measured and calculated appropriately and in accordance with GAAP. When transactions are recorded in enough detail to properly classify and present them in the financial reports, and to support related disclosures, the presentation assertion is accomplished.

Rapid technological change increases both an auditee's business risk and the risk that auditors will not detect critical business risks and/or control weaknesses. If an information system is fully manual, the transaction processing can be followed and is supported by paper documents: approvals, invoices, and other records of accountability, such as perpetual inventory records. Many aspects of IT-based systems are designed along similar lines, so similar "documents" may exist. However, in many cases these documents are available only in electronic form. Further, the basic records (ledgers and journals) of an IT-based accounting system are electronic data files that cannot be read or changed without a computer and may be deleted so that there is no paper trail for tracing transactions. When these or other complex aspects of IT-based systems are present—remote access by many users, use of customized software, dependency on a continuously operating website—risk is increased. In these cases, the auditor will likely need to include an IT

[2] The auditor may choose another accepted framework to guide this evaluation. Appendix 7A on the OLC outlines the control frameworks organizations and auditors can select to use in practice.

expert on the audit team. Appendix 9A on the OLC gives more detail on the risks and controls found in IT-based systems for students who are interested in understanding computerized accounting information systems from an auditor's perspective.

- -

**R E V I E W
CHECKPOINTS**

8 Why does the auditor evaluate the auditee's internal controls?

9 Why does an inventory of Rolex watches have a high inherent risk, and why does the auditor expect management to have strong controls over this inventory?

10 What are two processes auditors use to describe their control risk assessments?

11 What is the impact on audit work of a clean audit as compared with a dirty audit?

12 Why can it be efficient for the auditor to rely on internal controls?

13 If internal controls are weak, in what situations could an audit still be done and in what situations would it not be possible to do an audit?

- -

How Control Risk Assessment Affects the Audit Plan

Examining the business processes and related accounting processes allows the auditor to design audit procedures to test controls and financial statement transactions and balances. Tests of controls are performed if it is a less costly way to obtain audit evidence or if effective control is necessary to get sufficient appropriate audit evidence about one or more assertions. Auditors might try to design dual-purpose tests—tests of controls that also provide substantive evidence. For example, a test verifying the control that all payments have been properly authorized could also trace each payment amount to the cash records and the general ledger for substantive evidence of correct recording.

The auditor's control risk assessment will affect the procedures included in the detailed audit programs of the audit plan. As explained in Chapter 8, an audit program is a list of specific audit procedures designed to produce evidence about the assertions in financial statements. Each procedure's description should indicate its nature, timing, and extent, as well as a direct association with one or more financial statement assertions. The nature of procedures refers to the six general techniques: recalculation/reperformance, confirmation, enquiry, inspection, observation, and analysis. The timing of procedures is when they are performed: at "interim," before the balance sheet date, or at "year-end," shortly before and after the balance sheet date. The extent of procedures refers to the amount of work done, such as the sample size, when the procedures are performed.

Exhibit 9–3 lists five procedures for auditing two of the accounts receivable assertions as part of the account balance audit program. The existence and completeness subheadings and columns in the exhibit indicate connections to financial statement assertions and to the nature, timing, and extent of the procedures. Some decisions about the timing and extent of work shown in this exhibit suggest the auditor has assessed control risk to be low; for example

- confirmation of a sample of customer accounts receivable before year-end, instead of confirmation of all accounts as of December 31;
- vouching the last 5 days' recorded sales to bills of lading for cutoff evidence, instead of vouching the last 15 days' sales; and
- tracing the last 5 days' shipments to recorded sales invoices for cutoff evidence, instead of tracing the last 15 days' shipments.

You should assume the auditors found the controls to be strong and, thus, think the preceding program is efficient. If they found control weaknesses, the risk of material

EXHIBIT 9–3   ACCOUNT RECEIVABLE BALANCE AUDIT PROGRAM (PARTIAL ILLUSTRATION)

Assertions/Procedures	Nature	Timing	Extent
Existence/Cutoff: Accounts receivable are authentic obligations owed to the company and represent sales made before December 31.			
1. Obtain a trial balance of customers' accounts. Select 75 for positive confirmation.	Confirmation	November 1 (interim date)	Limited sample
2. Obtain a year-end trial balance of customer accounts. Compare to the November 1 trial balance and investigate significant changes by vouching large increases to sales invoices and bills of lading.	Analytical procedures Document vouching	December 31 (year-end)	All customer accounts
3. Select all the sales invoices recorded in the last five days of the year, and vouch to bills of lading for December shipping date.	Document vouching	December 31 (year-end)	Last five days' sales
Completeness/Cutoff: Accounts receivable include all amounts owed to the company at December 31.			
4. Send positive confirmations to customers with zero balances.	Confirmation	December 31 (year-end)	All zero balance accounts
5. Select all the bills of lading dated in the last five days of the year, and trace to sales invoices recorded in December.	Document tracing	December 31 (year-end)	Last five days' shipments

misstatement is increased and a different program would be more appropriate, but it would probably take more time and cost more, too. For example, it might require the auditor to

- confirm the customer accounts as of year end, December 31, rather than an earlier date;
- confirm a larger sample of customer accounts;
- select all the sales invoices recorded in the last 15 days for vouching to December bills of lading; and
- select all bills of lading dated in the last 15 days for tracing to December sales invoices.

Note that, in this higher risk situation, more substantive evidence is needed to provide assurance about whether or not there is a material financial statement misstatement.

The preliminary audit program in Exhibit 9–3, therefore, depends on a low control risk related to the company's internal control structure. The task is to assess the inherent and internal control risks that there is a material misstatement (error or irregularity) in the accounts receivable total. If the risks are too high, procedures are changed to provide for greater extent (larger samples) and better timing (confirmation moved to December 31). Likewise, if the risk is not high less work needs to be done (e.g., the confirmation of zero-balance receivables might be omitted). In general, a good system of internal control should result in less audit work than a bad system of internal control. Thus, audit efficiencies come from good internal controls: less testing and spreading the audit work out over more convenient times.

REVIEW CHECKPOINTS

14 How does the auditor's control risk assessment affect the preliminary audit program?

15 What audit planning activities are performed to lead up to the control risk evaluation?

16 Give two reasons why controls would be tested.

17 In what situation(s) would controls not be tested?

CONTROL OBJECTIVES AND PROCEDURES

· · · · · · · · · · · · · · · ·

The objective of control procedures is to process transactions correctly. Correctly processed transactions produce accurate account balances, which in turn help produce reliable assertions in the financial statements, as shown in Exhibit 9–4. The exhibit gives an example of two revenue transaction streams, sales invoicing and cash receipts, and links these to the control objectives. These control objectives then link to the impact of the transaction streams on increasing (sales) and decreasing (cash receipts) the Accounts Receivable account balance. If the control objectives over the transaction streams are met, this should ensure that the assertions in the final account balance are true.

Control Objectives

Note that each control objective is the flip side of one of the seven errors and irregularities shown in Exhibit 9–1 (page 317). The seven objectives are listed in Exhibit 9–5, with a general statement of each objective along with a specific example for the revenue transaction process. The explanations that follow this exhibit tell you more about these objectives and give examples of auditee procedures designed to accomplish them.

Validity is ensuring that recorded transactions are ones that should be recorded, that is, they really exist. The auditee's procedure might require matching shipping documents with sales invoices before a sale is recorded. This procedure prevents the recording of undocumented (possibly fictitious) sales.

Completeness is ensuring that valid transactions are not missing from the accounting records. If sales are represented by shipments, then every shipment should be matched with a sales invoice. Transaction documents (e.g., shipping documents) are often prenumbered, and accounting for their numerical sequence is a control procedure designed to achieve the completeness objective.

Authorization is ensuring that transactions are approved before they are recorded, that is, they are "owned" by the company. Management establishes criteria for recognizing transactions in the accounting system and for supervisory approval of them, much as credit sales must be preapproved. A control system should stop any unauthorized transactions from entering the accounting records.

The nature of authorization for transactions may vary. For example, authorization is not usually needed to record a cash receipt from a regular customer as companies are happy to accept payments, but a sales manager may need to approve giving a discount after the end of the discount period. Unauthorized transactions of any kind are a source of risk that

EXHIBIT   9–4   CONTROL OBJECTIVES AND FINANCIAL STATEMENT ASSERTIONS—REVENUE TRANSACTIONS

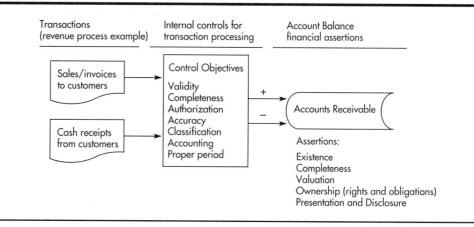

EXHIBIT 9–5   INTERNAL CONTROL OBJECTIVES

Objective	General Statement	Specific Example (revenue process)
Validity	Recorded transactions are valid and documented.	Recorded sales are supported by invoices, shipping documents, and customer orders.
Completeness	All valid transactions are recorded, and none are omitted.	All shipping documents are prenumbered and matched with sales invoices daily.
Authorization	Transactions are authorized according to company policy.	Credit sales over $1,000 are given prior approval by the credit manager.
Accuracy	Transaction dollar amounts are properly calculated.	Sales invoices contain correct quantities and are mathematically correct.
Classification	Transactions are properly classified in the accounts.	Sales to subsidiaries and affiliates are classified as intercompany transactions.
Accounting	Transaction accounting is complete.	All sales on credit are charged to customers' individual accounts.
Proper period	Transactions are recorded in the proper period.	Sales of the current period are charged to customers in the current period, and sales of the next period are charged in the next period.

the auditor needs to understand. For example, unauthorized cash receipts may be part of a fraud cover-up or an illegal money laundering scheme.

Authorization for routine transactions may be delegated to a fairly low level of management. For example, (1) all shipments with a value of more than $1,000 require credit approval, (2) all sales are recorded in the accounting department upon receipt of a copy of a shipping document, and (3) the receptionist's listing of payments received on account when the mail is opened may be sufficient authorization for cash receipts. Some authorizations have to come from a high level of the company's governance structure, such as the board of directors. For example, significant non-routine transactions, like sales of major assets and acquisition of another business, or signing the company name to a loan agreement, usually will be authorized specifically in the minutes of a board of directors' meeting.

Accuracy is ensuring that dollar amounts are calculated correctly. A manual or computer check that the quantity invoiced equals the quantity shipped and the correct list price is used, with a correctly calculated total, is a control procedure for accuracy.

Classification is ensuring that transactions are recorded in the right accounts, charged or credited to the right customers (including classification of sales to subsidiaries and affiliates, as mentioned in Exhibit 9–5), entered in the correct segment product line or inventory description, and so forth. Classification errors between balance sheet and income statement accounts present the greatest risk of misstatement because they will change the net income. For example, before its bankruptcy WorldCom misstated its income by misclassifying operating expenses as assets, thereby concealing its poor financial performance from financial statement users.

Accounting is a general category concerned with ensuring that the accounting process for a transaction is performed completely and in conformity with GAAP. For example, a clerk can balance the total of individual receivables with the control account to determine if all entries to the control account have also been entered in individual customers' accounts. Bank reconciliation could be done by a person who is independent of cash recording. Balancing and reconciliation procedures like these can meet more than one control objective. Control over accounting, in general, is a useful category if you cannot identify a control problem in one of the other categories.

Proper period refers to ensuring that transactions are accounted for in the period they occurred in. This control objective relates to cut-off—part of the existence and completeness assertions. The auditee's accountants must be alert to the dates of transactions in

EXHIBIT 9-6   HOW CONTROL OBJECTIVES RELATE TO FINANCIAL STATEMENT ASSERTIONS

Control Objective	Financial Statement Assertions				
	Existence	Completeness	Valuation	Ownership	Presentation and Disclosure
Validity	X			X	
Completeness		X		X	
Authorization	X		X	X	
Accuracy			X		
Classification			X		X
Accounting					X
Proper Period	X	X			

relation to month-, quarter-, and year-end. Proper period accounting (cut-off) is a pervasive problem. It is mentioned in relation to all kinds of transactions—sales, purchases, inventories, expense accruals, income accruals, and others. The risk of errors in cut-off is high because they are complex and non-routine events, but they can also be used to manipulate income, for example, by using accruals to record sales too early or expenses too late.

Control Objectives and Assertions
The control objectives are closely connected to the assertions in management's financial statements. For example, the accuracy control objective relates to the existence, completeness, and valuation assertions, as mechanical errors will result in overstated, understated, or incorrectly measured balances. However, recognizing that the control objective is to assess accuracy is more helpful in designing appropriate tests, such as tests for errors of billing at too low or too high a price, or for a smaller or larger quantity than shipped, or using price lists in U.S. dollars when the financial statement information should be in Canadian dollars.

The grid in Exhibit 9–6 shows how the control objectives are related to the assertions, the Xs showing the primary relevance. To interpret Exhibit 9–6, link the achievement of control objectives with the probability that an assertion may be materially misstated. For example, a strong control over the validity of recorded sales and cash receipts transactions, an effective system of credit authorization, and a system ensuring that transactions are recorded in the proper period, allows control risk related to the existence/occurrence assertions for accounts receivable and sales balances to be assessed as low.

However, an auditor may find that some, but not all, of the control objectives for a particular account balance (i.e., set of assertions) are achieved. For example, the above situation may coexist with failure to achieve control over the completeness of recording sales transactions and accounts receivable amounts. In this case, the preliminary audit program may be changed to require more work related to the completeness of accounts receivable (the assertion which had high control risk) and be unchanged for the work on the existence of accounts receivable (which had low control risk).

The final evaluation of a company's internal control is the assessment of the control risk (CR) related to each assertion. (The audit risk model AR = IR × CR × DR is explained in Chapter 7.) In this assessment, an auditor expresses the effectiveness of the control system for preventing, detecting, and correcting specific errors and irregularities in management's financial statement assertions.

REVIEW CHECKPOINTS

18 Why do control procedures affect management's financial statement assertions?

19 List the control objectives and the misstatement risk that each one relates to.

20 Why can some authorization procedures be performed by low-level managers? What kinds of authorizations need to come from the board of directors?

21   What are the risks related to cut-off procedures?

22   Match the seven control objectives to the five principal assertions.

23   Can control risk be high for one assertion and low for another assertion for the same account balance? Explain.

24   How does the auditor's control risk assessment relate to audit risk?

. . . .

Phases of a Control Evaluation

LEARNING OBJECTIVE

4 Describe general and application control activities, document accounting systems, identify key controls and weaknesses, and write key control tests for an audit program (3 phases).

As discussed in Chapters 7 and 8, the auditee's controls need to be understood to assess the risk of material misstatement, develop the overall audit strategy, and make preliminary planning decisions to use a combined or substantive audit approach. As the audit work proceeds, new knowledge allows the audit team to continuously refine and improve the planned audit work, but in many audits the detailed internal control work will follow the initial plan. We now will look at the detailed audit work done to assess and test internal control, noting that the findings of this work may result in some revisions to the original strategy and plan.

This section describes the three phases of control evaluation:

- understanding control (expanding on the discussion in Chapter 7)
- assessing control risk by identifying control strengths and weaknesses in the accounting information system
- testing controls (The main coverage of this topic is in this chapter, and Chapter 10 covers sampling aspects. Testing controls also will be integrated with the planned substantive audit procedures included in audit programs that will be covered in detail in Part III.)

Audits aim to be efficient. This means doing high-quality work to obtain sufficient appropriate evidence with minimum time and cost expenditure. The time allocation between control evaluation and "substantive audit work" (e.g., the procedures in Exhibit 9–3) is a cost-benefit trade-off. Generally, the more auditors know about good controls, the less substantive year-end work they need to do. They might not need to evaluate or test the entire internal control structure for this, but they need to understand it well enough to assess if there are any significant risks of material misstatement that the audit work needs to address.

If there are significant risks and certain controls are essential to preventing or detecting these risks, those would be key controls. These are evaluated by testing their effectiveness during the audit period in preventing material misstatement in the financial statements. Auditors may only obtain a minimum understanding on non-key controls and instead rely primarily on substantive audit work on the financial statement balance or transactions. If the risk of misstatement in a particular financial statement account is very low, they may perform very little substantive work. Some examples of transaction processing risks and the importance of controls in the audit are provided in the following box.

Auditors must make a trade-off between costs of evaluating internal control and costs of substantive audit tests. A decision to obtain a high level of assurance from controls will cause the costs of control evaluation and testing to be high but should be offset by lower costs for substantive testing as less substantive evidence is required. On the other hand, obtaining a low level of assurance from testing controls may mean that substantive testing costs will be higher. An efficient audit program looks for the combination of control evaluation and substantive work that provides an acceptable level of assurance at the lowest total cost.

The three phases of control evaluation work are described as if they are distinct programs completed before any substantive audit work begins. In practice, work on the phases overlaps. The understanding phase and the control risk assessment phase are each made

KEY AND NON-KEY CONTROLS

Examples	**Control importance (Key vs. Non-key)**
The business processes a high volume of cash sales transactions through retail stores (e.g., Canadian Tire). There is a significant risk that not all sales will be recorded.	Controls over sales completeness will be considered key controls because a material misstatement could occur and there is no other reliable substantive procedure that auditors can use to verify that all sales have been recorded. If these were absent, it would present a material risk of misstatement.
The inventory controller performs a monthly variance analysis to ensure production costs are staying within budget. There is a risk that avoidable cost overruns will occur if timely action is not taken when variances from budget occur.	Because the auditor plans to obtain evidence at year-end by extensive inventory valuation testing, controls over monthly production costs would be considered non-key.
The company's petty cash fund of $200 is kept in a locked box by the receptionist, who must present valid signed receipts for all expenditures to the controller when the fund runs low. The controller authorizes the payables manager to issue a cheque to "cash" to replenish the fund back up to $200. There is a risk that petty cash funds will be misappropriated.	The controls here—reconciliation, supervision, and segregation—are non-key because the auditor plans to scrutinize the petty cash expenditure records for the whole year and expects the total value of these transactions to be immaterial. Thus there is no need to evaluate these controls. If a material amount of expenditures is found to have been processed through petty cash, this may suggest a fraud and this possibility will need to be investigated substantively. In either case, these controls will not be relevant to the audit work planned.
The company uses an Internet-based sales order system. Customers enter order details online and pay online by entering their credit card information. The order entry system automatically checks that order details are correct and the goods are in stock, calculates the price, and verifies the validity of the credit card payment online with the credit card company. After these control routines are run, a shipping order is automatically created which simultaneously creates entries in the accounting system to recognize the revenue and costs of sales.	Since the automated controls are necessary to ensure the sale information recorded is valid and accurate and that the customer's payment is valid, these automated controls are considered key. The accounting entries are made automatically once the controls have been performed so there is no paper trail or other documented evidence of performance of the control procedures. The auditor will need to test these automated controls for assurance that all sales are valid and accurately recorded, and that the credit payments have been authorized through online verification with the credit card company.

distinct to help you to comprehend the purpose of this part of the audit work. However, in practice most auditors do the two together, since the purpose of understanding the controls is to assess control risk. Understanding and assessment can both involve control testing. For example, auditors learn more about the existence and operating effectiveness of controls when they actually start testing them. The control evaluation phase can also overlap substantive work. For example, account balance audit work may be done at an interim date (before the company's fiscal year-end) while some of the control evaluation work is being done. However, the three phases described here are a simple way to explain the analytical thinking that auditors follow to decide on the best approach for collecting sufficient appropriate audit evidence to support their opinion.

25 Why is there a cost-benefit trade-off involved in evaluating internal controls for planning the audit?

26 What is a key control? Give a specific example.

27 What is a non-key control? Give a specific example.

28 Why do key controls always need to be evaluated in an audit?

Phase 1: Understanding the Internal Control

Nature and Timing of Phase 1 Work

Understanding controls is a key part of understanding the business and risk of misstatement introduced in Chapters 6 and 7. Done early in the engagement, this work acquaints auditors with the overall control environment and the flow of transactions through the accounting system. We now will apply this understanding to identify significant risks at the assertion level in account balances, transaction streams, and disclosures. These risks will correspond to the key control activities that should be in place to minimize them, as described in the following section.

Control Activities: General Controls and Application Control Procedures

The internal control framework presented earlier showed that management implements control activities to achieve the organization's control objectives. Control activities are classified as either general or application controls. General controls are those that have an overall impact on accounting processes. Applications controls address the control objectives relating to input, processing, and output of data in each accounting process. All detail control procedures are directed, one way or another, toward preventing or detecting and correcting errors, irregularities, frauds, and misstatements. Exhibit 9–7 provides an overview of control activities, which are further explained below.

General Controls

Organizational features like capable personnel, segregation of responsibilities, controlled access, and periodic comparison are general controls. Like environmental controls, general controls are primarily preventive in nature and pervasively impact the various accounting cycles. For these reasons, auditors tend to focus on environmental

EXHIBIT 9–7   OVERVIEW OF CONTROL ACTIVITIES

General Controls	Application Controls		
	Applications	System Functions to Be Controlled	Control Objectives
• Capable personnel	Revenues/Receivables/Receipts	Transaction input	Specific procedures to ensure:
• Performance reviews	Purchases/Payables/Payments	Transaction processing	• validity • completeness
• Segregation of responsibilities	Production and Payroll		• authorization • accuracy
• Supervision	Investment and Finance	Transactions, balances, and disclosure output	• classification
• Controlled access	Other applications		• accounting
• Periodic comparison			• proper period
• IT controls			

and general controls in the preliminary evaluation of internal controls. Some of the general controls are discussed below.

Capable Personnel.   The people who make the system work are the most important aspect of control. Personnel problems might result in internal control problems. High turnover in accounting jobs means that inexperienced people are doing the accounting and control tasks, and they generally make more mistakes than experienced people. New accounting officers and managers (e.g., financial vice-president, controller, chief accountant, plant accountant, or data processing manager) are not familiar with company accounting and may make technical and judgmental errors. Accounting officers and employees may be fired because they refuse to go along with improper accounting procedures desired by a higher level of management. In general, accounting personnel changes may be a warning signal.

Performance Reviews.   Management reviews of how reported performance compares with expectations are an effective general control. Comparing reported performance with budgets and prior years is an important part of management's risk assessment process. Management should follow up on any discrepancies and, if errors or other irregularities are uncovered, take appropriate action to implement corrections and solutions. Performance review procedures can be reperformed by auditors as part of their analytical procedures to reveal significant control weaknesses, risks, or actual errors and fraud.

Segregation of Responsibilities.   An important characteristic of reliable internal control is the appropriate segregation of functional responsibilities. Sometimes called division of duties, proper segregation of responsibilities is necessary for making detailed clerical control procedures effective. Examples of duties that should be done by separate individuals include reports, review and approval of reconciliations, and approval and control of documents. These are four kinds of functional responsibilities that should each be performed by different departments, or at least by different people on the company's accounting staff:

1. *Authorization to execute transactions.* This duty belongs to people who have authority and responsibility for initiating the recordkeeping for transactions. Authorization may be general, referring to a class of transactions (e.g., all purchases), or it may be specific (e.g., sale of a major asset).

2. *Recording of transactions.* This is the accounting and recordkeeping function (bookkeeping) that in most organizations is performed by a computerized process.

3. *Custody of assets involved in the transactions.* This is the actual physical possession or effective physical control of property.

4. *Periodic reconciliation of existing assets to recorded amounts.* This duty refers to making comparisons at regular intervals and taking appropriate action with respect to any differences.

Responsibilities are incompatible when they place a single person in a position to create and conceal errors, irregularities, and misstatements. No one person should control two or more functional responsibilities. The first and fourth responsibilities are management functions, the second is an accounting function, and the third is a custodial (physical access) function. If different departments or persons deal with the different transactions, two benefits are obtained: (1) irregularities would require collusion of two or more people, and most people hesitate to ask for help when conducting wrongful acts, and (2) innocent errors are more likely to be found and flagged for correction. The saying that two heads are better than one is as true as its flip side; the more people assigned to control duties, the better the controls are. The costs, however, would be higher as well. Any control system will reflect a cost-benefit compromise.

Separation of the duties is also an important IT control. Work performed by analysts, programmers, and operators should be segregated. Anyone who designs a processing system should not do the technical programming work, and anyone who performs either of these tasks should not be the computer operator when "live" data are being processed. People performing each function should not have access to each other's work, and only the computer operators should have access to the equipment. Lack of separation of duties along these lines should be considered a serious weakness in general control. A lack of segregation here could be compensated for by having a separate information control group, or monitoring by the user departments. The following box gives an example of what can happen when incompatible IT functions are performed by the same individual.

Programmer and Operator Combined

A programmer employed by a large U.S. savings and loan association wrote a special subroutine that could be activated by a command from the computer console. The computation of interest on deposits and certificates was programmed to truncate calculations at the third decimal place. The special subroutine instructed the program to accumulate the truncated mills, and, when processing was complete, to credit the amount to the programmer-operator's savings account. Whenever this person was on duty for the interest calculation run, she could "make" several hundred dollars! She had to be on duty to manipulate the control figures "properly" so the error of overpaying interest on her account would not be detected by the control group. She was a programmer with computer operation duties.

Supervision.   Supervision is an important element of control. Management's supervision of the work of clerks and computers carrying out the accounting and control procedures is important. A supervisor could, for example, oversee the credit manager's performance or could periodically compare the sum of customers' balances with the accounts receivable control account total. Supervisors or department heads can correct errors found by the clerical staff and make or approve accounting decisions. Supervision is an important means used by management for monitoring and maintaining a system of internal control.

Controlled Access.   Access to assets, important records, documents, and blank forms should be limited to authorized personnel. Inventory and securities should not be available to people who have no need to handle them. Likewise, access to cost records and accounts receivable records should be denied to people who do not have a recordkeeping responsibility for them. Access to blank forms is the equivalent of access to, or custody of, an important asset. For example, someone who has access to blank cheques has a measure of actual custody of and access to cash. Blank sales invoices and shipping orders are very important for accounting and control, and their availability should be restricted to those involved in accounting for sales.

In IT-based systems, controlled access is achieved through locating hardware, software, and data in secured facilities, and through use of user identity codes and passwords to restrict online access for networks, programs, and data to authorized personnel. Determining who should have access to which IT functions should be done on the basis of keeping incompatible functions separate.

A physical control's relevance to financial statement reliability and the audit depends on the auditee's accounting system. For example, if management uses periodic physical counts to detect any inventory losses and records all these losses in the financial statements, the physical controls would not be highly relevant to the audit. However, if management relies on perpetual inventory records for financial reporting purposes and inventory is physically counted at a date other than year end, then the physical security controls would be relevant to the audit. In this case, the auditor needs assurance that controls operated effectively throughout the period between the physical count and the financial statement date to have sufficient appropriate audit evidence about the reported ending inventory balance.

Periodic Comparison.   Management has responsibility for the recorded accountability of assets and liabilities. The recorded amounts should be periodically compared with independent evidence of existence and valuation. This is done by periodic counting of cash, securities, and inventory and then comparing the results with control totals in the accounting records. Internal auditors and others on an accounting staff could do this on a regular basis, but the same people should not also have responsibility for authorization of related transactions, accounting or recordkeeping, or custodial responsibility for the assets.

Periodic comparisons include counts of cash on hand, reconciliation of bank statements, counts of securities, confirmation of accounts receivable balances, reconciling customer account balances to the general ledger accounts receivable control balance, reconciling accounts payable to supplier statements, and other comparisons to determine if accounting records—the recorded accountability—represent real assets and liabilities. Frequent comparisons give management more opportunities to detect errors in the records than infrequent ones do, and these can also motivate employees to work more accurately. Like all control procedures, frequency of comparisons is governed by the costs and benefits. Very frequent comparisons are worthwhile for assets especially susceptible to loss or error, or ones that are highly valuable. In other words, if the inherent risk is high, the controls should be strengthened to compensate and lower the control risk.

Follow-up to correct differences found by periodic comparisons is also important. This lowers the risk that material misstatements will remain in the accounts. Accounting data error-checking techniques can be categorized as (1) input controls, (2) processing controls, and (3) output controls. The weakest point in computer systems is input—the point at which transaction data are transformed from hard-copy source documents or online order keying into machine-readable form. When undetected errors are entered originally, they may not be detected during processing, and, if detected, they can be costly to correct. For this reason, preventive controls at input are the most cost effective. Processing controls are error-condition check routines written into the computer program. Output control refers primarily to control over the distribution of reports, but it includes feedback on errors and comparison of input totals to output totals. Error-checking techniques are closely related to application controls, but, because errors compound if they are not corrected quickly and appropriately, they have a pervasive impact on the accounting system's integrity. The auditor should consider the overall effectiveness of error-correction procedures as a key part of the general IT control activities.

IT Controls.   General IT controls are policies and procedures that relate to IT-based systems and support the effective functioning of IT application controls by helping to ensure the continued proper operation of information systems. These controls apply to mainframe, server, and end-user environments. General IT controls over computer operations commonly include

- operating system and application software acquisition, change, and maintenance;
- access security, authorization for access to systems, programs, and data files;
- system and application development and maintenance;
- routine data and system backup procedures;
- disaster recovery plans to restore systems and data, or to provide backup processing capability; and
- physical security of assets, including adequate safeguards such as secured facilities over access to assets and records with appropriate environmental controls.

REVIEW CHECKPOINTS

29 What risks are addressed by controlled access?

30 Give some examples of periodic comparisons a company can perform. How do they control the accuracy of its financial records?

31 List general controls related to IT.

32 Which duties should be segregated within the information system? Why?

. . . .

Applications Control Activities

Applications control activities are specific procedures used in each accounting process to meet the relevant control objectives. Auditors evaluate the activities in terms of how they address financial reporting risk at the assertion level. The audit approach starts with documenting the accounting processes and information systems, and then it identifies the application controls within each system. Methods of documenting accounting systems and controls are discussed next.

Documentation of Internal Control. Auditors' understanding of the internal controls comes through several sources of information: (1) last year's audit experience with the company, (2) auditee personnel responses to enquiries, (3) documents and records inspection, (4) walk-through observation of the activities and operations of a single transaction. Such walk-through tests have traditionally been used to verify the accuracy of the auditor's narrative or flow chart description of the system.

Working paper documentation should include records showing the audit team's understanding of the internal controls. It can be summarized in the form of questionnaires, narratives, and flow charts. The decision on how much reliance to place on controls and how much to place on substantive work should also be documented by a memorandum explaining underlying reasons, for instance, to increase effectiveness and efficiency. This is helpful for reference in next year's audit.

Internal Control Questionnaire and Narrative The most efficient means of gathering evidence about internal control is to conduct formal interviews with knowledgeable managers using a checklist guide such as the **internal control questionnaire** shown in Exhibit 9–8. This questionnaire is organized under headings identifying the questions related to the environment and general controls and those related to each of the seven control objectives. In creating a questionnaire, using these seven categories helps to ensure it will cover all the assertions.

Internal control questionnaires are designed to help the audit team obtain evidence about the control environment as well as about the general and application control activities that can reduce risks of error and fraud. Answers to the questions, however, should not be taken as final and definitive evidence about how well control actually functions. Evidence obtained through the interview-questionnaire process is hearsay as its source is an individual who, while knowledgeable, may not be the person who actually performs the control work. They may give answers reflecting what they believe the system should be, rather than what it really is. They may be unaware of informal ways that have been changed or be innocently ignorant of the system details. Nevertheless, interviews and questionnaires are useful as a starting point. If a manager admits to a weak control, it is important to document and follow up in subsequent audit work.

One strength of questionnaires is that they minimize the risk that an important point will be forgotten. Questions are usually worded so that a "no" answer points out some weakness or control deficiency, thus making analysis easier. These enquiry procedures can be tailored to a particular company by writing descriptions of each important control subsystem. It would simply describe all the environmental elements, the accounting system, and the control procedures. The narrative description may be efficient in audits of small businesses or simple systems within larger organizations.

Accounting and Control System Flow Charts Flow charts are one technique used by auditors to document their understanding of accounting and control systems. Many control-conscious companies have their own flow charts, usually prepared by internal auditors, that external auditors can use instead of constructing their own. The advantages of flow charts can be

EXHIBIT 9-8   INTERNAL CONTROL QUESTIONNAIRE—REVENUE TRANSACTION PROCESSING

Auditee _____   Audit Date _____

Auditee Personnel Interviewed _____

_____

Auditor _____   Date Completed _____

Reviewed by _____   Date Reviewed _____

Question	Answer			
	NA	Yes	No	Remarks
Environment and General Controls Related to Sales Transaction Processing				
1. Is the credit department independent of the marketing department?				
2. Are sales accounting staff properly trained in and subject to supervisory reviews? Are they independent of marketing and credit departments?				
3. Are nonroutine sales of the following types controlled by the same procedures described below? Sales to employees, COD sales, disposals of property, cash sales, and scrap sales.				
4. Are policies in place to ensure effective IT management and IT staff supervision?				
5. Are IT systems general controls in place to ensure				
– accurate data and processing of sales transactions?				
– authorized access to data and application software?				
Assertion-based Control Evaluation				
Validity Objective				
6. Are procedures in place to				
– prevent fictitious sales being recorded in accounts?				
– ensure approved revenue recognition policies are followed?				
7. Is access to sales invoice blanks, or online order entry restricted to authorized personnel?				
8. Are prenumbered bills of lading or other shipping documents prepared or completed in the shipping department?				
Completeness Objective				
9. Are procedures in place to ensure				
– all goods shipped/services performed are invoiced?				
– no fictitious sales credits are recorded?				
10. Are sales invoice blanks or online orders numbered sequentially?				
11. Is the sequence checked for missing invoices by appropriate personnel?				
12. Is the shipping document numerical sequence checked for missing bills of lading numbers by appropriate personnel?				
Authorization Objective				
13. Are all credit sales approved by the credit department prior to shipment?				
14. Are sales prices and terms based on approved standards?				
15. Are returned sales credits and other credits supported by documentation as to receipt, condition, and quantity and approved by a responsible officer?				
Accuracy Objective				
16. Are shipped quantities compared with invoice quantities by appropriate personnel?				
17. Are sales invoices checked for error in quantities, prices, extensions and footing, and freight allowances as well as checked with customer's orders?				
18. Is there an overall check on arithmetic accuracy of period sales data by a statistical or product-line analysis?				
19. Are periodic sales data reported directly to general ledger accounting independent of accounts receivable accounting?				
Classification Objective				
20. Does the accounting manual contain instructions for classifying revenues according to the company's revenue recognition policies?				
21. Are accounting supervisors aware of related parties and are related party transactions flagged in the accounting system?				
Accounting Objective				
22. Are summary journal entries approved before posting?				

EXHIBIT 9–8 Continued

Question	Answer			
	NA	Yes	No	Remarks
Proper Period Objective				
23. Does the accounting manual contain instructions to date sales invoices on the shipment date?				
24. Do accounting staff understand proper period end cut-off procedures for sales and cash receipts?				
25. Does the information system correctly age receivables to provide information about doubtful accounts?				

summarized by an old cliché, "A picture is worth a thousand words." They enhance auditors' evaluations and are easy to update—simply add or delete symbols and lines.

Flowchart construction takes time because an auditor must learn about the operating of personnel involved in the system and gather samples of relevant documents. Thus, the information for the flow chart, like the narrative description, involves a lot of legwork and observation. When the flow chart is complete, however, the result is an easily evaluated, informative description of the system. Flowcharting software that saves time and produces more readable output is available.

Exhibit 9–9 contains a few simple flowchart symbols. An audit supervisor should be able to understand the chart without consulting a lengthy index of symbols. It should be legible and drawn with a template and ruler or with computer software. The starting point in the system should, if possible, be placed at the upper left-hand corner, with the flow of procedures and documents moving from left to right and from top to bottom, as much as is possible. Narrative explanations should be written on the chart as annotations, or be part of a readily available reference key.

The flow chart should communicate all relevant information and evidence about segregation of responsibilities, authorization, and accounting and control procedures in an understandable, visual form. Exhibit 9–10 shows a partial flowchart representation of the beginning stages of a sales and delivery processing system. The out-connectors shown by the circled A and B indicate continuation on other flow charts. Ultimately, the flow chart ends by showing entries in accounting journals and inventory ledgers.

In Exhibit 9–10 you can see both some characteristics of flow chart construction and some characteristics of this accounting system.[3] Minimizing the number of flow lines that cross each other is helpful for following the chart. Reading down each department's column shows that initiation authority for transactions (both credit approval and sales invoice preparation) and custody of assets are separated. All documents have an intermediate or final resting place in a file (some of these files are in the flow charts connected to A and B), thus giving auditors information about where to find audit evidence later.

Technology such as workflow charting software tools allows businesses to describe their processes, integrate various processes, automate routine management activities, and integrate information systems. The SOX regulation in the U.S. requires public companies to document their controls, and tools like these help businesses comply.

Regardless of the method used to develop the flow chart, its accuracy can be verified by performing a walk-through test of the documents and procedures to see if they are processed as described in the flow chart. An understanding of the flow of transactions through the accounting system supports the design of substantive audit procedures, and it begins with referring to the auditee's description of the accounting processes. Descriptions could include user's manuals and instructions, file descriptions, system flow charts, and narrative descriptions.

[3] Accounting firms have various methods for constructing flow charts. The illustrations in this book take the approach of describing an accounting subsystem completely. Some accounting firms use more efficient methods of charting only the documents, information flows, and controls considered important for the audit.

EXHIBIT 9-9 STANDARD FLOWCHART SYMBOLS

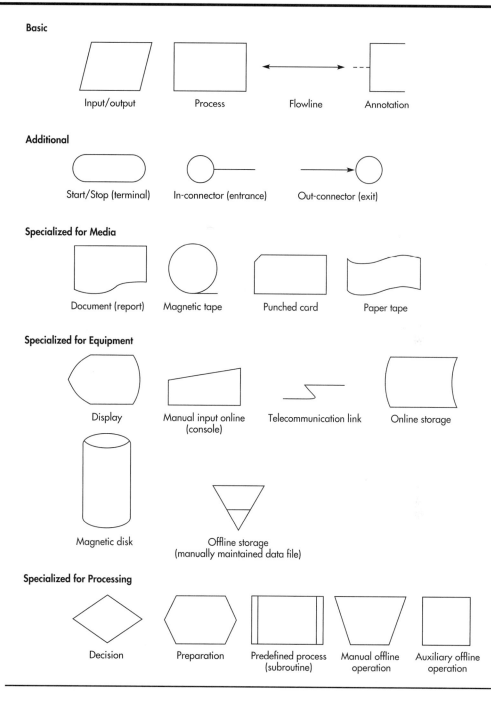

The audit team may find that there already is documentation related to the flow of transactions that may be adequate for understanding the accounting system. Early in the audit planning, the internal auditors and other auditee personnel should be consulted to determine whether they have documentation that can be useful.

Internal Control and Planned Audit Approach
A brief overview of how internal controls affect the audit approach to be used in the detailed audit programs for each significant transaction stream and account balance concludes this section.

EXHIBIT 9-10   CREDIT APPROVAL AND REVENUE PROCESSING, SHIPMENT AND DELIVERY

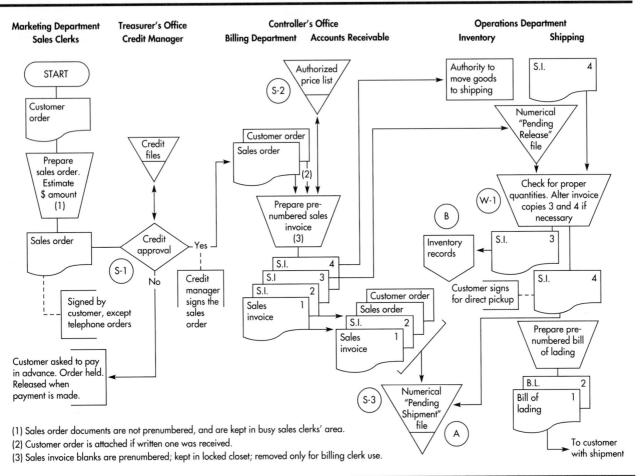

(1) Sales order documents are not prenumbered, and are kept in busy sales clerks' area.

(2) Customer order is attached if written one was received.

(3) Sales invoice blanks are prenumbered; kept in locked closet; removed only for billing clerk use.

1. All audit engagements involve some evaluation of internal controls, even if only on environmental controls affecting all cycles (for example, reconciliation of general ledger to subsidiary ledgers). Under GAAS, auditors are required to understand internal controls in order to assess the risk of material misstatement for all audits.[4]

2. Internal control is documented through narratives, questionnaires, and flow charts. These are corroborated with walk-through tests or tracing of a representative transaction.

3. In reaching a preliminary evaluation of internal control, the auditor must consider
   (a) errors that may arise
   (b) controls that exist to prevent or detect those errors
   Professional judgment is applied to knowledge gained in point (b).

4. The review, preliminary evaluation, and documentation must be applied to specific internal controls within an individual accounting process. The specific controls activities, not the system as a whole, are assessed. Only the specific controls which auditors intend to obtain audit assurance from need to be tested.

5. If the auditor wishes to use internal controls as a component of audit evidence, tests of control need to be planned and executed. The decision to test the controls is a function of
   (a) evaluation of the design of the system
   (b) cost-benefit trade-offs of control testing, assuming the design is adequate

[4] CAS 200 (5100) and 315 (5141).

In summary, if the auditor decides not to test internal controls, the **substantive audit approach** is being used. If, on a preliminary basis, the auditor does decide to test internal controls, and the tests confirm that the controls are operating effectively, then the auditor may reduce the extent of substantive audit procedures. Finally, in the case where the auditor cannot obtain sufficient appropriate audit evidence on the basis of substantive tests alone, testing controls and finding them effective increases the evidence sufficiency to an acceptable level to support the audit opinion. These last two approaches are referred to as the **combined audit approach**.[5]

**R E V I E W
C H E C K P O I N T S**

33 What does the auditor need to understand about the auditee's control environment?

34 What does the auditor need to understand about the flow of transactions in the auditee's information systems?

35 What sources of information can auditors use to gain knowledge about the auditee's internal controls?

36 What internal control documentation needs to be included in the audit files?

37 Why is audit file documentation required for the auditor's decision on whether to rely on controls in the audit planning?

38 What is an audit internal control questionnaire?

39 What is an internal control system narrative and what is it used for in an audit?

40 What is the purpose of an internal control systems flow chart? How does it differ from a narrative?

41 Why do many organizations have documentation of their internal control system?

42 What is a walk-through and why is this procedure used in an audit?

43 What role can internal auditors play in internal control system documentation?

44 What is a substantive audit approach and how does it differ from a combined audit approach?

Phase 2: Assessing the Control Risk

After phase 1—obtaining an understanding of the internal control and making a preliminary decision on an audit approach—the audit team assesses the control risk at the assertion level. Control risk assessment involves

- identifying specific control objectives based on the risks of misstatements that may be present in significant accounting applications,
- identifying the points in the flow of transactions where specific types of misstatements could occur,
- identifying specific control procedures designed to prevent or detect misstatements,
- identifying the control procedures that must function to prevent or detect misstatements, and
- evaluating the design of control procedures to determine whether it suggests the auditee has strong control procedures in place and whether it may be cost effective to test these controls as part of the audit.

A useful assessment technique is to analyze control strengths and weaknesses. **Strengths** are specific features of effective control procedures that would prevent, detect, or correct material misstatements. **Weaknesses** are a lack of controls in particular areas that would allow material errors to get by undetected. The auditors' findings and preliminary conclusions on control strengths and weaknesses should be written up for the working paper files

[5] CAS 330.

EXHIBIT 9-11   BRIDGE WORKING PAPER

Index _____   By _____   Date _____
                  Reviewed _____   Date _____

KINGSTON COMPANY
Credit Approval, Sales Processing, Shipment and Delivery Control
December 31, 20X2

	Strength/Weakness	Audit Implication	Audit Program
S-1	Credit approval on sales order.	Credit authorization reduces risk of bad debt loss and helps check on validity of customer identification.	Select a sample of recorded sales invoices, and look for credit manager signature on attached sales order.
S-2	Unit prices are taken from an authorized list.	Prices are in accordance with company policy, minimizing customer disputes.	Using the S-1 sample of sales invoices, vouch prices used thereon to the price lists.
S-3	Sales are not recorded until goods are shipped.	Cut-off will be proper and sales will not be recorded too early.	Using the S-1 sample of sales invoices, compare the recording date with the shipment date on attached bill of lading or copy 4. (Also, scan the "pending shipment" file for old invoices that might represent unrecorded shipments.)
W-1	Shipping personnel have transaction alteration (initiation) authority to change the quantities on invoices, as well as custody of the goods.	Dishonest shipping personnel can alone let accomplices receive large quantities and alter the invoice to charge them for small quantities. If this happened, sales and accounts receivable would be understated, and inventory could be overstated.	The physical count of inventory will need to be observed carefully (extensive work) to detect material overstatement.

S = Strength
W = Weakness

in a document called a **bridge working paper**—so called because it connects (bridges) the control evaluation to subsequent audit procedures. The major strengths and weaknesses apparent in the flow chart of Exhibit 9–10 are summarized in the bridge working paper in Exhibit 9–11. On the flow chart, the strengths are indicated by S-, and the weakness by W-. In Exhibit 9–11, the "audit program" column contains procedures for auditing the control strengths and suggestions about substantive account balance audit procedures related to the weaknesses (the last column in the exhibit). Auditors do not need to test control weaknesses just to prove they are weak places as this would be inefficient. However, auditors do always need to take control weaknesses into account in assessing the risk of material misstatements in the financial statements.

At this stage in the control risk assessment, the control risk related to the inventory balance might be set very high (e.g., 0.8 or 0.9 in probability terms). The three control strengths, however, relate to good control over sales validity and accounts receivable accuracy. The auditors probably will want to rely on these controls to reduce audit work on the accounts receivable balance. Tests of these control procedures ought to be performed to obtain evidence about whether the apparent strengths actually are performed well. The "audit program" segment of Exhibit 9–11 for each of the strengths describes specific control tests of the relevant control procedure. Testing controls (phase 3) consists of tests designed to produce evidence of how well the controls worked in practice. If they pass the auditor's criteria (the required degree of compliance), control risk can be assessed low, but, if they fail the test, a high control risk is assessed and the audit plan revised to take the control weakness into account. Control tests only provide indirect evidence of the monetary accuracy of financial statement balances, because not all monetary misstatements are caused by control weaknesses. Substantive testing provides more direct evidence about monetary accuracy.

R E V I E W
C H E C K P O I N T S

45 What steps are involved in a control risk assessment?

46 What is a control strength? What is a control weakness? How do control strengths relate to control testing?

47 What is the purpose of a bridge working paper and what information does it contain?

48 Why is it not necessary to test control weaknesses? What action does the auditor need to take when control evaluation work indicates a control weakness?

49 What are the implications for the audit program if tests of key controls indicate they are operating effectively for the whole period being audited? What are the implications if a key control is tested and a high degree of noncompliance is found?

This section on control risk assessment concludes with a special note on assessing risks in complex IT and ecommerce environments as well as considerations of manual and IT controls in information systems.

Special Note: Assessing the Control Risk in Complex IT and Ecommerce Environments

Business Internet and IT use have a big impact on control risk. There are many business models that incorporate the Internet. In addition to **business to business (B2B)**, **business to consumer (B2C)**, and **consumer to consumer (C2C)** (discussed in Appendix 7E on the OLC), some models include **business to employee (B2E)**, for example, a system allowing intracompany (intragroup) emails to be directed to the correct department. Internal uses of Internet technology are referred to as **Intranets.** Other models include **business to government (B2G)**—electronic submission of corporate tax returns and regulatory filings—and **customer to government (C2G)**—electronic submission of individual tax returns.

Auditors are mainly concerned with the security of IT processing, especially as it affects the accuracy and reliability of the accounting function. In a business with complex IT use and ecommerce activities, it is challenging to maintain the integrity of control systems and to ensure access to relevant records for management and audit purposes in a rapidly changing environment. In some circumstances (e.g., when ecommerce systems are highly automated, when transaction volumes are high, or when electronic evidence comprising the audit trail is not retained), the auditor may determine that controls are critical to reducing financial reporting risks as it may not be possible to reduce audit risk to an acceptably low level using only substantive procedures. It will be necessary to assess and test effectiveness of key controls to determine their adequacy in ensuring that the requirements relevant to the financial statement assertions, information's authorization, authenticity, confidentiality, integrity, nonrepudiation, and availability are met.

When the auditee engages in ecommerce, the following aspects of internal control are particularly relevant:

- security
- transaction integrity
- process alignment

These aspects are explained in the following paragraphs.

Security.   External parties' ability to access the auditee's information system using the Internet creates security risks. The security infrastructure and related controls include an information security policy, an information security risk assessment process, and security procedures, which incorporate both physical measures and logical or other technical safeguards such as user identities, passwords, firewalls, and encryption including both authorization and safeguarding of decryption keys. The control environment ensures systems are updated so that risk posed by new technologies is addressed.

Security concerns and controls can be broken down into the components shown in the following box.

SEVEN CORNERSTONES OF BASIC SECURITY

Security concerns	**Controls**
1. Network security	• network segmentation, intrusion detection software, all network devices at current patch level
2. Database security	• control administrator access accounts, update access restrictions
3. Operating system security	• upgrade Windows O/S to eliminate NetBIOS, penetration audits
4. External security	• firewalls, modem and wireless access, monitor trading partner access accounts
5. Application security	• rule of least access for users, review transaction routing, application triggers for unusual items, purge old users
6. Physical security	• annual physical security audit, surprise intrusion tests
7. Business continuance and disaster preparedness security	• server, applications, firewall and ISP redundancy, business continuance plan stored off-site at key employees' homes

Source: Adapted from Gordon E. Smith, "Information Security: Is Your Auditing Up to the Task?" *The Journal of Corporate Accounting and Finance*, 15 (4), May/June 2004, p. 13.

In addition to internal risks, information security breaches in ecommerce applications can lead to unauthorized access to private information, customer credit card numbers and social insurance numbers, for example. Privacy laws require all businesses to have control over privacy of information in place, and weaknesses can result in legal action against a company, as well as action by private individuals whose information was improperly given out. A weakness in privacy controls could thus mean that a material misstatement of the financial statements exists in the form of an undisclosed contingent liability. Rapid and radical technological changes are risk factors that can expose the organization to control risks such as unauthorized access to their proprietary or confidential information, as shown in the following box.

SCRAP YARD RECEIVING CIBC CUSTOMERS' PRIVATE DATA

HOST: Beverly Thomson
GUESTS: David Akin, CTV News; Wade Peer, Junkyard Owner

THOMSON: It's one of the worst security-breach scenarios imaginable. Your personal banking information, information you think is being kept confidential, is mistakenly sent to the wrong person. And that's exactly what happened to hundreds of CIBC customers. Instead of being sent to bank offices, their financial records were accidentally faxed to a junkyard man in West Virginia. And the faxes kept on coming, despite pleas from the frustrated yard owner to stop. CTV's David Akin has this exclusive.

[Taped segment begins]

DAVID AKIN (CTV News): The first faxes came through in 2001; confidential documents never intended to be seen outside a CIBC branch. And yet, they have ended up here, at Wade Peer's scrap yard in rural West Virginia.

WADE PEER (Junkyard Owner): I feel that CIBC's customers should know. I think that had that been my information I would be highly upset. I'd be livid.

AKIN: Here is why. Many faxes that Peer received contain some of the most sensitive data a bank has about its customers: names, phone numbers, social insurance numbers, bank account numbers, and even signatures. Peer needed his fax machine to talk to customers of his auto-accessories wholesale business. But a flood of faxes from the CIBC overwhelmed the phone system, Peer says, and he had to shut the accessories business down.

PEER: We couldn't even use them. We couldn't get calls in, we couldn't get calls out.

AKIN: But he didn't close down the fax number. And even as recently as this week the faxes sent by CIBC continue to arrive at this West Virginia scrap yard.

PEER: Cooksville, Edmonton, Calgary, Burlington, Port Hope, Toronto.

AKIN: Both he and the bank used similar toll-free 1-877 lines for their faxes. But neither he nor the bank can say how they got mixed up. Frustrated by the bank's response, Peer filed a lawsuit last spring. He wants $3 million U.S. for the damage he says CIBC did to his business. The bank denies his allegations.

AKIN: The CIBC said it thought the problem of misdirected faxes was resolved in 2002. And in a statement issued to CTV News it said it takes the confidentiality of its customers' personal information very seriously; and that it was a disturbing revelation to learn that the faxes continue. It went on to say that "we are undertaking a full review of this matter."

[Taped segment ends]

THOMSON: . . . And wow. I mean, Wade Peer is an honest guy . . . who has not done anything sinister with this. What happens if it falls into the wrong hands?

AKIN: Well, you hit on it. I mean, by lucky chance this went to a responsible guy. He shredded a lot of the documents he first got. He knew exactly what he had at first. But when he started to get in this contest with the bank, he has kept many of the documents. They're locked up in a filing cabinet you saw in that piece. Experts say this is exactly the sort of information that online fraud artists, identity thieves could use to go to a bank and get a debit card, get a new PIN number, and away they go.

THOMSON: False ID.

AKIN: I think it's important to point out, so far as we know, no CIBC customer has come to any harm or lost any money as a result of this.

THOMSON: And David, just very quickly, is it normal business practice to be faxing these kinds of pieces of information?

AKIN: The banks need your signature on these documents. So they have a central fax unit in Toronto, most banks do, so that the transaction will happen electronically. And this is just the backup document to authenticate it. So it's routine for banks to do this but, presumably, they're triple-checking fax numbers. And I'm sure all the banks this morning are triple-checking their fax numbers to make sure that the documents are going to where they're supposed to be going.

Source: "Scrap Yard Receiving CIBC Customers' Private Data," Canada AM—CTV Television, Transcript, Toronto: November 26, 2004. p. 1. CTV Television Inc.

The auditor needs to consider whether the entity has implemented general IT and application controls that respond adequately to the risks arising from IT. Auditors consider these controls effective if they maintain the integrity of information and the security of the data processed.[6] This is another reason for audit teams to include up-to-date IT experts.

Transaction Integrity.   Risks related to the recording and processing of ecommerce transactions include the completeness, accuracy, timeliness, and authorization of information in the entity's financial records. Control activities relating to transaction integrity in an ecommerce environment are often designed to do the following:

(a) validate input

(b) prevent duplication or omission of transactions

(c) ensure the terms of trade have been agreed before an order is processed; usually payment is obtained when an order is placed

---

[6] CAS 315 (5141).

(*d*) distinguish between customer browsing and orders placed, ensure a party to a transaction cannot later deny having agreed to specified terms (nonrepudiation), and ensure transactions are with approved parties when appropriate

(*e*) prevent incomplete processing by rejecting the order if all steps are not completed and recorded (for example, for a B2C transaction: order accepted, payment received, goods delivered, and accounting system updated)

(*f*) ensure the proper distribution of transaction details across multiple systems in a network (for example, when data are collected centrally and communicated to various resource managers to execute the transaction)

(*g*) ensure records are properly retained, backed up, and secured

Weaknesses in IT and ecommerce controls can increase the company's vulnerability to fraudulent activities by both inside employees and outside customers, suppliers or strangers, as described in the following box.

FRAUD RISKS IN ECOMMERCE

Possible fraudulent activities include the following:
- unauthorized movement of money, such as payments to fictitious suppliers located in jurisdictions where recovery of money will be difficult
- misrepresentations of company tenders
- corruption of electronic ordering or invoicing systems
- duplication of payments
- denying an order was placed
- denying an order was received
- denying receipt of goods
- denying that payment was received
- falsely declaring that a payment was made

Source: Adapted from Jagdish Pathak, "A Conceptual Risk Framework for Internal Auditing in E-commerce," *Managerial Auditing Journal* 19 (4), 2004, p. 560.

Process Alignment. Process alignment refers the integration of IT systems so that they operate as one system. Transactions generated on the business website should be processed properly by the entity's various internal systems, such as the accounting, customer relationship management, and inventory management systems (often known as "back office" systems). Many websites are not automatically integrated with internal systems, increasing the risk of inconsistent recording and other errors.

Identifying specific control objectives is the same in both manual and IT-based data processing procedures. However, the points in the flow of transactions where misstatements could occur may be different, as is seen in Exhibit 9–12, which gives a flow chart of a basic IT-based accounting system indicating the points in the process where misstatements could occur.

The points in the system where misstatements might occur are:

Input

1. Activities related to source data preparation are performed, causing the flow of transactions to include authorization and initial execution.

2. Manual procedures are applied to source data, such as a manual summarization of accounting data (preparation of batch totals).

3. Source data are converted into computer-readable form.

4. Input files are identified for use in processing.

Processing

5. Information is transferred from one computer program to another.

EXHIBIT 9–12   IT ACCOUNTING: POINTS OF VULNERABILITY TO MISSTATEMENT ERRORS

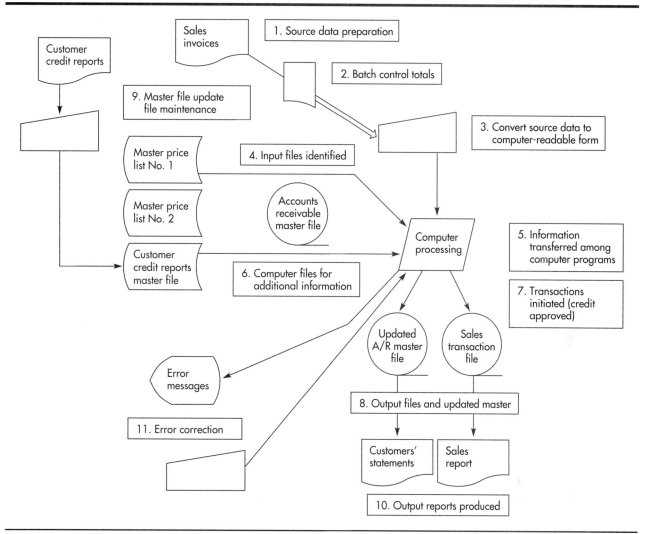

6. Computer-readable files are used to supply additional information relating to individual transactions (e.g., customer credit reports).

7. Transactions are initiated by the computer.

Output

8. Output files are created or master files are updated.

9. Master files are changed (records added, deleted, or modified) outside the normal flow of transactions within each cycle through file maintenance procedures.

10. Output reports or files are produced.

11. Errors identified by control procedures are corrected.

Once the audit team has identified the risks, specific control objectives can be related to such points. For example, invoicing customers with incorrect prices if the wrong price list file has been used would lead to a misstatement. The control objective for this type of misstatement is "Appropriate price information should be used during the invoicing process." The controls associated with prevention, detection, and correction of misstatements can be grouped into three broad categories: input, processing, and output controls. Input controls are associated with preventing misstatements related to the points numbered 1 through 4 above. Processing controls are primarily designed to detect misstatements related to points 5 through 8 above. Output controls are designed to correct misstatements related to points 9 through 11 above.

Control procedures should be related to specific control objectives. For example, for the objective of using appropriate price information, one control procedure might be "The invoicing program should use the most up-to-date price list file and the price list file date should appear on the invoicing summary management report. The accounts receivable manager should review the invoicing summary report and verify that the correct price list has been used to calculate the invoice amounts prior to issuing and sending the invoices to customers."

Manual control procedures may differ from IT controls that are designed to accomplish the same control objectives. For example, in a manual system, credit approval usually is indicated by an authorized person putting their signature on a source document, such as a customer's order or invoice. In a computerized system, however, approval can be accomplished by the authorized person using an approved password that releases a credit sale transaction by assigning a special code to it. Even though the objectives are the same, because the methods used to achieve the objectives and the visible evidence differ, different audit approaches may be required as well. The following section will describe manual and IT control components in detail and discuss the benefits and risk of each type of control.

Manual and IT Controls over Information Processing. Most entities use IT systems for financial reporting and operational purposes, but even so there will also be manual elements to the systems. The system of internal control is also likely to contain manual and automated procedures, the characteristics of which will affect the auditor's risk assessment and design of further audit procedures. The methods used to process accounting transactions will affect a company's organizational structure and influence the procedures and techniques used to accomplish the objectives of internal control.

Controls in a manual system include approvals, management reviews of reports and activities, reconciliations, and follow-up of reconciling items. Controls in IT systems will typically be a combination of automated controls (e.g., controls embedded in computer programs) and manual controls, which may either use information produced by IT or be independent of IT. In order to understand internal control, the auditor has to understand the risks of IT or manual systems and whether management has responded adequately by establishing effective controls. Some of the risks and benefits of manual versus IT procedures in internal control are noted in the following box.

MANUAL VERSUS IT CONTROLS: RISKS AND BENEFITS

IT Control Benefits
IT can enhance internal control effectiveness and efficiency by the following:
- consistently processing large volumes of transactions or data by applying predefined business rules and performing complex calculations
- enhancing the timeliness, availability, and accuracy of information
- facilitating the further information analysis
- enhancing the entity's performance monitoring
- reducing the risk of controls being overridden
- allowing effective segregation of duties by implementing security controls in applications, databases, and operating systems

IT Control Risks
IT also can create specific internal control risks, including:
- reliance on inaccurate systems, programs, or data
- unauthorized data access allowing data destruction, improper changes, recording unauthorized, inaccurate, or non-existent transactions, particularly when multiple users access a common database
- IT personnel gaining inappropriate or unnecessary access privileges that undermine segregation of duties, or allow unauthorized changes to master file data, systems, or programs
- failure to make necessary updates to systems or programs
- inappropriate manual intervention
- potential loss of data or inability to access data as required

Manual Control Benefits

Manual systems can be beneficial when judgment and discretion are required, such as for the following circumstances:

- large, unusual, or non-recurring transactions
- circumstances where errors are difficult to define, anticipate, or predict
- changing circumstances that require a control response outside the scope of an existing automated control
- monitoring the effectiveness of automated controls

Manual Control Risks

Manual controls tend to raise the following risks:

- human error is always possible, so mistakes can occur and consistent application cannot be assumed
- relatively easy to bypass, ignore, or override
- less effective for high volume or recurring transactions, or other situations where typical errors can be anticipated, prevented, or detected by control parameters that can be automated.

Source: Adapted from CAS 315.

Regardless of whether it is manual or automated, every accounting system must contain procedures ensuring proper recording of transactions, prevention or detection of errors and irregularities, and monitoring of control effectiveness. It is management's responsibility to establish and maintain internal controls, and the information system policies and procedures are part of this. The audit team's responsibility is to make an assessment of the control risk in the system. Management can meet its responsibility and assist auditors by (1) ensuring that documentation of the system is complete and up to date, (2) maintaining a system of transaction processing that includes an audit trail, and (3) making IT resources and knowledgeable personnel available to the auditors. Appendix 9A on the OLC provides a detailed description of the characteristics of IT-based information systems, and of the auditors' risk and control assessment, for students who are interested in applying the concepts and techniques from their management information systems courses.

REVIEW CHECKPOINTS

50 What are the main purposes of control procedures in an information system?

51 Explain the difference between manual controls and IT controls. Give an example of each.

52 In which situations are manual controls preferable and in which are IT controls preferable?

Summary of Phases 1 and 2

According to GAAS, the auditor is required to assess control risk for the different classes of transactions and account balances at the assertion level. The information gathered about the auditee's control environment, the accounting information systems, and the control procedures should enable the auditor to reach one of the following conclusions about control risk.

- Control risk may be assessed low. The auditor believes the control procedures designed to prevent or detect misstatements can be audited for compliance in a cost-effective manner, reducing the amount of substantive evidence needed for reasonable assurance. Alternatively, when certain control procedures are essential for reducing risk of material misstatement, and substantive procedures alone won't provide sufficient appropriate evidence about the assertion(s), controls must be tested to support the audit opinion. In this case, the auditor plans an audit approach that combines control testing and substantive evidence gathering.

or

- Control risk may be assessed low. Control policies and procedures appear to be good, but testing controls is not cost effective because substantive procedures can provide sufficient appropriate evidence and are more efficient than a combined approach. In this case the auditors would concentrate attention on the substantive audit procedures.

or

- Control risk may be assessed high. Control policies and procedures do not appear to be sufficient to prevent or detect material misstatements. In this case the auditors will concentrate on substantive audit procedures. The auditor also has additional responsibilities to report the control weaknesses to management and those charged with governance. If the effective operation of controls is essential to reduce the risk of material misstatement, and substantive procedures alone won't provide sufficient appropriate evidence about the assertion(s), a scope limitation exists that may prevent the auditor from obtaining reasonable assurance that no material misstatement has occurred.

The control risk conclusion determines the approach that will be followed in planning the audit. The first conclusion above will result in the auditor's choosing a combined audit approach using both control and substantive testing, and the second and third conclusions will result in choosing an approach based on obtaining substantive evidence. Since the auditor is required to make the control assessment at the assertion level, it may be possible to identify specific control procedures that provide a low risk assessment with regard to some but not all assertions, leading the auditor to use a combination of tests of controls and substantive auditing. Other audit objectives may be achieved through substantive procedures alone.

To summarize the auditor's control assessment up to this point, phases 1 and 2 can be described as dealing with the evaluation of the design of the system that operates properly. Now we move on to phase 3 where we test the actual operation of the system.

REVIEW CHECKPOINTS

53 What challenges arise for management and the auditor when an auditee uses complex IT and/or is involved in ecommerce?

54 What is information security risk? What are its components?

55 Give examples of controls related to information security concerns.

56 Why are an auditee's privacy controls relevant to the audit?

57 What risks and controls relate to recording and processing ecommerce transactions?

58 List fraud risks that exist in ecommerce activities.

59 What risk arises if IT processes are not aligned properly?

60 Identify the three main components in the flow of transactions.

61 Categorize the 11 points of vulnerability to misstatement errors related to manual input, computer processing, and error correction activities in a computerized information system.

62 Why are the control objectives the same regardless of whether manual or computerized controls procedures are used?

63 Why might manual control procedures differ from computerized control procedures even if both are directed at the same control objective?

64 Describe one manual and one computerized control procedure designed to prevent a credit sale being processed without proper authorization by the credit manager.

65 What three conclusions about control risk can be reached based on internal control evaluation? What are the implications of each on the audit approach selected?

Phase 3: Testing Controls

By the third phase of an internal control evaluation, auditors will have assessed individual controls. To reach a conclusion on control risk, auditors must determine (a) what degree of compliance with the control policies and procedures is required, and then (b) what degree of control compliance is actually present. The degree of compliance required is the criterion that control performance is assessed against. Knowing that compliance cannot be perfect, auditors might decide, for example, that using shipping documents to validate sales invoice recordings 96 percent of the time is sufficient to assess a low control risk for the audit of accounts receivable (controls relating to the existence assertion in receivables and sales). Auditors perform control tests to determine how well the company's control procedures actually worked during the period under audit.

A control test has two parts. The first part is identifying the data population from which to select a sample of items for audit. Part two is describing the action that was taken to produce relevant evidence. Basically, the action determines whether the selected items both correspond to a standard (e.g., mathematical accuracy) and agree with information in another data population. The control tests in the audit program in Exhibit 9–11 show this two-part design.

One other important aspect of these audit procedures is known as the direction of the test. The procedures described in Exhibit 9–11 provide evidence about control over the validity of sales transactions. However, they do not provide evidence about control over completeness of recording all shipments. Another data population, the shipping documents, can be sampled to provide evidence about completeness. The direction of the test idea is illustrated in Exhibit 9–13. For example, if the completeness control is found to be strong, the auditors could omit the year-end procedure of confirming customers' zero-balance accounts receivable to search for unrecorded assets (understatements).

If control tests involve recalculation/reperformance, auditors redo the arithmetic calculations and comparisons that employees were supposed to have performed. This control could be tested by inspection alone—looking to see if the documents were marked with an initial, signature, or stamp indicating they had been checked. Recalculation/ reperfomance provides more reliable, first-hand evidence that the control operates effectively. Merely inspecting the control only provides evidence that it exists, not that it operates effectively. Performing both procedures with dual purpose tests is very cost-effective. Much of the cost of control testing is in designing the procedures and selecting the sample to inspect. The marginal cost of extending the work to reperform the calculation or comparison can often be worthwhile. The additional evidence is also substantive in nature since it would actually detect any material misstatement—hence the term dual purpose; that is, providing evidence of both control effectiveness and whether any monetary errors have occurred.

EXHIBIT 9–13   DIRECTION OF CONTROL TESTING

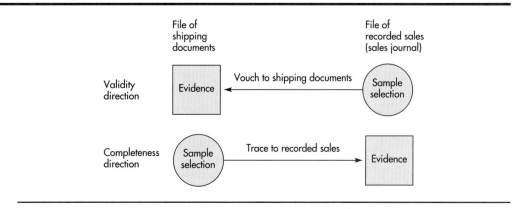

Control tests that depend on documentary evidence, such as signatures, initials, checklists, reconciliation working papers, and the like, provide better evidence than procedures that leave no documentary traces. Some control elements, such as segregation of employees' duties, may produce no documents. Since reperformance of these control operations cannot be done, a less reliable procedure, observation, must be used; an auditor performs unobtrusive eyewitness observation of employees at their jobs performing control operations.

Control tests should be applied to samples of transactions and control procedures executed throughout the whole period being audited. This is required because the auditor's conclusions about whether controls operated effectively must apply to the whole period covered by the financial statements under audit.

Audit procedures relating to the integrity of ecommerce transactions in the accounting process largely evaluate the reliability of the systems for capturing and processing information, unlike procedures for traditional business activities where the focus is on separate control processes relating to each stage of transaction capture and processing. In ecommerce transactions, the originating action (e.g., receipt of a customer order over the Internet) typically initiates all other steps in processing the transaction automatically.

REVIEW CHECKPOINTS

66   What do the terms "required degree of control compliance" and "actual degree of control compliance" mean?

67   How does the degree of control reliance relate to the auditor's control risk assessment?

68   What is a control test? Why do auditors perform control tests? What audit evidence is produced by control tests?

69   What two parts are important in writing out a control test for an audit program?

70   How does the direction of a control test relate to control objectives?

71   What is the difference between inspection and reperformance in control testing?

72   What is a dual purpose test?

73   How are control procedures with no documentary evidence tested?

74   Why are controls tested for the whole period being audited?

AUDITOR'S RESPONSIBILITY TO REPORT INTERNAL CONTROL DEFICIENCIES AND FRAUD RISKS

LEARNING OBJECTIVE

5 Outline the auditor's responsibility when internal control evaluation work detects or indicates a significant control weakness or high risk of fraudulent misstatement.

After the auditor has evaluated and tested internal controls, he or she is in a strong position to assess the likelihood of material misstatements. This is a good point to review auditor responsibilities for detecting and communicating misstatements.

Financial misstatements can arise from either error or fraud. A **financial error** is defined as an unintentional misstatement, whereas **fraud** is intentional. Intent is not something that the auditor can observe, so it is often difficult to determine, particularly in the case of accounting estimates or the choice and application of accounting principles. Unreasonable accounting estimates may be unintentional or may have been deliberately done to manipulate and misstate the financial statements. Although an audit cannot determine intent, the auditor still has a responsibility to plan and perform the audit to obtain reasonable assurance that there is no material misstatement, whether intentional or not.[7]

The auditor is responsible for reporting all identified deficiencies in internal control, other than obviously trivial ones, to an appropriate level of management as soon as

[7] CAS 240 (5135).

possible. The appropriate level of management is usually the one at least one level above those responsible for the deficient controls. If the auditor finds that there is an alternative, effective control that achieves the same purpose as the missing one, then there might not be a deficiency or a need to communicate it.

If the auditor believes an identified control deficiency or combination of deficiencies exposes the entity to a serious risk of material misstatement, it is considered to be a **significant deficiency**. The auditor has a responsibility to report all significant deficiencies in writing to those charged with governance (audit committee or equivalent). Examples of such deficiencies are a control environment weakness indicating a lack of management competence or integrity, a lack of effective controls over critical accounting processes, a weakness allowing a material misstatement or fraud, or one that increases the entity's susceptibility to fraud. The auditor is required to communicate material weaknesses or other important issues, such as discovery of a fraud or material misstatement, to management and those charged with governance, at various stages of the audit.[8] These communications are two-way; the auditor provides entity officials with information they need to discharge their responsibilities, and the entity officials provide the auditor with any information they have that is relevant to the audit.

While the auditor's communication to management can be oral rather than written when the control deficiencies are not significant, serious control weaknesses uncovered during the normal performance of the audit are usually communicated in writing to management in a **management letter**. A copy of the written communication, or a memorandum summarizing the discussion if reported orally, should be placed in the working papers.

Whenever written communication is made there is potential for misinterpretation, so it is important for the auditor to include a very clear description of the deficiencies identified, their potential effects, and the reasons for the communication. He should also explain that the audit's objective was to express an opinion on the financial statements as a whole, not to provide assurance on internal control; therefore, other deficiencies may exist and other controls not mentioned may not be effective.

Audit requirements for listed public companies in the U.S. include management reports on internal control effectiveness. This may lead to more audit reporting related to internal control in Canada, although at the time of writing those were not in place. The CICA has issued practice guidance (s. 5925) based on U.S. PCAOB Auditing Standard No. 5 for integrated audits of financial statements and internal control effectiveness, but these audits are voluntary in Canada at this time.

Under financial institution regulations, Canadian auditors have a "well-being" reporting requirement that includes reporting on significant internal control weaknesses, as described in CICA Guideline AuG–17 (to be renumbered CAPS 1117-C). The matters that need to be reported are shown in the box following.

Examples of Reportable Conditions in Federal Institutions Legislation

- significant weaknesses in internal control, or transactions or events that create risks potentially jeopardizing the institution's ability to continue as a going concern
- going-concern uncertainties that require disclosure or change in accounting basis
- reservations in the auditor's opinion
- indicators of lack of good faith by management
- contraventions of legislated capital requirements

Source: CICA Guideline AuG–17 (CAPS 1117-C), "Transactions or Conditions Reportable Under the Well-Being Reporting Requirement in Federal Institutions Legislation."

---

[8] CAS 260 (5751), 265 (5220), 315 (5141), 330 (5143).

These communication responsibilities highlight the need for the audit to be performed with professional skepticism, which means the auditor should

1. be aware of factors that increase the risk of misstatement and take these into account in performing the audit, and

2. take appropriate action if there is evidence that contradicts the assumption of management integrity.

Note that many risk factors relate to poor internal controls. If there are enough "red flags" present, the auditor will assess a higher inherent risk, and, if control risk is also high, these higher assessments will cause the auditor to

– obtain more reliable evidence;

– expand the extent of audit procedures performed;

– apply audit procedures closer to, or as of, the balance sheet date; and

– require more extensive supervision of assistants and/or assigning assistants with more experience and training.

In essence, if the auditor suspects that the financial statements are misstated, she or he should perform procedures to confirm or dispel that suspicion.

To summarize, the auditor should inform the appropriate level of management whenever there is evidence of a non-trivial misstatement and weaknesses in internal control that could allow a material misstatement to occur. The audit committee or board of directors should be informed of all significant misstatements and any that appear to be intentional and fraud related. Generally, an auditor is less likely to detect those arising from fraud as there is deliberate concealment involved. (Procedures for fraud detection are discussed in more detail later in Chapter 17 and in various examples.)

The auditor should consider obtaining legal advice if he or she has doubts about communicating misstatements to third parties, particularly if the auditor resigned, was removed, or was unable to report on the financial statements.

REVIEW CHECKPOINTS

75 What are the auditor's reporting responsibilities for internal control deficiencies?

76 What is the financial statement auditor's responsibility for detecting and communicating misstatements?

77 What is professional skepticism? How does it help financial statement auditors meet their responsibilities?

78 How does control risk relate to the risk of material misstatement?

79 What action should an auditor take if he suspects the financial statements are materially misstated?

80 What findings are auditors required to communicate to management? to the audit committee or board of directors?

CONTROL EVALUATION, FURTHER AUDIT PROCEDURES, AND REASONABLE ASSURANCE

LEARNING OBJECTIVE

6 Explain reasonable assurance and cost benefit in the context of control risk assessment and development of the audit approach.

Now that you have studied control tests and their relation to substantive tests of account balances, it may be helpful for you to think about the overall purposes of all audit procedures. The purpose of all audit work is to obtain reasonable assurance about whether the financial statements as a whole are free from material misstatement, whether due to fraud or error, to be able to express an opinion on whether the financial statements are fairly presented, in all material respects, in accordance with GAAP. In turn, the purpose of audit procedures is to obtain sufficient appropriate audit evidence about the assessed risks of material misstatement by designing and implementing appropriate procedures in response to those risks. The most effective approach integrates all aspects of the auditee's business and systems into the overall design of the audit. The choice of control reliance and substantive evidence should maximize efficiency and minimize auditing costs.

For study purposes, we tend to discuss control tests and substantive tests of balances as if these are easily distinguishable. The six general audit techniques described in Chapter 8 can be used in both tests of controls and in substantive procedures. The auditor's goal at the planning stage is to select the most cost-effective set of evidence gathering procedures to provide reasonable assurance to support the audit opinion. As discussed earlier, a single procedure may produce both control and substantive evidence that serves both purposes: dual-purpose tests. For example, a selection of recorded sales entries could be used to both vouch sales to supporting shipping documents and calculate the correct dollar amount of sales. The first part of the test provides information about control compliance, while the second is dollar-value information that may help measure the amount of misstatement in the general ledger balance of sales. The confirmation of accounts receivable procedure is another example. Its purpose is mainly substantive, but when confirmation replies indicate significant or systematic errors, the evidence is relevant to control evaluation as well as to measuring the dollar-value of misstatements. Since dual purpose tests provide both compliance and substantive evidence, they can lower the cost of obtaining audit evidence.

Many audit procedures can be designed to serve dual purposes and yield evidence about both controls and financial statement assertions. This allows the auditor to select an audit approach combining control reliance and substantive evidence as the basis for a cost-effective overall audit plan, and one that provides sufficient appropriate evidence from both control and substantive testing.

The audit standards that result in the auditor's obtaining reasonable assurance on fair presentation of the financial statements are summarized in the box below.

AUDIT PROCEDURES RESPONSIVE TO THE ASSESSED RISKS OF MATERIAL MISSTATEMENT AT THE ASSERTION LEVEL

OVERVIEW

The purpose of the auditor's inherent and control risk assessment is to allow the auditor to design and perform appropriate audit procedures that reflect the risks of material misstatement at the assertion level for each class of transaction, account balance, and disclosure.

When the auditor intends to rely on the operating effectiveness of controls in determining the nature, timing, and extent of substantive procedures, the auditor must obtain audit evidence to determine whether the controls are operating effectively. Control testing would also be required in situations when substantive procedures alone cannot provide sufficient appropriate audit evidence at the assertion level.

CONTROL TESTING

When the auditor plans to rely on controls over a risk the auditor has determined to be a significant risk, the auditor shall test those controls in the current period.

In designing and performing tests of controls, the auditor shall obtain more persuasive audit evidence the greater the reliance the auditor places on the effectiveness of a control.

The auditor shall test controls for the particular time, or throughout the period, for which the auditor intends to rely on those controls.

If the auditor plans to use audit evidence from a previous audit about the operating effectiveness of specific controls, the auditor shall establish the continuing relevance of that evidence by obtaining audit evidence about whether significant changes in those controls have occurred subsequent to the previous audit. The auditor shall obtain this evidence by performing inquiry combined with observation or inspection, to confirm the understanding of those specific controls, and

a. if there have been changes that affect the continuing relevance of the audit evidence from the previous audit, the auditor shall test the controls in the current audit.

b. if there have not been such changes, the auditor shall test the controls at least once in every third audit, and shall test some controls in each audit to avoid the possibility of testing all the controls on which the auditor intends to rely in a single audit period with no testing of controls in the subsequent two audit periods.

EVALUATING THE OPERATING EFFECTIVENESS OF CONTROLS

When evaluating the operating effectiveness of relevant controls, the auditor shall evaluate whether misstatements that have been detected by substantive procedures indicate that controls are not operating effectively. The absence of misstatements detected by substantive procedures, however, does not provide audit evidence that controls related to the assertion being tested are effective.

When deviations from controls upon which the auditor intends to rely are detected, the auditor shall make specific inquiries to understand these matters and their potential consequences, and shall determine whether

a. the tests of controls that have been performed provide an appropriate basis for reliance on the controls;

b. additional tests of controls are necessary; or

c. the potential risks of misstatement need to be addressed using substantive procedures.

MATERIAL CONTROL WEAKNESSES

The auditor shall evaluate whether, on the basis of the audit work performed, the auditor has identified a material weakness in the operating effectiveness of controls.

The auditor shall communicate material weaknesses in internal control identified during the audit on a timely basis to management at an appropriate level of responsibility and, as required by CAS 260, "Communication with Those Charged with Governance," with those charged with governance (unless all of those charged with governance are involved in managing the entity).

SUBSTANTIVE PROCEDURES

Irrespective of the assessed risks of material misstatement, the auditor shall design and perform substantive procedures for each material class of transactions, account balance, and disclosure.

When the auditor has determined that an assessed risk of material misstatement at the assertion level is a significant risk, the auditor shall perform substantive procedures that are specifically responsive to that risk. When the approach to a significant risk consists only of substantive procedures, those procedures shall include tests of details.

The auditor's substantive procedures shall include the following audit procedures related to the financial statement closing process:

a. Agreeing or reconciling the financial statements with the underlying accounting records, and

b. Examining material journal entries and other adjustments made during the course of preparing the financial statements.

Source: Extracts from CAS 330.

REVIEW CHECKPOINTS

81 Why do internal controls provide reasonable, but not absolute, assurance that control objectives are met?

82 How can management's cost-benefit judgments lead to internal control deficiencies?

83 Explain how using dual-purpose tests can lower audit costs.

84 What does it mean if an overall audit plan is said to be cost-effective? How do auditors develop a cost-effective overall audit plan?

85 If the auditee's revenue transactions for the year are material but the auditor assesses the risk of material mistatement to be low, why do the audit standards require the auditor to design and perform substantive procedures for these transactions regardless of the low risk assessment?

86 What procedures is the auditor required to perform related to the financial statement closing process? Why are these procedures required? What can they find? If the auditor assessed the risk of material mistatement to be low, why would these procedures still be required?

APPLICATION CASE AND ANALYSIS
INFORMATION SYSTEMS AND CONTROLS IN A SMALL BUSINESS

LEARNING OBJECTIVE

7 Apply and integrate the chapter topics to analyze a practical auditing situation/case/scenario.

Discussion Case

After only a year as an audit manager in a mid-sized public accounting firm, Hilda has brought in her first new audit client, Ming Auto Perfection Inc. (Ming). The firm's audit partners are happy that Hilda has shown such initiative so early in her career. Also, the firm recently lost some larger audits clients to the Big Four companies after mergers or buyouts, so the partners now believe their best opportunity for growing their auditing practice is in the small and medium enterprise (SME) sector.

Chi Ming started his business 12 years ago as a car wash in a busy part of the city. A few years later he married Jin and she joined in the business, with Chi keeping 51% of the shares and Jin receiving 49%. Thanks to Jin's outstanding marketing skills and Chi's strength in operating management, Ming soon expanded from individual car washes to operating a full car cleaning and detailing service for several taxi companies and other businesses in the city. Recently, Ming expanded further, designing and applying advertising material to the sides of taxis and buses. The company has grown successfully and now has six full-time employees and several part-timers.

Chi and Jin have recently separated, making shareholder meetings quite tense. Jin decided to leave the business but retain her 49% interest, so they decided that an independent audit of the company's financial statements would minimize concerns about the fairness of the reported profits. Hilda knows the Mings personally because their sons play in the same hockey league. The Mings have an excellent reputation in the business community, so it was an easy decision for the firm to accept Ming as a new auditee.

However, since the firm is fairly new to SME auditing, and the partners want to develop this area of practice, they have asked Hilda to use the Ming audit as a basis for developing a robust audit methodology that addresses special concerns in audits of smaller enterprises. Hilda has always been impressed by Jack's grasp of audit theory and his ability to apply it practically, and she thinks it would be both an excellent learning experience for him to draft up the small business considerations that the firm can use as a general practice guidance and a great opportunity for him to impress the partners right before bonus and promotion time.

Jack meets with Chi to learn about Ming's operations and information systems, and a few key differences from larger organization become apparent. Chi is actively involved, understands all the systems, and can do anyone else's job. Most employees do a number of different accounting tasks, sometimes ones that are incompatible from a control perspective. Most of the accounting information is captured and processed by manual processes and ad hoc computer programs like Excel, Word, and Access. An off-the-shelf accounting package called QuickBooks is used to generate the general ledger and draft financial statements. The office PCs are networked, but there are no user access restrictions; however, they are all in plain sight.

Jack's observations raise a number of questions about the differences between Ming and the larger companies Jack has audited. A good way to begin the SME guidance document for the practice is to consider some key questions Jack will try to answer in this case.

Analysis

Some key questions and related considerations are as follows.

What aspects of good internal control differ between large organizations and small ones?

A company must be large and employ several people (about 10 or more) to have a theoretically appropriate segregation of functional responsibilities and its accompanying high degree of specialization of work. Supervision requires people. There is extensive necessary paperwork and computer control necessary in most large systems. Large organization control theory and practice suggests that people performing in accounting and control roles do not engage in frequent personal interaction across functional responsibility boundaries.

What are the two main features of internal control in a small business?

The small number of people engaged in the accounting and control systems make segregation of functional responsibilities very difficult. Also, the owner-manager is actively involved in the operation of the accounting and control system, making the owner-manager's competence and integrity important considerations for the auditor.

How does the cost of implementing controls affect large businesses differently than small ones?

The theoretical dimensions of good control tend to fit large, not small, businesses. A large company employs enough people to have appropriate segregation of functional responsibilities along with its high degree of specialization of work. There are also enough people to provide supervision and to prepare the paperwork and perform other controls such as reviews and reconciliations. The computer control necessary in most large systems is extensive and also requires staff to design and implement them. The theory of large organization control also suggests that people performing accounting and control roles do not engage in frequent personal interaction across functional responsibility boundaries, as they usually do in a small business. Small businesses' costs will be affected as they are unlikely to enjoy economies of scale in implementing controls, whereas large business will likely be able to justify the cost of the suggested ideal control policies, procedures, and staffing.

The theory of internal control applies to both large and small businesses as long as the underlying behavioural assumptions are met. However, the fact that small businesses employ only a few people usually means that the required separation of duties is not met, and the entire general theory is less applicable for practical reasons; strict separation of duties, tight authority structure, extensive system of rules and files, and impersonality are harder to satisfy when there are only a few employees operating in an informal manner. The costs of controls are more easily absorbed in a large business, and the benefits of elaborate control structures are also likely to be greater in a large business. In a small business, communications and observation, particularly by the owner-manager, can be highly effective control components.

What impact do the owner-manager role and the lack of complexity have on the internal control requirements of a small business?

Internal control questionnaires designed specifically for small businesses contain more items related to the owner-manager and other key personnel than do large-business questionnaires.

What control risks are related to rapid growth in a small business?

As a small business grows, the transition to more formalized internal control tends to lag behind. For example, the owner-manager may become overburdened with control duties and tacitly delegate these to others, but fail to monitor these duties adequately. The need to hire a controller may not be apparent in time to prevent serious and costly breakdowns in the internal controls over financial reporting. The intermediate-size stage represents a turning point where both owner-manager and auditor need to be very careful. At this point, such measures as limited specialization and surety bonding of employees may help make the transition.

What cost-effectiveness considerations tend to be important in planning small business audits?

Most auditors rely primarily on substantive evidence with small business audits. The minimum documentation required in a small business audit is an internal control memorandum with a narrative description of the control system and the results of internal control evaluation. The description should include weaknesses, implications, and recommendations. Generalized audit software applications can be a major advantage because it allows the auditor to obtain a higher degree of audit assurance, at little additional cost.

How are PCs used in small business audits?

Auditors can use trial balance and financial statement software, preparation of audit programs, planning and administration tools, and computer-assisted audit techniques (most often using generalized audit software).

Which important duties are generally not segregated in small business computer systems?

Accounting Functions—people in user departments may initiate and authorize source documents, enter data, operate the computer, and distribute output reports.

Computer Functions—functions of programming and operating the computer might not be separated; programs and data are often resident on disk at all times and accessible by any operator.

What control techniques can a company use to achieve control over the operation of a PC-based accounting system?

Restricting access to input devices
Standard screens and computer prompting
Online editing and sight verification

What control techniques can a company use to achieve control over the computer processing of accounting data in a PC system?

Transaction logs
Control totals
Balancing input to output
Audit trail

What are the major characteristics and control problems in PC installations?
   Characteristics:
       Staff and location of the computer—operated by small staff located within the user department and
       without physical security
       Programs—supplied by computer manufacturers or software houses
       Processing mode—interactive data entry by users with most of the master files accessible for inquiry
       and direct update
   Control Problems:
       Lack of segregation of duties
       Lack of controls on the operating system and application programs
       Unlimited access to data files and programs
       No record of usage
       No backup of essential files
       No audit trail of processing
       No authorization or record of program changes

SUMMARY

This chapter explained the theory and practice of auditors' involvement with an auditee's internal control. The auditors' involvement is meant to assess the control risk in order to plan the substantive audit program and report control deficiencies to management and the audit committee or board of directors. It was shown that understanding the auditee's business and information systems is relevant to control understanding. The distinction between management's and the auditor's responsibilities with respect to internal control was explained.

Elements of the accounting system were described in conjunction with control procedures designed to prevent, detect, and correct misstatements that occur in transactions. These misstatements were systematized in a set of seven categories of errors and irregularities that can occur. A reverse expression of them yielded the seven control objectives an organization wishes to achieve. These control objectives were related to management's assertions found in financial statements.

Control activities were organized under the headings of general controls and application controls procedures for addressing the control objectives as they relate to input, processing, and output of data in each accounting process. The explanations of these integrated IT-based accounting systems with control consideration.

Documentation of a control system included reference to control questionnaires, flow charts, and narratives. Questionnaires and flow charts were demonstrated. This then led to the test of controls decisions and the cost reduction reasons for doing work to obtain a low control risk assessment. The assessed control risk was connected to the control risk component in the audit risk model (covered in Chapter 7). Control evidence was linked to audit programs by presenting a bridge working paper. The chapter also reviewed considerations for auditing IT-based information systems and controls.

The chapter discussed the auditor's responsibilities for communicating with management and those charged with governance when control work reveals a fraudulent misstatement or a high risk of one occurring. It presented the cost-benefit and reasonable assurance considerations that affect the auditor's choice of audit approach with respect to relying on controls and the extent to which substantive work will be used in forming the audit opinion. The chapter provides a summary of key auditing standards requirements related to control risk assessment, control testing, and their relation to substantive procedures. The discussion of control risk assessment provided some basis for the theory and practice of audit sampling, which is covered next in Chapter 10.

To be able to summarize the role of information systems and control in (a) capturing relevant information from the organization's business environment and activities and (b) processing it into the financial statements and disclosures that contain management assertions about the organization's performance and financial position, it may be helpful to review the big picture overview of the financial reporting process presented in Exhibit 7–19 of Chapter 7 (page 258). This chapter finished with the application case given above showing how control theory and evaluations apply to small businesses.

MULTIPLE-CHOICE QUESTIONS FOR PRACTICE AND REVIEW

MC 1 Which of the following can an auditor observe as a general control procedure used by companies?
a. Segregation of functional responsibilities
b. Management philosophy and operating style
c. Open lines of communication to the audit committee of the board of directors
d. External influences such as federal bank examiner audits

MC 2 A company's control procedure is:
a. an action taken by auditors to obtain evidence.
b. an action taken by company personnel for the purpose of preventing, detecting, and correcting errors and irregularities in transactions.
c. a method for recording, summarizing, and reporting financial information.
d. the functioning of the board of directors in support of its audit committee.

MC 3 The control objective intended to reduce the probability that fictitious transactions get recorded in the accounts is:
a. completeness.
b. authorization.
c. proper period.
d. validity.

MC 4 The control objective intended to reduce the probability that a credit sale transaction will get debited to cash instead of accounts receivable is:
a. validity.
b. classification.
c. accuracy.
d. completeness.

MC 5 Which of the following employees normally would be assigned the operating responsibility for designing a computerized accounting system, including documentation of application systems?
a. Computer programmer
b. Data processing manager
c. Systems analyst
d. Internal auditor

MC 6 When erroneous data are detected by computer program controls, such data may be excluded from processing and printed on an error report. The error report should most probably be reviewed and followed up by the:
a. control group.
b. systems analyst.
c. supervisor of computer operations.
d. computer programmer.

MC 7 Totals of amounts in computer-record data fields that are not usually added but are used only for data processing control purposes are called:
a. record totals.
b. hash totals.
c. processing data totals.
d. field totals.

MC 8 In updating a computerized accounts receivable file, which one of the following would be used as a batch control to verify the accuracy of the posting of cash receipts remittances?
a. The sum of the cash deposits plus the discounts less the sales returns
b. The sum of the cash deposits
c. The sum of the cash deposits less the discounts taken by customers
d. The sum of the cash deposits plus the discounts taken by customers

MC 9 In most audits of large companies, internal control risk assessment contributes to audit efficiency, which means:
a. the cost of year-end audit work will exceed the cost of control evaluation work.
b. auditors will be able to reduce the cost of year-end audit work by an amount more than the control evaluation costs.
c. the cost of control evaluation work will exceed the cost of year-end audit work.
d. auditors will be able to reduce the cost of year-end audit work by an amount less than the control evaluation costs.

MC 10 Which of the following is a device designed to help the audit team obtain evidence about the control environment and about the accounting and control procedures of an audit client:
a. A narrative memorandum describing the control system
b. An internal control questionnaire
c. A flowchart of the documents and procedures used by the company
d. A well-indexed file of working papers

MC 11 A bridge working paper shows the connection between:
a. control evaluation findings and subsequent audit procedures.
b. control objectives and accounting system procedures.
c. control objectives and company control procedures.
d. financial statement assertions and test of control procedures.

MC 12 Control tests are required for:
a. obtaining evidence about the financial statement assertions.
b. accomplishing control over the validity of recorded transactions.
c. analytical review of financial statement balances.
d. obtaining evidence about the operating effectiveness of company control procedures.

MC 13 In an IT-based information system, automated equipment controls or hardware controls are designed to:
a. arrange data in a logical sequential manner for processing purposes.
b. correct errors in the computer programs.

c. monitor and detect errors in source documents.

d. detect and control errors arising from use of equipment.

MC 14 A good example of application (user) computer software is:

a. payroll processing program.

b. operating system program.

c. data management system software.

d. utility programs.

MC 15 Which of the following statements most likely represents a disadvantage for a company that performs its accounting using PCs?

a. It is usually difficult to detect arithmetic errors.

b. Unauthorized persons find it easy to access the computer and alter the data files.

c. Transactions are coded for account classifications before they are processed on the computer.

d. Random errors in report printing are rare in packaged software systems.

MC 16 A procedural control used in the management of a computer centre to minimize the possibility of data or program file destruction through operator error includes:

a. control figures.

b. crossfooting tests.

c. limit checks.

d. external labels.

MC 17 Which of the following is not a characteristic of a batch-processed computer system?

a. The collection of like transactions that are sorted and processed sequentially against a master file

b. Keyboard input of transactions, followed by machine processing

c. The production of numerous printouts

d. The posting of a transaction, as it occurs, to several files, without intermediate printouts

MC 18 What is the computer process called when data processing is performed concurrently with a particular activity and the results are available soon enough to influence the particular course of action being taken or the decision being made?

a. Batch processing

b. Real-time processing

c. Integrated data processing

d. Random access processing

MC 19 The auditee's computerized exception-reporting system helps an auditor to conduct a more efficient audit because it:

a. condenses data significantly.

b. highlights abnormal conditions.

c. decreases the tests of computer controls requirements.

d. is efficient computer input control.

MC 20 Auditors often make use of computer programs that perform routine processing functions, such as sorting and merging. These programs are made available by software companies and are specifically referred to as:

a. compiler programs.

b. supervisory programs.

c. utility programs.

d. user programs.

MC 21 In the weekly computer run to prepare payroll cheques, a cheque was printed for an employee who had been terminated the previous week. Which of the following controls, if properly utilized, would have been most effective in preventing the error or ensuring its prompt detection?

a. A control total for hours worked, prepared from time cards collected by the timekeeping department

b. Requiring the treasurer's office to account for the numbers of the prenumbered cheques issued to the computer department for the processing of the payroll

c. Use of the check digit for employee numbers

d. Use of a header label for the payroll input sheet

EXERCISES AND PROBLEMS

EP 1
LO.1
LO.3
LO.4
LO.6
Internal Control Understanding and Assessment. Assume that, when conducting procedures to obtain an understanding of the control structure in the Denton Seed Company, you checked "No" to the following internal control questionnaire items (selected from those illustrated in the chapter):

• Does access to online files require specific passwords to be entered to identify and validate the terminal user?

• Are control totals established by the user prior to submitting data for processing? (Order entry application subsystem)

• Are input control totals reconciled to output control totals? (Order entry application subsystem)

Required:

a. Describe the errors, irregularities, or misstatements that could occur because of the weaknesses indicated by the lack of controls.

b. Explain the impact these control weaknesses would have on the audit approach selected and on the design of the audit programs.

EP 2
LO.1
LO.2
LO.3
Approach for Internal Control Assessment. One of the things you can do in a logical approach to the assessment of internal control is to imagine what types of errors or irregularities could occur with regard to each significant class of transactions. Assume a company has the significant classes of transactions listed below. For each one,

identify one or more errors or irregularities that could occur and specify the accounts that would be affected if proper controls were not specified or were not followed satisfactorily.

1. Credit sales transactions
2. Raw materials purchase transactions
3. Payroll transactions
4. Equipment acquisition transactions
5. Cash receipts transactions
6. Leasing transactions
7. Dividend transactions
8. Investment transactions (short term)

EP 3 **Key Control, Control Test Evaluation.** The auditor learns
LO.2 that the auditee has a control procedure in place that
LO.4 addresses the validity of sales and existence of accounts
LO.6 receivable. When a truck driver picks up goods from the warehouse, the warehouse employee has the driver sign a "shipper's receipt" showing the quantities and item numbers shipped, and the customer information. The shipper's receipts are filed in date order in the warehouse office. A copy of the signed shipper's receipt is sent to the accounting office where it is used to record the reduction in inventory and issue a sales invoice. The invoice number is noted on the shipper's receipt and it is filed by invoice number in the accounting area. Since the auditee has a large number of customers, the auditor decides this is a key control that will be tested.

Required:

a. Why would the auditor decide this is a key control?
b. What will the auditor achieve by testing this control?
c. Design a control test the auditor could perform for this control procedure. Describe the two parts of the test in detail.
d. Assume the auditor performs a control test and finds the control procedure operated properly 95 percent of the time. How does this evidence affect the auditor's control risk assessment? What if the control operated 60 percent of the time? What if it operated 99 percent of the time?

EP 4 **Online Sales, Audit Procedures.** Online retailers, such
LO.3 as Amazon.com or Grocerygateway.com, make use of
and online customer order forms to allow customers to input
LO.4 all the required sale, delivery, and payment data.

Required:

a. Identify control procedures that can be used in an online sales order system and the risk(s) each addresses.
b. How would the revenue control objectives be audited in an online retail sales business?

EP 5 **Auditee's Control Procedures and Audit Programs.** To
LO.3 test an organization's internal control procedures, auditors
and design a test of controls audit program. This audit program
LO.4 is a list of control tests to be performed, and each is directly related to an important auditee control procedure. Auditors perform the tests to obtain evidence about the operating effectiveness of the auditee's control procedures.

The controls listed below in (b) relate to a system for processing sales transactions. Each numbered item

indicates an error or irregularity that could occur and specifies a control procedure that could prevent or detect it.

Required:

a. Identify the control objective satisfied by the auditee's control procedure.
b. Write the test of controls audit program by specifying an effective control test to produce evidence about the auditee's performance of the control procedure. [*Hint:* A control test is a two-part statement consisting of (1) identification of a data population from which a sample can be drawn and (2) expression of an action to take.]

1. The company wants to avoid selling goods on credit to bad credit risks. Poor credit control could create problems with estimating the allowance for bad debts and a potential error by overstating the realizable value of accounts receivable. Therefore, the control procedure is: Each customer order is to be reviewed and approved for 30-day credit by the credit department supervisor. The supervisor then notes the decision on the customer order, which eventually is attached to copy 2 of the sales invoice and filed by date in the accounts receivable department. The company used sales invoices numbered 20,001 through 30,000 during the period under review.

2. The company considers sales transactions complete when shipment is made. The control procedures are: Shipping department personnel prepare prenumbered shipping documents in duplicate (sending one copy to the customer and filing the other copy in numerical order in the shipping department file). The shipping clerk marks up copy 3 of the invoice, indicating the quantity shipped, the date, and the shipping document number, and sends it to the billing department where it is taken as authorization to complete the sales recording. Copy 3 is then filed in a daily batch in the billing department file. These procedures are designed to prevent the recording of sales (1) for which no shipment is made, or (2) before the date of shipment.

3. The company wants to control unit pricing and mathematical errors that could result in overcharging or undercharging customers, thus producing the errors of overstatement or understatement of sales revenue and accounts receivable. The accounting procedures are: Billing clerks use a catalogue list price to price the shipment on invoice copies 1, 2, and 3. They compute the dollar amount of the invoice. Copy 1 is sent to the customer. Copy 2 is used to record the sale and later is filed in the accounts receivable department by date. Copy 3 is filed in the billing department by date.

4. The company needs to classify sales to subsidiaries apart from other sales so the consolidated financial statement eliminations will be accurate. That is, the company wants to avoid the error of understating the elimination of intercompany profit and, therefore, overstating net income and inventory. The control procedure is: A billing supervisor reviews

EXHIBIT   EP   6

	a.	Sales recorded, goods not shipped
	b.	Goods shipped, sales not recorded
	c.	Goods shipped to a bad credit risk customer
	d.	Sales billed at the wrong price or wrong quantity
	e.	Product line A sales recorded as Product line B
	f.	Failure to post charges to customers for sales
	g.	January sales recorded in December

Control Procedures

1. Sales order approved for credit
2. Prenumbered shipping doc prepared, sequence checked
3. Shipping document quantity compared to sales invoice
4. Prenumbered sales invoices, sequence checked
5. Sales invoice checked to sales order
6. Invoiced prices compared to approved price list
7. General ledger code checked for sales product lines
8. Sales dollar batch totals compared to sales journal
9. Periodic sales total compared to same period accounts receivable postings
10. Accountants have instructions to date sales on the date of shipment
11. Sales entry date compared to shipping document date
12. Accounts receivable subsidiary totalled and reconciled to accounts receivable control account
13. Intercompany accounts reconciled with subsidiary company records
14. Credit files updated for customer payment history
15. Overdue customer accounts investigated for collection

each invoice copy 2 to see whether the billing clerk imprinted sales to the company's four subsidiaries with a big red "9" (the code for intercompany sales). The supervisor does not initial or sign the invoices.

EP 6
LO.3
and
LO.4

Control Objectives, Procedures, Assertions, and Tests. Exhibit EP–6 contains an arrangement of examples of transaction errors (lettered *a–g*) and a set of auditee control procedures and devices (numbered 1–15). You could photocopy the Exhibit EP–6 to use for the following requirements.

Required:

a. Opposite the examples of transaction errors lettered a–g, write the name of the control objective organizations wish to achieve to prevent, detect, or correct the error.
b. Opposite each numbered control procedure, place an X in the column that identifies the error(s) the procedure is likely to control by prevention, detection, or correction.
c. For each error/control objective, identify the financial statement assertion most benefitted by the control.
d. For each company control procedure numbered 1–15, write an auditor's control test that could produce

evidence on the question of whether the company's control procedure has been installed and is operating effectively.

EP 7
LO.3
and
LO.4

Controls and Control Weaknesses in Purchasing System

Part A.

The following are internal control procedures found in the purchases and payment process of your auditee, Integrated Measurement Systems Inc.

Required:

For each control procedure:

a. Explain the type of control that is being applied.
b. Identify the control objective(s) that the control procedure meets.
c. Describe in detail one test of controls the auditor could perform to test the effectiveness of the control.

Control 1

Purchase Requests from operating departments are authorized by the appropriate person in the requesting department.

Control 2

The Purchasing Clerk verifies that there is a signature on the Purchase Request (PR) and then issues a pre-numbered Purchase Order (PO) for the items required. The Purchasing Clerk retains copies of the PR and the PO and files them by PO number.

Control 3

The Purchasing Manager reviews the Purchase Order to see whether the Purchase Request is authorized, and, if so, approves it and forwards it to the Buyer.

Control 4

The Buyer must select a vendor from a pre-approved list for all Purchase Orders over $5,000. For POs under $5,000 the Buyer can select any vendor.

Control 5

The Receiver who accepts the goods into the warehouse verifies that the quantity received matches the Bill of Lading (BL), and signs on behalf of IMS for receipt of the goods listed on the BL. If there is a discrepancy in the quantity received, the receiver does not sign the BL; the BL is sent to the Buyer to resolve the problem with the vendor.

Control 6

The Purchasing Clerk matches the signed BL with the filed copies of the PO and PR

Part B.

The following are internal control weaknesses found in the purchases and payment process of your auditee, Integrated Measurement Systems Inc.

Required:

For each control weakness;
- *d.* Describe the control risk that exists because of the weakness—what could go wrong?
- *e.* Explain whether a monetary financial statement misstatement could result because of the weakness, and, if so, what it would be.
- *f.* Describe in detail the impact the weakness will have on your other audit procedures.

Control Weakness 1

The Purchasing Clerk does not verify that the Purchase Requests are authorized by an appropriate person in the operating department, but only checks that there is a signature on the document.

Control Weakness 2

Access to the warehouse is not controlled and anyone can enter and leave anytime.

Control Weakness 3

The receiver does not match the Bill of Lading to an authorized Purchase Order.

EP 8
LO.3 and LO.4
Explain Computer Control Procedures. At a meeting of the corporate audit committee attended by the general manager of the products division and you, representing the internal audit department, the following dialogue took place:

Jiang (committee chair): Mr. Marks has suggested that the internal audit department conduct an audit of the computer activities of the products division.
Smith (general manager): I don't know much about the technicalities of computers, but the division has some of the best computer people in the company.
Jiang: Do you know whether the internal controls protecting the system are satisfactory?
Smith: I suppose they are. No one has complained. What's so important about controls anyway, as long as the system works?
Jiang turns to you and asks you to explain IT control policies and procedures.

Required:

Address your response to the following points:
- *a.* State the principal objective of achieving control over (1) input, (2) processing, and (3) output.
- *b.* Give at least three methods of achieving control over (1) source data, (2) processing, and (3) output.

EP 9
LO.3 and LO.4
Testing Computer Processing. An experienced auditor remarked that it is only necessary to check the additions and extensions on one invoice generated by an IT-based system because if the computer program does one invoice correctly it will do them all correctly, so there is no point in testing a statistical sample of invoices.

Required:

- *a.* Comment on whether or not you agree with this statement. Give your reasons.
- *b.* Assume that a company had effective controls over program changes in prior years, but during the current year a new programmer was hired who was not qualified for the job and did not document changes to the programs that were made during the year. Would this fact have an impact on your response for (*a*)?

EP 10
LO.4
Controls Tests and Errors/Irregularities. The four questions below are taken from an internal control questionnaire. For each question, state (*a*) one control test you could use to find out whether the control technique was really used, and (*b*) what error or irregularity could occur if the question were answered "no," or if you found the control was not effective.
1. Are blank (sales) invoices available only to authorized personnel?
2. Are (sales) invoices checked for the accuracy of quantities billed? Prices used? Mathematical calculations?
3. Are the duties of the accounts receivable bookkeeper separate from any cash functions?
4. Are customer accounts regularly balanced with the control account?

EP 11
LO.4
Control Risk Assessment, Online Input. The Canada Revenue Agency has introduced "e-filing." Registered tax professionals can submit taxpayers' annual income tax returns online over the Internet. The taxpayer's annual return information is automatically entered into the tax department's computer system. No paper forms or receipts

need to be submitted, but the taxpayer must retain them because tax department auditors might ask to see them in the future. The tax return, and any refund due, are processed much more quickly than when paper forms are mailed in. A refund can be electronically deposited to the taxpayer's bank account, sometimes within one week.

Required:

Comment on the control strengths and weaknesses of the "e-file" system. In the case of weaknesses, provide recommendations on how they can be compensated for.

EP 12 **IT Risks and Controls.** The strengths of the IT general
LO.4   controls collectively provide an appropriate foundation for maintaining the integrity of information, the security of data, and the efficient operation of application controls. Weaknesses in IT general controls increase the risk of material misstatement at the financial statement level, and undermine the effectiveness of specific IT application controls.

Required:

For each of the following four IT control risks, describe one control that an organization could have in place to reduce the risk of material misstatement, and explain specifically how the risk is reduced.

1. No policies/procedures exist to ensure effective IT management or IT staff supervision.
2. No alignment exists between business objectives, risks, and IT plans.
3. Reliance is placed on systems/programs that are inaccurately processing data or processing inaccurate data.
4. Unauthorized access to data. Possible destruction of data, improper changes, unauthorized or non-existent transactions, or inaccurate recording of transactions

DISCUSSION CASES

. . . .

DC 1   **Back-Up Procedures, Availability of Data for Audit**
LO.1   **tests.** Whistler Corp. is a new audit engagement for your
LO.2   firm. Whistler backs up all its sales transaction detailed
LO.3   data for each month on a portable hand-held disk drive.
LO.4   The drive is retained offsite for three months and then reused. This system is used because the company only has four drives, which cost over $100 each, and offsite storage charges are on a per-drive basis. The Whistler information system manager considers this to be a cost-effective back-up procedure. Following the request of their former auditors, Whistler retains back-up drives for December (the year-end) and the following January until the financial statement audit is completed. The audit is usually completed by the end of April.

Required:

a. Discuss the impact of this back-up procedure on Whistler's control risk. Suggest alternate feasible approaches Whistler's management could use to improve internal control and explain fully how your recommendations improve control and reduce risk. How would you communicate such recommendations to management?

b. Discuss the impact Whistler's back-up procedure has on your audit approach. Consider any limitations it may impose on audit tests or analytical procedures, or the possibility of your firm's using a combined audit approach. Suggest alternate feasible approaches that may improve your audit scope.

DC 2   **Control Risk Assessment and Testing Costs and Ben-**
LO.1   **efits.** The following are narrative descriptions of sales
LO.2   systems and controls for these two different businesses.
LO.3
LO.4   **Avocet Inc.**
LO.6   Avocet is a franchise fast food restaurant business. When customers order food, the counter person presses the appropriate buttons on the cash register. There is a button for each menu item. The point of sale (POS) system retrieves the current item prices from the price files, extends for quantities ordered, and displays the sale total on the cash register screen. A sales entry is also generated in the daily sales register. The customer's payment is then entered and their food order is displayed on a screen in the food preparation area. The POS system generates a cash receipt entry for the cash register and also in the daily cash receipts register. Food preparation staff put together the order and place it in the pick-up area behind the front counter. When the food order is filled, the staff clears the order from the system; this generates an entry in the inventory system to remove the food and packaging items sold from the perpetual inventory listing.

A restaurant manager is on duty at all times. The manager circulates between the counter and food services areas, observing that cash received is placed in the register and spot-checking that food orders match with cash sales. If a customer receives an incorrect order, the manager can void the sale entry using a special key in the cash register and a secret password for the POS entries. A corrected order is then input by the usual method, if required. At the close of each day's business, the cash in the register is totalled and agreed to the cash, debit card, and credit card slips collected in the register during the day. Differences of less than $10 are recorded in an account named "Cash over/under." Larger discrepancies will be investigated by scrutinizing the day's entries and interviewing all counter people using the register. The sales and cash information from the POS is then uploaded over a phone line to the franchise company head office, where it is consolidated with the reports from all the restaurants in the system. On a weekly basis, the food and packaging inventory on hand in the restaurant is counted and reconciled to the inventory system. The inventory usage is also compared with the sales records for reasonability.

Boblink Limited

Boblink is a new-car dealership. Once a customer has decided to buy a car, the car salesperson fills out a purchase agreement form, including the description of the car, the serial number, and the name and address of the purchaser. The agreed sale price is entered, along with any extras such as options or extended warranties, any allowance for a used car traded in, additional dealer preparation fees, licensing fees, and various taxes. A second form is used outlining the car purchase financing. The financing can be cash, a bank loan prearranged by the customer, or a lease arranged by Bobolink's financing company. Both forms are reviewed by the customer, and, if they are satisfactory, the customer signs. The salesperson then takes the signed forms to the dealership's general manager for review and approval. If payment is by cash, the cash is given to the general manager at this point. Any discrepancies in the payment or paperwork are corrected and must be agreed to by the customer. Once the sales documents are completed, the ownership papers and keys are handed over to the customer, who drives away with the car. The sales documents are faxed to the car manufacturer's sales head office for inventory and warranty purposes, and to the bank or leasing company, if applicable. The sales information is entered by the Bobolink bookkeeper to the financial system and the inventory system. The bookkeeper follows up on collection of the funds from the bank or leasing company, which usually takes two to three days. The sales information is also set up in the dealership management system for purposes of sales incentives and commissions, future service work, and sales follow-up.

Required:

a. Compare and contrast the control risks in these two businesses.

b. Identify input, processing, and output control procedures that exist in each business, including the control objective for each.

c. Comment on whether each business control system relies on prevention of errors, early detection of errors, or later detection and correction. Do you think the control method designed by management in each business is the most effective and efficient system for its particular control risks? Can you recommend any more cost-effective control techniques?

d. Identify control strengths and weaknesses in the two sales systems in relation to the seven control objectives described in the chapter.

e. Assume you are required to test controls in both these audits. Write controls tests that address all the control objectives. Also indicate which financial statement assertion(s) each control test addresses.

f. Assume that it is your responsibility to decide whether to rely on controls in these two audits. Evaluate the cost-benefit trade-off of testing controls in both businesses and recommend an audit approach for each, giving your reasons.

DC 3 Costs and Benefits of Control. The following questions
LO.1 and cases deal with the subject of cost-benefit analysis of
LO.2 internal control. Some important concepts in cost-benefit
LO.3 analysis are:
LO.5 1. Measurable benefit. Benefits or cost savings may be measured directly or may be based on estimates of expected value. An expected loss is an estimate of the amount of a probable loss multiplied by the frequency or probability of the loss-causing event. A measurable benefit can arise from the reduction of an expected loss.

2. Qualitative benefit. Some gains or cost savings may not be measurable, such as company public image, reputation for regulatory compliance, customer satisfaction, and employee morale.

3. Measurable costs. Controls may have direct costs such as wages and equipment expenses.

4. Qualitative cost factors. Some costs may be indirect, such as lower employee morale created by overcontrolled work restrictions.

5. Marginal analysis. Each successive control feature may have marginal cost and benefit effects on the control problem.

Case A

Porterhouse Company has numerous bank accounts. Why might management hesitate to spend $20,000 (half of a clerical salary) to assign someone the responsibility of reconciling each account every month for the purpose of catching the banks' accounting errors? Do other good reasons exist to justify spending $20,000 each year to reconcile bank accounts monthly?

Case B

Harper Hoe Company keeps a large inventory of hardware products in a warehouse. Last year, $500,000 was lost to thieves who broke in through windows and doors. Josh Harper figures that installing steel doors with special locks and burglar bars on the windows at a cost of $25,000 would eliminate 90 percent of the loss. Hiring armed guards to patrol the building 16 hours a day at a current annual cost of $75,000 would eliminate all the loss, according to officials of the Holmes Security Agency. Should Josh arrange for one, both, or neither of the control measures?

Case C

The Merry Mound Cafeteria formerly collected from each customer as he or she reached the end of the food line. A cashier, seated at a cash register, rang up the amount (displayed on a digital screen) and collected money. Management changed the system, and now a clerk at the end of the line operates a calculator/printer machine and gives each customer a paper tape. The machine accumulates a running total internally. The customer presents the tape at the cash register on the way out and pays.

The cafeteria manager justified the direct cost of $30,000 annually for the additional salary and $500 for the new machine by pointing out that he could serve 4 more people each weekday (Monday through Friday) and 10 more people on Saturday and Sunday. The food line now moves faster and customers are more satisfied. (The average meal tab is $12, and total costs of food and service are considered fixed.) "Besides," he said, "my internal control is better." Evaluate the manager's assertions.

Case D

Assume, in the Merry Mound situation cited above, that the better control of separating cash custody from the end-of-food-line recording function was not cost beneficial, even after taking all measurable benefits into consideration. As an auditor, you believe the cash collection system deficiency is a material weakness in internal control, and you have written it as such in your letter concerning reportable conditions, which you delivered to Merry Mound's central administration. The local manager insists on inserting his own opinion on the cost-benefit analysis in the preface to the document that contains your report. Should you, in your report, express any opinion or evaluation on the manager's statement?

DC 4 **Controls, Irregularities.** The SB Construction Com-
LO.2 pany has two divisions. The president, Su, manages the
and roofing division. Su has delegated authority and responsi-
LO.5 bility for management of the modular manufacturing division to Jon Gee. The company has a competent accounting staff and a full-time internal auditor. Unlike Su, however, Gee and his secretary handle all the bids for manufacturing jobs, purchase all the materials without competitive bids, control the physical inventory of materials, contract for shipping, supervise the construction work, bill the customers, approve all bid changes, and collect the payment from customers. With Su's tacit approval, Gee has asked the internal auditor not to interfere with his busy schedule.

Required:
a. Discuss the internal control in this fact situation and identify irregularities that could occur.
b. Assume you are the independent external auditor of SB. Explain your responsibilities to report on this situation to SB's management and board of directors.

DC 5 **Cash Receipts Control.** Sally's Craft Corner was opened
LO.3 in 1993 by Sally Moore, a fashion designer employed by
LO.4 Bundy's Department Store. Sally is employed full-time
LO.5 at Bundy's and travels frequently to shows and marts in Vancouver, Montreal, and Toronto. She enjoys crafts, wanted a business of her own, and saw an opportunity in Vancouver. The Corner now sells regularly to about 300 customers, but business only began to pick up in 2000. The staff presently includes two salespeople and four office personnel, and Sally herself helps out on weekends.

Sales have grown, as has the Corner's reputation for quality crafts. The history is as follows:

	Sales	Discounts and Allowances	Net Sales
1996	$164,950	$5,000	$159,950
1997	185,750	5,500	180,250
1998	176,100	5,200	170,900
1999	183,800	5,700	178,100
2000	239,500	9,500	230,000
2001	294,700	14,800	279,900
2002	372,300	$22,300	350,000

With an expanding business and a need for inventory, the Corner is now cash poor. Prices are getting higher every month, and Sally is a little worried. The net cash flow is only about $400 per month after allowance of a 3 percent discount for timely payments on account. So she has engaged you as auditor and also asks for recommendations you might have about the cash flow situation. The Corner has never been audited.

During your review of internal control, you have learned the following about the four office personnel:

Janet Bundy is the receptionist and also helps customers. She is the daughter of the Bundy Department Store owner and a longtime friend of Sally. Janet helped Sally start the Corner. They run around together when Sally is in town. She opens all the mail, answers most of it herself, but turns over payments on account to Sue Kenmore.

Sue Kenmore graduated from high school and started working as a bookkeeper-secretary at the Corner in 2000. She wants to go to university but cannot afford it right now. She is very quiet in the office, but you have noticed she has some fun with her friends in her new BMW. In the office she gets the mailed-in payments on account from Janet, takes payments over the counter in the store, checks the calculations of discounts allowed, enters the cash collections in the cash receipts journal, prepares a weekly bank deposit (and mails it), and prepares a list (remittance list) of the payments on account. The list shows amounts received from each customer, discount allowed, and amount to be credited to customer's account. She is also responsible for approving the discounts and credits for merchandise returned.

Ken Murphy has been the bookkeeper-clerk since 1996. He also handles other duties. Among them, he receives the remittance list from Sue, posts the customers' accounts in the subsidiary ledger, and gives the remittance list to David Roberts. Ken also prepares and mails customers' monthly statements. Ken is rather dull, interested mostly in hunting on weekends, but is a steady worker. He always comes to work in a beat-up pickup truck—an eyesore in the parking lot.

David Roberts is the bookkeeping supervisor. He started work in 1997 after giving up his small practice as a PA. He posts the general ledger (using the remittance list as a basis for cash received entries) and prepares monthly financial statements. He also approves and makes all other ledger entries and reconciles the monthly bank statement. He reconciles the customer subsidiary records to the accounts receivable control each month. David is very happy not to have to contend with the pressures he experienced in his practice as a PA.

Required:
a. Draw a simple flow chart of the cash collection and bookkeeping procedures.
b. Identify any reportable conditions or material weakness in internal control. Explain any reasons why you might suspect that errors or irregularities may have occurred.
c. Recommend corrective measures you believe necessary and efficient in this business.

DC 6 **Tests of Controls, IT-Based Sales System.** Garganey
LO.4 Corp. manufactures automobile dashboards and interior components for Big Motors Inc. (BMI). BMI requires that all its suppliers be connected to its computerized procurement and manufacturing system. BMI's production planning system generates components requirements lists, which are then transferred electronically to various suppliers' computers for them to bid on. Garganey's production system calculates the cost of manufacturing the components at the required times,

including materials, labour, overtime charges, overhead, and profit. Garganey makes a bid on the order and, if its bid is accepted by BMI, BMI's production schedule for that component is downloaded to Garganey's production system so that the required parts will be manufactured and delivered to BMI's plants at the times they are required in the BMI assembly lines. When the components are completed, Garganey's system generates a shipping instructions document, which is signed by the trucking company that picks up the components and delivers them to BMI. When the components arrive at BMI, they are inspected and, if approved, payment for the order is automatically transferred from BMI's bank account to Garganey's bank account. Any adjustments for quantities short-shipped are deducted from the amount BMI transfers and an adjustment memo is communicated electronically to Garganey's sales system.

Required:

Develop an internal control audit program that will generate evidence about the effectiveness of Garganey's internal controls. Using the tests of controls procedures described in the chapter as a starting point, adapt the procedures to be suitable for the IT-based sales system used by Garganey.

DC 7   **Flowchart Control Points.** Each number of the flow-
LO.4   chart in Exhibit DC 7 locates a control point in the labour processing system of your auditee, Alouette Inc.

EXHIBIT   DC   7

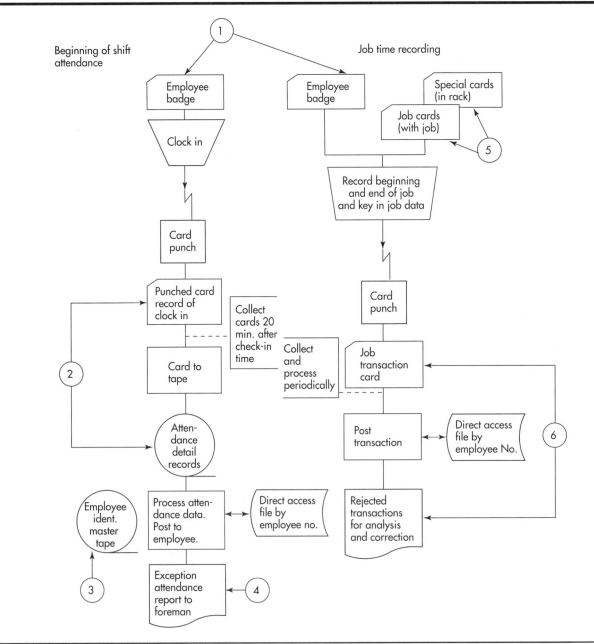

Required:

a. Make a list of the control points, and, for each point, describe the type or kind of internal control procedure that ought to be specified.

b. Assume that Exhibit DC 7 is the system description in Alouette's prior year's audit file. During the current year, the company converted to a magnetic security card system. Each employee is issued a security card with a magnetic stripe containing his or her identity code. At the start of the shift the employee swipes his or her security card to enter the factory floor. Using an internal clock, the scanner generates a start time entry in the system's attendance detail records file. The employee then reports to the floor supervisor to be assigned to a job for his or her shift. The supervisor uses a terminal that displays a real-time list of checked-in employees, and enters the job number assignment beside the employee's name. The job costing system automatically creates an open daily job transaction entry. At the end of the shift the employee swipes his or her card to exit the factory floor and the total shift time is entered to the open job transaction. The daily job transaction entry is then closed and a labour charge entry for the employee's shift is generated in the job costing system and in the payroll file.

You have been assigned to assess controls for the current year audit. Update Exhibit DC 7 to reflect the new employee attendance and job costing systems described above. Identify control points in the new systems, and indicate control procedures that should be used to prevent errors in payroll and job costing.

DC 8
LO.4

Audit Approach, Computer Service Organization. Eider Equipment Leasing Limited is in the financing lease business. It uses a service organization to compute lease payment schedules. Eider's customers sign standard equipment leases ranging from 3 to 15 years. The details of the leases are summarized and sent to the service organization for generating the schedules. Hard copy reports from the service organization are delivered to Eider monthly and used by its bookkeeper to generate entries in the company's general ledger system, which is run on a popular accounting software package.

Required:

a. Design two or more appropriate audit approaches for verifying leasing revenues in this auditee.

b. List factors that would indicate which approach will be most efficient and effective.

CHAPTER 10

Audit Sampling

In this chapter, we review the general topic of audit sampling, which relies heavily on the concepts of materiality and risk—audit risk, inherent risk, control risk, and detection risk. Audit sampling is not an audit procedure in the same class as the procedures explained in previous chapters. Instead, it is a method of organizing the application of audit procedures, as well as a method of organizing the auditor's decision-making process.

LEARNING OBJECTIVES

After completing this chapter, you will be able to do the following:

1 Explain the role of professional judgment in audit sampling decisions.

2 Distinguish audit sampling work from non-sampling work.

3 Compare and contrast statistical and nonstatistical sampling.

4 Differentiate between sampling and nonsampling risk.

5 Develop a simple audit program for test of a client's internal control procedures.

a. Specify objectives, deviation conditions, populations, and sampling units.
b. Demonstrate some basic audit sampling calculations.
c. Evaluate evidence from control testing.

6 Develop a simple audit program for an account balance, considering the influences of risk and tolerable misstatement.

a. Specify objectives and a population of data.
b. Determine sample size and select sample units.
c. Evaluate monetary error evidence from a balance audit sample.

7 Apply and integrate the chapter topics to analyze a practical auditing situation/case/scenario.

Note: Appendix 10A gives the tables needed to do the statistical auditing problems in the chapter review section. Appendix 10B gives more details and theory underlying the above objectives and is located on the text Online Learning Centre (OLC).

INTRODUCTION TO AUDIT SAMPLING

LEARNING OBJECTIVE

1 Explain the role of professional judgment in audit sampling decisions.

Audit sampling is the application of an audit procedure to less than 100 percent of the items within an account balance population or class of transactions in order to evaluate some characteristic of the group.[1] Testing is synonymous with sampling.[2] Sampling was part of the explanation of a control test, which was defined as (1) identifying the data population from which to select a sample of items and (2) describing an action to produce relevant evidence.

To understand the definition of audit sampling, you must keep the following definitions in mind. **Audit procedures** are the general audit techniques of Chapter 8 (recalculation/reperformance, observation, confirmation, enquiry, inspection, and analysis). An **account balance** is a control account made up of many constituent items; for example, an accounts receivable control account represents the sum of customers' accounts. A **class of transactions** refers to a group of transactions with common characteristics, such as cash receipts or cash disbursements, but not added together as an account balance in GAAP financial statements. A **population** is the set of all the elements that constitute an account balance or class of transactions; each of the elements within it is a **population unit**. When an auditor selects a sample of the population, each element selected is called a **sampling unit** (e.g., a customer's account, an inventory item, a debt issue, a cash receipt, a cancelled cheque, and so forth). A **sample** is a set of such sampling units. Note that populations, population units, and sampling units represent factual information about the auditee. In particular, in the sampling process there is no need to predict future events that might affect the auditee.

How Risk and Materiality Are Used in Audit Sampling

Materiality and risk are key concepts in statistical sampling and auditing. This is indicated in CAS 530 (5300, 5142) by quotes such as the following:

> The determination of an appropriate sample on a representative basis may be made using either statistical or non-statistical methods. Whether statistical or non-statistical methods are used, their common purpose is to enable the auditor to reach a conclusion about an entire set of data by examining only a part of it. Statistical sampling methods allow the auditor to express in mathematical terms the uncertainty he or she is willing to accept and the conclusions of his or her test. The use of statistical methods does not eliminate the need for the auditor to exercise judgment. For example, the auditor has to determine the degree of audit risk he or she is willing to accept and make a judgment as to materiality.

The following box shows how the auditor's professional judgment is applied when deciding how much audit work is required and how the audit finding will be interpreted.

PROFESSIONAL JUDGMENT AND THE EXTENT OF AUDIT TESTING

Handbook 5142.08 states, "decisions concerning materiality and audit risk are the most significant made in the course of an audit because they form the basis for determining the extent of the auditing procedures to be undertaken." Also see CAS 320.06. This illustrates that professional judgment is critical to audit practice.

---

[1] CAS 530.05 (a).
[2] *Terminology for Accountants*, 4th Ed. (CICA; Toronto, 1992).

To better understand why this is, imagine that the audit is a purely scientific endeavour in which the management assertions are hypotheses that have to be either supported (verified) or contradicted by the evidence. An analogy, but not one to be taken too literally, is to think of auditor opinions as being similar to a media opinion poll.

An opinion poll in *The Toronto Star* reported that a mayoral candidate M.L. led with 51 percent of the decided vote, over candidate B.H. who had 46 percent support. This poll was the result of surveying 400 Toronto residents. A sample of this size is considered accurate to within 5 percentage points, 19 times out of 20. In other words, because of the uncertainties associated with the representatives of the sample of 400, the best the statistician can conclude about M.L.'s prospects is that there is a 95 percent confidence level that his actual support is in the range 51% ± 5% = 46–56%. The width of this band around M.L.'s best point estimate of 51 percent is referred to as **sampling precision**, which is related to materiality. The confidence level is related to audit assurance.

Conceptually, an auditor might do the same with the financial statements. For example, after audit testing, the auditor may conclude that a client's net income number is $200,000 ± $10,000, 19 times out of 20. The auditor could make this kind of declaration if the appropriate statistical samples were drawn from all the accounting components that make up net income. In this statistical sampling framework, materiality is the degree of accuracy or precision of the sample, that is, the ± $10,000 (or ± 5% in the *Star* poll). Audit assurance is the statistical confidence; that is, 19 times out of 20, which is equal to 95 percent. Thus, if an auditor's report were interpreted purely statistically, "presents fairly in all material respects" means that the difference between the audit estimate (audit value, or AV) based on audit testing and the reported amount (book value, or BV) is less than material. The level of audit assurance is captured by the words *in our opinion* in the auditor's report. Under this view, the standard audit report indicates, therefore, that there is a high level of assurance that there are no material factual misstatements in the financial statements. We can also look at the complement of assurance, audit risk discussed in paragraph CAS 200 (5095), and interpret the standard audit report to mean there is a low level of risk that there are material misstatements in the financial statements after the audit.

Using a statistical sampling framework, the audit report decision will be based on a sufficient amount of testing so that the confidence interval around the auditor's best estimate AV will both include BV *and* be smaller than materiality; that is, the auditor will have achieved the planned level of assurance from the testing. For example, assume the auditor has done enough testing of a client with a reported net income of $198,000 to conclude with 95 percent confidence (assurance) that GAAP income is in the interval $198,000 ± $10,000. If materiality is set at 8 percent of reported income, it equals 0.08 × $198,000 = $15,840. As the achieved precision of $10,000 is less than materiality of $15,840, the auditor can conclude with at least 95 percent assurance that there is no material error in the reported net income of $198,000.

To reach such a conclusion, the auditor will have to plan the testing so that achieved precision is no larger than materiality. If BV − AV is greater than materiality, the auditor has not obtained the 95 percent assurance from testing and will either have to do more audit work or insist on an adjustment.

Sampling and the Extent of Auditing

Three aspects of auditing procedures are important—nature, timing, and extent. **Nature** refers to the six general techniques (recalculation/reperformance, observation, confirmation, enquiry, inspection, and analysis). Timing considers when procedures are performed. More will be said about timing later in this chapter. Audit sampling is concerned primarily with matters of extent—the amount of work done when the procedures are performed. In the context of auditing standards, nature and timing relate most closely to the appropriateness of the evidence, while extent relates most closely to its sufficiency (sample size). Since client files on inventory and accounts receivable contain thousands of accounting records, it is uneconomical to test them exhaustively and auditors consider the concept of testing carefully.

Testing is a means of gaining assurance that the amount of error in large files is not material. Statistical sampling is the formal theory supporting the concept of testing, but courts approved it long before statistical theories were introduced to auditing. The majority of testing in auditing was once done on a judgmental basis, but as accounting populations grew, auditors realized that statistical sample sizes could be much smaller than intuition would suggest. For this reason, statistical sampling became increasingly popular in the 1970s and 1980s. While both testing methods are equally acceptable by auditing standards, the focus here is on statistics, as the theory underlying it formalizes the reasoning used in pure judgmental testing. The two types of audit programs introduced in Chapter 8 are summarized below. Note that both of these can be performed on a statistical or non-statistical basis.

TWO KINDS OF AUDIT PROGRAMS: TWO PURPOSES FOR AUDIT SAMPLING

Internal Control Program	Balance Audit Program
Purpose	Purpose
Obtain evidence about client's control objective Compliance	Obtain evidence about client's financial statement Assertions
Validity	Existence (Occurrence)
Completeness	Completeness
Authorization	Valuation
Accuracy	Ownership (Rights and obligations)
Classification	Presentation and disclosure
Accounting	
Proper period	
Sample	Sample
Usually from a class of transactions (population), such as	Usually from items in an asset or liability balance (population), such as
Cash receipts	Accounts receivable
Cash disbursements	Loans receivable
Purchases (inventory additions)	Inventory
Inventory issues	Small tool fixed assets
Sales on credit	Depositors' savings accounts
Expense details	Accounts payable
Welfare payments (eligibility)	Unexpired magazine subscriptions

REVIEW CHECKPOINTS

1 Define the following terms: audit sampling, population, population unit, and sample.
2 What role does professional judgment play in audit decisions regarding materiality, risk, and sampling?
3 How does audit assurance relate to audit risk?
4 How does sampling relate to forming an audit opinion on financial statements?

Inclusions and Exclusions Related to Audit Sampling

LEARNING OBJECTIVE
2 Distinguish audit sampling work from nonsampling work.

Look again at the audit sampling definition, specifically the statement "for the purpose of evaluating some characteristics of the balance or class." This means that an audit procedure is considered audit sampling only if the auditor's objective is to reach a conclusion about the entire account balance or transaction class (the population) on the basis of the evidence obtained from sample. If the entire population is audited, or if it is only done to gain general familiarity, the work is not considered audit sampling.

Perhaps the distinction between audit sampling and other methods can be seen when considered against the following work that is *not* considered audit sampling:

- Complete (100 percent) audit of all the elements in a balance or class
- Analytical procedures that are overall comparisons, ratio calculations, and the like
- A **walk-through**—following one or a few transactions through the accounting and control systems in order to obtain a general understanding of the client's systems
- Methods such as enquiry of employees, obtaining written representations, obtaining enquiry responses via an internal control questionnaire, scanning accounting records for unusual items, and observation of personnel and procedures[3]
- Selecting specific items because of their high or key value or some other characteristic of special interest, such as suspected fraud (CAS 530)

Several procedures *are* typically used in audit sampling applications: recalculation, physical observation of tangible assets, confirmation, and document examination. These procedures most often are applied to the audit of the details of transactions and balances.

REVIEW CHECKPOINTS

5   Give examples of auditing procedures that are not sampling applications.

6   List audit procedures likely to be applied on a sample basis.

Why Auditors Sample

LEARNING OBJECTIVE

3 Compare and contrast statistical and nonstatistical sampling.

Auditors use audit sampling when (1) the nature and materiality of the balance or class does not demand a 100 percent audit, (2) a decision must be made about the balance or class, and (3) the time and cost to audit 100 percent of the population would be too great. The two sampling designs used are statistical and nonstatistical sampling. Exhibit 10–1 provides an overview of the different choices auditors can make about the extent of their testing.

EXHIBIT 10 – 1   EXTENT OF AUDIT TESTING

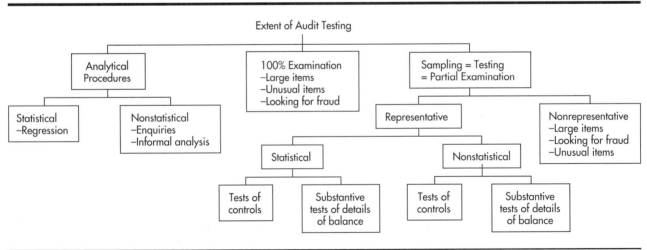

---

[3] "Audit Sampling," *Audit and Accounting Guide* (AICPA, 1983), pp. 1–3.

Statistical Sampling

Statistical sampling uses the laws of probability for selecting and evaluating a sample from a population for the purpose of reaching a conclusion about the population. The essential points of this definition are that (1) a statistical sample is selected at random, and (2) statistical calculations are used to measure and express the results. Both conditions are necessary for a method to be considered statistical sampling rather than nonstatistical sampling.

A **random sample** is chosen so that each population item has an equal likelihood of being selected in the sample. You cannot use statistical calculations with a nonrandom sample. The mathematical laws of probability don't apply to nonrandom samples, and basing such calculations on a nonrandom sample would be wrong.

Any appropriate sample size may be considered a statistical sampling. However, a preliminary estimate of sample size can be made using statistical models. A sampling method is statistical by virtue of random selection of the sample coupled with statistical calculation of the results (CAS 530).

Nonstatistical Sampling

Nonstatistical (judgmental) sampling is audit sampling in which auditors do not use statistical calculations to express the results. Sample selection can be random sampling or some other nonmathematical selection technique. Auditors are fond of saying that nonstatistical sampling involves "consideration of sampling risk in evaluating an audit sample without using statistical theory to measure that risk." In this context, "consideration" means giving sampling risk some thoughtful attention without directly knowing or measuring its magnitude. Do not confuse sampling and nonsampling risk with statistical and nonstatistical sampling. They are not the same, as is further explained in the next learning objective.

USE STATISTICAL SAMPLING WHEN

- random numbers can be associated with population items.
- objective results that can be defended mathematically are desired.
- the auditor has insufficient knowledge about the population to justify a nonstatistical sample.
- a representative (random) sample is required.
- staff are adequately trained in statistical auditing.

STATISTICAL SAMPLING IS ADVANTAGEOUS BECAUSE IT

- requires a precise and definite approach to the audit problem.
- incorporates evaluation showing a direct relation between the sample results and the entire population under audit.
- requires auditors to specify, and even quantify, particular judgments on risk and materiality.
- does not eliminate or reduce auditors' professional judgment.
- allows more objective control of audit risks.
- results in better planning and documentation when properly implemented (but can be more time-consuming and costly because of the greater formalism required).

REVIEW CHECKPOINTS

7 Give three reasons why auditors may choose to use sampling.

8 What three choices are available to the auditor for deciding on the extent of audit procedures?

9 Are testing, partial examination, and sampling the same thing? Explain your response.

10 Distinguish between statistical and nonstatistical sampling.

11 Differentiate between representative and nonrepresentative testing. What client factors determine which is most appropriate in planning audit procedures?

12 What is the difference between a statistical representative test and a nonstatistical representative test?

13 Why can a nonrepresentative test *not* be done statistically?

Sampling and Nonsampling Risk

LEARNING OBJECTIVE
④ Differentiate between sampling and nonsampling risk.

Even when procedures are performed on a sample basis and sufficient evidence is obtained, a conclusion about the population characteristic can still be wrong. For example, suppose an auditor selected 100 sales invoices for audit and found no errors or irregularities in any of them. To conclude from this that there is no significant incidence of errors and irregularities in the entire population of sales invoices might be wrong. How, you ask? The sample might not reflect the actual condition of the population. No matter how randomly or carefully the sample was selected, it might not be a good representation of the extent of errors and irregularities actually in the population.

Sampling risk is the probability that an auditor's conclusion based on a sample might be different from a conclusion based on an audit of the entire population. If an auditor with more time went through all the invoices and found multiple errors, your sample-based decision will be proven wrong. Apparently, your sample did not represent the population very well. Sampling risk expresses the probability of a wrong decision based on sample evidence, and it is a fact in both statistical and nonstatistical sampling methods. With statistical sampling, you can both measure and control it by auditing sufficiently large samples. With nonstatistical sampling, you can "consider" it without measuring it, something that requires experience and expertise. Other special aspects of sampling risk are discussed later in the sections on auditing control compliance and account balances.

Two types of sampling risk are alpha and beta risk. **Alpha risk** is also frequently referred to as **Type I error risk** while **beta risk** is frequently referred to as **Type II error risk**, and they apply to *all* statistical procedures. Alpha risk is the risk that the auditor concludes that the population is worse in terms of errors than it really is. Beta risk is the risk that the auditor concludes that the population is better than it really is. Now, which risk covers the situation of the auditor's failing to detect a material misstatement? If you said beta risk you are correct. Beta risk covers the situation where the auditor concludes the population is better (i.e., immaterial misstatements) than it actually is (i.e., material misstatements). Auditors have developed more specific risk terms for various types of testing, but they are all either alpha- or beta-type risks. Keep this basic classification in mind to help you better follow the subsequent terminology.

USE NONSTATISTICAL SAMPLING WHEN

- association of population items with random numbers is difficult and expensive.
- strictly defensible results based on mathematics are not necessary.
- the auditor's knowledge about the population justifies a nonstatistical sample with expectation of a reasonable conclusion about the population.
- a representative (random) sample is not required; for example, when an efficient nonstatistical sample of large items leaves an immaterial amount unaudited.
- the population is known to be diverse, with some segments especially error prone.

NONSTATISTICAL SAMPLING IS ADVANTAGEOUS BECAUSE IT

- permits a less rigidly defined approach to unique problems that might not fit into a statistical method.
- permits the auditors to reapply evaluation judgments based on factors in addition to the sample evidence.
- permits auditors to be less than definite about, and omit quantification of, particular judgments on risk and materiality.
- permits auditors to assert standards of subjective judgment. (Thus, the alternative name is judgment sampling.)

EXAMPLES OF NONSAMPLING RISK

Performing inappropriate procedures: Auditor based the evaluation of inventory obsolescence on forecast sales without adequately evaluating the reasonability of the forecast assumptions.

Failure to consider test results appropriately: Auditor did not adequately investigate discrepancies in inventory counts and pricing, failing to note misstatements.

Neglecting the importance of analytical review: Auditor might have discovered client's failure to eliminate intercompany profits if year-to-year product mix, gross profit, and recorded eliminations had been analyzed.

Failure to maintain control over audit procedures: Auditor's lax attitude permitted client employees to tamper with records selected for confirmation.

Lack of professional skepticism: Auditor accepted client's unsupported verbal representations instead of gathering independent evidence to support management's assertions.

Accounting risk: Risks related to predicting the future (risk of forecast errors), typically affecting the measurement or valuation assertions, and unable to be eliminated by gathering more evidence as they are related to auditee business risks not affected by audit procedures. The accounting risk concept helps in identifying accounting deficiencies that result in misleading financial reporting.

Nonsampling risk is all risk other than sampling risk. The audit risk (AR) model given in Chapter 8 is necessary to understanding the breadth of this definition:

Risk Model: $AR = IR \times CR \times DR$

Nonsampling risk can arise from any of the following:

- Misjudging the inherent risk (IR). An auditor who, in the first place, mistakenly believes that few material errors or irregularities occur will tend to do less work and, therefore, may fail to detect problems.
- Misjudging the control risk (CR). An auditor who is too optimistic about the ability of controls to prevent, detect, and correct errors and irregularities will tend to do less work, with the same results as misjudging the inherent risk.
- Poor choice of procedures and mistakes in execution—related to detection risk (DR). Auditors can select procedures inappropriate for the objective (e.g., confirming recorded accounts receivable when the objective is to find unrecorded accounts receivable), fail to recognize errors or irregularities when vouching supporting documents, or sign off on procedures when the work actually was not done.

EXHIBIT 10-2

Summary of Risks in Audit Testing
(categorized by type of test)

Risk	Tests of Controls	Substantive Tests of Balance
Audit risk (AR)	CR* component of AR	RIA** or APR*** component of AR
Sampling risk	Risk of selecting a nonrepresentative sample in tests of controls	Risk of selecting a nonrepresentative sample in substantive tests
Alpha risk	Controlled indirectly via tests of controls	Controlled indirectly via substantive tests
Beta risk	Controlled directly via value for CR	Controlled directly via values for RIA and APR
Nonsampling risk	All other risks associated with testing of controls	All other risks associated with substantive testing

*CR: Control risk, **RIA: Risk of incorrect acceptance, ***APR: Analytical procedures risk

Nonsampling risk includes the possibility of making a wrong decision, which exists in both statistical and nonstatistical sampling. Nonsampling risk's problem is that it cannot be measured. Auditors control it and believe they have reduced it to a negligible level through adequate planning and supervision of the audit, by having policies and procedures for quality control of their auditing practices, and by having internal monitoring and external peer review of their own quality control systems. Auditors are also more open to criticism and fault-finding when erroneous audit decisions result from nonsampling risk. External critics (judges, juries, peer reviewers) have few grounds for criticizing auditors who fall victim to sampling risk, provided that an audit sampling application is planned and executed reasonably well.

The various risks in auditing are summarized in Exhibit 10–2. Exhibit 10–2 focuses on sampling and nonsampling risks associated with gathering evidence. If these risks are at unacceptably high levels, then an audit deficiency occurs. By contrast, unacceptably high levels of accounting risks, discussed earlier, result in accounting deficiencies. This distinction is important because it relates to the two major categories of audit report reservations discussed in Chapter 3.

Sampling Methods and Applications

Audit sampling concerns the amount of work performed and the sufficiency of audit evidence obtained. The terminology of it includes many new concepts and definitions. The ones presented in earlier chapters, however, are general and apply to all phases of audit sampling. Knowing them allows you to "speak the language."

Auditors design audit samples to (1) evaluate control effectiveness in assessing control risk and (2) audit account balances in gathering direct evidence about financial statement assertions. These two parts will be covered in the next sections of the chapter. Each design is organized in terms of planning, performing, and evaluating audit sampling.

This chapter is presented in general terms, avoiding the mathematics of sampling, along the same lines as the *CICA Handbook* section 5300, the auditing guideline "Applying the Concept of Materiality," CAS 530, and the AICPA audit and accounting guide entitled "Auditing Sampling."

. . . .

REVIEW
CHECKPOINTS

14 What is nonsampling risk? Give some examples.

15 Define sampling risk.

16 Does sampling risk always exist in both statistical and nonstatistical sampling? Explain your response.

17 Can sampling risk be avoided? Explain.

18 Can nonsampling risk be avoided? Explain.

19 Are auditors most likely to be sued successfully for sampling risk or for nonsampling risk?

20 What two types of audit programs are ordinarily used as written plans for audit procedures?

21 What are control tests? What purpose do they serve?

TEST OF CONTROLS FOR ASSESSING CONTROL RISK

LEARNING OBJECTIVE

5 Develop a simple audit program for a test of a client's internal control procedures.

Auditors must assess control risk to determine the nature, timing, and extent of other audit procedures. Final evaluations of internal control are based on evidence obtained in the review and testing phases of an evaluation. It is difficult to describe control risk assessments as they depend entirely on judgments made in the circumstances of each specific situation. For example, an auditor might learn that a company requires the bookkeeper to match a shipping order with each sales invoice before recording a sale, as a control against the recording of fictitious sales. Now suppose this control test shows a number of invoices without supporting shipping orders, causing sales possibly to be overstated. More extensive work on accounts receivable using confirmation, enquiries, and analytical review related to collectability would deal with this control deficiency. This shows how control testing provides only indirect evidence of the monetary accuracy of the accounts. Failure to have a matching shipping order only increases the probability of a monetary misstatement but is not guarantee of a misstatement; the shipping orders might have been misplaced and the recorded sales invoice might still be correct. Only further substantive work such as direct confirmation with the customer would provide convincing evidence of a misstatement.

This example related a specific control (matching sales invoices with shipping orders) to a specific set of audit procedures directed toward a possible problem (overstatement of sales and receivables). Generally, auditors reach judgments about control risk as shown in Exhibit 10–3. Some situations call for a nonquantitative expression, and some for a quantitative expression. The quantitative ranges overlap, communicating that auditors cannot put exact numbers on these kinds of evaluations.

Audit sampling is a structured, formal approach and plan for conducting control. The seven-step framework helps auditors plan, perform, and evaluate control test results. It also helps auditors accomplish an eighth step—careful documentation of the work—by showing

EXHIBIT 10-3 | **AUDITOR'S ASSESSMENT OF CONTROL RISK**

Evaluation of Internal Control	*Judgment Expression of Control Risk*	
	Nonquantitative	Quantitative
Excellent control, both as specified and in compliance	Low (1)	10%–30%
Good control, but lacks something in specification or compliance	Moderate (2)	20%–70%
Deficient control, either in specification or compliance or both	High (3)	60%–95%
Little or no control	Maximum	100%

If combining inherent and control risk evaluation is easier, then "low," "moderate," and "high" mean the following:
1. Low combined inherent and control risk.
2. Moderate combined inherent and control risk.
3. High combined inherent and control risk.

each of the seven areas to be described in the working papers. The first seven steps are as follows:

1. Specify the audit objectives.
2. Define the deviation conditions.
3. Define the population.
4. Determine the sample size.
5. Select the sample.
6. Perform the control tests.
7. Evaluate the evidence.

Plan the Procedures

LEARNING OBJECTIVE

5a Specify objectives, deviation conditions, populations, and sampling units.

The first three steps are the phase of **problem recognition**. When a client describes the control system, the implicit assertion is, "These controls work; people comply with the control procedures and achieve the control objectives." The auditors' question (problem) is, "Is it so? Are the validity (and other) control objectives achieved satisfactorily?"

Test of controls is always directed towards producing evidence of the client's performance of its own control procedures. Thus, auditors' procedures should produce evidence about the client's achievement of the seven control objectives.

1. Specify the Audit Objectives

A validity control procedure—namely, the client's procedure of requiring a shipping order to be matched with a sales invoice before a valid sale is recorded—is an example. The specific objective of an auditor's test of controls audit procedure could be, "determine whether recorded sales invoices are supported by matched shipping orders." The audit procedure itself would be, "select a sample of recorded sales invoices and vouch them to supporting shipping orders."

The matching of sales invoices to shipping orders is a **key control** and important here. Auditors should identify and audit only the key controls. Incidental controls are not relied on to reduce control risk, and auditing them for compliance just wastes time.

2. Define the Deviation Conditions

The terms deviation, error, occurrence, and exception are synonyms in test of controls sampling. They all refer to departure from a prescribed internal control procedure; for example, an invoice is recorded with no supporting shipping order (bill of lading). Deviation conditions need to be defined at the outset so the auditors will know a deviation when they see one. As an assistant accountant, you would prefer to be instructed to "select a sample of recorded sales invoices, vouch them to supporting shipping orders, and document cases where the shipping order is missing," rather than, "check recorded sales invoices for mistakes." The latter instruction does not clearly define the deviation conditions and can increase nonsampling risk.

This example is oversimplified, but this vouching procedure for compliance evidence might be used to obtain evidence about several control objectives at the same time. The invoice can be compared with the shipping order for evidence of actual shipment (validity), reviewed for credit approval (authorization), prices compared with the price list (authorization and accuracy), quantity billed compared with quantity shipped (accuracy), recalculated (arithmetic accuracy), compared for correspondence of shipment date and record date (proper period), and traced to postings in the general ledger and subsidiary accounts (accounting).

Exhibit 10–4 shows some deviation conditions laid out in a working paper designed to record the control testing results for a sample of sales invoices.

Test of controls audit sampling is also called **attribute sampling**—sampling in which auditors look for the presence or absence of a control condition. In response to the audit question, "For each sales invoice in the sample, can a matched shipping order be found?" the answer can be only yes or no. With this definition, auditors can count the number of

EXHIBIT 10-4   TEST OF CONTROLS AUDIT DOCUMENTATION

Index *M 10.3*

By *JC*   Date *11-11-20X2*
Review *J.D.*   Date *11-15-20X2*

KINGSTON COMPANY
Test of Controls over Recorded Sales
December 31, 20X2

Invoice number	Date	Amount	Bill of lading	Credit approved	Approved prices	Quantities match	Arithmetic accurate	Dates match	Posted to customer
35000	Mar. 30	$ 3,000							
35050	Mar. 31	$ 800			X				
35100	Apr. 2	$ 1,200					Y		
35150	Apr. 3	$ 1,500			Y				
35200	Apr. 5	$ 400							
35250	Apr. 6	$ 300	X			X	Y	X	
32100	Jan. 3	$ 1,000							
32150	Jan. 4	$ 200							
34850	Mar. 25	Missing	X	X	X	X	X	X	
34900	Mar. 26	$ 100			Y				
34950	Mar. 27	$ 200							
Sample = 200		$98,000							
Uncorrected deviations			4	9	5	6	3	7	0

X = Uncorrected deviation
Y = Deviation occurred but was detected and corrected later.

deviations and use the count when evaluating the evidence. Attribute sampling can also be useful in balance auditing; an example is shown in the box on page 378.

3. Define the Population

Specifying the control test (compliance) audit objectives and the deviation conditions usually defines the population; that is, the set of all elements in the balance or class of transactions. In our example, the population consists of all the recorded sales invoices, and each invoice is a population unit. In **classical attribute sampling**, a sampling unit is the same thing as a population unit.[4]

Population definition is important because audit conclusions can only be made about the population the sample was selected from. For example, evidence from a sample of recorded sales invoices cannot be used for a conclusion about completeness. Controls related to the completeness objective (in this case, control over failure to record an invoice for goods shipped) can only be audited by sampling from a population representing goods shipped (the shipping order file) and not by sampling from the population of recorded invoices.

The timing of the audit work complicates population definition. Control tests ideally should be applied to transactions executed throughout the entire period under audit. However, auditors often perform control tests at an **interim date**—a date some weeks or months before the client's year-end date—when the entire population is not available for audit. Doing the work at an interim date is fine, but auditors cannot ignore the period

[4] Dollar-unit sampling, however, defines a different sampling unit. Dollar-unit sampling (DUS) is explained in detail in Appendix 10B on the Online Learning Centre.

between the interim date and the year-end. Strategies for control in the period after the interim date are explained later.

The question of how well the **physical representation of the population** corresponds to the population itself also complicates the population definition. The physical representation of the population is the auditor's frame of reference for selecting a sample. It can be a journal listing of recorded sales invoices, a file drawer full of invoice copies, a computer file of invoices, or another physical representation. The sample actually will be selected from the physical representation, so it must be complete and correspond with the actual population. The physical representation of the recorded sales invoices as a list in a journal is fairly easy to visualize. However, an auditor should make sure that periodic listings (e.g., monthly sales journals) are added correctly and posted to the general ledger sales accounts. In our example, a selection of individual sales invoices from the sales journal is known to be from the complete population of recorded sales invoices, but some physical representations are not so easy to assess for the completeness of correspondence to their population.

A BALANCE AUDIT APPLICATION OF ATTRIBUTE SAMPLING

Attribute control test samples usually are drawn from a class of transactions in order to obtain evidence about compliance with control objectives. Attribute samples may be used for balance audit purposes. This example suggests an attribute sample to obtain evidence about an ownership (rights) financial statement assertion.

Question: A lessor is in the business of leasing autos, large trucks, tractors, and trailers. Is it necessary for the auditors to examine the titles to all the equipment?

Answer: It is not necessary, unless some extraordinary situation or circumstance is brought to light, for the auditors to examine titles to all the equipment. Random test verification of title certificates or proper registration of vehicles should be made.

Source: AICPA Technical Practice Aids, 8330.02.

The Procedures

LEARNING OBJECTIVE
5b Demonstrate some basic audit sampling calculations.

The next three performance steps represent the phase of **evidence collection** of the sampling method. These steps are performed to obtain the evidence.

4. Determine the Sample Size

Sample size—the number of population units to audit—should be determined thoughtfully. Some auditors operate on the "magic number theory" (e.g., select 30, because that's what we've always used on this audit). But a magic number may not provide enough evidence, or it may be too large a sample. Auditors must consider four influences on sample size: sampling risk, tolerable deviation rate, expected population deviation rate, and population size.

Sampling Risk Sampling risk was defined as the probability that a conclusion based on the audit of a sample might be different from a conclusion based on an audit of the entire population. In other words, when using evidence from a sample, an auditor might decide that (1) control risk is very low when, in fact, it is not, or (2) control risk is very high when, in fact, it is not so bad. The more you know about a population (from a larger sample), the less likely you are to reach a wrong conclusion, or the lower the sampling risk will be of making either of the two decision errors. More will be said about these risks in the section on evaluation.

In terms of our example, the important sampling risk is the probability that the sample will reveal few or no recorded sales invoices without supporting shipping orders when, in fact, the population contains many such deviations. This result would lead to the erroneous conclusion that the control worked well. Auditing a larger sample reduces the probability of finding few deviations when many exist. Thus, sample size varies inversely with the amount of sampling risk an auditor is willing to take.

Tolerable Deviation Rate   Auditors should have an idea of how rates of deviation in the population correspond with control risk assessments. Perfect control compliance is not necessary, so the question is rather what rate of deviation in the population signals control risk of 10 percent? 20 percent? 30 percent? and so forth, up to 100 percent. Suppose an auditor believes that $90,000 of sales invoices could contain control deviations without causing a minimum material misstatement in the sales and accounts receivable balances. If the total gross sales is $8.5 million, this judgment implies a **tolerable deviation rate** of about 1 percent ($90,000/$8.5 million). Since this 1 percent rate marks the minimum material misstatement, it indicates a low control risk (say, 0.05), and it justifies a great deal of reliance on internal control in the audit of the sales and accounts receivable balances.

However, there can be more than one tolerable deviation rate. Each successively higher rate is associated with a higher control risk. Continuing with our example, higher tolerable deviation rates could be associated with higher control risks as follows:[5]

Deviation Rate (%)	Control Risk
1	0.05
2	0.10
4	0.20
6	0.30
8	0.40
10	0.50
12	0.60
14	0.70
16	0.80
18	0.90
20	1.00

Since sample size varies inversely with the tolerable deviation rate, the auditor who wants to assess control risk at 0.05 (tolerable rate = 1%) will need to audit a larger sample of sales transactions than another auditor who is willing to assess control risk at 0.40 (tolerable rate = 8%). The desired control risk level and its tolerable rate are a matter of auditor choice.

The tolerable rate is not a fixed rate until the auditor decides what control risk assessment suits the audit plan, at which point it becomes a decision criterion involved in the sampling application. Some auditors express the tolerable rate as a number (necessary for statistical calculation of sample size), while others do not put a number on it. Appendix 10B on the Online Learning Centre contains more explanation about determining various tolerable rates.

Expected Population Deviation Rate   Auditors usually know of or suspect some control performance conditions. They could have last year's audit experience with the client or information from a predecessor auditor, which informs them about the client's personnel, working conditions, and general control environment. This knowledge contributes to an **expectation about the population deviation rate**, an estimate of the ratio of the number of expected deviations to population size. If there was a 1 percent deviation in last year's audit, this year's expected rate could be 1 percent as well. Auditors can also stipulate a zero expected deviation rate, which will produce a minimum sample size for audit.

From a common-sense perspective, the expected rate of deviation must be less than the tolerable rate, as there would be no reason to perform any test of controls if the auditor expected to find more. Also, the closer the expected rate is to the tolerable rate, the larger is the sample needed to reach a conclusion that deviations do not exceed the tolerable rate.

---

[5] Accounting firms have different policies for associating tolerable deviation rates with control risk categories. Some start with a minimum rate of 1 percent, and others start with higher rates.

Thus, sample size varies directly with the expected deviation rate. Some auditors will express the expected rate as a number (necessary for statistical calculations of sample size), while others will not put a number on it.

The simplified approach we use does not quantify the expected population deviation—effectively, the expected rate is zero. This expected error rate results in use of the smallest statistical sample sizes possible, consistent with auditor risk and materiality objectives. Some auditors use these smallest statistical sample sizes as a guide to the minimal amount of testing even for nonstatistical sampling (e.g., see AICPA, "Audit Sampling Guide," May 1, 2008, edition, page 34). Statistical sample size calculations can, thus, be an important guide in all audit sampling situations (CAS 530). Appendix 10B on the Online Learning Centre explains how to work with nonzero expected population deviation rates.

Population Size   Common sense probably tells you that samples should be larger for bigger populations (a direct relationship). While your common sense is accurate, practically speaking, the appropriate sample size for a population of 100,000 units may be only 2 or 3 sampling units larger than that for a 10,000-unit population. Not much difference! By using the same calculation for both populations, your sample size for the 10,000 population is proportionally bigger, and thus more conservative. The general principle is that if you use the simplified formulas for very large populations, you end up with slightly conservative results. Many practising auditors find this trade-off worthwhile.

The four influences on sample size in this section, and summarized in Exhibit 10–5, are applicable to both statistical and nonstatistical sampling.

Calculating Sample Size   The preceding discussion of sample-size determinants gives you a general understanding of the four influences on sample size. Next, we consider the simplified way of calculating sample sizes with a brief overview of basic formulas and tables used in statistical auditing.

Some basic formulas provide an overview of the most fundamental mechanics of statistical auditing. Two key points at which the formulas and tables are used in statistical sampling are (1) sample size planning and (2) sample evaluation. With one commonly used approach, called dollar-unit sampling (DUS), the same formula and table can be applied to both tests of controls and substantive tests of balances. DUS is common because it is effective, efficient, and the easiest approach to use. We begin by illustrating its use in sample-size planning for tests of control.

For planning audit sample sizes, the equation $n = R/P$ summarizes the key factors affecting the sufficiency of audit evidence: the relationship between confidence level (R value) and materiality (P value), and the extent of audit testing (sample size n). That is, the amount of audit work is directly proportional to the confidence level and inversely proportional to the materiality level used.

For tests of controls and substantive tests, solve for n in the formula $R = nP$, where $R = {}_{CL}R_K$ is a confidence-level factor that is unique for each combination of confidence

---

EXHIBIT 10-5   SAMPLE-SIZE RELATIONSHIPS: TEST OF CONTROLS AUDITING

	Predetermined Sample Size Will Be		
Sample Size Influence	High Rate or Large Population	Low Rate or Small Population	Sample Size Relationship
1. Acceptable sampling risk	Smaller	Larger	Inverse
2. Tolerable deviation rate	Smaller	Larger	Inverse
3. Expected population deviation rate	Larger**	Smaller	Direct
4. Population	Larger*	Smaller*	Direct

*Effect on sample size is quite small for population of 1,000 or more.
**Effect of this is explained in Appendix 10B on the Online Learning Centre. Many auditors do not quantify the expected rate. This results in the simplified approach described in this section.

level (CL) and acceptable number of errors (K) from the table of values for R given in Appendix 10A (page 412), and P is materiality, or something based on materiality, which is represented as a rate or proportion. P is also referred to as UEL (upper error limit). The auditor must use professional judgment in specifying K, CL, and P.

P is the amount, as a rate, that the auditor considers material for the population being tested. When being set, it has to take into consideration the additive effect of errors in other accounting populations representing other balances or transaction streams. In this stage of sampling, the planned P might be an amount lower than materiality so that the auditor can reduce alpha risk. Firm practice varies: alpha risk can be indirectly controlled through the *planned* K value, the *planned* P value, or a combination of the two. The most common strategy is to use K = 0 and a *planned* P in the range of half to full materiality. We discuss these options in the online Appendix 10B. Here the calculations are simplified by assuming that P is set equal to materiality or tolerable deviation rate. This results in the smallest sample size possible for the stated confidence level and precision. This smallest sample size is used by many firms as a guide to sufficient sample sizes for all representative sampling, whether statistical or nonstatistical (e.g., see AICPA, "Audit Sampling Guide," May 1, 2008, edition, p. 34).

When a planned P lower than materiality is used in planning the extent of testing, the term *scope* distinguishes it from the tolerable amount the after-testing sample evaluation decision will be based on. If detected errors exceed the scope amount after sampling, the results may still be acceptable if the errors are nevertheless below the tolerable amount. The key after-sampling decision rule is based on the tolerable or material amount, not on any other amount.

In the formula CL = 1 − beta risk, beta risk is the risk that the test will fail to detect a material misstatement when it exists—the risk of incorrect acceptance (RIA). Alpha risk is the risk of concluding that there is a material misstatement when in fact the misstatements are immaterial—the risk of incorrect rejection. Beta risk is the more serious as it relates directly to the audit risk model and its components, depending on whether we are talking about tests of controls or substantive tests. It relates to audit effectiveness because the audit fails if it fails to detect a material misstatement. Alpha risk, instead, relates to audit efficiency; it results in the auditors' doing unnecessary work to clear up their mistake, something they are aware of by the end of the audit. This risk is implicitly controlled by the K value, as the higher the K value used in sample-size planning, the lower the alpha risk and the larger the sample size.

To illustrate the calculations using the table of R values in Appendix 10A, let us assume the auditor wants a confidence level of 95 percent, uses K = 0 to make the sample planning as simple as possible (this results in the smallest sample size for the planned confidence level), and sets P so that it equals the tolerable deviation rate, which we assume here is 0.05, so that P = 0.05. Using our formula $n = R/P$ and the table, you should get the following results: $n = 3.0/0.05 = 60$, so that your planned sample size, given these objectives, is 60.

Working with tables based on the above formulas will minimize the use of formulas. For example, the simplified table titled "Table to Determine Sample Sizes for Tests of Control Using the DUS Approach" in Appendix 10A is constructed using the calculations with formulas in the preceding paragraph. A table is usually based on some formula or algorithm. When using such a table, the auditor only needs to identify the required beta risk (= 1 minus the confidence level) and tolerable deviation rate (material rate). In constructing the table, the expected error rate is zero (K = 0), thereby leading to the smallest sample size possible for the stated confidence level and tolerable rate. This table is restricted to the most common beta risk levels of .10 and .05 and the most commonly used tolerable deviation rates. Thus the table is quite small. To figure out the sample size, the auditor looks up the number in the table that is at the intersection of the desired beta risk and tolerable rate. Using a desired risk of .05 (or, equivalently, a desired confidence level of .95) and tolerable rate for tests of controls of .05, then the table gives 60 as the desired sample size. The same size sample could have been calculated using the formula. Your instructor will indicate to you which approach is to be used in your course.

A Note on Testing of Controls for Audits of Internal Control Statements

Section 404 of the Sarbanes-Oxley Act introduced a requirement for management to prepare internal control statements and have them audited. This requirement led to PCAOB's Auditing Standard No. 2.

What does testing of controls mean in this new context? First, internal control statements focus on company-level control objectives such as "tone at the top," corporate codes of conduct, and corporate governance in general. Second, the focus is on the design of internal control at a specific point in time. Third, auditors need to utilize an authoritative framework for evaluating the design. For example, the PCAOB requires that the following be considered as part of the framework of suitable internal control criteria for purposes of reporting on internal control: control environment, risk assessment, control activities, information and communication, and monitoring. The rest of this chapter stresses testing of detailed control activities, while the other components of PCAOB's framework are broader, company-level controls as summarized below.

Company-Level Control Objectives

Control Environment
- Through its attitudes and actions, management demonstrates character, integrity, and ethical values.
- Management's philosophy and operating style are consistent with a sound control environment.
- Management assigns authority and responsibility.
- Human resource policies and procedures are consistent with and reinforce the control environment.
- The audit committee and overall board of directors are actively involved and have significant influence over the organization.

Risk Assessment
- Management has established practices for identifying, evaluating, and appropriately mitigating risks.

Information and Communication
- Management gathers information from and disseminates information to the appropriate people on a timely basis.
- Management has established an effective "whistle-blower" program as it relates to financial reporting.

Monitoring
- Management has established effective ongoing monitoring activities.
- Management performs separate evaluations of the organization's internal control environment to confirm its effectiveness.

To effectively assess the broader corporate controls, auditors need to be more creative and use more critical thinking as discussed in Chapter 4. Generally, auditors need to rely less on detailed testing and more on observations and analytic-type procedures such as interviews of board members, surveys of employees, or tests of

> how effectively management responds to allegations of improprieties. Auditors will need to gauge employee awareness and comfort level with company-level controls. As you can imagine, assessing "comfort levels" and "tone at the top" will require auditors to evaluate character and ethical values of key people, with the result that critical thinking on these issues and its documentation will become more important than ever.
>
> Source: J. Stephen McNally, *Journal of Accountancy*, June 2005, p. 66.

5. Select the Sample

Auditing standards express two requirements for samples: (1) sampling units must be selected from the population an audit conclusion will apply to, ideally from transactions executed throughout the period under audit; and (2) a sample must be representative of the population it is drawn from. Thus, a sample mirrors the characteristics of the population, but auditors cannot guarantee its representativeness. After all, that is what sampling risk is all about—the probability that the sample might not mirror the population well enough.

Auditors can try to attain representativeness by selecting **random** samples—each unit in the population has an equal probability of being included in the sample. Intentionally or accidentally excluding a segment of a population can render a sample nonrepresentative. Random samples are often selected by assigning a number to each population unit (sometimes the units are prenumbered forms), and then choosing a selection of random numbers to make up the sample. A printed random number table (one is provided in Appendix 10A) or a computerized random number generator such as the RAND function in Excel will generate a list of random numbers. This method is known as **unrestricted random selection**.

Systematic random selection is another popular method. To use it, the population size and a predetermined sample size are needed. A random starting place in the physical representation (list of sales invoices recorded in a sales journal, for example) is chosen, and then every kth unit is selected, where the value for k is population size divided by sample size. For example, if 10,000 invoices, numbered from 32071 to 42070, were issued and you want a sample of 200, first randomly choose a starting place, say invoice 35000, then select every kth = 10,000 divided by 200 = 50th invoice. So the next invoice would be 35050, then 35100, then 35150, and so on. If the end of the list is reached before 200 are selected, cycle back to the sequence beginning invoice, 32071, and continue. Most systematic samples are selected using five or more random starts in the population.

With sample selection there is a critical distinction between statistical and nonstatistical audit sampling. In statistical sampling evaluation, the sample must be random, while in nonstatistical plans auditors sometimes use sample selection methods where randomness and representativeness cannot easily be evaluated. **Haphazard selection** refers to any unsystematic way of selecting sample units; for example, closing your eyes and dipping into a file drawer of sales invoices to pick items. You may pick only the crumpled ones that stick out, and they may be different from most of the other invoices in the drawer. Also, your method cannot be described so that someone can **replicate** it—reperform your selection procedure and get the same sample units. Some auditors describe haphazard sampling as choosing items without any special reason for including or excluding items, thus obtaining a **representative sample**. However, because it is hard to document and impossible to replicate, haphazard selection should be considered only as a last resort.

Block sampling is the practice of choosing segments of contiguous transactions; for example, choosing the sales invoices processed on randomly chosen days, say February 3, July 17, and September 29. Implicitly, the block-sampling auditor has defined the population unit as a business day (260 to 365 of them in a year) and has selected three—not much of a sample. Block sampling is undesirable because it is hard to get a representative sample of blocks efficiently; having enough blocks means there is a huge number of invoices to audit for compliance.

6. Perform the Control Tests

An **internal control program** consists of procedures designed to produce evidence about the effectiveness of a client's internal control performance, and now you are ready to obtain the evidence. The control tests listed in the following box determine how well the control procedures were followed on the transactions affecting accounts receivable. After each action, the parenthetical note tells you the control objective being tested.

TEST OF CONTROLS AUDITING

1. Select a sample of recorded sales invoices and perform the following:
   a. Determine whether a bill of lading is attached (evidence of validity).
   b. Determine whether credit was approved (evidence of authorization).
   c. Determine whether product prices on the invoice agree with the approved price list (evidence of authorization and accuracy).
   d. Compare the quantity billed with the quantity shipped (evidence of accuracy).
   e. Recalculate the invoice arithmetic (evidence of accuracy).
   f. Compare the shipment date with the invoice record date (evidence of proper period).
   g. Trace the invoice to posting in the general ledger control account and in the correct customer's account (evidence of accounting).
   h. Note the type of product shipped and determine proper classification in the right product-line revenue account (evidence of classification).

2. Select a sample of shipping orders and perform the following:
   a. Trace them to recorded sales invoices (evidence of completeness).
   b. The procedures in #1b, c, d, e, f, and h also could be performed on the sales invoices produced by this sample. However, the work need not be duplicated.

3. Select a sample of recorded cash receipts and perform the following:
   a. Trace them to deposits in the bank statement (evidence of validity).
   b. Vouch discounts taken by customers to proper approval or policy (evidence of authorization).
   c. Recalculate the cash summarized for a daily report or posting (evidence of accuracy).
   d. Trace the deposit to the right cash account (evidence of classification).
   e. Compare the date of receipt to the recording date (evidence of proper period).
   f. Trace the receipts to postings in the correct customers' accounts (evidence of accounting).

4. Select a sample of daily cash reports or another source of original cash records and perform the following:
   a. Trace to the cash receipts journal (evidence of completeness).
   b. The procedures in #3b, c, d, e, and f also could be performed on this cash receipts sample. However, the work need not be duplicated.

5. Scan the accounts receivable for postings from sources other than the sales and cash receipts journals (e.g., general journal adjusting entries, credit memos). Vouch a sample of such entries to supporting documents (evidence of validity, authorization, accuracy, and classification). This program describes the **nature** of the control testing procedures. Each is a specific application of one of the general control testing techniques.

REVIEW CHECKPOINTS

22 Why can poor controls over the existence of sales result in an overstated accounts receivable balance at year-end?

23 In control testing, why is it necessary to define a compliance deviation in advance? Give seven examples of compliance deviations.

24 Which judgments must an auditor make when deciding on a sample size?

25 Describe the influence of each judgment on sample size.

26 Name and describe four sample selection methods.

The Evidence

LEARNING OBJECTIVE

5c Evaluate evidence from control testing.

The final step is the **evidence-evaluation** phase of the sampling method. First, you determined whether each specified key control procedure worked satisfactorily. Then you gathered relevant compliance evidence. Now you need to evaluate the evidence and make justifiable decisions about the control risk.

7. Evaluate the Evidence

Test of controls audit sampling provides evidence of whether a client's internal control procedures are being followed satisfactorily. Compliance evidence, therefore, is very important for the conclusion about control risk. When auditors evaluate sample-based compliance evidence, there are two sampling risk decision errors they might make: assessing the control risk too low or assessing it too high. The **risk of assessing the control risk too low** is the probability that the compliance evidence in the sample indicates low control risk when the actual (but unknown) degree of compliance does not justify it. This can lead to failure to do the necessary additional work and threatens the effectiveness of the audit. It is also referred to as beta risk for tests of controls. On the other hand, the **risk of assessing the control risk too high** is the probability that the compliance evidence in the sample indicates high control risk when the actual (but unknown) degree of compliance justifies a lower control risk assessment. This is also referred to as the alpha risk for tests of controls. Assessing the control risk too high triggers more audit work than was planned and threatens the efficiency of the audit.

Audit efficiency is important, but audit effectiveness is more important. For this reason, auditing standards require only a low risk of assessing the control risk too low, especially when this decision error could cause an auditor to do significantly less work on the related account balances. These risks and decisions are illustrated in Exhibit 10–6. Keeping these risks in mind, evaluating evidence includes calculating the sample deviation rate, comparing it with the tolerable rate, and following up all the deviations discovered.

SUPERSEDED TERMINOLOGY: OVERRELIANCE AND UNDERRELIANCE

Several years ago, professional terminology was changed from "reliance on control" to "assessment of control risk." However, old habits die hard, and you will probably still encounter these uses of control terminology:

Overreliance is the result of realizing the risk of assessing control risk too low. If auditors think control risk is low when in fact it is higher, they will *overrely* on internal control and restrict other audit procedures when they actually should perform more work. Overreliance is the same as beta risk of tests of controls.

Underreliance is the result of realizing the risk of assessing control risk too high. If auditors think control risk is high when in fact it is lower, they will *underrely* on internal control and perform more audit work when less work would suffice. Underreliance risk is the same as alpha risk of tests of controls.

EXHIBIT 10-6   THE TEST OF CONTROLS AUDIT SAMPLING DECISION MATRIX

Actual State of Internal Controls (actual population deviation rate)	Sample Population Deviation Rate	
	Less than Tolerable Rate	Greater than Tolerable Rate
The deviation rate is less than the tolerable rate, so the control is performed satisfactorily.	Correct decision	Control risk too high decision error (Alpha risk for tests of controls)
The deviation rate is greater than the tolerable rate, so the control is not performed satisfactorily.	Control risk too low decision error (Beta risk for tests of controls)	Correct decision

Calculate the Sample Deviation Rate   The first piece of hard evidence is the sample deviation rate. Suppose an auditor selected 200 recorded sales invoices and vouched them to shipping orders (bills of lading), finding four without shipping orders. The sample deviation rate is 4/200 = 2 percent. This is the best single-point estimate of the actual, but unknown, deviation rate in the population. However, you cannot say that the deviation rate in the population is exactly 2 percent. Chances are the sample is not exactly representative; the actual but unknown population deviation rate could be lower or higher.

Judge the Deviation Rate in Relation to the Tolerable Rate and the Risk of Assessing the Control Risk Too Low   Suppose the auditor in the example believed the tolerable rate was 8 percent, justifying a control risk assessment of CR = 0.40. In a nonstatistical sampling case, this auditor is supposed to think of the sample deviation rate (2 percent) in relation to the tolerable rate (8 percent), and about the risk (of assessing control risk too low) that the actual, but unknown, deviation rate in the population exceeds 8 percent. The decision in this case depends on the auditor's experience and expertise. The nonstatistical auditor might conclude that the population deviation rate is probably 8 percent because the sample deviation rate of 2 percent is so much lower. *CICA Handbook* guideline, AuG-41, paragraph 42, suggests this logic. AuG-41 does not asume that the auditor is using statistical sampling. However, it must assume that the auditor used a minimal sample size, as discussed earlier, because the population is always rejected statistically when the sample size is too small.

Things are more explainable, in text, with a statistical sample evaluation, which explains why statistical sampling is more popular. The auditor establishes decision criteria by first assigning a number to the risk of assessing the control risk too low, say 10 percent, and then assigning a number to the tolerable rate, say 8 percent. A statistical table is then used to calculate a sampling error-adjusted upper limit, which is the sample deviation rate adjusted upward to allow for the idea that the actual population rate could be higher. In this example, the adjusted limit, the **UEL (upper error limit)**, can be calculated as 4 percent. This finding means "the probability is 10 percent that the actual but unknown population deviation rate is greater than 4 percent." The decision criterion was "the actual but unknown population deviation rate needs to be 8 percent or lower, with 10 percent risk of assessing the control risk too low." So the decision criterion is satisfied, and the control risk assessment (0.40) associated with the 8 percent tolerable rate can be justified.[6]

From a critical thinking perspective, this justification step (step 4 of Exhibit 4–1, page 98) uses statistical theory to support the conclusion. Many would view such a conclusion as better supported than one based on nonstatistical sampling. One of the advantages of statistical auditing is that it makes sample evaluation less ambiguous, as is illustrated next.

Sample Evaluation   Sample evaluation essentially involves solving for P in the formula R = nP so that P = R/n. Known as the achieved P or the achieved UEL, it is calculated after the sample has been taken and the results are known. This means that the number of errors (K)

---

[6] Changing the example to suppose 11 deviations were found creates a problem for the nonstatistical sampler. He or she must think harder about the evidence (a 5.5 percent sample rate) in relation to the tolerable rate (8 percent) and acceptable risk. The statistical sampler can measure the UEL at 8.3 percent, which is greater than the 8 percent tolerable rate at 10 percent risk of overreliance. The control fails the decision criterion test. Appendix 10B on the text Online Learning Centre contains more information about making these calculations using statistical tables and formulas.

detected by the sample is already known, the confidence level (CL = 1 – beta risk) is known, and the sample size taken is already known. Thus, we can solve for achieved UEL = achieved P = R/n, where R = $_{CL}R_K$, CL is the specified confidence level, and K is the number of errors *found* in the sample (not the number expected as in sample-size planning).

To illustrate sample evaluation for a test of controls, assume that two errors or deviations were found in a sample of 100 and you wish to calculate the achieved P at 95% CL; thus P = R/n = UEL. Plugging in the appropriate values from the table in Appendix 10A gives us the following: achieved P = R/n = UEL = 6.30/100 = 0.063. This is the maximum error at the specified confidence level. This is then compared with what is material or tolerable. The basic rule is that, if achieved P, or UEL, is greater than material or tolerable, reject the population—otherwise, accept it. Compare this rule with AuG-41, paragraph 42, and note that the dollar-unit sampling (DUS) rule is less ambiguous. In the case of tests of controls, rejection of the population is equivalent to assessing control risk as high; that is, there is no (or reduced) reliance on controls.

As in sample planning, the use of appropriate tables eliminates the need for the formulas. For example, Appendix 10A has tables entitled "Table to Evaluate Sample Results for Tests of Controls . . ." These tables provide for two widely used confidence levels: 95% and 90%, the equivalent to planned beta risk levels of 5% and 10%, respectively. The table values are the interaction of sample sizes (left-hand column) and number of errors. In our illustration we use .05 beta risk (= 1 – 95% confidence level) and a sample size of 100 to get a UEL of 7% (rounded up) for this confidence level. This conservative UEL of 7% can be interpreted as the maximum error rate at 95% confidence level. The decision rule is to accept reliance on the controls (or accept the population) if the UEL is less than tolerable; otherwise reject or reduce reliance (or reject the population error as unacceptable). This result is more conservative (higher UEL) than in the paragraph above, but done with tables, not formulas. You can get a more accurate value of 6.3% by dividing the R value at the top (6.3) by the sample size (100). Your instructor will tell you which approach to use in your course.

Achieved P can always be interpreted as the maximum error rate for the specified confidence level. There are additional complications for substantive testing, but these formulas are the only thing necessary for a conceptual understanding. These formulas or tables of **dollar-unit sampling (DUS)** are so simple and so effective that they are now the most widely used in audit practice.

DUS is also so widely used because taking an appropriate sample does not require advance knowledge of the recorded amount of the population, as the other statistical approaches do. This makes DUS particularly appropriate for audits involving continuous, online, real-time reporting of sales and purchases as might be demanded in ecommerce audits. This is further explained in Appendix 10B on the Online Learning Centre.

Follow-up All and the Deviations   The evaluation described so far has been mostly quantitative in nature, involving counts of deviations, deviation rates and tolerable rate, and risk judgment criteria. Qualitative evaluation through determining the nature and cause of the deviations is also necessary. A single deviation can be the tip of the iceberg—a sign of pervasive deficiency. Auditors are obligated by the standard of due audit care to investigate known deviations so that nothing important will be overlooked.

Qualitative evaluation is sometimes called **error analysis** because each deviation from a prescribed control procedure is investigated to determine its nature, cause, and probable effect on financial statements. The analysis is essentially judgmental and involves a decision on whether the deviation is (1) a pervasive error in principle affecting all like transactions or just the one; (2) a deliberate control breakdown or unintentional; (3) a result of misundersood instructions or careless inattention to control duties; or (4) directly or remotely related to a money amount measurement in the financial statements. Clearly, different qualitative perceptions of the seriousness of a deviation result from error analysis findings.

When the decision criteria are not satisfied and the preliminary conclusion is that the control risk is high, the auditors need to decide what to do next. The deviation follow-up can lead to more account balance audit work by making changes to the nature, timing, and extent of other audit procedures. If you suspect the sampling results overstate the actual population deviation rate (i.e., that alpha risk is occurring), you can perform the control tests on more sample units in hopes of deciding that the control risk is actually lower. However, when faced with the preliminary "nonreliance" decision, you should never manipulate the quantitative evaluation by raising the tolerable rate or setting the risk of assessing the control risk too low. Supposedly, these two decision criteria were carefully determined in the planning stage, and only new information is a good basis for easing them.

Timing of Test of Controls Audit Procedures

Earlier in the chapter, you learned that auditors can perform the control testing at an interim date—a date before the client's year-end date. When control testing is early, an audit manager must decide what to do about the remaining period (e.g., the period October through December after doing test of controls auditing in September for a December 31 year-end audit).

The decision turns on several factors: (1) the results of the work at interim might, for example, indicate poor control performance and high control risk; (2) enquiries made after interim may show that a particular control procedure has been abandoned or improved; (3) the length of the remaining period may be short enough to forego additional work or long enough to suggest a need for continuing the test of controls audit; (4) the dollar amounts affected by the control procedure may have been much larger or much smaller than before; (5) evidence obtained about control as a byproduct of performing substantive procedures for the remaining period may show enough about control performance that separate work on this is unnecessary; or (6) work performed by the company's internal auditors may be relied on for the remaining period.

Depending on these circumstances, an auditor can decide to (1) continue the test of controls because knowledge of control performance is necessary to justify restriction of other audit work or (2) stop further test of controls audit work because (*a*) there is enough evidence derived from other procedures or (*b*) information shows the control has failed, control risk is high, and other work will not be restricted. Whatever the judgment, audit effectiveness and efficiency should always be uppermost in the auditor's mind.

REVIEW CHECKPOINTS

27   In test of controls auditing, why should auditors be more concerned with the risk of assessing the control risk too low than with that of assessing it too high?

28   What important decision must be made when test of controls auditing is performed and control risk is evaluated at an interim date several weeks or months before the client's fiscal year-end?

SUBSTANTIVE PROCEDURES FOR AUDITING ACCOUNT BALANCES

LEARNING OBJECTIVE

6 Develop a simple audit program for an account balance, considering the influences of risk and tolerable misstatement.

When audit sampling is used for auditing the assertions in account balances, the monetary amount of the population units is the main interest, not the presence or absence of control deviations, as is the case with attribute sampling. **Substantive tests of details auditing** is done to obtain direct evidence about the dollar amounts and disclosures in the financial statements.

Substantive-purpose procedures include analytical procedures and test (audit) of details of transactions and balances. Analytical procedures involve overall comparisons of account balances with prior balances, financial relationships, nonfinancial information, budgeted or forecasted balances, and balances derived from estimates calculated by auditors (refer to the discussion of analytical procedures in Chapter 8). Analytical procedures are usually not applied on a sample basis. So, substantive procedures for auditing details are the normal procedures used in account balance audit sampling.

Risk Model Expansion

Up to now you have worked with a conceptual risk model that included **detection risk (DR)**. Detection risk is actually a combination of two risks: **analytical procedures risk (APR)** is the probability that analytical procedures will fail to detect material errors, and the **risk of incorrect acceptance (RIA)** is the probability that test-of-detail procedures will fail to detect material errors. The two types of procedures are considered independent, so detection risk is $DR = APR \times RIA$, and the expanded risk model is

$$AR = IR \times CR \times APR \times RIA$$

This model is still a conceptual tool. It can now be used to help you understand some elements of sampling for auditing the details of account balances. First, recognize that auditors exercise professional judgment in assessing the inherent risk (IR), control risk (CR), analytical procedures risk (APR), and audit risk (AR). If these four risks are given, you can then manipulate the model to express the RIA:

$$RIA = \frac{AR}{IR \times CR \times APR}$$

With AR, IR, and APR held constant, RIA varies inversely with CR; that is, the higher the planned CR, the lower the planned RIA, and vice versa. Furthermore, this is also true of the risk of material misstatement concept (RMM) of CAS 530, since $RMM = IR \times CR$.

More About Sampling Risk

Substantive-purpose procedures produce the evidence enabling an auditor to decide whether an account balance is fairly presented in conformity with GAAP. Thus, auditors run the sampling risks of making one of two decision errors. The RIA represents the decision to accept a balance as being materially accurate when, in fact (unknown to the auditor), the balance is materially misstated. This is the beta risk for a substantive test. The other decision error risk, the **risk of incorrect rejection**, represents the decision that a balance is materially misstated when, in fact, it is not. This is the alpha risk for a substantive test. These sampling risk relationships are shown in Exhibit 10–7.

Incorrect Acceptance (Beta Risk)

The risk of incorrect acceptance is considered the more important of the two decision error risks. When an auditor decides an account book balance is materially accurate (hence, needs no adjustment), the audit work on that account is considered finished, the decision is documented in the working papers, and the audit team proceeds to work on other accounts. If the account is, in fact, materially misstated, an unqualified opinion on the financial statements is unwarranted and the effectiveness of the audit is damaged.

EXHIBIT 10–7   THE ACCOUNT BALANCE AUDIT SAMPLING DECISION MATRIX

Audit Decision Alternatives (based on sample evidence)	Unknown Actual Account Balance is	
	Materially* accurate	Materially* misstated
The book value of the account is materially accurate.	Correct decision	Incorrect acceptance
The book value of the account is materially misstated.	Incorrect rejection	Correct decision

*Materially in this context refers to the "material misstatement" assigned to the account balance.

Incorrect Rejection (Alpha Risk)

When an auditor decides an account book balance is materially misstated, more audit work is performed to determine the adjustment. The risk is that the book balance really is a materially accurate representation of the (unknown) actual value, and the audit manager may recommend an unnecessary adjustment.

Incorrect rejection is not as serious as incorrect acceptance. When auditors first begin to think a balance may contain a material misstatement, they try to determine why this occurred. To estimate the amount, more evidence will be sought. The data will be reviewed for a source of systematic error and the amounts of errors will be analyzed carefully. Client personnel may do a complete analysis to determine a more accurate account balance.

If the initial decision was, in fact, an incorrect rejection, this other work allows the auditors to decide if the recorded amount is really misstated or the sample was not representative. Hence, steps will be taken to determine the amount of error and there is a chance for the error to be reversed. Incorrect rejection does affect the efficiency of an audit by causing unnecessary work.

Materiality and Tolerable Misstatement

Determining a threshold for the materiality of misstatements in financial statements is a tough problem under any circumstances. Audit sampling for substantive audits of particular account balances adds another wrinkle. Auditors must also decide on an amount of material misstatement—a judgment of the amount of monetary misstatement that may exist in an account balance or class of transactions. Audit risk (AR), therefore, is the risk that all the audit work on an account balance will not reveal material misstatement. This concept is further discussed in the online Appendix 10B.

SAMPLING STEPS FOR ACCOUNT BALANCE AUDIT

. . . .

Sampling for the audit of account balances is similar to the steps of test of controls audit sampling. An example related to auditing receivables illustrates these steps; test of controls sampling was illustrated with the audit of a control procedures for sales invoices. This work can produce independent evidence of sales overstatement resulting from a breakdown of the control or other causes. The seven-step framework helps auditors plan, perform, and evaluate account balance detail audit work. It also helps auditors accomplish an eighth step—careful documentation of the work—by showing each of the seven areas to be described in the working papers. The first seven steps are as follows:

1. Specify the audit objectives.
2. Define the population.
3. Choose an audit sampling method.
4. Determine the sample size.
5. Select the sample.
6. Perform the substantive-purpose procedures.
7. Evaluate the evidence.

Plan the Procedures

LEARNING OBJECTIVE
6a Specify objectives and a population of data.

The three planning steps are the problem-recognition phase of the sampling method. When a client presents the financial statements, they might make the following assertions: the trade accounts receivable exist (existence) and are *bona fide* obligations owed to the company (ownership); all the accounts receivable are recorded (completeness); they are stated at net realizable value (valuation); and they are properly classified as current assets, presented, and disclosed in conformity with GAAP (presentation). Each assertion represents a hypothesis (problem) to be tested.

1. Specify the Audit Objectives

When sampling to confirm accounts receivables, the specific objective is to decide whether the client's assertions about existence, rights (ownership), and valuation are materially accurate. This auditing is **hypothesis testing**—the auditors hypothesize that the book value is materially accurate about existence, ownership, and valuation. The evidence will enable them to accept or reject the hypothesis. The audit objective is to determine the monetary misstatement by comparing the recorded balances to the balances found through the evidence.

2. Define the Population

CAS 530 says that auditors must ensure that the population is appropriate for the specific objectives of the audit procedure, and that it is complete. A population of the recorded accounts receivable balances suits the objective of obtaining evidence about existence, ownership, and valuation. It also suits the related objective of obtaining evidence about sales overstatement. In the case of accounts receivable, each customer's account balance is a population unit. If obtaining evidence about completeness and sales understatement were the objectives, the recorded accounts receivable would be the wrong population.

Ordinarily, the sampling unit is the same as the population unit. Sometimes, however, it is easier to define the sampling unit as a smaller part of a population unit. For example, an auditor may want to audit samples of individual invoices for customers instead of working with each customer's balance.

Since a sample will be drawn from a physical representation of the population (e.g., a printed trial balance or computer file of customers' accounts), the auditors must determine whether it is complete. Re-adding the trial balance and reconciling it to the control account total does this.

Auditing standards (CAS 530) require auditors to use their judgment in deciding if any population units should be removed from the population and audited separately (not sampled) because sampling risk (risk of incorrect acceptance or incorrect rejection) with respect to them is not justified. Suppose, for example, the accounts receivable amounted to $400,000, but six of the customers had balances of $10,000 or more, for a sum of $100,000. The next-largest account balance is less than $10,000. If materiality is $10,000, the six accounts are considered **individually significant items** because each exceeds the material misstatement amount, and they should be removed from the population and audited completely.

In the jargon of audit sampling related to account balances, subdividing the population is known as **stratification**. The total population is subdivided by account balance size. For example, a small number of accounts totalling $75,000 may be the first (large balance) of, say, four strata. The remaining three strata might each contain a total of approximately $75,000 in recorded balances, but each is made up of a successively larger number of customer accounts with successively smaller account balances. Stratification can be used to increase audit efficiency (smaller total sample size). A stratification example appears in the next box.

STRATIFICATION EXAMPLE—SELECTING SAMPLE SIZES

The stratification below subdivides the population into a first stratum of six individually significant accounts and four other strata, each with approximately one-fourth ($75,000) of the remaining dollar balance. This is a typical situation where there is a greater number of accounts of smaller value.

The example allocates 90 items to the last four strata. This is referred to as *stratified sampling*. When each stratum gets one-fourth of the sample size, the sample is skewed toward the higher-value accounts: the second stratum has 23 out of 80 sample items, and the fifth stratum has 23 out of 910 items.

Stratum	Book Value	Number	Amount	Sample
1	Over $10,000	6	$100,000	6
2	$625–$9,999	80	75,068	23
3	$344–$624	168	75,008	22
4	$165–$343	342	75,412	22
5	$1–$164	910	74,512	23
		1,506	$400,000	96

This stratification deals with a normal situation in which the variability of the account balances and errors in them tend to be larger in the high-value accounts than in the low-value accounts. As a consequence, the sample includes a larger proportion of the high-value accounts (23/80) and a smaller proportion of the low-value accounts (23/910). In addition to size or variability, stratification can be based on other qualitative characteristics the auditor considers important, such as individual, location, date, product, and so forth.

3. Choose an Audit Sampling Method

An auditor must decide whether to use statistical or nonstatistical sampling methods. If statistical sampling is chosen, another choice needs to be made. In statistical sampling, classical variables sampling methods utilizing normal distribution theory are available. However, DUS, which uses attribute sampling theory, is used more widely in practice. Some of the technical characteristics of the statistical methods are explained more fully in the online Appendix 10B.

The calculation examples shown later in this chapter use the DUS method. This calculation is relatively simple and illustrates the important points.

Perform the Procedures

LEARNING OBJECTIVE
6b Determine sample size and select sample units.

The next three steps represent the evidence-collection phase of the sampling method. Figuring sample size correctly for account balance auditing is an important aspect of this and requires consideration of several influences. Figuring a sample size in advance helps guard against underauditing (not obtaining enough evidence) and overauditing (obtaining more evidence than needed). It also can control the cost of the audit. An arbitrary sample size could be used for the accounts receivable confirmation procedures, but if it turned out to be too small, processing more confirmations might be impossible before the audit report deadline. Alternative procedures could become costly and time-consuming. A predetermined sample size is not as important in other situations where the auditors can increase the sample simply by choosing more items from those available in the client's office.

4. Determine the Sample Size

Whether using statistical or nonstatistical sampling methods, auditors first need to establish decision criteria for the risk of incorrect acceptance (beta risk for substantive testing), the risk of incorrect rejection (alpha risk for substantive testing), and material misstatement. Also, auditors may want to estimate the expected dollar amount of misstatement. These decision criteria should be determined before any evidence is obtained from a sample.

Risk of Incorrect Acceptance (RIA)   The audit risk model can be your guide in assessing this risk. A suitable RIA depends on the assessments of inherent risk, control risk, and analytical procedures risk. The RIA varies inversely with the combined product of the other risks. The larger the combined product of the other risks, the smaller will be the allowable RIA.

Suppose, for example, two different auditors, both believing 0.05 is an acceptable level of audit risk (AR), independently assess the client's control risk and their own analytical procedures and arrive at the following conclusions.

Auditor A believes the inherent risk is high (IR = 1.0), the control risk is moderate (CR = 0.50), and analytical procedures will not be performed (APR = 1.0). Audit procedures need to be planned so that the risk of incorrect acceptance will be about 10 percent.

$$RIA = AR/(IR \times CR \times APR) = 0.05/(1.0 \times 0.50 \times 1.0) = 0.10$$

Auditor B believes the inherent risk is high (IR = 1.0), the control risk is very low (CR = 0.20), and analytical procedures will not be performed (APR = 1.0). Audit procedures need to be planned so that the risk of incorrect acceptance will be about 25 percent.

$$RIA = AR/(IR \times CR \times APR) = 0.05/(1.0 \times 0.20 \times 1.0) = 0.25$$

Use the model with caution. You can learn from these examples that auditor A's account balance sampling work must provide less risk than auditor B's. Since sample size varies inversely with the risk of incorrect acceptance, auditor A's sample will be larger. In fact, when the control risk is lower, as B's is, the acceptable RIA is higher. Thus, auditor B's sample of customers' accounts receivable can be smaller than auditor A's sample.

Risk of Incorrect Rejection   Like the risk of incorrect acceptance, the risk of incorrect rejection exists both in statistical and nonstatistical sampling. It can be controlled, usually by auditing a larger sample, and sample size varies inversely with the risk of incorrect rejection. DUS deals with incorrect rejection (alpha risk) by increasing sample size above the minimum associated with using K = 0 in sample planning. The simplified approach to sample planning we use here sets K = 0 so that the sample size is the smallest possible for the stated confidence level and materiality.

Material Misstatement   The material misstatement—usually the same as the overall materiality of misstatements—also must be considered in both nonstatistical and statistical sampling. In statistical sampling, material misstatement must be expressed as a dollar amount or as a proportion of the total recorded amount. The sample size varies inversely with the amount of misstatement considered material. The greater the materiality, the smaller the sample size needed.

Expected Dollar Misstatement   Auditors estimate an **expected dollar misstatement** amount based on last year's audit findings or on other knowledge of the accounting system. Expectations of dollar misstatement have the effect of increasing the sample size. The more dollar misstatement expected, the larger the sample size should be. So, sample size varies directly with the amount of expected dollar misstatement.

Variability Within the Population   Auditors using nonstatistical sampling must take into account the degree of dispersion, or typical skewness, of some accounting populations. **Skewness** is the concentration of a large proportion of the dollar amount in only a small number of the population items. For example, $100,000 (25 percent) of the total accounts receivable is in six customers' accounts, while the remaining $300,000 is in 1,500 customers' accounts.

As a general rule, auditors should be careful about populations whose unit values range widely, say from $1 to $10,000. In this case, for your population to be representative, you would need to take a larger sample than if the range were only from $1 to $500. Sample size should vary directly with the range of population unit values. Populations with high variability should be stratified, as shown in the stratification example.

When classical statistical sampling methods are used, there must be an estimate of the population **standard deviation**, which is a measure of the population variability. When using DUS, this estimate needn't be made separately as the unit of selection is each recorded dollar rather than the account balance. Thus there is no variability in the population of recorded dollars, as each dollar has the same value. (See the online Appendix 10B for more details.)

DUS sample sizes can be calculated as they are for tests of controls. The same sample planning formula can be applied as long as all monetary amounts are converted to a rate or percentage. Thus, for example, if you have an accounts receivable population with a balance of $10,000,000, you determine materiality to be $300,000, and you wish to plan a sample size for confirming receivables with 95 percent confidence level, then first convert materiality as a rate by calculating its proportion of the recorded value: $P = 300,000/10,000,000 = 0.03$. Now you can apply the formula as before to calculate the sample size: $n = R/P = 3.0/0.03 = 100$.

As you can see, the calculation of sample sizes under DUS are very similar for both tests of controls and tests of balances. The calculations for both are summarized in Exhibit 10–8.

You can now prove to yourself the efficiency effects of relying on internal controls using the audit risk model. In the above receivables example, assume you desired 95 percent confidence because you planned audit risk at 0.05, and you assessed inherent and control risk at the maximum of 1.0. Hence, you had to get all your assurance from the substantive test using a detective risk (DR) of 0.05. The DR is the same as beta risk or the risk of incorrect acceptance. Now assume that you assessed control risk below maximum at 0.50 (instead of at maximum at 1.0); then, using the risk model, you can prove to yourself that DR is revised to 0.10; that is, you accept more risk (get less assurance) from your substantive testing. This is reflected by the reduced sample size: $n = R/P = 2.31/0.03 = 77$ (always round up to ensure sample is large enough). You have thus reduced your substantive testing by 23 ($100 - 77$) as a result of your increased reliance on internal controls. This is a simple example, but it illustrates the basic principle of internal control reliance using the audit risk model.

These influences are summarized in Exhibit 10–9.

EXHIBIT 10-8

Sufficiency of Audit Evidence:
Summary of Simplified Calculations of Sample Size

Key Concepts	Tests of Controls	Substantive Tests of Balance
Basic Formula	$R = nP$	$R = nP$
Assessment of materiality or tolerable error rate	P = tolerable error rate	P = materiality as a proportion of the recorded balance
Assessment of beta risk = 1 confidence level = $1 - CL$	Beta risk is based on CR from Audit risk model	Beta risk is RIA of audit risk model
R value	From table use $K = 0$ and desired confidence level	From table use $K = 0$ and desired confidence level
Extent of testing = sample size	$n = \frac{clR_k}{P}$	$n = \frac{clR_k}{P}$

CR = control risk   n = sample size   RIA = risk of incorrect acceptance

EXHIBIT 10-9   SAMPLE SIZE RELATIONSHIPS: AUDIT OF ACCOUNT BALANCES USING DUS

| | Predetermined Sample Size Will Be | | |
Sample Size Influence	High Rate or Large Amount	Low Rate or Small Amount	Sample Size Relation
1. Risk of incorrect acceptance	Smaller	Larger	Inverse
2. Risk of incorrect rejection*	Smaller	Larger	Inverse
3. Tolerable misstatement	Smaller	Larger	Inverse
4. Expected misstatement*	Larger	Smaller	Direct

*These effects are discussed in the online Appendix 10B. They are ignored under the simplified approach used here, and many practitioners treat these effects as insignificant.

ACCOUNT BALANCE AUDITING

1. Confirm a sample of the receivables, investigate exceptions, and follow up non-respondents by vouching sales charges and cash receipts to supporting documents (evidence of existence, rights, and valuation).

2. Obtain an aged trial balance of the receivables. Audit the aging accuracy on a sample basis. Calculate and analyze the age status of the accounts and the allowance for uncollectible accounts in light of current economic conditions and the company's collection experience (evidence of valuation).

3. Discuss past-due accounts with the credit manager. Obtain credit reports and financial statements for independent analysis of large overdue accounts (evidence of valuation).

4. Vouch receivables balances to cash received after the cutoff date (evidence of existence, rights, and valuation).

5. Distinguish names of trade customers from others (officers, directors, employees, affiliates) and determine that the two classifications are reported separately (evidence of presentation and disclosure).

6. Read loan agreements and note any pledge of receivables, sales with recourse, or other restrictions or contingencies related to the receivables (evidence of presentation and disclosure).

7. Read sales contracts for evidence of customers' rights of return or price allowance terms (evidence of presentation and disclosure).

8. Obtain written representations from the client concerning pledges for collateral, related party receivables, collectability, and other matters relating to accounts receivable (detail assertions in writing).

In this program, each item is a specific application of one of the seven general procedures. However, no procedure deals explicitly with the completeness assertion. Completeness evidence can be obtained with the dual-purpose nature of the completeness procedures done in the test of controls procedures 2 and 4. The list also excludes analytical procedures based on interrelationships with budget, forecast, industry, or historical data. More specific facts are needed for analytical procedures work.

5. Select the Sample

As was the case with test of controls audit samples, account balance samples must be representative. The same selection methods as discussed for tests of controls can be used for DUS in substantive testing. Unrestricted random selection and systematic selection will obtain random samples for statistical applications. The online Appendix 10B outlines unique features of DUS selection in more detail. Haphazard and block selection methods have the same drawbacks as they have in test of controls audit samples.

6. Perform the Substantive-Purpose Procedures

The basic assertions in a presentation of accounts receivable are that they exist, they are complete (no receivables are unrecorded), the company has the right to collect the money, they are valued properly at net realizable value, and they are presented and disclosed properly in conformity with GAAP. A substantive-purpose audit program consists of account balance–related procedures designed to produce evidence about these assertions. The procedures listed in the preceding box will obtain the evidence related to each assertion (shown in parentheses).

The confirmation procedures should be performed for all the sampling units, and other procedures performed as necessary for evidence relating to existence, ownership, and valuation. It is important to audit all the sample units, even the hard ones. Auditing just those customers whose balances are easy might bias the sample. Sometimes, however, you will be unable to audit a sample unit; there may be no response to the confirmation requests, sales invoices supporting the balance can't be found, and no payment was received after the confirmation date. Auditing standards contain the following guidance in this situation:

- If your evaluation conclusion isn't affected by the misstated balance, then you can let it go. If your evaluation conclusion is to accept the book value, the account should not be big enough to change that. If your evaluation conclusion is already to reject the book value, this account misstatement just reinforces the decision.

- If considering the entire balance to be misstated would change an acceptance decision to a rejection decision, you may need to expand the sample, perform the procedures on them (other than confirmation), and re-evaluate the results.

- If control risk related to the balance was assessed to be low, you should consider whether this finding contradicts the low control risk assessment.

REVIEW CHECKPOINTS

29 Write the expanded risk model. What risk is implied for "test of detail risk" when IR = 1.0, CR = 0.40, APR = 0.60, AR = 0.048, tolerable misstatement = $10,000, and the estimated standard deviation in the population = $25?

30 Explain why control risk is inversely related to the risk of incorrect acceptance.

31 Why does the alpha risk affect audit efficiency and the beta risk affect audit effectiveness?

32 When auditing account balances, why is an incorrect acceptance decision considered more serious than an incorrect rejection decision?

33 What should be the relationship between tolerable misstatement in the audit of an account balance and the amount of monetary misstatement considered material to the overall financial statements?

34 What general set of audit objectives can you use as a frame of reference for specific objectives for the audit of an account balance?

35 What audit purpose is served by stratifying an account balance population and by selecting some units from the population for 100 percent audit verification?

The Evidence

LEARNING OBJECTIVE

6c Evaluate monetary error evidence from a balance audit sample.

The final step represents the evidence evaluation and decision-making phase of the sampling method. Your decisions about existence, ownership, and valuation need to be justifiable by sufficient, competent quantitative and qualitative evidence. You should be concerned first with the quantitative evaluation of the evidence. Qualitative follow-up is also important and is discussed later.

7. Evaluate the Evidence

Quantitative evaluation of substantive tests of balances using DUS is the same as that for tests of controls. For example, reject if achieved P is greater than or equal to materiality; otherwise accept the population total recorded amount. The complications arise from possible variability of the misstatements when calculating achieved P. The online Appendix 10B outlines how to deal with these complications. Exhibit 10–10 summarizes these statistical evaluations.

Auditing standards for this are not written with a particular approach, such as DUS, in mind. Instead, they deal with general features of quantitative evaluation already captured by the particular approaches of formulas, and we review these general considerations here. The reconciliation to particular calculations with DUS is given in the online Appendix 10B. These are the basic steps in quantitative evaluation:

- Figure the total amount of actual monetary error, the **known misstatement**, found in the sample.

- Project the known misstatement to the population. The projected amount is the **likely misstatement**.

- Compare the likely misstatement (also called the **projected misstatement**) to the material misstatement for the account and consider that (1) the risk of incorrect acceptance—that likely misstatement is calculated to be less than material misstatement even though the actual misstatement in the population is greater; or (2) the risk of incorrect rejection—that likely misstatement is calculated to be greater than material misstatement, even though the actual misstatement in the population is smaller.

Amount of Known Misstatement   Hypothetical audit evidence from the sample for the previous stratification example is shown in the box on page 398. In this example, total accounts receivable is $400,000, while $100,000 of the total is in six large balances, which are to be audited separately. The remainder is in 1,500 customer accounts whose balances range from $1 to $9,999. Suppose the audit team selected 90 of these accounts and applied the confirmation or vouching procedures to each of them and the evidence showed $136 of net overstatement of the recorded amounts. This amount is the known misstatement for this sample of 90 customer accounts.

EXHIBIT 10-10

Evaluating Sample Results (n is known and R is known based on detected errors K and confidence level planned)

Key Concepts	Tests of Control	Substantive Tests of Balance
Basic formula	$R = nP$	$R = nP$
Solve for achieved P	$P = \dfrac{R}{n}$	$P = \dfrac{R}{n}$
Basic decision rule	If achieved P≥ tolerable error rate, then reject; otherwise, accept reliance on control.	If achieved P≥ materiality, then reject; otherwise, accept the recorded total for the population.
Consequence of decision		
If accept	Can rely on controls to extent planned at stated confidence level.	Can accept clients recorded amount at stated confidence level.
If reject	Need to rely on controls less than expected.	Need to sample more or insist on an adjustment (adjust to most likely value as indicated by sample mean extrapolated to the population).

Project the Known Misstatement to the Population   To make a decision about the population, the known misstatement in the sample is projected to the population. The sample must be representative, because, if it is not, a projection can produce a misleading number. As an extreme example, suppose one of the six large accounts, which were all audited, contained a $600 disputed amount. Investigation showed the customer was right and management agreed, so the $600 is the amount of known misstatement. If an auditor takes this group of six accounts as being representative of the population, projecting the $100 average misstatement ($600/6) to 1,506 accounts ($100 × 1,506) would project a total misstatement of $150,600, compared with the recorded accounts receivable total of $400,000. This projection is neither reasonable nor appropriate. Nothing is wrong with the calculation method. The nonrepresentative "sample" is the culprit in this absurd result.

STRATIFICATION EXAMPLE—HYPOTHETICAL SAMPLE DATA

Assume the following differences were detected in the 90 audited items

Sample item	Stratum	Audited amount	Recorded amount	Difference** (Recorded – Audited)
1	2	$691	$691	$0
*		*	*	*
*		*	*	*
*		*	*	*
6	2	372	508	136
*		*	*	*
*		*	*	*
*		*	*	*
23	2	136	141	5
*		*	*	*
*		*	*	*
*		*	*	*
50	4	62	62	0
*		*	*	*
*		*	*	*
*		*	*	*
90	5	135	130	–5
Totals		$18,884	$19,020	$136
Averages:				
Audited amount		$209.82		
Recorded amount			$211.33	
Difference				$1.51

**A positive difference is an account overstatement, and a negative difference is an account understatement.

A projection based on a sample applies only to the population the sample was drawn from. Consider the sample of 90 accounts from the population of 1,500. The average difference is $1.51 (overstatement of the recorded amount), so the projected likely misstatement (PLM) is $2,267 (overstatement), provided the sample is representative. This projection method is called the average difference method, expressed in equation form as follows:

PLM (under the average difference method) =
[(Dollar amount of misstatement in the sample)/(Number of sampling units)] ×
(Number of population units)

In this example, if the population had not been stratified the calculation would be

PLM (under the average difference method) = ($136/90) × 1,500 = $2,267 (overstatement)

When the population is stratified, account sizes within each stratum are more homogeneous than in the population as a whole, and the known misstatement in each can be projected. A single projection, shown in the stratification calculation of the following box, results in a much smaller PLM.

You cannot guarantee representativeness, but you can try to attain it by selecting a random sample and by carefully subdividing (stratifying) the population according to an important characteristic, such as the size of individual customers' balances. You can also inspect the sample to see whether it shows the characteristics of the population. In the example, for instance, the average recorded amount of the population is $200 ($300,000 divided by 1,500); the average in the illustrative unstratified sample is $211.33 (a little high). You also can look to see whether the sample contains a range of recorded amounts similar to that of the population. With statistics, you can calculate the standard deviation of the sample recorded amounts and compare it with the standard deviation of the population.

STRATIFICATION EXAMPLE

Calculation of Projected Likely Misstatement by Average Difference Method

Stratification of a population is said to be more efficient because you can usually calculate a smaller projected likely misstatement with the same sample size than would have been used in an unstratified sample (as illustrated in this chapter), or you can usually calculate the same projected likely misstatement with a smaller stratified sample. The example below illustrates a typical situation of finding larger misstatements in the larger accounts, resulting in a projected likely misstatement smaller than the $2,267 illustrated in the chapter for an unstratified sample. The calculation of projected likely misstatements (PLM), using the difference method, is applied separately to each stratum. Then, the amounts are added to get the whole sample result.

Stratum	Number	Amount	Sample	Misstatement*	PLM
1	80	75,068	23	$141	$490
2	168	75,008	22	0	0
3	342	75,412	22	0	0
4	910	74,512	23	−5	−198
	1,506	$300,000	96	$136	$292

*A positive misstatement indicates overstatement of the book value, and a negative misstatement indicates understatement.

The DUS projection method automatically takes into account the stratification of the population. You can project using the dollar-unit sampling method, expressed in equation form as follows:

PLM (dollar-unit method) = (Sum of the proportionate
amount of misstatements or taintings of all dollar units in error in the sample) ×
(Recorded amount in the population)

Taintings are covered in more detail in the online Appendix 10B. In the example here,

PLM (dollar-unit method) =
$300,000 × (1/90) × [(136/508) + (5/141) − (5/130)] = $883 (overstatement)

The difference between the two projected likely misstatements illustrates the importance of having representative sampling. Auditors also need to be very careful about the adequacy of the sample size. You can see that small samples producing large or small dollar differences can distort both the average difference and the average dollar-unit ratio, thus distorting the projected likely misstatement. One way to exercise care is to take the sampling risks into account.

Consider Sampling Risks There are risks of making wrong decisions (incorrect acceptance or incorrect rejection) in both nonstatistical and statistical sampling. The smaller the sample, the greater both risks are. Common sense tells you that the less you know about a population because of a small sample, the more risk you run of making a wrong decision.

The problem is the risk that there could be a lower projected likely misstatement ($883 overstatement for the sample of 90 accounts in the example using the DUS method) even though the actual total misstatement in the population is greater than the material misstatement ($10,000 in the example). Auditing guidance suggests you can use your experience and professional judgment to consider the risk. If the projected likely misstatement is considerably less than tolerable misstatement, chances are good that the total actual misstatement in the population will be less than tolerable misstatement. However, when projected likely misstatement is close to tolerable misstatement (say, $9,000, compared with $10,000), the risk of incorrect acceptance may exceed the acceptable risk (RIA) that an auditor initially established as a decision criterion (see AuG-41, para. 42).

The risk of incorrect rejection is a similar situation. Suppose the sample results had produced a projected likely misstatement of $15,000 overstatement. What is the risk of calculating this PLM when the actual misstatement in the population is $10,000 or less? Again, the judgment depends on the size of the sample and the kinds and distribution of misstatements discovered.

Auditors take the rejection decision seriously and conduct enough additional investigation to determine the amount and adjustment required—extra work that mitigates the risk of incorrect rejection. In the example, if the sample of 90 customers' accounts had shown total misstatement of $900 (yielding the $15,000 projected misstatement using the average difference method), most auditors would consider the evidence insufficient to propose a significant adjustment. (However, correction of the $900 should not by itself be a sufficient action to satisfy the auditors.)

When using nonstatistical sampling, auditors use their experience and expertise to take risks into account. Statistical samplers can add statistical calculations to these considerations of sampling risk.

Qualitative Evaluation The numbers are not enough. Auditors are required to follow up each monetary difference to determine whether it arose from (a) misunderstanding of accounting principles, (b) simple mistakes or carelessness, (c) an intentional irregularity, or (d) management override of an internal control procedure. Auditors also need to relate the differences to their effect on other amounts in the financial statements. For example, overstatements in accounts receivable may indicate overstatement of sales revenue.

Likewise, you should not overlook the information that can be obtained in account balance auditing about the performance of internal control procedures—the dual-purpose characteristic of auditing procedures. Deviations (or absence of deviations) discovered when performing substantive procedures can help confirm or contradict an auditor's previous conclusion about control risk. If many more monetary differences than expected arise, the control risk conclusion may need to be revised and more account balance auditing work done.

Knowledge of the source, nature, and amount of monetary differences is very important in explaining the situation to management and directing additional work to areas where adjustments are needed. The audit work is not complete until the qualitative evaluation and follow-up is done.

Evaluate the Amount of Misstatement   The guideline AuG-41 requires the aggregation of known misstatement (identified misstatement, in the guideline) and projected likely misstatement (likely aggregate misstatement, in the guideline). The aggregation is the sum of (a) known misstatement in the population units identified for 100 percent audit (in the example, the six accounts totalling $100,000, with $600 overstatement discovered), and (b) the projected likely misstatement for the population sampled (in the example, the $883 overstatement projected using the DUS method). The theory underlying (b) is that the projected likely misstatement is the best single estimate of the amount that would be determined if all the accounts in the sampled population had been audited. You can see the importance of sample representativeness in this regard. This aggregation ($883 overstatement in the example) should be judged in combination with other misstatements found in the audit of other account balances to determine whether the financial statements taken as a whole need to be adjusted and, if so, in what amount.

The evaluation of amounts is not over yet, however. It cannot be said that the projected likely misstatement is the exact amount that would be found if all the units in the population were audited. The problem arises from **sampling error**—the amount by which a projected likely misstatement amount could differ from an actual (unknown) total as a result of the sample's not being exactly representative. Of course, auditors are mostly concerned with the possibility that the actual total misstatement might be considerably more than the projected likely misstatement.

This sampling phenomenon gives rise to the concept of **possible misstatement or maximum possible misstatement** (the third kind, in addition to known and likely misstatement), which is interpreted in AuG-41 as the further misstatement remaining undetected in the units not selected in the sample. Nonstatistical auditors use their experience and professional judgment in considering additional possible misstatement. Statistical auditors, however, use statistical calculations to measure possible misstatement.

In Appendix 10B on the text Online Learning Centre, the basic example shows how to calculate a possible misstatement. For the illustration here, the possible misstatement is $6,331—treat this as a given for now. Thus, the aggregation of known, projected, and possible misstatement is $600 + $884 + $6,331 = $7,814. This total suggests that the misstatement in the account does not exceed the amount considered material ($10,000). If the possible misstatement were higher, say $9,000, the total would be $10,483, and the evidence would suggest that the misstatement in the account exceeds $10,000. For a more complete discussion of the evaluation of statistical substantive testing of details results see Appendix 10B.

Timing of Substantive Audit Procedures

Account balances can be audited, at least in part, at an interim date. When this work is done before the company's year-end date, auditors must extend the interim-date audit conclusion to the balance sheet date. **Extending the audit conclusion** involves performing substantive-purpose audit procedures on the transactions in the remaining period and on the year-end balance to produce sufficient competent evidence for a decision about the year-end balance. It is unreasonable to audit a balance (say, accounts receivable) as of September 30, and then, without further work, accept the December 31 balance.

If the company's internal control over transactions that produce the balance under audit is not particularly strong, you should time the substantive detail work at year-end instead of at interim. Likewise, if rapidly changing business conditions predispose managers to misstate the accounts (try to slip one by the auditors), the work should be timed at year-end.

In most cases, careful scanning of transactions and analytical review comparisons should be performed on transactions that occur after the interim date.

As an example of the process, accounts receivable confirmation can be done at an interim date. Later, efforts must be made to ascertain whether controls continued to be reliable. You must scan the transactions of the remaining period, audit any new large balances and update work on collectability, especially with analysis of cash received after the year-end.

Audit work is performed at interim for two reasons: (1) to spread the accounting firms' workload so that not all the work on clients is crammed into December and January and (2) to make the work efficient and enable companies to report audited financial results soon after the year-end. Some well-organized companies with well-planned audits report their audited figures as early as five or six days after their fiscal year-ends.

BALANCE AUDIT SAMPLING FAILURE

The company owned surgical instruments that it lent and leased to customers. The auditors decided to audit the existence of the assets by confirming them with the customers who were supposed to be holding and using them. From the population of 880 instruments, the auditors selected eight for confirmation, using a sampling method that purported to produce a representative selection.

Two confirmations were never returned, and the auditors did not follow up on them. One returned confirmation indicated that the customer did not have the instrument in question; the auditors were never able to find it. Nevertheless, the auditors concluded that the $3.5 million recorded amount of the surgical instrument assets was materially accurate.

Judges who heard complaints on the quality of the audit work concluded that it was not performed in accordance with generally accepted auditing standards (GAAS) because the auditors did not gather sufficient evidence concerning the existence and valuation of the surgical instruments. GAAS requires auditors to project the sample findings to the population. The auditors did not do so. They never calculated (nonstatistical) the fact that $1,368,750 of the asset amount could not be confirmed or found to exist. The sample of eight was woefully inadequate, both in sample size and in the proportionately large number of exceptions reported. There was a wholly insufficient statistical basis for concluding that the account was fairly stated under generally accepted accounting principles.

Source: U.S. Securities and Exchange Commission, Administrative Proceeding File No. 3–6579 (Initial Decision, June 1990).

REVIEW
CHECKPOINTS

36   What kind of evidence evaluation consideration should an auditor give to the dollar amount of a population unit that cannot be audited?

37   What are the three basic steps in quantitative evaluation of monetary amount evidence when auditing an account balance?

38   The projected likely misstatement may be calculated, yet further misstatement may remain undetected in the population. How can auditors take the further misstatement under consideration when completing the quantitative evaluation of monetary evidence? How is this done by formula?

39   What additional considerations are in order when auditors plan to audit account balances at an interim date several weeks or months before the client's fiscal year-end date?

APPLICATION CASE AND ANALYSIS
DUS with Critical Thinking about Risk-Based Auditing

The DUS concepts introduced in this chapter are good illustrations of the application of critical thinking, although the issues of it may be hidden in the assumptions underlying the mechanics of applying DUS. Can you identify the critical thinking (CT) steps, as outlined in Exhibit 4–1, in the DUS decision making as described in this chapter?

Analysis

Through DUS, the auditor arrives at a value for an accounting population. This is done by a representative sampling, without 100 percent examination or selection for specific items of interest (CAS 530).

Step 1 of CT (learn the views of others): In the sampling context, this step is represented by obtaining from management the total amount recorded for the population or some other claim about a population (e.g., that proper internal controls have been applied to the transactions of the reporting period).

The auditor's views of the population for sampling purposes are relevant here. With DUS, the population is viewed as dollar units, with the total dollar amount recorded representing a population of individual dollars. The more traditional view, statistical sampling using normal distribution-based tests, is of a population consisting of individual accounts or physical units of varying values (e.g., a population of individual accounts receivable or inventory items). These differences in viewpoints have consequences for the two theories themselves.

The differing theories result in planning differences, most notably in whether or not materiality allocation is included in audit planning. Under DUS no allocation is needed. The DUS formula examples below show this. For other statistical approaches, the model requirements, not user needs, make materiality allocation necessary. DUS accommodates user needs by using lower performance materialities for any specific accounts as needed. Also, the results of individual tests can be combined, as shown below, and the results compared with materiality for financial statements as a whole. In general, the process of combining the results of multiple tests is simpler under DUS.

Step 2 (identify the claims at issue): Management claims (asserts) that the recorded amount is materially correct, and the main claim at issue is whether this is true or if, in fact, the population amount is materially in error. The auditor must verify the assertion with the help of the statistical test.

Step 3 (reasons for the competing claims). Management will refer to its system of internal controls, corporate governance, and past track record. The auditor must be skeptical and consider the alternative claim that there is a material misstatement in the recorded amount, and show that the risk of this claim is at an appropriately low level (i.e., at an acceptable level).

Step 4 (evaluate the arguments): An argument, essentially, gives good reasons for a claim or conclusion. In statistical decision making, logically structured reasoning (see Appendix 4A in OLC for more details) follows a pattern that is consistent with decision making throughout auditing and accounting.

The pattern of logical argumentation is as follows. First, identify assumptions (including theories), models, concepts, and principles that guide the overall reasoning process. DUS's distinctiveness is in viewing the population of interest as a population of dollar units and then applying attribute sampling theory to the dollar-unit population. With theories, many assumptions need to be made; some are more controversial than others and critical thinking focuses on the more controversial ones, aiming to demonstrate their reasonableness. Often the issues are a matter of firm policy and much of the justification is embedded in firm practice manuals and policies.

Second, gather the evidence in conformity with the theory and consistent with the goal of the audit procedure. This includes proper specification of the population to be evaluated, as discussed in the chapter. For example, in representative sampling, each unit of the population must have equal chance of being selected. This is absolutely essential for objectively controlling sampling risk, which is the primary advantage of statistical audit techniques.

Third, reach a conclusion about the population that is consistent with the theory. For DUS, the conclusion is reached using the following decision rule:

Decision Rule (1):

> If achieved P > materiality or tolerable deviation rate, then reject the recorded amount for the population; otherwise accept it.

This simple decision rule is effectively an evaluation of management's claim that there is no material error in the population or that no intolerable deviation rates exist in it.

Step 5 (reach a conclusion): The decision rule above indicates the quantitative result. The auditor must also consider qualitative aspects of the sample information, such as nature and cause of errors, before coming to a decision (CAS 530 and AuG-41). The decision rule has already incorporated risk and materiality considerations in the decision-making process.

Further elaboration of the critical thinking aspects of adopting DUS

Once a formal theory such as DUS has been accepted to assist in auditor decision making, it can be used to illustrate some basic concepts of auditing. For example, using our formulas and R value tables we can easily illustrate the law of diminishing returns on assurance as auditors gather additional sampling

LEARNING OBJECTIVE

7 Apply and integrate the chapter topics to analyze a practical auditing situation/case/scenario.

evidence. For example, assuming materiality has a value of .01 (1%), then the sample sizes ($n = R/P$) for confidence levels of 80%, 95%, and 99% respectively (equivalent beta risks of 20%, 5%, and 1%) are as follows: 161, 300, and 451. Confidence levels translate roughly to assurance levels obtained from these samples. Thus auditors using a materiality of 1% get assurance of 80% for sample size of 161, 95% assurance for sample size of 300, and 99% assurance for sample size of 451. These assurance levels relate to specific assertions, such as existence, depending on the audit purpose of the test. Testing is a generic term used for all types of sampling, whether representative or not.

The above calculations indicate the first 80% of assurance is achieved with a sample size of 161. To get an additional 15% assurance (to 95%), the necessary sample size almost doubles. In other words, the auditor gets less assurance for each additional item sampled. Note that to get an additional 4% assurance beyond 95%, the original sample size must almost triple. The final 1% assurance comes through testing the entire population. If, for instance, the population consisted of 10,000 items of varying amounts such as inventory items (not unusual for a medium-sized auditee), the final 1% assurance eliminating all uncertainties regarding existence involves testing an additional 9,549 (10,000 − 451) items! This explains why auditors use sampling and illustrates the diminishing law of assurance—it is rarely economical to eliminate the last bit of uncertainty in order to get 100% assurance. Since assurance equals 1 − risk, this also explains why auditors don't wish to fully eliminate risk (nor are clients willing to pay for it) but will settle for some acceptable level of it.

Illustration showing why there is no need to allocate materiality with DUS

With our formula, we can also show why there is no need to allocate materiality with DUS. For example, assume accounts receivable has a reported balance of $20 million, inventory has a balance of $10 million, and overall materiality is $1 million. If we wanted 95% confidence level to verify existence of accounts receivable via confirmation procedures, the sample size would be $n = R/P = 3/(1/20) = 60$. If we wanted 95% confidence level to verify existence of inventory via inventory counts, the sample size would be $n = R/P = 3/(1/10) = 30$. Note that the sum of these two sample sizes is the same as it would be if we treated inventory and receivables as one dollar-unit population, in which case the sample size for the combined population (at 95% confidence) would be $n = R/P = 3/(1/30) = 90$. Thus, by individually testing the populations associated with receivables and inventory using the same overall materiality of $1 million, the auditor can get the same 95% confidence for the combined population as for the separate populations. All the auditor needs to do is add up the errors from the two samples and evaluate as though one sample of a dollar-unit population of $90 million were tested. In this way, the auditor can also get 95% confidence on the overall conclusion for the combined population. The crucial point is that the same materiality is used for the overall evaluation as for the individual inventory and receivables valuations. There is no need to use different materialities for the components that are smaller than the overall materiality of $1 million with DUS. However, this is not the case for normal distribution-based tests, when materialities smaller than those overall would be required to get the same confidence level for the combined population. DUS can use smaller materialities for specific populations to meet specific user needs, but it does not require this whereas non-DUS models do require allocation. The need for complex materiality allocation rules has been introduced to auditing primarily because of normal distribution-based tests, further demonstrating how the needs of specific sampling models can affect audit reasoning about evidence gathering.

Auditing as a Bayesian reasoning process

Perhaps the most important influence on audit reasoning is the Bayesian view of evidence. This view permeates audit reasoning to the point of being reflected in the audit risk model. For our purposes, the importance of the Bayesian view is that it allows the assurance to correspond to the confidence level and the beta risk to the probability of material misstatement. Under the Bayesian view, it can be shown that decision rule (1) is equivalent to the following:

Decision Rule (2):
  If probability of material misstatement is greater than acceptable risk then reject; otherwise, accept the recorded amount.
The interesting aspect of decision rule (2) is that it can be applied to all types of risk, not just sampling risk. In particular, this decision rule can be applied to the accounting risk concept. Thus decision rule (2) provides a means for introducing consistency in reasoning for financial reporting involving estimates as well as for other auditing issues. Consistency in reasoning is important to good logic, and it is best that audit reasoning processes can be defended as logical. Inconsistencies in reasoning indicate that there is a contradiction, which, in turn, indicates flawed and illogical reasoning. It would be very difficult for an auditor to defend his work if the courts or CPAB can show there is an unresolved contradiction. In fact, philosophers have shown that contradictions can be used to represent lying (e.g., stated belief contradicts actual belief).

Chapter 3 distinguishes accounting deficiencies from audit deficiencies. If auditors are to deal with these deficiencies consistently, then a reasoning process like decision rule (2) is one way of doing so. Note that, since decision rule (2) focuses on risks, it is fully consistent with risk-based auditing and offers a way to deal with accounting risks of financial reporting as well as audit risk. We illustrate this in the application cases of Chapters 16 and 17 where suitability criteria for financial reporting and fraudulent reporting are discussed.

SUMMARY

Audit sampling was explained in this chapter as an organized method to make decisions. Two kinds of decisions were shown: assessment of control risk and the decision about whether financial statement assertions in an account balance are fairly presented. The method is organized by two kinds of audit programs to guide the work on these two decisions: the internal control program and the balance audit program. The audit sampling itself can be attribute sampling for test of controls and balance audit (variables) sampling for auditing the assertions in an account balance.

Audit sampling is a method of organizing the application of audit procedures and a disciplined approach to decision problems. Both types of sampling were explained in basic terms of planning the audit procedures, performing the audit procedures, and evaluating the evidence produced by the audit procedures. The latter process was reinforced with some differences and DUS projections of misstatement amounts. The mechanics were illustrated in the last section.

Risk in audit decisions was explained in the context of nonsampling and sampling risk, with sampling risk further subdivided into two types of decision errors: (1) assessing control risk too low and incorrect acceptance of a balance and (2) assessing control risk too high and incorrect rejection of an account balance. The first pair damages the effectiveness of audits, and the second pair damages the efficiency of audits.

Audit programs for test of controls procedures and balance audit procedures were illustrated. Separate sections explained the application of procedures at an interim date. Thus, the chapter covered the nature, timing, and extent of audit procedures. One of the goals of this chapter was to enable students to be able to understand these procedural programs in the context of audit sampling.

MULTIPLE-CHOICE QUESTIONS FOR PRACTICE AND REVIEW

MC 1 In an audit sampling application, an auditor performs procedures on which of the following?
  a. All the items in a balance and makes a conclusion about the whole balance.
  b. Less than 100 percent of the items in a balance and formulates a conclusion about the whole balance.
  c. Less than 100 percent of the items in a class of transactions for the purpose of becoming familiar with the client's accounting system.
  d. The client's unaudited financial statements as an analysis when planning the audit.

MC 2 Auditors consider statistical sampling to be characterized by which of the following?
  a. Representative sample selection and nonmathematical consideration of the results
  b. Carefully biased sample selection and statistical calculation of the results
  c. Representative sample selection and statistical calculation of the results
  d. Carefully biased sample selection and nonmathematical consideration of the results

MC 3 In audit sampling applications, what is sampling risk?

  a. A characteristic of statistical sampling applications but not of nonstatistical applications
  b. The probability that the auditor will fail to recognize erroneous accounting in the client's documentation
  c. The probability that accounting errors will arise in transactions and enter the accounting system
  d. The probability that an auditor's conclusion based on a sample might be different from the conclusion based on an audit of the entire population

MC 4 When auditing the client's performance of control for the completeness objective related to recording sales, auditors should draw sample items from which of the following?
  a. A sales journal list of recorded sales invoices
  b. A file of shipping documents
  c. A file of customer order copies
  d. A file of receiving reports for inventory additions

MC 5 Nelson Williams was considering the sample size needed for a selection of sales invoices for the test of controls audit of the LoHo Company's internal controls. He presented the following information for two alternative cases:

	Case A	Case B
Acceptable risk of underreliance	High	Low
Acceptable risk of overreliance	High	Low
Tolerable deviation rate	High	Low
Expected population deviation rate	Low	High

Nelson should expect the sample size for Case A to be which of the following?

a. Smaller than the sample size for Case B
b. Larger than the sample size for Case B
c. The same as the sample size for Case B
d. Not determinable relative to the Case B sample size

MC 6 Nelson next considered the sample size needed for a selection of customers' accounts receivable for the substantive audit of the total accounts receivable. He presented the following information for two alternative cases:

	Case X	Case Y
Acceptable risk of incorrect acceptance	Low	High
Acceptable risk of incorrect rejection	Low	High
Tolerable dollar misstatement in the account	Small	Large
Expected dollar misstatement in the account	Large	Small
Estimate of population variability	Large	Small

Nelson should expect the sample size for Case X to be which of the following?

a. Smaller than the sample size for Case Y
b. Larger than the sample size for Case Y
c. The same as the sample size for Case Y
d. Not determinable relative to the Case Y sample size

MC 7 Which of the following should be considered an audit procedure for obtaining evidence?

a. An audit sampling application in accounts receivable selection
b. The accounts receivable exist and are valued properly
c. Sending a written confirmation on a customer's account balance
d. Nonstatistical consideration of the amount of difference reported by a customer on a confirmation response

MC 8 When calculating the total amount of misstatement relevant to the analysis of an account balance, an auditor should add which of the following to the misstatement discovered in individually significant items?

a. The projected likely misstatement and the additional possible misstatement estimate
b. The known misstatement in the sampled items
c. The known misstatement in the sampled items, the projected likely misstatement, and the additional possible misstatement estimate
d. The additional possible misstatement estimate

MC 9 Eddie audited the LoHo Company's inventory on a sample basis. She audited 120 items from an inventory compilation list and discovered net overstatement of $480. The audited items had a book (recorded) value of $48,000. There were 1,200 inventory items listed, and the total inventory book amount was $490,000. Which of these calculations is (are) correct?

a. Known misstatement of $48000 using the average difference method
b. Projected likely misstatement of $480 using the sample stratification method
c. Projected likely misstatement of $49,000 using the taintings method
d. Projected likely misstatement of $4,800 using the average difference method

MC 10 Steve Katchy audited the client's accounts receivable, but he could not get any good information about customer 102's balance. The customer responded to the confirmation saying, "Our system does not provide detail for such a response." The sales invoice and shipping document papers have been lost, and the customer has not yet paid. What should Steve do?

a. Get another customer's account to consider in the sample.
b. Treat customer 102's account as being entirely wrong (overstated), if doing so will not affect his audit conclusion about the receivables taken altogether.
c. Require adjustment of the receivables to write off customer 102's balance.
d. Treat customer 102's account as accurate because there is no evidence saying it is fictitious.

MC 11 The risk of incorrect acceptance in balance audit sampling and the risk of assessing control risk too low in test of controls sampling both relate to which of the following?

a. Effectiveness of an audit
b. Efficiency of an audit
c. Control risk assessment decisions
d. Evidence about assertions in financial statements

MC 12 An advantage of statistical sampling is that it helps an auditor to do which of the following?

a. Eliminate nonsampling risk.
b. Reapply evaluation judgments based on factors in addition to the sample evidence.
c. Be precise and definite in the approach to an audit problem.
d. Omit quantification of risk and materiality judgments.

MC 13 To determine the sample size for a balance audit sampling application, an auditor should consider the tolerable misstatement, the risk of incorrect acceptance, the risk of incorrect rejection, the population size, plus which one of the following?

a. The expected monetary misstatement in the account
b. The overall materiality for the financial statements taken as a whole
c. The risk of assessing control risk too low
d. The risk of assessing control risk too high

EXERCISES AND PROBLEMS

EP 1
LO.3
Sampling and Nonsampling Audit Work. The accounting firm of Mason & Jarr performed the work described in each separate case below. The two partners are worried about properly applying standards regarding audit sampling. They have asked for your advice.

Required:

Write a report addressed to them, stating whether they did or did not observe the essential elements of audit sampling standards in each case:

a. Mason selected three purchase orders for raw materials from the LIZ Corporation files, and from there traced each one through the accounting system. He saw the receiving reports, purchasing agent's approvals, receiving clerks' approvals, the vendors' invoices (now stamped paid), the entry in the cash disbursement records and the cancelled cheques. This work gave him a firsthand familiarity with the cash disbursement system, and he felt confident about understanding related questions in the internal control questionnaire completed later.

b. Jarr observed the inventory taking at SER Corporation. She had an inventory list of the different inventory descriptions with the quantities taken from the perpetual inventory records. She selected the 200 items with the largest quantities and counted them after the client's shop foreman had completed his count. She decided not to check out the count accuracy on the other 800 items. The shop foreman miscounted in 16 cases. Jarr concluded the rate of miscount was 8 percent, so as many as 80 of the 1,000 items might be counted wrongly. She asked the foreman to recount everything.

c. CSR Corporation issued seven series of short-term commercial paper notes near the fiscal year-end to finance seasonal operations. Jarr confirmed the obligations under each series with the independent trustee for the holders, studied all seven indenture agreements and traced the proceeds of each issue to the cash receipts records.

d. At the completion of the EH&R Corporation audit, Mason obtained written representations, as required by auditing standards, from the president, the chief financial officer, and the controller. He did not ask the chief accountant at headquarters or the plant controllers in the three divisions for written representations.

EP 2
LO.5
Test of Controls Audit Procedure Objectives and Control Deviations. This exercise asks you to specify control test objectives and define deviations in connection with planning the test of controls audit of Kingston Company's internal controls.

Required:

a. For each control cited below, state the objective of an auditor's test of controls audit procedure.

b. For each control cited below, state the definition of a deviation from the control.

1. The credit department supervisor reviews each customer's order and approves credit by making a notation on the order.

2. The billing department must receive written notice from the shipping department of actual shipment to a customer before a sale is recorded. The sales record date is supposed to be the shipment date.

3. Billing clerks carefully look up the correct catalogue list prices for goods shipped and recheck the amounts billed on invoices for the quantities of goods shipped.

4. Billing clerks review invoices for intercompany sales and mark each one with the code "9," so that they will be posted to intercompany sales accounts.

EP 3
LO.5
Timing of Test of Controls Audit Procedures. Auditor Magann was auditing the authorization control over cash disbursements. She selected cash disbursement entries made throughout the year and vouched them to paid invoices and cancelled cheques bearing the initials and signatures of people authorized to approve the disbursements. She performed the work on September 30, when the company had issued cheques numbered from 43921 to 52920. Since 9,000 cheques had been issued in nine months, she reasoned that 3,000 more could be issued in the three months before the December 31 year-end. About 12,000 cheques had been issued last year. She wanted to take one sample of 100 disbursements for the entire year, so she selected 100 random numbers in the sequence 43921 to 55920. She audited the 80 cheques in the sample that were issued before September 30, and she held the other 20 randomly selected cheque numbers for later use. She found no deviations in the sample of 80—a finding that would, in the circumstances, cause her to assign a low (20 percent) control risk to the probability that the system would permit improper charges to be hidden away in expense and purchase/inventory accounts.

Required:

Take the role of Magann and write a memo to the audit manager (dated October 1) describing the audit team's options with respect to evaluating control performance for the remaining period, October through December.

EP 4
LO.5
Evaluation of Quantitative Test of Controls Evidence. Assume you audited control compliance in the Kingston Company for the deviations related to a random selection of sales transactions, as shown in Exhibit EP 4–1. For different sample sizes, the number of deviations was as Exhibit EP 4–1 on page 408.

Required:

For each deviation and each sample, calculate the rate of deviation in the sample (sample deviation rate).

EP 5
LO.6
Stratification Calculation of Projected Likely Misstatement Using the Ratio Method. The stratification calculation example in the chapter shows the results of

EXHIBIT EP 4-1

	Sample Sizes									
	30	60	80	90	120	160	220	240	260	300
Missing sales invoice	0	0	0	0	0	0	0	0	0	0
Missing bill of lading	0	0	0	0	0	1	2	2	3	3
No credit approval	0	3	6	8	10	14	17	23	26	31
Wrong prices used	0	0	0	0	2	4	8	9	9	12
Wrong quantity billed	1	2	4	4	4	5	5	5	5	5
Wrong invoice arithmetic	0	0	0	0	1	2	2	2	2	3
Wrong invoice date	0	0	0	0	0	2	2	2	2	2
Posted to wrong account	0	0	0	0	0	0	0	0	0	0

EXHIBIT EP 5-1

Stratum	Population Size	Recorded Amount	Sample Results		
			Sample	Recorded Amount	Misstatement Amount*
1	6	$100,000	6	$100,000	$ −600
2	80	75,068	23	21,700	−274
3	168	75,008	22	9,476	−66
4	342	75,412	22	4,692	−88
5	910	74,512	23	1,973	23
	1,506	$400,000	96	$137,841	$−1,005

*A negative misstatement indicates overstatement of the book value, and a positive misstatement indicates understatement.

calculating the projected likely misstatement using the difference method. Assume the results shown in Exhibit EP 5–1 were obtained from a stratified sample.

Required:
Apply the ratio calculation method to each stratum to calculate the projected likely misstatement (PLM). What is PLM for the entire sample?

EP 6
LO.6 **Determining Risk of Incorrect Acceptance.** In the dialogue between the Kingston auditors, Fred said, "Our analytical procedures related to receivables didn't show much. The total is down, consistent with the sales decline, so the turnover is up a little. If any misstatement is in the receivables total, it may be too small to be obvious in the ratios."

Jack replied, "That's good news if the problems are immaterial. Too bad we can't say analytical procedures reduce our audit risk. What about internal control?"
Fred responded: "I'd say it's about a 50–50 proposition. Sometimes control seemed to work well; sometimes it didn't. I noticed a few new people doing the invoice processing last week when we were here for a conference. Incidentally, I lump the inherent risk problems and internal control risk problems together when I think about internal control risk. Anyway, firm policy is to plan a sample for a low overall audit risk for the receivables."

Required:
Based on this dialogue information, use the expanded risk model to determine a test of detail risk. Relate this risk to sample size determination.

DISCUSSION CASES

DC 1
LO.6 **Application to Accounts Receivable.** Toni Tickmark has been assigned to plan the audit of the Cajuzzi Corporation, and is currently planning the circularization (confirmation) of accounts receivable. Cajuzzi sells a number of products in the personal health care field but its mainstay is a portable whirlpool unit for use in bathtubs called the "Ecstasizer." Offering the same therapeutic muscle-relaxing

benefits as built-in units costing up to four times more, the Ecstasizer has been an outstanding success and is largely responsible for the 14 percent jump in sales this year.

Cajuzzi has five major categories of customers: wholesalers, department store chains, drug stores, hardware stores, and sporting goods stores. Because the health care industry is highly competitive and a number of "clones"

EXHIBIT DC 1–1

SCHEDULE A
Cajuzzi—Five-Year Financial Summary
(in $1,000s)

	20X0	20X1	20X2	20X3	20X4
Sales	84,000	85,000	83,000	86,000	98,000
A/R (6/30)	11,000	12,500	12,000	13,000	18,000
Allowance for doubtful accounts	1,260	1,275	1,245	1,290	1,470
Pre-tax income	3,300	2,400	3,200	3,900	5,000
Total assets	25,000	25,000	26,000	26,000	29,000

SCHEDULE B
Cajuzzi—Accounts Receivable Summary
June 30, 20X4

Range	Number of Customers	Total $
$100,000–$500,000	6	$ 1,800,000
75,000–99,999	20	1,700,000
50,000–74,999	35	2,000,000
25,000–49,999	30	1,100,000
15,000–24,999	100	1,900,000
10,000–14,999	120	1,400,000
Less than 10,000	16,220	8,100,000
	16,531	$18,000,000

Cajuzzi—Aged Trial Balance at 06/30/X4

0–30 days	31–60 days	61–90 days	91–120 days	More than 120 days
$8,350,000	$5,740,000	$2,105,000	$1,350,000	$455,000

are appearing on the market, Cajuzzi has an aggressive sales strategy coupled with fairly liberal credit policies. Viewing onsite store displays as its primary advertising media, Cajuzzi actually gives each customer a display unit for demonstration purposes. These costs are charged to promotion expense. It is the stated objective of the company to have every store in the country displaying its products.

New customers are extended credit using a very liberal credit policy, and terms are net 30. Cajuzzi will not stop shipments unless balances are more than 120 days old. Customers' credit status is returned to normal as soon as the overdue balances are paid. Cajuzzi is loathe to write off any account unless the customer is actually insolvent or has given intent not to pay.

In Exhibit DC 1–1, Schedule A contains a five-year summary of key financial data, and Schedule B has a summary of accounts receivable at the year-end circularization date (06/30/X4). This is the second year that Toni's firm has been the auditor of Cajuzzi, and her first year on the engagement. Last year's working papers showed that the 50 largest accounts were circularized, which was coverage of 20 percent ($2,600,000). Overstatement of accounts receivable of $190,000 was dis-covered, but no adjustment was proposed as the error was deemed immaterial.

(ICAO adapted)

Required:

a. Critique last year's (20X3) approach to the circularization of receivables and the subsequent disposition of errors discovered.

b. What is meant by random (representative) selection, and why is it the most fundamental principle of sampling theory? Under what conditions is nonrandom selection appropriate?

c. What is meant by the terms *sampling error* and *nonsampling error?* What steps can the auditor take to control these?

d. Design a sampling plan for the circularization of receivables for Cajuzzi at 06/30/X4.
Cajuzzi's product line includes the following:
- bathtub whirlpool units
- exercise equipment (rowers, bikes, and mini-gyms)
- heating pads, massage units, and footbaths
- air purifiers and ionizers
- healthware" cooking utensils
- skin care products and vitamin supplements
- track suits, footwear, and sportswear

DC 2
LO.6

Statistical Confirmation of Receivables. You are about to commence the audit of Delta Ltd. (See Exhibit DC 2–1.) This is the first time you have worked in the field without direct supervision by a senior, and you are, of course, anxious to do a good job. The senior has preceded you in visiting the client and has left you an audit file containing the following:

- an internal control questionnaire indicating no serious deficiencies in internal control over accounts receivable
- an aged accounts receivable listing prepared by the client
- confirmation control schedule
- returned confirmations

The confirmation control shows the following information:

- number of accounts in the receivables subledger at December 31 = 65
- number of positive confirms mailed = 15
- number of negative confirms mailed = 30

The client year-end, December 31, was selected as the circulation date. Trade terms are 2/10, net/30. Confirmation results are as follows:

1. Eight positive confirms returned indicating full agreement
2. One positive confirm returned indicating the balance was correct but this is the outstanding balance as at November 30, 20X2, not December 31, 20X2
3. One positive confirm returned stating the balance was correct but should also reflect a credit memo issued January 5, 20X3
4. One positive confirm returned stating the company uses an open invoice system and is unable to respond
5. One positive confirm responding that the amount shown is incorrect because it does not reflect the 2 percent cash discount taken January 3, 20X3
6. One positive and three negative confirms returned by the post office marked "No Such Address"

7. One positive confirm stating that the balance was correct but that the company refuses to pay because of defective product quality
8. One positive confirm not returned, even after two follow-up requests
9. Two negative confirms returned with no notations made by customers
10. One negative confirm returned stating the customer owed more than the balance shown
11. One negative confirm returned stating that the balance was correct but asking for an extension of credit terms
12. One negative confirm returned stating "sue us"

The *first* page of the aged trial balance supplied by the client for Delta as at December 31 is shown in Exhibit DC 2–1.

Notes made by the senior indicate the following additional information:

- Abbey is an employee of Delta.
- The $700 Babbitt account represents a consignment shipment.
- The $500 October balance of Cabal has been formalized by a note receivable.
- The Cadenza balance represents a deposit. No shipments have been made to them yet.

Another note in the working paper file indicates that the client asked you not to send confirmation requests to Dacron Ltd. because they are worried about jeopardizing the ongoing collection efforts for the $3,000 past-due balance. Also, you were requested not to circularize Cadaver because Delta is extremely happy to have such a large account and wants to avoid bothering them in any way.

Required:

Analyze the evidence already obtained and describe any further procedures required to complete the audit of accounts receivable.

(ICAO adapted)

EXHIBIT DC 2–1

Delta Ltd.
Aged Trial Balance

Account	Balance	Dec	Nov	Oct	Prior
	(CR)				
Aardwark Enterprises	$4,200	$2,100	$2,100		
Abacus Inc.	900				$900
Abalone Co.	5,500	1,000	3,200	$1,200	
Abbey, Fred	(600)	(600)			
Abstract Enterprises	1,100	500	400		200
Babbitt Inc.	700	700			
Bacchus Co.	6,000	2,000	4,000		
Cabal Ltd.	1,000			500	500
Cacao Enterprises	(900)				(900)
Cadaver Inc.	30,000	30,000			
Cadenza Co.	(1,200)	(1,200)			
Dacron Ltd.	3,100	100		3,000	
Subtotal (first page)	$49,800	$34,600	$9,700	$4,700	$700

DC 3 **Projected Likely Misstatement.** When Marge
LO.6 Simpson, PA, audited the Candle Company inventory, a random sample of inventory types was chosen for physical observation and price testing. The sample size was 80 different types of candles and candle-making inventory. The entire inventory contained 1,740 types, and the amount in the inventory control account was $166,000. Simpson had already decided that a misstatement of as much as $6,000 in the account would not be material. The audit work revealed the following eight errors in the sample of 80.

Book Value	Audit Value	Error Amount
$ 600.00	$ 622.00	$ (22.00)
15.50	14.50	(1.00)
65.25	31.50	(33.75)
83.44	53.45	(29.99)
16.78	15.63	(1.15)
78.33	12.50	(65.83)
13.33	14.22	$ (.89)
93.87	39.87	(54.00)
$ 966.50	$ 803.67	$ (162.83)

The negative difference indicates overstatement of the recorded amount.

Required:
Calculate the projected likely misstatement using the difference method. Discuss the decision choice of accepting or rejecting the $166,000 book value (recorded amount) without adjustment.

DC 4 **Exercises in Applying the Basic Formula and Using
LO.5 the R Value Table in Appendix 10A.** The following Exhibit DC 4–1 gives auditor judgment and audit sampling results for six populations. Assume large population sizes.

Required:
a. For each population, did the auditor select a smaller sample size than is indicated by using the tables for determining sample size (assume K = 0 in sample size planning)? Explain the effect of selecting either a larger or a smaller size than those determined in the tables.
b. Calculate the sample deviation rate and the achieved P or upper error limit for each population.
c. For which of the six populations should the sample results be considered unacceptable? What options are available to the auditor?
d. Why is analysis of the deviations necessary even when the populations are considered acceptable?
e. For the following terms, identify which is an audit decision, a nonstatistical estimate made by the auditor, a sample result, and a statistical conclusion about the population:
   1. Estimated population deviation rate
   2. Tolerable deviation rate
   3. Acceptable risk of overreliance on internal control
   4. Actual sample size
   5. Actual number of deviations in the sample
   6. Sample deviation rate
   7. Achieved P or upper error limit

EXHIBIT DC 4–1

	1	2	3	4	5	6
Tolerable deviation rate or error rate as a percentage (equals materiality for the test)	6	3	8	5	20	15
Acceptable risk of overreliance on internal control in percentage = Beta Risk = 1 − Confidence Level	5	5	10	5	10	10
Actual sample size	100	100	60	100	20	60
Actual number of deviations (errors) in the sample	2	0	1	4	1	8

CRITICAL THINKING

CT 1 Does nonsampling risk include improper application of
LO.4 GAAP? Discuss.

CT 2 Do you think the general decision rule "if achieved P > materiality, then reject; otherwise accept the population"

should be applied to all estimates in financial reporting whether statistical or not? Discuss.

APPENDIX 10A

STATISTICAL SAMPLING TABLES

. . . .

R VALUE TABLE

Confidence Levels				K Value: Number of sample errors	Confidence Levels		
75% R	80% R	85% R	90% R		95% R	97.5% R	99% R
1.39	1.61	1.90	2.31	0	3.00	3.69	4.51
2.70	3.00	3.38	3.89	1	4.75	5.58	6.64
3.93	4.28	4.73	5.33	2	6.30	7.23	8.41
5.11	5.52	6.02	6.69	3	7.76	8.77	10.05
6.28	6.73	7.27	8.00	4	9.16	10.25	11.61
7.43	7.91	8.50	9.28	5	10.52	11.67	13.11
8.56	9.08	9.71	10.54	6	11.85	13.06	14.58
9.69	10.24	10.90	11.78	7	13.15	14.43	16.00
10.81	11.38	12.08	13.00	8	14.44	15.77	17.41
11.92	12.52	13.25	14.21	9	15.71	17.09	18.79
13.03	13.66	14.42	15.41	10	16.97	18.40	20.15

TABLE OF RANDOM DIGITS

32942	95416	42339	59045	26693	49057	87496	20624	14819
07410	99859	83828	21409	29094	65114	36701	25762	12827
59981	68155	45673	76210	58219	45738	29550	24736	09574
46251	25437	69654	99716	11563	08803	86027	51867	12116
65558	51904	93123	27887	53138	21488	09095	78777	71240
99187	19258	86421	16401	19397	83297	40111	49326	81686
35641	00301	16096	34775	21562	97983	45040	19200	16383
14031	00936	81518	48440	02218	04756	19506	60695	88494
60677	15076	92554	26042	23472	69869	62877	19584	39576
66314	05212	67859	89356	20056	30648	87349	20389	53805
20416	87410	75646	64176	82752	63606	37011	57346	69512
28701	56992	70423	62415	40807	98086	58850	28968	45297
74579	33844	33426	07570	00728	07079	19322	56325	84819
62615	52342	82968	75540	80045	53069	20665	21282	07768
93945	06293	22879	08161	01442	75071	21427	94842	26210
75689	76131	96837	67450	44511	50424	82848	41975	71663
02921	16919	35424	93209	52133	87327	95897	65171	20376
14295	34969	14216	03191	61647	30296	66667	10101	63203
05303	91109	82403	40312	62191	67023	90073	83205	71344
57071	90357	12901	08899	91039	67251	28701	03846	94589

Continued

78471	57741	13599	84390	32146	00871	09354	22745	65806
89242	79337	59293	47481	07740	43345	25716	70020	54005
14955	59592	97035	80430	87220	06392	79028	57123	52872
42446	41880	37415	47472	04513	49494	08860	08038	43624
18534	22346	54556	17558	73689	14894	05030	19561	56517
39284	33737	42512	86411	23753	29690	26096	81361	93099
33922	37329	89911	55876	28379	81031	22058	21487	54613
78355	54013	50774	30666	61205	42574	47773	36027	27174
08845	99145	94316	88974	29828	97069	90327	61842	29604
01769	71825	55957	98271	02784	66731	40311	88495	18821
17639	38284	59478	90409	21997	56199	30068	82800	69692
05851	58653	99949	63505	40409	85551	90729	64938	52403
42396	40112	11469	03476	03328	84238	26570	51790	42122
13318	14192	98167	75631	74141	22369	36757	89117	54998
60571	54786	26281	01855	30706	66578	32019	65884	58485
09531	81853	59334	70929	03544	18510	89541	13555	21168
72865	16829	86542	00396	20363	13010	69645	49608	54738
56324	31093	77924	28622	83543	28912	15059	80192	83964
78192	21626	91399	07235	07104	73652	64425	85149	75409
64666	34767	97298	92708	01994	53188	78476	07804	62404
82201	75694	02808	65983	74373	66693	13094	74183	73020
15360	73776	40914	85190	54278	99054	62944	47351	89098
68142	67957	70896	37983	20487	95350	16371	03426	13895
19138	31200	30616	14639	44406	44236	57360	81644	94761
28155	03521	36415	78452	92359	81091	56513	88321	97910
87971	29031	51780	27376	81056	86155	55488	50590	74514
58147	68841	53625	02059	75223	16783	19272	61994	71090
18875	52809	70594	41649	32935	26430	82096	01605	65846
75109	56474	74111	31966	29969	70093	98901	84550	25769
35983	03742	76822	12073	59463	84420	15868	99505	11426

Table for Determining Sample Size for Test of Control Using the DUS Approach

Tolerable Rate of Deviations or Errors

	.01	.02	.03	.04	.05	.06	.07	.08	.09	.10	.15	.20
Beta Risk = .05	300	150	100	75	60	50	43	38	34	30	20	15
Beta Risk = .10	231	116	77	58	47	39	33	29	26	24	16	12

Table to Evaluate Sample Results for Test of Controls Using DUS Approach: Computed UELs as a Percent (Achieved Ps) for Confidence Level = 95%

Beta Risk = .05										
R Value	3	4.75	6.3	7.76	9.16	10.52	11.85	13.15	14.44	15.71	16.97
Actual Number of Errors Found in the Sample										
Sample Size	0	1	2	3	4	5	6	7	8	9	10
20	15	*	*	*	*	*	*	*	*	*	*
25	12	19	*	*	*	*	*	*	*	*	*
30	10	16	*	*	*	*	*	*	*	*	*

35	9	14	18	*	*	*	*	*	*	*	*
40	8	12	16	20	*	*	*	*	*	*	*
45	7	11	14	18	*	*	*	*	*	*	*
50	6	10	13	16	19	*	*	*	*	*	*
55	6	9	12	15	17	20	*	*	*	*	*
60	5	8	11	13	16	18	20	*	*	*	*
65	5	8	10	12	15	17	19	*	*	*	*
70	5	7	9	12	14	16	17	19	*	*	*
75	4	7	9	11	13	15	16	18	20	*	*
80	4	6	8	10	12	14	15	17	19	20	*
90	4	6	7	9	11	12	14	15	17	18	19
100	3	5	7	8	10	11	12	14	15	16	17
125	3	4	6	7	8	9	10	11	12	13	14
150	2	4	5	6	7	8	8	9	10	11	12
175	2	3	4	5	6	7	7	8	9	9	10
200	2	3	4	4	5	6	6	7	8	8	9
250	2	2	3	4	4	5	5	6	6	7	7
300	1	2	3	3	4	4	4	5	5	6	6

Table to Evaluate Sample Results for Test of Controls Using DUS Approach: Computed UELs as a Percent (Achieved Ps) for Confidence Level = 90%

Beta Risk = .10										
R Values	2.31	3.89	5.33	6.69	8.00	9.28	10.54	11.78	13.00	14.21	15.41
Actual Number of Errors Found in the Sample										
Sample Size	**0**	**1**	**2**	**3**	**4**	**5**	**6**	**7**	**8**	**9**	**10**
20	12	20	*	*	*	*	*	*	*	*	*
25	10	16	*	*	*	*	*	*	*	*	*
30	8	13	18	*	*	*	*	*	*	*	*
35	7	12	16	20	*	*	*	*	*	*	*
40	6	10	14	17	20	*	*	*	*	*	*
45	6	9	12	15	18	*	*	*	*	*	*
50	5	8	11	14	16	19	*	*	*	*	*
55	5	8	10	13	15	17	20	*	*	*	*
60	4	7	9	12	14	16	18	20	*	*	*
65	4	6	9	11	13	15	17	19	20	*	*
70	4	6	8	10	12	14	16	17	19	*	*
75	4	6	8	9	11	13	15	16	18	19	*
80	3	5	7	9	10	12	14	15	17	18	20
90	3	5	6	8	9	11	12	14	15	16	18
100	3	4	6	7	8	10	11	12	13	15	16
125	2	4	5	6	7	8	9	10	11	12	13
150	2	3	4	5	6	7	8	8	9	10	11
175	2	3	4	4	5	6	7	7	8	9	9
200	2	2	3	4	4	5	6	6	7	8	8
250	1	2	3	3	4	4	5	5	6	6	7
300	1	2	2	3	3	4	4	4	5	5	6

PRELUDE TO PART III

PERFORMING THE AUDIT

Overview: Linking Audit Planning to Performance

You are about to begin Part III of the text, which illustrates how the audit activities, concepts, and tools presented in Part II are applied in practice to perform audits. Simplified business situations are used as examples.

Recall that the auditor's understanding of the auditee's business—its environment, risks, systems, and controls—were discussed in Chapters 6 to 9. This is the basis for developing an appropriate overall audit strategy, which should reflect the preliminary decisions on the scope of the audit. As covered in Chapter 3, the scope defines the entity and its financial information that is the subject of the audit opinion. The strategy also sets out the audit's timing and the approach to be used to gather sufficient appropriate evidence. As discussed in Chapter 6, the overall audit strategy also involves the following:

- determining appropriate materiality levels for planning purposes
- assessing the auditee's industry, legal, and regulatory environment; GAAP; and changes in the company's management, information systems, or operations that can affect financial reports
- identifying material financial statement components and high risk audit areas
- determining the audit evidence required to assess internal control effectiveness (If the auditor is required to provide an assurance report on management assertions about internal control effectiveness this additional responsibility is included here.)
- deciding, on a preliminary basis, if controls will be tested, what substantive evidence requirements there are, and what the timing for the procedures will be

Auditee resources and cooperation required in the overall strategy are communicated to auditee management and the audit committee so that arrangements for access to records and personnel for interim and final audit work can be made. The audit firm's internal resource needs are also specified in the overall strategy: How many audit staff are required and what experience levels do they need? Are audit staff with special expertise in IT or tax issues required? Will external experts be required for valuation assistance? Will other offices of the audit firm be involved for multilocation businesses or will the work of other audit firms be used?

Overall audit strategy development also sets out a schedule for audit team meetings, timing of the process, and experience levels required for working paper reviews. The auditor's assessment of management's internal controls is made at the company and application levels (transactions, balances, and disclosures, and the assertions of each). Details of this assessment are covered in Chapter 9, but this prelude provides a questionnaire guiding the auditor in this assessment for the overall strategy development stage of the audit.

The overall strategy is the basis for the detailed audit plan and the specific programs that make up the audit. A process view sees a business as being composed of several separate processes and related accounting cycles. This view of a business is useful for an organization's management and its systems development purposes, and it is likely also to be an effective approach in most audit engagements. The separate processes we will examine in Part III are as follows:

- revenues, receivables, and receipts process (Chapter 11)
- purchases, payables, and payments process (Chapter 12)
- production and payroll process (Chapter 13)
- finance and investment process (Chapter 14)

Even though each organization may view its processes differently from how others will, generally these are the key functions that need to be managed in every organization. In the detailed plan for each process, consideration is given to effectiveness and efficiency in (1) specifying the nature, extent, and timing of audit procedures to assess inherent and control risk, and (2) planning further audit procedures that will be done to reduce these risks to an acceptably low level in issuing an audit opinion.

The **detailed audit plan** also covers decisions about managing the audit team: direction for less-experienced staff, especially regarding the exercising of professional skepticism; supervision and review of their work; and the time budgets required.

Finally, the evidence gained from the audit procedures and other events uncovered will form feedback to the audit planning process and indicate how the current or future overall strategy and audit plan should be modified in their **scope**, timing, or extent. Exhibit PIII–1 summarizes the development process for the overall strategy and the detailed audit plan.

EXHIBIT PIII–1 RELATING AUDIT PLANNING TO AUDIT PERFORMANCE

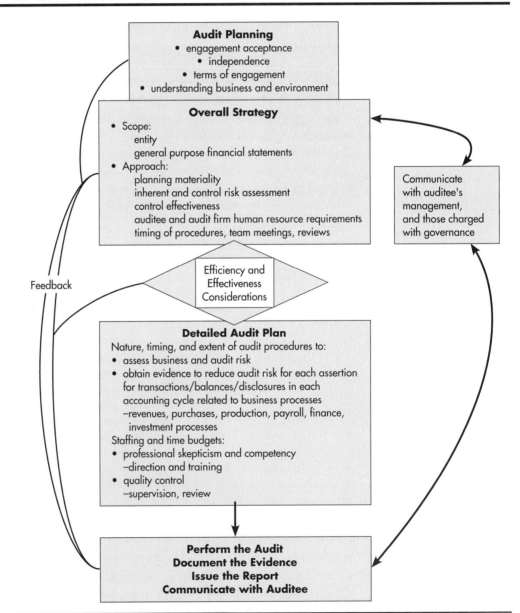

Business Processes and Accounting Cycles: The big picture

To keep things as simple as possible, the design and execution of audit programs for each business process will be focused on individually, even though the processes are all interrelated. Exhibit 7–13, shown earlier in the text, gave a "big picture" view of how the processes fit together in an organization. The shares and debt coming into the entity and being invested in capital assets are handled mainly in the financing and investing process (Chapter 14); creation of goods and services involves the purchases, payables, and payments process (Chapter 12) as well as the production and payroll processes (Chapter 13); and generation of revenues is handled in the revenue, receivables, and receipts process (Chapter 11).

The Balance Sheet Approach to Auditing

The financial statements covered by the auditor's opinion are part of the big picture approach as well. The full set of statements—that is, the balance sheet, income and retained earnings statement, cash flow statement, and statement of shareholders' equity—are all connected so that a change in one particular statement will flow through to all the related accounts in the other statements. This interrelationship mirrors that among the different business processes and is also the basis of what is known as the **balance sheet approach to auditing**. By focusing on balance sheet accounts and changes in them, we are also gaining assurance about the rest of the financial statement accounts that are connected to it.

As an example of this interrelationship, a high level of audit assurance about the change in net assets and shareholder transactions is also assurance that the net income amount is correct and that only the allocations within the income statement need to be verified as reasonable. This can be done by using analytical procedures rather than more costly vouching or confirmation. This illustrates the control provided by the double-entry accounting system and the financial statement definitions set out in generally accepted accounting principles. These strengths of the accounting and reporting framework are helpful in pulling all of the audit work together for completion of the audit.

Organization of Chapters 11 through 14

The organization of Chapters 11–14 illustrates how the audit plan is performed in the processes. Each chapter follows this pattern:

- An overview of the business risks and the transactions, balances, and disclosures in that process is given.
- Significant risks of misstatement at the assertion level are analyzed.
- An example of the process and the main accounts related to it is given.
- Key control assertions and risks, the types of control activities that would address those risks, and procedures auditors can use to assess controls are covered.
- Examples of alternative controls tests follow, should the auditors decide that reliance on effective controls would be cost-effective in reducing risk of not detecting a material misstatement.
- An application case with analysis illustrating accounting problems in that process and how audit procedures can uncover them is offered.
- An overview of the balance sheet approach to analyzing financial statement components and as a basis for developing analytical procedures concludes the chapter.
- Appendices to each of Chapters 11 through 14 give examples of audit programs, listing detailed audit procedures that are commonly used in each process.

Part III concludes with a chapter covering several issues that the auditor must address to complete the audit and form an audit opinion. These include audit procedures for revenues and expenses, auditing estimates, and procedures for auditing the cash flow statement. Other final stage issues include assessing misstatements and their materiality, financial statement adjustments, lawyers' letters, subsequent events, management representation letters, subsequent discovery of material facts, and management letters. Finally, the standards for documenting the audit work in the final audit file are reviewed.

Note that there are many references in Part III to details of generally accepted auditing standards issued in the *CICA Handbook* as CASs, as well as in ISAs. Since this text is aimed at students who will most likely be auditing under Canadian or international GAAS, the text refers, for the most part, to the auditing and assurance recommendations set out only by the CICA and IFAC. U.S. auditing standards are similar in principle to their Canadian and international counterparts, and U.S. standard-setting groups are moving towards a high degree of harmonization with international GAAS. However, U.S. pronouncements and standard setting are structured somewhat differently in response to unique U.S. legal, regulatory, and political circumstances. This text refers to U.S. standards when they are likely to lead to similar developments in future Canadian or international GAAS. For those of you who wish to learn more about U.S. GAAS, refer to the PCAOB and AICPA websites for specific details.

Following is Exhibit PIII–2, an example of an internal control questionnaire for company-level controls. Its points apply to all the processes and accounting cycles that will be covered in Chapters 11–14.

EXHIBIT PIII-2 INTERNAL CONTROL QUESTIONNAIRE FOR COMPANY-LEVEL CONTROLS AND CONTROL ACTIVITIES

This questionnaire is designed to assist the auditor in assessing the strength of internal control.

Internal control is divided into company-level controls and control activities. Company-level controls are: the overall control environment, management's risk assessment procedures, information systems and communication, and monitoring. Control activities include general and application controls.

General controls are policies and procedures that apply to all information systems and business processes.

Application controls are those that are specific to each of the main operating processes and their related accounting cycles.

In this text we will provide separate detailed questionnaires for each process in the relevant chapters, after the nature of each business process and accounting cycle has been explained: revenues/receivables/receipts (Chapter 11); purchases/payables/payments (Chapter 12); production and payroll (Chapter 13); and finance and investment (Chapter 14).

COMPANY-LEVEL CONTROLS

CONTROL ENVIRONMENT

The control environment refers to management's overall attitude, awareness, and actions concerning the importance of internal control to address the risks of the business and reduce inherent risks and the risk of a material misstatement. Consider the following aspects and evidence of strength.

"Tone at the Top"
- Do management actions and attitudes show character, integrity, and ethical values?
- Are audit committee and board of directors (or others responsible for governance of the organization) competent, knowlegable, actively involved, and influential in the organization?
- Does management have well-defined policies and objectives that communicate its commitment to integrity and ethical values?

Commitment to Competence
- Does management have sufficient experience to operate the business?
- Does management assign authority and responsibility appropriately?
- Does management provide accounting and key employees with the resources, training, and information necessary to discharge their duties?
- Do management's hiring and promotion policies emphasize competence and trustworthiness?

Management's Operating Style and Philosophy
- Does management encourage a strong control environment?
- Does the organizational structure provide a framework for establishing key areas of authority, responsibility, and reporting lines that promote strong internal control at all stages of planning, executing, and reviewing the organization's activities for achieving its objectives?
- Do management actions remove or reduce incentives and opportunities for employees to act dishonestly?

Continued

- Is there a mandatory vacation policy for employees performing key control functions?
- Does management implement controls over information systems?
- Does management maintain appropriate physical safeguards over cash, investments, inventory, and/or fixed assets?
- Does management establish adequate controls over accounting estimates and choice of accounting principles where applicable?

MANAGEMENT'S RISK ASSESSMENT PROCESS

For financial reporting purposes, management's risk assessment process should identify internal and external events and circumstances that can impair the organization's ability to initiate, record, process, and report financial data that is consistent with the assertions management makes in its financial statements.

Consider the following aspects:

- Has management established policies and assigned responsibility to personnel for identifying, evaluating, and mitigating risks?
- Does management have an ongoing process to identify risk and ensure exposure to such risks is minimized? Risks include:
  - changes in business and regulatory operating environment
  - new personnel
  - changes in information systems
  - rapid change in operations
  - new technology
  - new business models, products, or activities, including financial instruments/derivatives
  - organizational restructuring
  - foreign expansion
  - new accounting standards
- Does management independently evaluate the organization's internal control environment to assess its effectiveness?

INFORMATION AND COMMUNICATIONS

High-quality management information is an essential component of internal control. Creating and communicating information is relevant to operating decisions and to financial reporting objectives. The auditor is concerned mainly with the financial reporting information system, consisting of the procedures and records established to initiate, record, process, and report transactions, events, and conditions and to maintain accountability for the related assets, liabilities, and equity.

Consider the following aspects:

- Does management have documented policies and procedures to develop, operate, and maintain information systems, related business processes, and accounting cycles that produce reliable and timely financial information?
- Has management implemented an information system that is well designed to achieve the following financial reporting objectives?:
  - identify and record all valid transactions related to the organization in their proper reporting period;
  - capture sufficient detail to permit proper classification, measurement, and presentation of transactions in the financial statements and note disclosures in accordance with generally accepted accounting principles or other appropriate basis of accounting.
- Are appropriate lines of authority and reporting clearly established?
- Does management gather information from and communicate information to appropriate people on a timely basis?
- Is there a communication process available for people to report suspected improprieties? For example, has management established an effective whistle-blower program as it relates to financial reporting?
- Is there a disaster recovery plan in place to ensure minimum disruption should management information, accounting records, or other important data be destroyed, damaged, or stolen?

MONITORING

- Has management established effective monitoring procedures?
- Does management have a business plan that is monitored against actual results?

Continued

- Does management monitor compliance with internal control policies and procedures?
- Does management investigate variances and take proper and timely corrective action?

CONTROL ACTIVITIES

Control activities are the policies and procedures that ensure actions are taken to address risks that threaten the achievement of the entity's objectives.

Control activities are part of the information system, can be manual or IT-based, are directed toward the control objectives, and are applied at various organizational and functional levels. This questionnaire divides control activities into general controls and application controls.

General controls

General controls are pervasive policies and procedures that tend to apply to most or all processes in the information system and most or all organizational levels.

- Are there policies and procedures in place to:
  - prevent unauthorized access or changes to programs and data?
  - ensure the security and privacy of data?
  - control and maintain key systems?
  - protect assets susceptible to misappropriation?
- Is management's approach to IT planning and new systems development adequate to ensure new systems and systems changes protect the integrity of data and processing? In particular, note procedures that ensure the following: completeness, accuracy, and authorization of data and processing; the existence of adequate management trails; and the protection of the continuity of IT operations by back-up procedures and a formal disaster plan.
- Are appropriate procedures in place for software and hardware upgrades and other systems maintenance?
- Are day-to-day operations adequately controlled by IT support personnel to ensure data integrity?
- Are access controls adequate? Consider whether internal access is monitored across the information system such that appropriate personnel have access only to files they need to do their jobs, and unauthorized access is prohibited.
- For IT systems and applications run over the Internet or other telecommunications systems, is external access security adequately protected by firewalls, virus protection software, or other IT security features?

Application controls

Application controls relate to recording, processing, and reporting information. They will be specific to the business processes and related accounting cycles that generate financial information. Recording includes identifying and capturing the relevant information for transactions or events. Processing includes calculation, measurement, valuation, and summarization, whether performed by IT-based or manual procedures. Reporting relates to the preparation of financial reports, electronic or printed, that management uses for measuring and reviewing the entity's financial performance and reporting to stakeholders.

For each accounting cycle, a separate detailed questionnaire should be completed that assesses the following aspects of information processing:

- Are data integrity controls adequate? Identify and assess controls over data input to and processed in the accounting cycle that ensure data and processing are valid, complete, and accurate. Consider functions such as edit and validation checks, programmed reasonability checks, dollar limits, sequence numbering, internal confirmation of transaction data transferred from database files to the application, reconciliation, and other relevant control features.
- Are access and authorization controls adequate, e.g., are access points for data entry and enquiry (terminal, desktop, laptop, handheld device, etc.) set up to allow only designated functions to be performed and only authorized personnel to access data, processing, and output?

Based on the application-level assessment, the auditor will develop a detail plan setting out the planned approach, including decisions on whether to rely on controls as a component of audit evidence.

Refer to the detailed Internal Control Questionnaires for each business process/accounting cycle provided in Chapters 11 to 14.

PART 3
Performing the Audit

CHAPTER 11

Revenues, Receivables, and Receipts Process

This chapter offers a concise overview of the accounting cycle for the business processes related to accepting customer orders, delivering goods and services to customers, accounting for customer sales and accounts receivable, collecting and depositing cash received from customers, and reconciling bank statements. The chapter includes special technical notes on auditing the existence assertion using confirmations, and on auditing bank reconciliations. An application case with analysis is given at the end of the chapter to demonstrate the performance of audit procedures in situations where errors or frauds might be discovered in the revenues, receivables, and receipts process.

LEARNING OBJECTIVES

After completing this chapter, you will be able to do the following:

1 Describe the revenues, receivables, and receipts process, including typical risks, transactions, source documents, controls, and account balances.

2 Outline control tests for auditing control over customer credit approval, delivery, accounts receivable, cash receipts, and bank statements.

3 Explain the importance of the existence assertion for the audit of cash and accounts receivable.

4 Identify considerations for using confirmations when auditing cash and accounts receivable.

5 Perform substantive audit procedures for the audit of bank statement reconciliations, explaining how auditors can search for lapping and kiting.

6 Apply and integrate the chapter topics to design audit and investigative procedures for detecting misstatements due to error or fraud in the revenues, receivables, and receipts process.

Note: Appendices 11A Internal Control Questionnaires, 11B System Documentation Examples for the Revenues, Receivables, Receipts Process, and 11C Substantive Audit Programs accompany this chapter.

UNDERSTANDING THE REVENUES, RECEIVABLES, AND RECEIPTS PROCESS

LEARNING OBJECTIVE

1 Describe the revenues, receivables, and receipts process, including typical risks, transactions, source documents, controls, and account balances.

Revenue creation is the focus of strategy and business processes for any organization because revenues provide the cash flows that are its lifeblood. The auditor must understand the business's method of generating revenues and the use of them in the operation of the business in order to assess the business risk and the risk that the financial statements are misstated, as discussed in Chapter 6. Think of the business as a car: the revenue generating strategy is its engine and the cash flow is the gasoline that fuels it. In a for-profit business, costs incurred must generate enough sales revenue to provide profits to sustain operations and also provide investment returns to owners and creditors. A not-for-profit organization also must generate enough revenues to pay for the activities necessary to achieve its charitable or other purposes.

Risk Assessment for Revenues, Receivables, and Receipts

To assess risks in the revenue-generating processes, the auditor mainly considers the revenue and cash receipts transactions as well as the accounts receivable balances. Important disclosures relating to revenues include revenue recognition policies, related party transactions, commitments, and economic dependencies.

At the assertion level, risks related to the existence and ownership of revenues may arise if management chooses overly aggressive revenue recognition policies (e.g., Nortel), perhaps because of management incentives or pressure to meet performance targets. Ownership risks may exist where managers have the ability to transfer funds between related entities under their control (e.g., Enron, Hollinger). Completeness risks relate to recordkeeping and custodial controls over cash receipts; these must ensure that all revenues the business earns are received by the company and recorded in full. Fraudulent misappropriation of cash by employees is a key completeness risk in the revenue process. Two specific fraud techniques used by employees to cover up cash shortages, cheque kiting between banks and accounts receivable lapping between customer accounts, are explained in more detail later in the chapter. Because substantial flows of funds may be involved in the revenue processes of some businesses (e.g., financial services, banking), **money laundering**— processing monetary profits of crime to cover up their sources and convert them to "clean" cash—is also an ownership risk related to the revenue transactions. Valuation and ownership risks can exist when substantial revenues are generated in foreign countries, because of currency exchange risks and potential restrictions on removing money from those countries. Disclosure risks include revenue recognition policy explanations, reporting the extent of barter transactions (e.g., in ecommerce), or disclosing contractual commitments to sell inventory at fixed prices. These are only some examples of risks that may exist in a particular business. You can see how an auditor's in-depth understanding of the auditee's business, the revenue-generating strategy that drives it, and the environment it operates in are critical to a comprehensive assessment of business risks and the possible financial misstatements that these risks can lead to.

This chapter uses simple examples to outline the business processes and related accounting cycles for recording and controlling revenues, accounts receivable, and cash receipts. It explains the control activities that are important in these processes, how to evaluate and test these controls, and how to design and implement the substantive audit tests that provide evidence that the resulting financial statements are fairly reported. The risk of nonexistent or incorrectly valued revenues or receivables can often be addressed by confirmation and analytical procedures. Control tests in the revenue transaction processes may also provide assurance that the controls effectively lower the risk of material misstatement, thereby reducing the amount of assurance required from substantive evidence. Revenue completeness usually relies on controls and control testing; substantive testing alone may not provide sufficient evidence for the completeness assertion for revenues.

Revenues, Receivables, and Receipts Process: Typical Activities

Exhibit 11–1 is an overview of the revenues, receivables, and receipts process. The basic activities are as follows: (1) receiving and processing customer orders, including credit granting; (2) delivering goods and services to customers; (3) billing customers and accounting for accounts receivable; (4) collecting and depositing cash received from customers; and (5) reconciling bank statements. As you follow the exhibit, you can track some of the elements of the control structure.

Refer to Appendix 11A-2 for examples of controls related to this process. In practice, you would have obtained a detailed organizational chart as part of the audit planning. This chart identifies the specific auditee personnel responsible for the various functions in the process. These are the people you will work with to design and perform your audit work.

Revenues and Accounts Receivable: Processing and Controls

This section gives a narrative description of a system for processing customer sales orders. A flowchart diagram could be used for this description, and an example of a flowchart diagram is provided in Appendix 11B. At the starting point, company personnel receive

EXHIBIT   11–1   REVENUES, RECEIVABLES, AND RECEIPTS PROCESS EXAMPLE

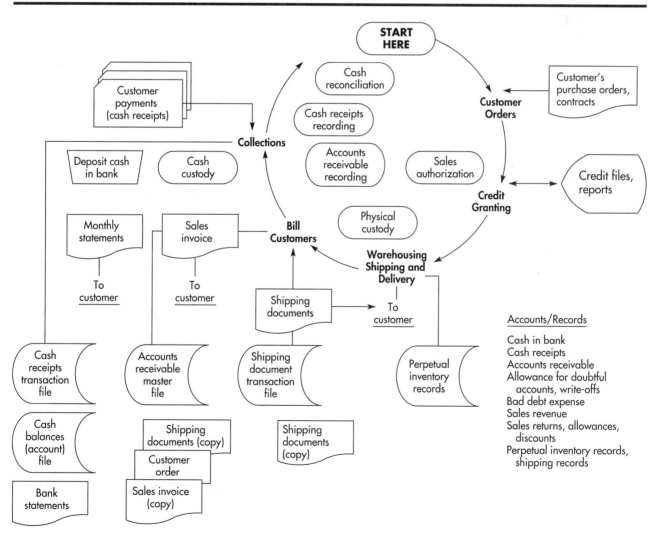

the customer's purchase order and create a sales order, entering it in a computer terminal. The computer system then performs automatic authorization procedures—determining whether the customer is a regular or new customer, approving credit, and checking the availability of inventory. (If inventory is short, a back order is entered.) Once these authorizations are in a computer system, access to the master files for additions, deletions, and other changes must be limited to responsible persons; otherwise it is possible that orders are processed for fictitious customers, credit is approved for bad credit risks, and packing slips are created for goods that do not exist in the inventory.

When a customer order passes the authorizations, the system (1) creates a record in the pending order master file, (2) transmits a packing slip to the stockroom and shipping department, and (3) updates the inventory master file to show the commitment (removal) of the inventory. The pending order and the packing slip should be numbered in a numerical sequence so that the system can determine if any transactions have not been completed (completeness objective of control). The packing slip is the stockkeeper's authorization to release inventory to the shipping department and the shipping department's authorization to release goods to a trucker or to the customer.

Custody

Physical custody of inventory starts with the stockroom or warehouse. Custody is transferred to the shipping department when the packing slip is authorized. As long as the system works, custody is under proper control. However, if the stockkeepers or the shipping department personnel have the power to change the quantity shown on the packing slip, they can cause errors in the system by billing the customer for too small or too large a quantity. (This is a combination of custody and recording functions, a segregation-of-duties control weakness. A computer record or log of such changes is a control procedure creating an electronic audit trail.)

PRICE FIXING

The company's computer programmer was paid off by a customer to cause the company to bill the customer at prices lower than list prices. The programmer wrote a subroutine that was invoked when the billing system detected the customer's regular code number. This subroutine instructed the customer billing system to reduce all unit prices 9.5 percent. The company relied on the computer billing system, and nobody ever rechecked the actual prices billed.

Custody of the accounts receivable records implies the power to alter those records directly or to enter transactions to alter them (e.g., transfers, returns, allowance credits, write-offs). Personnel with this power have a combination of authorization and recording responsibility that is another example of a control weakness due to a lack of segregation of incompatible duties.

Recording

When delivery or shipment is complete, the shipping personnel enter the completion of the transaction in the system, which (1) produces a bill of lading shipping document, evidence of an actual delivery or shipment; (2) removes the pending order from the inventory recording system; and (3) produces a sales invoice (prenumbered the same as the order and packing slip) that bills the customer for the quantity shipped, according to the bill of lading. Any personnel who have the power to enter or alter these transactions or to intercept the invoice that is supposed to be sent to the customer have undesirable combinations of authorization, custody, and recording responsibilities. This is a control weakness that provides an opportunity for employees to commit a fraud by misappropriating inventory and concealing it in the accounting records. Another authorization in the system is the price list master file containing product unit prices for billing customers. Those with power to alter this file have the ability to authorize price changes, so this function needs to be segregated from people who record customer receivables and receipts.

Periodic Reconciliation

The most frequent reconciliation is the comparison of the sum of customers' unpaid balances with the accounts receivable control account total in the general ledger. Usually, this reconciliation is done with an aged trial balance—a list of the customers and their balances—with the balances classified in columns indicating the different age categories (e.g., current, 10–30 days past due, 31–60 days past due, 61–90 days past due, and over 90 days past due). Internal auditors, or employees who are independent of the inventory and receivables recording functions, can perform periodic comparison of the customers' obligations (according to the customers) with the recorded amount by sending confirmations to the customers. (Refer to the special note on using confirmations later in this chapter.)

Cash Receipts and Cash Balances: Processing and Controls

There are numerous ways to receive payments: cash and cheques over the counter, through the mail, by receipt in a lockbox, and via electronic funds transfer. In a lockbox arrangement, a fiduciary (e.g., a bank) opens the box, lists the receipts, deposits the money, and sends the remittance advices showing the amount received from each customer to the company. While most companies need little authorization to accept a payment, authorization is important for approving discounts and allowances taken. Receiving cash and approving discounts is another example of incompatible duties that provide an opportunity for employees to defraud the company. A flowchart diagram of a manual system for processing cash receipts is shown in Appendix 11B-2.

Custody

In many organizations, someone takes the cash and cheques, which gives them custody of the physical cash for a time. Control over this custody can vary: responsibility can be rotated so that one person does not have this custody all the time; if there are teams of two or more people, they would need to collude to steal money; there could be arrangements outside the company for actual cash custody (e.g., the lockbox arrangement). Since initial custody cannot be avoided, it is good control to prepare a list of the cash receipts as early in the process as possible, and then separate the actual cash from the bookkeeping documents. The cash goes to a cashier or treasurer's office, where a bank deposit is prepared and made. The list goes to the accountants, who record the cash receipts. This list simply may be a stack of the remittance advices received with the customers' payments. Many organizations use electronic payment systems (e.g., debit and credit card readers in stores or for Internet sales). These systems reduce the amount of physical cash in custody, and rely instead on programmed systems control to ensure the payments transferred are authorized and complete.

CAREFUL RECONCILIATION

Suppose the cashier who prepares the remittance list had stolen and converted Customer A's cheques for personal use. The cashier knows this will work only until Customer A complains that the company has not given it credit for its payments. So, the cashier later puts Customer B's cheques in the bank deposit, but shows Customer A on the remittance list; thus, the accountants give Customer A credit. So far, so good for preventing Customer A's complaint, but now Customer B needs to be addressed.

This "lapping" of customer payments to hide an embezzlement can be detected by a bank reconciliation comparison of the cheques deposited (Customer B) with the remittance credit recorded (Customer A). Sometimes the lapping is covered by issuing a credit slip for Customer B. This illustrates the importance of proper authorization and control of credit slips.

SHIPPING EMPLOYEE CAUGHT BY COMPUTER!

A customer paid off a shipping department employee to change the quantity on the packing slip and bill of lading to a smaller quantity than was actually shipped. This caused the customer's invoices to be understated. The employee did not know that a computer log recorded all the entries altering the original packing slip record. An alert internal auditor noticed the pattern of "corrections" made by the shipping employee. A trap was laid by initiating fictitious orders for this customer, and the employee was observed making the alterations.

Recording

The accountants who record cash receipts and credits to customer accounts should not handle the cash. They should use the remittance list to make entries to the cash and accounts receivable control accounts and to the customers' accounts receivable subsidiary account records. In fact, a good error-checking procedure is to have control account and subsidiary account entries made by different people; then, later, the accounts receivable entries and balances can be compared (reconciled) to determine whether the proper source documents (remittance lists) were used to make error-free accounting entries. A further segregation prevents the person who receives and lists cheques from having access to cash, bank accounts, or receivables accounts. Some computerized accounting programs post the customers' accounts automatically by keying in the customer identification number.

Periodic Reconciliation

Bank account reconciliations should be prepared carefully. Deposit slips are compared with cash remittance lists, and the totals should be traced to the general ledger entries. Likewise, paid cheques should be traced to the cash disbursements listing (journal). This establishes that all receipts recorded in the books were deposited and that credit was given to the right customer. The reconciliation should be done by someone other than the accountant, such as the office manager or administrative assistant. (Refer to the special note on auditing bank reconciliations later in this chapter.)

REVIEW CHECKPOINTS

1 What is the basic sequence of activities and accounting in the revenues, receivables, and receipts process?

2 What purpose is served by prenumbering sales orders, shipping documents (packing slips and bills of lading), and sales invoices?

3 Why is controlled access to computer programs and master files (such as credit files and price lists) important in a control environment?

4 Why is it a control weakness if the same employee can authorize inventory transfers and record accounts receivable entries?

5 Why should a list of cash remittances be made and sent to the accounting department? Is it easier to send the cash and cheques to the accountants so that they can enter accurately the credits to customers' accounts?

Audit Evidence in Management Reports and Data Files

Management generates a variety of reports providing important audit evidence for revenues, accounts receivable, and cash receipts. Some examples follow.

Pending Order Master File

This file contains sales transactions started but not yet completed in the system, and thus not recorded as sales and accounts receivable. Old orders may represent shipments actually made, but for some reason the shipping department did not enter the shipping information (or entered an incorrect code that did not match the pending order file). The pending order backlog can be reviewed for evidence relating to the completeness assertion for recorded sales and accounts receivable.

Credit Check Files

The computer system may make automatic credit checks, but up-to-date maintenance of the credit information is very important. Customers' credit status is concerned with possibly uncollectible receivables, and this it is important audit evidence about the valuation assertion. Credit checks on old or incomplete information are not good credit checks. A sample of the files can be tested for current status, or the company's records can be reviewed for evidence of updating operations.

Price List Master File

The computer system may produce customer invoices automatically, but, if the master price list is wrong, the billings will be wrong. The computer file can be compared with an official price source for accuracy and authorization. (As a control, an employee should perform this comparison every time the prices are changed.) Incorrect pricing can lead to revenues and receivables being measured incorrectly, affecting the valuation assertion.

Sales Detail (Sales Journal) File

This file should contain the detailed sales entries, including the shipping references and dates. It can be scanned for entries without shipping references (fictitious sales) and for matching recording dates with shipment dates (sales recorded before shipment). This file also contains the population of debit entries to the accounts receivable, so this evidence is relevant to the existence/occurrence assertion for revenues and receivables. When there are high volumes of sales entries, these files can be tested with computer assisted auditing techniques (CAATs). Some examples of CAATs include the following:

- auditor designed analyses of customers or geographic regions assessed as high risk;
- scrutiny for unusually large entries that can indicate fraud or error;
- scrutiny for items in round numbers, same values, or just below some control dollar limit that occur more frequently than expected; and
- verification of numerical continuity of invoices and agreement to general ledger entries.

Sales Analysis Reports

The auditor can perform analytical procedures on a variety of sales analyses. Sales classified by product lines or region is information for the business segment disclosures. Those classified by period or by sales employee can show unusually high or low volume that may need investigation if error is suspected. This information can provide evidence related to completeness and existence, or occurrence, of revenues, and it is also useful for assessing the proper presentation or classification of revenue information in the financial statements, as shown in the following box relating to presentation of quarterly sales figures.

PEAKS AND VALLEYS

During the year-end audit, the independent auditors reviewed the weekly sales volume reports classified by region. They noticed that sales volume was very high in Region 2 the last two weeks of March, June, September, and December. The volume was unusually low in the first two weeks of April, July, October, and January. In fact, the peaks far exceeded the volume in all the other six regions. Further investigation revealed that the manager in Region 2 was holding open the sales recording at the end of each quarterly reporting period in an attempt to make the quarterly reports look good.

Aged Accounts Receivable Trial Balance

The list of accounts receivable balance details is called the **accounts receivable subsidiary ledger**. The summary of the subsidiary ledger by invoice dates is called the **aged A/R trial balance**. If the general ledger control account total is larger than the sum in the aged trial balance, too bad! A receivable amount not identified with a customer cannot be collected! The trial balance is the population used for confirmation. (See the special notes on the existence assertion and on using confirmations later in this chapter.) The aging information is used in assessing the allowance for doubtful accounts. (An aged trial balance is shown in Exhibit 11–6 on page 435.) The credit department uses the aged trial balance for follow-up of overdue and delinquent customer accounts. This is important evidence for assessing the existence, completeness, and valuation assertions for accounts receivable.

Cash Receipts Journal

The cash receipts journal contains all the detail for cash deposits and credits to various accounts and is the population of entries that should be the credits to accounts receivable for customer payments. It also contains any adjusting or correcting entries resulting from the bank account reconciliation. These entries may signal the types of accounting errors or manipulations that happen in the cash receipts accounting and provide evidence relating to existence and completeness of cash and accounts receivable.

REVIEW CHECKPOINTS

6   What accounting records and files could an auditor examine to find evidence of unrecorded sales, inadequate credit checks, and incorrect product unit prices?

7   Suppose you selected a sample of customers' accounts receivable and wanted to find supporting evidence for the entries in the accounts. Where would you go to vouch the debit entries? What would you expect to find? Where would you go to vouch the credit entries? What would you expect to find? What assertions are you finding evidence about?

CONTROL RISK ASSESSMENT

LEARNING OBJECTIVE

2 Outline control tests for auditing control over customer credit approval, delivery, accounts receivable, cash receipts, and bank statements.

Control risk assessment governs the nature, timing, and extent of substantive audit procedures that will be applied in the audit of account balances in the revenues, receivables, and receipts processes. These account balances (listed in the lower right corner of Exhibit 11–1, page 423) include the following:

- cash in bank
- cash receipts
- accounts receivable

- allowance for doubtful accounts
- bad debt expense
- sales revenue
- sales returns, allowances, and discounts
- perpetual inventory records and shipping records

Information about the control structure often is gathered though internal control questionnaires, introduced in Chapter 9. Refer to Exhibit 9–8 to review an internal control questionnaire for sales transaction control. A selection of other questionnaires for both general (manual) controls and computer controls over cash receipts and accounts receivable is found in Appendix 11A (page 460). These questionnaires provide details of desirable control policies and procedures. They are organized under headings that identify the important control objectives: environment, validity, completeness, authorization, accuracy, classification, accounting, and proper period recording.

General information about internal controls can also be gathered by a **walk-through**, or a **"sample" of one**. Here the auditors take a single example of a transaction and "walk it through" from its initiation to its recording in the accounting records. The revenue and collection cycle walk-through involves following a sale from the initial customer order through credit approval, billing, and delivery of goods, to the entry in the sales journal and subsidiary accounts receivable records, and finally to its subsequent collection and cash deposit. Sample documents are collected, and employees in each department are questioned about their specific duties. Walk-throughs (1) verify or update the auditors' understanding of the auditee's sales/accounts receivable accounting system and control procedures and (2) show whether the controls the auditee reported in the internal control questionnaire are actually in place. The walk-through, combined with enquiries, can contribute evidence about appropriate separation of duties, a basis for assessing control risk to be low. However, a walk-through is too limited in scope to provide sufficient evidence of whether the control procedures were operating effectively during the period under audit. A larger sample of transactions for detail testing is necessary to provide actual control performance evidence.

General Control Considerations

Control procedures for proper segregation of responsibilities should be in place and operating. Exhibit 11–1 shows that this involves authorization of sales and credit by persons who do not have custody, recording, or reconciliation duties. Custody of inventory and cash is by those who do not directly authorize credit, record the accounting entries, or reconcile the bank account. Recording (accounting) is performed by those who do not authorize sales or credit, handle the inventory or cash, or perform reconciliations. Periodic reconciliations should be performed by employees who do not have authorization, custody, or recording duties related to the same assets. Combinations of two or more of these responsibilities in one person, one office, or one computerized system may open the door for errors and fraud.

Cash management commonly requires people who handle cash to be insured under a **fidelity bond**—an insurance policy that covers most kinds of cash embezzlement losses. Fidelity bonds do not prevent or detect embezzlement, but failing to carry the insurance exposes the company to complete loss when embezzlement occurs. However, a company must prove its losses before it can collect on them—another good reason for internal controls.

The control structure should also provide for detail control checking procedures. The following set of procedures should take place:

1. sales orders entered only with a customer order;
2. credit-check code or manual signature recorded by authorized means;
3. inventory and the shipping area access restricted to authorized persons;
4. access to billing programs and blank invoice forms restricted to authorized personnel;

5. sales and accounts receivable recorded only when all supporting shipping documentation is in order (i.e., sales and receivables recorded as of the date the goods were shipped or services were provided, and cash receipts recorded as of the date the payments were received);

6. customer invoices compared with bills of lading and customer order detail to verify that quantities billed match quantities shipped, and that the goods were shipped in correct quantities and pricing to proper locations;

7. pending order files reviewed to ensure timely billing and recording; and

8. bank statements reconciled in detail, monthly.

The "Fictitious Revenue" box that follows contains an illustration of improper period recording. It is one of a class of widespread financial reporting problems commonly referred to as **revenue recognition problems**. Many of the financial restatements filed with the SEC by U.S. public companies involved revenue recognition, most of these dealing with inappropriate (too early) timing of recording revenue.

Timing is critical to many accounting issues. For example, major retailers that buy in bulk receive discounts from suppliers if they meet sales targets. But how are these rebates accounted for? The prudent practice is to wait until the targets are met. However, companies such as now-bankrupt Kmart in the U.S. and Royal Ahold in the Netherlands, once the world's third-largest food retailer, appear to have booked these payments before they were earned. In 2001–02, Ahold may have booked entire rebates as profit in the first-year of multi-year agreements, thereby overstating profits by as much as $500 million. Its chief executive officer and chief financial officer both resigned in February 2002. Ahold has been referred to as "Europe's Enron." Controls related to proper timing in the recording of transactions are becoming more important in the post-Enron environment.

FICTITIOUS REVENUE

A Mississauga computer peripheral equipment company was experiencing slow sales, so the sales manager entered some sales orders for customers who had not ordered anything. The invoices were marked "hold," while the delivery was to a warehouse owned by the company. The rationale was that these customers would buy the equipment eventually, so why not anticipate the orders! (However, it is a good idea not to send them the invoices until they actually make the orders, hence the "hold.") The "sales" and "receivables" were recorded in the accounts, and the financial statements contained overstated revenue and assets.

Control Tests

An organization should have input, processing, and output control procedures in place and operating in order to prevent, detect, and correct accounting errors. You studied the general control objectives in Chapter 9 (validity, completeness, authorization, accuracy, classification, accounting, and proper period recording). Exhibit 11–2 puts these in the perspective of the revenue process with examples of specific objectives. Study this exhibit carefully as it expresses the control objectives in specific examples rather than in the abstract.

The last general objective relates to recording sales in the proper period, a problem of timing, a growing concern to the profession. One of the most important audit procedures in this process is the **sales cutoff test**, concerning the proper allocation of transactions to the the correct period, either before or after a specific date. Allocation is essential to correctly including all period's revenues and expenses, and not including those of other periods. The shipment of goods at year-end is a critical component of this. Recognition of sales is tied to passage of title from seller to buyer—the point when the risks and

EXHIBIT 11-2   INTERNAL CONTROL OBJECTIVES: REVENUE CYCLE (SALES)

General Objectives	Examples of Specific Objectives
1. Recorded sales are *valid* and documented.	Customer purchase orders support invoices. Bills of lading or other shipping documentation exist for all invoices. Recorded sales in sales journal supported by invoices.
2. Valid sales transactions are *recorded* and none omitted.	Invoices, shipping documents, and sales orders are prenumbered and the numerical sequence is checked. Overall comparisons of sales are made periodically by a statistical or product-line analysis.
3. Sales are *authorized* according to company policy.	Credit sales approved by credit department. Prices used in preparing invoices are from authorized price schedule.
4. Sales invoices are *accurately* prepared.	Invoice quantities compared with shipment and customer order quantities. Prices checked and mathematical accuracy independently checked after invoice prepared.
5. Sales transactions are properly *classified*.	Sales to subsidiaries and affiliates classified as intercompany sales and receivables. Sales returns and allowances properly classified.
6. Sales transaction *accounting* is proper.	Credit sales posted to customer's individual accounts. Sales journal posted to general ledger account. Sales recognized in accordance with generally accepted accounting principles.
7. Sales transactions are recorded in the *proper period*.	Sales invoices recorded on shipment date.

rewards of ownership are transferred, and when the shipment or delivery of the auditee's inventory is made. Objective 7 in Exhibit 11–2 refers to shipment date.

Shipment of inventory is closely tied to the audit of inventory so we will defer that discussion to the next chapter. The relationship between all of these illustrates that the processes are not independent of each other, the important point here being that sales cutoff related to proper recording of sales for the period is closely linked to inventory shipments to customers and to the shipping terms (**FOB shipping point** or **FOB destination**). The effect of shipping terms on cutoff tests is explained in Chapter 12.

Some control tests can be used to effectively test procedures in more than one way at the same time. **Dual-direction testing**, for instance, audits both control over completeness in one direction and control over validity in the other. Completeness determines if all the sample transactions that occurred were recorded (none omitted), and validity determines if recorded transactions actually occurred (were real). An example of the first direction is examining a sample of shipping documents (from the file of all shipping documents) to determine whether invoices were prepared and recorded. The second direction is determining whether supporting shipping documents exist and verify the actual shipment. The content of each file is compared with the other. This is illustrated in Exhibit 11–3.

Exhibit 11–4 contains a selection of control tests, many of which are steps verifying the content and character of sample documents from one file against the content and character of documents in another file. This process leads to objective evidence about the effectiveness of controls and the reliability of accounting records. These samples are usually attribute samples similar to those you studied in Chapter 10.

Exhibit 11–4 shows the control objectives tested by the audit procedures. These test of controls procedures produce evidence that helps auditors determine whether the specific control objectives listed in Exhibit 11–2 were achieved. Appendix 11A illustrates internal control questionnaires used in deciding on the extent of the testing in Exhibit 11–4. (This exhibit is very general and not affected by whether manual or IT-based procedures are used to record a transaction.) Appendix 11C illustrates substantive audit programs that would be affected by the control testing results illustrated in Exhibit 11–4.

EXHIBIT 11–3   DUAL DIRECTION OF TEST AUDIT SAMPLES

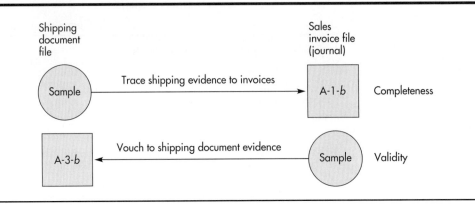

Note: The A-1-b and A-3-b codes refer to control tests listed in Exhibit 11–4.

EXHIBIT 11–4   CONTROL TESTS FOR SALES, CASH RECEIPTS, AND RECEIVABLES

	Control Objective
A. Sales	
1. Select a sample of shipping documents:	
a. Scan for missing numbers.	Completeness
b. Trace to related sales invoices.	Completeness
2. Scan sales invoices for missing numbers in the sequence.	Completeness
3. Select a sample of recorded sales invoices (sales journal):	
a. Perform recalculations to verify arithmetic accuracy.	Accuracy
b. Vouch to supporting shipping documents. Note dates and quantities.	Validity
	Accuracy
	Proper period
c. Vouch prices to approved price lists.	Authorization
d. Vouch credit approval.	Authorization
e. Trace posting to general ledger and proper customer account.	Accounting
4. Observe customer order handling and invoice preparation work.	Environment
B. Cash Receipts	
1. Select a sample of recorded cash receipts (cash receipts journal):	
a. Vouch to deposit slip and remittance list.	Validity
b. Trace to bank statement.	Validity
c. Trace posting to general ledger accounts.	Accounting
d. Trace posting to subsidiary accounts.	Accounting
2. Select a sample of remittance lists (or daily cash reports):	
a. Trace to cash receipts journal.	Completeness
b. Trace journal posting to general ledger.	Accounting
c. Trace to bank statement.	Accuracy
3. Observe the work habits of cashiers and their interactions with persons who keep cash records.	Environment
C. Accounts Receivable	
1. Trace sales invoices to accounts receivable posting (procedure A-3-*e* above).	Accounting
2. Trace cash receipts to accounts receivable posting (procedure B-1-*d* above).	Accounting
3. Select a sample of credit memos:	
a. Review for proper approval.	Authorization
b. Trace to posting in customers' accounts.	Accounting
4. Select a sample of customers' accounts:	
a. Vouch debits to supporting sales invoices.	Validity
b. Vouch credits to supporting cash receipts documents and approved credit memos.	Validity
5. Observe mailing of monthly customer statements.	Validity

Summary: Control Risk Assessment

The auditor must evaluate the evidence obtained from an understanding of the internal control structure and from control tests, two of the phases of control risk assessment work (see Chapter 9). If the control risk is assessed very low, the substantive audit procedures on the account balances can be limited in cost-saving ways. For example, the accounts receivable confirmations can be sent on a date prior to the year-end, and the sample size can be fairly small.

On the other hand, if tests of controls reveal weaknesses (such as posting sales without shipping documents, charging customers the wrong prices, and recording credits to customers without supporting credit memos), the substantive procedures will need to be designed to lower the risk of failing to detect material error in the account balances. For example, the confirmation procedure may need to be scheduled on the year-end date with a large sample of customer accounts. Descriptions of major deficiencies, control weaknesses, and inefficiencies are incorporated in a management letter to the auditee.

DUAL-PURPOSE NATURE OF ACCOUNTS RECEIVABLE CONFIRMATIONS

Accounts receivable confirmation is a substantive procedure designed to obtain evidence of the existence and gross amount (valuation) of customers' balances directly from the customer. If such confirmations show numerous exceptions, auditors will be concerned with the controls over the details of sales and cash receipts transactions even if previous control evaluations have seemed to show little control risk.

REVIEW CHECKPOINTS

8 What account balances are included in the revenues, receivables, and receipts process?

9 What specific control policies and procedures (in addition to separation of duties and responsibilities) should be in place and operating in a control structure governing revenue recognition and cash accounting?

10 What is a walk-through of a sales transaction? How can the walk-through work complement the use of an internal control questionnaire?

11 What are the two important characteristics of a control test? What actions are typically used to perform control tests?

12 What is dual-direction testing of controls sampling? What are the objectives of dual-direction testing in auditing the revenues, receivables, and receipts process?

SPECIAL NOTE: THE EXISTENCE ASSERTION

LEARNING OBJECTIVE

3 Explain the importance of the existence assertion for the audit of cash and accounts receivable.

When considering assertions and obtaining evidence about accounts receivable and other assets, auditors must put emphasis on the existence and ownership (rights) assertions. (For liability accounts, the emphasis is on the completeness assertion, as will be explained in Chapter 12.) This priority is placed on existence because companies and auditors have gotten into malpractice trouble by giving unqualified reports on financial statements that overstated assets and revenues and understated expenses. For example, credit sales recorded too early (fictitious sales) result in overstated accounts receivable and overstated sales revenue, and failure to amortize prepaid expenses results in understated expenses and overstated current assets.

Discerning the population of assets to audit for existence and ownership is easy because the company has asserted their existence by putting them on the balance sheet. The audit procedures described in the following sections can be used to obtain evidence about the existence and ownership of accounts receivable and other assets.

Computation

Assets that depend largely on calculations are amenable to auditors' recalculation procedures. For example, expired prepaid expenses are recalculated using vouching of basic documents, such as loan agreements (prepaid interest), rent contracts (prepaid rent), and insurance policies (prepaid insurance). Goodwill and deferred expenses are recalculated using original acquisition and payment documents and term (useful life) estimates. A bank reconciliation is a special kind of calculation, and it can be audited. (See the special note on auditing a bank reconciliation later in this chapter.)

Inspection of Physical Assets

Inventories and fixed assets can be inspected and counted (more on inventory observation is in Chapter 12). Titles to autos, land, and buildings can be vouched, sometimes using public records. Petty cash and undeposited receipts can be observed and counted, but the cash in the bank cannot. Securities held as investments can be inspected if documents are held by the auditee.

Confirmation

Letters of confirmation can be sent to banks and customers, asking for a report of the balances owed the company. Likewise, if securities held as investments are in the custody of banks or brokerage houses, the custodians can be asked to report the names, numbers, and quantity of the securities held for the company. In some cases, inventories held in public warehouses or out on consignment can be confirmed with the other party. (Refer to the special note on confirmations later in this chapter.)

Enquiry

While enquiries to management do not provide convincing evidence about existence and ownership, enquiries always should be made about the company's agreements to maintain compensating cash balances (these may not be classifiable as "cash" among the current assets), the pledge or sale of accounts receivable with recourse in connection with financings, and the pledge of other assets as collateral for loans.

Inspection of Documents: Vouching

Evidence of ownership can be obtained by studying the title documents for assets. Examination of loan documents may yield evidence of the need to disclose assets pledged as loan collateral.

Inspection of Documents: Scanning

Assets are supposed to have debit balances, and a computer can be used to scan large files of accounts receivable, inventory, and fixed assets for credit balances that usually reflect errors in the recordkeeping; for example, customer overpayments, failure to post purchases of inventory, and depreciation of assets more than cost. The names of debtors can be scanned for officers, directors, and other related parties, to identify amounts that need to be reported and disclosed separately in the financial statements.

Analysis

A variety of analytical comparisons may be employed, depending on the circumstances and the nature of the business. Comparisons of asset and revenue balances with recent history may help detect overstatements. Relationships such as receivables turnover, gross margin ratio, and sales-asset ratios can be compared with historical data and industry statistics for evidence of overall reasonableness. Account interrelationships also can be used in analytical review. For example, sales returns and allowances and sales commissions generally vary directly with dollar sales volume, bad debt expense usually varies directly with credit sales volume, and freight expense varies with the physical sales volume. Accounts receivable write-offs should be compared with earlier estimates of doubtful accounts.

R E V I E W
C H E C K P O I N T S

13   Why is it important to place emphasis on the existence and ownership (rights) assertions when auditing cash and accounts receivable?

14   Which audit procedures are usually the most useful for auditing and existence and ownership (rights) assertions? Give some examples.

SPECIAL NOTE: USING CONFIRMATIONS

LEARNING OBJECTIVE

④ Identify considerations for using confirmations when auditing cash and accounts receivable.

The confirmation audit procedure was introduced in Chapter 8. This special note gives some details about using confirmations in the audit of cash and accounts receivable. The use of confirmations for cash balances and trade accounts receivable is considered a generally accepted audit procedure.[1] However, auditors may decide not to use them if suitable alternative procedures are available and applicable in particular circumstances. Justifications for the decision not to use confirmations for trade accounts receivable in a particular audit should be documented. Acceptable reasons could be that (1) receivables are not material; (2) confirmations would be ineffective, based on prior-years' experience or knowledge that responses could be unreliable; and (3) other substantive test of details procedures provide sufficient appropriate evidence, and the assessed combined level of inherent risk and control risk associated with the financial statement assertions being audited is low.

SIMPLE ANALYTICAL COMPARISON

The auditors prepared a schedule of the monthly credit sales totals for the current and prior years. They noticed several variations, but one, in November of the current year, stood out in particular. The current-year credit sales were almost twice as large as in any prior November. Further investigation showed that a computer error had caused the November credit sales to be recorded twice in the control accounts. The accounts receivable and sales revenue were materially overstated as a result.

A DECISION NOT TO USE ACCOUNTS RECEIVABLE CONFIRMATIONS

Surepart Manufacturing Company sold all its production to three auto manufacturers and six aftermarket distributors. All nine of these customers were well-known companies that typically paid their accounts in full by the tenth day of the following month. The auditors were able to vouch the cash receipts for the full amount of the accounts receivable in the bank statements and cash receipts records in the month following the Surepart year-end. Confirmation evidence was not considered necessary in these circumstances as the risk of material misstatement was deemed to be very low.

Confirmations of Cash and Loan Balances

The standard bank confirmation form shown in Exhibit 11–5 is used to confirm deposit and loan balances. (Other confirmation letters are used to confirm contingent liabilities, endorsements, compensating balance agreements, lines of credit, and other financial instruments

---

[1] CAS 505 (5303).

EXHIBIT 11-5   BANK CONFIRMATION

Bank Confirmation

Areas to be completed by client are marked §, while those to be completed by the financial institution are marked †

FINANCIAL INSTITUTION § (Name, branch and full mailing address) CONFIRMATION DATE § (All information to be provided as of this date) (See Bank Confirmation Completion Instructions)	CLIENT (LEGAL NAME) § The financial institution is authorized to provide the details requested herein to the below-noted firm of accountants § _____ Client's authorized signature Please supply copy of the most recent credit facility agreement (initial if required) § _____

1. LOANS AND OTHER DIRECT AND CONTINGENT LIABILITIES (If balances are nil, please state.)

NATURE OF LIABILITY/ CONTINGENT LIABILITY †	INTEREST (Note rate per contract)		DUE DATE †	DATE OF CREDIT FACILITY AGREEMENT †	AMOUNT AND CURRENCY OUTSTANDING †
	RATE †	DATE PAID TO †			

ADDITIONAL CREDIT FACILITY AGREEMENT(S) _____
Note the date(s) of any credit facility agreement(s) not drawn upon and not referenced above † _____

2. DEPOSITS/OVERDRAFTS

TYPE OF ACCOUNT §	ACCOUNT NUMBER §	INTEREST RATE §	ISSUE DATE (If applicable) §	MATURITY DATE (If applicable) §	AMOUNT AND CURRENCY (Brackets if Overdraft) †

EXCEPTIONS AND COMMENTS (See Bank Confirmation Completion Instructions.)†

STATEMENT OF PROCEDURES PERFORMED BY FINANCIAL INSTITUTION †
The above information was completed in accordance with the Bank Confirmation Completion Instructions.

_____   BRANCH CONTACT _____
Authorized signature of financial institution   Name and telephone number

Please mail this form directly to our public accountant in the enclosed addressed envelope.

Name: Address: Telephone: Fax:

Source: Developed by the Canadian Bankers Association and The Canadian Public Accounting Associations.

and transactions. The standard form and illustrative letters are reproduced in the PA's professional engagement manuals.) A word of caution is in order: While financial institutions may note exceptions to the information typed in a confirmation and may confirm items omitted from it, the auditor should not rely solely on the form to satisfy the completeness assertion, insofar as cash and loan balances are concerned. Officers and employees of financial institutions cannot be expected to search their information systems for balances and loans that may not be immediately evident as assets and liabilities of the auditee company. However, it is a good idea to get bank confirmation of zero balances on accounts the company represents as closed during the year. (If a nonzero balance is confirmed, the auditors have evidence that some asset accounting has been omitted in the company records.)

The auditor should also be alert for evidence of transactions with banks or bank accounts other than those for which there are general ledger accounts. For example, loan documents or cheques written on other banks may come to light during scanning or other document examination procedures. Enquiries of management should be made to assess whether bank confirmations should be obtained from these banks and whether any financial statement impact exists.

Confirmation of Accounts and Notes Receivable

Confirmations provide evidence of existence and, to a limited extent, of valuation of accounts and notes receivable. Those to be confirmed should be documented in the working papers with an aged trial balance. An aged trial balance is shown in Exhibit 11–6,

---

E X H I B I T   1 1 – 6   AGED ACCOUNTS RECEIVABLE TRIAL BALANCE

```
D-2                           KINGSTON COMPANY              Prepared  JD
PG. 1 OF 15                   ACCOUNTS RECEIVABLE           Date      1-12-20X3
                              December 31, 20X2             Reviewed  Terri Tough
                                                            Date      1-17-X3


                        ----------  -------- Aged --------    Jan. 2003 Collection
                                    30-60   61-90   Over 90                   Past
                        Current     Days    Days    Days     Total   Current  Due
                        ------------------------------------------------------------
Able Hardware           12,337 X                             12,337 X PC "12,337
Baker Supply              712                                  712       712
Charley Company         1,486 X    420 X                     1,906 X PC 1,486    420
Dogg General Store                                755          755
                        ------------------------------------------------------------

                        ------------------------------------------------------------
Welsch Windows                             531 X              531 X NC           531
Zlat Stuff Place                                   214        214                214

Balance per books      335,000   30,000  20,000  15,000   400,000  320,000   25,000
                                                              ⑦
Billing errors         (11,000)          (1,000)          (12,000) ①

Adjusted balance       324,000   30,000  19,000  15,000   388,000
                        ------------------------------------------------------------
                        ------------------------------------------------------------

   X  Traced to accounts receivable subsidiary ledger.

   PC Positive confirmation mailed Jan. 4. Replies D-2.3

   NC Negative confirmation mailed Jan. 4. Replies D-2.4

   "  No reply to positive confirmation, vouched charges to invoices.

   ⑨  Traced to general ledger control account.

   ①  Billing error adjustment explained on working paper D-2.2

 Note: See D-2.2 for analysis of doubtful accounts and our test
       of reasonableness
```

annotated to show the auditor's work. Accounts for confirmation can be selected at random or in accordance with another plan consistent with the audit objectives. Statistical methods are useful for determining the sample size, and audit software accessing receivables files could be used to select and even print the confirmations.

However, confirmations of accounts, loans, and notes receivable may not produce sufficient evidence regarding the ownership (rights) assertion. Debtors may not be aware that the auditee has sold its accounts, notes, or loans receivable to financial institutions or to the public (as collateralized securities). Auditors need to perform additional enquiry and details procedures to get evidence of the ownership of the receivables and of the appropriateness of disclosures related to financing transactions secured by receivables.

Positive and Negative Confirmations

Confirmations can be either positive or negative type, and sometimes both forms are used, with positive confirmations being sent on some customers' accounts and negative confirmations on others. An example of a positive confirmation is shown in Exhibit 11–7. A variation of the positive confirmation is the blank form, which does not contain the balance; customers are asked to fill it in themselves. The blank positive confirmation may produce better evidence because the recipients need to get the

EXHIBIT 11–7 POSITIVE CONFIRMATION LETTER

D-2.3

KINGSTON COMPANY
Kingston, Ontario

January 5, 20X3

Charley Company
Lake and Adams
Chicago, Illinois

Gentlemen:

Our auditors, Anderson, Olds & Watershed, are making their regular audit of our financial statements. Part of this audit includes direct verification of customer balances.

PLEASE EXAMINE THE DATA BELOW CAREFULLY AND EITHER CONFIRM ITS ACCURACY OR REPORT ANY DIFFERENCES DIRECTLY TO OUR AUDITORS USING THE ENCLOSED REPLY ENVELOPE.

This is not a request for payment. Please do not send your remittance to our auditors.

Your prompt attention to this confirmation request will be appreciated.

Sandra Carboy
Sandra Carboy, Controller

The balance due Kingston Company as of December 31, 20X2, is $1,906. This balance is correct except as noted below:

It's correct. Will send payment as soon
as possible

Date: Jan. 7, 20X3   By: P. "Charley" O'Quirk

Title: President

EXHIBIT   11-8   NEGATIVE CONFIRMATION LETTER

KINGSTON COMPANY
Kingston, Ontario

January 5, 20X3

Charley Company
Lake and Adams
Chicago, Illinois

Gentlemen:

Our auditors, Anderson, Olds & Watershed, are making their regular audit of our financial statements. Part of this audit includes direct verification of customer balances.

PLEASE EXAMINE THE DATA BELOW CAREFULLY AND COMPARE THEM TO YOUR RECORDS OF YOUR ACCOUNT WITH US. IF OUR INFORMATION IS NOT IN AGREEMENT WITH YOUR RECORDS, PLEASE STATE ANY DIFFERENCES ON THE REVERSE SIDE OF THIS PAGE, AND RETURN DIRECTLY TO OUR AUDITORS IN THE RETURN ENVELOPE PROVIDED. IF THE INFORMATION IS CORRECT, NO REPLY IS NECESSARY.

This is not a request for payment. Please do not send your remittance to our auditors.

Your prompt attention to this confirmation request will be appreciated.

Sandra Carboy

Sandra Carboy, Controller

As of December 31, 20X2, balance due to Kingston Company: $1,906
Date of Origination: November and December, 20X2
Type: Open trade account

---

information directly from their own records instead of just signing the form and returning it with no exceptions noted. (However, the effort involved may result in a lower response rate.)

Exhibit 11-8 shows the negative confirmation form for the same request as in Exhibit 11-7. Note that the positive form asks for a response, while the negative form asks for a response only if something is wrong with the balance. Thus, lack of response to negative confirmations is considered evidence that nothing is wrong. For this reason, CAS 505 states that evidence from negative confirmations is less reliable than evidence from positive confirmations, and requires that negative confirmations be used only when the auditor has reason to believe the recipients will not disregard the request. For example, in the audit of an investment management business, if the balance of a customer's investment account has been understated, he or she would be very motivated to respond to a negative confirmation, to get this error corrected.

The positive form is used when individual balances are relatively large or when accounts are in dispute. They may ask for information about either the account balance or specific invoices, depending on knowledge about how customers maintain their accounting records. The negative form is used mostly when inherent risk and control risk are considered low, when a large number of small balances is involved, and when customers can be expected to consider the confirmations properly.

EXHIBIT 11-9   CONFIRMATION REQUEST FOR A BILL-AND-HOLD TRANSACTION

[Client Letterhead]

[Date]

[Name and address of customer
employee with sufficient
authority to commit customer]

Dear [Name]:

Our auditors [PA firm name and address] are auditing our financial statements at [balance sheet date]. Please compare the following information with your records and report directly to our auditors whether that information is correct:

We sold you [product description] on [date] for [total sales price] under your purchase order [date and number].

[Product description] has been sold to you on our normal payment terms as described in our invoice [number and date] and those terms have not been modified. There are no written or oral amendments to the terms specified in the purchase order.

At your request we are holding [product description] at your risk on our premises, and title has passed to you.

You requested us to hold [product description] for you because [description of business reason for delayed shipment].

There are no written or oral amendments to the terms specified in the purchase order.

You are obligated to pay us [total sales price] by [payment due date].

Please use the enclosed preaddressed, postage-paid reply envelope. Because this response is needed for our auditors to complete their audit, we would appreciate a prompt response.

Very truly yours,

[Signature and title of authorized client representative]

If the above information is correct, please confirm. If your understanding of anything described above differs in any respect, please explain.

_____
_____
_____

Date: _____

Signed: _____

Source: AICPA

A special positive confirmation form that may be used for possibly inappropriate bill-and-hold transactions is illustrated in Exhibit 11–9. While bill-and-hold sales transactions are not necessarily a GAAP violation when customers have requested this arrangement, they are often associated with financial fraud and should be investigated. It is the substance rather than the form of the transaction that is important. According to CICA EIC–141, Revenue Recognition, the following conditions should be met for revenue recognition to be appropriate in bill-and-hold sales arrangements:

- The risks of ownership must have passed to the buyer.
- The customer must have made a fixed commitment to purchase, in writing.
- A fixed delivery schedule must exist and must be reasonable for both the buyer and seller.
- The seller must not retain any significant performance obligations.
- The goods must be complete and ready for shipment and not subject to being used by the seller to fill other orders.
- The buyer, not the seller, must request the bill-and-hold transaction and substantiate a business purpose for it.

These points illustrate that auditors must have a good understanding of the auditee, its business, and its products in order to identify the warning signs of revenue recognition misstatements and fraud. The bill-and-hold confirmation is an example of a confirmation request to verify the substance of a transaction from the customer's point of view.

Controlling Delivery and Receipt of Confirmations

Delivering confirmations to the intended recipient is a problem that requires auditors' careful attention. Auditors need to control the confirmations, including the addresses to which they are sent, to ensure they were not mailed to company accomplices who provided false responses. Features of the reply, such as postmarks, fax responses, letterhead, email, telephone, or other characteristics that may suggest false responses should be carefully reviewed. Auditors should follow up electronic and telephone responses by returning the call if the number is known, looking up telephone numbers, or using a directory to determine the respondent's address to verify their origin. Furthermore, with the lack of response to a negative confirmation there is no guarantee that the intended recipient received it unless the auditor carefully controlled the mailing.

The **response rate** for positive confirmations is the proportion of the number returned to the number sent. This varies depending on from whom the confirmations are sought, but generally the auditor is aiming at a 100 percent response. Nonresponses are tolerated if the amounts can be verified by other audit procedures. The **detection rate** is the ratio of the number of misstatements reported to auditors to the number of actual account misstatements. Research indicates recipients detect account misstatements to varying degrees. Negative confirmations tend to have lower detection rates than positive confirmations, and detection rates for misstatements favouring recipients (i.e., an accounts receivable understatement) also tend to be less likely. Overall, positive confirmations appear to be more effective than negative confirmations, but results depend on the type of recipients, the size of the account, and the type of account being confirmed. Confirmation effectiveness depends on attention to these factors and on prior-years' experience with particular accounts.

Second and third requests for positive confirmations should be sent to nonrespondents. If there is no response or the response specifies an exception to the auditee's records, alternative substantive procedures should be done to audit the account. These procedures include finding sales invoice copies, shipping documents, and customer orders to verify the existence of sales transactions. They also include finding evidence of customer payments in cash receipts and bank statements.

When random sampling is used, all selected accounts in the sample should be audited rather than substituting an easier-to-audit customer account into the sample as a replacement for one that does not respond to a confirmation request. If the amount cannot be verified by confirmation or alternative procedures, the auditor has to consider that the account balance does not exist.

Confirmation at Dates Other Than Year-End

Confirmation of receivables may be performed at an interim date to help the audit firm spread work throughout the year and avoid the pressures that occur around December 31. Also, the audit can be completed sooner after the year-end date if confirmation has been done earlier. Internal control over transactions affecting receivables is the biggest concern when confirming accounts before the balance sheet date. The following additional procedures should be considered when confirmation is done at an interim date:

1. Obtain a summary of receivables transactions from the interim date to the year-end date.

2. Obtain a year-end trial balance of receivables, compare it with the interim trial balance and obtain evidence and explanations for large variations.

3. Consider additional confirmations as of the balance sheet date if balances have increased materially or a material new customer balance has been added.

Summary: Confirmations

Confirmations of cash balances, loans, accounts receivable, and notes receivable can provide very reliable audit evidence. Confirmation is usually required to provide sufficient appropriate audit evidence, unless auditors can justify substituting other procedures in a particular audit. The bank confirmation is a standard positive form. Confirmations for accounts and notes receivable can be in positive or negative form, and the positive form may be a blank confirmation.

Auditors must control confirmations to ensure that responses are received from the real debtors and not from persons intercepting the confirmations to give false responses. Responses by fax, email, telephone, or other means not written and signed by a recipient should be followed up. Second and third requests should be sent for positive confirmation responses, and nonresponding customers should be audited by alternative procedures. Accounts in a sample should not be left unaudited (e.g., "They didn't respond"), and easy-to-audit accounts should not be substituted for hard-to-audit ones in a sample. These techniques might raise the apparent response rate, but they do not increase the persuasiveness of the audit evidence obtained.

Confirmations yield evidence about existence and gross valuation. However, the fact that a debtor admits to owing the debt does not mean he can pay. While confirmations can give some clues about collectibility of accounts, other procedures must audit this. Confirmations of accounts, notes, and loans receivable provide only partial evidence of the ownership (rights) assertion of these financial assets, so other corroborating evidence of ownership must be obtained.

- -

REVIEW CHECKPOINTS

15 List the information an auditor should ask for in a standard bank confirmation sent to an auditee's bank.

16 Distinguish between positive and negative confirmations. Under what conditions would you expect each type of confirmation to be appropriate?

17 Distinguish between confirmation response rate and confirmation detection rate.

18 What are some of the justifications for not using confirmations of accounts receivable on a particular audit?

19 What special care should be taken with regard to examining the sources of accounts receivable confirmation responses?

- -

SPECIAL NOTE: AUDIT OF BANK RECONCILIATIONS WITH ATTENTION TO LAPPING AND KITING

LEARNING OBJECTIVE

5 Perform substantive audit procedures for the audit of bank statement reconciliations, explaining how auditors can search for lapping and kiting.

The company's bank reconciliation is the primary means of valuing cash in the financial statements. The amount of cash in the bank is almost always different from the amount in the books (financial statements), and the reconciliation purports to explain the difference. A company-prepared bank reconciliation is audited; auditors should not prepare the reconciliation as this is a company control function.

A bank reconciliation is shown in Exhibit 11–10. The bank balance is confirmed and cross-referenced to the bank confirmation working paper (Exhibit 11–5, page 436). The reconciliation is recalculated, the outstanding cheques and deposits in transit totals are recalculated, and the book balance is traced to the trial balance (which has been traced to the general ledger). The reconciling items should be vouched to determine whether outstanding cheques really were not paid and that deposits in transit actually were sent to the bank before the reconciliation date. The auditor vouches the bank reconciliation items against

EXHIBIT 11–10   BANK RECONCILIATION

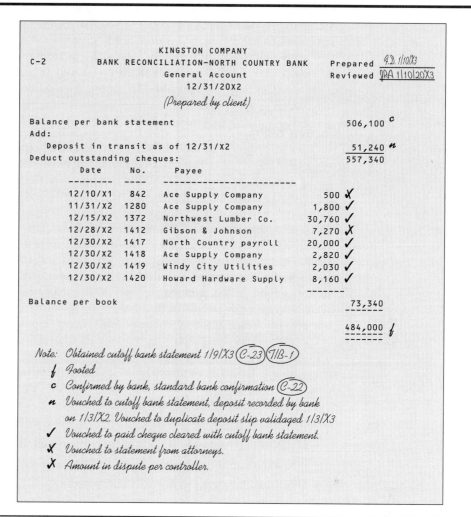

a **cutoff bank statement**—a complete bank statement including all paid cheques and deposit slips for a 10- to 20-day period following the reconciliation date, or the next regular monthly statement, received directly by the auditors.

Vouching outstanding cheques and deposits in transit is a matter of comparing cheques that cleared in the cutoff bank statement with the list of outstanding cheques, for evidence that all cheques written prior to the reconciliation date were on the list of outstanding cheques. The deposits shown in transit should be recorded by the bank in the first business days of the cutoff period. If otherwise, they may have been made up from receipts of the period after the reconciliation date. Other documents should be vouched for large outstanding cheques not cleared in the cutoff period. These procedures are keyed and described by tick marks in Exhibit 11–10.

Accounts Receivable Lapping

When the business receives many payments from customers, cheques listed on a sample of deposit slips (from the reconciliation month and other months) are compared with the detail of customer credits listed on the day's posting to customer accounts receivable (daily remittance list or other record of detail postings) in a detailed audit. This is a test for **accounts receivable lapping**—a manipulation of accounts receivable entries to hide a theft or fraud. For example, an employee steals a payment by collecting from customer A without recording the payment. Before customer A's account becomes past due and attracts attention of a credit manager, customer B's similar-sized payment is credited to customer A's account. Then, before customer B's account goes past due, a payment from customer C is credited to customer B's account, and so on. This fraud may grow and go on indefinitely. The audit procedure is to look for credits given to customers who did not make payments on the day in question. An example of this type of comparison is given in Audit 11.1 in the application case and analyis at the end of this chapter (page 446).

Cheque Kiting

Auditors also should be alert to the possibility of **cheque kiting**—building up apparent balances in one or more bank accounts based on uncollected (float) cheques drawn against similar accounts in other banks. Kiting involves depositing money from one bank account into another, using a hot cheque. There are insufficient funds to cover this cheque, but that is dealt with by another hot cheque from another bank account before the first cheque clears. The customer uses the time it takes for cheques to clear as an unauthorized loan without any interest charge. To continue, kites evolve to include more banks and more cheques until the number of banks involved and the distances between them make it difficult for the perpetrator to control the kite scheme. Within Canada, new technologies and procedures in the banking industry have greatly reduced the float time in clearing cheques between financial institutions, making kiting much more difficult to do. For example, electronic scans of cheques can process deposits before a kite can be started, and software detecting suspicious transactions can identify an attempted kite.

Professional money managers working for cash-conscious businesses try to have minimal unused balances in their accounts, and their efforts sometimes can look like cheque kites. Tight cash flows initiate kites, and when the kiting is done intentionally to take money from the bank, or to increase interest income, this can lead to criminal charges. These are some characteristic signs of cheque kiting schemes:

- Frequent deposits and cheques in the same accounts.
- Frequent deposits with cheques written on the same (other) banks.
- Short time lag between deposits and withdrawals.
- Many large deposits made on Thursdays or Fridays to take advantage of the weekend.
- Large periodic balances in individual accounts with no apparent business explanation.
- Low average balance compared with high level of deposits.
- Many cheques made payable to other banks.
- Bank willingness to pay against uncollected funds (bank has extended a line of credit on the company's bank account).
- Cash withdrawals with deposit cheques drawn on another bank.
- Cheques drawn on foreign banks with lax banking laws and regulations.

Auditors can detect the signs of cheque kiting in reviews of bank account activity. But criminal cheque kiters often destroy the banking documents. If a company cannot or will not produce its bank statements, with all deposit slips and cancelled cheques, the auditors should be wary. Since cash is the key account and most operating transactions run through it, an inability to obtain sufficient evidence to audit cash will probably result in a pervasive limitation on the audit scope, and an inability to form an audit opinion on the financial statements.

If cash transfers are recorded in the books, negative balances resulting from cheques drawn on insufficient funds will appear. Perpetrators may try to hide the kiting by not recording the deposits and cheques. Such manoeuvres may be detectable in a bank reconciliation audit. An audit test for kiting is preparing a bank transfer schedule in which all interbank transfers a few days before and after the year-end are traced to the accounting records. This schedule shows each cheque amount, the name of the paying bank (with the book recording date and the cheque clearing date), and the name of the receiving bank (with the book deposit date and the bank clearing date), using information taken from the cancelled cheques and the cleared deposits in the bank statements. The purpose of this schedule is to see that both sides of the transfer transaction are properly recorded in the same period.

Summary: Bank Reconciliations, Lapping, and Kiting

The combination of all the procedures performed on the bank reconciliation provides evidence of existence, valuation, and proper cutoff of the bank cash balances. Auditors use a cutoff bank statement to obtain independent evidence of the proper listing of outstanding cheques and deposits in transit on a bank reconciliation.

Note that, if the auditor reperforms the bank reconciliation, it is a substantive procedure because it yields direct evidence on monetary misstatements. However, if the auditor checks that bank reconciliations are performed on a regular basis, this is a test of controls that provides only indirect evidence on the risk of monetary misstatements.

Additional procedures might detect attempts at lapping accounts receivable collections and kiting cheques. Auditing the details of customer payments listed in bank deposits in comparison with details of customer payment postings (remittance lists) will show lapping. To detect kiting, auditors must be alert to the signs of kites and prepare schedules of interbank transfers.

· ·

REVIEW
CHECKPOINTS

20 What is a cutoff bank statement? How is it used by auditors?

21 What is lapping? What procedures can auditors employ for its detection?

22 What is cheque kiting? How might auditors detect kiting?

· ·

APPLICATION CASE AND ANALYSIS

This application case contains specific examples of tests of controls and **substantive audit procedures** used to gather evidence in the revenue, receivables, and receipts process. The purpose of substantive audit procedures differs from that of test of controls in that substantive procedures are designed to obtain direct evidence about the dollar amounts in account balances, while tests of controls obtain evidence about the company's performance of its own control procedures. Substantive procedures include tests of details of balances and transactions as well as focused analytical procedures. Substantive procedures must follow the assessment of control risk as auditors cannot rely exclusively on controls. Dual-purpose procedures can be designed that cover substantive and control testing purposes simultaneously.

LEARNING OBJECTIVE

6 Apply and integrate the chapter topics to design audit and investigative procedures for detecting misstatements due to error or fraud in the revenues, receivables, and receipts process.

In this application case, as well as in those of subsequent chapters, each audit case situation describes an error or fraud that occurred, followed by an audit approach analysis that explains the audit objective (assertion), controls relevant in the business process, tests of controls, and substantive procedures that could be considered in an approach to the case. The audit approach section presumes that the auditors do not know everything about the situation. (As a student of the case, you have inside information.) Each audit situation is set up with the following framework:

Case Description

This offers the background of what happened in the case; the dollar amount of overstated assets and revenue, or understated liabilities, and expenses that resulted; the method or cause of the misstatement (accidental error, intentional irregularity, or fraud attempt); the failure of controls that made it possible; and the amounts involved.

Audit Trail

The set of telltale signs of erroneous accounting and missing or altered documents.

Audit Approach Analysis

This section contains the following parts:

Audit objective

Recognition of a financial statement assertion for which evidence needs to be obtained. The assertions are about existence of assets, liabilities, revenues, and expenses; their valuation; their complete inclusion in the account balances; the rights and obligations inherent in them; and their proper presentation and disclosure in the financial statements. (These assertions were introduced in Chapter 6.)

Controls relevant in the process

Recognition of the control procedures that should be used by an organization to prevent and detect errors and fraud.

Audit Procedures

The evidence gathering procedures—Test of controls, Dual-purpose procedures, Tests of details of balance

Audit Results

This is a summary of the auditors' findings and their implications.

In the end-of-chapter review section, similar discussion cases allow you to test your ability to design audit procedures for the detection of errors or fraud.

Detecting Misstatements in the Revenue, Receivables, and Receipts Process

Jack's first year on the audit trail has been an exciting one. He has worked on many audits and gained experience in a wide variety of situations that have helped him develop his professional judgment. While meeting with some new junior audit staff members, Jack describes three very different experiences in auditing the revenue, receivables, and receipts process. The three audit situations he encountered provide a lot of insight into the risk of material misstatements. The first case involved misstatement due to employee embezzlement, the second involved fraudulent financial reporting by management, and the third was an unintentional error by the accounting department.

AUDIT 11.1
THE EMBEZZLING CASHIER

Case Description

Cash embezzlement by an employee at a new audit client, Sports Equipment Inc. (SEI), an equipment retailer, caused overstated accounts receivable, overstated customer discounts expense, and understated cash sales. SEI also failed to earn interest income on funds "borrowed." Over a six-year period, D. Bakel, the assistant controller of SEI, built up a $150,000 average balance in a Sport Equipment Company (SEC) account, which earned a total of $67,500 in interest that should have been earned by SEI. By approving the "extra" discounts, Bakel also skimmed 2 percent of about $1 million in annual sales, for a total of $120,000. Since SEI would have had net income before taxes of about $1.6 million over the six years, Bakel's embezzlement took about 12.5 percent of the income.

SEI maintained accounts receivable for school boards in the region; its other customers received credit only by using their own credit cards. Bakel was the company cashier, receiving all the incoming payments on school board accounts and credit card accounts, as well as all the other cash and cheques taken over the counter. Bakel prepared the bank deposit (and delivered the deposit to the bank), listing all the cheques and currency; prepared a remittance worksheet (daily cash report) that showed amounts received, discounts allowed on school board accounts, and amounts to credit to the accounts receivable; and reconciled the bank statement. No one else reviewed the deposits or the bank statements except the independent auditors.

Bakel opened the bank account in the name of Sport Equipment Company (SEC), after properly incorporating the company with the government Ministry of Commerce. He took over-the-counter cash and cheques and school board payments from the SEI receipts and deposited them in the SEC account. No one, including the bank, noticed the difference between the rubber stamp endorsements for the two similarly named corporations. Bakel kept the money in the SEC account, earning interest on it, and then wrote SEC cheques to SEI to replace the "borrowed" funds. In the meantime, new SEI receipts were being deposited to SEC. When Bakel deposited SEC cheques in SEI, giving the schools credit, an additional 2 percent customer discount was approved. Thus, the school boards received proper credit later, but SEC paid in a discounted amount.

Audit Trail

SEI's bank deposits showed fairly small currency deposits as Bakel was nervous about taking too many cheques, so preferred cash. As shown in the examples below, the deposit slips listed the SEC cheques Bakel deposited, as the bank tellers usually check this. The remittance worksheet, on the other hand, did not show SEC cheques but rather receipts from school boards and currency, and not many over-the-counter cheques from customers. The transactions became complicated enough that Bakel had to use the computer in the office to keep track of the school boards that needed to get credit. There were no vacations for this hard-working cashier because the discrepancies might be noticed by a substitute employee.

AUDIT APPROACH ANALYSIS

Audit objective

The auditor's objective was to obtain evidence determining whether the accounts receivable recorded on the books represented claims against real customers in the gross amounts recorded.

Controls relevant to the process

The authorization related to cash receipts, custody of cash, recording of cash transactions, and bank statement reconciliation should be separate duties assigned to different people. Independent review of one or more of these duties should be performed as a supervisory control designed to detect errors and fraud.

Unfortunately, at SEI Bakel had all these duties. (While recording was not actually performed, Bakel provided the source document, the remittance worksheet, that the other accountant used to make the cash and accounts receivable entries.) According to the company president, the only "control" was the diligence of "our long-time, trusted, hard-working assistant controller." Assessing the control risk on this new audit, Jack's audit team identified serious control weaknesses. By "thinking like a crook" to imagine ways these control weakness could allow Bakel to commit fraud, the auditors discovered the scheme for cash theft and accounts receivable lapping.

AUDIT PROCEDURES

Dual-purpose tests

Since Bakel's honest and diligent performance were the "control" of the accounting and control procedures that should have been performed by two or more people, the auditors performed a dual-purpose test of controls and substantive details of cash receipts transactions as they relate to accounts receivable credits. The samples and direction of test procedure are as follows:
(a) Validity direction—select a sample of customer accounts receivable, and reconcile payment credits to remittance worksheets and bank deposits, including recalculation of discounts allowed according to sales terms (2 percent), classification (customer name), identification, and correspondence of receipt date to recording date.
(b) Completeness direction—select a sample of remittance worksheets (or bank deposits), vouch details to bank deposit slips (trace details to remittance worksheets if the sample is bank deposits), and trace forward to complete accounting posting in customer accounts receivable.

Test of details of balance

The auditors sent positive confirmations on all 72 school board accounts. Since there was a control risk of incorrect accounting, the accounts receivable confirmation was performed at the year-end date, using positive confirmations. Blank confirmations were used, and the "sample" included all the accounts, since the number was not too large.

Audit results

The audit tests showed four cases of discrepancy where the responses stated that the boards had paid the balances before the confirmation date. Follow-up procedures on their accounts receivable credit in the next period showed they had received credit in remittance reports, and the bank deposits had shown no cheques from the school boards, but had contained a cheque from Sports Equipment Company. To further investigate, the auditors used the Internet, telephone book, chamber of commerce directory, and a visit to a local Ministry of Commerce office to determine the location and identity of Sport Equipment Company. Further investigation of SEC revealed the connection of Bakel, who was confronted and then confessed.

Bank Deposit Slip

Jones	25
Smith	35
Hill Dist.	980
Sport Equip	1,563
Currency	540
Deposit	3,143

Cash Remittance Report

Name	Amount	Discount	AR	Sales
Jones	25	0	0	25
Smith	35	0	0	35
Hill Dist.	980	20	1,000	0
Marlin Dist.	480	20	500	0
Waco Dist.	768	32	800	0
Currency	855	0	0	855
Totals	3,143	72	2,300	915

AUDIT 11.2
BILL EARLY, BILL OFTEN!

Case Description

McGossage Company is a long-time audit client of Jack's firm that had been experiencing profit pressures for two years now. A recessionary economy reduced profits, but the company reported net income decreases that were not as severe as other companies in its industry. In the audit it was discovered that employees were recording sales too early and failing to account for customer discounts taken, resulting in overstated sales and receivables, understated discounts expense, and overstated net income.

As misstatements go, some of these were on the materiality borderline. Sales were overstated 0.3 percent and 0.5 percent in the prior and current year, respectively. Accounts receivable were overstated 4 percent and 8 percent. But the combined effect was to overstate the division's net income by 6 percent and 17 percent. Selected data were as follows:

	One Year Ago		Current Year	
	Reported	Actual	Reported	Actual
Sales	$330.0	$329.0	$350.0	$348.0
Discounts expense	1.7	1.8	1.8	2.0
Net income	6.7	6.3	5.4	4.6

In McGossage's grocery products division, sales had been recorded for orders prepared for shipment but not actually shipped until later. Employees backdated the shipping documents. Gross profit on these "sales" was about 30 percent. Customers took discounts on payments, but the company did not record them, leaving the debit balances in the customers' accounts receivable instead of charging them to discounts and allowances expense. Company accountants were instructed to wait 60 days before recording discounts taken.

The division vice-president and general manager knew about these accounting practices, as did a significant number of the 2,500 employees in the division. The division managers were under orders to achieve profit objectives they considered unrealistic, thus creating pressure on them to misstate the financial results.

Audit Trail

The customers' accounts receivable balances contained amounts due for discounts the customers already had taken. The cash receipts records showed payments received without credit for discounts. Discounts were entered monthly by a special journal entry. The unshipped goods were on the shipping dock at year-end, with papers showing earlier shipping dates.

AUDIT APPROACH ANALYSIS

Audit objective

The auditors' objectives were to obtain evidence determining if sales were recorded in the proper period, if gross accounts receivable represented the amounts due from customers at year-end, and if discounts expenses were recognized in the proper amount in the proper period.

Controls relevant to the process

The accounting procedures manual should state that sales are to be recorded on the date of shipment (or when title passes, if later); management overrode this control procedure by having shipping employees date the shipping papers incorrectly. Cash receipts procedures call for discounts to be authorized and recorded when they are taken by customers; management overrode this control procedure by giving instructions to delay the recording.

AUDIT PROCEDURES

Tests of controls

Use questionnaires and enquiries to determine the company's accounting policies, as it is possible that employees and managers would conceal these from auditors. Pointed questions about revenue recognition and discount recording policies might elicit revealing answers as well.

Dual-purpose procedures

Select a sample of cash receipts, examine them for authorization, recalculate the customer discounts, and trace them to accounts receivable input for recording of the proper amount on the proper date. Select a sample of shipping documents and vouch them to customer orders, then trace them to invoices and to recording in the amounts receivable input with proper amounts on the proper dates. These tests follow the tracing direction—data representing the beginning of transactions (cash receipts, shipping) is traced through the company's accounting process.

Tests of details of balance

Confirm a sample of customer accounts. Use analytical relationships of past years' discount expense to a relevant base (sales, sales volume) to calculate an overall test of the discounts expense.

Audit Results

The managers lied to the auditors about their revenue and expense timing policies. The sample of shipping documents showed no dating discrepancies because the employees had inserted incorrect dates. The analytical procedures on discounts did not show the misstatement because the historical relationships were too erratic to show a deficient number (outlier). However, the sample of cash receipts transactions showed that discounts were not calculated and recorded at time of receipt. Additional enquiry led to discovery of the special journal entries and admission of the recording delay. Two customers in the sample of 65 confirmations responded with exceptions that turned out to be unrecorded discounts. Two other customers in the confirmation sample complained that they did not owe for late invoices on December 31. Follow-up showed the shipments were goods on the shipping dock noticed by auditors during the December 31 inventory taking. The shipping documents were dated December 26. The sales recording had them recorded as "bill and hold" on December 29.

AUDIT 11.3
THANK GOODNESS IT'S FRIDAY

Case Description

In the audit of Alpha Brewery Corporation (Alpha), Jack's audit team found that overstated sales caused net income, retained earnings, current assets, working capital, and total assets to be overstated. Overstated cash collections did not change the total current assets or total assets but they increased the amount of cash and decreased the amount of accounts receivable by an offsetting amount, affecting the quick ratio that Alpha's bank monitors. Alpha recorded sales of $672,000 and gross profit of $268,800 over the January 1–4 period. Cash collections on customers' accounts amounted to $800,000.

Alpha generally has good control policies and procedures related to authorization of transactions for accounting entry, and the accounting manual has instructions for recording sales transactions in the proper accounting period. The company regularly closes the accounting process each Friday at 5 p.m. to prepare weekly management reports. The year-end date (cutoff date) is December 31, and, in 20X0, December 31 was a Monday. However, the accounting was performed through Friday as usual, and the accounts were closed for the year on January 4.

Audit Trail

All the entries were properly dated after December 31, including the sales invoices, cash receipts, and shipping documents. However, the trial balance the financial statements were prepared from was dated December 31, 20X0, even though the accounts were actually closed on January 4. Nobody noticed the slip of a few days because the Friday closing was normal.

AUDIT APPROACH ANALYSIS

Audit objective

The auditors' objectives were to obtain evidence to determine the existence, completeness, and valuation of sales for the year ended December 31, 20X0, and of the cash and accounts receivable as of December 31, 20X0.

Controls relevant to the process

The company had in place proper instructions for dating transactions on the actual date they occurred, entering sales and cost of goods sold on the day of shipment, and entering cash receipts on the day received in the company offices. An accounting supervisor should have checked the entries through Friday to make sure the dates corresponded with the actual events and that the accounts for the year were closed with Monday's transactions.

AUDIT PROCEDURES

Tests of controls

In this case, the auditors needed to be aware of the company's weekly routine closing and of the possibility that the Monday occurrence of December 31 might cause a problem. Asking the question "Did you cut off the accounting on Monday night this week?" might elicit the "Oh, we forgot!" response. It would be normal to sample transactions around the year-end date to determine if they were recorded in the proper accounting period. To do this, they selected transactions from 10 days before and after the year-end date and inspected the dates on supporting documentation.

Tests of details of balance

For sales overstatements, the auditors confirmed a sample of accounts receivable. If the accounts were too large, the auditors expected the debtors to say so, thus leading to detection of sales overstatements. Cash overstatement was audited by examining the bank reconciliation to see whether deposits in transit (the deposits sent late in December) actually cleared the bank early in January. Obviously, the January 4 cash collections could not reach the bank until at least Monday, January 7. That's too long for a December 31 deposit to be in transit to a local bank.

The completeness of sales recordings was audited by selecting a sample of sales transactions (and supporting shipping documents) in the early part of the next accounting period (January 20X1). Sales of 20X0 could be incomplete if recording of December shipments had been postponed until January, and this procedure would detect them if the shipping documents were dated properly. The completeness of cash collections (and accounts receivable credits) was audited by examining the cash deposits early in January for any sign of holding cash without entry until January.

In this case the existence objective was more significant to discovering the problem than the completeness objective; after all, the January 1–4 sales, shipments, and cash collections did not "exist" in December 20X0.

Audit Results

The test of controls sample from the days before and after December 31 quickly revealed the problem. Company accounting personnel were embarrassed, but there was no intent to misstate the financial statements. This was a simple error. The company readily made the following adjustment:

	Debit	Credit
Sales	$672,000	
Inventory	403,200	
Accounts receivable	800,000	
Accounts receivable		$672,000
Cost of goods sold		403,200
Cash		800,000

REVIEW CHECKPOINTS

23   In the Audit 11.1 case, name one bank reconciliation control procedure that could have revealed signs of embezzlement.

24   What feature(s) of a cash receipts internal control system would be expected to prevent the cash receipts journal and recorded cash sales from reflecting more than the amount shown on the daily deposit slip?

25   In the Audit 11.2 case, what information might have been obtained from each of the following: enquiries, detail test of controls procedures, observations, and confirmations?

26   With reference to the Audit 11.3 case, how would an understanding of the business and management reporting system have contributed to discovery of the open cash receipts journal cutoff error?

SUMMARY

The revenue and collection cycle consists of customer order processing, credit checking, goods shipping, customer billing, accounts receivable accounting, cash receipts collection and accounting. Companies reduce control risk by having a suitable separation of authorization, custody, recording, and periodic reconciliation duties. Error-checking procedures of comparing customer orders and shipping documents are important for billing customers the right prices for the delivered quantities. Otherwise, many things could go wrong—from sales to fictitious customers or those with bad credit to billings for the wrong quantities at the wrong prices at the wrong time.

Cash collection is a critical point for asset control. Many cases of embezzlement occur in this process. This chapter's application case and analysis told the stories of some cash embezzlement schemes, including the practice of lapping accounts receivable.

Three topics were given special technical notes in the chapter. The existence assertion is very important in the audit of cash and receivables assets, as misleading financial statements often include overstated assets and revenue. A section was devoted to the use of confirmations for obtaining evidence of asset existence from outside parties. Bank reconciliations were shown to be an audit opportunity to recalculate the amount of cash reported in the financial statements and to look for signs of accounts receivable lapping and cheque kiting.

Analysis of Financial Statement Relationships

The audit of the revenues, receivables, and receipts processes verify that there is not a material misstatement in the balance of accounts receivable and the two transaction streams that run through it—revenues and cash receipts. In the balance sheet approach to auditing, we can analyze the accounts receivable balance changes and the financial statement items related to them by analyzing the continuity of the accounts receivable account over the period being audited. A **continuity schedule** is a working paper that shows the movements in the account balances and the other financial statement amounts that should tie in with them. Following is a continuity schedule for the accounts receivable balance:

Audited Amount	Financial Statement Where Amount Is Reported
Opening balance of accounts receivable	Balance sheet (prior year comparative figures)
Add: Revenues from credit sales	Income statement (component of total revenues)
Deduct: Cash received against accounts receivable	Cash flow statement (direct method)
Deduct: Uncollectible accounts written off	Balance sheet (change in allowance for doubtful Accounts)*
Ending balance of accounts receivable	Balance sheet (current year figures)

*Note: The bad debt expense and the allowance for doubtful accounts balance can be analyzed using the same technique. Question EP11.7 at the end of the chapter asks you to provide the continuity schedule for the allowance for doubtful accounts and to identify the related financial statement items that it will have to be agreed to in the audit file.

As these relationships illustrate, procedures to audit the revenues, receivables, and receipts allow assessment of whether all components of this system are reported accurately in the financial statements. These relationships also indicate analytical procedures that can detect material misstatements. For example, the ratios measuring collection period or number of days of sales in A/R can indicate nonexistent sales revenues or receivables that are not likely to be collected.

MULTIPLE-CHOICE QUESTIONS FOR PRACTICE AND REVIEW

MC 1 Which of the following would be the best protection for a company that wishes to prevent the lapping of trade accounts receivable?

a. Segregate duties so that the bookkeeper in charge of the general ledger has no access to incoming mail.

b. Segregate duties so that no employee has access to both cheques from customers and currency from daily cash receipts.

c. Have all customers send payments directly to the company's depository bank.

d. Request that customers' payment cheques be made payable to the company and addressed to the treasurer.

MC 2 Which of the following internal control procedures will most likely prevent the concealment of a cash shortage from the improper write-off of a trade account receivable?

a. Write-off must be approved by a responsible officer after review of credit department recommendations and supporting evidence.

b. Write-offs must be supported by an aging schedule showing that only receivables overdue several months have been written off.

c. Write-offs must be approved by the cashier who is in a position to know if the receivables have, in fact, been collected.

d. Write-offs must be authorized by company field sales employees who are in a position to determine the financial standing of the customers.

MC 3 Auditors sometimes use comparisons of ratios as audit evidence. For example, an unexplained decrease in the ratio of gross profit to sales suggests which of the following possibilities?

a. Unrecorded purchases

b. Unrecorded sales

c. Merchandise purchases charged to selling and general expense

d. Fictitious sales

MC 4 An auditor is auditing sales transactions. One step is to vouch a sample of debit entries from the accounts receivable subsidiary ledger back to the supporting sales invoices. What would the auditor intend to establish by this step?

a. Sales invoices represent bona fide sales.

b. All sales have been recorded.

c. All sales invoices have been properly posted to customer accounts.

d. Debit entries in the accounts receivable subsidiary ledger are properly supported by sales invoices.

MC 5 If a dishonest bookkeeper is trying to conceal defalcations involving receivables, which of the following accounts would the auditor most likely expect the bookkeeper to charge?

a. Miscellaneous income

b. Petty cash

c. Miscellaneous expense

d. Sales returns

MC 6 Which of the following would the auditor consider to be an incompatible operation if the cashier receives remittances?

a. The cashier prepares the daily deposit.

b. The cashier makes the daily deposit at a local bank.

c. The cashier posts the receipts to the accounts receivable subsidiary ledger cards.

d. The cashier endorses the cheques.

MC 7 The audit working papers often include an auditee-prepared, aged trial balance of accounts receivable as of the balance sheet date. The aging is best used by the auditor for which of the following?

a. Evaluating internal control over credit sales

b. Testing the accuracy of recorded charge sales

c. Estimating credit losses

d. Verifying the existence of the recorded receivables

MC 8 Which of the following might be detected by an auditor's cutoff review and examination of sales journal entries for several days prior to the balance sheet date?

a. Lapping year-end accounts receivable

b. Inflating sales for the year

c. Kiting bank balances

d. Misappropriating merchandise

MC 9 Confirmation of individual accounts receivable balances directly with debtors will, of itself, normally provide evidence concerning which of the following?

a. Collectability of the balances confirmed

b. Ownership of the balances confirmed

c. Existence of the balances confirmed

d. Internal control over balances confirmed

MC 10 Which of the following is one of the better auditing techniques for detecting kiting between intercompany banks?

a. Review composition of authenticated deposit slips.

b. Review subsequent bank statements.

c. Prepare a schedule of the bank transfers.

d. Prepare a year-end bank reconciliation.

MC 11 What is the best reason for prenumbering, in sequence, documents such as sales orders, shipping documents, and sales invoices?

a. Enables determination of the accuracy of each document.

b. Enables determination of the proper period recording of sales revenue and receivables.

c. Allows checking of the numerical sequence for missing documents and unrecorded transactions.

d. Enables determination of the validity of recorded transactions.

MC 12 When a sample of customer accounts receivable is selected for the purpose of vouching debits for evidence of existence, the auditors will vouch them to which other items?

a. Sales invoices with shipping documents and customer sales invoices

b. Records of accounts receivable write-offs

c. Cash remittance lists and bank deposit slips

d. Credit files and reports

MC 13 In the audit of cash and accounts receivable, the main emphasis should be on which assertion?

a. Completeness

b. Existence

c. Obligations

d. Presentation and disclosure

MC 14 When accounts receivable are confirmed at an interim date, the auditors are not concerned with which of the following?

a. Obtaining a summary of receivables transactions from the interim date to the year-end date

b. Obtaining a year-end trial balance of receivables, comparing it with the interim trial balance, and obtaining evidence and explanations for large variations

c. Sending negative confirmations to all the customers as of the year-end date

d. Considering the necessity for some additional confirmations as of the balance sheet date if balances have increased materially

MC 15 The negative request form of accounts receivable confirmation is most likely to be acceptable in which case?

	Assessed level of control risk relating to receivables is	Number of small balances is	Proper consideration by the recipient is
a.	Low	Many	Likely
b.	Low	Few	Unlikely
c.	High	Few	Likely
d.	High	Many	Likely

(AICPA adapted)

MC 16 When an auditor selects a sample of shipping documents and takes the tracing direction of a test to find the related sales invoice copies, the evidence is relevant for deciding which of the following?

a. If shipments to customers were invoiced
b. If shipments to customers were recorded as sales
c. If recorded sales were shipped
d. If invoiced sales were shipped

(AICPA adapted)

EXERCISES AND PROBLEMS

EP 1 **Cash Receipts: Control Objectives and Control**
LO.2 **Examples.** Prepare a table similar to Exhibit 11–4 on page 432 (internal control objectives) for cash receipts.

EP 2 **Cash: Substantive Audit Procedures on Bank Recon-**
LO.3 **ciliation.** The following auditee-prepared bank recon-
LO.5 ciliation is being examined by you during an audit of the financial statements of Cynthia Company:

CYNTHIA COMPANY
Bank Reconciliation
Village Bank Account 2
December 31, 20X0

Balance per bank **(a):**		$18,375.91
Deposits in transit **(b):**		
12/30	$1,471.10	
12/31	2,840.69	4,311.79
Subtotal		22,687.70
Outstanding cheques **(c):**		
837	6,000.00	
1941	671.80	
1966	320.00	
1984	1,855.42	
1985	3,621.22	
1987	2,576.89	
1991	4,420.88	(19,466.21)
Subtotal		3,221.49
NSF cheque Returned 12/29 **(d):**		200.00
Bank charges		5.50
Error: cheque no. 1932		148.10
Customer note collected by the bank ($2,750 plus $275 interest **(e):**		(3,025.00)
Balance per books **(f):**		$550.09

Required:
Indicate one or more audit procedures that should be performed in gathering evidence in support of each of the items *(a)* through *(f)* above.

(AICPA adapted)

EP 3 **Sales Cutoff and Cutoff Bank Statement.**
LO.2 a. You wish to test Houston Corporaton's sales cutoff
LO.3 at June 30. Describe the steps you should include in
LO.5 this test.
b. You obtain a July 10 bank statement directly from the bank. Explain how this cutoff bank statement should be used
   1. in your review of the June 30 bank reconciliation, and
   2. to obtain other audit information.

(AICPA adapted)

EP 4 **Alternative Accounts Receivable Procedures.** Several
LO.1 accounts receivable confirmations have been returned
LO.3 with the notation "verification of vendor statements is no
LO.6 longer possible because our data processing system does not accumulate each vendor's invoices." What alternative auditing procedures could be used to audit these accounts receivable?

(AICPA adapted)

EP 5 **Accounts Receivable Audit Procedures.** During the
LO.4 audit of the December 31, 20X5, financial statements,
and the auditor identifies cash amounts received subsequent
LO.6 to December 31, 20X5, and traces these amounts to the cash account in the general ledger and to the accounts receivable subledger balances at December 31, 20X5.

Required:
a. What kind of procedure is this? What evidence does it provide regarding which financial statement assertion?
b. What records or documents would the auditor need to look at to identify cash amounts received after the year-end?

EP 6 **Accounts Receivable Audit Procedures.** The auditor
LO.3 is considering confirming zero-balance accounts from
LO.4 the auditee's accounts receivable subledger to provide
LO.6 evidence concerning the completeness assertion for accounts receivables and sales.

Required:
a. What are the advantages and limitations of this procedure?
b. How would the decision to use this procedure relate to the auditor's control assessment? In particular, discuss the kinds of controls the auditee would be expected to have and the procedures the auditor could use to test them.

EP 7 **Continuity Schedule for Allowance for Doubtful**
LO.4 **Accounts.**

Required:
a. Complete the following continuity schedule indicating how the movements in the allowance for doubtful accounts tie into other amounts in the financial statements.
b. Prepare an audit program listing the procedures that can be used to audit the accounts in this system. Demonstrate how your audit program addresses all the relevant assertions.

Audited Amount	Financial Statement Where Amount Is Reported
Opening balance of allowance for doubtful accounts	
Add:	
Deduct:	
Ending balance of allowance for doubtful accounts	

DISCUSSION CASES

DC 1 **Internal Control Questionnaire for Book Buy-Back**
LO.2 **Cash Fund.** Taylor, a PA, has been engaged to audit the financial statements of University Books Incorporated. University Books maintains a large, revolving cash fund exclusively for the purpose of buying used books from students for cash. The cash fund is active all year because the nearby university offers a large variety of courses with varying start and completion dates throughout the year.

Receipts are prepared for each purchase. Reimbursement vouchers are periodically submitted to replenish the fund.

Required:
Construct an internal control questionnaire to be used in evaluating the system of internal control over University Books' use of the revolving cash fund to buy back books. The internal control questionnaire should elicit a yes or no response to each question. Do not discuss the internal controls over books that are purchased.

(AICPA adapted)

DC 2 **Test of Controls Audit Procedures for Cash Receipts.**
LO.2 You are the in-charge auditor examining the financial statements of the Gutzler Company for the year ended December 31. During late October you, with the help of Gutzler's controller, completed an internal control questionnaire and prepared the appropriate memoranda describing Gutzler's accounting procedures. Your comments relative to cash receipts are as follows:

All cash receipts are sent directly to the accounts receivable clerk with no processing by the mail department. This clerk keeps the cash receipts journal, prepares the bank deposit slip in duplicate, posts from the deposit slip to the subsidiary accounts receivable ledger, and mails the deposit to the bank.

The controller receives the validated deposit slips directly (unopened) from the bank. She also receives the monthly bank statement directly (unopened) from the bank and promptly reconciles it.

At the end of each month, the accounts receivable clerk notifies the general ledger clerk, by journal voucher, of the monthly totals of the cash receipts journal for posting to the general ledger.

Each month, the general ledger clerk records the total debits to cash from the cash receipts journal. The clerk also, on occasion, makes debit entries in the general ledger cash account from sources other than the cash receipts journal—for example, funds borrowed from the bank. Certain standard auditing procedures listed below already have been performed by you in the audit of cash receipts:

All columns in the cash receipts have been totalled and cross-totalled.

Postings from the cash receipts journal have been traced to the general ledger.

Remittance advices and related correspondence have been traced to entries in the cash receipts journal.

Required:
Considering Gutzler's internal control over cash receipts and the standard auditing procedures already performed, list all other auditing procedures that should be performed to obtain sufficient audit evidence regarding cash receipts control and give the reasons for each procedure. Do not discuss the procedures for cash disbursements and cash balances. Also, do not discuss the extent to which any of the procedures are to be performed. Assume adequate controls exist to ensure that all sales transactions are recorded. Organize your answer sheet as follows:

Other Audit Procedures	Reason for Other Audit Procedures

(AICPA adapted)

DC 3 **Cash Receipts: Weaknesses and Recommendations.**
LO.2 The Pottstown Art League operates a museum for the benefit and enjoyment of the community. During hours when the museum is open to the public, two volunteer

clerks positioned at the entrance collect a $5 admission fee from each nonmember patron. Members of the Art League are permitted to enter free of charge on presentation of their membership cards.

At the end of each day, one of the clerks delivers the proceeds to the treasurer. The treasurer counts the cash in the presence of the clerk and places it in a safe. Each Friday afternoon, the treasurer and one of the clerks deliver all cash held in the safe to the bank, and they receive an authenticated deposit slip that provides the basis for the weekly entry in the cash receipts journal.

The board of directors of the Pottstown Art League has identified a need to improve the system of internal control over cash admission fees. The board has determined that the cost of installing turnstiles or sales booths or otherwise altering the physical layout of the museum will greatly exceed any benefits that may be derived. However, the board has agreed that the sale of admission tickets must be an integral part of its improvement efforts.

Required:

The board of directors has requested your assistance. Prepare a report for presentation and discussion at their next board meeting that identifies the weaknesses in the existing system of cash admission fees and suggests recommendations.

(AICPA adapted)

DC 4 **Control Weaknesses: Shipping and Billing.** Ajax
LO.2 Inc. recently implemented a new accounting system to process the shipping, billing, and accounts receivable records more efficiently. During the interim work of Ajax's auditors, an assistant completed the review of the accounting system and the internal controls. The assistant determined the following information concerning the new computer systems and the processing and control of shipping notices and customer invoices.

The computer system documentation consists of the following items: program listings, error listings, logs, and database dictionaries. The system and documentation are maintained by the IT administrator. To increase efficiency, batch totals and processing controls are not used in the system.

Ajax ships its products directly from two warehouses, which forward shipping notices to general accounting. There, the billing clerk enters the price of the item and accounts for the numerical sequence of the shipping notices. The billing clerk also manually prepares daily adding machine tapes of the units shipped and the sales amounts. The computer processing output consists of the following:

a. A three-copy invoice that is forwarded to the billing clerk.
b. A daily sales register showing the aggregate totals of units shipped and sales amounts that the billing clerk compares with the adding machine tapes.

The billing clerk mails two copies of each invoice to the customer and retains the third copy in an open invoice file that serves as a detail accounts receivable record.

Required:

a. Prepare a list of weaknesses in internal control (manual and computer), and for each weakness make one or more recommendations.
b. Suggest how Ajax's computer processing over shipping and billing could be improved through the use of remote terminals to enter shipping notices. Describe appropriate controls for such an online data entry system.

DC 5 **Bank Reconciliation: Cash Shortage.** The Patrick
LO.5 Company had poor internal control over its cash transactions. Facts about its cash position at November 30 were the following:

The cash books showed a balance of $18,901.62, which included undeposited receipts. A credit of $100 on the bank statement did not appear on the books of the company. The balance according to the statement was $15,550.

When you received the cutoff bank statement on December 10, the following cancelled cheques were enclosed: No. 6500 for $116.25, No. 7126 for $150.00, No. 7815 for $253.25, No. 8621 for $190.71, No. 8623 for $206.80, and No. 8632 for $145.28. The only deposit was in the amount of $3,794.41 on December 7.

The cashier handles all incoming cash and makes the bank deposits personally. He also reconciles the monthly bank statement. His November 30 reconciliation is shown below.

Balance, per books, November 30		$18,901.62
Add: Outstanding cheques:		
8621	$190.71	
8623	206.80	
8632	145.28	442.79
		19,344.41
Less: Undeposited receipts		3,794.41
Balance per bank, November 30		15,550.00
Deduct: Unrecorded credit		100.00
True cash, November 30		$15,450.00

Required:

a. You suspect that the cashier has stolen some money. Prepare a schedule showing your estimate of the loss.
b. How did the cashier attempt to conceal the theft?
c. Based only on the information above, name two specific features of internal control that were missing.
d. If the cashier's October 31 reconciliation is known to be in order and you start your audit on December 5, what specific auditing procedures could you perform to discover the theft?

(AICPA adapted)

DC 6 **Receivables Audit Procedures.** The ABC Appliance
LO.4 Company, a manufacturer of small electrical appliances,
and deals exclusively with 20 distributors situated through-
LO.6 out the country. At December 31 (the balance sheet date)

receivables from these distributors aggregated $875,000.
Total current assets were $1.3 million.

With respect to receivables, the auditors followed the
procedures outlined below in the course of the annual
audit of financial statements:
1. Reviewed the system of internal control and found it
   to be exceptionally good.
2. Reconciled the subsidiary and control accounts at
   year-end.
3. Aged accounts—none were overdue.
4. Examined detail sales and collection transactions for
   February, July, and November.
5. Received positive confirmations of year-end balances.

Required:
Criticize the completeness or incompleteness of the above
program, giving reasons for your recommendations concerning the addition or omission of any procedures.

(AICPA adapted)

DC 7 **Rent Revenue.** You were engaged to conduct an audit of
LO.6 the financial statements of Clayton Realty Corporation
for the year ending January 31. The examination of the
annual rent reconciliation is a vital portion of the audit.
The following rent reconciliation was prepared by the
controller of Clayton Realty Corporation and was
presented to you. You subjected it to various audit procedures:

CLAYTON REALTY CORPORATION
Rent Reconciliation
For the Year Ended January 31

Gross apartment rents (Schedule A)	$1,600,800*
Less vacancies (Schedule B)	20,000*
Net apartment rentals	1,580,300
Less unpaid rents (Schedule C)	7,800*
Total	1,572,500
Add prepaid rent collected (Schedule D)	500*
Total cash collected	$1,573,000

Schedules A, B, C, and D are available to you but have
not been illustrated. You have conducted an assessment
of the control risk and found it to be low. Cash receipts
from rental operations are deposited in a special bank
account.

Required:
What substantive audit procedures should you employ
during the audit in order to substantiate the validity of
each of the dollar amounts marked by an asterisk(*)?

(AICPA adapted)

DC 8 **Business Risk, Evidence Analysis, Sales Detail.**
LO.1 Rosella is the senior in charge of the current-year audit
LO.4 of Harrier Limited, a company that designs and manu-
LO.6 factures highly sophisticated machines used to make
precision plastic parts and instruments. The machines
have a high dollar value (ranging from $500,000 to
over $1,000,000) and there is a long lead time between
receiving a customer's order and specifications, designing the machine, building it, and testing it. Because
of these business factors, sales do not tend to follow a
regular pattern, but certain constraints exist that can be
used to analyze the reasonability of sales for audit purposes. Customer orders are tracked as the "backlog"
file, and sales can be expected to follow the backlog
after allowing for design, manufacturing, and testing
time. This takes between two and three months, on average. Another factor is the physical limitation of the
factory and equipment: there are 12 job stations where
machines can be built, so a maximum of 12 machines
can be in the work-in-process inventory at any one
time.

Harrier's shares are privately held by its founder and
president, and several outside investors, but it issued
bonds to the public several years ago and is subject to
debt covenants that require it to maintain a working capital ratio of 1.5 to 1.0 and a debt to equity ratio of 0.5 to
1.0 at each year-end. In addition, no dividends or management bonuses can be paid out unless the net income
before taxes is at least $1,000,000. The draft statements
for the current year meet all covenants and show a net
income before taxes of $1,300,000.

In reviewing the monthly sales for the current year,
Rosella notices several anomalies. First, 15 machines
were shipped in December, the last month of the current year, while in December of the prior year only six
were shipped. The average monthly shipment volume is
between five and six machines. Also, the average gross
profit on sales in prior years, and in most months, is approximately 40 percent. The gross profit on the December
sales is 75 percent. The annual sales were $66 million,
with $15 million of this occurring in December. The an-
nual gross profit is $33 million, with $11 million of this
occurring in December. While scrutinizing the cash records for the first month of the new year to look for un-
accrued liabilities, Rosella notices some large amounts
paid for travel expenses for employees and for shipments of "spare parts" to customers. Enquiries of the
employees reveals that they are engineers and techni-
cians who were required to spend two or three weeks in
various cities where the December machine sales were
shipped in order to "work out the bugs" and add some
parts to these machines.

Required:
a. What are the main business risks in Harrier Limited?
   What are the risks of financial statement misstatements that Rosella should be aware of?
b. What types of evidence collection procedures were
   used and what assertions do they provide evidence
   about?

c. Analyze the information Rosella obtained and offer reasonable explanations for the sales anomalies noted. What additional enquiries should Rosella make to form an opinion on the operating results reported in Harrier's draft financial statements? What is your conclusion on the draft sales and gross profits amounts, based on your analysis of the facts given?

d. Harrier's revenue recognition policy is to recognize revenue when the machines are shipped and title passes to customers. This point occurs when the machines are loaded on the truck at Harrier's factory. Given this policy, what adjustment (if any) would be required in Harrier's current financial statements given the conclusion you reached in part c) above?

DC 9 **Negative Confirmations.** The auditor of a stock broker-
LO.1 age company, Roller Securities Inc., sends out negative
LO.4 confirmations of account details for a sample of about 50
LO.6 percent of the stock brokerage's customers, selected at random. Historically, between 2 and 5 percent of the confirmations have been returned, and the majority of the discrepancies reported have been understatements. Investigation of the discrepancies rarely indicates an error on Roller Securities Inc.'s part. Usually they are explained by transactions that are in progress or pending over the year-end, by late payments on the customer's part, or other mistakes in the customer's own records.

Required:

a. Describe the inherent risks and the internal control risks that exist for customer accounts at Roller Securities Inc.

b. Discuss the advantages and disadvantages of using negative confirmations to provide audit evidence about the assertions in this case. Comment on the persuasiveness of the evidence the negative confirmations provide; do you think it can be sufficient to support the auditor's opinion?

DC 10 **Controls Debit Card Fraud.** Read the following
LO.1 article on debit card theft and answer the questions
and that follow.
LO.6

THE STING

The first sign of trouble was the kind of minor glitch that's all too easy to ignore: My wife tried to pay for a pair of shoes with her debit card while we were on vacation. It didn't work. She tried again. Still no go. She borrowed mine, and moved on.

A short time later, Marian tried her debit card again. A message popped up on the screen, informing her that the card had been cancelled. I went on-line at our bank account. There wasn't much in it, but that's typical for a Toronto family with two kids, a mortgage, and a renovation tab. Then I noticed something odd—the bank had withdrawn $720 from our account to cover an "empty envelope deposit."

I didn't remember depositing $720. And why was the bank taking the money away from us? We called Toronto-Dominion. The news wasn't good. Bank staff believed that our account had been invaded. After their security software noticed a series of suspicious transactions involving my wife's debit card, they had cancelled it and left us a message on our home number.

We began combing through our account, and quickly found a series of payments and withdrawals that clearly weren't ours. They came to more than $1,200. Toronto-Dominion representatives told us that we would be paid back. That was a relief, but it was creepy to realize that someone had been able to breach our defences with such apparent ease.

My wife and I had long been aware of how easy it is to defraud a credit card. Ours had been raided several times, once to the tune of nearly $20,000. But we had always thought our debit card, which requires a PIN, was a virtual Fort Knox. We were wrong.

Debit-card fraud, the newest form of bank robbery, is on the rise in Toronto, I discovered. The banks don't like to talk about it, but Industry Canada figures show that in big cities like Toronto, a hotbed of card fraud, about 6 percent of bank accounts are raided.

Norman Inkster, a former RCMP commissioner who now runs his own security firm, said the true extent of debit-card fraud is unknown, since many thefts are reported to the banks, but not to police.

"Let's just say there's a lot of it," Mr. Inkster said.

Detective Ken Reimer of the Toronto Police fraud squad can confirm that personally. Just three weeks ago, several hundred dollars was drained from his own account. "That just shows you how much of it there really is," he said. "It's ridiculous."

The Toronto-Dominion security representative we dealt with gave us a quick primer on how it happens. Somewhere in our travels, he told us, the electronic information on my wife's card had probably been "skimmed." It could have been done by a clerk at a corner store or a gas station, who swiped our card through a small electronic machine called a card reader. (If a clerk tells you he needs to swipe your card again because the first try didn't work out, he may be running it for the second time through a reader, which then allows a duplicate to be made.)

After that, all he needed was the PIN, which he could get by watching us key it in, or by replaying the store's security tape.

The Toronto Police fraud squad now devotes a large percentage of its energies to debit-card fraud, which is growing at an exceptional rate. In 2003, reported debit-card fraud was estimated at $40 million across Canada. By the next year, it had risen 50 percent, to $60 million. (Although there are no figures for 2005, everyone in the field says it has risen significantly.)

One of Detective Reimer and Det. Sgt. White's biggest busts was Project Bam, a cooperative effort with other police agencies that resulted in more than 50 arrests in 2003. It exposed a network of criminals who had raked in more than $10 million. Sgt. White was another member of the squad.

The criminals had used a series of techniques. In some cases, they attached card readers over the slots of bank machines. The card readers looked like part of the official machine, but fed the electronic data on the cards into a memory chip. To get the PINs, they installed tiny spy cameras next to the machines or above them, enclosed in plastic hoods that had been spray-painted to match the bank colours. Another common technique is known as the Lebanese Loop (named after a Lebanese crime syndicate that invented it). The fraudsters install a plastic slot with a loop of tape inside it on bank machines. When a customer puts in his cards, the tape catches it. Then a gang member comes to the aid of the customer as he tries to retrieve his card, and suggests that he punch in his PIN to get the card back. When the customer leaves, the gang member retrieves the card and uses it.

Detective Sergeant John White says most of their investigations begin with information provided by banks, which have sophisticated software that makes it relatively easy to spot fraudulent transactions by highlighting deviations from customers' typical patterns. "They have excellent security systems," Det. Sgt. White says.

Toronto-Dominion's system had certainly been more vigilant than my wife and I were, shutting off her card after spotting three or four oddities—including the fact that the card was being used in Toronto while we were in Halifax.

Bank data play a key role in investigations. By sorting and matching data, banks can find locations where a number of fraud victims shopped or made withdrawals—this is known as a "point of common purchase," and is the likely location of a card-skimmer. (Gas stations, I was told, were particularly notorious.) In most cases, unfortunately, the guilty party is long gone. One common modus operandi for debit-card fraudsters is for a gang member to get hired at a store under a false name, collect card data for a few weeks, then quit. The card information is then used to manufacture new cards and to milk bank accounts.

According to Det. Sgt. White, banks often know where your card was skimmed, but refuse to divulge the names of businesses because of the potential consequences. "They're afraid of what might happen when people find out that someone at their local store or gas station was the culprit," Det. Sgt. White says. "Some people would probably head over with a baseball bat."

Det. Reimer says a large number of electronic frauds are executed with extremely low-tech methods. Criminals dig through garbage to find credit-card statements or banking documents. PINs are gleaned by looking over people's shoulders. (In some cases, store employees fasten portable keypads to the counter so shoppers can't shelter them next to their chest.)

Det. Reimer says there are three cardinal rules in the fight against electronic theft: First, hide the keypad when you punch in your PIN. Second, check your bank and credit account on-line, as often as possible. (He now checks his every day.) Third, shred all financial documents.

"Don't just use a regular shredder," he says. "You need a crosscut shredder. There are guys out there who will tape it all back together."

My wife and I will be shopping for our crosscut shredder this weekend.

Required:

a. What business processes in what business entities were used to perpetrate the debit card frauds described in the article?

b. What control weaknesses existed in these businesses that allowed these frauds to occur? Describe the weaknesses in terms of control objectives and explain how the weaknesses were exploited by the fraudsters.

c. Design control activities (policies and procedures) that could be implemented in these businesses to prevent and/or detect these types of frauds. Explain in detail how the control activities would be implemented and applied effectively.

d. Discuss the costs and benefits of the control activities you designed in (c). Do you think the benefits of these controls would exceed the costs? Why or why not?

DC 11 Municipal Government, Employee Theft. This case is
LO.2 modelled on the Application Case and Analysis in the
LO.3 chapter.
LO.6

Case Description: In the audit of a municipal government, the auditors discovered that receivables for property taxes were overstated because the tax assessor stole some taxpayers' payments. J. R. Shelstad had been the tax assessor–collector for 15 years in the Ridge Municipal District, a large metropolitan area. Known as a "good personnel manager" Shelstad pocketed 100–150 counter payments each year, in amounts of $500–$2,500, stealing about $200,000 a year for a total of approximately $2.5 million. The district had assessed about $800–$900 million per year in property tax revenues, so the annual theft was less than 1 percent. Nevertheless, the taxpayers got mad.

In Shelstad's assessor–collector office, staff processed tax notices on a computer system and generated 450,000 tax notices each October. An office copy was printed and used to check "paid" when payments were received. Payments were processed by computer and a master file of accounts receivable records (tax assessments, payments) was kept on the computer hard drive.

Shelstad was a good personnel manager, who often took over the front desk at lunchtime so the teller staff could enjoy lunch together. During these times, Shelstad took tax payments over the counter, gave the taxpayers a counter receipt, and pocketed some of the money, which was never entered in the computer system.

Shelstad eventually resigned when the District's assessor–collector office was eliminated upon the creation of a new region-wide tax agency.

Audit Trail: The computer records showed balances due from many taxpayers who had actually paid their taxes. The book of printed notices was not marked "paid" for many taxpayers who had received counter receipts. These records and the daily cash receipts reports (cash receipts journal) were available at the time the independent auditors performed the most recent annual audit in April. To keep his fraud going and prevent auditors from detecting it, Shelstad persuaded the auditors that the true "receivables" were the delinquencies turned over to the region's legal counsel. Their confirmation sample and other work were based on this population. Thus, confirmations were not sent to fictitious balances that Shelstad knew had been paid. When Shelstad resigned in August, a power surge permanently destroyed the hard drive where the receivables file was stored, and the cash receipts journals could not be found. When the new regional agency managers took over the tax assessment, they noticed that the total of delinquent taxes disclosed in the audited financial statements was much larger than the total turned over to the region's legal counsel for collection and foreclosure.

AUDIT APPROACH ANALYSIS

Audit objective: The auditors' objective is to obtain evidence determining if the receivables for taxes (delinquent taxes) represent genuine claims collectible from the taxpayers.

Controls relevant in the municipal tax revenue process: The municipal system for establishing the initial amounts of taxes receivable was fine. Professional staff appraisers and the independent appraisal review board established the tax base for each property, and the municipal council set the price (tax rate). The computer system authorization for billing was validated on these two inputs.

The cash receipts system was well designed, calling for preparation of a daily cash receipts report (cash receipts journal that served as a source input for computer entry). This report was always reviewed by the "boss," Shelstad.

Unfortunately, Shelstad had the opportunity and power to override the controls and become both cash handler and supervisor. He made the decisions about sending delinquent taxes to the region's legal counsel for collection, but the ones he knew to have been paid but stolen were withheld.

Required:

Describe in detail the audit procedures you would perform in this case. Consider tests of control, and substantive tests such as dual-purpose tests of transactions and/or tests of details of balance. In particular, identify the information that could have been obtained from confirmations directed to the real population of delinquent accounts receivable (i.e., including the ones that had been stolen by Shelstad). Which tests do you consider likely to detect Shelstad's theft? Why?

APPENDIX 11A

INTERNAL CONTROL QUESTIONNAIRES

··

EXHIBIT 11A-1 INTERNAL CONTROL QUESTIONNAIRES
REVENUES, RECEIVABLES, AND RECEIPTS PROCESS

OVERALL COMPANY-LEVEL CONTROL AND CONTROL ACTIVITIES ASSESSMENT
(Refer to responses recorded for questions in Exhibit PIII-3.)

Are company-level and general control activities adequate as they apply to the revenues, receivables, and receipts components of the information system?

- Consider the impact of any weakness in company-level and general control activities on planned audit approach and procedures.
- Assess the potential for weaknesses to result in a material misstatement of the financial information generated from this accounting cycle. If a significant risk of misstatement is assessed, perform procedures to determine extent of any misstatement.

Consider adequacy of the following general controls in place in the revenue, receivables, and receipts process to:
  — prevent unauthorized access or changes to programs and data
  — ensure the security and privacy of data
  — control and maintain key systems
  — protect assets susceptible to misappropriation
  — ensure completeness, accuracy, and authorization of data and processing
  — ensure that adequate management trails exist

CASH RECEIPTS PROCESSING APPLICATION
Environment and general control relevant to this application:
1. Are receipts deposited daily, intact, and without delay?
2. Does someone other than the cashier or accounts receivable bookkeeper take the deposits to the bank?
3. Are the duties of the cashier entirely separate from recordkeeping for notes and accounts receivable? From general ledger recordkeeping? Is the cashier denied access to receivables records or monthly statements?
4. Are employees with access to cash covered by fidelity insurance against embezzlement losses (also called "fidelity bonding" of employees)?

Assertion-Based Control Evaluation:
Validity objective:
5. Is a bank reconciliation performed monthly by someone who does not have cash custody or recordkeeping responsibility?
6. Are the cash receipts journal entries compared with the remittance lists and deposit slips regularly?

Completeness objective:
7. Does the person who opens the mail make a list of cash received (a remittance list)?
8. Are currency receipts controlled by mechanical devices? Are machine totals checked by the internal auditor?
9. Are prenumbered sales invoice or receipts books used? Is the numerical sequence checked for missing documents?

Authorization objective:
10. Does a responsible person approve discounts taken by customers with payments on account?

Accuracy objective:
11. Is a duplicate deposit slip retained by the internal auditor or someone other than the employee making up the deposit?
12. Is the remittance list compared with the deposit by someone other than the cashier?

Classification objective:
13. Does the accounting manual contain instructions for classifying cash receipts credits?

Accounting objective:
14. Does someone reconcile the accounts receivable subsidiary to the control account regularly (to determine whether all entries were made to customers' accounts)?

Proper period objective:
15. Does the accounting manual contain instructions for dating cash receipts entries the same day as the date of receipt?

SALES APPLICATION
Environment and general control evaluation relevant to this application:
1. Is the credit department independent of the marketing department?
2. Are nonroutine sales controlled by the same procedures described below? For example, sales to employees, COD sales, disposals of property, cash sales, and scrap sales.

Continued

EXHIBIT 11A–1 CONTINUED

Assertion-Based Control Evaluation:

Validity objective:

3. Is access to sales invoice blanks restricted?
4. Are prenumbered bills of lading or other shipping documents prepared or completed in the shipping department?

Completeness objective:

5. Are sales invoice blanks prenumbered?
6. Is the sequence checked for missing invoices?
7. Is the shipping document numerical sequence checked for missing bills of lading numbers?

Authorization objective:

8. Are all credit sales approved by the credit department prior to shipment?
9. Are sales prices and terms based on approved standards?
10. Are returned sales credits and other credits supported by documentation as to receipt, condition, and quantity and approved by a responsible officer?

Accuracy objective:

11. Are shipped quantities compared with invoice quantities?
12. Are sales invoices checked for error in quantities, prices, extensions and footing, freight allowances, and against customers' orders?
13. Is there an overall check on arithmetic accuracy of period sales data by a statistical or product-line analysis?
14. Are periodic sales data reported directly to general ledger accounting independent of accounts receivable accounting?

Classification objective:

15. Does the accounting manual contain instructions for classifying sales?

Accounting objective:

16. Are summary journal entries approved before posting?

Proper period objective:

17. Does the accounting manual contain instructions to date sales invoices on the shipment date?

ACCOUNTS RECEIVABLE APPLICATION

Environment and general controls relevant to this application:

1. Are customers' subsidiary records maintained by someone who has no access to cash?
2. Is the cashier denied access to the customers' records and monthly statements?
3. Are delinquent accounts listed periodically for review by someone other than the credit manager?
4. Are written-off accounts kept in a memo ledger or credit report file for periodic access?
5. Is the credit department separated from the sales department?
6. Are notes receivable in the custody of someone other than the cashier or accounts receivable recordkeeper?
7. Is custody of negotiable collateral in the hands of someone not responsible for handling cash or keeping records?

Assertion-Based Control Evaluation:

Validity objective:

8. Are customers' statements mailed monthly by the accounts receivable department?
9. Are direct confirmations of accounts and notes obtained periodically by the internal auditor?
10. Are differences reported by customers routed to someone outside the accounts receivable department for investigation?
11. Are returned goods checked against receiving reports?

Completeness objective:

(Refer to completeness questions in the sales and cash receipts questionnaires.)

12. Are credit memo documents prenumbered and the sequence checked for missing documents?

Authorization objective:

13. Is customer credit approved before orders are shipped?
14. Are write-offs, returns, and discounts allowed after discount date subject to approval by a responsible officer?
15. Are large loans or advances to related parties approved by the directors?

Accuracy objective:

16. Do the internal auditors confirm customer accounts periodically to determine accuracy?

Classification objective:

17. Are receivables from officers, directors, and affiliates identified separately in the accounts receivable records?

Accounting objective:

18. Does someone reconcile the accounts receivable subsidiary to the control account regularly?

Proper period objective:

(Refer to proper period objective questions in the sales and cash receipts questionnaires.)

EXHIBIT 11A-2 EXAMPLES OF SALES AND ACCOUNTS RECEIVABLE CONTROLS RELATING TO EXHIBIT 11-1

- Each terminal performs only designated functions. For example, the terminal at the shipping dock cannot be used to enter initial sales information or to access the payroll database.
- An identification number and password (issued on an individual person basis) are required to enter the sales and each command that a subsequent action has been completed. Unauthorized entry attempts are logged and immediately investigated. Further, certain passwords have "ready only" (cannot change any data) authorization. For example, the credit manager can determine the outstanding balance of any account or view online "reports" summarizing overdue accounts receivable, but cannot enter credit memos to change the balances.
- All input information is immediately logged to provide restart processing should any terminal become inoperative during the processing.
- A transaction code calls up on the terminals a full screen "form" that appears to the operator in the same format as the original paper documents. Each clerk must enter the information correctly or the computer will not accept the transaction. This is called **online input validation** and utilizes validation checks, such as missing data, check digit, and limit tests.
- All documents prepared by the computer are numbered, and the number is stored as part of the sales record in the accounts receivable database.
- A daily search of the pending order database is made by the computer, and sales orders outstanding more than seven days are listed on the terminal in marketing management.

APPENDIX 11B

SYSTEMS DOCUMENTATION EXAMPLES FOR THE REVENUES, RECEIVABLES, RECEIPTS PROCESS

This appendix provides examples of systems documentation prepared using flowchart-type diagrams. Exhibit 11B–1 diagrams an IT-based system for processing customer sales orders and accounts receivable. Exhibit 11B–2 show a manual system of processing cash receipts, and Exhibit 11B–3 shows the same sytems using a tabular documentation format. The narrative descriptions of these systems in the chapter correspond to the activities and records shown in these diagrams.

EXHIBIT 11B–1 SALES AND ACCOUNTS RECEIVABLE PROCESSING EXAMPLE: IT-BASED SYSTEM

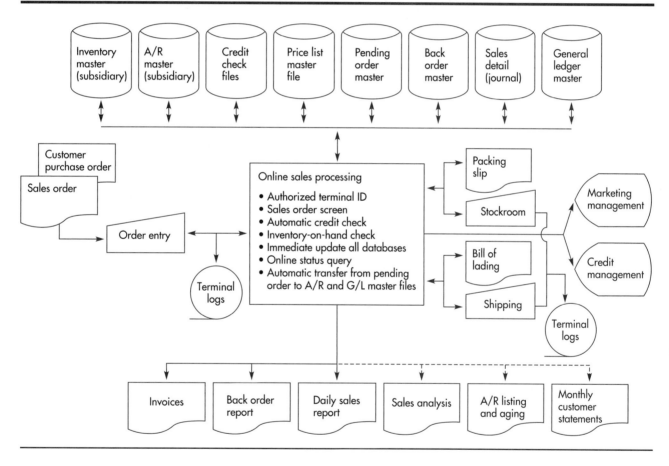

EXHIBIT 11B-2   CASH RECEIPTS PROCESSING EXAMPLE: MANUAL SYSTEM

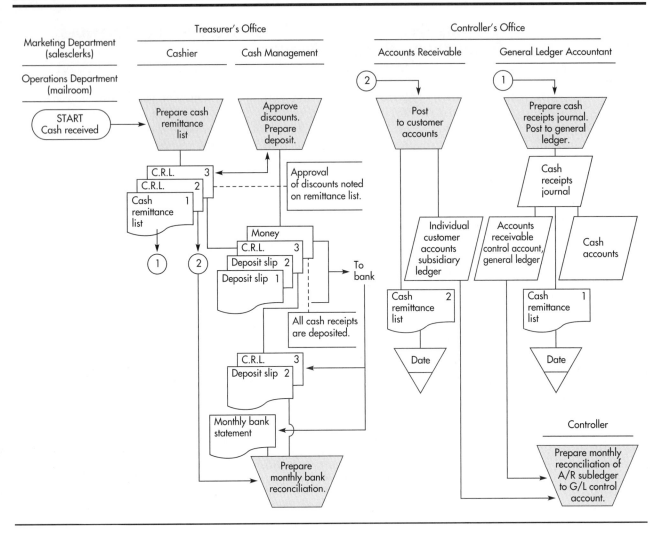

Another systems documentation technique that can be used is an input/process/output table. As an example, the same cash receipts processing system shown in the flowchart in Exhibit 11B–2 is documented in an input/process/output table below.

Input	Activity	Performed by	Frequency	Output
Customer payment collected	List Cash receipts by customer and invoice #	Cashier	Daily	Cash remittance list
Cash remittance list	Approve any discounts taken	Cash Management	Daily	Approved Cash remittance list [3 copies]
Approved Cash remittance list [1]	Prepare deposit slip for bank	Cashier	Daily	Deposit slip
Bank deposit slip	Take cash and deposit slip to bank	Cash management	Daily	Bank-stamped deposit slip
Approved Cash remittance list [2]	Post to customer accounts	Account receivable clerk	Daily	Accounts receivable subledger update
Approved Cash remittance list [3]	Post to Cash receipts journal	General ledger accountant	Daily	Accounts receivable subledger update
Accounts receivable subledger update	Post total cash receipts to General ledger A/R control account	General ledger accountant	Daily	General ledger update
Accounts receivable reconciliation	Agree total A/R subledger balance to balance of A/R control account in G/L	Controller	Monthly	Reconciliation summary with documented support for all reconciling items
Bank reconciliation	Reconcile Cash balance per G/L to balance per bank statement	Cash management	Monthly	Reconciliation summary with documented support for all reconciling items

APPENDIX 11C

SUBSTANTIVE AUDIT PROGRAMS

. . . .

EXHIBIT 11C-1   AUDIT PROGRAM FOR CASH: SELECTED SUBSTANTIVE PROCEDURES

1. Obtain confirmations from banks (standard bank confirmation).
2. Obtain reconciliations of all bank accounts.
   a. Trace the bank balance on the reconciliation to the bank confirmation.
   b. Trace the reconciled book balance to the general ledger.
   c. Recalculate the arithmetic on client-prepared bank reconciliations.
3. Review the bank confirmation for loans and collateral.
4. Ask the auditee to request cutoff bank statements to be mailed directly to the audit firm.
   a. Trace deposits in transit on the reconciliation to bank deposits early in the next period.
   b. Trace outstanding cheques on the reconciliation to cheques cleared in the next period.
5. Prepare a schedule of interbank transfers for a period of 10 business days before and after the year-end date. Document dates of book entry transfer and correspondence with bank entries and reconciliation items, if any.
6. Count cash funds in the presence of an auditee representative. Obtain a receipt for return of the funds.
7. Obtain written management representations concerning compensating balance agreements.

EXHIBIT 11C-2   AUDIT PROGRAM FOR ACCOUNTS AND NOTES RECEIVABLE AND REVENUE: SELECTED SUBSTANTIVE PROCEDURES.

A. Accounts and Notes Receivable
   1. Obtain an aged trial balance of individual customer accounts. Recalculate the total and trace to the general ledger control account.
   2. Send confirmations to all accounts over $X. Select a random sample of all remaining accounts for confirmation.
      a. Investigate differences reported by customers.
      b. Perform alternative procedures on accounts that do not respond to positive confirmation requests.
         (1) Vouch cash receipts after the confirmation date for subsequent payment.
         (2) Vouch sales invoices and shipping documents.
   3. Evaluate the adequacy of the allowance for doubtful accounts.
      a. Vouch a sample of *current* amounts in the aged trial balance to sales invoices to determine whether amounts aged current should be aged past due.
      b. Compare the current-year write-off experience to the prior-year allowance.
      c. Vouch cash receipts after the balance sheet date for collections on past-due accounts.
      d. Obtain financial statements or credit reports and discuss with the credit manager collections on large past-due accounts.
      e. Calculate an allowance estimate using prior relations of write-offs and sales, taking under consideration current economic events.
   4. Review the bank confirmations, loan agreements, and minutes of the board for indications of pledged, discounted, or assigned receivables.
   5. Inspect or obtain confirmation of notes receivable.
   6. Recalculate interest income and trace to the income account.
   7. Obtain written management representations regarding pledge, discount, or assignment of receivables, and about receivables from officers, directors, affiliates, or other related parties.
   8. Review the adequacy of control over recording of all charges to customers (completeness), audited in the sales transaction test of controls audit program.
B. Revenue
   1. Select a sample of recorded sales invoices and vouch to underlying shipping documents.
   2. Select a sample of shipping documents and trace to sales invoices.
   3. Obtain production records of physical quantities sold and calculate an estimate of sales dollars based on average sale prices.
   4. Compare revenue dollars and physical quantities with prior-year data and industry economic statistics.
   5. Select a sample of sales invoices prepared a few days before and after the balance sheet date and vouch to supporting documents for evidence of proper cutoff.

CHAPTER 12

Purchases, Payables, and Payments Process

This chapter summarizes the accounting cycle for business processes related to the acquisition of goods (inventory) and services (expenses), the acquisition of property, plant, and equipment (fixed assets), and the expenditure of cash (cash disbursements) to pay for purchases and acquisitions. The chapter provides special notes on inventory observation and accounts payable completeness. An application case and analysis is given at the end of the chapter to demonstrate the performance of audit procedures in situations where errors or frauds might be discovered in the purchases, payables, and payments process.

UNDERSTANDING THE PURCHASES, PAYABLES, AND PAYMENTS PROCESS

LEARNING OBJECTIVE

1 Describe the purchases, payables, and payments process, including typical risks, transactions, source documents, controls, and account balances.

Purchases of goods and services are a major part of cash outflow in most organizations. For this reason they will be subject to a fairly high level of management planning and control. Purchases may result in the organization's acquiring assets; for example, inventory, fixed assets (such as property, plant, and equipment), or intangibles (copyrights and customer lists). Some purchases of goods, such as supplies, are expensed, and purchases of services are mainly expensed. Costs of purchasing goods and services may be deferred in some cases, if they relate to producing inventory (see Chapter 13) or internally developed assets such as buildings and new products (deferred development costs).

Risk Assessment for Purchases, Payables, and Payments

To assess risks in the purchasing-related processes, the auditor focuses on purchasing and cash payment transaction streams and accounts payable balances. Important disclosures relating to purchases include asset capitalization policies, inventory cost flow assumption policies, contractual commitments, and related party transactions.

The auditors' understanding of the auditee's business and environment will point to specific business risks and the related financial misstatement risks that can arise from the auditee's purchasing, payables, and payments activities. Some examples of the risks at the assertion level are as follows.

A. Ownership risks:

Purchased assets and services may include improper capitalization of costs to increase reported profits (e.g., WorldCom).

Managers may be able to transfer funds between related entities under their control (e.g., Enron, Hollinger).

In an owner-managed business, some personal expenses of the owner may be run through the company to avoid income taxes.

Frauds relating to purchases and payables can arise from collusion between suppliers and employees; for example, via kickback schemes.

B. Completeness risks relating mainly to the possibility of unrecorded liabilities:

Goods or services received but not yet paid for at year-end may not have been accrued.

Provisions for future costs, such as warranties, may be missing or understated.

Improper cutoff can also lead to incomplete recording of liabilities.

C. Valuation risks can exist when purchases are denominated in foreign currency, and if inventory values decline because of market conditions, obsolescence, or improper storage.

D. Disclosure risks include inadequate capitalization policy notes and failure to disclose contractual commitments to make future purchases at fixed prices.

This chapter outlines simple examples of processes for purchasing services, inventory, and fixed assets, as well as the related accounting cycle and control activities. The main risk in these processes is incomplete recognition of expenses and liabilities. Control tests in the purchasing processes and physical inspection of inventory and fixed assets address existence, completeness, and valuation assertions, and some substantive evidence for completeness is obtained from examining payments subsequent to year-end. It may be necessary to further inspect documents and use confirmations for more evidence in assessing the ownership assertion.

Purchases, Payables, and Payments Process: Typical Activities

Exhibit 12–1 shows the activities and transactions involved in the purchases, payables, and payments process, and it also lists the accounts and records typically involved. The basic activities are (1) purchasing goods and services and (2) paying the bills. The exhibit tracks the elements of the control structure described in the following sections. The purchasing process involves meeting various departments' identification requirements for goods and services, issuing purchase orders to suppliers, receiving the goods and services, and taking custody of goods received. Accounts payable to suppliers are recorded once the goods have been received or the services have been used, usually at the time the supplier invoice is received. The payables are recorded in a subledger by supplier name and in a control account in the general ledger. Payments involve a cash disbursement to the supplier, which relieves the liability in both the supplier subledger and the general ledger control account. Frequently, suppliers provide monthly statements of the amount owing, and these are reconciled to the subledger balance to ensure the correct amounts are being paid.

Authorization

Purchases are requested (requisitioned) by people who know the needs of the organization. A purchasing department finds the best prices and quality and issues a purchase order. Obtaining competitive bids is a good practice because, by involving several suppliers, it

EXHIBIT 12–1 PURCHASES, PAYABLES, AND PAYMENTS PROCESS EXAMPLE

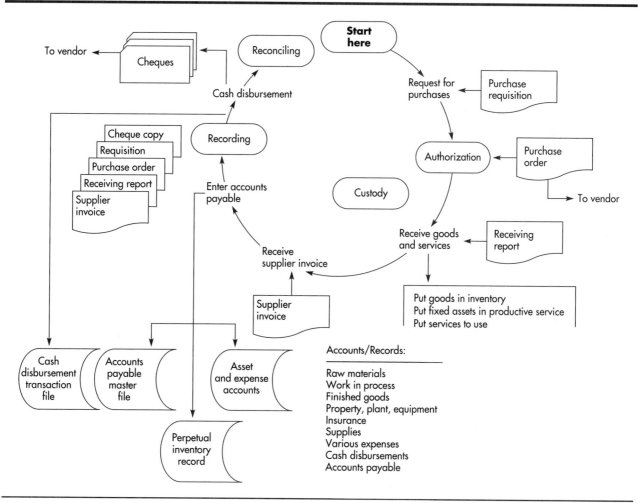

tends to produce the best prices. It also reduces the risk of frauds involving collusion between suppliers and purchasing department employees, such as inflating purchases to increase sales commissions to the supplier, who then kicks back some of these commissions to the purchasing employee.

Cash disbursements are authorized by an accounts payable department matching purchase orders, supplier invoices, and internal receiving reports to show a valid obligation to pay. Accounts payable obligations usually are recorded when the purchaser receives the goods or services ordered. Cheques are signed by an authorized person. Companies may have a policy requiring two signatures on cheques over a certain amount. Also, a company may have electronic funds transfer (ETF) arrangements with some suppliers that allow it to transfer money directly from its own bank account to the supplier's account. Invoices should be marked "paid" or otherwise stamped to show that they have been processed completely, so that they cannot be paid a second time.

Custody

The receiving department is responsible for inspecting received goods for quantity and quality (producing a receiving report) and passing them on (i.e., to inventory warehousing, fixed asset installation). Services are accepted by the people responsible for them. Cash custody belongs to those authorized to sign cheques or transfer funds.

Blank documents, such as purchase orders, receiving reports, and blank cheques, or access to a computerized purchase authorization program, are also custody issues. If unauthorized persons can access these or has authorization involving them, they can forge a purchase order to a fictitious supplier, forge a receiving report, send a false invoice from a fictitious supplier, and then prepare a company cheque in payment, which is embezzlement.

Recording

When the purchase order, supplier's invoice, and receiving report are matched, accountants enter the accounts payable with (1) debits to proper inventory, fixed asset, and expense accounts and (2) a credit to accounts payable. When cheques are prepared, entries are made to debit accounts payable and credit cash.

Periodic Reconciliation

A periodic reconciliation of existing assets to recorded amounts is not shown in Exhibit 12–1, but it occurs when (1) a physical inventory compares inventory on hand with perpetual inventory records, (2) a bank account reconciliation compares book cash balances with bank cash balances, (3) an inspection compares fixed assets with detail fixed asset records, (4) preparation of an accounts payable trial balance compares the detail of accounts payable with the control account in the general ledger, and (5) accounts payable personnel compare suppliers' reports and monthly statements to recorded liabilities.

TOO MUCH TROUBLE

A trucking company self-insured claims of damage to goods in transit, processed claims reports, and paid customers from its own bank accounts. Several persons were authorized to sign cheques. One person thought it "too much trouble" to stamp the claims reports as PAID and said, "That's textbook stuff anyway." Numerous claims were recycled to other cheque signers, and $80,000 in claims were paid in duplicate before the problem was discovered.

Audit Evidence in Management Reports

Computer processing of purchasing and payment transactions makes it possible for management to generate reports for control purposes, but they also can provide important audit evidence. Exhibit 12–2 shows how they might do this, and it is discussed in the following section.

EXHIBIT   12–2   MANAGEMENT CONTROL REPORTS USEFUL FOR AUDIT EVIDENCE

Management Report	Control Purpose	Potential Audit Evidence
Open purchase orders	Completeness of accounts payable	Purchase commitments, valuation of inventory
Unmatched receiving reports	Validity of purchases recorded	Unaccrued liabilities for purchases
Unmatched supplier invoices	Validity of purchases recorded	Unaccrued liabilities for purchases
Accounts payable trial balance	Proper accounting Cash flow management	Existence and completeness of payables
Purchases journal	Completeness and validity of inventory, purchases, expenses	Analysis of inventory changes and expense reasonability
Inventory reports	Completeness, validity, and valuation of inventory	Analysis of inventory balances, valuation, selection of samples for test counts, and valuation tests
Fixed asset reports	Completeness, validity, and valuation of fixed assets, accumulated depreciation and depreciation expense	Analysis of changes in fixed asset balances Selection of sample additions for vouching Recalculation of depreciation expense
Cash disbursements report	Expenditure reviews by management for validity, authorization	Selection of sample for testing existence, authorization, and proper cutoff of payments

Open Purchase Orders

Held in an open purchase order file, purchase orders are open from the time they are issued until the goods and services are received. Generally, no liability exists until the transactions are complete. However, auditors may find evidence of losses on purchase commitments in this file if market prices have fallen below the purchase order price.

Unmatched Receiving Reports

Normally, liabilities should be recorded on the date the goods and services are received and accepted. Sometimes, however, supplier invoices arrive later and the accounts payable department holds the receiving reports, unmatched with invoices, until the information for recording an accounting entry arrives. Auditors can inspect the unmatched receiving report file to see if the company has material unrecorded liabilities on the financial statement date.

Unmatched Supplier Invoices

Supplier invoices may arrive in the accounts payable department before the receiving processing is complete. These invoices are held, unmatched with receiving reports, until there is information that the goods and services were actually received and accepted. Systems failures and human coding errors can cause unmatched invoices and receiving reports to sit around unnoticed when all the information is actually at hand. Auditors can inspect the unmatched invoice file and compare it with the unmatched receiving report file to determine whether liabilities are unrecorded.

Accounts Payable Trial Balance

This trial balance is a list of payable amounts by supplier, and the sum should agree with the accounts payable control account in the general ledger. (Some organizations record by individual invoices instead of by supplier names, so the trial balance is a list of unpaid invoices, which still should agree with the control account balance.) The ideal trial balance for audit purposes contains the names of all of an organization's suppliers, even if their balances are zero. The audit "search for unrecorded liabilities" should include the small and zero balances, especially for regular suppliers, because these may be the places where liabilities are unrecorded. Major suppliers will send regular statements of amounts outstanding. These statement amounts can be reconciled with accounts payable, and the details can be audited to detect any unrecorded liabilities. All paid and unpaid accounts payable should have supporting documents—purchase requisition (if any), purchase order (if any), supplier invoice, receiving report (if any), and cheque copy (or notation of cheque number, date, and amount), as shown in Exhibit 12–1. Similar records should be available for audit verification in a computerized accounts payable system.

CLASSIFY THE DEBITS CORRECTLY

Invoices for expensive repairs were not clearly identified, so the accounts payable accountants entered the $125,000 as capitalized fixed assets instead of as repairs and maintenance expense. This initially understated expenses and overstated pre-tax income by $125,000 for one year, although the incorrectly capitalized expenses were written off as depreciation over the 10-year life of the assets. This spread the misstatement over many years, lowering its materiality.

THINKING AHEAD

Lone Moon Brewing purchased bulk aluminum sheets and manufactured its own cans. To ensure a source of raw materials, the company entered into a long-term purchase agreement for 3 million kilos of aluminum sheeting at 80 cents per kilo. At the end of this year, 1.5 million kilos have been purchased and used, but the market price had fallen to 64 cents per kilo. Lone Moon was on the hook for a $240,000 (1.5 million kilos × 16 cents) purchase commitment in excess of current market prices, so the auditors required this commitment to be disclosed in the company's financial statements.

Purchases Journal

This listing of all purchases may exist only in a computer transaction file, not in print. In either event, it provides raw material for (1) computer-audit analysis of purchasing patterns, which may exhibit characteristics of errors and irregularities, and (2) a sample selection of transactions for control tests of supporting documents for validity, authorization, accuracy, classification, accounting, and proper period recording. (A company may have already performed analyses of purchases, and auditors can use these for analytical evidence, provided the analyses are produced under reliable control conditions.)

Inventory Reports (Trial Balance)

A wide variety of inventory reports are useful for analytical evidence. An item-by-item trial balance should agree with a control account (if balances are kept in dollars). Auditors can use this trial balance (1) to scan for unusual conditions (e.g., negative item balances, overstocking, and valuation problems) and (2) as a population for sample selection for a physical inventory observation (audit procedures to obtain evidence about the existence of inventory included in the account). The scanning and sample selection may be computer-audit applications on a computerized inventory report file.

Fixed Asset Reports

These reports are similar to inventory reports because they show the details of fixed assets in control accounts, and they can be used for scanning and sample selection as well. A sample selection of fixed assets acquired can be verified against costs shown on purchase invoices. The information for depreciation calculation (cost, useful life, method, and salvage) can be audited by sampling, or a computer application could perform recalculations.

Cash Disbursements Report

The cash disbursements process produces a cash disbursements journal—sometimes printed, sometimes maintained only as a computer file. This journal should contain the date, cheque number, payee, amount, account debited for each cash disbursement, and a cross-reference to the supplier invoice number or other reason for the payment. A sample can be selected from the population of transactions in the cash disbursements journal for control tests of supporting documents for validity, authorization, accuracy, classification, accounting, and proper period recording of payments.

THE SIGN OF THE CREDIT BALANCE

Auto Parts & Repair Inc. kept perpetual inventory records and fixed assets records on a computer system. Because of the size of the files (8,000 parts in various locations and 1,500 asset records), the company never printed reports for visual inspection. Auditors ran a computer audit "sign test" on inventory balances and fixed asset net book balances. The test called for a printed report for all balances less than zero. The auditors discovered 320 negative inventory balances caused by failure to record purchases and 125 negative net asset balances caused by depreciating assets more than their cost.

R E V I E W
C H E C K P O I N T S

1 What is a purchase requisition?

2 How can the situation of duplicate payments made from the same supporting documents be prevented?

3 Where could an auditor look to find evidence of losses on purchase commitments? on unrecorded liabilities to suppliers?

4 List the main supporting source documents used in a purchases, payables, and payments process.

5 List the management reports that can be used for audit evidence. What information in them can be useful to auditors?

CONTROL RISK ASSESSMENT

LEARNING OBJECTIVE

2 Outline control tests for auditing control over the purchase of inventory, services, and fixed assets and for the disbursement of cash.

Control risk assessment is important because it governs the nature, timing, and extent of substantive audit procedures that will be applied in the audit of account balances in the purchases, payables, and payments process. These account balances include the following:

- inventory
- fixed and intangible assets
- depreciation expense
- accumulated depreciation

- accounts and notes payable
- cash
- expenses—administrative (supplies, legal fees, audit fees, taxes, insurance), selling (commissions, travel, delivery, advertising), manufacturing (maintenance, freight in, utilities), etc.

General Control Considerations

Control procedures for proper segregation of responsibilities should be in place and operating. Exhibit 12–1 shows proper segregation to mean that people with authorization (requisitioning, purchase ordering) responsibilities do not have custody, recording, or reconciliation duties. Custody of inventory, fixed assets, and cash belongs with people who do not directly authorize purchases or cash payments, record the accounting entries, or reconcile physical assets and cash to recorded amounts. Recording (accounting) is done by people who do not authorize transactions, have custody of assets, or perform reconciliations. Periodic reconciliations are performed by people who do not have authorization, custody, or recording duties related to the same assets. Combinations of two or more of these responsibilities in a single person, office, or computer system may open the door for errors or frauds.

PURCHASE ORDER SPLITTING

A school board's purchasing agent had authority to buy supplies in amounts of $1,000 or less without getting competitive bids for the best price. The purchasing agent wanted to favour local businesses owned by her friends instead of large chain stores, so she broke up the year's $350,000 supplies order into numerous $900–$950 orders, paying about 12 percent more to local stores than would have been paid to the large chains. In return, the purchasing agent received very generous discounts and gifts from these local businesses. The auditors discovered this practice by scanning the purchases journal and investigating the frequent small amounts that were being paid to the same payee. They informed management that a regular supervisor review of the purchases journal may improve control over authorization of purchases.

In addition, internal controls should provide for detail-checking control procedures. For example, (1) all purchase requisitions and purchase orders are approved by authorized personnel; (2) purchase order master files changes are made by authorized persons only; (3) physical security for inventory warehouses and fixed asset locations (storerooms, fences, locks, etc.) is adequate; (4) accounts payable are recorded only when all the supporting documentation is in order—purchases and payables as of the date goods and services were received, and cash disbursements on the date the cheques leave the organization's control; and (5) supplier invoices are compared with purchase orders and receiving reports to verify the price and that the quantity billed is the same as the quantity received. The next box offers an example of the consequences of weak management controls—in this case, when authorization controls for contract payments are inadequate in a government department.

Information gathering about the control structure often begins with an internal control questionnaire. Examples of questionnaires are provided in Appendix 12A. These questionnaires can be studied for details of desirable control policies and procedures as they are organized under headings that identify the important control objectives: environment, validity, completeness, authorization, accuracy, classification, accounting, and proper period recording.

WHERE TAX DOLLARS GO

The Auditor General of Canada had some harsh words for the federal government in an 83-page report released just days before an expected election call. The report criticized the way the government's departments and services spend money and was particularly critical of the Human Resources Department (HRDC), pointing out its sloppy paperwork, careless spending, and vague job creation figures.

HRDC was at the centre of a scandal starting in January 2000 when an internal audit found massive mismanagement in its $1-billion jobs grants program. The AG's report confirms that finding and condemns poor accountability between the department and its programs, and within HRDC itself. The audit cites breaches of authority, improper payment practices, and limited monitoring of recipient projects' finances and activities. It also found an inadequate process to decide which projects should get money, including examples of some that were not eligible for funding but received it anyway.

The jobs program administered by the HRDC was designed to create long-term jobs in areas of high unemployment by giving money to companies to hire workers. But HRDC counted some jobs twice, making it impossible to determine how successful a project really was.

Auditor General Sheila Fraser said in a 2002 speech:

"Our audit of HRDC grants and contributions showed what happens when there is no longer a balance between the insistence on performance and controls, and more emphasis is placed on one of these components.

"Management's priorities were to implement strategic initiatives and improve service. We found that it had not placed enough emphasis on maintaining vital control while it reduced red tape and improved service."

This audit also pointed out the importance of internal audit as a fundamental tool for management. Internal audits at HRDC had previously identified many of the problems, but management took little action in response.

Here are some of the major findings reported by the Auditor General in recent years.

In 2004: "Our recent investigation of the contracts awarded to Groupaction (in the federal government's advertising and sponsorship program) is another high-profile example of failure to comply with the basic rules of contract management. As a result, it is impossible to say whether taxpayers received value for the money spent."

Senior government officials running the federal government's advertising and sponsorship contracts in Quebec, as well as five Crown corporations—the RCMP, Via Rail, Canada Post, the Business Development Bank of Canada, and the Old Port of Montreal—wasted money and showed disregard for rules, mishandling millions of dollars since 1995.

More than $100 million was paid to various communications agencies in the form of fees and commissions. In most cases the agencies did little more than hand over the cheques. The sponsorship program was designed to generate commissions for private companies, while hiding the source of the funding, rather than providing any benefit for Canadians, Fraser said.

"I think this is such a blatant misuse of public funds that it is shocking. I am actually appalled by what we've found. I am deeply disturbed that such practices were allowed to happen in the first place. I don't think anybody can take this lightly."

In 2006: A sampling of seven of the 88 information technology projects launched in the federal government since 2003, worth $7.1 billion, found rampant mismanagement. Many were far over budget and long past deadline. The former Liberal government misinformed Parliament about millions of dollars in expenses incurred by the gun registry.

Sources: CBC News, Auditor General delivers stinging rebuke to Ottawa, October 22, 2000, www.cbc.ca/stories/2000/10/17/auditor001014 (accessed October 2005); Notes for an address by Sheila Fraser, FCA, Auditor General of Canada, to Canada Mortgage and Housing, June 11, 2002, Ottawa, Ontario, wwww.oag-bvg.gc.ca/domino/other.nsf/html/02sp06_e.html (accessed October 2005); CBC News, Auditor General's Report 2004, February 11, 2004, www.cbc.ca/news/background/auditorgeneral/report2004.html (accessed October 2005); www.cbc.ca/news/background/auditorgeneral (accessed July 2009)..

Control Tests

An organization should have detail control procedures in place and operating to prevent, detect, and correct accounting errors. You studied the general control objectives in Chapter 9 (validity, completeness, authorization, accuracy, classification, accounting, and proper period recording). Exhibit 12–3 demonstrates these in a purchasing activity situation, with examples related to specific purchasing objectives. Study this exhibit carefully.

EXHIBIT   12-3   INTERNAL CONTROL OBJECTIVES (PURCHASES)

General Objectives	Examples of Specific Objectives
1. Recorded purchases are *valid* and documented.	Purchases of inventory (or fixed assets) are supported by supplier invoices, receiving reports, purchase orders, and requisitions (or approved capital budget).
2. Valid purchase transactions are *recorded* and none omitted.	Requisitions, purchase orders, and receiving reports are prenumbered and numerical sequence is checked. Overall comparisons of purchases are made periodically by statistical or product-line analysis.
3. Purchases are *authorized* according to company policy.	All purchase orders are supported by requisitions from proper persons (or approved capital budgets). Purchases are made from approved suppliers only after bids are received and evaluated.
4. Purchase orders are *accurately* prepared.	Completed purchase order quantities and descriptions are independently compared with requisitions and suppliers' catalogues.
5. Purchase transactions are properly *classified*.	Purchases from subsidiaries and affiliates are classified as intercompany purchases and payables. Purchase returns and allowances are properly classified. Purchases for repairs and maintenance are segregated from purchases of fixed assets.
6. Purchase transaction *accounting* is complete and proper.	Account distributions for invoices are appropriate and reviewed independent of preparation. Freight-in is included as part of purchase and added to inventory (or fixed-assets) costs.
7. Purchase transactions are recorded in the *proper period*.	Perpetual inventory and fixed asset records are updated as of date goods are received or title of ownership is transferred.

Auditors can perform tests to determine whether controls said to be in place and operating actually are being performed properly by company personnel. Recall from Chapter 9 that a control test consists of (1) identification of the data population from which a sample of items will be selected for audit and (2) expression of the action that will produce relevant evidence. The actions involve vouching, tracing, observing, scanning, and recalculating—procedures for obtaining evidence used in a final control risk assessment. If control procedures are not well performed, auditors need to design substantive audit procedures to try to detect whether control failures have produced materially misleading account balances.

Proper timing is very important in the recording of the purchase transaction, and **purchase cutoff tests** provide assurance, as indicated in objective seven of Exhibit 12–3. In a perpetual inventory system, the inventory records are kept up-to-date continuously. In a periodic system, the inventory level is known only at the physical inventory count date. Even in perpetual systems, however, there should be an annual inventory count to reconcile records with actual inventory. The inventory count procedures are described in more detail later in this chapter. Thus, for both types of inventory systems, the inventory cutoff test date is the date the physical inventory is taken and accounting records are adjusted to distinguish between sales and purchases before the cutoff date and those after it.

A **cutoff error** is a failure to assign a transaction to the proper period. For example, the shipping terms "FOB destination" and "FOB shipping point" indicate the date that legal title to the inventory is transferred to the purchaser: when goods are received, in the case of FOB destination, and when goods leave the seller's premises, in the case of FOB shipping point. Delivery time can thus have a major impact on proper recording of purchases, payables, inventory, sales, and receivables. The appropriate accounting depends on the shipping terms and whether the auditee is the buyer or seller in the transaction. These are major considerations in cutoff procedures related to inventory. Note that the auditee control system's ability to detect and correct cutoff errors justifies the auditor's decision to perform more or fewer cutoff procedures.

The auditee may use a cutoff date other than the balance sheet date if controls are strong enough to ensure transactions between the cutoff and year-end are recorded accurately and

EXHIBIT 12-4   CONTROL TESTS FOR PURCHASES, CASH DISBURSEMENTS, AND ACCOUNTS PAYABLE

	Control Objective
Consider the control environment	
1. Observe whether purchasing department personnel understand and implement control activities assigned to them.	All control objectives
A. Purchases	
1. Select a sample of receiving reports:	
a. Vouch to related purchase orders, and note missing receiving reports (missing numbers).	Authorization Completeness
b. Trace to inventory record posting of additions.	Completeness
B. Cash Disbursements and Other Expenses	
1. Select a sample of cash disbursement cheque numbers:	
a. Scan for missing documents (missing numbers).	Completeness
b. Vouch supporting documentation for evidence of accurate arithmetic, correct classification, proper approval, and proper date of entry.	Accuracy Classification Authorization Proper period
c. Trace disbursement debits to general and subsidiary ledger accounts.	Accounting
2. Select a sample of recorded expenses from various accounts and vouch them to (a) cancelled cheques, and (b) supporting documentation.	Validity Classification
C. Accounts Payable	
1. Select a sample of open accounts payable and vouch to supporting documents of purchase (purchase orders, suppliers' invoices).	Validity
2. Trace debits arising from accounts payable transactions for proper classification.	Classification
3. Select a sample of accounts payable entries recorded after the balance sheet date and vouch to supporting documents for evidence of proper cutoff— evidence that a liability should have been recorded as of the balance sheet date.	Proper period

completely. In this situation, the auditor verifies both the cutoff and the transactions in the **rollforward period**, the period between cutoff and year-end, to ensure the year-end balance is not misstated.

Exhibit 12–4 shows a selection of tests for controls over purchase, cash disbursement, and accounts payable transactions. The samples are usually attribute samples designed along the lines studied in Chapter 10. On the right, the exhibit shows the control objectives tested by the audit procedures shown on the left.

Control Tests for Inventory Records

Many organizations have material investments in inventories. In some engagements, auditors need to determine whether they can rely on the accuracy of perpetual inventory records. For example, if inventory is to be physically counted at a date other than year-end, the controls need to be relied on to verify inventory changes in the rollforward period. Tests of controls over accuracy involve tests of the additions (purchases) to the inventory detail balances and tests of the reductions (issues) of the item balances.

Exhibit 12–5 pictures the dual direction of test audit samples. The source document samples (receiving reports, issue slips) meet the completeness direction requirement: everything received was recorded as an addition and everything issued as a reduction of the balance. The sample from the perpetual inventory transaction records meets the validity direction requirement: everything recorded as an addition or reduction is supported by receiving reports and issue documents.

EXHIBIT   12-5   DUAL DIRECTION OF TEST AUDIT SAMPLES

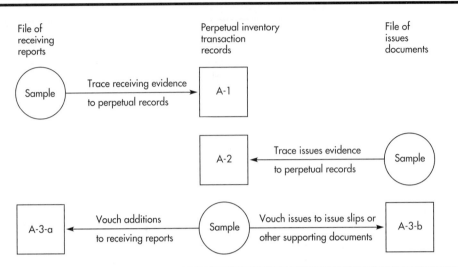

Note: The symbols A-1, A-2, A-3-a, and A-3-b are cross-references to the procedures in Exhibit 12-6.

Exhibit 12–6 contains a selection of tests for controls over perpetual inventory records similar to that of Exhibit 12–4. Note that some of these tests are dual purpose procedures as they also provide substantive evidence regarding the inventory balance. As before, the samples are usually attribute samples designed along the lines studied in Chapter 10. The control objectives tested are on the right side column.

EXHIBIT   12-6   CONTROL TESTS FOR INVENTORY RECORDS

	Control Objective
Consider the control environment	
1. Observe whether inventory department personnel understand and implement control activities assigned to them.	All control objectives
A. Inventory Receipts and Issues	
1. Select a sample of receiving reports:	
a. Trace to perpetual inventory record entry of receipt.	Authorization Completeness
2. Select a sample of sales invoices, bills of lading or other shipping documents, or production requisitions:	
a. Trace to perpetual inventory record entry of issue.	Authorization Completeness
3. Select a sample of inventory item perpetual records:	
a. Vouch additions to receiving reports.	Validity
b. Vouch issues to invoices, bills of lading or other shipping documents, or production requisitions.	Validity
B. Cost of Sales	
1. With the sample of issues in A-2 above:	
a. Review the accounting summary of quantities and prices for mathematical accuracy.	Accuracy
b. Trace posting of amounts to general ledger.	Completeness
2. Obtain a sample of cost of goods sold entries in the general ledger and vouch to supporting summaries of finished goods issues.	Validity
3. Review (recalculate) the appropriateness of standard costs, if used, to price inventory issues and cost of goods sold. Review the disposition of variances from standard costs.	Accuracy

Summary: Control Risk Assessment

The audit manager or senior in charge on the audit evaluates the evidence obtained from an understanding of the internal controls and from the control test procedures. If the control risk is assessed very low, the substantive audit procedures on the account balances can be limited for efficiency. For example, the inventory observation test counts could be done prior to year-end and with a small sample size. On the other hand, if tests of controls reveal weaknesses, the substantive procedures will be needed to lower the risk of failing to detect material error in the account balances. For example, the inventory observation may need to be done on the year-end date and with a large number of test counts. Descriptions of major deficiencies, control weaknesses, and inefficiencies may be incorporated in a management letter to the auditee.

REVIEW CHECKPOINTS

6 What are the functions that should be segregated in the purchases, payables, and payments process?

7 What control might prevent the embezzling of cash by creation of fictitious supplier invoices?

8 How could an auditor determine if the purchasing agent had practised purchase order splitting?

9 Describe the two general characteristics of a control test.

10 How is the information from the shipping department, receiving department, and warehouse used to update perpetual inventory records?

11 In fixed asset management and accounting, which functional responsibilities should be delegated to separate departments or management levels?

SPECIAL NOTE: THE COMPLETENESS ASSERTION FOR LIABILITIES

LEARNING OBJECTIVE

3 Explain the importance of the completion assertion for auditing the accounts payable liabilities, and the procedures used to search for unrecorded liabilities.

When considering assertions and obtaining evidence about accounts payable and other liabilities, auditors must emphasize the completeness assertion. (For asset accounts the emphasis is on the existence and ownership assertions.) This is necessary as companies are typically less concerned about timely recording of expenses and liabilities than they are about timely recording of revenues and assets. Of course, generally accepted accounting principles require timely accrual of liabilities and their associated expenses.

Evidence verifying the completeness assertion is more difficult to find than for the existence assertion. Auditors cannot rely entirely on a management assertion of completeness, even with a favourable assessment of control risk. Substantive procedures, tests of details, or analytical procedures should also provide corroborating evidence. The **search for unrecorded liabilities** is a set of procedures designed to yield audit evidence of liabilities that were not recorded in the reporting period. This search should normally be performed up to the audit report date in the period following the auditee's balance sheet date.

The following list of procedures is useful in the search for unrecorded liabilities. The audit objective is to search all the places where there might be evidence of them, and if none are revealed it is reasonable to conclude that all material liabilities were recorded.

- Scan the open purchase order file at year-end for purchase commitments at fixed prices. From current prices, determine if any adjustments for loss and liability are needed.

- List the unmatched supplier invoices and, from the unmatched receiving report file and receiving reports prepared after year-end, determine when the goods were received. Determine which invoices, if any, should be recorded.

- Trace the unmatched receiving reports to accounts payable entries, and determine if any recorded in the next accounting period need to be reported in the current accounting period under audit.

- Vouch a sample of cash disbursements from the accounting period following the balance sheet date against supporting documents (invoice, receiving report) to determine if the related liabilities were recorded in the proper accounting period. Select the sample from the post-year-end cutoff bank statement to audit the cash balance (see Chapter 11).

- Trace liabilities reported by financial institutions to the accounts. (See the bank confirmation in Exhibit 11–5, Chapter 11, page 436.) Since a bank may not report all auditee liabilities to auditors, other corroborating evidence for possible unrecorded debts should also be obtained.

- Canada Revenue Agency notices of assessment may contain evidence of income or other taxes in dispute that may need to be recorded as liabilities.

- Confirm accounts payable with suppliers, especially regular suppliers showing small or zero balances in the year-end accounts payable. (Suppliers' monthly statements controlled by the auditors also may be used.) Verify supplier addresses so confirmations will not be misdirected—perhaps deliberately.

- Study the accounts payable trial balance for dates showing fewer payables than are usually recorded near the year-end, evidence that invoices aren't being recorded.

- Review responses from auditee's lawyers to requests for information about pending or threatened litigation, and about unasserted claims and assessments. These may indicate a need for contingent liability accruals or disclosures. (As explained in Chapter 15, when the auditor assesses a risk of material misstatement due to litigation or claims, CAS 501(6560) requires that enquiry letters prepared by the auditee be sent to the auditee's lawyers by the auditor. These letters request the lawyer to communicate directly with the auditor.)

- A checklist of accrued expenses will help determine whether the company has been conscientious in expense and liability accruals, including accruals for wages, interest, utilities, sales and excise taxes, payroll taxes, income taxes, real property taxes, rent, sales commissions, royalties and warranties, and guarantee expense.

- When auditing the details of sales revenue, the terms of sales will help determine if any amounts should be deferred as unearned revenue. (Initial information is gained by enquiries to management about terms of sale, such as customers' rights of cancellation or return.)

- A schedule of casualty insurance on fixed assets is used to determine the adequacy of insurance in relation to asset market values. Inadequate insurance and self-insurance create risks that should be disclosed in the notes to the financial statements.

- Confirm life insurance policies with insurance companies to ask whether the company has any loans against the cash value of the insurance. Also request the names of the beneficiaries of the policies. If a party other than the company benefits from the insurance, it may be a creditor on unrecorded loans. Enquire about the business purpose of making insurance proceeds payable to other parties.

- Review terms of any debt due within one year but classified long-term because the company plans to refinance it on a long-term basis. This cannot be based on management's intent; holders of the debt or financial institutions must have shown (preferably in writing) a willingness to refinance the debt before it can be classified long-term.

- Apply analytical procedures appropriate in the circumstances. In general, accounts payable volume and period-end balances should increase when the company increases physical production volume or engages in inventory stockpiling. Some liabilities may be related to other activities; for example, sales taxes are functionally related to sales dollar totals, payroll taxes to payroll totals, excise taxes to sales dollars, or volume and income taxes to income.

R E V I E W
CHECKPOINTS

12 Describe the purpose of and give examples of audit procedures in the search for unrecorded liabilities.

13 Explain the difference in approach between confirmation of accounts receivable and confirmation of accounts payable.

14 In substantive auditing, why is the emphasis on the completeness assertion for liabilities instead of on the existence assertion as in the audit of assets?

SPECIAL NOTE: PHYSICAL INVENTORY OBSERVATION

LEARNING OBJECTIVE

4 Identify audit considerations for observing the physical inventory count.

The audit procedures for inventory and related cost of sales accounts can be extensive. A 96-page joint CICA–AICPA auditing technique study entitled *Audit of Inventories* published in 1986 describes many facets of inherent risk and control risk, and of the process of obtaining evidence about inventory financial statement assertions. The significance of inventories is acknowledged in the following statement:

> Generally, inventories reflect the characteristics of a business more than any other asset. Significant to manufacturing, wholesale, and retail organizations, inventories frequently are also material to the financial statements of service organizations. For some types of businesses, inventories constitute a significant percent of total assets and represent the largest current asset.

A material misstatement in inventory has a pervasive effect on financial statements. It will cause misstatements in current assets, working capital, total assets, cost of sales, gross margin, and net income. While analytical procedures can help indicate inventory presentation problems, physical observation of the auditee's inventory count is the best opportunity to detect inventory misstatements. Auditing standards (CAS 501 [6030]) require that auditors attend the physical inventory counting when inventory is material to the financial statements, to provide evidence of the existence and condition of inventory. While auditors rarely count the entire inventory, management's procedures for recording and controlling the count should be evaluated and observed, inventory inspected, and test counts performed. Later, the final inventory records should be tested to ensure they accurately reflect the evidence the auditor obtained at the physical counting.

In some audits, obtaining evidence about an inventory's existence and valuation requires expert knowledge in a field other than accounting or auditing, as described in CAS 620. Often experts employed by management will provide tests and reports for this purpose. An auditee will likely have employees with the expertise required; for example, able to assess the assembly stage of highly technical equipment or to calculate the quantity of raw material in containers or stockpiles based on measures of volume and density. An expert employed by the audit firm or an outside expert engaged by the audit firm to assist the team may be assigned to provide this evidence. In evaluating the need for an expert, the auditor first considers whether alternative sources of sufficient appropriate evidence are available and more cost effective. For example, an outside expert's report prepared for the auditee but for another purpose may also be relevant and reliable for the auditor's purposes.

The remainder of this special note covers details related to auditors' observation of physical inventory taking. The first task is to review the auditee's inventory-taking instructions. The instructions should include the following:

- Names of auditee personnel responsible for the count
- Dates, times, and locations of inventory taking
- Names of auditee personnel who will participate in the inventory taking
- Instructions for recording accurate descriptions of inventory items, for count and double count, and for measuring or translating physical quantities (such as counting by measures of litres, barrels, metres, dozens)

- Instructions for making notes of obsolete or worn items
- Instructions for the use of tags, cards, count sheets, or other media devices, and for their collection and control
- Plans for shutting down plant operations or for taking inventory after store closing hours, and plans for having goods in proper places (such as on store shelves instead of on the floor, or in a warehouse rather than in transit to a job)
- Plans for counting or controlling movement of goods in receiving and shipping areas if those operations are not shut down during the count
- Instructions for compilation of the count information (such as computer processing of scanned codes, or manual input of tags or count sheets) into final inventory listings or summaries
- Instructions for pricing the inventory items
- Instructions for review and approval of the inventory count and notations of obsolescence or other matters by supervisory personnel

These instructions characterize a well-planned counting operation. As the plan is carried out, the independent auditors should be present to hear the count instructions being given to the auditee's count teams and to observe the instructions being followed.

Many physical inventories are counted at year-end when the auditor is present to observe. The auditors can perform dual-direction testing by (1) selecting inventory items from a perpetual inventory master file and going to the location to obtain a test count, which produces evidence for the existence assertion; and (2) selecting inventory from locations on the warehouse floor, obtaining a test count, and tracing the count to the final inventory compilation, which produces evidence for the completeness assertion. If the company does not have perpetual records and a file to test for existence, the auditors must be careful to obtain a record of all the counts and to use it for the existence-direction tests.

However, other situations as described below frequently occur.

Physical Inventory Not on Period-End Date

Auditees sometimes count the inventory on a date other than the balance sheet date. The auditor observes this count, following the same procedures as for a period-end count. For the period between the count date and the balance sheet date, additional rollforward or rollback auditing procedures must be performed on inventory purchase (increasing) and issue (decreasing) transactions during that period. The inventory on the count date is reconciled to the period-end inventory by appropriate addition or subtraction of the receiving and issue transactions that have occurred in the rollforward or rollback period.

Cyclical Inventory Counting

Some companies count inventory on a cyclical basis or use a statistical counting plan but never take a complete count on a single date. Businesses that count inventory this way claim to have accurate perpetual records, and that they carry out the counting as a means of testing the records and maintaining their accuracy. In these cases, the auditors must understand management's counting plan and evaluate its appropriateness, and they should attend and perform tests whenever the value of inventory to be counted is material. They must be present during some counting operations to evaluate the counting plans and their execution. The procedures listed above for an annual count are used, test counts are made, and the audit team forms a conclusion concerning the accuracy (control) of perpetual records.

Auditors Not Present at Auditee's Inventory Count

It might happen on a first audit that the audit firm is appointed after the beginning inventory has already been counted. The auditors should still review the auditee's plan for the already completed count. Some test counts of current inventory should be made and traced to current records to form a conclusion about the reliability of perpetual records. If the actual count was recent, intervening transaction activity may be reconciled back to the beginning inventory.

However, it may be very difficult to reconcile more than a few months' transactions to an unobserved beginning inventory. Auditors may use the interrelationships between sales activity, physical volume, price variation, standard costs, and gross profit margins to form a conclusion about the reasonableness of the beginning inventory. This must be done very carefully, and, if the auditors cannot satisfy themselves as to the beginning inventory balance, a modification in the auditor's report is normally called for (CAS 501[6030]).

Inventories Located off the Auditee's Premises

The auditors must determine the locations and values of inventories that are located off the auditee's premises, perhaps in the custody of consignees or in public warehouses. If amounts are material and control is not exceptionally strong, the audit team may visit these locations and conduct on-site test counts. However, if amounts are not material or related evidence (periodic reports, cash receipts, receivables records, shipping records) is adequate and control risk is low, then direct confirmation with the inventory custodian may be sufficient appropriate evidence of existence (CAS 501 [6030]).

INVENTORY COUNT AND MEASUREMENT CHALLENGES

Examples	Challenges
Lumber	Identifying quality or grade
Piles of sugar, coal, scrap steel	Need geometric computations, aerial photos
Items weighed on scales	Accuracy of scales
Bulk materials (oil, grain, chemicals, liquids in storage tanks)	Dip measuring rods into tanks / Sample for assay or chemical analysis
Diamonds, jewellery	Identification and quality determination / Need an expert
Pulp wood	Quantity measurement estimation / Need aerial photos
Livestock	Movement not controllable (count critter's legs and divide by four—two for chickens).

Source: Adapted from CICA, Audit of Inventories, *Auditing Procedure Study* (1986), p. 28.

Summary: Inventory Observation

The physical observation procedures are designed to audit for existence and completeness (physical quantities) and also to provide support for audit valuation procedures (e.g., recalculation of appropriate FIFO, weighted average, specific item, or other pricing at cost, and evaluation of lower-of-cost-or-market write-down of obsolete or damaged inventory). After the observation is complete, auditors should have sufficient appropriate evidence of physical quantities and valuations to ensure the inventory compilation includes goods (a) owned, on hand, and counted; (b) owned but not on hand (consigned out or stored in outside warehouses); and (c) in transit (purchased and recorded but not yet received, or shipped FOB destination but not yet delivered to customers). The inventory compilation should exclude goods (a) in the perpetual records but not owned; (b) on hand, already sold, but not yet delivered; and (c) on hand but not owned (consigned in).

REVIEW CHECKPOINTS

15 In the review of an auditee's inventory-taking instructions, what characteristics are the auditors looking for?

16 Explain dual-direction sampling in the context of inventory test counts.

17 What procedures are followed to audit inventory when the physical inventory is taken on a cyclical basis or on a statistical plan but never as a complete count on a single date?

APPLICATION CASE AND ANALYSIS

In this application case, we will demonstrate tests of controls and substantive audit procedures in the evidence gathering process related to purchases, payables, and payments. The case situation for each audit presented parallels the framework shown in Chapter 11's application case (page 443). It provides context for the auditing decisions, rather than presenting a list of detection procedures in the abstract. Lists of detailed procedures, a selection of control tests, and detail substantive procedures for payables and payments are found in Appendices 12A and 12B.

LEARNING OBJECTIVE

5 Apply and integrate the chapter topics to design audit procedures for detecting misstatements due to error or fraud in the purchases, payables, and payments process.

Detecting Misstatements in the Purchases, Payables, and Payments Process

As Jack told the new junior auditors his stories about revenue-related misstatements, Syed, one of the audit firm's senior partners, joined in the conversation: "You really have had an interesting first year, Jack! Most people don't see two frauds and a material cutoff error in their first year on the audit trail. Next year you will move on to auditing more complex areas like accounts payable and inventory, so let me tell you some of the stories I have seen over many years in auditing. In some ways, fraud and other misstatements are even more likely in the purchases, payables, and payments process than in revenues. This is because there are complex accounts involved, but also because the main business purpose of the auditee's purchasing process is to move cash out of the organization. That means errors often result in cash outflows. Also, it can be easier to subvert the process fraudulently, and harder for management controls and auditors to detect it. One thing you will notice early on is that well-managed organizations tend to have the strongest controls in this part of their accounting system. But here are four stories of misstatements that I or my colleagues have experienced in practice. The first one involves an employee fraud in the cash payment process, the second is a supplier overcharging situation, the third is an inventory valuation scam by employees, and the fourth is a misstatement due to management's misestimating forecasts used to calculate amortization expense."

AUDIT 12.1
COPYING MONEY

Case Description

Argus Productions Inc. (Argus) is a motion picture and commercial production company. Improper expenditures for copy services were charged to production costs by an employee, Welby, who had the power to perform incompatible functions in the purchasing, payables, and payments process. Because of his authority at Argus, over a period of five years Welby was able to conduct a fraud that brought him $475,000 in false and inflated billings. (During this period, Argus's net income was understated a modest amount because copying costs were capitalized as part of production costs, then amortized over a 2–3 year period.)

Argus management had assigned Welby authority and responsibility for obtaining copies of scripts used in production. Established procedures permitted Welby to arrange for outside script-copying services, receive the copies, and approve the bills for payment. In effect, Welby was both the "purchasing department" and the "receiving department" for this particular service. To a certain extent, Welby was also the "accounting department" because he approved the bills for payment and coded them for assignment to projects. Welby did not make the actual accounting entries or sign the cheques.

Welby set up a fictitious company under the registered name of Quickprint Company with himself as the incorporator and shareholder. The company had a post office box number, letterhead stationery, and nicely printed invoices, but no printing equipment. Copy services were subcontracted by Quickprint to real printing businesses, which billed Quickprint. Welby then wrote Quickprint invoices to Argus, billing the production company at the legitimate shop's rate, but for a few extra copies each time. Welby also submitted Quickprint bills to Argus for fictitious copying jobs on scripts for movies and commercials that never went into production. As the owner of Quickprint, Welby endorsed Argus's cheques and deposited the money in the copy company's bank account, paid the legitimate printing bills of the subcontractors, and took the rest for personal use.

Audit Trail

Argus's production cost files contained all the Quickprint bills, sorted under the names of the movie and commercial production projects. Welby even created files for proposed films that never went into full production, and thus should not have had script copying costs. There were no copying service bills from any shop other than Quickprint.

AUDIT APPROACH ANALYSIS

Audit objective

The auditors' objective was to obtain evidence of the valid existence (occurrence) and valuation of copying charges capitalized as film production costs.

Controls relevant to the purchasing process

Authority to request copies and authority for purchasing should be assigned to different employees. The accounting, including the coding of cost assignments to production projects, also should be performed by someone else. A managerial review of production results might cause the excess costs to be noticed.

The request for a particular number of copies of a script should come from someone who would know the number needed. This person should act as the "receiving department," signing off on the requested number of copies and the payment. This procedure would prevent waste and excess cost, especially if the requesting person were held responsible for the project's profitability.

Purchasing is always done by a company agent—Welby, in this case. Purchasing agents generally have authority to look for the best service at the best price, with or without bids from competitors. A requirement to obtain bids is usually a good idea, but legitimate purchasing often is done with sole-source suppliers, without bidding. The accounting department should be responsible for coding invoices to the projects, thus making it possible to detect costs charged to projects that are not actually in production. Someone with managerial responsibility should review project costs and the purchasing practices. However, this is an expensive use of executive time. It was not spent in the Argus case, with unfortunate results.

AUDIT PROCEDURES

Tests of controls

While gaining their understanding of the control structure at Argus, auditors learned about all the trust and responsibility vested in Welby. The embezzlement was for about $95,000 per year, and total copying costs under Welby were around $1 million—inflating a cost by more than 10 percent might attract unwanted attention. (Note that the materiality concept even applies to the decisions of fraudsters!)

Company-level controls were very weak, especially in the combination of duties performed by Welby and in the lack of managerial review. For all practical purposes, there were no application controls to test since the weak company-level controls meant they would not be effective anyway. A test of proper classification to see whether Welby had approved the copying cost invoices and coded them to active projects might have uncovered Welby's payments for copying scripts of movies that never went into production, had this been verified against the list of authorized projects. Unfortunately, Welby also produced an "authorized production listing" that included the fictitious projects, which the auditors accepted.

Dual-purpose procedures

Vouching costs charged to projects against supporting source documents for a sample of movie project files tests validity of capitalized costs. Tracing a sample of payments to the project cost records is a test of completeness and proper classification of capitalized costs and, if traced to the approved list of productions, it tests authorization. Since Welby had used convincing falsified documents, these audit procedures might not indicate any control exceptions. This case also illustrates the effect and limitations in audit effectiveness relating to materiality levels; Welby deliberately kept this fraud "below the radar screen."

Tests of details of balance

Substantive procedures are directed toward obtaining evidence about the existence of film projects, the completeness of the costs charged to them, the ownership of copyrights, the valuation of the capitalized project costs, and the proper allocation and disclosure of amortization methods. The most important procedures are the same as the test of controls procedures; thus, when performed at the year-end date on the capitalized cost balances, they are dual-purpose audit procedures.

Any of the procedures described as test of controls procedures should show evidence of projects that had never gone into production. (Auditors should be careful to obtain a list of actual projects before they begin the procedures.) Chances are high that the discovery of bad project codes with copying cost would reveal a pattern of Quickprint bills.

Knowing that controls over copying costs are weak, auditors could be tipped off to the possibility of a Welby-Quickprint connection. Efforts to locate Quickprint should be taken. Enquiry with the provincial Ministry of Commerce for names of the Quickprint incorporators would reveal Welby's connection. The audit findings could then be turned over to a trained investigator to arrange an interview and confrontation with Welby.

Audit results

In this case, the manager of production, who was worried about profitability, requested that the internal auditors review project costs. They performed the procedures described above on 100 percent of the transactions and, thus, noticed the dummy projects and the Quickprint bills, investigated the ownership of Quickprint, and discovered Welby's association. First efforts to locate Quickprint's shop by telephone, chamber of commerce, or other city directories failed. They were careful not to direct any mail to the post office box for fear of alerting the then-unknown parties involved. Through a ruse at the post office, a sly internal auditor had already learned that Welby had rented the box, but they did not know if anyone else was involved. Alerted,

the internal auditors gathered all the Quickprint bills and determined, with witnesses, the total charged for nonexistent projects. Welby was interviewed by Argus managers and readily confessed.

AUDIT 12.2
RECEIVING THE MISSING OIL

Case Description

Johnson Chemical began a new contract with Madden Oil Distributors to supply fuel oil for the plant generators on a cost-plus contract. Madden delivered the oil weekly in a 20,000-litre-tank truck to Johnson's storage tanks. Because of short shipments by Madden, Johnson's fuel oil supplies inventory and fuel expense were inflated. During the first year, Madden shorted Johnson on quantity by 160,000 litres (loss = 160,000 × $.45 = $72,000) and charged 5 cents per litre more than competitors (loss = 940,000 litres × $0.05 = $47,000) for a total overcharge of $119,000—not to mention the inferior sludge mix occasionally delivered.

Johnson's receiving employees observed the pumping and recorded the quantity on a receiving report, which was forwarded to the accounts payable department and held pending arrival of Madden's invoice. The quantities received then were compared with the quantities billed by Madden, before the invoice was approved for payment and a cheque prepared for signature by the controller. Since it was a cost-plus contract, Madden's billing price was not checked against any standard price. The receiving employees were rather easily fooled by Madden's driver. He mixed sludge with the oil, but the receiving employees did not take samples to check for quality. He called out Johnson's storage tank content falsely at the beginning (e.g., 4,000 litres on hand when 8,000 were actually in the tank) and the receiving employees did not check the gauge themselves. The tank truck was not weighed at entry and exit to determine the amount delivered. During the winter months, when fuel oil use was high, Madden ran in extra trucks more than once a week, but pumped nothing when the receiving employees were not looking. Quantities "received" and paid during the first year of the contract were (in litres) as follows:

Jan.	124,000	May	72,000	Sept.	84,000
Feb.	112,000	June	56,000	Oct.	92,000
Mar.	92,000	July	60,000	Nov.	132,000
Apr.	76,000	Aug.	56,000	Dec.	144,000

Audit Trail

The receiving reports all agreed with the quantities billed by Madden. Each invoice had a receiving report attached in the Johnson accounts payable files. Even though Madden had many trucks, the same driver always came to the Johnson plant, as evidenced by his signature on the reports (along with the receiving employees' initials). At $.45 per litre, Madden charged $495,000 for 1,100,000 litres of fuel for the year. The previous year, Johnson paid a total of $360,000 for 900,000 litres, but nobody made a complete comparison with last year's quantity and cost.

AUDIT APPROACH ANALYSIS

Audit objective

The auditors' objective was to obtain evidence that all fuel oil billed and paid was actually received in the quality expected, at a fair price.

Controls relevant to the process

Receiving employees should be given the tools and techniques they need to do a good job. Scales at the plant entrance could weigh the trucks in and out,

determining the amount of fuel delivered. (Weight per litre is a well-known measure.) Sampling for simple chemical analysis would give evidence of the quality of the oil. Receiving employees should be instructed on the importance of their job, to encourage conscientiousness. They should have been instructed to read the storage tank gauges themselves instead of relying on Madden's driver. Lacking these tools and instructions, they were easy marks for the wily driver.

AUDIT PROCEDURES

Tests of controls

The information from the "understanding the control structure" phase would need to be very detailed if it is to alert the auditors to the poor receiving practices. Procedures will include making enquiries with the receiving employees to learn about their practices and work habits. The control procedure supposedly in place was the receiving report on the oil delivered. A control test procedure would be to take a sample of Madden's bills, and compare quantities billed with quantities received while verifying the price billed against the contract. Because of the deception by Madden's driver, this would not have shown anything unusual, unless perhaps the auditor became suspicious of the fact that the same driver made all the deliveries.

Tests of details of balance

The balances in question are the fuel oil supply inventory and the fuel expense. The inventory is easily audited by reading the tank storage gauge for the quantity. The price is found in Madden's invoices. However, a lower-of-cost-or-market test requires knowledge of market prices for the oil. Since Johnson Chemical apparently has no documentation of competing prices, the auditor will need to research with other oil distributors to get the prices. Presumably, the auditors would learn that the price is approximately $.40 per litre. The expense balance can be audited like a cost-of-goods-sold amount. With knowledge of the beginning fuel inventory, the quantity "purchased," and the quantity in the ending inventory, the fuel oil expense quantity can be calculated. This expense quantity can be priced at Madden's price per litre.

Substantive analytical procedures

Analytical procedures applied to the expense revealed the larger quantities used and the unusual pattern of deliveries, leading to suspicions of Madden and the driver. Aware of the current year's higher expense and the evidence of a lower market price, the auditors obtained the fuel oil delivery records from the prior year. They are shown below: (numbers in parentheses are the additional litres delivered in the current year)

Audit Results

Having found a consistent pattern of greater "use" in the current year, with no operational explanation for it, the auditors took to the field. With the cooperation of the receiving employees, the auditors read the storage tank measure before the Madden driver arrived. They hid in an adjoining building to watch (and film) the driver call out an incorrect reading, pump the oil, sign the receiving report, and depart. Then they took samples. These observations were repeated for three weeks. They saw short deliveries, tested inferior products, and built a case against Madden and the driver. Johnson recovered the overcharges from Madden and, of course, immediately switched to a different fuel supplier!

Jan.	112,000 (12,000)	May	52,000 (20,000)	Sept.	60,000 (24,000)
Feb.	96,000 (16,000)	June	44,000 (12,000)	Oct.	80,000 (12,000)
Mar.	80,000 (12,000)	July	40,000 (20,000)	Nov.	112,000 (20,000)
Apr.	68,000 (8,000)	Aug.	36,000 (20,000)	Dec.	120,000 (24,000)

AUDIT 12.3
RETREAD TIRES

Case Description

Ritter Tire Wholesale Company had a high-volume truck and passenger car tire business in Hamilton, Ontario (area population 500,000). J. Lock, the chief accountant, was a long-time trusted employee who had supervisory responsibility over the purchasing agent as well as general accounting duties. Lock had worked several years as a purchasing agent before moving into the accounting job. Lock carried out a fraudulent scheme for three years, diverting tires that cost Ritter $2.5 million, which Lock then sold for $2.9 million. Inventory and income were overstated by Lock's substitution of the new-tire inventory with lower-quality retread tires, which he valued at new tire prices. (Lock's cost for retread tires was approximately $500,000.)

Lock often prepared the purchase orders, and the manufacturers were directed to deliver the tires to a warehouse in Milton (a town of 60,000, about 30 kilometres north of Hamilton). Ritter Tire received the manufacturers' invoices, which Lock approved for payment. Lock and an accomplice (his brother-in-law) sold the tires from the Milton warehouse and pocketed the money. At night, Lock moved cheaper retread tires into the Ritter warehouse so the space would not be empty. As chief accountant, Lock could override controls (e.g., approving invoices for payment without a receiving report), and T. Ritter (president) never knew the difference because the cheques presented for his signature were not accompanied by the supporting documents.

Audit Trail

Ritter Tire's files were well organized. Each cheque copy had supporting documents attached (invoice, receiving report, purchase order), except for the misdirected tire purchases, which had no receiving reports. These purchase orders were all signed by Lock, and the shipping destination on them was the Milton address. There were no purchase requisition documents because "requisitions" were in the form of verbal requests from salespeople. There was no paper evidence of the retread tires because Lock simply bought them elsewhere and moved them in at night when nobody was around.

AUDIT APPROACH ANALYSIS

Audit objective

The auditors' objective was to obtain evidence of the existence and valuation of the inventory. (President Ritter engaged external auditors for the first time in the third year of Lock's scheme, after experiencing a severe cash squeeze.)

Controls relevant to the process

Competent personnel should perform the purchasing function. Lock and the other purchasing agents were competent and experienced. They prepared purchase orders, required by manufacturers for shipment, authorizing the purchase of tires. A receiving department prepared a receiving report, after counting and inspecting each shipment, by filling in the "quantity column" on a copy of the purchase order. (A common receiving report is a "blind" purchase order that has all the purchase information except the quantity, which the receiving department fills in after an independent inspection and count.) Receiving personnel made notes if the tires showed blemishes or damage. As chief accountant, Lock approved invoices from the manufacturers for payment after comparing the quantities with the receiving report and the prices with the purchase order. The cheques for payment were produced on the computerized accounting system when Lock entered the invoice payable in the system. The computer software did not void transactions without a receiving report reference because many expenses legitimately had no receiving reports. The key weaknesses in the control structure are that (1) no one on the accounting staff has the opportunity to notice missing receiving reports for invoices that should have had them, and (2) Ritter has no supporting documents when cheques are signed. Lock is a trusted employee.

AUDIT PROCEDURES

Tests of controls

Because the control procedures for cross-checking the supporting documents were said to be in place, the external auditors could test those controls by the following procedure:

Select a sample of purchases (manufacturers' invoices payable entered in the computer system), and

1. study the related purchase order for (a) valid manufacturer name and address; (b) date; (c) delivery address; (d) unit price, with reference to catalogue or price list; (e) correct arithmetic; and (f) approval signature. Then
2. compare purchase order information with the manufacturers' invoice, and
3. compare the purchase order and invoice with the receiving report for (a) date, (b) quantity and condition, (c) approval signature, and (d) location.

Tests of details of balance

Ritter Tire did not maintain perpetual inventory records, so the inventory was a periodic system—an inventory figure calculated from the annual physical inventory count and costing compilation. The basic audit procedure was to observe the count by taking a sample from different locations on the warehouse floor, recounting the employees' count, controlling the count sheets, and inspecting the tires for quality and condition (related to proper valuation). The auditors kept their own copy of all the count sheets with their test count notes and notes identifying tires as "new" or "retread." (They took many test counts in the physical inventory sample as a result of the test of controls work, described following.)

Audit Results

Forty manufacturers' invoices were selected at random for the test of controls procedure. The auditors were good. They had reviewed the business operations, and Ritter had said nothing about having operations or a warehouse in Milton, although a manufacturer might have been instructed to "drop-ship" tires to a customer there. The auditors noticed three missing receiving reports, all of them with purchase orders signed by Lock and requesting delivery to the same Milton address. They asked Lock about the missing receiving reports, and got this response: "It happens sometimes. I'll find them for you tomorrow." When Lock produced the receiving reports, the auditors noticed these were in a current numerical sequence (although dated much earlier), filled out with the same pen, and signed with an illegible scrawl not matching any of the other receiving reports they had seen.

The auditors knew the difference between new and retread tires when they saw them, and confirmed their observations with employees taking the physical inventory count. When Lock priced the inventory, new-tire prices were used, and the auditors knew the difference.

Ritter took the circumstantial evidence to a trained investigator who interviewed the manufacturers and obtained information about the Milton location. The case against Lock led to criminal theft charges and conviction.

AUDIT 12.4
AMORTIZE "THE DRUM" SLOWLY

Case Description

Candid Production Company was a major producer of theatrical movies. The company usually had 15–20 films in release at theatres across the nation and in foreign countries. Movies also generated revenue through video/DVD licences and product sales (T-shirts, toys, etc.). Over a four-year period, Candid's net asset value (unamortized cost of films) was overstated through taking too little amortization expense: Candid Productions postponed recognition of a $20 million amortization expense, thus inflating assets and income. Movie production costs are capitalized as assets and then amortized to expense as revenue is received from theatre ticket and DVD sales, and from other sources of revenue. The amortization depends on the total revenue forecast and the current-year revenue amount. As the success or failure of a movie unfolds at the box office, revenue estimates are revised. (The accounting amortization is similar to depletion of a mineral resource, which depends on estimates of recoverable minerals and current production.)

Candid Production was not too candid: its recent film, *Bang the Drum Slowly*, was forecast to produce $50 million total revenue over six years, while early box office returns showed only $10 million in the first eight months in the theatres. Revenue usually declines rapidly after initial openings, and DVD and other revenues depend on the box office success of a film. Accounting "control" with respect to film-cost amortization depends on the revenue forecasts, and the revision of them. In this case, these were overly optimistic, showing the expense recognition and overstating assets and income.

Audit Trail

Revenue forecasts are based on many factors, including facts and assumptions about number of theatres, ticket prices, receipt-sharing agreements, domestic and foreign reviews, and moviegoer tastes. Several publications track the box office records of movies. You can see them in entertainment websites, newspapers, and in the industry trade publications. Of course, the production companies themselves are the major source of the information, and company records do show the revenue realized from each movie. Revenue forecasts can be checked against actual results, and the company's history of forecasting accuracy can be determined by comparing actuals to forecasts over many films and many years.

AUDIT APPROACH ANALYSIS

Audit objective

The auditors' objective was to obtain evidence determining if revenue forecasts provide a sufficient basis for calculating film-cost amortization and net asset value of films.

Controls relevant to the process

Revenue forecasts need to be prepared by a systematic and methodical process that documents both the facts and the underlying assumptions of the forecast. Forecasts should break down the revenue estimate by years, and the accounting system should produce comparable actual revenue data so that forecast accuracy can be assessed after the fact. Forecast revisions should be prepared with as much detail and documentation as original forecasts.

AUDIT PROCEDURES

Tests of controls

The general procedures and methods used by personnel responsible for revenue forecasts should be studied (enquiries and review of documentation), including their sources of information—both internal and external. Procedures for review of mechanical aspects (arithmetic) should be tested by recalculating the final estimates for a sample of finished forecasts. Specific procedures for forecast revision should be studied in the same way. Reviewing the accuracy of the forecasts of other movies against actual revenues helps in a circumstantial way, but past accuracy on different film experiences may not be directly helpful to forecasting for a new, unique product.

Tests of details of balance

The audit of amortization expense concentrates on the content of the forecast itself. The forecasts used in the amortization calculation should be studied to distinguish underlying reasonable expectations from hypothetical assumptions. A hypothetical assumption states a condition that is not necessarily expected to occur, but it is nonetheless used to prepare an estimate—an if-then statement. For example, "If *Bang the Drum Slowly* sells 15 million tickets in the first 12 months of release, then domestic revenue and product sales will be $40 million, and foreign revenue can eventually reach $10 million." Auditors need to assess the reasonableness of the 15 million ticket assumption. It helps to have some early actual data from the film's release in hand before the financial statements need to be finished and distributed. For actual data, industry publications ought to be reviewed, with special attention paid to competing films and critics' reviews (yes, even movie reviews can be useful as audit evidence!).

Audit Results

The auditors were not skeptical enough about the revenue forecasts, and they did not weigh unfavourable actual-to-forecast history comparisons heavily enough. Apparently, they let themselves be convinced by exuberant company executives that the movies were comparable with the blockbuster *Titanic*! The audit of forecasts and estimates used in accounting determinations are very difficult to arrive at, especially when company personnel have incentives to hype the numbers, seemingly with conviction. The postponed amortization expense finally came home to roost in big write-offs when the company management changed.

REVIEW CHECKPOINTS

18 Give some examples of receiving departments in the audit application cases above.

19 In Audits 12.1 and 12.3, frauds involving fictitious people, businesses, and locations occurred. Where can auditors obtain information showing whether people, businesses, and locations are real or not?

20 How can analysis be used for discovery of excess costs (see Audit 12.2)?

21 How can analysis be used for discovery of understated expenses (see Audit 12.4)?

22 Why must auditors understand the physical characteristics of inventoried assets?

23 Why is professional skepticism important for auditors? Give two case examples.

24 What evidence could the verbal enquiry audit procedure produce in Audits 12.1, 12.2, and 12.3?

SUMMARY

The purchases, payables, and payments process consists of purchase requisitioning, purchase ordering, receiving goods and services, recording suppliers' invoices, accounting for accounts payable, and making disbursements of cash. Companies reduce control risk by having a suitable separation of authorization, custody, recording, and periodic reconciliation duties. Error-checking procedures of comparing purchase orders and receiving reports with supplier invoices are important for recording proper amounts of accounts payable liabilities. Supervisory control is provided by separating the duties of preparing cash disbursement cheques and actually signing them. Otherwise, many things could go wrong, ranging from processing false purchase orders to failing to record liabilities for goods and services received.

Two topics had special technical notes in the chapter. The completeness assertion is very important in the audit of liabilities because misleading financial statements often contain unrecorded liabilities and expenses. The search for unrecorded liabilities is an important set of audit procedures. The physical inventory observation audit work was a special section because actual contact with inventories (and fixed assets, for that matter) provides auditors with direct eyewitness evidence of important tangible assets.

Cash disbursement is a critical point for asset control. Many cases of embezzlement occur in this process. Illustrative cases in the chapter told of some embezzlement schemes involving payment of fictitious charges to dummy companies set up by employees.

Analysis of Financial Statement Relationships

The audit of the purchases, payables, and payments processes results in verifying the balance of accounts payables/accrued liabilities and the two transaction streams that run through it—purchases/expenses and cash payments. In the balance sheet approach to auditing, we can analyze balance changes and the financial statement items related to them by preparing a continuity schedule. The accrued legal fees balance shown on page 491 is one example of the purchases, payables, and payments process. (The relationship between inventory purchases and balance sheet amounts will be analyzed in Chapter 13.)

Audited Amount	Financial Statement where Amount is Reported
Opening balance of accrued liability for legal fees	Balance sheet (component of accrued liabilities in prior year comparative figures)
Add: New legal services expensed during the year	Income statement expense (e.g., legal services acquired)
Deduct: Cash paid against payables	Cash flow statement (direct method)
Ending balance of accrued liability for legal fees	Balance sheet (component of accrued liabilities in current year figures)

As these relationships illustrate, our procedures to audit the purchases, payables, and payments process allow us to assess whether all components of this system of related amounts are reported accurately in the financial statements. These relationships also indicate analytical procedures that can detect material misstatements. For example, the ratios that measure inventory turnover or expense-to-revenue ratios exploit these relationships and can indicate nonexistent inventory or misstatement in expense accounts and liabilities.

MULTIPLE-CHOICE QUESTIONS FOR PRACTICE AND REVIEW

MC 1 When verifying debits to the perpetual inventory records of a nonmanufacturing company, an auditor would be most interested in examining a sample of which of these purchasing documents?
  a. Approvals
  b. Requisitions
  c. Invoices
  d. Orders

MC 2 Which of the following is an internal control weakness for a company whose inventory of supplies consists of a large number of individual items?
  a. Supplies of relatively little value are expensed when purchased.
  b. The cycle basis is used for physical counts.
  c. The warehouse manager is responsible for maintenance of perpetual inventory records.
  d. Perpetual inventory records are maintained only for items of significant value.

MC 3 To protect against the preparation of improper or inaccurate cash disbursements, which effective internal control procedure would be required for all cheques?
  a. Signed by an officer after necessary supporting evidence has been examined
  b. Reviewed by a senior officer before mailing
  c. Sequentially numbered and accounted for by internal auditors
  d. Perforated or otherwise effectively cancelled when they are returned with the bank statement

MC 4 An auditee's purchasing system ends with the recording of a liability and its eventual payment. Which of the following best describes the auditor's primary concern with respect to liabilities resulting from the purchasing system?
  a. Accounts payable are not materially understated.
  b. Authority to incur liabilities is restricted to one designated person.
  c. Acquisition of materials is not made from one supplier or one group of suppliers.
  d. Commitments for all purchases are made only after established competitive bidding procedures are followed.

MC 5 Which of the following is an internal control procedure that would prevent a paid supplier invoice from being presented for payment a second time?
  a. Invoices should be prepared by individuals who are responsible for signing disbursement cheques.
  b. Disbursement cheques should be approved by a least two responsible management officials.
  c. The date on a supplier invoice should be within a few days of the date it is presented for payment.
  d. The official signing the cheque should compare it with the supplier invoice details and stamp "paid" on the invoice.

MC 6 Which of the following procedures would best detect the theft of valuable items from an inventory that consists of hundreds of different items selling for $1 to $10 and a few items selling for hundreds of dollars?
  a. Maintain a perpetual inventory of only the more valuable items with frequent periodic verification of the validity of the perpetual inventory record.
  b. Have an independent PA firm prepare an internal control report on the effectiveness of the administrative and accounting controls over inventory.

c. Have separate warehouse space for the more valuable items with frequent periodic physical counts and comparison with perpetual inventory records.

d. Trace items from the physical inventory count to the detailed year-end inventory compilation list.

MC 7 Budd, the purchasing agent of Lake Hardware Wholesalers, has a relative who owns a retail hardware store. Budd arranged for hardware to be delivered by Lake's suppliers/manufacturers to the relative's retail store on a COD basis, thereby enabling his relative to buy at Lake's wholesale prices. Budd was probably able to accomplish this because of Lake's poor internal control over which one of the items listed?

a. Disbursement cheques

b. Cash receipts

c. Perpetual inventory records

d. Purchase orders

MC 8 Which of the following is the best audit procedure for determining the existence of unrecorded liabilities?

a. Examine confirmation requests by creditors whose accounts appear on a subsidiary trial balance of accounts payable.

b. Examine a sample of cash disbursements in the period subsequent to the year-end.

c. Examine a sample of invoices a few days prior to and subsequent to the year-end to ascertain whether they have been properly recorded.

d. Examine unusual relationships between monthly accounts payable and recorded purchases.

MC 9 When evaluating inventory controls with respect to segregation of duties, which of the following would a PA be least likely to do?

a. Inspect documents.

b. Make enquiries.

c. Observe procedures.

d. Consider policy and procedure manuals.

MC 10 An auditor will usually trace the details of the test counts made during the observation of the physical inventory taking for a final inventory compilation. This audit procedure is undertaken to provide evidence that items physically present and observed by the auditor at the time of the physical inventory count are which of the following?

a. Owned by the auditee

b. Not obsolete

c. Physically present at the time of the preparation of the final inventory schedule

d. Included in the final inventory schedule

MC 11 Which of the following procedures is least likely to be performed before the balance sheet date?

a. Observation of inventory

b. Review of internal control over cash disbursements

c. Search for unrecorded liabilities

d. Confirmation of receivables

MC 12 The physical count of inventory of a retailer was higher than shown by the perpetual records. Which of the following could explain the difference?

a. Inventory items had been counted but the tags placed on the items had not been taken off the items and added to the inventory accumulation sheets.

b. Credit memos for several items returned by customers had not been recorded.

c. No journal entry had been made on the retailer's books for several items returned to its suppliers.

d. An item purchased "FOB shipping point" had not arrived at the date of the inventory count and was not reflected in the perpetual records.

MC 13 From the auditor's point of view, inventory counts are more acceptable prior to the year-end under which of the following circumstances?

a. Internal control is weak.

b. Accurate perpetual inventory records are maintained.

c. Inventory is slow moving.

d. Significant amounts of inventory are held on a consignment basis.

MC 14 To determine whether accounts payable are complete, an auditor performs a test to verify that all merchandise received is recorded. Which one of the following is the population for this test?

a. Suppliers' invoices

b. Purchase orders

c. Receiving reports

d. Cancelled cheques

MC 15 Which of the following internal control procedures most likely addresses the completeness assertion for inventory?

a. The work-in-process account is periodically reconciled with subsidiary inventory records.

b. Employees responsible for the custody of finished goods do not perform the receiving function.

c. Receiving reports are prenumbered and the numbering sequence is checked periodically.

d. There is a separation of duties between the payroll department and inventory accounting personnel.

(AICPA adapted)

EXERCISES AND PROBLEMS

EP 1
LO.1
and
LO.2
Liabilities: Authorization Control. The essential characteristic of the liabilities control system is to separate the authorization and approval to initiate a transaction from the responsibility for recordkeeping. What would constitute the authorization for accounts payable record-

ing? What documentary evidence could auditors examine as evidence of this authorization?

EP 2   **Cash Disbursements: Completeness Control.** The use of prenumbered documents is an important feature for

LO.1 and LO.2 control to ensure that all valid transactions are recorded and none are omitted. How could auditors gather evidence that the control for completeness of cash disbursements was being used properly by a company?

EP 3 **Automated Transactions: Authorization Control.** Two
LO.1 and LO.2 "automatic transactions" can be produced in a computerized accounting system: (1) cheque printing and signature and (2) purchase order at a preprogrammed stock reorder point. Assume management is uncomfortable with the computer creating transactions. How could management delay these transactions until they were "viewed" and authorized?

EP 4 **Liabilities: Insurance Coverage.** Why should auditors
LO.1 be concerned with the adequacy of casualty insurance coverage of a auditee's physical property?

EP 5 **Inventory: Enquiry-based Evidence.** What evidence
LO.4 and LO.5 regarding inventories and cost of sales can the auditor typically obtain from enquiry?

EP 6 **Specific Assertions: Fixed Assets.** Auditors plan their
LO.5 audit procedures to gather evidence about management's assertions in the financial statements. In addition to the broad assertions, such as existence and completeness, specific assertions are made for each major account area. List 9 or 10 examples of such specific assertions for the fixed assets and related accounts.

EP 7 **Repair and Maintenance Auditing.** Why should the re-
LO.5 pairs and maintenance expense account be audited at the same time as the fixed asset accounts?

EP 8 **Fixed Assets: Audit Procedures.** Audit procedures may
LO.5 be classified as:

    Recalculation/reperformance
    Observation
    Confirmation
    Enquiry
    Inspection of documents (vouching, tracing, scanning)
    Inspection of physical assets
    Analysis

Required:
Describe how each procedure may be used to gather evidence on fixed assets and which broad financial statement assertion(s) (existence, completeness, ownership [rights], valuation [allocation], and presentation and disclosure), are being addressed by the use of the procedure.

EP 9 **Payable Internal Control Questionnaire Items: Con-**
LO.1 **trol Objectives, Test of Controls Procedures, and Pos-**
LO.2 **sible Errors or Irregularities.** Listed below is a selection
LO.3 of items from the internal control questionnaire on payables shown in Appendix 12A.
1. Are invoices, receiving reports, and purchase orders reviewed by the cheque signer?
2. Are cheques dated in the cheque register with the date of the cheque?
3. Are quantity and quality of goods received determined at time of receipt by receiving personnel independent of the purchasing department?
4. Are suppliers' invoices matched against purchase orders and receiving reports before a liability is recorded?

Required:
For each one:
a. Identify the control objective to which it applies.
b. Specify one test of controls audit procedure an auditor could use to determine whether the control was operating effectively.
c. Using your business experience, your logic, your imagination, or all three, give an example of an error or fraud that could occur if the control was absent or ineffective.

EP 10 **Inventory Count, Measurement.** Consider the follow-
LO.1 ing examples of inventories in various businesses:
LO.4 1. Pharmaceuticals in a drug company
LO.5 2. Fine chemical compounds in a biotechnology company
3. Software in an information technology development company
4. New condominium office units in a commercial real estate developer
5. Fine art works in an interior design business

Required:
For each item indicate the challenges auditors would face in trying to count and measure the inventory, and suggest an approach to obtain sufficient audit evidence.

DISCUSSION CASES

DC 1 **Purchasing Control Procedures.** Long, PA, has been
LO.1 and LO.2 engaged to examine and report on the financial statements of Maylou Corporation. During the review phase of the study of Maylou's system of internal control over purchases, Long was given the following document flowchart for purchases (see Exhibit DC12.1–1).

Required:
Identify the procedures relating to purchase requisitions and purchase orders that Long would expect to find if Maylou's

system of internal control over purchases is effective. For example, purchase orders are prepared only after properly considering the time to order and quantity to order. Do not comment on the effectiveness of the flow of documents as presented in the flowchart or on separation of duties.

(AICPA adapted)

DC 2 **Control Tests for Cash Disbursements.** The Runge
LO.1 and LO.2 Controls Corporation manufactures and markets electrical control systems: temperature controls, machine controls,

EXHIBIT DC12.1-1   MAYLOU CORPORATION—DOCUMENT FLOWCHART FOR PURCHASES

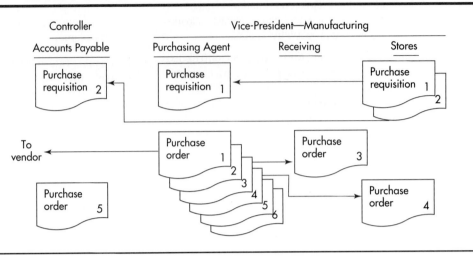

burglar alarms, and the like. Electrical and semiconductor parts are acquired from outside vendors, and systems are assembled in Runge's plant. The company incurs other administrative and operating expenditures. Liabilities for goods and services purchased are entered in an accounts payable journal, at which time the debits are classified to the asset and expense accounts they apply to. The company has specified control procedures for approving vendor invoices for payment, for signing cheques, for keeping records, and for reconciling the chequing accounts. The procedures appear to be well specified and placed in operation. You are the senior auditor on the engagement, and you need to specify a program (list) of control tests to audit the effectiveness of the controls over cash disbursements.

Required:
Using the seven general internal control objectives discussed in Chapter 9, specify two or more control tests to audit the effectiveness of typical control procedures. (*Hint:* From one sample of recorded cash disbursements, you can specify control tests related to several objectives. See Exhibit 12.4 for examples of control test procedures over cash disbursements.) Organize your list according to the example shown below for the "completeness" objective.

Completeness Objective	Test of Controls Program
All valid cash disbursements are recorded and none are omitted.	Determine the numerical sequence of cheques issued during the period and scan the sequence for missing numbers. (Scan the accounts payable records for amounts that appear to be too long outstanding, indicating liabilities for which payment may have been made but not recorded properly.)

DC 3
LO.3
and
LO.5

Unrecorded Liabilities Procedures. You were in the final stages of your audit of the financial statements of Ozine Corporation for the year ended December 31, 20X2, when you were consulted by the corporation's president. The president believes there is no point in your examining the 20X3 accounts payable records and testing data in support of 20X3 entries. He stated: (1) bills pertaining to 20X2 that were received too late to be included in the December accounts payable were recorded as of the year-end by the corporation by journal entry; (2) the internal auditor made tests after the year-end; and (3) he would furnish you with a letter certifying that there were no unrecorded liabilities.

Required:
a. Should your procedures for unrecorded liabilities be affected by the fact that the auditee made a journal entry to record 20X2 bills that were received later? Explain.
b. Should your test for unrecorded liabilities be affected by the fact that a letter is obtained in which a responsible management official certifies that to the best of his knowledge all liabilities have been recorded? Explain.
c. Should your test for unrecorded liabilities be eliminated or reduced because of the internal audit work? Explain.
d. What sources, in addition to the 20X3 accounts payable records, should you consider to locate possible unrecorded liabilities?

(AICPA adapted)

DC 4
LO.3
and
LO.5

Accounts Payable Confirmations. Clark and his partner, Kent, both PAs, are planning their audit program for the audit of accounts payable on the LeClair Corporation's annual audit. Saturday afternoon they reviewed the thick file of last year's working papers, and both of them remembered all too well the six days they spent last year on accounts payable.

Last year, Clark had suggested that they mail confirmations to 100 of LeClair's suppliers. The company regularly purchases from about 1,000 suppliers and these account payable balances fluctuate widely, depending on the volume of purchases and the terms LeClair's purchasing agent is able to negotiate. Clark's sample of 100 was designed to include accounts with large balances. In fact, the 100 accounts confirmed last year covered 80 percent of the total accounts payable.

Both Clark and Kent spent many hours tracking down minor differences reported in confirmation responses. Nonresponding accounts were investigated by comparing LeClair's balance with monthly statements received from suppliers.

Required:

a. Identify the accounts payable audit objectives that the auditors must consider in determining the audit procedures to be performed.
b. Identify situations when the auditors should use accounts payable confirmations, and discuss whether they are required to use them.
c. Discuss why the use of large dollar balances as the basis for selecting accounts payable for confirmation may not be the most efficient approach, and indicate a more efficient sample selection procedure that could be followed when choosing accounts payable for confirmation.

DC 5 **Inventory Count Observation: Planning and Sub-**
LO.3 **stantive Audit Procedures.** Cindy Li is the partner in
LO.4 charge of the audit of Blue Distributing Corporation, a
LO.5 wholesaler that owns one warehouse containing 80 percent of its inventory. Cindy is reviewing the working papers that were prepared to support the firm's opinion on Blue's financial statements. Cindy wants to be certain essential audit procedures are well documented in the working papers.

Required:

a. What evidence should Cindy expect to find that the audit observation of the auditee's physical count of inventory was well planned and that assistants were properly supervised?
b. What substantive audit procedures should Cindy find in the working papers that document management's assertions about existence and completeness of inventory quantities at the end of the year? (Refer to Appendix 12B for procedures.)

(AICPA adapted)

DC 6 **Sales/Inventory Cutoff.** Your auditee took a complete
LO.5 physical inventory count under your observation as of December 15 and adjusted the inventory control account (perpetual inventory method) to agree with the physical inventory. Based on the count adjustments as of December 15 and after review of the transactions recorded from December 16 to December 31, you are almost ready to accept the inventory balance as fairly stated.

However, your review of the sales cutoff as of December 15 and December 31 disclosed the following items not previously considered:

Cost	Sales Price	Shipped	Date Billed	Credited to Inventory Control
$28,400	$36,900	12/14	12/16	12/16
39,100	50,200	12/10	12/19	12/10
18,900	21,300	1/2	12/31	12/31

Required:

What adjusting journal entries, if any, would you make for each of these items? Explain why each adjustment is necessary.

(AICPA adapted)

DC 7 **Statistical Sampling Used to Estimate Inventory.** Ace
LO.4 Corporation does not conduct a complete annual physical
and count of purchased parts and supplies in its principal ware-
LO.5 house but, instead, uses statistical sampling to estimate the year-end inventory. Ace maintains a perpetual inventory record of parts and supplies. Management believes that statistical sampling is highly effective in determining inventory values and is sufficiently reliable that a physical count of each item of inventory is unnecessary.

Required:

a. List at least 10 normal audit procedures that should be performed to verify physical quantities whenever an auditee conducts a periodic physical count of all or part of its inventory (see Appendix 12B for procedures).
b. Identify the audit procedures you should use that change or are in addition to normal required audit procedures (in addition to those listed in your solution to part [a]) when a auditee utilizes statistical sampling to determine inventory value and does not conduct a 100 percent annual physical count of inventory items.

(AICPA adapted)

DC 8 **Inventory Procedures Using Generalized Audit Soft-**
LO.4 **ware.** You are conducting an audit of the financial state-
and ments of a wholesale cosmetics distributor with an
LO.5 inventory consisting of thousands of individual items. The distributor keeps its inventory in its own distribution centre and in two public warehouses. A perpetual inventory database is maintained on a computer system and is updated at the end of each business day. Each individual record of the perpetual inventory database contains the following data:

   item number
   location of item
   description of item
   quantity on hand
   cost per item
   date of last purchase
   date of last sale
   quantity sold during year

You are planning to observe the distributor's physical count of inventories as of a given date. You will have available a computer file, provided by the auditee, of the above items taken from their database as of the date of the physical count. Your firm has a generalized audit software package that can upload the auditee's computer data files.

Required:

List the basic inventory auditing procedures and, for each, describe how the use of the general-purpose audit software package and the perpetual inventory database might be helpful to the auditor in performing such auditing procedures. (See Appendix 12B for substantive audit procedures for inventory.)

Organize your answer as follows:

Basic inventory auditing procedures	How general purpose audit software package and the inventory file data might be helpful

(AICPA adapted)

DC 9
LO.5
Manufacturing Equipment and Accumulated Depreciation. In connection with a recurring examination of the financial statements of the Louis Manufacturing Company for the year ended December 31, you have been assigned the audit of the fixed assets accounts (Manufacturing Equipment, Manufacturing Equipment—Accumulated Depreciation, and Repairs to Manufacturing Equipment). Your review of Louis's policies and procedures has disclosed the following pertinent information:

1. The Manufacturing Equipment account includes the net invoice price plus related freight and installation costs for all of the equipment in Louis's manufacturing plant.
2. The Manufacturing Equipment—Accumulated Depreciation accounts are supported by a subsidiary ledger, which shows the cost and accumulated depreciation for each piece of equipment.
3. An annual budget for capital expenditures of $1,000 or more is prepared by the executive committee and approved by the board of directors. Capital expenditures over $1,000 that are not included in this budget must be approved by the board of directors, and variations of 20 percent or more must be explained to the board. Approval by the supervisor of production is required for capital expenditures under $1,000.
4. Company employees handle installation, removal, repair, and rebuilding of the machinery. Work orders are prepared for these activities and are subject to the same budgetary control as other expenditures. Work orders are not required for external expenditures.

Required:

a. Prepare a list of the major specific objectives (assertions) for your audit of the Manufacturing Equipment, Manufacturing Equipment—Accumulated Depreciation, and Repairs of Manufacturing Equipment accounts. Do not include in this listing the auditing procedures designed to accomplish these objectives.
b. Prepare the portion of your audit program applicable to the review of current-year additions to the Manufacturing Equipment account. (You will find Appendix

12B helpful, although it does not specifically mention manufacturing equipment.)

(AICPA adapted)

DC 10
LO.1
LO.2
LO.5
Peacock Company: Incomplete Flowchart of Inventory and Purchasing Control Procedures. Peacock Company is a wholesaler of soft goods. The inventory is composed of approximately 3,500 different items. The company employs a computerized batch processing system to maintain its perpetual inventory records. The system is run each weekend so that inventory reports are available on Monday morning for management use. The system has been functioning satisfactorily for the past 10 years, providing the company with accurate records and timely reports.

The preparation of purchase orders has been automatic as a part of the inventory system to ensure that the company will maintain enough inventory to meet customer demand. When an item of inventory falls below a predetermined level, a record of the inventory items is written. This record is used in conjunction with the vendor file to prepare the purchase orders.

Exception reports are prepared during the update of the inventory and the preparation of the purchase orders. These reports list any errors or exceptions identified during the processing. In addition, the system provides for management approval of all purchase orders exceeding a specified amount. Any exceptions or items requiring management approval are handled by supplemental runs on Monday morning and are combined with the weekend results.

A system flowchart of Peacock Company's inventory and purchase order procedure is in Exhibit DC 10–1.

Required:

a. The illustrated system flowchart (Exhibit DC 10–1) of Peacock Company's inventory and purchase order system was prepared, but several steps that are important to the successful operations of the system are omitted from the chart. Describe the steps that have been omitted and indicate where the omissions have occurred. The flowchart does not need to be redrawn.
b. In order for Peacock's inventory/purchase order system to function properly, control procedures should be included in the system. Describe the type of control procedures Peacock Company should use in its system to ensure proper functioning, and indicate where these procedures would be placed in the system.

(CMA adapted)

DC 11
LO.3
and
LO.5

Inventory Evidence and Long-Term Purchase Contracts. During the audit of Mason Company, Inc., for the calendar year 20X2, you noticed that the company produces aluminum cans at the rate of about 40 million units annually. On the plant tour, you noticed a large stockpile of raw aluminum in storage. Your inventory observation and pricing procedures showed this stockpile to be the raw materials inventory of 400 tons valued at $240,000 (average cost). Enquiry with the production

EXHIBIT DC 10-1 PEACOCK COMPANY—INVENTORY AND PURCHASE ORDER PROCEDURE

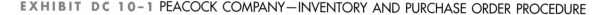

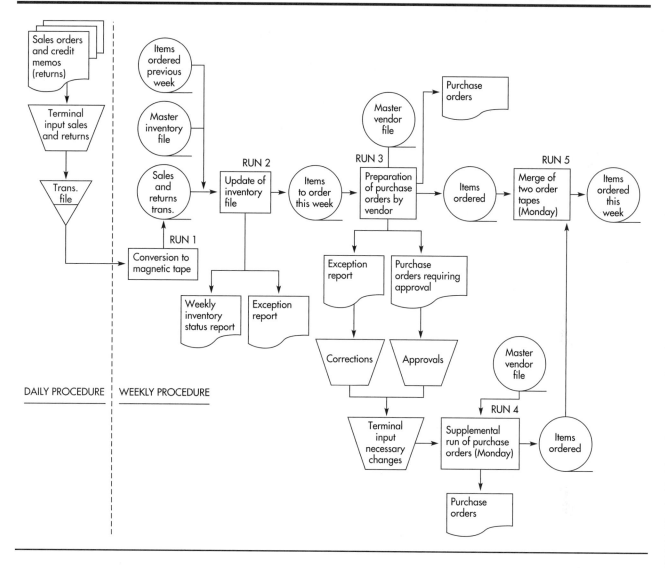

chief yielded the information that 400 tons was about a four-month supply of raw materials.

Suppose you learn that Mason had executed a firm long-term purchase contract with All Purpose Aluminum Company to purchase raw materials on the following schedule:

Delivery Date	Quantity (tons)	Total Price
January 30, 20X3	500	$300,000
June 30, 20X3	700	420,000
December 30, 20X3	1,000	500,000

Because of recent economic conditions, principally a decline in the demand for raw aluminum and a consequent oversupply, the price stood at $400 per ton (1 ton = 2,000 pounds) as of January 15, 20X3. Commodities

experts predict that this low price will prevail for 12 to 15 months or until there is a general economic recovery.

Required:

a. Describe the procedures you would employ to gather evidence about this contract (including its initial discovery).

b. What facts recited in the case are ones that you would have to discover for yourself in an audit?

c. Discuss the effect this contract has on the financial statements.

DC 12 Deake Corporation: Property Accounting System.
LO.1 Deake Corporation is a medium-sized, diversified manufacturing company. Recently, Jack Richards was promoted to manager of the property accounting section. Richards is having difficulty responding to some of the requests from individuals in other departments for information about the company's fixed assets. Some of the requests are:

1. The controller has requested schedules of individual fixed assets to support the balances in the general ledger. Richards has furnished the necessary information, but it was late. The manner in which the records are organized makes it difficult to obtain information easily.
2. The maintenance manager wishes to verify the existence of a punch press he thinks was repaired twice. He has asked Richards to confirm the asset number and location of the press.
3. The insurance department wants data on the cost and book values of assets to include in its review of current insurance coverage.
4. The tax department has requested data that can be used to calculate depreciation for tax purposes.
5. The company's internal auditors have spent a significant amount of time in the property accounting section recently, attempting to audit the annual depreciation expense.

The property account records consist of a set of manual books. These records show the date the asset was acquired, the account number for the asset, the dollar amount capitalized, and the estimated useful life of the asset for depreciation purposes.

After many frustrations, Richards has realized that his records are inadequate and that he cannot supply data when requested. He has decided to discuss his problem with the controller, Jim Castle.

Richards: Jim, something has got to give. My people are working overtime and can't keep up. You worked in property accounting before you became controller. You know I can't tell the tax, insurance, and maintenance people everything they need to know from my records. Also, that internal auditing team is coming back to check my area in a couple of weeks, and last year my group spent at least a hundred hours creating data to answer their questions. That really slows down the work pace. The requests of these people are reasonable, and we should be able to answer these questions and provide the needed data. I think we need a computerized property accounting system. I would like to talk to the information systems people to see if they can help me.

Castle: Jack, I think you have a good idea, but be sure you are personally involved in the design of any system so you get all the information you need.

Required:

a. Identify and justify four major objectives Deake Corporation's computerized property accounting system should meet to provide the data necessary to respond to requests for information by company personnel and auditors.

b. Identify the data that should be included in the computer record for each asset included in the property account.

(CMA adapted)

DC 13 **Grover Manufacturing—Purchasing Defalcation.** On
LO.5 January 11 at the beginning of your annual audit of the Grover Manufacturing Company's financial statements

for the year just ended December 31, the company president confides to you that an employee is living on a scale in excess of that which his salary would support.

The employee has been a buyer in the purchasing department for six years and has charge of purchasing all general materials and supplies. He is authorized to sign purchase orders for amounts up to $2,000. Purchase orders in excess of $2,000 require the countersignature of the general purchasing agent.

The president understands that the usual audit of financial statements is not designed to disclose immaterial fraud or conflicts of interest, although such events may be discovered. The president authorizes you, however, to expand your regular audit procedures and to apply additional audit procedures to determine whether there is any evidence that the buyer has been misappropriating company funds or has been engaged in activities that are a conflict of interest.

Required:

List the audit procedures that you would apply to the company records and documents in an attempt to:

1. Discover evidence within the purchasing department of defalcations being committed by the buyer. Give the purpose of each audit procedure.
2. Provide leads about possible collusion between the buyer and suppliers. Give the purpose of each audit procedure.

DC 14 **J. J. Barnicke Ltd.: Missing Millions and a Widow**
LO.5 **with a Lavish Lifestyle.**[4] Elizabeth (Liz) Lake lives in a million-dollar mansion in Don Mills. She spends time with her three children at a 1134-square-metre waterfront "cottage" in central Ontario. The slim, attractive widow also gets about $ 22,600 a month—or $270,000 a year—to maintain those properties and cover living expenses.

And prominent realtor Joe Barnicke says it's all possible with money her late husband stole from him, his firm J. J. Barnicke Ltd.—and a family trust fund. Liz Lake, who is in her mid-30s, has kept that lifestyle for almost two years since her husband jumped in front of a train at York Mills subway station. Jim Lake committed suicide on the morning of March 18, 1996, less than an hour after Barnicke confronted him at the firm's downtown office about a lot of missing money. Lake, the firm's star chief financial officer, excused himself and never returned.

Barnicke and his company immediately filed a lawsuit in court against Liz Lake and her husband's estate to recover what was left of $19.8 million Lake allegedly swiped over a decade. But Barnicke, the firm's 74-year-old chairman, has found it isn't easy trying to get any of the alleged stolen money back. The courts are slow and Liz Lake is fighting him all the way for the mansion, country estate, cars, boats, snowmobiles, and life insurance proceeds. Barnicke won't talk publicly about the case but acquaintances say he's bitter and disillusioned over Liz Lake's continuing monthly "allowances" and the lengthy court proceedings. In the battle over the estate,

[4] Tony Van Apphen, *The Toronto Star*, December 14, 1997, p. A1; Scott Burnside, *The Toronto Sun*, June 23, 1996, p. 45.

Barnicke figures there's now only about $4 million to $5 million left—including life insurance proceeds—after all the spending.

No wonder. One of Lake's own accounting reports filed with the court reveals the couple spent almost $7 million after tax in the three years before his death. Expenses included:

- $ 20,949.16 for booze,
- $ 110,577.25 for a BMW,
- $ 45,148.24 for his wife's clothes,
- $ 256,952.96 for vacations,
- $ 287,540.89 for gifts, and
- $ 720,550.38 for custom-made cottage furniture.

Lake fuelled that spending by jacking up his pay through misappropriation of Barnicke funds, according to documents filed in court. After a brief probe, Barnicke and top-flight forensic accountants Lindquist Avey McDonald Baskerville Inc. said a paper trail revealed that the likeable Lake moved money from the company's operating funds and the chairman's personal accounts to a payroll system. He then transferred the money into personal bank accounts at the Bank of Nova Scotia.

Lake ran the payroll system, from which he was paid. Investigators found a copy of Lake's T4 form to Revenue Canada in his briefcase showing a gross income of $2,468,938.63 for 1995. But Lake's annual salary never exceeded $110,000, Barnicke said in the claim. Barnicke's lawsuit also alleges Lake, who was 36 when he died, had improperly moved $1.5 million from a trust fund for Barnicke's three children to his own account. Barnicke said his signature on the transfer requests were forgeries.

Liz Lake, who is the estate's litigation guardian, denies her husband stole the money. If her husband did, it's Barnicke's own fault and he should suffer the losses, her statement of defence said. If the company had shown a minimal amount of diligence, it could have stopped any alleged losses and Lake might still be alive, she added. "The plaintiffs (Barnicke) by their gross negligence caused or contributed to the death of her husband and the father of her three children," the statement of defence said. "She and her children have been and will continue to be subjected to embarrassment, humiliation, and loss of reputation in the community." She noted that senior Barnicke executives visited the mansion on numerous occasions.

"Like other senior officers of J. J. Barnicke Limited, Mr. Lake openly lived an affluent lifestyle, which could only have been afforded by someone earning substantially in excess" of $100,000, Mrs. Lake alleges in the court documents. Barnicke has said Lake told co-workers he inherited the money.

She insists that all money received from the company was earned, "and was accurately recorded in J. J. Barnicke Ltd.'s books and records." Those books and records were kept at the company offices and in fact Lake paid taxes on the full amount. As well, Elizabeth Lake points out, the Barnicke books were made available to accountants Ernst & Young "at least annually" and that all her husband's earnings were deposited in their joint account at the Bank of Nova Scotia. (The bank is also named in the company's civil suit.)

Joe Barnicke, the blustery patriarch of the company, scoffs at the suggestion they are responsible for any financial loss. "He stole the money," he told *The Toronto Sun* this week. "He stole the money. That's all we can say."

Meanwhile, Barnicke's lawyer, Chris Osborne, said the cost of paying the mortgage, hydro, and other upkeep of the luxurious properties for Liz Lake is "bleeding" the estate of hundreds of thousands of dollars. But moments before Osborne could ask the Ontario Court, general division, to stop it by selling most of the property, Liz Lake surprised everyone. Her lawyer indicated she wished to change counsel again and needed more time for preparation. She is now dealing with her third legal firm in the case.

Reports finally appeared on the public record in connection with the receiver's requests for further direction on the propriety of some of Lake's spending and other matters. Personal documents and other information in the reports suggest Liz and Jim Lake didn't hold back in the last years of his life. Lake collected annual paycheques ranging from $2.2 million to $4.3 million in gross income from 1990 to 1995. Lake's own printout of "inflows" and "outflows" covering July 1993 to February 1996 disclosed that income from work, interest, and revenue on property sales totalled about $7 million. But the outflows or expenses left them with only $35,000. Furthermore, (the receiver) said at one point the couple regularly rang up credit card charges of more than $43,000 a month. The Lakes had "very lavish spending habits," the receiver noted.

There was the 558-square-metre Don Mills mansion, with five bedrooms, triple car garage and circular driveway near the exclusive Donalda Club at Don Mills and York Mills Rds. There was the cottage with six bedrooms and boathouse containing three slips at the northeast end of Balsam Lake. There were three autos, including a Cadillac and the BMW. There was a fleet of six boats featuring a 10-metre SeaRay luxury cruiser. There were five snowmobiles. There were country clubs, big parties, and skiing weekends. Lake bought a 7-metre wooden antique boat for $ 7,500 and then spent $ 131,000 restoring it, the receiver said.

Annual carrying costs for the house and cottage including mortgages and taxes are a whopping $124,000 and $150,000 respectively. In 18 months, the receiver has disbursed more than $1 million from the estate, he said. The receiver's own costs have topped $200,000. Liz Lake has spent more than $800,000, including mortgage payments and her monthly stipend. Her lawyers' costs alone have accounted for $300,000 of that amount.

Required:

a. Comment on the apparent control weaknesses at J. J. Barnicke suggested by the events in the above story. What general recommendations for the company's internal controls can you derive from this situation?

b. Assume the role of the judge. Which party's arguments do you think are more convincing? What additional evidence could each party provide to you that would strengthen their case?

c. What audit procedures might have been used to uncover the transfer of company funds to Mr. Lake's bank account?

DC 15 **Repairs Expense, Error Adjustment.** You are the audi-
LO.5 tor of Bittern Inc. Bittern's long-standing policy is to capitalize all repairs and maintenance payments that exceed $10,000, without assessing the nature of the expenditure. Many of Bittern's buildings and equipment are aging and repairs are becoming frequent and more expensive. You have concerns that a material amount of building repairs and maintenance expense is being capitalized, and undertake a detailed examination of all the building asset additions during the current year. Your analysis indicates that approximately $400,000 of repairs expense has been capitalized as buildings in the current year. Materiality for the audit is $500,000. In the prior year's audit, the staff noted approximately $100,000 of repairs expenses had been capitalized, but no adjustment was recorded. The estimated useful life of Bittern's buildings is 25 years, and the average remaining useful life of their buildings is approximately 8 years.

Required:

a. Describe the impact of the above error on the current year financial statements and the impact it will have on future periods' financial statements when the error reverses, if it is not adjusted.

b. Describe the impact the unadjusted error from the prior year will have on the current year's financial statements.

c. State whether you would require Bittern to adjust for this error, and support your conclusion. If you require an adjustment, provide the required journal entry.

d. What recommendation would you include in the management letter relating to the situation above?

DC 16 **Mining Properties, Using Work of Experts.** White Ice
LO.5 Mines Inc. is a mining company. During 20X4 White Ice acquired a diamond mine located in the far north for $800 million from Albatross Inc. The purchase price is based on the mine's inventory of extracted diamonds, with an appraised value of $300 million, plus diamond reserves estimated in the range of $600 million to over $2 billion. White Ice raised $100 million of the funds to acquire the mine by issuing public shares on the Canadian Adventure Exchange, with the remainder being lent by a consortium of three major Canadian banks. Shortly after the IPO, a shareholder resolution was passed to require White Ice to appoint new auditors from one of the large, national auditing firms. The previous auditor was a small firm that also was the auditor for Albatross for many years. The new auditor of White Ice is examining the existence, valuation, and ownership assertions for its mining assets for the year ended December 31, 20X4. White Ice informs the auditor that its mining specialists provided the appraisals for use in preparing the prospectus for their Initial Public Offering of shares, and to satisfy the due diligence enquiries of the three banks. The new auditor has determined that it will be necessary to rely on an independent expert to provide a valuation report to support the audit opinion.

Required:

a. Refer to CAS 620 (Using the Work of an Auditor's Expert) and develop an audit program for verifying White Ice's diamond mine investment.

b. White Ice's management is concerned that using another expert will drive up the audit cost. The managers (some of whom previously worked for a mining company called Bre-X) suggest it would be more efficient for the auditor to rely on the specialist reports already generated for the IPO and the bank financing. As the new auditor, how would you respond to this suggestion? You may want to refer to CAS 550 (Related Parties) for guidance.

DC 17 **Audit Issues in Internet Business.** TheShoppingMall.
LO.5 com (TSM) is an Internet business that provides a website with links to a variety of online shopping websites with which TSM has established "marketing partnerships." TSM also provides advertising, promotions, and discount coupons for its partner shopping sites. TSM was incorporated under the laws of Canada in early 1999. The original financing to start TSM came from its president, Mr. Fogg, and several outside venture capital investors. Mr. Fogg's plan is to issue common shares to the public after the business model has proven itself. The proceeds from this share issue will be used to repay the debt financing provided by Mr. Fogg and the venture capitalists. It is now late 20X2 and the financial results are being prepared for the year ended November 30, 20X2. Mr. Fogg believes that early 20X3 will be the right time to issue public shares

The preliminary financial statements for the year ended November 30, 20X2, include the following items:

TSM contracted with three partners for $103.5 million to develop all their online shopping systems, including customer relation management and payment processing. The partners are name-brand product manufacturers that want to start direct online retailing. TSM has never completed this type of system before, but expects to complete it by the end of 20X4. TSM recorded $36.5 million of the $103.5 as revenues, deferring the rest to be reported when the work was completed.

TSM also provides an online auction service where individuals and businesses can list items for sale and interested purchasers can bid on them. TSM provides the auction service, arranges delivery, and processes payments for a fee of 8 percent of the selling price. TSM recognized the full selling price of these auction items as revenue and the net 92 percent paid to the seller as "product costs."

TSM provided an online travel agency, selling airline tickets and hotel rooms and car rentals. It recorded as revenue the entire fee paid by a customer for an airline ticket or hotel room. The amount TSM paid the airline or hotel chain that supplied the ticket or room was classified as "product costs." TSM reported that it earned $152 million in revenues, and its product costs came to $134 million, leaving $18 million of "gross profits." TSM's other costs—like advertising and salaries—netted out to a loss of $102 million. While a traditional travel agency, which has a fixed commission, would show only the commission as revenue, Mr. Fogg believes it is appropriate to use the gross bookings amounts as revenue, because, unlike a traditional travel agency, TSM purchased the hotel room outright, so it assumed the full risk of ownership and could control the profit made on each sale.

To build awareness for its site, TSM purchased $1 million of advertising on several other companies' retailing websites. In exchange for advertising on these sites, TSM sold advertising worth $1million for these other companies on TSM's site. Mr. Fogg believes this bartering was an astute business move that "…saves us tons of cash and generates revenues at the same time."

TSM used promotions to bring people to its website. For example, customers who bought a pizza from a national pizza chain received a coupon for $10 off their next TSM purchase. TSM accounted for these costs as marketing expenses rather than recording them as a cost of goods sold. Mr. Fogg stated, "The gross profit line is very sensitive, so it is preferable to show these expenses below the gross profit line." Other expenses that TSM includes in "marketing expenses" are costs of warehousing, packaging, and shipping goods to customers.

Mr. Fogg and several top TSM executives have received options to purchase common shares of TSM at a fixed price of $1 per share.

Mr. Fogg realized the TSM financial statements must provide some disclosure of the accounting policies chosen. TSM's note on revenue recognition states, "Revenue is recognized when earned."

Required:

TSM plans to issue its Initial Public Offering of shares in early 20X4. It will require a set of audited financial statements. Assume the role of TSM's auditor. What is your position on the accounting matters listed above?

DC 18 **Comprehensive Audit Case: Tour Business.** On The
LO.5 Road Inc. (OTR) is a tour company owned by Joy Kerouak. OTR offers organized tours three weeks to six months long, targetted to early retirees 55 years old and over. OTR is in its third year of operations. Joy is not actively involved in the business and has hired a team of skilled managers to run the business. OTR is a private Canadian corporation, with Joy owning 100 percent of its common shares. The managers receive a bonus of 30 percent of monthly pretax profits.

OTR's tours are guided road trips across North America. Tour groups travel in brightly painted camper vans and visit sites of historic events of the 1950s and 1960s. The packages are sold online and through travel agents, under the following terms:

- A deposit of 40 percent is required upon booking, which is refundable until 14 days before the start of the tour and is nonrefundable after that point.
- The remaining 60 percent is due 14 days before the start of the tour. This is nonrefundable.
- If for some reason OTR is unable to offer the tour, 100 percent is refunded to the customer.

Online sales are paid by credit card. Travel agent sales are the same as those terms previously listed, except the agents receive payments from customers and forward these to OTR within seven days. Travel agents receive a commission of 10 percent of the tour selling price, which they deduct prior to forwarding the payments to OTR. During OTR's three years of operating, about half the tours have been sold through travel agents and the other half online, but the online portion has been increasing each year.

Economic conditions in the travel industry have been declining recently, and bankruptcies of travel agents are increasing. If travel agents that sell OTR tours go bankrupt, OTR would probably lose any customer payments the travel agents had not yet forwarded. Over its three year history, the company's bad debts from travel agents have been about 5 percent of sales. To date, only one tour has had to be cancelled by OTR due to Hurricane Katrina flooding New Orleans. This refund made up about 2 percent of the total 20X5 revenues of OTR.

The main assets of OTR are a fleet of 50 camper vans that were purchased when the business started up. Since these are high-quality VW vans in classic designs, management chose to depreciate the cost of the camper vans over 9.4 years. However, this winter management informed Joy that at least 35 of the vans are in poor condition and will need to be replaced at a cost of $40,000 each before the spring tour season begins. Joy has contacted her banker, Nik Beat, to arrange to borrow the cost of replacing the camper vans. Currently, OTR is debt-free. Mr. Beat requested audited financial statements prepared in accordance with generally accepted accounting principles for the first three years of OTR's operations. Since to date OTR has mainly prepared its financial statements for the purpose of computing the managers' monthly bonuses, Joy is not sure if these statements will meet Mr. Beat's requirements. Joy has hired you to advise her on accounting issues and on how to obtain the audit that her banker is requesting.

Required:

Assume the role of an advisor to Joy and answer the following questions:

a. Identify the main users of OTR's financial statements and the kinds of decisions/evaluations that each user will make based on these financial statements.

b. What are the main objectives of OTR's management that may affect the accounting choices it makes in preparing OTR's financial statements?

c. Describe four or more possible revenue and expense recognition points for OTR's tour business, indicating the most appropriate method in your judgement. Provide the reasons that support your judgement.

d. Outline the key issues that would need to be addressed by a prospective auditor in order to decide whether to accept the engagement.

e. Prepare a report to Joy describing in detail a preliminary audit plan for OTR. Include explanations for each component you include in the preliminary plan that will help Joy understand the audit objectives and procedures.

DC 19 **Cash Payments Fraud: Medical Benefits Claims.** This
LO.5 case is modelled on the Application Case and Analysis in
the chapter.

Case Description Beta Magnetic, a large company,
experienced a fraud in the cash payments processed for
employees' supplementary medical benefit claims.
Fictitious benefit claims were paid by the company,
which self-insured up to $50,000 per employee for sup-
plementary benefits costs (such as physiotherapy and
accupuncture) not covered by other medical and benefits
coverage plans. The expense account that included
legitimate and false charges was "employee supplementary medical benefits."

As manager of the claims payment department,
Martha Lee was considered one of Beta Magnetic's
best employees. She never missed a day of work in 10
years, and her department had one of the company's
best efficiency ratings. Controls were considered
good, including the verification by a claims processor
that (1) the patient was a Beta employee, (2) treatments were covered by the company-sponsored plan,
(3) the charges were within approved guidelines and
not covered by another plan, (4) the cumulative claims
for the employee did not exceed $50,000 (if over
$50,000, a claim was submitted to an insurance com-
pany), and (5) the calculation for payment was correct. After verification processing, claims were sent to
the claims payment department to pay the medical
practitioner directly. No payments ever went directly
to employees. Martha Lee prepared false claims on
real employees, forging the signature of various claims
processors, adding her own review approval, naming
bogus medical practitioners who would be paid by the
payment department. The payments were mailed to
various post office box addresses and to her husband's
business address.

Nobody ever verified claims information with the
employee. The employees received no reports of medical benefits paid on their behalf. While the department
had performance reports by claims processors, these
reports did not show claim-by-claim details. No one
verified the credentials of the medical practitioners.
Over the last seven years, Martha Lee and her husband
stole $3.5 million, and, until the last, no one noticed
anything unusual about the total amount of claims
paid.

Audit Trail The falsified claim forms were in Beta's
files, containing all the fictitious data on employee
names, processor signatures, medical practitioners'
bills, and phony medical practitioners addresses. The
cancelled cheques, "endorsed" by the doctors, were
returned by the bank and kept in Beta's files. Martha
Lee and her husband were somewhat clever: they deposited the cheques in various banks in accounts
opened in the names and identification of the "medical
practitioners."

Martha Lee did not make any mistakes in covering the
paper trail. She drew the attention of an auditor who saw
her take her 24 claims-processing employees out to an
annual staff appreciation luncheon in a fleet of stretch
limousines.

Audit Approach Analysis The auditor's objective is to
obtain evidence determing whether employee medical
benefits "existed" in the sense of being valid claims paid
to valid medical practitioners.

Controls relevant to the process are good as far as they
go. The claims processors used internal data in their
work—employee files for identification, treatment descriptions submitted by medical practitioners with comparisons to plan provisions and mathematical calculations.
This work amounted to all the approval necessary for the
claims payment department to prepare a cheque. There
were no controls that connected the claims data with outside sources, such as employee acknowledgment or medical practitioners investigation.

Required:
Describe in detail the audit procedures you would
perform in this case. Consider tests of control, and substantive tests such as dual-purpose tests of transactions
and/or tests of details of balance. Which tests do you
consider likely to detect Martha Lee's theft? Why?

DC 20 **Analysis of Purchasing Process and Controls.** Integrated Measurement Systems Inc. (IMS) is a Canadian
public company that manufactures high-end measuring
devices used primarily in the oil and natural gas industries. In 20X3, it had sales of $100 million and earnings
before income tax of $5 million. The company has a
December 31 year-end.

Ted Pollock, IMS's CEO, is a proponent of strong
corporate governance. He has spent the last year
strengthening IMS's internal control environment. He
believes that organizations that demonstrate good
corporate governance practices will be perceived
favourably by the markets. Ted wants to make a presentation to IMS's audit committee supporting the position
that throughout the year the company's internal controls
functioned in accordance with the company's control
objectives. Depending on the reaction of the audit committee, Ted would like to make the presentation an annual occurrence. IMS has hired your professional
services firm to assist Ted in preparing the content of his
presentation.

Your firm is currently assessing the purchasing process.
Accordingly, IMS has provided you with relevant material
and access to the company's resources (Exhibit II). As
part of the analysis of this process, IMS has asked
you to:

1. identify the existing key internal controls within the
   purchasing process,
2. describe the procedures that IMS could use to test the
   controls, and
3. identify the internal control weakness within the purchasing process and recommend improvements.

It is now the first week of March 20X4. The partner
responsible for the IMS audit engagement provides you
with her notes from a meeting with Ted Pollock (Exhibit I).
You have been asked by the partner to prepare the

analysis of IMS's purchasing process, addressing the three requirements, and to identify any additional issues and make any observations that would be relevant to the engagement.

Required:

Prepare an analysis of IMS's purchasing process, addressing the three requirements requested by the IMS CEO, in a report format suitable for the CEO's use.

EXHIBIT   I   **MEMO TO CA FROM PARTNER**

I met today with the CEO of IMS, Ted Pollock, for the purpose of discussing his needs. He provided the following information:

IMS's corporate governance framework

IMS has adopted an approach to establishing a strong corporate governance framework that includes:

1. Documentation of the existing processes and controls
2. Identification of the key controls in the process
3. Evaluation and testing of the internal controls and implementation of improvements

Control objectives that relate to the purchasing process

1. Proper approval of all transactions
2. Safeguarding of company assets
3. Prevention and detection of errors and irregularities
4. Accuracy and completeness of books and records
5. Appropriate use of information

EXHIBIT   II   **PURCHASING PROCESS DOCUMENTATION UPDATED NOVEMBER 20X3**

The purchasing process has four major components, namely:

1. Vendor prequalification
2. Purchase of goods and/or services
3. Receipt of goods
4. Settlement

Process description

The purchasing process begins when there is a requirement for goods or services. A manually completed purchase request form is sent from the operating department (e.g., Sales Marketing, Manufacturing, etc.) to the purchasing department. The purchasing clerk numbers these documents and reviews each purchase request form to verify that a signature is present.

Purchase request forms must be authorized by the signature of a person with the appropriate level of authority. The amount of the expenditure determines the level of authority required, and the expenditure authorization levels are organized in tiers. Because there are so many possible combinations of departments and authorization levels, the operating departments are responsible for ensuring that their purchase request forms are signed by individuals with the appropriate level of authority. This requirement eliminates the need for the purchasing clerk to check the specifics of their signatures.

The purchasing clerk sends the purchase requests to the purchasing manager for review and approval.

The approved purchase request is then sent to the buyer who sources the purchase. If the amount is below $5,000, selection of the vendor is left up to the buyer. For purchases in excess of $5,000 but less than $25,000, a vendor from the Prequalification Listing is selected, again at the discretion of the buyer. For purchases in excess of $25,000, a formal bidding process is performed. However, at the discretion of the buyer, the bid process can be waived if deemed to be cost inefficient.

Upon selection of the vendor, the buyer inputs the purchase request information into a purchase order form. The purchase order is forwarded to the purchasing manager for review, and a photocopy is made and filed, in numerical order, with the appropriate photocopy of the purchase request. The original purchase order is then sent back to the buyer who delivers it to the vendor.

All goods are received in the warehouse. All employees have access to the warehouse. The goods are checked against the packaging slip and are examined for damage, etc. If the goods are acceptable, the bill of lading is signed off by the receiver. A copy of the signed bill of lading is then forwarded to the purchasing clerk who matches it to the file copy of the purchase request and purchase order. If there are differences in the details (over/under shipment, wrong product, etc.), the bill of lading is forwarded to the buyer for resolution with the vendor. If no problems are noted, copies of the three documents are sent to the payables group for settlement.

The receiver, John Smith (who was hired 6 months ago), sends the goods to the user department that made the original purchase request along with a photocopy of the bill of lading. The user department agrees the quantities noted by the receiver and files the bill of lading. User departments have noted that, recently, there have been an increasing number of manual adjustments to the quantities shipped versus received.

Any unmatched purchase requests and purchase orders that remain outstanding for over 90 days are returned by the purchasing clerk to the user department that originally ordered the goods on the assumption that the goods have been received. It is then the responsibility of the user department to follow up and forward the paperwork to the payables group for settlement.

If a signed bill of lading is forwarded to the purchasing clerk for which there is no source documentation (i.e., no purchase request or purchase order exists), the purchasing clerk follows up with the buyer to understand the nature of the receipt. At the same time, a copy of the bill of lading is also sent to the payables group.

(CICA Adapted)

APPENDIX 12A

INTERNAL CONTROL QUESTIONNAIRES

· ·

EXHIBIT   12A-1   INTERNAL CONTROL QUESTIONNAIRE
PURCHASES, PAYABLES, AND PAYMENTS PROCESS

**OVERALL COMPANY-LEVEL CONTROL AND CONTROL ACTIVITIES ASSESSMENT
(Refer to responses recorded for questions in Exhibit PIII-2)**

Are company-level and general control activities adequate as they apply to the purchases, payables, and payments components of the information system?

- Consider the impact of any weakness in company-level and general control activities on planned audit approach and procedures.
- Assess the potential for weaknesses to result in a material misstatement of the financial information generated from this accounting cycle. If a significant risk of misstatement is assessed, perform procedures to determine extent of any misstatement.

Consider adequacy of the following general controls in place in the purchases, payables, and payments process to:

—prevent unauthorized access or changes to programs and data
—ensure the security and privacy of data
—control and maintain key systems
—protect assets susceptible to misappropriation
—ensure completeness, accuracy, and authorization of data and processing
—ensure adequate management trails exist

**PURCHASING AND ACCOUNTS PAYABLE APPLICATION
Environment and general controls relevant to this application:**

1. Is the purchasing department independent of the accounting department, receiving department, and shipping department?
2. Are receiving report copies transmitted to inventory custodians? to purchasing? to the accounting department?

Assertion-Based Control Evaluation:
Validity objective:

3. Are suppliers' invoices matched against purchase orders and receiving reports before a liability is recorded?

   Completeness objective:
4. Are the purchase order forms prenumbered and is the numerical sequence checked for missing documents?
5. Are receiving report forms prenumbered and is the numerical sequence checked for missing documents?
6. Is the accounts payable department notified of goods returned to vendors?
7. Are suppliers' invoices listed immediately upon receipt?
8. Are unmatched receiving reports reviewed frequently and investigated for proper recording?

EXHIBIT 12A-1   INTERNAL CONTROL QUESTIONNAIRE
PURCHASES, PAYABLES, AND PAYMENTS PROCESS (continued)

Authorization objective:
9. Are competitive bids received and reviewed for certain items?
10. Are all purchases made only on the basis of approved purchase requisitions?
11. Are purchases made for employees authorized through the regular purchases procedures?
12. Are purchase prices approved by a responsible purchasing officer?
13. Are all purchases, whether for inventory or expense, routed through the purchasing department for approval?
14. Are shipping documents authorized and prepared for goods returned to vendors?
15. Are invoices approved for payment by a responsible officer?

Accuracy objective:
16. Are quantity and quality of goods received determined at the time of receipt by receiving personnel independent of the purchasing department?
17. Are suppliers' monthly statements reconciled with individual accounts payable accounts?
18. In the accounts payable department, are invoices checked against purchase orders and receiving reports for quantities, prices, and terms?

Classification objective:
19. Does the chart of accounts and accounting manual give instructions for classifying debit entries when purchases are recorded?
20. Are account distributions recorded on supplier invoices and independently verified prior to being entered in the accounts payable system?

Accounting objective:
21. Is the accounts payable detail ledger balanced periodically with the general ledger control account?

Proper period objective:
22. Does the accounting manual give instructions to date purchase/payable entries on the date of receipt of goods?

CASH DISBURSEMENTS PROCESSING APPLICATION

Environment and general controls relevant to this application:
1. Are persons with cash custody or cheque-signing authority denied access to accounting journals, ledgers, and bank reconciliations?
2. Is access to blank cheques denied to unauthorized persons?
3. Are all disbursements except petty cash made by cheque?
4. Are cheque signers prohibited from drawing cheques to cash?
5. Is signing blank cheques prohibited?
6. Are voided cheques mutilated and retained for inspection?

Assertion-Based Control Evaluation:
Validity objective
7. Are invoices, receiving reports, and purchase orders reviewed by the cheque signer?
8. Are the supporting documents stamped "paid" (to prevent duplicate payment) before being returned to accounts payable for filing?
9. Are cheques mailed directly by the signer and not returned to accounts payable department for mailing?

Completeness objective:
10. Are blank cheques prenumbered and is the numerical sequence checked for missing documents?

Authorization objective:
11. Do cheques require two signatures? Is there dual control over machine signature plates?

Accuracy objective:
12. Are bank accounts reconciled by personnel independent of cash custody or recordkeeping?

Classification objective:
13. Do the chart of accounts and accounting manual give instructions for determining debit classifications of disbursements not charged to accounts payable?
14. Is the distribution of charges double-checked periodically by an official? Is the budget used to check on gross misclassification errors?
15. Are special disbursements (e.g., payroll and dividends) made from separate bank accounts?

Accounting objective:
16. Is the bank reconciliation reviewed by an accounting official with no conflicting cash receipts, cash disbursements or recordkeeping responsibilities?
17. Do internal auditors periodically conduct a surprise audit of bank reconciliations?

Proper period objective:
18. Are cheques dated in the cash disbursements journal with the date of the cheque?

**EXHIBIT   12A-2   EXAMPLES OF PURCHASES AND PAYABLES CONTROLS
RELATING TO EXHIBIT 12-1**

- Each terminal performs only designated functions. For example, the receiving clerk's terminal cannot accept a purchase order entry.
- An identification number and password (used on an individual basis) is required to enter the nonautomatic purchase orders, vendors' invoices, and the receiving report information. Further, certain passwords have "read only" authorization. These are issued to personnel authorized to determine the status of various records, such as an open voucher, but not authorized to enter data.
- All input immediately is logged to provide restart processing should any terminal become inoperative during the processing.
- The transaction codes call up a full-screen "form" on the terminals that appears to the operators in the same format as the original paper documents. Each clerk must enter the information correctly (online input validation) or the computer will not accept the data.
- All printed documents are computer numbered and the number is stored as part of the record. Further, all records in the open databases have the vendor's number as the primary search and matching field key. Of course, status searches could be made by another field. For example, the inventory number can be the search key to determine the status of a purchase of an item in short supply.
- A daily search of the open databases is made. Purchases outstanding for more than 10 days and the missing "document" records are printed out on a report for investigation of the delay.
- The cheque signature is printed, using a signature plate that is installed on the computer printer only when cheques are printed. A designated person in the treasurer's office maintains custody of this signature plate and must take it to the computer room to be installed when cheques are printed. This person also has the combination to the separate document storage room where the blank cheque stock is kept and is present at all cheque printing runs. The printed cheques are taken immediately from the computer room for mailing.

EXHIBIT   12A-3   INVENTORY TRANSACTION PROCESSING APPLICATION

Environment and general controls relevant to this application:
1. Are perpetual inventory records kept for raw materials? supplies? work in process? finished goods?
2. Are perpetual records subsidiary to general ledger control accounts?
3. Do the perpetual records show quantities only? quantities and prices?
4. Are inventory records maintained by someone other than the inventory stores custodian?
5. Is merchandise or materials on consignment-in (not the property of the company) physically segregated from goods owned by the company?

Assertion-Based Control Evaluation:
Validity objective:
6. Are additions to inventory quantity records made only on receipt of a receiving report copy?
7. Do inventory custodians notify the records department of additions to inventory?

Completeness objective:
8. Are reductions of inventory record quantities made only on receipt of inventory issuance documents?
9. Do inventory custodians notify inventory records of reductions of inventory?

Authorization objective:
 Refer to question 6 above (additions).
 Refer to question 8 above (reductions).

Accuracy objective:
10. If standard costs have been used for inventory pricing, have they been reviewed for current applicability?

Classification objective:
11. Are periodic counts of physical inventory made to correct errors in the individual perpetual records?

Accounting objective:
12. Is there a periodic review for overstocked, slow-moving, or obsolete inventory? Have any adjustments been made during the year?
13. Are perpetual inventory records kept in dollars periodically reconciled to general ledger control accounts?

Proper period objective:
14. Does the accounting manual give instructions to record inventory additions on the date of the receiving report?
15. Does the accounting manual give instructions to record inventory issues on the issuance date?

EXHIBIT 12A-4   FIXED ASSET AND RELATED TRANSACTIONS PROCESSING APPLICATION

Environment and general controls relevant to this application:
1. Are detailed property records maintained for the various fixed assets?

Assertion-Based Control Evaluation:

Validity objective:
2. Is the accounting department notified of actions of disposal, dismantling, or idling of a productive asset? for terminating a lease or rental?
3. Are fixed assets inspected periodically and physically counted?

Completeness objective:
4. Is casualty insurance carried? Is the coverage analyzed periodically? When was the last analysis?
5. Are property tax assessments periodically analyzed? When was the last analysis?

Authorization objective:
6. Are capital expenditure and leasing proposals prepared for review and approval by the board of directors or by responsible officers?
7. When actual expenditures exceed authorized amounts, is the excess approved?

Accuracy objective:
8. Is there a uniform policy for assigning depreciation rates, useful lives, and salvage values?
9. Are depreciation calculations checked by internal auditors or other officials?

Classification objective:
10. Does the accounting manual contain policies for capitalization of assets and for expensing repair and maintenance?
11. Are subsidiary fixed assets records periodically reconciled to the general ledger accounts?
12. Are memorandum records of leased assets maintained?

Proper period objective:
13. Does the accounting manual give instructions for recording fixed asset additions on a proper date of acquisition?

APPENDIX 12B

SUBSTANTIVE AUDIT PROGRAMS

EXHIBIT   12B-1   AUDIT PROGRAM FOR INVENTORY AND COST OF GOODS SOLD

A. Inventory
  1. Conduct an observation of the company's physical inventory count. Count a sample of inventory items and trace these counts to the final inventory compilation.
  2. Select a sample of inventory items. Vouch unit prices to vendors' invoices or other cost records. Recalculate the multiplication of unit times price.
  3. Scan the inventory compilation for items added from sources other than the physical count and items that appear to be large round numbers or systematic fictitious additions.
  4. Recalculate the extensions and footings of the final inventory compilation for clerical accuracy.
  5. For selected inventory items and categories, determine the replacement cost and the applicability of lower-of-cost-or-market valuation.
  6. Determine whether obsolete or damaged goods should be written down:
      a. Enquire about obsolete, damaged, unsalable, slow-moving items.
      b. Scan the perpetual records for slow-moving items.
      c. During the physical observation, be alert to notice damaged or scrap inventory.
      d. Compare the listing of obsolete, slow-moving, damaged, or unsalable inventory from last year's audit to the current inventory compilation.
  7. At year-end, obtain the numbers of the last shipping and receiving documents for the year. Use these to scan the sales, inventory/cost of sales, and accounts payable entries for proper cutoff.
  8. Read bank confirmations, debt agreements, and minutes of the board, and make enquiries about pledge or assignment of inventory to secure debt.
  9. Enquire about inventory out on consignment and about inventory on hand that is consigned in from vendors.
  10. Confirm or inspect inventories held in public warehouses.

EXHIBIT   12B-1   AUDIT PROGRAM FOR INVENTORY AND COST OF GOODS SOLD (continued)

11. Recalculate the amount of intercompany profit to be eliminated in consolidation.
12. Obtain written client representations concerning pledge of inventory as collateral, intercompany sales, and other related-party transactions.

B. Cost of Sales
1. Select a sample of recorded cost of sales entries and vouch to supporting documentation.
2. Select a sample of basic transaction documents (such as sales invoices, production reports) and determine whether the related cost of goods sold was figured and recorded properly.
3. Determine whether the accounting costing method used by the client (such as FIFO, LIFO, standard cost) was applied properly.
4. Compute the gross margin rate and compare with prior years.
5. Compute the ratio of cost elements (such as labour, material) to total cost of goods sold and compare with prior years.

EXHIBIT   12B-2   AUDIT PROGRAM FOR CAPITAL ASSETS (FIXED AND INTANGIBLE) AND RELATED ACCOUNTS

A. Capital Assets
1. Summarize and recalculate detail fixed and intangible asset subsidiary records and reconcile to general ledger control account(s).
2. Select a sample of capital asset subsidiary records:
   a. Perform a physical observation (inspection) of the fixed assets recorded.
   b. Inspect title documents, if any.
   c. Inspect supporting documention, (i.e., invoices, contracts, purchase agreements) or obtain written confirmation of acquisition and ownership.
3. Prepare, or have client prepare, a schedule of fixed asset additions and disposals for the period:
   a. Vouch to documents, indicating proper approval.
   b. Vouch costs to invoices, contracts, or other supporting documents.
   c. Determine whether all costs of shipment, installation, testing, and the like have been properly capitalized.
   d. Vouch proceeds (on dispositions) to cash receipts or other asset records.
   e. Recalculate gain or loss on dispositions.
   f. Trace amounts to detail fixed asset records and general ledger control account(s).
4. Prepare an analysis of fixed assets subject to investment tax credit for correlation with tax liability audit work.
5. Observe a physical inventory-taking of the fixed assets and compare with detail capital assets records.
6. Obtain written representations from management regarding pledge of assets as security for loans and leased assets.

B. Depreciation/Amortization
1. Analyze amortization expense for overall reasonableness with reference to costs of assets and average depreciation rates.
2. Prepare, or have client prepare, a schedule of accumulated amortization showing beginning balance, current amortization, disposals, and ending balance. Trace to amortization expense and asset disposition analyses. Trace amounts to general ledger account(s).
3. Recalculate amortization expense and trace to general ledger account(s).

C. Other Accounts
1. Analyze insurance for adequacy of coverage.
2. Analyze property taxes to determine whether taxes due on assets have been paid or accrued.
3. Recalculate prepaid and/or accrued insurance and tax expenses.
4. Select a sample of rental expense entries. Vouch to rent/lease contracts to determine whether any leases qualify for capitalization.
5. Select a sample of repair and maintenance expense entries and vouch them to supporting invoices for evidence of property that should be capitalized.

EXHIBIT   12B-3   AUDIT PROGRAM FOR ACCOUNTS PAYABLE

1. Obtain a trial balance of recorded accounts payable as of year-end. Recalculate its total and trace the total to the general ledger account. Vouch a sample of balances to vendors' statements. Review the trial balance for related-party payables.

2. When concerned about the possibility of unrecorded payables, send confirmations to creditors, especially those with small or zero balances and those with whom the company has done significant business.

3. Conduct a search for unrecorded liabilities by examining client reconciliations of suppliers statements to accounts payable control account and cash payments made for a period after year-end.

4. Enquire about terms that justify classifying payables as long term instead of current.

5. For estimated liabilities, such as warranties, determine and evaluate the basis of estimation, and recalculate the estimate.

6. Obtain written client representations about related-party payables and pledges of assets as collateral for liabilities.

EXHIBIT   12B-4   AUDIT PROGRAM FOR PREPAID, DEFERRED, AND ACCRUED EXPENSES

1. Obtain a schedule of all prepaid expenses, deferred costs, and accrued expenses.
2. Determine whether each item is properly allocated to the current or a future accounting period.
3. Select significant additions to deferred and accrued amounts, and vouch them to supporting invoices, contracts, or calculations.
4. Determine the basis for deferral and accrual, and recalculate the recorded amounts.
5. Study the nature of each item, discuss with management, and determine whether the remaining balance will be recovered from future operations.
6. In other audit work on income and expenses, be alert to notice items that should be considered prepaid, deferred, or accrued, and allocated to the current or a future accounting period.
7. Scan the expense accounts in the trial balance and compare to prior year. Investigate unusual differences that may indicate failure to account for a prepaid or accrual item.
8. Study each item to determine the proper current or noncurrent balance sheet classification.

CHAPTER 13

Production and Payroll Processes

This chapter offers an overview of the production and payroll process where materials, labour, and overhead are converted into finished goods and services. Our coverage separates this process into two distinct parts: Part I, which is the production process, including inventory valuation, amortization, and cost of goods sold; and Part 2, which covers the payroll process, including labour cost accounting. Application cases demonstrate the application of audit procedures in situations where errors or frauds might be discovered.

LEARNING OBJECTIVES

After completing this chapter, you will be able to do the following:

1 Describe the key risks of misstatement in production and payroll processes.

2 Describe the production process: typical transactions, source documents, controls, and account balances.

3 Outline control tests for auditing control over conversion of materials and labour in the production process.

4 Describe the payroll process: typical transactions, source documents, controls, and account balances.

5 Outline control tests for auditing control over the payroll process.

6 Apply and integrate the chapter topics to design audit procedures for detecting misstatements due to error or fraud in the production and payroll processes.

Note: Appendices 13A, Internal Control Questionnaires, and 13B, Substantive Audit Programs, accompany this chapter. Appendix 13C Just-in-Time Manufacturing and Supply Chain Management is on the text's Online Learning Centre.

RISK ASSESSMENT FOR THE PRODUCTION AND PAYROLL PROCESSES

· · · · · · · · · · · · · · · · ·

LEARNING OBJECTIVE

❶ Describe the key risks of misstatement in production and payroll processes.

For auditors, it is important to understand the production process of any businesses involved in manufacturing. Similarly, the payroll process is significant in virtually every business that has employees. Risk considerations are explained for each of these processes.

Production Process

The main function of inventory accounting within a manufacturing business is the allocation of material, labour, and overhead costs to inventory items being produced. Businesses produce many different types of tangible assets for sale or internal use, and all will have similar production accounting cycles that capture relevant costs and allocate them to asset accounts. Service businesses, on the other hand, bill customers for performing a specific job, such as a haircut or snowplowing, when the service is completed. Therefore, their productive activities are not inventoried. Professional service firms, such as lawyers and accountants, usually earn revenues based on the time spent on the assigned work; it could be hours, days, or weeks. For billing the customer, they have accounting systems that track hours spent on each job, giving them an intangible "inventory" of work in progresss showing hours worked that have not yet been billed.

The production accounting process discussed in this chapter generates important information for management decisions on setting product selling prices, product-line profitability, whether to produce or contract production out, and production volume decisions. The process also generates the reported balance sheet value of inventory or other assets. The flexibility and judgment involved in these costing processes leads to a risk of misstatement that the auditor has to assess. The inherent risk in this process also tends to be high because the information is complex and the transaction volumes involved can be large. This text focuses mainly on manufacturing businesses, while other types of production businesses have the same basic accounting requirements but with differing specific activities and costs.

Transaction streams in the production process are allocations from various material and overhead purchases, using accounts discussed in Chapter 12. Allocations are also made for labour costs, a payroll expenditure discussed later in this chapter. The main balances are finished inventory and work-in-process. **Cost of goods sold** expense is calculated from the changes in inventory, purchases, and other allocated costs, and from adjustments that result from reconciling booked quantities to a physical count of the inventory. The main disclosure is the inventory valuation policy, including lower-of-cost-or-market policy.

The audit risks for inventory relate to two components: physical quantities and valuation (or pricing). If the production process is the business's main activity, management should have strong controls over existence and completeness related to inventory quantities. Physical counts and reconciliation to booked quantities are very effective control procedures that auditors test substantively. Existence and completeness risks in inventory as well as related accounts receivable and payable balances are affected by cutoff errors. The valuation risk is affected by controls over pricing procedures for purchases and other manufacturing costs, and by the possibility that market values can fall below cost. Analytical procedures, often using detailed management reports, are useful for assessing risks related to the existence, completeness, and valuation assertions. Ownership risks relate to transfer of title to inventory, as it may not happen at the same time as the physical transfer. Ownership is assessed by enquiries, and by examining documents and inventory movements subsequent to year-end. Presentation risks include disclosure of inventory pledged as collateral.

Payroll Process

Payroll is the payments to hourly wage workers and salaried employees. Payments to employees involved in production are usually transferred to the cost of inventory (or self-constructed assets, etc.). Other wages and salaries will be expensed in the current period.

Payments to employees are the main transaction stream in the payroll process, and the main balances related to the process are relatively small year-end accruals for payroll liabilities. Ownership is the key assertion at risk here; the process involves small cash payments to individuals, so it is vulnerable to employee fraud. The major control risks are payments to fictitious employees (sometimes called ghosts on the payroll) and for more hours than are actually worked.

The assessment of payroll system control has to consider that the many transactions in this cycle add up to a large dollar amount, even though they result in small balance sheet account amounts at year-end. Because of this, reviews of control effectiveness and dual-purpose tests of controls and transaction details are used in many audit engagements, and the substantive audit procedures devoted to auditing the payroll-related year-end balances can be more limited.

Risk assessment involves ensuring that payroll processing duties are well segregated and that independent reviews and approvals are effective. Substantive evidence is available from reconciling to government income tax reports.

PART I: PRODUCTION PROCESS—TYPICAL ACTIVITIES

· · · · · · · · · · · · · · · ·

LEARNING OBJECTIVE

2 Describe the production process: typical transactions, source documents, controls, and account balances.

Exhibit 13–1 shows the activities and accounting involved in a production process. These begin with production planning, including inventory planning and management. Production planning can involve use of a sophisticated, computerized long-range plan with just-in-time (JIT) inventory management, or it can be done by a simple ad hoc method ("Hey, Joe, we got an order today. Go make 10 units!"). Most businesses try to estimate or forecast sales levels and seasonal effects, and they plan facilities and production schedules to meet forecast customer demand. As shown in Exhibit 13–1, the production cycle interacts with the purchasing process (Chapter 12) and the payroll process (later in this chapter) for the acquisition of fixed assets, materials, supplies, overhead, and labour.

The physical output of a production process is the inventory (from raw materials to work-in-process to finished goods). Inventory auditing and physical inventory taking were explained in Chapter 12, and Exhibit 11–1 (page 423) showed the connection of inventory to the revenue process in terms of orders and deliveries.

Most of the transactions in a production cycle are cost accounting allocations, unit cost determinations, and standard cost calculations. These are internal transactions, produced entirely within the company's accounting system. Exhibit 13–1 shows the elements of depreciation cost calculation, cost of goods sold determination, and job cost analysis as examples.

The audit of inventory consists of two phases: verifying the physical units and testing the unit costs. Physically observing the inventory count, including any equivalent units calculations for work-in-process, is the main procedure for verifying physical units. The unit costing of inventory (also referred to as price tests) for purchased inventory such as the inventory of retailers was partly covered in Chapter 12. In the cost testing procedures for produced or manufactured inventory, the cost allocations and computations are much more complex (as you may have noticed in your management accounting courses). For example, in process costing the following formula is used:

$$\text{Unit Cost of Production} = \frac{\text{Production Costs}}{\text{(Equivalent Units of Production)}}$$

Once the unit costs of production are known, the total inventory production costs for reporting purposes are unit cost times number of units. The total inventory production cost must be allocated between cost of sales (on the income statement) and inventory (on the balance sheet). This allocation of costs between inventory and cost of goods sold includes proper allocation of any cost variances. This is necessary because a budget system is a control system and for external reporting purposes the actual costs, not the standard or

EXHIBIT 13-1   PRODUCTION PROCESS

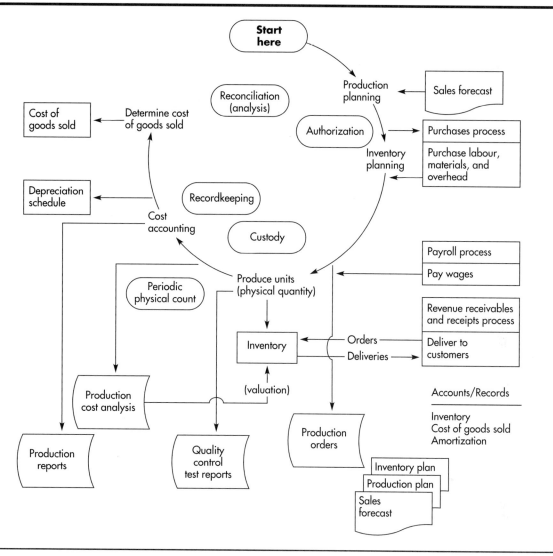

budgeted costs, must be disclosed. This allocation will affect the cost amounts the auditor uses in inventory valuation tests that assess whether recorded inventory costs are lower than market-based net realizable values. The box below shows how errors can arise in allocating standard overhead costs to inventory.

Valuation of manufactured inventory, manufactured cost of goods sold, and any self-constructed property, plant, and equipment assets are based on these internal cost allocations. Therefore, the appropriateness of such cost allocations is a critical part of the audit of the valuation assertion of inventory and fixed assets.

As you follow Exhibit 13–1, you can track the elements of the control structure below.

Authorization

Production authorization starts with production planning, which usually is based on a sales forecast. Production planning interacts with inventory planning to generate production orders. These production orders specify the materials and labour required as well as the timing for the start and end of production. Managers in the sales/marketing and production departments usually sign-off their approval on plans and production orders. Since sales volume and inventory requirements change with economic conditions and company success or failure, these plans and approvals are dynamic; they are amended according to changing needs. Authorization also can include plans and approvals for subcontracting work to other companies. The process of taking bids and executing contracts can be a part of the planning-authorization system.

The production order usually includes a **bill of materials** (a specification of the materials authorized for the production). The materials requisitions are prepared based on the authorization of the bill of materials, and these requisitions become the authorization for the inventory custodian to release raw materials and supplies to the production personnel. They then become the inventory recordkeepers' authorizations to update the raw materials inventory files to record reductions in the raw materials inventory.

Later, when production is complete, the production reports, the physical units, and the quality control test reports for them are the authorizations for the finished goods inventory custodian to place the units in the finished goods inventory. These same documents are the inventory recordkeepers' authorization to update the inventory record files with the additions.

OVERHEAD ALLOCATION

The cost accounting department at Pointed Publications Inc. routinely allocated overhead to book printing runs at the standard rate of 40 percent of materials and labour cost. The debit was initially to the finished books inventory, while the credit went to an "overhead allocated" account that was offset against other entries in the cost of goods sold calculation, which included all the actual overhead incurred. During the year, 10 million books were produced and $40 million of overhead was allocated to them. The auditors noticed that actual overhead expenditures were $32 million, and 3 million books remained in the ending inventory.

This finding resulted in the conclusion that the inventory was overstated by $2.4 million, and the cost of goods sold was understated by $2.4 million.

	Company Allocation (Using standard overhead rate)	Auditor Analysis (Using actual overhead)
Books produced	10 million	10 million
Labour and material cost	$100 million	$100 million
Overhead allocated	$ 40 million	$ 32 million
Cost per book	$ 14.00	$ 13.20
Cost of goods sold		
Labour and materials cost	$100 million	$100 million
Overhead allocated to books	40 million	
Overhead incurred	32 million	32 million
Overhead credited to cost	(40 million)	
Ending inventory	(42 million)	(39.6 million)
Total cost of goods sold	$ 90 million	$ 92.4 million

Custody

Supervisors and workers have physical custody of materials, equipment, and labour while production work is performed. They requisition materials from the raw materials inventory, assign people to jobs, and control the pace of work. In a sense, they have custody of a moving inventory. The work-in-process (an inventory category) is literally "moving" and changing form in the process of being transformed from raw materials into finished goods.

Control over this custody is more difficult than control over a closed warehouse full of raw materials or finished goods. It can be exercised by holding supervisors and workers accountable for the use of materials specified in the production orders, the timely completion of production, and the quality of the finished goods. This accountability can be achieved with good cost accounting, cost analysis, and quality control testing.

Recordkeeping (Cost Accounting)

When production is completed, production orders and the related records of material and labour used are forwarded to the cost accounting department. Since these accounting documents may come from the production personnel, the effective separation depends upon its receiving independent notices from other places, especially notifications of materials issued from the inventory custodian and of the labour costs assigned by the payroll department.

The cost accounting department calculates the cost-per-unit, standard cost, and variances. It also may determine the allocation of overhead to production in general, to production orders, and to finished units. Depending on the design of the company's accounting system, these costs are used in inventory valuation and ultimately in determining the cost of goods sold. Often this department is responsible for calculating the depreciation of production assets and the amortization of intangibles.

Periodic Reconciliation

Periodic reconciliation compares actual assets and liabilities with amounts recorded in the company accounts (e.g., the physical count of inventory with the perpetual inventory records, vendors' monthly statements with the recorded accounts payable). Exhibit 13–1 shows the periodic reconciliation of physical inventory to recorded amounts. The features and audit considerations of this reconciliation were covered in Chapter 12. The work-in-process inventory also can be observed, although the "count" of partially completed units is subjective. It can be costed based on the labour, materials, and overhead used at its stage of completion.

Most other periodic reconciliations in the production cycle are analyses of internal information. After all, other than physical inventory, no external transactions or physical units are unique to production and cost accounting. The analyses include costing the production orders, comparing the cost with prior experience or with standard costs, and determining **lower-of-cost-or-net-realizable-value (LCNRV)** valuations. In a sense, the LCNRV calculations are a reconciliation of product cost to the external market price of product units.

REVIEW CHECKPOINTS

1 What are the functions normally associated with the production process?

2 Why is an understanding of the production process, including the related data processing and cost accounting, important to auditors evaluating the control structure as part of their assessment of control risk?

3 Describe a walk-through of a production transaction from production orders to entry in the finished goods perpetual inventory records. What document copies would be collected? What controls noted? What duties separated?

4 Describe how the separation of (1) authorization of production transactions, (2) recording of these transactions, and (3) physical custody of inventories can be specified among the production, inventory, and cost accounting departments.

5 What features of the cost accounting system would be expected to prevent the omission of recording materials used in production?

Audit Evidence in Management Reports and Files

Most production accounting systems produce timely reports that managers use to supervise and control production. Auditors use them as supporting evidence for assertions about work-in-process and finished goods inventories and about cost of goods sold.

Sales Forecast

Several aspects of business planning, notably the planning of production and inventory levels, are based on management's sales forecasts. If the auditors want to use the forecast for substantive audit decisions, assurance about its reasonableness needs to be obtained, particularly about assumptions built into it. In addition, the mechanical accuracy of the forecast should be verified.

As much of the year under audit will have passed when the audit work begins, the forecasts can help the auditor to understand the nature and volume of production orders and the level of materials inventory on hand. Forecasts for the following year are used in valuing the inventory (e.g., lower-of-cost-or-net-realizable-value if forecast indicates slow-moving and potentially obsolete inventory). If a writedown from cost to market value is required, this increases the amount of cost of goods sold that is shown in the financial statements. Special care must be taken when using forecasts with inventory valuation because an overly optimistic forecast can lead to a failure to write down inventory.

THE SALY FORECAST

The auditors were reviewing the inventory items that had not been issued for thirty days or more, to assess whether any items need to be written down because their market values were lower than cost. The production manager showed them the SALY forecast that indicated a continuing need for the materials in products that were expected to have reasonable demand. The auditors agreed that the forecasts supported the prediction of future sales of products at prices that would cover the cost of the slow-moving material items.

Unfortunately, they neglected to ask the meaning of SALY in the designation of the forecast. They did not learn that it means "same as last year." It is not a forecast at all. The products did not sell at the prices expected, and the company experienced losses the following year that should have been charged to cost of goods sold earlier.

Production Plans and Reports

Management's plan for the amount and timing of production provides general information to the auditors, but the production orders and inventory plan associated with it are even more important. These carry the information about requirements for raw materials, labour, and overhead, including the requisitions for purchase and use of materials and labour. These documents are the initial authorizations for control of the inventory and production.

Production reports record the completion of production quantities. When coupled with the related cost accounting reports, they are the company's record of the cost of goods placed in the finished goods inventory. In most cases, auditors will audit the cost reports as part of determining the cost valuation of inventory and cost of goods sold.

Amortization Schedule

The cost accounting department may prepare the schedule of the amortization (depreciation) of production assets. Company accountants may prepare similar schedules for the company's other (nonproduction) fixed assets. These are often long and complicated, involving large dollar amounts of asset cost and calculated amortization expense. An abbreviated illustration of a production asset and amortization schedule follows.

| | Production Assets and Amortization | | | | | | | |
| | Asset Cost (000s) | | | | Accumulated Amortization (000s) | | | |
Description	Beginning Balance	Additions	Disposals	Ending Balance	Beginning Balance	Additions	Disposals	Ending Balance
Land	10,000			10,000				
Bldg 1	30,000			30,000	6,857	857		7,714
Bldg 2		42,000		42,000		800		800
Computer A	5,000		5,000	0	3,750	208	3,958	0
Computer B		3,500		3,500		583		583
Press	1,500			1,500	300	150		450
Auto 1	15		15	0	15		15	0
Auto 2		22		22		2		2
Total	46,515	45,522	5,015	87,022	10,922	2,600	3,973	9,549

The amortization schedule is audited by using the company's methods to recalculate the amortization expense, estimates of useful life, and estimates of residual value, and by verifying the additions and disposals recorded. When the schedule covers hundreds of assets and numerous additions and disposals, auditors can (a) use computer auditing methods to recalculate the amortization expense and (b) use sampling to choose additions and disposals for test of controls and substantive audits. The beginning balances of assets and accumulated amortization should be traced to the prior-year audit's working papers. This schedule can be made into an audit working paper and placed in the auditor's files for future reference.

REVIEW CHECKPOINTS

6 When auditors want to use an auditee's sales forecast for general familiarity with the production process or for evaluation of slow-moving inventory, what kind of work should be done on the forecast?

7 If the actual sales for the year are substantially lower than the sales forecast at the beginning of the year, what potential valuation problems may arise in the production cycle accounts?

8 What production documentation supports the valuation of manufactured finished goods inventory?

9 What items in an auditee's production asset and amortization schedule can auditors use for designing audit procedures? Describe these audit procedures.

CONTROL RISK ASSESSMENT

LEARNING OBJECTIVE

3 Outline control tests for auditing control over conversion of materials and labour in the production process.

Control risk assessment is important because it governs the nature, timing, and extent of substantive audit procedures that will be applied in the audit of account balances in the production accounting process. These account balances include the following:

- inventory—raw materials, work-in-process, finished goods
- cost of goods sold
- amortization—amortization expense, accumulated amortization

Several aspects of auditing purchased inventories and physical quantities are covered in Chapter 12. With respect to inventory valuation, this chapter points out the cost accounting function and its role in determining the cost valuation of manufactured finished goods.

General Control Considerations

Control procedures for proper segregation of responsibilities should be in place and operating. From Exhibit 13–1, you can see that proper segregation involves authorization (production planning and inventory planning) by those who do not have custody, recording, or cost accounting and reconciliation duties. Custody of inventories (raw materials, work-in-process, and finished goods) is in the hands of people who do not (a) authorize the amount or timing of production or the purchase of materials and labour, (b) perform the cost accounting recordkeeping, or (c) prepare cost analyses (reconciliations). Cost accounting (a recording function) is performed by those who do not authorize production or have custody of assets in the process of production. However, you usually will find that the cost accountants prepare various analyses and reconciliations directly related to production activities. Combinations of two or more of the duties of authorization, custody, or cost accounting in one person, one office, or one computerized system may open the door for errors or fraud.

In addition, the control structure includes the following detail-checking procedures:

1. Production orders contain a list of materials and their quantities, and they are approved by a production planner/scheduler.
2. Materials requisitions are (a) compared, in the cost accounting department, with the list of materials on the production order and (b) approved by the production operator and the materials inventory stockkeeper.
3. Job labour time records are signed by production supervisors, and the cost accounting department reconciles the amounts with the labour report from the payroll department.
4. Production reports of finished units are signed by the production supervisor and finished goods inventory custodian and then forwarded to cost accounting.

These control operations track the raw materials and labour through the production process. With each internal transaction, the responsibility and accountability for assets are passed to the next person or location.

Many companies have complex systems managing production and material flows. These information systems are customized as production processes vary considerably for different products and factories. Even within the same company, different information systems may be used to manage different products or different locations. Some parts of the production process and accounting may be done manually, while others may be automated. Paper source documents and authorization signatures may not exist for automated functions. Even though the information system and technology may be complex, the basic management and control functions of ensuring the flow of labour and materials to production and controlling waste should be in place. The feasibility of auditing within a computerized production information system is considered in Chapter 9.

Internal Control Questionnaire

Information about the production process control structure often is gathered initially by completing an internal control questionnaire (ICQ). Exhibit 13A–1 in Appendix 13A (page 547) is an example of an ICQ, and it can be studied for details of desirable control policies and procedures. The ICQ lists control activities found in the manual aspects of a production cost accounting system. The computerized parts that have no paper trail must be assessed to see whether each control objective is met through application controls or other verification procedures; for example, input/output checks.

Production Management: JIT

Just-in-time (JIT) manufacturing and supply chain management systems have expanded in many companies with the availability of electronic data interchange (EDI) and other information technologies. Auditors need to be familiar with the components and functions of these systems and their implications for auditing. Appendix 13C on the text Online Learning Centre provides further details on JIT manufacturing and supply chain management.

Control Tests

An organization should have funtioning control activities that prevent, detect, and correct accounting errors. You studied the general control objectives in Chapter 9 (validity, completeness, authorization, accuracy, classification, accounting, and proper period recording). Exhibit 13–2 puts these in the perspective of production activity, with examples of specific objectives. Study this exhibit carefully as it expresses the control objectives in examples specific to production.

Auditors perform control tests to determine whether controls said to be in place and operating actually are being performed properly by company personnel. Recall that a control test consists of (1) identification of the data population from which a sample of items will be selected for audit and (2) an expression of the action that will be taken to produce relevant evidence, such as vouching, tracing, observing, scanning, and recalculating.

Exhibit 13–3 contains a selection of control tests for auditing controls over the accumulation of costs for work-in-process inventory. This is the "inventory" of things in the production process. Upon completion, the accumulated costs become the cost valuation of the finished goods inventory. The exhibit presumes that there are production cost reports, which are updated as production takes place, labour reports assigning labour cost to the job, reports of materials used and materials requisitions charging raw materials to the production order, and overhead allocation calculations. Some or all of these documents may be in the form of computer records. The samples are usually attribute samples designed along the lines studied in Chapter 10. On the right-hand side, Exhibit 13–3 shows the control objectives tested by the audit procedures listed.

Dual Direction of the Test of Controls Procedures

The procedures listed in Exhibit 13–3 are designed to test the production accounting in two directions, the first being the completeness direction, testing whether all production

---

EXHIBIT 13-2   CONTROL OBJECTIVES (PRODUCTION PROCESS)

General Objectives	Examples of Specific Control Activities
1. Recorded production transactions are *valid* and documented.	Cost accounting separated from production, payroll, and inventory control Material use reports compared with raw material stores issue slips Labour use reports compared with job time tickets
2. Valid production transactions are *recorded* and none omitted.	All documents prenumbered and numerical sequence reviewed
3. Production transactions are *authorized*.	Material use and labour use prepared by foreman and approved by production supervisor
4. Production job cost transactions computations contain *accurate* figures.	Job cost sheet entries reviewed by person independent of preparation Costs of inventory used and labour used reviewed periodically
5. Labour and materials are *classified* correctly as direct or indirect.	Production supervisor required to account for all material and labour used as direct or indirect
6. Production *accounting* is complete.	Open job cost sheets periodically reconciled to the work-in-process inventory accounts
7. Production transactions are recorded in the *proper period*.	Production reports of material and labour used prepared weekly and transmitted to cost accounting Job cost sheets posted weekly and summary journal entries of work-in-process and work completed prepared monthly

EXHIBIT   13-3   CONTROL TESTS FOR WORK-IN-PROCESS INVENTORY

	Control Objective
1. Reconcile the open production cost reports to the work-in-process inventory control account.	Completeness
2. Select a sample of open and closed production cost reports:	
a. Recalculate all costs entered.	Accuracy
b. Vouch labour costs to labour reports.	Validity
c. Compare labour reports with summary of payroll.	Accounting
d. Vouch material costs to issue slips and materials-used reports.	Validity
e. Vouch overhead charges to overhead analysis schedules.	Accuracy
f. Trace selected overhead amounts from analysis schedules to cost allocations and to invoices or accounts payable vouchers.	Validity
3. Select a sample of issue slips from the raw materials stores file:	
a. Determine if a matching requisition is available for every issue slip.	Completeness
b. Trace materials-used reports into production cost reports.	Completeness
4. Select a sample of clock timecards from the payroll file. Trace to job time tickets, labour reports, and production cost reports.	Completeness
5. Select a sample of production orders:	
a. Determine whether production order was authorized.	Authorization
b. Match to bill of materials and labour hour needs.	Completeness
c. Trace bill of materials to material requisitions, material issue slips, materials-used reports, and production cost reports.	Completeness
d. Trace labour hour needs to labour reports and production cost reports.	Completeness

ordered to be started is recorded. Exhibit 13–4 shows that the sample for this testing direction is taken from the population of production orders found in the production planning department. The cost accumulation is traced forward into the production cost reports in the cost accounting department. The procedures keyed in the boxes (5-*a*, *b*, *c*, *d*) are cross-references to the procedures in Exhibit 13–3. Potentially, these procedures will find any scheduled production that has been cancelled because of technical or quality problems, which means there should be some writing off or scrapping of partially completed production units.

EXHIBIT   13-4   TEST OF PRODUCTION COST CONTROLS: COMPLETENESS DIRECTION

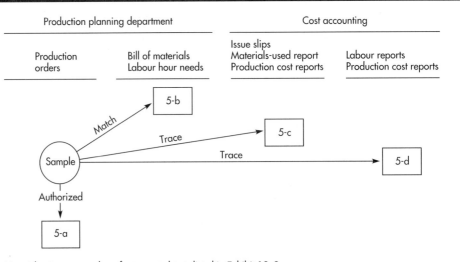

Note: The 5-a, etc., codes refer to control tests listed in Exhibit 13–3.

EXHIBIT   13-5   TEST OF PRODUCTION COST CONTROLS: VALIDITY DIRECTION

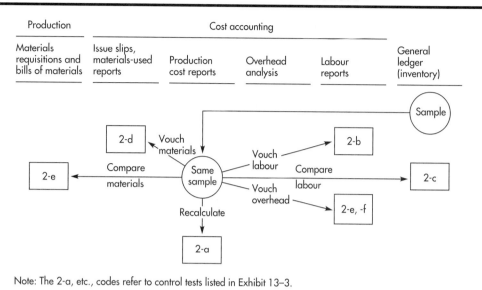

Note: The 2-a, etc., codes refer to control tests listed in Exhibit 13–3.

The other direction of the test is validity, which is concerned with the proper recording of work-in-process and finished goods in the general ledger. The Exhibit 13–5 sample for this test is from the production reports (quantity and cost) recorded in the inventory accounts. This sample references to production cost reports filed in the cost accounting department. From these basic records, the recorded costs can be recalculated, vouched to labour reports, compared with the payroll, and vouched to records of material used and overhead incurred. The procedures keyed in the boxes (2-a, b, c, d, e, f) are cross-references to the procedures in Exhibit 13–3. These procedures might reveal that there is improper valuation of the recorded inventory cost.

Summary: Control Risk Assessment

The audit manager or senior in charge of the audit should evaluate the evidence obtained from an understanding of the internal control structure and from the test of controls audit procedures. If the control risk is assessed very low, the substantive audit procedures on the account balances can be limited in cost-saving ways. For example, the inventory valuation substantive tests can be limited in scope (i.e., smaller sample sizes), and there can be more confidence that the overall analytical procedures will be able to detect material misstatements not otherwise evident in the accounting details.

On the other hand, if tests of controls reveal weaknesses, amortization calculation errors, and cost accumulation errors, the substantive procedures must be designed to lower the risk of failing to detect material error in the inventory and cost of goods sold account balances. For example, the amortization cost might be completely recalculated and reviewed again by the auditors, valuation calculations may need to be performed for a large number of the inventoried production reports, and contract terms related to cost overruns may need to be investigated to determine if they should be carried as assets (e.g., as inventory or unbilled receivables) or written off. Descriptions of major control deficiencies, control weaknesses, and inefficiencies may need to be communicated to the auditee management and those charged with governance.

Since inventory production accounting often involves processing high volumes of transactions and keeping track of items in different locations, computer assisted audit testing can be efficient. Computerized components of the production information system may range from simple batch systems, which automate the data processing, to transaction-driven integrated systems, which capture the production progress electronically from devices on the production line. Computer audit techniques, such as test data, may be used to audit controls in such systems. For tests of details of transactions and balances, auditor-created or -tested software for verifying all (or a sample) of the inventory transaction processing can include (a) selecting items for test counting based on auditor-determined criteria, (b) sorting inventory items by location to facilitate observations, (c) recalculating extensions on inventory quantities and pricing, and (d) comparing inventory test counts with perpetual records. Audit software can also perform analytical review procedures; for example, identify unusual fluctuations in current and prior inventory quantities in comparison with details of purchases and sales transactions, spot negative or unreasonably large inventory quantities, and summarize inventory turnover statistics for obsolescence analysis.

IMPROPER PRODUCTION LOSS DEFERRALS

Alton Corporation incurred cost overruns on its shipbuilding contracts. By classifying the cost overruns as an asset for financial reporting purposes, Alton postponed writing off an $18 million cost overrun. If it had been written off in the proper period, the company would have reported a large loss instead of a net income of $500,000 for the year. Alton wrote off the $18 million two years later by restating its financial statements.

****

International Technologies Corporation (ITC) experienced cost overruns on fixed price contracts, claims for price escalation, and kickback arrangements with suppliers. ITC recorded and reported these costs as "unbilled receivables," using the account to misrepresent the cost overruns as escalation payments due from the customer, while the contract did not provide for any such payment. ITC used the unbilled receivables account as a hiding place for improper and questionable payments on the contracts so it could show them as legitimate reimbursable contract costs in order to avoid (a) writing them off as expense and (b) showing the true nature of the items. ITC also buried uncollectible contract costs, which indicated losses on fixed price contracts, in other unrelated contracts that were still profitable. When ITC's auditor uncovered the materially overstated assets, it required a write-down. This revealed that ITC was insolvent, and it was acquired by another technology company that quickly fired ITC's management.

REVIEW CHECKPOINTS

10   What are the primary functions that should be segregated in the production process?

11   How does the production order document or record provide a control over the quantity of materials used in production?

12   Where might an auditor find accounting records of cost overruns on contracts? improper charges? improperly capitalized inventory?

13   Evaluate the following statement made by an auditing student: "I do not understand cost accounting; therefore, I want to get a job with an auditing firm where I will only have to know financial accounting."

14   Which population of documents or records would an auditor sample to determine whether (a) all authorized production was completed and placed in inventory or written off as scrap? and (b) finished goods inventory were actually produced and properly costed?

PART II: PAYROLL PROCESS—TYPICAL ACTIVITIES

LEARNING OBJECTIVE

4 Describe the payroll process: typical transactions, source documents, controls, and account balances.

Every company has a payroll. It may include manufacturing labour, research scientists, administrative personnel, or all of these. Subsidiary operations, partnerships, and joint ventures may call their payroll **management fees** charged by a parent company or general partner. Payroll can take different forms. Personnel management and the payroll accounting cycle includes transactions affecting the wage and salary accounts as well as those affecting pension benefits, deferred compensation contracts, compensatory stock option plans, employee benefits (such as health insurance), payroll taxes, and related liabilities for these costs. It is very important that auditors verify the payroll system's compliance with local, provincial, and federal laws regarding deductions, overtime rules (e.g., after 8 hours in a day or 40 in a week), and minimum hours, etc. Failures to comply can lead to large liabilities. Many companies find it cost effective to use an outside payroll service organization to process and distribute payroll directly to employees' bank accounts because income taxes, rates, and calculations change frequently, and service organizations are better able to keep up to date with these changes.

Exhibit 13–6 shows a payroll process. It starts with hiring (and firing) people, determining employee wage rates and deductions, recording attendance and work (timekeeping), payment of wages and salaries, and then ends with preparation of governmental (tax) and

EXHIBIT 13-6   PAYROLL PROCESS

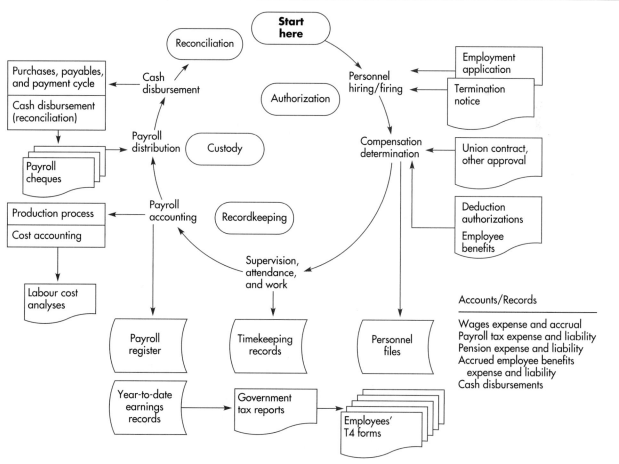

internal reports. One of these internal reports is a report of labour cost to the cost accounting department, which links the payroll cycle with cost accounting in the production cycle. Five functional responsibilities should be performed by separate people or departments. They are as follows:

- Human Resources—hiring and firing
- Supervision—approval of work time
- Timekeeping and Cost Accounting—payroll preparation and cost accounting
- Payroll Accounting—cheque preparation and related payroll reports
- Payroll Distribution—actual custody of cheques and distribution to employees by cash, cheque, or direct bank deposit

The elements that follow are part of the payroll control structure.

Authorization

A human resources department with authority to add new employees to the payroll, delete terminated employees, obtain authorizations for deductions (i.e., insurance, charitable donations, withholding tax exemptions), and transmit authority for pay rate changes to the payroll department should be independent of the other functions. The supervision function should include authorization power. All pay base data (hours, job number, absences, time off allowed for emergencies, and the like) should be approved by an employee's immediate supervisor. Authorization is also a feature of the timekeeping and cost accounting functions. The data that pay is based on (i.e., hours, piece-rate volume, and incentives) should be accumulated independent of other functions. Many of the functional duties and responsibilities described relate primarily to nonsalaried (hourly) employees. For salaried employees, no timekeeping data is collected.

Custody

The main custody item in the payroll cycle is possession of the paycheques, cash, or electronic transfer codes used to pay people. (**Electronic transfer codes** refer to the practice of transferring pay directly into employees' bank accounts.) A payroll distribution function should control the delivery of pay to employees so that unclaimed cheques, cash, or incomplete electronic transfers are not returned to persons involved in any of the other functions.

There are elements of custody of important documents in the supervision and timekeeping functions. Supervisors usually have access to time cards or time sheets that provide the basis for payment to hourly workers. Likewise, the timekeeping devices (e.g., time clocks, supervisory approval of time cards or time sheets, electronic punch-in systems) have a type of custody of employees' time-base for payroll calculations.

APPROVAL OF FICTITIOUS OVERTIME

A supervisor at Austin Stoneworks discovered that she could approve overtime hours even though an employee had not worked forty regular-time hours. She made a deal with several employees to alter their work time cards and split the extra payments. Over a 12-year period, the supervisor and her accomplices embezzled $107,000 in excess payments.

The employees' time cards were not reviewed after being approved by the supervisor. The company's payroll computer program did not have a valid data combination test that paid overtime only after forty regular-time hours were paid.

Recordkeeping

The **payroll accounting** function prepares individual paycheques, pay envelopes, or electronic transfers using rate and deduction information supplied by the human resources function and base data supplied by the timekeeping-supervision function. Those in charge of the authorization and custody functions should not also prepare the payroll, as they might be tempted to pay fictitious employees.

Payroll accounting maintains individual year-to-date earnings records and prepares the provincial and federal tax reports (income tax and Canada or Quebec Pension Plan withholding, employment insurance reports, and annual T4 forms). The payroll tax returns (e.g., the federal T4 summary reporting taxes withheld, employment insurance returns) and the annual T4 summary to employees are useful records for audit recalculation and overall testing (analytical) procedures. They should correspond to company records. When an outside payroll processing service is used, it usually will provide the detailed journal entries to record each payroll as well as the year-end T4 forms and summaries.

Periodic Reconciliation

The payroll bank account can be reconciled like any other bank account, and the transactions can also be reconciled to recorded wage cost and expense. Some companies send each supervisor a copy of the payroll register showing the employees paid under their authority and responsibility. The supervisor gets a chance to re-approve the payroll after it is completed. This provides an opportunity to notice whether any persons not approved have been paid and charged to the supervisor's accountability.

The payroll report sent to cost accounting can be reconciled to the labour records charging labour cost to production. The cost accounting function should determine whether the labour paid is the same as the labour cost used in the cost accounting calculations.

NOT ENOUGH CONTROL, NO FEEDBACK, BYE-BYE MONEY

Homer had been in payroll accounting for a long time. He knew it was not uncommon to pay a terminated employee severance benefits and partial pay after termination; Homer received the termination notices and the data for the final paycheques. But Homer also knew how to keep the terminated employee on the payroll for another week, pay a full week's compensation, change the electronic transfer code, and take the money for himself. The only things he could not change were the personnel department's copy of the termination notices, the payroll register, and the individual employee pay records used for withholding tax.

Fortunately for Homer, nobody reconciled the cost accounting labour charges to the payroll. The supervisors did not get a copy of the payroll register for postpayment approval, so they did not have any opportunity to notice the extra week. Nobody ever reviewed the payroll with reference to the termination notices. Former employees never complained about more pay and withholding reported on their T4s.

Homer and his wife, Marge, retired comfortably to a villa in Spain on a nest egg that had grown to $450,000. After Homer retired, the company experienced an unexpected decrease in labour costs and higher profits.

REVIEW CHECKPOINTS

15 What functional responsibilities are associated with the payroll process?

16 Describe a walk through of the payroll transaction flow from hiring authorization to payroll cheque disbursement. What document copies would be collected? What controls noted?

17 In a payroll system, which duties should be separated?

18 What features of a payroll system can be expected to prevent or detect (a) payment to a fictitious employee? (b) omission of payment to an employee?

. . . .

Audit Evidence in Management Reports and Files

Payroll systems produce numerous reports. Some are internal reports and bookkeeping records. Others are government tax reports.

Personnel Files

The human resources department keeps individual employee files. The contents usually include an employment application, background investigation report, notice of hiring, job classification with pay rate authorization, and authorizations for deductions (e.g., health benefits, life insurance, retirement contribution, union dues, and income tax exemptions). When employees retire, quit, or are otherwise terminated, appropriate notices of termination are filed. These files contain the raw data for important pension and post-retirement benefit accounting involving an employee's age, tenure with the company, wage record, and other information used in actuarial calculations.

A personnel file should establish the reality of a person's existence and employment. The background investigation report (prior employment, references, social insurance number validity check, credentials investigation, and perhaps a private investigator's report) is important for employees in sensitive positions such as accounting, finance, and asset custody. Capable personnel are a primary system control. Errors and frauds perpetrated by people who falsify their credentials (identification, education, prior experience, criminal record, and the like) abound. A fidelity bond for employees through an insurance company offers some protection from this risk.

Timekeeping Records

For employees paid by the hour or on various incentive systems, records of time, production, piecework, or other measures are the basis of their pay. These records are collected in a variety of ways. Old-fashioned time clocks still accept employee time cards and imprint the time when work started and ended. More sophisticated systems use card readers to perform the same function. Production employees may clock in for various jobs or production processes in a system that assigns labour costs to various stages of production.

Timekeeping records should be approved by supervisors to show that employees actually worked the hours (or produced the output) reported to the payroll department. A supervisor's signature or initials should be on the documents used by the payroll department as the basis for periodic pay. In computerized payroll systems, this approval comes in the form of the supervisory passwords used to input data.

WHERE DID HE COME FROM?

The controller defrauded the company for several million dollars. As it turned out, he was no controller at all. He didn't know a debit from a credit. The fraudster had been fired from five previous jobs where money had gone missing. He was discovered one evening when the president showed up unexpectedly at the company and found a stranger in the office with the controller. The stranger was doing all of the accounting for the bogus controller.

Source: "Auditing for Fraud," training course © 2006 Association of Certified Fraud Examiners.

Payroll Register

The payroll register typically contains a record for each employee, showing the gross regular pay, gross overtime pay, income tax withheld, Employment Insurance (EI) and Canada Pension Plan (CPP) or Quebec Pension Plan (QPP) withheld, other deductions, and net pay. The net pay amount usually is transferred from the general bank account to a special imprest payroll bank account. The journal entry for the transfer of net payroll, for example, is as follows:

Payroll Bank Account 25,774
     General Bank Account 25,774

When a payroll processing service is used, a cheque for the net payroll is usually issued to the payroll organization for distribution to employees' bank accounts; a separate payroll bank account is not required. The payroll amounts are accumulated to create the payroll posting to the general ledger, as in this example:

Wages clearing account 40,265
     Employee income taxes payable account 7,982
     Employee Canada Pension plan account 3,080
     Employment Insurance premium payable account 2,100
     Life insurance premium payable account 1,329
     Payroll bank account account 25,774

The payroll register is the primary original record for payroll accounting. It contains the implicit assertions that the employees are real company personnel (existence assertion), that they worked the time or production they were paid for (rights/ownership assertion), that the amount of the pay is calculated properly (valuation assertion), and that all the employees were paid (completeness assertion). The presentation and disclosure assertion depends on the labour cost analysis explained below.

Payroll department records also include the cancelled cheques (or a similar electronic-deposit record) containing the employees' endorsements.

Labour Cost Analysis

The cost accounting department can receive its information in more than one way. Systems may independently report time and production work data from the production floor directly to the cost accounting department. Cost accounting departments may receive labour cost data from the payroll department. When the information is received independently, it can be reconciled in quantity (time) or amount (dollars) with a report from the payroll department. This reconciliation makes sure that the cost accounting department is using actual payroll data and that the payroll department is paying only for work performed.

The cost accounting department (or a similar accounting function) is responsible for the cost distribution—the most important part of the payroll presentation and disclosure assertion. The cost distribution assigns payroll to the accounts where it belongs for internal and external reporting. Using its input data, the cost accounting department may make a distribution entry like the following:

Production job A 14,364
Production job B 3,999
Production process A 10,338
Selling expense 8,961
General and administrative expense 2,603
     Wages clearing account. 40,265

Payroll data flows from the hiring process, through the timekeeping function, into the payroll department, to the cost accounting department, and, finally, to the accounting entries that record the payroll for inventory cost determination and financial statement presentation. The same data are used for various governmental and tax reports.

Government and Tax Reports

Provincial and federal income and pension plan laws introduce complications into payroll systems. Several reports are produced that auditors can use in tests of controls and substantive tests of the balances produced by accumulating payroll transactions in year-to-date records.

Year-to-Date Earnings Records

The year-to-date (YTD) earnings records are the cumulative subsidiary records of each employee's gross pay, deductions, and net pay. Each time a periodic payroll is produced, the YTD earnings records are updated for the new information. The YTD earnings records are a subsidiary ledger of the wages and salaries cost and expense in the financial statements. Theoretically, like any subsidiary and control account relationship, their sum (e.g., the gross pay amounts) should be equal to the costs and expenses in the financial statements. The trouble with this reconciliation idea is that there are usually many payroll cost/ expense accounts in a company's chart of accounts. The production wages may be scattered in several different accounts, such as inventory (work-in-process and finished goods), selling, general, and administrative expenses.

The YTD records do, however, provide the data for periodic governmental and tax forms. They usually can be reconciled to the tax reports. Companies in financial difficulty have been known to try to postpone payment of employee taxes, EI, and CPP or QPP withheld. However, the consequences can be serious. The Canada Revenue Agency can and will padlock the business and seize the assets for nonpayment. After all, the withheld taxes belong to the employee's accounts with the government, and the employers are obligated to pay over the amounts withheld from employees along with a matching share for the Canada Pension Plan.

Employee Income Tax Reports

In Canada, the T4 slip is the annual report of gross salaries and wages as well as the income tax, pension plan, and employment insurance withheld. Copies are filed with the Canada (or Quebec) Pension Plan and the Canada Revenue Agency, and copies are sent to employees for preparing their income tax returns. The T4 contains the YTD accumulations for the employee, along with their address and social insurance number. In certain procedures (described later), auditors can use the name, address, social insurance number, and dollar amounts to obtain evidence about the existence of employees. The T4 can be reconciled to the payroll tax reports.

BEWARE THE "CLEARING ACCOUNT"

Clearing accounts are temporary storage places for transactions awaiting final accounting. Like the wages clearing account illustrated in the entries above, all clearing accounts should have zero balances after the accounting is completed.

A balance in a clearing account means that some amounts have not been classified properly in the accounting records. If the wages clearing account has a debit balance, some labour cost has not been properly classified in the expense accounts or cost accounting classifications. If the wages clearing account has a credit balance, the cost accountant has assigned more labour cost to expense accounts and cost accounting classifications than the amount actually paid.

REVIEW CHECKPOINTS

19 What important information can be found in employees' personnel files?

20 What is important about background checks using the employment applications submitted by prospective employees?

21 What payroll documentation supports the validity and accuracy of payroll transactions?

22 Which government tax returns can be reconciled in total with employees' year-to-date earnings records? Reconciled in total but not in detail?

23 What is the purpose of examining endorsements on the back of payroll cheques?

- -

CONTROL RISK ASSESSMENT

- - - - - - - - - - - - - - - -

The major risks in the payroll process are as follows:

- paying fictitious "employees" (employees that do not exist, invalid transactions)
- overpaying for time or production (inaccurate transactions, improper valuation)
- accounting for costs and expenses incorrectly (incorrect classification, improper or inconsistent presentation and disclosure)

The assessment of payroll system control risk is significant because there are so many transactions in this process, yet they result in small amounts in balance sheet accounts at year-end. Therefore, auditors often decide to use a combined audit approach, testing controls and transaction details using dual-purpose tests to lower assessed control risk so that less substantive testing is required.

General Control Considerations

Control procedures for proper segregation of responsibilities should be in place and operating. From Exhibit 13–6, you can see that proper segregation involves authorization (human resources department hiring and firing, pay rate, and deduction authorizations) by persons who do not have payroll preparation, paycheque distribution, or reconciliation duties. Payroll distribution (custody) is in the hands of those who neither authorize employees' pay rates or time, nor prepare the payroll cheques. Recordkeeping is performed by payroll and cost accounting personnel who do not make authorizations or distribute pay. Combinations of two or more of the duties of authorization, payroll preparation and recordkeeping, and payroll distribution in one person, office, or computerized system may open the door for errors and fraud.

In addition, the control structure should provide for detail-checking procedures: (1) periodic comparison of the payroll register with the human resources department files to check for hiring authorizations and terminated employees not deleted, (2) periodic rechecking of wage rate and deduction authorizations, (3) reconciliation of time and production paid to cost accounting calculations, (4) reconciliation of YTD earnings records with tax returns, and (5) payroll bank account reconciliation.

Many companies have IT-based systems to gather payroll data, calculate payroll amounts, print cheques, and transfer electronic deposits. Their complexity varies, however, from simply writing payroll cheques to an integrated system preparing management reports and cost analyses based on payroll and cost distribution inputs. Payroll accounting is frequently contracted out to specialized service organizations. Regardless of the technology, the basic management and control functions of ensuring a flow of data to the payroll department should be in place. Computer audit techniques, such as test data, can be used to audit general controls that may be embedded in a computerized payroll system, and penetration tests can be used to verify effectiveness of general controls over security and authorized access.

Internal Control Questionnaire (ICQ)

Information about the payroll process control structure often is gathered initially through an ICQ. Exhibit 13A–2 (page 548) in Appendix 13A shows details of desirable policies and procedures for the control environment and the important control objectives—validity, completeness, authorization, accuracy, classification, accounting, and proper period recording.

Control Tests

An organization should have detail control procedures in place and operating to prevent, detect, and correct accounting errors. The general control objectives were covered in Chapter 9. Exhibit 13–7 puts these in the perspective of the payroll functions with examples of specific objectives.

Auditors can perform control tests to determine whether controls that are said to be in place and operating actually are being performed properly by company personnel. Exhibit 13–8 contains a selection of procedures for testing controls over payroll with the control objective each tests. The samples are usually attribute samples designed along the lines you studied in Chapter 10.

COVERT SURVEILLANCE

This sounds like spy work, and it, indeed, includes certain elements of that.

Auditors can test controls over employees' clocking in for work shifts by making personal observations of the process—observing whether anybody clocks in with two time cards or with two or more electronic entries, or leaves the premises after clocking in.

The auditors need to be careful not to make themselves obvious. Standing around in a manufacturing plant at 6 a.m. in blue pinstripe suit is as good as printing "Beware of Auditor" on your forehead. People then will be on their best behaviour, and you will observe nothing unusual.

Find an unobtrusive observation post. Stay out of sight. Use a video camera. Get a knowledgeable office employee to accompany you to interpret various activities. Perform an observation that has a chance of producing evidence of improper behaviour.

Dual Direction of Control Tests

The control tests in Exhibit 13–8 are designed to test the payroll accounting in two directions. One is the completeness direction, which matches personnel file content to payroll department files and the payroll register. The procedures trace the human resources department authorizations to the payroll department files—procedure A-1–c in Exhibits 13–8

EXHIBIT 13-7   CONTROL OBJECTIVES (PAYROLL PROCESS)

General Objectives	Examples of Specific Control Activities
1. Recorded payroll transactions are *valid* and documented.	Payroll accounting separated from personnel and timekeeping Time cards approved by supervisor Payroll files compared with personnel files periodically
2. Valid payroll transactions are *recorded* and none are omitted.	Employees' complaints about paycheques investigated and resolved (written records maintained and reviewed by internal auditors)
3. Payroll names, rates, hours, and deductions are *authorized*.	Names of new hires or terminations reported immediately in writing to payroll by the personnel department Authorization for deductions kept on file Rate authorized by union contract, agreement, or written policy and approved by personnel officer
4. Payroll computations contain *accurate* gross pay, deductions, and net pay.	Payroll computations checked by person independent of preparation Totals of payroll register reconciled to totals of payroll distribution by cost accounting
5. Payroll transactions are *classified* correctly as direct or indirect labour or other expenses.	Employee classification reviewed periodically Overall charges to indirect labour compared with direct labour and total product costs periodically
6. Payroll transaction *accounting* is complete.	Details of employee withholding reconciled periodically to liability control accounts and tax returns Employee tax expense and liabilities prepared in conjunction with payroll
7. Payroll costs and expenses are recorded in the *proper period*.	Month-end accruals reviewed by internal auditors Payroll computed, paid, and booked in timely manner

EXHIBIT 13–8   CONTROL TESTS FOR PAYROLL

	Control Objective
A. Personnel Files and Compensation Documents	
1. Select a sample of personnel files:	
a. Review personnel files for complete information on employment date, authority to add to payroll, job classification, wage rate, and authorized deductions.	Authorization Classification Authorization
b. Trace pay rate to union or other contracts or other rate authorization. Trace salaries to directors' minutes for authorization.	Authorization
c. Trace pay rate and deduction information to payroll department files used in payroll preparation.	Completeness
2. Obtain copies of pension plans, stock options, profit sharing, and bonus plans. Review and extract relevant portions that relate to payroll deductions, fringe benefit expenses, accrued liabilities, and financial statement disclosure.	Validity Completeness
3. Trace management compensation schemes to minutes to verify board of directors approval.	Authorization Accuracy
B. Payroll	Accounting
1. Select a sample of payroll register entries:	
a. Vouch employee identification, pay rate, and deductions to personnel files or other authorizations.	Authorization
b. Vouch hours worked to time clock records and supervisor's approval.	Validity Authorization
c. Recalculate gross pay, deductions, net pay.	Accuracy
d. Recalculate a selection of periodic payrolls.	Accuracy
e. Vouch to cancelled payroll cheque. Examine employees' endorsement or payroll distribution report details.	Accuracy Validity
2. Select a sample of time clock entries. Note supervisor's approval and trace to periodic payroll registers.	Authorization Completeness
3. Vouch a sample of periodic payroll totals to payroll bank account transfer vouchers and vouch payroll bank account deposit slip for cash transfer.	Accounting
4. Trace a sample of employees' payroll entries to individual payroll records maintained for tax reporting purposes. Reconcile total of employees' payroll records with payrolls paid for the year.	Completeness Accuracy
5. Review computer-printed error messages for evidence of the use of check digits, valid codes, limit tests, and other input, processing, and output application controls. Investigate correction and resolution of errors.	Accuracy
6. Trace payroll information to management reports and to general ledger account postings.	Accounting
7. Obtain control of a periodic payroll and conduct a surprise distribution of paycheques.	Validity
C. Cost Distribution Reports	
1. Select a sample of cost accounting analyses of payroll:	
a. Reconcile periodic totals with payroll payments for the same periods.	Completeness
b. Vouch to time records.	Validity
2. Trace cost accounting labour cost distributions to management reports and postings in general ledger and subsidiary account(s).	Accounting Classification
3. Select a sample of labour cost items in (a) ledger accounts and/or (b) management reports. Vouch to supporting cost accounting analyses.	Validity

and 13–9. The other direction of the test is validity. The control performance of interest here is the preparation of the payroll register. Exhibit 13–9 shows that the sample for this test is from the completed payroll registers. The individual payroll calculations are vouched to the personnel files (procedure B-1–a).

Generalized audit software can be used to test controls in the payroll process. Files are matched (e.g., personnel master file and payroll master file), and unmatched records and differences in common fields can be printed out. Statistical samples of files can be printed for vouching to union contracts or other authorizations. Statistical samples can be selected for recalculation by the software or be printed out as working papers for tracing and vouching, using the procedures in Exhibit 13–8.

In both manual and computerized systems, the test of controls and transaction details are evidence of the reliability of internal management reports and analyses. In turn, reliance on these reports and analyses, along with other analytical relationships, is a major portion of the substantive audit of payroll, compensation costs, and labour costs assigned to inventory and costs of goods sold.

EXHIBIT 13-9   DUAL-DIRECTION TEST OF PAYROLL CONTROLS

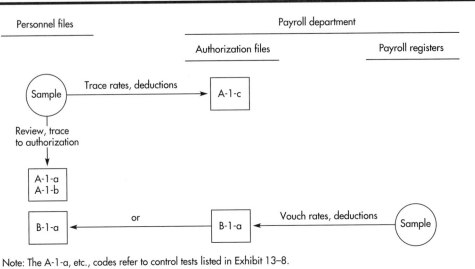

Note: The A-1-a, etc., codes refer to control tests listed in Exhibit 13–8.

The test of controls procedures are designed to produce evidence of the following items:

- Adequacy of personnel files, especially the authorizations of pay rate and deductions used in calculating pay.
- Accuracy of the periodic payrolls recorded in accounts and in employees' cumulative wage records; the procedures tend to centre on the periodic payroll registers.
- Accuracy of cost accounting distributions and management reports. (The cost accounting for labour costs must be reasonably accurate because good management reports contribute to cost control. The auditor who relies on the cost accounting system must determine whether it contains and transmits accurate information.)

OVERT SURVEILLANCE

SURPRISE PAYROLL DISTRIBUTION

Auditors may perform a surprise observation of a payroll distribution in connection with tests for overstatement. This involves taking control of paycheques and accompanying a company representative as the distribution takes place. The auditor ensures that each employee is identified and that only one cheque is given to each individual. Unclaimed cheques are controlled, and in this manner the auditor hopes to detect any fictitious persons on the payroll. Auditors need to be extremely careful to notice any duplication of employee identification or instance of one person attempting to pick up two or more cheques.

Summary: Control Risk Assessment

The audit manager or senior accountant in charge of the audit should evaluate the evidence obtained from an understanding of the internal control structure and from the test of controls audit procedures. If the control risk is assessed very low, the substantive audit procedures on the account balances can be limited. For example, it may be appropriate to rely on management reports generated by the payroll system.

On the other hand, if tests of controls reveal weaknesses, improper segregation of duties, inaccurate cost reports, inaccurate tax returns, or lax human resources policies, then substantive procedures will need to be designed to lower the risk of failing to detect material error in the financial statements. However, the irregularities of paying fictitious employees and overpaying for fraudulent time records do not normally misstate the financial statements, as long as the improper payments are expensed. (The losses are expensed, as they should be!) The misstatement is failing to distinguish and disclose "payroll fraud losses" from legitimate wages expense and cost of goods sold, but such losses are usually immaterial in a single year's financial statements, anyway. While it is not a crucial part of their work of detecting material misstatements in financial statements, auditors nevertheless do perform procedures that may find payroll fraud.

REVIEW CHECKPOINTS

24 What are common errors in the payroll process? Which control characteristics are auditors looking for to prevent or detect these errors?

25 Why is it unwise for an auditor to stand by the plant gate and time clock to observe employees checking in for work shifts?

26 How can an auditor determine whether the amount of labour cost charged to production was actually paid to employees?

27 Why might an auditor conduct a surprise observation of a payroll distribution? What should be observed?

28 Describe a control test using generalized audit software that can be performed in a computerized payroll system.

APPLICATION CASE AND ANALYSIS

LEARNING OBJECTIVE

6 Apply and integrate the chapter topics to design audit procedures for detecting misstatements due to error or fraud in the production and payroll processes.

In this application case we will demonstrate tests of controls and substantive audit procedures in the evidence gathering process related to the production and payroll processes. The case situation for each audit presented parallels the framework shown in Chapter 11's application case. The case situation provides context for the auditing decisions, rather than presenting a list of detection procedures in the abstract. Lists of detailed procedures, a selection of control tests, and detail substantive procedures for production and payroll are found in Appendices 13A and B.

Detecting Misstatements in Production and Payroll Processes

In his second year as an auditor, Jack is assigned to audit the payroll and inventory in Kromax Inc., a large manufacturing company. After the intial audit team meeting and his review of the prior years' audit files, Jack is starting to design his detailed audit programs for this year. Kromax is publicly traded and has been experiencing very poor profit results this year. Jack wants to make sure his procedures will address the risks of material misstatement, which may be higher this year than in the past, but he finds that many aspects of the payroll and manufacturing production processes are unfamiliar. Jack gets an opportunity to meet over lunch with Syed, one of his firm's senior partners. He knows Syed is always willing to help out less-experienced auditors by sharing stories about interesting audit situations. When Jack asks him specifically about audits where the auditors detected misstatements due to errors or frauds in payroll or production, Syed relates the following three audit stories showing errors in cost of sales recording, improper deferral of inventory costs, and payroll embezzlement through payment of fictitious employees.

AUDIT 13.1
UNBUNDLED BEFORE ITS TIME

Case Description

Western Corporation assembled and sold computer systems. A systems production order consisted of hardware and peripheral equipment specifications, and software specifications with associated performance criteria. Western brought in new auditors who discovered that items in production were being treated as finished goods "sold" before actual completion, which caused understated inventory, overstated cost of goods sold, overstated revenue, and overstated income. Western was routinely recording the hardware component of contracts too soon, recognizing revenue and cost of goods sold that should have been postponed until later when the customer accepted the entire system. In the last three years, the resulting income overstatement amounted to 12 percent, 15 percent, and 19 percent of the reported operating income before taxes.

Customer contracts always required that the unit be assembled to specifications, with hardware installation and testing as well as software installation and testing, before accepting the finished installation and paying for the entire package. Order completion usually took three to eight months. For internal accounting purposes, Western "unbundled" production orders into the hardware and software components of the customer orders so that production processing and cost accounting were performed as if the two were independent orders. When the hardware was installed and tested (with or without customer acceptance), Western recorded part of the contract price as sales revenue and the related cost of goods sold. The amount "due from customers" was carried in an asset account entitled "unbilled contract revenue," and no billing statement was sent to the customer at that time.

When the software component was completed, installed, tested, and accepted, the remainder of the contract price was recorded as revenue, the cost of the software was recorded as cost of goods sold, and a billing statement was sent to the customer. The "unbilled contract revenue," which now matched the customer's obligation, was moved to accounts receivable. While the two order components were in process (prior to installation at the customer's location), accumulated costs were carried in a work-in-process inventory account.

Audit Trail

Customer orders and contracts contained all the terms relating to technical specifications, acceptance testing, and the timing of the customer's obligation to pay. Copies of the technical specification sections of the contracts were attached to both the hardware and software production orders prepared and authorized in the production planning department. During production, installation, and testing, each of these orders was the basis of the production cost accumulation and subsidiary record of the work-in-process inventory. At the end, the production reports along with the accumulated costs became the production cost report and supporting documentation for the cost of goods sold entry.

AUDIT APPROACH ANALYSIS

Audit objective

The auditors' objective is to obtain evidence of the actual occurrence of cost of goods sold transactions, thereby yielding evidence of the completeness of recorded inventory.

Controls relevant to the process

The major control lies in the production planning department approval of orders identifying a total unit of production (in this case, the hardware and software components combined). Nothing is wrong with approving separate orders for efficiency of production, but they should be cross-referenced so that both production personnel and the cost accounting department see them as separate components of the same order unit.

AUDIT PROCEDURES

Tests of controls

While the company conducted a large business, it had relatively few production orders (200–250 charged to cost of goods sold during each year). A sample of completed production orders should be taken and vouched to the customer orders and contracts. This is done to determine the validity of the production orders in relation to customer orders and whether the cost of goods sold was recorded in the proper period. (Audit of accuracy and completeness of the cost accumulation can also be carried out on this sample, making it a dual-purpose test as further described below.)

Even though the auditors can read the customer contracts, enquiries should be made about the company's standard procedures for the timing of revenue and cost of goods sold recognition to determine what is actually being done in practice.

Tests of details of balance

The sample of completed production orders can also be used in a dual-purpose test of the cost of goods sold balance. For the balance audit, the primary points are the existence and completeness of the dollar amounts accumulated as cost of the contracts and the proper cutoff for recording the cost. The existence of the "unbilled contract revenue" asset account in the general ledger should raise a red flag. Such an account always means that management has estimated a revenue amount that has not been determined according to contract or billed to the customer according to contract terms. Even though the revenue is "unbilled," the related cost of goods sold still should be in the cost of goods sold account. While accounting theory and practice permit recognizing unbilled revenue in certain cases (e.g., percentage of completion for construction contracts), there have been abuses.

Audit Results

When the company decided to issue shares to the public, a new audit firm was engaged. The new auditor team performed the dual-purpose procedures already outlined, made the suggested enquiries, and investigated the unbilled contract revenue account. They learned about management's unbundling policy and insisted that it be changed so that revenue was recognized only when all the terms of the contract were met. (The investigation yielded the information about prior years' overstatements of revenue, cost of goods sold, and income.) Part of the reason for insisting on the change of policy was the finding that Western did not have a very good record of quality control and customer acceptance of software installation. Customer acceptance was often delayed several months while systems engineers debugged software. On several occasions Western solved the problems by purchasing complete software packages from other developers.

AUDIT 13.2
WHEN IN DOUBT, DEFER!

Case Description

SaCom was an auditor misconduct case that Syed had read about in the news. SaCom manufactured electronic and other equipment for private customers and government military defence contracts. The company was deferring costs under the headings of work-in-process, military contract claims, and R&D test equipment, thus overstating assets, understating cost of goods sold, and overstating income. Disclosure of the auditor's fees was manipulated and understated. SaCom reported net income of about $542,000 for the year, an overstatement of approximately 50 percent.

To achieve better reported profit, near the end of the year, the company used a journal entry to remove $170,000 from cost of goods sold and to defer it as tooling, leasehold improvements, and contract award and acquisition costs. The company capitalized certain expenditures as R&D test equipment ($140,000) and claims for reimbursement on defence contracts ($378,000).

In connection with a public offering of securities, the firm doing the audit billed SaCom $125,000 for professional fees. The underwriters objected so the auditors agreed to forgive $70,000 of the fees while SaCom agreed to pay higher fees the following year (150 percent of standard billing rates). SaCom disclosed audit fees in the registration statement in the amount of $55,000. This amount was paid from the proceeds of the offering.

Audit Trail

The $170,000 deferred costs were primarily labour costs, and the company altered the labour time records to be able to provide substantiating documentation. The auditors discovered the alterations as the jobs were left with labour costs that were too small, in light of the work performed. The R&D test equipment cost had already been charged to cost of goods sold with no indication of a reason for deferral when originally recorded. Deferral was accomplished with an adjusting journal entry. The company did not have documentation for the adjusting entry, except for an estimate of labour cost (44 percent of all labour cost in a subsidiary was capitalized during the period). The claim for reimbursement on defence contracts did not have documentation specifically identifying the costs as being related to the contract. (Auditors know that defence department auditors insist on documentation and justification before approving such a claim.) The audit fee arrangement was known to the audit firm, and it was recorded in an internal memorandum.

AUDIT APPROACH ANALYSIS

Audit objective

The auditors' objective is to obtain evidence of the validity of production costs deferred as tooling, leasehold improvements, contract award and acquisition costs, R&D test equipment, and claims for reimbursement on defence contracts.

Controls relevant to the process

The major control lies in the procedures for documenting the validity of cost deferral journal entries.

AUDIT PROCEDURES

Tests of controls

The procedure is to select a sample of journal entries, suspect ones in this case, and vouch them to supporting documentation and authorization. Experience has shown that nonstandard adjusting journal entries are the source of accounting errors and fraud more often than standard accounting for regular transactions. This makes adjusting journal entries a ripe field for control and substantive testing.

Tests of details of balance

The account balances created by the deferral journal entries can be audited in a dual-purpose procedure by auditing the supporting documentation. These balances were created entirely by the journal entries, and their "existence" as legitimate assets, deferrals, and reimbursement claims depends on the believability of the supporting explanations. In connection with the defence contract claim, auditors can review it knowing the extent of documentation required by government contract auditors. (As a separate matter, the auditors could "search for unrecorded liabilities," but they already knew about the deferred accounting fees anyway.)

Audit Results

By performing the procedures outlined, the audit team discovered all the questionable accounting. However, the partners in the auditing firm insisted on rendering unqualified opinions on the SaCom financial statements, without adjustment. One partner owned 300 shares of the company's stock in the name of a relative (without the consent or knowledge of the relative). Another audit partner later arranged a bank loan to the company to get $125,000 to pay past-due audit fees. This partner and another, along with their wives, guaranteed the loan. (When the bank later disclosed the guarantee in a bank confirmation, the confirmation was removed from the audit working paper file and destroyed.)

Regulatory Actions against the Auditors

The securities market regulator investigated the auditors' conduct in the SaCom audit, and, among other things, barred the audit firm for a period (about six months) from accepting new audit clients and also barred the partners involved in the SaCom audit work from involvement with new audit clients for various periods of time. The partners had violated several rules of professional conduct and were therefore subject to disciplinary action by their provincial institute (see Chapter 4 for discussion of rules of professional conduct).

AUDIT 13.3
GHOSTS ON THE PAYROLL

Case Description

Maybelle had responsibility for preparing personnel files for new hires, approving wages, verifying time cards, and distributing payroll cheques for the BlueBonnet Company. She embezzled funds by "hiring" fictitious employees, faking their records, and issuing cheques to them through the payroll system. She deposited some cheques in several personal bank accounts and cashed others, endorsing all of them with the names of the fictitious employees as well as her own. Maybelle stole $160,000 by creating these "ghosts," usually three to five of 112 people on the payroll, and paying them an average of $456 per week for three years. Sometimes the ghosts quit and were later replaced by others. But she stole "only" about 2 percent of the payroll funds during the period.

Audit Trail

Payroll creates a large paper trail with individual earnings records, T4 tax forms, payroll deductions for taxes, insurance and pension plans, and payroll tax reports. Maybelle mailed all the T4 forms to the same post office box.

AUDIT APPROACH ANALYSIS

Audit objective

The auditor's objective is to obtain evidence of the existence and validity of payroll transactions.

Controls relevant to the process

Different people should be responsible for hiring (preparing personnel files), approving wages, and distributing payroll cheques. "Thinking like a crook" in their fraud risk assessment led the audit team to suspect that Maybelle could put people on the payroll and obtain their cheques.

AUDIT PROCEDURES

Tests of controls

Audit for transaction authorization and validity. Random sampling may not work because of the small number of ghosts. Look for the obvious. Select several weeks' cheque blocks, account for numerical sequence (to see whether any cheques have been removed), and examine cancelled cheques for two endorsements.

Tests of details of balance

There may be no "balance" to audit other than the accumulated total of payroll transactions, and the total may not appear out of line with history because the fraud is small in relation to total payroll and has been going on for years. Scan cancelled payroll cheque endorsement details and trace these to personnel files. Observe a payroll distribution on a

surprise basis, noting any employees who do not collect their cheques and follow up by examining prior cancelled cheques for these missing employees. Scan personnel files for common addresses.

Audit Results

Both the surprise distribution observation and the scan for common addresses provided the names of

two to three exceptions. These led to prior cancelled cheques (which Maybelle had not removed and the bank reconciler had not noticed) that carried Maybelle's own name as endorser. Confronted, she confessed.

REVIEW
CHECKPOINTS

29 In a production situation similar to the Audit 13.1 case, what substantive audit work should be done on a sample of completed production orders (cost reports) recorded as cost of goods sold?

30 What red flag is raised when a company has an unbilled contract revenue account in its general ledger?

31 Why should auditors always select the auditee's adjusting journal entries for detail audit?

32 Is there anything wrong with auditors helping auditees obtain bank loans to pay their accounting firm's fees?

33 How can an auditor find out whether payroll control procedures were followed by company personnel?

34 Give some examples of payroll control omissions that would make it easy to "think like a crook" and see opportunities for errors and frauds.

SUMMARY

The production and payroll process consists of two parts that are closely related. Production involves production planning; inventory planning; acquisition of labour, materials, and overhead (purchases, payables, and payment process); custody of assets while work is in process and when finished products are stored in inventory; and cost accounting. Payroll is a part of every business and an important part of every production cycle. Management and control of labour costs are important. The payroll process consists of hiring, rate authorization, attendance and work supervision, payroll processing, and paycheque distribution.

Production and payroll information systems produce many internal documents, reports, and files that are sources of audit information. These systems mostly involve evidence made up of internal documentation, with relatively little external documentary evidence. Aside from physical inventory, the accounts in the production and payroll process are intangible: they cannot be observed, inspected, touched, or counted in any meaningful way. Most audit procedures for this cycle are analytical and dual-purpose procedures testing both the company's control procedures and the existence, valuation, and completeness assertions made by accumulating the results of numerous labour and overhead transactions.

Companies reduce control risk by separating authorization, custody, recording, and periodic reconciliation duties. Error-checking procedures of analyzing production orders and finished production cost reports are important for proper determination of inventory values and proper valuation of cost of goods sold. Without these procedures, many things could go wrong, ranging from overvaluing the inventory to understating costs of production by deferring costs that should be expensed. Cost accounting is a central feature of the production process and reports can be manipulated. Payroll accounting is critical to expenditure control as embezzlement often occurs during this process as well. Chapter application cases provided examples of these along with procedures for detecting them.

Analysis of Financial Statement Relationships

The audit of the production and payroll processes verifies the balances of inventory, various payroll liabilities, cost of goods sold, and wages/salary expense. In the balance sheet approach to auditing, we can analyze balance changes and the financial statement items related to them by preparing a continuity schedule. The finished goods inventory balance is used as an example for the production process:

Audited Amount	Financial Statement Where Amount Is Reported
Opening balance of finished goods inventory	Balance sheet (prior year comparative figure)
Add: Purchases of materials during the year Labour costs allocated Overhead costs allocated	Cash flow statement (direct method)
Deduct: Costs allocated to inventory work-in-process	Balance sheet (current year balance of work-in-process inventory, usually in inventory detail note)
Deduct: Cost of goods sold	Income statement expense
Ending balance of finished goods inventory	Balance sheet (current year figures)

Analytical procedures that use these relationships include inventory turnover ratios and gross margin analyses. Misstatements in the existence, completeness, and valuation assertions for inventory may result in unexplained fluctuations in these relationships.

MULTIPLE-CHOICE QUESTIONS FOR PRACTICE AND REVIEW

MC 1 When an auditor tests a company's cost accounting system, what are the auditor's procedures designed primarily to determine?
 a. Quantities on hand have been computed based on acceptable cost accounting techniques that reasonably approximate actual quantities on hand.
 b. Physical inventories are in substantial agreement with book inventories.
 c. The system is in accordance with generally accepted accounting principles and is functioning as planned.
 d. Costs have been properly assigned to finished goods, work-in-process, and cost of goods sold.

MC 2 The auditor tests the quantity of materials charged to work-in-process by vouching these quantities to which one of the following?
 a. Cost ledgers
 b. Perpetual inventory records
 c. Receiving reports
 d. Material requisition

MC 3 Effective internal control over the payroll function should include procedures that segregate the duties of making salary payments to employees and which of the following procedures?
 a. Controlling unemployment insurance claims
 b. Maintaining employee personnel records

 c. Approving employee fringe benefits
 d. Hiring new employees

MC 4 Which of the following is the best way for an auditor to determine that every name on a company's payroll is that of a bona fide employee presently on the job?
 a. Examine personnel records for accuracy and completeness.
 b. Examine employees' names listed on payroll tax returns for agreement with payroll accounting records.
 c. Make a surprise observation of the company's regular distribution of paycheques.
 d. Control the mailing of annual T4 tax forms to employee addresses in their personnel files.

MC 5 It would be appropriate for the payroll accounting department to be responsible for which of the following functions?
 a. Approval of employee time records
 b. Maintenance of records of employment, discharges, and pay increases
 c. Preparation of periodic governmental reports as to employees' earnings and withholding taxes
 d. Temporary retention of unclaimed employee paycheques

MC 6 To minimize the opportunities for fraud, unclaimed cash payroll should be handled by which of the following procedures?

    a. Deposited in a safe deposit box

    b. Held by the payroll custodian

    c. Deposited in a special bank account

    d. Held by the controller

MC 7 Which effective auditee internal control procedure prevents lack of agreement between the cost accounting for labour cost and the payroll paid?

    a. Reconciliation of totals on production job time tickets with job reports by the employees responsible for the specific jobs

    b. Verification of agreement of production job time tickets with employee time cards by a payroll department employee

    c. Preparation of payroll transaction journal entries by an employee who reports to the personnel department director

    d. Custody of pay rate authorization forms by the supervisor of the payroll department

(AICPA adapted)

MC 8 In a computerized payroll system, an auditor would be least likely to use test data to test controls related to which of the following?

    a. Missing employee numbers

    b. Proper signature approval of overtime by supervisors

    c. Time tickets with invalid job numbers

    d. Agreement of hours per clock card with hours on time tickets

EXERCISES AND PROBLEMS

· ·

PRODUCTION PROCESS

EP 1
LO.2
and
LO.3

ICQ Items: Possible Error Due to Weakness. Refer to the internal control questionnaire (Appendix 13A, Exhibit 13A–1, page 547) and assume the answer to each question is "no." Prepare a table matching questions to errors that could occur because of the absence of the control. Your column headings should be:

Question	Possible Error or Fraud Due to Weakness

EP 2
LO.2
and
LO.3

Control Tests Related to Controls and Objectives. Each of the following test of control audit procedures may be performed during the audit of the controls in the production and conversion cycle. For each procedure (a) identify the internal control procedure (strength) being tested, and (b) identify the internal control objective(s) being addressed.

  1. Balance and reconcile detail production cost sheets to the work-in-process inventory control account.

  2. Scan closed production cost sheets for missing numbers in the sequence.

  3. Vouch a sample of open and closed production cost sheet entries to (a) labour reports and (b) issue slips and materials-used reports.

  4. Locate the material issue forms. Are they prenumbered? kept in a secure location? available to unauthorized persons?

  5. Select several summary journal entries in the work-in-process inventory: (a) vouch to weekly labour and material reports and to production cost sheets, and (b) trace to control account.

  6. Select a sample of the material issue slips in the production department file. Examine for the following:

    a. Issue date/materials-used report date

    b. Production order number

    c. Supervisor's signature or initials

    d. Name and number of material

    e. Raw material stores clerk's signature or initials

    f. Matching material requisition in raw material stores file, noting date of requisition

  7. Determine by enquiry and inspection if cost clerks review dates on report of units completed for accounting in the proper period

EP 3
LO.1
and
LO.2

Cost Accounting Test of Controls. The diagram in Exhibit EP 3–1 describes several cost accounting test of control procedures. It shows the direction of the tests, leading from samples of cost accounting analyses, management reports, and the general ledger to blank squares.

Required:

For each blank square in Exhibit EP 3–1, write a cost accounting test of controls procedure and describe the evidence it can produce. (*Hint:* Refer to Exhibit 13–3.)

EP 4
LO.2

Work-in-Process Inventory, Tests of Control. Assume an auditor finds the following errors while performing tests of controls for work-in-process inventory in a custom machinery manufacturing business. For each finding, state which control objective is affected, what control deficiency is indicated, and what further investigation (if any) should be undertaken by the auditor.

    a. Budgeted labour hours are 30 percent lower than actual labour costs and production cost reports.

    b. Of 20 time-clock entries examined for July 14, three do not appear on the daily labour report or production cost report for that day.

    c. Weekly labour cost reports do not agree with the weekly payroll summary.

    d. The open production report used to cost work-in-process inventory contains costs of materials for which no matching amount and description are found on the material used reports and no material issue slip is on file in the material storage department.

EXHIBIT EP 3-1   DIAGRAM OF COST ACCOUNTING TEST OF CONTROLS

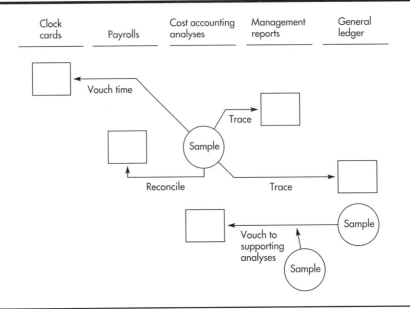

EP 5 **Auditor Independence.** Review the SaCom case given
LO.3 earlier (Audit 13.2). Discuss the auditor independence
issues in this case and how these issues may have contributed to the audit deficiencies that occurred. Discuss
whether the security market regulator's penalties were
appropriate in the circumstances, in your view.

PAYROLL PROCESS

EP 6 **ICQ Items: Misstatements That Could Occur from**
LO.4 **Control Weaknesses.** Refer to the internal control ques-
and tionnaire on a payroll system (Exhibit 13A–2 in Appen-
LO.5 dix 13A, page 548) and assume the answer to each
question is "no." Prepare a table matching each question
to an error or fraud that could occur because of the absence of the control. Your column headings should be:

Question	Possible Error or Fraud Due to Weakness

EP 7 **ICQ Items: Control Objectives, Control Tests,**
LO.4 **and Possible Misstatements.** Listed below is a selection
LO.5 of items from the payroll processing internal control
LO.6 questionnaire in Exhibit 13A–2.
1. Are names of terminated employees reported in writing to the payroll department?
2. Are authorizations for deductions, signed by the employees, on file?
3. Is the timekeeping department (function) independent
of the payroll department?
4. Are timekeeping and cost accounting records (such
as hours, dollars) reconciled with payroll department
calculations of wage and salaries?

Required:
For each question:
a. Identify the control objective the question applies to.
b. Specify one test of controls audit procedure an auditor could use to determine whether the control was
operating effectively (see Exhibit 13–8 on page 531
for procedures).
c. Using your business experience, your logic, and/or
your imagination, give an example of a misstatement
caused by error or fraud that could occur if the control
was absent or ineffective.

EP 8 **Major Risks in Payroll Process.** Prepare a schedule of
LO.1 the major risks in the payroll process. Identify the con-
LO.4 trol objectives and financial statement assertions related
LO.5 to each. Lay out a three-column schedule like this:

Payroll Process Risk	Control Objective	Assertion

EP 9 **Payroll Authorization in a Computerized System.** Two
LO.4 auditors were discussing control procedures and test of
and control auditing for payroll systems. The audit senior of
LO.5 the engagement said, "It seems almost impossible to determine who authorizes transactions when the payroll
account is computerized. Every system is so different."

Required:
Respond to the senior's remark. List the points in the
flow of payroll information where authorization can take
place in a computerized payroll system.

EP 10 **Payroll Processed by a Service Organization.** Assume
LO.5 that you are the audit senior conducting a review of the

EXHIBIT EP 11-1 DIAGRAM OF PAYROLL TEST OF CONTROLS

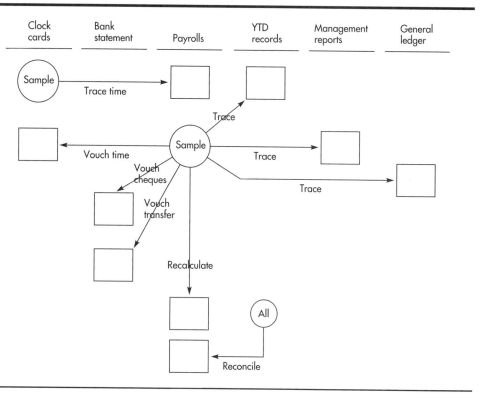

payroll system of a new auditee. While you are in the process of interviewing the payroll department manager, she makes the following statement, "We don't need many controls since our payroll is done outside the company by Automated Data Processing, a service organization."

Required:

Evaluate the payroll department manager's statement and describe how a service organization affects an auditors' review of controls. You may want to refer to Chapter 9.

EP 11
LO.4
and
LO.5

Payroll Test of Controls. The diagram in Exhibit EP 11–1 describes several payroll test of control procedures. It shows the direction of the tests, leading from samples of time cards, payrolls, and cumulative year-to-date earnings records to blank squares.

Required:

For each blank square in Exhibit EP 11–1, write a payroll test of controls procedure and describe the evidence it can produce. (*Hint:* Refer to Exhibit 13–8.)

DISCUSSION CASES

· ·

PRODUCTION PROCESS

DC 1
LO.1
LO.2
LO.3

Control over Departmental Labour Cost in a Job-Cost System. The Brown Printing Company accounts for the services it performs on a job-cost basis. Most jobs take a week or less to complete and involve two or more of Brown's five operating departments. Actual costs are accumulated by job. To ensure timely billing, however, the company prepares sales invoices based on cost estimates.

Recently, several printing jobs have incurred losses. To avoid future losses, management has decided to focus on cost control at the department level. Since labour is a

major element of cost, management proposes a department labour cost report. This report will originate in the payroll department as part of the biweekly payroll and then go to an accounting clerk for comparison with total labour cost estimates by department. If the actual total department labour costs in a payroll are not much more than the estimated total departmental labour cost during that period, the accounting clerk will send the report to the department foreman. If the accounting clerk concludes that a significant variance exists, the report will be sent to the assistant controller. The assistant controller will investigate the cause when time is available, and recommend corrective action to the production manager.

Required:

Evaluate the proposal:

a. Give at least three common aspects of control the department labour cost report proposal complies with. Give an example from the case to support each aspect cited.

b. Give at least three common aspects of control the departmental labour cost report proposal does not comply with. Give an example from the case to support each aspect cited.

(CIA adapted)

DC 2 **Audit the Fixed Asset and Amortization Schedule.**
LO.2 Bart's Company has prepared the fixed asset and amorti-
and   zation schedule shown in Exhibit DC 2–1. The following
LO.3 information is available:

- The land was purchased eight years ago when Building 1 was erected. The location was then remote but now is bordered by a major freeway. The appraised value is $35 million.
- Building 1 has an estimated useful life of 35 years and no residual value.
- Building 2 was built by a local contractor this year. It also has an estimated useful life of 35 years and no residual value. The company occupied it on May 1 this year.
- The Equipment A was purchased January 1 six years ago, when the estimated useful life was eight years with no residual value. It was sold on May 1 for $500,000.
- The Equipment B was placed in operation as soon as the Equipment A was sold. It is estimated to be in use for six years with no residual value at the end.
- The company estimated the useful life of the press at 20 years with no residual value.
- Auto 1 was sold during the year for $1,000.
- Auto 2 was purchased on July 1. The company expects to use it five years and then sell it for $2,000.
- All amortization is calculated on the straight-line method using months of service.

Required:

a. Audit the amortization calculations. Are there any errors? Put the errors in the form of an adjusting journal entry, assuming 90 percent of the amortization on the buildings and the press has been charged to cost of goods sold and 10 percent is still capitalized in the inventory, and the other amortization expense is classified as general and administrative expense.

b. List two audit procedures for auditing the fixed asset additions.

c. What will an auditor expect to find in the "gain and loss on sale of assets" account? What amount of cash flow from investing activities will be in the statement of cash flows?

DC 3 **Inventory Costing Errors, Standard Manufacturing**
LO.1 **Costs.** Thermox Inc. manufacturs heating elements and
LO.2 devices. One of its main raw material components is
LO.3 steel tubing. During the current year, Thermox's new raw material buyer began purchasing steel tubing from a U.S. supplier. The buyer found this supplier's prices to be considerably lower than the previous Canadian suppliers.

Thermox's cost accounting department uses standard manufacturing costs to determine its inventory cost and cost of goods sold. In her audit of the reasonability of the standard costs, the audit senior is vouching the raw materials components list to supplier invoices and supporting documents. She notes several steel tubing purchases in March that were invoiced in U.S. dollars (a U.S. dollar at this time was worth about $1.25 Canadian). However, the U.S. dollar amount, not the Canadian dollar amount, is used in the standard costing formula. Steel tubing comprises 70 percent of Thermox's standard manufacturing cost. The audit senior extends her vouching and discovers that all steel tubing purchases from March to the December year-end were from the same U.S. supplier, and were invoiced in U.S. dollars.

The audit senior then examines the U.S. supplier's monthly statements of account and discovers that

EXHIBIT DC 2–1

	Fixed Assets and Amortization							
	Asset Cost (000s)				Accumulated Amortization (000s)			
Description	Beginning Balance	Added	Sold	Ending Balance	Beginning Balance	Added	Sold	Ending Balance
Land	10,000			10,000				
Bldg. 1	30,000			30,000	6,857	857		7,714
Bldg. 2		42,000		42,000		800		800
Equipment A	5,000		5,000	0	3,750	208	3,958	0
Equipment B		3,500		3,500		583		583
Press	1,500			1,500	300	150		450
Auto 1	15		15	0	15		15	0
Auto 2		22		22		2		2
Total	46,515	45,522	5,015	87,022	10,922	2,600	3,973	9,549

Thermox's accounts payable department has been paying the U.S. steel tubing invoices in Canadian dollars. Thus Thermox has been short-paying the U.S. supplier by about 50 percent. Because of this related error, no significant cost variances appeared for raw materials, which would have alerted Thermox management to the problem.

Required:

a. What impact will this error have on Thermox's year-end inventory balance and its cost of sales if standard costs are used and no variances are adjusted? What impact will this error have on accounts payable? State any assumptions you make.

b. What records will the audit senior need to examine and what tests and analyses will she need to perform to assess the magnitude of the error in inventory, cost of goods sold, and accounts payable?

c. What control deficiency would allow this type of error to occur, and what kind of control procedure(s) could be implemented to prevent this type of error?

DC 4
LO.1
and
LO.2

Audit of Electronics Inventory. During his examination of the inventories and related accounts of Consumer Electronics Inc., a manufacturer and distributor of small appliances, a PA encountered the following:

a. During inventory observation, the PA noticed several trucks loaded with finished goods parked at the shipping dock. The contents of the trucks were excluded from the physical inventory.

b. The finished goods inventory included high volumes of several products, and many of their cartons were old and covered with dust. In response to the PA's questions, the plant manager stated that there was no problem as "all of these goods will eventually be sold although some price incentives may be necessary."

c. While reviewing the complex calculations used to develop the unit production costs of items in finished goods, the PA noted that the costs of the company's electrical engineering department had been treated as period expenses in previous years but were included in manufacturing overhead in the current year.

d. The company installed a new perpetual inventory system during the year. The PA noted that numerous of the company's recorded year-end quantities differed from the actual physical inventory counts. In part because of these problems, the company took a complete physical inventory at year-end.

Required:
Describe the additional audit procedures (if any) that the PA should perform to obtain sufficient appropriate evidence in each of the preceding situations.

(CGA-Canada adapted)

DC 5
LO.1
LO.2
LO.3

Audit of Real Estate Inventory. Desai Developments Limited (DDL) is in the business of buying undeveloped land in the regions outside of Calgary and holding it until it has development permits and market conditions are favourable for development. DDL began operations 12 years ago. Once a property is ready for development,

DDL contracts with various construction companies to build the houses. DDL handles all the promotions and sales of the houses once they are completed.

Because of recent changes in environmental laws and zoning restrictions, some of the sites DDL originally purchased for subdivisions can no longer be used for this purpose. However, golf courses are still permissible on these sites because they preserve wetlands and forests. DDL is, therefore now undertaking a new business model that involves developing and operating golf courses. DDL will also sell off the outer edges of the golf course properties as building lots for large "estate lot" homes, which are still permitted because they have a low impact on the environment.

The president of DDL, Mira Desai, owns 51 percent of the DDL common shares. Her relatives hold the remainder. DDL also has financed its operation by bank mortgages on the land. Mira Desai now wants to issue preferred shares in DDL to private investors, and use the proceeds to pay back the bank mortgages and fund the golf course developments. The plan is for the preferred shares to be nonvoting, to pay a 6 percent noncumulative dividend per year, and to provide the preferred share-holder with a life-long membership in one of the golf courses. She has found a securities firm to sell the preferred shares, but DDL will need to provide prospective investors with DDL's 20X5 financial statements prepared in accordance with generally accepted accounting principles (GAAP).

Mira Desai is considering engaging your audit firm to provide an audit opinion on DDL's GAAP financial statements. Up until now DDL has only prepared unaudited financial statements primarily for tax purposes, and has always used accounting methods that result in paying the minimum amount of tax. In discussions with Mira Desai, and from reviewing DDL's most recent annual financial statements (for the year ended December 31, 20X5), you learn the following:

1. DDL currently owns four properties that have been approved for golf course development. It has finalized the plans and will start development in the spring of 20X6. DDL owns five other properties that may be suitable for future golf course developments.

2. DDL owns another eight properties approved for residential subdivisions. Recently DDL received an offer from another property development company, Atim Corp., to purchase all eight of these properties for $50 million. The mortgages on these properties are $45 million. Mira Desai is interested in exiting from the subdivision development to allow DDL to focus on the golf course business. She is considering making a counter-offer in which DDL would form a 50:50 joint venture with Atim Corp. DDL would contribute the properties to this joint venture entity and Atim would contribute the cash and management skills to construct and sell the subdivision homes.

3. DDL has capitalized the purchase price of the land, legal fees relating to the purchase, and land transfer taxes. All other costs related to the properties, such as property taxes, interest, earth-moving costs, and fees for architectural and landscaping plans, have all been expensed to maximize tax deductions.

4. DDL's net income from the subdivision business has varied widely over the years, with profits in years when housing developments are completed and sold, and losses in other years. Revenue is recognized when each house is sold. The average subdivision development takes about 18 months to complete. A golf course development will take about two years because of the extensive landscaping and planting required.

5. The golf course development costs can be partly financed by selling the estate lots around the golf course site to the custom home builders. As part of its agreement with these construction companies, DDL will handle the sales promotions and marketing of the houses for a 10 percent commission on selling prices.

6. To date, DDL has completed five housing subdivision developments. The first development, completed about 10 years ago, has recently been in the news because methane and other noxious gases have been seeping into basements. Environmental assessments have determined that the subdivision was built on what was a landfill site in the 1950s. It was never properly sealed off prior to redevelopment and is now releasing gases that are dangerous to people. Environmental consultants estimate it will cost up to $2 million to remediate the properties so the houses will be safe to live in. The current owners of these homes have started legal action against DDL. DDL's lawyers believe that the company that sold DDL the land had fraudulently withheld relevant information about the prior use of the land, so that DDL will not be liable for the remediation costs.

7. DDL received a government loan of $6 million in early 20X5, under a program aimed at helping developers cope with the impact of the changes in environmental regulations The entire loan is forgivable if DDL produces a commercially viable golf course by the end of 20X7. Half of the government loan amount was recorded as revenue in 20X5 since, in DDL management's view, the golf course development is 50 percent complete.

8. Late in 20X5, DLL rented earth-moving equipment to start the golf course development work. The equipment lease agreement has a 10-year term and required a $200,000 payment at the start of the term, with payments of $200,000 thereafter at the start of each of the next nine years. The equipment could have been purchased for $1,265,650 in cash and has an expected useful life of 10 years. The relevant borrowing rate for assessing this lease is 12 percent per year.

Required:

a. Prepare a report outlining the considerations your firm would have to make before accepting the audit of DDL.

b. Assuming your firm accepts the engagement, prepare a detailed and complete audit plan that addresses the accounting and other information items noted previously. Also, suggest any other information that you would want for planning the audit.

PAYROLL PROCESS

DC 6 **Control Tests, Evaluation of Possible Diversion**
LO.4 **of Payroll Funds.** The Generous Loan Company has
LO.5 100 branch loan offices. Each office has a manager and
LO.6 four or five subordinates who are employed by the manager. Branch managers prepare the weekly payroll, including their own salaries, and pay employees from cash on hand. Employees sign the payroll sheet signifying receipt of their salary. Hours worked by hourly personnel are inserted in the payroll register sheet from time cards prepared by the employees and approved by the manager.

The weekly payroll register sheets are sent to the head office along with other accounting statements and reports. The head office compiles employee earnings records and prepares all federal and provincial salary reports from the weekly payroll sheets.

Salaries are established by head office job-evaluation schedules. Salary adjustments, promotions, and transfers of full-time employees are approved by a head office salary committee based on the recommendations of branch managers and area supervisors. Branch managers advise the salary committee of new full-time employees and terminated employees. Part-time and temporary employees are hired without advising the salary committee.

Required:

a. Prepare a payroll audit program to be used in the head office to audit the branch office payrolls of the Generous Loan Company. See Exhibit 13–8 (page 531) for sample audit procedures.

b. Based on your review of the payroll system, how might funds for payroll be diverted fraudulently?

(AICPA adapted)

DC 7 **Croyden Factory, Inc.: Evaluation of Flowchart for**
LO.4 **Payroll Control Weaknesses.** A PA's audit working pa-
LO.5 pers contain a narrative description of a segment of the Croyden Factory Inc. payroll system and an accompanying flow chart (Exhibit DC 7–1) as follows:

The internal control system, with respect to the personnel department, is well functioning and is not included in the accompanying flowchart.

At the beginning of each workweek, payroll clerk No. 1 reviews the payroll department files to determine the employment status of factory employees. Clerk No. 1 then prepares time cards and distributes them as each individual arrives at work. This payroll clerk, who also is responsible for custody of the cheque signature stamp machine, verifies the identity of each payee before delivering signed cheques to the supervisor.

At the end of each workweek, the supervisor distributes payroll cheques for the preceding workweek. Concurrent with this activity, the supervisor reviews the current week's employee timecards, notes the regular and overtime hours worked on a summary form, and initials the time cards. The supervisor then delivers all time cards and unclaimed payroll cheques to payroll clerk No. 2.

EXHIBIT DC 7-1   CROYDEN INC. FACTORY PAYROLL SYSTEM

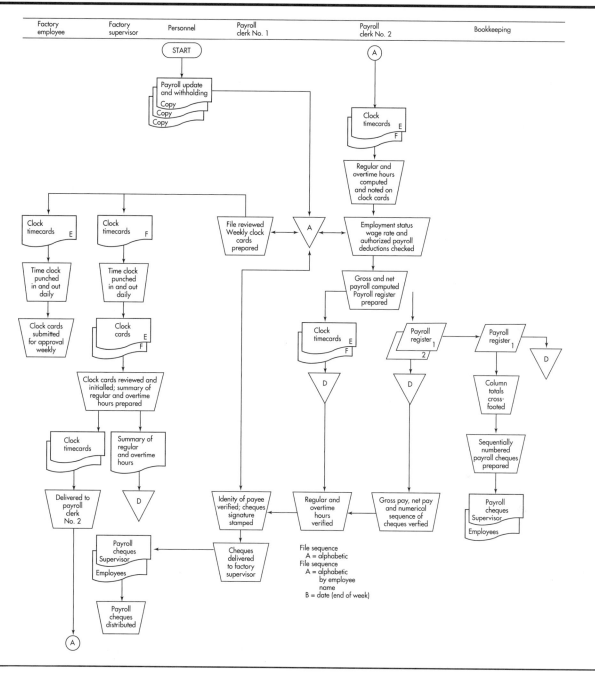

Required:

a. Based on the narrative and accompanying flow chart, what are the weaknesses in the system of internal control?

b. Based on the narrative and accompanying flow chart, what enquiries should be made with respect to clarifying the existence of possible additional weaknesses in the system of internal control?

Note: Do not discuss the internal control system of the personnel department.

(AICPA adapted)

DC 8 **Vane Corporation: Control Weaknesses in Comput-**
LO.5 **erized Payroll System.** The Vane Corporation is a manufacturing concern that has been in business for the past 18 years. During this period, the company has grown from a very small family-owned operation to a medium-sized company with several departments. Despite this growth, many procedures employed by Vane have been in effect since the business was started. Just recently, Vane has computerized its payroll function.

The payroll operation involves each worker picking up a weekly time card on Monday morning and writing in his or her name and identification number. These blank cards are kept near the factory entrance. Workers fill in their daily arrival and departure times each day on the card. Each Monday, the factory supervisor collects the time cards for the previous week and sends them to data processing.

In data processing the time cards are entered into the computerized payroll system. The system updates the payroll records and prints out the paycheques. The cheques are written on the regular chequing account, imprinted by a signature plate with the treasurer's signature, and sent to the factory supervisors who distribute them to the workers or hold them for absent workers to pick up later. Supervisors notify data processing of new employees, terminations, changes in hourly pay rates, or any other changes affecting payroll.

The workers also complete a job time ticket for each individual job they work on each day. These are collected daily and sent to cost accounting, where they are used to prepare a cost distribution analysis.

Further analysis of the payroll function reveals the following:
1. A worker's gross wages never exceed $300 per week.
2. Raises never exceed 55 cents per hour for the factory workers.
3. No more than 20 hours of overtime are allowed each week.
4. The factory employs 150 workers in 10 departments.

The payroll function had not been operating smoothly for some time, but even more problems have surfaced since the payroll was computerized. The factory supervisors would like a weekly report indicating worker tardiness, absenteeism, and idle time so that they can determine the amount of productive time lost and the reasons for the lost time. The following errors and inconsistencies have been encountered the past few pay periods:
1. A worker's paycheque was not processed properly because he had transposed two digits in his identification number on his time card.
2. A worker was issued a cheque for $1,531.80 when it should have been $153.18.
3. One worker's paycheque was not written, and this error was not detected until the paycheques for that department were distributed by the supervisor.
4. Some of the payroll register records were accidentally erased from the system when a data processing clerk tried to reorganize and rename the files in the hard drive. Data processing attempted to re-establish the destroyed portion from original source documents and other records.
5. One worker received a much larger paycheque than he should have. A clerk had keyed 84 instead of 48 for hours worked.
6. Several paycheques issued were not included in the totals posted to the payroll journal entry to the general ledger accounts. This was not detected for several pay periods.
7. In processing nonroutine changes, a data processing clerk included a pay rate increase for one of his friends in the factory. By chance, this was discovered by another employee.

Required:
Identify the control weaknesses in Vane's payroll procedures and in the computer processing as it is now conducted. Recommend the necessary changes to correct the system. Arrange your answer in the following columnar format:

Control Weaknesses	Recommendations
1	1

DC 9
LO.1
LO.2
LO.3
LO.6

Payroll Process: False Claims for Hours Worked. This case is modelled on the Application Case and Analysis in the chapter.

Case Description The case involves overpayment of wages to employees making false claims for hours worked. A temporary personnel agency assigned Nurse Jane to work at Municipal Hospital. The personnel agency paid Nurse Jane, then billed Municipal Hospital for the wages and benefits. Supporting documents were submitted with the personnel agency's bills.

Nurse Jane claimed payroll hours on agency time cards, which showed approval signatures of a hospital nursing shift supervisor. This shift supervisor had been terminated by the hospital several months prior to the periods covered by the time cards in question. Nurse Jane worked one or two days per week but submitted time cards for a full 40-hour work week.

Nurse Jane's wages and benefits were billed to the hospital at $22 per hour. False time cards charging about 24 extra hours per week cost the hospital $528 per week. Nurse Jane was assigned to Municipal Hospital for 15 weeks during the year, so she caused overcharges of about $7,900. However, she told three of her crooked friends about the procedure, and they overcharged the hospital another $24,000.

Audit Trail Each hospital work station keeps ward shift logs, which are sign-in sheets showing nurses on duty at all times. Nurses sign in and sign out when going on and off duty. Municipal Hospital maintains personnel records showing, among other things, the period of employment of its own nurses, supervisors, and other employees.

AUDIT APPROACH ANALYSIS

Audit objective The auditor's objective is to obtain evidence determining whether wages were paid to valid employees for actual time worked at the authorized pay rate.

Controls relevant to the process Control procedures in the payroll process should include a hiring authorization for putting employees on the payroll. For temporary employees, this authorization includes contracts for nursing time, conditions of employment, and terms, including the contract reimbursement rate. Control records of attendance and work should be kept (ward shift log). Supervisors should approve time cards or other records used by the payroll department to prepare paycheques.

In this case the contract with the personnel agency provided that approved time cards had to be submitted as supporting documentation for the agency billings.

Required:
Describe in detail the audit procedures you would perform in this case. Consider tests of control, and substantive tests such as dual purpose tests of transactions and/or tests of details of balance. Which tests do you consider likely to detect the overpayment of hourly wages? Why?

APPENDIX 13A

INTERNAL CONTROL QUESTIONNAIRES

· ·

EXHIBIT 13A-1   INTERNAL CONTROL QUESTIONNAIRES: PRODUCTION AND PAYROLL PROCESSES

Environment and general controls relevant to this application:
1. Is access to blank production order forms denied to unauthorized persons?
2. Is access to blank bills of materials and labour needs forms denied to unauthorized persons?
3. Is access to blank material requisitions forms denied to unauthorized persons?

Assertion-Based Control Evaluations:
Validity objective:
4. Are material requisitions and job time tickets reviewed by the production supervisor after the supervisor prepares them?
5. Are the weekly direct labour and materials-used reports reviewed by the production supervisor after preparation by the supervisor?

Completeness objective:
6. Are production orders prenumbered and the numerical sequence checked for missing documents?
7. Are bills of materials and labour needs forms prenumbered and the numerical sequence checked for missing documents?
8. Are material requisitions and job time tickets prenumbered and the numerical sequence checked for missing documents?
9. Are inventory issue slips prenumbered and the numerical sequence checked for missing documents?

Authorization objective:
10. Are production orders prepared by authorized persons?
11. Are bills of materials and labour needs prepared by authorized persons?

Accuracy objective:
12. Are differences between inventory issue slips and materials-used reports recorded and reported to the cost accounting supervisor?
13. Are differences between job time tickets and the labour report recorded and reported to the cost accounting supervisor?
14. Are standard costs used? If so, are they reviewed and revised periodically?
15. Are differences between reports of units completed and products-received reports recorded and reported to the cost accounting supervisor?

Classification objective:
16. Does the accounting manual give instructions for proper classification of cost accounting transactions?

Accounting objective:
17. Are summary entries reviewed and approved by the cost accounting supervisor?

Proper period objective:
18. Does the accounting manual give instructions to date cost entries on the date of use? Does an accounting supervisor review monthly, quarterly, and year-end cost accruals?

EXHIBIT 13A-2   PAYROLL APPLICATION

Environment and general controls relevant to this application:
1. Are all employees paid by cheque or direct deposit to their bank accounts?
2. If a special payroll bank account is used, is the payroll bank account reconciled by someone who does not prepare, sign, or deliver paycheques?
3. Are payroll cheques signed by persons who neither prepare cheques nor keep cash funds or accounting records?
4. If an outside payroll processing service is used, is the list of employees paid by the service reviewed by the employees' supervisor or someone else who cannot add or make changes to the employee payroll list submitted to the processing service?
5. Are payroll department personnel rotated in their duties? required to take vacations? bonded?
6. Is there a timekeeping department (function) independent of the payroll department?

Assertion-Based Control Evaluations:

Validity objective:
7. Are names of terminated employees reported in writing to the payroll department?
8. Is the payroll compared with personnel files periodically?
9. Are cheques distributed by someone other than the employee's immediate supervisor?
10. Are unclaimed wages deposited in a special bank account or otherwise controlled by a responsible officer?
11. Do internal auditors conduct occasional surprise distributions of paycheques?

Completeness objective:
12. Are names of newly hired employees reported in writing to the payroll department?
13. Are blank payroll cheques prenumbered and the numerical sequence checked for missing documents?

Authorization objective:
14. Are all wage rates determined by contract or approved by a personnel officer?
15. Are authorizations for deductions, signed by the employees, on file?
16. Are time cards or piecework reports prepared by the employee approved by his or her supervisor?
17. Is a time clock or other electromechanical or computer system used?
18. Is the payroll register sheet signed by the employee preparing it and approved prior to payment?

Accuracy objective:
19. Are timekeeping and cost accounting records (such as hours, dollars) reconciled with payroll department calculations of hours and wages?
20. Are payrolls audited periodically by internal auditors?

Classification objective:
21. Do payroll accounting personnel have instructions for classifying payroll debit entries?

Accounting objective:
22. Are payroll records reconciled with tax reports?

Proper period objective:
23. Are monthly, quarterly, and annual wage accruals reviewed by an accounting officer?

APPENDIX 13B

SUBSTANTIVE AUDIT PROGRAMS

EXHIBIT 13B-1   AUDIT PROGRAM FOR PRODUCTION COSTING

Analytical procedures
1. Obtain satisfactory explanations from management for relationships observed, based on the following:
   a) Compare gross profit margin (i.e., as a percentage of sales) by product and compare with prior periods.
   b) Compare gross profit margin by product with the standard mark-up.
   c) Compare gross profit margin by month for the last two fiscal periods. Note any differences in the gross profit margin in the months before and after the period end.

EXHIBIT 13B-1   AUDIT PROGRAM FOR PRODUCTION COSTING (continued)

Tests of details of transactions and balances

1. Select the significant items contained in the inventory balance and perform the following procedures:
   a) Raw material

      Agree cost to suppliers' invoices as well as shipper and customs brokers' charges.
   b) WIP and finished goods

      Review cost elements and costing calculations by product for accuracy and reasonableness.

      Compare labour rates used with the payroll records.
   c) Overhead applied to inventory

      Assess the reasonableness of overhead rates used by comparing amounts applied with actual overhead in the accounting records.
2. Ensure inventory costs in a foreign currency have been translated at the period-end exchange rate.
3. Assess reasonability of accounting policies chosen by the entity in relation to common practice in the industry, consistency with previous periods, and impact on net income.

EXHIBIT 13B-2   AUDIT PROGRAM FOR PAYROLL

Analytical procedures

1. Develop expectations for payroll expenses based on understanding the entity, including new product lines, labour union agreements, industry changes, etc.
   a) Enquire of management about changes to payroll policies and procedures, noting any changes from prior periods.
   b) Enquire of management whether there were any salary or rate increases, significant increases in staffing, and/or changes to the benefit plan or regulations.
2. Obtain satisfactory explanations from management for relationships observed, based on the following:
   a) Significant changes or trends in payroll expenses compared with prior period(s) and/or budgets in total and as a percentage of sales
   b) Payroll expenses compared with related accrued liabilities
   c) Average annual wage in comparison with work force, minimum wage rates, etc.
   d) Payroll expenses compared with nonfinancial information such as production volume, facility size, manufacturing process times, product-line changes
   e) Analyze payroll and benefits by employee type or class by comparing with prior period and budgets (e.g., benefits as a percentage of total payroll, average salary per employee, etc.)
   f) Calculate and assess the reasonableness of average hourly rates and average salary per employee when compared with normal rates or salary classes.

Tests of details of transactions and balances

For payroll and benefits:
   a) Scan the payroll journal for the period for large and unusual items and ascertain propriety of such items.
   b) Ask responsible payroll personnel about any instances of fictitious employees, employees with unusual contract terms or conditions, or unrecorded transactions.

For high assessed risk of misstatement of payroll and benefits

Select a sample of payroll payments and perform the following:
   a) Trace employee's name, job category, and employee number to authorized personnel records.
   b) Agree pay rate to authorized wage, union contract, or other authorized record.
   c) Agree hours worked to clock card or other time record.
   d) Agree hours worked to labour cost allocated to inventory cost accounting records.
   e) Recalculate gross and net pay using employee TD1 and current tax withholding tables for income tax withheld, Canada Pension Plan and Employment Insurance deduction rates, and by examining authorization forms for other payroll deductions such as company pension plan or group insurance.
   f) Examine paid and endorsed payroll cheques of selected employees and trace to data in the payroll journal.

CHAPTER 14

Finance and Investment Process

In essence, the finance and investment process is the manner in which a company plans for capital requirements and raises the money by borrowing, selling shares, and entering into acquisitions and joint ventures. Dividend, interest, and income tax payments are part of the related accounting cycle. This cycle also includes the accounting for investments in marketable securities, joint ventures and partnerships, and subsidiaries. The finance portion of the process deals with acquiring money to fund the company's activities. The investment portion deals with investing money in revenue-generating assets and other long-term investments. The process has become much more complex through the use of sophisticated financial engineering that better manages client financial and business risk. Auditors have to make sure that these complex risks are properly disclosed in financial reporting.

LEARNING OBJECTIVES

After completing this chapter, you will be able to do the following:

1 Describe the finance and investment process: risk assessment, typical transactions, source documents, controls, and account balances.

2 Outline control tests for auditing control over debt, owner's equity, and investment transactions.

3 Apply and integrate the chapter topics to design audit procedures for detecting misstatements

due to error or fraud in the finance and investment process. Some detailed programs are illustrated in Appendix 14A (page 587).

4* Describe the risks associated with derivative financial instruments (Appendix 14B).

5* Describe differential reporting requirements for qualifying enterprises (Appendix 14C).

Note: Appendix 14A accompanies this chapter and Appendices 14B and 14C are located on the text Online Learning Centre.

RISK ASSESSMENT FOR THE FINANCE AND INVESTMENT PROCESS

The finance and investment process involves the client company's legal structure, how it raises capital from shareholders and creditors, its intercorporate investments, and related parties. Each entity will have its own mix of these components. Understanding these important aspects of the corporate structure and their implications for financial statement misstatement risks requires the input of the most experienced audit team members. The corporate governance controls introduced in Chapter 9 are relevant to this risk assessment and are discussed in more detail in this chapter.

The account balances in the finance and investments process include those for financial instruments such as long-term investments and debt, share capital, and contributed surplus. Dividend and interest payments are regular transactions. Disclosure requirements in the finance and investment process are extensive and include accounting policies for intercorporate investments; valuation bases of financial instruments; continuity of financial instrument balances and share capital; detailed terms, interest rates, and repayment dates of debt; and details of any contingent liabilities.

The estimates that fair value accounting of financial instruments require have been blamed for helping cause the global credit crisis as shown in the Chapter 1 box entitled "Accounting Blamed for Global Credit Crisis." That article indicates how increasingly crucial the finance and investment process is to both individual auditees and the entire economy.

Paul Krugman, the 2008 winner of the Nobel Prize in economics, attributes the 2008/2009 economic crisis to widespread fraud on Wall Street: frauds carried out through the finance and investment process and based on risky gambles using other peoples' money. Here is what Krugman had to say shortly after he accepted the Nobel Prize.

THE MADOFF ECONOMY

The revelation that Bernard Madoff—brilliant investor (or so almost everyone thought), philanthropist, pillar of the community—was a phony has shocked the world, and understandably so. The scale of his alleged $50 billion Ponzi scheme is hard to comprehend.

Yet surely I'm not the only person to ask the obvious question: How different, really, is Mr. Madoff's tale from the story of the investment industry as a whole?

The financial services industry has claimed an ever-growing share of the nation's income over the past generation, making the people who run the industry incredibly rich. Yet, at this point, it looks as if much of the industry has been destroying value, not creating it. And it's not just a matter of money: the vast riches achieved by those who managed other people's money have had a corrupting effect on our society as a whole.

Let's start with those pay checks. Last year, the average salary of employees in "securities, commodity contracts, and investments" was more than four times the average salary in the rest of the economy. Earning a million dollars was nothing special, and even incomes of $20 million or more were fairly common. The incomes of the richest Americans have exploded over the past generation, even as wages of ordinary workers have stagnated; high pay on Wall Street was a major cause of that divergence.

But surely those financial superstars must have been earning their millions, right? No, not necessarily. The pay system on Wall Street lavishly rewards the appearance of profit, even if that appearance later turns out to have been an illusion.

Consider the hypothetical example of a money manager who leverages up his clients' money with lots of debt, then invests the bulked-up total in high-yielding but risky assets, such as dubious mortgage-backed securities. For a while—say, as long as a housing bubble continues to inflate—he (it's almost always a he) will make big profits and receive big bonuses. Then, when the bubble bursts and his investments turn into toxic waste, his investors will lose big—but he'll keep those bonuses.

O.K., maybe my example wasn't hypothetical after all.

So, how different is what Wall Street in general did from the Madoff affair? Well, Mr. Madoff allegedly skipped a few steps, simply stealing his clients' money rather than collecting big fees while exposing investors to risks they didn't understand. And, while Mr. Madoff was apparently a self-conscious fraud, many people on Wall Street believed their own hype. Still, the end result was the same (except for the house arrest): the money managers got rich; the investors saw their money disappear.

We're talking about a lot of money here. In recent years the finance sector accounted for 8 percent of America's GDP, up from less than 5 percent a generation earlier. If that extra 3 percent was money for nothing—and it probably was—we're talking about $400 billion a year in waste, fraud, and abuse.

But the costs of America's Ponzi era surely went beyond the direct waste of dollars and cents.

Meanwhile, how much has our nation's future been damaged by the magnetic pull of quick personal wealth, which for years has drawn many of our best and brightest young people into investment banking, at the expense of science, public service, and just about everything else?

Most of all, the vast riches being earned—or maybe that should be "earned"—in our bloated financial industry undermined our sense of reality and degraded our judgment.

Think of the way almost everyone important missed the warning signs of an impending crisis. How was that possible? How, for example, could Alan Greenspan have declared, just a few years ago, that "the financial system as a whole has become more resilient"—thanks to derivatives, no less? The answer, I believe, is that there's an innate tendency on the part of even the elite to idolize men who are making a lot of money, and assume that they know what they're doing.

After all, that's why so many people trusted Mr. Madoff.

Now, as we survey the wreckage and try to understand how things can have gone so wrong, so fast, the answer is actually quite simple: What we're looking at now are the consequences of a world gone Madoff.

Source: Paul Krugman. Op-Ed Columnist, "The Madoff Economy," *The New York Times,* Editorial Section. Dec. 19, 2008, page A45, Op-Ed Columnist.

We discuss the Madoff fraud in more detail in Chapter 17. For now we note that Krugman's view is consistent with PCAOB's observation, as early as 2005, that "Financial engineering, in general, involves structuring a transaction to achieve a desired accounting that is not consistent with the economics of the transaction." The PCAOB thus seems to view financial engineering via derivatives and other financial instruments of the finance and investment process as primarily a tool to create deceptive accounting.[1]

The credit crisis that started on Wall Street in 2007 spread globally and to the broader capital markets. Throughout 2007–2009 there was a cascading series of failures of financial institutions and government intervention, secondary effects on markets and individual corporations, all of which eventually impacted the global economy. The events will likely lead to calls for accounting and auditing changes. Many will come to question why those "fake profits" were so widespread and why auditing and accounting practices had allowed them to exist.

This brief summary of recent events illustrates why reporting of the finance and investment process is becoming increasingly important, and why this process is more and more

[1] Public Company Accounting Oversight Board (PCAOB), *Review of Existing Standards—Principles of Reporting,* Background Paper: Standards Advisory Group Meeting, October 5–6, 2005, p. 7 (www.pcaobus.org).

regarded as a risky part of the audit of financial statements. With this background we begin the detailed study of this process.

Many recently introduced accounting standards apply to accounts within the finance and investment process: measurement and recognition of financial instruments and derivatives at fair values, comprehensive income reporting, and consolidation of variable interest entreprises. There are differences between the risks in public companies and those "without public accountability." In particular, the latter group in Canada have the option to use **differential reporting**, which means they can use simpler accounting principles, such as cost basis for financial assets or taxes payable basis for income taxes. (See Appendix 14C.)

At the assertion level, the main risks are completeness of debt, valuation of financial instruments, disclosures of risks relating to financial instruments and derivatives, and presentation and disclosure of intercorporate investments. Controls in the finance and investment process involve the highest level of management, and auditors usually use substantive procedures to assess presentation and verify changes and balances. Since these are long-term (financing/investing) or permanent (shares issued) items in the financial statements, it is important to include copies of all legal documents relating to loans, partnerships, leases, joint venture (JV) investments, and other long-term legal arrangements in audit documentation. These legal documents must be retained in permanent audit files so auditors can check that the contracts are properly accounted for and disclosed in future audits. The same goes for **articles of incorporation** (which set out authorized classes of shares, their features, shareholder rights, etc.) and records of issuing shares approved by the board of directors in the minutes.

It is also important for auditors to document management's rationale and procedures for accounting estimates and the audit procedures used to verify them, both to help future auditors assess the methods and apply them consistently if there is no reason to change them. Note that changing economic and business conditions are risk factors and may indicate that estimation methods should be changed as well.

FINANCE AND INVESTMENT PROCESS—TYPICAL ACTIVITIES

· · · · · · · · · · · · · · · ·

LEARNING OBJECTIVE

1 Describe the finance and investment process: risk assessment, typical transactions, source documents, controls, and account balances.

The finance and investment process relates to a large number of accounts and records: assets that are either tangible or intangible, liabilities, deferred credits, shareholders' equity, gains and losses, expenses, and related taxes such as income tax, goods and services tax (GST), and provincial sales tax (PST). The major accounts and records are listed in Exhibit 14–1 and include some of the more complicated topics in accounting: equity method accounting for investments, consolidation accounting, goodwill, income taxes, and financial instruments, to name a few. We will not explain the accounting for these balances and transactions, but instead concentrate on a few important aspects of auditing them. Exhibit 14–1 shows a skeleton outline of the finance and investment process, the main functions of which are (1) financial planning and raising capital; (2) interacting with the processes of (i) purchases, payables, and payments; (ii) production and payroll; (iii) revenues, receivables, and receipts; and (3) entering into mergers, acquisitions, and other investments.

Good Corporate Governance: A Key Control for the Finance and Investment Process

According to CICA's "Guidance for Directors on Governance Processes for Control," the responsibilities of boards of directors are determined by the organization's legal and administrative framework.[2] This view considers the directors to be stewards of the organization and, as such, to have responsibility to oversee the conduct of the business and to monitor management, while giving all major issues affecting the business and affairs of

---

[2] CICA, Toronto, Canada, 1996.

EXHIBIT   14-1   FINANCE AND INVESTMENT PROCESS

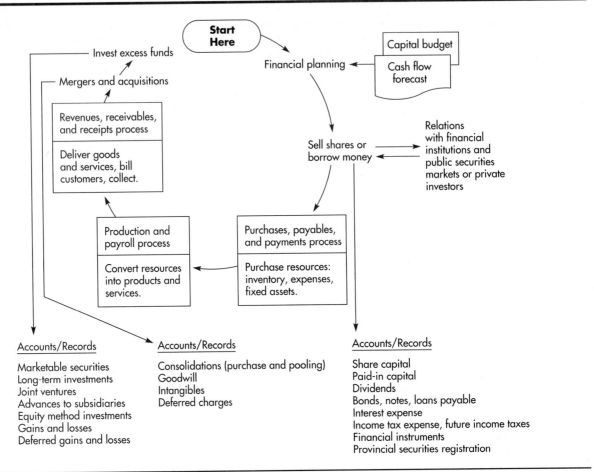

the organization proper consideration. The contributions by the board of directors to internal control are given as follows.

Approving and monitoring mission, vision, and strategy Endeavouring to see that the organization has the right approach in order to both add to shareholder and/or stakeholder value and improve its chances of viability and success.

Approving and monitoring the organization's ethical values Acting as guardian of the organization's values, and as its conscience.

Monitoring management control Overview of the systems whereby the chief executive officer and senior management exercise their power and influence over the rest of the organization.

Evaluating senior management Evaluation of the competence and integrity of the chief executive officer and other members of senior management, as it is primarily through them that the board exercises its power and influence.

Overseeing external communications Responsibility for the organization's communication of information to and from external parties.

Assessing the board's effectiveness Evaluation of how well it discharges its roles and responsibilities as part of the organization's overall control.

These make up a comprehensive, idealized role for the board, one which might not be fully realized in practice. Nevertheless, this guideline is an authoritative source on good corporate governance practices with respect to control of management activities, especially as they relate to the finance and investment process. These elements of board control, especially the last four, are a useful benchmark in auditor evaluation of internal controls in this cycle.

Debt and Shareholder Equity Capital

Transactions in debt and shareholder equity capital are typically few in number but large in monetary amount. They are handled by the highest levels of management, and the control-related duties and responsibilities reflect this high-level attention.

Authorization

Financial planning starts with the chief financial officer's (CFO) cash flow forecast. It informs the board of directors and management of the business plans, the prospects for cash inflows, and the needs for cash outflows. The forecast usually is integrated with the capital budget, which contains the plans for asset purchases and business acquisitions. A capital budget approved by the board of directors is the authorization for major asset acquisitions and investments.

Sales of share capital and debt financing transactions usually are authorized by the board of directors. All the directors must sign registration documents for public securities offerings. However, the CFO usually has authority to complete transactions such as periodic renewals of notes payable and other ordinary types of financing transactions without specific board approval of each transaction. Auditors should expect to find the authorizing signatures of the chief executive officer (CEO), CFO, chair of the board of directors, and perhaps other high-ranking officers on financing documents.

Many financing transactions are **off the balance sheet**. Companies can enter into obligations and commitments that are not required to be recorded in the accounts. Examples include various business and financing options such as leases, endorsements on discounted notes or on other companies' obligations, letters of credit, guarantees, repurchase or remarketing agreements, commitments to purchase at fixed prices, commitments to sell at fixed prices, and certain kinds of stock options. Many of these were discussed in previous chapters as part of the assessment of the risk of material misstatement related to the disclosure assertion.

Custody

In large companies, banks and trust companies serve as registrars and transfer agents of share certificates. A registrar keeps the shareholder list and, from time to time, determines the shareholders eligible to receive dividends (shareholders of record on a dividend record date) and those entitled to vote at the annual meeting. A transfer agent handles the exchange of shares, cancelling the shares surrendered by sellers, and issuing new certificates to buyers. The same bank or trust company might provide both services.

Small companies often keep their own shareholder records. A share certificate book looks like a chequebook, with perforated stubs for recording the number of shares, the owner's name and other identification, and the date of issue. Actual unissued share certificates are attached to the stubs, like unused cheques in a chequebook. The missing certificates have been sent to the share owners. Custody of the share certificate book is important because the unissued certificates are like money or collateral. Share certificates can be improperly sold to buyers who think they are genuinely issued or can be used as collateral with unsuspecting lenders.

Lenders have custody of **debt instruments** (e.g., leases, bonds, notes, and loans payable). A CFO may have copies, but they are just records. However, when a company repurchases its debt instruments, these become within the custody of trustees or company officials, usually the CFO. Until they are cancelled and destroyed, they can be misused by improperly reselling them to unsuspecting investors.

Recordkeeping

The accounting department and the CFO or controller keep records of notes, loans, and bonds payable. Recordkeeping procedures are similar to those used to account for vendor accounts payable: payment notices from lenders are compared with the accounting records, due dates are monitored, interest payments are set up for payment on due dates, and accruals for unpaid interest are made on financial reporting dates. If the company has only a few debt instruments outstanding, no subsidiary records of these are needed. All the information is in the general ledger accounts. (Companies with a large number of bonds, loans, and notes may keep control and subsidiary accounts, as is done for accounts receivable.) As all or some of the notes become due, the CFO and controller have the necessary information for properly classifying current and long-term amounts.

The functions of authorization, custody, and reconciliation for another class of credit balances, calculated liabilities, and credits are not easy to describe. These include lease obligations, future income taxes, pension and post-retirement benefit liabilities, and foreign currency translation gains and losses, to name a few. They are accounting creations, calculated according to accounting rules and using basic data from company plans and operations, and management usually enjoys considerable discretion in structuring them. These accounting calculations often involve significant accounting estimates by management. Company accountants should try to be realistic in these calculated liabilities by following generally accepted accounting principles and by paying careful attention to how these estimates may affect decisions of financial statement users.

Periodic Reconciliation

The share certificate book should be periodically inspected to ensure that only certificates in the possession of *bona fide* owners are outstanding. If necessary, company officials can confirm this with the holders of record. Reports with similar information can be obtained from registrars and transfer agents to verify that the numbers of outstanding shares agree. (Without this reconciliation, counterfeit shares handled by the transfer agent and recorded by the registrar might go unnoticed.)

A trustee with duties and responsibilities similar to those of registrars and transfer agents can handle ownership of bonds. Confirmations and reports from bond trustees can be reconciled to the company's records.

Investments and Intangibles

A company may have many or only a few investments, and these may include a large variety or a limited set of investments types. Intangible assets may be in the form of purchased assets (e.g., patents, trademarks) or of accounting allocations (e.g., goodwill, deferred charges). A manufacturing or service company is the context for the sections following, and investments and intangibles are fairly incidental in these businesses. Financial institutions (banks, trust companies), investment companies, mutual funds, insurance companies, and the like have more elaborate systems for managing their investments and intangibles.

Authorization

All investment policies and major individual investment transactions should be approved by the board of directors, executive committee, or its investment committee. However, there is a great deal of variety between companies in the nature and amount of transactions that must have specific high-level approval. The board of directors is always closely involved in major acquisitions, mergers, and share buy-back plans.

THE LITTLE LEASE THAT COULD

The Quick-Fly commuter airline was struggling. According to its existing debt covenants, it could not incur any more long-term liabilities. The company needed a new airplane to expand its services, so it "rented" one. The CFO pointed out that the deal for the $12 million airplane was a noncancellable operating lease because (1) Quick-Fly does not automatically own the plane at the end of the lease; (2) the purchase option of $1,500,000 is no bargain; (3) the lease term of 133 months is 74 percent, not 75 percent, of the plane's estimated 15-year economic life; and (4) the present

> value of the lease payments of $154,330 per month, discounted at the company's latest borrowing rate of 14 percent, is $10.4 million, which is less than the 90 percent of fair value (0.90 × $12 million = $10.8 million) criterion in the *CICA Handbook* in paragraph 3065.06.
>
> The CFO did not record a long-term lease obligation (liability). Do you agree with this accounting conclusion?

Custody

Custody of investments and other intangible assets varies. Some investments, such as shares and bonds, are represented by actual negotiable certificates that may be kept in a brokerage account in a "house name" (the brokerage company). In that case, custody rests with the company official who is authorized to order the buy, sell, and delivery transactions. They also may be in the possession of the owner (client company), in which case they should be in a safe or a bank safety deposit box. Only high-ranking officers (e.g., CFO, CEO, president, chair of board) should have combinations and keys.

Other kinds of investments such as joint ventures and partnerships do not have formal negotiable certificates, and custody may instead take the form of management responsibility. The venture and partnership agreements that are evidence of these investments are usually merely filed with other important documents as they are not readily negotiable. Management's supervision and monitoring of the operations is the true custody.

AUTHORIZATION: HERE TODAY, GONE TOMORROW

The treasurer of Travum County had many responsibilities as a chief financial officer. She invested several million dollars of county funds with a California-based investment money manager. Soon thereafter, news stories of the money manager's expensive personal lifestyle and questionable handling of client's funds began to circulate, indicating that clients could lose much of their investments. At the same time, news stories about the treasurer's own credit card spending habits were published locally, indicating that she had obtained a personal credit card by using the county's name.

Although no county funds were lost and no improper credit card bills were paid, the county commissioners temporarily suspended the treasurer's authority to choose investment vehicles for county funds.

Having custody of most intangibles is like trying to keep Jell-O in your pocket—good in theory but messy in practice. There are legal documents and contracts for patents, trademarks, copyrights, and similar legal intangibles. These seldom are negotiable, and are usually kept in ordinary company files. Company managers may be assigned responsibility to protect exclusive rights granted by various intangibles. Accounts like goodwill, deferred charges, and pension obligations are intangibles created by accountants' estimates and calculations. They have no physical substance, but they are "in the custody" of the accountants who calculate them.

Recordkeeping

Purchases of share and bond investments require authorization by the board of directors or other responsible officials. Because a higher level of approval is required for these, the cheque for the investment is signed by a higher ranking finance officer, such as the CFO or treasurer, as well. If the company has few investments, no subsidiary records are maintained and all information is kept in the general ledger accounts. If the company has many investments, a control account and subsidiary ledger may be maintained.

The recordkeeping for the maintenance of some investment and intangible accounts over time can be complicated. This is the place where complex accounting standards for equity method accounting, consolidations, goodwill, intangibles amortization and valuation, deferred charges, future income taxes, pension and post-retirement benefit liabilities, and various financial instruments enter the picture. High-level accountants who prepare financial statements get involved with the accounting rules and management estimates required. The accounting for these balances are influenced by management plans and estimates of future events and interpretations of the accounting standards. These decisions are risk areas for overstatement of assets, understatement of liabilities, and understatement of expenses because managers can exercise considerable discretion and auditors seldom have hard evidence confirming or refuting these management assessments.

Periodic Reconciliation

Inspection and count of negotiable securities certificates is the most significant reconciliation opportunity in the investments and intangibles accounts. Certificates on hand are inventoried, inspected, and compared with the information recorded in the accounts. (Written confirmations are requested for securities held by brokerage firms.)

A securities "inventory count" should include a record of the name of the company represented by the certificate, the interest rate for bonds, the dividend rate for preferred shares, the due date for bonds, the serial numbers on the certificates, the face value of bonds, the number or face amount of bonds and shares, and notes on the name of the owner shown on the face of the certificate or on the endorsements on the back (should be the client company). This reconciliation should happen reasonably often, and not wait until the independent auditors' annual visit. A securities count in a financial institution holding thousands of shares in multimillion-dollar asset accounts is a major undertaking.

The auditors should record the same information in the audit working papers when performing the securities inspection and count. If a security certificate has been pledged as collateral for a loan and is in the hands of a creditor, it can be confirmed or inspected only through a visit to the creditor. The fact that it has been pledged as collateral may be an important disclosure note. A securities count and reconciliation is important because companies do sometimes try to substitute others' securities for missing ones. If securities have been sold and replaced without any accounting entries, the serial numbers will show that the certificates recorded in the accounts are not the same as the ones on hand.

REVIEW CHECKPOINTS

1 When a management carefully crafts a lease agreement to barely fail the tests for lease capitalization and liability recognition, should the auditor insist on capitalization anyway?

2 What would constitute the authorization for loans payable? What documentation is evidence of this authorization?

3 Give five examples of off-balance-sheet information. Why should auditors be concerned with such items?

4 What features of a client's share capital are important in the audit?

5 What information about share capital could be confirmed with outside parties? How could auditors corroborate this information?

6 How can auditors verify the names of the issuers, the number of shares held, certificate numbers, maturity value, and interest and dividend rates in an audit of investment securities?

7 Describe the procedures and documentation of a controlled count of client's investment securities.

8 What information should be included in a working paper for the audit of investment securities?

CONTROL RISK ASSESSMENT

. . . .

LEARNING OBJECTIVE

2 Outline control tests for auditing control over debt, owner equity, and investment transactions.

In the finance and investment process, auditors enquire about and look for control procedures, such as authorization, custody, recordkeeping, and periodic reconciliation. They especially look for information about the level of management involved in these functions. Samples of transactions are not normally a part of the control risk assessment work as they can be in the other operations processes covered in Chapters 11 to 13. Because finance and investment transactions are usually individually material, each transaction is audited in detail. The extent of substantive audit work on finance and investment cycle accounts isn't reduced by relying on controls, but lack of controls can mean significant amounts of extended procedures as the risk of material misstatement from improper financing and investing transactions is high.

General Control Considerations

There should be control procedures for handling of responsibilities. Policies on this will vary greatly between companies, but the discussion related to Exhibit 14–1 indicates that these responsibilities are basically in the hands of senior management officials.

Segregation of incompatible duties does not really apply in the financing and investing functions. It is hard to have a strict segregation of functional responsibilities when the same principal officers authorize, execute, and control finance and investment activities. It is not realistic for a CEO to authorize investments but not have access to shareholder records, securities certificates, and the like. Real segregation of duties is found in middle management and lower ranks but is hard to create and enforce in upper-level management. A company should have compensating control procedures in place.

One compensating control could be involvement of two or more people in each important functional responsibility. Or, alternatively, oversight or review can be substituted. For example, if the board of directors authorized the purchase of securities or creation of a partnership, the CFO or CEO could carry out the transactions, have custody of certificates and agreements, manage the partnership or the portfolio of securities, oversee the recordkeeping, and make the decisions about valuations and accounting (authorizing the journal entries). These are rather normal management activities, and they combine several responsibilities. The compensating control could be periodic reports to the board of directors, oversight by the investment committee of the board, and a periodic reconciliation of securities certificates in a portfolio with the amounts and descriptions recorded in the accounts by internal auditors.

Control over Accounting Estimates

An accounting estimate amount showing the approximate effect of past business transactions or events on the present status of an asset or liability. Accounting estimates are common in financial statement reporting. Examples include such items as allowance for doubtful receivables, loss provisions, and valuation of stock options using a mathematical model. Accounting estimates can have a significant or pervasive effect on reported results, either individually or when considered in the aggregate.[3] They are included in basic financial statements because (1) the measurement of some values is uncertain, perhaps depending upon the outcome of future events, or (2) relevant data cannot be accumulated on a timely, cost-effective basis. Some examples of accounting estimates in the finance and investment process are shown in the box on page 560.

Management is responsible for making estimates and should have a process and control structure designed to reduce the likelihood of their material misstatement. The following are some items that this control structure should involve:

- management communication of the need for proper accounting estimates
- accumulation of relevant, sufficient, and reliable data for estimates

[3] *CICA Handbook*, paragraph 5305.02 and CAS 540.

- preparation of estimates by qualified personnel
- adequate review and approval by appropriate levels of authority
- comparison of estimates with subsequent results to assess the reliability of the estimation
- assessment by management of the consistency between accounting estimates and company operational plans

---

FINANCE AND INVESTMENT CYCLE ESTIMATES

Financial instruments: valuation of securities, classification into trading versus investment portfolios, probability of a correlated hedge, sales of securities with puts and calls

Accruals: compensation in stock option plans, actuarial assumptions in pension costs

Leases: initial direct costs, executory costs, residual values, capitalization interest rate

Rates: imputed interest rates on receivables and payables

Other: losses and net realizable value on segment disposal and business restructuring, fair values in nonmonetary exchanges

---

Auditors' test of controls of estimation procedures involves enquires about the process. They might ask who prepares estimates, when they are prepared, what data are used, who reviews and approves the estimates, and if the estimates are being compared with subsequent actual events. Auditors will also study data documentation, comparisons of prior estimates with subsequent actual experience, and intercompany correspondence concerning estimates and operational plans. Much of the audit test of controls of estimates has a bearing on the substantive quality of the estimation process and on the estimate itself. Further substantive audit procedures include recalculating the mathematical estimate, developing an auditor's own independent estimate based on reasonable alternative assumptions, and comparing the estimate to subsequent events, to the extent they are known before the end of the field work.

CAS 540 adopts a risk-based approach to the audit of accounting estimates including fair value accounting estimates. It addresses matters such as the auditor's evaluation of the effect of estimation uncertainty on risk assessments, management's estimation methods, the reasonableness of management assumptions, and the adequacy of disclosures. CAS 540 defines an accounting estimate as an approximation of a monetary amount in the absence of a precise means of measurement. Estimation uncertainty is the likelihood that the accounting estimate and related disclosures are not accurate.

Accounting estimates will have relatively high estimation uncertainty when they are based on significant assumptions and subjective judgment. Examples include fair value accounting estimates for derivative financial instruments not publicly traded, and fair value accounting estimates based on a highly specialized client-developed model, or for which there are assumptions or inputs that cannot be observed in the market place. When accounting estimates give rise to significant risks, the auditor should also evaluate how adequately the estimation uncertainty is disclosed in the financial statements. In some cases, the estimation uncertainty may be so great that the recognition criteria in the applicable financial reporting framework are not met and the accounting estimate cannot be made. In such situations, critical thinking involving integration of accounting and auditing theories is used to come up with appropriate reporting solutions. Conceivably, such reporting situations may also present new opportunities for management fraud. The box on pages 551 and 552 illustrates the extent to which estimation uncertainties have spread to the financial services sector.

Control Risk Assessment for Notes and Loans Payable

From the preceding discussion, you can tell that test of controls audit procedures take a variety of forms—enquiries, observations, study of documentation, comparison with related data (such as tax returns), and detail audit of some transactions. The detail audit of transactions, however, is a small part of the test of controls because finance and investment transactions are generally few in number while their amounts are large. However, some companies have numerous debt financing transactions, and in such cases a more detailed control risk assessment can be done that includes selecting a sample of transactions for control risk assessment evidence.

An internal control questionnaire for notes and loans payable is found in Exhibit 14–2. It illustrates typical questions about the control objectives. These enquiries give auditors insights into the review and approval procedures for major financing transactions, the accounting system for them, and the error-checking review procedures.

Auditors can select a sample of notes payable transactions for detail test of controls, provided that the population of notes is large enough to justify it. Exhibit 14–3 lists a selection of these procedures, with the relevant control objectives noted on the right.

EXHIBIT   14–2   INTERNAL CONTROL QUESTIONNAIRE: NOTES AND LOANS PAYABLE APPLICATION

Environment and general controls relevant to this application
1. Are records kept by someone who cannot sign notes or cheques?
Assertion-Based Control Evaluation
Validity objective:
2. Are paid notes cancelled and stamped "paid" and filed?
Completeness objective:
3. Is all borrowing authorization by the directors checked to determine whether all notes payable are recorded?
Authorization objective:
4. Are direct borrowings on notes payable authorized by the directors, the treasurer, or by the chief financial officer?
5. Are two or more authorized signatures required on notes?
Accuracy objective:
6. Are bank due notices compared with records of unpaid liabilities?
Classification objective:
7. Is sufficient information available in the accounts to enable financial statement preparers to classify current and long-term debt properly?
Accounting objective:
8. Is the subsidiary ledger of notes payable periodically reconciled with the general ledger control account(s)?
Proper period objective:
9. Are interest payments and accruals monitored for due dates and financial statement dates?

EXHIBIT   14–3   CONTROL TESTS FOR NOTES AND LOANS PAYABLE

	Control Objective
1. Read directors' and finance committee's minutes for authorization of financing transactions (such as short-term notes payable, bond offerings).	Authorization
2. Select a sample of paid notes:	
a. Recalculate interest expense for the period under audit.	Accuracy
b. Trace interest expense to the general ledger account.	Completeness
c. Vouch payment to cancelled cheques.	Validity
3. Select a sample of notes payable:	
a. Vouch to authorization by directors or finance committee.	Authorization
b. Vouch cash receipt to bank statement.	Validity

Control Risk Assessment for Derivatives

Derivative financial instruments can have a significant impact on audit procedures because they are becoming more complex and more commonplace. Accounting standards are also increasingly requiring that they be accounted for at fair value and other information about them is in financial statement notes.

In many cases, derivative financial instruments can reduce a company's exposures to risks, such as changes in exchange rates, interest rates, and commodity prices. On the other hand, the nature of activities involving derivative financial instruments, and derivative financial instruments themselves, also may result in increased business risk in some companies. This both increases and presents new inherent risk factors for the auditor to consider in terms of the values of derivative financial instruments. Their values are volatile and large, and unexpected decreases in their fair values can result in large losses to report in the income statement. The complexity of derivative activities increases the risk that management may not fully understand how to manage them, thus exposing the company to the risk of large losses.

The CICA Audit Guideline AuG-39 describes derivatives and the relevant accounting standards that apply as guidance for auditors of companies where derivative financial instruments are used. It sets out management's and auditor's responsibilities, and describes the risks and audit risk assessment in detail. AuG-39 paragraphs 24 and 40 describe internal control considerations specific to derivatives activities, including the control environment and control systems required to meet the control objectives. The following control objectives relate specifically to derivative financial instruments:

- Transactions are executed in accordance with approved policies.
- Information, including fair value information, is recorded on a timely basis, is complete and accurate, and has been properly classified, described, and disclosed.
- Misstatements in the processing of accounting information are prevented or detected in a timely manner.
- Activities are monitored on an ongoing basis to recognize and measure events affecting related financial statement assertions.
- Changes in the fair value are appropriately accounted for and disclosed to the right people from both an operational and a control viewpoint. Valuation may be a part of ongoing monitoring activities.
- Control systems for those designated as hedges should assure that these meet the criteria for hedge accounting, both at the inception and on an ongoing basis.

AuG-39 also deals with transaction records used for derivative financial instruments (database, register, or subsidiary ledger) and suggests the audit procedures of checking the transaction records for accuracy and independently confirming the derivative transactions with counterparties. The auditor needs to assess whether there are appropriate controls over input, processing, and maintenance of the transaction records because these often will be used to provide accounting information for disclosures in the financial statements and other risk management uses, such as exposure reports for comparison with company risk policy limits. Further detailed guidance in AuG-39 covers control testing, obtaining management representations, and communicating with those charged with governance relating to derivatives positions and trading.

Audit of derivative financial instruments is also covered in IAPS 1012 (International) and SAS No. 92 (AICPA). The latter lists the following as its key control procedures for derivatives:

- Derivatives activities are monitored by independent control staff.
- Approval (oral, at least) from members of senior management who are independent of derivatives activities is obtained by derivatives personnel prior to exceeding limits.

- Limit excesses and divergences from approved derivatives strategies are properly addressed by senior management.

- Accurate transmittals of derivatives positions are made to the risk measurement systems.

- Reconciliations are performed to ensure data integrity across a full range of derivatives.

- Constraints are designed, activities monitored, and identified excesses justified by traders, risk managers, and senior management.

- Regular review of the identifying controls and financial results of the derivatives activities are performed by senior management, an independent group, or an individual that management designates, to determine whether controls are being effectively implemented in the entity's business objectives and strategies are being achieved.

- Limits are reviewed in the context of changes and strategy, risk tolerance of the entity, conditions.

RISK FACTORS OF DERIVATIVES

The following are examples of unique, inherent risk factors associated with derivatives:
- Many derivatives are not recognized in the financial statements. As a result, there is an increased risk that derivatives, and related fees, premiums, commissions, receivables, and payables, will not be collected and recorded by control systems.
- Because derivatives are financial instruments whose values are derived from underlying market rates or indexes, their values change as those rates or indexes change. Increase in the volatility of interest rates, commodity prices, and foreign currency rates may cause wide fluctuations in the values of derivatives.
- Entities use derivatives to (a) manage risk—that is to hedge, and (b) to speculate. Derivatives used for hedging purposes must be accounted for differently from those used to speculate.

AUDIT CONSIDERATIONS FOR DERIVATIVES

The following are steps that the auditor might consider taking when auditing an entity involved with derivative financial instruments.
- Obtain an understanding of the nature and extent of the use of derivatives to determine whether they may have a significant effect on the audit or on the financial statements.
- Make preliminary decisions on the materiality of derivatives and the level of inherent risk during the planning stage of the audit.
- Ensure that audit staff who will be performing audit procedures on derivatives have an appropriate level of knowledge and experience.
- Consider whether it is necessary to use the work of a specialist (see "Using the work of a specialist," section 5360 of the *CICA Handbook* for guidance).
- Consider the extent to which it is appropriate to use the work of internal audit (see section 5230, "Using the work of internal audit").
- Obtain an understanding of the control-environment factors affecting derivative activities (see paragraph 5200.11 of the *Handbook* for examples).

Source: "Auditing Derivative Financial Instruments," Studies and Standards Alert, *CA Magazine*, January/February 1995, p. 66.

When applicable, auditors design tests of the preceding controls for derivatives to determine the extent of substantive tests needed. Key substantive procedures for derivatives include confirmations with issuers, brokers, or counterparties; physical inspection of derivatives contracts; inspection of underlying agreements and other supporting documentation in paper or electronic form; review of minutes of the board of directors' meetings; and confirmation of quoted prices from broker-dealers or from derivatives exchanges. For more background on the unique risks represented by derivatives activities, see Sample Letter 2 on page 568, which illustrates the important substantive procedure of a confirmation request detailing outstanding derivative instruments for a client.

Summary: Control Risk Assessment

The audit manager or senior accountant in charge of the audit should evaluate the evidence gathered through understanding the internal control structure and from test of controls procedures. These procedures can take many forms because management systems for finance and investment accounts vary between clients. Control risk assessment is tailored to each company's situation where senior officials are involved in the relatively small number of high-dollar transactions. The complexity of financing and investment transactions varies from one company to another as well.

AN ESTIMATED VALUATION BASED ON FUTURE DEVELOPMENT

Gulf & Western Industries (G&W) sold 450,000 shares of Pan American stock from its investment portfolio to Resorts International (Resorts). Resorts paid $8 million plus 250,000 shares of its unregistered common stock. G&W recorded the sale proceeds as $14,167,500, valuing the unregistered Resorts shares at $6,167,500, which was approximately 67 percent of the market price of Resorts shares at the time ($36.82 per share). G&W reported a gain of $3,365,000 on the sale.

Four years later, Resorts shares fell to $2.63. G&W sold its 250,000 shares back to Resorts in exchange for 1,100 acres of undeveloped land on Grand Bahamas Island. For its records, Resorts got a broker-dealer's opinion that its 250,000 shares were worth $460,000. For property tax assessment purposes, the Bahamian government valued the undeveloped land at $525,000.

G&W valued the land on its books at $6,167,500, which was the previous valuation of the Resorts shares. The justification was an appraisal of $6,300,000 based on the estimated value of the 1100 acres when ultimately developed (i.e., built into an operating resort and residential community). However, G&W also reported a loss of $5,527,000 in its tax return (effectively valuing the land at $640,500). The SEC accused G&W of failing to report a loss of $5.7 million in its financial statements. Do you think the loss should have appeared in the G&W income statement?

Source: Kellog, I., *How to Find Negligence and Misrepresentation in Financial Statements* (New York: Shepard's/ McGraw-Hill, 1983), p. 279.

Some control considerations can be generalized. There are common features characterizing control over management's production of accounting estimates. Detail testing through samples of transactions can produce evidence about compliance with control policies and procedures as well, for instance when there are numerous notes payable transactions.

In general, substantive audit procedures on finance and investment accounts are not limited in extent. It is very common for auditors to perform substantive audit procedures on 100 percent of these transactions and balances as there are not many transactions, and the audit cost for complete coverage is not high. But control deficiencies and unusual or complicated transactions might cause auditors to adjust the nature and timing of audit procedures. Complicated financial instruments, pension plans, exotic equity securities, related party transactions, and nonmonetary exchanges of investment assets call for procedures designed to find evidence of error and fraud. The next section deals with some of the finance and investment process assertions, and it has some cases for your review.

....

R E V I E W
CHECKPOINTS

9   What is a compensating control? Give some examples for finance and investment accounts.

10   What are some of the specific, relevant aspects of management's control over the production of accounting estimates? What are some enquiries auditors can make?

11   When a company has produced an estimate of an investment valuation based on a nonmonetary exchange, what source of comparative information can an auditor use?

12   If a company does not monitor notes and loans payable for due dates and interest payment dates in relation to financial statement dates, what misstatements can appear in the financial statements?

13   Generally, how much emphasis is placed on adequate internal control in the audit of each of long-term debt, share capital, contributed surplus, and retained earnings?

....

ASSERTIONS, SUBSTANTIVE PROCEDURES, AND AUDIT CASES FOR FINANCE AND INVESTMENT ACCOUNTS

....

Owners' Equity

Management makes assertions about the existence, completeness, rights and obligations, valuation and presentation, and disclosure of owners' equity. Typical specific assertions include the following:

1.   The number of shares shown as issued is in fact issued.

2.   No other shares (including options, warrants, and the like) have been issued and not recorded or reflected in the accounts and disclosures.

3.   The accounting is proper for options, warrants, and other share issue plans, and related disclosures are adequate.

4.   The valuation of shares issued for noncash consideration is proper, in conformity with accounting principles.

5.   All owners' equity transactions have been authorized by the board of directors.

An illustrative program of substantive audit procedures for owners' equity can be found in Exhibit 14A–1 in Appendix 14A (page 587). Some key substantive procedures are discussed below.

Documentation   Owners' equity transactions usually are well documented in board of directors meeting minutes, proxy statements, and securities offering registration statements. Transactions can be vouched to these documents, and the cash proceeds can be traced to the bank accounts.

Confirmation   Share capital may be subject to confirmation when independent registrars and transfer agents are employed. Agents are responsible for knowing the number of shares authorized and issued and for keeping lists of shareholders' names. The basic information about share capital—such as number of shares, classes of shares, preferred dividend rates, conversion terms, dividend payments, shares held in the company name, expiration dates and terms of warrants, and share dividends and splits—can be confirmed with them. Auditors corroborate many of these things by inspection and reading of share certificates, charter authorizations, directors' minutes, and registration statements. However, when there are no independent agents, most audit evidence is gathered by vouching share record documents (such as certificate book stubs). When circumstances call for extended procedures, information on outstanding shares is confirmed directly with the holders.

Long-Term Liabilities and Related Accounts

The primary audit concern with the verification of long-term liabilities is that all liabilities are recorded and that the interest expense is properly paid or accrued. This makes the completeness assertion paramount. During procedures in all areas, auditors are alert to the possibility of unrecorded liabilities. For example, when fixed assets are acquired during the year under audit, auditors should enquire about the source of funds for financing the new asset.

Management makes assertions about existence, completeness, rights and obligations, valuation and presentation, and disclosure. Typical specific assertions relating to long-term liabilities include the following:

1. All material long-term liabilities are recorded.
2. Liabilities are properly classified according to their current or long-term status. The current portion of long-term debt is properly valued and classified.
3. New long-term liabilities and debt extinguishments are properly authorized.
4. Terms, conditions, and restrictions relating to noncurrent debt are adequately disclosed.
5. Disclosures of maturities for the next five years and the capital and operating lease disclosures are accurate and adequate.
6. All important contingencies are either accrued in the accounts or disclosed in footnotes.

In Appendix 14A, Exhibit 14A–2 (page 587) illustrates some substantive audit procedures for notes and loans payable and for long-term debt. Below are some key audit procedures.

Confirmation When auditing long-term liabilities, auditors usually obtain independent written confirmations for notes, loans, and bonds payable. In the case of loans payable to banks, the standard bank confirmation may be used. The amount and terms of bonds payable, mortgages payable, and other formal debt instruments can be confirmed by requests to holders or a trustee. The confirmation request should include questions not only of amount, interest rate, and due date but also about collateral, restrictive covenants, and other items of agreement between lender and borrower. Confirmation requests should be sent to lenders the company has done business with in the recent past, even if no liability balance is shown at the confirmation date. This is part of the search for unrecorded liabilities. (Chapter 12 has more on this search.)

Off-Balance-Sheet Financing

Confirmation and enquiry procedures are used to obtain responses on a class of items loosely termed off-balance-sheet information. These items include terms of loan agreements, leases, endorsements, guarantees, and insurance policies (whether issued by a client insurance company or owned by the client). Among these items is the difficult-to-define set of "commitments and contingencies" that often pose evidence-gathering problems. Some common types of commitments are shown in Exhibit 14–4.

Footnote disclosure should be considered for the types of commitments shown in Exhibit 14–4. Some of them can be estimated and valued, allowing them to be recorded in the accounts and shown in the financial statements themselves (e.g., fixed price purchase commitments and losses on fixed price sales commitments).

EXHIBIT 14–4   OFF-BALANCE-SHEET COMMITMENTS

Type of Commitment	Typical Procedures and Sources of Evidence
1. Repurchase or remarketing agreements	1. Vouching of contracts, confirmation by customer, enquiry of client management
2. Commitments to purchase at fixed prices	2. Vouching of open purchase orders, enquiry of purchasing personnel, confirmation by supplier
3. Commitments to sell at fixed prices	3. Vouching of sales contracts, enquiry of sales personnel, confirmation by customer
4. Loan commitments	4. Vouching of open commitment file, enquiry of loan officers
5. Lease commitments	5. Vouching of lease agreement, confirmation with lessor or lessee

Analytical relationships are used to help verify interest expense, which generally is related item by item to interest-bearing liabilities. Interest expense amounts can be recalculated for long-term liability transactions (including those that have been retired during the year). The amount of debt, the interest rate, and the time period are used to determine whether the interest expense and accrued interest are properly recorded. The audit results are compared with the recorded interest expense and accrued interest accounts to detect (1) greater expense than audit calculations show, indicating some interest paid on an unknown debt, possibly an unrecorded liability; (2) lesser expense than audit calculations show, indicating misclassification, failure to accrue interest, or an interest payment default; or (3) interest expense equal to audit calculations. The first two possibilities raise questions for further study, while the third shows a correct correlation between debt and debt-related expense.

Deferred Credits: Calculated Balances

Existence and valuation of several types of deferred credits are calculated. Examples include (1) deferred profit on instalment sales involving the gross margin and the sale amount; (2) future income taxes and investment credits involving tax-book timing differences, tax rates, and amortization methods; and (3) deferred contract revenue involving contract provisions for prepayment, percentage-of-completion revenue recognition methods, or other terms unique to a contract. Auditors can check the calculations for accuracy.

Investments and Intangibles

There is a wide variety of investments and relationships a company might have with affiliates. Investment accounting for these may be on the cost or equity method, either without consolidation or with full consolidation, depending on the size and influence represented by the investment. Purchase method consolidations usually create problems of accounting for the fair value of acquired assets and the related goodwill. There are specific assertions typical of a variety of investment account balances:

1. Investment securities are on hand or are held in safekeeping by a trustee (existence).
2. Investment cost does not exceed market value (valuation).
3. Significant influence investments are accounted for by the equity method (valuation).
4. Purchased goodwill is properly valued (valuation).
5. Capitalized intangible costs relate to intangibles acquired in exchange transactions (valuation).
6. Research and development costs are properly classified (presentation).
7. Amortization is properly calculated (valuation).
8. Investment income has been received and recorded (completeness).
9. Investments are adequately classified and described in the balance sheet (presentation).

A program of substantive audit procedures for investments, intangibles, and related accounts is shown in Appendix 14A, Exhibit 14A–3 (page 588).

Unlike the current assets accounts, which typically include many small transactions, the noncurrent investment accounts usually consist of a few large entries. This difference has internal control and substantive audit procedure implications, and auditors will concentrate on the authorization of transactions, since each transaction is likely to be material in itself and the authorization will give significant information about the proper classification and accounting method. The controls usually are not reviewed, tested, or evaluated at an interim date but are included in year-end procedures when the transactions and their authorizations are audited. The following box shows a few of the trouble spots in audits of investments and intangibles.

TROUBLE SPOTS IN AUDITS OF INVESTMENTS AND INTANGIBLES

- Valuation of investments at cost or market and classification as held-to-maturity or financial assets held for trading or available for sale
- Determination of significant influence relationship for equity method investments
- Proper determination of goodwill in consolidations
- Capitalization and continuing valuation of intangibles
- Realistic distinctions of research, feasibility, and production milestones for capitalization of development costs
- Adequate disclosure of restrictions, pledges, or liens related to investment assets

---

Confirmation   Written confirmation obtained from outside parties is fairly limited for investments, intangibles, and related income and expense accounts. Securities held by trustees or brokers should be confirmed, and the confirmation should request the same descriptive information the auditor looks for in the physical count (described earlier in this chapter). The CICA recommends that the sample letter in the following box be used for confirming information related to derivative instruments.

SAMPLE LETTER 2

REQUEST FOR STATEMENT DETAILING OUTSTANDING DERIVATIVE INSTRUMENTS

[Client letterhead]

[Date]
[Financial institution official responsible for account]
[Financial institution name]
[Financial institution address]
Dear [financial institution official responsible for account]:

In connection with their audit of our financial statements for the year ended March 31, 20X9, our auditors, CA & Co., have requested a statement summarizing all derivative financial instruments entered into by the company and outstanding at March 11, 20X9. Derivative financial instruments include futures, foreign exchange contracts, forward rate agreements, interest rate swaps, and options contracts, or other financial instruments with similar characteristics.

   In your response, please include the following information for each instrument:

1. The principal, stated, face, or other similar amount (sometimes also referred to as the notional amount) on which future payments are based

2. The date of maturity, expiration, or execution

3. Any early settlement options, including the period in which, or date at which, the options may be exercised and the exercise price or range of prices

4. Any options to convert the instrument into, or exchange it for, another financial instrument or some other asset or liability, including the period in which, or date at which, the options may be exercised, and the conversion or exchange ratio(s)

5. The amount and timing of scheduled future cash receipts or payments of the principal amount of the instrument, including instalment repayments and any sinking fund or similar requirements

6. The stated rate or amount of interest, dividend, or other periodic return on principal and the timing of payments

7. Any collateral held or pledged

8. The currency of the cash flows if these are other than Canadian funds

9. Where the instrument provides for an exchange, information noted in 1 to 8 above for the instrument to be acquired in the exchange

10. Any condition of the instrument or an associated covenant that, if contravened, would significantly alter any of the other terms

Please mail the above noted information directly to our auditors in the enclosed addressed envelope. Should you wish to discuss any details of this confirmation request with our auditors, please contact (name of audit staff member) at (111) 222-3333, or by fax at (111) 222-3334.

Yours truly,

[Authorized signatory of the client]

Enquiries about Intangibles   Auditors query company counsel about any lawsuits or defects relating to patents, copyrights, trademarks, or trade names as a specific request in the enquiry letter to the law firm. (Chapter 15 contains more information about this enquiry letter.)

Income from Intangibles   Royalty income from patent licences received are confirmed. These income amounts are usually audited by examining licence agreements and vouching the licensee's reports and related cash payment.

Inspection   Investment property is inspected as the fixed assets are. The principal goal is to determine actual existence and condition of the property. Official documents of patents, copyrights, and trademark rights can be inspected to see that they are, in fact, in the name of the client.

Documentation Vouching   Investment costs should be vouched to brokers' reports, monthly statements, or other documentary evidence of cost. At the same time, the amounts of sales are traced to gain or loss accounts, and the amounts of sales prices and proceeds are vouched to the brokers' statements. Auditors should determine what method of cost-out assignment was used (i.e., FIFO, specific identification, or average cost) and whether it is consistent with prior-years' transactions. The cost of real and personal property likewise can be vouched to invoices or other documents of purchase, and title documents (such as on land, buildings) may be inspected.

Market valuation of securities may be required. Since 2006, companies must record financial assets and liabilities at their fair values at year end. The auditor will need to obtain evidence of market values or recent sales of investments to verify these fair values.

Vouching may be extensive in the areas of research and development (R&D) and deferred development costs. Evidence should determine whether costs are properly classified as assets or as R&D expense. A sample of recorded amounts is selected, and the purchase orders, receiving reports, payroll records, authorization notices, and management reports are compared with them. Some R&D costs may resemble non-R&D costs (such as supplies, payroll costs), so auditors must be alert for costs that appear to relate to other operations.

External Documentation   Auditors use quoted market values of securities to calculate market values. If quoted market values are not available, financial statements for investments are analyzed for evidence of basic value. If the financial statements are unaudited, the evidence indicated by them is considered to be extremely weak.

Income amounts can be verified by consulting published dividend records for dividends actually declared and paid during a period (e.g., Moody's and Standard & Poor's dividend records). Since auditors know the holding period of securities, dividend income can be calculated and compared with the amount in the account. Any difference could indicate a cutoff error, misclassification, defalcation, or failure to record a dividend receivable. Applying interest rates to bond or note investments produces a calculated interest income figure (making allowance for amortization of premium or discount if applicable).

Equity Method Investments

When equity method accounting is used for investments, auditors need the audited financial statements of the investee company. Inability to obtain these from a closely held investee may indicate that the client investor does not have the significant controlling influence required by *CICA Handbook* section 3051. These statements are used in recalculating the client's share of income to recognize in the accounts and to audit the disclosure of investees' assets, liabilities, and income presented in footnotes (a disclosure recommended when investments accounted for by the equity method are material).

Amortization Recalculation   Amortization expense owes its existence to a calculation, and recalculation based on audited costs and rates is sufficient audit evidence.[4]

The appraisals, judgments, and allocations within merger and acquisition transactions that are used to assign portions of the purchase price to tangible assets, intangible assets, liabilities, and goodwill should be reviewed. Inspection of transaction documentation is ideal, but verbal enquiries may help auditors to understand the circumstances of a merger.

Questions about lawsuits challenging patents, copyrights, or trade names may indicate problem areas for further investigation. Likewise, questions about research and development successes and failures may alert the audit team to problems of valuation of intangible assets and related amortization expense. Responses to questions about licensing of patents can be used in the audit of related royalty revenue accounts.

Enquiries about Management Intentions   Enquiries should deal with the nature of investments and the reasons for holding them. Management's expressed intention that a marketable security investment be considered a long-term investment may be the only evidence for classifying it as long term and not as a current asset. That classification will affect the accounting treatment of market values and the unrealized gains and losses on investments.

. . . .

REVIEW CHECKPOINTS

14   What are some of the typical assertions found in owners' equity descriptions and account balances?

15   How can confirmations be used in auditing shareholder capital accounts? auditing notes? loans and bonds payable?

---

[4] Under *CICA Handbook* section 3061, the official terminology is now "capital assets" and "amortization" although "depreciation" still receives common use when reference is to amortization of tangible (fixed) assets.

16   What are some of the typical assertions found in long-term liability accounts?

17   What procedures do auditors employ to obtain evidence of the cost of investments? investment gains and losses? investment income?

18   Why are auditors interested in substantial investment losses occurring early in the period following year-end?

19   What is the concept of "substance versus form" in relation to financing and investment transactions and balances? (Refer to the off-balance-sheet and application cases in the chapter.)

20   What are some of the trouble spots for auditors in the audits of investments and intangibles?

APPLICATION CASE AND ANALYSIS

LEARNING OBJECTIVE
3 Apply and integrate the chapter topics to design audit and investigative procedures for detecting misstatements due to error and fraud in the finance and investment process.

At the point in the chapter, we present an application case that contains specific examples of tests of controls and substantive audit procedures used to gather evidence in the finance and investment process. The case situation for each audit presented parallels the framework shown in Chapter 11's application case. Each case situation provides context for the auditing decisions, rather than presenting a list of detection procedures in the abstract. If you would like to review lists of detailed procedures, a selection of control tests and detail substantive procedures for cash and accounts receivable is found in Appendix 13A (page 547).

Detecting Misstatements in Finance and Investment Processes

While preparing to audit the investments and financing process of one of the firm's larger clients, Jack does some research work to become more knowledgeable about the risks in these areas. He finds news stories about four audits where misstatements occurred. These cases involved improper issue of securities, misstatement of tax loss carryforwards, misuse of related party transaction to keep liabilities off the balance sheet, and an example of nonconsolidation of a controlled company to conceal losses.

AUDIT 14.1
Unregistered Sale of Securities

Case Description

The Bliss Solar Heating Company (Bliss) sold investment contracts to the public in the form of limited partnership interests. These "securities" sales should have been under a public registration filing with the provincial securities regulator, but they were not. Under the terms of the deal, these investors purchased solar hot water heating systems for residential and commercial use from Bliss and then entered into arrangements to lease the equipment to Nationwide Corporation, which in turn rented the equipment to end users. The limited partnerships were, in effect, financing conduits for obtaining investors' money to pay for Bliss's equipment. The investors' return of capital and profit depended on Nationwide's business success and ability to pay under the lease terms. The amounts involved are not known, but all the money put up by the limited partnership investors was at risk and largely not disclosed to the investors.

Audit Trail

Bliss published false and misleading financial statements, which used a non-GAAP revenue recognition method and failed to disclose cost of goods sold. Bliss overstated Nationwide's record of equipment installation and failed to disclose that Nationwide had little cash flow from end users (resulting from rent-free periods and other inducements). Bliss knew, but failed to disclose to prospective investors, that a number of previous investors had filed petitions with the federal tax court to contest Canada Revenue Agency's disallowance of the tax credits and benefits claimed in connection with their investments in Bliss's tax-sheltered equipment lease partnerships.

AUDIT APPROACH ANALYSIS

Audit objective

The auditor's objective is to obtain evidence determining whether capital fundraising methods comply with provincial securities laws and whether financial statements and other disclosures are misleading.

Controls relevant to the process

Management should employ experts—lawyers, underwriters, and accountants—who can determine whether securities and investment contract sales require registration.

AUDIT PROCEDURES

Tests of controls

Auditors should learn about the business backgrounds and securities-industry expertise of the senior managers. Study the authorization of the fundraising method in the minutes of the board of directors meetings. Obtain and study opinions of lawyers and underwriters about the legality of the fundraising methods. Enquire about management's interaction with the provincial securities regulator in any presale clearance. (The securities regulator will give advice about the necessity for registration.)

Tests of details of balance

Auditors should study the offering documents and literature used in the sale of securities to determine whether financial information is being used properly. In this case, the close relationship with Nationwide and the experience of earlier partnerships give reasons for extended procedures to obtain

evidence about the representations concerning Nationwide's business success (in this case, lack of success).

Audit Results

The auditors gave unqualified reports on Bliss's materially misstated financial statements. They apparently did not question the legality of the sales of the limited partnership interests as a means of raising capital, nor did they perform procedures to verify representations made concerning Bliss or Nationwide finances. Two partners in the audit firm were enjoined for violations of the securities laws. They resigned from practice before the provincial securities regulator and were ordered not to perform any assurance services for companies making filings with the securities regulator. They later were expelled from the ICAO for failure to cooperate with the disciplinary committee in its investigation of alleged professional ethics violations.

AUDIT 14.2
Tax Loss Carryforwards

Case Description

Aetna Life & Casualty Insurance Company had losses in its taxable income operations in 2001 and 2002. Confident that future taxable income would absorb the losses, the company booked and reported a future income tax asset for the tax loss carryforward. The provincial securities regulator maintained that the company understated its tax expense and overstated its assets. Utilization of the loss carryforward was not "more likely than not to be realized," as required by *CICA Handbook*, paragraph 3465.24.

Aetna forecast several more years of taxable losses (aside from its nontaxable income from tax-exempt investments) followed by years of taxable income, which would eventually offset the losses and allow the company to utilize the benefit of the losses carried forward to offset against future taxable income. The company maintained there was no reasonable doubt that the forecasts would be achieved.

At first, the carryforward tax benefit was $25 million, soon growing to over $200 million, then forecast to become an estimated $1 billion before the losses would be reversed and absorbed by the forecast future taxable income. In 2003, the first full year in which these forecasts had an impact, Aetna's net income was 35 percent lower than it had been in 2001, instead of just 6 percent lower, as a result of the carryforward benefit recognized.

Audit Trail

The amounts of tax loss were clearly evident in the accounts and Aetna made no attempt to hide the facts. The portfolio of taxable investments and all sources of taxable income and deductions were well known to the company accountants, management, and independent auditors.

AUDIT APPROACH ANALYSIS

Audit objective

The auditor's objective is to obtain evidence determining whether realization of the benefits of the tax loss carryforward are "more likely than not to be realized."

Controls relevant to the process

The relevant control in this case concerns the assumptions and mathematics underlying the forecasts that justify recording the tax loss carryforward benefit. These forecasts are the basis for an accounting estimate of "more likely than not."

AUDIT PROCEDURES

Tests of controls

Auditors should make enquiries and determine the following. Who prepared the forecasts? When were they prepared? What data were used? Who reviewed and approved the forecast? Is there any way to test the accuracy of the forecast with actual experience?

Tests of details of balance

Aside from audit of the assumptions underlying the forecasts and recalculations of the compilation, the test of balances amounted to careful consideration of whether the forecast, or any forecast, could meet the test required by accounting standards. The decision was a judgment of whether the test of "more likely than not to be realized" was met.

The auditors should obtain information about other situations in which recognition of tax loss carryforward benefits were allowed in financial statements. Other companies have booked and reported such benefits when gains from sales of property were realized before the financial statement was issued and when the loss was from discontinuing a business line, leaving these businesses with long profit histories.

Audit Results

The provincial securities regulator was tipped off to Aetna's accounting recognition of the tax loss carryforward benefit by a story in *Financial Post* magazine, which described the accounting treatment. Aetna's defence was based on the forecasts. The securities regulator countered that the forecasts did not provide assurance beyond any reasonable doubt that future taxable income would be (1) sufficient to offset the loss carryforward and (2) earned during the prescribed carryforward period, as prescribed by paragraph 3465.28 of the *CICA Handbook*. For this reason, the securities regulator concluded that the "virtually certain realization" was not established. The securities regulator won the argument. Aetna revised its previously issued quarterly financial statements, and the company abandoned the attempt to report the tax benefit.

AUDIT 14.3
OFF-BALANCE-SHEET INVENTORY FINANCING

Case Description

Verity Distillery Company used the "product repurchase" ploy to convert its inventory to cash, failing to disclose the obligation to repurchase it later. Related party transactions were not disclosed. To do this, Verity's president formed Veritas Corporation, making himself and two other Verity officers the sole shareholders. The president arranged to sell $40 million of Verity's inventory of whiskey, still in the aging process, to Veritas, showing no gain or loss on the transaction. The officers negotiated a 36-month loan with a major bank to get the money Veritas needed for the purchase, pledging the inventory as collateral. Verity pledged to repurchase the inventory for $54.4 million, which amounted to the original $40 million plus 12 percent interest for three years.

The $40 million purchased 40 percent of Verity's normal inventory, and the company's cash balance was increased by 50 percent. While the current asset total was not changed, the inventory ratios (e.g., inventory turnover, day's sales in inventory) were materially altered. Long-term liabilities were understated by not recording the liability. The ploy was actually a secured loan with inventory pledged as collateral, but this reality was neither recorded nor disclosed. The total effect would be to keep debt off the books, avoid recording interest expense, and record inventory later at a higher cost. Subsequent sale of the whiskey at market prices would not affect the ultimate income results, but the unrecorded interest expense would be buried in the cost of goods sold. The net income in the year the "sale" was made was not changed, but the normal relationship of gross margin to sales was distorted by the zero-profit transaction.

Audit Trail

The contract of sale was in the files, specifying the name of the purchasing company, the $40 million amount, and the cash consideration. Nothing mentioned the relationship between Veritas and the officers. Nothing mentioned the repurchase obligation. However, the sale amount was unusually large.

	Before Transaction	Recorded Transaction	Should Have Recorded
Assets	$530	$530	$570
Liabilities	390	390	430
Shareholder Equity	140	140	140
Debt/Equity ratio	2.79	2.79	3.07

AUDIT APPROACH ANALYSIS

Audit objective

The auditors' objective is to obtain evidence determining whether all liabilities are recorded. Be alert to undisclosed related party transactions.

Controls relevant to the process

The relevant control in this case would rest with the integrity and accounting knowledge of the senior of-ficials who arranged the transaction. Authorization in the board minutes might detail the arrangements, but, if they wanted to hide it from the auditors, they also would suppress the telltale information in the board minutes.

AUDIT PROCEDURES

Tests of controls

Enquiries should be made about large and unusual financing transactions, although this may not elicit a response because the event is a sales transaction, according to Verity. Other audit work on controls in the revenues, receivables, and receipts process may turn up the large sale. Fortunately, this one stands out.

Tests of details of balance

Analytical procedures to compare monthly or seasonal sales probably will identify the sale as large and unusual, which should lead to an examination of the sales contract. Auditors should discuss the business purpose of the transaction with knowledgeable officials. If being this close to discovery does not bring out an admission of the loan and repurchase arrangement, the auditors nevertheless should investigate further. Even if the "customer" name is not a giveaway, a quick enquiry for corporation records at the relevant provincial ministry (online in some data-bases) will show the names of the officers, exposing the nature of the deal. Veritas's financial statements should be requested.

Audit Results

The auditors found the related party relationship between the officers and Veritas. Confronted, the president admitted the attempt to make the cash position and the debt-equity ratio look better than it was. The financial statements were adjusted to reflect the "should have recorded" set of figures shown previously.

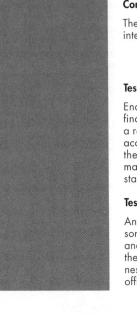

AUDIT 14.4
A CONSOLIDATION BY ANY OTHER NAME

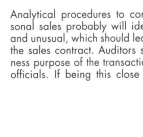

Case Description

Digilog Inc. formed a company named DBS International (DBSI) and controlled it, but did not consolidate its financial position and results of operations in the Digilog financial statements. Digilog income was overstated, and assets and liabilities were understated.

Digilog Inc. formed DBSI to market Digilog's computer equipment, but kept it separate to avoid the adverse impact of reporting expected startup losses in Digilog's financial statements. Instead of owning shares in DBSI, Digilog financed the company with loans convertible at will into 90 percent of DBSI's stock. (Otherwise, the share ownership was not in Digilog's name.) Since Digilog did not control DBSI (control is defined as 50 percent or more ownership), DBSI was not consolidated, and the initial losses were not reported in Digilog's financial statements. (See *Handbook* paragraph 1590.08 for the usual presumptions concerning the level of ownership leading to control.) Several hundred thousand dollars of losses in the first two years of DBSI operations were not consolidated. Ultimately, the venture became profitable and was absorbed into Digilog.

Audit Trail

DBSI's formation was not a secret. It was authorized and the incorporation papers were available. Loan documents showing the terms of Digilog's loans to DBSI were in the files.

AUDIT APPROACH ANALYSIS

Audit objective

The auditor's objective is to obtain evidence determining whether proper accounting methods (cost, equity, and consolidation) were used for investments.

Controls relevant to the process

The relevant control in this case would rest with the integrity and accounting knowledge of the senior officials who arranged the transaction. Proper documentation of authorization as well as financing and operating transactions between the two corporations should be in the companies' files.

AUDIT PROCEDURES

Tests of controls

Enquiries should be made about large and unusual financing transactions. Minutes of the board of directors meetings should be studied to find related authorizations. These authorizations and supporting papers signal the accounting issues and interpretations of generally accepted accounting principles required in the circumstances.

Tests of details of balance

The central issue in this case is the interpretation of accounting standards regarding required consolidation. Existence, completeness, valuation, and ownership were not problematic audit issues. Unless these are extenuating factors as per *CICA Handbook* paragraph 1590.08, accounting standards requires consolidation of subsidiaries over 50 percent owned, and prohibits consolidation of subsidiaries less than 50 percent owned. Digilog's purpose in financing DBSI with loans instead of direct share ownership was to skirt the 50 percent ownership criterion, thus keeping the DBSI losses out of the Digilog consoli-

dated financial statements. The "test of the balance" (decision of whether to require consolidation) amounted to an interpretation of the substance versus form of ownership through convertible notes instead of direct shareholding.

Audit Results

Digilog, with concurrence of its independent audit firm, adopted the narrow interpretation of ownership. Since Digilog did not "own" DBSI stock, DBSI was not "controlled," and its assets, liabilities, and results of operations were not consolidated. The regulator disagreed and acted on the position that the convertible feature of the loans and the business purpose of the DBSI formation were enough to attribute control to Digilog. The company was enjoined from activities resulting in violations of certain reporting and antifraud provisions of the provincial securities act and was required to amend its financial statements for the years in question. The regulator also took action against the audit firm partner in charge of the Digilog audit.

OTHER ASPECTS OF CLEVER ACCOUNTING AND FRAUD

Clever accounting and fraud that affect the fair presentation of material equity accounts, investments, and intangibles must be considered. Improper accounting presentations are engineered more frequently by senior officials than by middle management or those of lower ranks. Top management personnel who deal with the transactions involved in investments, long-term debt, and shareholders' equity are not subject to the kind of control that lower-level employees experience, and they often are able to override detail procedural controls.

Long-Term Liabilities and Owners' Equity

The clever accounting and fraud connected with liability and owners' equity accounts differ significantly from those associated with asset and revenue accounts. Few employees are tempted to steal a liability, although fictitious liabilities may be created as a means of misdirecting cash payments into the hands of an officer. Auditors should be alert for such fictions in the same sense that they are alert to the possibility of having fictitious accounts receivable. The area of liabilities and owners' equity also contains possibilities for company fraud against outsiders. This class of fraud is most often accomplished through material misrepresentations or omissions in financial statements and related disclosures.

Officers and employees can use share or bond instruments improperly. Unissued shares or bonds and treasury stock may be used as collateral for personal loans. Even though the company may not be damaged or suffer loss by this action (unless the employee defaults and the securities are seized), the practice is unauthorized and is contrary to company interests. Employees could gain access to shareholder lists and unissued coupons, using them for improper payments of dividends and interest on securities that are not outstanding.

Proper custodial control of securities (either by limited access vaults or an independent disbursing agent) prevents most such occurrences. Reconciling authorized dividend and interest payments to actual payments detects unauthorized payments. If the company did not perform this checking procedure, auditors should include it in their own analytical recalculation procedures. Many liability, equity, and off-balance-sheet transactions are outside the reach of normal internal control procedures, which can operate effectively over ordinary transactions (such as purchases and sales) processed by clerks and machines.

Auditors are justified in performing extensive substantive auditing of long-term liability, equity, and other high-level managed transactions and agreements as control depends in large part on the integrity and accounting knowledge of management.

Income tax evasion and fraud result from actions of managers. Evasion and fraud may be accomplished by (1) simple omission of income, (2) unlawful deductions (such as contributions to political campaigns, capital cost allowance on nonexistent assets or capital cost allowance in excess of cost), or (3) sham transactions for the sole purpose of avoiding taxation. Auditors should be able to detect errors of the first two categories if the actual income and expense data have been sufficiently audited in the financial statements. The last category, **contrived sham transactions**, is harder to detect because a dishonest management can skilfully disguise them. Some of the fraud awareness procedures outlined in Chapter 17 may be useful and effective.

Financial statements may be materially misstated through omission or understatement of liabilities and by failure to disclose technical defaults on loan agreement restrictions. These restrictions or test covenants are very important to the viability of the client because, if they are violated, creditors can force the client into bankruptcy. Auditor knowledge of these restrictions and comparison with the client's current financial condition pinpoints audit risk areas and helps assess the going concern assumption. The procedures for search for unrecorded liabilities may be used to discover such omissions and understatements (Chapter 12). If auditors discover that loan agreement terms have been violated, they should bring the information to the client's attention and insist on proper disclosure in notes to the financial statements. In both situations (liability understatement and loan default disclosure), management's actions, reactions, and willingness to adjust the financial figures and to make adverse disclosures are important insights for auditors' evaluation of managerial integrity, something that has an important bearing on the auditors' perceptions of risk for the audit engagement as a whole.

Misstatements in the financial statements can arise from error or fraud. According to CAS 240 (5135), the term "error" refers to an *unintentional* misstatement in financial statements, including the omission of an amount or a disclosure, or an incorrect accounting estimate arising from oversight or misinterpretation of facts. The term "fraud" refers to an *intentional* act by one or more individuals to misstate the financial statements to deceive users and obtain an unjust or illegal advantage. Although fraud is a broad legal concept, the auditor is only concerned with fraud that causes a material misstatement in the financial statements. Auditors do not make legal determinations of fraud.

Intent is difficult to prove, but if the auditor identifies a possible bias on the part of management in making accounting estimates, the auditor should consider whether there is a risk of material misstatement due to fraud.[5] For example, is it possible that the cumulative effect of bias in management's accounting estimates is designed to smooth earnings over two or more accounting periods, or to achieve designated earnings level to deceive financial statement users? The audit needs to be performed with professional skepticism, meaning the auditor (a) should be aware of factors that increase the risk of misstatement, and (b) should be sensitized to evidence that contradicts the assumption of management's good faith.

If there are enough red flags present, the auditor will assess a higher inherent risk resulting in the following actions:

(a) obtain more reliable evidence,

(b) expand the extent of audit procedures performed,

(c) apply audit procedures closer to or as of the balance sheet date,

(d) require more extensive supervision of assistants, and/or assistants with more experience and training.

In essence, if the auditor suspects that the financial statements are misstated, he should perform procedures to confirm or dispel that suspicion. Generally, however, the auditor is

---

[5] *CICA Handbook*, paragraph 5135.081.

less likely to detect material misstatements arising from fraud because of the deliberate concealment involved. When the auditor does obtain evidence of a nontrivial misstatement or fraud, he or she should inform the appropriate level of management, and the audit committee or board of directors should be informed.[6]

A company, its individual managers, and the auditors easily might violate securities regulations. Chapter 5 covers the general framework of regulation by provincial securities commissions. Auditors must know the provisions of the securities laws so that they can identify both situations that constitute obvious fraud and transactions that may be subject to the law. Having recognized or raised questions about a securities transaction, auditors should submit the facts to competent legal counsel for an opinion. Auditors are not expected to be legal experts, but they have the duty to recognize obvious instances of impropriety and to pursue investigations with the aid of legal experts.

Similarly, auditors should assist clients in observing securities commission rules and regulations on matters of timely disclosure. Timely disclosure rules are phrased as management's duties, and auditors aren't required to carry out any specific procedures or to make any specific disclosures. The regulations require management to disseminate any material information, favourable or unfavourable, so that investors can incorporate it in their decision making. Announcements and disclosures must be made very soon after information becomes known. If situations arise during the year when the independent auditors are not present they cannot be held responsible or liable. However, auditors may learn of the information inadvertently or the client may come to the auditor for advice. In such cases auditors should advise their clients according to the requirements of law and regulations.

Auditors are curently pressured to discover more information about off-balance-sheet contingencies and commitments and to discover the facts of management involvement with other parties to transactions. Auditors' knowledge of these things that are not in accounting records depends in large part on information the management and its legal counsel reveals. Nevertheless, certain investigative procedures are available (see Chapter 17). The expectation that auditors discover more information is a part of the public pressure on them to take more responsibility for fraud detection.

Investments and Intangibles

Theft, diversion, and unauthorized use of investment securities can occur in several ways. If safekeeping controls are weak, securities can simply be stolen, in which case it is a police problem rather than an auditing problem. Diversions, such as using securities as collateral during the year, returning them for a count, then giving them back to the creditor without disclosure to the auditor, are more common. If safekeeping methods require entry signatures (as for a safety deposit box), auditors may be able to detect the in-and-out movement. The best chance of discovery is creditor confirmation of the collateral arrangement. In a similar manner, securities may be removed by an officer and sold, then repurchased before the auditors' count. The auditors' record of the certificate numbers should reveal this change, since the returned certificates (and their serial numbers) will not be the same as the ones removed. The rapid growth in use of derivative securities as investments and hedges has created new and rather unique problems for auditors, not the least of which is lack of familiarity with these financial instruments. Appendix 14B (on the text Online Learning Centre) provides an overview of the recent global problems in this area.

Cash receipts from interest, royalties on patent licences, dividends, and sales proceeds may be stolen. The accounting records may or may not be manipulated to cover the theft. In general, this kind of defalcation should be prevented by cash receipts control; however, since these receipts usually are irregular and infrequent, the cash control system may not be as effective as it is for regular receipts on trade accounts.

---

[6] *CICA Handbook*, section 5135.

If the income accounts are not manipulated to hide stolen receipts, auditors will find less income in the account than their audit calculations based on other records tell them should be there. If sales of securities are not recorded, auditors will notice that securities are missing when they try to inspect or confirm them. If the income accounts have been manipulated to hide stolen receipts, vouching of cash receipts will detect the theft, or vouching may reveal some offsetting debit buried in some other account.

Accounting values may be manipulated in a number of ways: purchases of assets at inflated prices, leases with affiliates, acquisitions of patents for shares given to an inventor or promoter, sales to affiliates, and fallacious decisions about amortization. Business history has recorded several cases of non-arm's-length transactions with promoters, officers, directors, and controlled companies (even "dummy" companies) designed to drain the company's resources and fool the auditors.

In one case a company sold assets to a dummy purchaser set up by a director to bolster sagging income. The auditors did not know that the purchaser was a shell. All the documents of sale looked in order, and cash sales proceeds had been deposited. The auditors were not informed of a secret agreement by the seller to repurchase the assets at a later time. This situation illustrates a devious manipulation. All transactions with persons closely associated with the company (related parties) should be audited carefully with reference to market values, particularly when a nonmonetary transaction is involved (such as shares exchanged for patent rights). Sales and lease-back and straight lease transactions with insiders likewise should be audited carefully.

REVIEW CHECKPOINTS

21 What is the single most significant control consideration in connection with clever accounting and fraud in finance and investment accounts?

22 Which is more likely to exist in the finance and investment cycle accounts: (1) fraud against the company or (2) fraud by the company in financial or tax reporting? Explain.

23 What should an auditor do when violation of securities laws is suspected?

24 What is the danger for auditors when company officials engage in undisclosed related party transactions?

Analysis of Financial Statement Relationships

The audit of the finance and investment process verifies that there is not a material misstatement in the balance of long-term investments and liabilities (financial instruments) and share capital or in the transaction streams that are related to them, dividends and interest. As an example, the continuity of the share capital account is shown below.

Audited Amount	Financial Statement Where Amount Is Reported
Opening balance of share capital	Balance sheet (prior year comparative figures)
Add: Proceeds of shares issued during the year	Statement of Shareholders' Equity and Cash flow statement (financing activity)
Deduct: Reductions for shares redeemed during the year	Statement of Shareholders' Equity and Cash flow statement (financing activity)
Ending balance of share capital	Balance sheet (current year figures)

SUMMARY

The finance and investment process contains a wide variety of accounts—share capital, dividends, long-term debt, interest expense, tax expenses and future income taxes, financial instruments, derivatives, equity method investments, related gains and losses, consolidated subsidiaries, goodwill, and other intangibles. These accounts involve some of the most technically complex accounting standards. They create most of the difficult judgments for financial reporting.

Transactions in these accounts generally are controlled by senior officials. Therefore, internal control is centred on the integrity and accounting knowledge of these officials. The procedural controls over details of transactions are not very effective because senior managers can override them and order their own desired accounting presentations. As a consequence, auditors' work on the assessment of control risk is directed toward the senior managers, the board of directors and their authorizations, and the design of finance and investment deals.

Fraud and clever accounting in the finance and investment cycle get directed most often to producing misleading financial statements. While theft and embezzlement can occur, the accounts in this cycle frequently have been the ones manipulated and misvalued so that financial positions and results of operations look better than the company's reality. Off-balance-sheet financing and investment transactions with related parties are explained as areas easily targeted for fraudulent financial reporting.

This chapter ends the book's coverage of audit applications for various processes and their related accounts. Chapter 15 contains several topics involved in putting the finishing touches on an audit.

MULTIPLE-CHOICE QUESTIONS FOR PRACTICE AND REVIEW

MC 1 Jones was engaged to examine the financial statements of Gamma Corporation for the year ended June 30, 20X3. Having completed an examination of the investment securities, which of the following is the best method of verifying the accuracy of recorded dividend income?
- *a.* Tracing recorded dividend income to cash receipts records and validated deposit slips
- *b.* Utilizing analytical review techniques and statistical sampling
- *c.* Comparing recorded dividends with amounts appearing on federal tax returns
- *d.* Comparing recorded dividends with a standard financial reporting service's record of dividends

MC 2 When a large amount of negotiable securities is held by the client, planning by the auditor is necessary to guard against which of the following?
- *a.* Unauthorized negotiation of the securities before they are counted
- *b.* Unrecorded sales of securities after they are counted
- *c.* Substitution of securities already counted for other securities which should be on hand but are not
- *d.* Substitution of authentic securities with counterfeit securities

MC 3 Which of the following is the most important consideration of an auditor when examining the shareholders' equity section of a client's balance sheet?
- *a.* Changes in the share capital account are verified by an independent share transfer agent.

- *b.* Stock dividends and stock splits during the year under audit were approved by the shareholders.
- *c.* Stock dividends are capitalized at par or stated value on the dividend declaration date.
- *d.* Entries in the share capital account can be traced to resolutions in the minutes of the board of directors' meetings.

MC 4 If the auditor discovers that the carrying amount of a client's available-for-sale financial assets is greater than its market value at the balance sheet date, what should the auditor should insist on?
- *a.* The approximate market values of the investments are shown in parentheses on the face of the balance sheet.
- *b.* The investments are classified as long-term for balance sheet purposes with full disclosure in the footnotes.
- *c.* The decline in value is recognized in the financial statements.
- *d.* The liability section of the balance sheet separately shows a charge equal to the amount of the loss.

MC 5 Which of the following is the primary reason for preparing a reconciliation between interest-bearing obligations outstanding during the year and interest expense in the financial statements?
- *a.* Evaluating internal control over securities
- *b.* Determining the validity of prepaid interest expense
- *c.* Ascertaining the reasonableness of imputed interest
- *d.* Detecting unrecorded liabilities

MC 6 Why should the auditor insist that a representative of the client be present during the inspection and count of securities?

 a. To lend authority to the auditor's directives

 b. To detect forged securities

 c. To coordinate the return of all securities to proper locations

 d. To acknowledge the receipt of securities returned

MC 7 When independent share transfer agents are not employed and the corporation issues its own shares and maintains share records, how should cancelled share certificates be handled?

 a. Defaced to prevent re-issuance and attached to their corresponding stubs

 b. Not be defaced, but segregated from other share certificates and retained in a cancelled certificates file

 c. Destroyed to prevent fraudulent reissuance

 d. Defaced and sent to the federal finance minister

MC 8 When a client company does not maintain its own share capital records, the auditor should obtain written confirmation from the transfer agent and registrar concerning which of the following:

 a. Restrictions on the payment of dividends

 b. The number of shares issued and outstanding

 c. Guarantees of preferred share liquidation value

 d. The number of shares subject to agreements to repurchase

MC 9 Which item of all corporate share capital transactions should ultimately be traced?

 a. Minutes of the board of directors meetings

 b. Cash receipts journal

 c. Cash disbursements journal

 d. Numbered share certificates

MC 10 A corporate balance sheet indicates that one of the corporate assets is a patent. Where will an auditor most likely be able to obtain a written representation of this patent from?

 a. Patent lawyer

 b. Regional patent office

 c. Patent inventor

 d. Patent owner

MC 11 An audit program for the examination of the retained earnings account should include a step that requires verification of which of the following:

 a. Market value used to charge retained earnings to account for a two-for-one share split

 b. Approval of the adjustment to the beginning balance as a result of a write-down of account receivables

 c. Authorization for both cash and share dividends

 d. Gain or loss resulting from disposition of available-for-sale financial assets

(AICPA adapted)

EXERCISES AND PROBLEMS

. . . .

INVESTMENTS AND INTANGIBLES

EP 1
LO.1
and
LO.2
ICQ for Equity Investments. Cassandra Corporation, a manufacturing company, periodically invests large sums in marketable equity securities. The investment policy is established by the investment committee of the board of directors. The treasurer is responsible for carrying out the committee's directives. All securities are held by Cassandra's brokerage company.

 Your ICQ with respect to Cassandra's investments in equity securities contains the following three questions:

 1. Is investment policy established by the investment committee of the board of directors?

 2. Is the treasurer solely responsible for carrying out the investment committee's directive?

 3. Are all securities stored in a bank safety deposit box?

Required:

 a. What is the purpose of the above three questions?

 b. What additional questions should your ICQ include concerning the company's investment in marketable equity securities? (*Hint:* Prepare questions to cover the control objectives—validity, completeness, authorization, accuracy, classification, accounting, and proper period.)

(AICPA adapted)

EP 2
LO.3
Noncurrent Investment Securities. You are auditing the financial statements of Bass Corporation for the year ended December 31, and you are about to begin an audit of the noncurrent investment securities. Bass's records indicate that the company owns various bearer bonds, as well as 25 percent of the outstanding common shares of Commercial Industrial Inc. You are satisfied with evidence supporting the presumption of significant influence over Commercial. The various securities are at two locations as follows:

 a. Recently acquired securities are in the company's safe in the custody of the treasurer.

 b. All other securities are in a bank safety deposit box. All securities in Bass's portfolio are actively traded in a broad market.

Required:

 a. Assuming that the system of internal control over securities is satisfactory, what are the objectives (specific assertions) for the audit of the noncurrent securities?

 b. What audit procedures should you undertake with respect to the audit of Bass's investment securities?

(AICPA adapted)

EP 3
LO.3
Securities Examination and Count. You are in charge of the audit of the financial statements of the Demot

Corporation for the year ended December 31. The corporation has had the policy of investing its surplus funds in marketable securities. Its share and bond certificates are kept in a safety deposit box in a local bank. Only the president and the treasurer of the corporation have access to the box.

You were unable to obtain access to the safety deposit box on December 31 because neither the president nor the treasurer was available. Your assistant will accompany the treasurer to the bank on January 11 to examine the securities but he has never examined securities that were being kept in a safety deposit box and requires instructions. The inspection should only take an hour.

Required:

a. List the instructions you would give for examining the share and bond certificates in the safety deposit box. Include the details of the securities to be examined and the reasons for examining these details.

b. Your assistant reports that the treasurer had entered the box on January 4 to remove an old photograph of the corporation's original building. The photograph was lent to the local chamber of commerce. List the additional audit procedures required because of the treasurer's action.

(AICPA adapted)

EP 4 **Securities Procedures**. You were engaged to examine
LO.3 the financial statements of Ronlyn Corporation for the year ended June 30. On May 1 the corporation borrowed $500,000 from the Second National Bank to finance plant expansion. However, because of unexpected difficulties in acquiring the building site, the expansion had not begun as planned. To make use of the borrowed funds, management decided to invest in shares and bonds; on May 16 the $500,000 was invested in securities.

Required:

In your audit of investments, how would you

a. Audit the recorded dividend or interest income?

b. Determine market value?

c. Establish the authority for security purchases?

(AICPA adapted)

EP 5 **Research and Development**. The Hertle Engineering
LO.3 Company depends on new product development to maintain its position in the market for drilling tool equipment. The company conducts an extensive research and development program, and has charged all research and development costs to current operations in accordance with *CICA Handbook* requirements.

The company began a project called Project Able in January 20X1 with the goal of patenting a revolutionary drilling bit design. Work continued until October 20X2, when the company applied for a patent. Costs were charged to the research and development expense account in both years, except for the cost of a computer program that engineers plan to use in Project Baker, scheduled to start in December 20X2. The computer program was purchased from Computeering Inc. in January 20X1 for $45,000.

Required:

a. Give an audit program for the audit of research and development costs on Project Able. Assume that you are auditing the company for the first time at December 31, 20X2.

b. What evidence would you require for the audit of the computer program that has been capitalized as an intangible asset? As of December 31, 20X2, this account has a balance of $40,000 (cost less $5,000 amortized as a part of Project Able).

(AICPA adapted)

EP 6 **Intangibles**. Sorenson Manufacturing was incorporated
LO.1 on January 3, 20X1. The corporation's financial state-
and ments for its first year's operations were not examined by
LO.2 a PA. You have been engaged to audit the financial statements for the year ended December 31, 20X2, and your examination is substantially completed.

A partial trial balance of the company's accounts is given in Exhibit EP 6–1:

EXHIBIT EP 6-1

SORENSON MANUFACTURING CORPORATION
Partial Trial Balance at
December 31, 20X2

	Trial Balance	
	Debit	Credit
Cash	$11,000	
Accounts receivable	42,500	
Allowance for doubtful accounts		$ 500
Inventories	38,500	
Machinery	75,000	
Equipment	29,000	
Accumulated amortization		10,000
Patents	85,000	
Leasehold improvements	26,000	
Prepaid expenses	10,500	
Goodwill	24,000	

The following information relates to accounts which may yet require adjustment:

1. Patents for Sorenson's manufacturing process were purchased January 2, 20X2, at a cost of $68,000. An additional $17,000 was spent in December 20X2 to improve machinery covered by the patents and charged to the patents account. The patents had a remaining legal term of 17 years.

2. The balance in the goodwill account includes $24,000 paid December 30, 20X1, for an advertising program estimated to increase Sorenson's sales over a period of four years following the disbursement.

3. The leasehold improvement account includes (*a*) the $15,000 cost of improvements, with a total estimated useful life of 12 years, which Sorenson, as tenant,

made to leased premises in January 20X1; (*b*) movable assembly line equipment costing $8,500, which was installed in the leased premises in December 20X2; and (*c*) real estate taxes of $2,500 paid by Sorenson which, under the terms of the lease, should have been paid by the landlord. Sorenson paid its rent in full during 20X2. A 10-year nonrenewable lease was signed January 3, 20X1, for the leased building that Sorenson used in manufacturing operations. No amortization of the leasehold improvements has been recorded.

Required:

Prepare adjusting entries as necessary.

(AICPA adapted)

EP 7
LO.3

Long-Term Note. You were engaged to examine the financial statements of Ronlyn Corporation for the year ended June 30. On May 1 the corporation borrowed $500,000 from the Second National Bank to finance plant expansion. The long-term note agreement provided for the annual payment of principal and interest over five years. The existing plant was pledged as security for the loan.

Due to unexpected difficulties in acquiring the building site, the plant expansion had not begun as planned. To make use of the borrowed funds, on May 16 management invested the $500,000 was invested in securities.

Required:

a. What are the audit objectives in the examining of long-term debt?

b. Prepare an audit program for the examination of the long-term note agreement between Ronlyn and Second National Bank.

(AICPA adapted)

EP 8
LO.3

Long-Term Financing Agreement. You have been engaged to audit the financial statements of Broadwall Corporation for the year ended December 31, 20X2. During the year, Broadwall obtained a long-term loan from a local bank pursuant to the following financing agreement:

1. Loan was to be secured by the company's inventory and accounts receivable.
2. Company was to maintain a debt-to-equity ratio not to exceed 2:1.
3. Company was not to pay dividends without permission from the bank.
4. Monthly instalment payments were to commence July 1, 20X2.

In addition, the company also borrowed, on a short-term basis, substantial amounts from the president of the company just prior to the year-end.

Required:

a. For the purposes of your audit of the financial statements of Broadwall Corporation, what procedures should you employ in examining the described loans? Do not discuss internal control.

b. What financial statement disclosures should you expect to find with respect to the loan from the president?

EP 9
LO.3

Bond Indenture Covenants. The following covenants are extracted from the indenture of a bond issue. Failure

to comply with its terms in any respect automatically advances the due date of the loan to the date of noncompliance (the regular date is 20 years hence). Give any audit steps or reporting requirements you believe should be taken or recognized in connection with each of the following from the indenture:

1. The debtor company shall endeavour to maintain a working capital ratio of 2:1 at all times, and, in any fiscal year following a failure to maintain said ratio, the company shall restrict compensation of officers to a total of $500,000. Officers for this purpose shall include chairman of the board of directors, president, all vice presidents, secretary, and treasurer.
2. The debtor company shall keep all property which is security for this debt insured against loss by fire to the extent of 100 percent of its actual value. Policies of insurance comprising this protection shall be filed with the trustee.
3. The debtor company shall pay all taxes legally assessed against property that is security for this debt within the time provided by law for payment without penalty, and shall deposit receipted tax bills or equally acceptable evidence of payment of same with the trustee.
4. A sinking fund shall be deposited with the trustee by semiannual payments of $300,000, from which the trustee shall, at his discretion, purchase bonds of this issue.

(AICPA adapted)

EP 10
LO.1
and
LO.3

Shareholders' Equity. You are a PA examining the financial statements of Pate Corporation for the year ended December 31. The financial statements and records of Pate Corporation have not been audited by a PA in prior years.

The shareholders' equity section of the balance sheet at December 31 follows:

Shareholders' equity:

Share capital—10,000 no par value shares authorized; 5,000 shares issued and outstanding	$ 50,000
Contributed capital	32,580
Retained earnings	47,320
Total shareholders' equity	$129,900

Pate Corporation was founded in 1992. The corporation has 10 shareholders and serves as its own registrar and transfer agent. There are no capital share subscription contracts in effect.

Required:

a. Prepare the detailed audit program for the examination of the three accounts of the shareholders' equity section of the balance sheet. Organize the audit program under broad financial statement assertions. (Do not include in the audit program the audit of the results of the current year's operations.)

b. After every other figure on the balance sheet has been audited, it may appear that the retained earnings figure is a balancing figure and requires no further audit work. Why don't auditors audit retained earnings as they do the other figures on the balance sheet? Discuss.

(AICPA adapted)

DISCUSSION CASES

. . . .

DC 1   Intercompany and Interpersonal Investment Relations.

LO.3   You have been engaged to audit the financial statements of Hardy Hardware Distributors Inc., as of December 31. In your review of the corporate nonfinancial records, you have found that Hardy Hardware owns 15 percent of the outstanding voting common shares of Hardy Products Corporation. Upon further investigation, you learn that Hardy Products Corporation manufactures a line of hardware goods, 90 percent of which are sold to Hardy Hardware.

Mr. James L. Hardy, president of Hardy Hardware, has supplied you with objective evidence that he personally owns 30 percent of the Hardy Products voting shares and that the remaining 70 percent is owned by Mr. John L. Hardy, his brother and president of Hardy Products. James L. Hardy also owns 20 percent of the voting common shares of Hardy Hardware Distributors. Another 20 percent is held by an estate of which James and John are beneficiaries, and the remaining 60 percent is publicly held.

Hardy Hardware consistently has reported operating profits greater than the industry average. Hardy Products Corporation, however, has a net return on sales of only 1 percent. The Hardy Products investment always has been reported at cost, and no dividends have been paid by the company. During the course of your conversations with the Hardy brothers, you learn that you were appointed as auditor because the brothers had a heated disagreement with the former auditor over the issues of accounting for the Hardy Products investment and the prices at which goods have been sold to Hardy Hardware.

For Discussion

a. Identify the issues in this situation as they relate to (1) conflicts of interest and (2) controlling influences among individuals and corporations.

b. Should the investment in Hardy Products Corporation be accounted for on the equity method?

c. What evidence should the auditor seek with regard to the prices paid by Hardy Hardware for products purchased from Hardy Products Corporation?

d. What information would you consider necessary for adequate disclosure in the financial statements of Hardy Hardware Distributors?

INSTRUCTIONS FOR DISCUSSION CASES DC 2 AND DC 3

These cases are designed like the ones earlier in the chapter. They give the problem, the method, the audit trail, and the amount. Your assignment is to write the audit approach analysis portion of the case, organized around these sections:

Audit objectives: Express the objective in terms of the facts supposedly asserted in financial records, accounts, and statements. (Refer to discussion of assertions in Chapter 6.)

Control procedures relevant to the process: Write a brief explanation of control considerations, especially the kinds of manipulations that may arise from the situation described in the case.

Tests of controls: Write some procedures for getting evidence about existing controls, especially procedures that could discover management manipulations. If there are no controls to test, then there are no procedures to perform; go then to the

next section. A "procedure" should instruct someone about the source(s) of evidence to tap and the work to do.

Tests of details of balance: Write some procedures for getting evidence about the existence, completeness, valuation, ownership, or disclosure assertions identified in your objective section above.

Audit results: Write a short statement about the discovery you expect to accomplish with your procedures.

DC 2   Related Party Transaction "Goodwill."

LO.3   *Problem:* Gulwest Industries, a public company, used a contrived amount of goodwill to overstate assets and disguise a loss on discontinued operations. The company had decided to discontinue its unprofitable line of business of manufacturing sporting ammunition. They had capitalized the start-up cost of the business, and, with its discontinuance, the $7 million deferred cost should have been written off. Instead, Gulwest formed a new corporation named Amron and transferred the sporting ammunition assets (including the $7 million deferred cost) to it in exchange for all the Amron shares. In the Gulwest accounts, the Amron investment was carried at $12.4 million, which was the book value of the assets transferred (including the $7 million deferred cost).

In an agreement with a different public company (Big Industrial), Gulwest and Big created another company (BigShot Ammunition). Gulwest transferred all the Amron assets to BigShot in exchange for (1) common and preferred shares of Big, valued at $2 million, and (2) a note from BigShot in the amount of $3.4 million. Big Industrial thus acquired 100 percent of the shares of BigShot. Gulwest management reasoned that it had "given" Amron shares valued at $12.4 million to receive shares and notes valued at $5.4 million, so the difference must be goodwill. Thus, the Gulwest accounts carried amounts for Big Industrial shares ($2 million), BigShot note receivable ($3.4 million), and goodwill ($7 million).

Audit trail: Gulwest directors included in the minutes an analysis of the sporting ammunition business's lack of profitability. The minutes showed approval of a plan to dispose of the business, but they did not use the words "discontinue the business." The minutes also showed approval of the creation of Amron, the deal with Big Industrial along with the formation of BigShot, and the acceptance of Big's shares and Bigshot's note in connection with the final exchange and merger.

Amount: As explained above, Gulwest avoided reporting a write-off of $7 million by overstating the value of the assets given in exchange for the Big Industrial shares and the BigShot Ammunition note.

DC 3   Related Party Transaction Valuation. Follow the instructions preceding exercise, DC 2. Write the audit approach section of this case.

LO.3

IN PLANE VIEW

Problem: Whiz Corporation overstated the value of shares given in exchange for an airplane and, thereby, understated its loss on disposition of the shares. Income was overstated. Whiz owned 160,000 Wing Company shares, carried on the books as an investment in the amount of $6,250,000. Whiz bought a used airplane from Wing, giving in exchange (1) $480,000 cash and (2) the 160,000 Wing shares. Even though the quoted market value of the Wing shares was $2,520,000, Whiz valued the airplane received at $3,750,000, indicating a share valuation of $3,270,000. Thus, Whiz recognized a loss on disposition of the Wing shares in the amount of $2,980,000.

Whiz justified the airplane valuation with another transaction. On the same day it was purchased, Whiz sold the airplane to the Mexican subsidiary of one of its subsidiary companies (two layers down; but Whiz owned 100 percent of the first subsidiary, which in turn owned 100 percent of the Mexican subsidiary). The Mexican subsidiary paid Whiz with US$25,000 cash and a promissory note for US$3,725,000 (market rate of interest).

Audit trail: The transaction was within the authority of the chief executive officer, and company policy did not require a separate approval by the board of directors. A contract of sale and correspondence with Wing detailing the terms of the transaction were in the files. Likewise, a contract of sale to the Mexican subsidiary, along with a copy of the deposit slip, and a memorandum of the promissory note were on file. The note itself was kept in the company vault. None of the Wing papers cited a specific price for the airplane.

Amount: Whiz overvalued the Wing shares and justified this with a related party transaction with its own subsidiary company. The loss on the disposition of the Wing shares was understated by $750,000.

DC 4 Audit of Long-Term Debt. In Note 12 of its December
LO.3 2001 consolidated financial statements, Bell Canada reported long-term debt outstanding totalling $9,075 million. This amount is made up of 35 separate debentures, with maturity dates ranging from 2001 to 2054, in amounts ranging from $125 to $700 million, with interest rates ranging from 2.7 percent to 11.45 percent. The income statement for the year reports interest expense on this long-term debt of $725 million.[7]

Required:
List the assertions relating to Bell Canada's long-term debt and interest expense. Describe the audit procedures that you would perform to verify the debt and interest expense for 2001.

DC 5 Long-Term Debt Working Paper Review. The long-term debt working paper in Exhibit DC 5–1 was prepared by client personnel and audited by AA, an audit staff assistant, during the calendar year 20X2 audit of Canadian Widgets, Inc., a continuing audit client. You are the engagement supervisor, and your assignment is to review this working paper thoroughly.

Required:
Identify and prepare a list explaining the deficiencies that should be discovered in the supervisory review of the long-term debt working paper.

(AICPA adapted)

DC 6 Audit of Pension Expense. Clark, PA, has been engaged
LO.3 to perform the audit of Kent Ltd.'s financial statements for the current year. Clark is about to commence auditing Kent's employee pension expense. Her preliminary enquiries concerning Kent's pension plan lead her to believe that some of the actuarial computations and assumptions are so complex that they are beyond the competence ordinarily required of an auditor. Clark is considering engaging Lane, an actuary, to assist with this portion of the audit.

Required:
a. What are Clark's responsibilities with respect to the findings of Lane, if she wishes to rely on those findings?
b. Distinguish between the circumstances where it is and is not appropriate for Clark to refer to Lane in the auditor's report.

(CGA-Canada adapted)

DC 7 Board of Directors, Control Role. What is the role of
LO.2 the company's board of directors in controlling management's activities? Why is this particularly important in the financing and investing cycle? How does the board exercise this control and how can the auditor evaluate the board's effectiveness?

DC 8 Derivative Instruments, Controls, and Audit Proce-
LO.2 dures. Barrick Gold, a Canadian public corporation, has
and operations in six main countries. Barrick produces and
LO.3 sells gold, its primary product, as well as byproducts such as silver and copper. These activities expose Barrick to a variety of market risks, such as changes in commodity prices, foreign-currency exchange rates, and interest rates. Barrick has a risk-management program that seeks to reduce the potentially adverse effects of volatility in these markets on its operating results. It uses derivative instruments to mitigate significant unanticipated earnings and cash flow fluctuations that may arise. These instruments include spot deferred sales contracts, options contracts, interest-rate swaps, and foreign-currency forward exchange contracts. Barrick's derivatives activities are subject to the management, direction, and control of its finance committee as part of its oversight of Barrick's investment activities and treasury function. The finance committee, comprised of five members of Barrick's board of directors, including its CEO, approves corporate policy on risk-management objectives, provides guidance on derivative instrument use, reviews internal procedures relating to internal control and valuation of derivative instruments, monitors derivatives activities, and reports to the board. Implementation of these policies is delegated to Barrick's treasury function.[8]

[7] Bell Canada, 2001 Consolidated Financial Statements.
[8] Barrick Gold Corporation, 2001 Consolidated Financial Statements.

EXHIBIT   DC 5-1

CANADIAN WIDGETS, INC.
Working Papers December 31, 20X2

Index	K1	
	Initials	Date
Prepared by	AA	3/22/X2
Approved by		

Lender	Interest Rate	Payment Terms	Collateral	Balance 12/31/X1	20X2 Borrowings		20X2 Reductions		Balance 12/31/X2	Interest paid to	Accrued Interest Payable 12/31/X2	Comments
ⓘ First Commercial Bank	12%	Interest only on 25th of month, principal due in full 1/1/X6, no prepayment penalty	Inventories	$ 50,000 ✓	$300,000 1/31/X2	A	$100,000 6/30/X2	⊕	$ 250,000 CX	12/25/X2	$2,500 NR	Dividend of $80,000 paid 9/2/X2 (W/P N-3) violates a provision of the debt agreement, which thereby permits lender to demand immediate payment; lender has refused to waive this violation.
ⓘ Lender's Capital Corp.	Prime plus 1%	Interest only on last day of month, principal due in full 3/5/X4	2nd Mortgage on Park St. Building	100,000 ✓	50,000	A	—		200,000 C	12/31/02	—	
ⓘ Gigantic Building & Loan Assoc.	12%	$5,000 principal plus interest due on 5th of month, due in full 12/31/X13	1st Mortgage on Park St. Building	720,00 ✓	—		60,000	⊖	660,000 C	12/5/02	5,642 R	
ⓘ J. Lott, majority shareholder	0%	Due in full 12/13/X5	Unsecured	300,000 ✓	—		100,000	N	200,000 C			
				$1,170,000	$350,000		$260,000		$1,310,000 T/B		$8,142 T/B	
				F	F		F		F		F	

Comments column side notes:
- Prime rate was 8% to 9% during the year.
- Reclassification entry for current portion proposed (See RJE-3)
- Borrowed additional $100,000 from J. Lott on 1/7/X3.

Tick-mark legend
F   Readded, foots correctly.
C   Confirmed without exception, W/P K-2.
CX Confirmed with exception, W/P K-3.
NR Does not recompute correctly.
A   Agreed to loan agreement, validated bank deposit ticket, and board of directors authorization, W/P W-7.
⊖   Agreed to cancelled cheques and lender's monthly statements.
N   Agreed to cash disbursements journal and cancelled cheques dated 12/31/X2, clearing 1/8/X3.
T/B Traced to working trial balance.
✓   Agreed to 12/31/01 working papers.
ⓘ   Agreed interest rate, term, and collateral to copy of note and loan agreement.
⊕   Agreed to cancelled cheques and board of director's authorization, W/P W-7.

Interest costs for long-term debt

Interest expense for year	$ 281,333 T/B
Average loan balance outstanding	$1,406,667 R

Five year maturities (for disclosure purposes)

Year end		
12/31/X3	$	60,000
12/31/X4		260,000
12/31/X5		260,000
12/31/X6		310,000
12/31/X7		60,000
Thereafter		360,000
	$1,310,000	
	F	

Overall Conclusions
Long-term debt, accrued interest payable, and interest expense are correct and complete at 12/31/X2.

Required:

a. Identify the control risks in Barrick's derivatives activities and the key controls indicated in the above description. Provide a brief description of specific control procedures that likely are used by Barrick's treasury function to implement the risk-management policies.

b. Describe audit procedures that could be used to test these controls and substantive tests for derivatives activities at Barrick.

DC 9   Audit of Finance Transactions: Internet Business. City Search Inc. (CSI) is a technology company providing local search engine services in the Greater Toronto Area (GTA). CSI combines online search capability with a print directory (City Pages) focusing specifically on GTA websites. Consumers use the search engine and print directory to locate local businesses. Businesses use the search engine and print directory to attract potential customers to their places of business through paid advertisements. CSI began operations in March 20X3 and launched its first sales campaign for print and online search advertisements in June 20X3. Since that time, over 600,000 copies of the City Pages have been distributed to businesses and residences.

The original financing to start CSI came from several wealthy investors who purchased common shares. Additional common shares were issued to the public in late 20X4. These shares initially sold for $2.40, but, during 20X5, the share price fell to less than $1.00. The decline in price is mainly because two of the original investors sold large blocks of shares for whatever they could get as the business was not proving to be as successful as they expected. In early 20X5, the CSI board of directors hired a new president, Bill Dorado, to aggressively promote the CSI directory as a superior directory for local shopping and entertainment searches, and to find innovative ways to increase revenues and CSI's share price.

Businesses that are clients of CSI pay an advertising fee for print and online directory listings that include the business name, address, phone number, type of products/services offered, and website link. CSI will also create a website for clients for a one-time fee that varies depending on the number of pages, links, and type of content the client wants. CSI clients also can purchase banner advertising that pops up when users browse through the online directory. Clients sign a contract for the ad frequency they require, and are billed monthly. Clients can also purchase additional advertising features, such as moving graphics, audio, and a special patented "bull's eye target" (BT) feature, which concentrates the client's ads in directory locations they choose. For example, a home decorating service can sign up for BT service that will cause their ads to be shown whenever users are searching for home products businesses.

In February 20X6, CSI entered into an agreement with Flogg Investments Inc. (FII) in which FII agreed to sell newly issued common shares of the company for total gross proceeds of up to $8 million. The proceeds raised from the new common shares will be used by CSI to support its growth initiatives and for working capital and general corporate purposes, including repayment of loans from shareholders that amounted to approximately $4 million as of December 31, 20X5.

Your firm was recently engaged to audit CSI's 20X5 financial statements. The previous auditors that reported on the 20X3 and 20X4 financial statements have resigned. In communicating with the predecessor auditors, you find out that they resigned due to a change in circumstances that lead to their firm's partners not being independent of CSI. To date, CSI has provided the audit partner of your firm, who is in charge of the audit, with preliminary financial statements (prior to audit) for its most recent year end, December 31, 20X5. You are assigned to plan the audit. From reviewing these preliminary financial statements and talking to Bill Dorado you have learned the following:

1. CSI recognizes revenue on a straight-line basis as each service is provided over the terms of its individual client contracts. The contracts range in length from three months to four years, with the majority lasting for two years. Revenues from contracts ranging from one to four years are deferred and amortized as each service is provided. Upfront direct costs associated with these revenues, including the production costs and selling commissions, are deferred and amortized over the life of each client contract on a straight-line basis. Adjustments are made to deferred revenue and deferred production costs for cancellations at the time they are made. Cancellations are permitted if clients relocate outside the GTA or close their business. CSI management estimates the future value of contracts in progress and compares this value with deferred production costs to ensure these costs are fully recoverable.

2. CSI's revenue is generated mainly through the sale of advertising to local businesses, many of which are small- and medium-sized enterprises (up to 50 employees). In the ordinary course of operations,

CSI may extend credit to these advertisers for advertising purchases on a case-by-case basis, a practice that is common in the industry. CSI management evaluates the collectibility of its trade receivables from its clients based upon a combination of factors, including aging of receivables, on a periodic basis, and records a general allowance for doubtful accounts and bad debt expense. When management becomes aware of a client's inability to meet its financial obligations to CSI (such as in the case of bankruptcy or significant deterioration in the client's financial position and payment experience), a specific bad debt provision is recorded to reduce the client's related trade receivable to its estimated net realizable value.

3. CSI is a registered member of three barter networks serving the GTA marketplace. CSI sells its services and purchases goods and services through these networks. The full market value of a contract sale settled through a barter network is recorded in accounts receivable and deferred revenue at the time of the sale. Revenues are recognized in income on a straight-line basis over the term of the contract. Receivables are reduced when a good or service purchased through a barter network has been received. The president believes this bartering arrangement was an astute business move that "saves us tons of cash and increases revenues at the same time."

4. CSI has signed contracts with two well-known, local retail chains that want to start direct online retailing, and have paid CSI $13.5 million to develop all their online shopping systems, including customer relation management and payment processing. CSI has never completed this type of system before, but has the technical expertise from developing its own systems. CSI expects the contract to be completed by the end of 20X6. CSI recorded $6.5 million of the $13.5 million as revenues in 20X5, deferring the rest to be reported when the work is completed.

5. The president and several top CSI executives have received options to purchase common shares at a fixed price of $1 per share. None of the options have been exercised yet.

6. The BT technology was patented by CSI in early 20X4. In late 20X4 the BT patent was sold for $7 million to LivePatents Inc., which is owned by one of the original CSI investors, who is also a board member of CSI. CSI repurchased the patent in early 20X5 for $10 million, by paying $7 million in cash and issuing a loan payable to LivePatents Inc. for the remainder. The patent is shown on CSI balance sheet at its cost of $10 million, and is being amortized over 17 years.

7. Internal search engine development costs are recorded at cost. The company provides for amortization of these costs at the following annual rates:
   - Directory, research and design costs—30 percent declining-balance basis
   - Internal directory design costs—30 percent declining-balance basis

Required:
Prepare a detailed and complete audit plan that addresses the accounting and other information items noted in this case. Also, suggest any other information that you would want to obtain for planning the audit.

DC 10 Critical Thinking on the Estimation Uncertainty of CAS 540 and Appropriateness of Financial Reporting. Appendix 7D introduced you to critical thinking with accounting risks. What is the relationship between accounting risk and the estimation uncertainty of CAS 540? Using Appendix 7D, show how estimation uncertainty can be reduced via an adjusting entry. Explain how an adjusting entry can reflect the business risk. If the investment is valued as zero, under what conditions should it be disclosed in the notes to the financial statements? Under what conditions is no note disclosure required in order to meet the completeness criterion of the IASB/FASB financial reporting framework? Discuss in class.

APPENDIX 14A

SUBSTANTIVE AUDIT PROGRAMS

· ·

EXHIBIT 14A-1 AUDIT PROGRAM FOR OWNERS' EQUITY

1. Obtain an analysis of owners' equity transactions. Trace additions and reductions to the general ledger.
   a. Vouch additions to directors' minutes and cash receipts.
   b. Vouch reductions to directors' minutes and other supporting documents.
2. Read the directors' minutes for owners' equity authorization. Trace to entries in the accounts. Determine whether related disclosures are adequate.
3. Confirm outstanding common and preferred shares with share registrar agent.
4. Vouch stock option and profit-sharing plan disclosures to contracts and plan documents.
5. Vouch treasury stock transactions to cash receipts and cash disbursement records and to directors' authorization. Inspect treasury stock certificates.
6. When the company keeps its own share records
   a. inspect the share record stubs for certificate numbers and number of shares.
   b. inspect the unissued certificates.
   c. obtain written client representations about the number of shares issued and outstanding.

EXHIBIT 14A-2 AUDIT PROGRAM FOR NOTES AND LOANS PAYABLE AND LONG-TERM DEBT

1. Obtain a schedule of notes payable and other long-term debt (including capitalized lease obligations) showing beginning balances, new notes, repayments, and ending balances. Trace to general ledger accounts.
2. Confirm liabilities with creditor: amount, interest rate, due date, collateral, and other terms. Some of these confirmations may be standard bank confirmations.
3. Review the standard bank confirmation for evidence of assets pledged as collateral and for unrecorded obligations.
4. Read loan agreements for terms and conditions that need to be disclosed and for pledge of assets as collateral.
5. Recalculate the current portion of long-term debt and trace to the trial balance, classified as a current liability.
6. Study lease agreements for indications of need to capitalize leases. Recalculate the capital and operating lease amounts for required disclosures.
7. Recalculate interest expense on debts and trace to the interest expense and accrued interest accounts.
8. Obtain written representations from management concerning notes payable, collateral agreements, and restrictive covenants.

EXHIBIT 14A-3   AUDIT PROGRAM FOR INVESTMENTS AND RELATED ACCOUNTS

A. Investments and related accounts

1. Obtain a schedule of all investments, including purchase and disposition information for the period. Reconcile with investment accounts in the general ledger.
2. Inspect or confirm with a trustee or broker the name, number, identification, interest rate, and face amount (if applicable) of securities held as investments.
3. Vouch the cost of recorded investments to brokers' reports, contracts, cancelled cheques, and other supporting documentation.
4. Vouch recorded sales to brokers' reports and bank deposit slips and recalculate gain or loss on disposition.
5. Recalculate interest income and look up dividend income in a dividend reporting service (such as Moody's or Standard & Poor's annual dividend record).
6. Obtain market values of investments and determine whether any write-down or write-off is necessary. Scan transactions soon after the client's year-end to see if any investments were sold at a loss. Recalculate the unrealized gains and losses required for marketable equity securities disclosures.
7. Read loan agreements and minutes of the board, and enquire of management about pledge of investments as security for loans.
8. Obtain audited financial statements of joint ventures, investee companies (equity method of accounting), subsidiary companies, and other entities in which an investment interest is held. Evaluate indications of significant controlling influence. Determine proper balance sheet classification. Determine appropriate consolidation policy in conformity with accounting principles.
9. Obtain written representations from the client concerning pledge of investment assets as collateral.

B. Intangibles and related expenses

1. Review merger documents for proper calculation of purchased goodwill.
2. Enquire of management about legal status of patents, leases, copyrights, and other intangibles.
3. Review documentation of new patents, copyrights, leaseholds, and franchise agreements.
4. Vouch recorded costs of intangibles to supporting documentation and cancelled cheque(s).
5. Select a sample of recorded R&D expenses. Vouch to supporting documents for evidence of proper classification.
6. Recalculate amortization of copyrights, patents, and other intangibles.

CHAPTER 15

Completing the Audit

In this chapter, we will complete the field work, tying up the loose ends of the audit. The chapter covers the issues, techniques, procedures, and documents that are considered in completing an audit of financial statements. At the completion of the audit, the auditor must provide an opinion that is properly supported by the audit evidence and reflected in the audit files. The audit of the flow accounts that are reported in the income statement, the cash flow statement, and the statement of retained earnings can only be completed once all the period's transactions have been completed at the period end. The audit procedures related to revenue and expense accounts are covered in the first half of the chapter.

Other audit procedures relate to the year-end amounts on the balance sheet. The audit of many of these amounts has already been covered in Chapters 11 through 14. However, there are procedures—such as audit for subsequent events, contingencies, commitments or contractual obligations, overall evaluation of audit results, overall analysis of the financial statements, and presentation and disclosure issues—that still need to be considered after the balances have been audited but before forming a conclusion on whether the financial statements are fairly stated. These and related issues are covered in the second half of this chapter.

LEARNING OBJECTIVES

After completing this chapter, you will be able to:

1 Describe the balance sheet account groups that the major revenue and expense accounts are associated with, as well as the substantive analytical procedures applied to audit revenues and expenses.

2 Outline the overall analytical procedures to be performed at the final stage of the audit, including analysis of the income statement, cash flow statement, financial statement presentation, and disclosures.

③ Explain the purpose of lawyers' letters and how they are used at the completion stage of an audit to identify any contingencies.

④ Explain why written management representations are obtained and what items are generally included in the representation letter, including identification of related parties.

⑤ Given a set of facts and circumstances, classify a subsequent event by type and proper treatment in the financial statements, and outline the implications of the timing of discovery of the event for the auditor's report.

⑥ Explain the final evaluation and conclusion stage of the audit: adjustments resulting from the audit, evaluation of evidence and misstatements to form the audit opinion, and reviews of working paper files.

⑦ Summarize the auditor's communications throughout and at the conclusion of the engagement.

⑧ Apply and integrate the chapter topics to design audit procedures for detecting misstatements due to error or fraud at the overall completion stage of the audit.

The completion stage of the audit can be viewed as the nexus of all the audit work and judgments involved in reaching a final conclusion on whether the financial statements are fairly presented. All members of the audit team are involved in this final stage, but especially so the most experienced members such as the audit **engagement partner** who makes the final decision on the audit opinion. The activities and decisions taken at the completion stage are advanced topics in auditing, but in this introductory text we present them to finish the story of how the audit work supports that final and public product of the audit engagement, the auditor's report. Many of the procedures and decisions we will discuss occur concurrently. Exhibit 15–1 provides an overview, showing these activities as a framework for the discussion in this chapter.

EXHIBIT   15–1   AUDIT COMPLETION ACTIVITIES AND JUDGMENTS

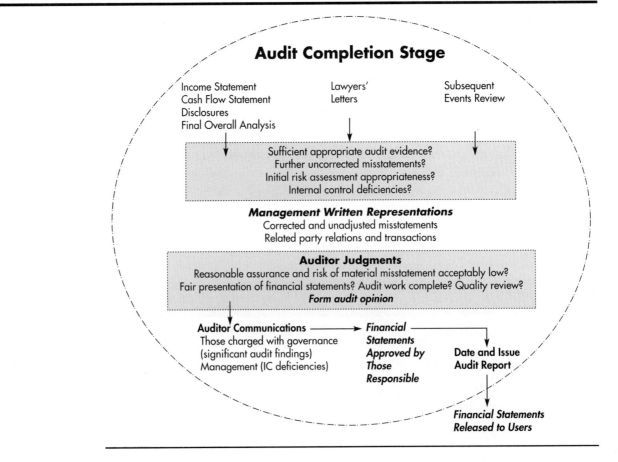

AUDIT OF REVENUES AND EXPENSES

· · · · · · · · · · · · · · · · ·

LEARNING OBJECTIVE

1 Describe the balance sheet account groups that the major revenue and expense accounts are associated with, as well as the substantive analytical procedures applied to audit revenues and expenses.

As the field work nears its end, the major revenue and expense accounts will have been audited in connection with related balance sheet accounts. Next, auditors need to consider other revenue and expense accounts. The broad financial statement assertions are the basis for specific assertions and audit objectives for these accounts. Those typical to the revenue and expense accounts are as follows:

1. Revenue accounts represent all the valid transactions recorded correctly in the proper account, amount, and period.
2. Revenue recognition policies are in accordance with established accounting principles and are consistent with the underlying economic substance of the earnings process.
3. Expense accounts represent all the valid expense transactions recorded correctly in the proper account, amount, and period.
4. Revenues, expenses, and cost of goods sold as well as extraordinary, unusual, or infrequent transactions are adequately classified and disclosed.

Exhibit 15–2 is an audit program for revenues and expenses.

Revenue

The following types of revenue and related topics have been audited, either in whole or in part, prior to the completion stage of the engagement:

Revenue and Related Topics	**Related Account Groups**
Sales and Sales returns	Receivables
Lease revenue	Fixed assets and Receivables
Franchise revenue	Receivables and Intangibles
Dividends and Interest	Receivables and Investments
Gain or Loss on asset disposals	Fixed assets, Receivables, and Investments
Rental revenue	Receivables and Investments
Royalty and Licence revenue	Receivables and Investments
Long-term sales commitments	Revenue and Receivables
Product line reporting	Revenue and Receivables
Accounting policy disclosure	Revenue and Receivables

The working paper's cross-references to the revenue accounts in the trial balance should reflect the extent to which the revenue items have already been audited with the related accounts, and revenues not audited completely should be evident. By reviewing the trial balance cross-references, auditors will verify that all revenue and gain or loss accounts and their amounts are listed.

Analytical procedures can be used as substantive procedures to compare the revenue accounts and amounts with prior-year data and with multiple-year trends, to look for unusual fluctuations. Comparisons with budgets, internal monthly reports and forecasts, and relevant nonfinancial data will determine whether any events need explanation or analysis. The explanations would then be verified by further audit procedures. For example, if management explains that the sales dollar increase is a consequence of a price increase, the auditor can corroborate that by referencing price lists used in the audit tests of sales transactions.

All miscellaneous or other revenue accounts and all clearing accounts with credit balances are analyzed by identifying each important item and amount in the account, followed by document vouching and enquiry to determine whether amounts should be classified elsewhere. All clearing accounts should be eliminated and the amounts classified as revenue, deferred revenue, liabilities, deposits, or contra-assets. Miscellaneous revenue and clearing accounts can harbour accounting errors, since accountants use them for

EXHIBIT 15-2   AUDIT PROGRAM FOR REVENUES AND EXPENSES

REVENUES

1. Obtain auditee's monthly analyses of sales, cost of goods sold, and gross profit by product line, department, division, or location.
   a. Trace amounts to the general ledger.
   b. Compare the analyses with prior years and seek explanations for significant variations.
   c. Determine one or more standard markup percentages and calculate expected gross profits. Enquire for explanations of significant variations compared with actual results.

2. Coordinate procedures for audit of revenue with evidence obtained in other audit programs:

Sales and sales returns	Sales control	Gain, loss on asset disposals	Fixed assets
	Cash receipts control		Investments
	Accounts receivable	Rental revenue	Accounts receivable
Lease revenue	Capital assets		Investments
	Accounts receivable	Royalty and licence revenue	Accounts receivable
Franchise revenue	Accounts receivable		Investments
	Intangibles	Long-term sales commitments	Accounts receivable
Dividends and interest	Accounts receivable		Inventory
	Investments		

3. Scan the revenue accounts for large or unusual items and for debit entries. Vouch any such items to supporting documentation.

4. Obtain written management representations about terms of sales, rights of return, consignments, and unusual or infrequent transactions.

EXPENSES

5. Obtain schedules of expense accounts comparing the current year with one or more prior years.
   a. Trace amounts to the general ledger.
   b. Compare the current expenses to prior years and seek explanations for significant variations.
   c. Be alert to notice significant variations that could indicate failure to defer or accrue expenses.

6. Compare the current expenses with the company budget, if any. Enquire and investigate explanations for significant variances.

7. Coordinate procedures for audit of expenses with evidence obtained in other audit programs:

Purchases, cost of goods sold	Acquisition control	Bad debt expense	Accounts receivable
	Cash disbursement control	Depreciation expense	Fixed assets
	Inventory	Property taxes, insurance	Prepaids and accruals
Inventory valuation losses	Inventory		Fixed assets
Warranty and guarantee expense	Inventory	Lease and rental expense	Fixed assets
	Prepaids and accruals	Repairs and maintenance	Fixed assets
	Accounts payable	Interest expense	Long-term liabilities
Royalty and licence expense	Inventory	Pension and retirement benefits	Liabilities
Marketing and product R&D	Investments		Payroll control
	Intangibles	Payroll and compensation	Payroll control
Investment value losses	Investments	Sales commissions	Payroll control
Rental property expenses	Investments		
Amortization of intangibles	Intangibles		

8. Prepare analyses of sensitive expense accounts, such as legal and professional fees, travel and entertainment, repairs and maintenance, taxes, and others unique to the company. Vouch significant items therein to supporting invoices, contracts, reimbursement forms, tax notices, and the like for proper support and documentation.

9. Scan the expense accounts for large or unusual items and for credit entries. Vouch items to supporting documentation.

10. Obtain written management representations about long-term purchase commitments, contingencies, and unusual or infrequent transactions.

---

unusual items they are not sure how to record; for example, proceeds from sale of assets, insurance premium refunds, and insurance proceeds.

Expenses

Most major expense items will have been audited in connection with other account groupings, but minor expenses may still be unaudited. As a brief review, the following major expenses may have been audited in whole or in part as the audit nears its end:

Expenses	Related Account Groups
Purchases and Cost of goods sold	Inventories
Inventory valuation losses	Inventories
Warranty and Guarantee expenses	Inventories and Liabilities
Royalty and Licence expenses	Inventories and Liabilities
Marketing and Product R&D	Investments and Intangibles

Investment value losses	Investments and Intangibles
Rental property expenses	Investments and Intangibles
Amortization of intangibles	Investments and Intangibles
Bad debt expenses	Receivables
Amortization expenses	Fixed assets
Property taxes and Insurance expenses	Fixed assets and Liabilities
Lease and Rental expenses	Fixed assets
Repairs and Maintenance expenses	Fixed assets and Liabilities
Legal and Professional fees	Liabilities
Interest expense	Liabilities
Pension and Retirement benefits	Liabilities and Payroll
Payroll and Compensation costs	Payroll
Sales commissions	Payroll

As with the revenue accounts mentioned in the previous section, if audit work is complete for expense accounts there will be cross-referencing from the working papers to the trial balance. Some significant expenses may not have been audited completely (such as property tax expense), and some finishing-touch vouching of supporting documents may be required.

Minor expenses, such as office supplies, telephone, utilities, and similar accounts are not audited until late in the engagement. Generally, the dollar amounts in these individual accounts are not material, and there is little relative risk that they will result in misleading financial statements. Auditors usually audit these kinds of accounts with substantive analytical procedures, such as comparing the balances with those of one or more prior periods. The dollar amounts are reviewed for unusual changes (or lack of, if reasons for change are known). Comparing balances and enquiring to get reasonable explanations may be enough to decide whether the amounts are fairly presented.

On the other hand, the questions may suggest a risk of misstatement. If more evidence is needed, auditors may vouch some expenses to supporting documents (invoices and cancelled cheques). If the auditors performed tests of controls on a sample of expenditure transactions in the purchases, payables, and payments process audit program, some of these expense transactions were selected for testing auditee compliance with control objectives (validity, completeness, authorization, accuracy, classification, accounting, and proper period). This evidence should be used. Analytical comparisons with budgets, internal reports and forecasts, and relevant nonfinancial data may also be made. Management may have already explained any variations from the budget, or the auditors may need to investigate variations.

All miscellaneous or other expense accounts and clearing accounts with debit balances should be analyzed by listing each important item on a working paper and vouching it to supporting documents. These may include abandonments of property, items not deductible for tax purposes, and payments that should be classified in other expense accounts. Clearing accounts should be analyzed and the contents classified by type or source and acounted for properly.

Advertising, travel and entertainment expense, and contributions accounts are analyzed in detail as they are particularly sensitive to management policy violations and income tax consequences. They must be documented carefully if they are to stand a Canada Revenue Agency auditor's examination. Questionable items may impact the income tax expense and liability. Minor embezzlements or falsification can be detected by careful auditors. A detailed audit of expense account payments may be of greater interest to the efficiency-minded internal auditor than to the independent auditor. The independent auditors are concerned that the paid-out amount is fairly presented, regardless of whether employees did overstate their expenses. Evidence of expense account falsification may be presented to management, but the overpayments are an expense of the business and need to be included in its financial statements.

1   Certain revenue and expense accounts usually are audited in conjunction with related balance sheet accounts. List the most likely related balance sheet accounts for these revenue and expense accounts: lease revenue, franchise revenue, royalty and licence revenue, amortization expense, repairs and maintenance expense, and interest expense.

2   Why are many of the revenue and expense accounts audited by analytical procedures only?

3   What procedures can be applied to audit minor expense accounts?

OVERALL ANALYTICAL PROCEDURES

LEARNING OBJECTIVE

2 Outline the overall analytical procedures to be performed at the final stage of the audit, including analysis of the income statement, cash flow statement, financial statement presentation, and disclosures.

Analytical procedures are used at these points during the audit:

1. for risk assessment at the planning stage (discussed in Chapter 6),

2. as a substantive test procedure (discussed in Chapter 8), and

3. during the overall evaluation of the financial statements at the end of the audit.

Auditing standards require the auditor to design and perform overall analytical procedures at the completion stage of the audit to help form a conclusion about whether the financial statements are a fair representation of what the auditors learned in the course of the audit (CAS 520 [5301]). Using analytical procedures to assess the reasonableness of reported results after most of the audit work has been performed is an effective means of obtaining assurance.

The results of the overall analytical procedures help the auditor reach reasonable conclusions to base the auditor's opinion on. The procedures are similar to those for risk assessment; for example, comparing financial and nonfinancial data and examining ratios and trends for unexpected relationships. However, by performing this analysis at a late stage in the audit, the auditors have the benefit of considerable knowledge about the auditee's business and a better basis on which to form expectations about the financial statement relationships, increasing their chances of noticing something out of line. This analysis can be sharper and more focused on finding potential misstatements than the preliminary risk assessment was. It may identify a risk of material misstatement not recognized at the early stage, in which case the planned audit procedures are revised to address this new risk.

The cash flow statement is prepared after the balance sheet and income statement are finalized, so it is audited at the completion stage of the audit. Verifying the cash flow statement explains the major changes in balance sheet accounts and thus provides analytical evidence that the financial statement relations are properly presented. It also bridges the balance sheet and income statement by explaining the relationship between net income and operating cash flow when the indirect method is used. These alternative presentations of the financial performance and changes in financial position should be evaluated by the auditors in relation to their knowledge of the year's activity. For example, a large financing inflow from new debt should match up with disclosure about the new loan. Also, many items of the cash flow will tie into audits of other balances; for example, cash flows for both additions to and proceeds from disposal of fixed assets should tie in to audit working paper information on fixed assets.

Auditors also verify the information presented in the statement of changes in retained earnings and shareholders' equity at this stage, to ascertain that account classifications, aggregations, and summarizations are comparable to those of the prior year in an assessment of the consistency of the financial reporting and the overall adequacy of disclosures. Certain other tests done later in the engagement, such as the search for contingent liabilities, commitments, and guarantees, will result in information that requires disclosure but no amounts recognized in the balance sheet. Auditors may use a checklist to ensure all disclosures required by GAAP are considered. An example of such a checklist is shown in the box that follows.

FINANCIAL STATEMENT PRESENTATION AND DISCLOSURE CHECKLIST

Auditee: _____

Period ended: _____

This checklist is to be used to assess whether the financial statements and the notes include all required disclosures for fair presentation.

Consider:	Response	File reference
Do the notes disclose, where relevant, all specific disclosure requirements, as per GAAP or applicable financial reporting framework, such as the following: • Contingent liabilities, commitments, guarantees • Accounting changes • Significant estimates • Going-concern considerations • Related party transactions • Measurement uncertainties • Restatements • Impaired assets • Other required information needed for fair presentation Do the notes accurately describe the policies used in preparing the financial statements? Is the comparative information provided appropriate? Are the financial statements and notes correctly cross-referenced? Do all events, transactions, and other information presented and disclosed in the financial statements pertain to the entity? Are the disclosures complete, based on the audit findings? Conclusion on appropriateness and completeness of overall financial statement presentation and disclosure: _____ _____ Prepared by/ Date: Reviewed by/ Date:		

Unusual Transactions

Significant audit evidence and reporting problems can arise if management transactions artificially create earnings. Generally, these transactions will run through a complicated structure of subsidiaries, affiliates, and related parties, and they involve large amounts of revenue. While transactions may not be concealed, there might be certain guarantees that management has not revealed to the auditors. The transactions may be carefully timed to provide the most favourable income result.

It is difficult to characterize these unusual transactions as they vary so widely. Controversies have arisen in the past over revenue recognized on bundled sales of hardware, software, and technology services; on the construction percentage-of-completion method; on sales of assets at inflated prices to management-controlled dummy corporations; on sales of real estate to independent parties with whom the seller later associates for development of the property (making guarantees on indemnification for losses); and on disclosure of revenues by source. These revenue issues pose a combination of evidence-gathering and reporting-disclosure problems. Three illustrations of such problems are given in the text box that follows.

UNUSUAL REVENUE TRANSACTIONS

MERGER

National Fried Chicken Inc., a large fast-food franchiser, began negotiations in August to purchase Provincial Hot Dog Company, a smaller convenience food chain. At August 1, 20X6, Provincial's net worth was $7 million, and National proposed to pay $8 million cash for all the outstanding shares. In June 20X7, the merger was consummated and National paid $8 million, even though Provincial's net worth had dropped to $6 million by that time. Consistent with prior years, Provincial lost $1 million in the 10 months ended June 1, 20X7, after showing a net profit of $1.5 million for June and July 20X7. At June 1, 20X7, the fair value of Provincial's net assets was $6 million, and National accounted for the acquisition as a purchase, recording $2 million goodwill. National proposed to show in consolidated financial statements the $1.5 million of post-acquisition income.

Audit Resolution. The auditors discovered that the purchase price was basically set at 16 times expected earnings and that management had carefully chosen the consummation date in order to maximize goodwill (and reportable net income in fiscal 20X7). The auditors required that $1 million of goodwill be treated as a goodwill impairment in the year ended July 31, 20X7, so that bottom-line income would be $500,000.

REAL ESTATE DEAL

In August, a company sold three real estate properties to BMC for $5,399,000 and recognized profit of $550,000. The agreement covering the sale committed the company to use its best efforts to obtain permanent financing and to pay underwriting costs for BMC. The agreement also provided BMC with an absolute guarantee against loss from ownership and a commitment by the company to complete construction of the properties.

Audit Resolution. The auditors determined that the terms of this agreement made the recognition of profit improper because the company had not shifted the risk of loss to BMC.

REAL ESTATE DEVELOPMENT, STRINGS ATTACHED

In December 20X6, Black Company sold one half of a tract of undeveloped land to Red Company in an apparent arms-length transaction. The portion sold had a book value of $1.5 million, and Red Company paid $2.5 million in cash. Red Company planned to build and sell apartment houses on the acquired land. In January 20X7, Black and Red formed a new joint venture to develop the entire tract. The two companies formed a partnership, each contributing its one half of the total tract of land. They agreed to share equally in future capital requirements and profits or losses.

Audit Resolution. The auditor discovered that Black and Red were both controlled by the same person. The $1 million profit from the sale was not recognized as income in Black's 20X6 financial statements, and Black's investment in the joint venture was valued at $1.5 million.

REVIEW CHECKPOINTS

4   How might usual revenue transactions cause significant audit evidence and reporting problems?

5   How are analytical procedures used for overall evaluation of the financial statements at the final stage of the audit? How does the use of analysis at this stage differ from its use at the risk assessment stage? at the substantive evidence gathering stage?

6   What procedures can be used to verify the accuracy of the information presented in the cash flow statement?

Sequencing of Audit Events

At this point it is helpful to note the sequencing of audit events. Based on the organization of the audit, some audit work might be done at an interim period sometime before the balance sheet date, followed by completion of the work on the exact balance sheet date. Often audit work is done months before the balance sheet date, with auditors working at the auditee's offices for a time, leaving, and then returning after the balance sheet date for the year-end field work. At year-end the auditor receives the final unaudited financial statements (or trial balance) prepared by the auditee personnel and can start where the interim work left off, completing the work on control risk assessment and audit of balances. Certain procedures, however, such as lawyers' letters and written management representation letters, discussed below, are always left to the final stages of the audit work.

LAWYER'S LETTERS TO DETECT CONTINGENCIES

LEARNING OBJECTIVE

3 Explain the purpose of lawyers' letters and how they are used at the completion stage of an audit to identify any contingencies.

The audit procedures of obtaining the lawyer's letter, and the written management representations discussed in this learning objective, are performed toward the end of the audit work. These written communications are dated at the audit report date because the auditors are responsible until that date for determining whether important events occurring after the balance sheet date are properly entered in the accounts or disclosed in the financial statement notes.

Communication with Auditee's Lawyer

The lawyer's letter is one of the most important audit confirmations. CAS 501 (6560) requires auditors to perform procedures identifying litigation and claims against the auditee, and, where there is a risk of material misstatement, auditors must communicate directly with the auditee's legal counsel. This is done by an enquiry letter from management to the lawyer, with the lawyer's response going directly from the lawyer to the auditor. The objective is to provide audit evidence about any potentially material litigation or claims against the auditee and to determine if management's estimates of the possible costs of these are reasonable. Exhibit 15–3.1 is an example of an enquiry letter. The auditor asks management to send enquiry letters to all lawyers who performed work for the auditee during the period under audit. This request informs the lawyer that their client, the auditee, is waiving the privilege of communications between lawyer and client, and gives the lawyer permission to give information to the auditors.

As implied by the letter in Exhibit 15–3.1, questions about contingencies, litigations, claims, and assessments should be directed to both legal counsel and management because an auditor has the right to expect to be informed by management about all material contingent liabilities. Audit procedures useful in this regard include the following:

- Enquire and discuss with management the policies and procedures for identifying, evaluating, and accounting for litigation, claims, and assessments.

- Obtain from management a description and evaluation of litigation, claims, and assessments.

EXHIBIT 15-3.1 SAMPLE LAWYER LETTERS[1]

Version 1—When there are claims or possible claims to be listed
(On client letterhead)

(To law firm)

(Date)

Dear Sir(s):

In connection with the preparation and audit of our financial statements for the fiscal period ended (date) (which include the accounts of the following entities)[2], we have made the following evaluations of claims and possible claims with respect to which your firm's advice or representation has been sought:

Description
(name of entity, name of other party, nature, amount claimed and current status)

Evaluation
(Indicate likelihood of loss (or gain) and estimated amount of ultimate loss (or gain), if any; or indicate that likelihood is not determinable or amount is not reasonably estimable.)

Would you please advise us, as of (effective date of response), on the following points:

(a) Are the claims and possible claims properly described?

(b) Do you consider that our evaluations are reasonable?

(c) Are you aware of any claims not listed above which are outstanding? If so, please include in your response letter the names of the parties and the amount claimed.

This enquiry is made in accordance with the Joint Policy Statement of January 1978 approved by The Canadian Bar Association and the Auditing and Assurance Standards Board of the Canadian Institute of Chartered Accountants.

Please address your reply, marked "Privileged and Confidential," to this company and send a signed copy of the reply directly to our auditor, (name and address of auditor).

Yours truly,

c.c. (name of auditor)

---

[1] The letter should be appropriately modified if the client advises that certain matters have been excluded in accordance with paragraph 12 of the Joint Policy Statement.

[2] Delete if inapplicable. If applicable, refer to paragraph 11 re signing of the enquiry letter.

Source: © CICA Handbook, CAS 501 (6560).

- Examine documents in the auditee's possession concerning litigation, claims, and assessments, including correspondence and invoices from lawyers.
- Obtain assurance from management that it has disclosed all material unasserted claims that the lawyer has advised them might result in litigation.
- Read minutes of meetings of shareholders, directors, and appropriate committees. Read contracts, loan agreements, leases, and correspondence from taxing or other governmental agencies.
- Obtain information concerning guarantees from bank confirmations.

The enquiry letter is a major means of learning about material contingencies. Even so, a devious or forgetful management or a careless lawyer may fail to tell the auditor of some important factor or development. Auditors have to be alert and sensitive to all possible contingencies so that they can ask the right questions at the right time. Auditors have a natural tendency to look out for adverse contingencies, but potentially favourable events should also be investigated and disclosed (such as the contingency of litigation for damages wherein the auditee is the plaintiff). If management or its lawyers fail to provide adequate information about lawsuit contingencies, the auditor should consider whether this represents a scope limitation on the audit. A serious audit scope limitation requires a qualification in the audit report or a disclaimer of opinion.

Auditors face other challenges when it comes to using lawyers' responses to audit contingency disclosures. The following box illustrates the kinds of wording lawyers provide in their letters.

INTERPRETING THE LAWYERS' LETTERS

Lawyers take great care in forming responses to auditees' requests for information to be transmitted to auditors. This care causes problems of interpretation for auditors. The difficulty arises over lawyers' desire to preserve lawyer-client confidentiality yet cooperate with auditors and the financial reporting process that seeks full disclosure.

The Canadian Bar Association policy statement observes that "[i]t is in the public interest that the confidentiality of lawyer-client communications be maintained."[1] Accordingly, any claims omitted from the enquiry letter will not be referred to by the law firm in the response letter.

Consequently, lawyers' responses to auditors may contain vague and ambiguous wording. Auditors need to determine whether a contingency is "likely, unlikely, or not determinable."[2] Although there are no comparable Canadian guidelines, in the United States the following lawyer responses can be properly interpreted to mean "remote," even though the word is not used:

- We are of the opinion that this action will not result in any liability to the company.
- It is our opinion that the possible liability to the company in this proceeding is nominal in amount.
- We believe the company will be able to defend this action successfully. We believe that the plaintiff's case against this company is without merit.
- Based on the facts known to us, after a full investigation, it is our opinion that no liability will be established against the company in these suits.

However, auditors should view the following response phrases as unclear, or providing no information, about the probable, reasonably possible, or remote likelihood of an unfavourable outcome for a litigation contingency:[3]

- We believe the plaintiff will have serious problems establishing the company's liability; nevertheless, if the plaintiff is successful, the damage award may be substantial.
- It is our opinion the company will be able to assert meritorious defences. ["Meritorious," in lawyer language, apparently means that the judge will not summarily throw out the defences.]
- We believe the lawsuit can be settled for less than the damages claimed.
- We are unable to express an opinion on the merits of the litigation, but the company believes there is absolutely no merit.
- In our opinion the company has a substantial chance of prevailing. ["Substantial chance," "reasonable opportunity," and similar phrases indicate uncertainty of success in a defence.]

Exhibit 15–3.2 shows an example of a lawyer's response letter.

[1] *CICA Handbook*, CAS 501, Appendix: "Joint Policy Statement Concerning Communications with Law Firms."
[2] Ibid., paragraph 3290.15.
[3] Adapted from AU 9337.

R E V I E W
C H E C K P O I N T S

7 The following was included in a letter auditors received from the auditee's lawyers, in response to a letter sent to them that was similar to Exhibit 15–3.2: "Several agreements and contracts to which the company is a party are not covered by this response since we have not advised or been consulted in their regard." How might the auditor's report be affected by that statement in the letter regarding a pending lawsuit against the auditee? Explain.

8 In addition to the lawyer's letter, what other procedures can be used to gather evidence regarding contingencies?

EXHIBIT 15-3.2   SAMPLE LAWYER'S RESPONSE LETTER

(On law firm letterhead)

Privileged and Confidential

(To auditee)

(Date – as close as possible to audit report date)

Dear Sir(s):

In connection with the preparation and audit of your financial statements for fiscal period ended (date), in response to your enquiries regarding the following claim and possible claim with respect to which our firm's advice of representation has been sought:

Description	Evaluation
A product liability claim has be made by a customer who was permanently injured while using a product purchased from the company.	Likelihood is not determinable and amount of claim is not likely to be significant.

We advise that, as of (effective date of response), the above claim is properly described, and the evaluation of the likehood of loss and amount of claim are reasonable.

(c) Are you aware of any claims not listed above which are outstanding? If so, please include in your response letter the names of the parties and the amounts claimed.

This response is made in accordance with the Joint Policy Statement of January 1978 approved by The Canadian Bar Association and the Auditing and Assurance Standards Board of the Canadian Institute of Chartered Accountants.

As requested, a signed copy of the reply has been sent directly to your auditor, (name and address of auditor).

Yours truly,

Lawyer representing auditee in the claim

c.c. (name of auditor)

Source: © *CICA Handbook*, section 6560.A, schedule A.

9   Why might companies and auditors experience difficulty making appropriate disclosures about litigation contingencies?

MANAGEMENT'S WRITTEN REPRESENTATIONS

LEARNING OBJECTIVE

4 Explain why written management representations are obtained and what items are generally included in the representation letter, including identification of related parties.

Management responds to numerous auditor enquiries during the course of an audit. These representations are very important components of audit evidence, but they are not sufficient by themselves. As much as possible, auditors should corroborate management representations with evidence from additional procedures.

Auditors should also obtain written representations from management on matters of audit importance (CAS 580 [5370]). These representations exist as a letter on the auditee's letterhead, addressed to the auditor, signed by responsible officers (normally the chief executive officer, chief financial officer, and other appropriate managers), and dated as of the date of the auditor's report. The letter, referred to as the **management representation letter,** covers events and representations running beyond the balance sheet date up to the audit report date.

In most cases, written management representations are assertions like the ones already in the financial statements, but perhaps more detailed. They are not sufficient evidence for auditors and not a good defence against criticism for failing to perform audit procedures independently. ("Management told us in writing that the inventory costing method was FIFO and adequate allowance for obsolescence was provided" is not a good excuse for failing to get the evidence from the records and other sources!) However, in some cases these are the only evidence about important matters of management intent; for example, (1) "We will discontinue the parachute manufacturing business, wind down the operations, and sell the remaining assets" (i.e., accounting for discontinued operations); and (2) "We will exercise our option to refinance the maturing debt on a long-term basis" (i.e., classifying maturing debt as long-term).

A primary purpose of the management representation letter is to impress upon the management its responsibility for the financial statements. They also may establish an auditor's defences against questions of management integrity: a management lie to the auditors will be captured in writing in the letter. Auditors draft the management representation letter to be prepared on the auditee's letterhead paper for signature by company representatives. This draft is reviewed with senior auditee personnel, and then finalized.

Auditing standards[1] indicate that the following written representations must be obtained in all audits:

- That management has fulfilled its responsibility for the preparation and presentation of the financial statements in accordance with the applicable financial reporting framework, as set out in the terms of the audit engagement
- That management has provided the auditor with all relevant information to conduct the audit engagement, as agreed in the terms of engagement
- That all transactions have been recorded and are reflected in the financial statements

The auditor may consider it necessary to get other written representations in some circumstances. These other representations could include the following:

- That the selection and application of accounting policies are appropriate
- That the financial statements have appropriately recognized, measured, presented, or disclosed
  - plans or intentions that may affect the carrying value or classification of assets and liabilities;
  - liabilities, both actual and contingent;
  - title to, or control over assets, liens or encumbrances on assets, and assets pledged as collateral; and
  - aspects of laws, regulations, and contractual agreements that may affect the financial statements, including noncompliance

In situations of fraud risk or known frauds, going concern uncertainty, correction of material misstatements uncovered in the audit, material estimates, related parties, and subsequent events, other written representations may be required. Several other representations may be relevant in particular businesses or industries; for example, environmental liabilities, derivative financial instruments, the appropriateness of accounting policies for complex areas of accounting, and areas involving management's judgment and estimates, such as revenue recognition, fair value measurements, transfers of receivables, hedging relationships, and consolidation of variable interest entities.

The representation letter provides management with a summary of the uncorrected financial statement misstatements found by the auditor during the audit, and it obtains management's representation of its belief that these are immaterial to the financial statements—a summary of such items is included in or attached to the letter. Management representations are also required for auditors involved with prospectuses[2] and for review engagements.[3] A written representation letter is shown in Exhibit 15–4.

Audit of Related Party Transactions

A representation letter answers these key questions: Has the auditee identified all its related parties to the auditor? and Has the auditee been involved in any related party transactions?

---

[1] *CICA Handbook,* CAS 580 (5370).
[2] *CICA Handbook,* section 7110.
[3] *CICA Handbook,* section 8200.

EXHIBIT 15-4   ILLUSTRATIVE WRITTEN REPRESENTATION LETTER

(Auditee Letterhead)

(To Auditor)   (Date)

This representation letter is provided in connection with your audit of the financial statements of ABC Company for the year ended December 31, 20XX for the purpose of expressing an opinion as to whether the financial statements are presented fairly, in all material respects, in accordance with International Financial Reporting Standards.

We confirm that:

Financial Statements
- We have fulfilled our responsibilities for the preparation and presentation of the financial statements as set out in the terms of the audit engagement dated [insert date] and, in particular, the financial statements are fairly presented in accordance with International Financial Reporting Standards.
- Significant assumptions used by us in making accounting estimates, including those measured at fair value, are reasonable.
- Related party relationships and transactions have been appropriately accounted for and disclosed in accordance with the requirements of International Financial Reporting Standards.
- All events subsequent to the date of the financial statements and for which International Financial Reporting Standards require adjustment or disclosure have been adjusted or disclosed.
- The effects of uncorrected misstatements are immaterial, both individually and in the aggregate, to the financial statements as a whole. A list of the uncorrected misstatements is attached to the representation letter.
- [Any other matters that the auditor may consider appropriate, such as whether financial statements have appropriately recognized, measured, presented, or disclosed:
  - Plans or intentions that may affect the carrying value or classification of assets and liabilities;
  - Liabilities, both actual and contingent;
  - Title to, or control over, assets, and the liens or encumbrances on assets, and assets pledged as collateral; and
  - Aspects of laws, regulations, and contractual agreements that may affect the financial statements, including noncompliance.
  - A going concern uncertainty, if any.]

Information Provided
- We have provided you with:
  - All information, such as records and documentation, and other matters that are relevant to the preparation and presentation of the financial statements;
  - Additional information that you have requested from us; and
  - Unrestricted access to those within the entity.
- All transactions have been recorded in the accounting records and are reflected in the financial statements.
- We have disclosed to you the results of our assessment of the risk that the financial statements may be materially misstated as a result of fraud.
- We have disclosed to you all information in relation to fraud or suspected fraud that we are aware of and that affects the entity and involves:
  - Management;
  - Employees who have significant roles in internal control; or
  - Others where the fraud could have a material effect on the financial statements.
- We have disclosed to you all information in relation to allegations of fraud, or suspected fraud, affecting the entity's financial statements communicated by employees, former employees, analysts, regulators, or others.
- We have disclosed to you all known actual or possible noncompliance with laws and regulations whose effects should be considered when preparing financial statements.
- We have disclosed to you the identity of the entity's related parties and all the related party relationships and transactions of which we are aware.
- [Any other matters that the auditor may consider necessary.]

{signed}   {signed}

Auditee CEO   Auditee CFO

Source: Adapted from CAS 580.

ROOM FOR IMPROVEMENT IN LITIGATION CONTINGENCY DISCLOSURES

American research on 126 lawsuits lost by public companies examined the disclosures about the suits in prior years' financial statements. The contingencies involved material, uninsured losses. Subsequent failure in the defence indicates the contingencies to have been "reasonably possible," calling for FASB 5 (comparable to section 3290) disclosure. For the 126 cases, wide disclosure diversity existed. As indicated in the table below, the majority of cases carried satisfactory disclosure while the lawsuits were in progress, but a significant minority did not.

	Number	Percent
Satisfactory disclosure:		
Disclosure conceded the possibility of liability	60	47.6%
Disclosure included an estimate of the related liability	5	4.0
Disclosure along with booked liability	7	5.6
Total	72	57.2%
Unsatisfactory disclosure:		
No mention of the litigation	45	35.7%
Litigation mentioned but with a strong disclaimer of liability	9	7.1
Total	54	42.8%

Among the types of lawsuits covered in the 126 cases, the ones dealing with securities law violations had the highest frequency of satisfactory disclosure (8 out of 11, or 73 percent). The ones dealing with fraud or misrepresentation had the lowest frequency of satisfactory disclosure (2 out of 8, or 25 percent). Speculations about the reasons company officials and lawyers have difficulty providing auditors with appropriate information include:

- High level of emotion surrounding the lawsuits.
- Fear that financial statement disclosure will be construed as an admission of guilt.
- The legal framework for evaluating litigation outcomes varies significantly from the framework used by auditors.
- More appropriate channels exist for disclosure of litigation information (e.g., business press).
- FASB 5 disclosure requirements are viewed as only a guide and, therefore, need not be taken literally.

Source: "Disclosure of Litigation Contingencies Faulted," *Journal of Accountancy*, July 1990, pp. 15–16. Copyright 1990. American Institute of Certified Public Accountants, Inc. All rights reserved. Used with permission.

(see Exhibit 15–4). Auditors have a responsibility to obtain reasonable assurance that related parties have been identified and that there is appropriate disclosure with such parties in the financial statements.[4] Related parties exist when one party has the ability to exercise either control or joint control, directly or indirectly, or has significant influence over the other. Parties are related when they are subject to common control, joint control, or common significant influence. Related parties could include management and immediate family members. Related party transactions are particularly important in Canada because of the high concentration of corporate ownership.

The problem with related party transactions is that, since they are not arm's length, they may not reflect the normal terms of trade that occur with most transactions with external parties. *CICA Handbook* section 3840 provides the measurement and disclosure standards for

[4] CAS 550 (6010).

related party transactions of profit-oriented enterprises. The auditor's main problem is identifying these transactions. Management enquiry is the main procedure (as in Exhibit 15–4), but others include reading the minutes of meetings of shareholders, directors, and executive and audit committees, as well as acquiring a general knowledge of the auditee's business.[5]

Unusual transactions might point to undisclosed relationships. The team discussions provide a good opportunity to ensure that the audit team is aware of related party relationships and transactions that could leave the financial statements susceptible to fraud or error. Some indications of the existence of undisclosed related parties are as a follows:

- abnormal terms of trade, such as unusually high or low selling prices, interest rates, and repayment terms;
- large, unusual transactions, particularly those recognized at or near the balance sheet date; and
- transactions that lack an apparent business reason, or where the legal form of the transactions seems to conceal its actual economic substance.

In addition to the auditor's business risk assessment, the following further procedures can help to identify the existence of related party transactions:[6]

- Review prior-year working papers for related party transactions.
- Review the entity's procedures for identifying related parties.
- Obtain written representation from management concerning identification and adequacy of related party disclosures.

Having identified related party transactions, the auditor can perform the following substantive procedures:

- Confirm the terms and amounts of the transactions with the related parties.
- Inspect evidence in possession of the related party.
- Confirm or discuss information with persons associated with the transactions, such as banks, lawyers, guarantors, and agents.

CAS 550 also requires the auditor to communicate significant matters identified during the audit that concern related party transactions or relationships to those charged with governance.

The next box illustrates how related party transactions can be used to significantly alter the financial statements. The illustration is based on an actual Canadian company trading on NASDAQ and the TSX.

Turning Expenses into Revenues

CB is a major biotechnology company in Canada that did not like the effect that expensing R&D had on its earnings. So, CB proceeded to create a related entity, CC, to which it made a capital contribution of $100 million. A series of share exchanges involving shares of both companies had the net effect of a debit to retained earnings and a credit to cash for $100 million on CB's financial statements. An agreement was then reached in which CC paid CB a fee in exchange for a technology licence. CC used the $100 million it had received from CB to repay CB for CB's R&D costs. CB accounted for the amounts received from CC as revenue.

In the words of CB's chairman of the Board, "This initiative will enable us to leverage our investment in R&D and pursue the ongoing development of exciting new products, without unduly affecting the company's baseline earnings."

---

[5] CAS 550 (6010), CAS 315 (5141).
[6] CAS 550 (6010).

10 What is the purpose of a management representation letter?

11 What representations would you request that management make in the representation letter with respect to related parties? receivables? inventories? minutes of meetings? subsequent events?

12 Why are written management representations and lawyers' letters obtained at the final stage of the audit and dated as close as possible to the audit report date?

EVENTS SUBSEQUENT TO THE BALANCE SHEET DATE

LEARNING OBJECTIVE

5 Given a set of facts and circumstances, classify a subsequent event by type and proper treatment in the financial statements, and outline the implications of the timing of discovery of the event for the auditor's report.

Material events that occur after the balance sheet date may require adjustments to or disclosures in the financial statements. Auditors (and management) are responsible for gathering evidence on these subsequent events and evaluating how they should be reflected in the financial statements (CAS 560 [5405]). Their impact on the audit report depends on whether they are discovered before or after the audit report date. This section first describes the two different types of subsequents that can occur, and then considers how the timing of discovery affects how the auditor addresses them in the audit report.

Two Types of Subsequent Events

Material subsequent events are classified into two types, which are treated differently in the financial statements. **Type I** are those that require adjustment of the dollar amounts in the financial statements and the addition of any related disclosure in the notes, while **Type II** adjustments require disclosure, and sometimes *pro forma* financial statements.

Type I: Adjustment of Financial Statement Amounts Required

Subsequent events that provide new information regarding financial conditions that existed at the date of the balance sheet affect the numbers on it. Amounts in the financial statements for the period under audit need to be changed as a result. The following are examples of Type I subsequent events:

- a loss on uncollectible trade accounts receivable resulting from the bankruptcy of a major customer (the customer's deteriorating financial condition existed prior to the balance sheet date), and

- litigation settled for an amount different than was estimated (the litigation had taken place prior to the balance sheet date).

Type II: No Adjustment of Financial Statements, but Disclosure Required

Subsequent events involving conditions arising after the balance sheet date are referred to as Type II. Recall that the auditor's responsibility for adequate disclosure runs to the audit report date. Consequently, even for events occurring after the balance sheet date, and thus not requiring financial statement adjustment as Type I events do, auditors consider their importance to users and then may insist on a disclosure. Type II events may be significant enough that disclosure is necessary to keep the financial statements from being misleading. Disclosure is normally in the form of a narrative note, but occasionally an event is so significant that the best disclosure is ***pro forma* financial data**—presentation of the financial statements "as if" the event had occurred on the date of the balance sheet. Such *pro forma* data are given in a note disclosure. For example, in addition to historical financial statements, *pro forma* financial data may be the best way to show the effect of a business purchase or other merger, or the sale of a major portion of assets.

Examples of Type II subsequent events are as follows:

- loss on an uncollectible trade receivable resulting from a customer's fire or flood loss subsequent to the balance sheet date (in contrast to a customer's slow decline into bankruptcy cited as a Type I event above),

- issue of bonds payable or share capital,
- settlement of litigation when the event giving rise to the claim took place subsequent to the balance sheet date, and
- loss of plant or inventories as a result of fire or flood.

Retroactive recognition of the effect of stock dividends and splits is an exception covered in the box following. The issue here is timely and informative communication to financial statement users; the stock dividend or split will have been completed by the time the financial statements reach users, and to report financial data as if they had not occurred might be considered misleading.

SUBSEQUENT EVENT STOCK SPLIT

The company approved on February 15 a two-for-one stock split to be effective on that date. The fiscal year-end was the previous December 31, and the financial statements as of December 31 showed 50 million shares authorized, 10 million shares issued and outstanding, and earnings per share of $3.

Audit Resolution. Note disclosure was made of the split and of the relevant dates. The equity section of the balance sheet showed 100 million shares authorized, 20 million shares issued and outstanding. The income statement reported earnings per share of $1.50. Earnings per share of prior years were adjusted accordingly. The note disclosed comparative earnings per share on the predividend shares. The audit report was dual dated, with February 1 as the report date except for the note disclosure, which was dated February 15.

Subsequent Events and the Audit Report

To understand the impact of subsequent events on the audit report, consider three possible scenarios and the responsibilities that follow from them.

These three situations and their different impact on the audit and audit report are illustrated in a timeline format in Exhibit 15–5.

Timing of subsequent event	Impact on audit and report
1. Events that occurred **between the date of the financial statements and the date of the auditor's report**	Auditors are responsible for actively searching for these to ensure they are properly reflected in the financial statements. Procedures to search for subsequent events are part of the audit plan.
2. Facts the auditor learns of **after the date of the auditor's report but before the date the financial statements are issued**	Auditors are responsible for making sure these are properly reflected in the financial statements. If it is appropriate to amend the financial statements just to reflect this specific event, the auditor updates the report by dual dating it, but is not required to extend the search for other possible subsequent events up to the second date.
3. Facts the auditor becomes aware of **after the financial statements and audit report have been issued**	If the auditors would have amended the auditor's report had the facts been known, they must determine with management whether financial statements need amendment. If so, and management amends, the auditor must extend procedures and issue a new audit report that emphasizes reasons for amended financial statements. If management does not amend, the auditor takes steps to prevent users from relying on the audit report.

EXHIBIT 15-5   TIMELINE FOR AUDITOR'S SUBSEQUENT EVENTS RESPONSIBILITIES

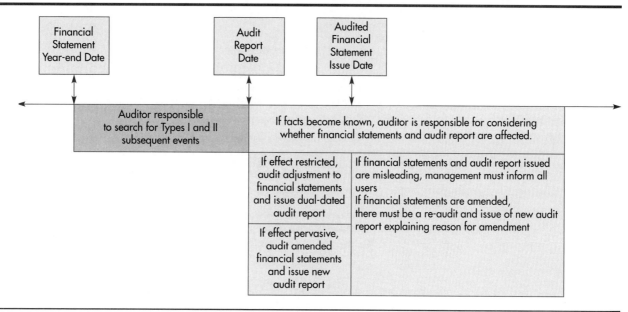

Special Note: Dual Dating in the Audit Report

Dual dating refers to instances of dating the audit report as of the date that financial statements are approved by the auditee's responsible parties (e.g., the company's board of directors) and attaching an additional later date to disclosure of a significant Type II subsequent event. Sometimes, after completion of the audit but before issuance of the report, a significant event comes to the audit team's attention. The purpose of dual dating is twofold: (1) to provide a means of inserting important information learned after the audit report date into the financial statement note disclosures, and (2) to inform users that the auditor takes full responsibility for discovering subsequent events only up to the audit report date and for the specifically identified later event. However, responsibility is not taken for other events that may have occurred after the audit report date. Dual dating is used to cut off the subsequent event procedural responsibility at the earlier date.

Audit Program for the Subsequent Period

An example of an audit program to search for subsequent events is given in Exhibit 15–6. Some audit procedures in the period subsequent to the balance sheet date may include those in the audit program for determining cutoff and proper valuation of balances as of the balance sheet date (Part A in Exhibit 15–6). However, procedures specifically designed for gathering evidence about the two types of subsequent events are different and separate from the rest of the audit program (Part B in Exhibit 15–6).

Summary of Subsequent Events in an Audit

Auditing standards for subsequent events consider two types of events. Type I are events that occurred or conditions that existed on or before the audit report date that would have caused the auditor to amend the audit report. Events and conditions that arise after the balance sheet date but that are important for understanding the financial statements nonetheless are known as Type II. The subsequent event or subsequently acquired knowledge may arise at three different times: (1) before the audit report date, (2) after the audit report date but before issuance of the report, or (3) after the audit report is issued. The most important things to remember are that auditors have an active,

EXHIBIT 15-6   AUDITING PROCEDURES FOR THE PERIOD SUBSEQUENT TO THE BALANCE SHEET DATE

A. Procedures performed in connection with other audit programs
  1. Use a cutoff bank statement to:
      a. Examine cheques paid after year-end that are, or should have been, listed on the bank reconciliation.
      b. Examine bank posting of deposits in transit listed on the bank reconciliation.
  2. Vouch collections on accounts receivable in the month following year-end for evidence of existence and collectibility of the year-end balances.
  3. Trace cash disbursements of the month after year-end to accounts payable for evidence of any liabilities unrecorded at year-end.
  4. Vouch write-downs of fixed assets after year-end evidence that such valuation problems existed at the year-end date.
  5. Vouch sales of investment securities, write-downs, or write-offs in the months after the audit date for evidence of valuation at the year-end date.
  6. Vouch and trace sales transactions in the month after year-end for evidence of proper sales and cost of sales cutoff.
B. Auditing procedures for subsequent events
  1. Read the latest available interim financial statements, compare them with the financial statements being reported on, and make any other comparisons considered appropriate in the circumstances.
  2. Enquire of officers and other executives having responsibility for financial and accounting matters about whether the interim statements have been prepared on the same basis as that used for the statements under examination.
  3. Enquire of and discuss with officers and other executives having responsibility for financial and accounting matters (limited where appropriate to major locations):
      a. Whether any substantial contingent liabilities or commitments existed at the date of the balance sheet being reported on or at the date of enquiry
      b. Whether there was any significant change in the share capital, long-term debt, or working capital to the date of enquiry
      c. The current status of items in the financial statements being reported on that were accounted for on the basis of tentative, preliminary, or inconclusive data
      d. Whether any unusual adjustments have been made during the period from the balance sheet date to the date of enquiry
  4. Read the available minutes of meetings of shareholders, directors, and appropriate committees; enquire about matters dealt with at meetings for which minutes are not available.
  5. Request that the client send a letter to legal counsel enquiring about outstanding claims, possible claims, and management's evaluation, with the reply to be sent directly to the auditor.
  6. Obtain written representations, dated as of the date of the auditor's report, from appropriate officials, generally the chief executive officer and chief financial officer, about whether any events occurred subsequent to the date of the financial statements that, in the officer's opinion, would require adjustment or disclosure in these statements.
  7. Make such additional enquiries or perform such procedures as considered necessary and appropriate to dispose of questions that arise in carrying out the foregoing procedures, enquiries, and discussions.

procedural responsibility for discovering Type I and Type II subsequent events up to the audit report date and for ensuring they are properly reported in the financial statements, but they are not required to perform procedures after the audit report date. However, because they are associated with financial statements they have given an audit opinion on, auditors have responsibilities once they become aware of the facts or omitted procedures.

While auditors are under no obligation to continue audit procedures past the report date, if they happen to learn of relevant facts they have an obligation to determine (1) if the information is reliable and (2) if the facts existed at the date of the report. When these conditions are affirmed and the auditors believe that people are relying on the report, steps should be taken to withdraw the first report, perform the additional procedures required, issue a new report, and inform anyone currently relying on the financial statements. Basically, the decisions relate to the importance and impact of the information, the cooperation of the auditee in taking necessary action, and the actions to be taken. The auditee's cooperation facilitates all of this, but the auditors have a duty to notify the public of an earlier, potentially misleading audit report even if the auditee does not cooperate.

REVIEW CHECKPOINTS

13 What are the two types of subsequent events? How are they treated differently in the financial statements?

14 What treatment is given stock dividends and splits occurring after the balance sheet date but before the audit report is issued? Explain.

15 What is the purpose of dual dating an audit report?

16 What is the difference between a subsequent event that occurs between the balance sheet date and the audit report date and the discovery after the audit report date of facts that existed at the report date? Describe the auditor's responsibility for each.

17 If, subsequent to issuing a report, the auditor discovers information that existed at the report date and materially affects the financial statements, what actions should the auditor take if the auditee consents to disclose the information? What action should be taken if the the auditee (including the board of directors) refuses to make disclosure?

18 After the audit report has been issued, someone discovers that the auditee had a material, unrecorded bank loan outstanding at year-end. There was no confirmation requested from that bank as the auditors were not aware of the auditee's relation with that bank. What steps should an auditor should take in this situation?

OVERALL EVALUATION OF EVIDENCE TO FORM THE AUDIT OPINION

LEARNING OBJECTIVE

6 Explain the final evaluation and conclusion stage of the audit: adjustments resulting from the audit, evaluation of evidence and misstatements to form the audit opinion, and reviews of working paper files.

At this stage the auditor does the final wrap-up of the audit evidence gathering and assesses the effect of identified and likely misstatements that could cause the financial statements not to be in accordance with GAAP (or another fair presentation framework), or to be misleading to users. Also, the remaining uncorrected misstatements must be discussed with the auditee management, and any necessary adjustments approved by them. The auditor then reaches a final conclusion on whether the audit has provided reasonable assurance that the risk of material misstatement is acceptably low. On this basis, the auditor will form an opinion on whether the financial statements are fairly presented. Before an audit can be considered finished, the audit working papers must be reviewed, including an engagement quality control review in the case of publicly listed companies.[7] At that point, the audit documentation files are assembled and stored for future reference.

Auditee Approval of Adjusting Entries and Financial Statement Disclosure

The financial statements, including adjustments to the draft version, are the responsibility of management. Some adjusting entries identified in the audit are approved by management as they are dealt with during the ongoing field work, and others are approved at the final wrap-up.

Exhibit 15–7 is a summary worksheet ("scoresheet") showing the end-of-audit proposed adjusting journal entries. Auditors prepare this summary to see how these adjustments will affect the financial statements, and to help decide which ones must be made to support an unqualified audit report and which ones may be passed. A passed adjustment is one the auditors decide not to insist on because the uncorrected misstatement does not materially effect the financial position and results of operations.

The proposed adjustments shown in Exhibit 15–7 are (1) recording cheques written and mailed but not in the books, (2) reversing recorded sales for goods shipped after the balance sheet date and reversing the 60 percent cost of goods sold, (3) writing off obsolete

[7] CAS 220 (5030).

EXHIBIT 15-7   PROPOSED ADJUSTING JOURNAL ENTRIES (ILLUSTRATIVE SCORESHEET WORKING PAPER)

	Income Statement		Balance Sheet	
	Debit	Credit	Debit	Credit
(1) Unrecorded cash disbursements:				
Accounts payable			$42,000	
Cash				$42,000
(2) Improper sales cutoff:				
Sales	$13,000			
Inventory			7,800	
Cost of goods sold (60%)		$7,800		
Accounts receivable				13,000
(3) Inventory write-off:				
Cost of goods sold	21,000			
Inventory				21,000
(4) Unrecorded liabilities:				
Utilities expense	700			
Commissions expense	3,000			
Wages	2,500			
Accounts payable				700
Accrued expenses payable				5,500
(5) Amortization calculation error:				
Accumulated amortization			17,000	
Amortization expense		17,000		
(6) Reclassify current portion of long-term debt:				
Notes payable			50,000	
Current portion of debt				50,000
(7) Income tax @ 40%:				
Income tax refund receivable			6,160	
Income tax expense		6,160		
	$40,200	$30,960	$122,960	$132,200
		($9,240)		
Net income change				
Current assets change				($62,040)
Current liabilities change				$14,200
Working capital change				($76,240)

Note: This exhibit illustrates a minimal method to assess whether misstatements aggregate to a material amount. This is referred to as "minimal" because it is based only on identified, factual misstatements. In this method, the uncorrected misstatements are aggregated in various ways to see if they total to a material amount. For example, if materiality is based on net income, the auditor must aggregate all misstatements affecting net income. This can be based on either (1) changes in net assets (assets less liabilities), or the equivalent, or (2) revenues less expenses. Given the nature of the double-entry system, either approach should yield the same number. In this exhibit's example, the net effect of uncorrected identified misstatements on net income is computed as follows:

misstatements in net income = misstatements in changes in net assets = misstatements in changes in assets − misstatements in changes in liabilities

Using the values in this exhibit,

42,000(A) + 13,000(A) + 21,000(A) − 7,800(A) − 17,000(A) − 6,160(A) − [+ 42,000(L) − 700(L) − 5,500(L) + 50,000(L) − 50,000(L)] = 9,240

= misstatements in revenues − misstatements in expenses

= 13,000(R) − [6,160(E) + 7,800(E) − 21,000(E) − 700(E) − 3,000(E) − 2,500(E) + 17,000(E)] = 9,240

= total net misstatements in net income (overstatement; i.e., to eliminate all the adjusting entries, auditee's proposed net income must be reduced by 9,240).

This total of 9,240 is then compared with the predetermined overall materiality. If 9,240 is less than material, the auditor may conclude that further adjustments are not necessary.

This analysis, in summary, is based on uncorrected, identified misstatements only, and it is perfectly appropriate in cases where the auditor tests 100 percent of the transactions. This level of testing is likely done for cash, capital assets, noncurrent liabilities, and owner's equity. For accounts such as inventory, receivables, and payables, which can represent large populations of individual items, the auditor may wish to use sampling theory concepts to include likely and possible misstatement in the assessment of whether the misstatements are material. Adjustments and decision making based on sampling situations are covered in Appendix 10A. Possible misstatements in the form of forecast errors that lead to accounting risk (as discussed in Appendix 7B) should also be considered by the auditor, especially for evaluating fairness of presentation in the circumstances.

and damaged inventory, (4) recording the amounts found in the search for unrecorded liabilities, (5) correcting an amortization calculation error, (6) reclassifying the current portion of long-term debt, and (7) recording a tax refund asset for overpaid income taxes (could be a debit to tax liability if all the taxes for the year had not already been paid). Summary effects on income, current assets, current liabilities, and working capital are shown at the bottom of the worksheet. These help auditors assess the potential impact of the adjustments on financial statement users; for example, lenders who are monitoring working capital ratio limits in debt covenants.

The adjusting entries shown in Exhibit 15–7 are labelled "proposed" as they are still subject to management's approval. A final list of all approved adjusting entries is given to the auditee accounting staff so that formal entries can be made, bringing the accounting records into balance with the financial statements.

The auditee must also approve all disclosure in the notes. Any additional disclosures auditors consider necessary usually are drafted as proposed notes. They must be considered carefully before being presented to management for acceptance as company disclosures.

Overall Evaluation of Audit Evidence and Misstatements

It is important to realize that the accumulated audit evidence is the main basis for deciding if the amount of uncorrected misstatement is material. Chapter 6 explained how the audit is planned with the objective of detecting misstatements that are material, either individually or in aggregate, to the financial statements as a whole. Recall that the auditor considers materiality at the planning stage, while performing the audit, and at the final evaluation stage when forming the audit opinion. The auditor uses professional judgment to determine a materiality level for planning and performing the audit, basing this on the amount of misstatement that would probably influence decisions of a person relying on the financial statements for making business and economic decisions. At the final evaluation stage, the auditor considers individual and aggregate misstatements discovered, their nature and cause, whether they indicate a possibility of further misstatements, and how they quantitatively and qualitatively affect the financial statements.

Misstatements have various causes, such as arithmetical mistakes (e.g., an addition error in a physical inventory count), use of inappropriate accounting principles, incorrect application of accounting principles, and disagreements about valuation or other estimates. They may occur accidentally or through misunderstanding, be the result of embezzlement, or be deliberate misrepresentations. As discussed in Chapter 6, a key qualitative factor in the auditor's assessment is evidence of deliberate misstatements intended to improve or defer earnings to achieve management's goals. These goals, such as obtaining an earnings-based bonus, may not be aligned with those of the company's capital providers, who are usually the most important users of the audited financial statements.

For evaluation, uncorrected misstatements can be classified into three main categories: known, likely, and further possible. **Known misstatements** are those actually identified during the audit, so there is no uncertainty about their existence. **Likely misstatements** are those that probably exist, based on audit evidence examined; for example, the projected effect of misstatements identified in representative samples or management accounting estimates or of policy choices that the auditor considers unreasonable. **Further possible misstatements** are those that could exist over and above the total of known and likely misstatements because of the fundamental limitations of auditing; for example, sampling and nonsampling risks (as discussed in Chapter 10), forecasting uncertainties in accounting estimates, and minimum review accounts (those subjected to minimal verification as they have a very low assessed risk of misstatement). The amount of possible misstatement cannot be precisely quantified, but the auditor must exercise professional judgment in addressing this possibility, particularly when the total approaches materiality, or when misstatements are due to general control breakdowns rather than isolated instances.[8]

---

[8] The approach described here is based on guidelines that were provided in the CICA *Handbook*, AuG-41: Applying the concept of materiality, prior to 2010.

EXHIBIT   15-8   RELATING MISSTATEMENTS TO MATERIALITY TO FORM THE AUDIT OPINION

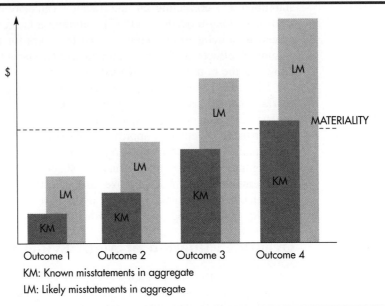

KM: Known misstatements in aggregate

LM: Likely misstatements in aggregate

Explanations

Outcome 1 – This outcome is frequently encountered in practice when auditees agree to correct most known misstatements. The level of known and likely aggregate misstatement is well below materiality, so the auditor may consider it very unlikely that the maximum possible misstatement (including further possible misstatements) would be quantitatively material. The auditor always also needs to consider the effect of the qualitative factors discussed in Chapter 6 when assessing whether the misstatement should be considered material, in order to reach a final conclusion on whether an unqualified or a qualified opinion should be given.

Outcome 2 – The sum of known and likely misstatements is close to, but below, materiality. This indicates that the auditor's best estimate is that financial statements are not materially misstated. The auditor still must assess whether further possible misstatements exist at a level that might cause the financial statements to be materially misstated. In this case, the auditor might propose that some or all known misstatements be corrected to bring the level of misstatement well below materiality, so that an unqualified opinion could be given. The auditor might also consider performing additional auditing procedures to reduce the assessment of likely and further possible misstatements. Ultimately, the auditor will have to consider qualitative factors and exercise professional judgment in deciding whether an unqualified opinion is appropriate in this case.

Outcome 3 – The known misstatements are less than materiality but, when combined with likely misstatements, the level exceeds materiality. In this case, the auditor's best estimate is that the financial statements are materially misstated. The auditor would need management to correct some or all misstatements to reduce the levels to sufficiently below materiality that an unqualified opinion can be given, subject also to consideration of qualitative factors.

Outcome 4 – The level of known misstatements exceeds materiality. In this case a qualified opinion is required, unless management will correct misstatements to reduce the levels of known and likely misstatements to be sufficiently below materiality to enable an unqualified opinion to be given. Again, the final decision is subject to consideration of qualitative factors.

The relationship between the known and likely misstatements and materiality is important as it determines the nature of the auditor's opinion on the financial statements.[9] Exhibit 15–8 (which is based on AuG-41) illustrates four possible outcomes of an audit and explains how professional judgment is applied in each case to determine the impact on the audit opinion.

Complications in audit evaluation can arise from measurements involving management estimates. Auditors are supposed to keep track of the differences between management estimates and the most reasonable estimates supported by audit evidence. They also identify estimates with high risk due to forecast errors, and assess whether these are fairly presented in the circumstances. In areas where GAAP are evolving, such as fair valuation of financial instruments (as discussed in Chapter 14), the accounting standards might not provide detailed implementation guidance, so the auditor needs to exercise judgment, guided by general principles and reporting objectives, to assess fair presentation.

Auditors are also supposed to evaluate the estimate differences as a group, for indications of a systematic bias (CAS 540), and examine the combination of differences and other likely misstatements found by other audit procedures. Accumulated uncorrected misstatements (passed adjustments) from prior periods may also have an impact as they may reverse and affect the materiality of current year's misstatements (CAS 450).

[9] Adjustments based on likely and possible misstatements are covered in Appendix 10A, and are less common in practice. The likely and further possible misstatements are auditor estimates, so it may be difficult for the auditor to make a defensible argument that they should be adjusted, and for the auditee to agree to adjust them.

Overall evaluation also connects materiality to assertions. Materiality is defined as the amount of misstatements from all sources that would affect a user decision. Thus, materiality may also presume that users mainly care that the aggregate misstatement for all assertions is less than material, rather than which particular assertions were affected. Again, review Exhibit 15–7 and note the assertions affected by the misstatements: completeness, valuation, existence, and presentation.

Forming an Opinion on the Financial Statements

To form an opinion on whether the financial statements are presented fairly in all material respects and in accordance with GAAP, the auditor must make a number of professional judgments as set out in CAS 700. He must decide whether the audit team has obtained sufficient appropriate audit evidence providing reasonable assurance that the financial statements as a whole are free from material misstatement due to fraud or error. This includes deciding if any uncorrected misstatements are material, either individually or in aggregate.

To assess fair presentation, the audit engagement partner considers the results of the final overall financial statement analysis, and assesses whether the overall presentation, structure, and content of the financial statements and notes represent the underlying transactions and events fairly, from the perspective of users (CAS 520 [5301]).

The auditor must be satisfied that the information presented in the financial statements is relevant, reliable, comparable, and understandable. Fair presentation also requires the financial statements to adequately disclose the significant accounting policies applied so that users can understand the effect of transactions and events on the information. The auditor assesses whether the terminology used and the titles of financial statements are appropriate and understandable. The final analysis considers the qualitative aspects of the accounting used, including indications of management bias in selecting accounting policies and making accounting estimates. The accounting risk concept is intended to help auditors guide reasonableness of forecasts in accounting estimates. For example, if management's assumption leads to an unacceptably high accounting risk estimate, the auditor may question the reasonableness of that assumption. An adjustment to the estimate, or at least note disclosure of the questionable assumption(s), may be necessary for fairness of presentation.

The trend in auditing is to replace qualitative analysis with more objective quantitative analysis or models. This parallels trends in other fields such as finance. Prime examples are the audit risk model and risk-based auditing generally, which are greatly influenced by statistical sampling theory. Under the right conditions, the analysis in Exhibit 15–8 can be reduced to a simple decision rule such as in the application case of Chapter 10. These right conditions include no important qualitative differences in the misstatements, such as evidence that there are intentional and unintentional misstatements. Different qualitative misstatements may require different concepts of risk, such as accounting risk or fraud risk, which are further devloped in later chapters.

Form of Opinion
As discussed in Chapter 3, when the auditor concludes that the financial statements are presented fairly in all material respects in accordance with GAAP, an unmodified opinion can be expressed. If, based on the audit evidence, the auditor concludes that the financial statements are not free from material misstatement (GAAP departure), or he is unable to obtain sufficient appropriate audit evidence to conclude that the financial statements are free from material misstatement (scope limitation), the auditor must give a modified opinion in the auditor's report in accordance with CAS 705 (5510).

Audit Documentation Working Paper Review

To wrap up the audit field work, the on-site audit supervisor makes a final review of the audit documentation working papers, which may be recorded in paper, electronic, or other media. This final review ensures that all accounts on the trial balance have a **working paper reference index**, the sign that audit work has been finished on that account, and that all procedures in the audit program are "signed off" with a date and initials. Soon after completion, the working papers are reviewed by the audit supervisor, and sometimes by the audit manager, to ensure that all tick-mark notations are clear, that all procedures performed are adequately documented, and that all necessary procedures were performed with due professional care.

The audit manager and engagement partner's review focuses more on the overall scope of the audit. They are very involved with the planning of the audit and may perform some of the field work on difficult areas, but they are usually not involved in preparing the detailed working papers. Even though the working papers are reviewed by the on-site audit supervisor, the partner who is going to sign the audit report should review them as well. To-do lists citing omissions or deficiencies that must be cleared before the final work is completed are prepared during these reviews.

Treatment of the to-do lists varies among audit firms. Some prefer to destroy the lists after the work is performed and documented in the working papers as a "clean up" of notes relating to loose ends. Other firms keep the lists as signed off, and cross-reference them for the work performed, believing the lists are evidence of careful review and completion of the audit. Sometimes, retained to-do lists backfire on auditors by showing questions raised but not resolved.

For **listed public entities**, an engagement-quality review of the working papers and financial statements, including notes, is performed by a partner not responsible for the client relationship. This **second-partner review** ensures that the quality of audit work and reporting is in keeping with the quality standards of the audit firm. This quality review must be complete before the audit report is issued (CAS 220 [5030]).

The completed working paper files are assembled for secure, long-term storage. Those retained in electronic files must have data integrity controls in place. Usually the files are completed within sixty days of the audit report date, and are retained for at least five years. When field work is complete, the final audit time reports for billing purposes and audit staff performance evaluation reports are prepared by the audit supervisor.

REVIEW CHECKPOINTS

19 Why are auditors' drafts of adjusting entries and note disclosures near the end of the audit always labelled "proposed"?

20 What are uncorrected misstatements and what role do they play in forming the audit opinion on the financial statements?

21 Outline the auditor's considerations at the end of the audit to form the opinion, especially referring to those requiring professional judgment.

22 What is the purpose of to-do lists in the audit documentaion? What is a good reason for keeping the to-do lists in the audit working paper files?

23 Describe an engagement quality control file review. Who performs it and what is its purpose?

AUDITOR COMMUNICATIONS

LEARNING OBJECTIVE

7 Summarize the auditor's communications throughout and at the conclusion of the engagement.

Once the auditor has concluded the audit work and the audit files are reviewed and complete, it is time for the auditor to communicate with those charged with governance regarding the significant audit findings and the planned audit report. Those charged with governance are responsible for ensuring that the organization is accountable to its stakeholders. The organization's financial statements are a key component of this accountability obligation, and those charged with governance must take responsibility for them before the auditor can issue her audit report. This section will review all the communications occurring throughout the audit and then discuss those carried out at the completion of the audit.

EXHIBIT 15-9 AUDIT CORRESPONDENCE

Type	From	To	Time
Engagement letter (acceptance)	Auditor (auditee)	Auditee (auditor)	Before engagement
Independence letter	Auditor	Auditee	Before engagement
Internal control deficiencies	Auditor	Auditee	Interim or after audit
Confirmations (replies)	Auditee (third parties)	Third parties (auditor)	Throughout the audit
Lawyer's letter (reply)	Auditee Lawyer	Lawyer (auditor)	Near end of audit
Management representation letter	Auditee management	Auditor	Audit report date
Communication with those charged with governance of auditee (e.g., audit committee)	Auditor	Directors	Planning, during audit, and after audit report

Summary of Audit Correspondence

Many types of formal correspondence have been mentioned in this text. Since you are learning the final procedures that complete the audit, this is a good place to summarize these correspondence items and when they typically occur. Exhibit 15–9 is a summary of audit correspondence. Refer also to Exhibit 6–1, which shows the communications that auditors are required to make throughout the audit process.

The two main communications occurring at the end report significant audit findings to those charged with governance (CAS 260) and report internal control weaknesses discovered during the audit to management (CAS 265). If the control deficiencies are significant, they are also reported in writing to those charged with governance (CAS 265).

Communications with Those Charged with Governance (Audit Committees or Equivalent)

The auditor and management should, in advance, review the information to be covered with the audit committee. On some matters (e.g., company operations), management should report and the auditor then comment. On other matters, such as audit findings, the auditor should report and management then comment. Both should be present in meetings with the audit committee to discuss these reports, which may be written or oral. When the auditor communicates in writing, the report should indicate that it is intended solely for use by the audit committee. In some instances the auditor may identify matters to discuss with the audit committee without the presence of management.

The auditor should keep notes of audit committee discussions, and these should be compared with the audit committee minutes of the meeting. Any inconsistencies shall be resolved with the audit committee or board of directors. The auditor should also communicate all matters affecting approval of the annual financial statements to the board of directors prior to such approval. Normally, the auditor would work within the audit committee's regular cycle of meetings.

The audit committee's expectations need to be clarified and put in writing. The most important matters arising from the audit of financial statements that should be communicated to the audit committee include the following:

1. Auditor responsibility under GAAS
2. Planning of the current audit
3. Material weaknesses in internal controls
4. Illegal acts

5. Fraud

6. Significant accounting principles and policies selected by management

7. Management judgments and accounting estimates

8. Misstatements, adjusted and uncorrected

9. Other information in annual reports (e.g., narrative information)

10. Disagreements with management

11. Consultation with other accountants by management

12. Significant findings of the audit

13. Difficulties encountered in performing the audit (e.g., unreasonable delays in obtaining information from management)

14. Effects of new developments in accounting standards, or of legislative or regulatory requirements, on the auditee's financial reporting

15. Use of experts

16. Audit and nonaudit services that the auditor is providing to the auditee

17. Summary of the audit approach

If the auditor considers that the audit committee's response to the matters communicated are seriously inappropriate, he or she may need to communicate directly with the board of directors, or even have an obligation to report to outside regulatory authorities. For example, the "well-being reporting requirement" under federal financial institutions legislation[10] may require the auditor to report to the Superintendent of Financial Institutions "any significant weaknesses in internal control which have the potential to jeopardize the financial institution's ability to continue as a going concern." As auditee confidentiality is an issue, the auditor should seek legal advice about the best manner of reporting to outside authorities.

. . . .

R E V I E W
CHECKPOINTS

24 What is the purpose of the auditor's communication with those charged with governance at the completion of the audit?

25 Why must the auditor communicate significant findings with those charged with governance prior to dating the audit report?

26 What information would the auditor communicate to management and to those charged with governance regarding internal control deficiencies discovered during the audit?

. . . .

[10] As described in the *CICA Handbook* Canadian Auditing Practice Statement, APS1117-C (formerly AuG–17, this statement numbering is proposed at the time of writing).

APPLICATION CASE AND ANALYSIS
FINAL OVERALL ANALYSIS UNCOVERS UNUSUAL RELATED PARTY TRANSACTIONS

LEARNING OBJECTIVE

8 Apply and integrate the chapter topics to design audit procedures for detecting misstatements due to error or fraud at the overall completion stage of the audit.

Discussion case

In his second year as an auditor, Jack assists an audit partner in completing the final analytical procedures and working paper review for a new audit of a group of mining companies. The audit file shows that in 20X9 Alta Gold Company, a public "shell" corporation, was purchased for $1,000 by the Blues brothers.

Operating under the corporate names of Diamond King and Pacific Gold, the brothers had also purchased numerous mining claims in auctions conducted by the Ministry of Natural Resources. They invested a total of $40,000 in 300 claims between the two companies. A series of transactions followed.

(a) Diamond King sold limited partnership interests in its 175 Northwest Territories diamond claims to local investors, raising $20 million to begin mining production.

(b) Pacific Gold then traded its 125 British Columbia gold mining claims for all the Diamond King assets and partnership interests, valuing the diamond claims at $20 million. Diamond King valued the gold claims received at $20 million as the fair value in the exchange.

(c) The brothers then put $3 million obtained from dividends into Alta Gold and, with the aid of a $15 million bank loan, Alta Gold purchased half of the Diamond King gold claims for $18 million.

(d) The Blues brothers then arranged for Alta Gold to obtain another bank loan of $38 million to purchase the remainder of Diamond King's assets and all of Pacific Gold's mining claims. They paid off the Diamond King limited partners.

(e) At the end of 20X9, Alta Gold had cash of $16 million and mining assets valued at $58 million, with liabilities on bank loans of $53 million.

Alta Gold had in its files the partnership offering documents, receipts and other papers showing partners' investment of $20 million in the Diamond King limited partnerships. The company also had Pacific Gold and Diamond King contracts for the exchange of mining claims. The $20 million value of the exchange was justified in light of the limited partners' investments.

Appraisals in the files showed one report that there was no basis for valuing the exchange of Diamond King claims other than the price limited partner investors had been willing to pay. The second appraiser reported a probable value of $20 million for the exchange, based on proven production elsewhere, but no geological data on the actual claims had been obtained. The $18 million paid by Alta Gold to Diamond King had similar appraisal reports.

Audit trail

The transactions occurred over a period of 10 months. The Blues brothers had $37 million cash in Diamond King and Pacific Gold, as well as the $16 million in Alta. All of the cash was borrowed from a bank that had granted the loan to Alta Gold with the mining claims and production as security. The mining claims that had cost $40,000 were now in Alta's balance sheet at $58 million; the $53 million in loans from the bank was secured by 300 mining claim papers.

AUDIT APPROACH ANALYSIS

The auditors' objective is to obtain evidence of the existence, valuation, and rights (ownership) in the mining claim assets. The review of the working papers indicated a number of audit issues and outstanding procedures still to be done.

Controls relevant to this process

The audit file documentation assessing of internal controls relevant to accounting for mining property investments indicated that Alta Gold, Pacific Gold, and Diamond King had no control structure. All transactions were engineered by the Blues brothers, including the hiring of friendly appraisers. The only control that might have been effective was the bank loan-granting process, but the bank failed to exercise appropriate procedures to evaluate the risk in the loans to Alta Gold.

Another effective control could have been engagement of competent, independent appraisers. Since the auditors will use (or try to use) the appraisers' reports, the procedures involve investigating the reputation, engagement terms, and independence of the appraisers. The auditors can use local business references, local financial institutions with lists of approved appraisers, membership directories of the professional appraisal associations, and interviews with the appraisers themselves.

AUDIT PROCEDURES

Test of details of balance

The procedures for auditing the asset values include tracing and analyzing the path of each transaction. This includes obtaining knowledge of the owners and managers of the several companies and the identities of the limited partner investors. If the Blues brothers have not disclosed their connection with the other companies (and perhaps with the limited partners), the auditors need to enquire at the Ministry of Commerce offices to discover the identities of the players in this flip game. Numerous complicated pre-merger transactions in small corporations and shells often signal manipulated valuations. Loan applications and supporting papers should be examined to determine the representations made by Alta Gold when obtaining the bank loans. These papers may reveal some contradictory or exaggerated information. Ownership of the mining claims might be confirmed with the Resources Ministry auctioneers or found in the local deed records (spread all over the Northwest Territories and British Columbia).

Audit results

Based on their final file review and analysis, Jack and the partner find that the audit staff assigned had documented the many transactions and loans, but they had not been able to unravel the complicated exchanges and they never questioned the relationship of Alta Gold to Diamond King and Pacific Gold. They never investigated and discovered the Blues brothers' involvement in the other side of the exchanges and the purchase transactions. They accepted the appraisers' reports as competent and independent but had not adequately supported these conclusions. The audit partners realize that the audit is far from complete. Attempting to contact the Blues brothers, the only directors of all the corporations, to communicate the findings at this point of the audit, it is learned that both have left the country on extended trips and cannot be contacted. Further investigation reveals the identities of the various related parties in the flips. The audit cannot be completed, and the initial decision to accept this new engagement is deemed not

appropriate based on the facts learned subsequently. Jack's audit firm withdraws from the engagement without issuing a report (a close call; the bank that lent the $53 million was not so lucky). The audit firm begins an investigation to find out how the inappropriate acceptance decision was made, so it can implement necessary improvements to its quality control procedures.

REVIEW CHECKPOINTS

27 What impact can related party transactions have in some cases of asset valuation?

SUMMARY

This chapter covered several aspects of completing an audit. As the work draws to a close, several income and expense accounts may still need to be audited. This work is largely done through analytical comparisons of these balances with those of prior years and with current expectations. While large and significant revenues and expenses usually have already been audited in connection with the audit of other accounts in the cycles, at this stage in the audit it is a good idea to step back and review large and unusual revenue and gain transactions recorded near the end of the year. Often these have been the vehicles for income statement manipulation. Some examples were given in the chapter.

Two of the most important topics for the audit completion work are the management's written representation letter and the lawyer's letter. These submissions to the auditors are requirements for an unqualified audit report, and without them the audit scope is considered limited. Several requirements for the management representation letter were specified in the chapter. A special insert described particular problems in interpreting lawyers' letters. Information from lawyers is especially important in evidence about litigation contingencies and their disclosure, according to *CICA Handbook,* section 3290. Some descriptive research on this *Handbook* section's disclosure experience in the United States was provided to emphasize the difficulties faced by managers and auditors.

Subsequent events were explained in detail that included (1) procedural responsibility for events following the balance sheet date; (2) the dual dating alternative for reporting on events that occurred between the audit report and the issue of the financial statements; and (3) auditors' discovery, after a report was delivered, of facts that existed at the balance sheet date.

The chapter ended this text's adventures in auditing with explanations of proposed adjusting journal entries and disclosure notes, assessment of audit evidence and findings to form the auditor's opinion, reviews of working papers, and communication of the audit findings with management and those charged with governance. All that remains is to write up the audit report itself, which was covered already in Chapter 3, the final objective and focal point of the whole financial statement audit engagement. The next chapter will discuss other types of engagements that are common in public practice.

MULTIPLE-CHOICE QUESTIONS FOR PRACTICE AND REVIEW

MC 1 When auditing the year-end balance of interest-bearing notes payable, which account are the auditors most likely to audit at the same time?
a. Interest income
b. Interest expense
c. Amortization of goodwill
d. Royalty revenue

MC 2 What is the main purpose of a written management representation letter?
a. Shift responsibility for financial statements from the management to the auditor.
b. Provide a substitute source of evidence for detail procedures auditors would otherwise perform.

c. Provide management a place to make assertions about the quantity and valuation of the physical inventory.

d. Obtain management's acknowledgement of its ultimate responsibility for the financial statements and disclosures.

MC 3 Which one of these procedures or sources is not likely to provide evidence about contingencies?

a. Scan expense accounts for credit entries.

b. Obtain a representation letter from the auditee's lawyer.

c. Read the minutes of the board of directors' meetings.

d. Examine terms of sale in sales contracts.

MC 4 A Type I subsequent event involves information about a condition that existed at the balance sheet date. Knowledge of which of the following subsequent events would cause the company to adjust its December 31 financial statements?

a. Sale of an issue of new shares for $500,000 on January 30

b. A $10,000 settlement of a damage lawsuit for a customer's injury sustained February 15

c. A February $100,000 settlement of litigation that had been estimated at $12,000 in the December 31 financial statements

d. Storm damage of $1 million to the company's buildings on March 1

MC 5 A. Griffin audited the financial statements of Dodger Magnificat Corporation for the year ended December 31, 20X2. She dated the audit report on January 30 when the board of directors approved the financial statements, and later learned of a stock split voted by the board of directors on February 5. The financial statements were changed to reflect the split, and she now needs to dual

date the audit report before it and the financial statements are issued to users. Which of the following is the proper form?

a. December 31, 20X2, except as to Note X, which is dated January 30, 20X3

b. January 30, 20X3, except as to Note X, which is dated February 5, 20X3

c. December 31, 20X2, except as to Note X, which is dated February 5, 20X3

d. February 5, 20X3, except for completion of audit work, the date of which is January 30, 20X3

MC 6 Until when do auditors have a responsibility to perform procedures to find subsequent events?

a. The year-end balance sheet date

b. The audit report date

c. The date the audited financial statements are delivered to the users

d. The end of audit field work

MC 7 The "subsequent discovery of facts that existed at the balance sheet date" refers to knowledge obtained after which date?

a. The date the audit report was delivered to the auditee

b. The audit report date

c. The company's year-end balance sheet date

d. The date interim audit work was complete

MC 8 Which of the following is not required by Canadian auditing standards?

a. Management representation letter

b. Lawyer's letter

c. Management letter

d. Engagement letter

EXERCISES AND PROBLEMS

EP 1
LO.4
Management Representation Letter. In connection with your audit, you request that management provide you with a letter containing certain representations such as the following:

1. The auditee has satisfactory title to all assets.

2. No contingent or unrecorded liabilities exist except as disclosed in the letter.

3. No shares of the company's stock are reserved for options, warrants, or other rights.

4. The company is not obligated to repurchase any of its outstanding shares under any circumstances.

Required:

a. Explain why you believe a letter of representation should be provided to you.

b. In what way, if any, do these management representations affect your audit procedures and responsibilities?

(AICPA adapted)

EP 2
LO.4
Engagement and Management Representation Letters. The two major written understandings between an auditor

and management, in connection with an audit of financial statements, are the engagement letter and the management representation letter.

Required:

a. (1) What are the objectives of the engagement letter?

(2) Who should prepare and sign the engagement letter?

(3) When should the engagement letter be sent?

(4) Why should the engagement letter be renewed periodically?

b. (1) What are the objectives of the management representation letter?

(2) Who should sign the management representation letter?

(3) When should the management representation letter be obtained?

(4) Why should the management representation letter be prepared for each examination?

c. An auditor's responsibilities for providing accounting services sometimes involve an association with unaudited financial statements. Discuss the need for each of the following in this circumstance:

(1) An engagement letter.
(2) Management representation letter.

(AICPA adapted)

EP 3
LO.4
and
LO.5

Subsequent Events and Contingent Liabilities. Crankwell Inc. is preparing its annual financial statements and report to shareholders. Management wants to be sure that all of the necessary and proper disclosures are incorporated into the financial statements and the annual report. Two classes of items that have an important bearing on the financial statements are subsequent events and contingent liabilities. The financial statements could be materially inaccurate or misleading if proper disclosure of these items is not made.

Required:

a. With respect to subsequent events:
   (1) Define subsequent events.
   (2) Identify the two types of subsequent events and explain the appropriate financial statement presentation of each type.

b. With respect to contingent liabilities:
   (1) Identify the essential elements of a contingent liability.
   (2) Explain how a contingent liability should be disclosed in the financial statements.

c. Explain how a subsequent event may relate to a contingent liability. Give an example to support your answer.

(CMA adapted)

EP 4
LO.3

Lawyer's Letters. Auditors are required to obtain representation letters from the auditee's lawyer to elicit information on claims and possible claims that may affect the financial statements.

Required:

a. Discuss the audit evidence provided by a lawyer's letter. Explain which assertions and which financial statement amounts the lawyer's letter relates to. What other audit evidence is available for these assertions, if any?

b. What other evidence may be available to an auditor that can corroborate the completeness of the claims the auditee has listed in the lawyer's letter?

c. What should be the effective date of the lawyer's letter? Why?

EP 5
LO.6

Misstatements, Adjustments. For the following findings, indicate the income statement and balance sheet accounts that are affected and whether these accounts are over or understated, and provide an adjusting entry to correct the misstatement, if required. Assume a December 31 year-end.

Required:

a. Outstanding cheques totalling $44,000 were deducted from the cash balance on December 23, but deliberately not mailed out to avoid a bank overdraft over the holidays. The cheques were in payment of various raw material supplier accounts.

b. Sales of $79,000 were recorded on goods that were shipped after year-end and included in the year-end inventory count. The cost of these goods is $53,000.

c. A lawyer's bill for services rendered in November was not paid or accrued.

d. The allowance for bad debts has a credit balance of $80,000. The accounts receivable balance is $150,000, and a reasonable estimate is that all but $10,000 of this will be collected.

e. As of December 31 the company has recognized $250,000 of revenue on a $750,000 contract to construct a bridge. The construction work has not yet started, but $40,000 of building materials for the job were received and expensed as contract costs.

EP 6
LO.4

Management Representation Letters. Refer to the example of a written management representation letter illustrated in Exhibit 15–4.

a. What are the assumptions about the audit engagement in this management representation letter?

b. Which of the representations in the example letter need to be provided regardless of their materiality?

c. If an event subsequent to the date of the balance sheet has been disclosed in the financial statements, what modification would be made to the example letter?

d. If management has received a communication regarding an allegation of fraud or suspected fraud, what modification would be made to the example letter?

EP 7
LO.6

Professional Judgment. Professional judgment is essential to auditors and the quality of audits.

Required:

a. Explain professional judgment in the context of an audit, giving three examples of situations in the audit process that require use of it.

b. The generally accepted auditing standards from the *CICA Handbook* include specific standards intended to enhance the quality and value of audits. Identify three requirements in CAS that relate to general, examination, and reporting standards and explain how each one can help junior auditors develop their professional judgment.

EP 8
LO.1
and
LO.2

Business Processes, Financial Statement Articulation, and XBRL Application. The final review stage of the audit involves taking an overall view of the financial statements and assessing how fairly they reflect the underlying economic events and conditions that occurred in the entity. This exercise involves pulling together difference aspects of the text material that help auditors take this overall integrated view.

a. For each of the items included in the entity's business processes in Exhibit 7–13 (page 242), identify which financial statement it will appear in and all the other financial statement items to which it is related.

b. XBRL is an Internet-based technology for presenting financial data on Web pages and exchanging it over the Internet with other users' systems. Companies are increasingly being required to provide their financial statements in XBRL format. Information on the underlying structure of XBRL and how it works can be found at the Web site XBRL.org. Further research can be done at other Web sites for reference: KOSDAC.com, ubmatrix.com. For the financial statement items you identified in part (a) above, describe how each data item could be defined/tagged in XBRL to appear in the financial statements. If the financial data item has been audited, can XBRL allow the auditor's assurance to be communicated to users at the same time as the data? How?

EP 9 **Auditor Communication with Entity and Liability.**
LO.7 Requirements set out in the auditing standard CAS 260 require an auditor to communicate certain issues and information to those charged with governance of the auditee entity as a financial statement audit proceeds.

Required:
Review the requirements in CAS 260 and discuss how they may affect the risk of an auditor's being liable to the auditee entity. Contrast this with the impact, if any, on the auditor's liability to shareholders (as discussed in Chapter 5). As an analytical perspective, consider the auditor's exposure to both sides as resulting from the three-party accountability relationship (discussed in Chapter 3). Provide your conclusion on whether this CAS requirement reduces auditor liability risk from either of these sides.

DISCUSSION CASES

. . . .

DC 1 **Management Representations Letter Omissions.**
LO.4 During the audit of the annual financial statements of Amis Manufacturing Inc., the company's president, Vance Molar, and Wayne Dweebins, the engagement partner, reviewed matters that were supposed to be included in a written representation letter. Upon receipt of the following representation letter, Dweebins contacted Molar to state that it was incomplete.

To John & Wayne, Public Accountants:
In connection with your examination of the balance sheet of Amis Manufacturing Inc., as of December 31, 20X2, and the related statements of income, retained earnings, and cash flows for the year then ended, for the purpose of expressing an opinion on whether the financial statements present fairly the financial position, results of operations, and cash flows of Amis Manufacturing Inc., in conformity with generally accepted accounting principles, we confirm, to the best of our knowledge and belief, the following representations made to you during your audit. The following were not present:

- Plans or intentions that may materially affect the carrying value or classification of assets or liabilities
- Communications from regulatory agencies concerning noncompliance with, or deficiencies in, financial reporting practices
- Agreements to repurchase assets previously sold
- Violations or possible violations of laws or regulations whose effects should be considered for disclosure in the financial statements or as a basis for recording a loss contingency
- Unasserted claims or assessments that our lawyer has advised are probable and that must be disclosed in accordance with Canadian GAAP
- Capital stock purchase options or agreements or capital stock reserved for options, warrants, conversions, or other requirements

- Compensating balance or other arrangements involving restrictions on cash balances

Vance Molar, President
Amis Manufacturing Inc.
March 14, 20X3

Required:
Identify the other matters that Molar's representation letter should specifically confirm.

(AICPA adapted)

DC 2 **Subsequent Events Procedures.** You are in the process of winding up the field work on Top Stove Corpo-
LO.5 ration, a company that manufactures and sells kerosene space heating stoves. To date there has been every indication that the financial statements of the company present fairly the position of the company at December 31 and the results of its operations for the year then ended. Top Stove had total assets at December 31 of $4 million and a net profit for the year (after deducting federal and provincial income taxes) of $285,000. The principal records of the company are a general ledger, cash receipts record, accounts payable register, sales register, cheque register, and general journal. Financial statements are prepared monthly. Your field work will be completed on February 20, and you expect the company's board to meet and approve the final financial statements on March 12.

Required:
a. Write a brief statement about the purpose and period to be covered in a review of subsequent events.
b. Outline the program you would follow to determine what transactions involving material amounts, if any, have occurred since the balance sheet date.

(AICPA adapted)

DC 3 **Subsequent Events: Cases.** The following events oc-
LO.5 curred in independent cases, but in each instance the event happened after the close of the fiscal year under audit but before all members of the audit team had left the office of the auditee. For each case, state what disclosure, if any, you would expect in the financial statements (and notes). The balance sheet date in each instance is December 31, 20X1.

1. On December 31, the commodities handled by the company had been traded in the open market for $1.40 per pound. This price had prevailed for two weeks, following an official market report that predicted vastly enlarged supplies; however, no purchases were made at $1.40. The price throughout the preceding year, and several prior years, had been about $2. On January 18, 20X2, the price returned to $2, following disclosure of an error in the official calculations of the prior December—correction of which destroyed the expectations of excessive supplies. Inventory at December 31, 20X1, had been valued on a lower-of-cost-or-market basis.

2. On February 1, 20X2, the board of directors adopted a resolution accepting an investment banker's offer to guarantee the marketing of $100 million of preferred shares.

3. On January 22, 20X2, one of the auditee's three major plants burned down, a $50 million loss that was covered to $40 million by insurance.

4. The auditee in this case is an open-end-type investment company. In January, 20X2, a new management took control. By February 20X2 it had sold 90 percent of the investments carried at December 31, 20X1, and had purchased substantially more speculative ones.

5. This company has a wholly owned but not consolidated subsidiary producing oil in a foreign country. A serious rebellion began in that country on January 18, 20X2, and continued beyond the completion of your audit work. There has been extensive coverage of the fighting here.

6. The auditee, Comtois Corp., sells property management software systems. Shortly before its December 31, 20X1, year-end, Comtois' president finalized a large sale to a provincial ministry. The contract has been completed and all the terms agreed to by the assistant deputy minister, but the minister herself is the only one authorized to sign the contract because of the large dollar amount involved. As of the last day of audit fieldwork, March 3, 20X2, Comtois has not yet received the signed contract because the minister has not been available. The president wants to recognize the revenue in Comtois' 20X1 fiscal year anyway so that the sales people and managers involved can be paid a bonus this year based on it. The auditee's stated accounting policy for revenue recognition on these types of sales, established five years earlier, is to recognize revenue when the sales contract is signed.

7. During its fiscal year ending December 31, 20X1, Noriker Inc. issued common shares to its vice-president of marketing. At the date of issuing these shares, the company also provided the vice-president with a non-interest bearing loan of $50,000 to purchase the shares. While reviewing the minutes of all the Noriker board of directors meetings during the audit fieldwork, Noriker's auditor notes that in a meeting on February 12, 20X2, the Noriker board agreed to forgive this loan, effective on that day.

(AICPA adapted)

DC 4 **Subsequent Events: Cases.** In connection with your ex-
LO.5 amination of the financial statements of Olars Manufacturing Corp. for the year ended December 31, your post-balance sheet audit procedures disclosed the following items:

1. January 3: The provincial government approved construction of an expressway. The plan will result in the expropriation of land owned by Olars Manufacturing Corp. Construction will begin late next year. No estimate of the expropriation award is available.

2. January 4: The funds for a $25,000 loan to the corporation made by Mr. Olars on July 15 were obtained by him with a loan on his personal life insurance policy. The loan was recorded in the account Loan payable to officers. Mr. Olars's source of the funds was not disclosed in the company records. The corporation pays the premiums on the life insurance policy, and Mrs. Olars, wife of the president, is the owner and beneficiary of the policy.

3. January 7: The mineral content of a shipment of ore en route on December 31 was determined to be 72 percent. The shipment was recorded at year-end at an estimated content of 50 percent by a debit to raw material inventory and a credit to accounts payable in the amount of $20,600. The final liability to the vendor is based on the actual mineral content of the shipment.

4. January 15: A series of personal disagreements have arisen between Mr. Olars, the president, and Mr. Tweedy, his brother-in-law, the treasurer. Mr. Tweedy resigned, effective immediately, under an agreement whereby the corporation would purchase his 10 percent share ownership at book value as of December 31. Payment is to be made in two equal amounts in cash on April 1 and October 1. In December the treasurer had obtained a divorce from Mr. Olars's sister.

5. January 31: As a result of reduced sales, production was curtailed in mid-January and some workers were laid off. On February 5 all the remaining workers went on strike. To date the strike is unsettled.

6. February 10: A contract was signed whereby Mammoth Enterprises purchased from Olars Manufacturing all of the latter's capital assets (including rights to receive the proceeds of any property expropriation), inventories, and the right to conduct business under the name "Olars Manufacturing Division." The transfer's effective date will be March 1. The sale price was $500,000, subject to adjustment after a physical inventory. Important factors contributing to the decision to enter into the contract were the policy of the board of directors of Mammoth Industries to diversify the firm's activities and the report of a survey conducted by an independent market appraisal firm, which revealed a declining market for Olars's products.

Required:

Assume that the above items came to your attention prior to completion of your audit work on February 15. For each of the above items:

a. Give the audit procedures, if any, that would have brought the item to your attention. Indicate other sources of information that may have revealed the item.

b. Discuss the disclosure that you would recommend for the item, listing all details. Indicate those, if any, that should not be disclosed. Give your reasons for recommending or not recommending disclosure of these.

(AICPA adapted)

DC 5 **Warranty Provision Audit Issues.** Breton Inc.
LO.6 manufactures industrial lighting fixtures with two main
and product lines: interior and exterior fixtures. The fixtures
LO.8 are sold with a one-year warranty on parts and labour. During 20X0, Breton's engineering group undertook a five-year review of its warranty claims history and costs, and established that an appropriate accounting policy for warranty costs is to accrue 3 percent of annual sales for exterior fixtures and 2 percent of annual sales for interior fixtures. PA, Breton's auditor, has used this analysis as the basis for evaluating provision for estimated warranty cost at year-end for the past two year's audits. During 20X3, Breton's competition increased as light fixtures from China entered the market, selling for prices 40 to 50 percent lower. To maintain its customer base, Breton's senior management decided to promote the higher quality of Breton's products, and expanded Breton warranty coverage to two years to support these quality claims. However, to keep costs in line, there were no changes to materials used or production methods. PA is now assessing the 20X3 year-end provision for estimated warranty costs and learns that there is no plan to change the approach for developing the estimate. Breton sales people receive commissions of 1 percent of gross sales. Senior managers, including the CFO, receive bonuses only if the company's pre-tax profit exceeds $300,000.

Required:

a. Discuss the implications of the changes in Breton's competitive environment and business strategy for the audit of its warranty liability estimate.

b. If you were the CFO, what arguments would you make to support not changing the method used to estimate warranty liability for the current year?

c. What actions do you recommend PA take in this case?

DC 6 **Fixed Asset Dispositions, Accounting Misstatements.**
LO.8 During the current year, Karabakh Limited sold off all the heating and air conditioning equipment in one of its buildings because it was being converted from an assembly plant to a warehouse. It was sold to a neighbouring business, which paid $400,000 cash. The equipment was about 10 years old, originally cost $1 million, and was approximately 80 percent depreciated. Karabakh's bookkeeper recorded the sale as follows:

dr Cash   400,000

  cr Sales revenue   400,000

Required:

a. What impact does the misstatement have on Karabakh's financial statements? Outline which accounts will be affected and the dollar amounts of these effects.

b. Assume this transaction is material to Karabakh's financial statements. What procedures would allow the Karabakh auditor to find this bookkeeping error?

c. Provide a draft adjusting journal entry to correct the entry.

DC 7 **Franchising Revenues.** You are an auditor with ZZ, a
LO.1 PA firm. Your firm has just accepted a new engagement
and to audit the annual financial statements of Chestnut Lim-
LO.2 ited, a medium-sized restaurant business. Chestnut operates a chain of specialty fast food restaurants. Most of the restaurants are franchised, and Chestnut receives franchise fees based on the franchisee store's net sales revenues.

Chestnut receives 4 percent of net sales as a base franchise fee, 1 percent as an advertising fee, and 0.5 percent as an administration fee for processing franchisee accounting information and issuing reports in standard format. Franchisee sales information is uploaded daily to Chestnut's central accounting system, where it is input into the franchise reporting system to generate daily, monthly, and year-end management reports.

Required:

Design an audit plan for franchise revenues at Chestnut. State any assumptions you make.

DC 8 **Lawyer's Letter Responses.** Omega Corporation is in-
LO.3 volved in a lawsuit brought by a competitor for patent infringement. The competitor is asking $14 million actual damages for lost profits and unspecified punitive damages. The lawsuit has been in progress for 15 months, and Omega has worked closely with its outside counsel preparing its defence. Omega recently requested its outside lawyers with the firm of Wolfe & Goodwin to provide information to the auditors.

The managing partner of Wolfe & Goodwin asked four different lawyers who have worked on the case to prepare a concise response to the auditors. They returned the following:

1. The action involves unique characteristics wherein authoritative legal precedents bearing directly on the plaintiff's claims do not seem to exist. We believe the plaintiff will have serious problems establishing Omega's liability; nevertheless, if the plaintiff is successful, the damage award may be substantial.

2. In our opinion, Omega will be able to defend this action successfully, and, if not, the possible liability to Omega in this proceeding is nominal in amount.

3. We believe the plaintiff's case against Omega is without merit.

4. In our opinion Omega will be able to assert meritorious defences and has a reasonable chance of sustaining an adequate defence, with a possible outcome of settling the case for less than the damages claimed.

Required:

a. Interpret each of the four responses separately. Decide whether each is (1) adequate to conclude that the likelihood of an adverse outcome is "remote," requiring no disclosure in financial statements, or (2) too vague to serve as adequate information for a decision, requiring more information from the lawyers or from management.

b. What kind of response do you think the auditors would get if they asked the plaintiff's counsel about the likely outcome of the lawsuit? Discuss.

DC 9
LO.1
and
LO.2
Revenue, Audit Procedures. While performing analytical procedures as part of her audit of the revenue and expense accounts at Galloway Inc., PA notes that Galloway's sales revenues in the current year have increased by 20 percent over the prior year. Galloway manufactures and sells business forms and has seen declining sales over the past few years as its customers have been changing to paperless, online process methods. In fact, in the prior year's audit there was concern about Galloway's ability to meet its long-term debt covenants which require at least a 2:1 current ratio and pretax earnings that are at least 10 times long-term debt interest charges. To meet these debt covenant restrictions, no bonuses were paid to management in the prior year. When PA discussed the current year sales figures with the sales manager, he informed her that Galloway had increased its prices by 50 percent in the third quarter of the current year, to offset the lower sales volumes. Management had determined that Galloway's remaining customers were restricted to using paper-based documentation for various business reasons and thus would accept higher prices. During this interview, the chief accountant was passing by and, overhearing the topic, made the following comments: "Note that accounts receivable balance is also much higher than last year, which is totally consistent with the higher sales. This should tie together your analysis, so your audit work on sales and AR must now be complete. We are looking forward to having our boardroom back when you auditors finally finish the job and leave!"

Required:

Discuss the nature and the persuasiveness of the audit evidence PA is gathering in the above scenario. What additional evidence would you recommend she obtain to support her conclusion on the sales revenue figure?

DC 10
LO.1
Revenues, General Journal Entries. Town & Country Cable Inc. (TCC) is a cable television provider servicing customers in small towns and rural areas. Its shares are privately held, but it issued a 20-year bond eight years ago to the public. The bond contains restrictive covenants, which include requirements for TCC to maintain a current ratio of at least 2:1 at each fiscal year-end, and a ratio of operating cash flow to current liabilities of at least 1:0. If the covenants are violated, the bond holders have the right to demand repayment, raise the interest rate, and/or liquidate the company. In recent years TCC has seen very little growth from new customer installations as most people are now choosing satellite service instead of cable. At the same time, TCC's existing installed customer base has been shrinking as many have switched to satellite for more channels and more reliable service. As a result of these changes in its operating environment, TCC has been close to violating its restrictive covenants in the past two years.

PA is the senior on the current-year audit. While scrutinizing a 300-page printout of the general journal entries for the year for material entries and seeing nothing but small adjustments for payroll and purchasing discounts, PA is about to sign off on the procedure. Then she notices ten journal entries in a row in the middle of November that debit account #22000 (current accrued liabilities) and credit account #54400 (other operating income). The entries are all for different immaterial amounts, but all are to the same two accounts, and all have the same explanatory note: "To adjust accrued liabilities as per instructions memo of Nov 2." On further investigation, PA finds 40 more entries to these accounts with the same explanation. The entries are all for different, immaterial amounts but add up to a large, material amount. The accountant who made these general journal entries is no longer employed by TCC, and no one else in the accounting department knows anything about the "memo of Nov 2."

Required:

a. What are some possible explanations for the PA's findings described above? How can the PA determine whether these entries result in a misstatement to the financial statements?

b. If these entries do result in financial statements that are materially misstated, what other procedures in the audit may have revealed these entries?

DC 11
LO.5
Subsequent Events, *Pro Forma* Disclosures. Assume that you are the financial statement auditor in the following independent cases, and you are completing your audit in February 20X2. For each of these subsequent events, indicate if you would require the auditee company to adjust its December 20X1 year-end financial statements, disclose the event in the 20X1 financial statements, and/or provide *pro forma* financial information in the 20X1 financial statements. Give reasons to support your responses. State any assumptions you make.

a. During January 20X2, the company's management decided to sell rental real estate properties that accounted for approximately 40 percent of its total revenues in 20X1.

b. The company's main factory was closed for six weeks in January and February of 20X2 because of ice storm damage. The factory resumed full operations in late February.

c. One of the company's factories was destroyed by a fire in January. The plant was old and will not be replaced, as production can be taken up by excess capacity in other plants.

d. In late February, the company's board of directors agreed to settle an outstanding claim by paying $15 million to former employees. The employees suffered health problems related to asbestos exposure during the years of their employment. A contingent liability was disclosed but not accrued as of December 31, 20X1, because of the uncertainty surrounding the outcome of the lawsuit.

    e. For the past four years, the company has made 90 percent of its revenues and profits from sales of specialty cable to computer manufacturers. Early in 20X2, it has become apparent that there is massive overcapacity in this industry, and demand for the product has fallen to almost zero. It is not expected to recover for several years, and may never recover if alternate technologies developed in the meantime make the product unnecessary.

DC 12 **Subsequent Discovery of Facts and Audit Reporting.**
LO.5 Refer to the application case and analysis at the end of
and the chapter (page 616). Assume that, instead of with-
LO.8 drawing from the engagement, the auditors in this case had issued a clean audit report on all the companies in the case for the 20X9 year-end. They used the appraisals and other representations from the Blues brothers as evidence that the mining properties were correctly valued and the financial statements were fairly presented. One month after the audited financial statements were issued to shareholders, the auditors contact the companies' accountant about their unpaid fees and learn that the companies have run out of cash and ceased operations. It is suspected that the Blues brothers took all the cash that the bank had lent to the companies and fled the country.

Required:

What are the auditors' responsibilities in this situation?

DC 13 **Going Concern Uncertainty and Audit Reporting**
LO.6 The auditors of the CRX Inc. (CRX) financial statements for the year ended December 31, 20X7, have decided that there is substantial doubt that CRX can continue to exist as a going concern, because the company has experienced significant operating losses since 20X5 and has

had to get permission from its lenders to postpone its debt payment requirements. CRX's management has agreed to describe the problems in the president's message to the shareholders in their annual report, but has decided not to reflect this situation in the notes to the financial statements.

Required:

Discuss fully the type of audit opinion to be issued in this situation, including a description of any modifications that would be necessary to the standard audit report. Describe what change(s) would be necessary for CRX to obtain an unqualified audit opinion in this case.

DC 14 **Scope Limitation and Audit Reporting.** Yue is audit-
LO.6 ing the accounts receivable for Slawson & Slawson, LLP, a large law partnership. The managing partner of the law firm has prohibited the auditor from confirming any of the law firm's accounts receivable. The lawyers are concerned that their clients would consider it a breach of confidentiality for the auditor to know they had engaged the lawyer's services and would not understand that the auditor is also operating under strict professional rules that require confidentiality. The accounts receivable balance is highly material. Yue is not able to satisfy himself as to the receivable balance by alternative means.

Required:

    a. Describe the type and format of audit report that should be issued in this case.
    b. Explain the type of evidence that Yue was trying to obtain by confirming the law firm's account receivable balances, and the assertion(s) and the specific audit objectives that this evidence relates to.
    c. Why do you think it was not possible to obtain this evidence by alternative means?

PART 4
Other Professional Services

CHAPTER 16

Other Public Accounting Services and Reports

Public accountants (PAs) offer assurance services on information other than the standard historical financial statements. These services grow out of business, government, and public consumer demand for the objective expert association offered by PAs. However, PAs need to be careful that they do not suggest more credibility than is warranted in their reports on the information.

As you study the topics in this chapter, you will see the standards for PA engagements other than audits of financial statements. The CICA has decided to adopt only the international *audit* standards at this time and will consider at a future date what, if any, other international standards it will adopt. Existing Canadian standards for other PA services and reports, as they are outlined at the beginning of Chapter 3, will remain in effect for the time being. In this chapter, we cover some of these other types of association in more detail: review engagements, compilation engagements, other engagements involving financial information, some assurance engagements other than financial statements, public sector assurance engagements, and the assurance engagement conceptual framework.

The standards in this chapter are covered under the original *CICA Handbook* system of numbered recommendations and thus does not refer to CASs. However, we do reference the most closely related international standard reference as well. As we will see, Canadian standards have had a significant influence on international standards for assurance engagements.

LEARNING OBJECTIVES

After completing this chapter, you will be able to do the following:

1 Prepare reports for review and compilation of unaudited financial statements, given specific facts.

2 Write a report on a review of interim financial information.

3* Describe the various reports on internal control and their connection with public reporting and reporting to a client's audit committee. (Partly in Appendix 16A)

4* Define the various financial presentations and levels of service involved in association with prospectuses, MD&A, and financial statements for use in other countries.

5* Describe the umbrella standards for assurance engagements, and relate them to an acceptable reporting framework.

6* Explain public sector auditing concepts.

7* Explain environmental auditing issues.

8* Identify assurance engagements unique to ebusiness. (Appendix 16A)

9* Give examples of another appropriate basis of accounting (AADBA), distinguishing it from GAAP. (Appendix 16A)

10* Contrast an audit report on supplementary current value financial statements with a standard report on historical cost financial statements. (Appendix 16A)

11* Define the various financial presentations and levels of service involved in association with financial forecasts and projections. (Appendix 16A)

Note: Those learning objectives marked with an asterisk (*) and their corresponding topics are considered advanced material. Appendix 16A is located on the text Online Learning Centre.

UNAUDITED FINANCIAL STATEMENTS

. . . .

LEARNING OBJECTIVE
1 Prepare reports for review and compilation of unaudited financial statements, given specific facts.

Many PA practices offer accounting and review services for small-business clients. These engagements include bookkeeping, financial statement preparation, and financial statement review to help small businesses prepare financial communications. Until the late 1970s, auditing standards concentrated on one level of assurance based on a full audit, and appeared to deny small clients the full benefit of PAs' services.

The investigations by the Adams Committee in Canada and the U.S. Congress during 1977–78 highlighted the problem by focusing attention on the idea that auditing standards handicapped the business of small public accounting firms and the services they offered small-business clients. The argument has become known as the "Big GAAS–Little GAAS" question. Big GAAS was portrayed as the villain in the play, with its proposal that existing standards were enacted under the influence of large PA firms whose practices are centred on big business. Even though this proposition is not true, the fact is that small PA firms want to give, and small businesses want to receive, some level of assurance as a result of accountants' work even though an audit in accordance with GAAS is not performed. As a result, a separate part of the *CICA Handbook*, the 8000 sections, and International Standard on Review Engagements (ISRE) 2400 have been set aside to deal with review engagements. *CICA Handbook,* section 9200, and International Standard on Related Services (ISRS) 4410 deal with compilation engagements.

Review Services

The review services explained in this section apply specifically to accountants' work on unaudited financial statements. In a review services engagement, an accountant performs some procedures to achieve a moderate level of assurance, not the same as that obtained by performing an audit in accordance with GAAS. *CICA Handbook* paragraph 8100.05 states the following:

> Reviews are distinguishable from audits in that the scope of a review is less than that of an audit and therefore the level of assurance provided is lower. A review consists primarily of enquiry, analytical procedures, and discussions related to information supplied to the public accountant by the enterprise, with the limited objective of assessing whether the information is being reported on appropriate criteria. In this section, the word *plausible* is used in the sense of appearing to be worthy of belief based on the information obtained by the public accountant in connection with the review.

Paragraph 8100.15 identifies standards applicable to a review engagement, and a similar set of standards is given in ISRE 2400. They are as follows:

General standard
The review should be performed and the review engagement report prepared by a person or persons having adequate technical training and proficiency in conducting reviews, with due care and with an objective state of mind.

Review standards
(*i*) The work should be adequately planned and properly executed. If assistants are employed, they should be properly supervised.

(*ii*) The public accountant should possess or acquire sufficient knowledge of the business carried on by the enterprise so that intelligent enquiry and assessment of information obtained can be made.

(*iii*) The public accountant should perform a review with the limited objective of assessing whether the information being reported on is plausible in the circumstances within the framework of appropriate criteria. Such a review should consist of

   (*a*) enquiry, analytical procedures, and discussion; and

   (*b*) additional or more extensive procedures when the public accountant's knowledge of the business carried on by the enterprise and the results of the enquiry, analytical procedures, and discussion cause him or her to doubt the plausibility of such information.

Reporting standards
(*i*) The review engagement report should indicate the scope of the review. The nature of the review engagement should be made evident and be clearly distinguished from an audit.

(*ii*) The report should indicate, based on the review

   (*a*) whether anything has come to the public accountant's attention that causes him or her to believe that the information being reported on is not, in all material respects, in accordance with appropriate criteria; or

   (*b*) that no assurance can be provided.

The report should provide an explanation of the nature of any reservations contained therein and, if readily determinable, the effect.

These standards suggest that auditors need special training and experience in conducting reviews, especially with respect to working within a plausibility framework. The second review standard shows that obtaining knowledge of the business is critical to the review engagement as it is necessary in determining whether the information gathered through the engagement process is plausible—or worth believing. Sufficient knowledge of the business (and industry) is required to make intelligent enquiries and a reasonable assessment of responses and other information obtained. However, the knowledge required for review engagements is normally less detailed than that required in an audit. The "plausible" concept also means that there is a higher risk of undetected material misstatement than there is in an audit engagement. This is why review engagements are considered to provide only moderate-level assurance, that is, in a 70–80 percent assurance range as compared with the 90–99 percent assurance looked for in an audit engagement.

When a PA doubts the plausibility of the information reported, sufficient additional or more extensive procedures should be carried out to resolve doubt or confirm the need for a reservation.

The review standards indicate that review work on unaudited financial statements consists primarily of enquiry and analytical procedures. The information gained is similar to audit evidence, but the limited procedures recommended suggest that typical auditing procedures of assessing control risk, conducting physical observation of tangible assets, sending confirmations, or examining documentary details of transactions are not performed. Following is a list of the recommended procedures:

- Obtain knowledge of the client's business. Know the accounting principles of the client's industry. Understand the client's organization and operations.
- Enquire about the accounting system and bookkeeping procedures.
- Perform analytical procedures to identify relationships and individual items that appear to be unusual.
- Enquire about actions taken at meetings of shareholders, directors, and other important executive committees.
- Read (study) the financial statements for indications that they conform with generally accepted accounting principles.
- Obtain reports from other accountants who audit or review significant components, from subsidiaries or from other investees.
- Enquire of officers and directors about the following: conformity with generally accepted accounting principles, consistent application of accounting principles, changes in the client's business or accounting practices, matters that raised questions when other procedures were applied (listed above), and events subsequent to the date of the financial statements.
- Perform any other procedures considered necessary if the financial statements appear to be incorrect, incomplete, or otherwise unsatisfactory.
- Prepare working papers showing the matters covered by the enquiry and analytical review procedures, especially the resolution of unusual problems and questions.
- Obtain written representation letters from the owner, manager, or chief executive officer and from the chief financial officer.

Many firms will perform more detailed procedures, such as bank reconciliations and bank confirmations, to corroborate information obtained by enquiry. However, current review standards do not require this. Reviews have traditionally provided negative assurance, or (in the words of the new assurance framework, to be discussed later in this chapter) a moderate level of assurance that indicates the financial information is "plausible" (paragraph 5025.12) or "moderate."[1] The term negative assurance has become traditional through use of the "nothing has come to my attention . . ." wording in the review report (see Exhibit 16–1).

A review service is not a basis for expressing an opinion on financial statements. Each page of the financial statements should be conspicuously marked as unaudited. The standards indicate that a report on a review services engagement should include the following statements:

- A review service was performed and the scope of the review engagement was in accordance with generally accepted standards for review engagement.
- Review procedures consist primarily of enquiries of company personnel and analytical procedures applied to financial data.
- A review service does not constitute an audit, and an opinion on financial statements is not expressed (a disclaimer of any audit opinion).
- The accountant is not aware of any material modifications that should be made; or, if aware, a disclosure is made of departure(s) from generally accepted accounting principles. (This is a negative assurance.)

When other independent accountants are involved in audit or review of parts of the business, the principal reviewer cannot divide responsibility by referring to the other accountants in the review report, unless the disclosure helps explain the reason for a reservation. In review engagements, PAs follow the spirit of the auditing standards to write

---

[1] *CICA Handbook*, paragraph 5025.12 or ISRE 2400.9.

EXHIBIT 16–1   PUBLIC ACCOUNTANT'S REPORT

To (person engaging the public accountant),

I have reviewed the balance sheet of Client Limited as at ...., 20..., and the statements of income, retained earnings, and changes in cash flow for the year then ended. My review was made in accordance with Canadian generally accepted standards for review engagements and accordingly consisted primarily of enquiry, analytical procedures, and discussion related to information supplied to me by the company.

A review does not constitute an audit and, consequently, I do not express an audit opinion on these financial statements.

Based on my review, nothing has come to my attention that causes me to believe that these financial statements are not, in all material respects, in accordance with Canadian generally accepted accounting principles.

City

Date

(signed).....................

CHARTERED ACCOUNTANT

Source: © *CICA Handbook*, paragraph 8200.42.

the form and content of the reference to the work and reports of other PAs.[2] An example of a review report is given in Exhibit 16–1.

Compilation Services

Compilation is a synonym for an older term—write-up work. Both terms refer to an accountant's helping a client to "write up" the financial information in the form of financial statements. In a compilation service, an accountant performs few, if any, procedures, and substantially less than in a review service. The description of a compilation of financial statements, according to *CICA Handbook* paragraph 9200.03, follows, and a similar description is given in ISRS 4410.3:

> [A compilation service is] one in which a public accountant receives information from a client and arranges it into the form of financial statements. The public accountant is concerned that the assembly of information is arithmetically correct; however, the public accountant does not attempt to verify the accuracy or completeness of the information provided. Unlike an audit or review engagement in which the public accountant does sufficient work to issue a communication that provides assurance regarding the financial statements, no expression of assurance is contemplated in a compilation engagement.

Since compilation engagements provide no assurance credibility, the PA is limited in the action she or he can take. They do, however, have a responsibility not to be associated with misleading information:

> When the public accountant is aware that there are matters which the public accountant believes would cause the financial statements to be false or misleading, she or he should request additional or revised information in order to complete the statements. If the client does not provide the information requested or agree with the statements, the public accountant should not release the statements and should withdraw from the engagement.[3]

Financial statements may be compiled on a basis other than GAAP if, in the auditor's judgment, this is appropriate for the circumstances. Appropriate non-GAAP bases are traditionally referred to as **another appropriate disclosed basis of accounting (AADBA)** in the literature. These are discussed later in the chapter as part of the suitable criteria of the assurance framework.

The best way to disclose AADBA statements is through their title (e.g., Statements Based on Income Tax Accounting) or in a note discussing the statements. Titles and notes are also the best method for indicating the reasons for the compilation. The presentation of the compiled financial statements can range from "bare bones" single column presentations to GAAP-form financial statement presentations with all known notes. If the PA is aware that

[2] CAS 626. A41–A2. *(CICA Handbook*, paragraphs 6930.22–23.)
[3] *CICA Handbook*, paragraph 9200.18, also see ISRS 4410.14.

EXHIBIT 16-2   NOTICE TO READER

I have compiled the balance sheet of Client Limited as at December 31, 20X1, and the statements of income, retained earnings, and cash flows for the (period) then ended from information provided by management (the proprietor). I have not audited, reviewed, or otherwise attempted to verify the accuracy or completeness of such information. Readers are cautioned that these statements may not be appropriate for their purposes.

I am not independent with respect to Client Limited.

City   (printed or signed).....................

Date   CHARTERED ACCOUNTANT

Source: © CICA Handbook, paragraph 9200.24.

the financial statements may be misleading and requests additional or revised information but the client does not provide the information or agree with the statements, then the PA should not release them and should withdraw from the engagement. The minimimum standard is that the financial statements not be "false or misleading." This, of course, includes arithmetic accuracy and conformity with the appropriate disclosed basis of accounting. This is accounting credibility or the "value added" that the PA association provides in compilation engagements.

At the outset, the PA should have an understanding and written agreement with the client as to the services that will be provided. An engagement letter is normally the clearest record of agreement. Although compilation engagements do not provide any attest assurance or credibility, they do provide accounting credibility—the reason to pay the extra cost to have a PA to do the compilation.

In a compilation service, an accountant should understand the client's business, read (study) the financial statements looking for obvious clerical or accounting principle errors, and follow up on information that is incorrect, incomplete, or otherwise unsatisfactory. Each page of the financial statements should be marked **unaudited—see Notice to Reader.** The report can be issued by an accountant who is not independent, provided the lack of independence and the reasons for it are disclosed in the financial statements and in the Notice to Reader (see Exhibit 16–2).

The report [or Notice to Reader] should contain the following:

- An assertion that the public accountant compiled the statement from information provided by management (or proprietor).

- A statement that the public accountant has not audited, reviewed, or otherwise attempted to verify the accuracy or completeness of such information.

- A caution to readers that the statement may not be appropriate for their purposes.

- No expression of any form of opinion or negative assurance

Note that the Notice to Reader is not a proper place to make non-GAAP AADBA disclosures because the Notice to Reader does not mention GAAP or any other basis of accounting. The proper place to make the necessary disclosures for nonmisleading financial statements, and possibly also the intended purpose of the financial statements, is in the financial statements.

Exhibit 16–2 illustrates that two kinds of reports on compiled financial statements can be given: (1) a report stating that the accountant is not independent (as in Exhibit 16–2), or (2) a report by a public accountant who is independent, and would therefore exclude the last sentence of the report in Exhibit 16–2. In either case, the basis of accounting may be an AADBA, just like other kinds of accounting services.

The possible components of a compilation file are as follows:

- financial statements and Notice to Reader,
- engagement letter,
- adjustments,
- working papers to support computations (e.g., capital asset schedule, etc.),

EXHIBIT 16-3   AUDIT VERSUS MAJOR NONAUDIT ENGAGEMENTS SUMMARY

Compilation	Review	Audit
Criteria: prepared for internal use of restricted users	Criteria: Plausibility, consistency	Criteria: present fairly in conformity with GAAP, GAAS
IC not evaluated	IC not evaluated	Evaluate IC
No independent corroborating evidence	Some evidence	Independent corroborating evidence
Compilation, bookkeeping	Enquiry-based review, discussions	Substantive and compliance testing
Accounting credibility	Negative or moderate assurance	Positive assurance or high assurance
Notice to reader	Public accountant's report or review engagement report	Auditor's report
IC = Internal control		

- documentation that the PA has resolved all matters leading to belief that the financial statements might be false or misleading,
- other working papers to meet the firm's quality control standards.

Exhibit 16–3 summarizes the major differences between audit, review, and compilation engagements.

OTHER REVIEW AND COMPILATION TOPICS

There are several other aspects of review and compilation engagements and of reports that differ from audit standards. The following topics point out some of the different problems in dealing with unaudited financial statements.

Prescribed Forms

Industry trade associations, banks, government agencies, and regulatory agencies often use prescribed forms (standard, reprinted documents) specifying the content and measurement of accounting information required for special purposes. These forms may not request disclosures or measurements required by or conforming to GAAP.

When such forms are compiled (but not when reviewed) by an accountant, the compilation report does not need to call attention to the GAAP departures or disclosure deficiencies. Nothing in either section 9200 or in the guideline, "Compilation Engagements—Financial Statement Disclosures," requires public accountants to disclose known departures from GAAP in either the compiled statements or the Notice to Reader.[4] In the latter case, the accountant specifically states that he or she has made no attempt to determine if the statements contain GAAP departures. In fact, disclosing known departures could be confusing or even misleading, as readers might assume the accountant was responsible for disclosing *all* GAAP departures, and that the only departures present are the ones disclosed. This responsibility is beyond the scope of a compilation engagement.

How should the auditor deal with situations of known departures from GAAP or other AADBA? The Notice to Reader does caution readers that the financial statements may not be appropriate for their purposes. Compiled statements may not be appropriate for general purposes and their use is restricted, depending on the purpose of the engagement. For example, compiled statements are frequently prepared for management, who are aware of the limitations. Moreover, "when the accountant is aware that the statements may be misleading for some users or purposes, then the public accountant may need to include appropriate disclosures (in the statements themselves, not the Notice to Reader) to prevent them from being misleading. Of course, if management will not allow the disclosures considered necessary, the public

[4] AuG-5.

accountant has no alternative but to withhold the statements and withdraw from the engagement."[5] Remember that, despite this responsibility, compilations are limited and there is no assurance that the PA can determine whether the financial statements achieve the specified intended purpose.

Personal Financial Plans

Personal financial planning has become a big source of business for PA firms. Most personal financial plan documentation includes personal financial statements. Ordinarily, an accountant associated with such statements would need to give the standard compilation report (disclaimer), which seems rather awkward when the client is the only one using the statements. In Canada, a PA who wishes to meet the requirements as a certified financial planner under the Financial Planning Standards Council of Canada must satisfy that body's rules of conduct by disclosing any potential conflicts of interest to his or her clients. In Canada there is no distinction for compilation of personal financial information. U.S. standards exempt personal financial statements from the reporting requirement; however, the following report must be given, with each page of the financial report marked "See accountant's report":

> The accompanying Statement of Financial Condition of Edward Beliveau, as of December 31, 2009, was prepared solely to help you develop your personal financial plan. Accordingly, it may be incomplete or contain other departures from generally accepted accounting principles and should not be used to obtain credit or for any purposes other than developing your financial plan. We have not audited, reviewed, or compiled the statements.

A Note on GAAP Departures and Review Engagement Reports

GAAP departures must be treated carefully in review reports. As in audit reports, the accountant can and should add an explanatory paragraph pointing out known departures, including omitted disclosures. Having knowledge of GAAP departures means that the accountant must make exception to them in the negative assurance sentence, such as the following: "Except for the failure, as described in the preceding paragraph, to (describe the departure), based on my review nothing has come to my attention . . ."

A separate paragraph describing the departure in more detail would be inserted as the next to last paragraph in the Review Engagement Report. See Exhibit 16–4 for the complete report.

EXHIBIT   16-4   QUALIFICATION RESULTING FROM A DEPARTURE FROM GENERALLY ACCEPTED ACCOUNTING PRINCIPLES WHEN THE EFFECTS ARE NOT READILY DETERMINABLE

REVIEW ENGAGEMENT REPORT

To (person engaging the public accountant)

I have reviewed the balance sheet of Client Limited as at ......, 20..., and the statements of income, retained earnings, and cash flows for the year then ended. My review was made in accordance with Canadian generally accepted standards for review engagements and accordingly consisted primarily of enquiry, analytical procedures, and discussion related to information supplied to me by the company.

A review does not constitute an audit and, consequently, I do not express an audit opinion on these financial statements.

Note .... indicates that the investments in companies subject to significant influence have not been accounted for on the equity basis. The effects of this departure from generally accepted accounting principles on the unaudited financial statements have not been determined.

Except for the failure, as described in the preceding paragraph, to account for the investments on an equity basis, based on my review, nothing has come to my attention that causes me to believe that these financial statements are not, in all material respects, in accordance with Canadian generally accepted accounting principles.

City

Date

(signed)...................

CHARTERED ACCOUNTANT

Source: © CICA Handbook, section 8200, Appendix B, Example C.

---

[5] R. J. Johnston, *CA Magazine*, May 1988, p. 53.

EXHIBIT 16-5   ADVERSE REPORT RESULTING FROM A DEPARTURE FROM GENERALLY ACCEPTED ACCOUNTING PRINCIPLES

REVIEW ENGAGEMENT REPORT

To (person engaging the public accountant),

I have reviewed the balance sheet of Client Limited as at ......, 20..., and the statements of income, retained earnings, and cash flows for the year then ended. My review was made in accordance with Canadian generally accepted standards for review engagements and accordingly consisted primarily of enquiry, analytical procedures, and discussion related to information supplied to me by the company.

A review does not constitute an audit and, consequently, I do not express an audit opinion on these financial statements.

Note .... indicates that commencing this year the company ceased to consolidate the financial statements of its subsidiary companies because management considers consolidation to be inappropriate when there are substantial noncontrolling interests. Under Canadian generally accepted accounting principles, the existence of such noncontrolling interests is not an acceptable reason for not consolidating the financial statements of subsidiary companies with those of the reporting enterprise. Had consolidated financial statements been prepared, virtually every account in, and the information provided by way of notes to, the accompanying financial statements would have been materially different. The effects of this departure from generally accepted accounting principles on the accompanying financial statements have not been determined.

My review indicates that, because the investment in subsidiary companies is not accounted for on a consolidated basis, as described in the preceding paragraph, these financial statements are not in accordance with Canadian generally accepted accounting principles.

City

Date

(signed).....................

CHARTERED ACCOUNTANT

Source: © CICA Handbook, section 8200, Appendix B, Example D.

EXHIBIT 16-6   DISCLAIMER OF ASSURANCE

REVIEW ENGAGEMENT REPORT

To (person engaging the public accountant),

I have reviewed the balance sheet of Client Limited as at ......, 20..., and the statements of income, retained earnings, and cash flows for the year then ended. My review was made in accordance with Canadian generally accepted standards for review engagements and accordingly consisted primarily of enquiry, analytical procedures, and discussion related to information supplied to me by the company, except as explained below.

A review does not constitute an audit and, consequently, I do not express an audit opinion on these financial statements.

My review indicated serious deficiencies in the accounting records of the company. As a consequence, I was unable to complete my review. Had I been able to complete my review, I might have determined adjustments to be necessary to these financial statements.

Because of my inability to complete a review, as described in the preceding paragraph, I am unable to express any assurance as to whether these financial statements are, in all material respects, in accordance with Canadian generally accepted accounting principles.

City

Date

(signed).....................

CHARTERED ACCOUNTANT

Source: © CICA Handbook, section 8200, Appendix B, Example F.

The range of possible review reports is similar to that for audit reports, and they arise for similar reasons. Exhibit 16–5 illustrates an adverse report resulting from a GAAP departure, and Exhibit 16–6 illustrates a disclaimer of assurance report as a result of a newer scope limitation.

REVIEW CHECKPOINTS

1   Explain what led to the creation of Review and Compilation Standards.

2   What considerations should a successor accountant make in accepting a new engagement?

3   How should a public accountant disclose misleading statements detected during a compilation engagement?

4   What is the difference between a review services engagement and a compilation service engagement regarding historical financial statements? Compare both of these with an audit engagement.

INTERIM FINANCIAL INFORMATION

LEARNING OBJECTIVE
2 Write a report on a review of interim financial information.

Interim financial information is not a basic and necessary element of financial statements that conform to GAAP. When interim information is presented, however, it should conform to the accounting Recommendations in the *CICA Handbook*.[6] Audited interim financial statements might be prepared for buy/sell situations for a business or to fulfill financial reporting requirements of regulatory authorities, particularly Canadian companies that are traded in U.S. capital markets and thus must comply with SEC requirements. On occasion, regulators such as the SEC insist that the interim financial information be audited, but interim statements are not normally audited.

A review of interim financial statements or information is a common type of review engagement. This review differs considerably from an audit. According to *CICA Handbook* section 7050, the key objective of a review of interim financial statements is to assess whether accounting principles have been applied on a basis that is consistent with the annual report and the corresponding interim financial statements of the previous year. In particular, the auditor is concerned that interim financial statements are not misleading relative to the annual report. The interim review does not require a complete assessment of internal control risk each quarter or that sufficient appropriate evidence is gathered for an opinion. The nature, timing, and extent of review procedures explained below presume that the reviewer has a knowledge base of the company from the audit of the most recent annual financial statements. A review done on this knowledge base is guided by significantly more information than one done without this, and it might, therefore, provide more assurance than a review without an audit knowledge base. For example, the public accountant with an existing audit knowledge base has familiarity with the system of internal controls.

Nature of Review Procedures

Reviews consist mainly of enquiry and analytical procedures. Paragraph 8200.23 and ISRE 2400.20 suggest checklists that include the following:

- Enquire about the accounting system.

- Obtain an understanding of the system. Determine whether there have been any significant changes in the system used to produce interim information.

- Perform analytical procedures to identify relationships and individual items that seem unusual.

- Read the minutes of shareholder, board of director, and board committee meetings to identify actions or events that may affect interim financial information.

- Read (study) the interim financial information and determine whether it conforms with generally accepted accounting principles.

- Obtain reports from other accountants who perform limited reviews of significant components, subsidiaries, or other investees.

- Enquire of officers and executives about the following: conformity with generally accepted accounting principles, consistent application of accounting principles,

---

[6] *CICA Handbook*, section 1751.

changes in the client's business or accounting practices, questions that have arisen as a result of applying other procedures (listed above), and events subsequent to the date of the interim information.

- Obtain written representations from management about interim information matters.

Timing of Review Procedures

Review procedures should be performed at or near the date of the interim information. Starting the engagement prior to the cutoff date will give auditors a chance to deal with problems and questions without undue deadline pressures.

Extent of Review Procedures

The accountant needs to acquire a sufficient knowledge of the client's business, as if it were a regular audit. The extent of review procedures depends on the accountant's professional judgment about problem areas in the system of internal control, the severity of unique accounting principles problems and the errors that have occurred in the past. With knowledge of these areas, the accountant can direct and fine-tune the review procedures in the interest of improving the quality of the interim information.

Review engagement working papers include the following:

- financial statements and review engagement report
- engagement letter
- evidence of planning
- documentation of knowledge of client's business
- names of persons requiring enquiries
- memoranda of enquiries and discussions
- analytical procedures
- details of documents examined
- lead schedules normally in comparative form; conclusion that the items dealt with are plausible in the circumstances, or, if not plausible, their effect on the report
- review engagement questionnaries
- letter of representation (failure to obtain one constitutes a scope restriction)

Reporting on a Review of Interim Information

An accountant may report on interim information presented separately from audited financial statements, provided that a review has been satisfactorily completed. The basic content of the report is as follows:[7]

- statement that a review was made in accordance with standards established for review engagements
- identification of the interim information reviewed
- description of the review procedures
- statement that a review is not an audit
- denial of opinion on the interim information
- negative assurance about material conformity with the disclosed basis of accounting
- mark indicating "unaudited" status on each page

When the interim information is presented, voluntarily under GAAP, as supplemental information in a note to audited annual financial statements and the client requests a review, the auditors give the standard audit report without mentioning the reviewed interim

---

[7] *CICA Handbook*, paragraph 8200.10.

EXHIBIT   16-7   REPORT ON INTERIM INFORMATION IN A COMPANY'S QUARTERLY REPORT
(SECTION 7050.61)

The Shareholders, XYZ Inc.:

At the request of the Board of Directors and Stockholders, we have made a review of the unaudited condensed balance sheets of Analog Devices Inc., at April 28, 20X6, and April 29, 20X5, the related unaudited consolidated statements of income for the three- and six-month periods ended April 28, 20X5, and April 29, 20X5, and the unaudited consolidated statements of cash flows for the six-month periods ending April 28, 20X6, and April 29, 20X5, in accordance with standards established by the CICA.

A review of interim financial information consists principally of obtaining an understanding of the system for the preparation of the interim financial information, applying analytical review procedures to financial data, and making inquiries to persons responsible for financial and accounting matters. It is substantially less in scope than an examination in accordance with generally accepted auditing standards, the objective of which is the expression of an opinion regarding the financial statements taken as a whole. Accordingly, we do not express such an opinion.

Based on our review, nothing has come to our attention that causes us to believe that the accompanying financial statements are not in all material respects in accordance with generally accepted accounting principles.

Public Accountants

Montreal, Quebec

May 16, 20X6

information, unless there is a reason to take exception. Under this exception-based reporting, interim information is mentioned in a modified standard audit report only if (1) it departs from section 1750 principles, (2) management indicates the auditor performed procedures without also saying they express no opinion, or (3) management fails to label interim information as "unaudited" in the note to annual audited financial statements.

An example report on reviewed interim information presented in a quarterly report (not within an annual report) is shown in Exhibit 16–7.

Additional Interim Information Communication

During the difficult economic times of the 1980s, especially in financial institutions, auditors in the United States were criticized for taking no action when they became aware of material problems with interim financial information. The auditors responded that they were not required to take any action because they were not engaged to perform an interim review and issue a report.

Several regulatory agencies were distressed that some companies issued misleading interim information—sometimes with auditors' knowledge—but nothing was done to inform the public or the regulators. The AICPA Auditing Standards Board responded with SAS 100, "Communication of Matters about Interim Financial Information Filed or to Be Filed with Specified Regulatory Agencies—An Amendment to SAS No. 36, Review of Interim Financial Information."

This AICPA standard requires auditors to act when they learn that interim information filed or to be filed with specified agencies is probably materially misstated as a result of a departure from GAAP. The required action is to (*a*) discuss the matter with management as soon as possible, (*b*) inform the company's audit committee if management does not take appropriate and timely action, and (*c*) if the audit committee does not respond appropriately, decide whether to resign from the interim review engagement or resign as the company's auditor. However, auditing standards do not require resignation or direct communication to the "specified agencies." This appears to be a compromise between regulators who probably wanted direct reporting and auditors who wanted to handle difficult problems within the affected companies. This requirement only affects Canadian companies falling within the jurisdiction of the SEC.

5 Must interim financial information required to be presented for annual financial statements be in conformity with GAAP?

6 In what ways is a review of the interim financial information similar to a review of the unaudited annual financial statements of a nonpublic company?

7 When interim information is presented in a note to annual financial statements, under what circumstances would an audit report on the annual financial statements be modified with respect to the interim financial information?

Special Reports—Additional Topics

Auditors may perform a variety of services acting in the capacity of auditor (not as tax adviser or management consultant) that require a report other than the standard unqualified audit report. Services involving special reports are engagements to report on specified elements, accounts, or items of a financial statement;[8] engagements to report on compliance with contractual agreements or regulatory requirements;[9] limited-scope engagements to perform procedures agreed on by the client.[10]

Specified Elements, Accounts, or Items

Auditors may be requested to render special reports on such things as rentals, royalties, profit participations, or a provision for income taxes. The third CICA reporting standard does not apply because these specified elements, accounts, or items do not purport to be statements of financial position or results of operations. The consistency disclosure should be made in the footnotes in all cases.

Special engagements with limited objectives allow auditors to provide needed services to clients. Section 5805 gives the standards for these engagements. Examples include grant application data, reports relating to amount of sales used in computing rental, reports relating to royalties, reports on a profit participation, and reports on the adequacy of a tax provision in financial statements. Exhibit 16–8 contains an illustrative report on a company's accounts receivable.

EXHIBIT   16–8   EXAMPLE OF A REPORT ON A SCHEDULE OF ACCOUNTS RECEIVABLE

AUDITOR'S REPORT
ON SCHEDULE OF ACCOUNTS RECEIVABLE

To the Directors of Client Limited,

I have audited the schedule of accounts receivable of Client Limited as at ...., 20... This financial information is the responsibility of the management of Client Limited. My responsibility is to express an opinion on this financial information based on my audit.

I conducted my audit in accordance with generally accepted auditing standards. Those standards require that I plan and perform an audit to obtain reasonable assurance whether the financial information is free of material misstatement. An audit includes examining, on a test basis, evidence supporting the amounts and disclosures in the financial information. An audit also includes assessing the accounting principles used and significant estimates made by management, as well as evaluating the overall presentation of the financial information.

In my opinion, this schedule presents fairly, in all material respects, the accounts receivable of Client Limited as at ...., 20..., in accordance with generally accepted accounting principles.

City

Date

(signed).....................

CHARTERED ACCOUNTANT

Source: © CICA Handbook, paragraph 5805.19.

[8] CICA Handbook, section 5805 or ISA 800.
[9] CICA Handbook, section 5815 or ISA 800.
[10] CICA Handbook, section 9100 or ISA 920.

Compliance with Contractual Agreements or Regulatory Requirements

Clients may have restrictive covenants in loan agreements. Lenders may require a periodic report on whether the client has complied with these. Following a scope paragraph referring to the report on the audited financial statements, the auditor may give a negative assurance of the following type:

> In connection with our audit, nothing came to our attention that caused us to believe that the company failed to comply with the terms, covenants, provisions, or conditions of sections 32 through 46 of the indenture dated January 1, 20×9, with North Country Bank. However, our audit examination was not directed primarily toward obtaining knowledge of such noncompliance.

Some federal and provincial regulatory requirements might call for such negative assurance; for example, limitations on investments for mutual funds and provincial insurance regulations about the nature of insurance company investments. When the auditor must provide an audit opinion on compliance with statutes or regulations, section 5815 provides guidance. In this case positive assurance is provided and, other than criteria and scope, the report is similar to that for audits of financial statements. An example of an opinion on compliance given in a separate report is provided in Exhibit 16–9.

The prescribed report language of regulatory agencies may push auditors into signing assertions that are beyond their reporting responsibilities and involve the auditors. In such cases, auditors should add their own wording into the prescribed report language or write a revised report that appropriately reflects their position and responsibility.

Applying Agreed-Upon Procedures

Clients might ask auditors to perform a specified set of procedures—the agreed-upon procedures—to examine a particular element, account, or item in a financial statement. This is not considered an audit because the set of agreed-upon procedures usually does not meet with generally accepted auditing standards. These special-purpose engagements have a limited scope, so the second and third GAAS examination standards (control risk assessment and sufficient competent evidence for an opinion) and the GAAS reporting standards do not apply.

EXHIBIT 16-9   EXAMPLE OF AN OPINION ON COMPLIANCE GIVEN IN A SEPARATE REPORT

AUDITOR'S REPORT
ON COMPLIANCE WITH AGREEMENT

To A Trust Company Limited,

I have audited Client Limited's compliance as at December 31, 20X1, with the criteria established by (describe nature of provisions to be complied with) described in Sections ...... to ...... inclusive of (name of agreement) dated ...., 20..., with (name of party to agreement) and the interpretation of such agreement as set out in note 1 attached. Compliance with the criteria established by the provisions of the agreement is the responsibility of the management of Client Limited. My responsibility is to express an opinion on this compliance based on my audit.

I conducted my audit in accordance with generally accepted auditing standards. Those standards require that I plan and perform an audit to obtain reasonable assurance whether Client Limited complied with the criteria established by the provisions of the agreement referred to above. Such an audit includes examining, on a test basis, evidence supporting compliance, evaluating the overall compliance with the agreement, and, where applicable, assessing the accounting principles used and significant estimates made by management.

In my opinion, Client Limited is in compliance, in all material respects, with the criteria established by (the provisions to be complied with) described in Sections ...... to ...... of this agreement.

City

Date

(signed)...................

CHARTERED ACCOUNTANT

Source: © CICA Handbook, paragraph 5815.11.

EXHIBIT 16–10   EXAMPLE OF A REPORT ON SPECIFIED AUDITING PROCEDURES CARRIED OUT ON LONG-TERM DEBT

To A. Trustee Limited,

As specifically agreed, I have performed the following procedures in connection with the above company's certificate dated ...., 20...., as to the amount of the company's Funded Obligations as at ...., 20....:

(list the procedures)

As a result of applying the above procedures, I found no (the following) exceptions (list of exceptions). However these procedures do not constitute an audit of the company's Funded Obligations and therefore I express no opinion on the amount of Funded Obligations as at ...., 20.....

This letter is for use solely in connection with the closing on ...., 20...., of the issue of .... securities of the company.

City

Date

(signed)...................

CHARTERED ACCOUNTANT

Source: © *CICA Handbook*, paragraph 9100.14.

For example, a client may request procedures on the long-term debt of a company it plans to acquire—not an audit of the company's complete financial statements. Section 9100, "Reports on the Results of Applying Specified Auditing Procedures," gives an example report on such an engagement. The scope paragraph, quoted in Exhibit 16–10, is clearly not a standard scope explanation describing an audit in accordance with generally accepted auditing standards.

The conclusions paragraph follows the recommendation in section 9100 by (1) denying an audit opinion on the accounts and items, (2) giving a negative assurance as to "no exceptions," (3) listing the procedures, and (4) stating that the report is for restricted use only. It is clear that the objectives of this kind of service are very limited and the report conclusions are limited also.

PUBLIC AND RESTRICTED REPORTS ON INTERNAL CONTROL

LEARNING OBJECTIVE

3 Describe the various reports on internal control and their connection with public reporting and reporting to a client's audit committee.

Several different kinds of reports on internal control, each based on a particular study of controls, have evolved in practice:

- Public reports on control in effect as of a specific date
- Public reports on control in effect during a specified time period
- Restricted-use reports based on the control risk assessment work during an audit, not sufficient for expressing an opinion on control
- Restricted-use reports based on regulatory agencies' pre-established criteria
- Restricted-use reports based on a review without tests of controls or based on application of agreed-upon procedures

In this section we focus on an unqualified report regarding the first bulleted item above. The other reports are covered in Appendix 16A of the OLC for this chapter. Exhibit 16–11 illustrates the AICPA recommended report applying to privately held companies. In that exhibit, the last paragraph expresses positive assurance (opinion) on the controls. We will discuss general assurance engagements later in this chapter.

The report in Exhibit 16–11 points to a problem with internal control evaluation. For example, should only accounting controls be evaluated? accounting controls plus operational controls? or accounting controls plus operational plus management controls? These questions point to issues regarding internal control objectives for publicly issued internal

EXHIBIT   16-11   REPORTING ON INTERNAL ACCOUNTING CONTROL

To the Company, Directors, Stockholders,
Management, a Regulatory Agency, or Specified Others:

We have made a study and evaluation of the system of internal accounting control of Anycompany and subsidiaries in effect at December 31, 20X5. Our study and evaluation were conducted in accordance with standards established by the American Institute of Certified Public Accountants.

The management of Anycompany is responsible for establishing and maintaining a system of internal accounting control. In fulfilling this responsibility, estimates and judgments by management are required to assess the expected benefits and related costs of control procedures. The objectives of a system are to provide management with reasonable, but not absolute, assurance that assets are safeguarded against loss from unauthorized use or disposition, and that transactions are executed in accordance with management's authorization and recorded properly to permit the preparation of financial statements in accordance with generally accepted accounting principles.

Because of inherent limitations in any system of internal accounting control, errors or irregularities may occur and not be detected. Also, projection of any evaluation of the system to future periods is subject to the risk that procedures may become inadequate because of changes in conditions, or that the degree of compliance with the procedures may deteriorate.

In our opinion, the system of internal accounting control of Anycompany and subsidiaries in effect at December 31, 20X5, taken as a whole, was sufficient to meet the objectives stated above insofar as those objectives pertain to the prevention or detection of errors or irregularities in amounts that would be material in relation to the consolidated financial statements.

/s/ Auditor signature, PA
February 18, 20X6

control reports. The criteria to be used in evaluating controls is another issue in public general-purpose internal control reports; for example, is management and operating control effectiveness too subjective to be measured and evaluated? Current standards focus on accounting controls. Also, what procedures should auditors perform to support such a report, and how should they distinguish between review and examination of internal controls? Some feel these issues can be addressed in a broader attestation/assurance framework rather than in a specific internal control framework.

In May 1990, the CICA sponsored a conference on "criteria of control." Its conclusion was that the CICA needed to develop systems criteria, similar to GAAP in accounting, for reporting on internal control. Only then would auditors be able to address Recommendation 49 of the Macdonald Commission Report (1988), which called for evaluation and reporting on the design and functioning of internal control systems of financial institutions. With this goal in mind, the CICA's board of governors established the Criteria of Control Committee in 1992. This committee's primary focus was financial reporting controls, but attempts were made to develop generic control principles applicable to operations also.

In November 1995, the Criteria of Control Committee of the CICA issued a publication in the control and governance series, *Guidance on Criteria on Control* (COCO). The executive summary of the exposure draft, shown below, provides a useful perspective on the committee's work efforts:

The guidance describes and defines control and sets out criteria for its effectiveness. The guidance is applicable to all kinds of organizations, and to a part of an organization.

The guidance adopts a broad understanding of control. It involves the coordination of activities toward the achievement of objectives, and includes the identification and mitigation of known risks, the identification and exploitation of opportunities, and the capacity to respond and adapt to the unexpected. Thus, control can provide assurance regarding a broad range of objectives in three general categories: the effectiveness and efficiency of operations, the reliability of financial and management reporting, and compliance with applicable laws and regulations and internal policies.

While people at all levels of an organization participate in control, the decisions and actions of senior management and the board of directors and their level of interest in control set the tone. Management is accountable for control, and therefore needs to assess its overall functioning.

The guidance sets out a control framework, which is a way of looking at an organization so that important aspects of control and relationships between them are apparent. The guidance acknowledges that no one control framework will be perfectly suited to all organizations. It also gives examples of how the criteria can be reorganized into other frameworks, and how other management approaches such as total quality management can be compared to the control framework.

The guidance sets out twenty-three control criteria, stated at a high level in order to be broadly applicable. They address areas such as the culture and values that support good control; objective-setting, risk assessment, and planning; control activities that provide assurance that necessary actions are performed; and the monitoring of all aspects of performance to learn what improvements are required. Considerable judgment will be required in applying the criteria, for example, in interpreting them into actionable steps that can be integrated with other management activities; in identifying indicators or early-warning signs so that timely reporting about control can be integrated with reporting about other aspects of performance; and in deciding on the acceptability of risk remaining after control processes have been taken into account.

The terms in COCO are general and abstract so that it provides a flexible framework for future guidelines. Auditors asked to provide assurance on the reliability of assertions about effectiveness of controls are the intended users of the guidelines. Control is defined as "those elements of an organization (including its resources, systems, processes, culture, structure, and taxes) that, taken together, support people in the achievement of the organization's objectives."

According to the guidance, key concepts in evaluating controls are as follows:

1. Control is effected by people throughout the organization, including the board of directors or its equivalent, management, and all other staff.[11]

2. People who are accountable, as individuals or teams, for achieving objectives should also be accountable for the effectiveness of control that supports achievement of those objectives.

3. Organizations are constantly interacting and adapting.

4. Control can be expected to provide only reasonable assurance, not absolute assurance.

5. Effective control demands that a balance be maintained:
   i) Between autonomy and integration—Keeping this balance often involves shifting between centralization and decentralization and between imposing constraints to achieve consistency and granting freedom to act.
   ii) Between the status quo and adapting to change—Keeping this balance often involves shifting between demanding greater consistency to gain efficiency and granting greater flexibility to respond to change.

Perhaps the most important features of the guidelines are the twenty control criteria they identify. They are quite detailed but can be summarized by the following categories or components:

1. Purpose groups criteria, which provide a sense of the organization's direction:
   - objectives (including mission, vision, and strategy)
   - risks (and opportunities)
   - policies
   - planning
   - performance targets and indicators

2. Commitment groups criteria, which provide a sense of the organization's identity and values:
   - ethical values, including integrity
   - human resource policies
   - authority, responsibility, and accountability
   - mutual trust

---

[11] The governing body of a government or not-for-profit entity may be called by a different name. In a unit within an organization, the equivalent to the board of directors is the senior management or other leadership group.

3. Capability groups criteria, which provide a sense of the organization's competence:
   * knowledge, skills, and tools
   * communication processes
   * information
   * coordination
   * control activities

4. Monitoring and learning groups criteria, which provide a sense of the organization's evolution:
   * monitoring internal and external environments
   * monitoring performance
   * challenging assumptions
   * reassessing information needs and information systems
   * follow-up procedures
   * assessing the effectiveness of control

The basic control framework consists of the definition of control and the criteria as summarized by the broad categories.

Response so far has been favourable toward the criteria. They are consistent with the Canadian philosophy of developing guidelines that are not so detailed that they resemble a "cookbook" for evaluating controls. The deliberately high level of the criteria allow them to be applied to all systems at all organizations. There is scope for experimentation and creativity with them, and auditors will have to use considerable professional judgment in applying the criteria to specific situations.

The United States has an equivalent document titled "Internal Control—An Integrated Framework," or **COSO**. Although COCO and COSO share the objective of providing guidance for control and criteria for control, COCO builds on COSO by expanding the concept of control and taking a particularly people-oriented approach towards it.

The guidance is not currently included in the *CICA Handbook*, and it therefore does not have the authority of *CICA Handbook* accounting or auditing recommendations. A member's decision to use the control guidance in assessing internal controls will depend on how useful and relevant they perceive the guidance to be. In this sense, the guidance is somewhat experimental.

A second project of the CICA Criteria of Control Committee is the document "Guidance for Directors—Governance Processes for Control," issued in December 1995. This is the second in a series addressing various aspects of control systems. The document sets out guidance on governance processes for meeting the control responsibilities of boards of directors.

It identifies six key areas of board control responsibility:

1. Establish and monitor the organization's ethical values.

2. Approve and monitor mission, vision, and strategy.

3. Oversee external communication.

4. Evaluate senior management.

5. Monitor management control systems.

6. Assess board effectiveness.

The primary focus of both the "Guidance for Directors" document and COCO is shown in Exhibit 16–12. This exhibit shows the framework for evaluating management and operational controls evolving within the internal control framework. To assist auditors in interpreting this guidance relative to other authorities on the topic, the Criteria of Control Committee prepared a framework for degree of authoritativeness, presented in Exhibit 16–13. This exhibit makes clear that the control and governance series are not intended to become *CICA Handbook* Recommendations. Rather, their intent is to get client organizations to experiment with the framework until a more finely tuned standard can be developed. First used for internal reporting, the framework might then develop sufficiently and support standards for external reporting.

EXHIBIT   16-12   CICA'S CRITERIA OF CONTROL GUIDANCE

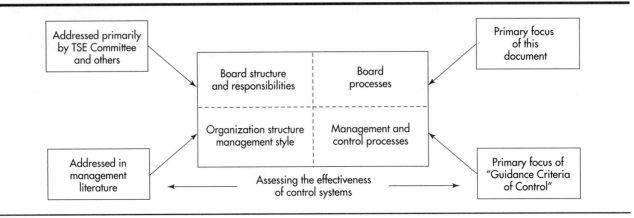

Source: © CICA, *Criteria of Control Guidance.*

EXHIBIT   16-13   DEGREE OF AUTHORITATIVENESS FRAMEWORK

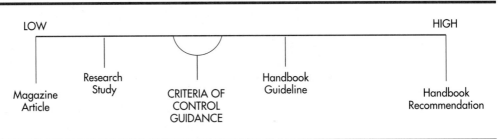

Source: © CICA, *Criteria of Control Guidance.*

SOX of 2002 has greatly accelerated the evolution of internal control reporting because it requires public companies in the United States to report on internal controls and to have these reports audited, just as financial statements are. COCO may provide suitable criteria for evaluating internal control, and it may evolve further, along with assurance engagements on internal control. The ongoing evolution of criteria and the dynamic nature of the audit environment underscore the need for the broad framework of critical thinking as a guide for professional judgment.

AUDIT REPORTS ON INTERNAL CONTROL

As explained in the first two chapters of the text, SOX in the United States and the increasing interest in corporate governance led to the additon of a new item in the audited financial statements: the internal controls statement called "Reporting on Internal Control over Financial Reporting."

Internal control can vary depending on the criteria used. However, for purposes of the internal control statement required by the CICA standard entitled "Reporting on Internal Control over Financial Reporting," they are limited to internal controls over financial reporting. This is consistent with U.S. requirements and is mainly concerned with accounting controls; that is, controls related to the accuracy of accounting recordkeeping and safeguarding of assets. This distinction was covered in more detail in Chapter 9. An example of an internal control statement by management follows in Exhibit 16–14.

EXHIBIT 16-14   REPORT OF MANAGEMENT

REPORT OF MANAGEMENT
Big Corporation and Subsidiary Companies

Management's Report on Internal Control over Financial Reporting

Management is responsible for establishing and maintaining adequate internal control over financial reporting of the company. Internal control over financial reporting is a process designed to provide reasonable assurance regarding the reliability of financial reporting and the preparation of financial statements for external purposes in accordance with accounting principles generally accepted in Canada.

The company's internal control over financial reporting includes those policies and procedures that (i) pertain to the maintenance of records that, in reasonable detail, accurately and fairly reflect the transactions and dispositions of the assets of the company; (ii) provide reasonable assurance that transactions are recorded as necessary to permit preparation of financial statements in accordance with accounting principles generally accepted in Canada, and that receipts and expenditures of the company are being made only in accordance with authorizations of management and directors of the company; and (iii) provide reasonable assurance regarding prevention or timely detection of unauthorized acquisition, use, or disposition of the company's assets that could have a material effect on the financial statements.

Because of its inherent limitations, internal control over financial reporting may not prevent or detect misstatements. Also, projections of any evaluation of effectiveness to future periods are subject to the risk that controls may become inadequate because of changes in conditions, or that the degree of compliance with the policies or procedures may deteriorate.

Management conducted an evaluation of the effectiveness of internal control over financial reporting based on the framework in Internal Control–Integrated Framework issued by the Committee of Sponsoring Organizations of the Treadway Commission. Based on this evaluation, management concluded that the company's internal control over financial reporting was effective as of December 31, 200X. Management's assessment of the effectiveness of the company's internal control over financial reporting as of December 31, 200X, has been audited by Big Four LLP, an independent registered public accounting firm, as stated in their report which is included herein.

Chief Executive Officer   Chief Financial Officer
March 17, 200X +1   March 17, 200X +1

Under CICA rules, the auditors verify the accuracy of the internal controls statement for public companies just as they verify the accuracy of financial statements. In fact, the proposed standards require that the audit of financial statements and the audit of the internal control statement be part of the same engagement—primarily because of the close link between accounting controls and accuracy of the financial statements.

In its *Handbook* section 5925, the CICA recommends the wording of a separate audit report on management's internal control shown in Exhibit 16–15.

Note that in Exhibit 16–15 there are six paragraphs. The first, like the introductory paragraph of the audit of financial statements (regular audit), identifies the statement covered and the responsibilities of the auditor and management. The second paragraph is similar to the scope paragraph in a regular report and explains the character of the auditor's examination. Note that reasonable (high) assurance on the effectiveness of internal control is required in the engagement. The third paragraph is a new one that defines the internal controls covered by the audit.

The opinion paragraph is fourth, but first we discuss the two paragraphs following it. The fifth covers inherent limitations indicating the risk that controls will not guarantee financial statements that are free of material misstatements, with an added caution that the current evaluation of controls will not necessarily apply to the future. There is nothing comparable in the regular report. The sixth paragraph indicates that the audit is done in conjunction with the financial statement audit.

In the fourth paragraph shown in Exhibit 16–15, the opinion paragraph, note the reference to conformity with established criteria as the basis of the opinion, the reference to materiality, and a direct reporting opinion on the effectiveness of internal controls. This paragraph also states that the opinions are given on the state of controls at a specific point in time ("as at"), that being the balance sheet date as is indicated in the sixth paragraph.

EXHIBIT   16-15   AUDITOR REPORT ON INTERNAL CONTROL OVER FINANCIAL REPORTING: UNQUALIFIED OPINION EXAMPLE FROM SECTION 5925, PARAGRAPH A82

We have audited the effectiveness of [name of entity]'s internal control over financial reporting as at December 31, 20X0. The entity's management is responsible for maintaining effective internal control over financial reporting. Our responsibility is to express an opinion based on our audit, whether the entity's internal control over financial reporting was effectively maintained in accordance with [identify control criteria, for example, "criteria established in 'Guidance on Control (COCO)' published by the Canadian Institute of Chartered Accountants or "Internal Control–Integrated Framework (COSO)" issued by the Committee of Sponsoring Organizations of the Treadway Commission."]

(Scope paragraph)

We conducted our audit in accordance with standards established by the Canadian Institute of Chartered Accountants (CICA) for audits of internal control over financial reporting. Those standards require that we plan and perform the audit to obtain reasonable assurance about whether effective internal control over financial reporting included obtaining an understanding of internal control over financial reporting, assessing the risk that a material weakness exists, testing and evaluating the design and operating effectiveness of internal control based on the assessed risk, and performing such other procedures as we considered necessary in the circumstances.

(Definition paragraph)

An entity's internal control over financial reporting is a process designed to provide reasonable assurance regarding the reliability of financial reporting and the preparation of financial statements for external purposes in accordance with generally accepted accounting principles. An entity's internal control over financial reporting includes those policies and procedures that (1) pertain to the maintenance of records that, in reasonable detail, accurately and fairly reflect the transactions and dispositions of the assets of the entity; (2) provide reasonable assurance that transactions are recorded as necessary to permit preparation of financial statements in accordance with generally accepted accounting principles, and that receipts and expenditures of the entity are being made only in accordance with authorizations of management and directors of the entity; and (3) provide reasonable assurance regarding prevention or timely detection of unauthorized acquisition, use, or disposition of the entity's assets that could have a material effect on the financial statements.

(Opinion paragraph)

In our opinion, the entity maintained, in all material respects, effective internal control over financial reporting as at December 31, 20X0, in accordance with [identify control criteria, for example, "criteria established in 'Guidance on Control (COCO)' published by The Canadian Institute of Chartered Accountants or 'Internal Control–Integrated Framework (COSO)' issued by the Committee of Sponsoring Organizations of the Treadway Commission."].

(Inherent limitations paragraph)

Because of its inherent limitations, internal control over financial reporting may not prevent or detect misstatements. Also, projections of any evaluation of effectiveness to future periods are subject to the risk that controls may become inadequate because of changes in conditions, or that the degree of compliance with the policies or procedures may deteriorate.

We have also audited, in accordance with Canadian generally accepted auditing standards, the [identify financial statements] of [name of entity] and issued our report dated [date of report, which is the same as the date of the report on the effectiveness of internal control over financial reporting].

City

Date

(signed)....................

CHARTERED ACCOUNTANT

The standard also requires that the financial statement auditor be the auditor of internal control over financial reporting. The term **audit of internal control over financial reporting** refers to the direct reporting audits of internal control. This standard is intended to meet the requirements of the Canadian Securities Administrators (CSA). Under current CSA rules, internal control statements are required for public companies, but the audits of internal controls are optional.

Note that under section 5925 there is no requirement for the auditor to refer to management's internal control statement. If there was, this could be an attest engagement on management's internal control statement.

Other Communication on Control and Other Matters

Regulators, federal and provincial governments, and the public have been concerned about auditors' communication of internal control and other matters to upper levels of public corporations, especially banks and other financial institutions. In response, the CICA issued

EXHIBIT   16–16   COMMUNICATION OF MATTERS IDENTIFIED DURING THE FINANCIAL STATEMENT AUDIT

During the course of my audit of .... for the year ended ...., I identified matters which may be of interest to management. The objective of an audit is to obtain reasonable assurance whether the financial statements are free of material misstatement, and it is not designed to identify matters that may be of interest to management in discharging its responsibilities. Accordingly an audit would not usually identify all such matters.

The matters identified were ....

This communication is prepared solely for the information of management and is not intended for any other purpose. I accept no responsibility to a third party who uses this communication.

Source: © *CICA Handbook,* paragraph 5750.08.

two recommendations addressing auditors' responsibilities to communicate both (1) internal control matters noted in an audit,[12] and (2) certain matters to those having financial reporting oversight responsibility (usually, the audit committee).[13] When performing audits, auditors may notice significant deficiencies in the design or operation of the internal control structure that could adversely affect the organization's ability to record, process, summarize, and report financial data in conformity with GAAP.[14] These problems are referred to as **reportable matters**. Auditing standards do not require auditors to search for reportable matters, but they do require auditors to report the ones that come to their attention.[15] The report, preferably in writing, is to be addressed to the management, or to the board of directors or its audit committee. An example of such a report is in Exhibit 16–16.

Auditors might also issue a report called a management letter. This letter may contain commentary and suggestions on a variety of matters in addition to internal control matters; for example, operational and administrative efficiency, business strategy, and profit-making possibilities. Management letters are not required by auditing standards but are advice to management offered as a part of an audit.

Concern about reporting control-related matters within a company has spilled over to a set of other important matters that auditors are required to report on to companies' audit committees or others with oversight responsibility.[16] The purpose of these communications is to enhance the audit committees' ability to oversee the audit functions (external and internal) in a company. The auditors are responsible for informing the audit committee about the following matters:

- Independent auditors' responsibilities regarding financial statements and other information in documents that include the audited financial statements (e.g., the annual report to shareholders and filings with the regulatory agencies such as the OSC or Superintendent of Financial Institutions)
- Management's significant accounting policies
- Management judgments about accounting estimates used in the financial statements
- Significant audit adjustments recommended by the auditors
- Disagreements with management about accounting principles, accounting estimates, scope of the audit, disclosures in the notes, and wording of the audit report
- The auditor's view on accounting matters on which management has consulted with other accountants
- Major accounting and auditing issues discussed with management in connection with beginning or continuing an auditor-client relationship

[12] CAS 265 *(CICA Handbook,* section 5750.)
[13] CAS 260 *(CICA Handbook,* section 5751.)
[14] AuG-13, "Special Reports on Regulated Financial Institutions."
[15] CAS 265 *(CICA Handbook,* section 5750.)
[16] CAS 260 *(CICA Handbook,* section 5751.)

- Illegal acts
- Difficulties with management encountered while performing the audit: delays in starting the audit or providing information, unreasonable time schedule, unavailability of client personnel, and failure of client personnel to complete data schedules

Auditors also have the responsibility to communicate, in a letter to the audit committee (or equivalent), on matters that bear on independence (covered in Chapter 15). CAS 260 (*CICA Handbook* paragraph 5751.32) requires a letter for the following:

- Confirmation of auditor's independence
- Disclosure of relationships that might impair independence
- Disclosure of total fees for audit and nonaudit services for clients having public accountability (such as companies whose securities are traded on regulated exchanges, public sector companies, and not-for-profit organizations)

REVIEW CHECKPOINTS

8   Does the standard public report on internal control give the opinion known as "positive assurance"?

9   What reports on control and other matters are auditors required to give to a company's management, board of directors, or audit committee?

10 What three types of engagements can produce an auditor's written internal control report intended for external use? Describe the reports in general terms.

Prospectuses

Whenever a client makes a new public offering of its securities (e.g., stock, bonds), it must provide a prospectus. The prospectus is meant to give prospective investors information for evaluating the merits of the proposed use of funds. Auditors' involvement with prospectuses can be quite extensive and is covered in sections 7110, 7115, and 7200 and in audit guidelines AuG–6, 16, and 30.

If a prospectus is issued shortly after the client's year-end, within 90 days, the auditor's involvement with the prospectus can be quite minimal. Minimal involvement includes auditing the financial statements, reading the prospectus for any "material inconsistencies" relative to the audited financial statements, and performing subsequent event review procedures.[17] If, on the other hand, a prospectus is issued after a specified period beyond the balance sheet date, then the auditor will need to become more involved with interim financial statements and any other financial information (such as forecasts). In such situations the auditor may be asked to prepare a comfort letter to securities regulators.[18]

If, after performing the required procedures outlined previously and listed in detail in paragraph 7110.07, the auditor finds no significant inconsistencies, the auditor consents to use their report in the prospectus. The recommended auditor's consent communication is given in Exhibit 16–17. If more than one auditor is involved in the audit, all auditors must issue a consent letter.

CICA's MD&A Guidance

With the increasing interest in corporate governance, the profession is becoming more involved in broader corporate disclosures and their relationship to the financial statements. This is reflected in the CICA's initiative on guidance concerning **management's discussion and analysis (MD&A)** accompanying the financial statements in the client's annual report.

[17] CAS 720.
[18] *CICA Handbook*, paragraph 7200.05.

EXHIBIT   16–17   AUDITOR'S CONSENT

I have read the [short form] prospectus of X Limited (Company) dated March 15, 20X5, relating to the issue and sale of [description of securities offered] of Company. I have complied with Canadian generally accepted standards for an auditor's involvement with offering documents.

I consent to the [use/incorporation by reference] in the above-mentioned prospectus of my report to the [directors/shareholders] of Company on the balance sheets of Company as at December 31, 20X4 and 20X3, and the statements of earnings, retained earnings, and cash flows for each of the years in the [three-/two-year] period ended December 31, 20X4. My report is dated February 15, 20X5 (except as to note . . . which is as of March 15, 20X5).

City   (signed)...................

Date   CHARTERED ACCOUNTANT

Source: © *CICA Handbook*, section 7110.69.

The guidance is primarily geared to directors and management, but auditors find it helpful in reviewing for consistency with the financial statements. No recommendations or standards have been issued yet, but a guidance document has been prepared, as shown in the box following.

CICA'S MD&A GUIDANCE

This Guidance breaks new ground by establishing six disclosure principles and a five-part framework for organizing and presenting Management's Discussion and Analysis (MD&A) disclosures, thus adding new dimensions to conventional MD&A reporting. Further, it reflects trends in the continuous disclosure requirements of Canadian securities jurisdictions and provides for updating of previous disclosures.

A significant feature of the Guidance is a series of questions audit committees and boards of directors might ask in reviewing the completeness and reliability of the MD&A—an important aspect of fulfilling their oversight and governance responsibilities. These questions should also assist management in determining the appropriateness of their MD&A disclosures and help officers of U.S. registered companies in making certifications specified under recent requirements.

Source: "CICA's MD&A Guidance," *CA Magazine*, January/February 2003, p. 30. Reproduced by permission from *CA Magazine*, published by the Canadian Institute of Chartered Accountants, Toronto, Canada.

The principles stress that MD&A is management's perspective and explanation for past performance results and future prospects. The MD&A should complement, as well as supplement, the financial statements and be clearly worded. Future guidance for auditors will likely focus on what constitutes material inconsistency between MD&A and the financial statements and how to detect such inconsistencies.

. . . .

REVIEW
CHECKPOINTS

11 How are prospective financial statements defined?

12 What are the similarities and differences between examination reports on forecasts and audit reports on historical financial statements? on compilation reports on forecasts? on compilation reports on historical financial statements?

13 What is the auditor's responsibility for information reported in MD&A in the audit of a public company?

. . . .

FINANCIAL STATEMENTS FOR USE IN OTHER COUNTRIES

· · · · · · · · · · · · · · · ·

Auditors practising in Canada are increasingly being asked to report on Canadian company financial statements intended for use in other countries, especially the United States. These financial statements might be used by foreign investors or by foreign parent companies for consolidation in foreign financial statements. For many years, American auditors have consolidated financial statements of foreign companies and subsidiaries of U.S.-based multinational companies in U.S. parent company financial statements. Non-American auditors have based these statements on U.S. GAAP, even though the same company's statements may also be prepared on the basis of non-Amercan country's GAAP for use in the country of origin. With increasing corporate globalization, many U.S. companies are now owned by non-Americans as well, and many U.S. company's financial statements must now be prepared on the basis of the accounting principles of other countries.

In engagements requiring use of foreign standards, Canadian auditors are expected to follow the Canadian general and field work auditing standards, just as they would in any audit. However, there may be differences in accounting that will change some of the audit objectives. For example, some South American countries permit or require general price-level adjusted measurements (because of high rates of inflation), and these management calculations applied to the Canadian company's account balances will need to be audited. Likewise, some countries do not permit recognition of deferred taxes, so no deferred tax account balances will exist for audit. Clearly, the auditors must know the accounting principles applied in the country the financial statements are intended for. The International Accounting Standards established by the International Accounting Standards Board is the place to begin.

In addition to knowing the foreign accounting principles, the Canadian auditor may be expected to apply foreign auditing standards and procedures. Some countries have codified their auditing standards in professional literature, as Canada has, while others put their auditing standards in statutes and legal-like regulations. More auditing of compliance with laws, regulations, or other procedures than Canadian standards require may be necessary. The audit report can take different forms, depending on the circumstances and the distribution of the foreign GAAP financial statements:

A. Option for foreign GAAP financial statements used only outside Canada:
   1. A Canadian-style report modified to refer to the GAAP of the other country (similar to an AADBA report)
   2. The report form used by auditors in the other country

B. Options for foreign GAAP financial statements that will have more than limited distribution in Canada:
   1. The CICA standard report, qualified or adverse for departures from Canadian GAAP, with another separate paragraph expressing an opinion on the fair presentation in conformity with the foreign GAAP.
   2. Both (*a*) the report form used by auditors in the other country (A2 above) or a Canadian-style report modified to refer to the GAAP of the other country (A1 above), and (*b*) the qualified or adverse Canadian standard report with an additional paragraph expressing an opinion on the foreign GAAP (B1 above).

C. Two options for sets of financial statements, foreign GAAP and Canadian GAAP, both of which may be distributed in both countries:
   1. A report on the foreign GAAP financial statements as in A1 above, with an additional paragraph notifying users that another report has been issued on Canadian GAAP financial statements.
   2. A report on Canadian GAAP financial statements as normally done for Canadian financial statements, but add a paragraph notifying users that another report has been issued on foreign GAAP financial statements.

When a Canadian client must file with the U.S.'s SEC *and* when there is either a disclaimer due to uncertainty or an explanatory paragraph resulting from a change in accounting principle, the CICA guideline on Canada–U.S. reporting conflicts has been followed.[19] This guideline recommends that a Canadian GAAS audit report be issued along with additional comments as additional information for American readers.

REVIEW CHECKPOINTS

14 Why do you think a Canadian-style report on foreign GAAP financial statements is similar to a report on AADBA financial statements?

15 What precautions should Canadian auditors take when reporting on foreign GAAP financial statements that will be distributed in the United States?

THE ASSURANCE FRAMEWORK

LEARNING OBJECTIVE

5 Describe the umbrella standards for assurance engagements, and relate them to an acceptable reporting framework.

Many of the engagements discussed in the preceding sections fall within the umbrella framework of the assurance engagements issued by the CICA in *Handbook* section 5025 in April 1997. This standard was introduced in Chapter 2 and compared with GAAS. You should begin this topic by reviewing that discussion.

The foundation of section 5025 is that of an accountability relationship: "An accountability relationship exists when one party (the accountable party) is answerable to and/or responsible to another party (the user) for a subject matter or voluntarily chooses to report to another party on a subject matter."[20] An assurance engagement can take place only when there is an accountability relationship. Therefore, paragraph 5025.21 makes clear that the auditor needs to obtain evidence of this relationship before taking on an assurance engagement. Typically, this evidence is acknowledgment of the existence of the relationship by the accountable party, usually management. Failure to obtain such acknowledgment should be disclosed in the practitioner's (auditor or assurer) report.

The accountability relationship is what distinguishes assurance engagements from other types of engagements, such as tax planning and consulting work.[21] The distinctions between assurance and nonassurance engagements can be very fine (see Appendix 16A), but they are important because assurance engagements of financial statements and the assurance standards are what distinguish the PA profession from other professional groups.

The nature of the assurance engagement determines the type of communication provided by the practitioner or assurer. According to CICA, there are two main categories of assurance engagements. In an **attestation engagements**, the practitioner offers a conclusion (attestation) on the accountable party's written assertion. The practioner evaluates, using suitable criteria and the written assertion, the things the accountable party (the asserter) is responsible for.

The other category of assurance engagement is a **direct reporting engagement**. "In a direct reporting engagement, the practitioners' conclusion will evaluate directly, using suitable criteria, the subject matter for which the accountable party is responsible."[22] Whereas in an assurance engagement the assertions are written out by the asserter, in a direct reporting engagement the assertions may only be implied. While this distinction seems straightforward, what exactly is meant in the current standard by the term "written assertion" is, for some, a controversial matter. Normally, written assertions are written management statements, like financial statements.

[19] AuG-21.
[20] *CICA Handbook*, paragraph 5025.04.
[21] *CICA Handbook*, paragraph 5025.15.
[22] *CICA Handbook*, paragraph 5025.05.

In order to understand how the preceding concepts operate, it is necessary to clarify additional concepts and relate them to the assurance framework. This is done in paragraphs 5025.08–13, as follows:

> The practitioner forms a conclusion concerning a subject matter by referring to suitable criteria. Criteria are benchmarks against which the subject matter and, in an attest engagement, mangement's written assertion on the subject matter, can be evaluated.
>
> In an assurance engagement, the practitioner reduces engagement risk to a level that is appropriate for the assurance provided in his or her report. The term engagement risk is the risk that the practitioner may express an inappropriate conclusion. The three components of engagement risk are inherent risk, control risk, and detection risk.
>
> Practitioners should in theory be able to vary infinitely the level of assurance provided in assurance engagements. However, in order to help users understand the level of assurance being provided by the practitioner, the standards in this Section limit assurance to two distinct levels—a high level and a moderate level.
>
> In an audit engagement, the practitioner provides a high, though not absolute, level of assurance by designing procedures so that, in the practitioner's professional judgment, the risk of an inappropriate conclusion is reduced to a low level through procedures such as inspection, observation, enquiry, confirmation, computation, analysis, and discussion. Use of the term "high level of assurance" refers to the highest reasonable level of assurance a practitioner can provide concerning a subject matter. Absolute assurance is not attainable as a result of factors such as the use of judgment, the use of testing, the inherent limitations of control, and the fact that much of the evidence available to the practitioner is persuasive rather than conclusive in nature. Assurance will also be influenced by the degree of precision associated with the subject matter itself.
>
> In a review engagement, the practitioner provides a moderate level of assurance by designing procedures so that, in the practitioner's professional judgment, the risk of an inappropriate conclusion is reduced to a moderate level through procedures which are normally limited to enquiry, analysis, and discussion. Such risk is reduced to a moderate level when the evidence obtained enables the practitioner to conclude the subject matter is plausible in the circumstances.
>
> Both attest engagements and direct reporting engagements can be completed with either a high or a moderate level of assurance. The level of assurance appropriate for a particular engagement will depend on the needs of users and the nature of the subject matter.

With these concepts and definitions, it is now possible to develop meaningful standards for assurance engagements. These have already been listed and compared with GAAS in Chapter 2. As noted there, the assurance standards are subdivided into (a) general standards of the practitioner and the use of suitable criteria in evaluating a subject matter (for example, criteria for control discussed in this chapter); (b) performance standards relating to obtaining sufficient appropriate evidence supporting the practitioner's conclusion, along with documentation, including the concepts of significance (materiality) and engagement risk; and (c) reporting standards prescribing the minimum requirements of the practitioner's report, including those for reservations and the conditions for issuing a reservation.

The truly novel aspects of these standards deal with suitability of criteria, significance, engagement risk, and the increasing reliance on specialists. As we will see later in this chapter, all of these concepts originated with public sector auditing standards. Given the variety of engagements contemplated by this standard, there could be far more reliance on specialists from other fields, thus making the practiioner responsible for understanding the specialists' work to the extent necessary to meet the engagement objectives.[23] Thus the standards contemplate using multidisciplinary audit team members to a much greater extent than is done in financial statement audits.

The standard's concept of significance appears to have been influenced by public sector standards, which use the same concept. Significance is materiality extended to include broader classes of users whose decisions may be influenced by nonfinancial factors, such as the effectiveness of health care, for example.

---

[23] *CICA Handbook*, paragraph 5025.34.

Engagement risk is defined in paragraphs 5025.51 and .52:

> [T]he risk that the practitioner will express an inappropriate conclusion in his or her report. This risk consists of (a) risks that are beyond the control of management and the practitioner (inherent risk), (b) the risks that are within control of management (control risk), and (c) risks that are within the control of the practitioner (detection risk). The extent to which the practitioner considers the relevant components of engagment risk will be affected by the nature of the subject matter and the level of assurance to be provided.

It is interesting that, in this definition of engagement risk and its components, risk is not limited to (*a*) risk of failing to detect significant misrepresentations or omissions, but also explicitly includes (*b*) the possibility that the practitioner may report significant items that in fact are not significant relative to the users. The traditional concept of audit risk is consistent with (*a*), but risk (*b*) has never before been explicitly considered in the audit risk model because of an assumption that this risk is self-correcting. In other words, if the auditor incorrectly concludes that there is a material misstatement, the assumption is that additional work will always point out the error. Risk (*a*) has traditionally been considered the more serious risk, because with this risk the auditor has no evidence to support the proposed material misstatement when in fact that is the case. Since the auditor's job is to find material misstatements, control of risk (*a*) is the reason the auditor was hired in the first place. By extending the risk definition to include (*b*)-type risks, the standard has potentially changed the risk model for generalized assurance engagements in a significant way that is not completely consistent with the traditional concept of audit risk. This may be justified by the significant changes in the assurance engagement environment. Auditors now need to be explicitly aware of what should be considered significant for various subject matters.

Perhaps the most important change introduced by section 5025 is the concept of suitable criteria. Paragraph 5025.38 identifies five characteristics of suitable criteria: relevance, reliability, neutrality, understandability, and completeness. Since these criteria are supposed to apply to all assurance engagements, including financial statement audits, they introduce a potentially revolutionary link to accounting theory in that new characteristics of accounting information may now be contemplated. For example, *CICA Handbook* section 1000 does not list completeness as a characteristic of financial statements, which is not a problem currently, as paragraph 5025.02 explicitly exempts existing *CICA Handbook* recommendations from the assurance engagement standard. In the longer term, however, it appears that some reconciliation may be necessary. What is remarkable in this is that assurance and accounting standards are for the first time being linked, albeit in a tentative way. It may indicate a closer coordination between accounting and auditing standard setting in the future—a development some consider long overdue in an increasingly complicated and interrelated business world. There is already a shared focus on accountability relations in assurance engagements and financial statements.

In the next section we will see that suitable criteria and accountability relations are also central concepts in public sector auditing. This is not surprising, since section 5025 is intended to provide a framework for all assurance engagements.

Suitable Criteria and the Fair Presentation Framework

The suitable criteria concept of section 5025 is clearly related to the acceptable reporting framework concept of CAS 200. An acceptable reporting framework is one that is required by law or regulation, or that meets the particular objectives of the entity's financial statements. AADBA discussed earlier in this chapter is the older Canadian term for the international concept of acceptable financial reporting framework. Acceptable financial reporting can be either special purpose or general purpose reporting. Acceptable reporting frameworks can also be classified according to whether they are compliance or fair presentation frameworks. These are summarized in the four categories in the following box.

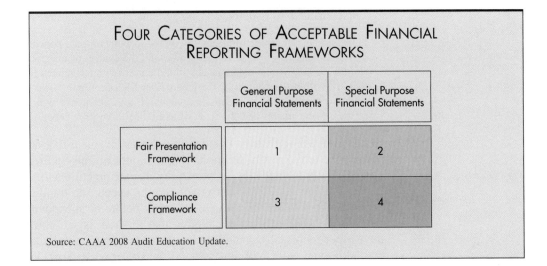

The most common reporting framework in Canada is the fair presentation framework, since Canadian GAAP is supposed to allow fairness of presentation for general purpose reporting. The importance of the fair presentation framework is that auditors can use the words "present fairly" only for fair reporting frameworks. This is summarized in the next box.

KEY CHANGES IN AUDITOR'S OPINION WORDING

FAIR PRESENTATION
FRAMEWORKS

COMPLIANCE
FRAMEWORKS

Wording of auditor's
standard opinion–general
purpose financial statements

Wording of auditor's
standard opinion–general
purpose financial statements

"the financial statements
present fairly, in all material
respects, the . . . in accordance
with Cdn GAAP" (CAS 700)

"the financial statements have
been prepared, in all material
respects, in accordance with
(applicable acceptable
general purpose
framework) . . . (CAS 700)

Source: CAAA 2008 Audit Education Update.

What exactly is a fairness framework? CAS 200 and CAS 700 together state that the following requirements need to be met for a fairness framework:

(i) The framework acknowledges explicitly or implicitly that, to achieve fair presentation of the financial statements, it may be necessary for management to provide disclosures beyond the specific requirements of the framework; or

(ii) The framework acknowledges explicitly that, in extremely rare circumstances, it may be necessary for management to depart from a specific requirement of the framework to achieve fair presentation of the financial statements.

(iii) CAS 700 (para. 10) specifies that a fair presentation framework (as opposed to a "compliance" framework) "embodies sufficiently broad principles *that can serve as a basis* for developing and applying accounting policies that are consistent with the underlying requirements of the framework" (emphasis added).

These distinctions show how complex suitable criteria can become in an international setting. The application case at the end of the chapter explains these distinctions in more detail.

The introduction to section 5025 makes it clear that existing *CICA Handbook* recommendations override the current standard. Nevertheless, the long-term objective is to provide guidelines where there are now no standards, and, in the future, to provide guidance on more specific recommendations in assurance engagements. The long-term objective is described in the scope of paragraph 5025.01 as follows:

> These standards establish a framework for all assurance engagements performed by practitioners and for the on-going development of related standards. The standards apply to
>
> *(a)* engagements in the private and public sectors;
>
> *(b)* attest engagements and direct reporting engagements;
>
> *(c)* engagements designed to provide a high (i.e., audit) level of assurance; and
>
> *(d)* engagements designed to provide a moderate (i.e., review) level of assurance.

The assurance standard appendix makes it clear that the standards apply only when the practitioner provides a conclusion on a subject matter. The following services are not considered to provide a conclusion on a subject matter:

(a) specified auditing procedure engagements,[24]

(b) compilation engagements,[25]

(c) derivative reporting,[26]

(d) reports on the application of accounting principles, auditing standards, or review standards.[27]

A good overview of the various services and the extent of the PA's involvement is provided as section 5020.B, which is reproduced in the following box.

The purpose of this . . . is to provide examples of information and the nature and extent of the public accountant's involvement with such information.

NOTE: In addition to the professional responsibilities outlined below, the public accountant would comply with the rules of professional conduct of his or her provincial institute and would therefore, in all cases, exercise due professional skill and care in the work he or she carries out.

TYPE OF INFORMATION RESPONSIBILITIES	NATURE AND EXTENT OF INVOLVEMENT	NATURE AND EXTENT OF ASSOCIATION	PROFESSIONAL WORK	REPORTING
Information that is the subject matter of an assurance.	Assurance engagement	The practitioner has associated himself or herself with the subject matter by virtue of the assurance engagement carried out (see paragraph 5020.04).	The practitioner discharges his or her responsibilities by complying with the Recommendations contained in STANDARDS FOR ASSURANCE ENGAGEMENTS, section 5025.	Reporting section of STANDARDS FOR ASSURANCE ENGAGEMENTS, section 5025.
Financial statements report	Audit	The auditor has associated himself or herself with the financial statements by virtue of the audit work carried out (see paragraph 5020.04).	The auditor discharges his or her responsibilities by complying with the Recommendations contained in GENERALLY ACCEPTED AUDITING STANDARDS, section 5100.	THE AUDITOR'S STANDARD, section 5400.

Continued

---

[24] *CICA Handbook,* paragraph 9100.
[25] *CICA Handbook,* paragraph 9200.
[26] *CICA Handbook,* section 5025, and AuG-13.
[27] *CICA Handbook,* section 7600.

TYPE OF INFORMATION RESPONSIBILITIES	NATURE AND EXTENT OF INVOLVEMENT	NATURE AND EXTENT OF ASSOCIATION	PROFESSIONAL WORK	REPORTING
Financial statements	Review	The public accountant has associated himself of herself with the financial statements by virtue of the review carried out (see paragraph 5020.04).	The public accountant discharges his or her responsibilities by complying with the relevant Recommendations contained in GENERAL REVIEW STANDARDS, section 8100, or REVIEWS OF FINANCIAL STATEMENTS, section 8200.	GENERAL REVIEW STANDARDS, section 8100, or REVIEWS OF FINANCIAL STATEMENTS, section 8200.
Financial statements	Compilation	The public accountant has associated himself or herself with the financial statements by virtue of compiling the financial statements (see paragraph 5020.04).	The public accountant discharges his or her responsibilities by complying with the relevant Recommendations contained in COMPILATION ENGAGEMENTS, section 9200.	COMPILATION ENGAGEMENTS, section 9200
Financing document containing financial information extracted from the audited financial statements.	Consent to use of the auditor's name in the document in connection with the condensed financial information, by consenting to a statement in the document such as, "This condensed financial information has been extracted from the audited financial statements for the year ended December 31, 1986, previously reported on by our auditors ZYX & Co."	The auditor has associated himself or herself with the financial information by consenting to the use of his or her name in connection with that information (see paragraph 5020.04).	The auditor discharges his or her responsibilities by complying with paragraph 5020.13.	No reporting standard. See paragraph 5020.10.
Financing document containing financial information prepared by the client and not reported on by the auditor.	Consent to the inclusion of the auditor's name in the document by, for example, consenting to a factual statement in the document naming lawyers, auditors, etc.	The auditor does not associate himself or herself with the information contained in the document by merely consenting to the inclusion of his or her name in the document (see paragraphs 5020.04 and 5020.16).	The auditor discharges his or her responsibilities by complying with paragraph 5020.17.	No reporting standard. See paragraph 5020.10.
Financial statements	Typing or reproduction services.	The public accountant has associated himself or herself with the financial statements by virtue of the typing or reproduction services carried out (see paragraph 5020.04).	No professional responsibilities other than those discussed in the Note on the first page of this Appendix.	No reporting standard. See paragraph 5020.10.
Annual report or other public documents containing audited or reviewed information.	To determine whether the financial statements and the auditor's report thereon are accurately reproduced in the annual report. To read the other information in the annual report and consider whether any of this information is inconsistent with the financial statements on which the auditor has reported.	The auditor has already associated himself or herself with the financial statements in the annual report by virtue of the audit work carried out. The auditor has also associated himself or herself with the other information in the annual report by virtue of the work carried out under section 7500 (see paragraph 5020.04).	The auditor discharges his or her responsibilities by complying with the Recommendations contained in THE AUDITOR'S ASSOCIATION WITH ANNUAL REPORTS OR OTHER PUBLIC DOCUMENTS, section 7500.	No reporting standard. See paragraph 5020.10.

Continued

TYPE OF INFORMATION RESPONSIBILITIES	NATURE AND EXTENT OF INVOLVEMENT	NATURE AND EXTENT OF ASSOCIATION	PROFESSIONAL WORK	REPORTING
Tax return and financial statements as attachments to the tax returns.	Preparation of tax return (financial statements were prepared by the client).	The public accountant has associated himself or herself with the tax return by virtue of preparing it and providing related tax advice (see paragraph 5020.04). The public accountant has not associated himself or herself with the financial statements because he or she has not performed services in respect of the financial statements or consented to the use of his or her name in connec tion with the financial state ments (see paragraph 5020.04).	No professional responsibilities other than those discussed in the Note on the first page of this Appendix.	No reporting standard. See paragraph 5020.10.

Audits of Public Sector and Not–for-Profit Financial Statements

Most public sector and not-for-profit organizations have their own accounting standards. The CICA provides public sector accounting standards, and *Handbook* sections 4400–447 are for not-for-profit organizations. In the *CICA Handbook*, fair presentation follows from the recommendations for the specified organizations. Some public sector organizations, however, are required under legislation to use other accounting policies. If the requirements are misleading and seem to be in conflict with *CICA Handbook* recommendations, the auditor is required to issue an opinion reservation. Under CICA Public Sector Recommendation 5200.04, the auditor must issue an opinion on fairness of presentation in accordance with GAAP or other basis of accounting "appropriate to public sector or not-for-profit organization."

Public Sector Auditing

Public sector auditors are auditors employed by federal, provincial, and municipal levels of government.

Public Sector Auditors

The Office of the Auditor General (OAG) is headed by the Auditor General of Canada. OAG auditors are the highest level of internal auditors for the federal government as a whole. Many provinces have provincial auditing offices similar to the OAG, and each answers to its provincial legislature. The OAG and the counterpart provincial agencies are actually external auditors with respect to the government agencies they audit because they are organizationally independent.

Many federal and provincial government agencies (e.g., the Canada Revenue Agency and Ontario's Ministry of Health and Long-term Care) and local governments have their own internal audit departments with an auditor general and internal auditors. In matters of scale and the positions they occupy, corporate and governmental auditors have much in common; many companies have revenues and assets as large as some governments, and corporate internal auditors have a relative position in their company similar to that of the auditor general in the federal government The discussion in this chapter contrasts and compares the activities of these two groups of auditors.

Compliance Auditing Applicable to Governmental Entities and Other Recipients of Governmental Financial Assistance

Federal and provincial governments and their agencies and local governments use the CICA Public Sector Standards to guide their audits. These standards are published in separate *CICA Handbook* sections. We will use the acronym **PS** for public sector auditing standards developed by the CICA. Public sector standards have been widely adopted and you will, therefore, be introduced to them in this chapter.

When independent accountants in public practice take engagements for the OAG, they are conducting the work in accordance with PSs. In fact, failure to follow PSs in such engagements is an "act discreditable to the profession." Some parliamentary regulatory laws require auditors to test and report on a public sector entity's compliance with laws and regulations. This work is a form of **compliance auditing**, which has a special relevance in government-standard audit engagements. Under the CICA's generally accepted auditing standards, external auditors are responsible for detecting material errors, irregularities, and certain illegal acts in their audits of private sector and not-for-profit financial statements. These are detailed in Chapter 17 in this text. However, governmental entities and recipients of government funds deal with laws and regulations concerned with eligibility, procedure, and payment of amounts under various entitlements and programs. After ensuring that management provided a list of the applicable laws and regulations, auditors study them and determine which specific procedures to perform in order to obtain evidence of compliance.

The public sector sometimes requires reports on compliance. The auditors can give positive assurance on areas tested with compliance procedures and negative assurance on those areas not tested. An example of part of a report on compliance test results is shown in the following box.

UNIVERSITY OF XYZ, PROVINCE OF XYZ

Finding: Of the 50 student records tested, for a $94,181 total dollar amount, fifteen loan application forms were completed incorrectly. These applications must be completed correctly to ensure that the students will not be overawarded. These errors resulted in one student overawarded a total amount of $1,387, two students underawarded a total of $631, and no effect on the awarded amount for the remaining 12 students.

Recommendations: To ensure that the costs and estimates are calculated correctly, management should review the loan applications.

University's response: The overaward resulted from late filing of one student's Student Aid Report. The award was based on preliminary information from the Comprehensive Financial Aid Report. Underawards were the result of clerical errors. Management will monitor the completion of the loan applications more closely.

Certain public sector agencies also require reports on internal control. These reports must describe the entity's control structure, the scope of the auditors' work, and any reportable conditions and material control weaknesses. The requirements for such reports can be very detailed and go beyond the scope of this text.

REVIEW CHECKPOINTS

18 Why do you think special attention is paid to compliance auditing for governmental-type audits when independent PAs may perform compliance procedures in all types of audits anyway?

Independence

Public sector auditors, like external and internal auditors, hold independence as a goal. PS 5000.04 and IFAC Public Sector Guidelines recommend that public sector auditors adhere to established rules of professional conduct: maintain integrity and objectivity and avoid the independence-damaging appearance of financial and managerial involvement. Public sector auditors must be aware that preconceived, personal ideas about programs, political or social convictions, and loyalties to certain levels of government may impair the integrity and objectivity that is foundational to independence. Like internal auditors, public sector auditors must be alert to external sources of independence impairment, such as interference and threats to job security by higher-level officials.

Separation from such influences is essential for independence; otherwise auditors cannot report directly to top management without fear of job or compensation retribution. Auditors of governmental units are presumed independent when they are (1) free from sources of personal impairment, (2) free from sources of external impairment, (3) organizationally independent, (4) independent under provincial rules of professional conduct, (5) elected or appointed and reporting to a legislative body of government, or (6) auditing in a level or branch of government other than the one to which they are normally assigned.

On any particular assignment, public sector auditors may perform services for the benefit of several interested parties—the management of the auditee, officials of the agency requiring the audit, officials of one or more agencies that fund the auditee's programs, members and committees of local governments, a provincial legislature, and/or the national Parliament, and the public. All such parties should receive the audit report unless laws or regulations restrict public distribution (e.g., for reasons of national security). In fact, the annual reports of the OAG and provincial auditors to their respective legislatures are widely reported media events—which suggests that public sector auditors do not face the expectations gap of external auditors. In contrast, standard audit reports on financial statements given by independent external auditors are addressed to the client and distributed only by the client to whomever the client wishes (except in the case of securities commission-registered companies, where the law usually requires the reports to be filed for public inspection).

Scope of Service

The objective of internal auditing is service to "the organization," not just to management or some narrow internal interest group. Internal auditors, exercising their objectivity, function for the benefit of the whole organization—whether represented by the board of directors, the chief executive officer, the chief financial officer, or other executives. The services provided by internal auditors include (1) audits of financial reports and accounting control systems; (2) reviews of control systems that ensure compliance with company policies, plans, and procedures and with laws and regulations; (3) appraisals of the economy and efficiency of operations; and (4) reviews of effectiveness in achieving program results in comparison with established objectives and goals. Internal auditors often make recommendations that result in additional profits or cost savings for their companies. In this capacity, they function like management consultants, and this is referred to as **operational auditing**.

The Office of the Auditor General of Canada shares these elements of expanded-scope services with internal auditors. The OAG, however, emphasizes the accountability of public officials for the efficient, economical, and effective use of public funds and other resources. It defines and describes expanded-scope governmental auditing in terms of the types of government audits that can be performed, which are as follows:

1. **Financial Statement Audits (PS 5200)**
   a. Financial statement audits determine (1) whether the financial statements of an audited entity present fairly the financial position, results of operations, and cash flows or changes in financial position in conformity with generally

accepted accounting principles; and (2) whether the entity has complied with laws and regulations for transactions and events that may have a material effect on the financial statements.

2. **Compliance Audits (PS 5300)**

    Compliance audits are those in which audit mandates are required to do one or more of the following:

    a. Express an opinion on whether an entity complied with specified authorities or whether its transactions were carried out in compliance with specified authorities.
    b. Express an opinion on whether the transactions that have come to their notice in the cause of discharging their other audit responsibilities were carried out in compliance with specified authorities.
    c. Report instances of noncompliance with authorities observed in the course of discharging their audit responsibilities.

3. **Value-for-Money (Performance) Audits (PS 5400)**

    a. Economy and efficiency audits include determining (1) whether the entity is acquiring, protecting, and using its resources (such as personnel, property, and space) economically and efficiently; (2) the causes of inefficiencies or uneconomical practices; and (3) whether the entity has complied with laws and regulations concerning matters of economy and efficiency.
    b. Effectiveness or program audits include determining (1) the extent to which the desired results or benefits established by the legislature or other authorizing body are being achieved; (2) the effectiveness of organizations, programs, activities, or functions; and (3) whether the agency has complied with laws and regulations applicable to the program.

Audits of a governmental organization, program, activity, or function may involve one or more of these types of audits. The term comprehensive audit describes engagements that include all three types of the audits described above. The OAG and other public sector auditors, however, do not require comprehensive audits, and the engagements involve just one or two of the three types. The scope of the work is supposed to be determined according to the needs of the users of the audit results. However, the OAG recommends observance of PS standards in audits of governmental units by external auditors as well as by governmental auditors at federal, provincial, and local levels.

REVIEW CHECKPOINTS

19 What is operational auditing, and why can it be called a type of consulting service?
20 How can internal auditors achieve practical independence?
21 What general auditing services do internal auditors provide?
22 What general auditing services do governmental auditors provide?
23 What factors should governmental auditors consider in determining whether they are independent?

ECONOMY, EFFICIENCY, AND EFFECTIVENESS AUDITS

Economy and efficiency measures are fairly straightforward. Auditors can use these tools and techniques to evaluate them: financial and organizational analysis, computer-assisted data analysis and EDP testing, value analysis, productivity measurement and quantitative analysis, methods analysis using work study techniques, work measurement, and productivity-opportunity matrices. Economy is related to the price variance, while efficiency is related to the efficiency variance of standard variance analysis in managerial accounting for control. The products here, however, are usually services or activities instead of tangible goods, and thus it may not be possible to measure them as discrete units.

Effectiveness is more difficult to define and evaluate, but it may be helpful to view it as a type of "volume" or "capacity" variance where volume(s) are measured relative to some objective or objectives of the organization. The Canadian Comprehensive Auditing Foundation (CCAF-FCVI Inc.) prepared a report called "Effectiveness Reporting and Auditing in the Public Sector" to deal with the question of effectiveness. This report enumerated 12 different attributes of effectiveness that the auditor must examine in performing a value-for-money (VFM) audit:

1. *Management direction.* How well integrated are the organization's objectives and component programs with management decision making?
2. *Relevance.* Does the program still serve the originally intended purpose?
3. *Appropriateness.* Is the program's structure appropriate, considering its purpose?
4. *Achievement of results.* Has the program realized its goals and objectives?
5. *Acceptance.* How well have constituents or customers received the service or output of the organization?
6. *Secondary impacts.* Has the organization caused any other intended or not-intended results?
7. *Costs and productivity.* How efficient has the organization been?
8. *Responsiveness.* Has the organization adapted well to changes in its environment?
9. *Financial results.* Has the organization accounted properly for revenues and expenses, and for valued assets and liabilities?
10. *Working environment.* Is the work environment appropriate, given the organization's purpose, and does it promote initiative and achievement?
11. *Protection of assets.* Does the organization safeguard valuable assets?
12. *Monitoring and reporting.* Does the organization know where it stands with regard to key performance indicators?

Effectiveness can mean much more than the extent to which program objectives are being met and encompass all the above characteristics. When defining effectiveness, the client (Parliament or other legislative bodies) may have completely different perceptions than the stakeholder (the program recipient).

Audit mandates specify what is required of auditors and provide auditors with the authority to carry out their work and report. The amount of discretion an auditor has in establishing the objectives and scope of the VFM audit varies. Mandates that are legislated may provide only general direction about objectives and scope, in which case the auditor decides on audit objectives and scope. Other legislated mandates, such as that for special examinations of federal Crown corporations, may be more specific in defining objectives and scope. In contractual mandates, audit objectives and scope are usually specified by the client. In those cases the auditor would assess the appropriateness of the audit objectives and scope before accepting the engagement.

VFM audit mandates also have different reporting requirements. Many mandates require direct reporting about the entity. For example, auditors may report deficiencies or provide an opinion on whether there is reasonable assurance, based on specified criteria, that there are no significant deficiencies in the systems and practices examined. Auditors may be asked to attest to management assertions. When the mandate does not specify reporting requirements, auditors choose, often in consultation with their clients, how the results of the audit will be reported. The reporting requirements affect the nature and extent of work performed in the audit.

Government audits require more work on compliance and reporting on internal control than external auditors might do in an audit of financial statements of a private business. The reason for this is the public's concern for laws, regulations, and control of expenditures. One-third of the Canadian economy and several $100 billion of federal funds is represented by the public sector, so the stakes are high.

We conclude with a summary of the differences between VFM audits (which have counterparts in internal audit via the performance or operational audit concepts) and traditional auditing, followed by environmental audits.

R E V I E W CHECKPOINTS

24 Identify the twelve attributes of effectiveness.

25 What is a comprehensive audit?

26 Explain the difference between compliance and VFM audits.

27 Compare and contrast economy, efficiency, and effectiveness measures of performance. Which of these is the hardest to audit? Explain.

Summary of the Differences between Traditional Auditing and VFM Auditing

LEARNING OBJECTIVE

6 Explain public sector auditing concepts.

1. In traditional audits, the objective is to render an opinion on the financial statements, and scope restrictions can result in qualification. In VFM audits, the auditor's mandate may provide the auditor with the discretion to establish the audit objectives and scope. In most cases VFM audits have mandates established through legislation or contracts. These mandates specify what is required for the auditor.

2. In VFM audits, the objectives and scope vary from one audit to another, depending on the function and characteristics of the organization being audited. According to PS 6410.07, an auditor always has to use his or her professional judgment when faced with a broad mandate, and define it in specific terms with specific objectives. In the case where the mandate is specific, an auditor must still assess the objectives' appropriateness.

3. In VFM audits, much of the audit focuses on matters that are not necessarily financial, such as human resource management.

4. There is no body of standards analogous to GAAP. Standards may be management-defined, legislative, or defined by professions and associations.

5. The nature and sources of evidence may differ from those in financial statement auditing. PS 6410.25 states that sufficient appropriate evidence should be obtained to afford a reasonable basis to support the content of the auditor's report. Since a VFM audit can be required to report deficiencies rather than to form an overall opinion, the amount of evidence needed may be lower. The fact that a VFM audit can focus more on processes than results also influences the nature of the evidence.

6. A VFM audit will tend to use a multidisciplinary audit team with expertise in different areas (like economics, statistics, engineering). The makeup of the group will depend on the type of organization being audited and the needs of the mandate.

7. VFM audits may not relate to a standard time period, such as a year-end.

8. There is no standard audit report for VFM audits. The form of the report will depend on the mandate and can take the form of a report on deficiencies or an overall opinion or an attestation of management assertions. By contrast, an audit of the financial statements of an entity has a standard report prescribed by the *CICA Handbook*.

9. VFM audits use the concept of "significance" rather than materiality. Significance, broadly defined, will include the following considerations:

   a. *Financial magnitude.* Areas with larger dollar amounts will receive greater attention.

   b. *Importance.* Some programs, operations, and activities are more important than others in the entity's strategy to achieve its objectives.

   c. *Economic, social, and environmental impact.* A project or program with a small budget may have a significant impact on the population or the environment.

   d. *Previous VFM recommendations.* The auditor may choose to emphasize deficient areas previously pointed out that appear not to have improved.

10. The concept of audit risk takes on unique meanings in a VFM audit. Inherent risk is the probability of lack of due regard to value-for-money. Control risk is the probability that a system, control, or practice is designed to ensure that VFM will fail. Detection risk is the risk that the auditor will fail to detect significant errors.

In summary, there are many differences between traditional financial statement audits and VFM audits. However, as noted in the preceding section, the assurance engagement concept introduced in *CICA Handbook* section 5025 incorporates, with modifications, many of the concepts of VFM audits. This is understandable, since an objective of section 5025 is to provide an umbrella framework for *all* audits, including VFM audits.

ENVIRONMENTAL AUDITS: ANOTHER POTENTIAL TYPE OF ASSURANCE ENGAGEMENT

. . . .

LEARNING OBJECTIVE

7 Explain environmental auditing issues.

The environmental audit evaluates a company's operations and performance in terms of conformity with federal, provincial, and municipal laws and regulations, and it identifies the risks of any noncompliance. It is used to compile and report all pertinent information related to the environment, and it can help in developing remedial plans aimed at mitigating environmental risks. Specifically, the results can be used in the following ways:

- Make managers and employees accountable for the environmental consequences of their activities.

- Assure the public and employees that environmental hazards are being adequately managed.

- Meet requirements of financial institutions and insurance companies.

- Evaluate compliance with government standards and legislation.

- Present a defence of due care if the company can show it took all reasonable precautions to avoid committing the offence in relation to environmental issues.

The actual environmental audit report will vary according to the specific terms of the mandate, the scope and complexity of the audit, and the audit findings. Although no standard guidelines exist in this field, every company should define its audit objectives and scope according to its own particular mandate, short- and long-term goals, and corporate culture. Some basic elements should be taken into consideration: size of the company and its operation and their effects on the environment, possibility of lawsuits, company role and image in the community, extent of management's commitment to environmental concerns, and government environmental laws and regulations affecting the company's operations.

Since the scope of an environmental audit is so broad, a multidisciplinary audit team should be carefully selected. Their knowledge of the industry and its equipment must be considered, as well as their training, experience, communication skills, and investigative techniques. At the planning stage, the auditors should gather preliminary documentation on the client's business and prepare analytical studies of the company's activities and operations in order to assess the inherent risk of misstatement in the financial statements resulting from environmental damage caused by the client. The auditors should determine the audit objectives and evaluation criteria and prepare an audit program.

The audit itself is done by inspecting the site and querying management and employees while compiling factual information about hazardous behaviour or situations. The audit team should also examine the company's efforts to provide reasonable prevention and control of the environmental risks, and ensure that environmental responsibilities have been appropriately assigned within the organization. By comparing the evidence gathered with the criteria, based on legal requirements and the company's own policies and management practices, the auditors should be able to express an opinion in an audit report as to whether environmental matters are fairly presented in the financial statements. This report must be accurate and concise and point out the problems detected, and its evaluations should be sufficiently and appropriately justified by the working papers.

Depending on the results of the audit, the audit team may be asked to prepare action plans, monitoring structures, directives, or recommendations, and then to discuss them with management or with an advisory committee. In essence, environmental auditing appears to conform to the characteristics of a VFM audit, especially the effectiveness characteristic.

A wide range of services have come to be described as environmental auditing, ranging from those meeting the assurance engagement criteria to consulting work. This is an area of practice that is still evolving. Environmental audits may develop further because of public interest in environmental issues such as global warming. There are many other types of assurance engagements possible. Some more are described in Appendix 16A.

APPLICATION CASE AND ANALYSIS
Suitable Criteria, GAAP, and Critical Thinking

In this chapter you were introduced to the suitable criteria concept that applies to all assurance engagements and to how this concept relates to the fairness of presentation framework of CAS 200 and 700. In earlier chapters you were introduced to the audit risk and accounting risk concepts. How are these concepts integrated in an assurance engagement? Specifically, how do audit and accounting risks relate to fairness of presentation frameworks of financial reporting?

Analysis

There is little authoritative guidance on these issues, so we must develop some reasonable interpretations to fill in the gaps. Suitable criteria are those that apply to the subject matter. The subject matter in financial statement auditing is financial reporting, and thus suitable criteria refer mainly to GAAP, not GAAS. In the case of financial information assurance engagements, the suitable criteria of relevance, reliability, neutrality, understandability, and completeness need to be compared with those of *CICA Handbook* section 1000.18–24: understandability, relevance (predictive value, timeliness), reliability (representational faithfulness, verifiability, neutrality, conservatism), and comparability. There is considerable overlap between these sets of terms, except for the completeness criterion of 5025. Any other differences found are relatively minor, and can be attributed to the more detailed explanations given in section 1000.

The now familiar assertions introduced in Chapter 6 are our starting point in this analysis. Note that all of them except valuation, and perhaps presentation, deal with fairly objective or factual information. GAAP presumes that the facts are presented truthfully as part of fair presentation. In other words, you may assume that GAAP does not condone lying in financial reporting. But auditors cannot assume that these facts are true. Instead, it is their responsibility to verify the facts through evidence. The various audit procedures verify facts such as existence, ownership, and completeness of assets and liabilities reported by the auditee.

However, GAAP accounting is more than just accurate recording of facts. To a considerable and increasing degree, GAAP accounting also involves forecasting of future events. Forecasting is the basis of most estimates in accounting; for example, for the allowance for doubtful accounts and other contra accounts that adjust for valuation, useful life, and disposal values of capital assets, pension assets and liabilities, leased assets and liabilities, contingencies, and going concern issues. In fact, the basic concept of asset is defined as a *future* benefit, which implies a forecast. In addition, the increasing use of fair value accounting in financial reporting requires frequent forecasting; market values are used when available because it is assumed that they are the best predictors of future benefits. The only account that does not require any type of forecsting is cash; cash and cash flows are matters of fact.

Forecasting introduces the most contentious issues within financial reporting. It strongly influences the valuation assertion of accounting. Uncertainty about the future can't be eliminated by facts as, under periodic reporting, auditors can't simply wait to see which forecasts will be realized on the balance sheet date. Auditors and management must be willing to make some reasonable asumptions about the future and incorporate those in the accounting estimates used in GAAP fiancial reporting.

The fundamental problem associated with forecasts in financial reporting is well illustrated by the concept of future oriented financial information (FOFI) in Appendix 16A to this chapter. Briefly, FOFI (also referred to as prospective financial information) is an acceptable form of financial reporting with a format similar to GAAP's but involving assumptions and projections concerning the future (sometimes the very far future) beyond those used in GAAP reporting. FOFI assurance engagements offer no assurance on the achievability of the prospective results. The standards on FOFI engagements also do not allow use of the words "present fairly" in high assurance FOFI engagements, and they are thus not treated as a fair presentation framework even though both types involve forecasts. What is the essential difference between FOFI and the forecasts used in GAAP financial reporting that are presumed to be achievable?

The most reasonable explanation for this difference appears to be that forecast risks are higher for FOFI than for the forecasts used in recording GAAP numbers, which introduces the concept of accounting risk. Although accounting risk applies as much to FOFI as it does to GAAP, those for FOFI are much higher (perhaps even as high as 100 percent risk) than they are for GAAP numbers. This suggests that it is the acceptability of accounting risk that characterizes a fair presentation framework. Specifically, in fairness of presentation frameworks, the acceptable level of accounting risk is lower. Accounting risk is "moderate" in fair presentation reporting and "high" in FOFI.

Figure 1 summarizes this information and attempts to capture all the information risks within assurance engagements involving financial information. The left-hand side of the figure shows the effects of the level of assurance, or 1 – evidence risk, which points to the amount of appropriate evidence gathered on the facts. For example, on audit (high) assurance engagements, the evidence risk is referred to as audit risk.

Levels of accounting risk lie across the top of Figure 1. Nothing currently captures the concept of 1 – accounting risk, except perhaps accounting reliability, which is incorporated in fair presentation reporting frameworks. An acceptable level of accounting reliability is a key judgment auditors make in financial reporting, although some guidance in accounting standards and in the accounting conceptual framework is preferred. By this analysis, the feature that distinguished FOFI forecasts from those of GAAP is their accounting risk levels, which are beyond what is considered acceptable for fairness reporting under GAAP. If their risk levels were not so high, they would not be labelled as FOFI.

An acceptable level of accounting risk not only establishes a fair presentation framework, as discussed above, but it also incorporates the completeness characteristic of suitable criteria.

The risk-based decision rule for accounting risk given in the application and analyis case at the end of Chapter 10 demonstrates this: the estimate is acceptable if the accounting estimate has an accounting risk less than or equal to an acceptable level of risk. For the example given in Appendix 7D, if we let acceptable accounting risk be set at .05, then the value of zero is accptable for financial reporting whereas the value $10 million or $1 billion is not. But should this contingent asset be disclosed?

The completeness is defined by the disclosure decision. In Chapter 10's demonstration of the statistical decision rule, any value that has a 1 – acceptable risk or greater probability of occurring should be

---

FIGURE   1   CLASSIFICATION OF ENGAGEMENTS BY ACCOUNTING AND EVIDENCE RISK

Level of Acceptable Accounting Risk → Level of Acceptable Evidence Risk ↓	LOW (High Accounting Reliability)	MEDIUM (Moderate Accounting Reliability)	HIGH (Low Accounting Reliability)
LOW (High or Reasonable Assurance)	Audit of cash flow information	Audit of GAAP financial statements	Audit of FOFI
MEDIUM (Moderate Assurance)	Review of cash flow information	Review of GAAP financial statements	Review of FOFI
HIGH (Low or no Assurance)	Compilation of cash flow information	Compilation of GAAP financial statements	Compilation of FOFI

recorded; otherwise, the value is ignored. Since financial reporting offers the option of disclosing future events in note disclosures, that is an option for values that are not recorded. Two good examples are note diclosure of contingencies and going concern. A natural cutoff probability for note disclosure is the probability of the acceptable risk level, because in sampling any material misstatement with probability less than acceptable risk is otherwise ignored. Therefore, applying consistent logic to accounting risk would ensure the completeness of dislosure of future events.

Completeness of financial reporting is implemented by requiring note disclosure of any material future event that falls in the range of acceptable risk to 1 – acceptable risk. For example, if the acceptable risk is .05, then any material future event having a probability between .05 to .95 should be dislosed in the notes to the financial statements. While auditors now decide on the acceptable risk for specific accounts, it would perhaps be better if accounting standard setters decided on such cutoff probabilities. They are a key feature of financial reporting, especially in determining which dislosures constitute fair presentation. One advantage would be a consistent, more rational way of dealing with key uncertainties of financial reporting in different assurance engagements summarized in Figure 1.

The left hand side of Figure 1 reflects the amount of evidence in relation to evidence risk: the more evidence there is on the facts, the lower the evidence risk, and the lower the evidence risk is the higher is the assurance provided. Evidence should be sufficient and appropriate for the the nature of the assurance engagement. Sufficiency of evidence relates to the amount of assurance provided by the engagement. High assurance results from persuasive evidence, while moderate assurance levels relate to the plausibility of the facts.

Reliability and relevance are the qualitative aspects of evidence that determine its appropriateness. Reliability relates to how persuasive the nature and source of the evidence are. For example, directly observing an inventory is the best proof of its existence. Relevance relates to how well the objectives of the engagement are met. It involves proving that every assertion for every line item in the financial statements is true, as is consistent with the presumption that GAAP does not present facts falsely. But relevance also relates to the valuation assertion. As already noted in this analysis, a key characteristic of valuation of GAAP accounting estimates is the accuracy of forecasts as reflected in accounting risk. If acceptable accounting risk is a key principle of a conceptual framework of financial reporting, it is understandable that detailed rules may not be adequate in all circumstances and the exceptions that characterize a general purpose fair presentation framework are necessary. Compliance reporting frameworks, on the other hand, tend to rely on detailed rules rather than general principles. This is because compliance frameworks, such as tax reporting rules, tend to have one specific user and one objective in mind.

SUMMARY

Public accountants are highly regarded providers of assurance services. Besides audits of historical financial statements, many other services have been offered or proposed. Company managers often develop innovative financial presentations and then engage auditors to give the public some assurance about them. Regulators are often interested in PAs' communications, and press for assurance involvement.

Guided by the general concepts of assurance as well as auditing, accounting, and review service standards, PAs offer services and render reports in several areas. These standards were summarized in Exhibit 3–1.

Unaudited financial statements have been around for a long time. In public practice these are known as review and compilation services. The difference between the two lies in the amount of work performed and the level of assurance given that each offers. Review engagements involve less work than an audit, and the report gives a low level of negative assurance. Compilation engagements involve the straightforward writing up of the financial statements, which is less work than a review, and the report gives an outright denial of assurance.

An accountants' review of interim financial information (e.g., quarterly financial reports) is another possiblity. Technically it is similar to a review of unaudited financial statements, and the report on this review of free-standing interim financial statements gives the negative assurance.

Financial statements fully in conformity with generally accepted accounting principles are not always the goal. Managers have the option to prepare their statements for public use on another appropriate disclosed basis of accounting (AADBA), and auditors may audit and report on such financial statements. In going this route, managers have an opportunity to avoid the complications of many of the GAAP rules. AADBA audits and reporting are in the auditing standards under the heading of "special reports."

Other special audit reports can be given on parts of financial statements and on current value financial statements. A certain engagement results in a positive assurance report on the internal control system. Regulators in some provinces, the SEC, and federal banking agencies have been interested in management reports and audit reports on internal control. The issue of reporting on internal control spills over into auditing standards that are designed to require annual auditors to report internally to managers and the board of directors in a company about internal control deficiencies and relations with management.

Auditors' responsibilities for reporting on financial statements prepared in accordance with the accounting principles generally accepted in other countries were outlined. The chapter then covered the CICA's recent attempt to develop an umbrella framework for many of the PA services via the assurance engagement concept. The chapter concluded with an overview of public sector auditing, which greatly influenced the assurance framework, and a brief review of environmental auditing.

MULTIPLE-CHOICE QUESTIONS FOR PRACTICE AND REVIEW

MC 1 Which of the following can be considered a prospective financial statement?
  a. Balance sheet based on current values of assets and liabilities
  b. Interim-date balance sheet for the first quarter of the fiscal year
  c. Forecast income statement based on assumptions about expected conditions and also expected conditions and expected courses of action
  d. Forecast valuation of securities held by a venture capital company

MC 2 Which of the following statements is correct?
  a. An examination report on prospective financial statements gives the same assurance as an audit report on historical financial statements.
  b. An examination report on prospective financial statements does not attest to the achievability of the forecast.
  c. In a compilation report on prospective financial statements, an accountant attests to the reasonableness of the underlying forecast assumptions.
  d. In reports on prospective financial statements, accountants undertake the obligation to update the reports for important subsequent events.

MC 3 Under the SEC "safe harbour" rule regarding financial forecasts, persons connected with a company's forecast can be liable for monetary damages in which case?
  a. The plaintiffs are able to prove that the persons connected with the forecast showed lack of good faith and lack of a reasonable basis for belief in the forecast.
  b. The plaintiffs are able to prove that the persons connected with the forecast were merely negligent.
  c. The persons connected with the forecast had good faith and a reasonable basis for belief in its presentation.
  d. The persons connected with a forecast cannot sustain the burden of proof that they acted in good faith and with a reasonable basis for belief in the forecast.

MC 4 In a current value presentation of the balance sheet of a manufacturing company:
  a. The basis of valuation must always be explained in notes to the financial statements.
  b. The basis of valuation is well known as a "comprehensive basis of accounting other than GAAP."
  c. An auditor can attest to the fair presentation of financial position in conformity with GAAP.
  d. The company must follow the AICPA guides for presentation of a financial forecast.

MC 5 Practice in connection with unaudited historical cost financial statements is conducted by which firms?
  a. International accounting firms only
  b. Regional- and local-size PA firms
  c. Local-size PA firms only
  d. All PA firms

MC 6 Which statements below are the official CICA Recommendations for Compilation and Review Services applicable to?
  a. Audited financial statements of public companies
  b. Unaudited financial statements of some companies
  c. Unaudited financial statements of all companies
  d. Audited financial statements of nonpublic companies

MC 7 A review service engagement for an accountant's association with unaudited financial statements involves which of the following:
  a. More work than a compilation, and more than an audit
  b. Less work than an audit, but more than a compilation
  c. Less work than a compilation, but more than an audit
  d. More work than an audit, but less than a compilation

MC 8 When an accountant is not independent, which following report can nevertheless be given?
  a. Compilation report
  b. Standard unqualified audit report
  c. Examination report on a forecast
  d. Review report on unaudited financial statements

MC 9 An accountant is permitted to express "negative assurance" in which of the following types of reports?
  a. Standard unqualified audit report on audited financial statements
  b. Compilation report on unaudited financial statements
  c. Review report on unaudited financial statements
  d. Adverse opinion report on audited financial statements

MC 10 When a company's financial statements in a review or compilation engagement contain a known material departure from GAAP, what should the accountant's report do?
  a. Make no mention of the departure in a compilation report because it contains an explicit disclaimer of opinion.
  b. Express the adverse conclusion, "The accompanying financial statements are not presented in conformity with generally accepted accounting principles."
  c. Explain the departure as necessary to make the statements not misleading, then gives the standard compilation report disclaimer.
  d. Explain the departure as necessary to make the statements not misleading; then give the standard review report negative assurance.

MC 11 When interim financial information is presented in a note to annual financial statements, the standard audit report on the annual financial statements should include which of the following?
  a. No mention of the interim information unless there is an exception the auditor needs to include in the report
  b. An audit opinion paragraph that specifically mentions the interim financial information if it is not in conformity with GAAP
  c. An extra paragraph that gives negative assurance on the interim information, if it has been reviewed
  d. An extra explanatory paragraph if the interim information note is labelled "unaudited"

MC 12 According to auditing standards, financial statements presented on another comprehensive basis of accounting should not do which of the following?
  a. Contain a note describing the other basis of accounting.
  b. Describe in general how the other basis of accounting differs from generally accepted accounting principles.
  c. Be accompanied by an audit report that gives an unqualified opinion with reference to the other basis of accounting.
  d. Contain a note with a quantified dollar reconciliation of the assets based on the other comprehensive basis of accounting with the assets based on generally accepted accounting principles.

MC 13 For which of the following reports is an expression of negative assurance not permitted?
  a. A review report on unaudited financial statements
  b. An audit report on financial statements prepared on a comprehensive basis of accounting other than GAAP
  c. A report based on applying selected procedures agreed upon by the client and the auditor
  d. A review report on interim financial information

MC 14 Which one of these events is an auditor not required to communicate to a company's audit committee or board of directors?
  a. Management's significant accounting policies
  b. Management judgments about accounting estimates used in the financial statements
  c. Immaterial errors in processing transactions discovered by the auditors
  d. Disagreements with management about accounting principles

EXERCISES AND PROBLEMS

EP 1 **Review of Forecast Assumptions.** You have been
LO.4 engaged by the Dodd Manufacturing Corporation to attest to the reasonableness of the assumptions underlying its forecast of revenues, costs, and net income for the next calendar year, 20X4. Four of the assumptions are shown below:
  a. The company intends to sell certain real estate and other facilities held by Division B at an after-tax profit of $600,000; the proceeds of this sale will be used to retire outstanding debt.
  b. The company will call and retire all outstanding 9 percent subordinated debentures (callable at 108). The debentures are expected to require the full call premium given present market interest rates of 8 percent on similar debt. A rise in market interest rates to 9 percent would reduce the loss on bond retirement from the projected $200,000 to $190,000.

  c. Current labour contracts expire on September 1, 20X4, and the new contract is expected to result in a wage increase of 5.5 percent. Given the forecast levels of production and sales, after-tax operating earnings would be reduced approximately $50,000 for each percentage-point wage increase in excess of the expected contract settlement.
  d. The sales forecast for Division A assumes that the new Portsmouth facility will be complete and operating at 40 percent of capacity on February 1, 20X4. It is highly improbable that the facility will be operational before January of 20X4. Each month's delay would reduce sales of Division A by approximately $80,000 and operating earnings by $30,000.

Required:
For each assumption, state the sources of evidence and procedures you would use to determine reasonableness.

EP 2 **Auditing a Current Value Balance Sheet.** Your client,
LO.10 the Neighbourhood Paper Company (NPC), has a fiscal
year-end of December 31. NPC needs to borrow money
from a local bank and believes current value financial
statements that report the appreciated value of its assets
would be helpful. A loan is needed for working capital
purposes.

NPC owns two paper-recycling processors. Old
paper is chemically processed, reduced to a wet mass,
and then pressed out into thick, semifinished paper
mats. The mats are sold to customers who use them for
packing material. Recycling processors are fairly complex pieces of integrated machinery and are built on a
customized basis by a few specialized engineering
companies.

NPC has owned one of the processors for five years.
It was appraised last year at $135,000 by a qualified
engineering appraiser. The second processor was purchased last month for $125,000—its appraised value—
and $10,000 was spent in bringing certain maintenance
up to date. Both processors have identical throughput
production capabilities.

The other major asset is a nine-hectare plot of land
NPC bought four years ago when management thought
the plant would be moved. The land was purchased for
$195,000 and was appraised by a qualified appraiser at
$250,000 only 20 months after the purchase date. The
nine hectares are located near a rapidly expanding industrial area.

Since the recycling processors were appraised/pur-
chased so recently, management does not want to bear
the expense of new appraisals this year. No plans have
been made to obtain a new appraisal on the land. NPC,
however, is a profitable operation. The unaudited income
statement for the current year (historical-cost basis)
shows net income of $46,000.

Required:

a. What practice standards are applicable to the engagement to review and report on the current value balance
sheet?

b. What primary auditing procedures should you apply
in addition to those necessary for the audit of the
historical-cost financial statements?

c. Will any additional disclosures in footnotes be necessary?

d. Are there any evidential problems in the NPC situation that might prevent your rendering a report on the
current value balance sheet?

EP 3 **Compilation Presentation Alternatives.** Jimmy C
LO.1 operates a large service station, garage, and truck stop on
Freeway 95 near Plainview. His brother, Bill, has recently
joined as a partner, even though he still keeps a small PA
practice. One slow afternoon, they were discussing
financial statements with Bert, the local PA who operates
the largest public practice in Plainview.

Jimmy: The business is growing, and sometimes I need
to show financial statements to parts suppliers
and to the loan officers at the bank. The problem
is, they don't like the way I put 'em together.

Bill: Jimmy, I know all about that. I can compile a jim-
dandy set of financial statements for us.

Bert: No, Jimmy. Bill can't do compiled financial statements for you. He's not independent.

Jimmy: I know, Momma didn't let him outa the house
'til he was 24.

Bert: That so?

Jimmy: But, Bert, those fellas are always asking me
about accounting policies, contingencies, and stuff
like that. Said something about "footnotes." I don't
want to fool with all that small print.

Required:

Think about the financial disclosure problems of Jimmy
and Bill's small business. What three kinds of compiled
financial statements can be prepared for them and by
whom?

EP 4 **Negative Assurance in Review Reports.** A PA states in
LO.1 the report on a review services engagement the following: Based on my review, I am not aware of any material
modifications that should be made to the accompanying
financial statements in order for them to be in conformity
with generally accepted accounting principles.

Required:

a. Is this paragraph a "negative assurance" given by the
PA?

b. Why is "negative assurance" generally prohibited in
audit reports?

c. What justification is there for permitting "negative
assurance" in a review services report on unaudited
financial statements and on interim financial information?

EP 5 **Reporting on a Forecast.** Kingston Company proposed
to sell to investors limited partnership interests in 40 new
hardware store buildings. Kingston Company would be
the general partner. The deal was structured to raise funds
for business expansion by offering a real estate investment. As part of the offering material, Kingston management produced a forecast based on the assumption of
$1.5 million gross annual revenue for each new location.
The lease income to the partnership is to be a base rental
fee plus 10 percent of gross revenue in excess of $1 mil-
lion. Kingston's existing stores have gross revenues
ranging from $800,000 to $1.75 million. Kingston also
produced related balance sheets and statements of
changes in financial position, all in conformity with
CICA forecast presentation guidelines.

Kingston engaged Anderson, Olds & Watershed to
examine the forecast and submit a report. One of the
assistant accountants on the engagement drafted the opinion paragraph of the report as follows:

In our opinion, the accompanying forecast is presented
in conformity with guidelines for presentation of a forecast established by the American Institute of Certified
Public Accountants, and the underlying assumption of
$1.5 million average revenue per store is sufficient to
cover the fixed and variable expenses of store maintenance, taxes, and insurance, which are the obligations of
the limited partners. However, there will usually be

differences between the forecast and actual results because store revenues frequently do not materialize as expected, and the shortfall may be material. We have no responsibility to update this report for events and circumstances occurring after the date of this report.

Required:

Identify and explain the errors, if any, in this portion of the forecast examination report.

EP 6
LO.1
Review Standards, Knowledge of Business. Two PAs are discussing review engagements.

A: As I see it, in a review we are providing a lower level of assurance and so we don't need the same extent of knowledge of the client's business and industry as we do in an audit.

B: That seems to be what the profession's review standards imply. But, at the same time, performing a review requires us to develop a "plausibility framework" that involves using enquiries and analytical procedures to assess whether the information being reported on is plausible in the circumstances. I don't see how this can be done unless I have an in-depth understanding of the client's business and its industry. To me this seems logically inconsistent: knowledge of the business and industry is critical in doing a review effectively, so how can I do a review with less knowledge than I need for an audit? And how do I know how much knowledge is "enough"?

A: I see your point. In some ways it seems knowledge of business is MORE critical in a review, not less, because in the audit you can rely on evidence. In a review you have to do it all by judgment.

B: And then, to make it even more confusing, there is also the "Strategic Systems Approach" to auditing that some auditors use; that seems to rely heavily on gathering knowledge of the business, its strategy, and its industry environment, but less on gathering hard, transaction-based audit evidence. So how does an SSA audit differ from a review?

Required:

Discuss the differences between these types of engagement, the assurance levels provided, and the knowledge and procedures required. Are the standards consistent in your view? What factors do PAs need to consider in deciding how much knowledge is enough and what procedures are required in a particular assurance engagement?

EP 7
LO.1
Review Procedures, Bank Confirmations. You have recently been hired as a junior accountant for a local PA firm. The firm's main practice involves reviews, compilations, and tax return preparation for small to medium business clients. The firm's policy for all review engagements is to always obtain a bank confirmation and reperform the client's year-end bank reconciliation. You have recently been studying about review engagement standards for one of your professional accounting exams, and point out to your senior that these procedures are not actually required by the standards. This means your firm could save some money by skipping them. The senior agrees because, in

her view, "Cash is a pretty low-risk account anyway. It's either right or wrong." But she notes that the firm's five partners are the ones who set the policy. "Maybe you should pull together a report on the advantages and disadvantages of this policy and present it to the partners—you might be able to make a big impression on them right away!"

Required:

a. Prepare the report suggested by your senior and include your conclusion on whether on not this policy is appropriate.

b. Why do you think the partners have this policy? How do you think they will respond to your report and your conclusion?

EP 8
LO.1
Compilations, Independence. PA has compiled the annual financial statements for her sister's pharmacy business since it started four years ago. The financial statements are attached to the pharmacy's corporate tax return, and are also provided to the company's banker to support the company's operating credit line. The banker has been satisfied with receiving tax-based financial statements compiled by PA.

Required:

a. Draft the report that PA should attach to the pharmacy company's financial statements.

b. Assume that, in the fifth year of the pharmacy's business, PA's sister decides to increase her bank credit line to renovate the pharmacy store and stock an expanded product line. To approve the higher credit line, the banker now requires financial statements prepared in accordance with GAAP. What actions must PA take under these new circumstances? How would these requirements differ if PA was not related to the pharmacy's owner?

EP 9
LO.7
Communications with Predecessor Auditor. Assume the role of the predecessor auditor and state what you would include in your communication with the successor auditor in the following independent situations.

a. You resigned from the audit because the client has not paid your fees for the previous year's audit.

b. You resigned from the audit because of concerns about management's integrity after discovering that many personal expenses of the senior managers had been improperly charged to the company's account.

c. The client dismissed you as auditor over a disagreement about the amount of inventory that should be written down for obsolescence.

d. The client dismissed you because your audit report in the previous year was a Denial of Opinion, resulting from serious deficiencies in the company's accounting records and internal controls

e. For each of the situations in *a)* to *d)* above, assume instead that you are the successor auditor and have received the above communications from the predecessor auditor. What action would you take on receiving the communication in each case?

EP 10 **Reviews, Interim Reports.** PA is the auditor of Shire
LO.2 Corp., a public company, and has also been engaged to
review Shire's third quarter interim financial statements.
Shire's third quarter financial statements will be filed
with the securities regulator within 30 days of the quarter
end, and will also be posted on Shire's corporate website
at that time.

Required:

a. Describe the procedures PA will use to review the
quarterly financial statements and the contents of PA's
review engagement report.

b. How might PA's work on the prior year-end audit relate
to and help with the review of the third quarter report?
(Consider what difficulties PA might have in conducting this review if PA did not also do the audit.)

EP 11 **Special Reports.** P. Nonius is the owner/manager of a
LO.2 company that owns several suburban shopping malls.
The retail store lease contracts require the store tenants
to pay a flat amount monthly, plus 1/2 percent of their
gross retail sales revenues quarterly. Nonius is concerned
that some of the lessees are understating their quarterly
gross retail sales. Nonius has contacted you, a PA, to
enquire about getting some assurance on the completeness of the retail sales reported by the tenants. You have
arranged to meet with Nonius next week to discuss this
engagement.

Required:

a. Prepare notes for your meeting with Nonius that
describe the assurance reporting options available
here (e.g., audit of the sales revenues, applying specified procedures, or other options) and outline the features of each option to help Nonius decide on the type
of assurance that will meet the objective in the most
cost-effective way.

b. You are aware that Nonius is very cost conscious and
will be reluctant to incur the additional cost of getting
assurance on the tenants' sales revenues. What additional points could you raise in the meeting with Nonius to show the value that can be provided to Nonius's
business by the assurance report itself, and by other
aspects of the assurance engagement?

EP 12 **Assurance Framework, Accountability Report.** In a
LO.5 recent round of federal-provincial healthcare funding
negotiations, the federal government took the position
that any additional funding it provides to the provinces
needs to be targeted to specific healthcare programs, such
as homecare. As a condition of funding, the federal government would require that the provincial governments
provide reports on their "accountability" for spending the
funds on the programs specified by the federal government. Consider the case of a hospital that is accountable
for implementing a homecare program, where people
who require medical care will be treated in their home by
hospital staff rather than being kept in the hospital.

Required:

a. Consider what information, or "subject matters," the
hospital would include in a "homecare accountability"

report. Give a brief list of general categories that would
be relevant in this report.

b. List the five characteristics of suitable criteria for
an assurance engagement provided in CICA section
5025 and in this chapter, and explain how each would
be applied to the categories of information that you
generated in part *a)* above.

c. Briefly describe some procedures you would perform to provide a high level of assurance on the subject matters reported. How would your procedures
differ if you were providing only a moderate level of
assurance?

EP 13 **Environmental Matters in a Financial Statement**
LO.7 **Audit.** PA is the senior in charge of the November 30,
20X1, audit of Baint's Paints Inc., a manufacturer of
various latex and oil-based paints. Baint's plant is
located on the banks of a river and was constructed on
this site in the 1930s because the river provided a ready
supply of water for manufacturing the paint, for cleaning out the manufacturing tanks, and for dumping surplus liquids produced in the manufacturing process.
With the passage of environmental legislation in the
1970s, Baint's was no longer permitted to use the river
water to clean its tanks and was required to have all
surplus manufacturing liquid removed for disposal elsewhere because many of these liquids were toxic to the
environment. While this environmental regulation
severely cut into Baint's profitability, it was able to
reduce costs in other aspects of the operation and remain in business, though at a somewhat lower level of
profitability. During her tour of the manufacturing operation, PA learns from Baint's production manager
that the plant produces approximately 80,000 litres of
paint per month from February to November. December
and January are too cold for paint manufacturing and the
two months are used for plant maintenance and clean
up. Baint's can sell all the paint it produces, and so production volumes are quite consistent from year to year.
The wastage in the paint manufacturing process ranges
from 5 to 6 percent of volume. The plant manager estimates that tank cleaning produces about 20,000 litres of
waste water a month during production, and about
100,000 litres in December and January as all the pipes
and pumping equipment are thoroughly flushed during
the plant shutdown. Waste water and paints are stored in
500 litre drums until the disposal company takes them
away. The empty drums are returned to Baint's plant for
refilling.

During her analytical review of the revenue and
expense accounts, PA notes that the processing costs
are significantly lower in the current year than in the
prior years. The main component of processing costs
contributing to the decline is the cost of waste disposal.
Suspecting a possible error in recording these costs,
PA finds out from the accounts payable clerk that the
disposal company charges $100 per drum. From this,
she estimates that Baint's has not paid for disposal of
approximately 80 percent of the year's waste liquid.
When she presents her analysis to the General Manager

for further explanation, he reports that, during the shutdown last year, he found a new disposal company that will take away the waste liquid for only $12 a drum, thus providing this substantial saving in the current year. While she is assessing the plausibility of all this analytical evidence, it occurs to PA that she has been working on the audit at the plant for two weeks now, arriving before light and leaving just at nightfall each day, and has never observed a disposal truck taking away the waste liquid drums.

Required:

a. Use the analytical information provided in the case to assess the approximate disposal costs and volumes. State any assumptions you make.

b. Does the General Manager's explanation make sense? What other possibilities might PA consider, and what additional information might she try to obtain.

c. To what extent is PA responsible for assessing the environmental compliance of Baint's Paints? Consider the implications of possible financial misstatements, as well as of possible illegal acts by management.

EP 14 **Association.** State whether PA is associated with the financial information in the following independent situations.
LO.10

a. PA compiles financial statements and prepares the corporate tax return for Appaloosa Inc.

b. PA advised Brumby Inc. on a sinking-fund amortization policy for its real estate investments; Brumby is the audit client of a different public accountant.

c. Criollo Inc. provides its banker with internal financial statements that have not been compiled, reviewed, or audited by PA, and informs the banker that PA is Criollo's independent accountant.

d. Fjord Company Ltd. is producing promotional material for its sales staff to use to get new customers. The promotional material includes a section titled "Fjord Company Facts" that lists company information such as the names of Fjord's CEO, CFP, COO, law firm, and accountant.

e. PA has performed an audit of Haflinger Inc. and has concluded that a denial of opinion is warranted because of severe internal control weaknesses and concerns about management's integrity.

f. PA prepares Hunter Inc.'s corporate tax return based solely on financial information produced by Hunter's accounting staff.

Discussion Cases

DC 1 **Internal Control Reports.** Do a class survey of internal control reports by auditors in 2006 at www.sec.gov. What is the most common criterion used to evaluate internal controls? Discuss.
LO.3

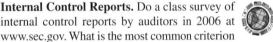

DC 2 **Controls and Financial Statements.** Should there be a relationship between audit reports on internal control statements and audit reports of financial statements? Discuss.
LO.3

DC 3 **Critical Thinking and the Assurance Framework.** CAS 700 notes a distinction between a fairness of presentation reporting framework and a compliance reporting framework. From the assurance framework perspective, what suitable criteria seem to be used for each framework?

DC 4 **Critical thinking and the GAAP hierarchy.** Is the FASB's 2008 GAAP hierarchy a fairness of presentation framework?

CHAPTER 17

Fraud Awareness Auditing

Fraud awareness auditing can be exciting with its aura of detectives investigating situations that people wish to keep hidden. However, fraud awareness auditing and examination are complex auditing activities that should not be pursued without proper training, experience, and care. This chapter is not intended to make you a fraud examiner or fraud auditor. Instead, its purpose is to heighten your familiarity with the nature, signs, prevention, detection, and reaction to fraud that can enable you to perform financial statement audits with awareness of fraud possibilities.

Users of audited financial statements generally believe that one of the main objectives of audits is fraud detection. External auditors know the issue is very complex, and they fear the general view that their work should ferret out all manner of fraud and misstatement in financial statements. This difference in viewpoints is one of the chronic expectation gaps between external auditors and users of published financial statements. However, in the post-Enron environment this expectation gap is increasingly being closed.

The gap exists partly because of the abilities and expertise needed by fraud examiners or fraud auditors. Most of the trained and experienced fraud examiners come from government agencies, such as the Canada Revenue Agency, the Royal Canadian Mounted Police (RCMP), the Office of the Auditor General of Canada (OAG), provincial securities commissions (especially the OSC), the Minister of Justice, and various police departments. Alumni of these agencies often practise as consultants and fraud examiners, but few of them enter public accounting to become financial statement auditors. So, what are most financial statement auditors to do? One option is to be more aware of fraud possibilities and able to perform a limited set of procedures determining when it is necessary to call on people with greater fraud examination expertise. Financial statement auditors need to understand fraud and potential fraud situations, and they need to know how to ask the right kinds of questions during an audit. We know this is possible because there have been occasional investigative jobs done by accountants. For example, one of the best known fraud auditors in Canada got started by doing an investigative audit of a former owner of the Toronto Maple Leafs hockey team.

DEFINITIONS RELATED TO FRAUD

LEARNING OBJECTIVE

1 Differentiate among frauds, errors, irregularities, and illegal acts that might occur in an organization.

There are several kinds of fraud. Some are defined in laws, while others are matters of general understanding. Exhibit 17–1 shows some acts and devices often involved in financial frauds. Collectively, these are known as **white-collar crime**—the misdeeds done by people who wear ties to work and steal with a pencil or a computer. White-collar crimes involve ink stains instead of bloodstains.

Fraud is knowingly making material misrepresentations of fact, with the intent of inducing someone believe the falsehood, act upon it, and thus suffer a loss or damage. This definition includes all the ways in which people can lie, cheat, steal, and dupe others.

Employee fraud is fraudulently taking money or other property from an employer. It usually involves falsifications of some kind—false documents, lying, exceeding authority, or violating an employer's policies. It consists of three phases: (1) the fraudulent act, (2) the conversion of the money or property to the fraudster's use, and (3) the cover-up.

Embezzlement is employees or nonemployees wrongfully taking money or property entrusted to their care, custody, and control. It is often accompanied by false accounting entries and other forms of lying and cover-up. **Defalcation** is another name for employee fraud and embezzlement. Technically, the term is used when somebody in charge of safekeeping the assets is doing the stealing.

Management fraud is deliberate fraud through exploitation of authority. Weaknesses in corporate governance create opportunities for management fraud. The perpetrators are management; the victims are investors and creditors; and the instruments of perpetration are corporations.[1] A special type of management fraud, **fraudulent financial reporting**, was defined by the United States National Commission on Fraudulent Financial Reporting (1987) as intentional or reckless conduct, whether by act or omission, that results in materially misleading financial statements.

---

[1] R. K. Ellott and J. J. Willingham, *Management Fraud: Detection and Deterrence* (New York: Petrocelli Books, Inc., 1980), p. 4.

EXHIBIT 17-1 AN ABUNDANCE OF FRAUDS

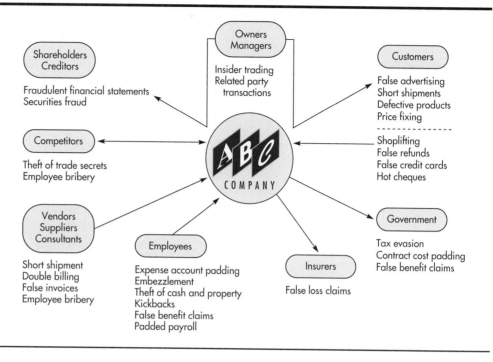

CAS 240 (section 5135), summarizes fraud and other irregularities as an intentional misstatement in financial statements, including an omission of amount or disclosure, or a misstatement arising from theft of the entity's assets. Fraud also involves:

(i) use of deception such as manipulation, falsification, or alteration of accounting records or documentation;

(ii) misrepresentation or intentional omission of events, transactions, or other significant information; or

(iii) intentional misapplication of accounting principles relating to amount, classification, or manner of presentation of disclosure.

The word *fraud* is used in this chapter, but in practice the auditor is concerned with a suspected fraud rather than a proven one. Final determination of whether fraud has occurred is a legal matter to be decided by a court of law.

Errors are unintentional misstatements or omissions of amounts or disclosures in financial statements. **Irregularities** are intentional misstatements or omissions in financial statements, including **fraudulent financial reporting** (usually a type of management fraud) and **misappropriations of assets** (defalcations). **Direct-effect illegal acts** are violations of laws or government regulations by the company, its management, or the employees that produce direct and material effects on dollar amounts in financial statements.

Fraud auditing is defined in Association of Certified Fraud Examiners course material as a proactive approach to detect financial frauds using accounting records and information, analytical relationships, and an awareness of fraud perpetration and concealment schemes. A good overview of the nature and scale of the fraud problem in Canada is provided by KPMG's Annual Fraud Report. For example, the 2004 report included the findings listed in the box following.

KPMG 2004 SURVEY ON THE RISK OF MANIPULATION OF FINANCIAL STATEMENTS

In a survey sent to the directors of 75 of Canada's largest corporations, 84 percent said that they think it is likely they will hear of a public company in Canada that has been involved in financial statement manipulation in 2004, according to the *2004 Survey on the Risk of Manipulation of Financial Statements* published by KPMG Forensic.

A further 46 percent thought it possible that such manipulation could occur in the company of the Board on which they themselves sit.

"It's illuminating that our survey results show that this type of fraudulent behaviour carried out as a conspiracy by a group of senior people to deceive corporate directors, auditors, lenders, and other stakeholders to line their own pockets, has come to be seen as commonplace," says James Hunter, President, KPMG Forensic.

Sixty-two percent of directors said that compensation models based on profitability encourage manipulation by CEOs and CFOs. However, directors also argued that the CEO and CFO both bear the greatest responsibility for protecting stakeholders against fraud.

Only 28 percent of respondents thought the Board of Directors are ultimately responsible for ensuring that financial statements have not been deliberately manipulated. However, 47 percent felt that it is the CEO who bears the greatest responsibility for protecting against such manipulations.

A more specific illustration of potential fraudulent financial reporting in Canada is given in the box below.

FRAUD CHARGES AGAINST NORTEL EXECUTIVES CONFIRM THEIR SPECTACULAR FAILURE OF CORPORATE GOVERNANCE

Nortel Networks Corp., Canada's former tech star and once the 12th most valuable company in the world, is now recognized as a spectacular failure in corporate governance with few equals in any nation or industry.

The RCMP made the status official yesterday, laying fraud and other criminal charges against former Nortel chief executive Frank Dunn, erstwhile chief financial officer Douglas Beatty, and Michael Gollogly, former corporate controller. Nortel thus joins the pantheon of disgraced high-fliers that includes WorldCom, Parmalat, Enron, and Tyco.

Dunn was one of seven top executives abruptly fired by Nortel in April 2004, setting off a long running financial scandal at the once revered firm.

Canadians need little reminding of the crash and burn of the widely held Nortel, whose shares peaked at $124.50 in July 2000 before nose-diving to a low of 67 cents by October 2002, erasing $385 billion in shareholder value—more than the GDP of Switzerland, Australia, or Malaysia.

Dunn was the obscure certified management accountant who joined Nortel after graduating from McGill University with a BCom and was tapped to replace retiring CEO John Roth in 2001.

Dunn's task was to revive an enterprise whose revenues had collapsed by two-thirds in the aftermath of the "irrational exuberance" of the late 1990s tech and telecom bubble, and that had laid off probably more employees more quickly—about 80,000—than any other firm in history.

In what turned out to be the false spring of 2004, with Nortel showing signs of recovery, Dunn was talking proud.

"We climbed a hill no one thought could be climbed," he boasted to the *Financial Times* early that year. "We've got a business model that everybody feels great about."

Dunn was in the habit of referring to himself as Nortel. "I am becoming a software/data company and less like a big car manufacturer," Dunn, said in 2003.

The career bookkeeper with no previous CEO or tech experience had broken ground on an Oakville lakefront castle with 10,800 sq. ft of living space, later dumped on the market with an asking price of $9.5 million after Dunn's firing.

What Nortel was becoming during Dunn's brief tenure was never clear. But Dunn undeniably was becoming rich; Nortel's board had agreed to a ludicrous bonus plan tied to profit targets designed to "incentivize" Dunn and his crew. In short order, Dunn obliged in January 2004 with a reported 2003 annual profit—Nortel's first in seven years, and, as agreed, Dunn, Beatty, and Gollogly pocketed a quick $13 million for meeting the target.

Alas, the "profits" justifying the bonus payouts turned out to be phantom, inflated by a staggering $3.4 billion (U.S.) between 1999 and 2005; during about half of that period, Dunn was chief financial officer, in charge of the firm's financial reporting. Today, Dunn claims he "rescued" Nortel, and that the accounting discrepancies over six years were all "innocent errors."

Nortel has paid a stunning $2.4 billion (U.S.) to settle class-action lawsuits and has spent many more millions of dollars in re-examining its own books.

But the principal culprit is a Nortel board of blue-chip luminaries so easily gulled into thinking Nortel was in vastly better shape than it was.

On June 19, 2008, there was a sort of "perp walk" scenario Nortel investors have waited years to see.

In a scene more reminiscent of high-profile U.S. fraud prosecutions against top executives from Enron to WorldCom, former Nortel chief executive Frank Dunn walked past a phalanx of cameras yesterday after facing criminal charges in a Newmarket courtroom.

Dunn is charged with two counts of falsifying accounts, three counts of being involved in issuing a false prospectus used to sell shares, and two counts of fraud affecting the public securities market.

After years of civil fraud allegations, investigations, lawsuits, and multi-million dollar settlements over the accounting scandal at Nortel Networks Corp., yesterday's move by the Royal Canadian Mounted Police marks the first criminal charges to be laid.

But it remains hotly debated whether the arrests will mark a turning point in Canada's reputation for loose oversight of stock markets and an inability to make prosecutions stick—what former Bank of Canada governor David Dodge once called our "wild west" notoriety among global investors.

It took police four years and more than more than 50 people sorting through some 20 million electronic documents to make the case against the former Nortel executives.

> Claude Lamoureux, former president of the Ontario Teachers' Pension Plan Board, said the fraud charges are a good sign.
>
> "Every investor should be happy these charges are being laid," he said. "Clearly it shows IMET (fraud unit of RCMP) was active and many of us had doubts about it."
>
> Source: *The Globe and Mail*, June 20, 2008, pp. 1, 15; *The Toronto Star*, June 20, 2008, p. 1; CTV News, June 19, 2008, at www.ctv.ca/servlet/ArticleNews/story/CTVNews/20080619/rcmp_nortel_080619/20080619?

Nortel's problems are not unique to Canada, or to the rest of the world, as the following PwC study indicates.

FRAUD—A MOST PROBLEMATIC BUSINESS RISK

Our 2007 survey reveals that fraud remains one of the most problematic issues for businesses worldwide, with no abatement, no matter what a company's country of operation, industry sector, or size. Of the 5,428 companies in 40 countries that took part in our research project[1], over 43% reported suffering one or more significant[2] economic crimes during the previous two years—an essentially static level compared with 2005 and an increase of six percentage points over 2003.[3]

Companies reporting fraud (2003–2007)

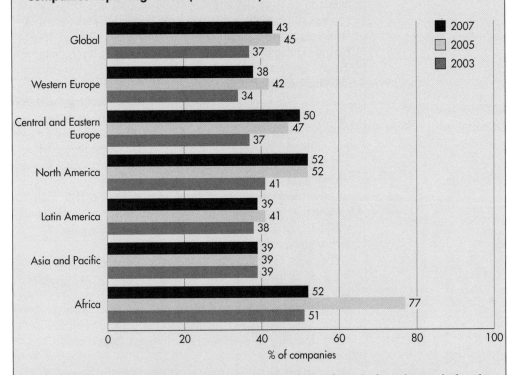

Source: © 2007 PricewaterhouseCoopers. All rights reserved. 'PricewaterhouseCoopers' refers to the network of member firms of PricewaterhouseCoopers International Limited, each of which is a separate and independent legal entity.

[1] The 2007 Crime survey is the fourth multinational survey conducted by PricewaterhouseCoopers and our data stretches over eight years.

[2] The term 'significant' was left to the discretion of the individual respondent with the proviso that it should relate to economic crimes that had a definite impact on the business, whether direct tangible damage or collateral and psychological damage.

[3] Copies of our previous global economic crime surveys can be found at www.pwc.com/crimesurvey

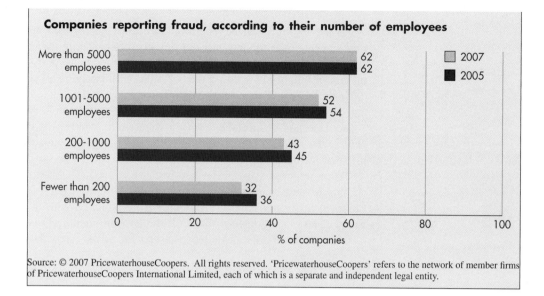

What may turn out to be one of the biggest frauds ever was first made public in December 2008. It was the Madoff fraud discussed in Chapter 14. It is described in more detail in the box below.

PONZI SCAM ARTISTS SHARE CHARM, RESPECTABILITY

BOSTON—They're smart and charming. They have an aura of success about them and exude respectability. Above all, they instill confidence.

Which is, after all, why they are called con men.

Bernard Madoff, the Wall Street trader accused of running the biggest Ponzi scheme in history—$50 billion—dealt in more astounding numbers than others but shares many of the basic qualities of Ponzi swindlers through history, according to law enforcement authorities and others who have studied such scams.

"They seem trustworthy because of their charm, their command of finance, and the unshakable confidence that they portray," said Jacob Frenkel, a former Securities and Exchange Commission enforcement lawyer. "The Bernie Madoffs of the world are the people you want to sit next to on an airplane."

Much like the original Ponzi schemer, Charles Ponzi. He was an Italian immigrant to Boston who worked as a waiter, bank teller, and nurse before he talked investors into sinking their money into a complex—and, it turned out, bogus—scheme involving postal currency.

His short-lived swindle in 1919–20 cheated thousands of people out of $10 million but was so wildly lucrative for some early investors that he was hailed as a hero in the Italian community. He was convicted of mail fraud and sent to prison before being deported in 1934.

A Ponzi scheme, or pyramid scheme, is a scam in which people are persuaded to invest in a fraudulent operation that promises unusually high returns. The early investors are paid their returns out of money put in by later investors.

"It used to be called 'robbing Peter to pay Paul,'" said Mitchell Zuckoff, a Boston University journalism professor who wrote a biography of Ponzi in 2005.

Ponzi's scheme became one of the most famous con games of his time, and his name has been attached to similar frauds ever since.

People who run Ponzis generally fall into two categories: hucksters like Ponzi who plan to cheat investors and get out quickly, often fleeing the country, and people who start a legitimate investment venture but lose money, then try desperately to cover it up and dig themselves into a deeper hole. Ultimately, it all comes crashing down.

Some have speculated that Madoff—once a highly respected figure on Wall Street and a former Nasdaq chairman—falls into the latter category.

Bookish and bespectacled with a wise smile, Madoff had multiple homes, fancy cars, and a membership at exclusive country clubs. He gave millions to charity from his own fortune.

"Looking successful is the key because everyone's first question is going to be, 'If this is such a great deal, then why are you wearing a cheap suit?'" said Eric Sussman, a former federal prosecutor from Chicago who helped on about a dozen Ponzi cases. "They have to have all the accoutrements of success."

One of the unanswered questions so far is precisely how much investors lost over all.

When Mr. Madoff confessed and was arrested last week, he told F.B.I. agents that the losses might be $50 billion, according to court filings. Various institutions and individuals so far have reported losses totalling more than $20 billion, but it is unclear how much of that is cash they actually invested and how much represents paper profits based on the falsified returns Mr. Madoff said investors were earning.

Mr. Madoff regularly delivered returns of 10 to 17 percent to investors, a very good year-in, year-out return but on the low end of the 10 to 100 percent a year typically dangled by promoters of Ponzi schemes.

But assets that can guarantee those returns year after year without risk simply do not exist. Instead of profitable investments, Ponzi schemes repay initial investors by raising more money from new investors. The schemes typically collapse when the promoter cannot bring in enough money to pay existing investors seeking redemptions.

Joel M. Cohen, the deputy head of litigation for the Clifford Chance law firm and a former federal prosecutor who specialized in business and securities fraud, said that payments to early investors were an integral part of any Ponzi scheme.

"You need to deliver returns in the range that you promised to attract investors," Mr. Cohen said.

Yet even Mr. Madoff's most fortunate clients may wind up having to give back some of their gains, as investors might have to do in another recent financial fraud, the collapse of the hedge fund Bayou Group in 2005.

In the Bayou case, in which investors lost $400 million, a bankruptcy judge ruled that investors who withdrew money even before Bayou collapsed might have to return their profits, and possibly some of the initial investments, to the bankruptcy trustee overseeing the unwinding of Bayou.

The returned money is to be distributed among all investors, who are expected to receive only about 20 to 40 percent of their original investments.

Mr. Madoff's winning clients are likely to face similar legal challenges. In fact, the Madoff client who profited from his investment spoke on the condition that he not be identified, out of concern that he might be sought out to repay some of his gains to the receiver or bankruptcy trustee for Mr. Madoff.

Jay B. Gould, a former lawyer at the Securities and Exchange Commission who now runs the hedge funds practice at Pillsbury Winthrop Shaw Pittman, said the client was correct to be concerned. New York State laws may allow the receiver or bankruptcy trustee to demand that Mr. Madoff's investors return money they received from the scheme any time in the last six years, Mr. Gould said.

Such so-called clawbacks may occur even if the client had no idea that the gains were fraudulent, he said.

> "The idea is that the whole thing was fraudulent undertaking, so nobody should profit from it, and everybody should be put on equitable footing," Mr. Gould said.
>
> Even determining which investors made money will be enormously complicated.
>
> Mr. Madoff's practices appear to have gone on for many years and entangled thousands, perhaps tens of thousands, of clients, who invested both directly with him and through third-party hedge funds. Some of those investors never took out a cent, while others took out only a fraction of what they invested and a few took out more than they put in.
>
> Sources: Denise Lavoie, Associated Press Writer accessed at news.yahoo.com on Dec. 19, 2008; Alex Berenson, *New York Times*, "Even Winners May Lose With Madoff," accessed at www.nytimes.com on Dec.19, 2008; and http://www.forbes.com/2008/12/12/madoff-ponzi-hedge-pf-ii-in_rl_1212croesus_inl.html.

DISCUSSION OF THE CONSEQUENCES AND SIGNIFICANCE OF THE MADOFF EVENT

The above box indicates how difficult it can be to sort losses from a Ponzi scheme such as those from the failure of the alleged scheme of Bernard L. Madoff Investment Securities LLC in December 2008. This Madoff box should be read in conjuction with the "Madoff Economy" box in Chapter 14 and the "Accounting Blamed for Global Credit Crisis" box early in Chapter 1. Ponzi schemes are frauds in which earlier investors are paid off with the money of later investors, until it is not possible to raise sufficient money to pay off earlier investors with promised returns, and the scheme collapses. If you think this sounds simple, then you might also consider it "simple" to calculate a company's net income. Ponzi schemes rely on investors' being unable to distinguish between a return *on* their capital and the return *of* their capital. One of the reasons for calculating a company's net income is so that investors can estimate the return on their capital investment. If this is impaired, then the whole system of capital markets begins unravelling because of lack of relevant information and loss of trust, as suggested in the above boxes.

Despite the name, Ponzi schemes were around long before Charles Ponzi. Other names for these schemes include pyramid, bubble, and mania, all of which are closely associated with phenomena such as asset price bubbles, market manias, and irrational exuberance. Interestingly, the history of accounting shows that the distinction between paid-in-capital and retained earnings developed to facilitate the detection of Ponzi schemes. Thus fundamental accounting concepts like capital maintenance, which is essential for determining the existence of earnings, were developed primarily to detect Ponzi-type financial reporting frauds.

Perhaps one reason the alleged Madoff fraud was not detected earlier is that Madoff's firm had been audited by a small, three-employee accounting firm. Thanks to loopholes in regulations, the accounting firm was not required to be monitored in any way nor registered with the PCAOB. The SEC had determined that not requiring small accounting firms with huge clients to be registered was "consistent with the public interest and protection of investors."

A further embarrassment to the SEC regarding Madoff was the revelation that it had received numerous complaints or red flags on Madoff going as far back as 1992, but failed to act on them. Most sensationally, Harry Markopolos testified at a U.S. Congressional hearing that he had sent "gift wrapped" to the SEC a list of 29 red flags indicating Madoff's fraud, and no action was taken in over three years. Markopolos was a securities industry executive with one of Madoff's competitors. On February 4, 2009, he testified that he had told the SEC's Boston office in May 1999 that they should investigate Madoff because "it was impossible for the kind of profit that Madoff was making to be gained legally." He further testified that "the SEC was never capable of catching Mr. Madoff. He could have gone $100 billion" without being discovered. Markopolos further testified, "It took me about five minutes to figure he was a fraud." This and further revelations of SEC incompetence led some to call February 4, 2009, the worst day in the agency's history, wrecking its reputation and sending its morale to new lows. At the time of writing, many knowledgeable observers are predicting the creation of a new regulatory framework in the United States, or a substantially reorganized SEC. There may be major repercussions for the accounting profession as well.

The financial crisis beginning in 2007 brought greater potential for Ponzi schemes within financial organizations because of the need to report gains that might not yet be realized (e.g., see Ari J. Officer "The Ponzi Scheme in Every Hedge Fund" at www.time. com, January 5, 2009). In financial reporting, the essence of the problem is verifying proper reporting of uncertainties in accounting estimates. We discuss and illustrate this fundamental problem of financial reporting in this chapter, especially in the application case at the end. But first we need to understand auditor responsibilies, other forms of frauds, and related audit procedures for detecting fraud.

AUDITORS' AND INVESTIGATORS' RESPONSIBILITIES

LEARNING OBJECTIVE

2 Explain the auditing standards related to external, internal, and governmental auditors' responsibilities to detect and report frauds, errors, irregularities, and illegal acts.

Audit standards from several sources explain responsibilities for errors, irregularities, and illegal acts. The term **external auditors** refers to independent PAs who audit financial statements for the purpose of rendering an opinion; **internal auditors** and **certified internal auditors** are persons, either independent or PAs, employed within organizations; **government auditors** are auditors whose work is governed by the public sector sections of the audit standards, whether they are audit employees of governments or of public accounting firms engaged to perform government audits; and **fraud examiners** are those engaged specifically for fraud investigation work. Forensic or investigative accounting relates and applies financial facts to legal problems, particularly those of trial findings. "The involvement of the forensic accountant is almost always on a reactive basis which distinguishes the forensic accountant from the fraud auditor, who more usually tends to be involved on an active basis with the aspects of prevention and detection in a corporate or regulatory environment."[2]

External Auditors' Responsibilities

In response to the growing problems of fraud, auditors have taken on increased responsibility for detecting fraud and other illegal acts in recent years. As indicated in the auditor's report (Chapter 3), auditors have the responsibility "to obtain reasonable (i.e., high) assurance whether the financial statements are free of material misstatements," including misstatements due to fraud. The CICA auditing standards are rigorous. Relevant standards concerning misstatements include CAS 240 (5135); misstatements due to illegal acts by clients, CAS 250 (5136); auditing accounting estimates, CAS 540 (5305); communication with those responsible for financial reporting, CAS 260 (5135 and 5751); and communicating matters identified during the financial statement audit, CAS 260 (5750). Most of these have been covered in previous chapters.

Auditors' Responsibility to Consider Fraud and Error in an Audit of Financial Statements

CICA Handbook section 5135 was revised in 2004 and again in 2006 in response to the post-Enron environment. These changes have been incorporated in CAS 240, which requires the auditor to make enquiries of management about fraud and to consider fraud risk factors on every audit engagement. Examples of such factors are given later in this chapter.

---

[2] G. J. Bologna and R. J. Lindquist, *Fraud Auditing and Forensic Accounting* (John Wiley & Sons, 1987), p. 85.

The auditor should document fraud risk factors identified as being present during the auditor's assessment process and document the auditor's response to any such factors. If, during the performance of the audit, fraud risk factors are identified that cause the auditor to believe that additional audit procedures are necessary, the auditor should document the presence of such risk factors and the auditor's response to them.[3]

Inherent and control risks should be assessed in conjunction with substantive tests so that the risk of material misstatement from fraud or error is appropriately low.[4] The auditor should also obtain written management representations about the extent of fraud. Findings should be communicated to management, the audit committee or equivalent, and, in some circumstances, to outside agencies. CAS 240 also makes clear that the primary responsibility for the prevention and detection of fraud rests with management and those charged with governance of the reporting entity. This responsibility includes designing and implementing internal controls and other corporate governance mechanisms to deter fraud. Misappropriation of assets fraud is frequently termed fraud against the company because it is usually carried out by lower-level employees, and management and auditors have a common interest in detecting such fraud. In contrast, fraudulent financial reporting (misreporting fraud) is a fraud *for* the company but against new investors that pits the auditor against management and its corporate governance. Ponzi schemes are a misreporting fraud.

CAS 240 (5135) requires auditors to ignore the traditional assumption of management's honesty.[5] Auditors must now presume a risk of fraudulent revenue recognition, a presumption that is "rebuttable" by the audit evidence. That is, if the auditors can convince themselves that the risk is appropriately low (the PCAOB suggests it should be "remote") then the presumption is rejected. This logic is similar to the burden of proof concept in law and critical thinking.

How does the auditor justify that the fraud risk is sufficiently low? Under CAS 240 (5135), the rebuttable presumption requires auditors to perform analytical procedures of revenues, make enquiries, and scan for unusual entries (especially at year-end), and the audit team should have brainstorming sessions to identify and share information on fraud risk factors during the audit. Auditors also need to identify biases in management accounting estimates and be able to understand the business rationale of transactions. If the auditors cannot reject the rebuttable presumption, then they need to raise the matter with the audit committee (or equivalent) and take it from there.

The traditional role of the investigative or forensic auditor was to get involved when the risk of fraud was not sufficiently low (i.e., when there was predication or cause for concern because there were too many fraud risk factors, the audit committee authorized further investigation). However, fraud auditors are increasingly being used to perform proactively the initial fraud risk assessments in planning the audit. They may be used to screen clients and be involved in the initial meetings with audit committees and management. There are several reasons for this trend. First, it acts as a fraud deterrent and makes the client aware of how seriously the profession takes its fraud detection responsibilities. Second, fraud examiners are specially trained in techniques to detect when people are lying. Finally, fraud auditors are more familiar with legal requirements regarding documentation of frauds, such as witness statements, confessions, control of chain of custody of evidence, and preparation of written reports for use as evidence in a court of law.

Illegal Acts by Clients

CAS 250 (5136) does not explicitly distinguish between the two kinds of illegal acts identified in U.S. SAS 54:

Direct-effect illegal acts have direct and material effects on financial statement amounts (e.g., violations of tax laws and government contracting regulations for cost and revenue recognition), and they are dealt with in the same manner as errors and irregularities. **Indirect-effect**

---

[3] *CICA Handbook,* section 5135.49.
[4] *CICA Handbook,* paragraph 5135.39.
[5] For example, see D. Selley and E. Turner, "Detecting Fraud and Error," *CA Magazine,* August 2004, p. 38.

illegal acts refer to violations of laws and regulations that are far removed from financial statements (e.g., those relating to securities trading, occupational health and safety, food and drug administration, environmental protection, and equal employment opportunity).

In the United States, indirect-effect illegal acts come under the general awareness responsibility, particularly in matters of contingent liability disclosure, but they are not part of the routine responsibility for detection and reporting. CAS 250 (5136), on the other hand, requires auditors to consider the consequences of the illegal acts and the best way of disclosing these. If failures to disclose would result in a material misstatement, then the auditor should attempt to reduce this risk to an appropriately low level. CAS 250 acknowledges that illegal acts may be difficult to detect because of (1) efforts made to conceal them and (2) questions about whether an act is illegal, which are complex and may only be resolved by a court of law. For these reasons, the engagement letter should inform management of the audit's limitations in detecting illegal acts.

The auditors' knowledge of the business and enquiries of management help to identify laws and regulations that, if violated and not reported, could result in material misstatements CAS 250.19 (paragraph 5136.11). In addition, auditors should enquire and obtain representations about awareness and disclosure of possibly illegal acts (paragraph 5136.21). Material, possibly illegal acts should be communicated to the audit committee and appropriate levels of management. Paragraph 5136.23 gives a list of circumstances that may indicate illegal acts.

From a critical thinking perspective, the most important development regarding CAS 240 and 250 sections was dropping the assumption that management is honest, a change that took place in 2004. Now auditors must explicitly address the risks of fraud in revenue recognition. If risk is present, the auditor must perform further procedures, but, even without this risk, auditors must now document the reasons (i.e., from a critical thinking perspective, the auditor must use audit evidence to argue that fraud risk is at an acceptable level). If sufficient risk of material fraud exists (i.e., fraud risk is higher than acceptable), then a fraud auditor would be called in, with the approval of the client's directors, audit committee, or management. If the risk of material fraud is not acceptably low, then the auditor cannot issue an unqualified audit report.

Auditing Accounting Estimates and Fair Value Accounting

CAS 540 and 545 (5306) relate to manipulation of estimates in fraudulent financial reporting. This is especially a concern in fair value accounting for securities in illiquid markets such as those of the global credit markets during the crisis in 2008 (see "Madoff Economy" box in Chapter 14). This area is difficult as accounting estimates are an approximation of a financial statement element, item, or account made by an organization's management; for example, for allowance for loan losses, net realizable value of inventory, percentage-of-completion revenue, and fair value accounting estimates.

CAS 540 deals with estimation uncertainty and the need to address significant risks associated with it by ensuring that they are adequately disclosed, either through appropriate accounting adjustments and/or in the notes to the financial statements, and possibly through emphasis of matter paragraphs in the auditor's report. Critical thinking concepts that make use of conceptual frameworks in accounting and auditing can help guide the appropriate auditor response.

Management is responsible for making the accounting estimates, and auditors are responsible for evaluating the reasonableness of these within the financial statements as a whole. Auditors are supposed to keep track of the differences between management's estimates and the closest reasonable estimates supported by the audit evidence. Uncorrected differences between the two increases estimation uncertainty. Auditors are also supposed to evaluate both the total of the differences for indications of a systematic bias and the combination of the differences along with other likely errors in the financial statements.

Communication with Audit Committees (or Equivalent)

CAS 260 (5751) gives requirements ensuring that audit committees (or equivalent) are informed about the scope and results of the independent audit. The auditing standards place great faith in audit committees and boards of directors, although their effectiveness has been questioned elsewhere.[6] This CAS requires oral or written communication from the auditors on the following: (a) misstatements other than trivial errors; (b) fraud; (c) misstatements that may cause future financial statements to be materially misstated; (d) illegal or possibly illegal acts, other than ones considered inconsequential; and (e) significant weaknesses in internal control.

There is some inconsistency in the CASs between responsibility for detecting material misstatements due to error and those due to fraud. Specifically, CAS 240 states, "The auditor seeks reasonable assurance whether the financial statements are free of material misstatement" without qualifying the sources of that misstatement, while later the same CAS 240 explains that an auditor is "less likely" (because of concealment) to detect misstatement due to fraud than he or she is to detect that resulting from error. In addition, CAS 250 suggests that some illegal acts, specifically those corresponding to indirect-effect illegal acts such as building code violations, may have an even lower chance of being detected by an external auditor.

AICPA standard SAS 99 was issued in the post-Enron environment of 2002. It is the first standard to require forensic procedures on all financial statement audit engagements. The AICPA views SAS 99 as the "cornerstone" of its comprehensive antifraud and corporate responsibility program. The goal of the program is to "rebuild the confidence of investors in our capital markets and re-establish audited financial statements as a clear picture window into corporate America." These words acknowledge the extensive harm done to the profession by Enron, Andersen, and WorldCom.

SAS 99 significantly extended audit requirements in a number of ways. These requirements have largely been incorporated in CAS 240 and can be summarized via the extensive documentation that now supports compliance with the standard. Auditors must document the following items in relation to the risk of material misstatement due to fraud:

- Discussion among audit team members regarding the entity's susceptibility to fraudulently misstated financial statements, including how and when the discussion occurred, who participated, and the subjects discussed

- Procedures to identify and assess the risks (This includes knowledge of client business risks and its effect on audit risk as per the international exposure draft on audit risk. This requirement suggests use of risk-based audit approaches as explained in Chapter 6.)

- Specific risks identified and a description of the auditor's response to those risks

- Reasons supporting that conclusion, unless a particular improper revenue recognition has been identified

- Results of procedures performed to address the risk of management override of controls

- Conditions and analytical relationships causing the auditor to believe additional auditing procedures were required, and any further responses deemed appropriate to addressing such risks

- Nature of communications about fraud made to management, the audit committee, and others[7]

External auditors assess the risk of fraud through warning signs. A study by American researchers provides guidance on these: "The lack of awareness of the warning signs of fraud is a frequently cited cause of audit failure. If auditors better understood the signs and applied professional scepticism, they would decrease their risk of not detecting fraud. Knowing the most important warning signs should help auditors do a better job of assessing

[6] Wechsler reported the findings of the National Commission on Fraudulent Financial Reporting: of the 120 fraudulent financial reporting cases brought by the SEC between 1981 and 1986, two-thirds involved companies that had audit committees. This caused Professor Briloff to remark, "Now I see that they are not functioning as they should." (D. Wechsler, "Giving the Watchdog Fangs," *Forbes*, November 13, 1989, p. 130.) However, these observations beg the question of the thousands of companies with and without audit committees that did not get involved in fraudulent financial reporting.
[7] M. Ramos, "Auditors' Responsibility for Fraud Detection," *Journal of Accountancy*, January 2003, pp. 29, 35–36.

fraud risk."[8] A survey of 130 auditors asked them to rank 30 commonly cited fraud warning signals according to their significance. The auditors ranked client dishonesty as the most important factor. The survey revealed that auditors generally perceived "attitude" factors to be more important warning signs of fraud than "situational" factors. The top 15 warning signs are listed in the following box.

AUDITORS' RANKING OF THE RELATIVE IMPORTANCE OF FRAUD WARNING SIGNS

1. Managers have lied to the auditors or have been overly evasive in response to audit enquiries.
2. The auditor's experience with management indicates a degree of dishonesty.
3. Management places undue emphasis on meeting earnings projections or the quantitative targets.
4. Management has engaged in frequent disputes with auditors, particularly about aggressive application of accounting principles that increase earnings.
5. The client has engaged in opinion shopping.
6. Management's attitude toward financial reporting is unduly aggressive.
7. The client has a weak control environment.
8. A substantial portion of management compensation depends on meeting quantified targets.
9. Management displays significant disrespect for regulatory bodies.
10. Management operating and financial decisions are dominated by a single person or a few persons acting in concert.
11. Client managers display a hostile attitude toward the auditors.
12. Management displays a propensity to take undue risks.
13. There are frequent and significant difficult-to-audit transactions.
14. Key managers are considered highly unreasonable.
15. The client's organization is decentralized without adequate monitoring.

Source: V. B. Heiman-Hoffman, K. P. Morgan, and J. M. Patton, "The Warning Signs of Fraudulent Financial Reporting," *Journal of Accountancy*, October 1996, pp. 76–77. Copyright 1996. American Institute of Certified Public Accountants, Inc. All rights reserved. Used with permission.

Internal Auditors' Responsibilities

Traditional internal auditor attitudes toward fraud responsibilities cannot be usefully generalized. Some believe that a watchdog role will damage their image and effectiveness as internal consultants. Others flock to the fraud investigation education programs run by the Association of Certified Fraud Examiners because they want to add fraud expertise to their skills.

The "Nature of Work" section of the internal audit standards charges internal auditors with basic fraud awareness in auditing: review reliability and integrity of financial and operating information; review systems established to ensure compliance with policies, plans, procedures, laws, and regulations; and review means of safeguarding assets and verify the existence of assets. This charge has been expanded as follows: "The internal

[8] V. B. Heiman-Hoffman, K. P. Morgan, and J. M. Patton, "The Warning Signs of Fraudulent Financial Reporting," *Journal of Accountancy*, October 1996, pp. 76–77.

auditor should have sufficient knowledge to identify indicators of fraud but is not expected to have the expertise of a person whose primary responsibility is detecting and investigating fraud." However, SOX is increasing the expectation for internal auditors to take greater responsibility for detecting fraud.

Currently, the internal auditing standards carefully impose no positive obligation for fraud detection and investigation work in the ordinary course of assignments. However, internal auditors are encouraged to be aware of the various types of frauds, their signs (red flags), and the need to follow up on signs and control weaknesses to determine whether a suspicion is justified; then, if necessary, to alert management to call in the experts. The standards caution that internal auditors are not expected to guarantee that fraud will be detected in the normal course of most internal audit assignments.

Public Sector Auditing Standards

Public sector standards apply to audits conducted by government employees and public accounting firms engaged to perform audits on governmental organizations, programs, activities, and functions. Consequently, the public sector standards control a significant portion of audits by public accountants. These audit requirements are to know the applicable laws and regulations, design the audit to detect abuse or illegal acts, and report to the proper level of authority.

Auditors should prepare a written report on their tests of compliance with applicable laws and regulations, including all material instances of noncompliance and all instances or indications of illegal acts that could result in criminal prosecution. (For more discussion of compliance auditing and reports relating to laws and regulations, see Chapter 16.) Reports should be directed to the top official of an organization and in some cases to an appropriate oversight body, including other government agencies and audit committees. Those receiving the audit reports are responsible for reporting to law enforcement agencies. The following box illustrates the dramatic impact that fraud can have in the public sector.

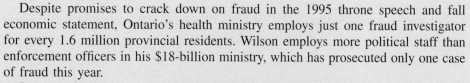

FORMER CHIEF MOUNTIE HIRED AFTER SUN EXPOSÉ BLITZ ON HEALTH CARE FRAUD

Ontario Health Minister Jim Wilson contracted Inkster, now president of KPMG Investigation and Security, after widespread cheating was exposed by *Sun* columnist Christie Blatchford yesterday.

"The number of reported fraud cases quoted in (*The*) *Toronto Sun* are of great concern to me," Wilson said in a statement hand-delivered by aide Cynthia Janzen yesterday.

Blatchford revealed every single day between 30 and 50 people show up at Ontario's hospitals and clinics seeking treatment with bogus health cards, and the government ignores it. In February, stolen health cards were presented for treatment 1,057 times, she wrote.

Despite promises to crack down on fraud in the 1995 throne speech and fall economic statement, Ontario's health ministry employs just one fraud investigator for every 1.6 million provincial residents. Wilson employs more political staff than enforcement officers in his $18-billion ministry, which has prosecuted only one case of fraud this year.

Janzen said Wilson was motivated after reading Blatchford's column. A 1993 internal governmental report found that fraud costs the health ministry $284 million a year. And, unfortunately, the Conservative government has failed in its promise to weed out health-care fraud, Tory and Liberal MPPs said.

> "Basically, there is no enforcement," Tory MPP and Crown attorney Toni Skarica said in an interview.
>
> "There are virtually no resources put into fraud investigations or prosecutions. As a result, we could get major frauds that undermine the economy," Skarica said.
>
> Liberal critic Dominic Agostino said the province is losing "hundreds of millions a year" to illegitimate hucksters.
>
> Source: Jeff Harder, "Former Chief Mountie Hired after Sun Exposé Blitz on Health Care Fraud," *The Toronto Sun,* May 31, 1997, p. 5. Sun Media Corporation.

Fraud Examiner Responsibilities

In an informal ranking of strength of commitment to fraud matters, external auditors come first, followed by public sector auditors, and then internal auditors. However, this situation is changing under SOX's increased reliance on internal controls to prevent both fraud and fraudulent reporting. Of course, fraud examiners have the strongest spirit of fraud detection and investigation. Their work differs significantly from that of other auditors in that, when they take an assignment, fraud is already known or strongly suspected. They do not look for fraud while performing "normal" work. In fact, the Association of Certified Fraud Examiners (ACFE) teaches that assignments do not begin without predication—a reason to believe fraud has occurred.

Fraud examiners' attitudes and responsibilities differ from those of other auditors in two additional respects: internal control and materiality. They evaluate the strengths, rather than the weaknesses, of internal control policies and procedures. Fraud examiners "think like crooks" to imagine fraud schemes for getting around an organization's internal controls. Where controls are not in place, they imagine possible scenarios of white-collar crime.

NO SEPARATION OF DUTIES

An electronic data processing employee instructed the company's computer to pay his wife rent for land she had allegedly leased to the company by assigning her an alphanumeric code as a lessor and then ordering the payments. The control lesson: Never let a data entry clerk who processes payment claims also have access to the approved vendor master file for additions or deletions.

Source: G. J. Bologna and R. J. Lindquist, *Fraud Auditing and Forensic Accounting* (New York: John Wiley & Sons, 1987), pp. 70–71.

MONEY, MONEY, MONEY CASE

Brian Molony, a 29-year-old assistant branch manager and lending officer of a large downtown Toronto bank, defrauded the bank of some $10.2 million over a 20-month period. He fabricated loans to real and fictitious customers and gambled away the proceeds at an Atlantic City casino. Molony was such a valued customer that the casino flew its corporate jet to Toronto to pick him up for weekend jaunts.

The defalcation came to light when Canadian law enforcement authorities arrested Molony for a traffic violation on his return from a trip to Atlantic City. A search of his person disclosed that he was carrying about $29,000 in currency. That information was passed on to the bank, which then conducted an audit and found the fictional loans and transfers of funds to the casino. The bank is suing the casino to recover at least part of its loss.

Molony used a *lapping scheme* to keep auditors off his trail—that is, he paid off earlier loans with subsequent loans so that no delinquencies would show. However, the fictional loan balances grew and grew. Molony's superior at the branch had approved the larger loans because "he had no reason to mistrust him." The branch manager was subsequently suspended, along with the assistant branch manager for administration, a credit officer, and an auditor.

Source: G. J. Bologna and R. J. Lindquist, *Fraud Auditing and Forensic Accounting, 2nd ed.* (New York: John Wiley & Sons, 1995), pp. 230–231. Reprinted by permission of John Wiley & Sons Inc.

Unlike other auditors, fraud examiners think of materiality as a cumulative amount. Other auditors' materiality criterion is a dollar amount that is big enough to matter, but fraud examiners have a much lower threshold. For them, an oddity is an oddity regardless of the amount, and small oddities ought not be passed by just because "$5,000 isn't material to the financial statements taken as a whole." External auditors weigh materiality in relation to each year's financial statements, while fraud examiners know that intentional misstatements are systematic and can accumulate to significant amounts over time. This distinction is discussed further in the next section.

REVIEW CHECKPOINTS

1 What are the Canadian auditing standards requirements regarding (*a*) awareness of fraud, (*b*) procedural audit work, (*c*) professional skepticism, and (*d*) reporting? Are these standards different for errors, irregularities, and direct-effect illegal acts than they are for indirect-effect illegal acts?

2 To what extent do internal auditors include fraud detection responsibility in their normal audit assignments?

3 How does the requirement for design of audit procedures in public sector audit work differ from external auditors' work on financial statement audits (not involving governmental auditing)? Consider errors, irregularities, and illegal acts.

4 Why is the order of strength of commitment to fraud matters as follows: (1) government auditors, (2) external auditors, (3) internal auditors?

5 Why might fraud examiners have attitudes about control systems and materiality that are different from those of other auditors?

Materiality and Fraud

Standards of materiality thresholds for external auditors are related to the reporting auditors' knowledge of errors, irregularities, and illegal acts. Immaterial errors are supposed to be reported to management at least one level above the people involved.[9] Small matters can be kept in the management family, but errors material to the financial statements must be adjusted and handled by management responsible for the financial statements, to the satisfaction of auditors, or else the audit report will be qualified.

Irregularities receive a slightly different treatment, but there is still a materiality standard in effect. The auditors should inform the audit committee of all irregularities, except those that are "clearly inconsequential." Those involving senior management are never inconsequential. In the CICA audit standards, discretion is used to determine whether

---

[9] CAS 260 (CICA *Handbook*, paragraph 5135.19.)

something is minor enough not to matter or report. However, auditors must be satisfied with how management and directors deal with irregularities. If uncertainties persist about the irregularities and management's actions, the audit report should be qualified, with reasons, or the auditors may withdraw from the engagement.

The "clearly inconsequential" materiality standard also applies to clients' illegal acts. Ones that are more than inconsequential are reported to the organization's audit committee and disclosed in the financial statements.[10] External auditors always have the option to withdraw from the engagement if management and directors do not take satisfactory action in the circumstances.

A study on the characterisitics of fraudulent reporting is summarized in the box below.

FRAUDULENT FINANCIAL REPORTING: 1987–1997 AN ANALYSIS OF U.S. PUBLIC COMPANIES

SUMMARY OF RESEARCH COMMISSIONED BY THE COMMITTEE OF SPONSORING ORGANIZATIONS (COSO) OF THE TREADWAY COMMISSION

- The companies committing fraud generally were small, and most were not listed on the New York or American Stock Exchanges.
- The frauds went to the very top of the organizations. In 72 percent of the cases, the CEO appeared to be associated with the fraud.
- The audit committees and boards of the fraud companies appeared to be weak. Most audit committees rarely met, and the companies' boards of directors were dominated by insiders and others with significant ties to the company.
- A significant portion of the companies was owned by the founders and board members.
- Severe consequences resulted when companies committed fraud, including bankruptcy, significant changes in ownership, and delisting by national exchanges.
- Cumulative amounts of fraud were relatively large for the many small companies involved; for example, resulting in an average financial misstatement of 25 percent total assets.

The study results highlight the need for an effective control environment, or "tone at the top." The risk of fraud is much higher in small companies. A strong CEO, with significant share ownership in a small organization, needs an experienced, independent board to insure objectivity.

COSO's mission is to improve the quality of financial reporting through internal controls, governance, and ethics. This study validates the need for continued focus on all three areas. We believe the study will provide a platform for those responsible for financial reporting to improve their effectiveness.

Source: "Fraudulent Financial Reporting: 1987–1997, An Analysis of U.S. Public Companies," source: www.AICPA. org as of April 15, 1999. © 1999 American Institute of Certified Public Accountants. All rights reserved. Reprinted with permission.

Under the CASs, disclosures of irregularities and clients' illegal acts to outside agencies are limited. If the auditors are fired, the provincial securities commission may require an explanation. A fired auditor can tell the successor auditor about the firm when the successor makes the enquiries required by professional ethics. Auditors must respond to a subpoena issued by a court or other agency with authority, which will happen in a lawsuit or prosecution. When performing work under public sector audit standards, auditors are required to report irregularities and illegal acts to the client agency under the audit contract, which may be an agency other than the one being audited.

[10] CAS 260 (CICA *Handbook*, paragraph 5136.04.)

Standards for internal auditors require them to inform management of suspected wrongdoing. Fraud findings are reported to management, the board of directors, or the audit committee of the board, but not to anyone who might be involved in a fraud scheme. But, as the preceding box indicates, much can still be done to improve the financial fraud record of companies even in the highly regulated securities markets of North America.

Former SEC chairman Arthur Levitt was critical of the profession for allowing **hocus-pocus accounting** that facilitates financial statement fraud. The following box summarizes the most common forms of hocus-pocus accounting.

HOCUS-POCUS ACCOUNTING

EXECUTIVE SUMMARY

- Public companies that fail to report quarterly earnings that meet or exceed analysts' expectations often experience a drop in their stock prices. This can lead to practices that sometimes include fraudulent overstatement of quarterly revenue.
- One of the most common schemes is the bill-and-hold sales transaction. While it's not necessarily a GAAP violation, it's often associated with financial frauds and calls for deeper investigation. The SEC says that all of the following conditions must be met for revenue recognition to be appropriate:
  - The risks of ownership must have passed to the buyer.
  - The customer must have a commitment to purchase, preferably in writing.
  - The buyer must request the bill-and-sale transaction and substantiate a business purpose for it.
  - A fixed delivery date must exist.
  - The seller must not retain any significant specific performance obligations.
  - The goods must be complete and ready for shipment and not subject to being used to fill other orders.
- Deals called sham transactions refer specifically to sales schemes that appear genuine but actually are rigged for the purpose of letting the seller recognize revenue. Other indicators that fraudulent financial reporting might exist include bogus shipping dates, revenue figures that always meet analysts' expectations, and transactions with unusual payment terms.
- Auditors with a good understanding of the client, the business, and its products are well prepared to see the warning signs of revenue-recognition fraud.

Source: D. R. Carmichael, "Hocus-Pocus Accounting," *Journal of Accountancy*, October 1999, p. 60. Copyright 1996. American Institute of Certified Public Accountants, Inc. All rights reserved. Used with permission.

Characteristics of Fraudsters

White-collar criminals are not like typical bank robbers, who are often described as "young and dumb" because of comical mistakes like writing the holdup note on the back of a probation identification card, leaving the getaway car keys on the convenience store counter, using a zucchini as a holdup weapon, and timing the holdup to get stuck in rush-hour traffic. Then there's the classic story about the robber who ran into his own mother at the bank (she turned him in!).

Burglars and robbers average about $400–$500 for each hit. Employee frauds average $20,000, or up to $500,000 if a computer is used. Yet employee frauds are not usually the intricate, well-disguised ploys of espionage novels. Who are these thieves wearing ties? What do they look like? Unfortunately, they look and are like most everybody else, including you and me: likely married, well-educated, between twenty and sixty-years old, and long-term employees. They are probably socially conforming, without an arrest record or visible tattoos, and possibly even a member of a church. In most instances, the fraudster will act alone.

White-collar criminals do not make themselves obvious, although there may be telltale signs, described later as behavioural "red flags." Unfortunately, the largest frauds are committed by people who hold high executive positions, have long tenure with an organization, and are respected and trusted employees. After all, these are the people who have access to the largest amounts of money and have the power to give orders and override controls.

The Art of Fraud Awareness Auditing

Fraud examination work combines the expertise of auditors and criminal investigators. Fraud examiners are fond of saying that their successes are the result of accidents, hunches, or luck. Nothing can be further from the truth; successes come from experience, application of logic, and the ability to see things that are not obvious (Sherlock Holmes noticed the dog that did not bark). Fraud awareness auditing, broadly speaking, involves familiarity with many elements: the human behaviour, organizational behaviour, knowledge of common fraud schemes, evidence and its sources, standards of proof, and sensitivity to red flags.[11]

Independent auditors of financial statements and fraud examiners approach their work differently. While there are many differences, these are some of the most important and obvious ones:

- Financial auditors follow a program or procedural approach designed to accomplish a fairly standard job; fraud examiners maintain a mindset of sensitivity to the unusual where nothing is standard.

- Financial auditors make note of errors and omissions; fraud examiners focus also on exceptions, oddities, and patterns of conduct.

- Financial auditors assess control risk in both general and specific terms to design other audit procedures; fraud examiners habitually "think like a crook" to imagine ways that controls could be subverted for fraudulent purposes.

- Financial auditors work to a higher level of materiality (dollar-size big enough to matter) and use materiality as a measure of importance one year at a time; fraud examiners consider smaller amounts and think in terms of cumulative materiality. (A theft of $20,000 may not be large for one year, but, over a 15-year fraud career, $300,000 is a considerable loss.)

- Financial audits are based on theories of financial accounting and auditing logic; fraud examination has theories of behavioural motive, opportunity, and integrity.

WHO DOES IT?

Alex W. was a 47-year-old treasurer of a credit union. Over a seven-year period, he stole $160,000. He was a good husband and the father of six children, and he was a highly reputed official of the credit union. His misappropriations came as a stunning surprise to his associates. He owed significant amounts on his home, cars, university for two children, two side investments, and five different credit cards. His monthly payments significantly exceeded his take-home pay.

[11] These and other aspects of the art of fraud auditing are more fully developed in G. J. Bologna and R. J. Lindquist, *Fraud Auditing and Forensic Accounting* (New York: John Wiley & Sons, 1987), pp. 27–42; W. S. Albrecht, M. B. Romney, D. J. Cherrington, I. R. Payne, and A. J. Roe, *How to Detect and Prevent Business Fraud* (New York: Prentice-Hall, 1982); R. White and W. G. Bishop, III, "The Role of the Internal Auditor in the Deterrence, Detection, and Reporting of Fraudulent Financial Reporting," The Institute of Internal Auditors; and M. J. Barrett and R. N. Carolus, "Control and Internal Auditing," The Institute of Internal Auditors.

THE CASE OF THE EXTRA CHECKOUT

The district grocery store manager could not understand why receipts and profitability had fallen and inventory was hard to manage at one of the largest stores in her area. She hired an investigator who covertly observed the checkout clerks and reported that no one had shown suspicious behaviour at any of the nine checkout counters. Nine? That store has only eight, she exclaimed! The store manager had installed another checkout aisle, not connected to the cash receipts and inventory maintenance central computer, and was pocketing all the receipts from that register.

External and internal auditors get credit for finding about 10–20 percent of discovered frauds. Voluntary confessions, anonymous tips, and other haphazard means uncover a larger percentage. Fraud examiners have a still higher success rate because they are called in for a specific purpose when fraud is known or highly suspected.

Some aspects of audit methodology make a big difference in fraud discovery success. Financial auditors use inductive reasoning: sample accounting data, derive audit findings, and project the finding to a conclusion about the population. Fraud examiners have the luxury of using deductive reasoning: identify the suspects from tipoffs, make clinical observations (stakeouts), conduct interviews and interrogations, eliminate dead-end results, and concentrate on running the fraudster to ground. They can conduct covert activities not in the financial auditors' tool kit. The luxury of the deductive approach involves surveying a wide array of information and sources, eliminating the extraneous, and retaining the selection that proves the fraud. However, as critical thinking recognizes, proof is a relative concept. While a signed confession to fraud may be considered the most conclusive evidence one can get, courts are skeptical of evidence that purports to evercome the presumption of innocence until proven guilty in the Ango-Saxon system of law. This aspect of fraud auditing and critical thinking is discussed later in this chapter.

. . . .

REVIEW
CHECKPOINTS

6 What are the defining characteristics of white-collar crime, employee fraud, embezzlement, defalcation, management fraud, errors, irregularities, and illegal acts?

7 What does a fraud perpetrator look like? How does he or she act?

8 Compare and contrast the type of work performed by external auditors (auditing financial statements to render an audit report) and fraud examiners.

. . . .

CONDITIONS THAT MAKE FRAUD POSSIBLE, EVEN EASY

. . . .

LEARNING OBJECTIVE

3 Outline some of the conditions that lead to frauds.

When can fraud occur? Imagine probability of fraud as a function of three factors: motive, opportunity, and lack of integrity. When one or two of these factors weigh heavily in the direction of fraud, the probability increases. When three of them lean in the direction of fraud, it almost certainly will occur.[12] As Bologna and Lindquist put it, some people are honest all the time, some people (fewer than the honest ones) are dishonest all the time, most people are honest some of the time, and some people are honest most of the time.[13]

[12] For further references, see D. R. Cressey, "Management Fraud, Accounting Controls, and Criminological Theory," pp. 117–147, and Albrecht et al., "Auditor Involvement in the Detection of Fraud," pp. 207–261, both in R. K. Elliott and J. J. Willingham, *Management Fraud: Detection and Deterrence* (New York: Petrocelli Books, Inc., 1980).; J. K. Loebbecke, M. M. Eining, and J. J. Willingham, "Auditors' Experience with Material Irregularities: Frequency, Nature, and Detectability," *Auditing: A Journal of Practice and Theory*, Fall 1989, pp. 1–28.

[13] Bologna and Lindquist, *Fraud Auditing and Forensic Accounting*, p. 8.

Motive

Pressure a person experiences and believes cannot be shared with friends and confidants is **motive**. *Psychotic* motivation is relatively rare and is experienced by "habitual" criminals who steal simply for the sake of stealing. *Egocentric* motivations drive people to steal to achieve more personal prestige. *Ideological* motivations are held by people who think that their cause is morally superior and that they are justified in making someone else a victim. *Economic* motive is far more common than the other three in business frauds, and is simply a need for money. At times it can be intertwined with egocentric and ideological motivations. Ordinarily honest people can fall into circumstances where there is a new or unexpected need for money and when the normal options for talking about it or going through legitimate channels seem to be closed. Consider these needs:

- college or university tuition
- gambling debts
- drugs
- alimony and child support
- expensive lifestyle (homes, cars, boats)
- business or stock speculation losses
- taxation on good financial results

Probably the most important motive that external auditors consider is compensation tied to accounting measures of performance. This situation creates incentives to manipulate the accounting measurements.

Opportunity

A **fraud opportunity** is an open door for solving the unshareable problem by violating a trust. The violation may be a circumvention of internal control policies and procedures, or it may be taking advantage of an absence or lapse of control procedures. Everyone has some degree of trust placed on them in their job, and the higher the position in an organization, the greater the degree of trust; hence, the greater the opportunity for larger frauds. Here are some examples of opportunities:

- Nobody counts the inventory, so losses are not known.
- The petty cash box is often left unattended.
- Supervisors set a bad example by taking supplies home.
- Upper management considered a written statement of ethics but decided not to publish one.
- Another employee was caught and fired, but not prosecuted.
- The finance vice-president has investment authority without any review.
- Frequent emergency jobs leave a lot of excess material just lying around.

I COULDN'T TELL ANYONE

An unmarried young woman stole $300 from her employer to pay for an abortion. Coming from a family that strongly disdained premarital sex, she felt that her only alternative was to have the secret abortion. Once she realized how easy it was to steal, however, she took another $86,000 before being caught.

Source: W. S. Albrecht, "How CPAs Can Help Clients Prevent Employee Fraud," *Journal of Accountancy*, December 1988, p. 113. Copyright 1988. American Institute of Certified Public Accountants, Inc. All rights reserved. Used with permission.

Probably the most significant opportunity as far as external auditors are concerned is lack of controls at the highest levels (corporate governance) to prevent management from overriding accounting controls.

Lack of Integrity

Practically everyone, even the most violent criminals, knows the difference between right and wrong. While unimpeachable integrity is the ability to act according to the highest moral and ethical values all the time, lapses and occasional **lack of integrity** permit motive and opportunity to take form as fraud. People normally do not make deliberate decisions to "lack integrity today while I steal some money," but they find ways to describe (rationalize) the act so that it is acceptable to their self-image: I need it more than they do (Robin Hood theory), I'll pay it back, I'm not hurting anybody, the company can afford it, and everybody does it.

As was evident from the auditor survey results presented earlier, lack of integrity appears to be the most important factor affecting the risk of management fraud. This should not be surprising since—given managers' authority, responsibilities, and incentives—the other factors of motive and opportunity are already largely present, and

SHE CAN DO EVERYTHING

Mrs. Lemon was the only bookkeeper for an electrical supply company. She wrote the cheques and reconciled the bank account. In the cash disbursements journal, she coded some cheques as inventory, but she wrote the cheques to herself, using her own true name. When the cheques were returned with the bank statement, she simply destroyed them. She stole $416,000 over five years. After being caught and sentenced to prison, she testified to having continuous guilt over doing something she knew was wrong.

Source: "Auditing for Internal Fraud" training course © 2006 Association of Certified Fraud Examiners.

THE MOST COMMON COMPUTER-RELATED CRIMES

Whereas computer hacking (pranksters breaking into computers) has received most of the recent media attention, the most prevalent computer crime is the fraudulent disbursement of funds, which is generally preceded by the submission of a spurious claim in one of the following forms:
- false vendor, supplier, or contractor invoice
- false governmental benefit claim
- false fringe benefit claim
- false refund or credit claim
- false payroll claim
- false expense claim

Fraudulent disbursement of funds usually requires a data entry clerk in accounts payable, payroll, or the benefits section, acting either alone or in collusion with an insider or outsider (depending on how tight the internal controls are). From an accountant's perspective, the claim is a false debit to an expense so that a corresponding credit can be posted to the cash account for the issuance of a cheque. Auditors assert that such disbursement frauds represent more than half of all frauds by lower-level employees.

At higher management levels, the typical fraud involves overstating profits by the fabrication of such data as sales, which are increased arbitrarily (sales booked before the sales transaction is completed), and the understatement of expenses, which are arbitrarily reduced or disguised as deferrals to the next accounting period. There are numerous variations on these two main themes: overstatement of sales, and understatement of expenses. One of the more common ploys to overstate profits is to arbitrarily increase the ending inventory of manufactured goods or merchandise held for sale. That ploy results in understating the cost of goods sold and thereby increasing the net profit.

The executive compensation system often provides the incentive to overstate profits. If bonus awards depend on profits, executives have an economic incentive to fudge the numbers. They may also be tempted to do so if they own a great many company shares, whose value depends on investors' perceptions of profitability. If profits are down, investors are unhappy and may rush to sell, thus causing a lowered share price and depressing the value of the executive's own shares.

Manipulations of this type often require line executives and personnel in accounting and data processing capacities to conspire together. Such conspiracies have become a recurring theme in business. The pressure on executives for high performance grows each year. We are therefore likely to see more such frauds in the future.

Source: G. J. Bologna and A. J. Lindquist, *Fraud Auditing and Forensic Accounting, 2nd ed.* (New York: John Wiley & Sons, 1995), pp. 176–179. Reprinted by permission of John Wiley & Sons, Inc.

---

integrity is the only thing preventing fraud at the top levels of the organization. This may be a reason that "tone at the top" is one of the most important aspects of good internal controls.

The importance of the three risk factors—motive, opportunity, and lack of integrity—has also been acknowledged in CAS 240 and SAS 99. Both standards use these factors as a framework for linking sources of these risks to audit procedures. CAS 240 and SAS 99 refer to motive as **incentives** or **pressures** and lack of integrity as **rationalization** or **attitude**. These can also be viewed as social, economic, and moral incentives. The three forms of incentives are referred to as the **fraud triangle** or **triangulation**. Evidence or signs of these incentives are the fraud risk factors. For fraud to occur, all three types of factors need to be present. Hence, auditors use these risk factors as guides for evaluating whether the risk of material fraud is at acceptable levels.

Appendix 2 of CAS 240 gives examples of audit procedures addressing higher than acceptable risks of fraud. These include revenue recognition procedures such as confirming relevant contract terms and absence of side agreements with customers, inventory quantity procedures, and procedures related to verifying management estimates. The applications case in this chapter illustrates some fundamental issues related to acceptability of management estimates.

R E V I E W
CHECKPOINTS

9 What are some of the pressures that can cause honest people to contemplate theft? List some egocentric and ideological pressures, as well as economic ones.

10 What kinds of conditions provide opportunities for employee fraud and financial statement fraud?

11 Give some examples of some rationalizations to excuse fraud. Would you be able to use them?

FRAUD PREVENTION

· · · · · · · · · · · · · · · · ·

LEARNING OBJECTIVE
④ Describe ways and means
   to prevent frauds.

Accountants and auditors are often exhorted to be the leaders in fraud prevention by designing tight control systems. This strategy is, at best, a short-run solution to a large and pervasive problem. Business activity is built on the trust that people at all levels will do their jobs properly, and control systems limit trust—sometimes even strangling business with bureaucracy. Imagine street crime being "prevented" by enrolling half the population in the police force to control the other half! Managers and employees must have freedom to do business, which means giving them freedom to commit frauds as well.[14] Effective long-run prevention measures are complex and involve eliminating the causes of fraud by mitigating the effects of motive, opportunity, and lack of integrity.

Managing People Pressures in the Workplace

From time to time, people will experience financial and other pressures. These cannot be eliminated, but facilities for sharing them can be created. Some companies have "ethics officers" who are available to talk over the ethical dilemmas faced in the workplace and help people adopt legitimate responses. However, the ethics officers are normally not psychological counsellors Many companies have "hot lines" for anonymously reporting ethical problems. The most effective agencies are outside the organization, coordinating their activities with the management of the auditee company.

The most effective long-run prevention, however, is a management practice of caring for people. Managers and supervisors at all levels can show genuine concern for the personal and professional needs of their employees and co-workers, and subordinates can show the same concern for one another and their managers. The approach is idealistic and calls for the elimination of interpersonal competition and office politics. Nevertheless, many organizations practise it in the form of staff meetings, personal counselling, and "quality circles" (groups of employees from all levels who plan production, selling, and administrative activities together). Some organizations have daycare centres, alcohol and drug counselling, financial counselling, and other programs to help people share their problems with experts.

During their audit of financial statements, external auditors must obtain an understanding of the company's control structure. This includes the control environment, which relates to the overall scheme of management activity in the company. Management that carefully considers the people pressures in the workplace and uses some of the devices mentioned has a good control environment and the beginnings of a good control structure.

Control Procedures and Employee Monitoring

Auditors would be properly horrified at an organization without control policies and procedures, and rightly so. Controls in the form of job descriptions and performance specifications help people know the jobs they are supposed to accomplish, and almost everyone needs some structure for their working hours. An organization whose only control is "trustworthy employees" has no control.[15] Unfortunately, "getting caught" is an important consideration for many people when coping with their problems, and controls provide the opportunity to get caught.

Without going into much detail about controls, procedures for recognizing and explaining red flags are important for stopping frauds before they get bigger. Controls that reveal the following kinds of symptoms are necessary:[16]

- missing documents
- second endorsements on cheques

---

[14] D. R. Cressey, "Management Fraud," p. 124.
[15] W. S. Albrecht, "How CPAs Can Help Clients Prevent Employee Fraud," *Journal of Accountancy*, December 1988, pp. 110–114.
[16] Albrecht, pp. 113–114.

- unusual endorsements
- unexplained adjustments to inventory balances
- unexplained adjustments to accounts receivable
- old items in bank reconciliations
- old outstanding cheques
- customer complaints
- unusual patterns in deposits in transit

As control systems are essentially restrictions on people, the ideal is to have a minimum of useful controls that avoid picky rules that are "fun to beat." The challenge of beating the system, which can lead to bigger and better things, is an invitation to fraudulent behaviours. (How many university students find ways to get into course registration before their scheduled times?)

Integrity by Example and Enforcement

The key to integrity in business is accountability—that is, each person must be willing to put his decisions and actions in the sunshine—and there must be norms for this. A published codes of conduct, which may be simple or elaborate, is a good beginning. Government agencies and defence contractors typically have the most elaborate rules for employee conduct. A code can be effective if the "tone at the top" supports it. When the chair of the board and the president make themselves visible examples of the code, then other people will follow that lead, thereby creating a positive workplace environment that deters fraud.

DISHONESTY IS BAD POLICY

Now be honest. When fixing your car following an accident, your body shop includes extra repairs and puts them on the insurance company's tab. Do you say thanks and let the insurer pay?

According to an ethics poll conducted recently for the **Canadian Coalition against Insurance Fraud,** 25 percent of those surveyed said they'd go along with the mechanic's bill padding.

For the property and casualty insurers who make up the membership of the coalition, this ethical laxity adds up to an estimated $1.3-billion-a-year problem, including the cost of police and fire officials' investigations.

That's how much is lost on fraudulent claims relating to homes. Insurance fraud is second only to illegal drug sales as a source of criminal profit.

Put another way, fraud accounts for 10 percent to 15 percent of all claims paid out—money that ends up being covered by honest policyholders in the form of increased premiums.

The coalition is conducting a study to analyze the kinds of insurance fraud that are most frequently perpetrated, says executive director Mary Lou O'Reilly.

She says a link has been found between the ethical decisions people make in their everyday lives and opportunistic fraud.

"Fraud for the average Canadian is an opportunity to 'get back' some of what they feel is rightfully theirs when they have a legitimate claim."

Sometimes, for example, they inflate a claim to cover the deductible. "But these are not seasoned criminals," she says. "These are honest people who just don't recognize that fraud is a crime."

Or people who get clumsy when they veer from the straight and narrow. Insurers have dozens of anecdotes about people whose 12-inch televisions suddenly develop 29-inch screens once they're lost. Then there was the one about the policyholder with the damaged 20-foot boat that turned out to have been stored in an 18-foot garage.

The coalition has helped cut down on fraud through an alliance with Crime Stoppers, which are volunteer-run, privately funded, anonymous telephone-tip services operated in cooperation with local police forces.

Under the arrangement, a tip called in to Crime Stoppers about a possible fraud is relayed to the Insurance Crime Prevention Bureau and investigated. Police may also be called in.

If a claim is denied, Crime Stoppers receives 5 percent of the damage claim up to $1,500, which is then passed on to the tipster at the discretion of Crime Stoppers.

Source: S. Yellin, "Dishonesty Is Bad Policy," *The Financial Post*, May 23, 1997, p. 10. Material reprinted with the express permission of "The National Post Company," a CanWest partnership.

Hiring and firing are important, and background checks on prospective employees are advisable. Someone with a questionable reputation in an earlier organization will probably be worthy of suspicion in a new place. Organizations have been known to hire private investigators to make these background checks. Fraudsters should be fired and, in most cases, prosecuted as they have a low rate of recidivism (repeat offences) if they are prosecuted but a high rate if not.[17] Prosecution delivers the message that management does not believe that "occasional dishonesty" is acceptable. Training employees is also important. Acceptable levels of behaviour and company standards should be communicated and taught so that employees can be expected to do what is required. Ask each employee to periodically confirm adherence to the company code of ethics.

HOW TO ENCOURAGE FRAUD

Practise autocratic management.
Orient management to power and low trust.
Manage by crisis.
Centralize authority in top management.
Measure performance on a short-term basis.
Make profits the only criterion for success.
Make rewards punitive, stingy, and political.
Give feedback that is always critical and negative.
Create a highly hostile, competitive workplace.
Insist that everything be documented with a rule for everything.

Source: Adapted from G. J. Bologna and R. J. Lindquist, *Fraud Auditing and Forensic Accounting* (New York: John Wiley & Sons, 1987), pp. 47–49.

REGULATORS UNITE TO FIGHT TELEMARKETING SCAMS

Two Canadian securities commissions have joined regulators from 21 U.S. states and the U.S. Federal Trade Commission in an offensive on telemarketing scams that cost investors about $40 billion a year.

[17] Albrecht, p. 114.

Securities regulators in Quebec and British Columbia are taking part in the campaign, "Project Field of Schemes," by publicizing some of the most significant cases of the past three months.

Frauds over the Internet are a new source of concern, an extension of the telemarketing campaigns that target old people.

"The Internet is like a huge classified ad section, with a money wanted column showing you where to invest, and it becomes a perfect medium for conveying investment offers," said Mark Griffin, president of the North American Securities Administrators Association.

The British Columbia Securities Commission supported the campaign because it knows all regulators deal with the same types of scams, often orchestrated by the same people.

"Frauds are similar wherever you go—and often the perpetrators have crossed jurisdictional boundaries so they can start fresh in a new place where they are not known," said Barbara Barry, communications manager at the BCSC.

"Basically, people and their greed are universal."

She noted a recent case involving a company called Goldman-Stanley consultants, which controlled four other firms. Its name was purposely similar to that of the well-known New York investment house and its stationery had a similar look.

"People who bought believed that Goldman-Stanley consultants were agents that were placing foreign exchange contract purchases for legitimate companies in other jurisdictions," Barry said.

Goldman-Stanley also used a storefront location to mimic a well-known Hong Kong investment firm in a successful attempt to solicit Asian clients.

Source: I. Karleff, "Regulations Unite to Fight Telemarketing Scams," *The Financial Post,* July 3, 1997, p. 8. Material reprinted with the express permission of *"The National Post Company,"* a CanWest partnership.

WHERE DID HE COME FROM?

The controller defrauded the company for several million dollars. As it turned out, he was no controller at all. He didn't know a debit from a credit. The fraudster had been fired from five previous jobs where money had turned up missing. He was discovered one evening when the president showed up unexpectedly at the company and found a stranger in the office with the controller. The stranger was doing all of the accounting for the bogus controller.

Source: "Auditing for Internal Fraud" training course © 2006 Association of Certified Fraud Examiners.

REVIEW CHECKPOINTS

12 Make a two-column list of management styles that show fraud-prevention characteristics in one column and, opposite each item, the management style that might lead to fraud.

FRAUD DETECTION

Since an organization cannot prevent all fraud, its auditors, accountants, and security personnel must be acquainted with some detection techniques. Frauds consist of the act itself, the conversion of assets to the fraudster's use, and the cover-up. Catching people in the fraud act is difficult and unusual. The act of conversion is equally difficult to observe, since it typically takes place in secret away from the organization's offices (e.g., fencing stolen inventory). Many frauds are investigated through noticing the signs and signals and then following the trail of missing, mutilated, or false documents that are part of the accounting records cover-up.

This chapter has already mentioned the red flags, oddities, and unusual events that are signs and signals. Being able to notice these takes some experience, but this text can give some starting places.

Red Flags

LEARNING OBJECTIVE

⑤ Explain the audit and investigative procedures for detecting common employee fraud schemes.

Employee Fraud. Employee fraud usually, but not always, involves people below the top executive levels. Observation of persons' habits and lifestyle as well as changes in these may reveal some red flags. Fraudsters frequently exhibit these characteristics: defensive, argumentative, and blame-shifting behaviours; tiredness; agitation; inability to make eye contact; irritability; and excessive sweating. Some of these symptoms might lead to suspicions of drug and or alchohol abuse by the individual.

HIGH STYLE IN THE MAILROOM

A female mailroom employee started wearing designer clothes (and making a big deal about it). She drove a new BMW to work. An observant manager, who had known her as an employee for seven years and knew she had no outside income, became suspicious. He asked the internal auditors to examine her responsibilities extra carefully. They discovered she had taken $97,000 over a two-year period.

Source: "Auditing for Internal Fraud" training course © 2006 Association of Certified Fraud Examiners.

Personality red flags are problematic because (1) honest people sometimes show them and (2) they often are hidden from view.[18] It is easier to notice changes, especially when a person adopts a new lifestyle or spends more money than the salary justifies; for example, on homes, furniture, jewellery, clothes, boats, autos, vacations, and the like.

Telltale hints of a cover-up often appear in the accounting records. The key is to notice exceptions and oddities, such as transactions that are at odd times of the day, month, or season; too many or too few of them; in the wrong branch location; and in amounts too high, too low, too consistent, or too inconsistent. Exceptions and oddities can appear in the following forms:

- missing documents
- cash shortages and overages
- excessive voids and credit memos
- customer complaints
- common names or addresses for refunds
- adjustments to receivables and payables
- general ledger that does not balance
- increased past due receivables
- inventory shortages
- increased scrap
- alterations on documents

---

[18] Long lists of red flags can be found in Bologna and Lindquist, *Fraud Auditing and Forensic Accounting*, pp. 49–56; Albrecht et. al., in *Management Fraud*, pp. 223–26; Statement on Auditing Standard 82; "Auditing for Fraud" courses of the Association of Certified Fraud Examiners; and courses offered by other organizations, such as the CICA and the Institute of Internal Auditors.

- duplicate payments
- employees who cannot be found
- second endorsements on cheques
- documents that are photocopied
- dormant accounts that have become active

Fraudulent Financial Reporting by Management

Fraud that affects financial statements and causes them to be materially misleading often arises from the perceived need to "get through a difficult period." These difficult periods may include a cash shortage, increased competition, cost overruns, and similar events. Managers usually view these conditions as temporary and believe they can overcome them by getting a new loan, selling shares, or otherwise buying time to recover. In the meantime, falsified financial statements are used to "benefit the company." Frauds have often accompanied the following conditions and circumstances:

- high debt
- unfavourable industry conditions
- excess capacity
- profit squeeze
- strong foreign competition
- lack of working capital
- rapid expansion
- product obsolescence
- slow customer collections
- related party transactions

Through fraud and "creative accounting," companies create financial statements that are materially misleading by either (1) overstating revenues and assets, (2) understating expenses and liabilities, or (3) giving disclosures that are misleading or that omit important information. Generally, fraudulent financial statements show financial performance and ratios that are better than current industry experience or better than the company's own history. Sometimes the performance exactly meets management targets announced months earlier.

Because of the double-entry bookkeeping system, fraudulent accounting entries always affect two accounts and two places in financial statements. Many frauds involve improper recognition of assets or a "dangling debit," which is an asset amount that is investigated and found to be false or questionable. Finding and investigating the "dangling credit" is normally very difficult, as these liabilities "dangle" off the books. Misleading disclosures are also difficult because they involve words and messages instead of numbers. Omissions may be hard to notice, and misleading inferences may be very subtle.

A client's far-removed illegal acts may cause financial misstatements, and external auditors should be aware of possible indications of them:

- unauthorized transactions
- government investigations
- regulatory reports of violations
- payments to consultants, affiliates, and employees for unspecified services
- excessive sales commissions and agent's fees
- unusually large cash payments
- unexplained payments to government officials
- failure to file tax returns or pay duties and fees

OVERSTATED REVENUE, RECEIVABLES, AND DEFERRED COSTS

Cali Computer Systems Inc. sold franchises enabling local entrepreneurs to open stores and sell Cali products. The company granted territorial franchises, in one instance recording revenue of $800,000 and in another $580,000. Unfortunately, the first of these "contracts" for a territorial franchise simply did not exist while the second was not executed and Cali had not performed its obligations by the time it was recorded. In both cases, the imaginary revenue was about 40 percent of reported revenues. These franchises were more in the nature of business hopes than completed transactions.

Cali was supposed to deliver computer software in connection with the contracts and had deferred $277,000 of software development cost in connection with the programs. However, this software did not work, and the contracts were fulfilled with software purchased from other suppliers.

Source: SEC Accounting and Auditing Enforcement Release 190, 1988.

Internal Control

A 2004 study by the Association of Certified Fraud Examiners showed that 40 percent of all frauds are detected through tips from employees. This explains why SOX requires audit committees to encourage anonymous whistle-blowing by employees. Almost 30 percent of frauds were detected by internal audit, 18 percent by other internal controls, 21 percent by accident, and 11 percent by external auditors.[19]

THE TRUSTED EMPLOYEE

The owner of a small business hired his best friend to work as his accountant. The friend was given full access to all aspects of the business and was completely responsible for the accounting. Five years later, the owner finally terminated the friend because the business was not profitable. Upon taking over the accounting, the owner's wife found that cash receipts from customers were twice the amounts formerly recorded by the accountant "friend." An investigation revealed that the friend had stolen $450,000 in cash sales receipts from the business, while the owner had never made more than $16,000 a year. (The friend had even used the stolen money to make loans to the owner and to keep the business going!)

NO LOCKS ON THE DOOR

Perini Corporation kept blank cheques in an unlocked storeroom, where every clerk and secretary had access. Also in the storeroom was the automatic cheque-signing machine. The prenumbered cheques were not logged or restricted to one person. The bookkeeper was very surprised to open the bank statement one month and find that $1.5 million in stolen cheques had been paid on the account.

Source: "Auditing for Internal Fraud" training course © 2006 Association of Certified Fraud Examiners.

---

[19] J. T. Wells, "Small Business, Big Losses" *Journal of Accountancy*, December 2004, pp. 42–47.

WHEN YOUR IDENTITY IS STOLEN

Even your utility bills can be turned to fraudulent use.

A 22-year-old secretary realizes she's got an evil twin travelling around the country when Canada Revenue Agency begins demanding she cough up unpaid taxes. Her imposter—who'd apparently applied for and received a social insurance number under her name years earlier—has been moving from job to job without paying taxes.

The names of children who died years ago are used to set up phony businesses that collect GST refunds. An Etobicoke man, who is eventually jailed for tax fraud, collected the names from tombstones.

Another con man opens a number of accounts at Vancouver-area banks using someone else's SIN and birth certificate. He defrauds the banks of more than $170,000 by depositing phony cheques and withdrawing the money from ATMs.

Identity thieves take over someone else's identity to commit fraud—either by applying for a credit card or loan, opening a bank account, or using social insurance numbers to hide from the taxman.

These are some of the stories on the growing list of Canadian cases involving identity theft as identified by privacy commissioner Ann Cavoukian.

The victim often doesn't find out what's happened until months later, and by that time his or her credit report is such a mess it can take years to sort out.

Cavoukian has just released a report on some of the steps she believes need to be taken to stop the crime. Some of the less obvious ones include the following:

TIPS TO PREVENT IDENTITY THEFT

- Shred or tear up sensitive documents before throwing them away. These include phone and utility bills, pre-approved credit applications and anything that provides credit card number, bank account number, tax information, your driver's licence number, or your birth date.
- Install a locked mailbox.
- Obtain a copy of your credit report regularly to check for fraudulent accounts and false address changes. Contact Equifax Canada Inc. at 1-800-465-7166.
- Don't leave a paper record behind after using bank machines.
- Avoid writing your credit card number or SIN on a cheque.
- Don't give your credit card number out over the phone unless you know the company you're dealing with well. It's especially important not to provide personal information over cordless or cellular phones.

Source: Valerie Lawton, *The Toronto Star,* July 6, 1997, p. B5. Reprinted with permission—Torstar Syndication Services.

Fraud awareness auditing involves awareness of employee perceptions of the controls in place (or not in place), plus "thinking like a crook" to imagine ways and means of stealing. When controls are absent, these may be obvious; otherwise, stealing from the company may take some scheming. Thinking like a crook involves critical thinking; it does not mean that you accept the crook's point of view, only that you understand it. It means visualizing how fraud risk factors become incentives for committing frauds, thereby putting the auditor in a better position to predict the fraud. This is also the essence of skepticism—requiring proof of management assertions. Insistence on proof is the essence of critical thinking.

REVIEW CHECKPOINTS

13 What might happen if a person could authorize medical insurance claims and enter them into the system for payment without supervisory review?

14 What might happen if the inventory warehouse manager also had responsibility for making the physical inventory observation and reconciling discrepancies to the perpetual inventory records?

SCHEMES AND DETECTION PROCEDURES

The importance of internal control in preventing and detecting fraud cannot be overestimated. In designing a system of controls, it's important to identify weaknesses or improper utilization of materials, people, or equipment. A good first step is investigating the company's history of losses and prevention of them, and designing a system of checks and balances to address these risks. To the extent possible, every transaction should be authorized, initiated, approved, executed, and recorded. No transaction should be handled by only one person. Preprinted, serial-numbered documents such as purchase orders, sales and purchases invoices, receiving reports, cheques, and debit or credit memos should be used. All policies and procedures should be documented, including procedures in the event of an internal control breakdown. Once implemented, the internal control system should be communicated orally and in writing to all employees. The policies should communicate firmly and clearly that fraud will not be tolerated and what the consequences of fraud involvement will be. The internal control system should be evaluated periodically for cost effectiveness, and employee feedback should be encouraged and rewarded. The following box gives a basic system of controls to deter common types of fraud.

---

1. FOCUS ON FRAUD POSSIBILITIES

Hard as it is to accept, most preventive controls can be beaten by a motivated thief. And, when thieves are inside the organization, they may be part of the control effort itself.

Ask yourself how management steps such as re-engineering, downsizing, outsourcing, computerization, and globalization affect the reliability of controls—as well as the attitudes of those who have access to the assets.

Other places to look are industry resources. Many industry organizations maintain data on fraud cases. Since banks, insurers, and others all support fraud prevention, contact your industry association's security professionals for guidance.

Keep files of news reports of fraud. These articles often contain enough detail to allow you to understand how the deed was done. But be careful not to get caught up in the drama of the fraud: Put less emphasis on the thieves and their reasons for stealing, focusing instead on the modus operandi.

Typical questions you should ask:
- What jobs are likely to provide opportunities for fraud?
- What opportunities exist for employees, executives, vendors, contractors' agents, customers, and others?
- How could they get around approval or transaction confirmation controls?
- What general ledger account and cost center could the fraud be charged to?
- How could the thief deceive the manager in charge of those cost centers when the month-end reports are reviewed?

2. KNOW THE SYMPTOMS

Here's a short list of some fraud symptoms:
- Multiple endorsements on commercial cheques
- The use of common or repetitive names for refunds—such as Smith or Jones or a commercial name that is very similar to one in your industry but is spelled slightly differently

- Line items in standard reconciliations that don't go away
- Customer complaints about having paid invoices for which they are being dunned
- Adjustments to either inventory records or customer accounts
- The addresses of vendors that are the same as employee addresses
- No proceeds from the disposition of used assets

When one of these symptoms appears, use caution. Often there are reasonable explanations and they usually don't lead to a thief—just an error or an ill-designed process. So don't jump to conclusions. Instead, track down the cause for the symptom.

Be especially cautious when reacting to a person's suspicious lifestyle. While such signs should sound an alarm, by themselves they prove nothing, but certainly more investigation is warranted.

3. DESIGN CONTROLS AND AUDIT PROCEDURES

In developing procedures, be sure to include specific steps calculated to look for fraud symptoms. And, while measuring fraud exposure, assess the reliability of such controls.

4. FOLLOW THROUGH ON ALL SYMPTOMS OBSERVED

Whoever finds a symptom of fraud—the external or internal auditor or a company manager—should resolve the situation before going on. Operate with an attitude of healthy professional skepticism. Beware of pressures to complete work within unreasonable deadlines. Be aware that the single symptom you are looking at may not be an isolated occurrence; it may be one of many.

If you believe the follow-up is beyond your capabilities, consider giving the problem to a professional investigator. There are legal liability dangers inherent in mishandling possible fraud cases.

Source: J. Hall, "How to Spot Fraud," *Journal of Accountancy*, October 1996. Copyright 1996. American Institute of Certified Public Accountants, Inc. All rights reserved. Used with permission.

THE REBATE SCAM

A construction company's project manager engineered a simple scam that earned him about $250,000 before he was unmasked. Here's how he did it—and how he was tripped up.

The project manager opened a bank account using a name very similar to the name of the construction project he was managing. He then approached three major suppliers and requested cash rebates in excess of normal industry practice. In exchange, he guaranteed each would be the sole source for their respective products. In addition, he promised they would be paid promptly for all materials delivered. He told them the rebates were due on the first of each month for all transactions of the preceding month. The cheques were to be made payable to the name on the bogus bank account.

The suppliers agreed to the unusual terms in order to secure the business. None questioned the name on the cheques because it was close enough to the actual project name.

The arrangement worked smoothly for several months. Rebate cheques were delivered to the project manager each month and he deposited them into his account. After the cheques cleared, he withdrew most of the funds using cashier's cheques.

The scheme came to light when a supervisor in the construction company's accounts payable department questioned why prompt-payment discounts weren't being made to the three suppliers. She had just attended a fraud-awareness seminar and remembered that such an unusual arrangement might be a symptom of fraud. Rather than question either the project manager or the suppliers, she correctly referred the matter to the corporate audit department for investigation.

The auditors made simultaneous unannounced visits to all three suppliers. Two wouldn't talk, but the third explained the relationship and provided copies of the cancelled rebate cheques.

Lessons learned from the case:
- It's relatively easy to open unauthorized bank accounts because most banks have limited ability to verify the identity of the person opening an account.
- Scam artists know how to cash cheques—to any payee, in any amount.
- Schemes that involve relationships with suppliers are particularly hard to prevent and detect.
- When contracting with suppliers, try to secure the right to review any appropriate records. While this is fairly common in the contracting environment, it's also something to consider for other relationships in which purchase orders are used.

Source: J. Hall, "How to Spot Fraud," *Journal of Accountancy*, October 1996. Copyright 1996. American Institute of Certified Public Accountants, Inc. All rights reserved. Used with permission.

A SIMPLE INTERNAL CONTROLS CHECKLIST FOR COMPANIES

- Allow for a system of checks and balances. Every transaction should be authorized, initiated, approved, executed, and recorded.
- Divide or segregate duties. Do not allow one person to handle all aspects of a transaction from beginning to end.
- Do not allow the same person to have custody of an asset (i.e., cash and inventory) and the responsibility to record transactions.
- Use serial numbers on debit or credit memos, sales and purchases invoices, cheques, tickets, purchase orders, and receiving reports.
- Use a safe, and maintain adequate safekeeping of all assets. Make deposits on a daily basis, and, if necessary, several times per day.
- Use a budget or forecast to detect whether goals are achieved. Investigate the differences—what happened and why.
- Incorporate hiring policies and practices that include drug testing and background checks. Subscribe to an ethics hot line, such as the Association's *EthicsLine*, to provide a way for employees to report, anonymously, suspected infractions or violations within a company to an independent party.

SAFEGUARDING SMALL BUSINESSES

The minimum controls for a small organization are as follows:
- Deposit all cash receipts intact daily.
- Make all payments by serial-numbered cheques with the exception of small transactions by petty cash.
- Reconcile bank accounts monthly.
- Record all cash receipts immediately.
- Balance ledgers at regular intervals.
- Prepare comparative financial statements in sufficient detail every month to disclose significant variations in revenue and expense categories.

Source: D. A. Sebert, "Repeat After Me: Internal Controls, Internal Controls, Internal Controls ..." *The White Paper*, Association of Certified Fraud Examiners, September/October 1998, p. 33.

SOME NEWER APPROACHES TO FRAUD DETECTION

. . . .

The auditor's understanding of the business that was discussed in previous chapters has been promoted as a means of increasing the auditor's effectiveness in detecting fraud: "The use of complex analytical procedures comprising a business knowledge acquisition framework, coupled with an assessment of other fraud risk factors, should improve the auditor's ability to detect and diagnose anomalies associated with management fraud. And, a comprehensive knowledge decision frame will serve to heighten the auditor's level of professional skepticism when appropriate, e.g., by enabling the auditor to develop his own hypotheses about unusual financial-statement trends and fluctuations without relying exclusively on management's explanations."[20]

Another recent development in fraud detection is the use of Benford's Law to detect anomalies in the accounting records, as indicated in the box following.

BENFORD'S LAW AND AUDITING

Do financial statements universally "favour" some numbers over others? The idea seems to defy logic. In a random string of numbers pulled from a company's books, each digit, 1–9, would seem to have one chance in nine of starting a given number. But, according to a 60-year-old formula making its way into the accounting field, some numbers really *are* more "popular" than others. A disruption in the pattern may reveal an inefficient process, an honest mistake, or outright fraud. Benford's Law is the newest tool in the auditor's arsenal.

According to Mark J. Nigrini, PhD, "Benford's Law gives us the expected patterns of the digits in a list of numbers. . . . These patterns would appear in accounts payable invoices and accounts receivable numbers, for example." When patterns vary from those set down by Benford, there may be a problem. "Variations may reveal employees are listing expenses as $24 to avoid a $25 voucher limit. Or consider a manager who has a $3,000 signing authority. Benford's Law tells me that, say, only 0.6 percent of all numbers should start with 29. If I get more than that, maybe a manager is approving too many $2,900 invoices right under his limit." . . . "Maybe managers are breaking down one project into several pieces to circumvent a higher level of oversight for some reason. Clients want to know when employees are going around their control systems." . . . Sometimes, said Nigrini, patterns change because of an error. "Invoices entered more than once will change the frequencies."

"At other times we see spikes—digit frequencies that violate Benford's Law—at $15 or $25," said Ernst & Young partner James Searing. "Even though these are low-dollar items, that might mean a client is writing a separate cheque for each express-mail delivery. That is a very expensive way to process invoices and write cheques." By advising the client to arrange for monthly billing for express mail, E&Y can make the audit a value-added service.

Benford's Law may also catch fraud, thanks to psychology, said Nigrini. "People just don't think 'Benford-like.' If someone is cutting a $400 cheque every week for nonexistent janitorial services, those cheques will skew the digit distribution. A thorough application of the law will find the fraud."

E&Y has developed proprietary software that applies Benford's Law to a client's data. "The more we use such analytical tools, the more we find," said Searing. "In the long term, advanced analytical tools, such as application of Benford's Law, will be part of the audit. They may very well help us reduce the overall risk of auditing, increase the reliability of the audit opinion, and increase value to the client."

Source: "Numerology for Accountants," *Journal of Accountancy*, November 1998, p. 15. Copyright © 1998, 1999 from the *Journal of Accountancy* by the American Institute of Certified Public Accountants, Inc. Opinions of the authors are their own and do not reflect policies of the AICPA. All rights reserved. Used with permission.

---

[20] T. Bell, F. Marrs, I. Solomon, and H. Thomas, *Auditing Organizations Through a Strategic-Systems Lens*, KPMG, 1997, p. 69.

In this section of the chapter we will consider some cases. They will follow a standard format of case description and audit approach analysis. In similar problems at the end of the chapter, you will be asked to write the audit approach section for a case situation. The first three cases here deal with employee fraud, and the last two deal with management fraud. With the first three, you will practise Learning Objective 5, and with the last two, Learning Objective 6.

AUDIT CASE 17.1
THE MISSING PETTY CASH

Case description

The petty cash custodian brought postage receipts from home and paid them from the fund. He persuaded the supervisor to sign blank authorization slips the custodian could use when the supervisor was away, and he used these to pay for fictitious meals and minor supplies. He took cash to get through the weekend, replacing it the next week.

Audit trail

The postage receipts were from a distant post office the company did not use. The blank slips were dated on days the supervisor was absent. The fund was cash short during the weekend and for a few days in the following week. The fund was small ($100), but the custodian replenished it about every two working days, stealing about $20 each time. With about 260 working days per year and 130 reimbursements, the custodian was stealing about $2,600 per year. The custodian was looking forward to getting promoted to general cashier and bigger and better things!

AUDIT APPROACH ANALYSIS

Audit objective

Obtain evidence of the existence and validity of petty cash transactions.

Controls relevant to the process

A supervisor is assigned to approve petty cash disbursements by examining them for validity and signing an authorization slip.

AUDIT PROCEDURES

Tests of controls

Audit for transaction authorization and validity. Select a sample of petty cash reimbursement cheque copies with receipts and authorization slips attached; study them for evidence of authorization and validity (vouching procedure). Notice the nature and content of the receipts. Obtain supervisor's vacation schedule and compare dates with authorization slip dates.

Tests of details of balance

On a Friday, count the petty cash and receipts to see that they add up to $100. Then, count the fund again later in the afternoon. (Be sure the second count is a surprise and that the custodian and supervisor sign off on the count working paper so the auditor will not be accused of theft.)

Audit results

Knowing the location of the nearby post office used by the company, the auditor noticed the pattern of many receipts from a distant post office, which was near the custodian's apartment. Several authorizations were dated during the supervisor's vacation, and he readily admitted signing the forms in blank so his own supervisor "wouldn't be bothered." The second count on the same day was a real surprise, and the fund was found $35 short.

AUDIT CASE 17.2
THE LAUNDRY MONEY SKIM

Case description

Albert owned and operated forty coin laundries around town. As the business grew, he could no longer visit each one to empty the cash boxes and deposit the receipts. Each location grossed about $140 to $160 per day, operating 365 days per year. (Gross income was about $2 million per year.) Four part-time employees each visited ten locations, collecting the cash boxes and delivering them to Albert's office, where he would count the coins and currency (from the change machine) and prepare a bank deposit. One of the employees skimmed $5 to $10 from each location visited each day.

Audit trail

There was no trail, unfortunately. The first paper that gets produced is Albert's bank deposit, and the money is gone by then. The daily theft does not seem like much, but, at an average of $7.50 per day from each of ten locations, it was about $27,000 per year. If all four of the employees had stolen the same amount, the loss could have been about $100,000 per year.

AUDIT APPROACH ANALYSIS

Audit objective

Obtain evidence of the completeness of cash receipts—that is, that all the cash received is delivered to Albert for deposit.

Controls relevant to the process

Controls over the part-time employees were nonexistent. There was no overt or covert observation and

no times when two people went to collect cash (thereby needing to agree, be in collusion, to steal). There was no rotation of locations or other indications to the employees that Albert was concerned about control.

AUDIT PROCEDURES

Tests of controls

With no controls there are no tests of control procedures. Obviously, "thinking like a crook" leads to the conclusion that the employees could simply pocket money.

Tests of details of balance

The "balance" in this case is the total revenue that should have been deposited, and auditing for completeness

is always difficult. Albert marked a quantity of coins with an etching tool and marked some $5 bills with ink. Without the employees knowing, he put these in all the locations, carefully noting the coins and bills left in each.

Audit results

Sure enough, a pattern of missing money emerged. When confronted, the employee confessed.

AUDIT 17.3
THE WELL-PADDED PAYROLL

Case description

Maybelle had responsibility for preparing personnel files for new hires, approving wages, verifying time cards, and distributing payroll cheques. She "hired" fictitious employees, faked their records, and ordered cheques through the payroll system. She deposited some cheques in several personal bank accounts and cashed others, endorsing all of them with the names of the fictitious employees and her own name.

Audit Trail

Payroll creates a large paper trail with individual earnings records, T4 tax forms, payroll deductions for taxes and insurance, and payroll tax reports. Maybelle mailed all the T4 forms to the same post office box. She stole $160,000 by creating these "ghost" employees, usually three to five out of 112 people on the payroll, and paying them an average of $256 per week for three years. Sometimes the ghosts quit and were later replaced by others. But she stole "only" about 2 percent of the payroll funds during the period.

AUDIT APPROACH ANALYSIS

Audit objective

Obtain evidence of the existence and validity of payroll transactions.

Controls relevant to the process

Different people should be responsible for each task of hiring (preparing personnel files), approving wages, and distributing payroll cheques. "Thinking like a crook" leads an auditor to see that Maybelle could put people on the payroll and obtain their cheques.

AUDIT PROCEDURES

Tests of Controls

Audit for transaction authorization and validity. Random sampling might not work because of the small number of ghost employees. Look for the obvious. Select several weeks' cheque blocks, account for numerical sequence (to see whether any cheques have been removed), and examine cancelled cheques for two endorsements.

Tests of details of balance

There may be no "balance" to audit, other than the accumulated total of payroll transactions, and the total may not appear out of line with history because the

fraud is small in relation to total payroll, and has been going on for years. Conduct a surprise payroll distribution; follow up by examining prior cancelled cheques for the missing employees. Scan personnel files for common addresses.

Audit results

Both the surprise distribution and the scan for common addresses provided the names of two or three exceptions. Both led to prior cancelled cheques (which Maybelle had not removed and the bank reconciler had not noticed), which carried Maybelle's own name as endorser. Confronted, she confessed.

AUDIT 17.4
FALSE SALES, ACCOUNTS RECEIVABLE, AND INVENTORY

Case description

Q. T. Wilson was a turnaround specialist who took the challenge at MiniMarc Corporation, a manufacturer of computer peripheral equipment. He set high goals for sales and profits, and to meet these goals, managers shipped bricks to distributors and recorded some as sales of equipment to retail distributors and some as inventory out on consignment. No real product left the plant. The theory was that actual sales would grow, and the bricks would be replaced later with real products. In the meantime, the distributors may have thought they were holding consignment inventory in the unopened cartons. Overstated sales and accounts receivable caused overstated net income, retained earnings, current assets, working capital, and total assets.

Audit Trail

All the paperwork was in order because the managers had falsified the sales and consignment invoices; but they did not have customer purchase orders for all the false sales. Shipping papers were in order, and several shipping employees knew the boxes did not contain disk drives.

Prior to the manipulation, annual sales were $135 million. During the two falsification years, sales were $185 million and $362 million. Net income went up from a loss of $20 million to $23 million (income), then to $31 million (income), and the gross margin percent went from 6 percent to 28 percent. The revenue and profit figures outpaced the industry performance. The accounts receivable collection period grew to 94 days, while it was 70 days elsewhere in the industry.

AUDIT APPROACH ANALYSIS

Audit objective

Obtain evidence about the existence and valuation of sales, accounts receivable, and inventory.

Controls relevant to the process

Company accounting and control procedures required customer purchase orders or contracts as evidence of

real orders. A sales invoice was supposed to indicate the products and their prices, and shipping documents were supposed to indicate actual shipment. Sales were always charged to the customer's account receivable.

AUDIT PROCEDURES

Tests of controls

There were no glaring control omissions such that "thinking like a crook" would have pointed to fraud possibilities. Sensitive auditors might have noticed the high tension among employees caused by the focus on profit goals. Normal selection of sales transactions with vouching to customer orders and shipping documents might turn up a missing customer order. Otherwise, the paperwork would seem to be in order. The problem lay in the managers' power to

override controls and instruct shipping people to send bricks. Most auditors do not ask the question, "Have you shipped anything other than company products this year?"

Tests of details of balance

Confirmations of distributors' accounts receivable might have elicited exception responses. The problem was in having a confirmation sample large enough to pick up some of these distributors or in

being skeptical enough to send a special sample of confirmations to distributors who took the "sales" near the end of the accounting period. Observation of inventory should include some inspection of goods not on the company's premises.

Audit results

The overstatements were not detected. The confirmation sample was small and did not contain any of the false shipments. Tests of detail transactions did not turn up any missing customer orders. The inventory out on consignment was audited by obtaining a written confirmation from the holders, who apparently had not opened the boxes. The remarkable financial performance was attributed to good management.

AUDIT 17.5
OVERSTATE THE INVENTORY, UNDERSTATE THE COST OF GOODS SOLD

Case description

A division manager at Doughboy Foods wanted to meet his profit goals, and simply submitted overstated quantities in inventory reports. The manager *(a)* inserted fictitious count sheets in the independent auditors' working papers, *(b)* handed additional count sheets to the independent auditors after the count was completed, saying "these got left out of your set," and *(c)* inserted false data into the computer system that produced a final inventory compilation (even though this ploy caused the computer-generated inventory not to match with the count sheets). Overstated inventory caused understated cost of goods sold, overstated net income and retained earnings, and overstated current assets, working capital, and total assets.

Audit trail

In general, management reports should correspond to accounting records. The manager's inventory reports showed amounts larger than those in the accounts. He fixed the problem by showing false inventory that was "not recorded on the books." The food products inventory was overstated by $650,000. Through a two-year period, the false reports caused an income overstatement of 15 percent in the first year and would have caused a 39 percent overstatement the second year.

AUDIT APPROACH ANALYSIS

Audit objective

Obtain evidence of the existence, completeness, and valuation of inventory.

Controls relevant to the process

Inventory counts should be taken under controlled conditions, but not under the control of managers who might benefit from manipulation. (However, if these managers are present, auditors should nevertheless be prepared to perform the audit work.) Inventory takers should be trained and follow instructions for recording quantities and condition.

AUDIT PROCEDURES

Tests of controls

Auditors should attend the inventory-taking training sessions and study the instructions for adequacy. Observation of the inventory taking should be conducted by managers and by auditors to ensure compliance with the instructions.

Tests of details of balance

For evidence of existence, select a sample of inventory items from the perpetual records and test-count them in the warehouse. For evidence of completeness, select a sample of inventory items in the warehouse, test-count them, and trace them to the final inventory compilation. For evidence of valuation, find the proper prices of inventory for one or both of the samples, calculate the total cost for the items, and compare this with the amounts recorded in the books. Compare book inventory amounts with management reports. Control the working papers so that only members of the audit team have access. Analytical procedures gave some signals. The particular manager's division had the lowest inventory turnover rate (6.3%) among all the company divisions (comparable turnover, about 11.1%) and its inventory had consistently increased from year to year (227% over the two-year period).

Audit results

In the second year, when the manager handed over the count sheets "that got left out of your set," the auditor thanked him and then went to the warehouse to check them out. Finding them inaccurate, she compared book inventories with his management reports and found an overstatement in the reports. This prompted further comparison of the computer-generated inventory with the count sheets and more evidence of overstated quantities on 22 of the 99 count sheets.

REVIEW
CHECKPOINTS

15 If the petty cash custodian were replaced and the frequency of fund reimbursement decreased from every two days to every four days, what might you suspect?

16 Give some examples of control omissions that would make it easy to "think like a crook" and see opportunities for fraud.

17 If sales and income were overstated by recording a false cash sale at the end of the year, what "dangling debit" might give the scheme away?

18 What three general descriptions can be given to manipulations that produce materially misleading financial statements?

DOCUMENTS, SOURCES, AND "EXTENDED PROCEDURES"

Auditing literature often refers to "extended procedures" that are rarely defined and listed. Authorities fear that a list will limit the range of such procedures, so "extended procedures" are left undefined as an open-ended set referring to "whatever is necessary in the circumstances." This section describes some of these procedures with the proviso that (1) some auditors may consider them ordinary and (2) other auditors may consider them unnecessary in any circumstances. They are useful detective procedures in either event.

Content of Common Documents

Textbooks on auditing often advise beginner auditors to "examine cheques," and to "check the employees on a payroll." It helps to know something about these common documents and the information that can be seen on them.

Cheques

Exhibit 17–2 describes the information found on a typical cheque. Knowledge of the codes for the Canadian banking system's identification numbers could enable an auditor to spot a crude cheque forgery. Similarly, mistakes with the optical identification printing or the magnetic cheque number might be a tipoff. If the amount of a cheque is altered after it has cleared the bank, the change would be noted by comparing the magnetic imprint of the amount paid (in the bank's records) against the amount written on the cheque face. The back of a cheque carries the endorsement(s) of the payee and others to whom the payee may have endorsed the cheque; and, in due course, the date, name, and routing number of the bank where the cheque was deposited; and the date, identification of the bank office, and its routing number for the cheque clearing. (There is no bank clearing identification when local cheques are cleared locally without going through a Bank of Canada office.) Auditors can follow the path of a cancelled cheque to note if it corresponds with the characteristics of the payee; for example, why would a cheque to a local business in Mississauga, Ontario, be deposited in a small Missouri bank and cleared through the St. Louis federal reserve office?

Bank Statements

Most of the information shown on the bank statement in Exhibit 17–3 is self-explanatory. However, auditors should be aware that the bank's count and dollar amount of deposits and cheques can be compared with the detail data on the statement; the account holder's business identification number is on the statement, and this can be used in other databases (for individuals, this is a place to get a person's social insurance number); and the statement itself can be studied for alterations.

EXHIBIT 17-2   HOW TO READ A CANCELLED CHEQUE AND ENDORSEMENT

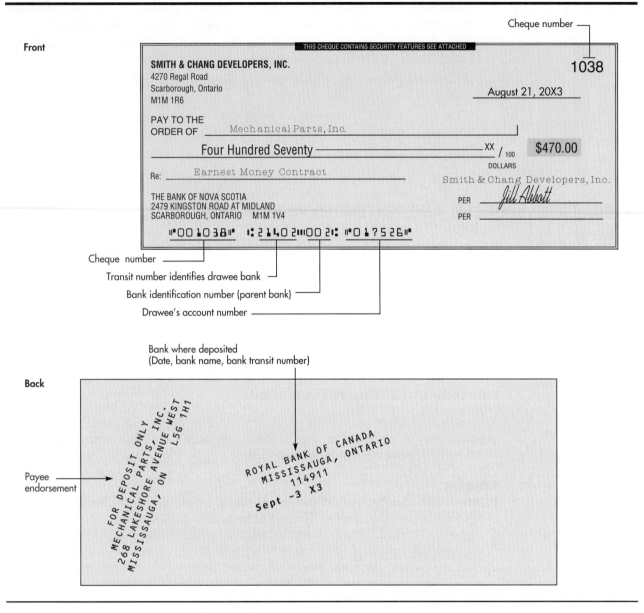

Valid Social Insurance Numbers

In Canada, **social insurance numbers** (**SIN**s) have become universal identification numbers. They can be useful to auditors when checking the personnel files and the validity of people on the payroll. Here are some characteristics of SINs:[21]

- The SIN is a nine-digit number; the ninth digit is a check digit that is calculated using the first eight digits.

- There are two types of SINs: regular numbers and distinctive numbers. Regular numbers are issued to Canadian citizens, registered Native peoples, and permanent residents. Distinctive numbers start with digit 9 and are issued to people who do not have status as above, e.g., foreign workers, visitors.

---

[21] Caution: Human Resources Development Canada periodically adds numbers that have been issued and may use numbers assigned to one geographic area for another. If the validity of a SIN becomes important in an audit, check with Human Resources Development Canada to ascertain the current status of numbers issued. For further reference, see M. L. Levy, "Financial Fraud: Schemes and Indicia," *Journal of Accountancy*, August 1985, p. 85; E. J. Pankau, *Check it Out* (Houston: Cloak & Data Press, 1990), pp. 20–27.

EXHIBIT 17-3   SMALL BUSINESS BANK STATEMENT

```
                                                                    27

        ⊠ North Country Bank
        MISSISSAUGA, ON                                      ACCOUNT
        P.O. BOX 908                      ---          604017-526-5
        MISSISSAUGA, ON L5G 2H3           ---    ---
                                          ---                  PAGE
                                                ---              1


        CAULCO INC                                         SIN/TAX ID
        BLDG 1 OFFICE F                                    74-2076251
        5450 BEE CAVE RD
        MISSISSAUGA, ON                                  CYC MC FREQ
        L5G 1H2                                          01 01 M0000

        **  YOUR CHEQUING ACCOUNT      01-29-X3 THRU 02-29-X3 **

   TO YOUR PREVIOUS BALANCE OF - - - - - - - - -        7,559.06
   YOU ADDED          1 DEPOSITS FOR  - - - - - -        5,654.16
   YOU SUBTRACTED   26 WITHDRAWALS FOR - - - - -        10,838.29
   GIVING YOU A CURRENT BALANCE OF - - - - - - -         7,374.93

   NUMBER OF DAYS USED FOR AVERAGES  - - - - - -               31
   YOUR AVERAGE LEDGER BALANCE - - - - - - - - -         4,014.67
   YOUR LOW BALANCE OCCURRED ON 02-22 AND WAS  -         2,374.93

                       THANK YOU

   -------------------------------------------------------------
   -------------------------------------------------------------
                 DEPOSITS AND OTHER ADDITIONS

        DATE     AMOUNT
        0204     5654.16 ✓
   -------------------------------------------------------------
                 CHEQUES AND OTHER WITHDRAWALS

   CHEQUE DATE     AMOUNT CHEQUE DATE    AMOUNT CHEQUE DATE   AMOUNT
    2201  0211      57.83✓ 2214  0203    403.92✓ 2225  0217 ✓ 182.77
     **                   2215  0203    135.59✓  **
    2205  0222      16.72✓ 2216  0216      6.16✓ 2231  0205 ✓ 254.37
    2206  0203     533.28✓ 2217  0217    138.43✓ 2232  0210 ✓  60.61
    2207  0203    1312.15✓ 2218  0217    131.92✓
     **                   2219  0217     82.97✓ 2234  0217 ✓  64.69
    2209  0203     247.10✓ 2220  0217     87.49✓ 2235  0218 ✓ 279.97
    2210  0203     249.98✓ 2221  0217     85.68✓  **
    2211  0203     255.26✓ 2222  0217     84.69✓ 2238  0219 ✓  90.00
    2212  0203     242.09✓  **
    2213  0203     384.91✓ 2224  0217    449.71✓
```

- The first digit, other than 9, indicates the province or territory where the number was issued.
- The middle seven digits are issued in generally ascending numerical order, making it feasible to apply Benford's Law to analyzing these digits.
- Working with Human Resources Development Canada, an auditor may be able to detect fictitious SINs.

REVIEW CHECKPOINTS

19 How could you tell whether the amount on a cheque has been increased after it was paid by a bank?

20 If a false SIN for a new employee is entered in the payroll system and the employee receives a paycheque, what control in the system is not being used?

Sources of Information

A wide variety of records and information is available for investigations ranging from personal background checks to business enquiries. Our concern here is with public records and ways to get them. A few of the hundreds of sources are described briefly following.

General Business Sources

City and regional tax assessor–collectors keep files on real property by address and legal description, owner, taxable value, improvements, and amount of taxes and delinquencies. Provincial (and some city) regulatory agencies have directories of liquor licences and various professionals (e.g., PAs, dentists, doctors, plumbers, electricians). Provincial building ministries and ministries of public housing may have a central index file of appraisers, real estate brokers, and most components of the building industry. The industry and trade ministries have data on companies that apply for import and export licences. The federal Ministry of Transportation maintains files on the chain of ownership of all civil aircraft in Canada. Provincial securities commissions have extensive financial information on registered companies and their properties, principal officers, directors, and owners. Local Better Business Bureaus keep information about criminal rackets, cons, and their operators, and can provide information about the business reputations of local businesses. Standard & Poor's Register of Corporations, Directors, and Executives lists about 37,000 public and private companies and the names and titles of over 400,000 officials. The Internet and various online information sources are becoming increasingly important, not only in investigative accounting, but also as part of gaining familiarity with a new client in a normal audit.[22]

Business and Asset Identification Sources

Each region and province has a system for registering businesses—corporations, joint ventures, sole proprietorships, and partnerships—where they keep files on registered "assumed names" (**DBA**, or **doing business as** names). Some businesses may be registered with a province and not a region, or with a region and not a province. All real corporations are registered by a province or federal government, and each province's ministry of consumer and corporate affairs keeps corporate record information, such as the date of registration and the initial officers and owners. (Using these sources, you can find the assets or businesses "hidden" in the spouse's name.) Crooks often work through a labyrinth of business entities, and you can find all the registered companies here, including the phony vendor companies created by employees to bilk employers with false billings. Banks, finance companies, and other creditors often file **Uniform Commercial Code (UCC)** records of creditor interest in assets already used as collateral for a loan (e.g., boats, business equipment, appliances). UCCs are found in regional clerks' offices and in the province's office of the ministry of consumer and/or commercial affairs. (They are also online in some commercial databases.)[23] The following boxes provide illustrations of procedures used in public sector auditing and by insurance fraud auditors, respectively.

QUOTA REPORTS FISHY?

HALIFAX—New recruits to the ranks of the federal fisheries enforcement program are to be given courses in accounting so they can net fishermen who have been cooking their books. And inspectors currently on the payroll of the Fisheries and

---

[22] Hundreds of sources and directories under the categories of business, finance, people, property, and electronic databases are listed and described in the U.S. General Accounting Office publication *Investigators' Guide to Sources of Information* (GAO/OSI-88-1, March 1988, updated periodically). Also, insider information is increasingly difficult to "keep under the lid" as investors form online investor forums to assist each other in passing on "hot tips." (See J. A. Abbey, "Fools and Their Money," *Time*, June 17, 1996, pp. 51–54). Auditors may find these online services useful sources of information on risks and uncertainties facing their clients.

[23] These and other sources of business and personal information are described in Pankau, *Check It Out*.

Oceans Department will be given crash courses in audit procedures over the next several months that will teach them to focus on crooked practices in the fishing industry. A 1994 audit suggested that much of the fish caught on the country's coasts slips through the federal quota system as a result of misreporting of black market trading. The report by federal auditors was obtained by The Canadian Press news service under the Access to Information Act.

It is said the inspectors, who tend to concentrate on the mesh sizes of nets and the species and volumes of fish in a trawler's hold, should focus more on the records and catch reports maintained by fishermen. Authors of the report suggested the inspectors attend commercial-crime courses conducted by the RCMP. The audit pointed to some fishermen, provided with individual quotas, as possible villains who have taken advantage of procedural gaps in enforcement to cheat the quota system.

Over the last few years, individual quotas have replaced the shared quota system, which set overall limits on catches within designated fisheries. The new system reduced competition for the total allowable catches and extended the season for fishermen who survived devastation of the east coast cod fishery. It was eventually extended to the west coast and Lake Erie fisheries.

Despite its shortcomings, however, the bureaucrats who reviewed the process hailed the individual quota system as a stabilizing factor in the fragile fishing industry.

Source: "Quota Reports Fishy?" *The Bottom Line*, September 1996, p. 6.

Federal and Provincial Revenue Agencies

The following are possible sources for big audit findings: (1) police arrest records may indicate those who may have illicit unreported income; (2) real estate sales records may identify people who "forget" to put their sales in a tax return; (3) registrations of expensive cars point to people with a lot of money to spend—perhaps unreported income; (4) comparison of provincial sales tax returns with income tax revenue amounts may reveal discrepancies (depending on which tax collector is feared the most); and (5) university-town newspaper rental ads may identify people who rent rooms, garage apartments, duplex halves, and the like, but forget to report the income.

FORENSICS ON FRONT LINES IN WAR ON INSURANCE FRAUDS

TORONTO—Forensic accountants play an increasingly important role in documenting, proving, and reducing insurance fraud.

Insurance adjusters and lawyers have long used accountants to document clearly fraudulent claims. However, many insurance companies, concerned about huge losses to fraud—about $1.3 billion a year in property and casualty (P&C) claims alone—have recently set up their own fraud-busting Special Investigation Units (SIUs).

The SIUs, staffed mostly by ex commercial crime unit police officers, work proactively to reduce fraud by investigating all claims above a certain amount, as well as suspicious claims.

Once they have established the possibility of fraud, the SIUs (or insurance counsel, if the claim has already progressed to the litigation stage) turn to forensic accountants for the hard proof. "It's just starting to happen," said Ted Baskerville of Lindquist Avey MacDonald Baskerville. "Our role up to now has always been to deal with claims that are overstated—or appear to be—or with arson, or staged theft."

In suspected arson or staged theft cases, Lindquist Avey's forensic specialists determine the insured's possible financial motive by looking at details of ownership or management, historical financial results, past and future obligations, profitability, and cash flow.

They prepare a general profile of the company, including its relationship with creditors, and try to answer the following: Do owners have financial needs they can't satisfy legitimately through the business? What do the owners withdraw from the company, or how do they benefit from it in other ways?

In cases of possible theft, it's important to look at other businesses owned by the insured; maybe they're trying to run down one business for the benefit of another.

The growing use of electronic document storage systems can have unexpected benefits for the forensic sleuth.

According to Ken Gibson of Mintz & Partners in Toronto, "People sometimes don't realize what they have stored." Many systems automatically back up computer communications like email.

Aspiring fraud perpetrators may destroy the email record in their own computers, but forget, or don't know, that investigators can read the backup disk.

Gibson typically deals with commercial damage claims—theft, for example, where inventory appears to be gone, but there's little evidence of a break-in.

In those sorts of cases, he said, investigators try to establish whether anything is in fact missing and, if so, whether it had any real value.

Often, a line of goods, such as video or electronic products, isn't selling, and then it allegedly disappears.

The forensic investigator looks at sales figures and dealings with suppliers, and interviews employees or others involved.

Fraud by employees, leading to fidelity bond claims, is a growth industry, according to Ivor Gottschalk of Ernst & Young's Toronto-based forensic and litigation accounting group.

Often, an employee in a company's purchasing department orders an unnecessary or nonexistent material or service, and gets a kickback for the order.

Other types of fraud include setting up fake suppliers, fictitious employees on a payroll, or phony accounts payable.

"People are getting more and more creative," said Gottschalk.

"We're seeing fraud on the other side, where there's actually fraud in collusion with customers. Companies will normally control their purchasing departments quite closely because they're aware that purchasing is very vulnerable to outside forces."

"But, generally, you wouldn't think of your accounts receivable clerk as being in a position to benefit somebody outside the company, writing off invoices to customers, for example."

Many forensic accountants are members of the Association of Certified Fraud Examiners, based in the United States but with more than 900 Canadian members in nine chapters.

Source: Copyright 1996 by Derek Lundy. Reprinted with permission.

REVIEW CHECKPOINTS

21 Where could you find information about real estate valuation, aircraft ownership, names of licensed doctors, assumed (fictitious) business names, and liens on personal property?

Extended Procedures

LEARNING OBJECTIVE

7 Explain the use of extended audit procedures for detecting fraud.

The nature of extended procedures is limited only by an auditor's imagination and, sometimes, the willingness of management to cooperate in extraordinary audit activities. Next is a short series of extended procedures, with some brief explanations.[24]

Enquire, ask questions Be careful not to discuss fraud possibilities with the managers who might be involved. It gives them a chance to cover up or run. Wells described **fraud audit questioning (FAQ)** as a nonaccusatory method of asking key questions during a regular audit to give personnel an opportunity to supply information about possible misdeeds. Fraud possibilities are addressed in a direct manner, so the FAQ approach must have the

---

[24] Further explanation of these and other procedures can be found in the books and articles cited in preceding footnotes and in these sources: AICPA Technical Practice Aids (TPA 8200.02); D. Churbuck, "Desktop Forgery," *Forbes*, November 27, 1989, pp. 246–254; O. Hilton, *Scientific Examination of Questioned Documents, rev. ed.* (New York: Elsevier North Holland, 1982); A. C. Levinston, "40 Years of Embezzlement Tracking," *Internal Auditor*, April 1991, pp. 51–55.

support of management. Some example questions: Do you think fraud is a problem for business in general? Do you think this company has any particular problem with fraud? Who is beyond suspicion in your department? Is there any information you would like to give regarding possible fraud within this organization? [25]

Count the petty cash twice in a day A second count is unexpected and might catch an embezzling custodian short.

Investigate suppliers (vendors) Check with the Better Business Bureau for a reputation, the telephone book for a listing and address, and the provincial corporation records for owners and assumed names. You may find fictitious vendors making false billings or companies related to purchasing department employees.

Investigate customers As with vendors, investigation may reveal companies set up by insiders, with billings at below-list prices so that the insiders can buy goods and resell them at a profit.

Examine endorsements on cancelled cheques Look for second endorsements, especially by employees; most business payments are deposited with only one. Include those payable to "cash" or to a bank, for purchase of cashiers' cheques. The second endorsee indicates that the payee may not have received the benefit of the payment.

Add up the accounts receivable subsidiary Cash payments on customer accounts have been stolen with credit entries to the customer account, but with no cash deposit or entry made to the control account.

Audit general journal entries Experience has shown that the largest number of accounting errors requiring adjustment are found in nonroutine, nonsystematic journal entries. (Systematic accounting is the processing of large volumes of day-to-day ordinary transactions.)

Match payroll to life and medical insurance deductions Ghosts on the payroll seldom elect these insurance coverages. Doing so reduces the embezzler's take and complicates the cover-up.

Match payroll to Social Insurance Numbers Fictitious SINs may be chosen at random. If so, the fraudster may have made the mistake of using an unissued number or one that does not match with the birth date. Sort the payroll SINs in numerical order and look for false, duplicate, or unlikely (e.g., consecutive) numbers.

Match payroll with addresses Look for multiple persons at the same address.

Retrieve customers' cheques If an employee has diverted customer payments, the cancelled cheques are not available for examination because they are returned to the customer. Ask the customer to give originals or copies, or to provide access for examination.

Use marked coins and currency Plant marked money in locations where cash collections are gathered for turning over for deposit.

Measure deposit lag time Compare the dates of cash debit recording and deposit slip dates with dates credited by the bank. Someone who takes cash and then holds it so that the next cash receipts can make up the difference causes a delay between the date of recording and the bank's date of deposit.

[25] J. T. Wells, "From the Chairman: Fraud Audit Questioning," *The White Paper*, National Association of Certified Fraud Examiners, May–June 1991, p. 2. This technique must be used with extreme care and practice.

Document examination   Look for erasures, alterations, copies where originals should be filed, telltale lines from a copier when a document has been pieced together, handwriting, and other oddities. Professional document examination is a technical activity that requires special training (e.g., the RCMP), but crude alterations may be observed, at least enough to bring them to specialists' attention.

Covert surveillance   Observe activities while hidden. External auditors might watch employees clocking onto a work shift, observing whether they use only one time card. Travelling hotel auditors may check in unannounced, use the restaurant and entertainment facilities, and watch the employees skimming receipts and tickets. (Trailing people on streets and maintaining a "stakeout" should be left to trained investigators.)

Horizontal and vertical analyses   This is analytical review ratio analysis and is very similar to the preliminary analytical procedures explained in Chapter 8. **Horizontal analysis** looks at changes of financial statement numbers and ratios across several years. Examining each year's financial statement as proportions of a base, such as sales for the income statement accounts and total assets for the balance sheet accounts, is **vertical analysis**. Relationships that do not make sense may be indicators of large misstatement and fraud.

Net worth analysis   When fraud has been discovered or strongly suspected, and a suspect's asset and liability records or bank accounts can be obtained, a **net worth analysis** can be done. To do this, calculate the suspect's net worth (known assets less known liabilities) at the beginning and end of a period (months or years), then try to account for the difference as (1) known income less living expenses and (2) unidentified difference. The unidentified difference could be the amount of a theft.

Expenditure analysis   Comparing the data on the suspect's spending with known income is **expenditure analysis**. If spending exceeds legitimate and explainable income, the difference may be the amount of a theft. An analysis like this, however, normally represents only indirect (circumstantial) evidence in a court of law and won't by itself prove the "guilt beyond a reasonable doubt" that is required in criminal cases.

Valuation services   Forensic accounting and fraud auditing frequently involve quantification of economic losses resulting from illegal activities. This may require the specialized services of chartered business valuators.[26]

REVIEW CHECKPOINTS

22   What is the difference between a normal procedure and an extended procedure?

23   What might two endorsements on a cancelled cheque mean?

24   What three oddities might indicate ghosts on a payroll?

25   What can an auditor find using horizontal analysis, vertical analysis, net worth analysis, and expenditure analysis?

AFTER DISCOVERING A FRAUD

Building a case against a fraudster is a task for trained investigators. Internal and external auditors act as assistants to fraud examiners who conduct interviews and interrogations, perform surveillance, use informants, and obtain usable confessions. In almost all cases, the post-discovery activity proceeds with a special prosecutorial assignment with the cooperation

[26] For example, see the CICA practice aid, "Investigative and Forensic Accounting Practice Issues," (1995).

or under the leadership of management. A Crown attorney and the police may be involved. It is advisable to prosecute fraudsters as, otherwise, they often steal again. This is no place for "normal" auditing, but there are guidlelines for auditors on relevant communications.

Consulting and Assisting

LEARNING OBJECTIVE

8 Summarize how PAs can assist in prosecuting fraud perpetrators.

While engaged in the audit work, auditors should preserve the chain of custody of evidence linking the evidence to the suspect—what lawyers and judges call the "relevance" of evidence. If documents are lost, mutilated, or compromised (so that a defence lawyer can argue that they were altered to frame the suspect), they can lose their effectiveness for the prosecution. Auditors should mark the evidence, identifying the location, condition, date, time, and circumstances, as soon as it appears to be a signal of fraud. This marking should be on a separate tag or page, the original document protected in a plastic envelope, and the audit work proceed with copies instead of originals. There should be a record of the safekeeping and of all persons who use the original. Eyewitness observations should be recorded in a memorandum or on tape (audio or video), with corroboration, if possible. Other features in the chain of custody—interviews, interrogations, confessions, documents obtained by subpoena, and other matters—usually are not conducted by auditors.

Independent PAs often accept engagements for litigation support and expert witnessing. This work is called **forensic accounting**—applying accounting and auditing skills to either civil or criminal legal problems. Litigation support is usually consulting work that helps lawyers document cases and determine damages. Expert witness work involves testifying to findings determined during litigation support and testifying about accounting principles and auditing standards. The CICA and the Institute of Internal Auditors conduct continuing education courses for auditors who want to become experts in these fields. The CICA now offers a specialization certificate in investigative and forensic accounting (IFA).

FIRMS SHOULD TAKE FRAUD SERIOUSLY

Company managers are increasingly aware of fraud and have taken initiatives to address its costly consequences, but there is no reason for complacency.

KPMG Investigation and Security Inc. says 62 percent of respondents to its survey of 1,000 of the country's largest companies as ranked by FP reported that fraud had taken place in their organization in the past year, up from 52 percent in the 1996 survey. Better detection is responsible for some of the rise, KPMG says, but a large part is attributable to an actual increase in the incidence of fraud.

Those surveyed see a host of factors as key in allowing fraud to take place, such as poor hiring practices, management override of internal controls, and collusion between employees and third parties. However, poor internal controls are viewed as the leading factor.

Internal fraud remains a huge problem. The survey indicates that, based on dollar losses, 55 percent of all scams are from inside companies. Management accounts for 17 percent of all fraud—usually phoney expense accounts. Employee fraud—38 percent—is predominantly cheque forgery or counterfeiting. What is equally disturbing is that almost half the respondents conduct business in such a way as to be vulnerable to money laundering.

The sad fact is many companies—25 percent of those surveyed—haven't taken even basic measures to shrink the possibility of fraud. These include devising a corporate code of conduct and checking new employees. With the incidence of fraud rising, this is hardly a responsible way to manage a company.

Source: Editorial. "Firms Should Take Fraud Seriously," *The Financial Post,* May 16, 1997, p. 14. Material reprinted with the express permission of "The National Post Company," a CanWest partnership.

FRAUD AUDITS AS ASSURANCE ENGAGEMENTS: A CRITICAL THINKING ISSUE

Are the types of investigations and audits discussed in this chapter assurance or consulting engagements? This depends on the nature of the engagement and whether an accountability relationship exists. But if we view every employee, including management, as being accountable for resources entrusted to them by the company, many fraud audits are the direct reporting type, with an implied assertion that defalcations are not occurring.

Currently, the Association of Certified Fraud Examiners' *Fraud Examiners Manual* is the only authoritative guidance on fraud audit reports. Exhibit 17–4 illustrates a "clean" opinion on a fraud audit. Although the term *opinion* used in it suggests high assurance for the assertion that "there is no fraud," the opinion paragraph offers more of a moderate-assurance, with its "nothing came to our attention" wording that is used in review engagements. This is probably because there is no agreed-upon set of procedures such as GAAS that can provide high assurance for this particular type of assertion.

On the other hand, the equivalent of an adverse opinion, shown in Exhibit 17–5, provides much higher assurance for the assertion that a fraud did occur (especially if there is a signed confession satisfying all legal requirements). But note that the high assurance is due in part to the way the opinion is worded. It does not state that the fraud can be proven legally, "beyond a reasonable doubt," as would be required in a criminal court. Instead, the conclusion is much milder: "if proven in a court of law," the actions would be considered fraudulent. In other words, the fraud auditor is not claiming that there is fraud beyond a reasonable doubt, something only the courts can decide, but rather he or she is providing high assurance that a fraud may have taken place. Thus, by properly wording the conclusion, the auditor can provide high assurance for it, and the use of the word "opinion" is warranted in this case, under section 5025.

EXHIBIT 17–4   FRAUD EXAMINATION OPINION (EVIDENCE DOES NOT SUPPORT ALLEGATION)

Investigation Appendix	**Engagement Contracts/Opinion Letters**

[Date]

[   ], Esq.
[Law Department]
[Company Name]
[Address]
[City, State, Zip Code]

RE: [Fraud Examination]

Dear Mr./Mrs. [   ]:

We have conducted a fraud examination concerning a possible misappropriation of assets of the [Company Name]. This examination was predicated upon information resulting from a routine audit of the company's books by the company's internal auditors.

Our examination was conducted in accordance with lawful fraud examination techniques, which include, but are not limited to: examination of books and records; voluntary interviews of appropriate personnel; and other such evidence-gathering procedures as necessary under the circumstances.

Because concealment and trickery are elements of fraud, no assurance can be given that fraud does not exist. However, based on the results of our examination, we have found no evidence to indicate a violation of criminal and/or civil fraud-related statutes in connection with this matter.

Very truly yours,

Source: *The Fraud Examiners Manual* © 2006 Association of Certified Fraud Examiners.

EXHIBIT   17-5   FRAUD EXAMINATION OPINION (EVIDENCE SUPPORTS ALLEGATION)

Investigation Appendix	**Engagement Contracts/Opinion Letters**

[Date]

[[   ], Esq.
[Law Department]
[Company Name]
[Address]
[City, State, Zip Code]

RE: [Fraud Examination]

Dear Mr./Mrs. [   ]:

We have conducted a fraud examination concerning a possible misappropriation of assets of the [Company Name]. This examination was predicated upon information resulting from a routine audit of the company's books by the company's internal auditors.

Our examination was conducted in accordance with lawful fraud examination techniques, which include, but are not limited to: examination of books and records; voluntary interviews of appropriate witnesses/personnel; and other such evidence-gathering procedures as necessary under the circumstances.

During the pendency of this fraud examination, Mr. [   ] voluntarily furnished a signed statement indicating that he misappropriated $ [amount] to his personal benefit.

Based on the results of our examination and the confession of Mr. [ ], it is our opinion that his actions, if proven in a court of law, could constitute a violation of relevant criminal and/or civil fraud-related statutes.

Very truly yours,

Source: *The Fraud Examiners Manual* © 2006 Association of Certified Fraud Examiners.

There are two important lessons to be learned from these illustrative reports: the level of assurance depends both on identifying suitable criteria (e.g., a signed confession) and on the phrasing of the conclusion. For example, if in Exhibit 17–5 the auditor had concluded that fraud had taken place, such an opinion would provide only low assurance because fraud is a legal matter that must be proven in the courts. In addition, because the fraud assertion has not yet been proven in the courts, and because fraud is a matter to be proven under criminal law, the auditor might even be accused of defamation! Even if the auditor *does* have high assurance that a fraud has been perpetrated, high audit assurance does not necessarily equate to the "beyond a reasonable doubt" burden of proof required by the Criminal Code. On the other hand, if, for example, the client's company is expecting to recover only damages or is trying to obtain sufficient cause to fire the employee under civil law, then the burden of proof is considerably lower. In civil law the burden of proof is "on balance of probabilities," and an opinion, such as in Exhibit 17–5, may very well satisfy this requirement. Thus, the amount of assurance depends on the circumstances, and the wording should properly reflect the circumstances.

Since fraud is a legal term and legal conditions must be met before the term is assigned to anyone, perhaps a word for an assurance report is "irregularities," a term defined by the PA profession. An auditor can reach a conclusion about the likelihood of irregularities occurring (including but not limited to fraud) without being encumbered with legal definitions and the responsibilities inherent in using specific legal terms, such as fraud. As long as there is ambiguity between the level of assurance provided by the assurance engagement and legal assurance required by terms such as "on balance of probabilities" and "proof beyond a reasonable doubt," it is likely in the auditor's best interest to use terminology reflecting the standards of the PA profession but not having a precise legal meaning.

We hope this section has illustrated some of the complexities of expanding assurance engagements into new areas not familiar to most PAs.

REVIEW CHECKPOINTS

26 Why is prosecution of fraud perpetrators generally a good idea?

27 What are the CICA materiality guidelines for reporting errors, irregularities, and illegal acts?

28 Why must care be taken with evidence of fraudulent activity?

BRIBERY AND CORRUPTION: A NEW GLOBAL SOCIAL CONCERN

A White Paper published by the Association of Certified Fraud Examiners entitled "The Global Explosion of Corruption" identifies corruption as a major challenge in the new global, high-tech economy. A long section of this paper discusses Transparency International, a unique organization dedicated to fighting global corruption. This section of the Paper is reproduced in full here.

TRANSPARENCY INTERNATIONAL ENCOURAGES GOVERNMENTS TO FIGHT CORRUPTION

In 1993, Dr. Peter Eigen, former World Bank director, founded Transparency International (TI) in Berlin as a not-for-profit, nongovernmental organization, "to counter corruption . . . in international business transactions," according to its mission statement.

The small group, which has organized over 60 chapters throughout the world, says that it encourages governments to establish laws, policies, and anti-corruption programs. TI is funded by multilateral groups (including the World Bank), national programs, and private companies.

TI says that corruption is causing vast sums of money to be misallocated by public officials in dozens of countries. The group says that funds which were originally earmarked for new schools, hospitals, and institutions to serve the most needy are often channelled into projects of negligible social value by officials receiving kickbacks from commercial contractors.

Corruption is also the enemy of progress, TI says. Corrupt leaders cling to power, opposing efforts to open government, curbing personal freedoms, and abusing human rights, the group says. Also, the honest business person goes broke, the rules of a healthy economic system become twisted, and companies addicted to paying bribes become rotten, TI says.

The group says there are too many countries where corporations can pay bribes abroad and claim these as tax deductible expenses in their home countries. "We will do our best to get our house in order," said Ethiopian Prime Minister Meles Zenawi at an international conference a year ago, "but our Northern friends: please do not support the bribery by your exporters by giving them tax deductions for their bribes."

One of the most effective ways that TI has publicized the corruption problem is through its annual Corruption Perception Index based on the experience of multinational corporations. This index is increasingly used to develop international efforts to fight worldwide corruption and bribery.

The Transparency International Corruption Perception Index (CPI), 2008

Country rank	Selected countries	CPI score (out of 10)
1	Denmark	9.3
9	Canada	8.7
16	U.K.	7.7
18	USA	7.3
23	France	6.9
40	South Korea	5.6

Higher-risk countries (5.0 or less) in which Canadian companies are most likely to do business

55	Italy	4.8
72	China	3.6
72	Mexico	3.6
80	Brazil	3.5
85	India	3.4
109	Argentina	2.9
126	Indonesia	2.6
134	Pakistan	2.5
141	Philippines	2.3
147	Russia	2.1

Source: www.transparency.org/cpi 2008 table

"The mounting support for anti-corruption action in the international organizations is a vital requirement in raising this issue to highest political levels in governments around the globe," said Eigen. "But these initiatives only have an impact if they are followed up at the national level and if organizations like TI constantly monitor the official agencies to see their bold rhetoric is matched by meaningful action."

Electronic trading and funds transfer systems combined with offshore banking havens and new financial instruments have facilitated the laundering of criminal and illegal funds. It has been estimated that up to 25 percent of financial instruments and foreign currency trading involves some kind of illegal money laundering scheme. Cross border capital flows now amount to $1.25 trillion per day. The illegitimate amounts are so huge that they threaten world financial markets. The only way to deal with money laundering of this scale is through international efforts.

Source: Excerpt taken from "The Global Explosion of Corruption—the Misuse of Public Power for Private Profit or Political Gain," *The White Paper*, May/June 1997, a publication of the Association of Certified Fraud Examiners.

As part of an international fight against bribery, sponsored by TI and the Organization for Economic Cooperation and Development (OECD), early in 1999 Canada made it illegal to pay foreign bribes. Modelled on the U.S.'s Foreign Corrupt Practices Act, Canada's Corruption of Foreign Public Officials Act makes foreign bribes illegal and a nondeductible business expense. Thus foreign bribes now fall under CAS 250 (5136: Misstatements—Illegal Acts). This makes auditors responsible for the detection of foreign bribes that can have a material effect on the financial statements. Auditors now need to assess the risk of such material misstatements by, for example, checking to see both how much and the nature of business done in "high risk" countries in the corruption index. Other risk factors to consider include a past record of having to pay bribes and unnecessarily complex or unusual payment methods.[27]

Controls to compensate for these high inherent risks include a corporate code of conduct containing specific policies and procedures designed to avoid violating the Corruption of

[27] S. Chester and D. Selley, "Giving Kickbacks the Boot," *CA Magazine*, August 1999, pp. 20–24.

Worth a Closer Look

CONSIDER THE FOLLOWING AUDIT PROCEDURES WHEN THE COMBINED INHERENT AND CONTROL RISK IS ASSESSED AS "NOT LOW"

- Examine all relevant contracts and source documents thoroughly. Discuss them with management to assess whether they reflect the transaction's substance.
- When applicable, check documentation concerning the bidding process for major contracts in foreign countries, including the inclusion of unusually large agency fees or other amounts that do not appear to relate directly to the contract's substance.
- Review banking records for large and unusual transactions or cash transactions. Consider using analytical procedures such as data-mining techniques.
- If local auditors are involved (whether affiliates of the Canadian auditor or not), discuss the risk assessment with them and obtain their views of the likelihood of a bribe having been paid; also discuss the procedures they have carried out or might perform. Be aware, too, that the position of such auditors may be very sensitive in their local environment and that telephone and other communications may not be secure. It may be appropriate to visit the locations concerned.
- If payments are made through offshore companies or bank accounts, obtain information about the companies and financial institutions to assess their legitimacy.
- If inexplicably large payments are made to an agent, attempt to contact the agent to determine how the fees were disbursed. This will often be a fruitless exercise, but a refusal to answer on the agent's part significantly increases the likelihood that the Corruption of Foreign Public Officials Act has been breached. An agent should not be contacted without the client's permission.

Source: S. Chester and D. Selley, "Giving Kickbacks the Boot," *CA Magazine*, August 1999, Exhibit 2, p. 23. Reproduced by permission from *CA Magazine* published by the Canadian Institute of Chartered Accountants, Toronto, Canada.

Foreign Public Officials Act and effective monitoring and communication of these procedures. If combined inherent and control risks are assessed as too high, then the auditor would consider additional procedures as listed in the preceding box.

In June 2000, the PCMLTA legislation discussed in Chapter 5 became law. It was passed as a measure to combat the international problem of money laundering—the conversion of funds from criminal activities to legitimate ones. Canada was among the last of the industrialized countries to pass such legislation.

PAs are affected by these issues because, unknowingly, they may be manipulated into recycling funds through complex transactions. Moreover, the PAs' association helps legitimize racketeers' criminal activities:

> Under the new law, accountants need to be careful not to be considered accomplices under the concept of "willful blindness," which is very close to actual knowledge. This is said to occur when a person prefers to remain ignorant despite having well-founded suspicions that something is amiss. Accordingly, the refusal of the CA to investigate or ask relevant questions because he or she suspects the existence of an illegal or dishonest situation can be considered an act of complicity.[28]

The best way to avoid this risk is to be knowledgeable about the client and the client's business. The PA needs to be skeptical about unusual transactions that are inconsistent with industry standards and do not make economic sense. The PA should be especially cautious when asked to carry out transactions for third parties. In short, the same skepticism and responsibilities apply to money laundering activities as to fraud and other illegal acts involving deception.

[28] E. Lavoie and G. Leclerc, "Keeping Your Hands Clean," *CA Magazine*, October 2001, p. 36.

REVIEW CHECKPOINTS

29 Is there anything odd about these situations? (1) Auditors performed a surprise payroll distribution, and J. Jones, S. Smith, and D. Douglas were absent from work. (2) A cheque to Larson Lectric Supply was endorsed with Larson Lectric above the signature of Eloise Garfunkle. (3) Numerous cheques were issued dated January 1, May 22, July 1, September 4, October 9, and December 25, 2000.

30 What account could you audit to determine whether a company had recorded fictitious sales?

APPLICATION CASE AND ANALYSIS
DETECTING FRAUDULENT REPORTING IN ACCOUNTING ESTIMATES

Appendix 7D introduced applications of accounting risk. The investment shown there is an example of estimating a future benefit. Consider the analysis of item 8 in that instance. To review: recording zero results is an accounting risk of 0.01, while recording a $1 billion asset results in an accounting risk of 0.99. But what is the risk of fraudulent reporting? We propose to answer that question in this application case, where the focus will be determining how much of this accounting risk is intentional (i.e., fraudulent) and how much is unintentional. Being able to answer these questions is the key to successfully detecting fraud in accounting estimates. For example, virtually everyone agrees that reporting the investment from the Appendix 7D case as a $1 billion asset on the balance sheet is not fairly presenting the "asset." Many would even say it is misleading or even fraudulent reporting, and especially so if large management bonuses were based on such unrealized gains. (Accounting research has not considered this potential for manipulation in forecasts.) To clarify further, consider the question of how the payment of close to $1 billion for such an investment should be recorded. Should the debit go to an asset account? an expense account? a loss account? This is the problem of dealing with extreme values when considering forecast estimation uncertainties.

Analysis

In Appendix 7D, we can assume management recorded the asset on the financial statements at $1 billion in value well before the payoff determination date and after paying something closer to its expected value of $10 million for it. This would result in reported earnings growth of about $990 million, which might allow management to reward itself for the great investment with a bonus of $500 million. Many readers would feel that such a bonus is fraudulent. They might view it as an illustration of a "real bonus based on a fake profit" that economics Nobel Prize winner Krugman criticizes in his article at the beginning of Chapter 14. But on what basis can they argue that a fraud took place?

Risk-based reasoning (RBR) in reporting of estimates, as described in the application case for Chapter 10, would explain that the fraud is in recognizing the $1 billion payoff as an asset. If acceptable accounting risk for this investment were set at, say, 0.05, then the only asset value acceptable is zero. In other words, under RBR there is no recordable asset here. Note that asset recognition is a fundamental issue in financial reporting, because, if there is an asset increase, it affects the balance sheet and possibly the income statement, and, therefore, the amount available for distribution as dividends. Thus, proper asset (and liabilities, which can be viewed as negative assets) measurement is a key to preventing Ponzi schemes and fraudulent reporting. (The issue of whether such a payoff possibility should be disclosed is discussed in the application case for Chapter 16.)

If, on the other hand, acceptable accounting risk was set at 0.99, then recording an asset of $1 billion for this investment is acceptable (zero would also be acceptable, but the reader can imagine which acceptable estimate management would prefer). Allowing the recording of either extreme is a consequence of the high acceptable accounting risk of 0.99. This illustrates that the higher the acceptable accounting risk, the more difficult it is to detect fraud. (CAS 540 has flagged such high risk estimates as "significant estimation uncertainties.")

But many readers, upon seeing the potential consequences of allowing high accounting risks in accounting estimates, might argue that such high risk levels are unrealistic. If that is the reader's view, then he or she might want to reconsider the expected value of $10 million as well, because it has an even higher accounting risk of 1.00. Yet the expected value is widely associated with fair value accounting (e.g., *expected* future cash flows). Why is fair value accounting considered realistic in the case of $10 million, but not for $1 billion? The potential problem in using expected values for valuation, referred to by some as the "flaw of averages," is well recognized by portfolio managers.

The point of this exercise is to show that acceptable accounting risk levels can be important for detecting fraud, and they, therefore, should be used in developing benchmarks for identifying appropriate accounting estimates. Note that an acceptable accounting risk of 1.00 means *any* forecast value is acceptable for financial reporting purposes. It also means that intentional and unintentional misstatements are indistinguishable. Thus, to prevent expected values from hiding high-risk estimates (resulting in mispricing of risk problems as in the economic crisis of 2008/2009), the risk effects demonstrated via RBR, or some similar logic, should be incorporated into financial reporting.

To illustrate the effect of using a benchmark based on RBR, let us continue with this investment example and assume that the appropriate benchmark (B) for the investment is zero. If we record zero for the lottery ticket, then the accounting risk is 0.01 and, by definition, an unintentional risk. The auditor or accounting standards should define the benchmark after considering both the accounting risk consequences and what is acceptable accounting risk. If the client records $1 billion, the accounting risk of 0.99 is considered, by definition, intentional because $1 billion is not the benchmark. Thus, recording a $1 billion asset (and related gains) is considered a 0.99 risk of fraudulent reporting. In fact, recording anything materially different from the zero benchmark has a very high 1.00 risk of being fraudulent reporting. But that is the exact purpose of RBR benchmarks!

Some might argue that it is more realistic to have a benchmark allowing a range of possible future values. This is compatible with RBR benchmarks, as long as the acceptable accounting risk conditions (as determined by the auditor or accounting standard setters) are met for the range of values. To illustrate, we use the following excerpt from *CICA Handbook* AuG-41, paragraph 30:

> For example, the auditor's analysis of specific accounts receivable and recent trends in bad debt losses as a percent of sales may cause the auditor to conclude that the allowance for doubtful accounts should be between $130,000 and $160,000. If management's recorded estimate falls within that range, the auditor ordinarily would conclude that the recorded amount is *reasonable*, and no difference would be aggregated. If management's recorded estimate falls outside the auditor's range of acceptable amounts, the difference between the recorded amount and the amount at the closest end of the auditor's range would be aggregated as a misstatement. For example, if management has recorded $110,000 as the allowance, the amount by which the recorded estimate falls outside the range (i.e., $20,000) would be aggregated as a misstatement. [emphasis added]

Note that accounting risks are ignored in the above analysis. The future is treated as if it were deterministic (more specifically, AuG-41 assumes that the accounting risk is zero). This excerpt is very useful as it is the only place in the standards where an "unreasonable" estimate is made very specific (the AICPA uses this example in its standards as well). Don Cockburn identified some of the problems associated with using reasonable ranges to verify the reasonableness of estimates.[29] He suggested that in the most extreme cases the estimates be treated as a type of contingency. However, through RBR and viewing the CICA's reasonable range as a type of confidence interval but without the confidence level, accounting risks can be incorporated in the analysis.

Introducing accounting risk requires us to make assumptions about the distribution within possible forecasts for the allowance for doubtful accounts. We use the same reasonable range in the AuG-41 example, but with two additional assumptions: materiality is $15,000 and uniform distribution can represent the uncertainty within the reasonable range. Uniform distribution assumes that any value within the "range of reasonable outcomes" is equally likely to occur. The use of the uniform distribution is most consistent with the AICPA (2005: AUI 312.04) and CICA (2007: AuG-41.29) idea that a range of reasonableness is used when no estimate is better than any amount within the range, as otherwise a point estimate would be used. Thus, based on the concepts used in the guidelines and standards, the uniform distribution is the best basis to model the forecast uncertainties on. The uniform probabilities are also relatively easy to work with since they are simply proportional to the length of the reasonable range, and thus no formulas or tables are needed as the following calculations will illustrate.

First, let us assume the logic of AuG-41 and ignore the accounting risk. With a materiality of $15,000, the client's proposed reporting of $110,000 is clearly unacceptable as it results in a misstatement of $20,000. Under AuG-41, the auditor would insist on an adjustment to at least $115,000. If the auditor could convince the client to adjust to $130,000 there would be no misstatement.

If we were to recognize the accounting risk through the uniform distribution (this is a situation where no one can predict the allowance account with certainty), recording $130,000 gives us an accounting risk of 0.5! This is because the reasonable range of $130,000–$160,000 is two materialities wide, so recording at the bottom edge of the range means that half of the range is more than a material amount away. Specifically, all the equally likely values between $145,000 and $160,000 are materially different from $130,000. If the auditor in this case, as in any other, finds that the accounting risk is unacceptable, he or she needs to find a range with acceptable risk.

If the auditor felt that acceptable risk for forecast uncertainties is about 0.17 or 1/6, then it can be shown that the appropriate benchmark to use, along with the above assumptions, is a range of $140–$150,000. This range is 1/3 the size of the original one, and is smaller than materiality because the auditor is willing to tolerate less accounting risk in an estimate. This illustrates that RBR can address Cockburn's concerns as outlined above. Such a benchmark also allows the auditor to better distinguish between fraudulent forecasts and legitimate ones, and to measure the risks of fraud with such forecasts. For a more complete discussion of the use of reasoning and risk models in detecting fraudulent reporting, see the Smieliauskas work discussed earlier.[30]

On a historical note, the reasoning used here is fully consistent with the classical accounting measurement theory that current conceptual frameworks of financial reporting are based on. For example, the very influential article by Yuji Ijiri and Robert Jaedicke entitled "Reliability and Objectivity of Accounting Measurements" defines the basic concepts of relevance and reliability in financial reporting.[31] Our

[29] D. Cockburn, "At home on the range," *CA Magazine.* CICA. May 1992, pp. 38–39)

[30] W. Smieliauskas, "A framework for identifying (and avoiding) fraudulent financial reporting," *Accounting Perspectives* 7(3), 2008, pp. 189–226.

[31] Y. Ijiri and R. Jaedicke, "Reliability and Objectivity of Accounting Measurements," *The Accounting Review*, July 1966, pp. 474–483.

discussion of the accounting risk concept captures the inherent lack of reliability. Relevance within RBR considers the truth about the facts and uses acceptable forecasts in accounting estimates, as demonstrated by the benchmark concept. Ijiri and Jaedicke also deal with the concept of relevance. Perhaps most importantly for this chapter, Ijiri and Jaedicke's consideration of bias is dealt with in our discussion of the risk of fraudulent reporting when an auditee insists on recording an estimate outside the auditor determined benchmark. The logic presented here is similar to that in the AuG-41 excerpt given above, except that, when a client refuses to adjust to what the auditor considers appropriate in the circumstances, and as is contained in the benchmark, the auditor treats it as an intentional misstatement. This is consistent with SEC guidance concerning fraud identification.

This RBR approach to estimates is new for auditors. We have found it useful in our classes to offer practice using the uniform distribution reasonable ranges identified by auditors. Many feel such practice exercises provide a useful supplement to traditional risk assessment. The exercises below are all based on the AuG-41 example given above.

Further Illustrations of Accounting Risk Calculations

The following examples have been developed to give you a better understanding of how RBR can be used to construct "reasonable ranges" that address both the concerns expressed in Cockburn's 1992 discussion and the use of benchmarks to detect fraudulent forecasts within the estimates in financial reporting. With the AuG-41 example as our base, we progress from the simple to the more complex issues.

Assumptions from AuG-41: the auditor identifies a reasonable range of $130,000–$160,000. Only numbers outside the range are considered to be misstatements. AuG-41 ignores accounting risk (uncertainty due to forecast errors) and treats any misstatements as factual. Using RBR reasoning, the auditor assesses materiality of $15,000. The use of RBR reasoning means the auditor must make an additional assumption about the forecast error distribution affecting the reasonable range. The definition of reasonable range in AuG-41 indicates that all future realizations must be within that range and all values in this range are equally likely. Thus, it is logical to assume uniform distribution across the $130,000–$140,000 range for future realized values, and also to use it as a basis for calculating accounting risk (AccR) for any recorded amount.

With the above assumptions made explicit, we can now calculate the various AccRs discussed in this chapter. The exercises below are arranged in order of increasing difficulty, and the answers to all of them are given. An inability to understand these exercises indicates an incomplete grasp of the basic concepts of RBR and reasonable ranges, and of detecting fraudulent financial forecasts in today's economic environment.

Exercise 1: What is AccR for the client recorded amount of $110,000? What is the misstatement of this recorded amount under AuG-41? Note that the misstatement at $110,000 is material under AuG-41 definition of misstatement.

Exercise 2: What is AccR for a recorded amount of $125,000? What is the misstatement of this recorded amount under AuG-41? Note that the misstatement at $125,000 is not material under AuG-41 definition of misstatement.

Exercise 3: What is AccR for a recorded amount of $130,000? What is the misstatement of this recorded amount under AuG-41?

Exercise 4: What is AccR for a recorded amount of $140,000? What is the misstatement of this recorded amount under AuG-41?

Exercise 5: What is AccR for a recorded amount of $145,000? What is the misstatement of this recorded amount under AuG-41?

Exercise 6: Assume that the auditor decides that the AccR associated with the AuG-41 reasonable range is too high and judges that acceptable risk for AccR in this situation should be 1/6. Calculate the benchmark range that results in acceptable risk. Once a benchmark is introduced, we can distinguish between $AccR_U$ and $AccR_I$ as discussed below. These two risks are not additive but must be reconciled another way as indicated in Smieliauskas (2008). This reconciliation is consistent with the Ijiri/Jaedicke accounting measurement concepts.

Exercise 7: Assume the range identified in Exercise 6 is the benchmark value(s) *(B)* for distinguishing between intentional and unintentional misstatements. What is $AccR_U$ (risk associated with the benchmark—this is defined as the maximum accounting risk at the benchmark) and $AccR_I$ (this is the risk of intentional forecast error; i.e., the risk of a fraudulent forecast), when the client records $140,000?

Exercise 8: Same requirements as in exercise 7, but the client records $135,000.

Exercise 9: Same requirements as in exercise 7, but the client records $130,000.

Exercise 10: Same requirements as in exercise 7, but the client records $110,000.

Exercise 11: Same requirements as in exercise 7, but the client records $155,000.

Exercise 12: Assume that the auditor decides that the AccR associated with the AuG-41 reasonable range is too high and judges that acceptable risk for AccR in this situation should be zero. Calculate the new reasonable range that results in acceptable risk.

Exercise 13: Assume the range identified in Exercise 12 is the benchmark value(s) *(B)* for distinguishing between intentional and unintentional misstatements. What is $AccR_U$ and $AccR_I$, assuming the client records $140,000?

Exercise 14: Same requirements as in Exercise 13, but the client records $130,000.

Exercise 15: Same requirements as in Exercise 13, but the client records $110,000.

We hope you found that these exercises helped to clarify the concepts. Now you should better understand the effects of acceptable risk in defining reasonable ranges, and the effects of more precise benchmarks in identifying fraudulent financial reporting.

Solutions

Exercise 1: AccR = $30,000/$30,000 = 1.0. AuG-41 misstatement = $20,000 which is greater than materiality (of $15,000) and therefore unacceptable. Note: If the client would refuse to make the correcting entry, then this $20,000 misstatement could be considered intentional and thus fraudulent by section 5135.

Exercise 2: AccR = $20,000/$30,000 = 2/3. AuG-41 misstatement = $5,000 which is immaterial.

Exercise 3: AccR = $15,000/$30,000 = ½. AuG-41 misstatement is zero.

Exercise 4: AccR = $5,000/$30,000 = 1/6. AuG-41 misstatement is zero.

Exercise 5: AccR = $0/$30,000 = 0. AuG-41 misstatement is zero.

Exercise 6: Reasonable range = $140,000–$150,000. Note that this new range is 1/3 the size of the original, and is smaller than materiality. That is because the auditor is willing to tolerate less risk. This illustrates that RBR can help address Cockburn's 1992 article concerns.

Exercise 7: $AccR_U$ = 1/6, $AccR_I$ = 0. Note: $AccR_U$ is *defined* as the maximum in the benchmark. This is consistent with the way we treat all acceptable risks in auditing, i.e., *maximum* acceptable risk.

Exercise 8: $AccR_U$ = 1/6, $AccR_I$ = 2/6.

Exercise 9: $AccR_U$ = 1/6, $AccR_I$ = 3/6.

Exercise 10: $AccR_U$ = 1/6, $AccR_I$ = 6/6.

Exercise 11: $AccR_U$ = 1/6, $AccR_I$ = 2/6.

Exercise 12: The new reasonable range is now the single point estimate of 145. The acceptable accounting risk is zero, and recording a value other than $145,000 is considered a misstatement.

Exercise 13: = $AccR_U$ = 0, $AccR_I$ = 5k/30k = 1/6.

Exercise 14: = $AccR_U$ = 0, $AccR_I$ = 15k/30k = 3/6.

Exercise 15: = $AccR_U$ = 0, $AccR_I$ = 30k/30k = 6/6.

These calculations illustrate that introducing an appropriate benchmark makes it clearer when fraud is taking place. The challenge is in maintaining the relevance of financial statement auditing in today's more volatile and complex reporting environment. Accounting standard setters' primary role is to establish as a basic principle that reasonable ranges for accounting estimates be based on accounting risk, as demonstrated here, and not just on materiality. This proposal is consistent with CAS/IFA 540.

SUMMARY

Under the new CASs, Canadian auditors need to take more responsibility for detecting fraud. This means being more aware of fraud. Fraud awareness auditing starts with knowledge of the types of errors, irregularities, illegal acts, and frauds that can be perpetrated. External, internal, and governmental auditors all have standards for care, attention, planning, detection, and reporting of some kinds of errors, irregularities, and illegal acts. Fraud examiners, on the other hand, have little in the way of standard programs or materiality guidelines to limit their attention for fraud possibilities. They float on a sea of observations of exceptions and oddities that may only hint at the fraud beneath the surface.

Individuals may contemplate fraud when they have a motive, usually a financial need, for stealing money or property. When there is a combination of motive with opportunity and a lapse of integrity, there is a high probability of fraud or theft. Opportunities arise when an organization's management is lax in setting an example of good behaviour and in maintaining a supportive control environment. The fear of getting caught by control procedures deters some fraudsters. Also, attentive management of personnel can ease the pressures people feel and, thus, reduce the incidence of fraud.

Auditors need to know the red flags, the signs and indications that accompany many fraudulent activities. When studying a business operation, auditors need to "think like a crook" to uncover possiblities for theft, as this can help in the planning of procedures designed to determine whether fraud has occurred. Often, imaginative extended procedures will unearth evidence of fraudulent activity. However, technical and personal care must always be exercised because accusations of fraud are always taken very seriously. For this reason, after preliminary findings indicate possible fraud, auditors should enlist the cooperation of management and assist fraud examination professionals in bringing an investigation to a conclusion.

For information on the Association of Certified Fraud Examiners (CFEs), visit their website at www.acfe.com. For information on the CA-IFA specialist designation see their website at www.rotman.cfenet.com.

MULTIPLE-CHOICE QUESTIONS FOR PRACTICE AND REVIEW

MC 1 Which of the following is characteristic of management fraud?
a. Falsification of documents in order to steal money from an employer
b. Victimization of investors through the use of materially misleading financial statements
c. Illegal acts committed by management to evade laws and regulations
d. Conversion of stolen inventory to cash deposited in a falsified bank account

MC 2 Canadian auditing standards do not require auditors of financial statements to do which of the following?
a. Understand the nature of errors and irregularities.
b. Assess the risk of occurrence of errors and irregularities.
c. Design audits to provide reasonable assurance of detecting errors and irregularities.
d. Report all finding of errors and irregularities to police authorities.

MC 3 Which of the following types of auditors have the highest expectations in their audit standards regarding the detection of fraud?
a. External auditors of financial statements
b. Government auditors of financial statements, programs, activities, and functions
c. Internal auditors employed by companies
d. Management advisory consultants engaged to design a company's information system

MC 4 Which two of the following characterize the work of fraud examiners and are different from the typical attitude of external auditors?
a. Analysis of control weaknesses for opportunities to commit fraud
b. Analysis of control strengths as a basis for planning other audit procedures
c. Determination of a materiality amount that represents a significant misstatement of the current-year financial statements
d. Thinking of materiality as a cumulative amount—that is, growing over a number of years

MC 5 When auditing with "fraud awareness," auditors should especially notice and follow up employee activities under which of these conditions?
a. The company always estimates the inventory but never takes a complete physical count.
b. The petty cash box is always locked in the desk of the custodian.
c. Management has published a company code of ethics and sends frequent communication newsletters about it.
d. The board of directors reviews and approves all investment transactions.

MC 6 Which is the best way to enact a broad fraud-prevention program?
a. Install airtight control systems of checks and supervision.
b. Name an "ethics officer" who is responsible for receiving and acting upon fraud tips.
c. Place dedicated "hot line" telephones on walls around the workplace with direct communication to the company ethics officer.
d. Practise management "of the people and for the people" to help them share personal and professional problems.

MC 7 Which of the following gives the least indication of fraudulent activity?
a. Numerous cash refunds have been made to different people at the same post office box address.
b. Internal auditor cannot locate several credit memos to support reductions of customers' balances.
c. Bank reconciliation has no outstanding cheques or deposits older than 15 days.
d. Three people were absent the day the auditors handed out the paycheques and have not picked them up four weeks later.

MC 8 Which of the following combinations is a good means of hiding employee fraud but a poor means of carrying out management (financial reporting) fraud?
a. Overstating sales revenue and overstating customer accounts receivable balances
b. Overstating sales revenue and overstating bad debt expense
c. Understating interest expense and understating accrued interest payable
d. Omit the disclosure information about related party sales to the president's relatives at below-market prices

MC 9 Which of these arrangements of duties could most likely lead to an embezzlement or theft?
a. Inventory warehouse manager has responsibility for making the physical inventory observation and reconciling discrepancies to the perpetual inventory records.
b. Cashier prepared the bank deposit, endorsed the cheques with a company stamp, and took the cash and cheques to the bank for deposit (no other bookkeeping duties).
c. Accounts receivable clerk received a list of payments received by the cashier so that he could make entries in the customers' accounts receivable subsidiary accounts.
d. Financial vice-president received cheques made out to suppliers and the supporting invoices, signed the cheques, and put them in the mail to the payees.

MC 10 If sales and income were overstated by recording a false credit sale at the end of the year, in which account could you find the false "dangling debit?"
a. Inventory
b. Cost of goods sold

c. Bad debt expense
d. Accounts receivable

MC 11 Which of these is an invalid social insurance number?
a. 462 003 335
b. 473 09 7787
c. 506 98 5529
d. 700 051 135

MC 12 Records from which of the following sources could be used to find the owner of an office building?
a. Ministry of Industry and Trade export/import licence files
b. Transport Canada records
c. City and county tax assessor-collector files
d. Securities commission filings

MC 13 Where has experience shown that most accounting errors requiring adjustment can be found?
a. Systematic processing of large volumes of day-to-day ordinary transactions
b. Payroll fraudsters' mistakes in using unissued social insurance numbers
c. Petty cash embezzlements
d. Nonroutine, nonsystematic journal entries

MC 14 Which of these is known as the financial analysis that expresses balance sheet accounts as percentages of total assets?
a. Horizontal analysis
b. Vertical analysis
c. Net worth analysis
d. Expenditure analysis

EXERCISES AND PROBLEMS

EP 1
LO.1
Give Examples of Errors, Irregularities, and Frauds. This is an exercise concerning financial reporting misstatements, not employee theft. Give an example of an error, irregularity, or fraud that would misstate financial statements to affect the accounts as follows, taken one case at a time. (Note: "overstate" means the account has a higher value than would be appropriate under GAAP, and "understate" means it has a lower value.)
a. Overstate an asset, state another asset.
b. Overstate an asset, overstate shareholder equity.
c. Overstate an asset, overstate revenue.
d. Overstate an asset, understate an expense.
e. Overstate a liability, overstate an expense.
f. Understate an asset, overstate an expense.
g. Understate a liability, understate an expense.

EP 2
LO.1
Overall Analysis of Accounting Estimates. Oak Industries, a manufacturer of radio and cable TV equipment and an operator of subscription TV systems, had a multitude of problems. Subscription services in a market area, for which $12 million cost had been deferred, were being terminated, and the customers were not paying on time ($4 million receivables in doubt). The chances are 50–50 that the business will survive another two years.

An electronic part turned out to have defects that needed correction. Warranty expenses are estimated to range from $2 million to $6 million. The inventory of the part ($10 million) is obsolete, but $1 million can be recovered as salvage or the parts in inventory can be rebuilt at a cost of $2 million (selling price of the inventory on hand would then be $8 million, with 20 percent of selling price required to market and ship the products, and the normal profit expected is 5 percent of the selling price). If the inventory were scrapped, the company would manufacture a replacement inventory at a cost of $6 million, excluding marketing and shipping costs and normal profit.

The company has defaulted on completion of a military contract, and the government is claiming a $2 million refund. Company lawyers think the dispute might be settled for as little as $1 million.

The auditors had previously determined that an overstatement of income before taxes of $7 million would be material to the financial statements. These items were the only ones left for audit decisions about possible adjustment. Management has presented the analysis below for the determination of loss recognition:

Provide for expected warranty expense	2,000,000
Lower of cost or market inventory write-down	2,000,000
Loss on government contract refund	—
Total write-offs and losses	$11,000,000

Required:
Prepare your own analysis of the amount of adjustment to the financial statements. Assume that none of these estimates have been recorded yet, and give the adjusting entry you would recommend. Give any supplementary explanations you believe necessary to support your recommendation.

EP 3
LO.7
Select Effective Extended Procedures. Below are some "suspicions." You have been requested to select some effective extended procedures designed to confirm or deny the suspicions.

Required:
Write out the procedure you would suggest for each case so that another person would know what to do.
a. The custodian of the petty cash fund may be removing cash on Friday afternoon to pay for his weekend activities.
b. A manager has noticed that eight new vendors have been added to the purchasing department approved list since the assistant purchasing agent was promoted to chief agent three weeks ago. She suspects that all or some of them may be phony companies set up by the new chief purchasing agent.

c. The payroll supervisor may be stealing unclaimed paycheques of people who quit work and don't pick up the last cheque.

d. Although no customers have complained, cash collections on accounts receivable are down, and the counter clerks may have stolen customers' payments.

e. The cashier may have "borrowed" money, covering it by holding each day's deposit until there is enough cash from the daily collection to make up the shortage, before sending the deposit to the bank.

EP 4
LO.6
Horizontal and Vertical Analysis. Horizontal analysis refers to changes in financial statement numbers and ratios across two or more years. Vertical analysis refers to financial statement amounts expressed each year as proportions of a base, such as sales for the income statement accounts, and total assets for the balance sheet accounts. Exhibit EP 5–1 contains the Retail Company's prior year (audited) and current year (unaudited) financial statements, along with amounts and percentages of change from year to year (horizontal analysis) and common-size percentages (vertical analysis). Exhibit EP 5–2 contains

selected financial ratios based on these financial statements. Analysis of these data may enable auditors to discern relationships that raise questions about misleading financial statements.

Required:
Study the data in Exhibits EP 5–1 and EP 5–2. Write a memo identifying and explaining potential problem areas where misstatements in the current year financial statements might exist. Additional information about Retail Company is as follows:

• The new bank loan, obtained on July 1 of the current year, requires maintenance of a 2:1 current ratio.
• Principal of $100,000 plus interest on the 10 percent long-term note obtained several years ago in the original amount of $800,000 is due each January 1.
• The company has never paid dividends on its common shares and has no plans for a dividend.

EP 5
LO.5
Expenditure Analysis. Expenditure analysis is used when fraud has been discovered or strongly suspected, and the information to calculate a suspect's income and

EXHIBIT EP 5–1   RETAIL COMPANY

	Prior Year Audited		Current Year		Change	
	Balance	Common Size	Balance	Common Size	Amount	Percent
Assets:						
Cash	$ 600,000	14.78%	$ 484,000	9.69%	(116,000)	–19.33%
Accounts receivable	500,000	12.32	400,000	8.01	(100,000)	–20.00
Allowance doubt accts.	(40,000)	–0.99	(30,000)	–0.60	10,000	–25.00
Inventory	1,500,000	36.95	1,940,000	38.85	440,000	29.33
Total current assets	$2,560,000	63.05	2,794,000	55.95	234,000	9.14
Capital assets	3,000,000	73.89	4,000,000	80.10	1,000,000	33.33
Accum. depreciation	(1,500,000)	–36.95	(1,800,000)	–36.04	(300,000)	20.00
Total assets	$4,060,000	100.00%	$4,994,000	100.00%	934,000	23.00%
Liabilities and equity:						
Accounts payable	$ 450,000	11.08%	$ 600,000	12.01%	150,000	33.33%
Bank loans, 11%	0	0.00	750,000	15.02	750,000	NA
Accrued interest	50,000	1.23	40,000	0.80	(10,000)	–20.00
Accurals and other	60,000	1.48	10,000	0.20	(50,000)	–83.33
Total current liab.	560,000	13.79	1,400,000	28.03	840,000	150.00
Long-term debt, 10%	500,000	12.32	400,000	8.01	(100,000)	–20.00
Total liabilities	1,060,000	26.11	1,800,000	36.04	740,000	69.81
Share capital	2,000,000	49.26	2,000,000	40.05	0	0
Retained earnings	1,000,000	24.63	1,194,000	23.91	194,000	19.40
Total liabilities and equity	$4,060,000	100.00%	$4,994,000	100.00%	934,000	23.00%
Statement of operations:						
Sales (net)	$9,000,000	100.00%	$8,100,000	100.00%	(900,000)	–10.00%
Cost of goods sold	6,296,000	69.96	5,265,000	65.00	(1,031,000)	–16.38
Gross margin	2,704,000	30.04	2,835,000	35.00	131,000	4.84
General expense	2,044,000	22.71	2,005,000	24.75	(39,000)	–1.91
Amortization	300,000	3.33	300,000	3.70	0	0
Operating income	360,000	4.00	530,000	6.54	170,000	47.22
Interest expense	50,000	0.56	40,000	0.49	(10,000)	–20.00
Income taxes (40%)	124,000	1.38	196,000	2.42	72,000	58.06
Net income	$ 186,000	2.07%	$ 294,000	3.63%	108,000	58.06%

NA means not applicable.

EXHIBIT EP 5-2   RETAIL COMPANY

	Prior Year	Current Year	Percent Change
Balance sheet ratios:			
Current ratio	4.57	2.0	−56.34%
Days' sales in receivables	18.40	16.44	−10.63
Doubtful accounts ratio	0.08	0.075	−6.25
Days' sales in inventory	85.77	132.65	54.66
Debt/equity ratio	0.35	0.56	40.89
Operations ratios:			
Receivables turnover	19.57	21.89	11.89
Inventory turnover	4.20	2.71	−35.34
Cost of goods sold/sales	69.96%	65.00%	−7.08
Gross margin %	30.04%	35.00%	16.49
Return on equity	6.61%	9.80%	48.26

expenditures can be obtained (e.g., asset and liability records, bank accounts). Expenditure analysis consists of establishing the suspect's known expenditures for all purposes for the relevant period, subtracting all known sources of funds (e.g., wages, gifts, inheritances, bank balances, and the like), and calling the difference the expenditures financed by unknown sources of income.

FORENSIC ACCOUNTING
CONSULTING ENGAGEMENT 1

You have been hired by the law firm of Gleckel and Morris. The lawyers have been retained by Blade Manufacturing Company in a case involving a suspected kickback by a purchasing employee, E. J. Cunningham.

Cunningham is suspected of taking kickbacks from Mason Varner, a salesman for Tanco Metals. He has denied the charges, but Lanier Gleckel, the lawyer in charge of the case, is convinced the kickbacks have occurred.

Gleckel filed a civil action and subpoenaed Cunningham's books and records, including his last year's bank statements. The beginning bank balance January 1 was $3,463, and the ending bank balance December 31 was $2,050. Over the intervening 12 months, Cunningham's gross salary was $3,600 per month, with a net of $2,950. His wife doesn't work at a paying job. His house payments were $1,377 per month. In addition, he paid $2,361 per month on a new Mercedes 500 SEL and paid a total of $9,444 last year toward a new Nissan Maxima (including $5,000 down payment). He also purchased new state-of-the-art audio and video equipment for $18,763, with no down payment, and total payments on the equipment last year of $5,532. A reasonable estimate of his household expenses during the period is $900 per month ($400 for food, $200 for utilities, and $300 for other items).

Required:

Using expenditure analysis, calculate the amount of income, if any, from "unknown sources."

EP 6   **Net Worth Analysis.** Net worth analysis is used when
LO.5   fraud has been discovered or strongly suspected, and the information to calculate a suspect's net worth can be

obtained (e.g., asset and liability records, bank accounts). The procedure is to calculate the person's change in net worth (excluding changes in market values of assets), and to identify the known sources of funds to finance the changes. Any difference between the change in net worth and the known sources of funds is called "funds from unknown sources," which may be ill-gotten gains.

FORENSIC ACCOUNTING
CONSULTING ENGAGEMENT 2

C. Nero has worked for Bonne Consulting Group (BCG) as the executive secretary for administration for nearly 10 years. His dedication has earned him a reputation as an outstanding employee and has resulted in increasing responsibilities. C. Nero is a suspect in fraud.

This is the hindsight story. During Nero's first five years of employment, BCG subcontracted all of its feasibility and marketing studies through Jackson & Company. This relationship was terminated because Jackson & Company merged with a larger, more expensive consulting group. At the time of termination, Nero and his supervisor were forced to select a new firm to conduct BCG's market research. However, Nero never informed the accounting department that the Jackson & Company account had been closed.

Since his supervisor allowed Nero to sign the payment voucher for services rendered, Nero was able to continue to process cheques made payable to Jackson's account. Nero was trusted to be the only signature authorizing payments less than $10,000. The accounting department continued to write the cheques and Nero would take responsibility for delivering them. Nero opened a bank account in a nearby city under the name of Jackson & Company, where he would make the deposit.

Required:

C. Nero's financial records (see Exhibit EP 6–1) have been obtained by subpoena. You have been hired to estimate the amount of loss by estimating Nero's "funds from unknown sources" that financed his comfortable lifestyle. Below is a summary of the data obtained from Nero's records.

EXHIBIT EP 6-1   NERO'S RECORDS

	Year One	Year Two	Year Three
Assets:			
Residence	$100,000	$100,000	$100,000
Shares and bonds	30,000	30,000	42,000
Automobiles	20,000	20,000	40,000
Certificate of deposit	50,000	50,000	50,000
Cash	6,000	12,000	14,000
Liabilities:			
Mortgage balance	90,000	50,000	—
Auto loan	10,000	—	—
Income:			
Salary		34,000	36,000
Other		6,000	6,000
Expenses:			
Scheduled mortgage payments		6,000	6,000
Auto loan payments		4,800	—
Other living expenses		20,000	22,000
Hint:			
Set up a working paper like this:			
	End Year 1	End Year 2	End Year 3

Assets (list)
Liabilities (list)
Net worth (difference)
Change in net worth
Add total expenses
= Change plus expenses
Subtract known income
= Funds from unknown sources

DISCUSSION CASES

DC 1   Famous Fraud Case Analysis: Enron. Given the successful prosecution of CEOs in Worldcom, Tyco, and Adelphia through 2006, do a Web search on one of these cases and answer the following:

a. How was the fraud detected?

b. How was the fraud perpetrated? Was it a financial statement fraud?

c. What was the weakness in internal control or corporate governance that allowed the fraud to occur?

d. Should a financial statement audit have detected this fraud? Discuss.

e. Would an internal control audit have detected this fraud? Discuss.

DC 2:   Critical Thinking and Fraudulent Reporting: What is a fraudulent forecast in an accounting estimate? Appendix 7D and Chapter 14 introduced you to the concept of accounting risk and distinguished it from other risks relevant to fraudulent reporting. These different risks introduce the possibility that forecasts and estimates made by management may be fraudulent. But how to distinguish a fraudulent forecast from all others, including those associated with FOFI as discussed in Chapter 16? In other words, what is the acceptable accounting risk for FOFI, and how does that compare with acceptable accounting risk for comparable GAAP estimates? Standards are vague on how much risk is acceptable in estimation uncertainty for the majority of accounts in the financial statements. The complexity is increased when fraud risk is incorporated in estimation uncertainty. For example, in the situation described in Appendix 7D, assume management insisted on recording $1 billion. How much of the accounting risk would be due to fraud? Would or should your answer differ if management wanted to record the $1 billion in an audited forecast set of financial statements? Should fairness of presentation be influenced by the level of accounting risk? Discuss these issues in class after reading the latest version of the FASB/IASB conceptual framework for financial reporting

KEY TERMS

accountability relationship a relationship in which at least one of the parties needs to be able to justify its actions or claims to another party in the relationship *(Chapter 1)*

accounting the process of recording, classifying, and summarizing into financial statements a company's transactions that create assets, liabilities, equities, revenues, and expenses *(Chapter 1)*

accounting deficiency reservations a review of audit file documentation to check if audit standards were adhered to in a situation where the auditor failed to detect an accounting deficiency in audited financial statements *(Chapter 3)*

Accounting Standards Oversight Council (AcSOC) *(Chapter 4)*

accounts receivable lapping a manipulation of the accounts receivable entries to hide a theft or fraud *(Chapter 11)*

accounts receivable subsidiary ledger a detailed listing of outstanding accounts receivable balances by individual customer that adds up to the total balance in the general ledger accounts receivable "control" account; reconciliation of the subsidiary ledger and the control account is an important control procedure and a key audit test *(Chapter 11)*

adverse opinion states that financial statements are not in accordance with GAAP *(Chapter 2)*

aged A/R trial balance a list of all outstanding accounts receivable balances organized by how long they have been outstanding; used to manage collection and assess the accounting requirement to provide an allowance for possible uncollectible accounts *(Chapter 11)*

alpha risk the risk that the auditor will incorrectly reject an account balance that is not materially misstated; a type of sampling risk *(Chapter 10)*

American Institute of Certified Public Accountants (AICPA) *(Chapter 1)*

analysis techniques for identifying unusual changes and relations in financial statement data that alert the audit team to problems (errors, fraud) that may exist in the account balances and disclosures to guide the design of further audit work; involves developing expectations and designing procedures to assess whether the data conform to expectations *(Chapter 8)*

analytical procedures specific methods and tests used to perform analysis on client account balances, such as: comparison of current-year account balances to balances for one or more comparable periods; comparison of the actual balances to budgets; evaluation of the relationships between different current-year account balances for conformity with predictable patterns and expectations; comparison of current-year account balances and financial relationships (e.g., ratios) with similar information for the client's industry; study of the relationships of current-year account balances with relevant nonfinancial information *(Chapter 6)*

analytical procedures risk (APR) *(Chapter 10)*

anchoring preconceived notions about control risk that auditors carry over when they perform an audit on a client year after year, a potential pitfall if conditions have changed *(Chapter 7)*

another appropriate disclosed basis of accounting (AADBA) *(Chapter 16)*

application control procedures individual computerized accounting applications, for example, programmed validation controls for verifying customers' account numbers and credit limits *(Chapter 7)*

articles of incorporation a corporation's legal documents that set out its purpose, classes of shares that can be issued, etc. *(Chapter 14)*

assertions claims that management makes on financial statements *(Chapter 6)*

associated with financial statements any involvement of a public accountant with financial statements issued by a client *(Chapter 3)*

association a term used within the profession to indicate a public accountant's involvement with an enterprise or with information issued by that enterprise *(Chapter 3)*

assurance verifying the truthfulness of an assertion by an accountable party with independent corroborating evidence *(Chapter 1)*

assurance engagement an engagement in which the auditor adds either reasonable (high) or moderate (negative) levels of assurance *(Chapter 1)*

attestation engagement when a public accountant is hired to perform procedures and issue a report resulting from those procedures that affirms the validity of an assertion *(Chapters 1, 2, and 16)*

attribute sampling in control testing this is the type of audit sampling in which auditors look for the presence or absence of a control condition *(Chapter 10)*

audit committees monitor management's financial reporting responsibilities, including meeting with the external auditors and dealing with various audit and accounting matters that may arise *(Chapter 1)*

Audit Guidelines (AuGs) the part of the *CICA Handbook* that provides procedural guidance on implementing GAAS *(Chapter 2)*

audit of internal control over financial reportings the engagement that results in an audit report on the effectiveness of a client's internal control over financial reporting *(Chapter 16)*

audit program a list of the audit procedures auditors need to perform to produce sufficient, competent evidence as the basis for good audit decisions *(Chapters 2 and 6)*

audit risk (account level) the probability that an auditor will fail to find a material misstatement that exists in an account balance *(Chapters 1, 2, and 7)*

audit risk (global) (AR) the probability that an auditor will give an inappropriate opinion on financial statements *(Chapter 5)*

audit sampling testing less than 100 percent of a population (items in an account balance or class of transactions) to form a conclusion about some characteristic of the balance or class of transactions *(Chapter 10)*

audit societies the term coined by Michael Power for societies in which there is extensive examination by auditors of economic and other politically important activities *(Chapter 1)*

audit trail the series of accounting operations in a client's system that goes from transaction analyses to entry to output reports; in auditing work the trail starts with the source documents and proceeds through the information system processes to the final financial statement amounts *(Chapter 7)*

auditee the entity (company, proprietorship, organization, department, etc.) being audited; usually it refers to the entity whose financial statements are being audited *(Chapter 1)*

auditing the verification of information by someone other than the one providing it *(Chapter 1)*

Auditing and Assurance Standards Oversight Council (AASOC) *(Chapter 4)*

auditing standards the subset of assurance standards dealing with "high" or "positive" levels of assurance in assurance engagements *(Chapters 1 and 2)*

authorization ensuring that transactions are approved before they are recorded *(Chapter 9)*

balance audit program lists the substantive procedures for gathering direct evidence on the assertions (i.e., existence, completeness, valuation, ownership, presentation) about dollar amounts in the account balances and related discourses *(Chapter 8)*

balance sheet approach to auditing a view of the audit that takes into account the articulation of the financial statements in that the changes in each balance sheet account are made up of changes in the income statement and cash flow statement; using this articulation as the basis for identifying the transactions that need to be verified to prove the ending balance is correct *(Prelude to Part III)*

balanced scorecard a tool used to analyze business performance that measures resources (learning and growth), processes (internal business), and markets (customer relations), relating all three to financial performance; an approach that the auditor can use for benchmarking the client firm with others in its industry *(Chapter 7)*

beta risk the risk that the auditor will incorrectly accept an account balance that is materially misstated; it can result in audit failure and so is considered to be a more serious problem for the audit than incorrect rejection; a type of sampling risk *(Chapter 10)*

block sampling the practice of choosing segments of contiguous transactions; undesirable because it is hard to get a representative sample of blocks efficiently *(Chapter 10)*

bridge working papers audit documentation that connects (bridges) the control evaluation to subsequent audit procedures by summarizing the major control strengths and weaknesses, listing test of controls procedures for auditing the control strengths, and suggesting substantive audit procedures related to the weaknesses *(Chapter 9)*

business risk the chance a company takes when it engages in any economic activity, such as taxes increasing or customers buying from competitors *(Chapter 1)*

business risk–based approach the requirement for the auditor to understand the client's business risks and strategy in order to assess the risks of material misstatement in the financial statements and design appropriate audit procedures in response to those risks *(Chapter 7)*

business to business (B2B) when commercial transactions are conducted over the Internet between business entities, such as a manufacturer and its suppliers *(Chapter 9)*

business to consumer (B2C) when commercial transactions are conducted over the Internet between business entities and their end customers, such as online book sales *(Chapter 9)*

business to employee (B2E) when administrative transactions are conducted over the Internet between a business and its employees, such as payroll and benefits *(Chapter 9)*

business to government (B2G) when transactions between businesses and government are conducted over the Internet, such as electronic submission of corporate tax returns and regulatory filings *(Chapter 9)*

Canadian Audit Standard (CAS) *(Chapter 1)*

Canadian Coalition Against Insurance Fraud (CCAIF) *(Chapter 17)*

Canadian Coalition for Good Governance (CCGG) group of the largest pension and mutual funds whose purpose is to monitor executives and boards of directors to comply with good corporate governance and financial reporting practices *(Chapter 1)*

Canadian Institute of Chartered Accountants (CICA) *(Chapter 1 and throughout text)*

Canadian Public Accountability Board (CPAB) board that oversees auditors of public companies in Canada, created by the CICA *(Chapter 1)*

Canadian Securities Administrators (CSA) *(Chapter 5)*

Certified Internal Auditors (CIA) persons who have met the Institute of Internal Auditors' criteria for professional CIA credentials *(Chapter 17)*

cheque kiting the practice of building up apparent balances in one or more bank accounts based on uncollected (float) cheques drawn against similar accounts in other banks *(Chapter 11)*

class of transactions groups of accounting entries that have the same source or purpose, for example credit sales, cash sales, and cash receipts are three different classes *(Chapter 10)*

classical attribute sampling when a sampling unit is the same thing as an invoice or population unit *(Chapter 10)*

clean audit an audit of a client where the accounting records are accurate and easy to verify and there are good controls *(Chapter 9)*

clean opinion the highest level of assurance with an opinion sentence that reads, "In our opinion, the accompanying financial statements present fairly, in all material respects" *(Chapter 3)*

client the person or company who retains the auditor and pays the fee *(Chapter 1)*

commission a percentage fee charged for professional services for executing a transaction or performing some other business activity *(Chapter 4)*

completeness ensuring that valid transactions are not missing from the accounting records *(Chapter 9)*

compliance auditing when an audit engagement is being done for the sole purpose of reporting on compliance with laws, regulations, or rules *(Chapters 6 and 16)*

comprehensive governmental auditing auditing that goes beyond an audit of financial reports to include economy, efficiency, and effectiveness audits *(Chapter 1)*

conflict of interest reason for society's demand for audit services because financial decision makers usually obtain accounting information from companies that want to obtain loans or sell stock *(Chapter 1)*

consequentialism the moral theory that an action is right if it produces at least as much good (utility) as any other action. Also referred to as **utilitarianism** or **utility theory**. Note that economics and business are based on this theory *(Chapter 4)*

continuing professional education (CPE) *(Chapter 4)*

continuity schedule a working paper that shows the movements in an account balance from the beginning to the end of the period under audit, used to analyze the account balance changes and the other financial statement items related to them *(Chapter 11)*

continuous auditing auditing real-time transaction processing systems, using techniques such as audit programming codes that continuously select and monitor the processing of data; more recently can refer to auditing the continuous disclosures of public companies that are required by securities market regulations *(Chapter 7)*

contrived sham transactions fictitious transactions created for illegal purposes such as evading taxes *(Chapter 14)*

control documentation client's documentation of its control procedures, including computer and manual controls; a reference auditors use to understand and assess a client's internal control *(Chapter 7)*

control risk (CR) the risk that the client's internal control will not prevent or detect a material misstatement *(Chapters 2 and 7)*

control risk assessment the process the auditor uses to understand the client's internal control that will be sufficient to identify and assess the risks of material misstatement of the financial statements whether due to fraud or error, and to design and perform further audit procedures; required to comply with the second examination standard of generally accepted auditing standards *(Chapter 11)*

control testing (compliance testing) performing procedures to assess whether controls are operating effectively *(Chapter 7)*

corporate governance the ways in which the suppliers of capital to corporations assure themselves of getting a return on their investment. More generally, under the corporate social responsibility view, corporate governance is the system set up to hold a corporation accountable to employees, communities, the environment, and similar broader social concerns, in addition to being accountable to the capital providers *(Chapter 1)*

COSO (Committee of Sponsoring Organizations of the Treadway Commission) an organization that investigated corporate fraud and developed a control framework that has become the standard for the design of controls by companies and evaluation of controls by auditors; the COSO control framework is cited by the PCAOB in its auditing standards on internal control as an acceptable framework against which control design and effectiveness should be evaluated *(Chapter 16)*

cost of goods sold includes costs such as materials, labour, overheads, freight, etc., that are necessary to get goods to the stage when they can be sold; calculated as the beginning inventory plus costs added during the period less the ending inventory; offset against sales revenues it indicates the gross profit or gross margin on sales on which analytical expectations can be based *(Chapter 13)*

critical-thinking framework principles and concepts to help structure your thinking so that your conclusions will be better justified *(Chapter 4)*

current file the administrative and evidence audit working papers that relate to the audit work for the year being audited *(Chapter 8)*

customer to government (C2G) when transactions between individuals or organizations and government are conducted over the Internet, such as electronic tax return filing *(Chapter 9)*

cutoff bank statement a complete bank statement including all paid cheques and deposit slips for a 10- to 20-day period following the reconciliation date *(Chapter 11)*

cutoff error when transactions are recorded in the wrong period, either by postponing to the next period or accelerating next period transactions into the current period *(Chapter 12)*

dangling debit a false or erroneous debit balance that exists because one or more accounts are misstated *(Chapter 11)*

debt instrument a legally documented obligation between a borrower and a lender, such as a bond payable, lease, mortgage payable *(Chapter 14)*

defalcation when somebody in charge of safekeeping the assets is stealing them; another name for employee fraud and embezzlement *(Chapter 17)*

deontological (Kantian) ethics the moral theory that an action is right if it is based on a sense of duty or obligation *(Chapter 4)*

derivative report a report that results as a side-product of another engagement, such as an auditor providing a report on internal control deficiencies that were uncovered in the process of providing an audit report on the financial statements *(Chapter 16)*

detailed audit plan an audit planning document outlining the nature timing and extent of audit procedures to assess risk of financial statement misstatement, obtain the necessary audit evidence for each assertion for all significant transactions/balances/disclosures, including staffing decisions and time budget *(Prelude to Part III)*

detection rate the ratio of the number of misstatements reported to auditors to the number of actual account misstatements *(Chapter 11)*

detection risk (DR) the risk that the auditor's procedures will fail to find a material misstatement that exists in the accounts *(Chapters 7 and 10)*

differential reporting a reporting option under current Canadian GAAP that allows private companies to use less complex accounting policies than other companies if there is unanimous shareholder approval; special wording is required in the audit report when differential reporting options are used *(Chapter 14)*

direct-effect illegal acts are violations of laws or government regulations by the company, its management, or the employees that produce direct and material effects on dollar amounts in financial statements *(Chapter 17)*

direct reporting engagement a type of assurance engagement in which the assertions are implied and not written down in some form *(Chapters 1, 2, and 16)*

disclaimer of opinion auditor's declaration that no opinion is given on financial statements and the reasons why this is so, usually due to a scope limitation; also called a **denial of opinion** *(Chapter 2)*

doing business as (DBA) *(Chapter 17)*

dual dating refers to instances of dating the audit report as of the date that financial statements are approved by the auditee's responsible parties and attaching an additional later date to disclosure of a significant Type II subsequent event *(Chapter 15)*

dual-direction testing audits both control over completeness in one direction and control over validity in the other *(Chapter 11)*

dual-purpose procedure an audit procedure which is used simultaneously for testing controls over a transaction and to provide substantive audit evidence about its amount *(Chapter 11)*

electronic transfer codes used by companies to transfer pay amounts directly to employees' bank accounts *(Chapter 13)*

embezzlement type of fraud involving employees' or non-employees' wrongfully taking money or property entrusted to their care, custody, and control; often accompanied by false accounting entries and other forms of lying and cover-up *(Chapter 17)*

employee fraud the use of fraudulent means to take money or other property from an employer *(Chapter 17)*

engagement letter sets forth terms of engagement, including an agreement about the fee when a new audit client is accepted *(Chapter 6)*

engagement partner one of the most experienced members of the audit team who makes the final decision on the audit opinion *(Chapter 15)*

enterprise resource planning systems (ERPS) an information system in which inputs and outputs from many or all the business processes will be processed in an integrated manner, so the accounting component of the information system will be closely related to many other functional areas such as sales, inventory, human resources, cash management, etc. *(Chapters 6 and 7)*

entity's risk assessment process management's process for identifying business risks that could affect financial reporting objectives and for deciding on actions to address and minimize these risks; understanding this process helps auditors to assess the risk that the financial statements could be materially misstated *(Chapter 7)*

error synonym of deviation in test of controls sampling *(Chapter 17)*

error analysis qualitative evaluation of control risk *(Chapter 10)*

evidence all the influences on auditors' minds that ultimately guide their decisions *(Chapter 2)*

evidence collection steps 4, 5, and 6 of the sampling method, which are performed to get the evidence *(Chapter 10)*

evidence evaluation the final step of the sampling method, to evaluate the evidence and make justifiable decisions about the control risk *(Chapter 10)*

expectation about the population deviation rate an estimate of the ratio of the number of expected deviations to population size *(Chapter 10)*

expenditure analysis   comparing the suspect's spending with known income *(Chapter 17)*

extending the audit conclusion performing substantive-purpose audit procedures on the transactions in the remaining period and on the year-end balance to produce sufficient competent evidence for a decision about the year-end balance *(Chapter 10)*

external auditor   an auditor who is an outsider and independent of the entity being audited *(Chapters 1, 2, and 17)*

fidelity bond   a type of insurance policy that covers theft of cash by employees *(Chapter 11)*

financial error   an unintentional misstatement of the financial statements; in contrast, is defined as intentional misstatement *(Chapter 9)*

financial reporting   broad-based process of providing statements of financial position (balance sheets), statements of results of operations (income statements), statements of results of changes in financial position (cash flow statements), and accompanying disclosure notes (footnotes) to outside decision makers who have no internal source of information like the management of the company has *(Chapter 1)*

FOB destination   terms of sale indicating that title to goods sold transfers from seller to buyer when the goods reach the buyer's destination, can give rise to an amount of inventory-in-transit at year end that is owned by a client but not physically on hand at the client's premises *(Chapter 11)*

FOB shipping   terms of sale indicating that title to goods sold transfers from seller to buyer when the goods are handed over from the seller to the shipping company that will ultimately deliver them to the buyer; can give rise to an amount of inventory-in-transit at year end that is owned by a client but not physically on hand at the client's premises *(Chapter 11)*

forensic accounting   application of accounting and auditing skills to legal problems, both civil and criminal *(Chapters 1 and 17)*

fraud   an intentional misstatement of the financial statements *(Chapter 9)*

fraud audit questioning (FAQ)   a nonaccusatory method of asking key questions during a regular audit to give personnel an opportunity to supply information about possible misdeeds *(Chapter 17)*

fraud auditing   a proactive approach to detect financial frauds using accounting records and information, analytical relationships, and an awareness of fraud perpetration and concealment efforts (ACFE) *(Chapter 1)*

fraud examiners   those engaged specifically for fraud investigation work *(Chapter 17)*

fraud opportunity   an open door for solving the unshareable problem by violating a trust *(Chapter 17)*

fraudulent financial reporting   intentional or reckless conduct, whether by act or omission, that results in materially misleading financial statements *(Chapter 17)*

further possible misstatements   those that could exist over and above the total of known and likely misstatements because of the fundamental limitations of auditing *(Chapter 15)*

general control procedures   relate to many or all of computerized and manual accounting activities, for example, controls over access to data files and division of duties *(Chapter 7)*

generally accepted accounting principles (GAAP)   those accounting methods that have been established in a particular jurisdiction by formal recognition by a standard-setting body, or by authoritative support or precedent such as the accounting recommendations of the *CICA Handbook (Chapter 1)*

generally accepted auditing standards (GAAS)   those auditing recommendations that have been established in a particular jurisdiction by formal recognition by a standard-setting body, or by authoritative support or precedent such as the auditing and assurance recommendations of the *CICA Handbook*; also refers to the general, examination and reporting standards included in *CICA Handbook*, section 5100; the minimum standards for performing an acceptable audit *(Chapter 2)*

haphazard selection   unsystematic way of selecting sample units *(Chapter 10)*

high assurance   highest level of conclusion of an audit report, which states that the financial statements present fairly in all material respects; also known as **positive assurance** *(Chapter 3)*

horizontal analysis   comparison of changes of financial statement numbers and ratios across two or more years *(Chapters 6 and 17)*

hypothesis testing   when auditors hypothesize that the book value is materially accurate regarding existence, ownership, and valuation *(Chapter 10)*

imperative   a universal principle assumed by monistic moral theories *(Chapter 4)*

indirect-effect illegal acts refer to violations of laws and regulations that are far removed from financial statements *(Chapter 17)*

individually significant items   items in account balances that exceed the material misstatement amount; in audit sampling these should be removed from the population and audited completely *(Chapter 10)*

information risk   the failure of financial statements to appropriately reflect the economic substance of business activities *(Chapter 1)*

information technology (IT)   the hardware and software needed to process data *(Chapters 1 and 7)*

inherent risk (IR)   the probability that material misstatements have occurred *(Chapters 2 and 7)*

initial public offering (IPO)   a first time offering of a corporation's shares to the public *(Chapter 1)*

Institute of Internal Auditors (IIA)   *(Chapter 18)*

Intranet internal communications network using Internet technology, such as an employee e-mail system *(Chapter 7)*

interim audit work covers procedures performed several weeks or months before the balance sheet date *(Chapter 6)*

interim date a date before the end of the period under audit when some of the audit procedures might be performed, such as control evaluation and testing *(Chapters 2 and 10)*

internal auditing verification work performed by company employees who are trained in auditing procedures, mainly used for internal control purposes but external auditors can rely on internal audit work if certain criteria are met *(Chapter 1)*

internal control the system of policies and procedures needed to maintain adherence to a company's objectives; especially the accuracy of recordkeeping and safegarding of assets *(Chapter 1)*

internal control program an audit planning document listing the specific procedures for obtaining an understanding of the client's business and management's control system, and for assessing the inherent risk and the control risk related to the financial account balances. *(Chapters 8 and 10)*

internal control questionnaire (ICQ) checklist to gather evidence about the control environment *(Chapter 9)*

International Auditing Assurance and Standards Board (IAASB) the audit standard-setting body for International Standards on Auditing (ISAs) *(Chapter 1)*

International Federation of Accountants (IFAC) an organization dedicated to developing international auditing standards *(Chapter 1)*

international harmonization international convergence of national auditing standards with ISAs, including going concern, fraud, and the audit risk model *(Chapter 1)*

International Standards on Auditing (ISAs) the auditing standards of IFAC *(Chapter 1)*

irregularities intentional misstatements or omissions in financial statements, including fraudulent financial reporting *(Chapter 17)*

joint and several liability a legal liability regime in which one party found to be liable can be required to pay the full amount of the damages even if there are other parties that are partially liable but they are bankrupt or otherwise unable to pay a proportionate share of the damages *(Chapter 5)*

just-in-time (JIT) an inventory production system where inventory holding is minimized by having raw materials and supplies delivered as close as possible to the time that they will be used in the production process *(Chapter 13)*

key control important control procedure; auditors should identify and audit only these controls *(Chapter 10)*

known misstatement the total amount of actual monetary error found in a sample *(Chapters 10 and 15)*

legal responsibilities auditor responsibilities imposed by the legal system *(Chapter 5)*

levels of assurance the amount of credibility provided by accountants and auditors *(Chapter 3)*

likely misstatement the projected amount of the known misstatement in the population of a sample *(Chapters 10 and 15)*

limited liability partnership (LLP) company whose partners' liability is limited to the capital they have invested in the business *(Chapters 1 and 5)*

lower of cost or market (LCM) accounting valuation test that assesses whether the recorded cost of inventory exceeds its market value in which case the value needs to be written down to the lower market value *(Chapters 6 and 12)*

lower-of-cost-or-net-realizable-value (LCNRV) *(Chapter 13)*

management auditing auditors' study of business operations for the purpose of making recommendations about economic and efficient use of resources, effective achievement of business objectives and compliance with company policies; see **operational auditing** *(Chapters 1 and 16)*

management controls aspects of internal control that operate at the company level including the control environment; the entity's risk assessment process; the information system, including the related business processes, relevant to financial reporting, and communication; monitoring of controls *(Chapter 7)*

management fraud deliberate fraud committed by management that injures investors and creditors through materially misleading financial statements *(Chapter 17)*

management representation letter communication sent to client in which recommendations are noted and evaluated *(Chapters 9 and 15)*

management's discussion and analysis (MD&A) a section of the annual report that includes management's analysis of past operating and financial results, can also include forward-looking information; the financial statement auditor reviews the information to ensure there is nothing that is inconsistent with the audited financial statements but the MD&A itself is not audited *(Chapter 16)*

materiality amount of misstatement that would likely affect a user's decision *(Chapter 6)*

mitigating factors elements of financial flexibility (saleability of assets, lines of credit, debt extension, dividend elimination) available as survival strategies in circumstances of going concern uncertainty which may reduce the financial difficulty problems *(Chapter 3)*

money laundering engaging in specific financial transactions in order to conceal the identity, source, and/or destination of money resulting from an illegal act, which may involve organized crime, tax evasion, or false accounting *(Chapter 11)*

monistic theories ethical theories that assume universal principles apply regardless of the specific facts of a situation *(Chapter 4)*

moral imagination   part of ethical reasoning where one has the ability to imagine others' feelings about the consequences of a decision *(Chapter 4)*

moral responsibilities   auditor responsibilities to conform to broad social norms of behaviour *(Chapter 4)*

nature (of audit procedures)   refers to the six general techniques of an account balance audit program: computation, confirmation, enquiry, inspection, observation, and analysis *(Chapter 10)*

negative assurance   synonym for moderate assurance *(Chapter 3)*

no assurance   an engagement in which the PA provides zero assurance credibility because there is no independent verification of the data provided by the client; a prime example involving financial information is a compilation engagement *(Chapter 3)*

nonstatistical (judgmental) sampling   choosing items in a population for audit testing and evaluating the findings based on the auditor's own knowledge and experience rather than statistical methods *(Chapter 10)*

occurrence   (as in **control failure**, also **deviation**, **error**, and **exception**) synonym of deviation in test of controls sampling *(Chapter 10)*

off the balance sheet   refers to how certain obligations and commitments do not have to be reported on the balance sheet, such as purchase commitments and operating leases *(Chapter 14)*

online input validation   inputting information correctly or computer will not accept the transaction; uses validation checks, such as missing data, check digit and limit tests *(Chapter 11)*

operational auditing   see **management auditing** *(Chapters 1 and 16)*

overall strategy   audit planning decisions about the scope and approach to the audit outline, the materiality, the risk assessment control evaluation, planned procedures, and related decisions on staffing, supervision, and timing *(Chapter 6)*

overreliance   the result of assessing control risk too low *(Chapter 10)*

peer review   study of a firm's quality control policies and procedures, followed by a report on a firm's quality of audit practice *(Chapters 2 and 15)*

performance auditing   see **management auditing** and **operational auditing** *(Chapters 1 and 8)*

permanent file   audit working papers that are of continuing interest from year to year, including the client company's articles of incorporation, shareholder agreements, major contracts, minutes *(Chapter 8)*

pervasive materiality   occurs if the GAAP departures are either so significant that they overshadow the financial statements, or pervasive, affecting numerous accounts and financial statement relationships *(Chapter 3)*

physical representation of the population   the auditor's frame of reference for selecting a sample, for example, a journal listing of recorded sales invoices *(Chapter 10)*

planning memorandum   where all planning activities are recorded and summarized *(Chapter 8)*

pluralistic theories   ethical theories that assume that there are no universal principles and that the best approach is to use the principles that are most relevant in a particular case *(Chapter 4)*

population   the set of all the elements that constitute an account balance or class of transactions *(Chapter 10)*

population unit   each element of a population *(Chapter 10)*

positive assurance   see **high assurance** *(Chapter 3)*

possible misstatement   the further misstatement remaining undetected in the units not selected in the sample *(Chapter 10)*

post-Enron world   the audit environment characterized by the failure of the Enron Corporation in December 2001 and its consequences since then *(Chapter 1)*

practice inspection   the system of reviewing and evaluating practice units' audit files and other documentation by an independent external party *(Chapter 2)*

pre-audit risk management activities   procedures auditors perform before accepting an audit engagement to ensure the client and the engagement do not pose an unacceptably high risk of audit failure *(Chapter 6)*

predecessor   the auditor that held the engagement previously, before a new successor auditor took on the engagement *(Chapter 6)*

preventive maintenance   auditors should determine whether maintenance is scheduled and whether the schedule is followed and documented, and also review contract with computer vendor *(Chapter 7)*

primary beneficiaries   third parties for whose primary benefit the audit or other accounting service is performed *(Chapter 5)*

private placement   sale of securities to a small number of persons or institutional investors (usually not more than 35), who can demand and obtain sufficient information without the formality of registration *(Chapter 17)*

pro forma financial data   the presentation of financial statements as if the event had occurred on the date of the balance sheet; for example, perhaps the best way to show the effect of a business purchase or other merger *(Chapter 15)*

problem recognition   the first three steps of the sampling method *(Chapter 10)*

professional judgment   the application of relevant training, knowledge, and experience, within the context provided by auditing, accounting, and ethical standards, in making informed decisions about the courses of action that are appropriate in the circumstances of the audit engagement *(Chapter 1)*

professional responsibilities (or ethics) the rules and principles for the proper conduct of an auditor in her work, necessary to obtain the respect and confidence of the public, achieve order within the profession, and to provide a means of self-policing the profession *(Chapter 4)*

professional skepticism an auditor's tendency to question management representations and look for corroborating evidence before accepting them *(Chapter 2)*

projected misstatement the estimated amount of likely misstatement in a population based on extrapolating a misstatement discovered in a sample (known/identified misstatement) over the whole population *(Chapter 10)*

proper period refers to ensuring that transactions are accounted for in the period they occurred in *(Chapter 9)*

proportionate liability a legal liability regime where a party found to be partly liable is only responsible for paying a part of the damages in proportion to their share of the blame *(Chapter 5)*

prospectus set of financial statements and disclosures distributed to all purchasers in an offering registered under Securities Law *(Chapter 1)*

providing assurance the "lending of credibility" to financial information by objective intermediaries *(Chapter 1)*

Provincial Institutes of Chartered Accountants (PICA) *(Chapter 4)*

Public Company Accounting Oversight Board (PCAOB) *(Chapter 1)*

public sector activities of all levels of government *(Chapter 1)*

purchase cutoff recording purchase transactions in the proper period, including accruals of payments not due until the following period *(Chapter 12)*

qualified reports audit reports that contain an opinion paragraph that does not give the positive assurance that everything in the financial statements is in conformity with GAAP *(Chapter 3)*

quality earnings reported accounting earnings that are highly correlated with the underlying economic performance of the business and free of management bias or manipulation *(Chapter 7)*

quality inspection an examination and evaluation of the quality of the overall practice *(Chapter 2)*

random sample a set of sampling units so chosen that each population item has an equal likelihood of being selected in the sample *(Chapter 10)*

reliance letter where accountants sign that they have been notified that a particular recipient of the financial statements and audit report intends to rely upon them for particular purposes *(Chapter 5)*

replication process of re-performing a selection procedure and getting the same sample units *(Chapter 10)*

reportable matters significant deficiencies in the design or operation of the company's internal control structure, which could adversely affect its ability to report financial data in conformity with GAAP *(Chapters 9 and 16)*

representative sample sample that mirrors the characteristics of the population being studied *(Chapter 10)*

reservations major variations on the standard audit report *(Chapter 3)*

response rate the proportion of the number of confirmations for bill-and-hold transactions returned to the number sent *(Chapter 11)*

revenue recognition problems techniques used by financial statement preparers to manipulate reported revenues resulting in low-quality earnings *(Chapter 11)*

risk model $AR = IR \times CR \times DR$ *(Chapter 10)* $AR = IR \times CR \times APR \times RIA$ *(Chapter 10)*

risk of assessing the control risk too high the probability that the compliance evidence in the sample indicates high control risk when the actual (but unknown) degree of compliance would justify a lower control-risk assessment *(Chapter 10)*

risk of assessing the control risk too low the probability that the compliance evidence in the sample indicates low control risk when the actual (but unknown) degree of compliance does not justify it *(Chapter 10)*

risk of incorrect acceptance (RIA) the decision to accept a balance as being materially accurate when the balance is materially misstated *(Chapter 10)*

risk of incorrect rejection the decision to accept a balance as being materially misstated when it is not *(Chapter 10)*

risk of material misstatement the auditor's assessment of combined inherent and control risk *(Chapter 7)*

rollforward period the period between the cutoff and year-end *(Chapter 12)*

sales cutoff recording sales transactions in the proper period *(Chapter 11)*

sample a set of sampling units *(Chapter 10)*

sample of one see **walk-through** *(Chapter 11)*

sampling error the amount by which a projected likely misstatement amount could differ from an actual (unknown) total as a result of the sample not being exactly representative *(Chapter 10)*

sampling risk the probability that an auditor's conclusion based on a sample might be different from the conclusion based on an audit of the entire population *(Chapter 10)*

sampling unit unit used for testing a client's population, for example, a customer's account, an inventory item, a debt issue, or a cash receipt *(Chapter 10)*

scope   the entity and its financial statements that will be covered by the audit engagement, the client documents and records to be examined to provide the necessary audit evidence *(Prelude to Part III)*

scope limitations   conditions where auditors are unable to obtain sufficient appropriate evidence *(Chapter 3)*

search for unrecorded liabilities   set of procedures designed to yield audit evidence of liabilities that were not recorded in the period following the audit client's balance sheet date *(Chapter 12)*

second audit partner   one who reviews the work of the audit team *(Chapter 4)*

second-partner review   review of working papers and financial statements by a partner not responsible for client relations; ensures that quality of audit work is in keeping with the standards of the audit firm *(Chapter 15)*

Securities and Exchange Commission (SEC)   *(Chapter 1)*

self-regulation   refers to a situation where a professional group is given the power to monitor and discipline its members by the government *(Chapters 1 and 4)*

service organization   a business other than the client's that executes or records transactions on behalf of the client *(Chapter 16)*

significant deficiency   when the auditor believes that an identified control deficiency or combination of deficiencies exposes the entity to a serious risk of material misstatement *(Chapter 9)*

skewness   the concentration of a large proportion of the dollar amount in only a small number of the population items *(Chapter 10)*

Society of Management Accountants of Canada (SMAC) *(Chapter 1)*

standard deviation   a measure of population variability *(Chapter 10)*

statistical sampling   audit sampling that uses the laws of probability for selecting and evaluating a sample from a population for the purpose of reaching a conclusion about the population *(Chapter 10)*

strategic systems auditing (SSA audits)   an auditing approach that has a top-down focus, starting with an in-depth understanding of the auditee's business. This focus enables the auditor to understand the strategic objectives of the auditee, the risks the auditee faces in relation to these objectives, and the controls necessary for the business to respond to these risks. After obtaining an understanding of the business as a whole, the SSA auditor then proceeds to look at the details of the risky transactions in the context of the knowledge gained at the broader level *(Chapter 7)*

stratification   subdividing the population in an audit sample by, for example, account balance size *(Chapter 10)*

strengths   specific features of good detail controls that would prevent, detect, or correct material misstatements *(Chapter 9)*

substantive audit approach   is being used if the auditor decides not to test internal controls *(Chapter 9)*

substantive tests of details auditing   the performance of procedures to obtain direct evidence about the dollar amounts and disclosures in the financial statements *(Chapter 10)*

successor auditor   a new auditor who takes over the engagement from the predecessor *(Chapter 6)*

supply chain management   system for organizing all the entities and activites involved in supplying the requirements of a business operation *(Chapter 13)*

systematic random selection   using a predetermined population and sample size and random starting places *(Chapter 10)*

three-party accountability   an accountability relationship in which there are three distinct parties (individuals): an asserter, an assurer, and a user of the asserted information *(Chapter 1)*

tolerable deviation rate   rate of deviation that can exist without causing a minimum material misstatement in the sales and accounts receivable balances *(Chapter 10)*

tolerable misstatement   can be set by using an amount lower than whole materiality for a certain account *(Chapter 6)*

tort   legal action covering civil complaints other than breach of contract; normally initiated by users of financial statements *(Chapter 5)*

Type 1 error risk   see **alpha risk** *(Chapter 10)*

Type 2 error risks   see **beta risk** *(Chapter 10)*

Type I (subsequent events)   those that require adjustment of the dollar amounts in the financial statements and the addition of any related disclosure in the notes *(Chapter 15)*

Type II (subsequent events)   those that require disclosure, but no adjustment of dollar amounts *(Chapter 15)*

unaudited   note accountant places on each page of financial statements in performing write-up or compilation work *(Chapter 16)*

underreliance   the result of realizing the risk of assessing control risk too high *(Chapter 10)*

Uniform Commercial Code (UCC)   *(Chapter 17)*

unqualified reports   reports in which auditors are not calling attention to anything wrong with the audit work or financial statements *(Chapter 2)*

unrestricted random selection   using a printed random number table or computerized random number generator to obtain a list of random numbers *(Chapter 10)*

utilitarianism   the moral theory that an action is right if it produces at least as much good (utility) as any other action. It relies on the principle of utility; also referred to as **consequentialism**. *(Chapter 4)*

validity   ensuring that the recorded transactions are ones that should be recorded, i.e., that they exist *(Chapter 9)*

value-for-money (VFM) audit   audit concept from public sector that incorporates audits of economy, efficiency, and effectiveness *(Chapter 1)*

vertical analysis   analytical procedure of comparing all financial statement items to a common base, for example, total assets or total sales *(Chapters 6 and 17)*

walk-through   following one or more transactions through the accounting and control systems to obtain a general understanding of the client's systems *(Chapters 10 and 11)*

weaknesses   the lack of controls in particular areas that would allow material errors to get by undetected *(Chapter 9)*

white-collar crime   the misdeeds done by people who wear ties to work and steal with a pencil or a computer *(Chapter 17)*

working paper reference index   table of contents listing all the index numbers used to identify section of the audit working paper files *(Chapter 15)*

work-in-progress   inventory in a manufacturing operation that is partly completed *(Chapter 13)*

year-end audit work   audit procedures performed shortly before and after the balance sheet date *(Chapter 6)*

INDEX

INTERNATIONAL FEDERATION OF ACCOUNTANTS

CODE OF ETHICS FOR PROFESSIONAL ACCOUNTANTS

CONTENTS